THE FREUD READER

EDITED BY
Peter Gay

✔
VINTAGE

Published by Vintage 1995

4 6 8 10 9 7 5

Selections on pages 55, 89 and 111 are excerpted by permission
of the publishers from *The Complete Letters of Sigmund
Freud to Wilhelm Fliess, 1887–1904*, Jeffrey Moussaief Masson,
ed., Cambridge, Mass.: The Belknap Press of
Harvard University Press, © 1985 Sigmund Freud
Copyright Ltd., and Jeffrey Moussaief Masson.
Selections on pages 86, 129, 539 and 772 are excerpted by
permission of the publishers Hogarth Press Ltd.
Selections on pages 48, 60, 78, 96, 117, 172, 239, 293, 297,
301, 309, 351, 356, 363, 378, 387, 394, 400, 429, 436, 514, 522,
545, 562, 568, 572, 584, 589, 661, 666 and 670 are excerpted
by permission of the publishers Basic Books, Inc.

First published in the States of America by
W.W.Norton & Company, Inc
and simultaneously in Canada by
Penguin Books Canada Ltd, 1989

Vintage
Random House, 20 Vauxhall Bridge Road, London SW1V 2SA

Random House Australia (Pty) Limited
20 Alfred Street, Milsons Point, Sydney
New South Wales 2061, Australia

Random House New Zealand Limited
18 Poland Road, Glenfield,
Auckland 10, New Zealand

Random House South Africa (Pty) Limited
PO Box 337, Bergvlei, South Africa

Random House UK Limited Reg. No. 954009

A CIP catalogue record for this book
is available from the British Library

ISBN 0 09 957711 9

Printed and bound in Great Britain by
Cox & Wyman, Reading, Berkshire

A VINTAGE ORIGINAL

THE FREUD READER

Peter Gay's first volume of his two-volume work, *The Enlightenment: An Interpretation*, won a National Book Award, and his bestselling *Freud: A Life for Our Time* was finalist for the National Book Award. His other numerous works include studies on the eighteenth century, *Voltaire's Politics* and *The Party of Humanity*, and essays on the writing of history, *Style in History* and *Art and Act*. The recipient of Guggenheim and Rockefeller Foundation Fellowships, an Overseas Fellowship at Churchill College, Cambridge, and the Heineken Prize for Historical Study, Peter Gay is Sterling Professor of History at Yale University.

BY PETER GAY

The Dilemma Of Democratic Socialism:
Eduard Bernstein's Challenge

Voltaire's Politics: The Poet As Realist

The Party Of Humanity:
Essays In The French Enlightenment

The Enlightenment: An Interpretation/
The Rise Of Modern Paganism

A Loss Of Mastery:
Puritan Historians In Colonial America

Weimar Culture: The Outsider As Insider

The Enlightenment: An Interpretation/
The Science Of Freedom

The Bridge Of Criticism:
Dialogues On The Enlightenment

Modern Europe (with R.K.Webb)

Style In History

Art And Act: On Causes
In History - Manet, Gropius, Mondrian

Freud, Jews And Other Germans:
Masters And Victims In Modernist Culture

The Bourgeois Experience:
Victoria To Freud/ Education Of The Senses

Freud For Historians

The Bourgeois Experience:
Victoria To Freud/The Tender Passion

A Godless Jew: Freud, Atheism
And The Making Of Psychoanalysis

Freud: A Life For Our Time

The Freud Reader

To
Gladys Topkis

Reader—and Friend

Contents

Preface

Sigmund Freud—along with Karl Marx, Charles Darwin, and Albert Einstein—is among that small handful of supreme makers of the twentieth-century mind whose works should be our prized possession. Yet, voluminous, diverse, and at times technical, Freud's writings have not been as widely read as they deserve to be; most of those who may claim direct acquaintance with them have limited their acquaintance to his late essay *Civilization and Its Discontents*. Others have contented themselves with compendia, popularizations, even comic books attempting to make Freud and his ideas palatable, even easy. That is a pity, for he was a great stylist and equally great scientist. Hence it can be pleasurable, and it is certainly essential, to know Freud, not merely to know about him.

The Freud Reader is designed to repair such unmerited and unfortunate neglect. It is the first truly comprehensive survey of Freud's writings, using not some dated and discredited translations but the authoritative versions in the twenty-four-volume Standard Edition of Freud's Psychological Writings. It is the Standard Edition, the Bible for psychoanalysts in the English-speaking world, to which students of Freud, whether psychiatrists or social workers, philosophers or aestheticians, literary critics or cultural anthropologists, historians or political scientists, inescapably turn. For psychoanalysts, psychoanalytically inclined psychiatrists and social workers in the English-speaking world, the Standard Edition is the Bible. Its notes have proved so copious and so dependable that a recent twelve-volume German edition of Freud, the *Studienausgabe*, has simply copied them; in this *Freud Reader*, I have supplemented them only wherever it seemed necessary to offer an even fuller explanation.

To make Freud all the more accessible, I have furnished this Reader with a substantial general introduction designed to place the man and his work in his time and culture and with a no less substantial chronology recording not merely all the significant dates in Freud's life but equally significant dates in European culture and politics. In addition, I have supplied each selection with introductory paragraphs and conclude the Reader with a selected bibliography that contains all the titles I mention in my introductions, and more. All this explanatory material should help to pierce the barriers that have hitherto kept a wider public from appreciating Freud's originality, savoring his wit, and recognizing his versatility.

That versatility is positively awe-inspiring: though, of course, principally known as the founder of psychoanalysis, Freud did not confine his thinking, and writing, to the suffering men and women he saw before him on the couch day after day. It is true that his case histories, his papers on psychoanalytic technique, and his theoretical papers are at the heart of his thought. But he developed a theory of mind that he thought explained all of mental activity, normal and neurotic alike, and he applied that theory to virtually every aspect of culture: to the arts, to literature, to biography, to mythology, to religion, to politics, to education, to the law, to prehistory. *The Freud Reader*, in addition to covering Freud's psychoanalytic evolution, also faithfully reflects these wider concerns. It does so not with anemic snippets but with lengthy excerpts, at times with complete papers. Each of the more than fifty selections in this Reader is a facet of a complex whole—Freud's thought. All together they should give a fair, far from fragmentary sense of that whole.

Since Freud's thought developed, matured, and changed, the only responsible way into that thought, it seems to me, is chronological. Hence I have chosen to present Freud's writings in strict sequence—with one exception: I have enlisted substantial excerpts from his "Autobiographical Study," published in 1925 when Freud was sixty-nine, to serve as a lively and trustworthy overture to the rest of his work from the 1880s to the 1930s.

I owe particular thanks to two friends for helping me shape this Reader: Richard Kuhns, my former colleague at Columbia University, and Donald Lamm, my publisher and editor.

PETER GAY

Introduction

Freud is inescapable. It may be a commonplace by now that we all speak Freud whether we know it or not, but the commonplace remains both true and important. Freud's terminology and his essential ideas pervade contemporary ways of thinking about human feelings and conduct. Even critics who find psychoanalysis both as a therapy and as a theory of mind fatally flawed will catch themselves borrowing such Freudian categories as repression and narcissism to make knowing comments about the deeper meanings of slips, or resorting to the Oedipus complex to interpret family tensions. All this psychoanalytic talk is often imprecise in the extreme.[1] And the definitive outlines of Freud's legacy remain uncertain. But they could not be anything else: Freud covered so much ground in developing his theories of the mind, and inevitably left so much of his work unfinished, that even those who firmly call themselves psychoanalysts sometimes disagree with Freud, and often disagree with one another. No matter: ignorant or well-informed, our culture has found Freud's vision of mind compelling enough to live with it, whether comfortably or not.

Yet while modern culture has largely absorbed Freud's ideas, and given them enormous influence, they are, strangely enough, really not very well known or fully appreciated. Freud wrote a great deal, and it takes considerable patience to work one's way through his books and papers. After all, much of what he wrote is highly technical, and hence requires not just patience but close attention. Freud was a master of exposition, an unsurpassed persuader, but he touched on matters that even his most felicitous metaphors cannot make easy. Most troubling of all, Freud's estimate of the human animal is far from flattering, and his message is sobering in the extreme. To expose oneself to the full gravity of Freud's thought is therefore risky and unsettling, and many have found it more soothing by far to soak up fragments of that thought through bland popularizations, or to rely on the doubtful wisdom of common discourse. Freud took some pride in disturbing the sleep of mankind, and mankind has responded by trivializing him, watering him

---

1. Thus many diagnose themselves, or others, as suffering from an "inferiority complex" as though they had learned that term from Freud when it is actually the property of Freud's rival Alfred Adler; others freely use the term "subconscious" as a synonym for "unconscious," even though Freud explicitly refused to commit himself to the vague word "subconscious."

down, or finding reasons—whether by denouncing his theories or denigrating his character—for disregarding him altogether.[2]

This *Freud Reader*, a comprehensive survey of Freud's writings equipped with introductory comments and notes, has been compiled to provide a more than casual, or fragmentary, overview of his work for those who choose *not* to trivialize or disregard him. It covers his publications across more than forty years, and across an impressive range, of activity: scientific papers; case histories; papers on psychoanalytic technique; fundamental texts on dreams, sexuality, anxiety, and mental structure; speculative flights in his letters; polemical sallies in the combat zone of psychoanalytic politics; essays in biography, cultural criticism, sociology, literary analysis. Except for Freud's "Autobiographical Study" of 1925, placed at the head of this anthology as an overture, the sequence of the selections is chronological. Freud's thought virtually commands such a procedure; his ideas evolved, and his changes of mind, though never amounting to a conversion, were drastic enough. What is more, Freud's writings were more closely implicated in his personal situation than has been generally recognized; hence an arrangement that follows the calendar of his life is highly appropriate.[3] The early Freud is recognizable in the late Freud, but it is a momentous matter just which Freud one is reading. The chronology preceding the selections has been designed to orient the reader in the stages of Freud's life. And the pages that follow discuss some themes that pervaded that life.

I. THE OUTSIDER

Throughout all his career, Freud regarded himself as an outsider and derived his intellectual daring from his peculiarly exposed position on the margins of society. He was, to be sure, anything but a pariah. As a Jew growing up in the 1860s in a Roman Catholic country, Freud was buoyed by the liberal interlude in Austrian history, a time when ambitious Jewish youngsters cultivated fantasies about the most exalted careers. In the *Interpretation of Dreams*, he recounts an instructive anecdote demonstrating just what sort of realistic experiences fed the "thirst for grandeur" he developed during these heady years. "My parents had been in the habit, when I was a boy of eleven or twelve, of taking me with them to the Prater. One evening, while we were sitting in a restaurant there, our attention had been attracted by a man who was moving from one table to another and, for a small consideration, improvising a verse upon any topic presented to him. I was dispatched to bring the poet to our table and he showed his gratitude to the messenger.

2. College students are likely to have dipped into only one of Freud's texts, the late essay *Civilization and Its Discontents* (1930). That little book, as explosive as it is terse, can be upsetting enough, for it shows Freud at his most disenchanted. But by itself, it provides only very limited access to Freud's thought; its background in that thought is impossible to tease out without some knowledge of the writings that preceded it.

3. I have tried to argue this point in some detail in *Freud: A Life for Our Time* (1988).

Before enquiring what the chosen topic was to be, he had dedicated a few lines to myself; and he had been inspired to declare that I should probably grow up to be a Cabinet Minister." Freud took this forecast to be anything but utopian. "Those were the days"—the late 1860s—"of the *'Bürger'* Ministry. Shortly before, my father had brought home portraits of these middle-class professional men . . . and we had illuminated the house in their honour. There had even been some Jews among them." Hence, "every industrious Jewish schoolboy carried a Cabinet Minister's portfolio in his satchel."[4]

But in the course of time, whatever fantasies of this kind Freud may have entertained were first tempered, then wiped out, by political realities. Outbursts of anti-Semitism, growing more frequent and more virulent from the days of the stock market crash of 1873—a decisive year for him—cast doubts on any prominent future for a Jew in Austrian public life. "When, in 1873, I first joined the University," Freud recalled half a century later, "I experienced some appreciable disappointments. Above all, I found that I was expected to feel myself inferior and an alien because I was a Jew." He indignantly refused to accept the sorry status that anti-Semites wanted to assign to him *as* a Jew, and he did not object to being seen as someone who does not fit in. "These first impressions at the University," in fact, "had one consequence which was afterwards to prove important; for at an early age I was made familiar with the fate of being in the Opposition and of being put under the ban of the 'compact majority.' " He intended, in short, to be as brave in face of powerful and persecuting public opinion as the honest and courageous Dr. Stockmann, in Ibsen's drama *The Enemy of the People.* "The foundations were thus laid for a certain degree of independence of judgment."[5]

Freud, indeed, was an outsider in more ways than one. He would neither try to join, nor observe the verdict of, the "compact majority" of his fellow-Austrians. Beyond that, he was an outsider no less in rejecting completely, even vehemently, the religion of his forefathers. Freud had been educated for atheism. His father, though knowledgeable in the Jewish scriptures, who "spoke the sacred language as well as German or better," had yet let Freud "grow up in complete ignorance of everything that concerned Judaism."[6] To be sure, Freud felt at home among Jews: in the mid-1890s, he joined a newly formed lodge of B'nai B'rith, a Jewish fraternal organization, in Vienna. Moreover, nearly all of his intimates and card-playing friends were Jews, as were his Austrian, Hungarian, and German adherents—though no less firmly atheists than he. Yet Freud stood outside the Jewish faith. Once he had a family of his own, he celebrated Christmas and Easter, and his children never

4. *Interpretation of Dreams* (1900), *SE* IV, 193.
5. "An Autobiographical Study" (1925), *SE* XX, 9.
6. Freud to J. Dwossis, December 15, 1930.

Typed transcription, Freud Museum, London. See Peter Gay, *A Godless Jew: Freud, Atheism, and the Making of Psychoanalysis* (1987), 125.

attended a synagogue. In 1930, in the preface to the Hebrew translation of *Totem and Taboo,* he described himself, as he had often done before, as a man "completely estranged from the religion of his fathers—as well as from every other religion."[7] He was proud of his Jewish identity, but his definition of his Jewishness was purely, aggressively, secular. Thus, as far as his two cultures, religious-Jewish and nationalist-Austrian, were concerned, Freud was doubly marginal. Yet Freud was ambivalent about his exposed position and half welcomed it. He persuaded himself that it had proved immensely productive for him.

Freud was something of an outsider in still other ways, notably in his chosen medical specialty. A promising researcher during, and after, his medical training, highly regarded by his eminent professors, he began in the mid-1880s to expound views that could only make him unpopular—or at least controversial. In the spring of 1886, after his return from his study trip to Paris, where he had worked with the celebrated neurologist Jean Martin Charcot for several months, he tried to convert his fellow physicians in Vienna to Charcot's radical ideas—most notoriously to Charcot's respect for hypnotism, and to Charcot's unconventional claim that men, too, suffer from hysteria. Far from accepting Freud's enthusiastic missionary insistence that these were important insights destined to revolutionize mental healing, his colleagues refused to abandon their traditional ways. Hypnotism was a fraud, a technique best left to charlatans at fairs. And hysteria, as the etymology of the word showed to their satisfaction, deriving as it does from "womb," must be a woman's ailment. Again, a decade later, Freud dared to present to those colleagues his subversive "seduction theory" of neuroses—the theory that all neuroses originate in sexual assaults, whether persuasion or rape, in childhood—only to have them dismiss it as nothing better than a fairy tale.[8] Freud was to abandon that theory soon after, but that is not the issue here. The point is that he was willing to stand up before fellow physicians to offer ideas that appeared to be not merely absurd but obscene.

Indeed, the ideas that Freud came to champion after he had discarded the seduction theory were, if anything, more unrespectable still: the origins of neuroses in sexual fantasies, the roots of adult erotic life in childhood sexuality, the disposition of children to "polymorphous perversion," to say nothing of Freud's conviction that a homosexual is neither a sinner, nor a madman, nor a criminal, nor a degenerate. Again, as Freud pointed out in his first, still most astonishing, masterpiece, *The Interpretation of Dreams,* in arguing that dreams have meanings that can be understood and interpreted, he was taking the side of the unlettered and the superstitious against blind philosophers and obtuse psychologists. Over and over, Freud joined his audacious championship of innovative and troubling ideas to the lament that he had been for a long time a general without an army, a pioneer wholly alone and wholly unappreciated. "For more than ten years," he wrote in his self-portrait in a characteristic reminiscence, speaking of the 1890s when he was developing the rudiments of his psychoanalytic system, "I had no followers. I was completely isolated."[9]

The historian must offer some corrections to this stark appraisal. While Freud's sense of his audacity in radically refashioning the science of mind is perfectly justified, his grievance against his scientific colleagues is rather more problematic. To be sure, contemporary reviews of his papers and books offer persuasive evidence of widespread incomprehension. In fact, in the first decade of the twentieth century, as Freud increasingly captured the attention—even the admiration—of a handful of fascinated followers, hostility to his ideas markedly grew in volume and volubility. Neurologists and psychiatrists assailed Freud's theories mercilessly, calling them ludicrous, filthy, a matter for the police rather than scientific congresses. And Freud's reviewers, though some of them were perfectly polite, did not for years fully understand, or acknowledge, the import of his innovations. Still, one might have expected Freud to tell himself that he should have anticipated nothing less: the relatively sparse attention his *Interpretation of Dreams* received, and the outright animosity his *Three Essays on the Theory of Sexuality* aroused, were wry tributes to his subversion of contemporary mental science.

After all, if Freud was right, respected professors of psychiatry and neurology would have to disavow their work of a lifetime, work that had brought them prestigious, highly visible posts at universities and in editorial offices. More than once, Freud boasted that psychoanalysis had been the third insult that intrepid investigators had offered mankind's megalomania. Copernicus had shown that the earth, and hence man, is not at the center of the universe; Darwin had linked mankind to the animal kingdom; and now he, Freud, had demonstrated that reason is not master in its own house. How else was the public, learned or lay, to respond to such offensive views except to be offended? One must not forget that Freud was himself a highly respectable nineteenth-century professional man. His preferences in furniture, entertainment, art, domestic and social life all attest to a solid bourgeois taste that did not differentiate him from other educated professional men of his time. Among those whom he frightened with his portrait of man, the insatiable animal pushed and pulled by unrespectable, largely unconscious, desires and aversions, was himself. It will not do to dismiss Freud's sense of alienation from nationalist Austrians, devout Jews, and the medical community as a mere self-indulgent pose. No doubt he derived a degree of sheer pleasure as well as intellectual profit from his self-portrait as the solitary explorer, all alone on the frontier of knowledge, his eyes fixed on unknown terrain. Surely he chose the fate under which he

9. "An Autobiographical Study," *SE* XX, 48.

labored. But the paradox of the lonely pioneer at once creating, and deploring, his loneliness is more apparent than real. Yet his self-portrait served him well. Besides it is, though somewhat simplified and distorted, largely accurate.

II. THE *PHILOSOPHE*

Freud's self-portrait as a reluctant revolutionary seems paradoxical enough. At first glance, Freud's contradictory self-definition as a philosopher and anti-philosopher appears no less paradoxical. Yet this paradox, too, will not stand up to investigation. As a young student, Freud had passionately wrestled with philosophical questions; looking back in his late years, he asserted that "after forty-one years of medical activity, my self-knowledge tells me that I have never really been a doctor in the proper sense. I became a doctor through being compelled to deviate from my original purpose; and the triumph of my life lies in my having, after a long and roundabout journey, found my way back to my earliest path," which was to "understand something of the riddles of the world in which we live and perhaps even to contribute something to their solution."[1] In a word, he was returning to philosophy at last. At the same time, Freud never tired of denigrating philosophers, all of them, by his lights, shallow men. They dismissed the unconscious from their deliberations. They departed from fruitful inquiry by investing their energies in arid logical manipulations or equally arid intuitive speculations. They played, in short, irresponsible intellectual games. Ridiculing the contemporary philosopher Hans Vaihinger for his doctrine of "as if," which advocates treating fictions as true if they are useful, Freud could think of nothing more derisive than to call this a doctrine "that only a philosopher could put forward."[2]

The resolution of these apparently paradoxical attitudes lies in Freud's largely implicit, but nonetheless sharp, distinction between true and false philosophy. A loyal son of the eighteenth-century Enlightenment, and of its seventeenth-century precursors and nineteenth-century heirs, he had only contempt for the linguistic acrobatics of metaphysicians that the pioneering ideologist of science, Francis Bacon, had already pilloried nearly three centuries before him. Like Bacon, and like the eighteenth-century *philosophes*, Freud could see nothing in metaphysical systems but dogmatic and ostentatious verbal constructions that in no way advance knowledge. Quite the contrary, precisely by pretending to advance knowledge, metaphysicians retarded it. The "spirit of system" to which such seventeenth-century thinkers as Descartes or Malebranche seemed addicted was, he thought, infinitely less effective in securing man's conquest of the world and understanding of himself than the Enlightenment's "systematic spirit."

1. "Postscript" to *The Question of Lay Analysis* (1927), SE XX, 253.   2. *The Future of an Illusion* (1927), SE XXI, 29.

This enlightened spirit is easy to define though hard to practice. It is in essence the critical spirit that humbly salutes experience as its master, corrects its conclusions by observations, tests, experiments, and exempts no dimension of life and nature—not even religion, in fact *especially* not religion—from candid, fearless examination. This was the true philosophy, the way, as the eighteenth-century *philosophes* insisted, of the natural sciences. It was the philosophy that Newton had preached and supremely embodied. The abbé de Condillac, the eighteenth century's leading philosopher of language, spoke for the whole international family of *philosophes* when he advised his fellow researchers to "avoid the mania for systems" by imitating the scientists.[3] The true philosophy needs no world view of its own.

It is essential to an understanding of Freud's thought that this is precisely how Freud read the nature of psychoanalysis. For, in his view, psychoanalysis is not theology, not metaphysics, but quite simply part of natural philosophy. His paper on "The Question of a *Weltanschauung*," the concluding selection in this anthology, which sums up a lifetime of thought, is therefore a cardinal document. It *places* Freud's creation with impressive—some might say, excessive—precision. "Psycho-analysis," Freud concludes, "in my opinion, is incapable of creating a *Weltanschauung* of its own. It does not need one; it is a part of science and can adhere to the scientific *Weltanschauung*."[4]

Freud's dismissive, unvaryingly antagonistic attitude toward religion, all religion, is at once cause, sign, and consequence of this total commitment to science. To be sure, Freud had been a declared atheist before he became a psychoanalyst. "Neither in my private life nor in my writings," he told a correspondent a year before he died, "have I ever made a secret of being an out-and-out unbeliever." But being an atheist helped him to become a psychoanalyst and mattered to his work: "Every scientific investigation of religion has unbelief as its presupposition."[5] And not just, one might add, of religion. Freud's unbelief, then, was more than mere indifference; it was an active, persistent, bellicose aversion to any religious belief or ritual whatever and the precondition for his investigations.

Not surprisingly, once again displaying his debt to the Enlightenment, Freud visualized the relation of science and religion, with a certain sublime simplicity, as war to the end. Religion, he said flatly, is the enemy, far more emotionally gripping, far more widespread and pernicious in its effects, than philosophy can ever be. It is thus characteristic of his scientific stance that Freud should devote much psychoanalytic ingenuity to a dissection of the religious impulse, its manifestations and repercussions. As a schoolboy he made jokes about it. In his early paper

3. Condillac, *Traité des systèmes*, in *Oeuvres*, ed. Georges Le Roy, 3 vols. (1947–51), I, 127. See Peter Gay, A *Godless Jew*, 52.
4. "The Question of a *Weltanschauung*," New In-troductory Lectures on Psycho-Analysis (1933), SE XXII, 181.
5. Freud to Charles Singer, October 31, 1938. Briefe, 469.

"Obsessive Actions and Religious Practices" (1907), as in *Totem and Taboo* or in his mature essay *The Future of an Illusion*, he anatomized it. In sharply observing his patients in the grip of theological ruminations, he sought to penetrate to the origins of religion in childish helplessness.

But since religion was, and had long been, at war with science, it was, for Freud, far more than an interesting and important psychological phenomenon to be observed, studied, and explained. Employing its powerful diagnostic instruments, psychoanalysis could serve at the front lines as reason's most interesting, perhaps most effective ally. Freud thought that reason, beyond which there should be no appeal, appeared to be making inroads in the domains of superstition. Yet he acknowledged that the great struggle for freedom from faith was far from won. One of Freud's self-identifications was therefore that of soldier in the brave army of rationality, wielding weapons he himself had forged. To be sure, as Freud insisted more than once, psychoanalysis was a piece of science and hence anything but tendentious. But to the extent that the advance of science meant the retreat of religion, progress in psychoanalysis could only aid the cause of reason as it tries to storm the well-fortified citadel of unreason.[6]

III. THE SCIENTIST

The professors at the University of Vienna to whose lectures he listened and in whose laboratories he worked gave Freud's youthful atheism the scientific grounding he had needed and desired. No wonder he should scatter through his writings grateful tributes to these eloquent and eminent scientists to whom he owed so much. Ernst Brücke, the famous physiologist, "who carried more weight with me than any one else in my whole life,"[7] was a characteristic nineteenth-century positivist, a scientist who had no use for vague, occult forces, for what the romantics had called "Nature Philosophy"—let alone for religion. Rather, he insisted on reducing natural phenomena to phenomena of motion. And Brücke's colleagues were no less materialist in their scientific stance. Freud would in the 1890s complicate their materialism, which made psychology into the servant of physiology. He would seek out psychological causes for psychological effects. But the essential antimetaphysical thrust of his teachers' thought remained his guide through his life.

One of the difficulties in placing Freud precisely within the community of scientists stems from his unmatched eminence as a founder. No other innovator—not Copernicus or Galileo, not Newton or Darwin or Einstein—had so few direct ancestors. Freud, of course, was not wholly alone and he knew it. While he took pride in his originality and

---

6. Here, too, an apparent paradox lies concealed: Freud, who more than any other psychologist concentrated on the workings of unreason, detecting sexual motives and death wishes behind the masks of polite manners and untroubled affection, was one of the great rationalists of the modern age. He waded into the sewers of irrationality not to wallow in them, but to clean them out.

7. Postscript to *The Question of Lay Analysis*, SE XX, 253.

never thought blushing modesty a virtue, he wryly admitted more than once that he had been anticipated by philosophers or psychologists or, even more, poëts and novelists. Thus, in his *Future of an Illusion*, after anatomizing religion as mankind's supreme illusion he conceded: "I have said nothing which other and better men have not said before me in a much more complete, forcible and expressive manner."[8] Again, on the opening page of his book on jokes he mentioned four students of the subject, and noted that Theodor Lipps's book *The Comic and Humor* of 1898 had "given me the courage to undertake this attempt as well as the possibility of doing so."[9] And, to give another instance, in a note to his essay on "Sexual Aberrations"—the first of the *Three Essays on the Theory of Sexuality*—he listed no fewer than nine investigators whose "well-known writings" had supplied him with information.[1] As he told the Austrian playwright and novelist Arthur Schnitzler, whose work he followed with admiration, he envied creative writers who discover intuitively what it had taken him years of tedious research to establish. He stayed away from Nietzsche, and from Schopenhauer, precisely because he sensed how relevant they were to his terrain, and how much of it they had already visited. Besides, there can be little doubt that Freud lived in an intellectual climate in which self-scrutiny was growing increasingly common, subjectivity increasingly scientific, and sexuality increasingly open to investigation.

For all these debts, Freud's originality remains impressive, almost unique. While, as I have noted, he was thoroughly at home in the positivist tradition and the scientific stance of Brücke and his other professors at the University of Vienna, he drastically modified their physiological psychology to devise an unprecedented dynamic psychology of his own. The immense prestige of Freud among his followers, the authority that permitted, virtually compelled, them to start their papers by invoking some appropriate texts from him, stems at least in part from his stature as an astonishing pioneer.

Yet, while the attitude of his followers has often seemed—and often enough was—anything but that of a scientist encountering theories he must test before judging them, Freud never wavered in his claim that he had indeed founded a new branch of science—a new psychology. He recognized that it was still in its infancy and thus less securely grounded than a mature science could be. He recognized, too, even insisted, that it was by its nature inhospitable to experimentation and difficult to verify. But these were parts of the price one had to pay for developing a method of penetrating to the depths of the mind—a mind, after all, whose operations are largely unconscious, which is to say, inaccessible to direct inspection.

---

8. *Future of an Illusion*, SE XXI, 35.
9. *Jokes and Their Relation to the Unconscious* (1905), SE VIII, 9.

1. *Three Essays on the Theory of Sexuality* (1905), SE VII, 135n.

IV. THE PIONEER

In 1913, at the request of an Italian scientific journal, Freud put together an extensive account of what psychoanalysis had achieved so far and promised to achieve in the future. The claims he made were far-reaching. "Psycho-analysis," he began, "is a medical procedure which aims at the cure of certain forms of nervous disease (the neuroses) by a psychological technique."[2] But this was not all that psychoanalysis had done and could do: novel as they still were, his ideas, he wrote not without some pride, had already begun to make interesting contributions to general psychology. And, Freud added, they had reached beyond psychology to such disciplines as philology, philosophy, biology, the history of culture, aesthetics, sociology, and pedagogy. He acknowledged that this Freudian invasion of other domains of inquiry had not gone unresisted. "It has not been the fate of psycho-analysis," he wrote, "to be greeted (like other young sciences) with the sympathetic encouragement of those who are interested in the advance of knowledge."[3] Still, his essay breathed a certain confidence. Psychoanalytic studies of pre-history or sociology or aesthetics might be at their very beginning, but he had little doubt that in the years ahead, psychoanalysis would widen its beach-head in cultural as much as in psychological or biological studies. And indeed, as several selections in this *Reader* demonstrate, his own work in what came to be called applied psychoanalysis proved an important impetus for extending this invasion.[4]

His measured optimism has proved largely justified. Had he written this paper a decade or more later, he could have adduced ample new evidence for the uses of psychoanalysis in fields that at first glance appeared to be quite remote from it. And he would have had to add at least two disciplines he had omitted from his enumeration of 1913: literary criticism and the arts. To say this is not to forget that the resistance to psychoanalysis remained tenacious, in psychology probably even more thorough-going than elsewhere. History, to name but one humane study, did not develop a serious interest in the uses of psychoanalysis until the mid-1950s, and for every historian confessing himself attracted to Freud's thought, there must be ten or more who continue to find themselves indifferent or openly hostile.[5] They, too, I should hope, could profit from this *Reader*.

For all this rejection of Freud, from the 1920s on, social scientists, humanists, and philosophers took a steadily increasing interest in his theories. A number of avant-garde painters and poets, the Surrealists most prominent among them, took what they wanted from psychoanalysis to perform their experiments in prompting the unconscious to

---

2. "The Claims of Psycho-Analysis to Scientific Interest," SE XIII, 165.
3. Ibid., 179.

4. See below, Part Four.
5. See Peter Gay, *Freud for Historians* (1985).

guide their productions.[6] Similarly, and with more visible results, literary critics, following the lead of Freud's paper on "Creative Writers and Daydreaming,"[7] and of such psychoanalytic publicists as Ernest Jones and Otto Rank, began working with Freudian ideas to explicate the psychology of the writer, of fictional characters, and of audiences. A few critics, indeed, ventured to psychoanalyze imaginary figures, like Hamlet, as though they were living human beings.[8] Others, among them so distinguished a literary essayist as Lionel Trilling, wholly sympathetic to Freud, once again canvassed the old question whether artistic creativity must spring from neurotic suffering.[9] D. H. Lawrence, though he never accepted Freud as a whole, did not escape his influence and translated Freud's thought, especially about sexuality, into his own excited, mystical irrationalism. For his part, Franz Kafka came to Freud largely through fragmentary readings, but his diary for September 1912, after he had completed the important, chilling story "The Judgment," firmly notes, "Thoughts of Freud, of course."[1] One of Kafka's recent biographers, Ronald Hayman, justly observes that Kafka's fascination with his dreams stemmed from his reading of Freud.[2]

The influence of Freud on untold numbers of other imaginative writers has by and large followed quite similar paths: with reading that ranged from scattered to systematic, with verdicts that ranged from vigorous (but productive) dissent to partial agreement to wholesale appropriation. In May 1936, in a speech celebrating Freud's eightieth birthday, Thomas Mann asserted that the spheres of psychoanalytic science and literary art had long enjoyed a "profound sympathy," though "for a long time unperceived." Their bond, he added, was twofold, "a love of truth," a "sensitiveness and receptivity for truth's sweet and bitter," and a "clarity of vision," combined with "an understanding of disease, a certain affinity with it, outweighed by fundamental health, and an understanding of its productive significance." And he added: "We shall one day recognize in Freud's life-work the cornerstone for the building of a new anthropology and therewith of a new structure, to which many stones are being brought up today, which shall be the future dwelling of a wiser and freer humanity."[3] In a birthday tribute, one might say, paraphrasing Samuel Johnson on epitaphs, an author is not an oath. But the evidence shows that Thomas Mann was speaking sincerely, and not only for himself.

6. See the fine study by Jack J. Spector, *The Aesthetics of Freud: A Study in Psychoanalysis and Art* (1972), esp. ch. 4.

7. See below, pp. 436–43.

8. Among a number of anthologies, perhaps the most comprehensive is *Literature and Psychoanalysis*, ed. Edith Kurzweil and William Phillips (1983).

9. See Trilling's "Art and Neurosis" (1945), conveniently reprinted in Kurzweil and Phillips,

op. cit.

1. Kafka, September 23, 1912. *Tagebücher*, ed. Max Brod (ed. 1967), 210.

2. "Without Freud he might never have come to take so much interest in his own dreams." Hayman, *Kafka: A Biography* (1981), 1.

3. Thomas Mann, "Freud and the Future" (1936), in *Essays of Three Decades*, tr. H. T. Lowe-Porter (1947), 412–13, 417.

For their part, especially from the 1930s on, eminent social scientists—notably sociologists, political scientists, and cultural anthropologists—welcomed psychoanalytic ideas as a particularly useful aide in the examination of group behavior, primitive ritual, religious bigotry, political fanaticism, and social cohesion or social conflict in general. In these disciplines, as in others, psychoanalysis has remained controversial, and some of the enthusiasm for the simple answers that Freud was expected to supply has rather faded. Still, the *relevance* of Freud to the social sciences remains unquestioned. If, as Freud and his followers have argued with a good show of justification, his fundamental description of human nature holds true not just for the patients he saw in his consulting room, but for all humanity—not just for late-nineteenth-century Viennese, but for ancient Greeks and contemporary Trobriand Islanders as well—psychoanalysis must of necessity have much of value for those disciplines that study human nature at work in culture. It may be, as a good deal of still highly tentative scholarship suggests, that some of Freud's theories may require careful reexamination, serious modification, perhaps even replacement. But his general model of the mind—the central role of the dynamic unconscious and of defensive maneuvers in mental work, the continuing impact of infantile sexuality and aggressiveness on adult life, the inescapability of inner conflict—remains a solid, indeed indispensable, contribution to our knowledge of the human mind.

The gradual return to Freud that the spread of sober, less polemical literature is fostering is particularly dramatic in a field that has long had a somewhat embittered, largely adversarial relationship to his ideas: academic psychology. For a number of years, American or English undergraduates seeking clarity, or even the most basic information, about Freud could obtain it only in departments of literature. To be sure, several critics of Freud among psychologists adopted the somewhat conciliatory line taken in 1935 by the well-known and prolific social psychologist William McDougall in a series of lectures at the University of London: McDougall professed his great respect for Freud on both moral and intellectual grounds and launched what he called his "ruthless" critique of psychoanalysis with the proviso that he did so because the Freudian "system" was, in his judgment, the one "most deserving of honest criticism."[4] But other behaviorist psychologists, like the prominent English experimental psychologist H. J. Eysenck, went much further to argue flatly, and often, that Freud's ideas were neither new nor true, and in any event wholly untestable.[5]

This outright dismissive attitude is changing and changing drastically. Nowadays, more psychologists, it would appear, take their cue from McDougall than from Eysenck. A leading recent textbook like Henry

4. McDougall, *Psycho-Analysis and Social Psychology* (1936), vi.
5. See, for one instance, the Pelican paperback addressed to a general audience, *Sense and Nonsense in Psychology* (1957).

Gleitman's *Psychology* (first published in 1981 and in a second edition in 1986), which covers every aspect of psychology from action and cognition to social behavior, personal development, and individual differences, devotes an entire—and entirely respectful—chapter to "The Contributions of Sigmund Freud." Freud's views, Gleitman observes, looking back, "were to revolutionize all subsequent accounts of what humans are really like."[6] He is far from wholly uncritical: without being able to proffer a new theory of his own, Gleitman expresses some serious reservations about Freud's dream theory, his therapeutic techniques, and his way of demonstrating psychoanalytic theoretical claims. Despite it all, Gleitman remains convinced, largely on the basis of experimental evidence gathered outside the psychoanalytic setting, that such fundamental Freudian ideas as "unconscious conflict and defense are probably genuine phenomena."[7] In this context, it is interesting to observe that psychologists who have rejected a Freudian theory and are proposing a rival theory of their own still find it necessary to attack Freud in considerable detail and with an almost anxious vehemence. Whatever the individual style of those psychologists who remain unpersuaded by Freud, his recent opponents have left no doubt that Freud remains the classic figure in psychology—the man to beat. Somewhat unintentionally, this posture helps to shore up a stature that Freud has, of course, never lost among his admirers, whether they are psychoanalysts or not.

V. THE ORGANIZER

Psychoanalysis was not a machine that went by itself. As I have noted, after surmounting limited attention and deliberate silence, Freud's ideas aroused continuous, often envenomed, disputes. Psychologists, psychiatrists, neurologists, and, after a time, pedagogues, social scientists, editorial writers, and theologians thought it necessary to have opinions about psychoanalytic theories of the unconscious, the sexual roots of aesthetics and morality, the infantile origins of neuroses, and other scandals like them. There came a time, around 1910, when Freud, who had earlier complained of being ostracized, wryly thought back to his first quiet days, the days of neglect, with some nostalgia.

Still, with considerable combative energy and a lively taste for polemics, Freud entered the fray. He expanded his activities. If, before 1900, his sole concern had been the cultivation of his ideas, after that date, he plunged with a will into popularization and into controversy. He delivered—and published—lectures designed to be accessible to wider audiences; he grudgingly but diligently took precious time to write articles on psychoanalysis for encyclopedias and medical compendia; he harangued adversaries beyond, and dissidents within, the psychoanalytic fold. One characteristic product of Freud the fighter at work was his

6. Gleitman, *Psychology* (2nd ed., 1986), 412.   7. Ibid., 432.

polemical and tendentious *History of the Psycho-Analytic Movement*, which appeared in June 1914. It was directed against Alfred Adler and Carl Jung, who both, in his view, each in his way, had tried to substitute watered-down psychological theories for the hard truths of psychoanalysis. The pamphlet was known affectionately, to Freud and to his delighted adherents, as "the bomb." Another, far more popular, venture was the series of lectures he gave at the University of Vienna between 1915 and 1917, in the midst of the First World War. He spoke, as he put it, to "a mixed audience of physicians and laymen of both sexes."[8] Cunningly, he began with ordinary experiences—slips of the tongue and pen and other "caused" mental accidents, then moved on to dreams, and finally to the more technical subject of the neuroses. The lectures, once published, proved an immense success: some fifty thousand copies appear to have been sold in Freud's lifetime, in at least fifteen languages.[9]

All these pointed acts of explanation and aggression were part of Freud's effort at mobilizing and molding his followers, who were thinly scattered across Western culture, chiefly concentrated in metropolitan centers like Vienna, Berlin, Budapest, London, and New York. Under his alert, indefatigable leadership, exercised at home as he called in his lieutenants for urgent consultations, at psychoanalytic congresses in sessions devoted to organizational detail, and, perhaps most important, by mail—Freud was a prompt, one may say obsessive, correspondent—psychoanalysis grew from a cluster of scientific ideas into a movement. Freud has left accounts of all these activities: the founding of the Wednesday night group meeting at his house from late 1902, the transformation of this informal association into the Vienna Psychoanalytic Society six years later, his part in founding psychoanalytic periodicals, his collaboration and conflicts with Adler and Jung. Hence it is not necessary to dwell on them here.[1] But some observations are in order. Above all, it will be useful to confront the argument that Freud's supremacy made psychoanalysis into a sect, indeed into a religion.

The charge is an old one and finds some support in occasional, infelicitous metaphors used by Freud and by his closest adherents. He could speak of "the religion of science."[2] And his friend, the Swiss pastor Oskar Pfister, called Freud's set of ideas a "substitute religion."[3] But for the most part it has been Freud's critics—and, let me not shy away from the word, enemies—who have enjoyed this game. It is easy to play: Freud is the pope or a prophet. His most eminent followers have formed a submissive college of cardinals or a band of high priests. His constructions are the sacred doctrine to which everyone must slavishly subscribe or be banished into outer darkness. His pronouncements have the authority of a papal encyclical. His public controversies amount to heresy

8. "Preface" to *Introductory Lectures on Psycho-Analysis,* SE XV, 9.
9. See Peter Gay, *Freud: A Life for Our Time* (1988), 369.
1. See above all his "Autobiographical Study," be-

low, pp. 3–41.
2. Freud to Fliess, February 6, 1899. *Freud-Fliess,* 376.
3. Pfister to Freud, November 24, 1927. *Freud-Pfister, Briefe,* 123.

trials. His zealous work of popularization is a mission to the heathen.[4] His "god logos," whom he apostrophizes in *The Future of an Illusion,* is a theological entity no less than any of the gods that other religions produce. And so forth.

All this is amusing and seductive. Nor is it pure absurdity. The psychoanalysts delivering papers who, during Freud's late years and for decades after his death, sought to prove their points by finding some suitable quotations in the Founder, more or less unwittingly contributed to the legend of Freud the infallible authority. At the same time, the record shows that Freud repeatedly, insistently, and quite sincerely refused the mantle of final arbiter. He worried over followers who took his word for everything and encouraged them to explore the depths of the mind in their own way. He was not only sensitive, but also open, to criticism, and capable of revising some of his most cherished ideas: the etiology of the neuroses, the nature of anxiety, the psychology of women, the very structure of the mind. Ernest Jones could vocally dissent from Freud's late papers on female sexuality without being read out of the psychoanalytic clan. Melanie Klein could advocate radical revisions of Freud's theory of aggression and his schedule for the onset of the Oedipus complex—and, for that matter, savage his cherished daughter Anna's practice of child analysis—without being damned as an enemy to the clan. The reproach that Freud found it necessary to quarrel with everyone because he was intolerant of dissent seems to have touched a raw spot in him. Otherwise he would not have troubled to list, in his "Autobiographical Study," the names of those, like Karl Abraham, Ernest Jones, Oskar Pfister, Max Eitingon, and a half dozen others, with whom he had worked "in loyal collaboration and for the most part in uninterrupted friendship." He was virtually pleading for understanding when he added, "I think I can say in my defense that an intolerant man, dominated by an arrogant belief in his own infallibility, would never have been able to maintain his hold upon so large a number of intellectually eminent people, especially if he had at his command as few practical attractions as I had."[5]

But Freud also clearly recognized, reasonably enough, that this collaboration must necessarily be grounded in agreement on fundamentals. He had across the years arrived at a small number of essential principles— he called them the shibboleths—that define psychoanalysis. The departure of Adler and Jung, the two most spectacular defectors from the Freudian camp, were not excommunications: both men saw the disputes that in the end led to an irreparable rift with Freud as something of a liberation—an opportunity to found psychologies of their own. Hence they were no longer psychoanalysts. "If a community is based on agree-

4. This is not mere fancy. For detailed documentation, see Peter Gay, *A Godless Jew,* esp. pp. 17–21.
5. "Autobiographical Study," *SE* XX, 53 (see below, pp. 33–34.) It is interesting to note that when one or another of his followers showed signs of departing from the indispensable tenets of psychoanalysis—like Otto Rank in 1923—Freud would be the last of his inner circle to brand him another Jung or Adler: if Freud was the pope, Jones or Abraham were more papist than he.

ment upon a few cardinal points," Freud observed in his "Auto-biographical Study," "it is obvious that people who have abandoned that common ground will cease to belong to it."[6] To call oneself a Roman Catholic while, at the same time, denying the Trinity or the Resurrection, would be a transparent inconsistency. The same must hold true of psychoanalysis: one cannot logically claim to belong to its camp while denying the existence of a dynamic unconscious, of infantile sexuality, of a libidinal drive separate from aggression, of repression and other defenses. At the same time, the psychoanalytic literature of the last half century has amply demonstrated that the Freudian school of thought allows elbow room for divergent views, and, above all, for development. To be sure, there have been some vehement, even ugly factional fights within the psychoanalytic establishment. But, to repeat, the Freudian legacy remains open.

Indeed, as I have observed, Freud left it open. In a long lifetime of psychoanalytic theorizing, he shifted from one fundamental theoretical conception, the so-called "topographic" theory, to another, the "structural" theory. In the first, he laid down as fundamental the relation of thoughts to consciousness: thoughts are conscious, on the surface of the mind; preconscious, not immediately available but, as it were, buried so shallowly that access to them offers no particular difficulty; and unconscious, driven back into remote regions of the mind from which they try to escape. Freud's theory of the drives that accompanied this conception was constructed on the confrontation of sexual with egotistical drives.[7] Then he was assailed by doubts, doubts he canvassed brilliantly if still somewhat tentatively, in his crucial paper on "Narcissism."[8] Finally, after the war, he offered a revised theory of the drives, first in *Beyond the Pleasure Principle* in 1920, and three years later in his epochal *The Ego and the Id*.[9] His somber rumination on culture, his *Civilization and Its Discontents* of 1930, which remains one of his most widely read books, rests completely on this new structural view. Having long delayed the recognition of aggression as a fundamental human endowment, Freud, in his late years, confessed that he could no longer conceive of the mind without it. While in this new phase he retained his traditional division of conscious, preconscious, and unconscious, he now postulated a no less dramatic confrontation of drives: the drive toward life and that toward death. Such revisions, and others like them, made his followers uneasy, but they pointed to the next assignment of theoretically minded psychoanalysts: to examine, test, and, if necessary, revise the very fundamentals of psychoanalytic thought.

Freud's theory, then, does remain open. Yet it is not formless, chaotic. No doubt, the student of the mind working half a century after Freud's

6. Ibid.
7. See below, pp. 562–68.

8. See below, pp. 545–62.
9. See below, pp. 594–626, 628–58.

death must look at the progress of psychoanalysis by studying the developments that have enriched, and sometimes confused, the picture. The most promising new terrain is the observation, and analysis, of children, with their magnificent opportunities for the close study of psychological development. And the controversies, even over such fundamental ideas as the status of aggression as an independent drive, continue. But they are all based, quite directly, on the work of the founder, who remains one of the most influential spirits of the modern age. It is to the sweeping survey of this work that I have devoted this *Reader*.

Sigmund Freud: A Chronology

1855   (July 29) Jacob Freud marries Amalia Nathansohn, his third wife, in Vienna and takes her to Freiberg in Moravia, where two sons from his first marriage, Emanuel and Philipp, live.

1856   (May 6) Sigismund Schlomo Freud born.
(May 13) Freud is circumcised.

1857   (October) Julius Freud, Freud's first brother, is born.

1858   (April 15) Julius Freud dies.
(December 15) Anna, Freud's first sister, is born.

1859   (August) The Freuds leave Freiberg and first go to Leipzig.

1860   (March) The Freuds settle in Vienna, under most impecunious circumstances.
(March 21) Regine Debora (Rosa), Freud's second sister, is born.
(June 28) Sam Freud, son of Emanuel and Maria Freud, is born in Manchester, to which Emanuel and Philipp Freud had moved. Sam Freud would become a welcome and assiduous resource to the hungry and cold Freuds after the First World War.

1861   (March 22) Maria (Mitzi), Freud's third sister, is born.
(July 26) Martha Bernays (Freud's future wife) is born in Wandsbek near Hamburg.

1862   (July 23) Esther Adolfine (Dolfi), Freud's fourth sister, is born.

1864   (May 3) Pauline Regine (Paula), Freud's fifth and last sister, is born.

1865   (July 20) Josef, Freud's uncle, is arrested in Vienna for circulating forged ruble notes, tried, convicted, and sentenced (February 22, 1866) to ten years in prison. The event, Freud later recalled, turned his father's hair gray.
(Fall) Freud is enrolled in the Leopoldstädter Real- und Obergymnasium. He does brilliantly from the outset. The family is beginning to be somewhat better off.

1866   (April 19) Alexander, Freud's brother, is born. This completes the Freud family.

1870   (Winter) Freud and his intimate school friend, Eduard Silberstein, visit the family of another school friend, Emil Fluss, in his birthplace, Freiberg.

1872   (Early August to mid-September) Freud makes a second visit to the Fluss family and undergoes an adolescent infatuation with Emil's sister Gisela.

1873 (July) Freud graduates from his Gymnasium by passing (most impressively) his examinations.

(Fall) Freud enrolls in the medical faculty at Vienna University after changing his choice of career from the law. At first, he scatters the courses across a wide humanistic spectrum.

Henrik Ibsen (1828–1906), the great Norwegian dramatist whom Freud repeatedly quotes, moves to Germany (to stay until 1891). There he writes some of his most important plays: *The Pillars of Society* (1877), *A Doll's House* (1879), *Ghosts* (1881), and *An Enemy of the People* (1882).

1875 Freud makes his first foray to his beloved England, visiting his half-brothers in Manchester.

1876 (Spring) Freud obtains a coveted grant to do research on the gonads of eels at the Zoological Experimental Station his university maintains at Trieste. His work is creditable, though scarcely sensational.

1877 Freud joins the formidable Ernst Brücke, the celebrated German physiologist teaching at the University of Vienna, by Freud's testimony the most important teacher in his life.

Emile Zola (1840–1902), the noted French Realist whose writings Freud highly recommended, publishes *L'Assommoir*, one of the two or three best-known of his twenty-volume Rougon-Macquart cycle. Others are *Nana* (1880) and *Germinal* (1885).

1880 (July) "Fräulein Anna O.,"—really Bertha Pappenheim—a most intelligent and sensitive young woman of twenty-one, falls ill with a set of spectacular and increasingly bizarre hysterical symptoms. Late that year, Josef Breuer, a prominent and highly respected internist whom Freud had met some time before, begins to treat her. More or less unwittingly, in developing the "talking cure," Breuer makes Anna O. into the founding patient of psychoanalysis. In years to come, Freud will press Breuer again and again for intimate clinical details concerning this fascinating patient.

1881 Freud finally obtains his medical degree, after delays caused by his passion for research.

1882 (April) Freud meets and quickly falls in love with Martha Bernays.

(June 17) The couple, too poor to marry, become secretly engaged.

(Fall) Freud decides (upon Brücke's urging) to prepare himself for medical practice, to permit him to marry. He begins to train himself in the Vienna General Hospital, moving from department to department.

1883 Freud leaves home and moves into the hospital.

(October) Freud's sister Anna marries Eli Bernays. The couple will later emigrate to the United States and prosper there.

1884 (April) Freud starts research on cocaine, whose properties were still virtually unknown.

(July) Freud publishes an enthusiastic paper, "On Coca." But the credit for discovering—among its other properties—its possible role as an anesthetic for minor operations on the eye largely goes to Freud's colleagues.

Johan August Strindberg (1849–1912), Swedish playwright and novelist, publishes the first volume of his autobiographical "novels," *Married*, to be followed by others down to 1909.

1885 (September 5) Freud is appointed Privatdozent, the first step on the long, steep ladder of academic preferment.

(Early October) After receiving a skimpy grant to study in Paris with the famous innovative French neurologist Jean-Martin Charcot, Freud visits his fiancée, her mother and sister, in Wandsbek (he has been there before).

(October 11) Freud arrives in Paris and begins work under Charcot's supervision at the Salpêtrière, the mental hospital where Charcot, who takes both hysteria and hypnosis seriously, "demonstrates" his hysterical patients.

1886 (February 28) Freud leaves Paris after a most fruitful stay and closer acquaintance with Charcot and returns via Berlin, where he studies children's diseases for some weeks.

(April 15) Freud opens his private practice.

(September 13) Freud and Martha Bernays marry.

(October 15) Freud lectures to the Imperial and Royal Society of Physicians on male hysteria and is challenged by one of his teachers, the eminent professor Theodor Meynert, to present cases of male hysteria.

(November 26) Freud takes up Meynert's challenge before the same medical society. His presentation is printed in the *Wiener Medizinische Wochenschrift*.

1887 (October 16) Mathilde, the Freuds' first child, is born, named after Frau Breuer.

(November) Freud meets the Berlin ear-nose-and-throat specialist Wilhelm Fliess, the most intimate—only intimate—friend for the next decade, with whom he carries on an immensely revealing emotional and scientific correspondence.

1888 Freud begins to publish papers on a variety of neurological and psychiatric subjects in A. Villaret's *Handlexicon of All Medicine*.

1889 (May 1) Freud starts the treatment of "Frau Emmy von N.," who will be one of his case histories in *Studies on Hysteria* (see below, 1895).

Freud returns to France, to Nancy, accompanied by a patient (probably Emmy von N.), to discuss hypnotic technique with Professor Hippolyte Bernheim.

(December 6) Jean Martin, known as Martin, the Freuds' second child, is born, named after Charcot.

1890   (August) Freud has one of his refreshing conferences (the two called them "congresses") with Fliess.

1891   (February 19) Oliver, the Freuds' third child, named after Cromwell, is born.

(September 20, 1891) Freud moves with his family to Berggasse 19, a house in which he will live for forty-seven years.

Freud publishes, with his friend Oskar Rie, a clinical study on infantile cerebral paralysis.

He also publishes an original brief "critical study" on the aphasias, which, despite its concern with neurology, begins to show an interest in the psychological side of mental functioning.

1892   As he has done several times before, Freud brings out translations of French scientific texts—this year, Bernheim's study on hypnotism and suggestion.

(April 6) Ernst, the Freuds' fourth child, is born; he is named after Brücke.

As his friendship with Fliess intensifies, the two men adopt the familiar "du," and he begins to flood Fliess with long memoranda detailing his radical psychological conjectures.

(Fall) Freud takes into treatment "Elisabeth von R.," another of his case histories in Studies on Hysteria. He treats her with little hypnosis. The listening cure is on its way.

Arthur Schnitzler (1862–1931), the Viennese physician, novelist, and playwright whose work Freud greatly appreciated, publishes Anatol.

1893   (January) Freud publishes, with Breuer, a "preliminary communication," two years later to be incorporated into the Studies on Hysteria, on the mechanisms of hysterical phenomena.

(April 12) Sophie, the Freuds' fifth child, is born, named after a niece of Samuel Hammerschlag, his cherished religion teacher at Gymnasium.

(August) Charcot dies. Freud publishes a detailed and illuminating appreciation in September.

(Fall) Freud suffers from cardiac symptoms that will intermittently trouble him across the decades. On Fliess's emphatic recommendation, Freud tries to quit smoking—more or less in vain—with frequent relapses.

1894   (January) Freud publishes "The Neuro-Psychoses of Defense," which stresses the sexual etiology of hysteria and serves to widen the breach with his good friend Breuer, which had begun somewhat earlier.

(March, through the spring) Cardiac symptoms and "death deliria."

(May–June) Freud plans a monograph on the neuroses, defines anxiety as transformed libido, and begins to classify the neuroses, hitherto loosely called "neurasthenia," in a more discriminating way.

Alfred Dreyfus (1859–1935), a French-Jewish general staff officer, is accused (on forged evidence) and convicted of treason for passing secret documents to the Germans. The case, at once the consequence and the cause of anti-semitism, achieves international notoriety.

1895   (January) Publishes the fruit of his thoughts with "On the Grounds for Detaching a Particular Syndrome from Neurasthenia under the Description 'Anxiety Neurosis.' "

(Late February) Fliess operates on Freud's patient Emma Eckstein's nose and, with spectacular incompetence, nearly kills her by leaving a strip of gauze in it. Freud spends valuable time, into 1896, seeking an alibi for his friend.

(May) Breuer and Freud's *Studies on Hysteria*, a collaborative effort, containing papers on theory and therapy, and important case histories, including Anna O., is published, though the two men no longer see eye to eye.

(July 24) Living in his summer headquarters, Bellevue, just outside Vienna, Freud dreams and then fully interprets the classic dream of psychoanalysis, the "dream of Irma's injection." It takes pride of place in Freud's *Interpretation of Dreams*, published a little more than four years later.

(Early September) With his brother Alexander, Freud goes sightseeing in Italy for the first time, confining himself to Venice, Bologna, Florence, and other north-Italian cities, but, haunted by a neurotic inhibition, stopping short of the city he wants to see most: Rome.

(September 4) Freud has one of his stimulating "congresses" with Fliess, this time in Berlin. On the train to Vienna, he starts on his so-called "Project," an ambitious "psychology for neurologists" that he will leave unfinished and unpublished.

(October 8) Freud sends the fragmentary "Project" to Fliess.

(October 15, 16) Freud, writing to Fliess, argues that hysteria is caused by a sexual shock, obsessional neurosis by premature sexual pleasure.

(October 31) Freud doubts his earlier theorizing on the etiology of the neuroses, but remains committed to it.

(December 3) Anna, the Freuds' sixth, last, and eventually only famous child is born. Had it been a boy, Freud tell Fliess, the infant would have been called "Wilhelm." Since it is a girl, Freud names it after a daughter of Samuel Hammerschlag.

(December) Minna Bernays, Martha Freud's unmarried sister, who has been a frequent and welcome visitor at Berggasse 19, moves in permanently.

Through the year, Freud develops his ideas on melancholia, paranoia, migraine, obsessive rituals, and phobias in long memoranda to Fliess.

William Butler Yeats (1865–1939), first collected poems.

1896   (March 30) Freud publishes "Heredity and the Aetiology of the Neuroses" (in French); the word "psychoanalysis" appears here for the first time.

(April 21) Freud lectures to the Society for Psychiatry and Neurology in Vienna on "The Aetiology of Hysteria," published the end of May. His paper, detailing the so-called "seduction theory" of the neuroses, receives a notably unfriendly reception.

(mid-June) His aged father falls ill, and Freud cancels a congress with Fliess.

(October 23) Jacob Freud dies, a crucial moment in Freud's life, with which he wrestles for years.

(Fall) Freud's psychological speculations continue, but he also broods on his own early death.

Theodor Herzl (1860–1902) publishes his epochal pamphlet, *Der Judenstaat—The State of the Jews*, an eloquent plea for Zionism.

1897   (January) Freud continues to work on the "seduction theory."

(February) Hermann Nothnagel, one of Freud's professors, recommends him for an "extraordinary" (roughly associate) professorship.

(Summer and fall) Freud reports to Fliess, at once exhilarated and exhausted, that he has been carrying on the hardest of analyses—his self-analysis—and that it is making intermittent but dramatic progress.

(September 21) Freud, returning from his summer holiday, informs Fliess that he has abandoned the "seduction theory." The way to an understanding of fantasy is now open.

(October 15) Freud writes Fliess that he has understood the "gripping power" of Sophocles' *Oedipus Rex*: the tragedy enshrines the universal experience of the boy loving his mother and being jealous of his father.

(December 3) Freud tells Fliess that his reluctance to visit Rome is "deeply neurotic." Other self-analytical insights abound.

1898   A year of intense labor on the manuscript of *The Interpretation of Dreams*.

Frequent congresses with Fliess.

1899   Working to complete his "dream book," Freud attempts to analyze his inhibition against visiting Rome.

(September) Freud's revealing, partly autobiographical paper "Screen Memories" is published.

(September 11) Freud announces that he has completed the book.

(October 11) Freud informs Fliess that his next project will probably be a theory of sexuality.

(November 4) *The Interpretation of Dreams* is published, bearing the date 1900.

Karl Kraus (1874–1936), the great satirist and guardian of the German language whom Freud respected, begins to publish (and largely write) his periodical, *Die Fackel* (*The Torch*).

Captain Dreyfus wins a retrial but is convicted once again.

1900   (Early part of the year) Freud responds rather grimly to the mixed reception of his dream book.

(June 12) Freud, at Bellevue, wonders in a letter to Fliess whether some day it will bear a plaque, "In This House, on July 24th, 1895 the Secret of Dreams was Revealed to Dr. Sigm. Freud."

(August) Freud and Fliess, on holiday at Achensee, quarrel bitterly.

(October 14) "Dora" enters analysis with Freud.

Thomas Mann (1875–1955) publishes *Buddenbrooks*.

Pablo Picasso (1881–1973), the great Spanish painter, moves to Paris; he launches on his "Blue Period" the following year.

1901   (January 25) Freud completes "Fragment of an Analysis of a Case of Hysteria," the Dora case (see 1905).

(July and August) *The Psychopathology of Everyday Life* published in two issues of a psychiatric journal (the book will appear in 1904).

(Late August—early September) Freud finally goes to Rome, accompanied by his brother Alexander. It is a breakthrough for him.

1902   (March) Freud is appointed *Ausserordentlicher Professor* after using some of his connections.

(October) Following the suggestion of his (later wayward) disciple Wilhelm Stekel, Freud founds the Psychological Wednesday Society, which includes, in addition to these two, Alfred Adler (1870–1937), Max Kahane, and Rudolf Reitler.

Dmitri Sergeyevich Merezhkovsky (1865–1941), Russian utopian novelist, publishes *The Romance of Leonardo da Vinci*, on which Freud will rely in his paper on Leonardo.

1904   (July 27) Freud writes his last letter to Fliess; their correspondence had been dwindling.

Ivan Petrovich Pavlov (1849–1936), experimental psychologist and physiologist, awarded the Nobel Prize for Physiology and Medicine.

1905   Freud publishes *Jokes and Their Relation to the Unconscious,*
and, more important, *Three Essays on the Theory of Sexuality,*
the latter a worthy companion to *The Interpretation of Dreams.*
Albert Einstein (1879–1955) develops special theory of relativity.
(October and November) The Dora case is published.

1906   (April 11) Freud writes his first letter to Carl G. Jung (1875–
1961), gratefully acknowledging a copy of Jung's *Diagnostic As-
sociation Studies.*
(May 6) Freud is fifty.
(September) Freud's first collection of papers on neuroses pub-
lished, including material from 1893 to 1906.
(October 10) The first session of the Wednesday Psychological
Society at which Freud's young protégé Otto Rank takes notes.
Dreyfus is completely rehabilitated, reinstated, and decorated.

1907   (Late January) Max Eitingon, the first of the "Zurichers," calls
on Freud.
(March) Jung's first visit to Berggasse 19.
(April) "Obsessive Actions and Religious Practices," Freud's
opening gun in the psychoanalysis of religion.
(June 25) Karl Abraham sends his first letter to Freud.
(June) "The Sexual Enlightenment of Children," a brief analytic
plea for frankness with children.
Freud publishes "Delusions and Dreams in Jensen's *Gradiva,*"
his first published analysis of a literary work.
(December) Karl Abraham visits Freud for the first time.
Picasso paints, but does not exhibit, his revolutionary canvas,
Les demoiselles d'Avignon.

1908   (February 2) Sandor Ferenczi calls on Freud for the first time,
and the two rapidly become close friends.
(March) "Creative Writers and Day-Dreaming," a paper earlier
delivered to a lay audience on December 6, 1907, published.
(March) Freud publishes one of his few ventures into psychoanalytic characterology, "Character and Anal Erotism."
(March) " 'Civilized' Sexual Morality and Modern Nervous Illness," the first paper in the psychoanalysis of culture.
(Late April) The first international congress of psychoanalysts at
Salzburg. Freud lectures for more than four hours on his patient,
the "Rat Man" (see 1909); Ernest Jones meets, and is dazzled
by, Freud.
(April) The Wednesday Psychological Society is transformed into
the more formal Vienna Psychoanalytical Society.
(September) Freud's second visit to England, and he stops off
to see Jung in Zurich.
(December) "On the Sexual Theories of Children."
Schnitzler publishes *Der Weg ins Freie (The Road to the Open),*
his most remarkable novel.

With Georges Braque (1881–1963), Picasso moves into his experimental Cubist period.

1909   (January) Jung becomes editor of the newly founded *Yearbook for Psychosomatic and Psychopathological Investigations*. The lead piece is Freud's case history of "Little Hans"—"Analysis of a Phobia in a Five-Year-Old Boy."

(January 18) Freud writes his first letter to the Zurich pastor Oskar Pfister, acknowledging an offprint; the two men will become fast friends soon.

(February 7) Mathilde, Freud's eldest, the first to leave the household, marries Robert Hollitscher.

Freud's case history of the Rat Man, "Notes Upon a Case of Obsessional Neurosis," is published in the second number of the *Yearbook*.

(September) Freud visits, to lecture and receive an honorary doctorate of laws, Clark University at Worcester, Massachusetts, in the company of Jung and Ferenczi.

1910   (February) A wealthy young Russian patient, who will become famous as the "Wolf Man" (see 1918), enters analysis with Freud.

(March) Second international psychoanalytic congress meets in Nürnberg. Jung is elected president of the newly founded International Psychoanalytic Association; his relative and colleague Franz Riklin becomes secretary. The Viennese, seeing themselves (quite accurately) eclipsed by Zurich, especially by Freud's "son" and "crown prince," Jung, protest vehemently but largely in vain.

(April) Reconciliation in Vienna; Stekel and Adler are made editors of a new professional periodical, the *Zentralblatt*. But Freud is becoming irritated with Adler, whose theories seem increasingly remote from his own.

(May) Publication of Freud's long essay "Leonardo da Vinci and a Memory of his Childhood," a venture into fragmentary psychobiography.

(September) Freud takes a long, emotionally unsatisfying, holiday tour, chiefly to Sicily with Ferenczi, who is excessively filial.

Five Lectures on Psychoanalysis, the English version of Freud's lectures at Clark (delivered in German).

Freud publishes, in the *Yearbook*, the first of three "Contributions to the Psychology of Love," titled "A Special Type of Choice of Object Made by Men." The second, "On the Universal Tendency to Debasement in the Sphere of Love," will follow in 1912; the third, "The Taboo of Virginity," in 1917.

Yeats publishes *The Green Helmet and Other Poems*.

1911   Freud publishes an important short paper, "Formulations on

the Two Principles of Mental Functioning," followed by the
"Schreber case," officially called "Psycho-Analytic Notes on an
Autobiographical Account of a Case of Paranoia (Dementia Par-
anoides)," in the first number of the third volume of the
Yearbook.

(June) Adler resigns from the Vienna Psychoanalytic Society;
his adherents will follow him in October. The gap between
Freud and Jung, at first imperceptible, is beginning to widen.

(September 21–22) Third international congress of psychoanalysts, at Weimar; Freud speaks on a "postscript" to the recently
published Schreber case.

(December) Freud brings out the first of his epochal series of
papers on psychoanalytic technique, "The Handling of Dream-
Interpretation." Others, on transference, on beginning the treatment, on working through, on transference love, will follow
between 1912 and 1915. They take the place of a book on
technique Freud never wrote.

1912   (Through the early part of the year) Dissensions in the Vienna
Society, notably with Stekel, continue. Tensions between Freud
and Jung mount.

(March) Publication of "The Horror of Incest," the first of four
linked papers (published together in 1913 under the collective
title *Totem and Taboo*).

(April 24) The Vienna Psychoanalytic Society successfully concludes a set of discussions on masturbation, initiated in November 22, 1911; later published with a contribution by Freud.

Freud and his colleagues found *Imago*, a psychoanalytic journal
devoted to cultural questions, edited by Otto Rank and Hanns
Sachs.

(Summer) Ernest Jones, sensing that Freud needs protection
from the rising storms emerging from Zurich, sets up the "Committee," a Pretorian Guard consisting of Freud, Jones, Rank,
Ferenczi, Abraham, Sachs (and, from 1919 on, Eitingon).

(Fall) The formidable intellectual and "muse," Lou Andreas-
Salomé, to become one of Freud's (and Anna Freud's) closest
friends, comes to Vienna to study psychoanalysis.

(October) Stekel resigns, leaving the Vienna Psychoanalytic Society entirely to Freud and his loyal adherents.

(November) Freud founds *Internationale Zeitschrift für ärztliche
Psychoanalyse (International Journal for Medical Psychoanalysis)*.

(December) After a most uneasy summer and a fleeting reconciliation, Freud and Jung virtually cease speaking to one
another.

Jung publishes *Theory of Psychoanalysis*.

Schnitzler's play *Dr. Bernhardi*, a tragic story of a Jewish physician in Vienna.

Gerhart Hauptmann (1862–1946), German playwright and novelist, awarded the Nobel Prize for Literature.

1913 (September) The fourth international congress of psychoanalysts, disagreeable to all parties, is held in Munich; Jung, though he and Freud now have broken on matters of psychoanalytic theory (and after intolerable personal tensions), is reelected president of the International Psychoanalytic Association. But Freud now works to oust Jung from his organizational and editorial positions.

(October) Jung resigns as editor of the *Yearbook*.

Marcel Proust (1871–1922) publishes *Du côté de chez Swann* (*Swann's Way*), the first volume of his cycle *Remembrance of Things Past*.

1914 Freud publishes "The Moses of Michelangelo" (anonymously) in *Imago*.

(March 13) Sophie Halberstadt's first child, Ernst, Freud's first grandchild, is born.

(March) Freud completes "On Narcissism: An Introduction," a pivotal paper in the evolution of Freud's thought, not to be completed until his publication of *Beyond the Pleasure Principle* in 1920.

(April) Jung resigns as president of the International Psychoanalytic Association, and, as in Vienna before, now internationally, Freud has regained control.

(June) Freud's polemical "History of the Psycho-Analytic Movement," his reckoning with Adler and Jung, known among his friends as "the bomb," is published.

(June 28) Austria's Archduke Franz Ferdinand and his consort are assassinated at Sarajevo. The Wolf Man's analysis, begun four and a half years before, is complete.

(July) Anna Freud goes on a visit to England, where she will be caught by the outbreak of war.

(July 23) Austria issues an uncompromising ultimatum to Serbia, and war between the two countries follows.

(End of July, early August) The worsening international situation catches Freud on vacation in Karlsbad.

(August 4) The war becomes general. Freud returns to Vienna a few days later. His daughter Anna reaches home via a circuitous route late in August. In the course of the summer and early fall, Freud's three sons volunteer for the army.

(Late in the year) Freud's early patriotic enthusiasm slowly wanes as he watches the general slaughter with increasing gloom.

Arnold Schönberg (1874–1951), radical Austrian composer, who has been experimenting with atonality in his compositions, declares his twelve-tone scale to be thought through.

1915   (March 15) Freud writes "Instincts and their Vicissitudes," designed as the introductory chapter for an ambitious book on metapsychology. By summer, all twelve papers are complete, but Freud releases only "Instincts," "Repression," and "The Unconscious" to the *International Journal* in 1915, with two further papers, "A Metapsychological Supplement to the Theory of Dreams" and "Mourning and Melancholia," appearing in 1917. The others he destroys.

(March, April) Freud writes two linked papers, "Thoughts for the Times on War and Death," published later that year.

(October) Freud begins a series of three sets of immensely successful introductory lectures on psychoanalysis—on slips, on dreams, and on the theory of neuroses—at the University of Vienna. Parts one and two will be published separately in 1916, the whole in 1917.

Romain Rolland (1866–1944), French biographer, novelist, and musicologist, who will become Freud's much appreciated correspondent in the 1920s, awarded the Nobel Prize for Literature.

1918   Freud publishes his case history of the Wolf Man, "From the History of an Infantile Neurosis," written down in 1914.

(September 28 and 29) Fifth international congress of psychoanalysts at Budapest, the first since the Munich congress five years earlier. Among those invited is Anna Freud, then a teacher but aspiring to become a psychoanalyst. Her father has taken her into analysis this year.

(Early November) The war comes to an end. The Freuds are mired in Vienna, hungry and cold like everyone else.

1919   (January) The International Psychoanalytic Press is founded in Vienna with a munificent gift from a rich Hungarian ex-patient of Freud's, Anton von Freund.

Freud organizes supplies for his families by mobilizing friends and relatives abroad.

(September) Ernest Jones (who had stayed in touch with his "enemy" Freud through neutral channels) sees Freud again.

John B. Watson (1878–1958) publishes a major statement, *Psychology from the Standpoint of a Behaviorist.*

1920   (January 20) Anton von Freund dies.

(January 25) Sophie Halberstadt, Freud's beloved "Sunday child," dies in Hamburg in the influenza epidemic.

(January) Jones founds the *International Journal of Psycho-Analysis.*

(February) Founding of the Berlin psychoanalytic policlinic.

(September 8–11) Sixth international congress of psychoanalysts at The Hague, at which analysts from hitherto belligerent countries cordially meet again. Anna Freud accompanies her father. (Fall) *Beyond the Pleasure Principle,* which offers the first published revision of Freud's drive theory.

1921   (Early summer) *Group Psychology and the Analysis of the Ego,* Freud's most sustained venture into social psychology.

(August) "Psycho-Analysis and Telepathy," a paper addressed to Freud's intimates (not published until 1941), takes up the vexed question of thought transference and its possible relation to psychoanalysis.

Einstein wins the Nobel Prize for Physics.

Anatole France, pseudonym of Jacques Anatone Thibault (1844–1924), wins the Nobel Prize for Literature. Freud admired his outspoken liberal fiction.

Jung publishes *Psychological Types,* outlining a psychological classification stressing "extroversion" and "introversion."

1922   With "Dreams and Telepathy," Freud continues his interest in the subject.

(May) Opening of a psychoanalytic clinic in Vienna.

(End of September) Seventh international psychoanalytic congress in Berlin, the last Freud will attend.

T. S. Eliot (1888–1965) publishes *The Waste Land.*

1923   (Late April) Freud publishes *The Ego and the Id,* a continuation of *Beyond the Pleasure Principle,* and the central work in his postwar output.

(April 20) First operation on Freud's jaw and palate for what the doctors falsely call a leukoplakia, a benign growth associated with smoking. Actually, Freud is suffering from cancer.

(June 19) Heinz Halberstadt ("Heinele"), Freud's cherished little grandson, dies of miliary tuberculosis, a loss he finds hard to recover from.

(Early September) Freud visits Rome, showing his favorite city to his daughter Anna.

(October 4 and 12) Professor Hans Pichler, the best possible choice of surgeon, performs two drastic operations to excise Freud's cancer. The prosthesis inserted into his mouth (and repeatedly changed for a new model) is uncomfortable at best and painful much of the time.

(November 12) Follow-up operation.

Yeats wins the Nobel Prize for Literature.

Alfred Adler publishes *The Practice and Theory of Individual Psychology,* perhaps the best summary of his psychological position.

1924   Otto Rank, hitherto among Freud's most dependable disciples, publishes *The Trauma of Birth,* exalting the birth trauma at the expense of the Oedipus complex. Freud, at first interested and indulgent, becomes increasingly skeptical (see *Inhibitions, Symptoms and Anxiety,* 1926).

Freud publishes several shorter papers, mainly elaborating his structural theory and, in some, introducing innovations: "The Economic Problem of Masochism" and "The Loss of Reality in Neurosis and Psychosis."

"The Dissolution of the Oedipus Complex," the first paper in which Freud discusses his recent researches into the differential sexual evolution of boys and girls.

Thomas Mann publishes *Zauberberg (The Magic Mountain).*

1925   (June 20) Freud's former friend and mentor Josef Breuer dies at the age of eighty-four.

(August 18) Amalia Freud, Freud's mother, is ninety.

(September 2–5) International congress at Bad Homburg; Freud does not attend, and his daughter Anna reads his controversial paper "Some Psychical Consequences of the Anatomical Distinction Between the Sexes," promptly published in the fall.

(September) Freud publishes, in a volume of self-portraits by prominent physicians, "An Autobiographical Study."

(December 25) Karl Abraham, who had been ailing all summer, dies in Berlin—an inestimable loss to Freud and psychoanalysis.

George Bernard Shaw (1856–1950), playwright, music critic, political maverick whose work Freud knew well, is awarded the Nobel Prize for Literature.

1926   (May 6) Freud is seventy.

Inhibitions, Symptoms and Anxiety, Freud's response to Rank's theory of the birth trauma and a complete revision of his own theory of anxiety.

(June) Freud writes *The Question of Lay Analysis,* his defense of lay analysis in general and of his younger follower Theodor Reik, accused of quackery, in particular.

1927   (July 15) Riots and general strike in Vienna, with many dead on the Socialists' side. Freud is neutral.

(November) *The Future of an Illusion,* Freud's most sustained psychoanalytic assault on religion.

The Austrian neurologist Julius Wagner-Jauregg (1857–1940), Freud's long-time acquaintance, superior, and colleague, wins the Nobel Prize for Physiology and Medicine.

1928   (August) Freud goes to Berlin to consult another oral surgeon, Professor Schroeder.

(Fall) "Dostoevsky and Parricide," a psychoanalytic study of Dostoevsky the neurotic.

1929   (July) Freud completes *Civilization and Its Discontents,* partially published in late 1929, and completely early in 1930.

(Late October) Stock market crash in New York has rapid re-
verberations in Europe, including Austria.

Thomas Mann awarded the Nobel Prize for Literature.

1930   (July 26) Freud is informed that he has been awarded the prestigious Goethe Prize of the city of Frankfurt.

(August 28) On Goethe's birthday, Anna Freud reads, in the
Goethe House, a message from her father.

(September 12) Freud's mother dies at ninety-five.

(September 14) The Nazis score an impressive triumph in the
elections to the German Reichstag. In Austria, too, the Nazis
are becoming a formidable force.

(Fall) Freud works with William Bullitt on *Thomas Woodrow
Wilson: A Psychological Study*, a hostile dissection not published
until 1966; Freud's exact share in the book remains uncertain.

1931   (May 6) Freud is seventy-five.

(May 11) The once-powerful Austrian Credit-Anstalt is threatened with total collapse despite state intervention; the great
depression has hit Austria as badly as any country.

(June) Ominous symptoms that Freud's cancer may be active
once again.

(Summer) Freud completes "Female Sexuality," continuing
the argument published in 1925 in "Some Psychical Consequences."

(October 25) Unveiling of a plaque on Freud's birth house in
Příbor; Anna Freud reads to the celebrants a short letter Freud
had written to the mayor.

1932   (July and August) Einstein and Freud correspond, at the instance
of the League of Nations, on the possible prevention of war.
Their letters are published together as "Why War?" in March
1933.

(December 6) Publication of Freud's *New Introductory Lectures on Psycho-Analysis*, dated 1933; Freud designed these
"lectures," not meant to be delivered, to help out the psycho-
analytic publishing house, which is (as so often) facing bank-
ruptcy.

John Galsworthy (1867–1933), English playwright and novelist
whose writings Freud valued, wins the Nobel Prize for
Literature.

1933   (January 30) Adolf Hitler is appointed Chancellor of Germany.
The Nazi regime is launched.

(May 10) Burning of the books in Berlin; Freud's writings are
included in the *auto-da-fé*.

(May 22) Sandor Ferenczi dies in Budapest, almost sixty. Despite
periods of mistrust and estrangement, Freud retained cordial
feelings for Ferenczi.

(August) Freud starts on the essays that will become *Moses and Monotheism*.

(Fall and winter) With the dissolution of the (mainly Jewish) German Psychoanalytic Society, a number of German psychoanalysts leave the country.

(December) Max Eitingon emigrates from Berlin to Jerusalem.

1934 Freud keeps busy by working on *Moses and Monotheism*.

(July 25) An attempted Nazi coup fails, but Chancellor Engelbert Dollfuss is murdered. Kurt Schuschnigg becomes chancellor. Freud thinks him a decent man.

1935 Austria repeals the anti-Habsburg laws enacted with the founding of the republic, restoring part of the old imperial family's property; rumors of a restoration.

1936 (May 6) Freud cannot wholly evade the storm of congratulations that breaks over him on his eightieth birthday.

(July) Freud's cancer recurs (for the first time since 1923) and calls for a major operation—as distinct from the many minor operations he had been compelled to endure during the years.

(September 13) The Freuds' golden wedding anniversary.

(December) Freud's former analysand, now close friend and general benefactress, Princess Marie Bonaparte, is offered Freud's letters to Fliess, a treasure that she grabs with both hands despite Freud's plea that she destroy them.

1937 (February 5) Lou Andreas-Salomé dies, nearly seventy-six; Freud writes a brief, affectionate obituary.

(Early spring) Publication of "Moses an Egyptian," the first of the three linked essays making up *Moses and Monotheism*.

(June) "Analysis Terminable and Interminable."

(Late in the year) Publication of "If Moses Was an Egyptian . . . ," the second part of *Moses and Monotheism*.

Picasso paints his major protest against Franco's fascism, *Guernica*.

1938 (January) Another cancer operation.

(February) Despite most ominous signs that a Nazi invasion is imminent, Freud refuses quite to believe it; in any event, he says, he is too old to leave the country.

(February 12) Schuschnigg, under increasing pressure from Nazi Germany, pays a visit to Hitler at Berchtesgaden.

(March 9) Schuschnigg defiantly announces a plebiscite on Austrian independence.

(March 11) German ultimatum to Austria to postpone plebiscite. Schuschnigg resigns; the Nazi Arthur Seyss-Inquart becomes chancellor. Freud's laconic entry in his diary: "Finis Austriae."

(March 12) Nazis march into Austria, greeted by cheering

throngs. Spontaneous acts of vandalism and violence against Austrian Jews, which astonishes German observers.

(March 13) Anschluss with Germany proclaimed. Vienna Psychoanalytic Society votes to dissolve and counsels immediate emigration.

(March 14) Hitler in Vienna.

(March 15) Ernest Jones reaches Vienna, persuades a most reluctant Freud that it is time for him and his family to leave.

(March 17) Marie Bonaparte arrives from Paris; she will prove invaluable through the spring.

(March 22) Anna Freud summoned to Gestapo; released unharmed that evening. But the trauma persuades Freud to make every effort now.

(March through May) While waiting for permission to leave, Freud works sporadically on "Moses, His People and Monotheist Religion," the third and most provocative essay in *Moses and Monotheism*.

(June 4) After other members of his family have left, Freud, his wife, and his daughter Anna take the train to Paris.

(June 5) After a short stay at Marie Bonaparte's villa, the Freud party leaves on the night boat for England.

(June 6) The Freuds reach London.

(July 22) Freud starts work on what will remain a substantial fragment to be published posthumously in 1940, *An Outline of Psychoanalysis*.

(August) *Moses and Monotheism* published in Amsterdam.

(September 16) The Freuds move to 20 Maresfield Gardens in Hampstead, Freud's last home.

(November 9–10) The so-called "Kristallnacht" in Nazi Germany: looting of Jewish stores, transportation of thousands of Jews to concentration camps, wholesale burnings of synagogues.

1939   (February) The cancer recurs and proves inoperable.

(May 6) Freud is eighty-three. There are no festivities.

(August) Freud officially closes his practice. His condition visibly worsens.

(September 1) The Germans invade Poland. Freud is alert enough to follow the news.

(September 3) France and Britain declare war on Germany.

(September 21) Freud reminds Max Schur of the promise Schur had made ten years before upon becoming his personal physician not to let him suffer unduly. Schur complies with several injections of morphine.

(September 23) Freud dies at 3 A.M.

A Note on Symbols
and Abbreviations

( ) = notes on publishing details (such as added footnotes) supplied by the editors of the Standard Edition.
[ ] = notes to the text supplied by the editors of the Standard Edition.
{ } = notes added by the present editor.

Briefe = Sigmund Freud, *Briefe 1873–1939*, ed. Ernst and Lucie Freud (1960; 2nd enlarged ed., 1968).

Freud = Peter Gay, *Freud: A Life for Our Time* (1988).

Freud-Fliess = Sigmund Freud, *Briefe an Wilhelm Fliess, 1887–1904*, ed. Jeffrey Moussaieff Masson, German version by Michael Schrö-ter, transcription by Gerhard Fichtner (1986); the English version, *The Complete Letters of Sigmund Freud to Wilhelm Fliess, 1887–1904*, same editor, appeared in 1985.

GW = Sigmund Freud, *Gesammelte Werke*, ed. Anna Freud, Edward Bibring, Willi Hoffer, Ernst Kris, and Otto Isakower, in collaboration with Marie Bonaparte, 18 vols. (1940–68).

SE = *Standard Edition of the Complete Psychological Works of Sigmund Freud*, tr. under the general editorship of James Strachey in collaboration with Anna Freud, assisted by Alix Strachey and Alan Tyson, 24 vols. (1953–74).

OVERTURE

An Autobiographical Study

In 1924, when Freud was sixty-eight and had done most (though not all) of his original work, he was invited to contribute a "self-portrait" to a collection of autobiographical statements supplied by eminent physicians. Freud's contribution to that collection, which appeared between 1923 and 1925 in four volumes under the general title *Die Medizin der Gegenwart in Selbstdarstellungen*, was published in 1925. Neither its format nor, for that matter, Freud's inclination made his "Autobiographical Study" a very personal document; he revealed far more of himself in the readings he gave his own dreams in the *Interpretation of Dreams*. Yet there is much of Freud in this document: his attitudes toward Judaism and philosophy, his feelings of isolation in the early years and about the not wholly gratifying spread of his ideas, and his views on science and religion—all emerge clearly, in Freud's characteristically energetic and informal style. So do the summary accounts of his intellectual development and of the ideas fundamental to psychoanalysis: repression, resistance, transference, infantile sexuality, and the rest. There is no better introduction to Freud's work, seen chronologically, than this highly partial "autobiography."

* * *

I was born on May 6th, 1856, at Freiberg in Moravia, a small town in what is now Czechoslovakia. My parents were Jews, and I have remained a Jew myself. I have reason to believe that my father's family were settled for a long time on the Rhine (at Cologne), that, as a result of a persecution of the Jews during the fourteenth or fifteenth century, they fled eastwards, and that, in the course of the nineteenth century, they migrated back from Lithuania through Galicia into German Austria. When I was a child of four I came to Vienna, and I went through the whole of my education there. At the 'Gymnasium' I was at the top of my class for seven years; I enjoyed special privileges there, and had scarcely ever to be examined in class. Although we lived in very limited circumstances, my father insisted that, in my choice of a profession, I should follow my own inclinations alone. Neither at that time, nor indeed in my later life, did I feel any particular predilection for the career of a doctor.[1] I was moved, rather, by a sort of curiosity, which was, however, directed more towards human concerns than towards natural objects; nor had I grasped the importance of observation as one of the best means of gratifying it. My deep engrossment in the Bible story (almost as soon as I had learnt the art of reading) had, as I recognized much later, an enduring effect upon the direction of my interest. Under the powerful influence of a school friendship with a boy rather my senior

1. {See below, p. 681.}

who grew up to be a well-known politician, I developed a wish to study law like him and to engage in social activities. At the same time, the theories of Darwin, which were then of topical interest, strongly attracted me, for they held out hopes of an extraordinary advance in our understanding of the world; and it was hearing Goethe's beautiful essay on Nature read aloud at a popular lecture by Professor Carl Brühl[2] just before I left school that decided me to become a medical student.

When in 1873, I first joined the University, I experienced some appreciable disappointments. Above all, I found that I was expected to feel myself inferior and an alien because I was a Jew. I refused absolutely to do the first of these things. I have never been able to see why I should feel ashamed of my descent or, as people were beginning to say, of my 'race'. I put up, without much regret, with my non-acceptance into the community; for it seemed to me that in spite of this exclusion an active fellow-worker could not fail to find some nook or cranny in the framework of humanity. These first impressions at the University, however, had one consequence which was afterwards to prove important; for at an early age I was made familiar with the fate of being in the Opposition and of being put under the ban of the 'compact majority'.[3] The foundations were thus laid for a certain degree of independence of judgement.

I was compelled, moreover, during my first years at the University, to make the discovery that the peculiarities and limitations of my gifts denied me all success in many of the departments of science into which my youthful eagerness had plunged me. Thus I learned the truth of Mephistopheles' warning:

> Vergebens, dass ihr ringsum wissenschaftlich schweift,
> Ein jeder lernt nur, was er lernen kann.[4]

At length, in Ernst Brücke's physiological laboratory, I found rest and full satisfaction—and men, too, whom I could respect and take as my models: the great Brücke himself, and his assistants, Sigmund Exner and Ernst Fleischl von Marxow.[5] With the last of these, a brilliant man, I was privileged to be upon terms of friendship. Brücke gave me a problem to work out in the histology of the nervous system; I succeeded in solving it to his satisfaction and in carrying the work further on my own account. I worked at this Institute, with short interruptions, from 1876 to 1882, and it was generally thought that I was marked out to fill the next post of Assistant that might fall vacant there. The various branches of med-

---

2. {It is now generally agreed that the author of this essay was one of Goethe's Swiss acquaintances, G. C. Tobler, and that Goethe later mistakenly included this emotional hymn to nature among his own writings.}

3. {Freud is here quoting, and allying himself with, the brave Dr. Stockmann in Ibsen's *Enemy of the People*.}

4. {Freud is quoting Goethe's Mephistopheles in *Faust*, Part I, scene four: "In vain you roam around

scientifically / Everyone learns only what he can learn."}

5. {Ernst Brücke—later Ernst von Brücke—(1819–92), the great German physiologist imported to Vienna, remained Freud's admired and unforgettable model. Sigmund Exner (1846–1926), a gifted physiologist, succeeded Brücke as Professor of Physiology at the University of Vienna. Ernst Fleischl von Marxow (1840–91), a brilliant young physiologist and Freud's friend, died young.}

icine proper, apart from psychiatry, had no attraction for me. I was decidedly negligent in pursuing my medical studies, and it was not until 1881 that I took my somewhat belated degree as a Doctor of Medicine.

The turning-point came in 1882, when my teacher, for whom I felt the highest possible esteem, corrected my father's generous improvidence by strongly advising me, in view of my bad financial position, to abandon my theoretical career. I followed his advice, left the physiological laboratory and entered the General Hospital as an *Aspirant* [Clinical Assistant]. I was soon afterwards promoted to being a *Sekundararzt* [Junior or House Physician], and worked in various departments of the hospital, among others for more than six months under Meynert,[6] by whose work and personality I had been greatly struck while I was still a student.

In a certain sense I nevertheless remained faithful to the line of work upon which I had originally started. The subject which Brücke had proposed for my investigations had been the spinal cord of one of the lowest of the fishes (*Ammocoetes Petromyzon*); and I now passed on to the human central nervous system. Just at this time Flechsig's discoveries of the non-simultaneity of the formation of the medullary sheaths were throwing a revealing light upon the intricate course of its tracts. The fact that I began by choosing the medulla oblongata as the one and only subject of my work was another sign of the continuity of my development. In complete contrast to the diffuse character of my studies during my earlier years at the University, I was now developing an inclination to concentrate my work exclusively upon a single subject or problem. This inclination has persisted and has since led to my being accused of one-sidedness.

I now became as active a worker in the Institute of Cerebral Anatomy as I had previously been in the physiological one. Some short papers upon the course of the tracts and the nuclear origins in the medulla oblongata date from these hospital years, and some notice was taken of my findings by Edinger.[7] One day Meynert, who had given me access to the laboratory even during the times when I was not actually working under him, proposed that I should definitely devote myself to the anatomy of the brain, and promised to hand over his lecturing work to me, as he felt he was too old to manage the newer methods. This I declined, in alarm at the magnitude of the task; it is possible, too, that I had guessed already that this great man was by no means kindly disposed towards me.

From the material point of view, brain anatomy was certainly no better than physiology, and, with an eye to pecuniary considerations, I began to study nervous diseases. There were, at that time, few specialists in that branch of medicine in Vienna, the material for its study was distributed over a number of different departments of the hospital, there

---

6. {Theodor Meynert (1833–92), the eminent Professor of Psychiatry at Freud's university, later quarreled with Freud.}

7. [Ludwig Edinger (1855–1918), the well-known Berlin Professor of Neuro-Anatomy.]

was no satisfactory opportunity of learning the subject, and one was forced to be one's own teacher. Even Nothnagel,[8] who had been appointed a short time before, on account of his book upon cerebral localization, did not single out neuropathology from among the other subdivisions of medicine. In the distance shone the great name of Charcot; so I formed a plan of first obtaining an appointment as University Lecturer [Dozent] on Nervous Diseases in Vienna and of then going to Paris to continue my studies.

In the course of the following years, while I continued to work as a junior physician, I published a number of clinical observations on organic diseases of the nervous system. I gradually became familiar with the ground; I was able to localize the site of a lesion in the medulla oblongata so accurately that the pathological anatomist had no further information to add; I was the first person in Vienna to send a case for autopsy with a diagnosis of polyneuritis acuta.

The fame of my diagnoses and of their *post-mortem* confirmation brought me an influx of American physicians, to whom I lectured upon the patients in my department in a sort of pidgin-English. About the neuroses I understood nothing. On one occasion I introduced to my audience a neurotic suffering from a persistent headache as a case of chronic localized meningitis; they all quite rightly rose in revolt and deserted me, and my premature activities as a teacher came to an end. By way of excuse I may add that this happened at a time when greater authorities than myself in Vienna were in the habit of diagnosing neurasthenia as cerebral tumour.

In the spring of 1885 I was appointed Lecturer [Dozent] in Neuropathology on the ground of my histological and clinical publications. Soon afterwards, as the result of a warm testimonial from Brücke, I was awarded a Travelling Bursary of considerable value. In the autumn of the same year I made the journey to Paris.

I became a student [élève] at the Salpêtrière, but, as one of the crowd of foreign visitors, I had little attention paid me to begin with. One day in my hearing Charcot expressed his regret that since the war he had heard nothing from the German translator of his lectures; he went on to say that he would be glad if someone would undertake to translate the new volume of his lectures into German. I wrote to him and offered to do so; I can still remember a phrase in the letter, to the effect that I suffered only from 'l'aphasie motrice' and not from 'l'aphasie sensorielle du français'. Charcot accepted the offer, I was admitted to the circle of his personal acquaintances, and from that time forward I took a full part in all that went on at the Clinic.

As I write these lines, a number of papers and newspaper articles have reached me from France, which give evidence of a violent objection to the acceptance of psycho-analysis, and which often make the most in-

---

8. {Hermann Nothnagel (1841–1905), a distinguished internist, Professor of Medicine at the University of Vienna, particularly endeared himself to Freud with his philo-Semitism.}

accurate assertions in regard to my relations with the French school. I read, for instance, that I made use of my visit to Paris to familiarize myself with the theories of Pierre Janet and then made off with my booty. I should therefore like to say explicitly that during the whole of my visit to the Salpêtrière Janet's name was never so much as mentioned.

What impressed me most of all while I was with Charcot were his latest investigations upon hysteria, some of which were carried out under my own eyes. He had proved, for instance, the genuineness of hysterical phenomena and their conformity to laws (*'introite et hic dii sunt'* {'Enter, for here too are gods'}), the frequent occurrence of hysteria in men, the production of hysterical paralyses and contractures by hypnotic suggestion and the fact that such artificial products showed, down to their smallest details, the same features as spontaneous attacks, which were often brought on traumatically. Many of Charcot's demonstrations began by provoking in me and in other visitors a sense of astonishment and an inclination to scepticism, which we tried to justify by an appeal to one of the theories of the day. He was always friendly and patient in dealing with such doubts, but he was also most decided; it was in one of these discussions that (speaking of theory) he remarked, *'Ça n'empêche pas d'exister'*, a *mot* which left an indelible mark upon my mind.

No doubt not the whole of what Charcot taught us at that time holds good to-day: some of it has become doubtful, some has definitely failed to withstand the test of time. But enough is left over that has found a permanent place in the storehouse of science. Before leaving Paris I discussed with the great man a plan for a comparative study of hysterical and organic paralyses. I wished to establish the thesis that in hysteria paralyses and anaesthesias of the various parts of the body are demarcated according to the popular idea of their limits and not according to anatomical facts. He agreed with this view, but it was easy to see that in reality he took no special interest in penetrating more deeply into the psychology of the neuroses. When all is said and done, it was from pathological anatomy that his work had started.

Before I returned to Vienna I stopped for a few weeks in Berlin, in order to gain a little knowledge of the general disorders of childhood. {Max} Kassowitz, who was at the head of a public institute in Vienna for the treatment of children's diseases, had promised to put me in charge of a department for the nervous diseases of children. In Berlin I was given assistance and a friendly reception by {Adolf} Baginsky. In the course of the next few years I published, from the Kassowitz Institute, several monographs of considerable size on unilateral and bilateral cerebral palsies in children. And for that reason, at a later date (in 1897), Nothnagel made me responsible for dealing with the same subject in his great *Handbuch der allgemeinen und speziellen Therapie*.

In the autumn of 1886 I settled down in Vienna as a physician, and married the girl who had been waiting for me in a distant city for more than four years. I may here go back a little and explain how it was the fault of my *fiancée* that I was not already famous at that youthful age. A side interest, though it was a deep one, had led me in 1884 to obtain from Merck[9] some of what was then the little-known alkaloid cocaine and to study its physiological action. While I was in the middle of this work, an opportunity arose for making a journey to visit my *fiancée*, from whom I had been parted for two years. I hastily wound up my investigation of cocaine and contented myself in my monograph on the subject with prophesying that further uses for it would soon be found. I suggested, however, to my friend Königstein,[1] the ophthalmologist, that he should investigate the question of how far the anaesthetizing properties of cocaine were applicable in diseases of the eye. When I returned from my holiday I found that not he, but another of my friends, Carl Koller (now in New York), whom I had also spoken to about cocaine, had made the decisive experiments upon animals' eyes and had demonstrated them at the Ophthalmological Congress at Heidelberg. Koller is therefore rightly regarded as the discoverer of local anaesthesia by cocaine, which has become so important in minor surgery; but I bore my *fiancée* no grudge for the interruption.

I will now return to the year 1886, the time of my settling down in Vienna as a specialist in nervous diseases. The duty devolved upon me of giving a report before the 'Gesellschaft der Aerzte' [Society of Medicine] upon what I had seen and learnt with Charcot. But I met with a bad reception. Persons of authority, such as the chairman (Bamberger, the physician), declared that what I said was incredible. Meynert challenged me to find some cases in Vienna similar to those which I had described and to present them before the Society. I tried to do so; but the senior physicians in whose departments I found any such cases refused to allow me to observe them or to work at them. One of them, an old surgeon, actually broke out with the exclamation: 'But, my dear sir, how can you talk such nonsense? *Hysteron* (*sic*) means the uterus. So how can a man be hysterical?' I objected in vain that what I wanted was not to have my diagnosis approved, but to have the case put at my disposal. At length, outside the hospital, I came upon a case of classical hysterical hemi-anaesthesia in a man, and demonstrated it before the 'Gesellschaft der Aerzte' [1886d]. This time I was applauded, but no further interest was taken in me. The impression that the high authorities had rejected my innovations remained unshaken; and, with my hysteria in men and my production of hysterical paralyses by suggestion, I found myself forced into the Opposition. As I was soon afterwards excluded from the laboratory of cerebral anatomy and for terms on end had nowhere to deliver my lectures, I withdrew from academic life and ceased to attend the learned societies. It is a whole generation since I have visited the 'Gesellschaft der Aerzte'.

9. [A chemical firm in Darmstadt.]   1. [Leopold Königstein (1850–1924), Professor of Ophthalmology, was a lifelong friend of Freud's.]

Anyone who wants to make a living from the treatment of nervous patients must clearly be able to do something to help them. My therapeutic arsenal contained only two weapons, electrotherapy and hypnotism, for prescribing a visit to a hydropathic establishment after a single consultation was an inadequate source of income. My knowledge of electrotherapy was derived from W. Erb's text-book [1882], which provided detailed instructions for the treatment of all the symptoms of nervous diseases. Unluckily I was soon driven to see that following these instructions was of no help whatever and that what I had taken for an epitome of exact observations was merely the construction of phantasy. The realization that the work of the greateset name in German neuropathology had no more relation to reality than some 'Egyptian' dreambook, such as is sold in cheap book-shops, was painful, but it helped to rid me of another shred of the innocent faith in authority from which I was not yet free. So I put my electrical apparatus aside, even before Moebius had saved the situation by explaining that the successes of electric treatment in nervous disorders (in so far as there were any) were the effect of suggestion on the part of the physician.

With hypnotism the case was better. While I was still a student I had attended a public exhibition given by Hansen the 'magnetist', and had noticed that one of the subjects experimented upon had become deathly pale at the onset of cataleptic rigidity and had remained so as long as that condition lasted. This firmly convinced me of the genuineness of the phenomena of hypnosis. Scientific support was soon afterwards given to this view by Heidenhain; but that did not restrain the professors of psychiatry from declaring for a long time to come that hypnotism was not only fraudulent but dangerous and from regarding hypnotists with contempt. In Paris I had seen hypnotism used freely as a method for producing symptoms in patients and then removing them again. And now the news reached us that a school had arisen at Nancy which made an extensive and remarkably successful use of suggestion, with or without hypnosis, for therapeutic purposes. It thus came about, as a matter of course, that in the first years of my activity as a physician my principal instrument of work, apart from haphazard and unsystematic psychotherapeutic methods, was hypnotic suggestion.

This implied, of course, that I abandoned the treatment of organic nervous diseases; but that was of little importance. For on the one hand the prospects in the treatment of such disorders were in any case never promising, while, on the other hand, in the private practice of a physician working in a large town, the quantity of such patients was nothing compared to the crowds of neurotics, whose number seemed further multiplied by the way in which they hurried, with their troubles unsolved, from one physician to another. And, apart from this, there was something positively seductive in working with hypnotism. For the first time there was a sense of having overcome one's helplessness; and it was highly flattering to enjoy the reputation of being a miracle-worker. It was not until later that I was to discover the drawbacks of the procedure. At the moment there were only two points to complain of: first, that I could not succeed in hypnotizing every patient, and secondly, that I was unable to put individual patients into as deep a state of hypnosis as I should have wished. With the idea of perfecting my hypnotic technique, I made a journey to Nancy in the summer of 1889 and spent several weeks there. I witnessed the moving spectacle of old {Auguste} Liébeault working among the poor women and children of the labouring classes. I was a spectator of {Professor Hippolyte} Bernheim's astonishing experiments upon his hospital patients, and I received the profoundest impression of the possibility that there could be powerful mental processes which nevertheless remained hidden from the consciousness of men. Thinking it would be instructive, I had persuaded one of my patients to follow me to Nancy. This patient was a very highly gifted hysteric, a woman of good birth, who had been handed over to me because no one knew what to do with her. By hypnotic influence I had made it possible for her to lead a tolerable existence and I was always able to take her out of the misery of her condition. But she always relapsed again after a short time, and in my ignorance I attributed this to the fact that her hypnosis had never reached the stage of somnambulism with amnesia. Bernheim now attempted several times to bring this about, but he too failed. He frankly admitted to me that his great therapeutic successes by means of suggestion were only achieved in his hospital practice and not with his private patients. * * *

During the period from 1886 to 1891 I did little scientific work, and published scarcely anything. I was occupied with establishing myself in my new profession and with assuring my own material existence as well as that of a rapidly increasing family. In 1891 there appeared the first of my studies on the cerebral palsies of children, which was written in collaboration with my friend and assistant, Dr. Oskar Rie. An invitation which I received in the same year to contribute to an encyclopaedia of medicine led me to investigate the theory of aphasia. This was at the time dominated by the views of Wernicke and Lichtheim, which laid stress exclusively upon localization. The fruit of this enquiry was a small critical and speculative book, *Zur Auffassung der Aphasien*.

* * *

II

I must supplement what I have just said by explaining that from the very first I made use of hypnosis in *another* manner, apart from hypnotic suggestion. I used it for questioning the patient upon the origin of his symptom, which in his waking state he could often describe only very imperfectly or not at all. Not only did this method seem more effective than mere suggestive commands or prohibitions, but it also satisfied the curiosity of the physician, who, after all, had a right to learn something of the origin of the phenomenon which he was striving to remove by the monotonous procedure of suggestion.

The manner in which I arrived at this other procedure was as follows. While I was still working in Brücke's laboratory I had made the acquaintance of Dr. Josef Breuer,[2] who was one of the most respected family physicians in Vienna, but who also had a scientific past, since he had produced several works of permanent value upon the physiology of respiration and upon the organ of equilibrium. He was a man of striking intelligence and fourteen years older than myself. Our relations soon became more intimate and he became my friend and helper in my difficult circumstances. We grew accustomed to share all our scientific interests with each other. In this relationship the gain was naturally mine. The development of psycho-analysis afterwards cost me his friendship. It was not easy for me to pay such a price, but I could not escape it.

Even before I went to Paris, Breuer had told me about a case of hysteria which, between 1880 and 1882, he had treated in a peculiar manner which had allowed him to penetrate deeply into the causation and significance of hysterical symptoms. This was at a time, therefore, when Janet's works still belonged to the future. He repeatedly read me pieces of the case history, and I had an impression that it accomplished more towards an understanding of neuroses than any previous observation. I determined to inform Charcot of these discoveries when I reached Paris, and I actually did so. But the great man showed no interest in my first outline of the subject, so that I never returned to it and allowed it to pass from my mind.

When I was back in Vienna I turned once more to Breuer's observation and made him tell me more about it. The patient had been a young girl of unusual education and gifts, who had fallen ill while she was nursing her father, of whom she was devotedly fond. When Breuer took over her case it presented a variegated picture of paralyses with contractures, inhibitions and states of mental confusion. A chance observation showed her physician that she could be relieved of these clouded states of consciousness if she was induced to express in words the affective phantasy by which she was at the moment dominated. From this discovery, Breuer arrived at a new method of treatment. He put her into deep hypnosis and made her tell him each time what it was that was oppressing her mind. After the attacks of depressive confusion had been overcome in this way, he employed the same procedure for removing her inhibitions and physical disorders. In her waking state the girl could no more describe than other patients how her symptoms had arisen, and

2. {Breuer (1842–1925), a leading internist in Vienna; probably the most decisive influence on Freud's development as a psychoanalyst.}

she could discover no link between them and any experiences of her life. In hypnosis she immediately discovered the missing connection. It turned out that all her symptoms went back to moving events which she had experienced while nursing her father; that is to say, her symptoms had a meaning and were residues or reminiscences of those emotional situations. It was found in most instances that there had been some thought or impulse which she had had to suppress while she was by her father's sick-bed, and that, in place of it, as a substitute for it, the symptom had afterwards appeared. But as a rule the symptom was not the precipitate of a single such 'traumatic' scene, but the result of a summation of a number of similar situations. When the patient recalled a situation of this kind in a hallucinatory way under hypnosis and carried through to its conclusion, with a free expression of emotion, the mental act which she had originally suppressed, the symptom was abolished and did not return. By this procedure Breuer succeeded, after long and painful efforts, in relieving his patient of all her symptoms.

The patient had recovered and had remained well and, in fact, had become capable of doing serious work. But over the final stage of this hypnotic treatment there rested a veil of obscurity, which Breuer never raised for me; and I could not understand why he had so long kept secret what seemed to me an invaluable discovery instead of making science the richer by it. The immediate question, however, was whether it was possible to generalize from what he had found in a single case. The state of things which he had discovered seemed to me to be of so fundamental a nature that I could not believe it could fail to be present in any case of hysteria if it had been proved to occur in a single one. But the question could only be decided by experience. I therefore began to repeat Breuer's investigations with my own patients and eventually, especially after my visit to Bernheim in 1889 had taught me the limitations of hypnotic suggestion, I worked at nothing else. After observing for several years that his findings were invariably confirmed in every case of hysteria that was accessible to such treatment, and after having accumulated a considerable amount of material in the shape of observations analogous to his, I proposed to him that we should issue a joint publication. At first he objected vehemently, but in the end he gave way, especially since, in the meantime, Janet's works had anticipated some of his results, such as the tracing back of hysterical symptoms to events in the patient's life, and their removal by means of hypnotic reproduction *in statu nascendi*. In 1893 we issued a preliminary communication, 'On the Psychical Mechanism of Hysterical Phenomena', and in 1895 there followed our book, *Studies on Hysteria*.

If the account I have so far given has led the reader to expect that the *Studies on Hysteria* must, in all essentials of their material content, be the product of Breuer's mind, that is precisely what I myself have always maintained and what it has been my aim to repeat here. As regards the *theory* put forward in the book, I was partly responsible, but to an extent which it is to-day no longer possible to determine. That theory was in any case unpretentious and hardly went beyond the direct description of the observations. It did not seek to establish the nature of hysteria but merely to throw light upon the origin of its symptoms. Thus it laid stress upon the significance of the life of the emotions and upon the importance of distinguishing between mental acts which are unconscious and those which are conscious (or rather capable of being conscious); it introduced a dynamic factor, by supposing that a symptom arises through the damming-up of an affect, and an economic factor, by regarding that same symptom as the product of the transformation of an amount of energy which would otherwise have been employed in some other way. (This latter process was described as *conversion*.) Breuer spoke of our method as *cathartic*; its therapeutic aim was explained as being to provide that the quota of affect used for maintaining the symptom, which had got on to the wrong lines and had, as it were, become strangulated there, should be directed on to the normal path along which it could obtain discharge (or *abreaction*). The practical results of the cathartic procedure were excellent. Its defects, which became evident later, were those of all forms of hypnotic treatment. * * * Its value as an abridged method of treatment was shown afresh by Simmel [1918] in his treatment of war neuroses in the German army during the Great War. The theory of catharsis had not much to say on the subject of sexuality. In the case histories which I contributed to the *Studies* sexual factors played a certain part, but scarcely more attention was paid to them than to other emotional excitations. Breuer wrote of the girl, who has since become famous as his first patient, that her sexual side was extraordinarily undeveloped. It would have been difficult to guess from the *Studies on Hysteria* what an importance sexuality has in the aetiology of the neuroses.

* * * The event which formed the opening of this {transitional} period {from catharsis to psycho-analysis} was Breuer's retirement from our common work, so that I became the sole administrator of his legacy. There had been differences of opinion between us at quite an early stage, but they had not been a ground for our separating. In answering the question of when it is that a mental process becomes pathogenic—that is, when it is that it becomes impossible for it to be dealt with normally— Breuer preferred what might be called a physiological theory: he thought that the processes which could not find a normal outcome were such as had originated during unusual, 'hypnoid', mental states. This opened the further question of the origin of these hypnoid states. I, on the other hand, was inclined to suspect the existence of an interplay of forces and the operation of intentions and purposes such as are to be observed in normal life. Thus it was a case of 'hypnoid hysteria' versus 'neuroses of defence'. But such differences as this would scarcely have alienated him

from the subject if there had not been other factors at work. One of these was undoubtedly that his work as a physician and family doctor took up much of his time, and that he could not, like me, devote his whole strength to the work of catharsis. Again, he was affected by the reception which our book had received both in Vienna and in Germany. His self-confidence and powers of resistance were not developed so fully as the rest of his mental organization. When, for instance, the *Studies* met with a severe rebuff from {Adolf von} Strümpell, I was able to laugh at the lack of comprehension which his criticism showed, but Breuer felt hurt and grew discouraged. But what contributed chiefly to his decision was that my own further work led in a direction to which he found it impossible to reconcile himself.

The theory which we had attempted to construct in the *Studies* remained, as I have said, very incomplete; and in particular we had scarcely touched on the problem of aetiology, on the question of the ground in which the pathogenic process takes root. I now learned from my rapidly increasing experience that it was not *any* kind of emotional excitation that was in action behind the phenomena of neurosis but habitually one of a sexual nature, whether it was a current sexual conflict or the effect of earlier sexual experiences. I was not prepared for this conclusion and my expectations played no part in it, for I had begun my investigation of neurotics quite unsuspectingly. While I was writing my 'History of the Psycho-Analytic Movement' in 1914, there recurred to my mind some remarks that had been made to me by Breuer, Charcot, and Chrobak, which might have led me to this discovery earlier. But at the time I heard them I did not understand what these authorities meant; indeed they had told me more than they knew themselves or were prepared to defend. What I heard from them lay dormant and inactive within me, until the chance of my cathartic experiments brought it out as an apparently original discovery. Nor was I then aware that in deriving hysteria from sexuality I was going back to the very beginnings of medicine and following up a thought of Plato's. It was not until later that I learnt this from an essay by Havelock Ellis.

Under the influence of my surprising discovery, I now took a momentous step. I went beyond the domain of hysteria and began to investigate the sexual life of the so-called neurasthenics who used to visit me in numbers during my consultation hours. This experiment cost me, it is true, my popularity as a doctor, but it brought me convictions which to-day, almost thirty years later, have lost none of their force. There was a great deal of equivocation and mystery-making to be overcome, but, once that had been done, it turned out that in all of these patients grave abuses of the sexual function were present. Considering how extremely widespread are these abuses on the one hand and neurasthenia on the other, a frequent coincidence between the two would not have proved much; but there was more in it than that one bald fact. Closer observation suggested to me that it was possible to pick out from the confused jumble of clinical pictures covered by the name of neurasthenia two fundamentally different types, which might appear in any degree of mixture but which were nevertheless to be observed in their pure forms. In the one type the central phenomenon was the anxiety attack with its equivalents, rudimentary forms and chronic substitutive symptoms; I consequently gave it the name of *anxiety neurosis*, and limited the term *neurasthenia* to the other type. Now it was easy to establish the fact that each of these types had a different abnormality of sexual life as its corresponding aetiological factor: in the former, *coitus interruptus*, unconsummated excitation and sexual abstinence, and in the latter, excessive masturbation and too numerous nocturnal emissions. In a few specially instructive cases, which had shown a surprising alteration in the clinical picture from one type to the other, it could be proved that there had been a corresponding change in the underlying sexual régime. If it was possible to put an end to the abuse and allow its place to be taken by normal sexual activity, a striking improvement in the condition was the reward.

I was thus led into regarding the neuroses as being without exception disturbances of the sexual function, the so-called '*actual neuroses*' being the direct toxic expression of such disturbances and the *psychoneuroses* their mental expression. My medical conscience felt pleased at my having arrived at this conclusion. I hoped that I had filled up a gap in medical science, which, in dealing with a function of such great biological importance, had failed to take into account any injuries beyond those caused by infection or by gross anatomical lesions. The medical aspect of the matter was, moreover, supported by the fact that sexuality was not something purely mental. It had a somatic side as well, and it was possible to assign special chemical processes to it and to attribute sexual excitation to the presence of some particular, though at present unknown, substances. There must also have been some good reason why the true spontaneous neuroses resembled no group of diseases more closely than the phenomena of intoxication and abstinence, which are produced by the administration or privation of certain toxic substances, or than exophthalmic goitre, which is known to depend upon the product of the thyroid gland.

Since that time I have had no opportunity of returning to the investigation of the 'actual neuroses'; nor has this part of my work been continued by anyone else. If I look back to-day at my early findings, they strike me as being the first rough outlines of what is probably a far more complicated subject. But on the whole they seem to me still to hold good. I should have been very glad if I had been able, later on, to make a psycho-analytic examination of some more cases of simple juvenile neurasthenia, but unluckily the occasion did not arise. To avoid misconceptions, I should like to make it clear that I am far from denying the existence of mental conflicts and of neurotic complexes in neurasthenia. All that I am asserting is that the symptoms of these patients are not mentally determined or removable by analysis, but that they must be regarded as direct toxic consequences of disturbed sexual chemical processes.

During the years that followed the publication of the *Studies*, having reached these conclusions upon the part played by sexuality in the aetiology of the neuroses, I read some papers on the subject before various medical societies, but was only met with incredulity and contradiction. Breuer did what he could for some time longer to throw the great weight of his personal influence into the scales in my favour, but he effected nothing and it was easy to see that he too shrank from recognizing the sexual aetiology of the neuroses. He might have crushed me or at least disconcerted me by pointing to his own first patient, in whose case sexual factors had ostensibly played no part whatever. But he never did so, and I could not understand why this was, until I came to interpret the case correctly and to reconstruct, from some remarks which he had made, the conclusion of his treatment of it. After the work of catharsis had seemed to be completed, the girl had suddenly developed a condition of 'transference love'; he had not connected this with her illness, and had therefore retired in dismay. It was obviously painful to him to be reminded of this apparent *contretemps*. His attitude towards me oscillated for some time between appreciation and sharp criticism; then accidental difficulties arose, as they never fail to do in a strained situation, and we parted.

Another result of my taking up the study of nervous disorders in general was that I altered the technique of catharsis. I abandoned hypnotism and sought to replace it by some other method, because I was anxious not to be restricted to treating hysteriform conditions. Increasing experience had also given rise to two grave doubts in my mind as to the use of hypnotism even as a means to catharsis. The first was that even the most brilliant results were liable to be suddenly wiped away if my personal relation with the patient became disturbed. It was true that they would be re-established if a reconciliation could be effected; but such an occurrence proved that the personal emotional relation between doctor and patient was after all stronger than the whole cathartic process, and it was precisely that factor which escaped every effort at control. And one day I had an experience which showed me in the crudest light what I had long suspected. It related to one of my most acquiescent patients, with whom hypnotism had enabled me to bring about the most marvellous results, and whom I was engaged in relieving of her suffering by tracing back her attacks of pain to their origins. As she woke up on one occasion, she threw her arms round my neck. The unexpected entrance of a servant relieved us from a painful discussion, but from that time onwards there was a tacit understanding between us that the hypnotic treatment should be discontinued. I was modest enough not to attribute the event to my own irresistible personal attraction, and I felt that I had now grasped the nature of the mysterious element that was at work behind hypnotism. In order to exclude it, or at all events to isolate it, it was necessary to abandon hypnotism.

But hypnotism had been of immense help in the cathartic treatment, by widening the field of the patient's consciousness and putting within his reach knowledge which he did not possess in his waking life. It seemed no easy task to find a substitute for it. While I was in this perplexity there came to my help the recollection of an experiment which I had often witnessed while I was with Bernheim. When the subject awoke from the state of somnambulism, he seemed to have lost all memory of what had happened while he was in that state. But Bernheim maintained that the memory was present all the same; and if he insisted on the subject remembering, if he asseverated that the subject knew it all and had only to say it, and if at the same time he laid his hand on the subject's forehead, then the forgotten memories used in fact to return, hesitatingly at first, but eventually in a flood and with complete clarity. I determined that I would act in the same way. My patients, I reflected, must in fact 'know' all the things which had hitherto only been made accessible to them in hypnosis; and assurances and encouragement on my part, assisted perhaps by the touch of my hand, would, I thought, have the power of forcing the forgotten facts and connections into consciousness. No doubt this seemed a more laborious process than putting the patients into hypnosis, but it might prove highly instructive. So I abandoned hypnotism, only retaining my practice of requiring the patient to lie upon a sofa while I sat behind him, seeing him, but not seen myself.

III

My expectations were fulfilled; I was set free from hypnotism. But along with the change in technique the work of catharsis took on a new complexion. Hypnosis had screened from view an interplay of forces which now came in sight and the understanding of which gave a solid foundation to my theory.

How had it come about that the patients had forgotten so many of the facts of their external and internal lives but could nevertheless recollect them if a particular technique was applied? Observation supplied an exhaustive answer to these questions. Everything that had been forgotten had in some way or other been distressing; it had been either alarming or painful or shameful by the standards of the subject's personality. It was impossible not to conclude that that was precisely why it had been forgotten—that is, why it had not remained conscious. In order to make it conscious again in spite of this, it was necessary to overcome something that fought against one in the patient; it was necessary to make efforts on one's own part so as to urge and compel him to remember. The amount of effort required of the physician varied in different cases; it increased in direct proportion to the difficulty of what had to be remembered. The expenditure of force on the part of the physician was evidently the measure of a *resistance* on the part of the patient. It was only necessary to translate into words what I myself had observed, and I was in possession of the theory of *repression*.

It was now easy to reconstruct the pathogenic process. Let us keep to a simple example, in which a particular impulsion had arisen in the subject's mind but was opposed by other powerful impulsions. We should have expected the mental *conflict* which now arose to take the following course. The two dynamic quantities—for our present purposes let us call them 'the instinct' and 'the resistance'—would struggle with each other for some time in the fullest light of consciousness, until the instinct was repudiated and the cathexis of energy withdrawn from its impulsion. This would have been the normal solution. In a neurosis, however (for reasons which were still unknown), the conflict found a different outcome. The ego drew back, as it were, on its first collision with the objectionable instinctual impulse; it debarred the impulse from access to consciousness and to direct motor discharge, but at the same time the impulse retained its full cathexis of energy. I named this process *repression*; it was a novelty, and nothing like it had ever before been recognized in mental life. It was obviously a primary mechanism of defence, comparable to an attempt at flight, and was only a forerunner of the later-developed normal condemning judgement. The first act of repression involved further consequences. In the first place the ego was obliged to protect itself against the constant threat of a renewed advance on the part of the repressed impulse by making a permanent expenditure of energy, an *anticathexis*, and it thus impoverished itself. On the other hand, the repressed impulse, which was now *unconscious*, was able to find means of discharge and of substitutive satisfaction by circuitous routes and thus to bring the whole purpose of the repression to nothing. In the case of conversion hysteria the circuitous route led to the somatic innervation; the repressed impulse broke its way through at some point or other and produced *symptoms*. The symptoms were thus results of a compromise, for although they were substitutive satisfactions they were nevertheless distorted and deflected from their aim owing to the resistance of the ego.

The theory of repression became the corner-stone of our understanding of the neuroses. A different view had now to be taken of the task of therapy. Its aim was no longer to 'abreact' an affect which had got on to the wrong lines but to uncover repressions and replace them by acts of judgement which might result either in the accepting or in the condemning of what had formerly been repudiated. I showed my recognition of the new situation by no longer calling my method of investigation and treatment *catharsis* but *psycho-analysis*.

* * *

But the study of pathogenic repressions and of other phenomena which have still to be mentioned compelled psycho-analysis to take the concept of the 'unconscious' seriously. Psycho-analysis regarded everything mental as being in the first instance unconscious; the further quality of 'consciousness' might also be present, or again it might be absent. This of course provoked a denial from the philosophers, for whom 'conscious' and 'mental' were identical, and who protested that they could not conceive of such an absurdity as the 'unconscious mental'. There was no help for it, however, and this idiosyncrasy of the philosophers could only be disregarded with a shrug. Experience (gained from pathological material, of which the philosophers were ignorant) of the frequency and power of impulses of which one knew nothing directly, and whose existence had to be inferred like some fact in the external world, left no alternative open. It could be pointed out, incidentally, that this was only treating one's own mental life as one had always treated other people's. One did not hesitate to ascribe mental processes to other people, although one had no immediate consciousness of them and could only infer them from their words and actions. But what held good for other people must be applicable to oneself. Anyone who tried to push the argument further and to conclude from it that one's own hidden processes belonged actually to a second *consciousness* would be faced with the concept of a consciousness of which one knew nothing, of an 'unconscious consciousness'—and this would scarcely be preferable to the assumption of an 'unconscious mental'. If on the other hand one declared, like some other philosophers, that one was prepared to take pathological phenomena into account, but that the processes underlying them ought not to be described as mental but as 'psychoid', the difference of opinion would degenerate into an unfruitful dispute about words, though even so expediency would decide in favour of keeping the expression 'unconscious mental'. The further question as to the ultimate nature of this unconscious is no more sensible or profitable than the older one as to the nature of the conscious.

It would be more difficult to explain concisely how it came about that psycho-analysis made a further distinction in the unconscious, and separated it into a *preconscious* and an unconscious proper. It will be sufficient to say that it appeared a legitimate course to supplement the theories that were a direct expression of experience with hypotheses that were designed to facilitate the handling of the material and related to matters which could not be a subject of immediate observation. The very same procedure is adopted by the older sciences. The subdivision of the unconscious is part of an attempt to picture the apparatus of the mind as being built up of a number of *agencies* or *systems* whose relations to one another are expressed in spatial terms, without, however, implying any connection with the actual anatomy of the brain. (I have described this as the *topographical* method of approach.) Such ideas as these are part of a speculative superstructure of psycho-analysis, any portion of which can be abandoned or changed without loss or regret the moment its inadequacy has been proved. But there is still plenty to be described that lies closer to actual experience.

I have already mentioned that my investigation of the precipitating and underlying causes of the neuroses led me more and more frequently to conflicts between the subject's sexual impulses and his resistances to sexuality. In my search for the pathogenic situations in which the repressions of sexuality had set in and in which the symptoms, as substitutes for what was repressed, had had their origin, I was carried further and further back into the patient's life and ended by reaching the first years of his childhood. What poets and students of human nature had always asserted turned out to be true: the impressions of that early period of life, though they were for the most part buried in amnesia, left ineradicable traces upon the individual's growth and in particular laid down the disposition to any nervous disorder that was to follow. But since these experiences of childhood were always concerned with sexual excitations and the reaction against them, I found myself faced by the fact of *infantile sexuality*—once again a novelty and a contradiction of one of the strongest of human prejudices. Childhood was looked upon as 'innocent' and free from the lusts of sex, and the fight with the demon of 'sensuality' was not thought to begin until the troubled age of puberty. Such occasional sexual activities as it had been impossible to overlook in children were put down as signs of degeneracy or premature depravity or as a curious freak of nature. Few of the findings of psycho-analysis have met with such universal contradiction or have aroused such an outburst of indignation as the assertion that the sexual function starts at the beginning of life and reveals its presence by important signs even in childhood. And yet no other finding of analysis can be demonstrated so easily and so completely.

Before going further into the question of infantile sexuality I must mention an error into which I fell for a while and which might well have had fatal consequences for the whole of my work. Under the influence of the technical procedure which I used at that time, the majority of my patients reproduced from their childhood scenes in which they were sexually seduced by some grown-up person. With female patients the part of seducer was almost always assigned to their father. I believed these stories, and consequently supposed that I had discovered the roots of the subsequent neurosis in these experiences of sexual seduction in childhood. My confidence was strengthened by a few cases in which relations of this kind with a father, uncle, or elder brother had continued up to an age at which memory was to be trusted. If the reader feels inclined to shake his head at my credulity, I cannot altogether blame him; though I may plead that this was at a time when I was intentionally keeping my critical faculty in abeyance so as to preserve an unprejudiced and receptive attitude towards the many novelties which were coming to my notice every day. When, however, I was at last obliged to recognize that these scenes of seduction had never taken place, and that they were only phantasies which my patients had made up or which I myself had perhaps forced on them, I was for some time completely at a loss.[3] My confidence alike in my technique and in its results suffered a severe blow; it could not be disputed that I had arrived at these scenes by a technical method which I considered correct, and their subject-matter was unquestionably related to the symptoms from which my investigation had started. When I had pulled myself together, I was able to draw the right conclusions from my discovery: namely, that the neurotic symptoms were not related directly to actual events but to wishful phantasies, and that as far as the neurosis was concerned psychical reality was of more importance than material reality. I do not believe even now that I forced the seduction-phantasies on my patients, that I 'suggested' them. I had in fact stumbled for the first time upon the *Oedipus complex*, which was later to assume such an overwhelming importance, but which I did not recognize as yet in its disguise of phantasy. Moreover, seduction during childhood retained a certain share, though a humbler one, in the aetiology of neuroses. But the seducers turned out as a rule to have been older children.

It will be seen, then, that my mistake was of the same kind as would be made by someone who believed that the legendary story of the early kings of Rome (as told by Livy) was historical truth instead of what it is in fact—a reaction against the memory of times and circumstances that were insignificant and occasionally, perhaps, inglorious. When the mistake had been cleared up, the path to the study of the sexual life of children lay open. It thus became possible to apply psycho-analysis to another field of science and to use its data as a means of discovering a new piece of biological knowledge.

The sexual function, as I found, is in existence from the very beginning of the individual's life, though at first it is attached to the other vital functions and does not become independent of them until later; it has to pass through a long and complicated process of development before it becomes what we are familiar with as the normal sexual life of the adult. It begins by manifesting itself in the activity of a whole number of *component instincts*. These are dependent upon *erotogenic zones* in the body; some of them make their appearance in pairs of opposite impulses (such as sadism and masochism or the impulses to look and to be looked at); they operate independently of one another in a search for pleasure, and they find their object for the most part in the subject's

3. {See below. pp. 111–13, for Freud's important letter to his close friend Wilhelm Fliess of September 21, 1897.}

own body. Thus at first the sexual function is non-centralized and pre-dominately *auto-erotic*. Later, syntheses begin to appear in it; a first stage of organization is reached under the dominance of the *oral* components, an *anal-sadistic* stage follows, and it is only after the third stage has at last been reached that the primacy of the *genitals* is established and that the sexual function begins to serve the ends of reproduction. In the course of this process of development a number of elements of the various component instincts turn out to be unserviceable for this last end and are therefore left on one side or turned to other uses, while others are diverted from their aims and carried over into the genital organization. I gave the name of *libido* to the energy of the sexual instincts and to that form of energy alone. I was next driven to suppose that the libido does not always pass through its prescribed course of development smoothly. As a result either of the excessive strength of certain of the components or of experiences involving premature satisfaction, *fixations* of the libido may occur at various points in the course of its development. If subsequently a repression takes place, the libido flows back to these points (a process described as *regression*), and it is from them that the energy breaks through in the form of a symptom. Later on it further became clear that the localization of the point of fixation is what de-termines the *choice of neurosis*, that is, the form in which the subsequent illness makes its appearance.

The process of arriving at an *object*, which plays such an important part in mental life, takes place alongside of the organization of the libido. After the stage of *auto-erotism*, the first love-object in the case of both sexes is the mother; and it seems probable that to begin with a child does not distinguish its mother's organ of nutrition from its own body. Later, but still in the first years of infancy, the relation known as the *Oedipus complex* becomes established: boys concentrate their sexual wishes upon their mother and develop hostile impulses against their father as being a rival, while girls adopt an analogous attitude.[4] All of the different variations and consequences of the Oedipus complex are important; and the innately bisexual constitution of human beings makes itself felt and increases the number of simultaneously active tendencies. Children do not become clear for quite a long time about the differences between the sexes; and during this period of *sexual researches* they pro-duce typical *sexual theories* which, being circumscribed by the incom-pleteness of their authors' own physical development, are a mixture of truth and error and fail to solve the problems of sexual life (the riddle of the Sphinx—that is, the question of where babies come from). We see, then, that a child's first object-choice is an *incestuous* one. The

4. (*Footnote added* 1935:) The information about sexuality was obtained from the study of men and the theory deduced from it was concerned with male children. It was natural enough to expect to find a complete parallel between the two sexes; but this turned out not to hold. Further investigations and reflections revealed profound differences be-tween the sexual development of men and women. {In fact, while Freud was writing the text of this "Self-Portrait," in 1924, he was already severely amending his earlier views. See below, pp. 661–66, 670–78.}

whole course of development that I have described is run through rapidly. For the most remarkable feature of the sexual life of man is its *diphasic* onset, its onset in two waves, with an interval between them. It reaches a first climax in the fourth or fifth year of a child's life. But thereafter this early efflorescence of sexuality passes off; the sexual impulses which have shown such liveliness are overcome by repression, and a *period of latency* follows, which lasts until puberty and during which the *reaction-formations* of morality, shame, and disgust are built up. Of all living creatures man alone seems to show this diphasic onset of sexual growth, and it may perhaps be the biological determinant of his predisposition to neuroses. At puberty the impulses and object-relations of a child's early years become re-animated, and amongst them the emotional ties of its Oedipus complex. In the sexual life of puberty there is a struggle between the urges of early years and the inhibitions of the latency period. Before this, and while the child is at the highest point of its infantile sexual development, a genital organization of a sort is established; but only the male genitals play a part in it, and the female ones remain undiscovered. (I have described this as the period of *phallic* primacy.) At this stage the contrast between the sexes is not stated in terms of 'male' or 'female' but of 'possessing a penis' or 'castrated'. The *castration complex* which arises in this connection is of the profoundest importance in the formation alike of character and of neuroses.

In order to make this condensed account of my discoveries upon the sexual life of man more intelligible, I have brought together conclusions which I reached at different dates and incorporated by way of supplement or correction in the successive editions of my *Three Essays on the Theory of Sexuality*. I hope it will have been easy to gather the nature of my extension (on which so much stress has been laid and which has excited so much opposition) of the concept of sexuality. That extension is of a twofold kind. In the first place sexuality is divorced from its too close connection with the genitals and is regarded as a more comprehensive bodily function, having pleasure as its goal and only secondarily coming to serve the ends of reproduction. In the second place the sexual impulses are regarded as including all of those merely affectionate and friendly impulses to which usage applies the exceedingly ambiguous word 'love'. I do not, however, consider that these extensions are innovations but rather restorations: they signify the removal of inexpedient limitations of the concept into which we had allowed ourselves to be led.

The detaching of sexuality from the genitals has the advantage of allowing us to bring the sexual activities of children and of perverts into the same scope as those of normal adults. The sexual activities of children have hitherto been entirely neglected and though those of perverts have been recognized it has been with moral indignation and without understanding. Looked at from the psycho-analytic standpoint, even the most eccentric and repellent perversions are explicable as manifestations of component instincts of sexuality which have freed themselves from the primacy of the genitals and are now in pursuit of pleasure on their own account as they were in the very early days of the libido's development. The most important of these perversions, homosexuality, scarcely deserves the name. It can be traced back to the constitutional bisexuality of all human beings and to the after-effects of the phallic primacy. Psycho-analysis enables us to point to some trace or other of a homosexual object-choice in everyone. If I have described children as 'polymorphously perverse', I was only using a terminology that was generally current; no moral judgement was implied by the phrase. Psycho-analysis has no concern whatever with such judgements of value.

The second of my alleged extensions of the concept of sexuality finds its justification in the fact revealed by psycho-analytic investigation that all of these affectionate impulses were originally of a completely sexual nature but have become *inhibited in their aim* or *sublimated*. The manner in which the sexual instincts can thus be influenced and diverted enables them to be employed for cultural activities of every kind, to which indeed they bring the most important contributions.

My surprising discoveries as to the sexuality of children were made in the first instance through the analysis of adults. But later (from about 1908 onwards) it became possible to confirm them fully and in every detail by direct observations upon children. Indeed, it is so easy to convince oneself of the regular sexual activities of children that one cannot help asking in astonishment how the human race can have succeeded in overlooking the facts and in maintaining for so long the wishful legend of the asexuality of childhood. This surprising circumstance must be connected with the amnesia which, with the majority of adults, hides their own infancy.

IV

*   *   *

The means which I first adopted for overcoming the patient's resistance, by insistence and encouragement, had been indispensable for the purpose of giving me a first general survey of what was to be expected. But in the long run it proved to be too much of a strain on both sides, and further, it seemed open to certain obvious criticisms. It therefore gave place to another method which was in one sense its opposite. Instead of urging the patient to say something upon some particular subject, I now asked him to abandon himself to a process of *free association*—that is, to say whatever came into his head, while ceasing to give any conscious direction to his thoughts. It was essential, however, that he should bind himself to report literally everything that occurred to his self-perception and not to give way to critical objections which sought to put certain associations on one side on the ground that they were not sufficiently important or that they were irrelevant or that they were altogether meaningless. There was no necessity to repeat explicitly the demand for candour on the patient's part in reporting his thoughts, for it was the precondition of the whole analytic treatment.

It may seem surprising that this method of free association, carried out subject to the observation of the *fundamental rule of psycho-analysis*, should have achieved what was expected of it, namely the bringing into consciousness of the repressed material which was held back by resistances. We must, however, bear in mind that free association is not really free. The patient remains under the influence of the analytic situation even though he is not directing his mental activities on to a particular subject. We shall be justified in assuming that nothing will occur to him that has not some reference to that situation. His resistance against reproducing the repressed material will now be expressed in two ways. Firstly it will be shown by critical objections; and it was to deal with these that the fundamental rule of psycho-analysis was invented. But if the patient observes that rule and so overcomes his reticences, the resistance will find another means of expression. It will so arrange it that the repressed material itself will never occur to the patient but only something which approximates to it in an allusive way; and the greater the resistance, the more remote from the actual idea that the analyst is in search of will be the substitutive association which the patient has to report. The analyst, who listens composedly but without any constrained effort to the stream of associations and who, from his experience, has a general notion of what to expect, can make use of the material brought to light by the patient according to two possibilities. If the resistance is slight he will be able from the patient's allusions to infer the unconscious material itself; or if the resistance is stronger he will be able to recognize its character from the associations, as they seem to become more remote from the topic in hand, and will explain it to the patient. Uncovering the resistance, however, is the first step towards overcoming it. Thus the work of analysis involves an *art of interpretation*, the successful handling of which may require tact and practice but which is not hard to acquire. But it is not only in the saving of labour that the method of free association has an advantage over the earlier method. It exposes the patient to the least possible amount of compulsion, it never allows of contact being lost with the actual current situation, it guarantees to a great extent that no factor in the structure of the neurosis will be overlooked and that nothing will be introduced into it by the expectations of the analyst. It is left to the patient in all essentials to determine the course of the analysis and the arrangement of the material; any systematic handling of particular symptoms or complexes thus becomes impossible. In complete contrast to what happened with hypnotism and with the urging method, interrelated material makes its appearance at different times and at different points in the treatment. To a spectator, therefore—though in fact there must be none—an analytic treatment would seem completely obscure.

Another advantage of the method is that it need never break down. It must theoretically always be possible to have an association, provided that no conditions are made as to its character. Yet there is one case in which in fact a breakdown occurs with absolute regularity; from its very uniqueness, however, this case too can be interpreted.

I now come to the description of a factor which adds an essential feature to my picture of analysis and which can claim, alike technically and theoretically, to be regarded as of the first importance. In every analytic treatment there arises, without the physician's agency, an intense emotional relationship between the patient and the analyst which is not to be accounted for by the actual situation. It can be of a positive or of a negative character and can vary between the extremes of a passionate, completely sensual love and the unbridled expression of an embittered defiance and hatred. This *transference*—to give it its short name—soon replaces in the patient's mind the desire to be cured, and, so long as it is affectionate and moderate, becomes the agent of the physician's influence and neither more nor less than the mainspring of the joint work of analysis. Later on, when it has become passionate or has been converted into hostility, it becomes the principal tool of the resistance. It may then happen that it will paralyse the patient's powers of associating and endanger the success of the treatment. Yet it would be senseless to try to evade it; for an analysis without transference is an impossibility. It must not be supposed, however, that transference is created by analysis and does not occur apart from it. Transference is merely uncovered and isolated by analysis. It is a universal phenomenon of the human mind, it decides the success of all medical influence, and in fact dominates the whole of each person's relations to his human environment. We can easily recognize it as the same dynamic factor which the hypnotists have named 'suggestibility', which is the agent of hypnotic *rapport* and whose incalculable behaviour led to difficulties with the cathartic method as well. When there is no inclination to a transference of emotion such as this, or when it has become entirely negative, as happens in dementia praecox or paranoia, then there is also no possibility of influencing the patient by psychological means.

It is perfectly true that psycho-analysis, like other psychotherapeutic methods, employs the instrument of suggestion (or transference). But the difference is this: that in analysis it is not allowed to play the decisive part in determining the therapeutic results. It is used instead to induce the patient to perform a piece of psychical work—the overcoming of his transference-resistances—which involves a permanent alteration in his mental economy. The transference is made conscious to the patient by the analyst, and it is resolved by convincing him that in his transference-attitude he is *re-experiencing* emotional relations which had their origin in his earliest object-attachments during the repressed period of his childhood. In this way the transference is changed from the strongest weapon of the resistance into the best instrument of the analytic treatment. Nevertheless its handling remains the most difficult as well as the most important part of the technique of analysis.

With the help of the method of free association and of the related art of interpretation, psycho-analysis succeeded in achieving one thing which appeared to be of no practical importance but which in fact necessarily led to a totally fresh attitude and a fresh scale of values in scientific thought. It became possible to prove that *dreams* have a meaning, and to discover it. In classical antiquity great importance was attached to dreams as foretelling the future; but modern science would have nothing to do with them, it handed them over to superstition, declaring them to be purely 'somatic' processes—a kind of twitching of a mind that is otherwise asleep. It seemed quite inconceivable that anyone who had done serious scientific work could make his appearance as an 'interpreter of dreams'. But by disregarding the excommunication pronounced upon dreams, by treating them as unexplained neurotic symptoms, as delusional or obsessional ideas, by neglecting their apparent content and by making their separate component images into subjects for free association, psycho-analysis arrived at a different conclusion. The numerous associations produced by the dreamer led to the discovery of a thought-structure which could no longer be described as absurd or confused, which ranked as a completely valid psychical product, and of which the *manifest* dream was no more than a distorted, abbreviated, and misunderstood translation, and for the most part a translation into visual images. These *latent dream-thoughts* contained the meaning of the dream, while its manifest content was simply a make-believe, a façade, which could serve as a starting-point for the associations but not for the interpretation.

There were now a whole series of questions to be answered, among the most important of them being whether the formation of dreams had a motive, under what conditions it took place, by what methods the dream-thoughts (which are invariably full of sense) become converted into the dream (which is often senseless), and others besides. I attempted to solve all of these problems in *The Interpretation of Dreams*, which I published in the year 1900. I can only find space here for the briefest abstract of my investigation. When the latent dream-thoughts that are revealed by the analysis of a dream are examined, one of them is found to stand out from among the rest, which are intelligible and well known to the dreamer. These latter thoughts are residues of waking life (the *day's residues*, as they are called technically); but the isolated thought is found to be a wishful impulse, often of a very repellent kind, which is foreign to the waking life of the dreamer and is consequently disavowed by him with surprise or indignation. This impulse is the actual constructor of the dream: it provides the energy for its production and makes use of the day's residues as material. The dream which thus originates represents a situation of satisfaction for the impulse, it is the fulfilment of its wish. It would not be possible for this process to take place without being favoured by the presence of something in the nature of a state of sleep. The necessary mental precondition of sleep is the concentration of the ego upon the wish to sleep and the withdrawal of psychical energy from all the interests of life. Since at the same time all the paths of approach to motility are blocked, the ego is also able to reduce the expenditure [of energy] by which at other times it maintains the repressions. The unconscious impulse makes use of this nocturnal relaxation of repression in order to push its way into consciousness with the dream. But the repressive resistance of the ego is not abolished in sleep but merely reduced. Some of it remains in the shape of a *censorship of dreams* and forbids the unconscious impulse to express itself in the forms which it would properly assume. In consequence of the severity of the censorship of dreams, the latent dream-thoughts are obliged to submit to being altered and softened so as to make the forbidden meaning of the dream unrecognizable. This is the explanation of *dream-distortion*, which accounts for the most striking characteristics of the manifest dream. We are therefore justified in asserting that *a dream is the (disguised) fulfilment of a (repressed) wish*. It will now be seen that dreams are constructed like a neurotic symptom: they are compromises between the demands of a repressed impulse and the resistance of a censoring force in the ego. Since they have a similar origin they are equally unintelligible and stand in equal need of interpretation.

There is no difficulty in discovering the general function of dreaming. It serves the purpose of fending off, by a kind of soothing action, external or internal stimuli which would tend to arouse the sleeper, and thus of securing sleep against interruption. External stimuli are fended off by being given a new interpretation and by being woven into some harmless situation; internal stimuli, caused by instinctual demands, are given free play by the sleeper and allowed to find satisfaction in the formation of dreams, so long as the latent dream-thoughts submit to the control of the censorship. But if they threaten to break free and the meaning of the dream becomes too plain, the sleeper cuts short the dream and wakes in a fright. (Dreams of this class are known as *anxiety-dreams*.) A similar failure in the function of dreaming occurs if an external stimulus becomes too strong to be fended off. (This is the class of *arousal-dreams*.) I have given the name of *dream-work* to the process which, with the co-operation of the censorship, converts the latent thoughts into the manifest content of the dream. It consists of a peculiar way of treating the preconscious material of thought, so that its component parts become *condensed*, its psychical emphasis becomes *displaced*, and the whole of it is translated into visual images or *dramatized*, and completed by a deceptive *secondary revision*. The dream-work is an excellent example of the processes occurring in the deeper, unconscious layers of the mind, which differ considerably from the familiar normal processes of thought. It also displays a number of archaic characteristics, such as the use of a *symbolism* (in this case of a predominantly sexual kind) which it has since also been possible to discover in other spheres of mental activity.

We have explained that the unconscious instinctual impulse of the dream connects itself with a residue of the day, with some interest of waking life which has not been disposed of; it thus gives the dream which it constructs a double value for the work of analysis. For on the one hand a dream that has been analysed reveals itself as the fulfilment of a repressed wish; but on the other hand it may be a continuation of some preconscious activity of the day before and may contain every kind of subject-matter and give expression to an intention, a warning, a reflection, or once more to the fulfilment of a wish. Analysis exploits the dream in both directions, as a means of obtaining knowledge alike of the patient's conscious and of his unconscious processes. It also profits from the fact that dreams have access to the forgotten material of childhood, and so it happens that infantile amnesia is for the most part overcome in connection with the interpretation of dreams. In this respect dreams achieve a part of what was previously the task of hypnotism. On the other hand, I have never maintained the assertion which has so often been ascribed to me that dream-interpretation shows that all dreams have a sexual content or are derived from sexual motive forces. It is easy to see that hunger, thirst, or the need to excrete, can produce dreams of satisfaction just as well as any repressed sexual or egoistic impulse. The case of young children affords us a convenient test of the validity of our theory of dreams. In them the various psychical systems are not yet sharply divided and the repressions have not yet grown deep, so that we often come upon dreams which are nothing more than undisguised fulfilments of wishful impulses left over from waking life. Under the influence of imperative needs, adults may also produce dreams of this infantile type.

In the same way that psycho-analysis makes use of dream-interpretation, it also profits by the study of the numerous little slips and mistakes which people make—symptomatic actions, as they are called. I investigated this subject in a series of papers which were published for the first time in book form in 1904 under the title of *The Psychopathology of Everyday Life* [Freud, 1901b]. In this widely circulated work I have pointed out that these phenomena are not accidental, that they require more than physiological explanations, that they have a meaning and can be interpreted, and that one is justified in inferring from them the presence of restrained or repressed impulses and intentions. But what constitutes the enormous importance of dream-interpretation, as well as of this latter study, is not the assistance they give to the work of analysis but another of their attributes. Previously psycho-analysis had only been concerned with solving pathological phenomena and in order to explain them it had often been driven into making assumptions whose comprehensiveness was out of all proportion to the importance of the actual material under consideration. But when it came to dreams, it was no longer dealing with a pathological symptom, but with a phenomenon of normal mental life which might occur in any healthy person. If dreams turned out to be constructed like symptoms, if their explanation required the same assumptions—the repression of impulses, substitutive formation, compromise-formation, the dividing of the conscious and the unconscious into various psychical systems—then psycho-analysis was no longer an auxiliary science in the field of psychopathology, it was rather the starting-point of a new and deeper science of the mind which would be equally indispensable for the understanding of the normal. Its postulates and findings could be carried over to other regions of mental happening; a path lay open to it that led far afield, into spheres of universal interest.

V

I must interrupt my account of the internal growth of psycho-analysis and turn to its external history. What I have so far described of its discoveries has related for the most part to the results of my own work; but I have also filled in my story with material from later dates and have not distinguished between my own contributions and those of my pupils and followers.

For more than ten years after my separation from Breuer I had no followers. I was completely isolated. In Vienna I was shunned; abroad no notice was taken of me. My Interpretation of Dreams, published in 1900, was scarcely reviewed in the technical journals. In my paper 'On the History of the Psycho-Analytic Movement' I mentioned as an instance of the attitude adopted by psychiatric circles in Vienna a conversation with an assistant at the clinic [at which I lectured], who had written a book against my theories but had never read my Interpretation of Dreams. He had been told at the clinic that it was not worth while. The man in question, who has since become a professor, has gone so far as to repudiate my report of the conversation and to throw doubts in general upon the accuracy of my recollection. I can only say that I stand by every word of the account I then gave.

As soon as I realized the inevitable nature of what I had come up against, my sensitiveness greatly diminished. Moreover my isolation gradually came to an end. To begin with, a small circle of pupils gathered round me in Vienna; and then, after 1906, came the news that the psychiatrists at Zurich, E. Bleuler,[5] his assistant C. G. Jung, and others, were taking a lively interest in psycho-analysis. We got into personal touch with one another, and at Easter 1908 the friends of the young science met at Salzburg, agreed upon the regular repetition of similar informal congresses and arranged for the publication of a journal which

5. {Eugen Bleuler (1857–1939), celebrated chief of the Burghölzli, the mental hospital in Zurich that was also the university hospital.}

was edited by Jung and was given the title of *Jahrbuch für psychoanalytische und psychopathologische Forschungen* [*Yearbook for Psycho-Analytic and Psychopathological Researches*]. It was brought out under the direction of Bleuler and myself and ceased publication at the beginning of the [first] World War. At the same time that the Swiss psychiatrists joined the movement, interest in psycho-analysis began to be aroused all over Germany as well; it became the subject of a large number of written comments and of lively discussions at scientific congresses. But its reception was nowhere friendly or even benevolently non-committal. After the briefest acquaintance with psycho-analysis German science was united in rejecting it.

* * *

One of my opponents boasted of silencing his patients as soon as they began to talk of anything sexual and evidently thought that this technique gave him a right to judge the part played by sexuality in the aetiology of the neuroses. Apart from emotional resistances, which were so easily explicable by the psycho-analytic theory that it was impossible to be misled by them, it seemed to me that the main obstacle to agreement lay in the fact that my opponents regarded psycho-analysis as a product of my speculative imagination and were unwilling to believe in the long, patient and unbiased work which had gone to its making. Since in their opinion analysis had nothing to do with observation or experience, they believed that they themselves were justified in rejecting it without experience. Others again, who did not feel so strongly convinced of this, repeated in their resistance the classical manœuvre of not looking through the microscope so as to avoid seeing what they had denied. It is remarkable, indeed, how incorrectly most people act when they are obliged to form a judgement of their own on some new subject. For years I have been told by 'benevolent' critics—and I hear the same thing even to-day—that psycho-analysis is right up to such-and-such a point but that there it begins to exaggerate and to generalize without justification. And I know that, though nothing is more difficult than to decide where such a point lies, these critics had been completely ignorant of the whole subject only a few weeks or days earlier.

The result of the official anathema against psycho-analysis was that the analysts began to come closer together. At the second Congress, held at Nuremberg in 1910, they formed themselves, on the proposal of Ferenczi, into an 'International Psycho-Analytical Association' divided into a number of local societies but under a common President. The Association survived the Great War and still exists, consisting to-day of branch societies in Austria, Germany, Hungary, Switzerland, Great Britain, Holland, Russia, and India, as well as two in the United States. I arranged that C. G. Jung should be appointed as the first President, which turned out later to have been a most unfortunate step. At the same time a second journal devoted to psycho-analysis was started, the *Zentralblatt für Psychoanalyse* [*Central Journal for Psycho-Analysis*], edited by Adler and Stekel, and a little later a third, *Imago*, edited by two nonmedical analysts, H. Sachs and O. Rank, and intended to deal with the application of analysis to the mental sciences. Soon afterwards Bleuler [1910] published a paper in defence of psycho-analysis. Though it was a relief to find honesty and straightforward logic for once taking part in the dispute, yet I could not feel completely satisfied by Bleuler's essay. He strove too eagerly after an appearance of impartiality; nor is it a matter of chance that it is to him that our science owes the valuable concept of *ambivalence*. In later papers Bleuler adopted such a critical attitude towards the theoretical structure of analysis and rejected or threw doubts upon such essential parts of it that I could not help asking myself in astonishment what could be left of it for him to admire. Yet not only has he subsequently uttered the strongest pleas in favour of 'depth psychology' but he based his comprehensive study of schizophrenia upon it. Nevertheless Bleuler did not for long remain a member of the International Psycho-Analytical Association; he resigned from it as a result of misunderstandings with Jung, and the Burghölzli was lost to analysis.

* * * In 1909 G. Stanley Hall invited Jung and me to America to go to Clark University, Worcester, Mass., of which he was President, and to spend a week giving lectures (in German) at the celebration of the twentieth anniversary of that body's foundation. Hall was justly esteemed as a psychologist and educationalist, and had introduced psycho-analysis into his courses several years earlier; there was a touch of the 'king-maker' about him, a pleasure in setting up authorities and in then deposing them. We also met James J. Putnam there, the Harvard neurologist, who in spite of his age was an enthusiastic supporter of psycho-analysis and threw the whole weight of a personality that was universally respected into the defence of the cultural value of analysis and the purity of its aims. He was an estimable man, in whom, as a reaction against a predisposition to obsessional neurosis, an ethical bias predominated; and the only thing in him that was disquieting was his inclination to attach psycho-analysis to a particular philosophical system and to make it the servant of moral aims. Another event of this time which made a lasting impression on me was a meeting with William James the philosopher. I shall never forget one little scene that occurred as we were on a walk together. He stopped suddenly, handed me a bag he was carrying and asked me to walk on, saying that he would catch me up as soon as he had got through an attack of angina pectoris which was just coming on. He died of that disease a year later; and I have always wished that I might be as fearless as he was in the face of approaching death.

At that time I was only fifty-three. I felt young and healthy, and my short visit to the new world encouraged my self-respect in every way. In Europe I felt as though I were despised; but over there I found myself received by the foremost men as an equal. As I stepped on to the platform at Worcester to deliver my *Five Lectures on Psycho-Analysis* [1910] it seemed like the realization of some incredible day-dream: psycho-analysis was no longer a product of delusion, it had become a valuable part of reality. It has not lost ground in America since our visit; it is extremely popular among the lay public and is recognized by a number of official psychiatrists as an important element in medical training. Unfortunately, however, it has suffered a great deal from being watered down. Moreover, many abuses which have no relation to it find a cover under its name, and there are few opportunities for any thorough training in technique or theory. In America, too, it has come in conflict with Behaviourism, a theory which is naïve enough to boast that it has put the whole problem of psychology completely out of court.

In Europe during the years 1911–13 two secessionist movements from psycho-analysis took place, led by men who had previously played a considerable part in the young science, Alfred Adler and C. G. Jung. Both movements seemed most threatening and quickly obtained a large following. But their strength lay, not in their own content, but in the temptation which they offered of being freed from what were felt as the repellent findings of psycho-analysis even though its actual material was no longer rejected. Jung attempted to give to the facts of analysis a fresh interpretation of an abstract, impersonal and non-historical character, and thus hoped to escape the need for recognizing the importance of infantile sexuality and of the Oedipus complex as well as the necessity for any analysis of childhood. Adler seemed to depart still further from psycho-analysis; he entirely repudiated the importance of sexuality, traced back the formation both of character and of the neuroses solely to men's desire for power and to their need to compensate for their constitutional inferiorities, and threw all the psychological discoveries of psycho-analysis to the winds. But what he had rejected forced its way back into his closed system under other names; his 'masculine protest' is nothing else than repression unjustifiably sexualized. The criticism with which the two heretics were met was a mild one; I only insisted that both Adler and Jung should cease to describe their theories as 'psycho-analysis'. After a lapse of ten years it can be asserted that both of these attempts against psycho-analysis have blown over without doing any harm.

If a community is based on agreement upon a few cardinal points, it is obvious that people who have abandoned that common ground will cease to belong to it. Yet the secession of former pupils has often been brought up against me as a sign of my intolerance or has been regarded as evidence of some special fatality that hangs over me. It is a sufficient answer to point out that in contrast to those who have left me, like Jung, Adler, Stekel, and a few besides, there are a great number of men, like Abraham, Eitingon, Ferenczi, Rank, Jones, Brill, Sachs, Pfister, van Emden, Reik, and others, who have worked with me for some fifteen years in loyal collaboration and for the most part in uninterrupted friendship. I have only mentioned the oldest of my pupils, who have already made a distinguished name for themselves in the literature of psycho-analysis; if I have passed over others, that is not to be taken as a slight, and indeed among those who are young and have joined me lately talents are to be found on which great hopes may be set. But I think I can say in my defence that an intolerant man, dominated by an arrogant belief in his own infallibility, would never have been able to maintain his hold upon so large a number of intellectually eminent people, especially if he had at his command as few practical attractions as I had.

The World War, which broke up so many other organizations, could do nothing against our 'International'. The first meeting after the war took place in 1920, at The Hague, on neutral ground. It was moving to see how hospitably the Dutch welcomed the starving and impoverished subjects of the Central European states; and I believe this was the first occasion in a ruined world on which Englishmen and Germans sat at the same table for the friendly discussion of scientific interests. Both in Germany and in the countries of Western Europe the war had actually stimulated interest in psycho-analysis. The observation of war neuroses had at last opened the eyes of the medical profession to the importance of psychogenesis in neurotic disturbances, and some of our psychological conceptions, such as the 'gain from illness' and the 'flight into illness', quickly became popular. The last Congress before the German collapse, which was held at Budapest in 1918, was attended by official represen-tatives of the allied governments of the Central European powers, and they agreed to the establishment of psycho-analytic Centres for the treat-ment of war neuroses. But this point was never reached. Similarly too the comprehensive plans made by one of our leading members, Dr. Anton von Freund, for establishing in Budapest a centre for analytic study and treatment came to grief as a result of the political upheavals that followed soon afterwards and of the premature death of their irre-placeable author. At a later date some of his ideas were put into execution by Max Eitingon, who in 1920 founded a psycho-analytical clinic in Berlin. During the brief period of Bolshevik rule in Hungary, Ferenczi was still able to carry on a successful course of instruction as the official representative of psycho-analysis at the University of Budapest. After the war our opponents were pleased to announce that events had produced a conclusive argument against the validity of the theses of analysis. The war neuroses, they said, had proved that sexual factors were unnecessary to the aetiology of neurotic disorders. But their triumph was frivolous and premature. For on the one hand no one had been able to carry out a thorough analysis of a case of war neurosis, so that in fact nothing whatever was known for certain as to their motivation and no conclusions could be drawn from this uncertainty; while on the other hand psycho-analysis had long before arrived at the concept of narcissism and of narcissistic neuroses, in which the subject's libido is attached to his own ego instead of to an object. Though on other occasions, therefore, the charge was brought against psycho-analysis of having made an unjustifiable extension of the concept of sexuality, yet, when it became convenient for controversial ends, this crime was forgotten and we were once more held down to the narrowest meaning of the word.

* * *

I must begin by adding that increasing experience showed more and more plainly that the Oedipus complex was the nucleus of the neurosis. It was at once the climax of infantile sexual life and the point of junction from which all of its later developments proceeded. But if so, it was no longer possible to expect analysis to discover a factor that was specific in the aetiology of the neuroses. It must be true, as Jung expressed it so well in the early days when he was still an analyst, that neuroses have no peculiar content which belongs exclusively to them but that neurotics break down at the same difficulties that are successfully overcome by normal people. This discovery was very far from being a disappointment. It was in complete harmony with another one: that the depth-psychology revealed by psycho-analysis was in fact the psychology of the normal mind. Our path had been like that of chemistry: the great qualitative differences between substances were traced back to quantitative variations in the proportions in which the same elements were combined.

In the Oedipus complex the libido was seen to be attached to the image of the parental figures. But earlier there was a period in which there were no such objects. There followed from this fact the concept (of fundamental importance for the libido theory) of a state in which the subject's libido filled his own ego and had that for its object. This state could be called *narcissism* or self-love. A moment's reflection showed that this state never completely ceases. All through the subject's life his ego remains the great reservoir of his libido, from which object-cathexes are sent out and into which the libido can stream back again from the objects. Thus narcissistic libido is constantly being transformed into object-libido, and *vice versa*. An excellent instance of the length to which this transformation can go is afforded by the state of being in love, whether in a sexual or sublimated manner, which goes so far as involving a sacrifice of the self. Whereas hitherto in considering the process of repression attention had only been paid to what was repressed, these ideas made it possible to form a correct estimate of the repressing forces too. It had been said that repression was set in action by the instincts of self-preservation operating in the ego (the 'ego-instincts') and that it was brought to bear upon the libidinal instincts. But since the instincts of self-preservation were now recognized as also being of a libidinal nature, as being narcissistic libido, the process of repression was seen to be a process occurring within the libido itself; narcissistic libido was opposed to object-libido, the interest of self-preservation was defending itself against the demands of object-love, and therefore against the demands of sexuality in the narrower sense as well.

There is no more urgent need in psychology than for a securely founded theory of the instincts on which it might then be possible to build further. Nothing of the sort exists, however, and psycho-analysis is driven to making tentative efforts towards some such theory. It began by drawing a contrast between the ego-instincts (the instinct of self-preservation, hunger) and the libidinal instincts (love), but later replaced it by a new contrast between naricissistic and object-libido. This was clearly not the last word on the subject; biological considerations seemed to make it impossible to remain content with assuming the existence of only a single class of instincts.

In the works of my later years (*Beyond the Pleasure Principle* [1920], *Group Psychology and the Analysis of the Ego* [1921], and *The Ego and the Id* [1923], I have given free rein to the inclination, which I kept down for so long, to speculation, and I have also contemplated a new solution of the problem of the instincts. I have combined the instincts for self-preservation and for the preservation of the species under the concept of *Eros* and have contrasted with it an *instinct of death* or *destruction* which works in silence. Instinct in general is regarded as a kind of elasticity of living things, an impulsion towards the restoration of a situation which once existed but was brought to an end by some external disturbance. This essentially conservative character of instincts is exemplified by the phenomena of the *compulsion to repeat*. The picture which life presents to us is the result of the concurrent and mutually opposing action of Eros and the death instinct.

It remains to be seen whether this construction will turn out to be serviceable. Although it arose from a desire to fix some of the most important theoretical ideas of psycho-analysis, it goes far beyond psycho-analysis. I have repeatedly heard it said contemptuously that it is impossible to take a science seriously whose most general concepts are as lacking in precision as those of libido and of instinct in psycho-analysis. But this reproach rests on a complete misconception of the facts. Clear basic concepts and sharply drawn definitions are only possible in the mental sciences in so far as the latter seek to fit a region of facts into the frame of a logical system. In the natural sciences, of which psychology is one, such clear-cut general concepts are superfluous and indeed impossible. Zoology and Botany did not start from correct and adequate definitions of an animal and a plant; to this very day biology has been unable to give any certain meaning to the concept of life. Physics itself, indeed, would never have made any advance if it had had to wait until its concepts of matter, force, gravitation, and so on, had reached the desirable degree of clarity and precision. The basic ideas or most general concepts in any of the disciplines of science are always left indeterminate at first and are only explained to begin with by reference to the realm of phenomena from which they were derived; it is only by means of a progressive analysis of the material of observation that they can be made clear and can find a significant and consistent meaning. I have always felt it as a gross injustice that people have refused to treat psycho-analysis like any other science. This refusal found an expression in the raising of the most obstinate objections. Psycho-analysis was constantly reproached for its incompleteness and insufficiencies; though it is plain that a science based upon observation has no alternative but to work out its findings piecemeal and to solve its problems step by step. Again, when I endeavoured to obtain for the sexual function the recognition which had so long been withheld from it, psycho-analytic theory was branded as 'pan-sexualism'. And when I laid stress on the hitherto neglected importance of the part played by the accidental impressions of early youth, I was told that psycho-analysis was denying constitutional and hereditary factors—a thing which I had never dreamt of doing. It was a case of contradiction at any price and by any methods.

I had already made attempts at earlier stages of my work to arrive at some more general points of view on the basis of psycho-analytic observation. In a short essay, 'Formulations on the Two Principles of Mental Functioning' [1911], I drew attention (and there was, of course, nothing original in this) to the domination of the *pleasure-unpleasure principle* in mental life and to its displacement by what is called the *reality principle*. Later on [in 1915] I made an attempt to produce a 'Meta-psychology'. By this I meant a method of approach according to which every mental process is considered in relation to three coordinates, which I described as *dynamic, topographical,* and *economic* respectively; and this seemed to me to represent the furthest goal that psychology could attain. The attempt remained no more than a torso; after writing two or three papers—'Instincts and their Vicissitudes' [1915], 'Repression' [1915], 'The Unconscious' [1915], 'Mourning and Melancholia' [1917], etc.—I broke off, wisely perhaps, since the time for theoretical predications of this kind had not yet come.[6] In my latest speculative works I have set about the task of dissecting our mental apparatus on the basis of the analytic view of pathological facts and have divided it into an *ego,* an *id,* and a *super-ego.*[7] The super-ego is the heir of the Oedipus complex and represents the ethical standards of mankind.

I should not like to create an impression that during this last period of my work I have turned my back upon patient observation and have abandoned myself entirely to speculation. I have on the contrary always remained in the closest touch with the analytic material and have never ceased working at detailed points of clinical or technical importance. Even when I have moved away from observation, I have carefully avoided any contact with philosophy proper. This avoidance has been greatly

6. {See below, p. 545.}

7. *The Ego and the Id* [1923]. {See below, pp. 628–61.}

facilitated by constitutional incapacity. I was always open to the ideas of G. T. Fechner and have followed that thinker upon many important points. The large extent to which psycho-analysis coincides with the philosophy of Schopenhauer—not only did he assert the dominance of the emotions and the supreme importance of sexuality but he was even aware of the mechanism of repression—is not to be traced to my acquaintance with his teaching. I read Schopenhauer very late in my life. Nietzsche, another philosopher whose guesses and intuitions often agree in the most astonishing way with the laborious findings of psycho-analysis, was for a long time avoided by me on that very account; I was less concerned with the question of priority than with keeping my mind unembarrassed.

* * *

VI

* * *

The beginnings of the majority of these applications of psycho-analysis {to folklore, religion, and other fields} will be found in my works. Here and there I have gone a little way along the path in order to gratify my non-medical interests. Later on, others (not only doctors, but specialists in the various fields as well) have followed in my tracks and penetrated far into the different subjects. But since my programme limits me to a mention of my own share in these applications of psycho-analysis, I can only give a quite inadequate picture of their extent and importance.

A number of suggestions came to me out of the Oedipus complex, the ubiquity of which gradually dawned on me. The poet's choice, or his invention, of such a terrible subject seemed puzzling; and so too did the overwhelming effect of its dramatic treatment, and the general nature of such tragedies of destiny. But all of this became intelligible when one realized that a universal law of mental life had here been captured in all its emotional significance. Fate and the oracle were no more than materializations of an internal necessity; and the fact of the hero's sinning without his knowledge and against his intentions was evidently a right expression of the *unconscious* nature of his criminal tendencies. From understanding this tragedy of destiny it was only a step further to understanding a tragedy of character—*Hamlet*, which had been admired for three hundred years without its meaning being discovered or its author's motives guessed. It could scarcely be a chance that this neurotic creation of the poet should have come to grief, like his numberless fellows in the real world, over the Oedipus complex. For Hamlet was faced with the task of taking vengeance on another for the two deeds which are the subject of the Oedipus desires; and before that task his arm was paralysed by his own obscure sense of guilt. Shakespeare wrote

Hamlet very soon after his father's death.[8] The suggestions made by me for the analysis of this tragedy[9] were fully worked out later on by Ernest Jones [1910]. And the same example was afterwards used by Otto Rank as the starting-point for his investigation of the choice of material made by dramatists. In his large volume on the incest theme (Rank, 1912) he was able to show how often imaginative writers have taken as their subject the themes of the Oedipus situation, and traced in the different literatures of the world the way in which the material has been transformed, modified, and softened.

It was tempting to go on from there to an attempt at an analysis of poetic and artistic creation in general. The realm of imagination was seen to be a 'reservation' made during the painful transition from the pleasure principle to the reality principle in order to provide a substitute for instinctual satisfactions which had to be given up in real life. The artist, like the neurotic, had withdrawn from an unsatisfying reality into this world of imagination; but, unlike the neurotic, he knew how to find a way back from it and once more to get a firm foothold in reality. His creations, works of art, were the imaginary satisfactions of unconscious wishes, just as dreams are; and like them they were in the nature of compromises, since they too were forced to avoid any open conflict with the forces of repression. But they differed from the asocial, narcissistic products of dreaming in that they were calculated to arouse sympathetic interest in other people and were able to evoke and to satisfy the same unconscious wishful impulses in them too. Besides this, they made use of the perceptual pleasure of formal beauty as what I have called an 'incentive bonus.' What psycho-analysis was able to do was to take the interrelations between the impressions of the artist's life, his chance experiences, and his works, and from them to construct his [mental] constitution and the instinctual impulses at work in it—that is to say, that part of him which he shared with all men. With this aim in view, for instance, I made Leonardo da Vinci the subject of a study [1910], which is based on a single memory of childhood related by him and which aims chiefly at explaining his picture of 'The Madonna and Child with St. Anne'. Since then my friends and pupils have undertaken numerous analyses of artists and their works. It does not appear that the enjoyment of a work of art is spoiled by the knowledge gained from such an analysis. The layman may perhaps expect too much from analysis in this respect, for it must be admitted that it throws no light on the two problems which probably interest him the most. It can do nothing

---

8. (*Footnote added* 1935:) This is a construction which I should like explicitly to withdraw. I no longer believe that William Shakespeare the actor from Stratford was the author of the works which have so long been attributed to him. Since the publication of J. T. Looney's volume '*Shakespeare' Identified* [1920], I am almost convinced that in fact Edward de Vere, Earl of Oxford, is concealed behind this pseudonym. {Freud's most devoted English supporters, including Ernest Jones, were appalled by this crotchet, but could not talk him out of it.}

9. {First adumbrated in a letter to his intimate Wilhelm Fliess—see below, p. 116—and developed in *The Interpretation of Dreams, SE* IV, 264–66.}

towards elucidating the nature of the artistic gift, nor can it explain the means by which the artist works—artistic technique.

I was able to show from a short story by W. Jensen called *Gradiva* [1907], which has no particular merit in itself, that invented dreams can be interpreted in the same way as real ones and that the unconscious mechanisms familiar to us in the 'dream-work' are thus also operative in the processes of imaginative writing. My book on *Jokes and their Relation to the Unconscious* [1905] was a side-issue directly derived from *The Interpretation of Dreams*. The only friend of mine who was at that time interested in my work {, Wilhelm Fliess,} remarked to me that my interpretations of dreams often impressed him as being like jokes. In order to throw some light on this impression, I began to investigate jokes and found that their essence lay in the technical methods employed in them, and that these were the same as the means used in the 'dream-work'—that is to say, condensation, displacement, the representation of a thing by its opposite or by something very small, and so on. This led to an economic enquiry into the origin of the high degree of pleasure obtained from hearing a joke. And to this the answer was that it was due to the momentary suspension of the expenditure of energy upon maintaining repression, owing to the attraction exercised by the offer of a bonus of pleasure (*fore-pleasure*).

I myself set a higher value on my contributions to the psychology of religion, which began with the establishment of a remarkable similarity between obsessive actions and religious practices or ritual (1907).[1] Without as yet understanding the deeper connections, I described the obsessional neurosis as a distorted private religion and religion as a kind of universal obsessional neurosis. Later on, in 1912, Jung's forcible indication of the far-reaching analogies between the mental products of neurotics and of primitive peoples led me to turn my attention to that subject. In four essays, which were collected into a book with the title of *Totem and Taboo* [1912–13], I showed that the horror of incest was even more marked among primitive than among civilized races and had given rise to very special measures of defence against it. I examined the relations between taboo-prohibitions (the earliest form in which moral restrictions make their appearance) and emotional ambivalence; and I discovered under the primitive scheme of the universe known as 'animism' the principle of the over-estimation of the importance of psychical reality—the belief in 'the omnipotence of thoughts'—which lies at the root of magic as well. I developed the comparison with the obsessional neurosis at every point, and showed how many of the postulates of primitive mental life are still in force in that remarkable illness. Above all, however, I was attracted by totemism, the first system of organization in primitive tribes, a system in which the beginnings of social order are united with a rudimentary religion and the implacable domination of a

1. {See below, pp. 429–36.}

small number of taboo-prohibitions. The being that is revered is ultimately always an animal, from which the clan also claims to be descended. Many indications pointed to the conclusion that every race, even the most highly developed, had once passed through the stage of totemism.[2]

* * *

I have taken but little direct part in certain other applications of psychoanalysis, though they are none the less of general interest. It is only a step from the phantasies of individual neurotics to the imaginative creations of groups and peoples as we find them in myths, legends, and fairy tales. Mythology became the special province of Otto Rank; the interpretation of myths, the tracing of them back to the familiar unconscious complexes of early childhood, the replacing of astral explanations by a discovery of human motives, all of this is to a large extent due to his analytic efforts. The subject of symbolism, too, has found many students among my followers. Symbolism has brought psychoanalysis many enemies; many enquirers with unduly prosaic minds have never been able to forgive it the recognition of symbolism, which followed from the interpretation of dreams. But analysis is guiltless of the discovery of symbolism, for it had long been known in other regions of thought (such as folklore, legends, and myths) and plays an even larger part in them than in the 'language of dreams'.

* * *

By a process of development against which it would have been useless to struggle, the word 'psycho-analysis' has itself become ambiguous. While it was originally the name of a particular therapeutic method, it has now also become the name of a science—the science of unconscious mental processes. By itself this science is seldom able to deal with a problem completely, but it seems destined to give valuable contributory help in the most varied regions of knowledge. The sphere of application of psycho-analysis extends as far as that of psychology, to which it forms a complement of the greatest moment.

Looking back, then, over the patchwork of my life's labours, I can say that I have made many beginnings and thrown out many suggestions. Something will come of them in the future, though I cannot myself tell whether it will be much or little. I can, however, express a hope that I have opened up a pathway for an important advance in our knowledge.

2. {See below, pp. 481–513.}

PART ONE: MAKING OF A PSYCHOANALYST

Preface to the Translation of Bernheim's *Suggestion*

From the mid-1880s on, after foraging among a variety of medical subjects, Freud increasingly concentrated on mental illnesses. His months of study in Paris with the great French neurologist Jean-Martin Charcot (from October 1885 to the end of February 1886) only strengthened his resolve to specialize in "neurasthenia." One of Charcot's contributions to Freud's development as an independent, unconventional healer was Charcot's willingness to take hypnosis, hitherto the province of charlatans, seriously and to use it on his patients. Freud followed that lead. Acquainting himself with the subject, he found another group of French hypnotists, most eloquently represented by Professor Hippolyte Bernheim. These two French theorists and practitioners of hypnosis, Charcot and Bernheim, founded two rival schools. Freud summed up Charcot's views as a "somatic" theory that "explains hypnotic phenomena on the pattern of spinal reflexes; it regards hypnosis as a physiologically altered condition of the nervous system brought about by external stimuli" that "only have a 'hypnogenic' effect when there is a particular disposition of the nervous system and therefore that only neuropaths (especially hysterics) are hypnotizable." In contrast, Bernheim's theory, derived in part from a local physician at Nancy, Ambroise Liébeault, saw "all the phenomena of hypnosis" as "physical effects, effects of ideas which are provoked in the hypnotized subject or not" (Freud, "Review of Forel's *Hypnotism*" [1889], SE I, 91–102; quotation at 97). Freud's own views fluctuated, and in the end he gave up hypnosis, which he used with a number of patients in these early years, altogether. In 1888, he translated Bernheim's seminal *De la suggestion et de ses applications à la thérapeutique* (1886; 2nd ed. 1887) under the German title, *Die Suggestion und ihre Heilwirkung*. The preface displays Freud's willingness to confront—and affront—the Viennese medical establishment and to expose them to the two French schools.

This book has already received warm commendation from Professor Forel of Zurich, and it is to be hoped that its readers will discover in it all the qualities which have led the translator to present it in German. They will find that the work of Dr. Bernheim of Nancy provides an admirable introduction to the study of hypnotism (a subject which can no longer be neglected by physicians), that it is in many respects stimulating and in some positively illuminating, and that it is well calculated to destroy the belief that the problem of hypnosis is still surrounded, as Meynert asserts, by a 'halo of absurdity'.

The achievement of Bernheim (and of his colleagues at Nancy who are working along the same lines) consists precisely in stripping the manifestations of hypnotism of their strangeness by linking them up with familiar phenomena of normal psychological life and of sleep. The principal value of this book seems to me to lie in the proof it gives of the relations which link hypnotic phenomena with ordinary processes of waking and sleeping, and in its bringing to light the psychological laws that apply to both classes of events. In this way the problem of hypnosis is carried over completely into the sphere of psychology, and 'suggestion' is established as the nucleus of hypnotism and the key to its understanding. Moreover in the last chapters the importance of suggestion is traced in fields other than that of hypnosis. In the second part of the book convincing evidence is offered that the use of hypnotic suggestion provides the physician with a powerful therapeutic method, which seems indeed to be the most suitable for combating certain nervous disorders and the most appropriate to their mechanism. This lends the volume a quite unusual practical importance. And its insistence upon the fact that both hypnosis and hypnotic suggestion can be applied, not only to hysterical and to seriously neuropathic patients, but also to the majority of healthy people, is calculated to extend the interest of physicians in this therapeutic method beyond the narrow circle of neuropathologists.

The subject of hypnotism has had a most unfavourable reception among the leaders of German medical science (apart from such few exceptions as Krafft-Ebing, Forel, etc.). Yet, in spite of this, one may venture to express a wish that German physicians may turn their attention to this problem and to this therapeutic procedure, since it remains true that in scientific matters it is always experience, and never authority without experience, that gives the final verdict, whether in favour or against. * * *

Some ten years ago the prevalent view in Germany was still one which doubted the reality of hypnotic phenomena and sought to explain the accounts given of them as due to a combination of credulity on the part of the observers and of simulation on the part of the subjects of the experiments. This position is to-day no longer tenable, thanks to the works of Heidenhain[1] and Charcot, to name only the greatest of those who have lent their unimpeachable support to the reality of hypnotism. Even the most violent opponents of hypnotism have become aware of this, and consequently their writings, though they still betray a clear inclination to deny the reality of hypnosis, habitually include as well attempts at explaining it and thus in fact recognize the existence of these phenomena.

Another line of argument hostile to hypnosis rejects it as being dangerous to the mental health of the subject and labels it as 'an experimentally produced psychosis'. Evidence that hypnosis leads to injurious results in a few cases would no more decide against its general usefulness than, for instance, does the occurrence of isolated instances of death under chloroform narcosis forbid the use of chloroform for the purposes

1. [Rudolf Peter Heinrich Heidenhain (1834-97) was Professor of Physiology and Histology at Breslau University from 1859.]

of surgical anaesthesia. It is a very remarkable fact, however, that this analogy cannot be carried any further. The largest number of accidents in chloroform narcosis are experienced by the surgeons who carry out the largest number of operations. But the majority of reports of the injurious effects of hypnosis are derived from observers who have worked very little with hypnosis, whereas all those workers who have had a large amount of hypnotic experience are united in their belief in the harmlessness of the procedure. In order, therefore, to avoid any injurious effects in hypnosis, all that is probably necessary is to carry out the procedure with care, with a sufficiently sure touch and upon correctly selected cases. It must be added that there is little to be gained by calling suggestions 'obsessional ideas' and hypnosis 'an experimental psychosis'. It seems likely that more light will be thrown on obsessional ideas by comparing them with suggestions than the other way round. And anyone who is scared by the abusive term 'psychosis' may well ask himself whether our natural sleep has any less claim to that description—if, indeed, there is anything at all to be gained from transporting technical names out of their proper spheres. No, the cause of hypnotism is in no danger from this quarter. And as soon as a large enough number of doctors are in a position to report observations of the kind that are to be found in the second part of Bernheim's book, it will become an established fact that hypnosis is a harmless condition and that to induce it is a procedure 'worthy' of a physician.

This book also discusses another question, which at the present time divides the supporters of hypnotism into two opposing camps. One party, whose opinions are voiced by Dr. Bernheim in these pages, maintains that all the phenomena of hypnotism have the same origin: they arise, that is, from a suggestion, a conscious idea, which has been introduced into the brain of the hypnotized person by an external influence and has been accepted by him as though it had arisen spontaneously. On this view all hypnotic manifestations would be psychical phenomena, effects of suggestions. The other party, on the contrary, stand by the view that the mechanism of some at least of the manifestations of hypnotism is based upon physiological changes—that is, upon displacements of excitability in the nervous system, occurring without the participation of those parts of it which operate with consciousness; they speak, therefore, of the physical or physiological phenomena of hypnosis.

The principal subject of this dispute is *'grand hypnotisme'* ['major hypnotism']—the phenomena described by Charcot in the case of hypnotized hysterical patients. Unlike normal hypnotized subjects, these hysterical patients are said to exhibit three stages of hypnosis, each of which is distinguished by special physical signs of a most remarkable kind (such as enormous neuro-muscular hyper-excitability, somnambulistic contractures, etc.). It will easily be understood what an important bearing, in connection with this region of facts, the difference of opinion that has just been indicated must have. If the supporters of the suggestion theory are right, all the observations made at the Salpêtrière are worthless; indeed, they become errors in observation. The hypnosis of hysterical patients would have no characteristics of its own; but every physician would be free to produce any symptomatology that he liked in the patients he hypnotized. We should not learn from the study of major hypnotism what alterations in excitability succeed one another in the nervous system of hysterical patients in response to certain kinds of intervention; we should merely learn what intentions Charcot suggested (in a manner of which he himself was unconscious) to the subjects of his experiments—a thing entirely irrelevant to our understanding alike of hypnosis and of hysteria.

* * *

I am convinced that this view will be most welcome to those who feel an inclination—and it is still the predominant one in Germany to-day—to overlook the fact that hysterical phenomena are governed by laws. Here we should have a splendid example of how neglect of the psychical factor of suggestion has misled a great observer into the artificial and false creation of a clinical type as a result of the capriciousness and easy malleability of a neurosis.

Nevertheless there is no difficulty in proving piece by piece the objectivity of the symptomatology of hysteria. * * * But the principal points of the symptomatology of hysteria are safe from the suspicion of having originated from suggestion by a physician. Reports coming from past times and from distant lands, which have been collected by Charcot and his pupils, leave no room for doubt that the peculiarities of hysterical attacks, of hysterogenic zones, of anaesthesia, paralyses and contractures, have been manifested at every time and place just as they were at the Salpêtrière when Charcot carried out his memorable investigation of that major neurosis. * * *

* * *

Charcot

Freud was anything but a hero worshipper, but in the lonely and difficult years between ca. 1885 and 1900, when he worked his way toward psycho-analysis, he leaned on friends to supply him with ideas and encouragement. Charcot, as this affectionate obituary of August 1893 amply demonstrates, remained Freud's model even after Freud developed strong reservations about some of Charcot's theories. Charcot's elegance and eloquence, his imagination at once luxuriant and controlled, his bold readiness to entertain and propagate unfashionable ideas, above all his willingness to see and to listen, made an indelible mark on Freud. This was the kind of scientist Freud wanted to become—and became.

On the 16th of August of this year, J.-M Charcot died suddenly, without pain or illness, after a life of happiness and fame. In him, all too soon, the young science of neurology has lost its greatest leader, neurologists of every country have lost their master teacher and France has lost one of her foremost men. He was only sixty-eight years old; his physical strength and mental vigour, together with the hopes he so frankly expressed, seemed to promise him the long life which has been granted to not a few mental workers of this century. The nine imposing volumes of his *Œuvres complètes*, in which his pupils had collected his contributions to medicine and neuropathology, his *Leçons du mardi*, the yearly reports of his clinic at the Salpêtrière, and other works besides—all these publications will remain precious to science and to his pupils; but they cannot take the place of the man, who had still much more to give and to teach and whose person or whose writings no one has yet approached without learning something from them.

He took an honest, human delight in his own great success and used to enjoy talking of his beginnings and the road he had travelled. His scientific curiosity, he said, had been aroused early, when he was still a young *interne*, by the mass of material presented by the facts of neuropathology, material which was not in the least understood at the time. In those days, whenever he went the rounds with his senior in one of the departments of the Salpêtrière (the institution for the care of women) amid all the wilderness of paralyses, spasms and convulsions for which forty years ago there was neither name nor understanding, he would say: '*Faudrait y retourner et y rester*',[1] and he kept his word. When he became *médecin des hôpitaux*, he at once took steps to enter the Salpêtrière in one of the departments for nervous patients. Having got there, he stayed where he was instead of doing what French senior physicians are entitled to do—transferring in regular succession from one department to another and from hospital to hospital, and at the same time changing their specialty as well.

Thus his first impression and the resolution it led him to were decisive for the whole of his further development. His having a great number of chronic nervous patients at his disposal enabled him to make use of his own special gifts. He was not a reflective man, not a thinker: he had the nature of an artist—he was, as he himself said, a '*visuel*', a man who sees. Here is what he himself told us about his method of working. He used to look again and again at the things he did not understand, to deepen his impression of them day by day, till suddenly an understanding of them dawned on him. In his mind's eye the apparent chaos

1. ["I shall have to come back here and stop here."]

presented by the continual repetition of the same symptoms then gave
way to order: the new nosological pictures emerged, characterized by
the constant combination of certain groups of symptoms. The complete
and extreme cases, the 'types', could be brought into prominence with
the help of a certain sort of schematic planning, and, with these types
as a point of departure, the eye could travel over the long series of ill-
defined cases—the *formes frustes*—which, branching off from one or
other characteristic feature of the type, melt away into indistinctness.
He called this kind of intellectual work, in which he had no equal,
'practising nosography', and he took pride in it. He might be heard to
say that the greatest satisfaction a man could have was to see something
new—that is, to recognize it as new; and he remarked again and again
on the difficulty and value of this kind of 'seeing'. He would ask why it
was that in medicine people only see what they have already learned to
see. He would say that it was wonderful how one was suddenly able to
see new things—new states of illness—which must probably be as old
as the human race; and that he had to confess to himself that he now
saw a number of things which he had overlooked for thirty years in his
hospital wards. No physician needs to be told what a wealth of forms
were acquired by neuropathology through him, and what increased
precision and sureness of diagnosis were made possible by his observations. But the pupil who spent many hours with him going round the
wards of the Salpêtrière—that museum of clinical facts, the names and
peculiar characteristics of which were for the most part derived from
him—would be reminded of Cuvier, whose statue, standing in front of
the Jardin des Plantes, shows that great comprehender and describer of
the animal world surrounded by a multitude of animal forms; or else
he would recall the myth of Adam, who, when God brought the creatures
of Paradise before him to be distinguished and named, may have experienced to the fullest degree that intellectual enjoyment which Charcot
praised so highly.

Charcot, indeed, never tired of defending the rights of purely clinical
work, which consists in seeing and ordering things, against the encroachments of theoretical medicine. On one occasion there was a small
group of us, all students from abroad, who, brought up on German
academic physiology, were trying his patience with our doubts about
his clinical innovations. 'But that can't be true,' one of us objected, 'it
contradicts the Young-Helmholtz theory.' He did not reply 'So much
the worse for the theory, clinical facts come first' or words to that effect;
but he did say something which made a great impression on us: '*La
théorie, c'est bon, mais ça n'empêche pas d'exister.*'{—'Theory is good,
but that doesn't prevent things from existing.'}

For a whole number of years Charcot occupied the Chair of Pathological Anatomy in Paris, and he carried on his neuropathological studies
and lectures, which quickly made him famous abroad as well as in

France, on a voluntary basis and as a secondary occupation. It was a piece of good fortune for neuropathology that the same man could undertake the discharge of two functions: on the one hand he created the nosological picture through clinical observation, and on the other he demonstrated that the same anatomical changes underlay the disease whether it appeared as a type or as a *forme fruste*. * * *

* * *

In Vienna we have repeatedly had occasion to realize that the intellectual significance of an academic teacher is not necessarily combined with a direct personal influence on younger men which leads to the creation of a large and important school. If Charcot was so much more fortunate in this respect we must put it down to the personal qualities of the man—to the magic that emanated from his looks and from his voice, to the kindly openness which characterized his manner as soon as his relations with someone had overcome the stage of initial strangeness, to the willingness with which he put everything at the disposal of his pupils, and to his life-long loyalty to them. The hours he spent in his wards were hours of companionship and of an exchange of ideas with the whole of his medical staff. He never shut himself away from them there. The youngest newly-qualified physician walking the wards had a chance of seeing him at his work and might interrupt him at it; and the same freedom was enjoyed by students from abroad, who, in later years, were never lacking at his rounds. And, lastly, on the evenings when Madame Charcot was at home to a distinguished company, assisted by a highly-gifted daughter who was growing up in the likeness of her father, the pupils and medical assistants who were always present met the guests as part of the family.

In 1882 or 1883, the circumstances of Charcot's life and work took on their final form. People had come to realize that the activities of this man were a part of the assets of the nation's *'gloire'*, which, after the unfortunate war of 1870–1, was all the more jealously guarded. The government, at the head of which was Charcot's old friend, Gambetta, created a Chair of Neuropathology for him in the Faculty of Medicine (so that he could give up the Chair of Pathological Anatomy) and also a clinic, with auxiliary scientific departments, at the Salpêtrière. *'Le service de M. Charcot'* now included, in addition to the old wards for chronic female patients, several clinical rooms where male patients, too, were received, a huge out-patient department—the *'consultation externe'*—, a histological laboratory, a museum, an electro-therapeutic department, an eye and ear department and a special photographic studio. All these things were so many means of keeping former assistants and pupils permanently at the clinic in secure posts. The two-storeyed, weathered-looking buildings and the courtyards which they enclosed reminded the stranger vividly of our *Allgemeines Krankenhaus*; but no doubt the resemblance did not go far enough. 'It may not be beautiful here, perhaps,' Charcot would say when he showed a visitor his domain, 'but there is room for everything you want to do.'

Charcot was in the very prime of life when this abundance of facilities for teaching and research were placed at his disposal. He was a tireless worker, and always, I believe, the busiest in the whole institute. * * * There is no doubt that this throng of people did not turn to him solely because he was a famous discoverer but quite as much because he was a great physician and friend of man, who could always find an answer to a problem and who, when the present state of science did not allow him to *know*, was able to make a good guess. He has often been blamed for his therapeutic method which, with its multiplicity of prescriptions, could not but offend a rationalistic conscience. But he was simply continuing the procedures which were customary at that time and place, without deceiving himself much about their efficacy. He was, however, not pessimistic in his therapeutic expectations, and repeatedly showed readiness to try new methods of treatment in his clinic: their short-lived success was to find its explanation elsewhere.

As a teacher, Charcot was positively fascinating. Each of his lectures was a little work of art in construction and composition; it was perfect in form and made such an impression that for the rest of the day one could not get the sound of what he had said out of one's ears or the thought of what he had demonstrated out of one's mind. He seldom demonstrated a single patient, but mostly a series of similar or contrasting cases which he compared with one another. In the hall in which he gave his lectures there hung a picture which showed 'citizen' Pinel having the chains taken off the poor madmen in the Salpêtrière.[2] The Salpêtrière, which had witnessed so many horrors during the Revolution had also been the scene of this most humane of all revolutions. At such lectures Maître Charcot himself made a curious impression. He, who at other times bubbled over with vivacity and cheerfulness and who always had a joke on his lips, now looked serious and solemn under his little velvet cap; indeed, he even seemed to have grown older. His voice sounded subdued. We could almost understand how ill-disposed strangers could reproach the whole lecture with being theatrical. Those who spoke like this were doubtless accustomed to the formlessness of German clinical lectures, or else forgot that Charcot gave only *one* lecture in the week and could therefore prepare it carefully.

In this formal lecture, in which everything was prepared and everything had to have its place, Charcot was no doubt following a deeply-rooted tradition; but he also felt the need to give his audience a less elaborated picture of his activities. This purpose was served by his out-patient clinic of which he took personal charge in what were known as

2. {Philippe Pinel (1745–1826), the hero of reformers looking to a more humane treatment of the mentally ill, became chief physician of the Salpêtrière in 1794; the extent of his humaneness has recently become the subject of intense research and no less intense controversy.}

his '*Leçons du mardi*'. There he took up cases which were completely unknown to him; he exposed himself to all the chances of an examination, all the errors of a first investigation; he would put aside his authority on occasion and admit—in one case that he could arrive at no diagnosis and in another that he had been deceived by appearances; and he never appeared greater to his audience than when, by giving the most detailed account of his processes of thought and by showing the greatest frankness about his doubts and hesitations, he had thus sought to narrow the gulf between teacher and pupil. The publication of these improvised lectures, given in the year 1887 and 1888, at first in French and now in German as well, has also immeasurably widened the circle of his admirers; and never before has a work on neuropathology had such a success with the medical public as this.

At about the time at which the clinic was established and at which he gave up the Chair of Pathological Anatomy, a change occurred in the direction of Charcot's scientific pursuits, and to this we owe the finest of his work. He now pronounced that the theory of organic nervous illnesses was for the time being fairly complete, and he began to turn his attention almost exclusively to hysteria, which thus all at once became the focus of general interest. This, the most enigmatic of all nervous diseases, for the evaluation of which medicine had not yet found a serviceable angle of approach, had just then fallen into thorough discredit; and this discredit extended not only to the patients but to the physicians who concerned themselves with the neurosis. It was held that in hysteria anything was possible, and no credence was given to a hysteric about anything. The first thing that Charcot's work did was to restore its dignity to the topic. Little by little, people gave up the scornful smile with which the patient could at that time feel certain of being met. She was no longer necessarily a malingerer, for Charcot had thrown the whole weight of his authority on the side of the genuineness and objectivity of hysterical phenomena. * * * He treated hysteria as just another topic in neuropathology; he gave a complete description of its phenomena, demonstrated that these had their own laws and uniformities, and showed how to recognize the symptoms which enable a diagnosis of hysteria to be made. The most painstaking investigations, initiated by himself and his pupils, extended over hysterical disturbances of sensibility in the skin and deeper tissues, over the behaviour of the sense organs, and over the peculiarities of hysterical contractures and paralyses, and of trophic disturbances and changes in metabolism. The many different forms of hysterical attack were described, and a schematic plan was drawn up by depicting the typical configuration of the major hysterical attack ['*grande hystérie*'] as occurring in four stages, which made it possible to trace the commonly observed 'minor' attacks ['*petite hystérie*'] back to this same typical configuration. The localization and frequency of occurrence of the so-called 'hysterogenic zones' and their relationship to the attacks were also studied, and so on. Once all this information about the manifestations of hysteria had been arrived at, a number of surprising discoveries were made. Hysteria in males, and especially in men of the working class, was found far more often than had been expected; it was convincingly shown that certain conditions which had been put down to alcoholic intoxication or lead-poisoning were of a hysterical nature; it was possible to subsume under hysteria a whole number of affections which had hitherto not been understood and which had remained unclassified; and where the neurosis had become joined with other disorders to form complex pictures, it was possible to separate out the part played by hysteria. Most far-reaching of all were the investigations into nervous illnesses which followed upon severe traumas—the 'traumatic neuroses'—views about which are still under discussion and in connection with which Charcot has successfully put forward the arguments in favour of hysteria.

*   *   *

The construction of this great edifice was naturally not achieved without violent opposition. But it was the sterile opposition of an old generation who did not want to have their views changed. The younger among the neuropathologists, including those in Germany, accepted Charcot's teaching to a greater or lesser degree. Charcot himself was completely certain that his theories about hysteria would triumph. When it was objected that the four stages of hysteria, hysteria in men, and so on, were not observable outside France, he pointed out how long he himself had overlooked these things, and he said once more that hysteria was the same in all places and at every time. He was very sensitive about the accusation that the French were a far more neurotic nation than any other and that hysteria was a kind of national bad habit; and he was much pleased when a paper 'On a Case of Reflex Epilepsy', which dealt with a Prussian Grenadier, enabled him to make a long-range diagnosis of hysteria.

At one point in his work Charcot rose to a level higher even than that of his usual treatment of hysteria. The step he took assured him for all time, too, the fame of having been the first to explain hysteria. While he was engaged in the study of hysterical paralyses arising after traumas, he had the idea of artificially reproducing those paralyses, which he had earlier differentiated with care from organic ones. For this purpose he made use of hysterical patients whom he put into a state of somnambulism by hypnotizing them. He succeeded in proving, by an unbroken chain of argument, that these paralyses were the result of ideas which had dominated the patient's brain at moments of a special disposition. In this way, the mechanism of a hysterical phenomenon was explained for the first time. This incomparably fine piece of clinical research was afterwards taken up by his own pupil, Pierre Janet, as well as by Breuer and others, who developed from it a theory of neurosis which coincided with the mediaeval view—when once they had replaced the 'demon' of clerical phantasy by a psychological formula.

Charcot's concern with hypnotic phenomena in hysterical patients led to very great advances in this important field of hitherto neglected and despised facts, for the weight of his name put an end once and for all to any doubt about the reality of hypnotic manifestations. But the exclusively nosographical approach adopted at the School of the Salpêtrière was not suitable for a purely psychological subject. The restriction of the study of hypnosis to hysterical patients, the differentiation between major and minor hypnotism, the hypothesis of three stages of 'major hypnosis', and their characterization by somatic phenomena—all this sank in the estimation of Charcot's contemporaries when Liébeault's pupil, Bernheim, set about constructing the theory of hypnotism on a more comprehensive psychological foundation and making suggestion the central point of hypnosis. It is only the opponents of hypnotism who, content to conceal their lack of personal experience behind an appeal to authority, still cling to Charcot's assertions and who like to take advantage of a pronouncement made by him in his last years, in which he denied to hypnosis any value as a therapeutic method.

Furthermore, the aetiological theories supported by Charcot in his doctrine of the *'famillé névropathique'*, which he made the basis of his whole concept of nervous disorders, will no doubt soon require sifting and emending. So greatly did Charcot overestimate heredity as a causative agent that he left no room for the acquisition of nervous illness. To syphilis he merely allotted a modest place among the *'agents provocateurs'*; nor did he make a sufficiently sharp distinction between organic nervous affections and neuroses, either as regards their aetiology or in other respects. It is inevitable that the advance of our science, as it increases our knowledge, must at the same time lessen the value of a number of things that Charcot taught us; but neither changing times nor changing views can diminish the fame of the man whom—in France and elsewhere—we are mourning to-day.

VIENNA, August 1893.

Draft B

Freud met Wilhelm Fliess (1858–1926), a reputable nose and throat specialist from Berlin, in November 1887, and the two men soon became fast friends, sharing the most intimate personal and professional secrets. They remained friends until they quarreled irreparably in 1900 and, though their correspondence lingered on for several years, never saw one another again. The importance of Fliess for Freud cannot be overestimated: during the 1890s, the decade that Freud scouted out unknown terrains of the mind,

Fliess was Freud's reliable and imaginative supporter, critic, inspiration. In a rather loose sense, he acted as Freud's analyst; there was no one—no one—whom Freud trusted so completely and on whom he transferred more passionate feelings. Fliess was enamored of highly unconventional notions concerning the influence of the nose on other bodily organs, and propagated speculations about male and female cycles of twenty-three and twenty-eight days respectively, which, he thought, determined moods, creativity, and the recurrence of ailments. For years, though, Freud was wholly uncritical of his friend from Berlin, met him at occasional "congresses" where the two men canvassed their latest discoveries, and sent him confidential letters and long exploratory memoranda in which he developed his burgeoning theories of mental functioning—and malfunctioning. The following draft, enclosed in a letter of February 8, 1893, is a good instance of such a memorandum. It shows Freud experimenting with ideas about what he would later call "anxiety neurosis." It also shows the importance that sexuality had begun to assume as a causative factor in "neurasthenia."

THE AETIOLOGY OF THE NEUROSES

I am writing the whole thing down a second time, for you, my dear friend, and for the sake of our common labours. You will of course keep the draft away from your young wife.

I. It may be taken as a recognized fact that *neurasthenia* is a frequent consequence of an abnormal sexual life. The assertion, however, which I wish to make and to test by my observations is that neurasthenia is always *only* a sexual neurosis.

I have adopted a similar point of view (along with Breuer) in regard to hysteria. Traumatic hysteria was well known; what we asserted beyond this was that *every* hysteria that is not hereditary is traumatic. In the same way I am now asserting that *every* neurasthenia is sexual.

We will for the moment leave on one side the question of whether hereditary disposition and, secondarily, toxic influences can produce genuine neurasthenia, or whether what appears to be hereditary neurasthenia in fact also goes back to early sexual exhaustion. If there is such a thing as hereditary neurasthenia, the questions arise of whether the *status nervosus* in the hereditary cases should not be distinguished from neurasthenia, what relation at all it has to the corresponding symptoms in childhood, and so on.

In the first instance, therefore, my contention will be restricted to *acquired* neurasthenia. What I am asserting can accordingly be formulated as follows. In the aetiology of a nervous affection we must distinguish (1) the necessary precondition without which the state cannot come about at all, and (2) the precipitating factors. The relation between these two can be pictured thus. If the necessary precondition has operated sufficiently, the affection sets in as an inevitable consequence; if it has not operated sufficiently, the result of its operation is in the first place a disposition to the affection which ceases to be latent as soon as a sufficient amount of one of the secondary factors supervenes. Thus what is lacking for full effect in the first aetiology can be replaced by the aetiology of the second order. The aetiology of the second order can, however, be dispensed with, while that of the first order is indispensable.

If this aetiological formula is applied to our present case, we arrive at this. Sexual exhaustion can by itself alone provoke neurasthenia. If it fails to achieve this by itself, it has such an effect on the disposition of the nervous system that physical illness, depressive affects and overwork (toxic influences) can no longer be tolerated without [leading to] neurasthenia. Without sexual exhaustion, however, all these factors are incapable of generating neurasthenia. They bring about normal fatigue, normal sorrow, normal physical weakness, but they only continue to give evidence of how much 'of these detrimental influences a normal person can tolerate'.

I will consider neurasthenia in men and in women separately.

Neurasthenia in males is acquired at puberty and becomes manifest in the patient's twenties. Its source is masturbation, the frequency of which runs completely parallel with the frequency of male neurasthenia. One can observe in the circle of one's acquaintances that (at all events in urban populations) those who have been seduced by women at an early age have escaped neurasthenia. When this noxa has operated long and intensely, it turns the person concerned into a sexual neurasthenic, whose potency, too, has been impaired; the intensity of the cause is paralleled by a life-long persistence of the condition. Further evidence of the causal connection lies in the fact that a sexual neurasthenic is always a general neurasthenic at the same time.

If the noxa has not been sufficiently intense, it will have (in accordance with the formula given above) an effect on the patient's disposition; so that later, if provoking factors supervene, it will produce neurasthenia, which those factors alone would not have produced. Intellectual work— cerebral neurasthenia; normal sexual activity—spinal neurasthenia, etc.

In intermediate cases we find the neurasthenia of youth, which typically begins and runs its course accompanied by dyspepsia, etc., and which terminates at marriage.

The second noxa, which affects men at a later age, makes its impact on a nervous system which is either intact or which has been disposed to neurasthenia through masturbation. The question is whether it can lead to detrimental results even in the former case; probably it can. Its effect is manifest in the second case, where it revives the neurasthenia of youth and creates new symptoms. This second noxa is *onanismus conjugalis*—incomplete coition in order to prevent conception. In the case of men all the methods of achieving this seem to fall into line: they operate with varying intensity according to the subject's earlier disposition, but do not actually differ qualitatively. Even normal coition is not tolerated by those with a strong disposition or by chronic neurasthenics; and beyond this, intolerance of the condom, of extra-vaginal coition and of coitus interruptus take their toll. A healthy man will tolerate all of these for quite a long time, but even so not indefinitely. After a certain time he behaves like the disposed subject. His only advantage over the masturbator is the privilege of a longer latency or the fact that on every occasion he needs a provoking cause. Here coitus interruptus proves to be the main noxa and produces its characteristic effect even in non-disposed subjects.

Neurasthenia in females. Normally, girls are sound and not neurasthenic; and this is true as well of young married women, in spite of all the sexual traumas of this period of life. In comparatively rare cases neurasthenia appears in married women and in older unmarried ones in its pure form; it is then to be regarded as having arisen spontaneously and in the same manner [? as is men]. Far more often neurasthenia in a married woman is derived from neurasthenia in a man or is produced simultaneously. In that case there is almost always an admixture of hysteria and we have the common mixed neurosis of women.

The *mixed neurosis* of women is derived from neurasthenia in men in all those not infrequent cases in which the man, being a sexual neurasthenic, suffers from impaired potency. The admixture of hysteria results directly from the *holding-back* of the excitation of the act. The poorer the man's potency, the more the woman's hysteria predominates; so that in reality a sexually neurasthenic man makes his wife not so much neurasthenic as hysterical.

This neurosis arises, with neurasthenia in males, during the second onset of sexual noxae, which is of far the greater significance for a woman, assuming that she is sound. Thus we come across far more neurotic men during the first decade of puberty and far more neurotic women during the second. In the latter case this is the result of the noxae due to the prevention of conception. It is not easy to arrange them in order and in general none of them should be regarded as entirely innocuous to women; so that even in the most favorable case (a condom) women, being the more exacting partners, will scarcely escape slight neurasthenia. A great deal will obviously depend on the two dispositions: whether (1) she herself was neurasthenic before marriage or whether (2) she was made hysterico-neurasthenic during the period of free intercourse [without preventives].

II. *Anxiety neurosis.* Every case of neurasthenia is no doubt marked by a certain lowering of self-confidence, by pessimistic expectation and an inclination to distressing antithetic ideas. But the question is whether the prominent emergence of this factor [anxiety], without the other symptoms being specially developed, should not be detached as an independent 'anxiety neurosis', especially as this is to be met with no less frequently in hysteria than in neurasthenia.

Anxiety neurosis appears in two forms: as a *chronic state* and as an *attack of anxiety*. The two may readily be combined: and an anxiety attack never occurs without chronic symptoms. Anxiety attacks are commoner in the forms connected with hysteria—more frequent, therefore, in women. The chronic symptoms are commoner in neurasthenic men.

The chronic symptoms are: (1) anxiety relating to the body (hypochondria); (2) anxiety relating to the functioning of the body (agoraphobia, claustrophobia, giddiness on heights); (3) anxiety relating to decisions and memory (*folie du doute*, obsessive brooding, etc.). So far, I have found no occasion for not treating these symptoms as equivalent. Again, the question is (1) to what extent this condition emerges in hereditary cases, without any sexual noxa, (2) whether it is released in hereditary cases by any chance sexual noxa, (3) whether it supervenes as an intensification in common neurasthenia. There is no question but that it is acquired, and specially by men and women in marriage, during the second period of sexual noxae, through coitus interruptus. I do not believe that disposition owing to earlier neurasthenia is necessary for this; but where disposition is lacking, latency is longer. The causal formula is the same as in neurasthenia.

The rarer cases of anxiety neurosis outside marriage are met with especially in men. They turn out to be cases of congressus interruptus in which the man is strongly involved psychically with women whose well-being is a matter of concern to him. This procedure in these conditions is a greater noxa for a man than coitus interruptus in marriage, for this is often corrected, as it were, by normal coitus outside marriage.

I must look upon *periodic depression*, an attack of anxiety lasting for weeks or months, as a third form of anxiety neurosis. This, in contrast to melancholia proper, almost always has an apparently rational connection with a psychical trauma. The latter is, however, only the provoking cause. Moreover, this periodic depression is without psychical [sexual] anaesthesia, which is characteristic of melancholia.

I have been able to trace back a number of such cases to coitus interruptus; their onset was a late one, during marriage, after the birth of the last child. In a case of tormenting hypochondria which began at puberty, I was able to prove an assault in the eighth year of life. Another case from childhood turned out to be a hysterical reaction to a masturbatory assault. Thus I cannot tell whether we have here truly hereditary forms without a sexual cause; and on the other hand I cannot tell whether coitus interruptus alone is to be blamed here, whether hereditary disposition can always be dispensed with.

I will omit occupational neuroses, since, as I have told you, changes in the muscular parts have been demonstrated in them.

CONCLUSIONS

It follows from what I have said that neuroses are entirely preventible as well as entirely incurable. The physician's task is wholly shifted on to prophylaxis.

The first part of this task, the prevention of the sexual noxa of the first period, coincides with prophylaxis against syphilis and gonorrhoea, since they are the noxae which threaten anyone who gives up masturbation. The only alternative would be free sexual intercourse between young men and respectable girls; but this could only be adopted if there were innocuous methods of preventing conception. Otherwise, the alternatives are: masturbation, neurasthenia in the male, hystero-neurasthenia in the female, or syphilis in the male, syphilis in the next generation, gonorrhoea in the male, gonorrhoea and sterility in the female.

The same problem—an innocuous means of controlling conception— is set by the sexual trauma of the second period; since the condom provides neither a safe solution nor one acceptable to someone who is already neurasthenic.

In the absence of such a solution, society appears doomed to fall a victim to incurable neuroses, which reduce the enjoyment of life to a minimum, destroy the marriage relation and bring hereditary ruin on the whole coming generation. The lower strata of society know nothing of Malthusianism, but they are in full pursuit, and in the course of things will reach the same point and fall victim to the same fatality.

Thus the physician is faced by a problem whose solution is worthy of all his efforts.

JOSEF BREUER

Anna O.

During the early 1890s, as Freud's intimacy with Fliess grew, his intimacy with his older friend Josef Breuer began to wane. Through the previous decade, the home of Breuer, and of his wife Mathilde, had been a warm, hospitable, generous, and always interesting refuge for the still unknown, immensely ambitious Freud. When Freud's oldest child, a daughter, was born in October 1887, he named her after Frau Breuer as a matter of course. And it was during these congenial years that Breuer told Freud about a fascinating hysteric he had treated some time earlier, between 1880 and 1882. The case had its embarrassing aspects, notably Anna O.'s infatuation with her physician (Freud would later call this a case of "transference love"), but precisely these interested Freud, and he pressed Breuer again and again for more details. While Breuer refused to follow the implications of "Anna

O.," Freud had the courage of Breuer's discoveries. Many years later, in his "Autobiographical Study," Freud would incorporate the essence of the case and be rather scathing about what he thought Breuer's genteel, nonsexual interpretation of Anna O.'s hysteria (see above, p. 13). Still, in a very real sense, Anna O. (really Bertha Pappenheim, later to become a prominent social worker and energetic leader in Jewish feminist causes) may claim the distinction of being the founding patient of psychoanalysis. That is why Freud more than once gave Breuer credit for originating psychoanalysis, and why this text, even if it is not by Freud, is essential to this anthology. In *Studies on Hysteria*, a collection of case histories and theoretical papers that Breuer and Freud published jointly in 1895, Anna O. has pride of place.

II
CASE HISTORIES

(BREUER AND FREUD)

CASE 1

FRÄULEIN ANNA O. (Breuer)

At the time of her falling ill (in 1880) Fräulein Anna O. was twenty-one years old. She may be regarded as having had a moderately severe neuropathic heredity, since some psychoses had occurred among her more distant relatives. Her parents were normal in this respect. She herself had hitherto been consistently healthy and had shown no signs of neurosis during her period of growth. She was markedly intelligent, with an astonishingly quick grasp of things and penetrating intuition. She possessed a powerful intellect which would have been capable of digesting solid mental pabulum and which stood in need of it—though without receiving it after she had left school. She had great poetic and imaginative gifts, which were under the control of a sharp and critical common sense. Owing to this latter quality she was *completely unsuggestible*; she was only influenced by arguments, never by mere assertions. Her will-power was energetic, tenacious and persistent; sometimes it reached the pitch of an obstinacy which only gave way out of kindness and regard for other people.

One of her essential character traits was sympathetic kindness. Even during her illness she herself was greatly assisted by being able to look after a number of poor, sick people, for she was thus able to satisfy a powerful instinct. Her states of feeling always tended to a slight exaggeration, alike of cheerfulness and gloom; hence she was sometimes subject to moods. The element of sexuality was astonishingly undeveloped in her. The patient, whose life became known to me to an extent to which one person's life is seldom known to another, had never been in love; and in all the enormous number of hallucinations which occurred during her illness that element of mental life never emerged.

This girl, who was bubbling over with intellectual vitality, led an extremely monotonous existence in her puritanically-minded family. She embellished her life in a manner which probably influenced her decisively in the direction of her illness, by indulging in systematic daydreaming, which she described as her 'private theatre'. While everyone thought she was attending, she was living through fairy tales in her imagination; but she was always on the spot when she was spoken to, so that no one was aware of it. She pursued this activity almost continuously while she was engaged on her household duties, which she discharged unexceptionably. I shall presently have to describe the way in which this habitual day-dreaming while she was well passed over into illness without a break.

The course of the illness fell into several clearly separable phases:

(A) Latent incubation. From the middle of July, 1880, till about December 10. This phase of an illness is usually hidden from us; but in this case, owing to its peculiar character, it was completely accessible; and this in itself lends no small pathological interest to the history. I shall describe this phase presently.

(B) The manifest illness. A psychosis of a peculiar kind, paraphasia, a convergent squint, severe disturbances of vision, paralyses (in the form of contractures), complete in the right upper and both lower extremities, partial in the left upper extremity, paresis of the neck muscles. A gradual reduction of the contracture to the right-hand extremities. Some improvement, interrupted by a severe psychical trauma (the death of the patient's father) in April, after which there followed

(C) A period of persisting somnambulism, subsequently alternating with more normal states. A number of chronic symptoms persisted till December, 1881.

(D) Gradual cessation of the pathological states and symptoms up to June, 1882.

In July, 1880, the patient's father, of whom she was passionately fond, fell ill of a peripleuritic abscess which failed to clear up and to which he succumbed in April, 1881. During the first months of the illness Anna devoted her whole energy to nursing her father, and no one was much surprised when by degrees her own health greatly deteriorated. No one, perhaps not even the patient herself, knew what was happening to her; but eventually the state of weakness, anaemia and distaste for food became so bad that to her great sorrow she was no longer allowed to continue nursing the patient. The immediate cause of this was a very severe cough, on account of which I examined her for the first time. It was a typical *tussis nervosa*. She soon began to display a marked craving for rest during the afternoon, followed in the evening by a sleep-like state and afterwards a highly excited condition.

At the beginning of December a convergent squint appeared. An ophthalmic surgeon explained this (mistakenly) as being due to paresis of one abducens. On December 11 the patient took to her bed and remained there until April 1.

There developed in rapid succession a series of severe disturbances which were *apparently* quite new: left-sided occipital headache; convergent squint (diplopia), markedly increased by excitement; complaints that the walls of the room seemed to be falling over (affection of the obliquus); disturbances of vision which it was hard to analyse; paresis of the muscles of the front of the neck, so that finally the patient could only move her head by pressing it backwards between her raised shoulders and moving her whole back; contracture and anaesthesia of the right upper, and, after a time, of the right lower extremity. The latter was fully extended, adducted and rotated inwards. Later the same symptom appeared in the left lower extremity and finally in the left arm, of which, however, the fingers to some extent retained the power of movement. So, too, there was no complete rigidity in the shoulder-joints. The contracture reached its maximum in the muscles of the upper arms. In the same way, the region of the elbows turned out to be the most affected by anaesthesia when, at a later stage, it became possible to make a more careful test of this. At the beginning of the illness the anaesthesia could not be efficiently tested, owing to the patient's resistance arising from feelings of anxiety.

It was while the patient was in this condition that I undertook her treatment, and I at once recognized the seriousness of the psychical disturbance with which I had to deal. Two entirely distinct states of consciousness were present which alternated very frequently and without warning and which became more and more differentiated in the course of the illness. In one of these states she recognized her surroundings; she was melancholy and anxious, but relatively normal. In the other state she hallucinated and was 'naughty'—that is to say, she was abusive, used to throw the cushions at people, so far as the contractures at various times allowed, tore buttons off her bedclothes and linen with those of her fingers which she could move, and so on. At this stage of her illness if something had been moved in the room or someone had entered or left it [during her other state of consciousness] she would complain of having 'lost' some time and would remark upon the gap in her train of conscious thoughts. Since those about her tried to deny this and to soothe her when she complained that she was going mad, she would, after throwing the pillows about, accuse people of doing things to her and leaving her in a muddle, etc.

These '*absences*' had already been observed before she took to her bed; she used then to stop in the middle of a sentence, repeat her last words and after a short pause go on talking. These interruptions gradually increased till they reached the dimensions that have just been described; and during the climax of the illness, when the contractures had extended to the left side of her body, it was only for a short time during the day that she was to any degree normal. But the disturbances invaded even her moments of relatively clear consciousness. There were extremely rapid changes of mood leading to excessive but quite temporary high spirits, and at other times severe anxiety, stubborn opposition to every therapeutic effort and frightening hallucinations of black snakes, which was how she saw her hair, ribbons and similar things. At the same time she kept on telling herself not to be so silly: what she was seeing was really only her hair, etc. At moments when her mind was quite clear she would complain of the profound darkness in her head, of not being able to think, of becoming blind and deaf, of having two selves, a real one and an evil one which forced her to behave badly, and so on.

In the afternoons she would fall into a somnolent state which lasted till about an hour after sunset. She would then wake up and complain that something was tormenting her—or rather, she would keep repeating in the impersonal form 'tormenting, tormenting'. For alongside of the development of the contractures there appeared a deep-going functional disorganization of her speech. It first became noticeable that she was at a loss to find words, and this difficulty gradually increased. Later she lost her command of grammar and syntax; she no longer conjugated verbs, and eventually she used only infinitives, for the most part incorrectly formed from weak past participles; and she omitted both the definite and indefinite article. In the process of time she became almost completely deprived of words. She put them together laboriously out of four or five languages and became almost unintelligible. When she tried to write (until her contractures entirely prevented her doing so) she employed the same jargon. For two weeks she became completely dumb and in spite of making great and continuous efforts to speak she was unable to say a syllable. And now for the first time the psychical mechanism of the disorder became clear. As I knew, she had felt very much offended over something and had determined not to speak about it. When I guessed this and obliged her to talk about it, the inhibition, which had made any other kind of utterance impossible as well, disappeared.

This change coincided with a return of the power of movement to the extremities of the left side of her body, in March, 1881. Her paraphasia receded; but thenceforward she spoke only in English—apparently, however, without knowing that she was doing so. She had disputes with her nurse who was, of course, unable to understand her. It was only some months later that I was able to convince her that she was talking English. Nevertheless, she herself could still understand the people about her who talked German. Only in moments of extreme anxiety did her power of speech desert her entirely, or else she would use a mixture of all sorts of languages. At times when she was at her very best and most free, she talked French and Italian. There was complete amnesia between these times and those at which she talked English. At this point, too, her squint began to diminish and made its appearance only at moments of great excitement. She was once again able to support her head. On the first of April she got up for the first time.

On the fifth of April her adored father died. During her illness she had seen him very rarely and for short periods. This was the most severe psychical trauma that she could possibly have experienced. A violent outburst of excitement was succeeded by profound stupor which lasted about two days and from which she emerged in a greatly changed state. At first she was far quieter and her feelings of anxiety were much diminished. The contracture of her right arm and leg persisted as well as their anaesthesia, though this was not deep. There was a high degree of restriction of the field of vision: in a bunch of flowers which gave her much pleasure she could only see one flower at a time. She complained of not being able to recognize people. Normally, she said, she had been able to recognize faces without having to make any deliberate effort; now she was obliged to do laborious 'recognizing work'[1] and had to say to herself 'this person's nose is such-and-such, his hair is such-and-such, so he must be so-and-so'. All the people she saw seemed like wax figures without any connection with her. She found the presence of some of her close relatives very distressing and this negative attitude grew continually stronger. If someone whom she was ordinarily pleased to see came into the room, she would recognize him and would be aware of things for a short time, but would soon sink back into her own broodings and her visitor was blotted out. I was the only person whom she always recognized when I came in; so long as I was talking to her she was always in contact with things and lively, except for the sudden interruptions caused by one of her hallucinatory '*absences*'.

She now spoke only English and could not understand what was said to her in German. Those about her were obliged to talk to her in English; even the nurse learned to make herself to some extent understood in this way. She was, however, able to read French and Italian. If she had to read one of these aloud, what she produced, with extraordinary fluency, was an admirable extempore English translation.

She began writing again, but in a peculiar fashion. She wrote with her left hand, the less stiff one, and she used Roman printed letters, copying the alphabet from her edition of Shakespeare.

She had eaten extremely little previously, but now she refused nourishment altogether. However, she allowed me to feed her, so that she very soon began to take more food. But she never consented to eat bread.

1. [In English in the original.]

After her meal she invariably rinsed out her mouth and even did so if, for any reason, she had not eaten anything—which shows how absent-minded she was about such things.

Her somnolent states in the afternoon and her deep sleep after sunset persisted. If, after this, she had talked herself out (I shall have to explain what is meant by this later) she was clear in mind, calm and cheerful.

This comparatively tolerable state did not last long. Some ten days after her father's death a consultant was brought in, whom, like all strangers, she completely ignored while I demonstrated all her peculiarities to him. 'That's like an examination,'[2] she said, laughing, when I got her to read a French text aloud in English. The other physician intervened in the conversation and tried to attract her attention, but in vain. It was a genuine 'negative hallucination' of the kind which has since so often been produced experimentally. In the end he succeeded in breaking through it by blowing smoke in her face. She suddenly saw a stranger before her, rushed to the door to take away the key and fell unconscious to the ground. There followed a short fit of anger and then a severe attack of anxiety which I had great difficulty in calming down. Unluckily I had to leave Vienna that evening, and when I came back several days later I found the patient much worse. She had gone entirely without food the whole time, was full of anxiety and her hallucinatory *absences* were filled with terrifying figures, death's heads and skeletons. Since she acted these things through as though she was experiencing them and in part put them into words, the people around her became aware to a great extent of the content of these hallucinations.

The regular order of things was: the somnolent state in the afternoon, followed after sunset by the deep hypnosis for which she invented the technical name of 'clouds'.[3] If during this she was able to narrate the hallucinations she had had in the course of the day, she would wake up clear in mind, calm and cheerful. She would sit down to work and write or draw far into the night quite rationally. At about four she would go to bed. Next day the whole series of events would be repeated. It was a truly remarkable contrast: in the day-time the irresponsible patient pursued by hallucinations, and at night the girl with her mind completely clear.

In spite of her euphoria at night, her psychical condition deteriorated steadily. Strong suicidal impulses appeared which made it seem inadvisable for her to continue living on the third floor. Against her will, therefore, she was transferred to a country house in the neighbourhood of Vienna (on June 7, 1881). I had never threatened her with this removal from her home, which she regarded with horror, but she herself had, without saying so, expected and dreaded it. This event made it clear once more how much the affect of anxiety dominated her psychical disorder. Just as after her father's death a calmer condition had set in,

2. [In English in the original.]   3. [In English in the original.]

so now, when what she feared had actually taken place, she once more became calmer. Nevertheless, the move was immediately followed by three days and nights completely without sleep or nourishment, by numerous attempts at suicide (though, so long as she was in a garden, these were not dangerous), by smashing windows and so on, and by hallucinations unaccompanied by *absences*—which she was able to distinguish easily from her other hallucinations. After this she grew quieter, let the nurse feed her and even took chloral at night.

Before continuing my account of the case, I must go back once more and describe one of its peculiarities which I have hitherto mentioned only in passing. I have already said that throughout the illness up to this point the patient fell into a somnolent state every afternoon and that after sunset this period passed into a deeper sleep—'clouds'. (It seems plausible to attribute this regular sequence of events merely to her experience while she was nursing her father, which she had had to do for several months. During the nights she had watched by the patient's bedside or had been awake anxiously listening till the morning; in the afternoons she had lain down for a short rest, as is the usual habit of nurses. This pattern of waking at night and sleeping in the afternoons seems to have been carried over into her own illness and to have persisted long after the sleep had been replaced by a hypnotic state.) After the deep sleep had lasted about an hour she grew restless, tossed to and fro and kept repeating 'tormenting, tormenting', with her eyes shut all the time. It was also noticed how, during her *absences* in day-time she was obviously creating some situation or episode to which she gave a clue with a few muttered words. It happened then—to begin with accidentally but later intentionally—that someone near her repeated one of these phrases of hers while she was complaining about the 'tormenting'. She at once joined in and began to paint some situation or tell some story, hesitatingly at first and in her paraphasic jargon; but the longer she went on the more fluent she became, till at last she was speaking quite correct German. (This applies to the early period before she began talking English only.) The stories were always sad and some of them very charming, in the style of Hans Andersen's *Picture-book without Pictures*, and, indeed, they were probably constructed on that model. As a rule their starting-point or central situation was of a girl anxiously sitting by a sick-bed. But she also built up her stories on quite other topics.—A few moments after she had finished her narrative she would wake up, obviously calmed down, or, as she called it, *'gehäglich'*.[4] During the night she would again become restless, and in the morning, after a couple of hours' sleep, she was visibly involved in some other set of ideas.—If for any reason she was unable to tell me the story during her evening hypnosis she failed to calm down afterwards, and on the fol-

4. [She used this made-up word instead of the regular German *'behaglich,'* meaning 'comfortable.']

lowing day she had to tell me *two* stories in order for this to happen.

The essential features of this phenomenon—the mounting up and intensification of her *absences* into her auto-hypnosis in the evening, the effect of the products of her imagination as psychical stimuli and the easing and removal of her state of stimulation when she gave utterance to them in her hypnosis—remained constant throughout the whole eighteen months during which she was under observation.

The stories naturally became still more tragic after her father's death. It was not, however, until the deterioration of her mental condition, which followed when her state of somnambulism was forcibly broken into in the way already described, that her evening narratives ceased to have the character of more or less freely-created poetical compositions and changed into a string of frightful and terrifying hallucinations. (It was already possible to arrive at these from the patient's behaviour during the day.) I have already described how completely her mind was relieved when, shaking with fear and horror, she had reproduced these frightful images and given verbal utterance to them.

While she was in the country, when I was unable to pay her daily visits, the situation developed as follows. I used to visit her in the evening, when I knew I should find her in her hypnosis, and I then relieved her of the whole stock of imaginative products which she had accumulated since my last visit. It was essential that this should be effected completely if good results were to follow. When this was done she became perfectly calm, and next day she would be agreeable, easy to manage, industrious and even cheerful; but on the second day she would be increasingly moody, contrary and unpleasant, and this would become still more marked on the third day. When she was like this it was not always easy to get her to talk, even in her hypnosis. She aptly described this procedure, speaking seriously, as a 'talking cure', while she referred to it jokingly as 'chimney-sweeping'.[5] She knew that after she had given utterance to her hallucinations she would lose all her obstinacy and what she described as her 'energy'; and when, after some comparatively long interval, she was in a bad temper, she would refuse to talk, and I was obliged to overcome her unwillingness by urging and pleading and using devices such as repeating a formula with which she was in the habit of introducing her stories. But she would never begin to talk until she had satisfied herself of my identity by carefully feeling my hands. On those nights on which she had not been calmed by verbal utterance it was necessary to fall back upon chloral. I had tried it on a few earlier occasions, but I was obliged to give her 5 grammes, and sleep was preceded by a state of intoxication which lasted for some hours. When I was present this state was euphoric, but in my absence it was highly disagreeable and characterized by anxiety as well as excitement. (It may

5. [These two phrases are in English in the original.]

be remarked incidentally that this severe state of intoxication made no difference to her constractures.) I had been able to avoid the use of narcotics, since the verbal utterance of her hallucinations calmed her even though it might not induce sleep; but when she was in the country the nights on which she had not obtained hypnotic relief were so unbearable that in spite of everything it was necessary to have recourse to chloral. But it became possible gradually to reduce the dose.

The persisting somnambulism did not return. But on the other hand the alternation between two states of consciousness persisted. She used to hallucinate in the middle of a conversation, run off, start climbing up a tree, etc. If one caught hold of her, she would very quickly take up her interrupted sentence without knowing anything about what had happened in the interval. All these hallucinations, however, came up and were reported on in her hypnosis.

Her condition improved on the whole. She took nourishment without difficulty and allowed the nurse to feed her; except that she asked for bread but rejected it the moment it touched her lips. The paralytic contracture of the leg diminished greatly. There was also an improvement in her power of judgement and she became much attached to my friend Dr. B., the physician who visited her. She derived much benefit from a Newfoundland dog which was given to her and of which she was passionately fond. On one occasion, though, her pet made an attack on a cat, and it was splendid to see the way in which the frail girl seized a whip in her left hand and beat off the huge beast with it to rescue his victim. Later, she looked after some poor, sick people, and this helped her greatly.

It was after I returned from a holiday trip which lasted several weeks that I received the most convincing evidence of the pathogenic and exciting effect brought about by the ideational complexes which were produced during her *absences*, or *condition seconde*, and of the fact that these complexes were disposed of by being given verbal expression during hypnosis. During this interval no 'talking cure' had been carried out, for it was impossible to persuade her to confide what she had to say to anyone but me—not even to Dr. B. to whom she had in other respects become devoted. I found her in a wretched moral state, inert, unamenable, ill-tempered, even malicious. It became plain from her evening stories that her imaginative and poetic vein was drying up. What she reported was more and more concerned with her hallucinations and, for instance, the things that had annoyed her during the past days. These were clothed in imaginative shape, but were merely formulated in stereotyped images rather than elaborated into poetic productions. But the situation only became tolerable after I had arranged for the patient to be brought back to Vienna for a week and evening after evening made her tell me three to five stories. When I had accomplished this, everything that had accumulated during the weeks of my absence had been worked off. It was only now that the former rhythm was re-established:

on the day after her giving verbal utterance to her phantasies she was amiable and cheerful, on the second day she was more irritable and less agreeable and on the third positively 'nasty'. Her moral state was a function of the time that had elapsed since her last utterance. This was because every one of the spontaneous products of her imagination and every event which had been assimilated by the pathological part of her mind persisted as a psychical stimulus until it had been narrated in her hypnosis, after which it completely ceased to operate.

When, in the autumn, the patient returned to Vienna (though to a different house from the one in which she had fallen ill), her condition was bearable, both physically and mentally; for very few of her experiences—in fact only her more striking ones—were made into psychical stimuli in a pathological manner. I was hoping for a continuous and increasing improvement, provided that the permanent burdening of her mind with fresh stimuli could be prevented by her giving regular verbal expression to them. But to begin with I was disappointed. In December there was a marked deterioration of her psychical condition. She once more became excited, gloomy and irritable. She had no more 'really good days' even when it was impossible to detect anything that was remaining 'stuck' inside her. Towards the end of December, at Christmas time, she was particularly restless, and for a whole week in the evenings she told me nothing new but only the imaginative products which she had elaborated under the stress of great anxiety and emotion during the Christmas of 1880 [a year earlier]. When the scenes had been completed she was greatly relieved.

A year had now passed since she had been separated from her father and had taken to her bed, and from this time on her condition became clearer and was systematized in a very peculiar manner. Her alternating states of consciousness, which were characterized by the fact that, from morning onwards, her *absences* (that is to say, the emergence of her *condition seconde*) always became more frequent as the day advanced and took entire possession by the evening—these alternating states had differed from each other previously in that one (the first) was normal and the second alienated; now, however, they differed further in that in the first she lived, like the rest of us, in the winter of 1881–2, whereas in the second she lived in the winter of 1880–1, and had completely forgotten all the subsequent events. The one thing that nevertheless seemed to remain conscious most of the time was the fact that her father had died. She was carried back to the previous year with such intensity that in the new house she hallucinated her old room, so that when she wanted to go to the door she knocked up against the stove which stood in the same relation to the window as the door did in the old room. The change-over from one state to another occurred spontaneously but could also be very easily brought about by any sense-impression which vividly recalled the previous year. One had only to hold up an orange before her eyes (oranges were what she had chiefly lived on during the

first part of her illness) in order to carry her over from the year 1882 to
the year 1881. But this transfer into the past did not take place in a
general or indefinite manner; she lived through the previous winter day
by day. I should only have been able to *suspect* that this was happening,
had it not been that every evening during the hypnosis she talked through
whatever it was that had excited her on the same day in 1881, and had
it not been that a private diary kept by her mother in 1881 confirmed
beyond a doubt the occurrence of the underlying events. This re-living
of the previous year continued till the illness came to its final close in
June, 1882.

It was interesting here, too, to observe the way in which these revived
psychical stimuli belonging to her secondary state made their way over
into her first, more normal one. It happened, for instance, that one
morning the patient said to me laughingly that she had no idea what
was the matter but she was angry with me. Thanks to the diary I knew
what was happening; and, sure enough, this was gone through again in
the evening hypnosis: I had annoyed the patient very much on the same
evening in 1881. Or another time she told me there was something the
matter with her eyes; she was seeing colours wrong. She knew she was
wearing a brown dress but she saw it as a blue one. We soon found that
she could distinguish all the colours of the visual test-sheets correctly
and clearly, and that the disturbance only related to the dress-material.
The reason was that during the same period in 1881 she had been very
busy with a dressing-gown for her father, which was made with the same
material as her present dress, but was blue instead of brown. Incidentally,
it was often to be seen that these emergent memories showed their effect
in advance; the disturbance of her normal state would occur earlier on,
and the memory would only gradually be awakened in her *condition
seconde*.

Her evening hypnosis was thus heavily burdened, for we had to talk
off not only her contemporary imaginative products but also the events
and 'vexations'[6] of 1881. (Fortunately I had already relieved her at the
time of the imaginative products of that year.) But in addition to all this
the work that had to be done by the patient and her physician was
immensely increased by a third group of separate disturbances which
had to be disposed of in the same manner. These were the psychical
events involved in the period of incubation of the illness between July
and December, 1880; it was they that had produced the whole of the
hysterical phenomena, and when they were brought to verbal utterance
the symptoms disappeared.

When this happened for the first time—when, as a result of an accidental and spontaneous utterance of this kind, during the evening
hypnosis, a disturbance which had persisted for a considerable time
vanished—I was greatly surprised. It was in the summer during a period

6. [In English in the original.]

of extreme heat, and the patient was suffering very badly from thirst; for, without being able to account for it in any way, she suddenly found it impossible to drink. She would take up the glass of water she longed for, but as soon as it touched her lips she would push it away like someone suffering from hydrophobia. As she did this, she was obviously in an *absence* for a couple of seconds. She lived only on fruit, such as melons, etc., so as to lessen her tormenting thirst. This had lasted for some six weeks, when one day during hypnosis she grumbled about her English lady-companion whom she did not care for, and went on to describe, with every sign of disgust, how she had once gone into that lady's room and how her little dog—horrid creature!—had drunk out of a glass there. The patient had said nothing, as she had wanted to be polite. After giving further energetic expression to the anger she had held back, she asked for something to drink, drank a large quantity of water without any difficulty and woke from her hypnosis with the glass at her lips; and thereupon the disturbance vanished, never to return. A number of extremely obstinate whims were similarly removed after she had described the experiences which had given rise to them. She took a great step forward when the first of her chronic symptoms disappeared in the same way—the contracture of her right leg, which, it is true, had already diminished a great deal. These findings—that in the case of this patient the hysterical phenomena disappeared as soon as the event which had given rise to them was reproduced in her hypnosis—made it possible to arrive at a therapeutic technical procedure which left nothing to be desired in its logical consistency and systematic application. Each individual symptom in this complicated case was taken separately in hand; all the occasions on which it had appeared were described in reverse order, starting before the time when the patient became bed-ridden and going back to the event which had led to its first appearance. When this had been described the symptom was permanently removed.

In this way her paralytic contractures and anaesthesias, disorders of vision and hearing of every sort, neuralgias, coughing, tremors, etc., and finally her disturbances of speech were 'talked away'. Amongst the disorders of vision, the following, for instance, were disposed of separately: the convergent squint with diplopia; deviation of both eyes to the right, so that when her hand reached out for something it always went to the left of the object; restriction of the visual field; central amblyopia; macropsia; seeing a death's head instead of her father; inability to read. Only a few scattered phenomena (such, for instance, as the extension of the paralytic contractures to the left side of her body) which had developed while she was confined to bed, were untouched by this process of analysis, and it is probable, indeed, that they had in fact no immediate psychical cause.

It turned out to be quite impracticable to shorten the work by trying to elicit in her memory straight away the first provoking cause of her symptoms. She was unable to find it, grew confused, and things proceeded even more slowly than if she was allowed quietly and steadily to follow back the thread of memories on which she had embarked. Since the latter method, however, took too long in the evening hypnosis, owing to her being over-strained and distraught by 'talking out' the two other sets of experiences—and owing, too, to the reminiscences needing time before they could attain sufficient vividness—we evolved the following procedure. I used to visit her in the morning and hypnotize her. (Very simple methods of doing this were arrived at empirically.) I would next ask her to concentrate her thoughts on the symptom we were treating at the moment and to tell me the occasions on which it had appeared. The patient would proceed to describe in rapid succession and under brief headings the external events concerned and these I would jot down. During her subsequent evening hypnosis she would then, with the help of my notes, give me a fairly detailed account of these circumstances.

An example will show the exhaustive manner in which she accomplished this. It was our regular experience that the patient did not hear when she was spoken to. It was possible to differentiate this passing habit of not hearing as follows:

(a) Not hearing when someone came in, while her thoughts were abstracted. 108 separate detailed instances of this, mentioning the persons and circumstances, often with dates. First instance: not hearing her father come in.

(b) Not understanding when several people were talking. 27 instances. First instance: her father, once more, and an acquaintance.

(c) Not hearing when she was alone and directly addressed. 50 instances. Origin: her father having vainly asked her for some wine.

(d) Deafness brought on by being shaken (in a carriage, etc.). 15 instances. Origin: having been shaken angrily by her young brother when he caught her one night listening at the sickroom door.

(e) Deafness brought on by fright at a noise. 37 instances. Origin: a choking fit of her father's, caused by swallowing the wrong way.

(f) Deafness during deep *absence*. 12 instances.

(g) Deafness brought on by listening hard for a long time, so that when she was spoken to she failed to hear. 54 instances.

Of course all these episodes were to a great extent identical in so far as they could be traced back to states of abstraction or *absences* or to fright. But in the patient's memory they were so clearly differentiated, that if she happened to make a mistake in their sequence she would be obliged to correct herself and put them in the right order; if this was not done her report came to a standstill. The events she described were so lacking in interest and significance and were told in such detail that there could be no suspicion of their having been invented. Many of these incidents consisted of purely internal experiences and so could not be verified; others of them (or circumstances attending them) were within the recollection of people in her environment.

This example, too, exhibited a feature that was always observable when a symptom was being 'talked away': the particular symptom emerged with greater force while she was discussing it. Thus during the analysis of her not being able to hear she was so deaf that for part of the time I was obliged to communicate with her in writing. The first provoking cause was habitually a fright of some kind, experienced while she was nursing her father—some oversight on her part, for instance.

The work of remembering was not always an easy matter and sometimes the patient had to make great efforts. On one occasion our whole progress was obstructed for some time because a recollection refused to emerge. It was a question of a particularly terrifying hallucination. While she was nursing her father she had seen him with a death's head. She and the people with her remembered that once, while she still appeared to be in good health, she had paid a visit to one of her relatives. She had opened the door and all at once fallen down unconscious. In order to get over the obstruction to our progress she visited the same place again and, on entering the room, again fell to the ground unconscious. During her subsequent evening hypnosis the obstacle was surmounted. As she came into the room, she had seen her pale face reflected in a mirror hanging opposite the door; but it was not herself that she saw but her father with a death's head.—We often noticed that her dread of a memory, as in the present instance, inhibited its emergence, and this had to be brought about forcibly by the patient or physician.

The following incident, among others, illustrates the high degree of logical consistency of her states. During this period, as has already been explained, the patient was always in her *condition seconde*—that is, in the year 1881—at night. On one occasion she woke up during the night, declaring that she had been taken away from home once again, and became so seriously excited that the whole household was alarmed. The reason was simple. During the previous evening the talking cure had cleared up her disorder of vision, and this applied also to her *condition seconde*. Thus when she woke up in the night she found herself in a strange room, for her family had moved house in the spring of 1881. Disagreeable events of this kind were avoided by my always (at her request) shutting her eyes in the evening and giving her a suggestion that she would not be able to open them till I did so myself on the following morning. The disturbance was only repeated once, when the patient cried in a dream and opened her eyes on waking up from it.

Since this laborious analysis for her symptoms dealt with the summer months of 1880, which was the preparatory period of her illness, I obtained complete insight into the incubation and pathogenesis of this case of hysteria, and I will now describe them briefly.

In July, 1880, while he was in the country, her father fell seriously ill of a sub-pleural abscess. Anna shared the duties of nursing him with her mother. She once woke up during the night in great anxiety about the patient, who was in a high fever; and she was under the strain of expecting the arrival of a surgeon from Vienna who was to operate. Her mother had gone away for a short time and Anna was sitting at the bedside with her right arm over the back of her chair. She fell into a waking dream and saw a black snake coming towards the sick man from the wall to bite him. (It is most likely that there were in fact snakes in the field behind the house and that these had previously given the girl a fright; they would thus have provided the material for her hallucination.) She tried to keep the snake off, but it was as though she was paralysed. Her right arm, over the back of the chair, had gone to sleep and had become anaesthetic and paretic; and when she looked at it the fingers turned into little snakes with death's heads (the nails). (It seems probable that she had tried to use her paralysed right arm to drive off the snake and that its anaesthesia and paralysis had consequently become associated with the hallucination of the snake.) When the snake vanished, in her terror she tried to pray. But language failed her: she could find no tongue in which to speak, till at last she thought of some children's verses in English and then found herself able to think and pray in that language. The whistle of the train that was bringing the doctor whom she expected broke the spell.

Next day, in the course of a game, she threw a quoit into some bushes; and when she went to pick it out, a bent branch revived her hallucination of the snake, and simultaneously her right arm became rigidly extended. Thenceforward the same thing invariably occurred whenever the hallucination was recalled by some object with a more or less snake-like appearance. This hallucination, however, as well as the contracture only appeared during the short *absences* which became more and more frequent from that night onwards. (The contracture did not become stabilized until December, when the patient broke down completely and took to her bed permanently.) As a result of some particular event which I cannot find recorded in my notes and which I no longer recall, the contracture of the right leg was added to that of the right arm.

Her tendency to auto-hypnotic *absences* was from now on established. On the morning after the night I have described, while she was waiting for the surgeon's arrival, she fell into such a fit of abstraction that he finally arrived in the room without her having heard his approach. Her persistent anxiety interfered with her eating and gradually led to intense feelings of nausea. Apart from this, indeed, each of her hysterical symptoms arose during an affect. It is not quite certain whether in every case a momentary state of *absence* was involved, but this seems probable in view of the fact that in her waking state the patient was totally unaware of what had been going on.

* * *

I cannot feel much regret that the incompleteness of my notes makes it impossible for me to enumerate all the occasions on which her various hysterical symptoms appeared. She herself told me them in every single case, with the one exception I have mentioned; and, as I have already said, each symptom disappeared after she had described its first occurrence.

In this way, too, the whole illness was brought to a close. The patient herself had formed a strong determination that the whole treatment should be finished by the anniversary of the day on which she was moved into the country [June 7]. At the beginning of June, accordingly, she entered into the 'talking cure' with the greatest energy. On the last day— by the help of re-arranging the room so as to resemble her father's sickroom—she reproduced the terrifying hallucination which I have described above and which constituted the root of her whole illness. During the original scene she had only been able to think and pray in English; but immediately after its reproduction she was able to speak German. She was moreover free from the innumerable disturbances which she had previously exhibited.[7] After this she left Vienna and travelled for a while; but it was a considerable time before she regained her mental balance entirely. Since then she has enjoyed complete health.

* * *

There were two psychical characteristics present in the girl while she was still completely healthy which acted as predisposing causes for her subsequent hysterical illness:

(1) Her monotonous family life and the absence of adequate intellectual occupation left her with an unemployed surplus of mental liveliness and energy, and this found an outlet in the constant activity of her imagination.

(2) This led to a habit of day-dreaming (her 'private theatre'), which laid the foundations for a dissociation of her mental personality. Nevertheless a dissociation of this degree is still within the bounds of normality. Reveries and reflections during a more or less mechanical occupation do not in themselves imply a pathological splitting of consciousness, since if they are interrupted—if, for instance, the subject is spoken to —the normal unity of consciousness is restored; nor, presumably, is any amnesia present. In the case of Anna O., however, this habit prepared the ground upon which the affect of anxiety and dread was able to establish itself in the way I have described, when once that affect had transformed the patient's habitual day-dreaming into a hallucinatory

7. [At this point (so Freud once told the present editor {James Strachey}, with his finger on an open copy of the book) there is a hiatus in the text. What he had in mind and went on to describe was the occurrence which marked the end of Anna O.'s treatment. . . . [I]t is enough to say here that, when the treatment had apparently reached a successful end, the patient suddenly made manifest to Breuer the presence of a strong unanalyzed positive transference of an unmistakably sexual nature. {Behind these technical terms lies a dramatic story: after Breuer had said good-bye to his patient, about to go off on a trip with his wife who had become jealous of her husband's interesting patient, he was suddenly called back that very evening to discover that she was in the throes of a hysterical pregnancy, claiming to be carrying Breuer's child.} It was this occurrence, Freud believed, that caused Breuer to hold back the publication of the case history for so many years and that led ultimately to his abandonment of all further collaboration in Freud's researches.]

absence. It is remarkable how completely the earliest manifestation of her illness in its beginnings already exhibited its main characteristics, which afterwards remained unchanged for almost two years. * * *

* * *

The question now arises how far the patient's statements are to be trusted and whether the occasions and mode of origin of the phenomena were really as she represented them. So far as the more important and fundamental events are concerned, the trustworthiness of her account seems to me to be beyond question. As regards the symptoms disappearing after being 'talked away', I cannot use this as evidence; it may very well be explained by suggestion. But I always found the patient entirely truthful and trustworthy. The things she told me were intimately bound up with what was most sacred to her. Whatever could be checked by other people was fully confirmed. Even the most highly gifted girl would be incapable of concocting a tissue of data with such a degree of internal consistency as was exhibited in the history of this case. It cannot be disputed, however, that precisely her consistency may have led her (in perfectly good faith) to assign to some of her symptoms a precipitating cause which they did not in fact possess. But this suspicion, too, I consider unjustified. The very insignificance of so many of those causes, the irrational character of so many of the connections involved, argue in favour of their reality. The patient could not understand how it was that dance music made her cough; such a construction is too meaningless to have been deliberate. (It seemed very likely to me, incidentally, that each of her twinges of conscience brought on one of her regular spasms of the glottis and that the motor impulses which she felt—for she was very fond of dancing—transformed the spasm into a *tussis nervosa*.) Accordingly, in my view the patient's statements were entirely trustworthy and corresponded to the facts.

* * *

* * * Every one of her hypnoses in the evening afforded evidence that the patient was entirely clear and well-ordered in her mind and normal as regards her feeling and volition so long as none of the products of her secondary state was acting as a stimulus 'in the unconscious'. The extremely marked psychosis which appeared whenever there was any considerable interval in this unburdening process showed the degree to which those products influenced the psychical events of her 'normal' state. It is hard to avoid expressing the situation by saying that the patient was split into two personalities of which one was mentally normal and the other insane. The sharp division between the two states in the present patient only exhibits more clearly, in my opinion, what has given rise to a number of unexplained problems in many other hysterical patients. It was especially noticeable in Anna O. how much the products of her 'bad self', as she herself called it, affected her moral habit of mind. If these products had not been continually disposed of, we should have been faced by a hysteric of the malicious type—refractory, lazy, disagreeable and ill-natured; but, as it was, after the removal of those stimuli her true character, which was the opposite of all these, always reappeared at once.

* * *

The final cure of the hysteria deserves a few more words. It was accompanied, as I have already said, by considerable disturbances and a deterioration in the patient's mental condition. I had a very strong impression that the numerous products of her secondary state which had been quiescent were now forcing their way into consciousness; and though in the first instance they were being remembered only in her secondary state, they were nevertheless burdening and disturbing her normal one. It remains to be seen whether it may not be that the same origin is to be traced in other cases in which a chronic hysteria terminates in a psychosis.[8]

Katharina

There were a total of five extended case histories in Breuer and Freud's *Studies on Hysteria*: Breuer's epoch-making report on Anna O. (just above), and four cases by Freud. These patients—and others, like "Cäcilie M.," mentioned in passing—were Freud's highly appreciated instructors in what was rapidly becoming psychoanalytic technique. "Emmy von N.," a wealthy middle-aged widow whom Freud treated in 1889 and 1890 with Breuer's hypnoanalytic method for her tics and terrifying hallucinations, instructed Freud in the virtue of patience: rather crossly she told him as he kept interrupting that he should let her finish and tell her story in her own way. "Fräulein Elisabeth von R.," whom Freud hypnotized only briefly during her treatment in 1892, taught him the value of free association, of letting the patient's thoughts and speech ramble without rational control, and of working through symptoms over and over. "Miss Lucy R.," whom Freud treated late that same year, an English governess suffering from bizarre and apparently trivial symptoms—she was haunted by such olfactory hallucinations as the smell of burnt pudding—made Freud see (as he was already suspecting) that every symptom is meaningful, none is wholly arbitrary or absurd. Moreover, she confirmed in her treatment the lesson that Elisabeth von R. had already inculcated: the value of free association. In comparison, the case of "Katharina" appears almost like an anecdote. It illustrates Freud's early excessive self-confidence; he was later compelled by his clinical experience to abandon any hope that a single "session" might wholly cure a hysteria. It also dramatizes (see the concluding footnote) the tension between

8. {It remains to be said that Anna O.'s cure was by no means so complete as this concluding paragraph of Breuer's intimates. She had to spend time in a sanatorium, still addicted to morphine and still frequently subject to the loss of her German language. It was only after a time that most of her symptoms abated and she began to lead an active, highly productive life.}

the physician's need to respect his patient's privacy and to publicize his cases in the interest of science.

CASE 4

KATHARINA——(Freud)

In the summer vacation of the year 189– I made an excursion into the Hohe Tauern[1] so that for a while I might forget medicine and more particularly the neuroses. I had almost succeeded in this when one day I turned aside from the main road to climb mountain which lay somewhat apart and which was renowned for its views and for its well-run refuge hut. I reached the top after a strenuous climb and, feeling refreshed and rested, was sitting deep in contemplation of the charm of the distant prospect. I was so lost in thought that at first I did not connect it with myself when these words reached my ears: 'Are you a doctor, sir?' But the question was addressed to me, and by the rather sulky-looking girl of perhaps eighteen who had served my meal and had been spoken to by the landlady as 'Katharina'. To judge by her dress and bearing, she could not be a servant, but must no doubt be a daughter or relative of the landlady's.

Coming to myself I replied: 'Yes, I'm a doctor: but how did you know that?'

'You wrote your name in the Visitors' Book, sir. And I thought if you had a few moments to spare . . . The truth is, sir, my nerves are bad. I went to see a doctor in L—— about them and he gave me something for them; but I'm not well yet.'

So there I was with the neuroses once again—for nothing else could very well be the matter with this strong, well-built girl with her unhappy look. I was interested to find that neuroses could flourish in this way at a height of over 6,000 feet; I questioned her further therefore. I report the conversation that followed between us just as it is impressed on my memory. * * *

'Well, what is it you suffer from?'

'I get so out of breath. Not always. But sometimes it catches me so that I think I shall suffocate.'

This did not, at first sight, sound like a nervous symptom. But soon it occurred to me that probably it was only a description that stood for an anxiety attack: she was choosing shortness of breath out of the complex of sensations arising from anxiety and laying undue stress on that single factor.

'Sit down here. What is it like when you get "out of breath"?'

'It comes over me all at once. First of all it's like something pressing

1. [One of the highest ranges in the Eastern Alps.]

on my eyes. My head gets so heavy, there's a dreadful buzzing, and I feel so giddy that I almost fall over. Then there's something crushing my chest so that I can't get my breath.'

'And you don't notice anything in your throat?'

'My throat's squeezed together as though I were going to choke.'

'Does anything else happen in your head?'

'Yes, there's a hammering, enough to burst it.'

'And don't you feel at all frightened while this is going on?'

'I always think I'm going to die. I'm brave as a rule and go about everywhere by myself—into the cellar and all over the mountain. But on a day when that happens I don't dare to go anywhere; I think all the time someone's standing behind me and going to catch hold of me all at once.'

So it was in fact an anxiety attack, and introduced by the signs of a hysterical 'aura'[2]—or, more correctly, it was a hysterical attack the content of which was anxiety. Might there not probably be some other content as well?

'When you have an attack do you think of something? and always the same thing? or do you see something in front of you?'

'Yes. I always see an awful face that looks at me in a dreadful way, so that I'm frightened.'

Perhaps this might offer a quick means of getting to the heart of the matter.

'Do you recognize the face? I mean, is it a face that you've really seen some time?'

'No.'

'Do you know what your attacks come from?'

'No.'

'When did you first have them?'

'Two years ago, while I was still living on the other mountain with my aunt. (She used to run a refuge hut there, and we moved here eighteen months ago.) But they keep on happening.'

Was I to make an attempt at an analysis? I could not venture to transplant hypnosis to these altitudes, but perhaps I might succeed with a simple talk. I should have to try a lucky guess. I had found often enough that in girls anxiety was a consequence of the horror by which a virginal mind is overcome when it is faced for the first time with the world of sexuality.[3]

So I said: 'If you don't know, I'll tell you how I think you got your

---

2. [The premonitory sensations preceding an epileptic or hysterical attack.]

3. I will quote here the case in which I first recognized this causal connection. I was treating a young married woman who was suffering from a complicated neurosis and . . . was unable to admit that her illness arose from her married life. She objected that while she was still a girl she had had attacks of anxiety, ending in fainting fits. I remained firm. When we had come to know each other better she suddenly said to me one day: 'I'll tell you now how I came by my attacks of anxiety when I was a girl. At that time I used to sleep in a room next to my parents'; the door was left open and a night-light used to burn on the table. So more than once I saw my father get into bed with my mother and heard sounds that greatly excited me. It was then that my attacks came on.'

attacks. At that time, two years ago, you must have seen or heard something that very much embarrassed you, and that you'd much rather not have seen.'

'Heavens, yes!' she replied, 'that was when I caught my uncle with the girl, with Franziska, my cousin.'

'What's this story about a girl? Won't you tell me all about it?'

'You can say *anything* to a doctor, I suppose. Well, at that time, you know, my uncle—the husband of the aunt you've seen here—kept the inn on the——kogel. Now they're divorced, and it's my fault they were divorced, because it was through me that it came out that he was carrying on with Franziska.'

'And how did you discover it?'

'This way. One day two years ago some gentlemen had climbed the mountain and asked for something to eat. My aunt wasn't at home, and Franziska, who always did the cooking, was nowhere to be found. And my uncle was not to be found either. We looked everywhere, and at last Alois, the little boy, my cousin, said: "Why, Franziska must be in Father's room!" And we both laughed; but we weren't thinking anything bad. Then we went to my uncle's room but found it locked. That seemed strange to me. Then Alois said: "There's a window in the passage where you can look into the room." We went into the passage; but Alois wouldn't go to the window and said he was afraid. So I said: "You silly boy! I'll go. I'm not a bit afraid." And I had nothing bad in my mind. I looked in. The room was rather dark, but I saw my uncle and Franziska; he was lying on her.'

'Well?'

'I came away from the window at once, and leant up against the wall and couldn't get my breath—just what happens to me since. Everything went blank, my eyelids were forced together and there was a hammering and buzzing in my head.'

'Did you tell your aunt that very same day?'

'Oh no, I said nothing.'

'Then why were you so frightened when you found them together? Did you understand it? Did you know what was going on?'

'Oh no. I didn't understand anything at that time. I was only sixteen. I don't know what I was frightened about.'

'Fräulein Katharina, if you could remember now what was happening in you at that time, when you had your first attack, what you thought about it—it would help you.'

'Yes, if I could. But I was so frightened that I've forgotten everything.'

* * *

'Tell me, Fräulein. Can it be that the head that you always see when you lose your breath is Franziska's head, as you saw it then?'

'Oh no, she didn't look so awful. Besides, it's a man's head.'

'Or perhaps your uncle's?'

'I didn't see his face as clearly as that. It was too dark in the room. And why should he have been making such a dreadful face just then?'

'You're quite right.'

(The road suddenly seemed blocked. Perhaps something might turn up in the rest of her story.)

'And what happened then?'

'Well, those two must have heard a noise, because they came out soon afterwards. I felt very bad the whole time. I always kept thinking about it. Then two days later it was a Sunday and there was a great deal to do and I worked all day long. And on the Monday morning I felt giddy again and was sick, and I stopped in bed and was sick without stopping for three days.'

We [Breuer and I] had often compared the symptomatology of hysteria with a pictographic script which has become intelligible after the discovery of a few bilingual inscriptions. In that alphabet being sick means disgust. So I said: 'If you were sick three days later, I believe that means that when you looked into the room you felt disgusted.'

'Yes, I'm sure I felt digusted,' she said reflectively, 'but disgusted at what?'

'Perhaps you saw something naked? What sort of state were they in?'

'It was too dark to see anything; besides they both of them had their clothes on. Oh, if only I knew what it was I felt disgusted at!'

I had no idea either. But I told her to go on and tell me whatever occurred to her, in the confident expectation that she would think of precisely what I needed to explain the case.

Well, she went on to describe how at last she reported her discovery to her aunt, who found that she was changed and suspected her of concealing some secret. There followed some very disagreeable scenes between her uncle and aunt, in the course of which the children came to hear a number of things which opened their eyes in many ways and which it would have been better for them not to have heard. At last her aunt decided to move with her children and niece and take over the present inn, leaving her uncle alone with Franziska, who had meanwhile become pregnant. After this, however, to my astonishment she dropped these threads and began to tell me two sets of older stories, which went back two or three years earlier than the traumatic moment. The first set related to occasions on which the same uncle had made sexual advances to her herself, when she was only fourteen years old. She described how she had once gone with him on an expedition down into the valley in the winter and had spent the night in the inn there. He sat in the bar drinking and playing cards, but she felt sleepy and went up to bed early in the room they were to share on the upper floor. She was not quite asleep when he came up; then she fell asleep again and woke up suddenly 'feeling his body' in the bed. She jumped up and remonstrated with him: 'What are you up to, Uncle? Why don't you stay in your own bed?' He tried to pacify her: 'Go on, you silly girl, keep still. You don't know how nice it is.'—'I don't like your "nice" things; you don't even let one sleep in peace.' She remained standing by the door, ready to take refuge outside in the passage, till at last he gave up and went to sleep himself. Then she went back to her own bed and slept till morning. From the way in which she reported having defended herself it seems to follow that she did not clearly recognize the attack as a sexual one. When I asked her if she knew what he was trying to do to her, she replied: 'Not at the time.' It had become clear to her much later on, she said; she had resisted because it was unpleasant to be disturbed in one's sleep and 'because it wasn't nice'.

I have been obliged to relate this in detail, because of its great importance for understanding everything that followed.—She went on to tell me of yet other experiences of somewhat later date: how she had once again had to defend herself against him in an inn when he was completely drunk, and similar stories. In answer to a question as to whether on these occasions she had felt anything resembling her later loss of breath, she answered with decision that she had every time felt the pressure on her eyes and chest, but with nothing like the strength that had characterized the scene of discovery.

Immediately she had finished this set of memories she began to tell me a second set, which dealt with occasions on which she had noticed something between her uncle and Franziska. Once the whole family had spent the night in their clothes in a hay loft and she was woken up suddenly by a noise; she thought she noticed that her uncle, who had been lying between her and Franziska, was turning away, and that Franziska was just lying down. Another time they were stopping the night at an inn at the village of N——; she and her uncle were in one room and Franziska in an adjoining one. She woke up suddenly in the night and saw a tall white figure by the door, on the point of turning the handle: 'Goodness, is that you, Uncle? What are you doing at the door?'—'Keep quiet. I was only looking for something.'—'But the way out's by the *other* door,'—'I'd just made a mistake' . . . and so on.

I asked her if she had been suspicious at that time. 'No, I didn't think anything about it; I only just noticed it and thought no more about it.' When I enquired whether she had been frightened on these occasions too, she replied that she thought so, but she was not so sure of it this time.

At the end of these two sets of memories she came to a stop. She was like someone transformed. The sulky, unhappy face had grown lively, her eyes were bright, she was lightened and exalted. Meanwhile the understanding of her case had become clear to me. The later part of what she had told me, in an apparently aimless fashion, provided an admirable explanation of her behaviour at the scene of the discovery. At that time she had carried about with her two sets of experiences which she remembered but did not understand, and from which she drew no inferences. When she caught sight of the couple in intercourse, she at once established a connection between the new impression and these two sets of recollections, she began to understand them and at the same time to fend them off. There then followed a short period of working-out, of 'incubation', after which the symptoms of conversion set in, the vomiting as a substitute for moral and physical disgust. This solved the riddle. She had not been disgusted by the sight of the two people but by the memory which that sight had stirred up in her. And, taking everything into account, this could only be the memory of the attempt on her at night when she had 'felt her uncle's body'.

So when she had finished her confession I said to her: 'I know now what it was you thought when you looked into the room. You thought: "Now he's doing with her what he wanted to do with me that night and those other times." That was what you were disgusted at, because you remembered the feeling when you woke up in the night and felt his body.'

'It may well be,' she replied, 'that that was what I was disgusted at and that that was what I thought.'

'Tell me just one thing more. You're a grown-up girl now and know all sorts of things . . .'

'Yes, now I am.'

'Tell me just one thing. What part of his body was it that you felt that night?'

But she gave me no more definite answer. She smiled in an embarrassed way, as though she had been found out, like someone who is obliged to admit that a fundamental position has been reached where there is not much more to be said. I could imagine what the tactile sensation was which she had later learnt to interpret. Her facial expression seemed to me to be saying that she supposed that I was right in my conjecture. But I could not penetrate further, and in any case I owed her a debt of gratitude for having made it so much easier for me to talk to her than to the prudish ladies of my city practice, who regard whatever is natural as shameful.

Thus the case was cleared up.—But stop a moment! What about the recurrent hallucination of the head, which appeared during her attacks and struck terror into her? Where did it come from? I proceeded to ask her about it, and, as though *her* knowledge, too, had been extended by our conversation, she promptly replied: 'Yes, I know now. The head is my uncle's head—I recognize it now—but not from *that* time. Later, when all the disputes had broken out, my uncle gave way to a senseless rage against me. He kept saying that it was all my fault: if I hadn't chattered, it would never have come to a divorce. He kept threatening he would do something to me; and if he caught sight of me at a distance his face would get distorted with rage and he would make for me with his hand raised. I always ran away from him, and always felt terrified that he would catch me some time unawares. The face I always see now is his face when he was in a rage.'

This information reminded me that her first hysterical symptom, the vomiting, had passed away; the anxiety attack remained and acquired a fresh content. Accordingly, what we were dealing with was a hysteria which had to a considerable extent been abreacted. And in fact she had reported her discovery to her aunt soon after it happened.

'Did you tell your aunt the other stories—about his making advances to you?'

'Yes. Not at once, but later on, when there was already talk of a divorce. My aunt said: "We'll keep that in reserve. If he causes trouble in the Court, we'll say that too." '

I can well understand that it should have been precisely this last period—when there were more and more agitating scenes in the house and when her own state ceased to interest her aunt, who was entirely occupied with the dispute—that it should have been this period of accumulation and retention that left her the legacy of the mnemic symbol [of the hallucinated face].

I hope this girl, whose sexual sensibility had been injured at such an early age, derived some benefit from our conversation. I have not seen her since.

DISCUSSION

If someone were to assert that the present case history is not so much an analysed case of hysteria as a case solved by guessing, I should have nothing to say against him. It is true that the patient agreed that what I interpolated into her story was probably true; but she was not in a position to recognize it as something she had experienced. I believe it would have required hypnosis to bring that about. Assuming that my guesses were correct, I will now attempt to fit the case into the schematic picture of an 'acquired' hysteria on the lines suggested by Case 3. It seems plausible, then, to compare the two sets of erotic experiences with 'traumatic' moments and the scene of discovering the couple with an 'auxiliary' moment. The similarity lies in the fact that in the former experiences an element of consciousness was created which was excluded from the thought-activity of the ego and remained, as it were, in storage, while in the latter scene a new impression forcibly brought about an associative connection between this separated group and the ego. On the other hand there are dissimilarities which cannot be overlooked. The cause of the isolation was not, as in Case 3, an act of will on the part of the ego but *ignorance* on the part of the ego, which was not yet capable of coping with sexual experiences. In this respect the case of Katharina is typical. In every analysis of a case of hysteria based on sexual traumas we find that impressions from the pre-sexual period which produced no effect on the child attain traumatic power at a later date as memories, when the girl or married woman has acquired an understanding of sexual life. The splitting-off of psychical groups may be said to be a normal process in adolescent development; and it is easy to see that their later reception into the ego affords frequent opportunities for psychical disturbances. Moreover, I should like at this point to express a doubt as to whether a splitting of consciousness due to ignorance is really different from one due to conscious rejection, and whether even adolescents do not possess sexual knowledge far oftener than is supposed or than they themselves believe.

A further distinction in the psychical mechanism of this case lies in the fact that the scene of discovery, which we have described as 'auxiliary', deserves equally to be called 'traumatic'. It was operative on account of its own content and not merely as something that revived previous traumatic experiences. It combined the characteristics of an 'auxiliary' and a 'traumatic' moment. There seems no reason, however, why this coincidence should lead us to abandon a conceptual separation which in other cases corresponds also to a separation in time. Another peculiarity of Katharina's case, which, incidentally, has long been familiar to us, is seen in the circumstance that the conversion, the production of the hysterical phenomena, did not occur immediately after the trauma but after an interval of incubation. Charcot liked to describe this interval as the 'period of psychical working-out' [élaboration].

The anxiety from which Katharina suffered in her attacks was a hysterical one; that is, it was a reproduction of the anxiety which had appeared in connection with each of the sexual traumas. I shall not here comment on the fact which I have found regularly present in a very large number of cases—namely that a mere suspicion of sexual relations calls up the affect of anxiety in virginal individuals.[4]

Project for a Scientific Psychology

From the spring of 1895 on, Freud was working intensely on what he called, to Fliess, his "psychology for neurologists." He had two aims in view: to discover and describe "a kind of economics of nervous force," and to utilize his experience with psychopathology in constructing a general theory of mind. Even then, and increasingly after, Freud saw neuroses as on a continuum of mental functioning, and neurotics as displaying in exaggerated (and hence extremely instructive) form the traits and troubles of "normal" humans. In September 1895, after a "congress" with Fliess in Berlin, Freud set to work rapidly, starting on the train, to draft his project. It owes much to the researches he had conducted in previous years, but it is also a way station to his turn away from the neurological, physiological view of mind then dominant, and toward his psychology for psychologists. He never fin-

4. (Footnote added 1924:) I venture after the lapse of so many years to lift the veil of discretion and reveal the fact that Katharina was not the niece but the daughter of the landlady. The girl fell ill, therefore, as a result of sexual attempts on the part of her own father. Distortions like the one which I introduced in the present instance should be altogether avoided in a case history. From the point of view of understanding the case, a distortion of this kind is not, of course, a matter of such indifference as would be shifting the scene from one mountain to another.

ished, or published, his draft, but the editors of the Standard Edition of Freud's psychological writings are correct to say that "the *Project*, in spite of being ostensibly a neurological document, contains within itself the nucleus of a great part of Freud's later psychological theories. . . . The *Project*, or rather its invisible ghost, haunts the whole series of Freud's theoretical writings to the very end" (*SE* I, 290). The short extract here reproduced should give an inkling of Freud's scientific style in 1895, on the verge of his breakthrough to what he would call the following year, for the first time, "psychoanalysis."

[PART I]

GENERAL SCHEME

Introduction

The intention is to furnish a psychology that shall be a natural science: that is, to represent psychical processes as quantitatively determinate states of specifiable material particles, thus making those processes perspicuous and free from contradiction. Two principal ideas are involved: [1] What distinguishes activity from rest is to be regarded as Q, subject to the general laws of motion. (2) The neurones[1] are to be taken as the material particles.

* * *

[1] (a) First Principal Theorem
The Quantitative Conception

This is derived directly from pathological clinical observation especially where excessively intense ideas were concerned—in hysteria and obsessions, in which, as we shall see, the quantitative characteristic emerges more plainly than in the normal. Processes such as stimulus, substitution, conversion and discharge, which had to be described there [in connection with those disorders], directly suggested the conception of neuronal excitation as quantity in a state of flow. It seemed legitimate to attempt to generalize what was recognized there. Starting from this consideration, it was possible to lay down a basic principle of neuronal activity in relation to Q, which promised to be highly enlightening, since it appeared to comprise the entire function. This is the principle of neuronal inertia: that neurones tend to divest themselves of Q. On

---

1. [The term 'neurone', as a description of the ultimate unit of the nervous system, had been introduced by W. Waldeyer in 1891. Freud's own histological researches had led him towards the same finding.]

this basis the structure and development as well as the functions [of neurones] are to be understood.[2]

In the first place, the principle of *inertia* explains the structural dichotomy [of neurones] into motor and sensory as a contrivance for neutralizing the reception of $Q\acute{\eta}$ by giving it off. Reflex movement is now intelligible as an established form of this giving-off: the principle provides the motive for reflex movement. If we go further back from here, we can in the first instance link the nervous system, as inheritor of the general irritability of protoplasm, with the irritable external surface [of an organism], which is interrupted by considerable stretches of non-irritable surface. A primary nervous system makes use of this $Q\acute{\eta}$ which it has thus acquired, by giving it off through a connecting path to the muscular mechanisms, and in that way keeps itself free from stimulus. This discharge represents the primary function of the nervous system. Here is room for the development of a secondary function. For among the paths of discharge those are preferred and retained which involve a cessation of the stimulus: *flight from the stimulus*. Here in general there is a proportion between the Q of excitation and the effort necessary for the flight from the stimulus, so that the principle of *inertia* is not upset by this.

The principle of inertia is, however, broken through from the first owing to another circumstance. With an [increasing] complexity of the interior [of the organism], the nervous system receives stimuli from the somatic element itself—endogenous stimuli—which have equally to be discharged. These have their origin in the cells of the body and give rise to the major needs: hunger, respiration, sexuality. From these the organism cannot withdraw as it does from external stimuli; it cannot employ their Q for flight from the stimulus. They only cease subject to particular conditions, which must be realized in the external world. (Cf., for instance, the need for nourishment.) In order to accomplish such an action (which deserves to be named 'specific'), an effort is required which is independent of endogenous $Q\acute{\eta}$ and in general greater, since the individual is being subjected to conditions which may be described as *the exigencies of life*. In consequence, the nervous system is obliged to abandon its original trend to inertia (that is, to bringing the level [of $Q\acute{\eta}$] to zero). It must put up with [maintaining] a store of $Q\acute{\eta}$ sufficient to meet the demand for a specific action. Nevertheless, the manner in which it does this shows that the same trend persists, modified into an endeavour at least to keep the $Q\acute{\eta}$ as low as possible and to guard against any increase of it—that is, to keep it constant. All the functions of the nervous system can be comprised either under the aspect of the primary function or of the secondary one imposed by the exigencies of life.

2. [. . . this is what was later known as the 'principle of constancy' and attributed by Freud to {the German philosopher and physicist Gustav Theoder} Fechner {1801–87}.]

[2] [b] Second Principal Theorem
The Neurone Theory

The idea of combining with this $Q\dot\eta$ theory the knowledge of the neurones arrived at by recent histology is the second pillar of this thesis. The main substance of these new discoveries is that the nervous system consists of distinct and similarly constructed neurones, which have contact with one another through the medium of a foreign substance, which terminate upon one another as they do upon portions of foreign tissue, [and] in which certain lines of conduction are laid down in so far as they [the neurones] receive [excitations] through cell-processes [dendrites] and [give them off] through an axis-cylinder [axon]. They have in addition numerous ramifications of varying calibre.

If we combine this account of the neurones with the conception of the $Q\dot\eta$ theory, we arrive at the idea of a *cathected* neurone filled with a certain $Q\dot\eta$ while at other times it may be empty.[3] The principle of inertia [p. 296] finds its expression in the hypothesis of a *current* passing from the cell's paths of conduction or processes [dendrites] to the axis-cylinder. A single neurone is thus a model of the whole nervous system with its dichotomy of structure, the axis-cylinder being the organ of discharge. The secondary function [of the nervous system], however, which calls for the accumulation of $Q\dot\eta$ [p. 297], is made possible by the assumption of resistances which oppose discharge; and the structure of neurones makes it probable that the resistances are all to be located in the *contacts* [between one neurone and another], which in this way assume the value of *barriers*. The hypothesis of *contact-barriers* is fruitful in many directions.

* * *

Draft K

Here is another memorandum Freud enclosed in a letter to Fliess (January 1, 1896). It was certainly, as Freud indicates by calling it a "Christmas Fairy Tale," written the week before. Draft K deals with the vexed question of "choice of neurosis," to which Freud returned again and again, and it utilizes in preliminary but recognizable form such fundamental psychoanalytic ideas as defensive activity (particularly repression) and the nature of symptoms as compromises. Freud indicates in describing "the course taken by the illness in neuroses of repression" that he thinks their origins go back to traumatic sexual experiences. He later felt compelled to complicate, indeed largely

3. [The notion of 'cathexis' ("*Besetzung*') had been used by Freud already, but not much earlier, in *Studies on Hysteria*.] {It is worth adding that Freud himself thought a good translation for his "Besetzung," which means occupation (as by troops) or charge (as in electrical charge) would be "interest." In general, Freud used common rather than technical terms, a habit that his English translators only imperfectly respected.}

abandon, this etiology (see below, pp. 111–13), but the sequence of events leading to neurosis he proposes in this draft remained largely intact in his thought. The memorandum also makes it apparent that after years of concentrating on clinical work with hysterics, Freud is now turning to obsessional neuroses, though he does not neglect hysteria. His inclusion of paranoia among the neuroses of defense is also of interest.

THE NEUROSES OF DEFENCE

(A *Christmas Fairy Tale*)

There are four types of these and many forms. I can only make a comparison between hysteria, obsessional neurosis and one form of paranoia. They have various things in common. They are pathological aberrations of normal psychical affective states: of *conflict* (hysteria), of *self-reproach* (obsessional neurosis), of *mortification* (paranoia), of *mourning* (acute hallucinatory amentia). They differ from these affects in that they do not lead to anything being settled but to permanent damage to the ego. They come about subject to the same precipitating causes as their affective prototypes, provided that the cause fulfils two more preconditions—that it is of a sexual kind and that it occurs during the period before sexual maturity (the preconditions of *sexuality and infantilism*). About preconditions applying to the individual concerned I have no fresh knowledge. In general I should say that heredity is a further precondition, in that it facilitates and increases the pathological affect—the precondition, that is, which mainly makes possible the gradations between the normal and the extreme case. I do not believe that heredity determines the choice of the particular defensive neurosis.

There is a normal trend towards defence—that is, an aversion to direction psychical energy in such a way that unpleasure results. This trend, which is linked to the most fundamental conditions of the psychical mechanism (the law of constancy), cannot be employed against perceptions, for these are able to compel attention (as is evidenced by their consciousness); it only comes in question against memories and thoughts. It is innocuous where it is a matter of ideas to which unpleasure was at one time attached but which are unable to acquire any contemporary unpleasure (other than remembered unpleasure), and in such cases too it can be over-ridden by psychical interest.

The trend towards defence becomes detrimental, however, if it is directed against ideas which are also able, in the form of memories, to release fresh unpleasure—as is the case with sexual ideas. Here, indeed, the one possibility is realized of a memory having a greater releasing power subsequently than had been produced by the experience corresponding to it. Only one thing is necessary for this: that puberty should be interpolated between the experience and its repetition in memory—an event which so greatly increases the effect of the revival. The psychical mechanism seems unprepared for this exception, and it is for that reason a necessary precondition of freedom from neuroses of defence that no considerable sexual irritation should occur before puberty, though it is true that the effect of such an experience must be increased by hereditary disposition before it can reach a pitch capable of causing illness.

(Here a subsidiary problem branches off: how does it come about that under analogous conditions, perversion or simple immorality emerges instead of neurosis?)

We shall be plunged deep into psychological riddles if we enquire into the origin of the unpleasure which seems to be released by premature sexual stimulation and without which, after all, a repression cannot be explained. The most plausible answer will appeal to the fact that shame and morality are the repressing forces and that the neighbourhood in which the sexual organs are naturally placed must inevitably arouse disgust along with sexual experiences. Where there is no shame (as in a male person), or where no morality comes about (as in the lower classes of society), or where disgust is blunted by the conditions of life (as in the country), there too no repression and therefore no neurosis will result from sexual stimulation in infancy. I fear, nevertheless, that this explanation will not stand up to deeper testing. I do not think that the release of unpleasure during sexual experiences is the consequence of the chance admixture of certain unpleasurable factors. Everyday experience teaches us that if libido reaches a sufficient height disgust is not felt and morality is over-ridden; and I believe that the generation of shame is connected with sexual experience by deeper links. In my opinion there must be an independent source for the release of unpleasure in sexual life: once that source is present, it can activate sensations of disgust, lend force to morality, and so on. I hold to the model of anxiety neurosis in adults, where a quantity deriving from sexual life similarly causes a disturbance in the psychical sphere, though it would ordinarily have found another use in the sexual process. So long as there is no correct theory of the sexual process, the question of the origin of the unpleasure operating in repression remains unanswered.

The course taken by the illness in neuroses of repression is in general always the same: (1) the sexual experience (or series of experiences) which is traumatic and premature and is to be repressed. (2) Its repression on some later occasion which arouses a memory of it; at the same time the formation of a primary symptom. (3) A stage of successful defence, which is equivalent to health except for the existence of the primary symptom. (4) The stage in which the repressed ideas return, and in which, during the struggle between them and the ego, new symptoms are formed which are those of the illness proper: that is, a stage of adjustment, of being overwhelmed, or of recovery with a malformation.

The main differences between the various neuroses are shown in the way in which the repressed ideas return; others are seen in the manner in which the symptoms are formed and in the course taken by the illness. But the specific character of a particular neurosis lies in the fashion in which the repression is accomplished.

The course of events in obsessional neurosis is what is clearest to me, because I have come to know it the best.

OBSESSIONAL NEUROSIS

Here the primary experience has been accompanied by pleasure. Whether an active one (in boys) or a passive one (in girls), it was without pain or any admixture of disgust; and this in the case of girls implies a comparatively high age in general (about 8 years). When this experience is remembered later, it gives rise to a release of unpleasure; and, in particular, there first emerges a self-reproach, which is conscious. It seems, indeed, as though the whole psychical complex—memory and self-reproach—is conscious to start with. Later, both of them, without anything fresh supervening, are repressed and in their place an *antithetic symptom*, some nuance of *conscientiousness*, is formed in consciousness.

The repression may come about owing to the memory of the pleasure itself releasing unpleasure when it is reproduced in later years; this should be explicable by a theory of sexuality. But things may happen differently as well. In *all* my cases of obsessional neurosis, at a very early age, years before the experience of pleasure, there had been a *purely passive* experience; and this can hardly be accidental. If so, we may suppose that it is the later convergence of this passive experience with the experience of pleasure that adds the unpleasure to the pleasurable memory and makes repression possible. So that it would be a necessary clinical precondition of obsessional neurosis that the passive experience should happen early enough not to be able to prevent the spontaneous occurrence of the experience of pleasure. The formula would therefore run:

Unpleasure—Pleasure—Repression.

The determining factor would be the chronological relations of the two experiences to each other and to the date of sexual maturity.

At the stage of the return of the repressed, it turns out that the *self-reproach* returns unaltered, but rarely in such a way as to draw attention to itself; for a while, therefore, it emerges as a pure sense of guilt without any content. It usually becomes linked with a content which is distorted in two ways—in time and in content: the former in so far as it relates to a contemporary or future action, and the latter in so far as it signifies not the real event but a surrogate chosen from the category of what is analogous—a substitution. An obsessional idea is accordingly a product of compromise, correct as regards affect and category but false owing to chronological displacement and substitution by analogy.

The affect of the self-reproach may be transformed by various psychical processes into other affects, which then enter consciousness more clearly than the affect itself: for instance, into *anxiety* (fear of the consequences of the action to which the self-reproach applies), *hypochondria* (fear of its bodily effects), *delusions of persecution* (fear of its social effects), *shame* (fear of other people knowing about it), and so on.

The conscious ego regards the obsession as something alien to itself: it withholds belief from it, by the help, it seems, of the antithetic idea of conscientiousness, formed long before. But at this stage it may at times happen that the ego is overwhelmed by the obsession—for instance, if the ego is affected by an episodic melancholia. Apart from this, the stage of illness is occupied by the defensive struggle of the ego against the obsession; and this may itself produce new symptoms—those of the *secondary defence*. The obsessional idea, like any other, is attacked by logic, though its compulsive force is unshakable. The secondary symptoms are an intensification of conscientiousness, and a compulsion to examine things and to hoard them. Other secondary symptoms arise if the compulsion is transferred to motor impulses against the obsession— for instance, to brooding, drinking (*dipsomania*), protective ceremonials, *folie du doute*.

Here, then, we arrive at the formation of three species of symptoms:

(*a*) the primary symptom of defence—*conscientiousness*,

(*b*) the compromise symptoms of the illness—*obsessional ideas* or *obsessional affects*,

(*c*) the secondary symptoms of defence—*obsessional brooding, obsessional hoarding, dipsomania, obsessional ceremonials*.

Those cases in which the content of the memory has not become admissible to consciousness through substitution, but in which the affect of self-reproach has become admissible through transformation, give one the impression of a displacement having occurred along a chain of inferences: I reproach myself on account of an event—I am afraid other people know about it—therefore I feel ashamed in front of other people. As soon as the first link in this chain is repressed, the obsession jumps on to the second or third link, and leads to two forms of delusions of reference, which, however, are in fact part of the obsessional neurosis. The defensive struggle terminates in general doubting mania or in the development of the life of an eccentric with an indefinite number of secondary defensive symptoms—that is, if such a termination is reached at all.

It further remains an open question whether the repressed ideas return of their own accord, without the assistance of any contemporary psychical force, or whether they need this kind of assistance at every fresh wave of their return. My experiences indicate the latter alternative. States of contemporary unsatisfied libido, it seems, are what employ the force of their unpleasure to arouse the repressed self-reproach. Once this arousal has occurred and symptoms have arisen through the impact of the repressed on the ego, then, no doubt the repressed ideational material continues to operate on its own account; but in the oscillations of its quantitative power it always remains dependent on the quota of libidinal tension present at the moment. Sexual tension which, owing to being satisfied, has no time to turn into unpleasure remains harmless. Obsessional neurotics are people who are subject to the danger that eventually the whole of the sexual tension generated in them daily may turn into self-reproach or rather into the symptoms resulting from it, although at the present time they would not recognize the primary self-reproach afresh.

Obsessional neurosis can be cured if we undo all the substitutions and affective transformations that have taken place, till the primary self-reproach and the experience belonging to it can be laid bare and placed before the conscious ego for judging anew. In doing this we have to work through an incredible number of intermediate or compromise ideas which become obsessional ideas temporarily. We gain the liveliest conviction that it is impossible for the ego to direct on to the repressed material the part of the psychical energy to which conscious thought is linked. The repressed ideas—so we must believe—are present in and enter without inhibition into the most rational trains of thought; and the memory of them is aroused too by the merest allusions. The suspicion that 'morality' is put forward as the repressing force only as a pretext is confirmed by the experience that resistance during the therapeutic work avails itself of every possible motive of defence.

PARANOIA

The clinical determinants and chronological relations of pleasure and unpleasure in the primary experience are still unknown to me. What I have distinguished is the fact of repression, the primary symptom and the stage of illness as determined by the return of the repressed ideas.

The primary experience seems to be of a similar nature to that in obsessional neurosis; repression occurs after the memory of it has released unpleasure—it is unknown how. No self-reproach, however, is formed and afterwards repressed; but the unpleasure generated is referred to the patient's fellow-men in accordance with the psychical formula of projection. The primary symptom formed is *distrust* (sensitiveness to other people). In this, belief has been withheld from a self-reproach.

We may suspect the existence of different forms, according to whether only the affect is repressed by projection or the content of the experience too, along with it. So, again, what returns may be merely the distressing affect or the memory as well. In the second case, which is the only one I am closely acquainted with, the content of the experience returns as a thought that occurs to the patient or as a visual or sensory hallucination. The repressed affect seems invariably to return in hallucinations of voices.

The returning portions of the memory are distorted by being replaced by analogous images from the present day—that is, they are simply distorted by a chronological replacement and not by the formation of a surrogate. The voices, too, bring back the self-reproach as a compromise symptom and they do so, firstly, distorted in its wording to the pitch of being indefinite and changed into a threat; and, secondly, related not to the primary experience but precisely to the distrust—that is, to the primary symptom.

Since belief has been withheld from the primary self-reproach, it is at the unrestricted command of the compromise symptoms. The ego does not regard them as alien to itself but is incited by them to make attempts at explaining them which may be described as *assimilatory delusions*.

At this point, with the return of the repressed in distorted form, the defence has at once failed; and the assimilatory delusions cannot be interpreted as a symptom of secondary defence but as the beginning of an *alteration of the ego*, an expression of its having been overwhelmed. The process reaches its conclusion either in melancholia (a sense of the ego's littleness), which, in a secondary manner, attaches to the distortions the belief which has been withheld from the pimary self-reproach, or—what is more frequent and more serious—in *protective delusions* (megalomania), till the ego has been completely remodelled.

The determining element of paranoia is the mechanism of projection involving the refusal of belief in the self-reproach. Hence the common characteristic features of the neurosis: the significance of the voices as the means by which other people affect us, and also of gestures, which reveal other people's mental life to us; and the importance of the *tone* of remarks and *allusions* in them—since a direct reference from the *content* of remarks to the repressed memory is inadmissible to consciousness.

In paranoia repression takes place after a complicated conscious process of thought (the withholding of belief). This may perhaps be an indication that it first sets in at a later age than in obsessional neurosis and hysteria. The preconditions of repression are no doubt the same. It remains a completely open question whether the mechanism of projection is entirely a matter of individual disposition or whether it is selected by particular temporal and accidental factors.

Four species of symptoms:

(*a*) primary symptoms of defence,
(*b*) compromise symptoms of the return,
(*c*) secondary symptoms of defence,
(*d*) symptoms of the overwhelming of the ego.

HYSTERIA

Hysteria necessarily presupposes a primary experience of unpleasure—that is, of a passive nature. The natural sexual passivity of women explains their being more inclined to hysteria. Where I have found hysteria in men, I have been able to prove the presence of abundant sexual passivity in their anamneses. A further condition of hysteria is that the primary experience of unpleasure shall not occur at too early a time, at which the release of unpleasure is still too slight and at which, of course, pleasurable events may still follow independently. Otherwise what will follow will be only the formation of obsessions. For this reason we often find in men a combination of the two neuroses or the replacement of an initial hysteria by a later obsessional neurosis. Hysteria begins with the ovewhelming of the ego, which is what paranoia leads to. The raising of tension at the primary experience of unpleasure is so great that the ego does not resist it and forms no psychical symptom but is obliged to allow a manifestation of discharge—usually an excessive expression of excitation. This first stage of hysteria may be described as 'fright hysteria'; its primary symptom is the *manifestation of fright* accompanied by a *gap* in the psyche. It is still unknown up to how late an age this first hysterical overwhelming of the ego can occur.

Repression and the formation of defensive symptoms only occur subsequently, in connection with the memory; and thenceforward *defence* and *overwhelming* (that is, the formation of symptoms and the outbreak of attacks) may be combined to any extent in hysteria.

Repression does not take place by the construction of an excessively strong antithetic idea but by the intensification of a boundary idea, which thereafter represents the repressed memory in the passage of thought. It may be called a *boundary idea* because on the one hand it belongs to the ego and on the other hand forms an undistorted portion of the traumatic memory. So, once again, it is the result of a compromise; this, however, is not manifested in a replacement on the basis of some category of subject-matter, but by a displacement of attention along a series of ideas linked by temporal simultaneity. If the traumatic event found an outlet for itself in a motor manifestation, it will be this that becomes the boundary idea and the first symbol of the repressed material. There is thus no need to assume that some idea is being suppressed at each repetition of the primary attack; it is a question in the first instance of a *gap in the psyche*.

The Aetiology of Hysteria

This is the much-discussed paper that Freud read to the Viennese Society for Psychiatry and Neurology in late April 1896. It is at once elegant and eloquent, but it advocates an untenable theory—that neuroses are almost invariably caused by sexual aggression of adults against children, whether subtle seduction or rude rape. Richard Freiherr von Krafft-Ebing (1840–1902), the celebrated neurologist who specialized in sexual pathology (and who in general thought well enough of Freud to advance his career through the maze of the Austrian bureaucracy), dismissed the talk as "a scientific fairy tale." Before long, Freud would think so, too, but the lecture is a splendid instance of his forensic skill.

[I]

Gentlemen,—When we set out to form an opinion about the causation of a pathological state such as hysteria, we begin by adopting the method of anamnestic investigation: we question the patient or those about him in order to find out to what harmful influences they themselves attribute his having fallen ill and developed these neurotic symptoms. What we discover in this way is, of course, falsified by all the factors which commonly hide the knowledge of his own state from a patient—by his lack of scientific understanding of aetiological influences, by the fallacy of *post hoc, propter hoc*, by his reluctance to think about or mention certain noxae and traumas. Thus in making an anamnestic investigation of this sort, we keep to the principle of not adopting the patients' belief without a thorough critical examination, of not allowing them to lay down our scientific opinion for us on the aetiology of the neurosis. Although we do, on the one hand, acknowledge the truth of certain constantly repeated assertions, such as that the hysterical state is a long-persisting after-effect of an emotion experienced in the past, we have, on the other hand, introduced into the aetiology of hysteria a factor which the patient himself never brings forward and whose validity he only reluctantly admits—namely, the hereditary disposition derived from his progenitors. As you know, in the view of the influential school of Charcot heredity alone deserves to be recognized as the true cause of hysteria, while all other noxae of the most various nature and intensity only play the part of incidental causes, of 'agents provocateurs'.

You will readily admit that it would be a good thing to have a second method of arriving at the aetiology of hysteria, one in which we should feel less dependent on the assertions of the patients themselves. * * *

Imagine that an explorer arrives in a little-known region where his interest is aroused by an expanse of ruins, with remains of walls, fragments of columns, and tablets with half-effaced and unreadable inscriptions. He may content himself with inspecting what lies exposed to view, with questioning the inhabitants—perhaps semi-barbaric people—who live in the vicinity, about what tradition tells them of the history and meaning of these archaeological remains, and with noting down what they tell him—and he may then proceed on his journey. But he may act differently. He may have brought picks, shovels and spades with him, and he may set the inhabitants to work with these implements. Together with them he may start upon the ruins, clear away the rubbish, and, beginning from the visible remains, uncover what is buried. If his work is crowned with success, the discoveries are self-explanatory: the ruined walls are part of the ramparts of a palace or a treasure-house; the fragments of columns can be filled out into a temple; the numerous inscriptions, which, by good luck, may be bilingual, reveal an alphabet and a language, and, when they have been deciphered and translated, yield undreamed-of information about the events of the remote past, to commemorate which the monuments were built. *Saxa loquuntur!* {*Stones talk!*}

If we try, in an approximately similar way, to induce the symptoms of a hysteria to make themselves heard as witnesses to the history of the origin of the illness, we must take our start from Josef Breuer's momentous discovery: *the symptoms of hysteria* (apart from the stigmata) *are determined by certain experiences of the patient's which have operated in a traumatic fashion and which are being reproduced in his psychical life in the form of mnemic symbols*. What we have to do is to apply Breuer's method—or one which is essentially the same—so as to lead the patient's attention back from his symptom to the scene in which and through which that symptom arose; and, having thus located the scene, we remove the symptom by bringing about, during the reproduction of the traumatic scene, a subsequent correction of the psychical course of events which took place at the time.

It is no part of my intention to-day to discuss the difficult technique of this therapeutic procedure or the psychological discoveries which have been obtained by its means. I have been obliged to start from this point only because the analyses conducted on Breuer's lines seem at the same time to open up the path to the causes of hysteria. If we subject a fairly large number of symptoms in a great number of subjects to such an analysis, we shall, of course, arrive at a knowledge of a correspondingly large number of traumatically operative scenes. It was in these experiences that the efficient causes of hysteria came into action. Hence we may hope to discover from the study of these traumatic scenes what the influences are which produce hysterical symptoms and in what way they do so.

This expectation proves true; and it cannot fail to, since Breuer's theses, when put to the test in a considerable number of cases, have turned out to be correct. But the path from the symptoms of hysteria to its aetiology is more laborious and leads through other connections than one would have imagined.

For let us be clear on this point. Tracing a hysterical symptom back to a traumatic scene assists our understanding only if the scene satisfies two conditions; if it possesses the relevant *suitability to serve as a determinant* and if it recognizably possesses the necessary *traumatic force*. Instead of a verbal explanation, here is an example. Let us suppose that the symptom under consideration is hysterical vomiting; in that case we shall feel that we have been able to understand its causation (except for a certain residue) if the analysis traces the symptom back to an experience which *justifiably produced a high amount of disgust*—for instance, the sight of a decomposing dead body. But if, instead of this, the analysis shows us that the vomiting arose from a great fright, e.g. from a railway accident, we shall feel dissatisfied and will have to ask ourselves how it is that the fright has led to the particular symptom of vomiting. This derivation lacks *suitability as a determinant*. We shall have another instance of an insufficient explanation if the vomiting is supposed to have arisen from, let us say, eating a fruit which had partly gone bad. Here, it is true, the vomiting *is* determined by disgust, but we cannot understand how, in this instance, the disgust could have become so powerful as to be perpetuated in a hysterical symptom; the experience lacks *traumatic force*.

Let us now consider how far the traumatic scenes of hysteria which are uncovered by analysis fulfil, in a fairly large number of symptoms and cases, the two requirements which I have named. Here we meet with our first great disappointment. It is true, indeed, that the traumatic scene in which the symptom originated does in fact occasionally possess both the qualities—suitability as a determinant and traumatic force—which we require for an understanding of the symptom. But far more frequently, incomparably more frequently, we find one of the three other possibilities realized, which are so unfavourable to an understanding. Either the scene to which we are led by analysis and in which the symptom first appeared seems to us unsuited for determining the symptom, in that its content bears no relation to the nature of the symptom; or the allegedly traumatic experience, though it *does* have a relation to the symptom, proves to be an impression which is normally innocuous and incapable as a rule of producing any effect; or, lastly, the 'traumatic scene' leaves us in the lurch in both respects, appearing at once innocuous and unrelated to the character of the hysterical symptom.

* * *

Moreover, Gentlemen, this first disappointment we meet with in following Breuer's method is immediately succeeded by another, and one that must be especially painful to us as physicians. When our procedure leads, as in the cases described above, to findings which are insufficient as an explanation both in respect to their suitability as determinants and to their traumatic effectiveness, we also fail to secure any therapeutic gain; the patient retains his symptoms unaltered, in spite of the initial result yielded by the analysis. You can understand how great the temptation is at this point to proceed no further with what is in any case a laborious piece of work.

But perhaps all we need is a new idea in order to help us out of our dilemma and lead to valuable results. The idea is this. As we know from

Breuer, hysterical symptoms can be resolved if, starting from them, we are able to find the path back to the memory of a traumatic experience. If the memory which we have uncovered does not answer our expectations, it may be that we ought to pursue the same path a little further; perhaps behind the first traumatic scene there may be concealed the memory of a second, which satisfies our requirements better and whose reproduction has a greater therapeutic effect; so that the scene that was first discovered only has the significance of a connecting link in the chain of associations. And perhaps this situation may repeat itself; inoperative scenes may be interpolated more than once, as necessary transitions in the process of reproduction, until we finally make our way from the hysterical symptom to the scene which is really operative traumatically and which is satisfactory in every respect, both therapeutically and analytically. Well, Gentlemen, this supposition is correct. If the first-discovered scene is unsatisfactory, we tell our patient that this experience explains nothing, but that behind it there must be hidden a more significant, earlier, experience; and we direct his attention by the same technique to the associative thread which connects the two memories—the one that has been discovered and the one that has still to be discovered. A continuation of the analysis then leads in every instance to the reproduction of new scenes of the character we expect. * * *

But we must not fail to lay special emphasis on one conclusion to which analytic work along these chains of memory has unexpectedly led. We have learned that *no hysterical symptom can arise from a real experience alone, but that in every case the memory of earlier experiences awakened in association to it plays a part in causing the symptom.* If—as I believe—this proposition holds good *without exception*, it furthermore shows us the basis on which a psychological theory of hysteria must be built.

* * *

But the most important finding that is arrived at if an analysis is thus consistently pursued is this. Whatever case and whatever symptom we take as our point of departure, *in the end we infallibly come to the field of sexual experience.* So here for the first time we seem to have discovered an aetiological precondition for hysterical symptoms.

From previous experience I can foresee that it is precisely against this assertion or against its universal validity that your contradiction, Gentlemen, will be directed. Perhaps it would be better to say, your *inclination* to contradict; for none of you, no doubt, have as yet any investigations at your disposal which, based upon the same procedure, might have yielded a different result. As regards the controversial matter itself, I will only remark that the singling out of the sexual factor in the aetiology of hysteria springs at least from no preconceived opinion on my part. The two investigators as whose pupil I began my studies of hysteria, Charcot and Breuer, were far from having any such presupposition; in fact they had a personal disinclination to it which I originally shared. Only the most laborious and detailed investigations have converted me, and that slowly enough, to the view I hold to-day. If you submit my assertion that the aetiology of hysteria lies in sexual life to the strictest examination, you will find that it is supported by the fact that in some eighteen cases of hysteria I have been able to discover this connection in every single symptom, and, where the circumstances allowed, to confirm it by therapeutic success. * * *

Eventually, then, after the chains of memories have converged, we come to the field of sexuality and to a small number of experiences which occur for the most part at the same period of life—namely, at puberty. It is in these experiences, it seems, that we are to look for the aetiology of hysteria, and through them that we are to learn to understand the origin of hysterical symptoms. But here we meet with a fresh disappointment and a very serious one. It is true that these experiences, which have been discovered with so much trouble and extracted out of all the mnemic material, and which seemed to be the ultimate traumatic experiences, have in common the two characteristics of being sexual and of occurring at puberty; but in every other respect they are very different from each other both in *kind* and in *importance*. In some cases, no doubt, we are concerned with experiences which must be regarded as severe traumas—an attempted rape, perhaps, which reveals to the immature girl at a blow all the brutality of sexual desire, or the involuntary witnessing of sexual acts between parents, which at one and the same time uncovers unsuspected ugliness and wounds childish and moral sensibilities alike, and so on. But in other cases the experiences are astonishingly trivial. In one of my women patients it turned out that her neurosis was based on the experience of a boy of her acquaintance stroking her hand tenderly and, at another time, pressing his knee against her dress as they sat side by side at table, while his expression let her see that he was doing something forbidden. For another young lady, simply hearing a riddle which suggested an obscene answer had been enough to provoke the first anxiety attack and with it to start the illness. Such findings are clearly not favourable to an understanding of the causation of hysterical symptoms. If serious and trifling events alike, and if not only experiences affecting the subject's own body but visual impressions too and information received through the ears are to be recognized as the ultimate traumas of hysteria, then we may be tempted to hazard the explanation that hysterics are peculiarly constituted creatures—probably on account of some hereditary disposition or degenerative atrophy— in whom a shrinking from sexuality, which normally plays some part at puberty, is raised to a pathological pitch and is permanently retained; that they are, as it were, people who are psychically inadequate to meeting the demands of sexuality. This view, of course, leaves hysteria in men out of account. But even without blatant objections such as that, we should scarcely be tempted to be satisfied with this solution. We are only too distinctly conscious of an intellectual sense of something half-understood, unclear and insufficient.

Luckily for our explanation, some of these sexual experiences at puberty exhibit a further inadequacy, which is calculated to stimulate us into continuing our analytic work. For it sometimes happens that they, too, lack suitability as determinants—although this is much more rarely so than with the traumatic scenes belonging to later life. Thus, for instance, let us take the two women patients whom I have just spoken of as cases in which the experiences at puberty were actually innocent ones. As a result of those experiences the patients had become subject to peculiar painful sensations in the genitals which had established themselves as the main symptoms of the neurosis. I was unable to find indications that they had been determined either by the scenes at puberty or by later scenes; but they were certainly not normal organic sensations nor signs of sexual excitement. It seemed an obvious thing, then, to say to ourselves that we must look for the determinants of these symptoms in yet other experiences, in experiences which went still further back—and that we must, for the second time, follow the saving notion which had earlier led us from the first traumatic scenes to the chains of memories behind them. In doing so, to be sure, we arrive at the period of earliest childhood, a period before the development of sexual life; and this would seem to involve the abandonment of a sexual aetiology. But have we not a right to assume that even the age of childhood is not wanting in slight sexual excitations, that later sexual development may perhaps be decisively influenced by childhood experiences? Injuries sustained by an organ which is as yet immature, or by a function which is in process of developing, often cause more severe and lasting effects than they could do in maturer years. Perhaps the abnormal reaction to sexual impressions which surprises us in hysterical subjects at the age of puberty is quite generally based on sexual experiences of this sort in childhood, in which case those experiences must be of a similar nature to one another, and must be of an important kind. If this is so, the prospect is opened up that what has hitherto had to be laid at the door of a still unexplained hereditary predisposition may be accounted for as having been acquired at an early age. And since infantile experiences with a sexual content could after all only exert a psychical effect through their *memory-traces*, would not this view be a welcome amplification of the finding of psycho-analysis which tells *us that hysterical symptoms can only arise with the co-operation of memories?*

II

* * * If we have the perseverance to press on with the analysis into early childhood, as far back as a human memory is capable of reaching, we invariably bring the patient to reproduce experiences which, on account both of their peculiar features and of their relations to the

symptoms of his later illness, must be regarded as the aetiology of his neurosis for which we have been looking. These *infantile* experiences are once more *sexual* in content, but they are of a far more uniform kind than the scenes at puberty that had been discovered earlier. It is now no longer a question of sexual topics having been aroused by some sense impression or other, but of sexual experiences affecting the subject's own body—of *sexual intercourse* (in the wider sense). You will admit that the *importance* of such scenes needs no further proof; to this may now be added that, in every instance, you will be able to discover in the details of the scenes the *determining* factors which you may have found lacking in the other scenes—the scenes which occurred later and were reproduced earlier.

I therefore put forward the thesis that at the bottom of every case of hysteria there are *one or more occurrences of premature sexual experience*, occurrences which belong to the earliest years of childhood but which can be reproduced through the work of psycho-analysis in spite of the intervening decades. I believe that this is an important finding, the discovery of a *caput Nili* {source of the Nile} in neuropathology * * *.

* * * Doubts about the genuineness of the infantile sexual scenes can, however, be deprived of their force here and now by more than one argument. In the first place, the behaviour of patients while they are reproducing these infantile experiences is in every respect incompatible with the assumption that the scenes are anything else than a reality which is being felt with distress and reproduced with the greatest reluctance. Before they come for analysis the patients know nothing about these scenes. They are indignant as a rule if we warn them that such scenes are going to emerge. Only the strongest compulsion of the treatment can induce them to embark on a reproduction of them. While they are recalling these infantile experiences to consciousness, they suffer under the most violent sensations, of which they are ashamed and which they try to conceal; and, even after they have gone through them once more in such a convincing manner, they still attempt to withhold belief from them, by emphasizing the fact that, unlike what happens in the case of other forgotten material, they have no feeling of remembering the scenes.

* * *

There are * * * a whole number of * * * things that vouch for the reality of infantile sexual scenes. In the first place there is the uniformity which they exhibit in certain details, which is a necessary consequence if the preconditions of these experiences are always of the same kind, but which would otherwise lead us to believe that there were secret understandings between the various patients. In the second place, patients sometimes describe as harmless events whose significance they obviously do not understand, since they would be bound otherwise to be horrified by them. Or again, they mention details, without laying any stress on them, which only someone of experience in life can understand and appreciate as subtle traits of reality.

Events of this sort strengthen our impression that the patients must really have experienced what they reproduce under the compulsion of analysis as scenes from their childhood. But another and stronger proof of this is furnished by the relationship of the infantile scenes to the content of the whole of the rest of the case history. It is exactly like putting together a child's picture-puzzle: after many attempts, we become absolutely certain in the end which piece belongs in the empty gap; for only that one piece fills out the picture and at the same time allows its irregular edges to be fitted into the edges of the other pieces in such a manner as to leave no free space and to entail no overlapping. In the same way, the contents of the infantile scenes turn out to be indispensable supplements to the associative and logical framework of the neurosis, whose insertion makes its course of development for the first time evident, or even, as we might often say, self-evident.

*   *   *

Sexual experiences in childhood consisting in stimulation of the genitals, coitus-like acts, and so on, must therefore be recognized, in the last analysis, as being the traumas which lead to a hysterical reaction to events at puberty and to the development of hysterical symptoms. This statement is certain to be met from different directions by two mutually contradictory objections. Some people will say that sexual abuses of this kind, whether practised upon children or between them, happen too seldom for it to be possible to regard them as the determinant of such a common neurosis as hysteria. Others will perhaps argue that, on the contrary, such experiences are very frequent—much too frequent for us to be able to attribute an aetiological significance to the fact of their occurrence. They will further maintain that it is easy, by making a few enquiries, to find people who remember scenes of sexual seduction and sexual abuse in their childhood years, and yet who have never been hysterical. Finally we shall be told, as a weighty argument, that in the lower strata of the population hysteria is certainly no more common than in the highest ones, whereas everything goes to show that the injunction for the sexual safeguarding of childhood is far more frequently transgressed in the case of the children of the proletariat.

Let us begin our defence with the easier part of the task. It seems to me certain that our children are far more often exposed to sexual assaults than the few precautions taken by parents in this connection would lead us to expect. When I first made enquiries about what was known on the subject, I learnt from colleagues that there are several publications by paediatricians which stigmatize the frequency of sexual practices by nurses and nursery maids, carried out even on infants in arms; and in the last few weeks I have come across a discussion of 'Coitus in Childhood' by Dr. Stekel (1895) in Vienna. I have not had time to collect other published evidence; but even it if were only scanty, it is to be expected that increased attention to the subject will very soon confirm the great frequency of sexual experiences and sexual activity in childhood.

Lastly, the findings of my analysis are in a position to speak for themselves. In all eighteen cases (cases of pure hysteria and of hysteria combined with obsessions, and comprising six men and twelve women) I have, as I have said, come to learn of sexual experiences of this kind in childhood. I can divide my cases into three groups, according to the origin of the sexual stimulation. In the first group it is a question of assaults—of single, or at any rate isolated, instances of abuse, mostly practised on female children, by adults who were strangers, and who, incidentally, knew how to avoid inflicting gross, mechanical injury. In these assaults there was no question of the child's consent, and the first effect of the experience was preponderantly one of fright. The second group consists of the much more numerous cases in which some adult looking after the child—a nursery maid or governess or tutor, or, unhappily all too often, a close relative—has initiated the child into sexual intercourse and has maintained a regular love relationship with it—a love relationship, moreover, with its mental side developed—which has often lasted for years. The third group, finally, contains child-relationships proper—sexual relations between two children of different sexes, mostly a brother and sister, which are often prolonged beyond puberty and which have the most far-reaching consequences for the pair. In most of my cases I found that two or more of these aetiologies were in operation together; in a few instances the accumulation of sexual experiences coming from different quarters was truly amazing. You will easily understand this peculiar feature of my observations, however, when you consider that the patients I was treating were all cases of severe neurotic illness which threatened to make life impossible.

* * *

It is true that if infantile sexual activity were an almost universal occurrence the demonstration of its presence in every case would carry no weight. But, to begin with, to assert such a thing would certainly be a gross exaggeration; and secondly, the aetiological pretensions of the infantile scenes rest not only on the regularity of their appearance in the anamneses of hysterics, but, above all, on the evidence of there being associative and logical ties between those scenes and the hysterical symptoms—evidence which, if you were given the complete history of a case, would be as clear as daylight to you.

What can the other factors be which the 'specific aetiology' of hysteria still needs in order actually to produce the neurosis? * * * To-day I need only indicate the point of contact at which the two parts of the topic—the specific and the auxiliary aetiology—fit into one another. No doubt a considerable quantity of factors will have to be taken into account. There will be the subject's inherited and personal constitution, the inherent importance of the infantile sexual experiences, and, above all, their number: a brief relationship with a strange boy, who afterwards becomes indifferent, will leave a less powerful effect on a girl than intimate sexual relations of several years' standing with her own brother. In the aetiology of the neuroses quantitative preconditions are as important as qualitative ones: there are threshold-values which have to be crossed before the illness can become manifest. Moreover, I do not myself regard this aetiological series as complete; nor does it solve the riddle of why hysteria is not more common among the lower classes. (You will remember, by the way, what a surprisingly large incidence of hysteria was reported by Charcot among working-class *men*). * * *

* * *

* * * We have heard and have acknowledged that there are numerous people who have a very clear recollection of infantile sexual experiences and who nevertheless do not suffer from hysteria. This objection has no weight; but it provides an occasion for making a valuable comment. According to our understanding of the neurosis, people of this kind *ought* not to be hysterical at all, or at any rate, not hysterical as a result of the scenes which they consciously remember. With our patients, those memories are never conscious; but we cure them of their hysteria by transforming their unconscious memories of the infantile scenes into conscious ones. There was nothing that we could have done or needed to do about the fact that they have had such experiences. From this you will perceive that the matter is not merely one of the existence of the sexual experiences, but that a psychological precondition enters in as well. The scenes must be present as *unconscious memories*; only so long as, and in so far as, they are unconscious are they able to create and maintain hysterical symptoms. But what decides whether those experiences produce conscious or unconscious memories—whether that is conditioned by the content of the experiences, or by the time at which they occur, or by later influences—that is a fresh problem, which we shall prudently avoid. Let me merely remind you that, as its first conclusion, analysis has arrived at the proposition that *hysterical symptoms are derivatives of memories which are operating unconsciously.*

Our view then is that infantile sexual experiences are the fundamental precondition for hysteria, are, as it were, the *disposition* for it and that it is they which create the hysterical symptoms, but that they do not do so immediately, but remain without effect to begin with and only exercise a pathogenic action later, when they have been aroused after puberty in the form of unconscious memories. * * *

In this way we obtain an indication that a certain *infantile* state of the psychical functions, as well as of the sexual system, is required in order that a sexual experience occurring during this period shall later on, in the form of a memory, produce a pathogenic effect. I do not venture as yet, however, to make any more precise statement on the nature of this psychical infantilism or on its chronological limits.

* * *

III

Gentlemen, the problem, the approaches to which I have just formulated, concerns the *mechanism* of the formation of hysterical symptoms. We find ourselves obliged, however, to describe the *causation* of those symptoms without taking that mechanism into account, and this involves an inevitable loss of completeness and clarity in our discussion. Let us go back to the part played by the infantile sexual scenes. I am afraid that I may have misled you into over-estimating their power to form symptoms. Let me, therefore, once more stress the fact that every case of hysteria exhibits symptoms which are determined, not by infantile but by later, often by recent, experiences. Other symptoms, it is true, go back to the very earliest experiences and belong, so to speak, to the most ancient nobility. Among these latter are above all to be found the numerous and diverse sensations and paraesthesias of the genital organs and other parts of the body, these sensations and paraesthesias being phenomena which simply correspond to the sensory content of the infantile scenes, reproduced in a hallucinatory fashion, often painfully intensified.

Another set of exceedingly common hysterical phenomena—painful need to urinate, the sensation accompanying defaecation, intestinal disturbances, choking and vomiting, indigestion and disgust at food—were also shown in my analyses (and with surprising regularity) to be derivatives of the same childhood experiences and were explained without difficulty by certain invariable peculiarities of those experiences. For the idea of these infantile sexual scenes is very repellent to the feelings of a sexually normal individual; they include all the abuses known to debauched and impotent persons, among whom the buccal cavity and the rectum are misused for sexual purposes. For physicians, astonishment at this soon gives way to a complete understanding. People who have no hesitation in satisfying their sexual desires upon children cannot be expected to jib a finer shades in the methods of obtaining that satisfaction; and the sexual impotence which is inherent in children inevitably forces them into the same substitutive actions as those to which adults descend if they become impotent. All the singular conditions under which the ill-matched pair conduct their love-relations—on the one hand the adult, who cannot escape his share in the mutual dependence necessarily entailed by a sexual relationship, and who is yet armed with complete authority and the right to punish, and can exchange the one role for the other to the uninhibited satisfaction of his moods, and on the other hand the child, who in his helplessness is at the mercy of this arbitrary will, who is prematurely aroused to every kind of sensibility and exposed to every sort of disappointment, and whose performance of the sexual activities assigned to him is often interrupted by his imperfect control of his natural needs—all these grotesque and yet tragic incongruities reveal themselves as stamped upon the later development of the individual and of his neurosis, in countless permanent effects which deserve to be traced in the greatest detail. Where the relation is between two children, the character of the sexual scenes is none the less of the same repulsive sort, since every such relationship between children postulates a previous seduction of one of them by an adult. The psychical consequences of these child-relations are quite extraordinarily far-reaching; the two individuals remain linked by an invisible bond throughout the whole of their lives.

Sometimes it is the accidental circumstances of these infantile sexual scenes which in later years acquire a determining power over the symptoms of the neurosis. Thus, in one of my cases the circumstance that the child was required to stimulate the genitals of a grown-up woman with his foot was enough to fixate his neurotic attention for years on to his legs and to their function, and finally to produce a hysterical paraplegia. In another case, a woman patient suffering from anxiety attacks which tended to come on at certain hours of the day could not be calmed unless a particular one of her many sisters stayed by her side all the time. Why this was so would have remained a riddle if analysis had not shown that the man who had committed the assaults on her used to enquire at every visit whether this sister, who he was afraid might interrupt him, was at home.

It may happen that the determining power of the infantile scenes is so much concealed that, in a superficial analysis, it is bound to be overlooked. In such instances we imagine that we have found the explanation of some particular symptom in the content of one of the later scenes—until, in the course of our work, we come upon the same content in one of the *infantile* scenes, so that in the end we are obliged to recognize that, after all, the later scene only owes its power of determining symptoms to its agreement with the earlier one. I do not wish because of this to represent the later scene as being unimportant; if it was my task to put before you the rules that govern the formation of hysterical symptoms, I should have to include as one of them that the idea which is selected for the production of a symptom is one which has been called up by a combination of several factors and which has been aroused from various directions simultaneously. I have elsewhere tried to express this in the formula: *hysterical symptoms are over-determined*.

* * * There is *one* fact above all which leads us astray in the psychological understanding of hysterical phenomena, and which seems to warn us against measuring psychical acts in hysterics and in normal people with the same yardstick. That fact is the descrepancy between psychically exciting stimuli and psychical reactions which we come upon in hysterical subjects. * * * The main part of the phenomenon—of the abnormal, exaggerated, hysterical reaction to psychical stimuli— admits of another explanation, an explanation which is supported by countless examples from the analyses of patients. And this is as follows: *The reaction of hysterics is only apparently exaggerated; it is bound to appear exaggerated to us because we only know a small part of the motives from which it arises.*

In reality, this reaction is proportionate to the exciting stimulus; thus it is normal and psychologically understandable. We see this at once when the analysis has added to the manifest motives, of which the patient is conscious, those other motives, which have been operative without his knowing about them, so that he could not tell us of them.

* * *

* * * It is not the latest slight— which, in itself, is minimal—that produces the fit of crying, the outburst of despair or the attempt at suicide, in disregard of the axiom that an effect must be proportionate to its cause; the small slight of the present moment has aroused and set working the memories of very many, more intense, earlier slights, behind all of which there lies in addition the memory of a serious slight in childhood which has never been overcome. Or again, let us take the instance of a young girl who blames herself most frightfully for having allowed a boy to stroke her hand in secret, and who from that time on has been overtaken by a neurosis. You can, of course, answer the puzzle by pronouncing her an abnormal, eccentrically disposed and over-sensitive person; but you will think differently when analysis shows you that the touching of her hand reminded her of another, similar touching, which had happened very early in her childhood and which formed part of a less innocent whole, so that her self-reproaches were actually reproaches about that old occasion. * * *

To this psychology, which has yet to be created to meet our needs— to this future *psychology of the neuroses*—I must also refer you when, in conclusion, I tell you something which will at first make you afraid that it may disturb our dawning comprehension of the aetiology of hysteria. For I must affirm that the aetiological role of infantile sexual experience is not confined to hysteria but holds good equally for the remarkable neurosis of obsessions, and perhaps also, indeed, for the various forms of chronic paranoia and other functional psychoses. I express myself on this with less definiteness, because I have as yet an-alysed far fewer cases of obsessional neurosis than of hysteria; and as regards paranoia, I have at my disposal only a single full analysis and a few fragmentary ones. But what I discovered in these cases seemed to be reliable and filled me with confident expectations for other cases. You will perhaps remember that already, at an earlier date, I recommended that hysteria and obsessions should be grouped together under the name of *'neuroses of defence'*, even before I had come to know of their common infantile aetiology. I must now add that—although this need not be expected to happen in general—every one of my cases of obsessions revealed a substratum of hysterical symptoms, mostly sensations and pains, which went back precisely to the earliest childhood experiences. What, then, determines whether the infantile sexual scenes which have remained unconscious will later on, when the other pathogenic factors are super-added, give rise to hysterical or to obsessional neurosis or even to paranoia? This increase in our knowledge seems, as you see, to prejudice the aetiological value of these scenes, since it removes the specificity of the aetiological relation.

I am not yet in a position, Gentlemen, to give a reliable answer to this question. The number of cases I have analysed is not large enough nor have the determining factors in them been sufficiently various. So far, I have observed that obsessions can be regularly shown by analysis to be disguised and transformed *self-reproaches about acts of sexual aggression in childhood*, and are therefore more often met with in men than in women, and that men develop obsessions more often than hysteria. From this I might conclude that the character of the infantile scenes—whether they were experienced with pleasure or only passively–has a determining influence on the choice of the later neurosis; but I do not want to underestimate the significance of the age at which these childhood actions occur, and other factors as well. Only a discussion of further analyses can throw light on these points. But when it becomes clear which are the decisive factors in the choice between the possible forms of the neuro-psychoses of defence, the question of what the mechanism is in virtue of which that particular form takes shape will once again be a purely psychological problem.

I have now come to the end of what I have to say to-day. Prepared as I am to meet with contradiction and disbelief, I should like to say one thing more in support of my position. Whatever you may think about the conclusions I have come to, I must ask you not to regard them as the fruit of idle speculation. They are based on a laborious individual examination of patients which has in most cases taken up a hundred or more hours of work. What is even more important to me than the value you put on my results is the attention you give to the procedure I have employed. This procedure is new and difficult to handle, but it is nevertheless irreplaceable for scientific and therapeutic purposes. You will realize, I am sure, that one cannot properly deny the findings which follow from this modification of Breuer's procedure so long as one puts it aside and uses only the customary method of questioning patients. To do so would be like trying to refute the findings of histological technique by relying upon macroscopic examination. The new method of research gives wide access to a new element in the psychical field of events, namely, to processes of thought which have remained unconscious—which, to use Breuer's expression, are 'inadmissible to consciousness'. Thus it inspires us with the hope of a new and better understanding of all functional psychical disturbances. I cannot believe that psychiatry will long hold back from making use of this new pathway to knowledge.

Letters to Fliess

On September 21, 1897, after returning from his summer holiday in the country, Freud reported to Fliess, in one of the most significant communications he ever sent to his intimate friend, that he could no longer sustain the "seduction theory" of the neuroses on which he had founded his hopes for fame. He did not give it up wholly—on December 12 of the same year he told Fliess that his confidence in the theory had considerably increased—but with the passage of time, his decision announced in the letter excerpted here became final. He was deeply disappointed, but rallied quickly and drew great profit from his "mistake": if the tales his women patients had told him about being seduced or raped by a parent or brother were not true, this did not mean that they had simply lied to him. It must mean that they were reporting on their fantasies. By taking such mental activity seriously, and (as he put it in his "Autobiographical Study") after he had "pulled myself together," he could "draw the right conclusions from my discovery: namely, that the neurotic symptoms were not related to actual events but to wishful phantasies, and that as far as the neurosis was concerned psychical reality was of more importance than material reality." Freud could now leap forward to the psychoanalytic theory of the mind. The way to the Oedipus complex lay open. (see above, p. 21).

Freud's abandonment of the "seduction theory" has been vigorously debated, but it would seem that the reasons he offered for his change of mind are cogent enough. It is important to insist that Freud never denied that child abuse was an appalling reality. The case of Katharina (see above, pp. 78–86) and others left no doubt in his mind on that score. "Seduction during childhood," he noted in his "Autobiographical Study," retained a certain share, though a humbler one, in the aetiology of neuroses" (see above, p. 21).

These were extraordinarily difficult and exciting times for Freud. His father had died on October 23, 1896, and the event had let loose in him forces of which he had been only dimly aware—or not aware at all. His self-analysis, the unsparing examination of his dreams, slips of the tongue, forgetfulness, and other "minor" events, the deepest, wholly unprecedented self-examination on which he had informally started somewhat earlier, now became a principal preoccupation, and he dredged up significant memories of his earliest days. His mother could confirm and elaborate on at least some of them. Thus, on October 3 and 4, 1897, not long after the shock of abandoning his "seduction theory," he reported to Fliess some of the fascinating material he had recovered. In later letters, the rush of self-discovery went on. Much of what he wrote Fliess in 1897 would find a place in his

Interpretation of Dreams. And what Freud thought most exciting about this work of self-scrutiny was that his discoveries characterized not just his own private history: everyone, it seemed, had been a little Oedipus.

. . . I will confide in you at once the great secret that has been slowly dawning on me in the last few months. I no longer believe in my *neurotica* [theory of the neuroses]. This is probably not intelligible without an explanation; after all, you yourself found what I could tell you credible. So I will begin historically from the question of the origin of my reasons for disbelief. The continual disappointments in my attempts at bringing my analysis to a real conclusion, the running-away of people who had for a time seemed most in my grasp, the absence of the complete successes on which I had reckoned, the possibility of explaining the partial successes in other ways, on ordinary lines,—this was the first group. Then came surprise at the fact that in every case the father, not excluding my own, had to be blamed as a pervert—the realization of the unexpected frequency of hysteria, in which the same determinant is invariably established, though such a widespread extent of perversity towards children is, after all, not very probable. (The perversity would have to be immeasurably more frequent than the hysteria, since the illness only arises where there has been an accumulation of events and where a factor that weakens defence has supervened.) Then, thirdly, the certain discovery that there are no indications of reality in the unconscious, so that one cannot distinguish between the truth and fiction that is cathected with affect. (Thus, the possibility remained open that sexual phantasy invariably seizes upon the theme of the parents.) Fourthly, the reflection that in the most deep-going psychosis the unconscious memory does not break through, so that the secret of the childhood experiences is not betrayed even in the most confused delirium. If in this way we see that the unconscious never overcomes the resistance of the conscious, then, too, we lose our expectation that in treatment the opposite will happen, to the extent of the unconscious being completely tamed by the conscious.

I was influenced so far by this that I was prepared to give up two things: the complete resolution of a neurosis and the certain knowledge of its aetiology in childhood. I have no idea now where I have got to, since I have not achieved a theoretical understanding of repression and its interplay of forces. It seems to have become once again arguable that it is only later experiences that give the impetus to phantasies, which then hark back to childhood; and with this the factor of a hereditary disposition regains a sphere of influence from which I had made it my task to expel it—in the interest of throwing a flood of light on neurosis.

If I were depressed, confused, or exhausted, doubts of this kind would no doubt have to be interpreted as signs of weakness. Since I am in an opposite state, I must recognize them as the result of honest and forcible intellectual work and must be proud that after going so deep I am still capable of such criticism. Can it be that this doubt merely represents an episode in advance towards further knowledge?

It is remarkable, too, that there has been an absence of any feeling of shame, for which, after all, there might be occasion. Certainly I shall not tell it in Dan or speak of it in Askelon, in the land of the Philistines. But in your eyes and my own I have more of the feeling of a victory than of a defeat—and, after all, that is not right.

. . . [October 3] Very little is still happening to me externally, but internally something most interesting. For the last four days my self-analysis, which I consider indispensable for throwing light upon the whole problem, has proceeded in dreams and has presented me with the most valuable inferences and clues. At some points I have a feeling of being at the end, and so far, too, I have always known where the dream of the next night would take things up. To describe it in writing is more difficult than anything else, and also it would be far too diffuse. I can only say shortly that *der Alte* [my father] played no active part in my case, but that no doubt I drew an inference by analogy from myself on to him; that the 'prime originator' [of my troubles] was a woman, ugly, elderly, but clever, who told me a great deal about God Almighty and Hell and who gave me a high opinion of my own capacities; that later (between the ages of two and two-and-a-half) my libido was stirred up towards *matrem*, namely on the occasion of a journey with her from Leipzig to Vienna, during which we must have spent the night together and I must have had an opportunity of seeing her *nudam*[1]—you drew the conclusion from this long ago for your own son, as a remark of yours revealed to me—; that I greeted my brother (who was a year my junior and died after a few months) with ill-wishes and genuine childish jealousy, and that his death left the germ of self-reproaches in me. I have also long known the companion in my evil deeds between the ages of one and two. It was my nephew, a year older than myself, who is now living in Manchester and who visited us in Vienna when I was fourteen. The two of us seem occasionally to have behaved in a cruel fashion to my niece, who was a year younger. This nephew and this younger brother have determined what is neurotic, but also what is intense, in all my friendships. You yourself have seen my travel-anxiety in full swing.

I have not yet found out anything about the scenes which underlie the whole business. If they come to light and if I succeed in resolving my own hysteria, I shall be grateful to the memory of the old woman who provided me at such an early age with the means for living and

1. [Freud seems in fact to have been four years old at the time of this journey.]

going on living. As you see, my old liking for her is breaking through again. I can give you no idea of the intellectual beauty of the work. . . .

October 4. . . . To-day's dream has produced what follows, under the strangest disguises.

She was my teacher in sexual matters and scolded me for being clumsy and not being able to do anything. (This is always how neurotic impotence comes about; it is thus that fear of incapacity at school obtains its sexual substratum.) At the same time I saw the skull of a small animal and in the dream I thought 'Pig!' But in the analysis I associated it with your wish two years ago that I might find a skull on the Lido to enlighten me, as Goethe once did. But I failed to find one. So I was a little fool. The whole dream was full of the most mortifying allusions to my present powerlessness as a therapist. Perhaps this is where an inclination to believe that hysteria is incurable has its start. Besides this, she washed me in reddish water, in which she had previously washed herself. (The interpretation is not difficult; I find nothing like this in the chain of my memories, so I regard it as a genuine ancient discovery.) And she made me carry off 'zehners' (ten kreuzer pieces) and give them to her. There is a long chain from these first silver zehners to the heap of paper ten-florin notes which I saw in the dream as Martha's housekeeping money. The dream can be summed up a 'bad treatment'. Just as the old woman got money from me for her bad treatment of me, so to-day I get money for my bad treatment of my patients. A special part was played by Frau Qu., whose remark you reported to me: I ought not to take anything from her as she was the wife of a colleague. (Of course he made it a condition that I should.)

A severe critic might say of all this that it was retrogressively phantasied and not progressively determined. Experimenta crucis [crucial experiments] would have to decide against him. The reddish water seems to be one such already. Where do all patients get the frightful perverse details which are often as remote from their experience as from their knowledge?

{October 15, 1897} . . . My self-analysis is in fact the most essential thing I have at present and it promises to become of the greatest value to me if it reaches its end. In the middle of it, it suddenly ceased for three days and I had the feeling of being tied up inside which patients complain of so much, and I was really inconsolable . . .

It is an uncanny fact that my practice still allows me a great deal of time.

The whole thing is all the more valuable for my purposes since I have succeeded in finding a few real points of reference for the story. I asked my mother whether she still recollected the nurse. 'Of course', she said, 'an elderly person, very clever. She was always taking you to church: when you came back afterwards you used to preach sermons and tell us

all about God Almighty. During my confinement when Anna was born,'
(she is two and a half years my junior) 'it was discovered that she was a
thief, and all the shiny new kreuzers and zehners and all the toys that
had been given to you were found in her possession. Your brother Philipp
[see below] himself went for the policeman and she was given ten months
in prison.' Now just see how this confirms the conclusions of my dream-
interpretation. I have found a simple explanation of my own possible
mistake. I wrote to you that she led me into stealing zehners and giving
them to her. The dream really meant that she stole them herself. For
the dream-picture was a memory of my taking money from the mother
of a doctor—that is, wrongfully. The correct interpretation is: I = she,
and the mother of a doctor equals my mother. So far was I from knowing
that she was a thief that I made a wrong interpretation.

I also made enquiries about the doctor we had in Freiberg, because
a dream showed a great deal of resentment against him. In the analysis
of the figure in the dream behind which he was concealed I thought
also of a Professor von K., who was my history master at school. He did
not seem to fit in at all, as my relations with him were indifferent or,
rather, agreeable. My mother then told me that the doctor in my childhood had only one eye, and of all my schoolmasters Professor K. too
was the only one with that same defect.

The evidential value of these coincidences might be invalidated by
the objection that on some occasion in my later childhood I had heard
that the nurse was a thief, and that I had then apparently forgotten it
till it finally emerged in the dream. I think myself that that is so. But I
have another unexceptionable and amusing piece of evidence. I said to
myself that if the old woman disappeared so suddenly, it must be possible
to point to the impression this made on me. Where is that impression,
then? A scene then occurred to me which, for the last 29 years, has
occasionally emerged in my conscious memory without my understanding it. My mother was nowhere to be found: I was screaming my head
off. My brother Philipp, twenty years older than me, was holding open
a cupboard [Kasten] for me, and, when I found that my mother was
not inside it either, I began crying still more, till, looking slim and
beautiful, she came in by the door. What can this mean? Why was my
brother opening the cupboard, though he knew that my mother was not
in it, so that this could not pacify me? And then suddenly I understood.
I had asked him to do it. When I missed my mother, I had been afraid
she had vanished from me just as the old woman had a short time before.
Now I must have heard that the old woman had been locked up and
consequently I must have thought that my mother had been too—or
rather had been 'boxed up' ['eingekastelt']; for my brother Philipp, who
is 63 now, is fond to this very day of talking in this punning fashion.
The fact that it was to him in particular that I turned proves that I knew
quite well of his share in the nurse's disappearance.

Since then I have got much further, but have not yet reached any real stopping-point. Communicating what is unfinished is so diffuse and laborious that I hope you will excuse me from it and content yourself with a knowledge of the portions that are established with certainty. If the analysis contains what I expect from it, I will work it over systematically and put it before you afterwards. So far I have found nothing completely new, only complications, to which I am ordinarily accustomed. It is not quite easy. To be completely honest with oneself is good practice. One single thought of general value has been revealed to me. I have found, in my own case too, falling in love with the mother and jealousy of the father, and I now regard it as a universal event of early childhood, even if not so early as in children who have been made hysterical. (Similarly with the romance of parentage in paranoia—heroes, founders of religions.) If that is so, we can understand the riveting power of *Oedipus Rex*, in spite of all the objections raised by reason against its presupposition of destiny; and we can understand why the later 'dramas of destiny' were bound to fail so miserably. Our feelings rise against any arbitrary, individual compulsion [of fate], such as is presupposed in [Grillparzer's] *Die Ahnfrau*, etc. But the Greek legend seizes on a compulsion which everyone recognizes because he feels its existence within himself. Each member of the audience was once, in germ and in phantasy, just such an Oedipus, and each one recoils in horror from the dream-fulfilment here transplanted into reality, with the whole quota of repression which separates his infantile state from his present one.

A fleeting idea has passed through my head of whether the same thing may not lie at the bottom of *Hamlet* as well. I am not thinking of Shakespeare's conscious intention, but I believe rather that here some real event instigated the poet to his representation, in that the unconscious in him understood the unconscious in his hero. How can Hamlet the hysteric justify his words 'Thus conscience does make cowards of us all', how can he explain his hesitation in avenging his father by the murder of his uncle—he, the same man who sends his courtiers to their death without a scruple and who is positively precipitate in killing Laertes? How better could he justify himself than by the torment he suffers from the obscure memory that he himself had meditated the same deed against his father from passion for his mother, and—'use every man after his desert, and who should 'scape whipping?' His conscience is his unconscious sense of guilt. And is not his sexual alienation in his conversation with Ophelia typically hysterical? and his rejection of the instinct which seeks to beget children? and, finally, his transferring the deed from his own father to Ophelia's? And does he not in the end, in the same remarkable way as my hysterical patients, bring down punishment on himself by suffering the same fate as his father of being poisoned by the same rival?

Screen Memories

This paper of 1899, a charming but pointed set of disguised reminiscences, is evidence and part of the self-exploration that occupied Freud day and night in those years and that was indispensable to his work on *The Interpretation of Dreams*. Just how much autobiography is concealed in the stories attributed to third persons remains a matter of some dispute.

---

* * *

We are so much accustomed to this lack of memory of the impressions of childhood that we are apt to overlook the problem underlying it and are inclined to explain it as a self-evident consequence of the rudimentary character of the mental activities of children. Actually, however, a normally developed child of three or four already exhibits an enormous amount of highly organized mental functioning in the comparisons and inferences which he makes and in the expression of his feelings; and there is no obvious reason why amnesia should overtake these psychical acts, which carry no less weight than those of a later age.

* * * I have no intention at present of discussing the subject as a whole, and I shall therefore content myself with emphasizing the few points which will enable me to introduce the notion of what I have termed 'screen memories'.

The age to which the content of the earliest memories of childhood is usually referred back is the period between the ages of two and four. * * * There are some, however, whose memory reaches back further— even to the time before the completion of their first year; and, on the other hand, there are some whose earliest recollections go back only to their sixth, seventh, or even eighth year. * * *

Quite special interest attaches to the question of what is the usual *content* of these earliest memories of childhood. The psychology of adults would necessarily lead us to expect that those experiences would be selected as worth remembering which had aroused some powerful emotion or which, owing to their consequences, had been recognized as important soon after their occurrence. And some indeed of the observations collected by the Henris appear to fulfil this expectation. They report that the most frequent content of the first memories of childhood are on the one hand occasions of fear, shame, physical pain, etc., and on the other hand important events such as illnesses, deaths, fires, births of brothers and sisters, etc. We might therefore be inclined to assume that the principle governing the choice of memories is the same in the case of children as in that of adults. It is intelligible—though the fact deserves to be explicitly mentioned—that the memories retained from childhood should necessarily show evidence of the difference between what attracts the interest of a child and of an adult. * * *

* * *

Further investigation of these indifferent childhood memories has taught me that they can originate in other ways as well and that an unsuspected wealth of meaning lies concealed behind their apparent innocence. But on this point I shall not content myself with a mere assertion but shall give a detailed report of one particular instance which seems to me the most instructive out of a considerable number of similar ones. Its value is certainly increased by the fact that it relates to someone who is not at all or only very slightly neurotic.

The subject of this observation is a man of university education, aged thirty-eight.[1] Though his own profession lies in a very different field, he has taken an interest in psychological questions ever since I was able to relieve him of a slight phobia by means of psycho-analysis. Last year he drew my attention to his childhood memories, which had already played some part in his analysis. After studying the investigation made by V. and C. Henri, he gave me the following summarized account of his own experience.

'I have at my disposal a fair number of early memories of childhood which I can date with great certainty. For at the age of three I left the small place where I was born and moved to a large town; and all these memories of mine relate to my birthplace and therefore date from my second and third years. They are mostly short scenes, but they are very well preserved and furnished with every detail of sense-perception, in complete contrast to my memories of adult years, which are entirely lacking in the visual element. From my third year onwards my recollections grow scantier and less clear; there are gaps in them which must cover more than a year; and it is not, I believe, until my sixth or seventh year that the stream of my memories becomes continuous. My memories up to the time of my leaving my first place of residence fall into three groups. The first group consists of scenes which my parents have repeatedly since described to me. As regards these, I feel uncertain whether I have had the mnemic image from the beginning or whether I only construed it after hearing one of these descriptions. I may remark, however, that there are also events of which I have no mnemic image in spite of their having been frequently retailed by my parents. I attach more importance to the second group. It comprises scenes which have not (so far as I know) been described to me and some of which, indeed, could not have been described to me, as I have not met the other participants in them (my nurse and playmates) since their occurrence. I shall come to the third group presently. As regards the content of these scenes and their consequent claim to being recollected, I should like to say that I am not entirely at sea. I cannot maintain, indeed, that what I have retained are memories of the most important events of the period,

1. [There can be no doubt that what follows is autobiographical material only thinly disguised. . . . At the date at which this paper was sent in for publication in May 1899, Freud was in fact just forty-three years old.]

or what I should to-day judge to be the most important. I have no knowledge of the birth of a sister, who is two and a half years younger than I am; my departure, my first sight of the railway and the long carriage-drive before it—none of these has left a trace in my memory. On the other hand, I can remember two small occurrences during the railway-journey; these, as you will recollect, came up in the analysis of my phobia. But what should have made most impression on me was an injury to my face which caused a considerable loss of blood and for which I had to have some stitches put in by a surgeon. I can still feel the scar resulting from this accident, but I know of no recollection which points to it, either directly or indirectly. It is true that I may perhaps have been under two years old at the time.

'It follows from this that I feel no surprise at the pictures and scenes of these first two groups. No doubt they are displaced memories from which the essential element has for the most part been omitted. But in a few of them it is at least hinted at, and in others it is easy for me to complete them by following certain pointers. By doing so I can establish a sound connection between the separate fragments of memories and arrive at a clear understanding of what the childish interest was that recommended these particular occurrences to my memory. This does not apply, however, to the content of the third group, which I have not so far discussed. There I am met by material—one rather long scene and several smaller pictures—with which I can make no headway at all. The scene appears to me fairly indifferent and I cannot understand why it should have become fixed in my memory. Let me describe it to you. I see a rectangular, rather steeply sloping piece of meadow-land, green and thickly grown; in the green there are a great number of yellow flowers—evidently common dandelions. At the top end of the meadow there is a cottage and in front of the cottage door two women are standing chatting busily, a peasant-woman with a handkerchief on her head and a children's nurse. Three children are playing in the grass. One of them is myself (between the age of two and three); the two others are my boy cousin, who is a year older than me, and his sister, who is almost exactly the same age as I am. We are picking the yellow flowers and each of us is holding a bunch of flowers we have already picked. The little girl has the best bunch; and, as though by mutual agreement, we—the two boys—fall on her and snatch away her flowers. She runs up the meadow in tears and as a consolation the peasant-woman gives her a big piece of black bread. Hardly have we seen this than we throw the flowers away, hurry to the cottage and ask to be given some bread too. And we are in fact given some; the peasant-woman cuts the loaf with a long knife. In my memory the bread tastes quite delicious—and at that point the scene breaks off.

'Now what is there in this occurrence to justify the expenditure of memory which it has occasioned me? I have racked my brains in vain over it. Does the emphasis lie in our disagreeable behaviour to the little girl? Did the yellow colour of the dandelions—a flower which I am, of course, far from admiring to-day—so greatly please me? Or, as a result of my careering round the grass, did the bread taste so much nicer than usual that it made an unforgettable impression on me? Nor can I find any connection between this scene and the interest which (as I was able to discover without any difficulty) bound together the other scenes from my childhood. Altogether, there seems to me something not quite right about this scene. The yellow of the flowers is a disporportionately prominent element in the situation as a whole, and the nice taste of the bread seems to me exaggerated in an almost hallucinatory fashion. I cannot help being reminded of some pictures that I once saw in a burlesque exhibition. Certain portions of these pictures, and of course the most inappropriate ones, instead of being painted, were built up in three dimensions—for instance, the ladies' bustles. Well, can you point out any way of finding an explanation or interpretation of this redundant memory of my childhood?'

I thought it advisable to ask him since when he had been occupied with this recollection: whether he was of opinion that it had recurred to his memory periodically since his childhood, or whether it had perhaps emerged at some later time on some occasion that could be recalled. This question was all that it was necessary for me to contribute to the solution of the problem; the rest was found by my collaborator himself, who was no novice at jobs of this kind.

'I have not yet considered that point,' he replied. 'Now that you have raised the question, it seems to me almost a certainty that this childhood memory never occurred to me at all in my earlier years. But I can also recall the occasion which led to my recovering this and many other recollections of my earliest childhood. When I was seventeen and at my secondary school, I returned for the first time to my birthplace for the holidays, to stay with a family who had been our friends ever since that remote date. I know quite well what a wealth of impressions overwhelmed me at that time. But I see now that I shall have to tell you a whole big piece of my history: it belongs here, and you have brought it upon yourself by your question. So listen. I was the child of people who were originally well-to-do and who, I fancy, lived comfortably enough in that little corner of the provinces. When I was about three, the branch of industry in which my father was concerned met with a catastrophe. He lost all his means and we were forced to leave the place and move to a large town. Long and difficult years followed, of which, as it seems to me, nothing was worth remembering. I never felt really comfortable in the town. I believe now that I was never free from a longing for the beautiful woods near our home, in which (as one of my memories from those days tells me) I used to run off from my father, almost before I had learnt to walk. Those holidays, when I was seventeen, were my first holidays in the country, and, as I have said, I stayed with a family with whom we were friends and who had risen greatly in the world since our move. I could compare the comfort reigning there with our own style of living at home in the town. But it is no use evading the subject any longer: I must admit that there was something else that excited me powerfully. I was seventeen, and in the family where I was staying there was a daughter of fifteen, with whom I immediately fell in love. It was my first calf-love and sufficiently intense, but I kept it completely secret. After a few days the girl went off to her school (from which she too was home for the holidays) and it was this separation after such a short acquaintance that brought my longings to a really high pitch. I passed many hours in solitary walks through the lovely woods that I had found once more and spent my time building castles in the air. These, strangely enough, were not concerned with the future but sought to improve the past. If only the smash had not occurred! If only I had stopped at home and grown up in the country and grown as strong as the young men in the house, the brothers of my love! And then if only I had followed my father's profession and if I had finally married her—for I should have known her intimately all those years! I had not the slightest doubt, of course, that in the circumstances created by my imagination I should have loved her just as passionately as I really seemed to then. A strange thing. For when I see her now from time to time—she happens to have married someone here—she is quite exceptionally indifferent to me. Yet I can remember quite well for what a long time afterwards I was affected by the yellow colour of the dress she was wearing when we first met, whenever I saw the same colour anywhere else.'

That sounds very much like your parenthetical remark to the effect that you are no longer fond of the common dandelion. Do you not suspect that there may be a connection between the yellow of the girl's dress and the ultra-clear yellow of the flowers in your childhood scene?

'Possibly. But it was not the same yellow. The dress was more of a yellowish brown, more like the colour of wallflowers. However, I can at least let you have an intermediate idea which may serve your purpose. At a later date, while I was in the Alps, I saw how certain flowers which have light colouring in the lowlands take on darker shades at high altitudes. Unless I am greatly mistaken, there is frequently to be found in mountainous regions a flower which is very similar to the dandelion but which is dark yellow and would exactly agree in colour with the dress of the girl I was so fond of. But I have not finished yet. I now come to a second occasion which stirred up in me the impressions of my childhood and which dates from a time not far distant from the first. I was seventeen when I revisited my birthplace. Three years later during my holidays I visited my uncle and met once again the children who had been my first playmates, the same two cousins, the boy a year older than I am and the girl of the same age as myself, who appear in the childhood scene with the dandelions. This family had left my birthplace at the same time as we did and had become prosperous in a far-distant city.'

And did you once more fall in love—with your cousin this time—
and indulge in a new set of phantasies?

'No, this time things turned out differently. By then I was at the
University and I was a slave to my books. I had nothing left over for
my cousin. So far as I know I had no similar phantasies on that occasion.
But I believe that my father and my uncle had concocted a plan by
which I was to exchange the abstruse subject of my studies for one of
more practical value, settle down, after my studies were completed, in
the place where my uncle lived, and marry my cousin. No doubt when
they saw how absorbed I was in my own intentions the plan was dropped;
but I fancy I must certainly have been aware of its existence. It was not
until later, when I was a newly-fledged man of science and hard pressed
by the exigencies of life and when I had to wait so long before finding
a post here, that I must sometimes have reflected that my father had
meant well in planning this marriage for me, to make good the loss in
which the original catastrophe had involved my whole existence.'

Then I am inclined to believe that the childhood scene we are considering emerged at this time, when you were struggling for your daily
bread—provided, that is, that you can confirm my idea that it was during
this same period that you first made the acquaintance of the Alps.

'Yes, that is so: mountaineering was the one enjoyment that I allowed
myself at that time. But I still cannot grasp your point.'

I am coming to it at once. The element on which you put most stress
in your childhood scene was the fact of the country-made bread tasting
so delicious. It seems clear that this idea, which amounted almost to a
hallucination, corresponded to your phantasy of the comfortable life you
would have led if you had stayed at home and married this girl [in the
yellow dress]—or, in symbolic language, of how sweet the bread would
have tasted for which you had to struggle so hard in your later years.
The yellow of the flowers, too, points to the same girl. But there are
also elements in the childhood scene which can only be related to the
second phantasy—of being married to your cousin. Throwing away
the flowers in exchange for bread strikes me as not a bad disguise for
the scheme your father had for you: you were to give up your unpractical
ideals and take on a 'bread-and-butter' occupation, were you not?

'It seems then that I amalgamated the two sets of phantasies of how
my life could have been more comfortable—the "yellow" and the
"country-made bread" from the one and the throwing-away of the flowers
and the actual people concerned from the other.'

Yes. You projected the two phantasies on to one another and made
a childhood memory of them. The element about the alpine flowers is
as it were a stamp giving the date of manufacture. I can assure you that
people often construct such things unconsciously—almost like works of
fiction.

'But if that is so, there was *no* childhood memory, but only a phantasy put back into childhood. A feeling tells me, though, that the scene is genuine. How does that fit in?'

There is in general no guarantee of the data produced by our memory. But I am ready to agree with you that the scene is genuine. If so, you selected it from innumerable others of a similar or another kind because, on account of its content (which in itself was indifferent) it was well adapted to represent the two phantasies, which were important enough to you.

Recollection of this kind, whose value lies in the fact that it represents in the memory impressions and thoughts of a later date whose content is connected with its own by symbolic or similar links, may appropriately be called a 'screen memory'. In any case you will cease to feel any surprise that this scene should so often recur to your mind. It can no longer be regarded as an innocent one since, as we have discovered, it is calculated to illustrate the most momentous turning-points in your life, the influence of the two most powerful motive forces—hunger and love.[2]

'Yes, it represented hunger well enough. But what about love?"

In the yellow of the flowers, I mean. But I cannot deny that in this childhood scene of yours love is represented far less prominently than I should have expected from my previous experience.

'No. You are mistaken. This essence of it is its representation of love. Now I understand for the first time. Think for a moment! Taking flowers away from a girl means to deflower her. What a contrast between the boldness of this phantasy and my bashfulness on the first occasion and my indifference on the second.'

I can assure you that youthful bashfulness habitually has as its complement bold phantasies of that sort.

'But in that case the phantasy that has transformed itself into these childhood memories would not be a conscious one that I can remember, but an unconscious one?'

Unconscious thoughts which are a prolongation of conscious ones. You think to yourself 'If I had married so-and-so', and behind the thought there is an impulse to form a picture of what the 'being married' really is.

'I can go on with it now myself. The most seductive part of the whole subject for a young scapegrace is the picture of the marriage night. (What does he care about what comes afterwards?) But that picture cannot venture out into the light of day: the dominating mood of diffidence and of respect towards the girl keeps it suppressed. So it remains unconscious—'

And slips away into a childhood memory. You are quite right. It is

2. {This thought borrows from Schiller's poem "Die Weltweisen." The idea, which is an early version of Freud's first theory of the drives—sexual and self-preservative—recurs in his writings for some years. Indeed, he had quoted it in his letter of February 12, 1884, to his fiancée Martha Bernays (see Peter Gay, Freud, p. 46.)}

precisely the coarsely sensual element in the phantasy which explains why it does not develop into a *conscious* phantasy but must be content to find its way allusively and under a flowery disguise into a childhood scene.

'But why precisely, into a *childhood* scene, I should like to know?'

For the sake of its innocence, perhaps. Can you imagine a greater contrast to these designs for gross sexual aggression than childish pranks? However, there are more general grounds that have a decisive influence in bringing about the slipping away of repressed thoughts and wishes into childhood memories: for you will find the same thing invariably happening in hysterical patients. It seems, moreover, as though the recollection of the remote past is in itself facilitated by some pleasurable motive: *forsan et haec olim meminisse juvabit.*[3]

'If that is so, I have lost all faith in the genuineness of the dandelion scene. This is how I look at it: On the two occasions in question, and with the support of very comprehensible realistic motives, the thought occurred to me: "If you had married this or that girl, your life would have become much pleasanter." The sensual current in my mind took hold of the thought which is contained in the protasis and repeated it in images of a kind capable of giving that same sensual current satisfaction. This second version of the thought remained unconscious on account of its incompatibility with the dominant sexual disposition; but this very fact of its remaining unconscious enabled it to persist in my mind long after changes in the real situation had quite got rid of the conscious version. In accordance, as you say, with a general law, the clause that had remained unconscious sought to transform itself into a childhood scene which, on account of its innocence, would be able to become conscious. With this end in view it had to undergo a fresh transformation, or rather two fresh transformations. One of these removed the objectionable element from the protasis by expressing it figuratively; the second forced the apodosis into a shape capable of visual representation—using for the purpose the intermediary ideas of "bread" and "bread-and-butter occupations". I see that by producing a phantasy like this I was providing, as it were, a fulfilment of the two suppressed wishes—for deflowering a girl and for material comfort. But now that I have given such a complete account of the motives that led to my producing the dandelion phantasy, I cannot help concluding that what I am dealing with is something that never happened at all but has been unjustifiably smuggled in among my childhood memories.'

I see that I must take up the defence of its genuineness. You are going too far. You have accepted my assertion that every suppressed phantasy of this kind tends to slip away into a childhood scene. But suppose now that this cannot occur unless there is a memory-trace the content of which offers the phantasy a point of contact—comes, as it were, half

---

3. ['Some day, perhaps, it will be a joy to remember even these things.' Virgil, *Aeneid*, I, 203.]

way to meet it. Once a point of contact of this kind has been found—in the present instance it was the deflowering, the taking away of the flowers—the remaining content of the phantasy is remodelled with the help of every legitimate intermediate idea—take the bread as an example—till it can find further points of contact with the content of the childhood scene. It is very possible that in the course of this process the childhood scene itself also undergoes changes; I regard it as certain that falsifications of memory may be brought about in this way too. In your case the childhood scene seems only to have had some of its lines engraved more deeply: think of the over-emphasis on the yellow and the exaggerated niceness of the bread. But the raw material was utilizable. If that had not been so, it would not have been possible for this particular memory, rather than any others, to make its way forward into consciousness. No such scene would have occurred to you as a childhood memory, or perhaps some other one would have—for you know how easily our ingenuity can build connecting bridges from any one point to any other. And apart from your own subjective feeling which I am not inclined to under-estimate, there is another thing that speaks in favour of the genuineness of your dandelion memory. It contains elements which have not been solved by what you have told me and which do not in fact fit in with the sense required by the phantasy. For instance, your boy cousin helping you to rob the little girl of her flowers—can you make any sense of the idea of being helped in deflowering someone? or of the peasant-woman and the nurse in front of the cottage?

'Not that I can see.'

So the phantasy does not coincide completely with the childhood scene. It is only based on it at certain points. That argues in favour of the childhood memory being genuine.

'Do you think an interpretation like this of an apparently innocent childhood memory is often applicable?

Very often, in my experience. Shall we amuse ourselves by seeing whether the two examples given by the Henris can be interpreted as screen memories concealing subsequent experiences and wishes? I mean the memory of a table laid for a meal with a basin of ice on it, which was supposed to have some connection with the death of the subject's grandmother, and the other memory, of a child breaking off a branch from a tree while he was on a walk and of his being helped to do it by someone.

He reflected for a little and then answered: 'I can make nothing of the first one. It is most probably a case of displacement at work; but the intermediate steps are beyond guessing. As for the second case, I should be prepared to give an interpretation, if only the person concerned had not been a Frenchman.'

I cannot follow you there. What difference would that make?

'A great deal of difference, since what provides the intermediate step between a screen memory and what it conceals is likely to be a verbal expression. In German "to pull one out" is a very common vulgar term for masturbation. The scene would then be putting back into early childhood a seduction to masturbation—someone was helping him to do it—which in fact occurred at a later period. But even so, it does not fit, for in the childhood scene there were a number of other people present.'

Whereas his seduction to masturbate must have occurred in solitude and secrecy. It is just that contrast that inclines me to accept your view: it serves once again to make the scene innocent. Do you know what it means when in a dream we see 'a lot of strangers', as happens so often in dreams of nakedness in which we feel so terribly embarrassed? Nothing more nor less than secrecy, which there again is expressed by its opposite. However, our interpretation remains a jest, since we have no idea whether a Frenchman would recognize an allusion to masturbation in the words *casser une branche d'un arbre* or in some suitably emended phrase.

This analysis, which I have reproduced as accurately as possible, will, I hope, have to some extent clarified the concept of a 'screen memory' as one which owes its value as a memory not to its own content but to the relation existing between that content and some other, that has been suppressed. * * *

Our earliest childhood memories will always be a subject of special interest because the problem mentioned at the beginning of this paper (of how it comes about that the impressions which are of most significance for our whole future usually leave no mnemic images behind) leads us to reflect upon the origin of conscious memories in general.

* * *

* * * It may indeed be questioned whether we have any memories at all *from* our childhood: memories *relating to* our childhood may be all that we possess. Our childhood memories show us our earliest years not as they were but as they appeared at the later periods when the memories were aroused. In these periods of arousal, the childhood memories did not, as people are accustomed to say, *emerge*; they were *formed* at that time. And a number of motives, with no concern for historical accuracy, had a part in forming them, as well as in the selection of the memories themselves.

PART TWO: THE CLASSIC THEORY

The Interpretation of Dreams

Freud's *Interpretation of Dreams*, published in November 1899 but dated 1900 by the publisher (and by Freud, too, in his references to it), is still, after all these decades, an astonishing performance. The author's pride in it remained undimmed. As he put it three decades after its publication, in 1931, prefacing the third, revised, English edition: "Insight such as this falls to one's lot but once in a lifetime." The book is so rich as to be virtually unclassifiable. It is partly open and partly concealed autobiography, partly an account of what it meant to be a Jew in Habsburg Austria-Hungary, partly an analysis of the considerable literature on dreaming from antiquity to the nineteenth century, but also, and mainly, the working out of a theory of dreams and (in the difficult, famous last chapter, the seventh) a more general theory of mind. In one way or another, Freud had been working on the book since about 1892, when he began to take particular account of dreams. The most celebrated of the dreams he uses in the book (reprinted below), the so-called "Irma dream," was dreamt in mid-July 1895, years before Freud had precisely determined what to do with the material he was amassing. The preface to the second edition, just below, shows how intimately entangled this work was with Freud's deepest feelings. In short, *The Interpretation of Dreams* is impossible really to excerpt. The reader should permit the whole book to work on him.

Preface to the Second Edition

If within ten years of the publication of this book (which is very far from being an easy one to read) a second edition is called for, this is not due to the interest taken in it by the professional circles to whom my original preface was addressed. My psychiatric colleagues seem to have taken no trouble to overcome the initial bewilderment created by my new approach to dreams. The professional philosophers have become accustomed to polishing off the problems of dream-life (which they treat as a mere appendix to conscious states) in a few sentences—and usually in the same ones; and they have evidently failed to notice that we have something here from which a number of inferences can be drawn that are bound to transform our psychological theories. The attitude adopted by reviewers in the scientific periodicals could only lead one to suppose that my work was doomed to be sunk into complete silence; while the small group of gallant supporters, who practise medical psycho-analysis under my guidance and who follow my example in interpreting dreams and make use of their interpretations in treating neurotics, would never have exhausted the first edition of the book. Thus it is that I feel indebted to a wider circle of educated and curious-minded readers, whose interest has led me to take up once more after nine years this difficult, but in many respects fundamental, work.

I am glad to say that I have found little to change in it. Here and there I have inserted some new material, added some fresh points of detail derived from my increased experience, and at some few points recast my statements. But the essence of what I have written about dreams and their interpretation, as well as about the psychological theorems to be deduced from them—all this remains unaltered: subjectively at all events, it has stood the test of time. Anyone who is acquainted with my other writings (on the aetiology and mechanism of the psycho-neuroses) will know that I have never put forward inconclusive opinions as though they were established facts, and that I have always sought to modify my statements so that they may keep in step with my advancing knowledge. In the sphere of dream-life I have been able to leave my original assertions unchanged. During the long years in which I have been working at the problems of the neuroses I have often been in doubt and sometimes been shaken in my convictions. At such times it has always been the *Interpretation of Dreams* that has given me back my certainty. It is thus a sure instinct which has led my many scientific opponents to refuse to follow me more especially in my researches upon dreams.

An equal durability and power to withstand any far-reaching alterations during the process of revision has been shown by the *material* of the book, consisting as it does of dreams of my own which have for the most part been overtaken or made valueless by the march of events and by which I illustrated the rules of dream-interpretation. For this book has a further subjective significance for me personally—a significance which I only grasped after I had completed it. It was, I found, a portion of my own self-analysis, my reaction to my father's death—that is to say, to the most important event, the most poignant loss, of a man's life. Having discovered that this was so, I felt unable to obliterate the traces of the experience. To my readers, however, it will be a matter of indifference upon what particular material they learn to appreciate the importance of dreams and how to interpret them.

Wherever I have found it impossible to incorporate some essential addition into the original context, I have indicated its more recent date by enclosing it in square brackets.

BERCHTESGADEN, *Summer* 1908

PREAMBLE

During the summer of 1895 I had been giving psycho-analytic treatment to a young lady who was on very friendly terms with me and my family. It will be readily understood that a mixed relationship such as this may be a source of many disturbed feelings in a physician and particularly in a psychotherapist. While the physician's personal interest is greater, his authority is less; any failure would bring a threat to the old-established friendship with the patient's family. This treatment had ended in a partial success; the patient was relieved of her hysterical anxiety but did not lose all her somatic symptoms. At that time I was not yet quite clear in my mind as to the criteria indicating that a hysterical case history was finally closed, and I proposed a solution to the patient which she seemed unwilling to accept. While we were thus at variance, we had broken off the treatment for the summer vacation.—One day I had a visit from a junior colleague, one of my oldest friends, who had been staying with my patient, Irma, and her family at their country resort. I asked him how he had found her and he answered: 'She's better, but not quite well.' I was conscious that my friend Otto's words, or the tone in which he spoke them, annoyed me. I fancied I detected a reproof in them, such as to the effect that I had promised the patient too much; and, whether rightly or wrongly, I attributed the supposed fact of Otto's siding against me to the influence of my patient's relatives, who, as it seemed to me, had never looked with favour on the treatment. However, my disagreeable impression was not clear to me and I gave no outward sign of it. The same evening I wrote out Irma's case history, with the idea of giving it to Dr. M. (a common friend who was at that time the leading figure in our circle) in order to justify myself. That night (or more probably the next morning) I had the following dream, which I noted down immediately after waking.[1]

DREAM OF JULY 23RD–24TH, 1895

A large hall—numerous guests, whom we were receiving.—Among them was Irma. I at once took her on one side, as though to answer her letter and to reproach her for not having accepted my 'solution' yet. I said to her: 'If you still get pains, it's really only your fault.' She replied: 'If you only knew what pains I've got now in my throat and stomach and abdomen—it's choking me'—I was alarmed and looked at her. She looked pale and puffy. I thought to myself that after all I must be missing some organic trouble. I took her to the window and looked down her throat, and she showed signs of recalcitrance, like women with artificial dentures. I thought to myself that there was really no need for her to do that.—She then opened her mouth properly and on the right I found a big white patch; at another place I saw extensive whitish grey scabs upon some remarkable curly structures which were evidently modelled on the turbinal bones of the nose.—I at once called in Dr. M., and he repeated the examination and confirmed it. . . . Dr. M. looked quite different from usual; he was very pale, he walked with a limp and his chin was clean-shaven. . . . My friend Otto was now standing beside her as well, and my friend Leopold was percussing her through her bodice and saying: 'She has a dull area low down on the left.' He also indicated that a

1. [*Footnote added* 1914:] This is the first dream which I submitted to a detailed interpretation.

portion of the skin on the left shoulder was infiltrated. (I noticed this, just as he did, in spite of her dress.) . . . M. said: 'There's no doubt it's an infection, but no matter; dysentery will supervene and the toxin will be eliminated.' . . . We were directly aware, too, of the origin of the infection. Not long before, when she was feeling unwell, my friend Otto had given her an injection of a preparation of propyl, propyls . . . propionic acid . . . trimethylamin (and I saw before me the formula for this printed in heavy type). . . . Injections of that sort ought not to be made so thoughtlessly. . . . And probably the syringe had not been clean.

This dream has one advantage over many others. It was immediately clear what events of the previous day provided its starting-point. My preamble makes that plain. The news which Otto had given me of Irma's condition and the case history which I had been engaged in writing till far into the night continued to occupy my mental activity even after I was asleep. Nevertheless, no one who had only read the preamble and the content of the dream itself could have the slightest notion of what the dream meant. I myself had no notion. I was astonished at the symptoms of which Irma complained to me in the dream, since they were not the same as those for which I had treated her. I smiled at the senseless idea of an injection of propionic acid and at Dr. M.'s consoling reflections. Towards its end the dream seemed to me to be more obscure and compressed than it was at the beginning. In order to discover the meaning of all this it was necessary to undertake a detailed analysis.

Analysis

The hall—numerous guests, whom we were receiving. We were spending that summer at Bellevue, a house standing by itself on one of the hills adjoining the Kahlenberg.[2] The house had formerly been designed as a place of entertainment and its reception-rooms were in consequence unusually lofty and hall-like. It was at Bellevue that I had the dream, a few days before my wife's birthday. On the previous day my wife had told me that she expected that a number of friends, including Irma, would be coming out to visit us on her birthday. My dream was thus anticipating this occasion: it was my wife's birthday and a number of guests, including Irma, were being received by us in the large hall at Bellevue.

I reproached Irma for not having accepted my solution; I said: 'If you still get pains, it's your own fault.' I might have said this to her in waking life, and I may actually have done so. It was my view at that time (though I have since recognized it as a wrong one) that my task was fulfilled when I had informed a patient of the hidden meaning of his symptoms: I considered that I was not responsible for whether he accepted the solution or not—though this was what success depended on. I owe it to

---

2. [A hill which is a favourite resort in the immediate neighborhood of Vienna.]

this mistake, which I have now fortunately corrected, that my life was made easier at a time when, in spite of all my inevitable ignorance, I was expected to produce therapeutic successes.—I noticed, however, that the words which I spoke to Irma in the dream showed that I was specially anxious not to be responsible for the pains which she still had. If they were her fault they could not be mine. Could it be that the purpose of the dream lay in this direction?

Irma's complaint: pains in her throat and abdomen and stomach; it was choking her. Pains in the stomach were among my patient's symptoms but were not very prominent; she complained more of feelings of nausea and disgust. Pains in the throat and abdomen and constriction of the throat played scarcely any part in her illness. I wondered why I decided upon this choice of symptoms in the dream but could not think of an explanation at the moment.

She looked pale and puffy. My patient always had a rosy complexion. I began to suspect that someone else was being substituted for her.

I was alarmed at the idea that I had missed an organic illness. This, as may well be believed, is a perpetual source of anxiety to a specialist whose practice is almost limited to neurotic patients and who is in the habit of attributing to hysteria a great number of symptoms which other physicians treat as organic. On the other hand, a faint doubt crept into my mind—from where, I could not tell—that my alarm was not entirely genuine. If Irma's pains had an organic basis, once again I could not be held responsible for curing them; my treatment only set out to get rid of *hysterical* pains. It occurred to me, in fact, that I was actually *wishing* that there had been a wrong diagnosis; for, if so, the blame for my lack of success would also have been got rid of.

I took her to the window to look down her throat. She showed some recalcitrance, like women with false teeth. I thought to myself that really there was no need for her to do that. I had never had any occasion to examine Irma's oral cavity. What happened in the dream reminded me of an examination I had carried out some time before of a governess: at a first glance she had seemed a picture of youthful beauty, but when it came to opening her mouth she had taken measures to conceal her plates. This led to recollections of other medical examinations and of little secrets revealed in the course of them—to the satisfaction of neither party. *'There was really no need for her to do that'* was no doubt intended in the first place as a compliment to Irma; but I suspected that it had another meaning besides. (If one carries out an analysis attentively, one gets a feeling of whether or not one has exhausted all the background thoughts that are to be expected.) The way in which Irma stood by the window suddenly reminded me of another experience. Irma had an intimate woman friend of whom I had a very high opinion. When I visited this lady one evening I had found her by a window in the situation reproduced in the dream, and her physician, the same Dr. M., had pronounced that she had a diphtheritic membrane. The figure of Dr.

M. and the membrane reappear later in the dream. It now occurred to me that for the last few months I had had every reason to suppose that this other lady was also a hysteric. Indeed, Irma herself had betrayed the fact to me. What did I know of her condition? One thing precisely: that, like my Irma of the dream, she suffered from hysterical choking. So in the dream I had replaced my patient by her friend. I now recollected that I had often played with the idea that she too might ask me to relieve her of her symptoms. I myself, however, had thought this unlikely, since she was of a very reserved nature. She was *recalcitrant*, as was shown in the dream. Another reason was that *there was no need for her to do it*: she had so far shown herself strong enough to master her condition without outside help. There still remained a few features that I could not attach either to Irma or to her friend: *pale; puffy; false teeth*. The false teeth took me to the governess whom I have already mentioned; I now felt inclined to be satisfied with *bad* teeth. I then thought of someone else to whom these features might be alluding. She again was not one of my patients, nor should I have liked to have her as a patient, since I had noticed that she was bashful in my presence and I could not think she would make an amenable patient. She was usually pale, and once, while she had been in specially good health, she had looked puffy.[3] Thus I had been comparing my patient Irma with two other people who would also have been recalcitrant to treatment. What could the reason have been for my having exchanged her in the dream for her friend? Perhaps it was that I should have *liked* to exchange her: either I felt more sympathetic towards her friend or had a higher opinion of her intelligence. For Irma seemed to me foolish because she had not accepted my solution. Her friend would have been wiser, that is to say she would have yielded sooner. She would then have *opened her mouth properly*, and have told me more than Irma.[4]

What I saw in her throat: a white patch and turbinal bones with scabs on them. The white patch reminded me of diphtheritis and so of Irma's friend, but also of a serious illness of my eldest daughter's almost two years earlier and of the fright I had had in those anxious days. The scabs on the turbinal bones recalled a worry about my own state of health. I was making frequent use of cocaine at that time to reduce some troublesome nasal swellings, and I had heard a few days earlier that one of my women patients who had followed my example had developed an extensive necrosis of the nasal mucous membrane. I had been the first

3. The still-unexplained complaints about *pains in the abdomen* could also be traced back to this third figure. The person in question was, of course, my own wife; the pains in the abdomen reminded me of one of the occasions on which I had noticed her bashfulness. I was forced to admit to myself that I was not treating either Irma or my wife very kindly in this dream; but it should be observed by way of excuse that I was measuring them both by the standard of the good and amenable patient.
4. I had a feeling that the interpretation of this part of the dream was not carried far enough to make it possible to follow the whole of its concealed meaning. If I had pursued my comparison between the three women, it would have taken me far afield.—There is at least one spot in every dream at which it is unplumbable—a navel, as it were, that is its point of contact with the unknown.

to recommend the use of cocaine, in 1885, [5] and this recommendation had brought serious reproaches down on me. The misuse of that drug had hastened the death of a dear friend of mine. This had been before 1895 [the date of the dream].

I at once called in Dr. M., and he repeated the examination. This simply corresponded to the position occupied by M. in our circle. But the *'at once'* was sufficiently striking to require a special explanation. It reminded me of a tragic event in my practice. I had on one occasion produced a severe toxic state in a woman patient by repeatedly prescribing what was at that time regarded as a harmless remedy (sulphonal), and had hurriedly turned for assistance and support to my experienced senior colleague. There was a subsidiary detail which confirmed the idea that I had this incident in mind. My patient—who succumbed to the poison—had the same name as my eldest daughter. It had never occurred to me before, but it struck me now almost like an act of retribution on the part of destiny. It was as though the replacement of one person by another was to be continued in another sense: this Mathilde for that Mathilde, an eye for an eye and a tooth for a tooth. It seemed as if I had been collecting all the occasions which I could bring up against myself as evidence of lack of medical conscientiousness.

Dr. M. was pale, had a clean-shaven chin and walked with a limp. This was true to the extent that his unhealthy appearance often caused his friends anxiety. The two other features could only apply to someone else. I thought of my elder brother, who lives abroad, who is clean-shaven and whom, if I remembered right, the M. of the dream closely resembled. We had had news a few days earlier that he was walking with a limp owing to an arthritic affection of his hip. There must, I reflected, have been some reason for my fusing into one the two figures in the dream. I then remembered that I had a similar reason for being in an ill-humour with each of them: they had both rejected a certain suggestion I had recently laid before them.

My friend Otto was now standing beside the patient and my friend Leopold was examining her and indicated that there was a dull area low down on the left. My friend Leopold was also a physician and a relative of Otto's. Since they both specialized in the same branch of medicine, it was their fate to be in competition with each other, and comparisons were constantly being drawn between them. Both of them acted as my assistants for years while I was still in charge of the neurological out-patients' department of a children's hospital. Scenes such as the one represented in the dream used often to occur there. While I was discussing the diagnosis of a case with Otto, Leopold would be examining the child once more and would make an unexpected contribution to our decision. The difference between their characters was like that be-

5. [This is a misprint . . . for '1884', the date of Freud's first paper on cocaine.]

tween the bailiff Bräsig and his friend Karl:[6] one was distinguished for his quickness, while the other was slow but sure. If in the dream I was contrasting Otto with the prudent Leopold, I was evidently doing so to the advantage of the latter. The comparison was similar to the one between my disobedient patient Irma and the friend whom I regarded as wiser than she was. I now perceived another of the lines along which the chain of thought in the dream branched off: from the sick child to the children's hospital.—*The dull area low down on the left* seemed to me to agree in every detail with one particular case in which Leopold had struck me by his thoroughness. I also had a vague notion of something in the nature of a metastatic affection; but this may also have been a reference to the patient whom I should have liked to have in the place of Irma. So far as I had been able to judge, she had produced an imitation of a tuberculosis.

A *portion of the skin on the left shoulder was infiltrated*. I saw at once that this was the rheumatism in my own shoulder, which I invariably notice if I sit up late into the night. Moreover the wording in the dream was most ambiguous: '*I noticed this, just as he did. . . .*' I noticed it in my own body, that is. I was struck, too, by the unusual phrasing: 'a portion of the skin was infiltrated'. We are in the habit of speaking of 'a left upper posterior infiltration', and this would refer to the lung and so once more to tuberculosis.

In spite of her dress. This was in any case only an interpolation. We naturally used to examine the children in the hospital undressed: and this would be a contrast to the manner in which adult female patients have to be examined. I remembered that it was said of a celebrated clinician that he never made a physical examination of his patients except through their clothes. Further than this I could not see. Frankly, I had no desire to penetrate more deeply at this point.

Dr. M. said: 'It's an infection, but no matter. Dysentery will supervene and the toxin will be eliminated.' At first this struck me as ridiculous. But nevertheless, like all the rest, it had to be carefully analysed. When I came to look at it more closely it seemed to have some sort of meaning all the same. What I discovered in the patient was a local diphtheritis. I remembered from the time of my daughter's illness a discussion on diphtheritis and diphtheria, the latter being the general infection that arises from the local diphtheritis. Leopold indicated the presence of a general infection of this kind from the existence of a dull area, which might thus be regarded as a metastatic focus. I seemed to think, it is true, that metastases like this do not in fact occur with diphtheria: it made me think rather of pyaemia.

No matter. This was intended as a consolation. It seemed to fit into

6. [The two chief figures in the once popular novel, *Ut mine Stromtid*, written in Mecklenburg dialect, by Fritz Reuter (1862–64.) There is an English translation, *An Old Story of my Farming Days* (London, 1878).]

the context as follows. The content of the preceding part of the dream had been that my patient's pains were due to a severe organic affection. I had a feeling that I was only trying in that way to shift the blame from myself. Psychological treatment could not be held responsible for the persistence of diphtheritic pains. Nevertheless I had a sense of awkwardness at having invented such a severe illness for Irma simply in order to clear myself. It looked so cruel. Thus I was in need of an assurance that all would be well in the end, and it seemed to me that to have put the consolation into the mouth precisely of Dr. M. had not been a bad choice. But here I was taking up a superior attitude towards the dream, and this itself required explanation.

And why was the consolation so nonsensical?

Dysentery. There seemed to be some remote theoretical notion that morbid matter can be eliminated through the bowels. Could it be that I was trying to make fun of Dr. M.'s fertility in producing far-fetched explanations and making unexpected pathological connections? Something else now occurred to me in relation to dysentery. A few months earlier I had taken on the case of a young man with remarkable difficulties associated with defaecating, who had been treated by other physicians as a case of 'anaemia accompanied by malnutrition'. I had recognized it as a hysteria, but had been unwilling to try him with my psychotherapeutic treatment and had sent him on a sea voyage. Some days before, I had had a despairing letter from him from Egypt, saying that he had had a fresh attack there which a doctor had declared was dysentery. I suspected that the diagnosis was an error on the part of an ignorant practitioner who had allowed himself to be taken in by the hysteria. But I could not help reproaching myself for having put my patient in a situation in which he might have contracted some organic trouble on top of his hysterical intestinal disorder. Moreover, 'dysentery' sounds not unlike 'diphtheria'—a word of ill omen which did not occur in the dream.[7]

Yes, I thought to myself, I must have been making fun of Dr. M. with the consoling prognosis 'Dysentery will supervene, etc.': for it came back to me that, years before, he himself had told an amusing story of a similar kind about another doctor. Dr. M. had been called in by him for consultation over a patient who was seriously ill, and had felt obliged to point out, in view of the very optimistic view taken by his colleague, that he had found albumen in the patient's urine. The other, however, was not in the least put out: 'No matter', he had said, 'the albumen will soon be eliminated!'—I could no longer feel any doubt, therefore, that this part of the dream was expressing derision at physicians who are ignorant of hysteria. And, as though to confirm this, a further idea crossed my mind: 'Does Dr. M. realize that the symptoms in his patient

7. [The German words *'Dysenterie'* and *'Dyphtherie'* are more alike than the English ones.]

(Irma's friend) which give grounds for fearing tuberculosis also have a hysterical basis? Has he spotted this hysteria? or has he been taken in by it?'

But what could be my motive for treating this friend of mine so badly? That was a very simple matter. Dr. M. was just as little in agreement with my 'solution' as Irma herself. So I had already revenged myself in this dream on two people: on Irma with the words 'If you still get pains, it's your own fault', and on Dr. M. by the wording of the nonsensical consolation that I put into his mouth.

We were directly aware of the origin of the infection. This direct knowledge in the dream was remarkable. Only just before we had had no knowledge of it, for the infection was only revealed by Leopold.

When she was feeling unwell, my friend Otto had given her an injection. Otto had in fact told me that during his short stay with Irma's family he had been called in to a neighbouring hotel to give an injection to someone who had suddenly felt unwell. These injections reminded me once more of my unfortunate friend who had poisoned himself with cocaine. I had advised him to use the drug internally [i.e. orally] only, while morphia was being withdrawn; but he had at once given himself cocaine *injections.*

A preparation of propyl . . . propyls . . . propionic acid. How could I have come to think of this? During the previous evening, before I wrote out the case history and had the dream, my wife had opened a bottle of liqueur, on which the word 'Ananas'[8] appeared and which was a gift from our friend Otto: for he has a habit of making presents on every possible occasion. It was to be hoped, I thought to myself, that some day he would find a wife to cure him of the habit. This liqueur gave off such a strong smell of fusel oil that I refused to touch it. My wife suggested our giving the bottle to the servants, but I—with even greater prudence—vetoed the suggestion, adding in a philanthropic spirit that there was no need for *them* to be poisoned either. The smell of fusel oil (amyl . . .) evidently stirred up in my mind a recollection of the whole series—propyl, methyl, and so on—and this accounted for the propyl preparation in the dream. It is true that I carried out a substitution in the process: I dreamt of propyl after having smelt amyl. But substitutions of this kind are perhaps legitimate in organic chemistry.

Trimethylamin. I saw the chemical formula of this substance in my dream, which bears witness to a great effort on the part of my memory. Moreover, the formula was printed in heavy type, as though there had been a desire to lay emphasis on some part of the context as being of quite special importance. What was it, then, to which my attention was to be directed in this way by trimethylamin? It was to a conversation with another friend who had for many years been familiar with all my

8. I must add that the sound of the word 'Ananas' bears a remarkable resemblance to that of my patient Irma's family name.

writings during the period of their gestation, just as I had been with his.[9] He had at that time confided some ideas to me on the subject of the chemistry of the sexual processes, and had mentioned among other things that he believed that one of the products of sexual metabolism was trimethylamin. Thus this substance led me to sexuality, the factor to which I attributed the greatest importance in the origin of the nervous disorders which it was my aim to cure. My patient Irma was a young widow; if I wanted to find an excuse for the failure of my treatment in her case, what I could best appeal to would no doubt be this fact of her widowhood, which her friends would be so glad to see changed. And how strangely, I thought to myself, a dream like this is put together! The other woman, whom I had as a patient in the dream instead of Irma, was also a young widow.

I began to guess why the formula for trimethylamin had been so prominent in the dream. So many important subjects converged upon that one word. Trimethylamin was an allusion not only to the immensely powerful factor of sexuality, but also to a person whose agreement I recalled with satisfaction whenever I felt isolated in my opinions. Surely this friend who played so large a part in my life must appear again elsewhere in these trains of thought. Yes. For he had a special knowledge of the consequences of affections of the nose and its accessory cavities; and he had drawn scientific attention to some very remarkable connections between the turbinal bones and the female organs of sex. (Cf. the three curly structures in Irma's throat.) I had had Irma examined by him to see whether her gastric pains might be of nasal origin. But he suffered himself from suppurative rhinitis, which caused me anxiety; and no doubt there was an allusion to this in the pyaemia which vaguely came into my mind in connection with the metastases in the dream.

Injections of that sort ought not to be made so thoughtlessly. Here an accusation of thoughtlessness was being made directly against my friend Otto. I seemed to remember thinking something of the same kind that afternoon when his words and looks had appeared to show that he was siding against me. It had been some such notion as: 'How easily his thoughts are influenced! How thoughtlessly he jumps to conclusions!'— Apart from this, this sentence in the dream reminded me once more of my dead friend who had so hastily resorted to cocaine injections. As I have said, I had never contemplated the drug being given by injection. I noticed too that in accusing Otto of thoughtlessness in handling chemical substances I was once more touching upon the story of the unfortunate Mathilde, which gave grounds for the same accusation against

9. {This, as the editors correctly point out, was Wilhelm Fliess. In fact, Fliess played a far larger part in the making of this dream than either Freud, or his editors, acknowledge. Shortly before Freud dreamt this dream, Fliess had been involved in an appalling piece of malpractice: operating on the nose of one of Freud's patients, he had left a piece of gauze in her nose and nearly killed her. One motive for this famous dream was the exculpation not just of himself, but of Fliess. (For details, see Peter Gay, *Freud*, pp. 83–87.)}

myself. Here I was evidently collecting instances of my conscientiousness, but also of the reverse.

And probably the syringe had not been clean. This was yet another
accusation against Otto, but derived from a different source. I had
happened the day before to meet the son of an old lady of eighty-two,
to whom I had to give an injection of morphia twice a day. At the
moment she was in the country and he told me that she was suffering
from phlebitis. I had at once thought it must be an infiltration caused
by a dirty syringe. I was proud of the fact that in two years I had not
caused a single infiltration; I took constant pains to be sure that the
syringe was clean. In short, I was conscientious. The phlebitis brought
me back once more to my wife, who had suffered from thrombosis
during one of her pregnancies; and now three similar situations came
to my recollection involving my wife, Irma and the dead Mathilde. The
identity of these situations had evidently enabled me to substitute the
three figures for one another in the dream.

I have now completed the interpretation of the dream.[1] While I was
carrying it out I had some difficulty in keeping at bay all the ideas which
were bound to be provoked by a comparison between the content of the
dream and the concealed thoughts lying behind it. And in the meantime
the 'meaning' of the dream was borne in upon me. I became aware of
an intention which was carried into effect by the dream and which must
have been my motive for dreaming it. The dream fulfilled certain wishes
which were started in me by the events of the previous evening (the news
given me by Otto and my writing out of the case history). The conclusion
of the dream, that is to say, was that I was not responsible for the persistence of Irma's pains, but that Otto was. Otto had in fact annoyed me by
his remarks about Irma's incomplete cure, and the dream gave me my
revenge by throwing the reproach back on to him. The dream acquitted
me of the responsibility for Irma's condition by showing that it was due to
other factors—it produced a whole series of reasons. The dream represented a particular state of affairs as I should have wished it to be. *Thus its
content was the fulfilment of a wish and its motive was a wish.*

Thus much leapt to the eyes. But many of the details of the dream
also became intelligible to me from the point of view of wish-fulfilment.
Not only did I revenge myself on Otto for being too hasty in taking sides
against me by representing him as being too hasty in his medical treatment (in giving the injection); but I also revenged myself on him for
giving me the bad liqueur which had an aroma of fusel oil. And in the
dream I found an expression which united the two reproaches: the
injection was of a preparation of propyl. This did not satisfy me and I

1. [*Footnote added* 1909:] Though it will be
understood that I have not reported everything that
occurred to me during the process of interpretation. {As some of Freud's most alert early readers,
like Karl Abraham and Carl G. Jung, noted, he
had silently passed over all the sexual elements in
this dream interpretation.}

pursued my revenge further by contrasting him with his more trustworthy competitor. I seemed to be saying: 'I like *him* better than *you*.' But Otto was not the only person to suffer from the vials of my wrath. I took revenge as well on my disobedient patient by exchanging her for one who was wiser and less recalcitrant. Nor did I allow Dr. M. to escape the consequences of his contradiction but showed him by means of a clear allusion that he was an ignoramus on the subject. ('*Dysentery will supervene*, etc.') Indeed I seemed to be appealing from him to someone else with greater knowledge (to my friend who had told me of trimethylamin) just as I had turned from Irma to her friend and from Otto to Leopold. 'Take these people away! Give me three others of my choice instead! Then I shall be free of these undeserved reproaches!' The groundlessness of the reproaches was proved for me in the dream in the most elaborate fashion. *I* was not to blame for Irma's pains, since she herself was to blame for them by refusing to accept my solution. *I* was not concerned with Irma's pains, since they were of an organic nature and quite incurable by psychological treatment. Irma's pains could be satisfactorily explained by her widowhood (cf. the trimethylamin) which *I* had no means of altering. Irma's pains had been caused by Otto giving her an incautious injection of an unsuitable drug—a thing *I* should never have done. Irma's pains were the result of an injection with a dirty needle, like my old lady's phlebitis—whereas *I* never did any harm with my injections. I noticed, it is true, that these explanations of Irma's pains (which agreed in exculpating me) were not entirely consistent with one another, and indeed that they were mutually exclusive. The whole plea—for the dream was nothing else—reminded one vividly of the defence put forward by the man who was charged by one of his neighbours with having given him back a borrowed kettle in a damaged condition. The defendant asserted first, that he had given it back undamaged; secondly, that the kettle had a hole in it when he borrowed it; and thirdly, that he had never borrowed a kettle from his neighbour at all. So much the better: if only a single one of these three lines of defence were to be accepted as valid, the man would have to be acquitted.

Certain other themes played a part in the dream, which were not so obviously connected with my exculpation from Irma's illness: my daughter's illness and that of my patient who bore the same name, the injurious effect of cocaine, the disorder of my patient who was travelling in Egypt, my concern about my wife's health and about that of my brother and of Dr. M., my own physical ailments, my anxiety about my absent friend who suffered from suppurative rhinitis. But when I came to consider all of these, they could all be collected into a single group of ideas and labelled, as it were, 'concern about my own and other people's health—professional conscientiousness'. I called to mind the obscure disagreeable impression I had had when Otto brought me the news of Irma's condition. This group of thoughts that played a part in the dream enabled me retrospectively to put this transient impression into words.

It was as though he had said to me: 'You don't take your medical duties seriously enough. You're not conscientious; you don't carry out what you've undertaken.' Thereupon, this group of thoughts seemed to have put itself at my disposal, so that I could produce evidence of how highly conscientious I was, of how deeply I was concerned about the health of my relations, my friends and my patients. It was a noteworthy fact that this material also included some disagreeable memories, which supported my friend Otto's accusation rather than my own vindication. The material was, as one might say, impartial; but nevertheless there was an unmistakable connection between this more extensive group of thoughts which underlay the dream and the narrower subject of the dream which gave rise to the wish to be innocent of Irma's illness.

I will not pretend that I have completely uncovered the meaning of this dream or that its interpretation is without a gap. I could spend much more time over it, derive further information from it and discuss fresh problems raised by it. I myself know the points from which further trains of thought could be followed. But considerations which arise in the case of every dream of my own restrain me from pursuing my interpretative work. If anyone should feel tempted to express a hasty condemnation of my reticence, I would advise him to make the experiment of being franker than I am. For the moment I am satisfied with the achievement of this one piece of fresh knowledge. If we adopt the method of interpreting dreams which I have indicated here, we shall find that dreams really have a meaning and are far from being the expression of a fragmentary activity of the brain, as the authorities have claimed. *When the work of interpretation has been completed, we perceive that a dream is the fulfilment of a wish.*[2]

On Dreams

Aware that his *Interpretation of Dreams* was both very substantial and (in parts) very difficult, Freud, though exhausted by his labor on that book, rather unwillingly undertook to condense his theory of dreams into an accessible popularization. Freud was always his best expounder and advocate: as reported before, he wrote articles for encyclopedias and compendia on mental illness. The lectures he delivered at Clark University in 1909, published the following year as *Five Lectures on Psycho-Analysis*, or the more extensive series of lectures published from 1916 on as *Introductory Lectures on Psycho-Analysis*, would enjoy worldwide circulation and have lasting appeal. "On Dreams" works admirably as a lucid account of Freudian dream

---

2. [In a letter to Fliess on June 12, 1900 . . . , Freud describes a later visit to Bellevue, the houses where he had this dream. 'Do you suppose,' he writes, 'that some day a marble tablet will be placed on the house, inscribed with these words?—

In This House, on July 24th, 1895
the Secret of Dreams was Revealed
to Dr. Sigm. Freud

At the moment there seems little prospect of it.']

theory, but it was not until 1911 that it appeared as an independent brochure: the original, slightly shorter, version of 1901 appeared as part of Löwenfeld and Kurella's *Grenzfragen des Nerven- und Seelenlebens.*

I

During the epoch which may be described as pre-scientific, men had no difficulty in finding an explanation of dreams. When they remembered a dream after waking up, they regarded it as either a favourable or a hostile manifestation by higher powers, daemonic and divine. When modes of thought belonging to natural science began to flourish, all this ingenious mythology was transformed into psychology, and to-day only a small minority of educated people doubt that dreams are a product of the dreamer's own mind.

Since the rejection of the mythological hypothesis, however, dreams have stood in need of explanation. The conditions of their origin, their relation to waking mental life, their dependence upon stimuli which force their way upon perception during the state of sleep, the many peculiarities of their content which are repugnant to waking thought, the inconsistency between their ideational images and the affects attaching to them, and lastly their transitory character, the manner in which waking thought pushes them on one side as something alien to it, and mutilates or extinguishes them in memory—all of these and other problems besides have been awaiting clarification for many hundreds of years, and till now no satisfactory solution of them has been advanced. But what stands in the foreground of our interest is the question of the *significance* of dreams, a question which bears a double sense. It enquires in the first place as to the psychical significance of dreaming, as to the relation of dreams to other mental processes, and as to any biological function that they may have; in the second place it seeks to discover whether dreams can be interpreted, whether the content of individual dreams has a 'meaning', such as we are accustomed to find in other psychical structures.

* * *

II

One day I discovered to my great astonishment that the view of dreams which came nearest to the truth was not the medical but the popular one, half involved though it still was in superstition. For I had been led to fresh conclusions on the subject of dreams by applying to them a new method of psychological investigation which had done excellent service in the solution of phobias, obsessions and delusions, etc. Since then, under the name of 'psycho-analysis', it has found acceptance by a whole school of research workers. * * *

This procedure is easily described, although instruction and practice would be necessary before it could be put into effect.

If we make use of it on someone else, let us say on a patient with a phobia, we require him to direct his attention on to the idea in question, not, however, to reflect upon it as he has done so often already, but to take notice of *whatever occurs to his mind without any exception* and report it to the physician. If he should then assert that his attention is unable to grasp anything at all, we dismiss this with an energetic assurance that a complete absence of any ideational subject-matter is quite impossible. And in fact very soon numerous ideas will occur to him and will lead on to others; but they will invariably be prefaced by a judgement on the part of the self-observer to the effect that they are senseless or unimportant, that they are irrelevant, and that they occurred to him by chance and without any connection with the topic under consideration. We perceive at once that it was this critical attitude which prevented the subject from reporting any of these ideas, and which indeed had previously prevented them from becoming conscious. If we can induce him to abandon his criticism of the ideas that occur to him, and to continue pursuing the trains of thought which will emerge so long as he keeps his attention turned upon them, we find ourselves in possession of a quantity of psychical material, which we soon find is clearly connected with the pathological idea which was our starting-point; this material will soon reveal connections between the pathological idea and other ideas, and will eventually enable us to replace the pathological idea by a new one which fits into the nexus of thought in an intelligible fashion.

* * *

If we make use of this procedure upon *ourselves*, we can best assist the investigation by at once writing down what are at first unintelligible associations.

I will now show what results follow if I apply this method of investigation to dreams. Any example of a dream should in fact be equally appropriate for the purpose; but for particular reasons I will choose some dream of my own, one which seems obscure and meaningless as I remember it, and one which has the advantage of brevity. A dream which I actually had last night will perhaps meet these requirements. Its content, as I noted it down immediately after waking up, was as follows:

'*Company at table or table d'hôte . . . spinach was being eaten . . . Frau E. L. was sitting beside me; she was turning her whole attention to me and laid her hand on my knee in an intimate manner. I removed her hand unresponsively. She then said: "But you've always had such*

*beautiful eyes." . . . I then had an indistinct picture of two eyes, as
though it were a drawing or like the outline of a pair of spectacles. . . .'*

This was the whole of the dream, or at least all that I could remember
of it. It seemed to me obscure and meaningless, but above all surprising.
Frau E. L. is a person with whom I have hardly at any time been on
friendly terms, nor, so far as I know, have I ever wished to have any
closer relations with her. I have not seen her for a long time, and her
name has not, I believe, been mentioned during the last few days. The
dream-process was not accompanied by affects of any kind.

Reflecting over this dream brought me no nearer to understanding it.
I determined, however, to set down without any premeditation or criticism the associations which presented themselves to my self-observation.
As I have found, it is advisable for this purpose to divide a dream into
its elements and to find the associations attaching to each of these
fragments separately.

Company at table or table d'hôte. This at once reminded me of an
episode which occurred late yesterday evening. I came away from a
small party in the company of a friend who offered to take a cab and
drive me home in it. 'I prefer taking a cab with a taximeter,' he said,
'it occupies one's mind so agreeably; one always has something to look
at.' When we had taken our places in the cab and the driver had set
the dial, so that the first charge of sixty hellers became visible, I carried
the joke further. 'We've only just got in,' I said, 'and already we owe
him sixty hellers. A cab with a taximeter always reminds me of a table
d'hôte. It makes me avaricious and selfish, because it keeps on reminding
me of what I owe. My debt seems to be growing too fast, and I'm afraid
of getting the worst of the bargain; and in just the same way at a table
d'hôte I can't avoid feeling in a comic way that I'm getting too little,
and must keep an eye on my own interests.' I went on to quote, somewhat
discursively:

> Ihr führt ins Leben uns hinein,
> Ihr lasst den Armen schuldig werden. [1]

And now a second association to 'table d'hôte'. A few weeks ago, while
we were at table in a hotel at a mountain resort in the Tyrol, I was very
much annoyed because I thought my wife was not being sufficiently
reserved towards some people sitting near us whose acquaintance I had
no desire at all to make. I asked her to concern herself more with me
than with these strangers. This was again *as though I were getting the*

1. [These lines are from one of the Harp-player's
songs in Goethe's *Wilhelm Meister*. In the original
the words are addressed to the Heavenly Powers
and may be translated literally: 'You lead us into
life, you make the poor creature guilty.' But the
words '*Armen*' and '*schuldig*' are both capable of
bearing another meaning. '*Armen*' might mean

'poor' in the financial sense and '*schuldig*' might
mean 'in debt.' So in the present context the last
line could be rendered: 'You make the poor man
fall into debt.' {When Freud quotes these lines
once again a couple of pages later, he might be
(as Freud's editors rightly observe) addressing them
to parents.}]

worst of the bargain at the table d'hôte. I was struck too by the contrast between my wife's behaviour at table and that of Frau E. L. in the dream, who 'turned her whole attention to me'.

To proceed. I now saw that the events in the dream were a reproduction of a small episode of a precisely similar kind which occurred between my wife and me at the time at which I was secretly courting her. The caress which she gave me under the table-cloth was her reply to a pressing love letter. In the dream, however, my wife was replaced by a comparative stranger—E. L.

Frau E. L. is the daughter of a man to whom I was once *in debt.* I could not help noticing that this revealed an unsuspected connection between parts of the content of the dream and my associations. If one follows the train of association starting out from one element of a dream's content, one is soon brought back to another of its elements. My associations to the dream were bringing to light connections which were not visible in the dream itself.

If a person expects one to keep an eye on his interests without any advantage to oneself, his artlessness is apt to provoke the scornful question: 'Do you suppose I'm going to do this or that for the sake of your *beaux yeux* [*beautiful eyes*]?' That being so, Frau E. L.'s speech in the dream, 'You've always had such beautiful eyes', can only have meant: 'People have always done everything for you for love; you have always had everything *without paying for it.*' The truth is, of course, just the contrary: I have always paid dearly for whatever advantage I have had from other people. The fact that my friend took me home yesterday in a cab *without my paying for it* must, after all, have made an impression on me.

Incidentally, the friend whose guests we were yesterday has often put me in his debt. Only recently I allowed an opportunity of repaying him to slip by. He has had only one present from me—an antique bowl, round which there are *eyes* painted: what is known as an '*occhiale*', to avert the *evil eye*. Moreover he is an *eye surgeon.* The same evening I asked him after a woman patient, whom I had sent on to him for a consultation to fit her with *spectacles.*

As I now perceived, almost all the elements of the dream's content had been brought into the new context. For the sake of consistency, however, the further question might be asked of why *spinach*, of all things, was being served in the dream. The answer was that *spinach* reminded me of an episode which occurred not long ago at our family table, when one of the children—and precisely the one who really deserves to be admired for his *beautiful eyes*—refused to eat any spinach. I myself behaved in just the same way when I was a child; for a long time I detested spinach, till eventually my taste changed and promoted that vegetable into one of my favourite foods. My own early life and my child's were thus brought together by the mention of this dish. 'You ought to be glad to have spinach,' the little *gourmet's* mother explained;

'there are children who would be only too pleased to have spinach.'
Thus I was reminded of the duties of parents to their children. Goethe's
words

> Ihr führt ins Leben uns hinein,
> Ihr lasst den Armen schuldig werden.

gained a fresh meaning in this connection.

I will pause here to survey the results I had so far reached in my
dream-analysis. By following the associations which arose from the separate elements of the dream divorced from their context, I arrived at a
number of thoughts and recollections, which I could not fail to recognize
as important products of my mental life. This material revealed by the
analysis of the dream was intimately connected with the dream's content,
yet the connection was of such a kind that I could never have inferred
the fresh material from that content. The dream was unemotional,
disconnected and unintelligible; but while I was producing the thoughts
behind the dream, I was aware of intense and well-founded affective
impulses; the thoughts themselves fell at once into logical chains, in
which certain central ideas made their appearance more than once.
Thus, the contrast between 'selfish' and 'unselfish', and the elements
'being in debt' and 'without paying for it' were central ideas of this kind,
not represented in the dream itself. I might draw closer together the
threads in the material revealed by the analysis, and I might then show
that they converge upon a single nodal point, but considerations of a
personal and not of a scientific nature prevent my doing so in public.
I should be obliged to betray many things which had better remain my
secret, for on my way to discovering the solution of the dream all kinds
of things were revealed which I was unwilling to admit even to myself.
Why then, it will be asked, have I not chosen some other dream, whose
analysis is better suited for reporting, so that I could produce more
convincing evidence of the meaning and connectedness of the material
uncovered by analysis? The answer is that *every* dream with which I
might try to deal would lead to things equally hard to report and would
impose an equal discretion upon me. Nor should I avoid this difficulty
by bringing up someone else's dream for analysis, unless circumstances
enabled me to drop all disguise without damage to the person who had
confided in me.

At the point which I have now reached, I am led to regard the dream
as a sort of *substitute* for the thought-processes, full of meaning and
emotion, at which I arrived after the completion of the analysis. * * *

Two other things are already clear. The content of the dream is very
much shorter than the thoughts for which I regard it as a substitute; and
analysis has revealed that the instigator of the dream was an unimportant
event of the evening before I dreamt it.

I should, of course, not draw such far-reaching conclusions if only a
single dream-analysis was at my disposal. If experience shows me, how-

ever, that by uncritically pursuing the associations arising from *any* dream I can arrive at a similar train of thoughts, among the elements of which the constituents of the dream re-appear and which are interconnected in a rational and intelligible manner, then it will be safe to disregard the slight possibility that the connections observed in a first experiment might be due to chance. I think I am justified, therefore, in adopting a terminology which will crystallize our new discovery. In order to contrast the dream as it is retained in my memory with the relevant material discovered by analysing it, I shall speak of the former as the *'manifest* content of the dream' and the latter—without, in the first instance, making any further distinction—as the *'latent* content of the dream.' I am now faced by two new problems which have not hitherto been formulated. (1) What is the psychical process which has transformed the latent content of the dream into the manifest one which is known to me from my memory? (2) What are the motive or motives which have necessitated this transformation? I shall describe the process which transforms the latent into the manifest content of dreams as the 'dreamwork'. The counterpart to this activity—one which brings about a transformation in the opposite direction—is already known to us as the work of analysis. * * * Since I attribute all the contradictory and incorrect views upon dream-life which appear in the literature of the subject to ignorance of the latent content of dreams as revealed by analysis, I shall be at the greatest pains henceforward to avoid confusing the *manifest dream* with the *latent dream-thoughts.*

III

The transformation of the latent dream-thoughts into the manifest dream-content deserves all our attention, since it is the first instance known to us of psychical material being changed over from one mode of expression to another, from a mode of expression which is immediately intelligible to us to another which we can only come to understand with the help of guidance and effort, though it too must be recognized as a function of our mental activity.

Dreams can be divided into three categories in respect of the relation between their latent and manifest content. In the first place, we may distinguish those dreams which *make sense* and are at the same time *intelligible*, which, that is to say, can be inserted without further difficulty into the context of our mental life. We have numbers of such dreams. * * * A second group is formed by those dreams which, though they are connected in themselves and have a clear sense, nevertheless have a *bewildering* effect, because we cannot see how to fit that sense into our mental life. Such would be the case if we were to dream, for instance, that a relative of whom we were fond had died of the plague, when we had no reason for expecting, fearing or assuming any such thing; we should ask in astonishment: 'How did I get hold of such an idea?' The third group, finally, contains those dreams which are without either sense or intelligibility, which seem *disconnected, confused* and *meaningless*. The preponderant majority of the products of our dreaming exhibit these characteristics, which are the basis of the low opinion in which dreams are held and of the medical theory that they are the outcome of a restricted mental activity. The most evident signs of incoherence are seldom absent, especially in dream-compositions of any considerable length and complexity.

The contrast between the manifest and latent content of dreams is clearly of significance only for dreams of the second and more particularly of the third category. It is there that we are faced by riddles which only disappear after we have replaced the manifest dream by the latent thoughts behind it; and it was on a specimen of the last category—a confused and unintelligible dream—that the analysis which I have just recorded was carried out. Contrary to our expectation, however, we came up against motives which prevented us from becoming fully acquainted with the latent dream-thoughts. A repetition of similar experiences may lead us to suspect that *there is an intimate and regular relation between the unintelligible and confused nature of dreams and the difficulty of reporting the thoughts behind them.* Before enquiring into the nature of this relation, we may with advantage turn our attention to the more easily intelligible dreams of the first category, in which the manifest and latent content coincide, and there appears to be a consequent saving in dream-work.

Moreover, an examination of these dreams offers advantages from another standpoint. For *children's* dreams are of that kind—significant and not puzzling. Here, incidentally, we have a further argument against tracing the origin of dreams to dissociated cerebral activity during sleep. For why should a reduction in psychical functioning of this kind be a characteristic of the state of sleep in the case of adults but not in that of children? On the other hand, we shall be fully justified in expecting that an explanation of psychical processes in children, in whom they may well be greatly simplified, may turn out to be an indispensable prelude to the investigation of the psychology of adults.

I will therefore record a few instances of dreams which I have collected from children. A little girl nineteen months old had been kept without food all day because she had had an attack of vomiting in the morning; her nurse declared that she had been upset by eating strawberries. During the night after this day of starvation she was heard saying her own name in her sleep and adding: '*Stwawbewwies, wild stwawbewwies, omblet, pudden!*' She was thus dreaming of eating a meal, and she laid special stress in her menu on the particular delicacy of which, as she had reason to expect, she would only be allowed scanty quantities in the near future.—A little boy of twenty-two months had a similar dream of a feast which he had been denied. The day before, he had been obliged to present his uncle with a gift of a basket of fresh cherries, of which he himself, of course, had only been allowed to taste a single sample. He awoke with this cheerful news: *'Hermann eaten all the chewwies!'*—

* * *

The common element in all these children's dreams is obvious. All of them fulfilled wishes which were active during the day but had remained unfulfilled. The dreams were simple and undisguised *wish-fulfilments*.

* * *

Even when the content of children's dreams becomes complicated and subtle, there is never any difficulty in recognizing them as wish-fulfilments. An eight-year-old boy had a dream that he was driving in a chariot with Achilles and that Diomede was the charioteer. It was shown that the day before he had been deep in a book of legends about the Greek heroes; and it was easy to see that he had taken the heroes as his models and was sorry not to be living in their days.

This small collection throws a direct light on a further characteristic of children's dreams: their connection with daytime life. The wishes which are fulfilled in them are carried over from daytime and as a rule from the day before, and in waking life they have been accompanied by intense emotion. Nothing unimportant or indifferent, or nothing which would strike a child as such, finds its way into the content of their dreams.

Numerous examples of dreams of this infantile type can be found occurring in adults as well, though, as I have said, they are usually brief in content. Thus a number of people regularly respond to a stimulus of thirst during the night with dreams of drinking, which thus endeavour to get rid of the stimulus and enable sleep to continue. * * * Under unusual or extreme conditions dreams of this infantile character are particularly common. Thus the leader of a polar expedition has recorded that the members of his expedition, while they were wintering in the ice-field and living on a monotonous diet and short rations, regularly dreamt like children of large meals, of mountains of tobacco, and of being back at home.

It by no means rarely happens that in the course of a comparatively long, complicated and on the whole confused dream one particularly clear portion stands out, which contains an unmistakable wish-fulfilment, but which is bound up with some other, unintelligible material. But in the case of adults, anyone with some experience in analysing their dreams will find to his surprise that even those dreams which have an appearance of being transparently clear are seldom as simple as those of children, and that behind the obvious wish-fulfilment some other meaning may lie concealed.

It would indeed be a simple and satisfactory solution of the riddle of dreams if the work of analysis were to enable us to trace even the meaningless and confused dreams of adults back to the infantile type of fulfilment of an intensely felt wish of the previous day. There can be no doubt, however, that appearances do not speak in favour of such an expectation. Dreams are usually full of the most indifferent and strangest material, and there is no sign in their content of the fulfilment of any wish.

But before taking leave of infantile dreams with their undisguised wish-fulfilments, I must not omit to mention one principal feature of dreams, which has long been evident and which emerges particularly clearly precisely in this group. Every one of these dreams can be replaced by an optative clause: 'Oh, if only the trip on the lake had lasted longer!'—'If only I were already washed and dressed!'—'If only I could have kept the cherries instead of giving them to Uncle!" But dreams give us more than such optative clauses. They show us the wish as already fulfilled; they represent its fulfilment as real and present; and the material employed in dream-representation consists principally, though not exclusively, of situations and of sensory images, mostly of a visual character. Thus, even in this infantile group, a species of transformation, which deserves to be described as dream-work, is not completely absent: *a thought expressed in the optative has been replaced by a representation in the present tense.*

IV

* * *

* * * Another achievement of the dream-work, tending as it does to produce incoherent dreams, is even more striking. If in any particular instance we compare the number of ideational elements or the space taken up in writing them down in the case of the dream and of the dream-thoughts to which the analysis leads us and of which traces are to be found in the dream itself, we shall be left in no doubt that the dream-work has carried out a work of compression or *condensation* on a large scale. It is impossible at first to form any judgement of the degree of this condensation; but the deeper we plunge into a dream-analysis the more impressive it seems. From every element in a dream's content associative threads branch out in two or more directions; every situation in a dream seems to be put together out of two or more impressions or experiences. For instance, I once had a dream of a sort of swimming-pool, in which the bathers were scattering in all directions; at one point on the edge of the pool someone was standing and bending towards one of the people bathing, as though to help her out of the water. The situation was put together from a memory of an experience I had had at puberty and from two paintings, one of which I had seen shortly before the dream. One was a picture from Schwind's series illustrating the legend of Mélusine, which showed the water-nymphs surprised in their pool (cf. the scattering bathers in the dream); the other was a picture of the Deluge by an Italian Master; while the little experience remembered from my puberty was of having seen the instructor at a swimming-school helping a lady out of the water who had stopped in until after the time set aside for men bathers.—In the case of the example which I chose for interpretation, an analysis of the situation led me to a small series of recollections each of which contributed something to the content of the dream. In the first place, there was the episode from the time of my engagement of which I have already spoken. The pressure upon my hand under the table, which was a part of that episode, provided the dream with the detail 'under the table'—a detail which I had to add as an afterthought to my memory of the dream. In the episode itself there was of course no question of 'turning to me'; the analysis showed that this element was the fulfilment of a wish by presenting the opposite of an actual event, and that it related to my wife's behaviour at the table d'hôte. But behind this recent recollection there lay concealed an exactly similar and far more important scene from the time of our engagement, which estranged us for a whole day. The intimate laying of a hand on my knee belonged to a quite different context and was concerned with quite other people. This element in the dream was in turn the starting-point of two separate sets of memories—and so on.

The material in the dream-thoughts which is packed together for the purpose of constructing a dream-situation must of course in itself be adaptable for that purpose. There must be one or more *common elements* in all the components. The dream-work then proceeds just as Francis Galton did in constructing his family photographs. It superimposes, as it were, the different components upon one another. The common element in them then stands out clearly in the composite picture, while contradictory details more or less wipe one another out. This method of production also explains to some extent the varying degrees of characteristic vagueness shown by so many elements in the content of dreams. Basing itself on this discovery, dream-interpretation has laid down the following rule: in analysing a dream, if an uncertainty can be resolved into an 'either—or', we must replace it for purposes of interpretation by an 'and', and take each of the apparent alternatives as an independent starting-point for a series of associations.

If a common element of this kind between the dream-thoughts is not present, the dream-work sets about *creating* one, so that it may be possible for the thoughts to be given a common representation in the dream. The most convenient way of bringing together two dream-thoughts which, to start with, have nothing in common, is to alter the verbal form of one of them, and thus bring it half-way to meet the other, which may be similarly clothed in a new form of words. A parallel process is involved in hammering out a rhyme, where a similar sound has to be sought for in the same way as a common element is in our present case. A large part of the dream-work consists in the creation of intermediate thoughts of this kind which are often highly ingenious, though they frequently appear far-fetched; these then form a link between the composite picture in the manifest content of the dream and the dream-thoughts, which are themselves diverse both in form and essence and have been determined by the exciting factors of the dream. The analysis of our sample dream affords us an instance of this kind in which a thought has been given a new form in order to bring it into contact with another which is essentially foreign to it. In carrying out the analysis I came upon the following thought: '*I should like to get something sometimes without paying for it.*' But in that form the thought could not be employed in the dream-content. It was therefore given a fresh form: '*I should like to get some enjoyment without cost* ["*Kosten*"].'[2] Now the word '*Kosten*' in its second sense fits into the 'table d'hôte' circle of ideas, and could thus be represented in the '*spinach*' which was served in the dream. When a dish appears at our table and the children refuse it, their mother begins by trying persuasion, and urges them '*just to taste* ["*kosten*"] *a bit of it*'. It may seem strange that the dream-work should make such free use of verbal ambiguity, but further experience will teach us that the occurrence is quite a common one.

The process of condensation further explains certain constituents of the content of dreams which are peculiar to them and are not found in waking ideation. What I have in mind are 'collective' and 'composite figures' and the strange 'composite structures', which are creations not unlike the composite animals invented by the folk-imagination of the Orient. The latter, however, have already assumed stereotyped shapes in our thought, whereas in dreams fresh composite forms are being perpetually constructed in an inexhaustible variety. We are all of us familiar with such structures from our own dreams.

* * *

The composite structures which occur in dreams in such immense numbers are put together in an equal variety of ways, and the same rules apply to their resolution. There is no need for me to quote any instances. Their strangeness disappears completely when once we have made up our minds not to class them with the objects of our waking perception, but to remember that they are products of dream-condensation and are emphasizing in an effectively abbreviated form some common characteristic of the objects which they are thus combining. Here again the common element has as a rule to be discovered by analysis. The content of the dream merely says as it were: 'All these things have an element *x* in common.' The dissection of these composite structures by means of analysis is often the shortest way to finding the meaning of a dream.—Thus, I dreamt on one occasion that I was sitting on a bench with one of my former University teachers, and that the bench, which was surrounded by other benches, was moving forward

2. [The German word '*Kosten*' means both 'cost' and 'to taste.']

at a rapid pace. This was a combination of a lecture theatre and a *trottoir roulant.* * * *

A good proportion of what we have learnt about condensation in dreams may be summarized in this formula: each element in the content of a dream is 'overdetermined' by material in the dream-thoughts; it is not derived from a *single* element in the dream-thoughts, but may be traced back to a whole number. These elements need not necessarily be closely related to each other in the dream-thoughts themselves; they may belong to the most widely separated regions of the fabric of those thoughts. A dream-element is, in the strictest sense of the word, the 'representative' of all this disparate material in the content of the dream. But analysis reveals yet another side of the complicated relation between the content of the dream and the dream-thoughts. Just as connections lead from each element of the dream to several dream-thoughts, so as a rule a single dream-thought is represented by more than one dream-element; the threads of association do not simply converge from the dream-thoughts to the dream-content, they cross and interweave with each other many times over in the course of their journey.

Condensation, together with the transformation of thoughts into situations ('dramatization'), is the most important and peculiar characteristic of the dream-work. So far, however, nothing has transpired as to any *motive* necessitating this compression of the material.

V

In the case of the complicated and confused dreams with which we are now concerned, condensation and dramatization alone are not enough to account for the whole of the impression that we gain of the dissimilarity between the content of the dream and the dream-thoughts. We have evidence of the operation of a third factor, and this evidence deserves careful sifting.

First and foremost, when by means of analysis we have arrived at a knowledge of the dream-thoughts, we observe that the manifest dream-content deals with quite different material from the latent thoughts. This, to be sure, is no more than an appearance, which evaporates under closer examination, for we find ultimately that the whole of the dream-content is derived from the dream-thoughts, and that almost all the dream-thoughts are represented in the dream-content. Nevertheless, something of the distinction still remains. What stands out boldly and clearly in the dream as its essential content must, after analysis, be satisfied with playing an extremely subordinate role among the dream-thoughts; and what, on the evidence of our feelings, can claim to be the most prominent among the dream-thoughts is either not present at all as ideational material in the content of the dream or is only remotely alluded to in some obscure region of it. We may put it in this way: *in the course of the dream-work the psychical intensity passes over from the thoughts and ideas to which it properly belongs on to others which in our judgement have no claim to any such emphasis.* No other process contributes so much to concealing the meaning of a dream and to making the connection between the dream-content and the dream-thoughts unrecognizable. In the course of this process, which I shall describe as 'dream-displacement', the psychical intensity, significance or affective potentiality of the thought is, as we further find, transformed into sensory vividness. We assume as a matter of course that the most distinct element in the manifest content of a dream is the most important one; but in fact [owing to the displacement that has occurred] it is often an *indistinct* element which turns out to be the most direct derivative of the essential dream-thought.

* * *

Our specimen dream exhibits displacement to this extent at least, that its content seems to have a different *centre* from its dream-thoughts. In the foreground of the dream-content a prominent place is taken by a situation in which a woman seems to be making advances to me; while in the dream-thoughts the chief emphasis is laid on a wish for once to enjoy unselfish love, love which 'costs nothing'—an idea concealed behind the phrase about 'beautiful eyes' and the far-fetched allusion to 'spinach'.

If we undo dream-displacement by means of analysis, we obtain what seems to be completely trustworthy information on two much-disputed problems concerning dreams: as to their instigators and as to their connection with waking life. There are dreams which immediately reveal their derivation from events of the day; there are others in which no trace of any such derivation is to be discovered. If we seek the help of analysis, we find that every dream without any possible exception goes back to an impression of the past few days, or, it is probably more correct to say, of the day immediately preceding the dream, of the 'dream-day'. The impression which plays the part of dream-instigator may be such an important one that we feel no surprise at being concerned with it in the daytime, and in that case we rightly speak of the dream as carrying on with the significant interests of our waking life. As a rule, however, if a connection is to be found in the content of the dream with any impression of the previous day, that impression is so trivial, insignificant and unmemorable, that it is only with difficulty that we ourselves can recall it. And in such cases the content of the dream itself, even if it is connected and intelligible, seems to be concerned with the most indifferent trivialities, which would be unworthy of our interest if we were awake. A good deal of the contempt in which dreams are held is due to the preference thus shown in their content for what is indifferent and trivial.

Analysis does away with the misleading appearance upon which this derogatory judgement is founded. If the content of a dream puts forward some indifferent impression as being its instigator, analysis invariably brings to light a significant experience, and one by which the dreamer has good reason to be stirred. This experience has been replaced by the indifferent one, with which it is connected by copious associative links. Where the content of the dream treats of insignificant and uninteresting ideational material, analysis uncovers the numerous associative paths connecting these trivialities with things that are of the highest psychical importance in the dreamer's estimation. *If what make their way into the content of dreams are impressions and material which are indifferent and trivial rather than justifiably stirring and interesting, that is only the effect of the process of displacement.* If we answer our questions about dream-instigators and the connection between dreaming and daily affairs on the basis of the new insight we have gained from replacing the manifest by the latent content of dreams, we arrive at these conclusions: *dreams are never concerned with things which we should not think it worth while to be concerned with during the day, and trivialities which do not affect us during the day are unable to pursue us in our sleep.*

What was the dream-instigator in the specimen that we have chosen for analysis? It was the definitely insignificant event of my friend giving me *a drive in a cab free of cost*. The situation in the dream at the table d'hôte contained an allusion to this insignificant precipitating cause, for in my conversation I had compared the taximeter cab with a table d'hôte. But I can also point to the important experience which was represented by this trivial one. A few days earlier I had paid out a considerable sum of money on behalf of a member of my family of whom I am fond. No wonder, said the dream-thoughts, if this person were to feel grateful to me: love of that sort would not be 'free of cost'. Love that is free of cost, however, stood in the forefront of the dream-thoughts. The fact that not long before I had had several *cab-drives* with the relative in question, made it possible for the cab-drive with my friend to remind me of my connections with this other person.

The indifferent impression which becomes a dream-instigator owing to associations of this kind is subject to a further condition which does not apply to the true source of the dream: it must always be a *recent* impression, derived from the dream-day.

I cannot leave the subject of dream-displacement without drawing attention to a remarkable process which occurs in the formation of dreams and in which condensation and displacement *combine* to produce the result. In considering condensation we have already seen the way in which two ideas in the dream-thoughts which have something in common, some point of contact, are replaced in the dream-content by a composite idea, in which a relatively distinct nucleus represents what they have in common, while indistinct subordinate details correspond to the respects in which they differ from each other. If displacement takes place in addition to condensation, what is constructed is not a composite idea but an 'intermediate common entity', which stands in a relation to the two different elements similar to that in which the resultant in a parallelogram of forces stands to its components. * * *

VI

It is the process of displacement which is chiefly responsible for our being unable to discover or recognize the dream-thoughts in the dream-content, unless we understand the reason for their distortion. Nevertheless, the dream-thoughts are also submitted to another and milder sort of transformation, which leads to our discovering a new achievement on the part of the dream-work—one, however, which is easily intelligible. The dream-thoughts which we first come across as we proceed with our analysis often strike us by the unusual form in which they are expressed; they are not clothed in the prosaic language usually employed by our thoughts, but are on the contrary represented symbolically by means of similes and metaphors, in images resembling those of poetic speech. There is no difficulty in accounting for the constraint imposed upon the form in which the dream-thoughts are expressed. The manifest content of dreams consists for the most part in pictorial situations; and the dream-thoughts must accordingly be submitted in the first place to a treatment which will make them suitable for a representation of this kind. If we imagine ourselves faced by the problem of representing the arguments in a political leading article or the speeches of counsel before a court of law in a series of pictures, we shall easily understand the modifications which must necessarily be carried out by the dream-work owing to *considerations of representability in the content of the dream.*

The psychical material of the dream-thoughts habitually includes recollections of impressive experiences—not infrequently dating back to early childhood—which are thus themselves perceived as a rule as situations having a visual subject-matter. Wherever the possibility arises, this portion of the dream-thoughts exercises a determining influence upon the form taken by the content of the dream; it constitutes, as it were, a nucleus of crystallization, attracting the material of the dream-thoughts to itself and thus affecting their distribution. The situation in a dream is often nothing other than a modified repetition, complicated by interpolations, of an impressive experience of this kind; on the other hand, faithful and straightforward reproductions of real scenes only rarely appear in dreams.

The content of dreams, however, does not consist entirely of situations, but also includes disconnected fragments of visual images, speeches and even bits of unmodified thoughts. It may therefore perhaps be of interest to enumerate very briefly the modes of representation available to the dream-work for reproducing the dream-thoughts in the peculiar form of expression necessary in dreams.

The dream-thoughts which we arrive at by means of analysis reveal themselves as a psychical complex of the most intricate possible structure.

Its portions stand in the most manifold logical relations to one another: they represent foreground and background, conditions, digressions and illustrations, chains of evidence and counter-arguments. Each train of thought is almost invariably accompanied by its contradictory counter-part. This material lacks none of the characteristics that are familiar to us from our waking thinking. If now all of this is to be turned into a dream, the psychical material will be submitted to a pressure which will condense it greatly, to an internal fragmentation and displacement which will, as it were, create new surfaces, and to a selective operation in favour of those portions of it which are the most appropriate for the construction of situations. If we take into account the genesis of the material, a process of this sort deserves to be described as a 'regression'. In the course of this transformation, however, the logical links which have hitherto held the psychical material together are lost. It is only, as it were, the substantive content of the dream-thoughts that the dream-work takes over and manipulates. The restoration of the connections which the dream-work has destroyed is a task which has to be performed by the work of analysis.

The modes of expression open to a dream may therefore be qualified as meagre by comparison with those of our intellectual speech; never-theless a dream need not wholly abandon the possibility of reproducing the logical relations present in the dream-thoughts. On the contrary, it succeeds often enough in replacing them by formal characteristics in its own texture.

In the first place, dreams take into account the connection which undeniably exists between all the portions of the dream-thoughts by combining the whole material into a single situation. They reproduce *logical connection* by *approximation in time and space*, just as a painter will represent all the poets in a single group in a picture of Parnassus. It is true that they were never in fact assembled on a single mountain-top; but they certainly form a conceptual group. Dreams carry this method of reproduction down to details; and often when they show us two elements in the dream-content close together, this indicates that there is some specially intimate connection between what correspond to them among the dream-thoughts. Incidentally, it is to be observed that all dreams produced during a single night will be found on analysis to be derived from the same circle of thoughts.

A *causal relation* between two thoughts is either left unrepresented or is replaced by a *sequence* of two pieces of dream of different lengths. Here the representation is often reversed, the beginning of the dream standing for the consequence and its conclusion for the premise. An immediate *transformation* of one thing into another in a dream seems to represent the relation of *cause and effect*.

The alternative '*either—or*' is never expressed in dreams, both of the alternatives being inserted in the text of the dream as though they were equally valid. I have already mentioned that an 'either—or' used in *recording* a dream is to be translated by 'and'.

Ideas which are contraries are by preference expressed in dreams by one and the same element. 'No' seems not to exist so far as dreams are concerned. Opposition between two thoughts, the relation of *reversal*, may be represented in dreams in a most remarkable way. It may be represented by some *other* piece of the dream-content being turned into its opposite—as it were by an afterthought. We shall hear presently of a further method of expressing contradiction. The sensation of *inhibition of movement* which is so common in dreams also serves to express a contradiction between two impulses, a *conflict of will*.

One and one only of these logical relations—that of *similarity, consonance, the possession of common attributes*—is very highly favoured by the mechanism of dream-formation. The dream-work makes use of such cases as a foundation for dream-condensation, by bringing together everything that shows an agreement of this kind into a new unity.

* * * Absurdity in a dream signifies the presence in the dream-thoughts of *contradiction, ridicule and derision*. Since this statement is in the most marked opposition to the view that dreams are the product of a dissociated and uncritical mental activity, I will emphasize it by means of an example.

One of my acquaintances, Herr M., had been attacked in an essay with an unjustifiable degree of violence, as we all thought—by no less a person than Goethe. Herr M. was naturally crushed by the attack. He complained of it bitterly to some company at table; his veneration for Goethe had not been affected, however, by this personal experience. I now tried to throw a little light on the chronological data, which seemed to me improbable. Goethe died in 1832. Since his attack on Herr M. must naturally have been made earlier than that, Herr M. must have been quite a young man at the time. It seemed to be a plausible notion that he was eighteen. I was not quite sure, however, what year we were actually in, so that my whole calculation melted into obscurity. Incidentally, the attack was contained in Goethe's well-known essay on 'Nature'.

The nonsensical character of this dream will be even more glaringly obvious, if I explain that Herr M. is a youngish business man, who is far removed from any poetical and literary interests. I have no doubt, however, that when I have entered into the analysis of the dream I shall succeed in showing how much 'method' there is in its nonsense.

The material of the dream was derived from three sources:

(1) Herr M., whom I had got to know among some *company at table*, asked me one day to examine his elder brother, who was showing signs of [general paralysis]. In the course of my conversation with the patient an awkward episode occurred, for he gave his brother away for no accountable reason by talking of his *youthful follies*. I had asked the patient

the *year of his birth* (cf. the *year of* Goethe's *death* in the dream) and had made him carry out a number of calculations in order to test the weakness of his memory.

(2) A medical journal, which bore my name among others on its title-page, had published a positively *'crushing'* criticism by a *youthful* reviewer of a book by my friend F. in Berlin. I took the editor to task over this; but, though he expressed his regret, he would not undertake to offer any redress. I therefore severed my connection with the journal, but in my letter of resignation expressed a hope that *our personal relations would not be affected by the event.* This was the true source of the dream. The unfavourable reception of my friend's work had made a profound impression on me. It contained, in my opinion, a fundamental biological discovery, which is only now—many years later—beginning to find favour with the experts.

(3) A woman patient of mine had given me an account a short time before of her brother's illness, and how he had broken out in a frenzy with cries of *'Nature! Nature!'* The doctors believed that his exclamation came from his having read Goethe's striking essay on that subject and that it showed he had been overworking at his studies. I had remarked that *it seemed to me more plausible* that his exclamation of the word 'Nature' should be taken in the sexual sense in which it is used by the less educated people here. This idea of mine was at least not disproved by the fact that the unfortunate young man subsequently mutilated his own genitals. He was *eighteen* at the time of his outbreak.

Behind my own ego in the dream-content there lay concealed, in the first instance, my friend who had been so badly treated by the critic. *'I tried to throw a little light on the chronological data.'* My friend's book dealt with the *chronological data* of life and among other things showed that the length of Goethe's life was a multiple of a number of days that has a significance in biology. But this ego was compared with a paralytic: *'I was not quite sure what year we were in.'* Thus the dream made out that my friend was behaving like a paralytic, and in this respect it was a mass of absurdities. The dream-thoughts, however, were saying ironically: 'Naturally, it's *he* [my friend F.] who is the crazy fool and it's *you* [the critics] who are the men of genius and know better. Surely it couldn't be the *reverse?'* There were plenty of examples of this *reversal* in the dream. For instance, Goethe attacked the young man, which is absurd, whereas it is still easy for quite a young man to attack the great Goethe.

I should like to lay it down that no dream is prompted by motives other than egoistic ones. In fact, the ego in the present dream does not stand only for my friend but for myself as well. I was identifying myself with him, because the fate of his discovery seemed to foreshadow the reception of my own findings. If I were to bring forward my theory emphasizing the part played by sexuality in the aetiology of psychoneurotic disorders (cf. the allusion to the eighteen-year-old patient's cry of

'Nature! Nature!'), I should come across the same criticisms; and I was already preparing to meet them with the same derision.

* * *

* * * In addition to condensation, displacement and pictorial arrangement of the psychical material, we are obliged to assign it yet another activity, though this is not to be found in operation in *every* dream. I shall not deal exhaustively with this part of the dream-work, and will therefore merely remark that the easiest way of forming an idea of its nature is to suppose—though the supposition probably does not meet the facts—that *it only comes into operation* AFTER *the dream-content has already been constructed*. Its function would then consist in arranging the constituents of the dream in such a way that they form an approximately connected whole, a dream-composition. In this way the dream is given a kind of façade (though this does not, it is true, hide its content at every point), and thus receives a first, preliminary interpretation, which is supported by interpolations and slight modifications. Incidentally, this revision of the dream-content is only possible if it is not too punctiliously carried out; nor does it present us with anything more than a glaring misunderstanding of the dream-thoughts. Before we start upon the analysis of a dream we have to clear the ground of this attempt at an interpretation.

The motive for this part of the dream-work is particularly obvious. *Considerations of intelligibility* are what lead to this final revision of a dream; and this reveals the origin of the activity. It behaves towards the dream-content lying before it just as our normal psychical activity behaves in general towards any perceptual content that may be presented to it. It understands that content on the basis of certain anticipatory ideas, and arranges it, even at the moment of perceiving it, on the presupposition of its being intelligible; in so doing it runs a risk of falsifying it, and in fact, if it cannot bring it into line with anything familiar, is a prey to the strangest misunderstandings. As is well known, we are incapable of seeing a series of unfamiliar signs or of hearing a succession of unknown words, without at once falsifying the perception from considerations of intelligibility, on the basis of something already known to us.

Dreams which have undergone a revision of this kind at the hands of a psychical activity completely analogous to waking thought may be described as 'well-constructed'. In the case of other dreams this activity has completely broken down; no attempt even has been made to arrange or interpret the material, and, since after we have woken up we feel ourselves identical with this last part of the dream-work, we make a judgement that the dream was 'hopelessly confused.' From the point of view of analysis, however, a dream that resembles a disordered heap of disconnected fragments is just as valuable as one that has been beautifully polished and provided with a surface. In the former case, indeed, we are saved the trouble of demolishing what has been superimposed upon the dream-content.

* * *

The dream-work exhibits no activities other than the four that have already been mentioned. If we keep to the definition of 'dream-work' as the process of transforming the dream-thoughts into the dream-content, it follows that the dream-work is not creative, that it develops no phantasies of its own, that it makes no judgements and draws no conclusions; it has no functions whatever other than condensation and displacement of the material and its modification into pictorial form, to which must be added as a variable factor the final bit of interpretative revision. It is true that we find various things in the dream-content which we should be inclined to regard as a product of some other and higher intellectual function; but in every case analysis shows convincingly that *these intellectual operations have already been performed in the dream-thoughts and have only been* TAKEN OVER *by the dream-content*. A conclusion drawn in a dream is nothing other than the repetition of a conclusion in the dream-thoughts; if the conclusion is taken over into the dream unmodified, it will appear impeccable; if the dream-work has displaced it on to some other material, it will appear nonsensical. A calculation in the dream-content signifies nothing more than that there is a calculation in the dream-thoughts; but while the latter is always rational, a dream-calculation may produce the wildest results if its factors are condensed or if its mathematical operations are displaced on to other material. Not even the speeches that occur in the dream-content are original compositions; they turn out to be a hotchpotch of speeches made, heard or read, which have been revived in the dream-thoughts and whose wording is exactly reproduced, while their origin is entirely disregarded and their meaning is violently changed.

It will perhaps be as well to support these last assertions by a few examples.

(I) Here is an innocent-sounding, well-constructed dream dreamt by a woman patient:

She dreamt she was going to the market with her cook, who was carrying the basket. After she had asked for something, the butcher said to her: 'That's not obtainable any longer,' and offered her something else, adding: 'This is good too.' She rejected it and went on to the woman who sells vegetables, who tried to get her to buy a peculiar vegetable that was tied up in bundles but was of a black colour. She said: 'I don't recognize that: I won't take it.'

The remark *'That's not obtainable any longer'* originated from the treatment itself. A few days earlier I had explained to the patient in those very words that the earliest memories of childhood were 'not obtainable any longer as such', but were replaced in analysis by 'transferences' and dreams. So I was the butcher.

The second speech—'I don't recognize that'—occurred in an entirely different connection. On the previous day she had reproved her cook, who incidentally also appeared in the dream, with the words: 'Behave yourself properly! I don't recognize that!' meaning, no doubt, that she did not understand such behaviour and would not put up with it. As the result of a displacement, it was the more innocent part of this speech which made its way into the content of the dream; but in the dream-thoughts it was only the other part of the speech that played a part. For the dream-work had reduced to complete unintelligibility and extreme innocence an imaginary situation in which I was behaving improperly to the lady in a particular way. But this situation which the patient was expecting in her imagination was itself only a new edition of something she had once actually experienced.

* * *

VIII

* * * The dream-work is only the first to be discovered of a whole series of psychical processes, responsible for the generation of hysterical symptoms, of phobias, obsessions and delusions. Condensation and, above all, displacement are invariable characteristics of these other processes as well. Modification into a pictorial form, on the other hand, remains a peculiarity of the dream-work. If this explanation places dreams in a single series alongside the structures produced by psychical illness, this makes it all the more important for us to discover the essential determining conditions of such processes as those of dream-formation. We shall probably be surprised to hear that neither the state of sleep nor illness is among these indispensable conditions. A whole number of the phenomena of the everyday life of healthy people—such as forgetting, slips of the tongue, bungled actions and a particular class of errors—owe their origin to a psychical mechanism analogous to that of dreams and of the other members of the series.

The heart of the problem lies in displacement, which is by far the most striking of the special achievements of the dream-work. If we enter deeply into the subject, we come to realize that the essential determining condition of displacement is a purely psychological one: something in the nature of a motive. One comes upon its track if one takes into consideration certain experiences which one cannot escape in analysing dreams. In analysing my specimen dream I was obliged to break off my report of the dream-thoughts * * * because, as I confessed, there were some among them which I should prefer to conceal from strangers and which I could not communicate to other people without doing serious mischief in important directions. I added that nothing would be gained if I were to choose another dream instead of that particular one with a view to reporting its analysis: I should come upon dream-thoughts which required to be kept secret in the case of *every* dream with an obscure or confused content. If, however, I were to continue the analysis on my own account, without any reference to other people (whom, indeed, an experience so personal as my dream cannot possibly have been intended to reach), I should eventually arrive at thoughts which would surprise me, whose presence in me I was unaware of, which were not only *alien* but also *disagreeable* to me, and which I should therefore feel inclined to dispute energetically, although the chain of thoughts running through the analysis insisted upon them remorselessly. There is only one way of accounting for this state of affairs, which is of quite universal occurrence; and that is to suppose that these thoughts really were present in my mind, and in possession of a certain amount of psychical intensity or energy, but that they were in a peculiar psychological situation, as a consequence of which they *could not become conscious* to me. (I describe this particular condition as one of 'repression'.) We cannot help concluding, then, that there is a causal connection between the obscurity of the dream-content and the state of repression (inadmissibility to consciousness) of certain of the dream-thoughts, and that the dream had to be obscure so as not to betray the proscribed dream-thoughts. Thus we are led to the concept of a 'dream-distortion', which is the product of the dream-work and serves the purpose of dissimulation, that is, of disguise.

I will test this on the specimen dream which I chose for analysis, and enquire what the thought was which made its way into that dream in a distorted form, and which I should be inclined to repudiate if it were undistorted. I recall that my free cab-drive reminded me of my recent expensive drive with a member of my family, that the interpretation of the dream was 'I wish I might for once experience love that cost me nothing', and that a short time before the dream I had been obliged to spend a considerable sum of money on this same person's account. Bearing this context in mind, I cannot escape the conclusion that *I regret having made that expenditure.* Not until I have recognized this impulse does my wish in the dream for the love which would call for *no* expenditure acquire a meaning. Yet I can honestly say that when I decided to spend this sum of money I did not hesitate for a moment. My regret at having to do so—the contrary current of feeling—did not become conscious to me. *Why* it did not, is another and a far-reaching question, the answer to which is known to me but belongs in another connection.

If the dream that I analyse is not my own, but someone else's, the conclusion will be the same, though the grounds for believing it will be different. If the dreamer is a healthy person, there is no other means open to me of obliging him to recognize the repressed ideas that have been discovered than by pointing out the context of the dream-thoughts; and I cannot help it if he refuses to recognize them. If, however, I am dealing with a neurotic patient, with a hysteric for instance, he will find the acceptance of the repressed thought forced upon him, owing to its connection with the symptoms of his illness, and owing to the improvement he experiences when he exchanges those symptoms for the repressed ideas. * * *

IX

Now that we have established the concept of repression and have brought dream-distortion into relation with repressed psychical material, we can express in general terms the principal finding to which we have been led by the analysis of dreams. In the case of dreams which are intelligible and have a meaning, we have found that they are undisguised wish-fulfilments; that is, that in their case the dream-situation represents as fulfilled a wish which is known to consciousness, which is left over from daytime life, and which is deservedly of interest. Analysis has taught us something entirely analogous in the case of obscure and confused dreams: once again the dream-situation represents a wish as fulfilled— a wish which invariably arises from the dream-thoughts, but one which is represented in an unrecognizable form and can only be explained when it has been traced back in analysis. The wish in such cases is either itself a repressed one and alien to consciousness, or it is intimately connected with repressed thoughts and is based upon them. Thus the formula for such dreams is as follows: *they are disguised fulfilments of repressed wishes*. It is interesting in this connection to observe that the popular belief that dreams always foretell the future is confirmed. Actually the future which the dream shows us is not the one which *will* occur but the one which we should *like* to occur. The popular mind is behaving here as it usually does: what it wishes, it believes.

* * *

X

Hitherto philosophers have had no occasion to concern themselves with a psychology of repression. We may therefore be permitted to make a first approach to this hitherto unknown topic by constructing a pictorial image of the course of events in dream-formation. It is true that the schematic picture we have arrived at—not only from the study of dreams—is a fairly complicated one; but we cannot manage with anything simpler. Our hypothesis is that in our mental apparatus there are two thought-constructing agencies, of which the second enjoys the privilege of having free access to consciousness for its products, whereas the activity of the first is in itself unconscious and can only reach consciousness by way of the second. On the frontier between the two agencies, where the first passes over to the second, there is a censorship, which only allows what is agreeable to it to pass through and holds back everything else. According to our definition, then, what is rejected by the censorship is in a state of repression. Under certain conditions, of which the state of sleep is one, the relation between the strength of the two agencies is modified in such a way that what is repressed can no longer be held back. In the state of sleep this probably occurs owing to a relaxation of the censorship; when this happens it becomes possible for what has hitherto been repressed to make a path for itself to consciousness. Since, however, the censorship is never completely eliminated but merely reduced, the repressed material must submit to certain alterations which mitigate its offensive features. What becomes conscious in such cases is a compromise between the intentions of one agency and the demands of the other. *Repression—relaxation of the censorship—the formation of a compromise,* this is the fundamental pattern for the generation not only of dreams but of many other psychopathological structures; and in the latter cases too we may observe that the formation of compromises is accompanied by processes of condensation and displacement and by the employment of superficial associations, which we have become familiar with in the dream-work.

We have no reason to disguise the fact that in the hypothesis which we have set up in order to explain the dream-work a part is played by what might be described as a 'daemonic' element. We have gathered an impression that the formation of obscure dreams occurs *as though* one person who was dependent upon a second person had to make a remark which was bound to be disagreeable in the ears of this second one; and it is on the basis of this simile that we have arrived at the concepts of dream-distortion and censorship, and have endeavoured to translate our impression into a psychological theory which is no doubt crude but is at least lucid. Whatever it may be with which a further investigation of the subject may enable us to identify our first and second agencies, we may safely expect to find a confirmation of some correlate of our hypothesis that the second agency controls access to consciousness and can bar the first agency from such access.

When the state of sleep is over, the censorship quickly recovers its full strength; and it can now wipe out all that was won from it during the period of its weakness. This must be one part at least of the explanation of the forgetting of dreams, as is shown by an observation which has been confirmed on countless occasions. It not infrequently happens that during the narration of a dream or during its analysis a fragment of the dream-content which had seemed to be forgotten re-emerges. This fragment which has been rescued from oblivion invariably affords us the best and most direct access to the meaning of the dream. And that, in all probability, must have been the only reason for its having been forgotten, that is, for its having been once more suppressed.

XI

When once we have recognized that the content of a dream is the representation of a fulfilled wish and that its obscurity is due to alterations in repressed material made by the censorship, we shall no longer have any difficulty in discovering the *function* of dreams. It is commonly said that sleep is disturbed by dreams; strangely enough, we are led to a contrary view and must regard dreams as *the guardians of sleep*.

In the case of children's dreams there should be no difficulty in accepting this statement. * * * We all know the amusing story told by Balduin Groller [a popular nineteenth-century Austrian novelist] of the bad little boy who woke up in the middle of the night and shouted across the night-nursery: 'I want the rhino!" A better behaved child, instead of shouting, would have *dreamt* that he was playing with the rhino. Since a dream that shows a wish as fulfilled is *believed* during sleep, it does away with the wish and makes sleep possible. It cannot be disputed that dream-images are believed in in this way, for they are clothed in the psychical appearance of perceptions, and children have not yet acquired the later faculty of distinguishing hallucinations or phantasies from reality.

Adults have learnt to make this distinction; they have also grasped the uselessness of wishing, and after lengthy practice know how to postpone their desires until they can find satisfaction by the long and roundabout path of altering the external world. In their case, accordingly, wish-fulfilments along the short psychical path are rare in sleep too; it is even possible, indeed, that they never occur at all, and that anything that may seem to us to be constructed on the pattern of a child's dream in fact requires a far more complicated solution. On the other hand, in the case of adults—and this no doubt applies without exception to everyone in full possession of his senses—a differentiation has occurred in the psychical material, which was not present in children. A psychical agency has come into being, which, taught by experience of life, exercises a dominating and inhibiting influence upon mental impulses and maintains that influence with jealous severity, and which, owing to its relation to consciousness and to voluntary movement, is armed with the strongest instruments of psychical power. A portion of the impulses of childhood has been suppressed by this agency as being useless to life, and any thought-material derived from those impulses is in a state of repression.

Now while this agency, in which we recognize our normal ego, is concentrated on the wish to sleep, it appears to be compelled by the psycho-physiological conditions of sleep to relax the energy with which it is accustomed to hold down the repressed material during the day. In itself, no doubt, this relaxation does no harm; however much the suppressed impulses of the childish mind may prance around, their access to consciousness is still difficult and their access to movement is barred, as the result of this same state of sleep. The danger of sleep being disturbed by them must, however, be guarded against. We must in any case suppose that even during deep sleep a certain amount of free attention is on duty as a guard against sensory stimuli, and that this guard may sometimes consider waking more advisable than a continuation of sleep. Otherwise there would be no explanation of how it is that we can be woken up at any moment by sensory stimuli of some particular *quality*. As the physiologist Burdach [1838, 486] insisted long ago, a mother, for instance, will be roused by the whimpering of her baby, or a miller if his mill comes to a stop, or most people if they are called softly by their own name. Now the attention which is thus on guard is also directed towards internal wishful stimuli arising from the repressed material, and combines with them to form the dream which, as a compromise, simultaneously satisfies both of the two agencies. The dream provides a kind of psychical consummation for the wish that has been suppressed (or formed with the help of repressed material) by representing it as fulfilled; but it also satisfies the other agency by allowing sleep to continue. In this respect our ego is ready to behave like a child; it gives credence to the dream-images, as though what it wanted to say was: 'Yes, yes! you're quite right, but let me go on sleeping!' The low estimate which we form of dreams when we are awake, and which we relate to their confused and apparently illogical character, is probably nothing other than the judgement passed by our sleeping ego upon the repressed impulses, a judgement based, with better right, upon the motor impotence of these disturbers of sleep. We are sometimes aware in our sleep of this contemptuous judgement. If the content of a dream goes too far in overstepping the censorship, we think: 'After all, it's only a dream!'—and go on sleeping.

This view is not traversed by the fact that there are marginal cases in which the dream—as happens with anxiety-dreams—can no longer perform its function of preventing an interruption of sleep, but assumes instead the other function of promptly bringing sleep to an end. In doing so it is merely behaving like a conscientious night-watchman, who first carries out his duty by suppressing disturbances so that the townsmen may not be woken up, but afterwards continues to do his duty by himself waking the townsmen up, if the causes of the disturbance seem to him serious and of a kind that he cannot cope with alone.

The function of the dream as a guardian of sleep becomes particularly evident when an external stimulus impinges upon the senses of a sleeper. It is generally recognized that sensory stimuli arising during sleep influence the content of dreams; this can be proved experimentally and is among the few certain (but, incidentally, greatly overvalued) findings of medical investigation into dreams. But this finding involves a puzzle which has hitherto proved insoluble. For the sensory stimulus which the experimenter causes to impinge upon the sleeper is not correctly recognized in the dream; it is subjected to one of an indefinite number of possible interpretations, the choice being apparently left to an arbitrary psychical determination. But there is, of course, no such thing as arbitrary determination in the mind. There are several ways in which a sleeper may react to an external sensory stimulus. He may wake up or he may succeed in continuing his sleep in spite of it. In the latter case he may make use of a dream in order to get rid of the external stimulus, and here again there is more than one method open to him. For instance, he may get rid of the stimulus by dreaming that he is in a situation which is absolutely incompatible with the stimulus. Such was the line taken by a sleeper who was subject to disturbance by a painful abscess on the perineum. He dreamt that he was riding on a horse, making use of the poultice that was intended to mitigate his pain as a saddle, and in this way he avoided being disturbed. Or, as happens more frequently, the external stimulus is given an interpretation which brings it into the context of a repressed wish which is at the moment awaiting fulfilment; in this way the external stimulus is robbed of its reality and is treated as though it were a portion of the psychical material. Thus someone dreamt that he had written a comedy with a particular plot; it was produced in a theatre, the first act was over, and there were thunders of applause; the clapping was terrific. . . . The dreamer must have succeeded in prolonging his sleep till after the interference had ceased; for when he woke up he no longer heard the noise, but rightly concluded that someone must have been beating a carpet or mattress. Every dream which occurs immediately before the sleeper is woken by a loud noise has made an attempt at explaining away the arousing stimulus by providing another explanation of it and has thus sought to prolong sleep, even if only for a moment.

XII[3]

No one who accepts the view that the censorship is the chief reason for dream-distortion will be surprised to learn from the results of dream-interpretation that most of the dreams of adults are traced back by analysis to *erotic wishes*. This assertion is not aimed at dreams with an *undisguised* sexual content, which are no doubt familiar to all dreamers from their own experience and are as a rule the only ones to be described as 'sexual dreams'. Even dreams of this latter kind offer enough surprises in their choice of the people whom they make into sexual objects, in their disregard of all the limitations which the dreamer imposes in his waking life upon his sexual desires, and by their many strange details, hinting at what are commonly known as 'perversions'. A great many other dreams, however, which show no sign of being erotic in their manifest

3. [The whole of this section was added in 1911.]

content, are revealed by the work of interpretation in analysis as sexual wish-fulfilments; and, on the other hand, analysis proves that a great many of the thoughts left over from the activity of waking life as 'residues of the previous day' only find their way to representation in dreams through the assistance of repressed erotic wishes.

There is no theoretical necessity why this should be so; but to explain the fact it may be pointed out that no other group of instincts has been submitted to such far-reaching suppression by the demands of cultural education, while at the same time the sexual instincts are also the ones which, in most people, find it easiest to escape from the control of the highest mental agencies. Since we have become acquainted with infantile sexuality, which is often so unobtrusive in its manifestations and is always overlooked and misunderstood, we are justified in saying that almost every civilized man retains the infantile forms of sexual life in some respect or other. We can thus understand how it is that repressed infantile sexual wishes provide the most frequent and strongest motive-forces for the construction of dreams.

There is only one method by which a dream which expresses erotic wishes can succeed in appearing innocently non-sexual in its manifest content. The material of the sexual ideas must not be represented as such, but must be replaced in the content of the dream by hints, allusions and similar forms of indirect representation. But, unlike other forms of indirect representation, that which is employed in dreams must not be immediately intelligible. The modes of representation which fulfil these conditions are usually described as 'symbols' of the things which they represent. Particular interest has been directed to them since it has been noticed that dreamers speaking the same language make use of the same symbols, and that in some cases, indeed, the use of the same symbols extends beyond the use of the same language. Since dreamers themselves are unaware of the meaning of the symbols they use, it is difficult at first sight to discover the source of the connection between the symbols and what they replace and represent. The fact itself, however, is beyond doubt, and it is important for the technique of dream-interpretation. For, with the help of a knowledge of dream-symbolism, it is possible to understand the meaning of separate elements of the content of a dream or separate pieces of a dream or in some cases even whole dreams, without having to ask the dreamer for his associations. Here we are approaching the popular ideal of translating dreams and on the other hand are returning to the technique of interpretation used by the ancients, to whom dream-interpretation was identical with interpretation by means of symbols.

Although the study of dream-symbols is far from being complete, we are in a position to lay down with certainty a number of general statements and a quantity of special information on the subject. There are some symbols which bear a single meaning almost universally: thus the Emperor and Empress (or the King and Queen) stand for the parents, rooms represent women[4] and their entrances and exits the openings of the body. The majority of dream-symbols serve to represent persons, parts of the body and activities invested with erotic interest; in particular, the genitals are represented by a number of often very surprising symbols, and the greatest variety of objects are employed to denote them symbolically. Sharp weapons, long and stiff objects, such as tree-trunks and sticks, stand for the male genital; while cupboards, boxes, carriages or ovens may represent the uterus. In such cases as these the *tertium comparationis*, the common element in these substitutions, is immediately intelligible; but there are other symbols in which it is not so easy to grasp the connection. Symbols such as a staircase or going upstairs to represent sexual intercourse, a tie or cravat for the male organ, or wood for the female one, provoke our unbelief until we can arrive at an understanding of the symbolic relation underlying them by some other means. Moreover a whole number of dream-symbols are bisexual and can relate to the male or female genitals according to the context.

Some symbols are universally disseminated and can be met with in all dreamers belonging to a single linguistic or cultural group; there are others which occur only within the most restricted and individual limits, symbols constructed by an individual out of his own ideational material. Of the former class we can distinguish some whose claim to represent sexual ideas is immediately justified by linguistic usage (such, for instance, as those derived from agriculture, e.g. 'fertilization' or 'seed') and others whose relation to sexual ideas appears to reach back into the very earliest ages and to the most obscure depths of our conceptual functioning. The power of constructing symbols has not been exhausted in our own days in the case of either of the two sorts of symbols which I have distinguished at the beginning of this paragraph. Newly discovered objects (such as airships) are, as we may observe, at once adopted as universally available sexual symbols.

It would, incidentally, be a mistake to expect that if we had a still profounder knowledge of dream-symbolism (of the 'language of dreams') we could do without asking the dreamer for his associations to the dream and go back entirely to the technique of dream-interpretation of antiquity. Quite apart from individual symbols and oscillations in the use of universal ones, one can never tell whether any particular element in the content of a dream is to be interpreted symbolically or in its proper sense, and one can be certain that the *whole* content of a dream is not to be interpreted symbolically. A knowledge of dream-symbolism will never do more than enable us to translate certain constituents of the dream-content, and will not relieve us of the necessity for applying the technical rules which I gave earlier. It will, however, afford the most valuable assistance to interpretation precisely at points at which the dreamer's associations are insufficient or fail altogether.

4. Cf. *'Frauenzimmer'* [literally 'women's apartment,' commonly used in German as a slightly derogatory word for 'woman'].

Dream-symbolism is also indispensable to an understanding of what are known as 'typical' dreams, which are common to everyone, and of 'recurrent' dreams in individuals.

* * * We must not suppose that dream-symbolism is a creation of the dream-work; it is in all probability a characteristic of the unconscious thinking which provides the dream-work with the material for condensation, displacement and dramatization.

Fragment of an Analysis
of a Case of Hysteria ("Dora")

In the course of his career as the first psychoanalyst, Freud presented in his published writings a good many vignettes from his clinical material. Many of them, though not explicitly mentioned, form the backdrop of, and enrich, his papers and monographs. It was not until he began to write speculative and comprehensive essays on religion and culture just before the First World War (starting with *Totem and Taboo* in 1913 and concluding with *Civilization and Its Discontents* in 1930) that he left the couch behind. Indeed, among his voluminous writings, his case histories loom large as expositions of the varieties of mental suffering amenable to psychoanalytic treatment and as instances of his technique—both successful and unsuccessful. Freud designed these subtle, beautifully designed reports (and they continue to work after all these years) as didactic devices of the first order. They remain impressive, and highly useful, even though later generations of psychoanalysts, freely employing the material that Freud offered them, have reanalyzed these cases and come to conclusions often at variance with Freud's own.

The famous and controversial "Dora" case is the first of Freud's five major case histories. Like the other four—"Little Hans," "The Rat Man," "Schreber," and "The Wolf Man"—it bears a sober technical title, "Fragment of an Analysis of a Case of Hysteria," but has since been known to the world under a nickname. "Dora" (her real name was Ida Bauer) went into analysis with Freud as an eighteen-year-old in October 1900 and abruptly ended her treatment eleven weeks later. Freud wrote up the case quickly in January 1901 but did not publish it, for a variety of reasons—alluded to, but not completely explained, in the "Prefatory Remarks"—until 1905. As the provisional title of the case, "Dreams and Hysteria," indicates, Freud had intended his exposition as an adjunct to his *Interpretation of Dreams* that would exhibit in a concrete instance the uses of dream interpretation. But, more consequential for the history of psychoanalysis, the case history was, as Freud acknowledges, the record of a failure. Accordingly, in the concluding passages he draws a lesson from that failure: he had been seriously remiss in not paying sufficient attention to his patient's transference on him. Dora had bestowed on him, her analyst, some of her most passionate feelings, at once amorous and furious. What is more, he had failed to appreciate the homosexual current in Dora's loves because he had not yet been fully aware of the share that homosexual urges play in neuroses. But Freud's critics have gone far beyond this. In the polemical feminist literature of the 1960s and beyond, Freud, the analyst of "Dora," has been charged with still another failure: a striking inability to set aside his male prejudices, a lack of empathy with a suffering adolescent girl being victimized by egoistic adults—including her father. There is a good deal to this charge, but Freud's attitude toward Dora remains susceptible to varying assessments, including his disappoint- ment at his inability to keep Dora in analysis and his habit of those days to push interpretations on his analysands—the men, too. What is demonstrated is that, as he had with his so-called seduction theory, so again with Dora, Freud was learning from his mistakes. After "Dora," psychoanalytic tech- nique was never the same.

PREFATORY REMARKS

In 1895 and 1896 I put forward certain views upon the pathogenesis of hysterical symptoms and upon the mental processes occurring in hys- teria. Since that time several years have passed. In now proposing, therefore, to substantiate those views by giving a detailed report of the history of a case and its treatment, I cannot avoid making a few intro- ductory remarks, for the purpose partly of justifying from various stand- points the step I am taking, and partly of diminishing the expectations to which it will give rise.

No doubt it was awkward that I was obliged to publish the results of my enquiries without there being any possibility of other workers in the field testing and checking them, particularly as those results were of a surprising and by no means gratifying character. But it will be scarcely less awkward now that I am beginning to bring forward some of the material upon which my conclusions were based and make it accessible to the judgement of the world. I shall not escape blame by this means. Only, whereas before I was accused of giving no information about my patients, now I shall be accused of giving information about my patients which ought not to be given. I can only hope that in both cases the critics will be the same, and that they will merely have shifted the pretext for their reproaches; if so, I can resign in advance any possibility of ever removing their objections.

Even if I ignore the ill-will of narrow-minded critics such as these, the presentation of my case histories remains a problem which is hard for me to solve. The difficulties are partly of a technical kind, but are partly due to the nature of the circumstances themselves. If it is true that the causes of hysterical disorders are to be found in the intimacies of the patients' psychosexual life, and that hysterical symptoms are the expression of their most secret and repressed wishes, then the complete elucidation of a case of hysteria is bound to involve the revelation of those intimacies and the betrayal of those secrets. It is certain that the patients would never have spoken if it had occurred to them that their admissions might possibly be put to scientific uses; and it is equally certain that to ask them themselves for leave to publish their case would be quite unavailing. In such circumstances persons of delicacy, as well as those who were merely timid, would give first place to the duty of medical discretion and would declare with regret that the matter was one upon which they could offer science no enlightenment. But in my opinion the physician has taken upon himself duties not only towards the individual patient but towards science as well; and his duties towards science mean ultimately nothing else than his duties towards the many other patients who are suffering or will some day suffer from the same disorder. Thus it becomes the physician's duty to publish what he believes he knows of the causes and structure of hysteria, and it becomes a disgraceful piece of cowardice on his part to neglect doing so, as long as he can avoid causing direct personal injury to the single patient concerned. I think I have taken every precaution to prevent my patient from suffering any such injury. I have picked out a person the scenes of whose life were laid not in Vienna but in a remote provincial town, and whose personal circumstances must therefore be practically unknown in Vienna. I have from the very beginning kept the fact of her being under my treatment such a careful secret that only one other physician—and one is whose discretion I have complete confidence {Wilhelm Fliess}—can be aware that the girl was a patient of mine. I have waited for four whole years since the end of the treatment and have postponed publication till hearing that a change has taken place in the patient's life of such a character as allows me to suppose that her own interest in the occurrences and psychological events which are to be related here may now have grown faint. Needless to say, I have allowed no name to stand which could put a non-medical reader upon the scent; and the publication of the case in a purely scientific and technical periodical should, further, afford a guarantee against unauthorized readers of this sort. I naturally cannot prevent the patient herself from being pained if her own case history should accidentally fall into her hands. But she will learn nothing from it that she does not already know; and she may ask herself who besides her could discover from it that she is the subject of this paper.

I am aware that—in this city, at least—there are many physicians who (revolting though it may seem) choose to read a case history of this kind not as a contribution to the psychopathology of the neuroses, but as a *roman à clef* designed for their private delectation. I can assure readers of this species that every case history which I may have occasion to publish in the future will be secured against their perspicacity by similar guarantees of secrecy, even though this resolution is bound to put quite extraordinary restrictions upon my choice of material.

Now in this case history—the only one which I have hitherto succeeded in forcing through the limitations imposed by medical discretion and unfavourable circumstances—sexual questions will be discussed with all possible frankness, the organs and functions of sexual life will be called by their proper names, and the pure-minded reader can convince himself from my description that I have not hesitated to converse upon such subjects in such language even with a young woman. Am I, then, to defend myself upon this score as well? I will simply claim for myself the rights of the gynaecologist—or rather, much more modest ones—and add that it would be the mark of a singular and perverse prurience to suppose that conversations of this kind are a good means of exciting or of gratifying sexual desires. For the rest, I feel inclined to express my opinion on this subject in a few borrowed words:

'It is deplorable to have to make room for protestations and declarations of this sort in a scientific work; but let no one reproach me on this account but rather accuse the spirit of the age, owing to which we have reached a state of things in which no serious book can any longer be sure of survival.' (Schmidt, 1902, Preface.)

I will now describe the way in which I have overcome the *technical* difficulties of drawing up the report of this case history. The difficulties are very considerable when the physician has to conduct six or eight psychotherapeutic treatments of the sort in a day, and cannot make notes during the actual session with the patient for fear of shaking the patient's confidence and of disturbing his own view of the material under observation. Indeed, I have not yet succeeded in solving the problem of how to record for publication the history of a treatment of long duration. As regards the present case, two circumstances have come to my assistance. In the first place the treatment did not last for more than three months; and in the second place the material which elucidated the case was grouped around two dreams (one related in the middle of the treatment and one at the end). The wording of these dreams was recorded immediately after the session, and they thus afforded a secure point of attachment for the chain of interpretations and recollections which proceeded from them. The case history itself was only committed to writing from memory after the treatment was at an end, but while my recollection of the case was still fresh and was heightened by my interest in its publication. Thus the record is not absolutely—phonographically—exact, but it can claim to possess a high degree of trustworthiness. Nothing of any importance has been altered in it except in some places the order in which the explanations are given; and this has been done for the sake of presenting the case in a more connected form.

I next proceed to mention more particularly what is to be found in this paper and what is not to be found in it. The title of the work was originally 'Dreams and Hysteria', for it seemed to me peculiarly well-adapted for showing how dream-interpretation is woven into the history of a treatment and how it can become the means of filling in amnesias and elucidating symptoms. It was not without good reasons that in the year 1900 I gave precedence to a laborious and exhaustive study of dreams (*The Interpretation of Dreams*) over the publications upon the psychology of the neuroses which I had in view. And incidentally I was able to judge from its reception with what an inadequate degree of comprehension such efforts are met by other specialists at the present time. In this instance there was no validity in the objection that the material upon which I had based my assertions had been withheld and that it was therefore impossible to become convinced of their truth by testing and checking them. For every one can submit his own dreams to analytic examination, and the technique of interpreting dreams may be easily learnt from the instructions and examples which I have given. I must once more insist, just as I did at that time, that a thorough investigation of the problems of dreams is an indispensable prerequisite for any comprehension of the mental processes in hysteria and the other psychoneuroses, and that no one who wishes to shirk that preparatory labour has the smallest prospect of advancing even a few steps into this region of knowledge. Since, therefore, this case history presupposes a knowledge of the interpretation of dreams, it will seem highly unsatisfactory to any reader to whom this presupposition does not apply. Such a reader will find only bewilderment in these pages instead of the enlightenment he is in search of, and he will certainly be inclined to project the cause of his bewilderment on to the author and to pronounce his views fantastic. But in reality this bewildering character attaches to the phenomena of the neurosis itself; its presence there is only concealed by the physician's familiarity with the facts, and it comes to light again with every attempt at explaining them. It could only be completely banished if we could succeed in tracing back every single element of a neurosis to factors with which we were already familiar. But everything tends to show that, on the contrary, we shall be driven by the study of neuroses to assume the existence of many new things which will later on gradually become the subject of more certain knowledge. What is new has always aroused bewilderment and resistance.

*   *   *

In face of the incompleteness of my analytic results, I had no choice but to follow the example of those discoverers whose good fortune it is to bring to the light of day after their long burial the priceless though mutilated relics of antiquity. I have restored what is missing, taking the best models known to me from other analyses; but, like a conscientious archaeologist, I have not omitted to mention in each case where the authentic parts end and my constructions begin.

There is another kind of incompleteness which I myself have intentionally introduced. I have as a rule not reproduced the process of interpretation to which the patient's associations and communications had to be subjected, but only the results of that process. Apart from the dreams, therefore, the technique of the analytic work has been revealed in only a very few places. * * *

For a third kind of incompleteness in this report neither the patient nor the author is responsible. It is, on the contrary, obvious that a single case history, even if it were complete and open to no doubt, cannot provide an answer to *all* the questions arising out of the problem of hysteria. It cannot give an insight into all the types of this disorder, into all the forms of internal structure of the neurosis, into all the possible kinds of relation between the mental and the somatic which are to be found in hysteria. It is not fair to expect from a single case more than it can offer. And any one who has hitherto been unwilling to believe that a psychosexual aetiology holds good generally and without exception for hysteria is scarcely likely to be convinced of the fact by taking stock of a single case history. He would do better to suspend his judgement until his own work has earned him the right to a conviction.

I

THE CLINICAL PICTURE

In my *Interpretation of Dreams*, published in 1900, I showed that dreams in general can be interpreted, and that after the work of interpretation has been completed they can be replaced by perfectly correctly constructed thoughts which can be assigned a recognizable position in the chain of mental events. I wish to give an example in the following pages of the only practical application of which the art of interpreting dreams seems to admit. I have already mentioned in {*The Interpretation of Dreams*} how it was that I came upon the problem of dreams. The problem crossed my path as I was endeavouring to cure psychoneuroses by means of a particular psychotherapeutic method. For, among their other mental experiences, my patients told me their dreams, and these dreams seemed to call for insertion in the long thread of connections which spun itself out between a symptom of the disease and a pathogenic idea. At that time I learnt how to translate the language of dreams into the forms of expression of our own thought-language, which can be understood without further help. And I may add that this knowledge is essential for the psycho-analyst; for the dream is one of the roads along which consciousness can be reached by the psychical material which, on account of the opposition aroused by its content, has been cut off from consciousness and repressed, and has thus become pathogenic. The dream, in short, is one of the *détours by which repression can be evaded*; it is one of the principal means employed by what is known as the indirect method of representation in the mind. The following fragment from the history of the treatment of a hysterical girl is intended to show the way in which the interpretation of dreams plays a part in the work of analysis. It will at the same time give me a first opportunity of publishing at sufficient length to prevent further misunderstanding some of my views upon the psychical processes of hysteria and upon its organic determinants. I need no longer apologize on the score of length, since it is now agreed that the exacting demands which hysteria makes upon physician and investigator can be met only by the most sympathetic spirit of inquiry and not by an attitude of superiority and contempt.

* * *

* * *

It follows from the nature of the facts which form the material of psycho-analysis that we are obliged to pay as much attention in our case histories to the purely human and social circumstances of our patients as to the somatic data and the symptoms of the disorder. Above all, our interest will be directed towards their family circumstances—and not only, as will be seen later, for the purpose of enquiring into their heredity.

The family circle of the eighteen-year-old girl who is the subject of this paper included, besides herself, her two parents and a brother who was one and a half years her senior. Her father was the dominating figure in this circle, owing to his intelligence and his character as much as to the circumstances of his life. It was those circumstances which provided the framework for the history of the patient's childhood and illness. At the time at which I began the girl's treatment her father was in his late forties, a man of rather unusual activity and talents, a large manufacturer in very comfortable circumstances. His daughter was most tenderly attached to him, and for that reason her critical powers, which developed early, took all the more offence at many of his actions and peculiarities.

Her affection for him was still further increased by the many severe illnesses which he had been through since her sixth year. At that time he had fallen ill with tuberculosis and the family had consequently moved to a small town in a good climate, situated in one of our southern provinces. There his lung trouble rapidly improved; but, on account of the precautions which were still considered necessary, both parents and children continued for the next ten years or so to reside chiefly in this spot, which I shall call B——. When her father's health was good, he used at times to be away, on visits to his factories. During the hottest part of the summer the family used to move to a health-resort in the hills.

When the girl was about ten years old, her father had to go through a course of treatment in a darkened room on account of a detached retina. As a result of this misfortune his vision was permanently impaired. His gravest illness occurred some two years later. It took the form of a confusional attack, followed by symptoms of paralysis and slight mental disturbances. A friend of his (who plays a part in the story with which we shall be concerned later on) persuaded him, while his condition had scarcely improved, to travel to Vienna with his physician and come to me for advice. I hesitated for some time as to whether I ought not to regard the case as one of tabo-paralysis, but I finally decided upon a diagnosis of a diffuse vascular affection; and since the patient admitted having had a specific infection before his marriage, I prescribed an energetic course of anti-luetic treatment, as a result of which all the remaining disturbances passed off. It is no doubt owing to this fortunate intervention of mine that four years later he brought his daughter, who had meanwhile grown unmistakably neurotic, and introduced her to me, and that after another two years he handed her over to me for psychotherapeutic treatment.

I had in the meantime also made the acquaintance in Vienna of a sister of his, who was a little older than himself. She gave clear evidence of a severe form of psychoneurosis without any characteristically hysterical symptoms. After a life which had been weighed down by an unhappy marriage, she died of a marasmus which made rapid advances and the symptoms of which were, as a matter of fact, never fully cleared up. An elder brother of the girl's father, whom I once happened to meet, was a hypochondriacal bachelor.

The sympathies of the girl herself, who, as I have said, became my patient at the age of eighteen, had always been with the father's side of the family, and ever since she had fallen ill she had taken as her model the aunt who has just been mentioned. There could be no doubt, too, that it was from her father's family that she had derived not only her natural gifts and her intellectual precocity but also the predisposition to her illness. I never made her mother's acquaintance. From the accounts given me by the girl and her father I was led to imagine her as an uncultivated woman and above all as a foolish one, who had concentrated all her interests upon domestic affairs, especially since her husband's illness and the estrangement to which it led. She presented the picture, in fact, of what might be called the 'housewife's psychosis'. She had no understanding of her children's more active interests, and was occupied all day long in cleaning the house with its furniture and utensils and in keeping them clean—to such an extent as to make it almost impossible to use or enjoy them. This condition, traces of which are to be found often enough in normal housewives, inevitably reminds one of forms of obsessional washing and other kinds of obsessional cleanliness. But such women (and this applied to the patient's mother) are entirely without insight into their illness, so that one essential characteristic of an 'obsessional neurosis' is lacking. The relations between the girl and her mother had been unfriendly for years. The daughter looked down on her mother and used to criticize her mercilessly, and she had withdrawn completely from her influence.[1]

During the girl's earlier years, her only brother (her elder by a year and a half) had been the model which her ambitions had striven to follow. But in the last few years the relations between the brother and

[1] I do not, it is true, adopt the position that heredity is the only aetiological factor in hysteria. But, on the other hand—and I say this with particular reference to some of my earlier publications, e.g. 'Heredity and the Aetiology of the Neuroses' (1896), in which I combated that view— I do not wish to give an impression of underestimating the importance of heredity, in the aetiology of hysteria or of asserting that it can be dispensed with. . . .

sister had grown more distant. The young man used to try so far as he could to keep out of the family disputes; but when he was obliged to take sides he would support his mother. So that the usual sexual attraction had drawn together the father and daughter on the one side and the mother and son on the other.

The patient, to whom I shall in future give the name of 'Dora', had even at the age of eight begun to develop neurotic symptoms. She became subject at that time to chronic dyspnoea with occasional accesses in which the symptom was very much aggravated. The first onset occurred after a short expedition in the mountains and was accordingly put down to over-exertion. In the course of six months, during which she was made to rest and was carefully looked after, this condition gradually passed off. The family doctor seems to have had not a moment's hesitation in diagnosing the disorder as purely nervous and in excluding any organic cause for the dyspnoea; but he evidently considered this diagnosis compatible with the aetiology of over-exertion.

The little girl went through the usual infectious diseases of childhood without suffering any lasting damage. As she herself told me—and her words were intended to convey a deeper meaning—her brother was as a rule the first to start the illness and used to have it very slightly, and she would then follow suit with a severe form of it. When she was about twelve she began to suffer from unilateral headaches in the nature of a migraine, and from attacks of nervous coughing. At first these two symptoms always appeared together, but they became separated later on and ran different courses. The migraine grew rarer, and by the time she was sixteen she had quite got over it. But attacks of *tussis nervosa*, which had no doubt been started by a common catarrh, continued to occur over the whole period. When, at the age of eighteen, she came to me for treatment, she was again coughing in a characteristic manner. The number of these attacks could not be determined; but they lasted from three to five weeks, and on one occasion for several months. The most troublesome symptom during the first half of an attack of this kind, at all events in the last few years, used to be a complete loss of voice. The diagnosis that this was once more a nervous complaint had been established long since; but the various methods of treatment which are usual, including hydrotherapy and the local application of electricity, had produced no result. It was in such circumstances as these that the child had developed into a mature young woman of very independent judgement, who had grown accustomed to laugh at the efforts of doctors, and in the end to renounce their help entirely. Moreover, she had always been against calling in medical advice, though she had no personal objection to her family doctor. Every proposal to consult a new physician aroused her resistance, and it was only her father's authority which induced her to come to me at all.

I first saw her when she was sixteen, in the early summer. She was suffering from a cough and from hoarseness, and even at that time I proposed giving her psychological treatment. My proposal was not adopted, since the attack in question, like the others, passed off spontaneously, though it had lasted unusually long. During the next winter she came and stayed in Vienna with her uncle and his daughters after the death of the aunt of whom she had been so fond. There she fell ill of a feverish disorder which was diagnosed at the time as appendicitis. In the following autumn, since her father's health seemed to justify the step, the family left the health-resort of B—— for good and all. They first moved to the town where her father's factory was situated, and then, scarcely a year later, settled in Vienna.

Dora was by that time in the first bloom of youth—a girl of intelligent and engaging looks. But she was a source of heavy trials for her parents. Low spirits and an alteration in her character had now become the main features of her illness. She was clearly satisfied neither with herself nor with her family; her attitude towards her father was unfriendly, and she was on very bad terms with her mother, who was bent upon drawing her into taking a share in the work of the house. She tried to avoid social intercourse, and employed herself—so far as she was allowed to by the fatigue and lack of concentration of which she complained— with attending lectures for women and with carrying on more or less serious studies. One day her parents were thrown into a state of great alarm by finding on the girl's writing-desk, or inside it, a letter in which she took leave of them because, as she said, she could no longer endure her life. Her father, indeed, being a man of some perspicacity, guessed that the girl had no serious suicidal intentions. But he was none the less very much shaken; and when one day, after a slight passage of words between him and his daughter, she had a first attack of loss of consciousness—an event which was subsequently covered by an amnesia— it was determined, in spite of her reluctance, that she should come to me for treatment.

No doubt this case history, as I have so far outlined it, does not upon the whole seem worth recording. It is merely a case of '*petite hystérie*' with the commonest of all somatic and mental symptoms: dyspnoea, *tussis nervosa*, aphonia, and possibly migraines, together with depression, hysterical unsociability, and a *taedium vitae* which was probably not entirely genuine. More interesting cases of hysteria have no doubt been published, and they have very often been more carefully described; for nothing will be found in the following pages on the subject of stigmata of cutaneous sensibility, limitation of the visual field, or similar matters. I may venture to remark, however, that all such collections of the strange and wonderful phenomena of hysteria have but slightly advanced our knowledge of a disease which still remains as great a puzzle as ever. What is wanted is precisely an elucidation of the *commonest* cases and of their most frequent and typical symptoms. I should have been very well satisfied if the circumstances had allowed me to give a complete elucidation of this case of *petite hystérie*. And my experiences with other patients leave me in no doubt that my analytic method would have enabled me to do so.

* * *

In Dora's case, thanks to her father's shrewdness which I have remarked upon more than once already, there was no need for me to look about for the points of contact between the circumstances of the patient's life and her illness, at all events in its most recent form. Her father told me that he and his family while they were at B—— had formed an intimate friendship with a married couple who had been settled there for several years. Frau K. had nursed him during his long illness, and had in that way, he said, earned a title to his undying gratitude. Herr K. had always been most kind to Dora. He had gone on walks with her when he was there, and had made her small presents; but no one had thought any harm of that. Dora had taken the greatest care of the K.'s two little children, and been almost a mother to them. When Dora and her father had come to see me two years before in the summer, they had been just on their way to stop with Herr and Frau K., who were spending the summer on one of our lakes in the Alps. Dora was to have spent several weeks at the K.'s, while her father had intended to return home after a few days. During that time Herr K. had been staying there as well. As her father was preparing for his departure the girl had suddenly declared with the greatest determination that she was going with him, and she had in fact put her decision into effect. It was not until some days later that she had thrown any light upon her strange behaviour. She had then told her mother—intending that what she said should be passed on to her father—that Herr K. had had the audacity to make her a proposal while they were on a walk after a trip upon the lake. Herr K. had been called to account by her father and uncle on the next occasion of their meeting, but he had denied in the most emphatic terms having on his side made any advances which could have been open to such a construction. He had then proceeded to throw suspicion upon the girl, saying that he had heard from Frau K. that she took no interest in anything but sexual matters, and that she used to read Mantegazza's *Physiology of Love* and books of that sort in their house on the lake. It was most likely, he had added, that she had been over-excited by such reading and had merely 'fancied' the whole scene she had described.

'I have no doubt', continued her father, 'that this incident is responsible for Dora's depression and irritability and suicidal ideas. She keeps pressing me to break off relations with Herr K. and more particularly with Frau K., whom she used positively to worship formerly. But that I cannot do. For, to begin with, I myself believe that Dora's tale of the man's immoral suggestions is a phantasy that has forced its way into her mind; and besides, I am bound to Frau K. by ties of honourable friendship and I do not wish to cause her pain. The poor woman is most unhappy with her husband, of whom, by the by, I have no very high opinion. She herself has suffered a great deal with her nerves, and I am her only support. With my state of health I need scarcely assure you that there is nothing wrong in our relations. We are just two poor wretches who give one another what comfort we can by an exchange of friendly sympathy. You know already that I get nothing out of my own wife. But Dora, who inherits my obstinacy, cannot be moved from her hatred of the K.'s. She had her last attack after a conversation in which she had again pressed me to break with them. Please try and bring her to reason.'

Her father's words did not always quite tally with this pronouncement; for on other occasions he tried to put the chief blame for Dora's impossible behaviour on her mother—whose peculiarities made the house unbearable for every one. But I had resolved from the first to suspend my judgement of the true state of affairs till I had heard the other side as well.

The experience with Herr K.—his making love to her and the insult to her honour which was involved—seems to provide in Dora's case the psychical trauma which Breuer and I declared long ago to be the indispensable prerequisite for the production of a hysterical disorder. But this new case also presents all the difficulties which have since led me to go beyond that theory, besides an additional difficulty of a special kind. For, as so often happens in histories of cases of hysteria, the trauma that we know of as having occurred in the patient's past life is insufficient to explain or to determine the *particular character* of the symptoms; we should understand just as much or just as little of the whole business if the result of the trauma had been symptoms quite other than *tussis nervosa*, aphonia, depression, and *taedium vitae*. But there is the further consideration that some of these symptoms (the cough and the loss of voice) had been produced by the patient years before the time of the trauma, and that their earliest appearances belong to her childhood, since they occurred in her eighth year. If, therefore, the trauma theory is not to be abandoned, we must go back to her childhood and look about there for any influences or impressions which might have had an effect analogous to that of a trauma. Moreover, it deserves to be remarked that in the investigation even of cases in which the first symptoms had not already set in in childhood I have been driven to trace back the patients' life history to their earliest years.

When the first difficulties of the treatment had been overcome, Dora told me of an earlier episode with Herr K., which was even better calculated to act as a sexual trauma. She was fourteen years old at the time. Herr K. had made an arrangement with her and his wife that they should meet him one afternoon at his place of business in the principal square of B—— so as to have a view of a church festival. He persuaded his wife, however, to stay at home, and sent away his clerks, so that he was alone when the girl arrived. When the time for the procession approached, he asked the girl to wait for him at the door which opened on to the staircase leading to the upper story, while he pulled down the outside shutters. He then came back, and, instead of going out by the open door, suddenly clasped the girl to him and pressed a kiss upon her lips. This was surely just the situation to call up a distinct feeling of sexual excitement in a girl of fourteen who had never before been approached. But Dora had at that moment a violent feeling of disgust, tore herself free from the man, and hurried past him to the staircase and from there to the street door. She nevertheless continued to meet Herr K. Neither of them ever mentioned the little scene; and according to her account Dora kept it a secret till her confession during the treatment. For some time afterwards, however, she avoided being alone with Herr K. The K.'s had just made plans for an expedition which was to last for some days and on which Dora was to have accompanied them. After the scene of the kiss she refused to join the party, without giving any reason.

In this scene—second in order of mention, but first in order of time—the behaviour of this child of fourteen was already entirely and completely hysterical. I should without question consider a person hysterical in whom an occasion for sexual excitement elicited feelings that were preponderantly or exclusively unpleasurable; and I should do so whether or no the person were capable of producing somatic symptoms. The elucidation of the mechanism of this *reversal of affect* is one of the most important and at the same time one of the most difficult problems in the psychology of the neuroses. In my own judgement I am still some way from having achieved this end; and I may add that within the limits of the present paper I shall be able to bring forward only a part of such knowledge on the subject as I do possess.

In order to particularize Dora's case it is not enough merely to draw attention to the reversal of affect; there has also been a *displacement* of sensation. Instead of the genital sensation which would certainly have been felt by a healthy girl in such circumstances, Dora was overcome by the unpleasurable feeling which is proper to the tract of mucous membrane at the entrance to the alimentary canal—that is by disgust. The stimulation of her lips by the kiss was no doubt of importance in localizing the feeling at that particular place; but I think I can also recognize another factor in operation.[2]

The disgust which Dora felt on that occasion did not become a permanent symptom, and even at the time of the treatment it was only, as it were, potentially present. She was a poor eater and confessed to some disinclination for food. On the other hand, the scene had left another consequence behind it in the shape of a sensory hallucination which

2. The causes of Dora's disgust at the kiss were certainly not adventitious, for in that case she could not have failed to remember and mention them. I happen to know Herr K., for he was the same person who had visited me with the patient's father, and he was still quite young and of prepossessing appearance.

occurred from time to time and even made its appearance while she was telling me her story. She declared that she could still feel upon the upper part of her body the pressure of Herr K.'s embrace. In accordance with certain rules of symptom-formation which I have come to know, and at the same time taking into account certain other of the patient's peculiarities, which were otherwise inexplicable,—such as her unwillingness to walk past any man whom she saw engaged in eager or affectionate conversation with a lady,—I have formed in my own mind the following reconstruction of the scene. I believe that during the man's passionate embrace she felt not merely his kiss upon her lips but also the pressure of his erect member against her body. This perception was revolting to her; it was dismissed from her memory, repressed, and replaced by the innocent sensation of pressure upon her thorax, which in turn derived an excessive intensity from its repressed source. Once more, therefore, we find a displacement from the lower part of the body to the upper.[3] On the other hand, the compulsive piece of behaviour which I have mentioned was formed as though it were derived from the undistorted recollection of the scene: she did not like walking past any man who she thought was in a state of sexual excitement, because she wanted to avoid seeing for a second time the somatic sign which accompanies it.

It is worth remarking that we have here three symptoms—the disgust, the sensation of pressure on the upper part of the body, and the avoidance of men engaged in affectionate conversation—all of them derived from a single experience, and that it is only by taking into account the interrelation of these three phenomena that we can understand the way in which the formation of the symptoms came about. The disgust is the symptom of repression in the erotogenic oral zone, which, as we shall hear, had been over-indulged in Dora's infancy by the habit of sensual sucking. The pressure of the erect member probably led to an analogous change in the corresponding female organ, the clitoris; and the excitation of this second erotogenic zone was referred by a process of displacement to the simultaneous pressure against the thorax and became fixed there. Her avoidance of men who might possibly be in a state of sexual excitement follows the mechanism of a phobia, its purpose being to safeguard her against any revival of the repressed perception.

In order to show that such a supplement to the story was possible, I questioned the patient very cautiously as to whether she knew anything of the physical signs of excitement in a man's body. Her answer, as touching the present, was 'Yes', but, as touching the time of the episode,

3. The occurrence of displacements of this kind has not been assumed for the purpose of this single explanation; the assumption has proved indispensable for the explanation of a large class of symptoms. Since treating Dora I have come across another instance of an embrace (this time without a kiss) causing a fright. It was a case of a young woman who had previously been devotedly fond of the man she was engaged to, but had suddenly begun to feel a coldness towards him, accompanied by severe depression, and on that account came to me for treatment. There was no difficulty in tracing the fright back to an erection on the man's part, which she had perceived but had dismissed from her consciousness.

'I think not'. From the very beginning I took the greatest pains with this patient not to introduce her to any fresh facts in the region of sexual knowledge; and I did this, not from any conscientious motives, but because I was anxious to subject my assumptions to a rigorous test in this case. Accordingly, I did not call a thing by its name until her allusions to it had become so unambiguous that there seemed very slight risk in translating them into direct speech. Her answer was always prompt and frank: she knew about it already. But the question of *where* her knowledge came from was a riddle which her memories were unable to solve. She had forgotten the source of all her information on this subject.

If I may suppose that the scene of the kiss took place in this way, I can arrive at the following derivation for the feelings of disgust.[4] Such feelings seem originally to be a reaction to the smell (and afterwards also to the sight) of excrement. But the genitals can act as a reminder of the excretory functions; and this applies especially to the male member, for that organ performs the function of micturition as well as the sexual function. Indeed, the function of micturition is the earlier known of the two, and the *only* one known during the pre-sexual period. Thus it happens that disgust becomes one of the means of affective expression in the sphere of sexual life. The Early Christian Father's '*inter urinas et faeces nascimur*' clings to sexual life and cannot be detached from it in spite of every effort at idealization. I should like, however, expressly to emphasize my opinion that the problem is not solved by the mere pointing out of this path of association. The fact that this association *can* be called up does not show that it actually *will* be called up. And indeed in normal circumstances it will not be. A knowledge of the paths does not render less necessary a knowledge of the forces which travel along them.

I did not find it easy, however, to direct the patient's attention to her relations with Herr K. She declared that she had done with him. The uppermost layer of all her associations during the sessions, and everything of which she was easily conscious and of which she remembered having been conscious the day before, was always connected with her father. It was quite true that she could not forgive her father for continuing his relations with Herr K. and more particularly with Frau K. But she viewed those relations in a very different light from that in which her father wished them to appear. In her mind there was no doubt that what bound her father to this young and beautiful woman was a common love-affair. Nothing that could help to confirm this view had escaped her perception, which in this connection was pitilessly sharp; *here there were no gaps to be found in her memory*. Their acquaintance with the K.'s had begun before her father's serious illness; but it had not become intimate until the young woman had officially taken on the position of nurse during

4. Here, as in all similar cases, the reader must be prepared to be met not only by one but by several causes—by *overdetermination*.

that illness, while Dora's mother had kept away from the sick-room. During the first summer holidays after his recovery things had happened which must have opened every one's eyes to the true character of this 'friendship'. The two families had taken a suite of rooms in common at the hotel. One day Frau K. had announced that she could not keep the bedroom which she had up till then shared with one of her children. A few days later Dora's father had given up his bedroom, and they had both moved into new rooms—the end rooms, which were only separated by the passage, while the rooms they had given up had not offered any such security against interruption. Later on, whenever she had reproached her father about Frau K., he had been in the habit of saying that he could not understand her hostility and that, on the contrary, his children had every reason for being grateful to Frau K. Her mother, whom she had asked for an explanation of this mysterious remark, had told her that her father had been so unhappy at that time that he had made up his mind to go into the wood and kill himself, and that Frau K., suspecting as much, had gone after him and had persuaded him by her entreaties to preserve his life for the sake of his family. Of course, Dora went on, she herself did not believe this story; no doubt the two of them had been seen together in the wood, and her father had thereupon invented this fairy tale of his suicide so as to account for their rendezvous.

When they had returned to B——, her father had visited Frau K. every day at definite hours, while her husband was at his business. Everybody had talked about it and had questioned her about it pointedly. Herr K. himself had often complained bitterly to her mother, though he had spared her herself any allusions to the subject—which she seemed to attribute to delicacy of feeling on his part. When they had all gone for walks together, her father and Frau K. had always known how to manage things so as to be alone with each other. There could be no doubt that she had taken money from him, for she spent more than she could possibly have afforded out of her own purse or her husband's. Dora added that her father had begun to make handsome presents to Frau K., and in order to make these less conspicuous had at the same time become especially liberal towards her mother and herself. And while previously Frau K. had been an invalid and had even been obliged to spend months in a sanatorium for nervous disorders because she had been unable to walk, she had now become a healthy and lively woman.

Even after they had left B—— for the manufacturing town, these relations, already of many years' standing, had been continued. From time to time her father used to declare that he could not endure the rawness of the climate, and that he must do something for himself; he would begin to cough and complain, until suddenly he would start off to B——, and from there write the most cheerful letters home. All these illnesses had only been pretexts for seeing his friend again. Then one day it had been decided that they were to move to Vienna and Dora began to suspect a hidden connection. And sure enough, they had scarcely been three weeks in Vienna when she heard that the K.'s had moved there as well. They were in Vienna, so she told me, at that very moment, and she frequently met her father with Frau K. in the street. She also met Herr K. very often, and he always used to turn round and look after her; and once when he had met her out by herself he had followed her for a long way, so as to make sure where she was going and whether she might not have a rendezvous.

On one occasion during the course of the treatment her father again felt worse, and went off to B—— for several weeks; and the sharp-sighted Dora had soon unearthed the fact that Frau K. had started off to the same place on a visit to her relatives there. It was at this time that Dora's criticisms of her father were the most frequent: he was insincere, he had a strain of falseness in his character, he only thought of his own enjoyment, and he had a gift for seeing things in the light which suited him best.

I could not in general dispute Dora's characterization of her father; and there was one particular respect in which it was easy to see that her reproaches were justified. When she was feeling embittered she used to be overcome by the idea that she had been handed over to Herr K. as the price of his tolerating the relations between her father and his wife; and her rage at her father's making such a use of her was visible behind her affection for him. At other times she was quite well aware that she had been guilty of exaggeration in talking like this. The two men had of course never made a formal agreement in which she was treated as an object for barter; her father in particular would have been horrified at any such suggestion. But he was one of those men who know how to evade a dilemma by falsifying their judgement upon one of the conflicting alternatives. If it had been pointed out to him that there might be danger for a growing girl in the constant and unsupervised companionship of a man who had no satisfaction from his own wife, he would have been certain to answer that he could rely upon his daughter, that a man like K. could never be dangerous to her, and that his friend was himself incapable of such intentions, or that Dora was still a child and was treated as a child by K. But as a matter of fact things were in a position in which each of the two men avoided drawing any conclusions from the other's behaviour which would have been awkward for his own plans. It was possible for Herr K. to send Dora flowers every day for a whole year while he was in the neighbourhood, to take every opportunity of giving her valuable presents, and to spend all his spare time in her company, without her parents noticing anything in his behaviour that was characteristic of love-making.

When a patient brings forward a sound and incontestable train of argument during psycho-analytic treatment, the physician is liable to feel a moment's embarrassment, and the patient may take advantage of it by asking: 'This is all perfectly correct and true, isn't it? What do you want to change in now that I've told it you?' But it soon becomes evident that the patient is using thoughts of this kind, which the analysis cannot attack, for the purpose of cloaking others which are anxious to escape from criticism and from consciousness. A string of reproaches against other people leads one to suspect the existence of a string of self-reproaches with the same content. All that need be done is to turn back each particular reproach on to the speaker himself. There is something undeniably automatic about this method of defending oneself against a self-reproach by making the same reproach against some one else. A model of it is to be found in the *tu quoque* arguments of children; if one of them is accused of being a liar, he will reply without an instant's hesitation: 'You're another.' A grown-up person who wanted to throw back abuse would look for some really exposed spot in his antagonist and would not lay the chief stress upon the same content being repeated. In paranoia the projection of a reproach on to another person without any alteration in its content and therefore without any consideration for reality becomes manifest as the process of forming delusions.

Dora's reproaches against her father had a 'lining' or 'backing' of self-reproaches of this kind with a corresponding content in every case, as I shall show in detail. She was right in thinking that her father did not wish to look too closely into Herr K.'s behaviour to his daughter, for fear of being disturbed in his own love-affair with Frau K. But Dora herself had done precisely the same thing. She had made herself an accomplice in the affair, and had dismissed from her mind every sign which tended to show its true character. It was not until after her adventure by the lake that her eyes were opened and that she began to apply such a severe standard to her father. During all the previous years she had given every possible assistance to her father's relations with Frau K. She would never go to see her if she thought her father was there; but, knowing that in that case the children would have been sent out, she would turn her steps in a direction where she would be sure to meet them, and would go for a walk with them. There had been some one in the house who had been anxious at an early stage to open her eyes to the nature of her father's relations with Frau K., and to induce her to take sides against her. This was her last governess, an unmarried woman, no longer young, who was well-read and of advanced views.[5] The teacher and her pupil were for a while upon excellent terms, until suddenly Dora became hostile to her and insisted on her dismissal. So long as the governess had any influence she used it for stirring up feeling against Frau K. She explained to Dora's mother that it was incompatible with her dignity to tolerate such an intimacy between her husband and

---

5. This governess used to read every sort of book on sexual life and similar subjects, and talked to the girl about them, at the same time asking her quite frankly not to mention their conversations to her parents, as one could never tell what line they might take about them. For some time I looked upon this woman as the source of all Dora's secret knowledge, and perhaps I was not entirely wrong in this.

another woman; and she drew Dora's attention to all the obvious features of their relations. But her efforts were vain. Dora remained devoted to Frau K. and would hear of nothing that might make her think ill of her relations with her father. On the other hand she very easily fathomed the motives by which her governess was actuated. She might be blind in one direction, but she was sharpsighted enough in the other. She saw that the governess was in love with her father. When he was there, she seemed to be quite another person: at such times she could be amusing and obliging. While the family were living in the manufacturing town and Frau K. was not on the horizon, her hostility was directed against Dora's mother, who was then her more immediate rival. Up to this point Dora bore her no ill-will. She did not become angry until she observed that she herself was a subject of complete indifference to the governess, whose pretended affection for her was really meant for her father. While her father was away from the manufacturing town the governess had no time to spare for her, would not go for walks with her, and took no interest in her studies. No sooner had her father returned from B—— than she was once more ready with every sort of service and assistance. Thereupon Dora dropped her.

The poor woman had thrown a most unwelcome light on a part of Dora's own behaviour. What the governess had from time to time been to Dora, Dora had been to Herr K.'s children. She had been a mother to them, she had taught them, she had gone for walks with them, she had offered them a complete substitute for the slight interest which their own mother showed in them. Herr K. and his wife had often talked of getting a divorce; but it never took place, because Herr K., who was an affectionate father, would not give up either of the two children. A common interest in the children had from the first been a bond between Herr K. and Dora. Her preoccupation with his children was evidently a cloak for something else that Dora was anxious to hide from herself and from other people.

The same inference was to be drawn both from her behaviour towards the children, regarded in the light of the governess's behaviour towards herself, and from her silent acquiescence in her father's relations with Frau K.—namely, that she had all these years been in love with Herr K. When I informed her of this conclusion she did not assent to it. It is true that she at once told me that other people besides (one of her cousins, for instance—a girl who had stopped with them for some time at B——) had said to her: 'Why you're simply wild about that man!' But she herself could not be got to recollect any feelings of the kind. Later on, when the quantity of material that had come up had made it difficult for her to persist in her denial, she admitted that she might have been in love with Herr K. at B——, but declared that since the scene by the lake it had all been over. In any case it was quite certain that the reproaches which she made against her father of having been deaf to the most imperative calls of duty and of having seen things in the light which was most convenient from the point of view of his own passions—these reproaches recoiled on her own head.[6]

Her other reproach against her father was that his ill-health was only a pretext and that he exploited it for his own purposes. This reproach, too, concealed a whole section of her own secret history. One day she complained of a professedly new symptom, which consisted of piercing gastric pains. 'Whom are you copying now?' I asked her, and found I had hit the mark. The day before she had visited her cousins, the daughters of the aunt who had died. The younger one had become engaged, and this had given occasion to the elder one for falling ill with gastric pains, and she was to be sent off to Semmering.[7] Dora thought it was all just envy on the part of the elder sister; she always got ill when she wanted something, and what she wanted now was to be away from home so as not to have to look on at her sister's happiness. But Dora's own gastric pains proclaimed the fact that she identified herself with her cousin, who, according to her, was a malingerer. Her grounds for this identification were either that she too envied the luckier girl her love, or that she saw her own story reflected in that of the elder sister, who had recently had a love-affair which had ended unhappily. But she had also learned from observing Frau K. what useful things illnesses could become. Herr K. spent part of the year in travelling. Whenever he came back, he used to find his wife in bad health, although, as Dora knew, she had been quite well only the day before. Dora realized that the presence of the husband had the effect of making his wife ill, and that she was glad to be ill so as to be able to escape the conjugal duties which she so much detested. At this point in the discussion Dora suddenly brought in an allusion to her own alternations between good and bad health during the first years of her girlhood at B——; and I was thus driven to suspect that her states of health were to be regarded as depending upon something else, in the same way as Frau K.'s. (It is a rule of psycho-analytic technique that an internal connection which is still undisclosed will announce its presence by means of a contiguity—a temporal proximity—of associations; just as in writing, if 'a' and 'b' are put side by side, it means that the syllable 'ab' is to be formed out of them.) Dora had had a very large number of attacks of coughing accompanied by loss of voice. Could it be that the presence or absence of the man she loved had had an influence upon the appearance and disappearance of the symptoms of her illness? If this were so, it must be possible to discover some coincidence or other which would betray the fact. I asked her what the average length of these attacks had been.

6. The question then arises: If Dora loved Herr K., what was the reason for her refusing him in the scene by the lake? Or at any rate, why did her refusal take such a brutal form, as though she were embittered against him? And how could a girl who was in love feel insulted by a proposal which was made in a manner neither tactless nor offensive? 7. [A fashionable health resort in the mountains, about fifty miles south of Vienna.]

'From three to six weeks, perhaps.' How long had Herr K.'s absences lasted? 'Three to six weeks, too', she was obliged to admit. Her illness was therefore a demonstration of her love for K just as his wife's was a demonstration of her *dislike*. It was only necessary to suppose that her behaviour had been the opposite of Frau K.'s and that she had been ill when he was absent and well when he had come back. And this really seemed to have been so, at least during the first period of the attacks. Later on it no doubt became necessary to obscure the coincidence between her attacks of illness and the absence of the man she secretly loved, lest its regularity should betray her secret. The length of the attacks would then remain as a trace of their original significance.

I remembered that long before, while I was working at Charcot's clinic, I had seen and heard how in cases of hysterical mutism writing operated vicariously in the place of speech Such patients were able to write more fluently, quicker, and better than others did or than they themselves had done previously. The same thing had happened with Dora. In the first days of her attacks of aphonia 'writing had always come specially easy to her'. No psychological elucidation was really required for this peculiarity, which was the expression of a physiological substitutive function enforced by necessity, it was noticeable, however, that such an elucidation was easily to be found. Herr K. used to write to her at length while he was travelling and to send her picture post-cards. It used to happen that she alone was informed as to the date of his return, and that his arrival took his wife by surprise. Moreover, that a person will correspond with an absent friend whom he cannot talk to is scarcely less obvious than that if he has lost his voice he will try to make himself understood in writing. Dora's aphonia, then, allowed of the following symbolic interpretation. When the man she loved was away she gave up speaking; speech had lost its value since she could not speak to *him*. On the other hand, writing gained in importance, as being the only means of communication with him in his absence.

Am I now going on to assert that in every instance in which there are periodical attacks of aphonia we are to diagnose the existence of a loved person who is at times away from the patient? Nothing could be further from my intention. The determination of Dora's symptoms is far too specific for it to be possible to expect a frequent recurrence of the same accidental aetiology. But, if so, what is the value of our elucidation of the aphonia in the present case? Have we not merely allowed ourselves to become the victims of a *jeu d'esprit*? I think not. In this connection we must recall the question which has so often been raised, whether the symptoms of hysteria are of psychical or of somatic origin, or whether, if the former is granted, they are necessarily *all* of them psychically determined. Like so many other questions to which we find investigators returning again and again without success, this question is not adequately framed. The alternatives stated in it do not cover the real essence of the matter. As far as I can see, every hysterical symptom involves the participation of *both* sides. It cannot occur without the presence of a certain degree of *somatic compliance* offered by some normal or pathological process in or connected with one of the bodily organs. And it cannot occur more than once—and the capacity for repeating itself is one of the characteristics of a hysterical symptom—unless it has a psychical significance, a *meaning*. The hysterical symptom does not carry this meaning with it, but the meaning is lent to it, soldered to it, as it were; and in every instance the meaning can be a different one, according to the nature of the suppressed thoughts which are struggling for expression. However, there are a number of factors at work which tend to make less arbitrary the relations between the unconscious thoughts and the somatic processes that are at their disposal as a means of expression, and which tend to make those relations approximate to a few typical forms. For therapeutic purposes the most important determinants are those given by the fortuitous psychical material; the clearing-up of the symptoms is achieved by looking for their psychical significance. When everything that can be got rid of by psycho-analysis has been cleared away, we are in a position to form all kinds of conjectures, which probably meet the facts, as regards the somatic basis of the symptoms—a basis which is as a rule constitutional and organic. Thus in Dora's case we shall not content ourselves with a psycho-analytic interpretation of her attacks of coughing and aphonia; but we shall also indicate the organic factor which was the source of the 'somatic compliance' that enabled her to express her love for a man who was periodically absent. And if the connection between the symptomatic expression and the unconscious mental content should strike us as being in this case a clever *tour de force*, we shall be relieved to hear that it succeeds in creating the same impression in every other case and in every other instance.

I am prepared to be told at this point that there is no very great advantage in having been taught by psycho-analysis that the clue to the problem of hysteria is to be found not in 'a peculiar instability of the molecules of the nerves' or in a liability to 'hypnoid states'—but in a 'somatic compliance'. But in reply to the objection I may remark that this new view has not only to some extent pushed the problem further back, but has also to some extent diminished it. We have no longer to deal with the *whole* problem, but only with the portion of it involving that particular characteristic of hysteria *which differentiates it* from other psychoneuroses. The mental events in all psychoneuroses proceed for a considerable distance along the same lines before any question arises of the 'somatic compliance' which may afford the unconscious mental processes a physical outlet. When this factor is not forthcoming, something other than a hysterical symptom will arise out of the total situation;

yet it will be something of an allied nature, a phobia, perhaps, or an obsession—in short, a psychical symptom.

I now return to the reproach of malingering which Dora brought against her father. It soon became evident that this reproach corresponded to self-reproaches not only concerning her earlier states of ill-health but also concerning the present time. At such points the physician is usually faced by the task of guessing and filling in what the analysis offers him in the shape only of hints and allusions. I was obliged to point out to the patient that her present ill-health was just as much actuated by motives and was just as tendentious as had been Frau K.'s illness, which she had understood so well. There could be no doubt, I said, that she had an aim in view which she hoped to gain by her illness. That aim could be none other than to detach her father from Frau K. She had been unable to achieve this by prayers or arguments; perhaps she hoped to succeed by frightening her father (there was her farewell letter), or by awakening his pity (there were her fainting-fits), or if all this was in vain, at least she would be taking her revenge on him. She knew very well, I went on, how much he was attached to her, and that tears used to come into his eyes whenever he was asked after his daughter's health. I felt quite convinced that she would recover at once if only her father were to tell her that he had sacrificed Frau K. for the sake of her health. But, I added, I hoped he would not let himself be persuaded to do this, for then she would have learned what a powerful weapon she had in her hands, and she would certainly not fail on every future occasion to make use once more of her liability to ill-health. Yet if her father refused to give way to her, I was quite sure she would not let herself be deprived of her illness so easily.

* * *

Motives that support the patient in being ill are probably to be found in all fully developed cases. But there are some in which the motives are purely internal—such as desire for self-punishment, that is, penitence and remorse. It will be found much easier to solve the therapeutic problem in such cases than in those in which the illness is related to the attainment of some external aim. In Dora's case that aim was clearly to touch her father's heart and to detach him from Frau K.

None of her father's actions seemed to have embittered her so much as his readiness to consider the scene by the lake as a product of her imagination. She was almost beside herself at the idea of its being supposed that she had merely fancied something on that occasion. For a long time I was in perplexity as to what the self-reproach could be which lay behind her passionate repudiation of this explanation of the episode. It was justifiable to suspect that there was something concealed, for a reproach which misses the mark gives no lasting offence. On the other hand, I came to the conclusion that Dora's story must correspond to the facts in every respect. No sooner had she grasped Herr K.'s intention than, without letting him finish what he had to say, she had given him a slap in the face and hurried away. Her behaviour must have seemed as incomprehensible to the man after she had left him as to us, for he must long before have gathered from innumerable small signs that he was secure of the girl's affections. In our discussion of Dora's second dream we shall come upon the solution of this riddle as well as upon the self-reproach which we have hitherto failed to discover.

As she kept on repeating her complaints against her father with a wearisome monotony, and as at the same time her cough continued, I was led to think that this symptom might have some meaning in connection with her father. And apart from this, the explanation of the symptom which I had hitherto obtained was far from fulfilling the requirements which I am accustomed to make of such explanations. According to a rule which I had found confirmed over and over again by experience, though I had not yet ventured to erect it into a general principle, a symptom signifies the representation—the realization—of a phantasy with a sexual content, that is to say, it signifies a sexual situation. It would be better to say that at least *one* of the meanings of a symptom is the representation of a sexual phantasy, but that no such limitation is imposed upon the content of its other meanings. Any one who takes up psycho-analytic work will quickly discover that a symptom has more than one meaning and serves to represent several unconscious mental processes simultaneously. And I should like to add that in my estimation a single unconscious mental process or phantasy will scarcely ever suffice for the production of a symptom.

An opportunity very soon occurred for interpreting Dora's nervous cough in this way by means of an imagined sexual situation. She had once again been insisting that Frau K. only loved her father because he was *'ein vermögender Mann'* ['a man of means']. Certain details of the way in which she expressed herself (which I pass over here, like most other purely technical parts of the analysis) led me to see that behind this phrase its opposite lay concealed, namely, that her father was *'ein unvermögender Mann'* ['a man without means']. This could only be meant in a sexual sense—that her father, as a man, was without means, was impotent.[8] Dora confirmed this interpretation from her conscious knowledge; whereupon I pointed out the contradiction she was involved in if on the one hand she continued to insist that her father's relation with Frau K. was a common love-affair, and on the other hand maintained that her father was impotent, or in other words incapable of carrying on an affair of such a kind. Her answer showed that she had no need to admit the contradiction. She knew very well, she said, that there was more than one way of obtaining sexual gratification. (The

8. ['*Unvermögend*' means literally 'unable,' and is commonly used in the sense of 'not rich' and 'impotent'.]

source of this piece of knowledge, however, was once more untraceable.)
I questioned her further, whether she referred to the use of organs other
than the genitals for the purpose of sexual intercourse, and she replied
in the affirmative. I could then go on to say that in that case she must
be thinking of precisely those parts of the body which in her case were
in a state of irritation,—the throat and the oral cavity. To be sure, she
would not hear of going so far as this in recognizing her own thoughts;
and indeed, if the occurrence of the symptom was to be made possible
at all, it was essential that she should not be completely clear on the
subject. But the conclusion was inevitable that with her spasmodic
cough, which, as is usual, was referred for its exciting stimulus to a
tickling in her throat, she pictured to herself a scene of sexual gratification
per os between the two people whose love-affair occupied her mind so
incessantly. A very short time after she had tacitly accepted this explanation her cough vanished—which fitted in very well with my view; but
I do not wish to lay too much stress upon this development, since her
cough had so often before disappeared spontaneously.

This short piece of the analysis may perhaps have excited in the
medical reader—apart from the scepticism to which he is entitled—
feelings of astonishment and horror; and I am prepared at this point to
look into these two reactions so as to discover whether they are justifiable.
The astonishment is probably caused by my daring to talk about such
delicate and unpleasant subjects to a young girl—or, for that matter, to
any woman who is sexually active. The horror is aroused, no doubt, by
the possibility that an inexperienced girl could know about practices of
such a kind and could occupy her imagination with them. I would
advise recourse to moderation and reasonableness upon both points.
There is no cause for indignation either in the one case or in the other.
It is possible for a man to talk to girls and women upon sexual matters
of every kind without doing them harm and without bringing suspicion
upon himself, so long as, in the first place, he adopts a particular way
of doing it, and, in the second place, can make them feel convinced
that it is unavoidable. A gynaecologist, after all, under the same conditions, does not hesitate to make them submit to uncovering every
possible part of their body. The best way of speaking about such things
is to be dry and direct; and that is at the same time the method furthest
removed from the prurience with which the same subjects are handled
in 'society', and to which girls and women alike are so thoroughly
accustomed. I call bodily organs and processes by their technical names,
and I tell these to the patient if they—the names, I mean—happen to
be unknown to her. *J'appelle un chat un chat.* I have certainly heard
of some people—doctors and laymen—who are scandalized by a therapeutic method in which conversations of this sort occur, and who appear
to envy either me or my patients the titillation which, according to their

notions, such a method must afford. But I am too well acquainted with the respectability of these gentry to excite myself over them. I shall avoid the temptation of writing a satire upon them. But there is one thing that I will mention: often, after I have for some time treated a patient who had not at first found it easy to be open about sexual matters, I have had the satisfaction of hearing her exclaim: 'Why, after all, your treatment is far more respectable than Mr. X.'s conversation!'

No one can undertake the treatment of a case of hysteria until he is convinced of the impossibility of avoiding the mention of sexual subjects, or unless he is prepared to allow himself to be convinced by experience. The right attitude is: '*pour faire une omelette il faut casser des œufs.*' The patients themselves are easy to convince; and there are only too many opportunities of doing so in the course of the treatment. There is no necessity for feeling any compunction at discussing the facts of normal or abnormal sexual life with them. With the exercise of a little caution all that is done is to translate into conscious ideas what was already known in the unconscious; and, after all, the whole effectiveness of the treatment is based upon our knowledge that the affect attached to an unconscious idea operates more strongly and, since it cannot be inhibited, more injuriously than the affect attached to a conscious one. There is never any danger of corrupting an inexperienced girl. For where there is no knowledge of sexual processes even in the unconscious, no hysterical symptom will arise; and where hysteria is found there can no longer be any question of 'innocence of mind' in the sense in which parents and educators use the phrase. With children of ten, of twelve, or of fourteen, with boys and girls alike, I have satisfied myself that the truth of this statement can invariably be relied upon.

As regards the second kind of emotional reaction, which is not directed against me this time, but against my patient—supposing that my view of her is correct—and which regards the perverse nature of her phantasies as horrible, I should like to say emphatically that a medical man has no business to indulge in such passionate condemnation. I may also remark in passing that it seems to me superfluous for a physician who is writing upon the aberrations of the sexual instincts to seize every opportunity of inserting into the test expressions of his personal repugnance at such revolting things. We are faced by a fact; and it is to be hoped that we shall grow accustomed to it, when we have put our own tastes on one side. We must learn to speak without indignation of what we call the sexual perversions—instances in which the sexual function has extended its limits in respect either to the part of the body concerned or to the sexual object chosen. The uncertainty in regard to the boundaries of what is to be called normal sexual life, when we take different races and different epochs into account, should in itself be enough to cool the zealot's ardour. We surely ought not to forget that the perversion which is the most repellent to us, the sensual love of a man for a man, was not only tolerated by a people so far our superiors in cultivation as were the Greeks, but was actually entrusted by them with important social functions. The sexual life of each one of us extends to a slight degree—now in this direction, now in that—beyond the narrow lines imposed as the standard of normality. The perversions are neither bestial nor degenerate in the emotional sense of the word. They are a development of germs all of which are contained in the undifferentiated sexual disposition of the child, and which, by being suppressed or by being diverted to higher, asexual aims—by being 'sublimated'—are destined to provide the energy for a great number of our cultural achievements. When, therefore, any one has *become* a gross and manifest pervert, it would be more correct to say that he has *remained* one, for he exhibits a certain stage of *inhibited development*. All psychoneurotics are persons with strongly marked perverse tendencies, which have been repressed in the course of their development and have become unconscious. Consequently their unconscious *phantasies* show precisely the same content as the documentarily recorded *actions* of perverts—even though they have not read Krafft-Ebing's *Psychopatha Sexualis*, to which simpleminded people attribute such a large share of the responsibility for the production of perverse tendencies. Psychoneuroses are, so to speak, the *negative* of perversions. In neurotics their sexual constitution, under which the effects of heredity are included, operates in combination with any accidental influences in their life which may disturb the development of normal sexuality. A stream of water which meets with an obstacle in the river-bed is dammed up and flows back into old channels which had formerly seemed fated to run dry. The motive forces leading to the formation of hysterical symptoms draw their strength not only from repressed *normal* sexuality but also from unconscious perverse activities.

The less repellent of the so-called sexual perversions are very widely diffused among the whole population, as every one knows except medical writers upon the subject. Or, I should rather say, they know it too; only they take care to forget it at the moment when they take up their pens to write about it. So it is not to be wondered at that this hysterical girl of nearly nineteen, who had heard of the occurrence of such a method of sexual intercourse (sucking at the male organ), should have developed an unconscious phantasy of this sort and should have given it expression by an irritation in her throat and by coughing. Nor would it have been very extraordinary if she had arrived at such a phantasy even without having had any enlightenment from external sources—an occurrence which I have quite certainly observed in other patients. For in her case a noteworthy fact afforded the necessary somatic prerequisite for this independent creation of a phantasy which would coincide with the practices of perverts. She remembered very well that in her childhood she had been a thumb-sucker. Her father, too, recollected breaking her of the habit after it had persisted into her fourth or fifth year. Dora herself had a clear picture of a scene from her early childhood in which she was sitting on the floor in a corner sucking her left thumb and at the same time tugging with her right hand at the lobe of her brother's ear as he sat quietly beside her. Here we have an instance of the complete form of self-gratification by sucking, as it has also been described to me by other patients, who had subsequently become anaesthetic and hysterical.

One of these patients gave me a piece of information which sheds a clear light on the origin of this curious habit. This young woman had never broken herself of the habit of sucking. She retained a memory of her childhood, dating back, according to her, to the first half of her second year, in which she saw herself sucking at her nurse's breast and at the same time pulling rhythmically at the lobe of her nurse's ear. No one will feel inclined to dispute, I think, that the mucous membrane of the lips and mouth is to be regarded as a primary 'erotogenic zone', since it preserves this earlier significance in the act of kissing, which is looked upon as normal. An intense activity of this erotogenic zone at an early age thus determines the subsequent presence of a somatic compliance on the part of the tract of mucous membrane which begins at the lips. Thus, at a time when the sexual object proper, that is, the male organ, has already become known, circumstances may arise which once more increase the excitation of the oral zone, whose erotogenic character has, as we have seen, been retained. It then needs very little creative power to substitute the sexual object of the moment (the penis) for the original object (the nipple) or for the finger which does duty for it, and to place the current sexual object in the situation in which gratification was originally obtained. So we see that this excessively repulsive and perverted phantasy of sucking at a penis has the most innocent origin. It is a new version of what may be described as a prehistoric impression of sucking at the mother's or nurse's breast—an impression which has usually been revived by contact with children who are being nursed. In most instances a cow's udder has aptly played the part of an image intermediate between a nipple and a penis.

* * *

Dora's incessant repetition of the same thoughts about her father's relations with Frau K. made it possible to derive still further important material from the analysis.

A train of thought such as this may be described as excessively intense, or better *reinforced*, or 'supervalent' ['*überwertig*'] in Wernicke's [1900, 140] sense. It shows its pathological character in spite of its apparently reasonable content, by the single peculiarity that no amount of conscious and voluntary effort of thought on the patient's part is able to dissipate or remove it. A normal train of thought, however intense it may be, can eventually be disposed of. Dora felt quite rightly that her thoughts about her father required to be judged in a special way. 'I can think of nothing else', she complained again and again. 'I know my brother says we children have no right to criticize this behaviour of Father's. He declares that we ought not to trouble ourselves about it, and ought even to be glad, perhaps, that he has found a woman he can love, since Mother understands him so little. I can quite see that, and I should like to think the same as my brother, but I can't. I can't forgive him for it.

Now what is one to do in the face of a supervalent thought like this, after one has heard what its conscious grounds are and listened to the ineffectual protests made against it? Reflection will suggest that *this excessively intense train of thought must owe its reinforcement to the unconscious*. It cannot be resolved by any effort of thought, either because it itself reaches with its root down into unconscious, repressed material, or because another unconscious thought lies concealed behind it. In the latter case, the concealed thought is usually the direct contrary of the supervalent one. Contrary thoughts are always closely connected with each other and are often paired off in such a way that *the one thought is excessively intensely conscious while its counterpart is repressed and unconscious*. This relation between the two thoughts is an effect of the process of repression. For repression is often achieved by means of an excessive reinforcement of the thought contrary to the one which is to be repressed. This process I call *reactive* reinforcement, and the thought which asserts itself with excessive intensity in consciousness and (in the same way as a prejudice) cannot be removed I call a *reactive thought*. The two thoughts then act towards each other much like the two needles of an astatic galvanometer. The reactive thought keeps the objectionable one under repression by means of a certain surplus of intensity; but for that reason it itself is 'damped' and proof against conscious efforts of thought. So that the way to deprive the excessively intense thought of its reinforcement is by bringing its repressed contrary into consciousness.

We must also be prepared to meet with instances in which the supervalence of a thought is due not to the presence of one only of these two causes but to a concurrence of both of them. Other complications, too, may arise, but they can easily be fitted into the general scheme.

Let us now apply our theory to the instance provided by Dora's case. We will begin with the first hypothesis, namely, that her preoccupation with her father's relations to Frau K., owed its obsessive character to the fact that its root was unknown to her and lay in the unconscious. It is not difficult to divine the nature of that root from her circumstances and her conduct. Her behaviour obviously went far beyond what would have been appropriate to filial concern. She felt and acted more like a jealous wife—in a way which would have been comprehensible in her mother. By her ultimatum to her father ('either her or me'), by the scenes she used to make, by the suicidal intentions she allowed to transpire,—by all this she was clearly putting herself in her mother's place. If we have rightly guessed the nature of the imaginary sexual situation which underlay her cough, in that phantasy she must have been putting herself in Frau K.'s place. She was therefore identifying herself both with the woman her father had once loved and with the woman he loved now. The inference is obvious that her affection for her father was a much stronger one than she knew or than she would have cared to admit: in fact, that she was in love with him.

I have learnt to look upon unconscious love relations like this (which are marked by their abnormal consequences)—between a father and a daughter, or between a mother and a son—as a revival of germs of feeling in infancy. * * * Distinct traces are probably to be found in most people of an early partiality of this kind—on the part of a daughter for her father, or on the part of a son for his mother; but it must be assumed to be more intense from the very first in the case of those children whose constitution marks them down for a neurosis, who develop prematurely and have a craving for love. At this point certain other influences, which need not be discussed here, come into play, and lead to a fixation of this rudimentary feeling of love or to a reinforcement of it; so that it turns into something (either while the child is still young or not until it has reached the age of puberty) which must be put on a par with a sexual inclination and which, like the latter, has the forces of the libido at its command. The external circumstances of our patient were by no means unfavourable to such an assumption. The nature of her disposition has always drawn her towards her father, and his numerous illnesses were bound to have increased her affection for him. In some of these illnesses he would allow no one but her to discharge the lighter duties of nursing. He had been so proud of the early growth of her intelligence that he had made her his confidante while she was still a child. It was really she and not her mother whom Frau K.'s appearance had driven out of more than one position.

When I told Dora that I could not avoid supposing that her affection for her father must at a very early moment have amounted to her being completely in love with him, she of course gave me her usual reply: 'I don't remember that.' But she immediately went on to tell me something analogous about a seven-year-old girl who was her cousin (on her mother's side) and in whom she often thought she saw a kind of reflection of her own childhood. This little girl had (not for the first time) been the witness of a heated dispute between her parents, and, when Dora happened to come in on a visit soon afterwards, whispered in her ear: 'You can't think how I hate that person!' (pointing to her mother), 'and when she's dead I shall marry Daddy.' I am in the habit of regarding associations such as this, which bring forward something that agrees with the content of an assertion of mine, as a confirmation from the unconscious of what I have said. No other kind of 'Yes' can be extracted from the unconscious; there is no such thing at all as an unconscious 'No'.[9]

For years on end she had given no expression to this passion for her father. On the contrary, she had for a long time been on the closest terms with the woman who had supplanted her with her father, and she had actually, as we know from her self-reproaches, facilitated this woman's relations with her father. Her own love for her father had therefore been recently revived; and, if so, the question arises to what end this had happened. Clearly as a reactive symptom, so as to suppress something else— something, that is, that still exercised power in the unconscious. Considering how things stood, I could not help supposing in the first instance that what was suppressed was her love of Herr K. I could not avoid the assumption that she was still in love with him, but that, for unknown reasons, since the scene by the lake her love had aroused in her violent feelings of opposition, and that the girl had brought forward and reinforced her old affection for her father in order to avoid any further necessity for paying conscious attention to the love which she had felt in the first years of her girlhood and which had now become distressing to her. In this way I gained an insight into a conflict which was well calculated to unhinge the girl's mind. On the one hand she was filled with regret at having rejected the man's proposal, and with longing for his company and all the little signs of his affection; while on the other hand these feelings of tenderness and longing were combated by powerful forces, amongst which her pride was one of the most obvious. Thus she had succeeded in persuading herself that she had done with Herr K.—that was the advantage she derived from this typical process of repression; and yet she was obliged to summon up her infantile affection for her father and to exaggerate it, in order to protect herself against the feelings of love which were constantly pressing forward into consciousness. The further fact that she was almost incessantly a prey to the most embittered jealousy seemed to admit of still another determination.

My expectations were by no means disappointed when this explanation

9. [*Footnote added* 1923:] There is another very remarkable and entirely trustworthy form of confirmation from the unconscious, which I had not recognized at the time this was written: namely, an explanation of the part of the patient of 'I didn't think that', or 'I didn't think of that'. This can be translated point-blank into: 'Yes, I was unconscious of that.' {Freud here deals rather casually with a tricky issue: in what way is it possible for anyone to disconfirm interpretations, or theoretical assertions, by a psychoanalyst? If Yes means Yes and No means Yes as well, if a theoretical assertion in psychoanalysis is proved correct by any sort of thought or response whatever, then the analyst is always right. And any theorist or clinician whose assertions cannot be falsified is propagating, as the philosopher Sir Karl Popper has been insisting for decades, not science but dogma. If only for the sake of the public reputation of psychoanalysis, whose assertions after all appear extravagant and far-fetched to common sense, Freud should have addressed this question more thoroughly, either here in the "Dora" case, or later. In fact Freud was aware, but perhaps insufficiently so, that there was a problem here. In one of his last papers, "Constructions in Analysis" (1937), he characterized the analyst's problem of proof with the English saying, "Heads I win, tails you lose." And he claimed—quite correctly—that this is not how the analyst proceeds. Yes *may* mean No, and so may No. In fact, psychoanalytic propositions *are* falsifiable. See Freud's paper on "Negation" of 1925 (below, pp. 666–69).}

of mine was met by Dora with a most emphatic negative. The 'No' uttered by a patient after a repressed thought has been presented to his conscious perception for the first time does no more than register the existence of a repression and its severity; it acts, as it were, as a gauge of the repression's strength. If this 'No', instead of being regarded as the expression of an impartial judgement (of which, indeed, the patient is incapable), is ignored, and if work is continued, the first evidence soon begins to appear that in such a case 'No' signifies the desired 'Yes'. Dora admitted that she found it impossible to be as angry with Herr K. as he had deserved. She told me that one day she had met Herr K. in the street while she was walking with a cousin of hers who did not know him. The other girl had exclaimed all at once: 'Why, Dora, what's wrong with you? You've gone as white as a sheet!' She herself had felt nothing of this change of colour; but I explained to her that the expression of emotion and the play of features obey the unconscious rather than the conscious, and are a means of betraying the former. Another time Dora came to me in the worst of tempers after having been uniformly cheerful for several days. She could give no explanation of this. She felt so contrary to-day, she said; it was her uncle's birthday, and she could not bring herself to congratulate him, she did not know why. My powers of interpretation were at a low ebb that day; I let her go on talking, and she suddenly recollected that it was Herr K.'s birthday too—a fact which I did not fail to use against her. And it was then no longer hard to explain why the handsome presents she had had on her own birthday a few days before had given her no pleasure. One gift was missing, and that was Herr K.'s, the gift which had plainly once been the most prized of all.

Nevertheless Dora persisted in denying my contention for some time longer, until, towards the end of the analysis, the conclusive proof of its correctness came to light.

I must now turn to consider a further complication to which I should certainly give no space if I were a man of letters engaged upon the creation of a mental state like this for a short story, instead of being a medical man engaged upon its dissection. The element to which I must now allude can only serve to obscure and efface the outlines of the fine poetic conflict which we have been able to ascribe to Dora. This element would rightly fall a sacrifice to the censorship of a writer, for he, after all, simplifies and abstracts when he appears in the character of a psychologist. But in the world of reality, which I am trying to depict here, a complication of motives, an accumulation and conjunction of mental activities—in a word, overdetermination—is the rule. For behind Dora's supervalent train of thought which was concerned with her father's relations with Frau K. there lay concealed a feeling of jealousy which had that lady as its *object*—a feeling, that is, which could only be based upon an affection on Dora's part for one of her own sex. It has long been known and often been pointed out that at the age of puberty boys and girls show clear signs, even in normal cases, of the existence of an affection for people of their own sex. A romantic and sentimental friendship with one of her school-friends, accompanied by vows, kisses, promises of eternal correspondence, and all the sensibility of jealousy, is the common precursor of a girl's first serious passion for a man. Thenceforward, in favourable circumstances, the homosexual current of feeling often runs completely dry. But if a girl is not happy in her love for a man, the current is often set flowing again by the libido in later years and is increased up to a greater or lesser degree of intensity. If this much can be established without difficulty of healthy persons, and if we take into account what has already been said about the fuller development in neurotics of the normal germs of perversion, we shall expect to find in these latter too a fairly strong homosexual predisposition. It must, indeed, be so; for I have never yet come through a single psycho-analysis of a man or woman without having to take into account a very considerable current of homosexuality. When, in a hysterical woman or girl, the sexual libido which is directed towards men has been energetically suppressed, it will regularly be found that the libido which is directed towards women has become vicariously reinforced and even to some extent conscious.

I shall not in this place go any further into this important subject, which is especially indispensable to an understanding of hysteria in men, because Dora's analysis came to an end before it could throw any light on this side of her mental life. But I should like to recall the governess, whom I have already mentioned, and with whom Dora had at first enjoyed the closest interchange of thought, until she discovered that she was being admired and fondly treated not for her own sake but for her father's; whereupon she had obliged the governess to leave. She used also to dwell with noticeable frequency and a peculiar emphasis on the story of another estrangement which appeared inexplicable even to herself. She had always been on particularly good terms with the younger of her two cousins—the girl who had later on become engaged—and had shared all sorts of secrets with her. When, for the first time after Dora had broken off her stay by the lake, her father was going back to B——, she had naturally refused to go with him. This cousin had then been asked to travel with him instead, and she had accepted the invitation. From that time forward Dora had felt a coldness towards her, and she herself was surprised to find how indifferent she had become, although, as she admitted, she had very little ground for complaint against her. These instances of sensitiveness led me to inquire what her relations with Frau K. had been up till the time of the breach. I then found that the young woman and the scarcely grown girl had lived for years on a footing of the closest intimacy. When Dora stayed with the K.'s she used to share a bedroom with Frau K., and the husband used to be quartered elsewhere. She had been the wife's confidante and adviser in all the difficulties of her married life. There was nothing they had not talked about Medea had been quite content that Creusa should make friends with her two children; and she certainly did nothing to interfere with the relations between the girl and the children's father. How Dora managed to fall in love with the man about whom her beloved friend had so many bad things to say is an interesting psychological problem. We shall not be far from solving it when we realize that thoughts in the unconscious live very comfortably side by side, and even contraries get on together without disputes—a state of things which persists often enough even in the conscious.

When Dora talked about Frau K., she used to praise her 'adorable white body' in accents more appropriate to a lover than to a defeated rival. Another time she told me, more in sorrow than in anger, that she was convinced the presents her father had brought her had been chosen by Frau K., for she recognized her taste. Another time, again, she pointed out that, evidently through the agency of Frau K., she had been given a present of some jewellery which was exactly like some that she had seen in Frau K.'s possession and had wished for aloud at the time. Indeed, I can say in general that I never heard her speak a harsh or angry word against the lady, although from the point of view of her supervalent thought she should have regarded her as the prime author of her misfortunes. She seemed to behave inconsequently; but her apparent inconsequence was precisely the manifestation of a complicating current of feeling. For how had this woman to whom Dora was so enthusiastically devoted behaved to her? After Dora had brought forward her accusation against Herr K., and her father had written to him and had asked for an explanation, Herr K. had replied in the first instance by protesting sentiments of the highest esteem for her and by proposing that he should come to the manufacturing town to clear up every misunderstanding. A few weeks later, when her father spoke to him at B——, there was no longer any question of esteem. On the contrary, Herr K. spoke of her with disparagement, and produced as his trump card the reflection that no girl who read such books and was interested in such things could have any title to a man's respect. Frau K., therefore, had betrayed her and had calumniated her; for it had only been with her that she had read Mantegazza and discussed forbidden topics. It was a repetition of what had happened with the governess: Frau K. had not loved her for her own sake but on account of her father. Frau K. had sacrificed her without a moment's hesitation so that her relations with her father might not be disturbed. This mortification touched her, perhaps, more nearly and had a greater pathogenic effect than the other one, which she tried to use as a screen for it,—the fact that she had been sacrificed by her father. Did not the obstinacy with which she retained the particular amnesia concerning the sources of her forbidden knowledge point directly to the great emotional importance for her of the accusation against her upon that score, and consequently to her betrayal by her friend?

I believe, therefore, that I am not mistaken in supposing that Dora's supervalent train of thought, which was concerned with her father's relations with Frau K., was designed not only for the purpose of suppressing her love for Herr K., which had once been conscious, but also to conceal her love for Frau K., which was in a deeper sense unconscious. The supervalent train of thought was directly contrary to the latter current of feeling. She told herself incessantly that her father had sacrificed her to this woman, and made noisy demonstrations to show that she grudged her the possession of her father; and in this way she concealed from herself the contrary fact, which was that she grudged her father Frau K.'s love, and had not forgiven the woman she loved for the disillusionment she had been caused by her betrayal. The jealous emotions of a woman were linked in the inconscious with a jealousy such as might have been felt by a man. These masculine or, more properly speaking, *gynaecophilic* currents of feeling are to be regarded as typical of the unconscious erotic life of hysterical girls.

II

THE FIRST DREAM

Just at a moment when there was a prospect that the material that was coming up for analysis would throw light upon an obscure point in Dora's childhood, she reported that a few nights earlier she had once again had a dream which she had already dreamt in exactly the same way on many previous occasions. A periodically recurrent dream was by its very nature particularly well calculated to arouse my curiosity; and in any case it was justifiable in the interests of the treatment to consider the way in which the dream worked into the analysis as a whole. I therefore determined to make an especially careful investigation of it.

Here is the dream as related by Dora: '*A house was on fire. My father was standing beside my bed and woke me up. I dressed quickly. Mother wanted to stop and save her jewel-case; but Father said: "I refuse to let myself and my two children be burnt for the sake of your jewel-case." We hurried downstairs, and as soon as I was outside I woke up.*'

As the dream was a recurrent one, I naturally asked her when she had first dreamt it. She told me she did not know. But she remembered having had the dream three nights in succession at L—— (the place on the lake where the scene with Herr K. had taken place), and it had now come back again a few nights earlier, here in Vienna. My expectations from the clearing-up of the dream were naturally heightened when I heard of its connection with the events at L——. But I wanted to discover first what had been the exciting cause of its recent recurrence, and I therefore asked Dora to take the dream bit by bit and tell me what occurred to her in connection with it. She had already had some training in dream interpretation from having previously analysed a few minor specimens.

'Something occurs to me,' she said, 'but it cannot belong to the dream, for it is quite recent, whereas I have certainly had the dream before.'

'That makes no difference,' I replied. 'Start away! It will simply turn out to be the most recent thing that fits in with the dream.'

'Very well, then. Father has been having a dispute with Mother in the last few days, because she locks the dining-room door at night. My brother's room, you see, has no separate entrance, but can only be reached through the dining-room. Father does not want my brother to be locked in like that at night. He says it will not do: something might happen in the night so that it might be necessary to leave the room.'

'And that made you think of the risk of fire?'

'Yes.'

'Now, I should like you to pay close attention to the exact words you used. We may have to come back to them. You said that "*something might happen in the night so that it might be necessary to leave the room.*" '[1]

But Dora had now discovered the connecting link between the recent exciting cause of the dream and the original one, for she continued:

'When we arrived at L—— that time, Father and I, he openly said he was afraid of fire. We arrived in a violent thunderstorm, and saw the small wooden house without any lightning-conductor. So his anxiety was quite natural.'

What I now had to do was to establish the relation between the events at L—— and the recurrent dreams which she had had there. I therefore said: 'Did you have the dream during your first nights at L—— or during your last ones? in other words, before or after the scene in the wood by the lake of which we have heard so much?' (I must explain that I knew that the scene had not occurred on the very first day, and that she had remained at L—— for a few days after it without giving any hint of the incident.)

Her first reply was that she did not know, but after a while she added: 'Yes. I think it was after the scene.'

So now I knew that the dream was a reaction to that experience. But why had it recurred there three times? I continued my questions: 'How long did you stop on at L—— after the scene?'

'Four more nights. On the following day I went away with Father.'

'Now I am certain that the dream was an immediate effect of your

---

1. I laid stress on these words because they took me aback. They seemed to have an ambiguous ring about them. Are not certain physical needs referred to in the same words? Now, in a line of associations ambiguous words (or, as we call them, 'switch-words') act like points at a junction. If the points are switched across from the position in which they appear to lie in the dream, then we find ourselves on another set of rails; and along this second track run the thoughts which we are in search of but which still lie concealed behind the dream.

experience with Herr K. It was at L—— that you dreamed it for the first time, and not before. You have only introduced this uncertainty in your memory so as to obliterate the connection in your mind. But the figures do not quite fit in to my satisfaction yet. If you stayed at L—— for four nights longer, the dream might have occurred four times over. Perhaps this was so?'

She no longer disputed my contention; but instead of answering my question she proceeded: 'In the afternoon after our trip on the lake, from which we (Herr K. and I) returned at midday, I had gone to lie down as usual on the sofa in the bedroom to have a short sleep. I suddenly awoke and saw Herr K. standing beside me. . . .'

'In fact, just as you saw your father standing beside your bed in the dream?'

'Yes. I asked him sharply what it was he wanted there. By way of reply he said he was not going to be prevented from coming into his own bedroom when he wanted; besides, there was something he wanted to fetch. This episode put me on my guard, and I asked Frau K. whether there was not a key to the bedroom door. The next morning I locked myself in while I was dressing. That afternoon, when I wanted to lock myself in so as to lie down again on the sofa, the key was gone. I was convinced that Herr K. had removed it.'

'Then here we have the theme of locking or not locking a room which appeared in the first association to the dream and also happened to occur in the exciting cause of the recent recurrence of the dream.[2] I wonder whether the phrase "*I dressed quickly*" may not also belong to this context?'

'It was then that I made up my mind not to stop on with the K.'s without Father. On the subsequent mornings I could not help feeling afraid that Herr K. would surprise me while I was dressing: *so I always dressed very quickly*. You see, Father lived at the hotel, and Frau K. used always to go out early so as to go on expeditions with him. But Herr K. did not annoy me again.'

'I understand. On the afternoon of the day after the scene in the wood you formed your intention of escaping from his persecution, and during the second, third, and fourth nights you had time to repeat that intention in your sleep. (You already knew on the second afternoon—before the dream, therefore—that you would not have the key on the following morning to lock yourself in with while you were dressing; and you could then form the design of dressing as quickly as possible.) But your dream recurred each night, for the very reason that it corresponded to an intention. An intention remains in existence until it has been carried out. You said to yourself, as it were: "I shall have no rest and I can get

2. I suspected, though I did not as yet say so to Dora, that she had seized upon this element on account of a symbolic meaning which it possessed. '*Zimmer*' {"room"} in dreams stands very frequently for '*Frauenzimmer*' {"female"}. The question whether a woman is 'open' or 'shut' can naturally not be a matter of indifference. It is well known, too, what sort of 'key' effects the opening in such a case.

no quiet sleep until I am out of this house." In your account of the dream you turned it the other way and said: "*As soon as I was outside I woke up.*" '

At this point I shall interrupt my report of the analysis in order to compare this small piece of dream-interpretation with the general statements I have made upon the mechanism of the formation of dreams. I argued in my book, *The Interpretation of Dreams* (1900), that every dream is a wish which is represented as fulfilled, that the representation acts as a disguise if the wish is a repressed one, belonging to the unconscious, and that except in the case of children's dreams only an unconscious wish or one which reaches down into the unconscious has the force necessary for the formation of a dream. I fancy my theory would have been more certain of general acceptance if I had contented myself with maintaining that every dream had a meaning, which could be discovered by means of a certain process of interpretation; and that when the interpretation had been completed the dream could be replaced by thoughts which would fall into place at an easily recognizable point in the waking mental life of the dreamer. I might then have gone on to say that the meaning of a dream turned out to be of as many different sorts as the processes of waking thought; that in one case it would be a fulfilled wish, in another a realized fear, or again a reflection persisting on into sleep, or an intention (as in the instance of Dora's dream), or a piece of creative thought during sleep, and so on. Such a theory would no doubt have proved attractive from its very simplicity, and it might have been supported by a great many examples of dreams that had been satisfactorily interpreted, as for instance by the one which has been analysed in these pages.

But instead of this I formulated a generalization according to which the meaning of dreams is limited to a single form, to the representation of *wishes*, and by so doing I aroused a universal inclination to dissent. I must, however, observe that I did not consider it either my right or my duty to simplify a psychological process so as to make it more acceptable to my readers, when my researches had shown me that it presented a complication which could not be reduced to uniformity until the inquiry had been carried into another field. It is therefore of special importance to me to show that apparent exceptions—such as this dream of Dora's, which has shown itself in the first instance to be the continuation into sleep of an intention formed during the day—nevertheless lend fresh support to the rule which is in dispute.

Much of the dream, however, still remained to be interpreted, and I proceeded with my questions: 'What is this about the jewel-case that your mother wanted to save?'

'Mother is very fond of jewellery and had had a lot given her by Father.'

'And you?'

'I used to be very fond of jewellery too, once; but I have not worn any since my illness.—Once, four years ago' (a year before the dream), 'Father and Mother had a great dispute about a piece of jewellery. Mother wanted to be given a particular thing—pearl drops to wear in her ears. But Father does not like that kind of thing, and he brought her a bracelet instead of the drops. She was furious, and told him that as he had spent so much money on a present she did not like he had better just give it to some one else.'

'I dare say you thought to yourself you would accept it with pleasure.'

'I don't know.[3] I don't in the least know how Mother comes into the dream; she was not with us at L—— at the time.'

'I will explain that to you presently. Does nothing else occur to you in connection with the jewel-case? So far you have only talked about jewellery and have said nothing about a case.'

'Yes, Herr K. had made me a present of an expensive jewel-case a little time before.'

'Then a return-present would have been very appropriate. Perhaps you do not know that "jewel-case" ["*Schmuckkästchen*"] is a favourite expression for the same thing that you alluded to not long ago by means of the reticule you were wearing—for the female genitals, I mean.'

'I knew you would say that.'

'That is to say, you knew that is *was* so.—The meaning of the dream is now becoming even clearer. You said to yourself: "This man is persecuting me; he wants to force his way into my room. My 'jewel-case' is in danger, and if anything happens it will be Father's fault." For that reason in the dream you chose a situation which expresses the opposite— a danger from which your father is *saving* you. In this part of the dream everything is turned into its opposite; you will soon discover why. As you say, the mystery turns upon your mother. You ask how she comes into the dream? She is, as you know, your former rival in your father's affections. In the incident of the bracelet, you would have been glad to accept what your mother had rejected. Now let us just put "give" instead of "accept" and "withhold" instead of "reject". Then it means that you were ready to give your father what your mother withheld from him; and the thing in question was connected with jewellery. Now bring your mind back to the jewel-case which Herr K. gave you. You have there the starting-point for a parallel line of thoughts, in which Herr K. is to be put in the place of your father just as he was in the matter of standing beside your bed. He gave you a jewel-case; so you are to give him your jewel-case. That was why I spoke just now of a "return-present". In this line of thoughts your mother must be replaced by Frau K. (You will not deny that she, at any rate, was present at the time.) So you are ready

3. The regular formula with which she confessed to anything that had been repressed.

to give Herr K. what his wife withholds from him. That is the thought which has had to be repressed with so much energy, and which has made it necessary for every one of its elements to be turned into its opposite. The dream confirms once more what I had already told you before you dreamt it—that you are summoning up your old love for your father in order to protect yourself against your love for Herr K. But what do all these efforts show? Not only that you are afraid of Herr K., but that you are still more afraid of yourself, and of the temptation you feel to yield to him. In short, these efforts prove once more how deeply you loved him.'[4]

Naturally Dora would not follow me in this part of the interpretation. I myself, however, had been able to arrive at a further step in the interpretation, which seemed to me indispensable both for the anamnesis of the case and for the theory of dreams. I promised to communicate this to Dora at the next session.

The fact was that I could not forget the hint which seemed to be conveyed by the ambiguous words already noticed—*that it might be necessary to leave the room; that an accident might happen in the night.* Added to this was the fact that the elucidation of the dream seemed to me incomplete so long as a particular requirement remained unsatisfied; for, though I do not wish to insist that this requirement is a universal one, I have a predilection for discovering a means of satisfying it. A regularly formed dream stands, as it were, upon two legs, one of which is in contact with the main and current exciting cause, and the other with some momentous event in the years of childhood. The dream sets up a connection between those two factors—the event during childhood and the event of the present day—and it endeavours to re-shape the present on the model of the remote past. For the wish which creates the dream always springs from the period of childhood; and it is continually trying to summon childhood back into reality and to correct the present day by the measure of childhood. I believed that I could already clearly detect those elements of Dora's dream which could be pieced together into an illusion to an event in childhood.

I opened the discussion of the subject with a little experiment, which was, as usual, successful. There happened to be a large match-stand on the table. I asked Dora to look round and see whether she noticed anything special on the table, something that was not there as a rule. She noticed nothing. I then asked her if she knew why children were forbidden to play with matches.

'Yes; on account of the risk of fire. My uncle's children are very fond of playing with matches.'

---

4. I added: 'Moreover, the re-appearance of the dream in the last few days forces me to the conclusion that you consider that the same situation has arisen once again, and that you have decided to give up the treatment—to which, after all, it is only your father who makes you come.' The sequel showed how correct my guess had been. . . .

'Not only on that account. They are warned not to "play with fire", and a particular belief is associated with the warning.'

She knew nothing about it.—'Very well, then; the fear is that if they do they will wet their bed. The antithesis of "water" and "fire" must be at the bottom of this. Perhaps it is believed that they will dream of fire and then try and put it out with water. I cannot say exactly. But I notice that the antithesis of water and fire has been extremely useful to you in the dream. Your mother wanted to save the jewel-case so that it should not be *burnt*; while in the dream-thoughts it is a question of the "jewel-case" not being *wetted*. But fire is not only used as the contrary of water, it also serves directly to represent love (as in the phrase "to be *consumed* with love"). So that from "fire" one set of rails runs by way of this symbolic meaning to thoughts of love; while the other set runs by way of the contrary "water", and, after sending off a branch line which provides another connection with "love" (for love also makes things wet), leads in a different direction. And what direction can that be? Think of the expressions you used: that *an accident might happen in the night*, and that *it might be necessary to leave the room*. Surely the allusion must be to a physical need? And if you transpose the accident into childhood what can it be but bed-wetting? But what is usually done to prevent children from wetting their bed? Are they not woken up in the night out of their sleep, *exactly as your father woke you up in the dream?* This, then, must be the actual occurrence which enabled you to substitute your father for Herr K., who really woke you up out of your sleep. I am accordingly driven to conclude that you were addicted to bed-wetting up to a later age than is usual with children. The same must also have been true of your brother; for your father said: "*I refuse to let my two children* go to their destruction. . . ." Your brother has no other sort of connection with the real situation at the K.'s; he had not gone with you to L——. And now, what have your recollections to say to this?'

'I know nothing about myself,' was her reply, 'but my brother used to wet his bed up till his sixth or seventh year; and it used sometimes to happen to him in the daytime too.'

I was on the point of remarking to her how much easier it is to remember things of that kind about one's brother than about oneself, when she continued the train of recollections which had been revived: 'Yes. I used to do it too, for some time, but not until my seventh or eighth year. It must have been serious, because I remember now that the doctor was called in. It lasted till a short time before my nervous asthma.'

'And what did the doctor say to it?'

'He explained it as nervous weakness; it would soon pass off, he thought; and he prescribed a tonic.[5]

---

5. The essence of the dream might perhaps be translated into words such as these: 'The temptation is so strong. Dear Father, protect me again as you used to in my childhood, and prevent my bed from being wetted!'

The interpretation of the dream now seemed to me to be complete. But Dora brought me an addendum to the dream on the very next day. She had forgotten to relate, she said, that each time after waking up she had smelt smoke. Smoke, of course, fitted in well with fire, but it also showed that the dream had a special relation to myself; for when she used to assert that there was nothing concealed behind this or that, I would often say by way of rejoinder: 'There can be no smoke without fire!' Dora objected, however, to such a purely personal interpretation, saying that Herr K. and her father were passionate smokers—as I am too, for the matter of that. She herself had smoked during her stay by the lake, and Herr K. had rolled a cigarette for her before he began his unlucky proposal. She thought, too, that she clearly remembered having noticed the smell of smoke on the three occasions of the dream's occurrence at L——, and not for the first time at its recent reappearance. As she would give me no further information, it was left to me to determine how this addendum was to be introduced into the texture of the dream-thoughts. One thing which I had to go upon was the fact that the smell of smoke had only come up as an addendum to the dream, and must therefore have had to overcome a particularly strong effort on the part of repression. Accordingly it was probably related to the thoughts which were the most obscurely presented and the most successfully repressed in the dream, to the thoughts, that is, concerned with the temptation to show herself willing to yield to the man. If that were so, the addendum to the dream could scarcely mean anything else than the longing for a kiss, which, with a smoker, would necessarily smell of smoke. But a kiss had passed between Herr K. and Dora some two years further back, and it would certainly have been repeated more than once if she had given way to him. So the thoughts of temptation seemed in this way to have harked back to the earlier scene, and to have revived the memory of the kiss against whose seductive influence the little 'thumb-sucker' had defended herself at the time, by the feeling of disgust. Taking into consideration, finally, the indications which seemed to point to there having been a transference on to me—since I am a smoker too—I came to the conclusion that the idea had probably occurred to her one day during a session that she would like to have a kiss from me. This would have been the exciting cause which led her to repeat the warning dream and to form her intention of stopping the treatment. Everything fits together very satisfactorily upon this view; but owing to the characteristics of 'transference' its validity is not susceptible of definite proof.

I might at this point hesitate whether I should first consider the light thrown by this dream on the history of the case, or whether I should rather begin by dealing with the objection to my theory of dreams which may be based on it. I shall take the former course.

The significance of enuresis in the early history of neurotics is worth going into thoroughly. For the sake of clearness I will confine myself to remarking that Dora's case of bed-wetting was not the usual one. The disorder was not simply that the habit had persisted beyond what is considered the normal period, but, according to her explicit account, it had begun by disappearing and had then returned at a relatively late age—after her sixth year. Bed-wetting of this kind has, to the best of my knowledge, no more likely cause than masturbation, a habit whose importance in the aetiology of bed-wetting in general is still insufficiently appreciated. In my experience, the children concerned have themselves at one time been very well aware of this connection, and all its psychological consequences follow from it as though they had never forgotten it. Now, at the time when Dora reported the dream, we were engaged upon a line of enquiry which led straight towards an admission that she had masturbated in childhood. A short while before, she had raised the question of why it was that precisely she had fallen ill, and, before I could answer, had put the blame on her father. The justification for this was forthcoming not out of her unconscious thoughts but from her conscious knowledge. It turned out, to my astonishment, that the girl knew what the nature of her father's illness had been. After his return from consulting me she had overheard a conversation in which the name of the disease had been mentioned. At a still earlier period—at the time of the detached retina—an oculist who was called in must have hinted at a luetic aetiology; for the inquisitive and anxious girl overheard an old aunt of hers saying to her mother: 'He was ill before his marriage, you know', and adding something which she could not understand, but which she subsequently connected in her mind with improper subjects.

Her father, then, had fallen ill through leading a loose life, and she assumed that he had handed on his bad health to her by heredity. I was careful not to tell her that, as I have already mentioned, I too was of opinion that the offspring of luetics were very specially predisposed to severe neuropsychoses. The line of thought in which she brought this accusation against her father was continued in her unconscious material. For several days on end she identified herself with her mother by means of slight symptoms and peculiarities of manner, which gave her an opportunity for some really remarkable achievements in the direction of intolerable behaviour. She then allowed it to transpire that she was thinking of a stay she had made at Franzensbad, which she had visited with her mother—I forget in what year. Her mother was suffering from abdominal pains and from a discharge (a catarrh) which necessitated a cure at Franzensbad. It was Dora's view—and here again she was probably right—that this illness was due to her father, who had thus handed on his venereal disease to her mother. It was quite natural that in drawing this conclusion she should, like the majority of laymen, have confused gonorrhoea and syphilis, as well as what is contagious and what is hereditary. The persistence with which she held to this identification with her mother almost forced me to ask her whether she too was suffering from a venereal disease; and I then learnt that she was afflicted with a catarrh (leucorrhoea) whose beginning, she said, she could not remember.

I then understood that behind the train of thought in which she brought these open accusations against her father there lay concealed as usual a *self*-accusation. I met her half-way by assuring her that in my view the occurrence of leucorrhoea in young girls pointed primarily to masturbation, and I considered that all the other causes which were commonly assigned to that complaint were put in the background by masturbation. I added that she was now on the way to finding an answer to her own question of why it was that precisely she had fallen ill—by confessing that she had masturbated, probably in childhood. Dora denied flatly that she could remember any such thing. But a few days later she did something which I could not help regarding as a further step towards the confession. For on that day she wore at her waist—a thing she never did on any other occasion before or after—a small reticule of a shape which had just come into fashion; and, as she lay on the sofa and talked, she kept playing with it—opening it, putting a finger into it, shutting it again, and so on. I looked on for some time, and then explained to her the nature of a 'symptomatic act'. * * *

* * *

There is a great deal of symbolism of this kind in life, but as a rule we pass it by without heeding it. When I set myself the task of bringing to light what human beings keep hidden within them, not by the compelling power of hypnosis, but by observing what they say and what they show, I thought the task was a harder one than it really is. He that has eyes to see and ears to hear may convince himself that no mortal can keep a secret. If his lips are silent, he chatters with his finger-tips; betrayal oozes out of him at every pore. And thus the task of making conscious the most hidden recesses of the mind is one which it is quite possible to accomplish.

Dora's symptomatic act with the reticule did not immediately precede the dream. She started the session which brought us the narrative of the dream with another symptomatic act. As I came into the room in which she was waiting she hurriedly concealed a letter which she was reading. I naturally asked her whom the letter was from, and at first she refused to tell me. Something then came out which was a matter of complete indifference and had no relation to the treatment. It was a letter from her grandmotherr, in which she begged Dora to write to her more often. I believe that Dora only wanted to play 'secrets' with me, and to hint that she was on the point of allowing her secret to be torn from her by the doctor. I was then in a position to explain her antipathy to every new doctor. She was afraid lest he might arrive at the foundation of her illness, either by examining her and discovering her catarrh, or by questioning her and eliciting the fact of her addiction to bed-wetting—lest he might guess, in short, that she had masturbated. And afterwards she would speak very contemptuously of the doctor whose perspicacity she had evidently over-estimated beforehand.

The reproaches against her father for having made her ill, together with the self-reproach underlying them, the leucorrhoea, the playing with the reticule, the bed-wetting after her sixth year, the secret which she would not allow the doctors to tear from her—the circumstantial evidence of her having masturbated in childhood seems to me complete and without a flaw. In the present case I had begun to suspect the masturbation when she had told me of her cousin's gastric pains and had then identified herself with her by complaining for days together of similar painful sensations. It is well known that gastric pains occur especially often in those who masturbate. According to a personal communication made to me by Wilhelm Fliess, it is precisely gastralgias of this character which can be interrupted by an application of cocaine to the 'gastric spot' discovered by him in the nose, and which can be cured by the cauterization of the same spot. In confirmation of my suspicion Dora gave me two facts from her conscious knowledge: she herself had frequently suffered from gastric pains, and she had good reasons for believing that her cousin was a masturbator. It is a very common thing for patients to recognize in other people a connection which, on account of their emotional resistances, they cannot perceive in themselves. And, indeed, Dora no longer denied my supposition, although she still remembered nothing. Even the date which she assigned to the bed-wetting, when she said that it lasted 'till a short time before the appearance of the nervous asthma', appears to me to be of clinical significance. Hysterical symptoms hardly ever appear so long as children are masturbating, but only afterwards, when a period of abstinence has set in; they form a substitute for masturbatory satisfaction, the desire for which continues to persist in the unconscious until another and more normal kind of satisfaction appears—where that is still attainable. For upon whether it is still attainable or not depends the possibility of a hysteria being cured by marriage and normal sexual intercourse. But if the satisfaction afforded in marriage is again removed—as it may be owing to *coitus interruptus*, psychological estrangement, or other causes—then the libido flows back again into its old channel and manifests itself once more in hysterical symptoms.

* * *

Let us next attempt to put together the various determinants that we have found for Dora's attacks of coughing and hoarseness. In the lowest stratum we must assume the presence of a real and organically determined irritation of the throat—which acted like the grain of sand around which an oyster forms its pearl. This irritation was susceptible to fixation, because it concerned a part of the body which in Dora had to a high degree retained its significance as an erotogenic zone. And the irritation was consequently well fitted to give expression to excited states of the libido. It was brought to fixation by what was probably its first psychical coating—her sympathetic imitation of her father—and by her subsequent self-reproaches on account of her 'catarrh'. The same group of symptoms, moreover, showed itself capable of representing her relations with Herr K.; it could express her regret at his absence and her wish to make him a better wife. After a part of her libido had once more turned towards her father, the symptom obtained what was perhaps its last meaning; it came to represent sexual intercourse with her father by means of Dora's identifying herself with Frau K. I can guarantee that this series is by no means complete. Unfortunately, an incomplete analysis cannot enable us to follow the chronological sequence of the changes in a symptom's meaning, or to display clearly the succession and coexistence of its various meanings. It may legitimately be expected of a complete analysis that it should fulfil these demands.

I must now proceed to touch upon some further relations existing between Dora's genital catarrh and her hysterical symptoms. At a time when any psychological elucidation of hysteria was still very remote, I used to hear experienced fellow-doctors who were my seniors maintain that in the case of hysterical patients suffering from leucorrhoea any increase in the catarrh was regularly followed by an intensification of the hysterical troubles, and especially of loss of appetite and vomiting. No one was very clear about the nature of the connection, but I fancy the general inclination was towards the opinion held by gynaecologists. According to their hypothesis, as is well known, disorders of the genitals exercise upon the nervous functions a direct and far-reaching influence in the nature of an organic disturbance—though a therapeutic test of this theory is apt to leave one in the lurch. In the light of our present knowledge we cannot exclude the possibility of the existence of a direct organic influence of this sort; but it is at all events easier to indicate its psychical coating. The pride taken by women in the appearance of their genitals is quite a special feature of their vanity; and disorders of the genitals which they think calculated to inspire feelings of repugnance or even disgust have an incredible power of humiliating them, of lowering their self-esteem, and of making them irritable, sensitive, and distrustful. An abnormal secretion of the mucous membrane of the vagina is looked upon as a source of disgust.

It will be remembered that Dora had a lively feeling of disgust after being kissed by Herr K., and that we saw grounds for completing her story of the scene of the kiss by supposing that, while she was being embraced, she noticed the pressure of the man's erect member against her body. We now learn further that the same governess whom Dora cast off on account of her faithlessness had, from her own experience of life, propounded to Dora the view that all men were frivolous and untrustworthy. To Dora that must mean that all men were like her father. But she thought her father suffered from venereal disease—for had he not handed it on to her and her mother? She might therefore have imagined to herself that all men suffered from venereal disease, and naturally her conception of venereal disease was modelled on her one experience of it—a personal one at that. To suffer from venereal disease, therefore, meant for her to be afflicted with a disgusting discharge. So may we not have here a further motive for the disgust she felt at the moment of the embrace? Thus the disgust which was transferred on to the contact of the man would be a feeling which had been projected according to the primitive mechanism I have already mentioned, and would be related ultimately to her own leucorrhoea.

I suspect that we are here concerned with unconscious processes of thought which are twined around a pre-existing structure of organic connections, much as festoons of flowers are twined around a wire; so that on another occasion one might find other lines of thought inserted between the same points of departure and termination. Yet a knowledge of the thought-connections which have been effective in the individual case is of a value which cannot be exaggerated for clearing up the symptoms. It is only because the analysis was prematurely broken off that we have been obliged in Dora's case to resort to framing conjectures and filling in deficiencies. Whatever I have brought forward for filling up the gaps is based upon other cases which have been more thoroughly analysed.

The dream from the analysis of which we have derived this information corresponded, as we have seen, to an intention which Dora carried with her into her sleep. It was therefore repeated each night until the intention had been carried out; and it reappeared years later when an occasion arose for forming an analogous intention. The intention might have been consciously expressed in some such words as these: 'I must fly from this house, for I see that my virginity is threatened here; I shall go away with my father, and I shall take precautions not to be surprised while I am dressing in the morning.' These thoughts were clearly expressed in the dream; they formed part of a mental current which had achieved consciousness and a dominating position in waking life. Behind them can be discerned obscure traces of a train of thought which formed part of a contrary current and had consequently been suppressed. This other train of thought culminated in the temptation to yield to the man, out of gratitude for the love and tenderness he had shown her during the last few years, and it may perhaps have revived the memory of the only kiss she had so far had from him. But according to the theory which I developed in my *Interpretation of Dreams* such elements as these are not enough for the formation of a dream. On that theory a dream is not an intention represented as having been carried out, but a wish represented as having been fulfilled, and, moreover, in most cases a wish dating from childhood. It is our business now to discover whether this principle may not be contradicted by the present dream.

The dream does not in fact contain infantile material, though it is impossible at a first glance to discover any connections between that material and Dora's intention of flying from Herr K.'s house and the temptation of his presence. Why should a recollection have emerged of her bed-wetting when she was a child and of the trouble her father used to take to teach the child clean habits? We may answer this by saying that it was only by the help of this train of thought that it was possible to suppress the other thoughts which were so intensely occupied with the temptation to yield or that it was possible to secure the dominance of the intention which had been formed of combating those other thoughts. The child decided to fly *with* her father; in reality she fled *to* her father because she was afraid of the man who was pursuing her; she summoned up an infantile affection for her father so that it might protect her against her present affection for a stranger. Her father was himself partly responsible for her present danger, for he had handed her over to this strange man in the interests of his own love-affair. And how much better it had been when that same father of hers had loved no one more than her, and had exerted all his strength to save her from the dangers that had then threatened her! The infantile, and now unconscious, wish to put her father in the strange man's place had the potency necessary for the formation of a dream. If there were a past situation similar to a present one, and differing from it only in being concerned with one instead of with the other of the two persons mentioned in the wish, that situation would become the main one in the dream. But there *had* been such a situation. Her father had once stood beside her bed, just as Herr K. had the day before, and had woken her up, with a kiss perhaps, as Herr K. may have meant to do. Thus her intention of flying from the house was not in itself capable of producing a dream; but it became so by being associated with another intention which was founded upon infantile wishes. The wish to replace Herr K. by her father provided the necessary motive power for the dream. Let me recall the interpretation I was led to adopt of Dora's reinforced train of thought about her father's relations with Frau K. My interpretation was that she had at that point summoned up an infantile affection for her father so as to be able to keep her repressed love for Herr K. in its state of repression. This same sudden revulsion in the patient's mental life was reflected in the dream.

* * *

Any one who has learnt to appreciate the delicacy of the fabric of structures such as dreams will not be surprised to find that Dora's wish that her father might take the place of the man who was her tempter called up in her memory not merely a casual collection of material from her childhood, but precisely such material as was most intimately bound up with the suppression of her temptation. For if Dora felt unable to yield to her love for the man, if in the end she repressed that love instead of surrendering to it, there was no factor upon which her decision depended more directly than upon her premature sexual enjoyment and its consequence—her bed-wetting, her catarrh, and her disgust. An early history of this kind can afford a basis for two kinds of behaviour in response to the demands of love in maturity—which of the two will depend upon the summation of constitutional determinants in the subject. He will either exhibit an abandonment to sexuality which is entirely without resistances and borders upon perversity; or there will be a reaction—he will repudiate sexuality, and will at the same time fall ill of a neurosis. In the case of our present patient, her constitution and the high level of her intellectual and moral upbringing decided in favour of the latter course.

I should like, further, to draw special attention to the fact that the analysis of this dream has given us access to certain details of the pathogenically operative events which had otherwise been inaccessible to memory, or at all events to reproduction. The recollection of the bedwetting in childhood had, as we have seen, already been repressed. And Dora had never mentioned the details of her persecution by Herr K.; they had never occured to her mind.

* * *

III

THE SECOND DREAM

A few weeks after the first dream the second occurred, and when it had been dealt with the analysis was broken off. It cannot be made as completely intelligible as the first, but it afforded a desirable confirmation of an assumption which had become necessary about the patient's mental state, it filled up a gap in her memory, and it made it possible to obtain a deep insight into the origin of another of her symptoms.

Dora described the dream as follows: '*I was walking about in a town which I did not know. I saw streets and squares which were strange to me.*[6] *Then I came into a house where I lived, went to my room, and found a letter from Mother lying there. She wrote saying that as I had left home without my parents' knowledge she had not wished to write to me to say that Father was ill. "Now he is dead, and if you like*[7] *you can come." I then went to the station* ["*Bahnhof*"] *and asked about a hundred times: "Where is the station?" I always got the answer: "Five minutes." I then saw a thick wood before me which I went into, and there I asked a man whom I met. He said to me: "Two and a half hours more."*[8] *He offered to accompany me. But I refused and went alone. I saw the station*

6. To this she subsequently made an important addendum: '*I saw a monument in one of the squares.*'

7. To this came the addendum: '*There was a question-mark after this word, thus "like?".*'

8. In repeating the dream she said: '*Two hours.*'

in front of me and could not reach it. At the same time I had the usual feeling of anxiety that one has in dreams when one cannot move forward. Then I was at home. I must have been travelling in the meantime, but I know nothing about that. I walked into the porter's lodge, and enquired for our flat. The maidservant opened the door to me and replied that Mother and the others were already at the cemetery ["Friedhof"].[9]

It was not without some difficulty that the interpretation of this dream proceeded. In consequence of the peculiar circumstances in which the analysis was broken off—circumstances connected with the content of the dream—the whole of it was not cleared up. And for this reason, too, I am not equally certain at every point of the order in which my conclusions were reached. I will begin by mentioning the subject-matter with which the current analysis was dealing at the time when the dream intervened. For some time Dora herself had been raising a number of questions about the connection between some of her actions and the motives which presumably underlay them. One of these questions was: 'Why did I say nothing about the scene by the lake for some days after it had happened?' Her second question was: 'Why did I then suddenly tell my parents about it?' Moreover, her having felt so deeply injured by Herr K.'s proposal seemed to me in general to need explanation, especially as I was beginning to realize that Herr K. himself had not regarded his proposal to Dora as a mere frivolous attempt at seduction. I looked upon her having told her parents of the episode as an action which she had taken when she was already under the influence of a morbid craving for revenge. A normal girl, I am inclined to think, will deal with a situation of this kind by herself.

I shall present the material produced during the analysis of this dream in the somewhat haphazard order in which it recurs to my mind.

She was wandering about alone in a strange town, and saw streets and squares. Dora assured me that it was certainly not B——, which I had first hit upon, but a town in which she had never been. It was natural to suggest that she might have seen some pictures or photographs and have taken the dream-pictures from them. After this remark of mine came the addendum about the monument in one of the squares and immediately afterwards her recognition of its source. At Christmas she had been sent an album from a German health-resort, containing views of the town; and the very day before the dream she had looked this out to show it to some relatives who were stopping with them. It had been put in a box for keeping pictures in, and she could not lay her hands on it at once. She had therefore said to her mother: 'Where is the box?' One of the pictures was of a square with a monument in it. The present

---

9. In the next session Dora brought me two addenda to this: '*I saw myself particularly distinctly going up the stairs,*' and *After she had answered I went to my room, but not the least sadly, and began reading a big book that lay on my writing-table.* {The precision with which Freud here reports this dream and Dora's subsequent amendment and additions is noteworthy.}

had been sent to her by a young engineer, with whom she had once had a passing acquaintance in the manufacturing town. The young man had accepted a post in Germany, so as to become sooner self-supporting; and he took every opportunity of reminding Dora of his existence. It was easy to guess that he intended to come forward as a suitor one day, when his position had improved. But that would take time, and it meant waiting.

The wandering about in a strange town was overdetermined. It led back to one of the exciting causes from the day before. A young cousin of Dora's had come to stay with them for the holidays, and Dora had had to show him round Vienna. This cause was, it is true, a matter of complete indifference to her. But her cousin's visit reminded her of her own first brief visit to Dresden. On that occasion she had been a stranger and had wandered about, not failing, of course, to visit the famous picture gallery. Another [male] cousin of hers, who was with them and knew Dresden, had wanted to act as a guide and take her round the gallery. *But she declined and went alone*, and stopped in front of the pictures that appealed to her. She remained *two hours* in front of the Sistine Madonna, rapt in silent admiration. When I asked her what had pleased her so much about the picture she could find no clear answer to make. At last she said: 'The Madonna.'

There could be no doubt that these associations really belonged to the material concerned in forming the dream. They included portions which reappeared in the dream unchanged ('she declined and went alone' and 'two hours'). I may remark at once that 'pictures' was a nodal point in the network of her dream-thoughts (the pictures in the album, the pictures at Dresden). I should also like to single out, with a view to subsequent investigation, the theme of the 'Madonna', of the virgin mother. But what was most evident was that in this first part of the dream she was identifying herself with a young man. This young man was wandering about in a strange place, he was striving to reach a goal, but he was being kept back, he needed patience and must wait. If in all this she had been thinking of the engineer, it would have been appropriate for the goal to have been the possession of a woman, of herself. But instead of this it was—a station. Nevertheless, the relation of the question in the dream to the questions which had been put in real life allows us to substitute '*box*' for 'station'.[1] A box and a woman: the notions begin to agree better.

She asked quite a hundred times. . . . This led to another exciting cause of the dream, and this time to one that was less indifferent. On the previous evening they had had company, and afterwards her father had asked her to fetch him the brandy: he could not get to sleep unless he had taken some brandy. She had asked her mother for the key of the sideboard; but the latter had been deep in conversation, and had not

---

1. ['Schachtel'], the word which was used for 'box' by Dora in her question, is a depreciatory term for 'woman'.]

answered her, until Dora had exclaimed with the exaggeration of impatience: 'I've asked you *a hundred times* already where the key is.' As a matter of fact, she had of course only repeated the question about *five times.*

'Where is the *key?*' seems to me to be the masculine counterpart to the question 'Where is the *box?*' They are therefore questions referring to—the genitals.

Dora went on to say that during this same family gathering some one had toasted her father and had expressed the hope that he might continue to enjoy the best of health for many years to come, etc. At this a strange quiver passed over her father's tired face, and she had understood what thoughts he was having to keep down. Poor sick man! who could tell what span of life was still to be his?

This brings us to the *contents of the letter* in the dream. Her father was dead, and she had left home by her own choice. In connection with this letter I at once reminded Dora of the farewell letter which she had written to her parents or had at least composed for their benefit. This letter had been intended to give her father a fright, so that he should give up Frau K.; or at any rate to take revenge on him if he could not be induced to do that. We are here concerned with the subject of her death and of her father's death. (Cf. 'cemetery' later on in the dream.) Shall we be going astray if we suppose that the situation which formed the façade of the dream was a phantasy of revenge directed against her father? The feelings of pity for him which she remembered from the day before would be quite in keeping with this. According to the phantasy she had left home and gone among strangers, and her father's heart had broken with grief and with longing for her. Thus she would be revenged. She understood very clearly what it was that her father needed when he could not get to sleep without a drink of brandy.[2] We will make a note of Dora's *craving for revenge* as a new element to be taken into account in any subsequent synthesis of her dream-thoughts.

But the contents of the letter must be capable of further determination. What was the source of the words 'if you like'? It was at this point that the addendum of there having been a question-mark after the word 'like' occurred to Dora, and she then recognized these words as a quotation out of the letter from Frau K. which had contained the invitation to L——, the place by the lake. In that letter there had been a question-mark placed, in a most unusual fashion, in the very middle of a sentence, after the intercalated words 'if you would like to come'.

So here we were back again at the scene by the lake and at the problems connected with it. I asked Dora to describe the scene to me in detail. At first she produced little that was new. Herr K.'s exordium had been somewhat serious; but she had not let him finish what he had to say.

2. There can be no doubt that sexual satisfaction is the best soporific, just as sleeplessness is almost always the consequence of lack of satisfaction. Her father could not sleep because he was debarred from sexual intercourse with the woman he loved. . . .

No sooner had she grasped the purport of his words than she had slapped him in the face and hurried away. I enquired what his actual words had been. Dora could only remember one of his pleas: 'You know I get nothing out of my wife.' In order to avoid meeting him again she had wanted to get back to L—— on foot, by walking round the lake, and *she had asked a man whom she met how far it was.* On his replying that it was *'Two and a half hours'*, she had given up her intention and had after all gone back to the boat, which left soon afterwards. Herr K. had been there too and had come up to her and begged her to forgive him and not to mention the incident. But she had made no reply.—Yes. The *wood* in the dream has been just like the wood by the shore of the lake, the wood in which the scene she had just described once more had taken place. But she had seen precisely the same thick wood the day before, in a picture at the Secessionist exhibition. In the background of the picture there were *nymphs*.[3]

At this point a certain suspicion of mine became a certainty. The use of *'Bahnhof'* ['station'; literally, 'railway-court']‌[4] and *'Friedhof'* ['cemetery'; literally, 'peace-court'] to represent the female genitals was striking enough in itself, but is also served to direct my awakened curiosity to the similarly formed *'Vorhof'* ['vestibulum'; literally, 'fore-court']—an anatomical term for a particular region of the female genitals. This might have been no more than mistaken ingenuity. But now, with the addition of 'nymphs' visible in the background of a 'thick wood', no further doubts could be entertained. Here was a symbolic geography of sex! 'Nymphae', as is known to physicians though not to laymen (and even by the former the term is not very commonly used), is the name given to the labia minora, which lie in the background of the 'thick wood' of the pubic hair. But any one who employed such technical names as 'vestibulum' and 'nymphae' must have derived his knowledge from books, and not from popular ones either, but from anatomical text-books or from an encyclopaedia—the common refuge of youth when it is devoured by sexual curiosity. If this interpretation were correct, therefore, there lay concealed behind the first situation in the dream a phantasy of defloration, the phantasy of a man seeking to force an entrance into the female genitals.[5]

I informed Dora of the conclusions I had reached. The impression made upon her must have been forcible, for there immediately appeared a piece of the dream which had been forgotten: *'she went calmly to her room, and began reading a big book that lay on her writing-table.'* The emphasis here was upon the two details 'calmly' and 'big' in connection

3. Here for the third time we come upon 'picture' (views of towns, the Dresden gallery), but in a much more significant connection. Because of what appears in the picture (the wood, the nymphs), the 'Bild' ['picture'] is turned into a *'Weibsbild'* [literally, 'picture of a woman'—a somewhat derogatory expression for 'woman'].

4. Moreover, a 'station' is used for purposes of *'Verkehr'* ['traffic', 'intercourse', 'sexual intercourse']: this fact determines the psychical coating in a number of cases of railway phobia.

5 This phantasy of defloration formed the second component of the situation. . . .

with 'book'. I asked whether the book was in encyclopaedia *format*, and she said it was. Now children never read about forbidden subjects in an encyclopaedia *calmly*. They do it in fear and trembling, with an uneasy look over their shoulder to see if some one may not be coming. Parents are very much in the way while reading of this kind is going on. But this uncomfortable situation had been radically improved, thanks to the dream's power of fulfilling wishes. Dora's father was dead, and the others had already gone to the cemetery. She might calmly read whatever she chose. Did not this mean that one of her motives for revenge was a revolt against her parents' constraint? If her father was dead she could read or love as she pleased.

At first she would not remember ever having read anything in an encyclopaedia; but she then admitted that a recollection of an occasion of the kind did occur to her, though it was of an innocent enough nature. At the time when the aunt she was so fond of had been so seriously ill and it had already been settled that Dora was to go to Vienna, a *letter* had come from another uncle, to say that they could not go to Vienna, as a boy of his, a cousin of Dora's therefore, had fallen dangerously ill with appendicitis. Dora had thereupon looked up in the encyclopaedia to see what the symptoms of appendicitis were. From what she had then read she still recollected the characteristic localization of the abdominal pain.

I then remembered that shortly after her aunt's death Dora had had an attack of what had been alleged to be appendicitis. Up till then I had not ventured to count that illness among her hysterical productions. She told me that during the first few days she had had high fever and had felt the pain in her abdomen that she had read about in the encyclopaedia. She had been given cold fomentations but had not been able to bear them. On the second day her period had set in, accompanied by violent pains. (Since her health had been bad, the periods had been very irregular.) At that time she used to suffer continually from constipation.

It was not really possible to regard this state as a purely hysterical one. Although hysterical fever does undoubtedly occur, yet it seemed too arbitrary to put down the fever accompanying this questionable illness to hysteria instead of to some organic cause operative at the time. I was on the point of abandoning the track, when she herself helped me along it by producing her last addendum to the dream: '*she saw herself particularly distinctly going up the stairs.*'

I naturally required a special determinant for this. Dora objected that she would anyhow have had to go upstairs if she had wanted to get to her flat, which was on an upper floor. It was easy to brush aside this objection (which was probably not very seriously intended) by pointing out that if she had been able to travel in her dream from the unknown town to Vienna without making a railway journey she ought also to have been able to leave out a flight of stairs. She then proceeded to relate that after the appendicitis she had not been able to walk properly and had dragged her right foot. This state of things had continued for a long time, and on that account she had been particularly glad to avoid stairs. Even now her foot sometimes dragged. The doctors whom she had consulted at her father's desire had been very much astonished at this most unusual after-effect of an appendicitis, especially as the abdominal pains had not recurred and did not in any way accompany the dragging of the foot.

Here, then, we have a true hysterical symptom. The fever may have been organically determined—perhaps by one of those very frequent attacks of influenza that are not localized in any particular part of the body. Nevertheless it was now established that the neurosis had seized upon this chance event and made use of it for an utterance of its own. Dora had therefore given herself an illness which she had read up about in the encyclopaedia, and she had punished herself for dipping into its pages. But she was forced to recognize that the punishment could not possibly apply to her reading the innocent article in question. It must have been inflicted as the result of a process of displacement, after another occasion of more guilty reading had become associated with this one; and the guilty occasion must lie concealed in her memory behind the contemporaneous innocent one. It might still be possible, perhaps, to discover the nature of the subjects she had read about on that other occasion.

What, then, was the meaning of this condition, of this attempted simulation of a perityphlitis? The remainder of the disorder, the dragging of one leg, was entirely out of keeping with perityphlitis. It must, no doubt, fit in better with the secret and possibly sexual meaning of the clinical picture; and if it were elucidated might in its turn throw light on the meaning which we were in search of. I looked about for a method of approaching the puzzle. Periods of time had been mentioned in the dream; and time is assuredly never a matter of indifference in any biological event. I therefore asked Dora when this attack of appendicitis had taken place; whether it had been before or after the scene by the lake. Every difficulty was resolved at a single blow by her prompt reply: 'Nine months later.' The period of time is sufficiently characteristic. Her supposed attack of appendicitis had thus enabled the patient with the modest means at her disposal (the pains and the menstrual flow) to realize a phantasy of *childbirth*. Dora was naturally aware of the significance of this period of time, and could not dispute the probability of her having, on the occasion under discussion, read up in the encyclopaedia about pregnancy and childbirth. But what was all this about her dragging her leg? I could now hazard a guess. That is how people walk when they have twisted a foot. So she had made a 'false step': which was true indeed if she could give birth to a child nine months after the scene by the lake. But there was still another requirement upon the fulfilment of which I had to insist. I am convinced that a symptom of this kind can only arise where it has an *infantile* prototype. All my experience hitherto has led me to hold firmly to the view that recollections derived from the impressions of later years do not possess sufficient force to enable them to establish themselves as symptoms. I scarcely dared hope that Dora would provide me with the material that I wanted from her childhood, for the fact is that I am not yet in a position to assert the general validity of this rule, much as I should like to be able to do so. But in this case there came an immediate confirmation of it. Yes, said Dora, once when she was a child she had twisted the same foot; she had slipped on one of the steps as she was going *downstairs*. The foot—and it was actually the same one that she afterwards dragged—had swelled up and had to be bandaged and she had to lie up for some weeks. This had been a short time before the attack of nervous asthma in her eighth year.

The next thing to do was to turn to account our knowledge of the existence of this phantasy: 'If it is true that you were delivered of a child nine months after the scene by the lake, and that you are going about to this very day carrying the consequences of your false step with you, then it follows that in your unconscious you must have regretted the upshot of the scene. In your unconscious thoughts, that is to say, you have made an emendation in it. The assumption that underlies your phantasy of childbirth is that on that occasion something took place,[6] that on that occasion you experienced and went through everything that you were in fact obliged to pick up later on from the encyclopaedia. So you see that your love for Herr K. did not come to an end with the scene, but that (as I maintained) it has persisted down to the present day—though it is true that you are unconscious of it.'—And Dora disputed the fact no longer.

The labour of elucidating the second dream had so far occupied two hours. At the end of the second session, when I expressed my satisfaction at the result, Dora replied in a depreciatory tone: 'Why, has anything so very remarkable come out?' These words prepared me for the advent of fresh revelations.

She opened the third session with these words: 'Do you know that I am here for the last time to-day?'—'How can I know, as you have said nothing to me about it?'—'Yes. I made up my mind to put up with it till the New Year. But I shall wait no longer than that to be cured.'—'You know that you are free to stop the treatment at any time. But for to-day we will go on with our work. When did you come to this decision?'—'A fortnight ago, I think.'—'That sounds just like a maidservant or a governess—a fortnight's warning.'—'There was a governess who gave warning with the K.'s, when I was on my visit to them that time

6. The phantasy of defloration is thus found to have an application to Herr K., and we begin to see why this part of the dream contained material taken from the scene by the lake—the refusal, two and a half hours, the wood, the invitation to L——.

L———, by the lake.'—'Really? You have never told me about her. Tell me.'

'Well, there was a young girl in the house, who was the children's governess; and she behaved in the most extraordinary way to Herr K. She never said good morning to him, never answered his remarks, never handed him anything at table when he asked for it, and in short treated him like thin air. For that matter he was hardly any politer to her. A day or two before the scene by the lake, the girl took me aside and said she had something to tell me. She then told me that Herr K. had made advances to her at a time when his wife was away for several weeks; he had made violent love to her and had implored her to yield to his entreaties, saying that he got nothing from his wife, and so on.'—'Why, those are the very words he used afterwards, when he made his proposal to you and you gave him the slap in his face'.—'Yes. She had given way to him, but after a little while he had ceased to care for her, and since then she hated him.'—'And this governess had given warning?'— 'No. She meant to give warning. She told me that as soon as she felt she was thrown over she had told her parents what had happened. They were respectable people living in Germany somewhere. Her parents said that she must leave the house instantly; and, as she failed to do so, they wrote to her saying that they would have nothing more to do with her, and that she was never to come home again.'—'And why had she not gone away?'—'She said she meant to wait a little longer, to see if there might not be some change in Herr K. She could not bear living like that any more, she said, and if she saw no change she should give warning and go away.'—'And what became of the girl?'—'I only know that she went away.'—'And she did not have a child as a result of the adventure?'—'No.'

Here, therefore (and quite in accordance with the rules), was a piece of material information coming to light in the middle of the analysis and helping to solve problems which had previously been raised. I was able to say to Dora: 'Now I know your motive for the slap in the face with which you answered Herr K.'s proposal. It was not that you were offended at his suggestions; you were actuated by jealousy and revenge. At the time when the governess was telling you her story you were still able to make use of your gift for putting on one side everything that is not agreeable to your feelings. But at the moment when Herr K. used the words "I get nothing out of my wife"—which were the same words he had used to the governess—fresh emotions were aroused in you and tipped the balance. "Does he dare", you said to yourself, "to treat me like a governess, like a servant?" Wounded pride added to jealousy and to the conscious motives of common sense—it was too much.[7] To prove to you how deeply impressed you were by the governess's story, let me

---

7. It is not a matter of indifference, perhaps, that Dora may have heard her father make the same complaint about his wife, just as I myself did from his own lips. She was perfectly well aware of its meaning.

draw your attention to the repeated occasions upon which you have identified yourself with her both in your dream and in your conduct. You told your parents what happened—a fact which we have hitherto been unable to account for—just as the governess wrote and told *her* parents. You give me a fortnight's warning, just like a governess. The letter in the dream which gave you leave to go home is the counterpart of the governess's letter from her parents forbidding her to do so.'

'Then why did I not tell my parents at once?'

'How much time did you allow to elapse?'

'The scene took place on the last day of June; I told my mother about it on July 14th.'

'Again a fortnight, then—the time characteristic for a person in service. Now I can answer your question. You understood the poor girl very well. She did not want to go away at once, because she still had hopes, because she expected that Herr K.'s affections would return to her again. So that must have been your motive too. You waited for that length of time so as to see whether he would repeat his proposals; if he had, you would have concluded that he was in earnest, and did not mean to play with you as he had done with the governess.'

'A few days after I had left he sent me a picture post-card.'

'Yes, but when after that nothing more came, you gave free rein to your feelings of revenge. I can even imagine that at that time you were still able to find room for a subsidiary intention, and thought that your accusation might be a means of inducing him to travel to the place where you were living.—'As he actually offered to do at first,' Dora threw in.—'In that way your longing for him would have been appeased'—here she nodded assent, a thing which I had not expected—'and he might have made you the amends you desired.'

'What amends?'

'The fact is, I am beginning to suspect that you took the affair with Herr K. much more seriously than you have been willing to admit so far. Had not the K.'s often talked of getting a divorce?'

'Yes, certainly: At first she did not want to, on account of the children. And now she wants to, but he no longer does.'

'May you not have thought that he wanted to get divorced from his wife so as to marry you? And that now he no longer wants to because he has no one to replace her? It is true that two years ago you were very young. But you told me yourself that your mother was engaged at seventeen and then waited two years for her husband. A daughter usually takes her mother's love-story as her model. So you too wanted to wait for him, and you took it that he was only waiting till you were grown up enough to be his wife. I imagine that this was a perfectly serious plan for the future in your eyes. You have not even got the right to assert that it was out of the question for Herr K. to have had any such intention; you have told me enough about him that points directly towards his having such an intention. Nor does his behaviour at L——

contradict this view. After all, you did not let him finish his speech and do not know what he meant to say to you. Incidentally, the scheme would by no means have been so impracticable. Your father's relations with Frau K.— and it was probably only for this reason that you lent them your support for so long—made it certain that her consent to a divorce could be obtained; and you can get anything you like out of your father. Indeed, if your temptation at L—— had had a different upshot, this would have been the only possible solution for all the parties concerned. And I think that is why you regretted the actual event so deeply and emended it in the phantasy which made its appearance in the shape of the appendicitis. So it must have been a bitter piece of disillusionment for you when the effect of your charges against Herr K. was not that he renewed his proposals but that he replied instead with denials and slanders. You will agree that nothing makes you so angry as having it thought that you merely fancied the scene by the lake. I know now—and this is what you do not want to be reminded of—that you *did* fancy that Herr K.'s proposals were serious, and that he would not leave off until you had married him.'

Dora had listened to me without any of her usual contradictions. She seemed to be moved; she said good-bye to me very warmly, with the heartiest wishes for the New Year, and—came no more. Her father, who called on me two or three times afterwards, assured me that she would come back again, and said it was easy to see that she was eager for the treatment to continue. But it must be confessed that Dora's father was never entirely straightforward. He had given his support to the treatment so long as he could hope that I should 'talk' Dora out of her belief that there was something more than a friendship between him and Frau K. His interest faded when he observed that it was not my intention to bring about that result. I knew Dora would not come back again. Her breaking off so unexpectedly, just when my hopes of a successful termination of the treatment were at their highest, and her thus bringing those hopes to nothing—this was an unmistakable act of vengeance on her part. Her purpose of self-injury also profited by this action. No one who, like me, conjures up the most evil of those half-tamed demons that inhabit the human breast, and seeks to wrestle with them, can expect to come through the struggle unscathed. Might I perhaps have kept the girl under my treatment if I myself had acted a part, if I had exaggerated the importance to me of her staying on, and had shown a warm personal interest in her—a course which, even after allowing for my position as her physician, would have been tantamount to providing her with a substitute for the affection she longed for? I do not know. Since in every case a portion of the factors that are encountered under the form of resistance remains unknown, I have always avoided acting a part, and have contented myself with practising the humbler arts of psychology. In spite of every theoretical interest and of every endeavour to be of assistance as a physician, I keep the fact in mind that there must be some limits set to the extent to which psychological influence may be used, and I respect as one of these limits the patient's own will and understanding.

Nor do I know whether Herr K. would have done any better if it had been revealed to him that the slap Dora gave him by no means signified a final 'No' on her part, but that it expressed the jealousy which had lately been roused in her, while her strongest feelings were still on his side. If he had disregarded that first 'No', and had continued to press his suit with a passion which left room for no doubts, the result might very well have been a triumph of the girl's affection for him over all her internal difficulties. But I think she might just as well have been merely provoked into satisfying her craving for revenge upon him all the more thoroughly. It is never possible to calculate towards which side the decision will incline in such a conflict of motives: whether towards the removal of the repression or towards its reinforcement. Incapacity for meeting a *real* erotic demand is one of the most essential features of a neurosis. Neurotics are dominated by the opposition between reality and phantasy. If what they long for the most intensely in their phantasies is presented to them in reality, they none the less flee from it; and they abandon themselves to their phantasies the most readily where they need no longer fear to see them realized. Nevertheless, the barrier erected by repression can fall before the onslaught of a violent emotional excitement produced by a real cause; it is possible for a neurosis to be overcome by reality. But we have no general means of calculating through what person or what event such a cure can be effected.

IV

POSTSCRIPT

It is true that I have introduced this paper as a fragment of an analysis; but the reader will have discovered that it is incomplete to a far greater degree than its title might have led him to expect. It is therefore only proper that I should attempt to give a reason for the omissions—which are by no means accidental.

A number of the results of the analysis have been omitted, because at the time when work was broken off they had either not been established with sufficient certainty or they required further study before any general statement could be made about them. At other points, where it seemed to be permissible, I have indicated the direction along which some particular solution would probably have been found to lie. I have in this paper left entirely out of account the technique, which does not at all follow as a matter of course, but by whose means alone the pure metal of valuable unconscious thoughts can be extracted from the raw material of the patient's associations. This brings with it the disadvantage of the reader being given no opportunity of testing the correctness of my procedure in the course of this exposition of the case. I found it quite impracticable, however, to deal simultaneously with the technique of analysis and with the internal structure of a case of hysteria: I could scarcely have accomplished such a task, and if I had, the result would have been almost unreadable. The technique of analysis demands an entirely separate exposition, which would have to be illustrated by numerous examples chosen from a very great variety of cases and which would not have to take the results obtained in each particular case into account. Nor have I attempted in this paper to substantiate the psychological postulates which will be seen to underlie my descriptions of mental phenomena. A cursory attempt to do so would have effected nothing; an exhaustive one would have been a volume in itself. I can only assure the reader that I approached the study of the phenomena revealed by observation of the psychoneuroses without being pledged to any particular psychological system, and that I then proceeded to adjust my views until they seemed adapted for giving an account of the collection of facts which had been observed. I take no pride in having avoided speculation; the material for my hypotheses was collected by the most extensive and laborious series of observations. The decidedness of my attitude on the subject of the unconscious is perhaps specially likely to cause offence, for I handle unconscious ideas, unconscious trains of thought, and unconscious impulses as though they were no less valid and unimpeachable psychological data than conscious ones. But of this I am certain—that any one who sets out to investigate the same region of phenomena and employs the same method will find himself compelled to take up the same position, however much philosophers may expostulate.

Some of my medical colleagues have looked upon my theory of hysteria as a purely psychological one, and have for that reason pronounced it *ipso facto* incapable of solving a pathological problem. They may perhaps discover from this paper that their objection was based upon their having unjustifiably transferred what is a characteristic of the technique on to the theory itself. It is the therapeutic technique alone that is purely psychological; the theory does not by any means fail to point out that neuroses have an organic basis—though it is true that it does not look for that basis in any pathological anatomical changes, and provisionally substitutes the conception of organic functions for the chemical changes which we should expect to find but which we are at present unable to apprehend. No one, probably, will be inclined to deny the sexual function the character of an organic factor, and it is the sexual function that I look upon as the foundation of hysteria and of the psychoneuroses in general. No theory of sexual life will, I suspect, be able to avoid assuming the existence of some definite sexual substances having an excitant action. Indeed, of all the clinical pictures which we meet with in clinical medicine, it is the phenomena of intoxication and abstinence in connection with the use of certain chronic poisons that most closely resemble the genuine psychoneuroses.

But, once again, in the present paper I have not gone fully into all that might be said to-day about 'somatic compliance', about the infantile germs of perversion, about the erotogenic zones, and about our predisposition towards bisexuality; I have merely drawn attention to the points at which the analysis comes into contact with these organic bases of the symptoms. More than this could not be done with a single case. And I had the same reasons that I have already mentioned for wishing to avoid a cursory discussion of these factors. There is a rich opportunity here for further works, based upon the study of a large number of analyses.

Nevertheless, in publishing this paper, incomplete though it is, I had two objects in view. In the first place, I wished to supplement my book on the interpretation of dreams by showing how an art, which would otherwise be useless, can be turned to account for the discovery of the hidden and repressed parts of mental life. (Incidentally, in the process of analysing the two dreams dealt with in the paper, the technique of dream-interpretation, which is similar to that of psycho-analysis, has come under consideration.) In the second place, I wished to stimulate interest in a whole group of phenomena of which science is still in complete ignorance to-day because they can only be brought to light by the use of this particular method. No one, I believe, can have had any true conception of the complexity of the psychological events in a case of hysteria—the juxtaposition of the most dissimilar tendencies, the mutual dependence of contrary ideas, the repressions and displacements, and so on. The emphasis laid by Janet upon the 'idée fixe' which becomes transformed into a symptom amounts to no more than an extremely meagre attempt at schematization. Moreover, it is impossible to avoid the suspicion that, when the ideas attaching to certain excitations are incapable of becoming conscious, those excitations must act upon one another differently, run a different course, and manifest themselves differently from those other excitations which we describe as 'normal' and which have ideas attaching to them of which we become conscious. When once things have been made clear up to this point, no obstacle can remain in the way of an understanding of a therapeutic method which removes neurotic symptoms by transforming ideas of the former kind into normal ones.

I was further anxious to show that sexuality does not simply intervene, like a *deus ex machina*, on one single occasion, at some point in the working of the processes which characterize hysteria, but that it provides the motive power for every single symptom, and for every single manifestation of a symptom. The symptoms of the disease are nothing else than *the patient's sexual activity*. A single case can never be capable of proving a theorem so general as this one; but I can only repeat over and over again—for I never find it otherwise—that sexuality is the key to the problem of the psychoneuroses and of the neuroses in general. No one who disdains the key will ever be able to unlock the door. I still await news of the investigations which are to make it possible to contradict this theorem or to limit its scope. What I have hitherto heard against it have been expressions of personal dislike or disbelief. To these it is enough to reply in the words of Charcot: 'Ça n'empêche pas d'exister.'

Nor is the case of whose history and treatment I have published a fragment in these pages well calculated to put the value of psycho-analytic therapy in its true light. Not only the briefness of the treatment (which hardly lasted three months) but another factor inherent in the nature of the case prevented results being brought about such as are attainable in other instances, where the improvement will be admitted by the patient and his relatives and will approximate more or less closely to a complete recovery. Satisfactory results of this kind are reached when the symptoms are maintained solely by the internal conflict between the impulses concerned with sexuality. In such cases the patient's condition will be seen improving in proportion as he is helped towards a solution of his mental problems by the translation of pathogenic into normal material. The course of events is very different when the symptoms have become enlisted in the service of external motives, as had happened with Dora during the two preceding years. It is surprising, and might easily be misleading, to find that the patient's condition shows no noticeable alteration even though considerable progress has been made with the work of analysis. But in reality things are not as bad as they seem. It is true that the symptoms do not disappear while the work is proceeding; but they disappear a little while later, when the relations between patient and physician have been dissolved. The postponement of recovery or improvement is really only caused by the physician's own person.

I must go back a little, in order to make the matter intelligible. It may be safely said that during psycho-analytic treatment the formation of new symptoms is invariably stopped. But the productive powers of the neurosis are by no means extinguished; they are occupied in the creation of a special class of mental structures, for the most part unconscious, to which the name of 'transferences' may be given.

What are transferences? They are new editions or facsimiles of the impulses and phantasies which are aroused and made conscious during the progress of the analysis; but they have this peculiarity, which is characteristic for their species, that they replace some earlier person by the person of the physician. To put it another way: a whole series of psychological experiences are revived, not as belonging to the past, but as applying to the person of the physician at the present moment. Some of these transferences have a content which differs from that of their model in no respect whatever except for the substitution. These then— to keep to the same metaphor—are merely new impressions or reprints. Others are more ingeniously constructed; their content has been subjected to a moderating influence—to *sublimation*, as I call it—and they may even become conscious, by cleverly taking advantage of some real peculiarity in the physician's person or circumstances and attaching themselves to that. These, then, will no longer be new impressions, but revised editions.

If the theory of analytic technique is gone into, it becomes evident that transference is an inevitable necessity. Practical experience, at all events, shows conclusively that there is no means of avoiding it, and that this latest creation of the disease must be combated like all the earlier ones. This happens, however, to be by far the hardest part of the whole task. It is easy to learn how to interpret dreams, to extract from the patient's associations his unconscious thoughts and memories, and to practise similar explanatory arts: for these the patient himself will always provide the text. Transference is the one thing the presence of which has to be detected almost without assistance and with only the slightest clues to go upon, while at the same time the risk of making arbitrary inferences has to be avoided. Nevertheless, transference cannot be evaded, since use is made of it in setting up all the obstacles that make the material inaccessible to treatment, and since it is only after the transference has been resolved that a patient arrives at a sense of conviction of the validity of the connections which have been constructed during the analysis.

Some people may feel inclined to look upon it as a serious objection to a method which is in any case troublesome enough that it itself should multiply the labours of the physician by creating a new species of pathological mental products. They may even be tempted to infer from the existence of transferences that the patient will be injured by analytic treatment. Both these suppositions would be mistaken. The physician's labours are not multiplied by transference; it need make no difference to him whether he has to overcome any particular impulse of the patient's in connection with himself or with some one else. Nor does the treatment force upon the patient, in the shape of transference, any new task which he would not otherwise have performed. It is true that neuroses may be cured in institutions from which psycho-analytic treatment is excluded, that hysteria may be said to be cured not by the method but by the physician, and that there is usually a sort of blind dependence and a permanent bond between a patient and the physician who has removed his symptoms by hypnotic suggestion; but the scientific explanation of all these facts is to be found in the existence of 'transferences' such as are regularly directed by patients on to their physicians. Psycho-analytic treatment does not *create* transferences, it merely brings them to light, like so many other hidden psychical factors. The only difference is this— that spontaneously a patient will only call up affectionate and friendly transferences to help towards his recovery; if they cannot be called up, he feels the physician is 'antipathetic' to him, and breaks away from him as fast as possible and without having been influenced by him. In psycho-analysis, on the other hand, since the play of motives is different, all the patient's tendencies, including hostile ones, are aroused; they are then turned to account for the purposes of the analysis by being made conscious, and in this way the transference is constantly being destroyed. Transference, which seems ordained to be the greatest obstacle to psycho-analysis, becomes its most powerful ally, if its presence can be detected each time and explained to the patient.

I have been obliged to speak of transference, for it is only by means of this factor that I can elucidate the peculiarities of Dora's analysis.[8] Its great merit, namely, the unusual clarity which makes it seem so suitable as a first introductory publication, is closely bound up with its great defect, which led to its being broken off prematurely. I did not succeed in mastering the transference in good time. Owing to the read-iness with which Dora put one part of the pathogenic material at my disposal during the treatment, I neglected the precaution of looking out for the first signs of transference, which was being prepared in connection with another part of the same material—a part of which I was in ig-norance. At the beginning it was clear that I was replacing her father in her imagination, which was not unlikely, in view of the difference between our ages. She was even constantly comparing me with him consciously, and kept anxiously trying to make sure whether I was being quite straightforward with her, for her father 'always preferred secrecy and roundabout ways'. But when the first dream came, in which she gave herself the warning that she had better leave my treatment just as she had formerly left Herr K.'s house, I ought to have listened to the warning myself. 'Now,' I ought to have said to her, 'it is from Herr K. that you have made a transference on to me. Have you noticed anything that leads you to suspect me of evil intentions similar (whether openly or in some sublimated form) to Herr K.'s? Or have you been struck by anything about me or got to know anything about me which has caught your fancy, as happened previously with Herr K.?' Her attention would then have been turned to some detail in our relations, or in my person or circumstances, behind which there lay concealed something analo-gous but immeasurably more important concerning Herr K. And when this transference had been cleared up, the analysis would have obtained access to new memories, dealing, probably, with actual events. But I was deaf to this first note of warning, thinking I had ample time before me, since no further stages of transference developed and the material for the analysis had not yet run dry. In this way the transference took me unawares, and, because of the unknown quantity in me which reminded Dora of Herr K., she took her revenge on me as she wanted to take her revenge on him, and deserted me as she believed herself to have been deceived and deserted by him. Thus she *acted out* an essential part of her recollections and phantasies instead of reproducing it in the treatment. What this unknown quantity was I naturally cannot tell. I

8. {For Freud's later treatment of this issue, see below, "Observations on Transference Love," pp. 378–87.}

suspect that it had to do with money, or with jealousy of another patient who had kept up relations with my family after her recovery. When it is possible to work transferences into the analysis at an early stage, the course of the analysis is retarded and obscured, but its existence is better guaranteed against sudden and overwhelming resistances.

In Dora's second dream there are several clear allusions to transference. At the time she was telling me the dream I was still unaware (and did not learn until two days later) that we had only *two hours* more work before us. This was the same length of time which she had spent in front of the Sistine Madonna, and which (by making a correction and putting 'two hours' instead of 'two and a half hours') she had taken as the length of the walk which she had not made round the lake. The striving and waiting in the dream, which related to the young man in Germany, and had their origin in her waiting till Herr K. could marry her, had been expressed in the transference a few days before. The treatment, she had thought, was too long for her; she would never have the patience to wait so long And yet in the first few weeks she had had discernment enough to listen without making any such objections when I informed her that her complete recovery would require perhaps a year. Her refusing in the dream to be accompanied, and preferring to go alone, also originated from her visit to the gallery at Dresden, and I was myself to experience them on the appointed day. What they meant was, no doubt: 'Men are all so detestable that I would rather not marry. This is my revenge.'9

If cruel impulses and revengeful motives, which have already been used in the patient's ordinary life for maintaining her symptoms, become transferred on to the physician during treatment, before he has had time to detach them from himself by tracing them back to their sources, then it is not to be wondered at if the patient's condition is unaffected by his therapeutic efforts. For how could the patient take a more effective revenge than by demonstrating upon her own person the helplessness and incapacity of the physician? Nevertheless, I am not inclined to put too low a value on the therapeutic results even of such a fragmentary treatment as Dora's.

9. The longer the interval of time that separates me from the end of this analysis, the more probable it seems to me that the fault in my technique lay in this omission: I failed to discover in time and to inform the patient that her homosexual (gynaecophilic) love for Frau K. was the strongest unconscious current in her mental life. I ought to have guessed that the main source of her knowledge of sexual matters could have been no one but Frau K.—the very person who later on charged her with being interested in those same subjects. Her knowing all about such things and, at the same time, her always pretending not to know where her knowledge came from was really too remarkable. I ought to have attacked this riddle and looked for the motive of such an extraordinary piece of repression. If I had done this, the second dream would have given me my answer. The remorseless craving for revenge expressed in that dream was suited as nothing else was to conceal the current of feeling that ran contrary to it—the magnanimity with which she forgave the treachery of the friend she loved and concealed from every one the fact that it was this friend who had herself revealed to her the knowledge which had later been the ground of the accusations against her. Before I had learned the importance of the homosexual current of feeling in psychoneurotics, I was often brought to a standstill in the treatment of my cases or found myself in complete perplexity.

It was not until fifteen months after the case was over and this paper composed that I had news of my patient's condition and the effects of my treatment. On a date which is not a matter of complete indifference, on the first of April (times and dates. as we know, were never without significance for her), Dora came to see me again: to finish her story and to ask for help once more. One glance at her face, however, was enough to tell me that she was not in earnest over her request. For four or five weeks after stopping the treatment she had been 'all in a muddle', as she said. A great improvement had then set in; her attacks had become less frequent and her spirits had risen. In the May of that year one of the K.'s two children (it had always been delicate) had died. She took the opportunity of their loss to pay them a visit of condolence, and they received her as though nothing had happened in the last three years. She made it up with them, she took her revenge on them, and she brought her own business to a satisfactory conclusion. To the wife she said: 'I know you have an affair with my father'; and the other did not deny it. From the husband she drew an admission of the scene by the lake which he had disputed, and brought the news of her vindication home to her father. Since then she had not resumed her relations with the family.

After this she had gone on quite well till the middle of October, when she had had another attack of aphonia which had lasted for six weeks. I was surprised at this news, and, on my asking her whether there had been any exciting cause, she told me that the attack had followed upon a violent fright. She had seen some one run over by a carriage. Finally she came out with the fact that the accident had occurred to no less a person than Herr K. himself. She had come across him in the street one day; they had met in a place where there was a great deal of traffic; he had stopped in front of her as though in bewilderment, and in his abstraction he had allowed himself to be knocked down by a carriage. She had been able to convince herself, however, that he escaped without serious injury. She still felt some slight emotion if she heard any one speak of her father's affair with Frau K., but otherwise she had no further concern with the matter. She was absorbed in her work, and had no thoughts of marrying.

She went on to tell me that she had come for help on account of a right-sided facial neuralgia, from which she was now suffering day and night. 'How long has it been going on?' 'Exactly a fortnight.' I could not help smiling; for I was able to show her that exactly a fortnight earlier she had read a piece of news that concerned me in the newspaper. (This was in 1902.)[1] And this she confirmed.

Her alleged facial neuralgia was thus a self-punishment—remorse at having once given Herr K. a box on the ear, and at having transferred

1. [No doubt the news was of Freud's appointment to a Professorship in March of that year.]

her feelings of revenge on to me. I do not know what kind of help she wanted from me, but I promised to forgive her for having deprived me of the satisfaction of affording her a far more radical cure for her troubles. Years have again gone by since her visit. In the meantime the girl has married, and indeed—unless all the signs mislead me—she has married the young man who came into her associations at the beginning of the analysis of the second dream.[2] Just as the first dream represented her turning away from the man she loved to her father—that is to say, her flight from life into disease—so the second dream announced that she was about to tear herself free from her father and had been reclaimed once more by the realities of life.

Three Essays on the Theory of Sexuality

If *The Interpretation of Dreams* is the first pillar on which the structure of psychoanalysis rests, the *Three Essays on the Theory of Sexuality* is the second. The brochure of some eighty pages of 1905, quite sparse and without some of its most celebrated sections, was steadily elaborated as edition after edition appeared. The last enlargement of the *Three Essays* came in 1924 (the so-called sixth edition of 1925 is identical with this publication), and it was then some forty pages longer than the little book of the first edition. One can follow the process of elaboration through the footnotes specifying the date that some paragraph or section was added to the original.

As earlier selections have made abundantly clear, Freud's interest in sexuality as the fundamental cause of neurosis and its prominence in mental life in general goes back to the early 1890s. His correspondence with Fliess, and especially the memoranda he enclosed with his letters, demonstrate his concentration on the erotic dimensions of the mind even before he had "invented" psychoanalysis. Fliess was most useful to Freud in this pursuit; the ideas of bisexuality, and of infant sexuality, owe much to Freud's intimate from Berlin. The abandonment of the "seduction theory" of the neuroses, which depended wholly on sexual etiologies, did not weaken Freud's commitment to the central import of sexuality. On the contrary, it allowed him to see its function in fantasy life. As soon as he had completed and published his *Interpretation of Dreams*, Freud accordingly turned to a theory of sexuality, and the *Three Essays* was the result.

---

2. [In the editions of 1909, 1912 and 1921 the following footnote appeared at this point: 'This, as I afterwards learnt, was a mistaken notion.']

I

THE SEXUAL ABERRATIONS[1]

The fact of the existence of sexual needs in human beings and animals is expressed in biology by the assumption of a 'sexual instinct', on the analogy of the instinct of nutrition, that is of hunger. Everyday language possesses no counterpart to the word 'hunger', but science makes use of the word 'libido' for that purpose.

Popular opinion has quite definite ideas about the nature and characteristics of this sexual instinct. It is generally understood to be absent in childhood, to set in at the time of puberty in connection with the process of coming to maturity and to be revealed in the manifestations of an irresistible attraction exercised by one sex upon the other; while its aim is presumed to be sexual union, or at all events actions leading in that direction. We have every reason to believe, however, that these views give a very false picture of the true situation. If we look into them more closely we shall find that they contain a number of errors, inaccuracies and hasty conclusions.

I shall at this point introduce two technical terms. Let us call the person from whom sexual attraction proceeds the *sexual object* and the act towards which the instinct tends the *sexual aim*. Scientifically sifted observation, then, shows that numerous deviations occur in respect of both of these—the sexual object and the sexual aim. The relation between these deviations and what is assumed to be normal requires thorough investigation.

(1) DEVIATIONS IN RESPECT OF THE
SEXUAL OBJECT

The popular view of the sexual instinct is beautifully reflected in the poetic fable which tells how the original human beings were cut up into two halves—man and woman—and how these are always striving to unite again in love. It comes as a great surprise therefore to learn that there are men whose sexual object is a man and not a woman, and women whose sexual object is a woman and not a man. People of this kind are described as having 'contrary sexual feelings', or better, as being 'inverts', and the fact is described as 'inversion'. The number of such

1. The information contained in this first essay is derived from the well-known writings of Krafft-Ebing, Moll, Moebius, Havelock Ellis, Schrenck-Notzing, Löwenfeld, Eulenburg, Bloch, and Hirschfeld, and from the *Jahrbuch für sexuelle Zwischenstufen*, published under the direction of the last-named author. * * * {This note, like some of the footnotes it has been necessary to omit, should serve as a reminder (as should the first chapter of *The Interpretation of Dreams* and the opening page of *Jokes and Their Relation to the Unconscious* [1905]) that Freud was only too ready to acknowledge the work of his precursors.}

people is very considerable, though there are difficulties in establishing it precisely.

(A) INVERSION

BEHAVIOUR
OF INVERTS

Such people vary greatly in their behaviour in several respects.

(a) They may be *absolute* inverts. In that case their sexual objects are exclusively of their own sex. Persons of the opposite sex are never the object of their sexual desire, but leave them cold, or even arouse sexual aversion in them. * * *

(b) They may be *amphigenic* inverts, that is psychosexual hermaphrodites. In that case their sexual objects may equally well be of their own or of the opposite sex: * * *

(c) They may be *contingent* inverts. In that case, under certain external conditions—of which inaccessibility of any normal sexual object and imitation are the chief—they are capable of taking as their sexual object someone of their own sex and of deriving satisfaction from sexual intercourse with him.

Again, inverts vary in their views as to the peculiarity of their sexual instinct. Some of them accept their inversion as something in the natural course of things, just as a normal person accepts the direction of *his* libido, and insist energetically that inversion is as legitimate as the normal attitude; others rebel against their inversion and feel it as a pathological compulsion.

Other variations occur which relate to questions of time. The trait of inversion may either date back to the very beginning, as far back as the subject's memory reaches, or it may not have become noticeable till some particular time before or after puberty. It may either persist throughout life, or it may go into temporary abeyance, or again it may constitute an episode on the way to a normal development. It may even make its first appearance late in life after a long period of normal sexual activity. A periodic oscillation between a normal and an inverted sexual object has also sometimes been observed. Those cases are of particular interest in which the libido changes over to an inverted sexual object after a distressing experience with a normal one.

As a rule these different kinds of variations are found side by side independently of one another. It is, however, safe to assume that the most extreme form of inversion will have been present from a very early age and that the person concerned will feel at one with his peculiarity.

* * *

NATURE OF
INVERSION

The earliest assessments regarded inversion as an innate indication of nervous degeneracy. This corresponded to the fact that medical observers first came across it in persons suffering, or appearing to suffer, from nervous diseases. This characterization of inversion involves two suppositions, which must be considered separately: that it is innate and that it is degenerate.

DEGENERACY   The attribution of degeneracy in this connection is open to the objections which can be raised against the indiscriminate use of the word in general. It has become the fashion to regard any symptom which is not obviously due to trauma or infection as a sign of degeneracy. * * * This being so, it may well be asked whether an attribution of 'degeneracy' is of any value or adds anything to our knowledge. It seems wiser only to speak of it where

(1) several serious deviations from the normal are found together, and

(2) the capacity for efficient functioning and survival seem to be severely impaired.[2]

Several facts go to show that in this legitimate sense of the word inverts cannot be regarded as degenerate:

(1) Inversion is found in people who exhibit no other serious deviations from the normal.

(2) It is similarly found in people whose efficiency is unimpaired, and who are indeed distinguished by specially high intellectual development and ethical culture.

(3) If we disregard the patients we come across in our medical practice, and cast our eyes round a wider horizon, we shall come in two directions upon facts which make it impossible to regard inversion as a sign of degeneracy:

(a) Account must be taken of the fact that inversion was a frequent phenomenon—one might almost say an institution charged with important functions—among the peoples of antiquity at the height of their civilization.

(b) It is remarkably widespread among many savage and primitive races, whereas the concept of degeneracy is usually restricted to states of high civilization (cf. Bloch); and, even amongst the civilized peoples of Europe, climate and race exercise the most powerful influence on the prevalence of inversion and upon the attitude adopted towards it.

INNATE   As may be supposed, innateness is only attributed to
CHARACTER   the first, most extreme, class of inverts, and the evidence for it rests upon assurances given by them that at no time in their lives has their sexual instinct shown any sign of taking another course. The very existence of the two other classes, and especially the third [the 'contingent' inverts], is difficult to reconcile with the hypothesis of the innateness of inversion. This explains why those who support this

2. Moebius {"Über Entartung," *Grenzfragen des Nerven- und Seelenlebens*, III} (1900) confirms the view that we should be chary in making a diagnosis of degeneracy and that it has very little practical value: 'If we survey the field of degeneracy upon which some glimpses of revealing light have been thrown in these pages, it will at once be clear that there is small value in ever making a diagnosis of degeneracy.'

view tend to separate out the group of absolute inverts from all the rest, thus abandoning any attempt at giving an account of inversion which shall have universal application. In the view of these authorities inversion is innate in one group of cases, while in others it may have come about in other ways.

The reverse of this view is represented by the alternative one that inversion is an acquired character of the sexual instinct. This second view is based on the following considerations:

(1) In the case of many inverts, even absolute ones, it is possible to show that very early in their lives a sexual impression occurred which left a permanent after-effect in the shape of a tendency to homosexuality.

(2) In the case of many others, it is possible to point to external influences in their lives, whether of a favourable or inhibiting character, which have led sooner or later to a fixation of their inversion. (Such influences are exclusive relations with persons of their own sex, comradeship in war, detention in prison, the dangers of heterosexual intercourse, celibacy, sexual weakness, etc.)

(3) Inversion can be removed by hypnotic suggestion, which would be astonishing in an innate characteristic.

In view of these considerations it is even possible to doubt the very existence of such a thing as innate inversion. * * *

The apparent certainty of this conclusion is, however, completely countered by the reflection that many people are subjected to the same sexual influences (e.g. to seduction or mutual masturbation, which may occur in early youth) without becoming inverted or without remaining so permanently. We are therefore forced to a suspicion that the choice between 'innate' and 'acquired' is not an exclusive one or that it does not cover all the issues involved in inversion.

* * *

BISEXUALITY   A fresh contradiction of popular views is involved in the considerations put forward by Lydston [1889], Kiernan [1888] and Chevalier [1893] in an endeavour to account for the possibility of sexual inversion. It is popularly believed that a human being is either a man or a woman. Science, however, knows of cases in which the sexual characters are obscured, and in which it is consequently difficult to determine the sex. This arises in the first instance in the field of anatomy. The genitals of the individuals concerned combine male and female characteristics. (This condition is known as hermaphroditism.) In rare cases both kinds of sexual apparatus are found side by side fully developed (true hermaphroditism); but far more frequently both sets of organs are found in an atrophied condition.

The importance of these abnormalities lies in the unexpected fact that they facilitate our understanding of normal development. For it appears that a certain degree of anatomical hermaphroditism occurs normally. In every normal male or female individual, traces are found of the apparatus of the opposite sex. These either persist without function as rudimentary organs or become modified and take on other functions.

These long-familiar facts of anatomy lead us to suppose that an originally bisexual physical disposition has, in the course of evolution, become modified into a unisexual one, leaving behind only a few traces of the sex that has become atrophied.

* * *

The theory of bisexuality has been expressed in its crudest form by a spokesman of the male inverts: 'a feminine brain in a masculine body'. But we are ignorant of what characterizes a feminine brain. There is neither need nor justification for replacing the psychological problem by the anatomical one. Krafft-Ebing's attempted explanation seems to be more exactly framed than that of Ulrichs but does not differ from it in essentials. According to Krafft-Ebing * * * every individual's bisexual disposition endows him with masculine and feminine brain centres as well as with somatic organs of sex; these centres develop only at puberty, for the most part under the influence of the sex-gland, which is independent of them in the original disposition. But what has just been said of masculine and feminine brains applies equally to masculine and feminine 'centres'; and incidentally we have not even any grounds for assuming that certain areas of the brain ('centres') are set aside for the functions of sex, as is the case, for instance, with those of speech.

Nevertheless, two things emerge from these discussions. In the first place, a bisexual disposition is somehow concerned in inversion, though we do not know in what that disposition consists, beyond anatomical structure. And secondly, we have to deal with disturbances that affect the sexual instinct in the course of its development.

SEXUAL OBJECT   The theory of psychical hermaphroditism presup-
OF INVERTS   poses that the sexual object of an invert is the opposite
of that of a normal person. An inverted man, it holds, is like a woman in being subject to the charm that proceeds from masculine attributes both physical and mental: he feels he is a woman in search of a man.

But however well this applies to quite a number of inverts, it is, nevertheless, far from revealing a universal characteristic of inversion. There can be no doubt that a large proportion of male inverts retain the mental quality of masculinity, that they possess relatively few of the secondary characters of the opposite sex and that what they look for in their sexual object are in fact feminine mental traits. If this were not so, how would it be possible to explain the fact that male prostitutes who offer themselves to inverts—to-day just as they did in ancient times—imitate women in all the externals of their clothing and behaviour? Such imitation would otherwise inevitably clash with the ideal of the inverts. It is clear that in Greece, where the most masculine men were numbered among the inverts, what excited a man's love was not the *masculine* character of a boy, but his physical resemblance to a woman as well as his feminine mental qualities—his shyness, his modesty and his need for instruction and assistance. As soon as the boy became a man he ceased to be a sexual object for men and himself, perhaps, became a lover of boys. In this instance, therefore, as in many others, the sexual object is not someone of the same sex but someone who combines the characters of both sexes; there is, as it were, a compromise between an impulse that seeks for a man and one that seeks for a woman, while it remains a paramount condition that the object's body (i.e. genitals) shall be masculine. Thus the sexual object is a kind of reflection of the subject's own bisexual nature.[3]

The position in the case of women is less ambiguous; for among them the active inverts exhibit masculine characteristics, both physical and mental, with peculiar frequency and look for femininity in their sexual objects—though here again a closer knowledge of the facts might reveal greater variety.

SEXUAL AIM   The important fact to bear in mind is that no one single
OF INVERTS   aim can be laid down as applying in cases of inversion.

Among men, intercourse *per anum* by no means coincides with inversion; masturbation is quite as frequently their exclusive aim, and it is even true that restrictions of sexual aim—to the point of its being limited to simple outpourings of emotion—are commoner among them than among heterosexual lovers. Among women, too, the sexual aims of inverts are various: there seems to be a special preference for contact with the mucous membrane of the mouth.

CONCLUSION   It will be seen that we are not in a position to base a
                    satisfactory explanation of the origin of inversion upon

3. [This last sentence was added in 1915.—*Footnote added* 1910:] It is true that psycho-analysis has not yet produced a complete explanation of the origin of inversion; nevertheless, it has discovered the psychical mechanism of its development, and has made essential contributions to the statement of the problems involved. In all the cases we have examined we have established the fact that future inverts, in the earliest years of their childhood, pass through a phase of very intense but short-lived fixation to a woman (usually their mother), and that, after leaving this behind, they identify themselves with a woman and take *themselves* as their sexual object. * * * [*Added* 1915:] Psycho-analytic research is most decidedly opposed to any attempt at separating off homosexuals from the rest of mankind as a group of a special character. By studying sexual excitations other than those that are manifestly displayed, it has found that all human beings are capable of making a homosexual object-choice and have in fact made one in their unconscious. Indeed, libidinal attachments to persons of the same sex play no less a part as factors in normal mental life, and a greater part as a motive force for illness, than do similar attachments to the opposite sex. On the contrary, psycho-analysis considers that a choice of an object independently of its sex—freedom to range equally over male and female objects—as it is found in childhood, in primitive states of society and early periods of history, is the original basis from which, as a result of restriction in one direction or the other, both the normal and the inverted types develop. Thus from the point of view of psycho-analysis the exclusive sexual interest felt by men for women is also a problem that needs elucidating and is not a self-evident fact based upon an attraction that is ultimately of a chemical nature. * * * [*Added* 1920:] Ferenczi (1914) has brought forward a number of interesting points on the subject of inversion. He rightly protests that, because they have in common the symptom of inversion, a large number of conditions, which are very different from one another and which are of unequal importance both in organic and psychical respects, have been thrown together under the name of 'homosexuality.' * * *

the material at present before us. Nevertheless our investigation has put us in possession of a piece of knowledge which may turn out to be of greater importance to us than the solution of that problem. It has been brought to our notice that we have been in the habit of regarding the connection between the sexual instinct and the sexual object as more intimate than it in fact is. Experience of the cases that are considered abnormal has shown us that in them the sexual instinct and the sexual object are merely soldered together—a fact which we have been in danger of overlooking in consequence of the uniformity of the normal picture, where the object appears to form part and parcel of the instinct. We are thus warned to loosen the bond that exists in our thoughts between instinct and object. It seems probable that the sexual instinct is in the first instance independent of its object; nor is its origin likely to be due to its object's attractions.

(B) SEXUALLY IMMATURE PERSONS AND ANIMALS AS SEXUAL OBJECTS

People whose sexual objects belong to the normally inappropriate sex—that is, inverts—strike the observer as a collection of individuals who may be quite sound in other respects. On the other hand, cases in which sexually immature persons (children) are chosen as sexual objects are instantly judged as sporadic aberrations. It is only exceptionally that children are the exclusive sexual objects in such a case. They usually come to play that part when someone who is cowardly or has become impotent adopts them as a substitute, or when an urgent instinct (one which will not allow of postponement) cannot at the moment get possession of any more appropriate object. Nevertheless, a light is thrown on the nature of the sexual instinct by the fact that it permits of so much variation in its objects and such a cheapening of them—which hunger, with its far more energetic retention of its objects, would only permit in the most extreme instances. A similar consideration applies to sexual intercourse with animals, which is by no means rare, especially among country people, and in which sexual attraction seems to override the barriers of species.

One would be glad on aesthetic grounds to be able to ascribe these and other severe aberrations of the sexual instinct to insanity; but that cannot be done. Experience shows that disturbances of the sexual instinct among the insane do not differ from those that occur among the healthy and in whole races or occupations. Thus the sexual abuse of children is found with uncanny frequency among school teachers and child attendants, simply because they have the best opportunity for it. The insane merely exhibit any such aberration to an intensified degree; or, what is particularly significant, it may become exclusive and replace normal sexual satisfaction entirely.

The very remarkable relation which thus holds between sexual variations and the descending scale from health to insanity gives us plenty of material for thought. I am inclined to believe that it may be explained by the fact that the impulses of sexual life are among those which, even normally, are the least controlled by the higher activities of the mind. In my experience anyone who is in any way, whether socially or ethically, abnormal mentally is invariably abnormal also in his sexual life. But many people are abnormal in their sexual life who in every other respect approximate to the average, and have, along with the rest, passed through the process of human cultural development, in which sexuality remains the weak spot.

* * *

(2) DEVIATIONS IN RESPECT OF THE SEXUAL AIM

The normal sexual aim is regarded as being the union of the genitals in the act known as copulation, which leads to a release of the sexual tension and a temporary extinction of the sexual instinct—a satisfaction analogous to the sating of hunger. But even in the most normal sexual process we may detect rudiments which, if they had developed, would have led to the deviations described as 'perversions'. For there are certain intermediate relations to the sexual object, such as touching and looking at it, which lie on the road towards copulation and are recognized as being preliminary sexual aims. On the one hand these activities are themselves accompanied by pleasure, and on the other hand they intensify the excitation, which should persist until the final sexual aim is attained. Moreover, the kiss, one particular contact of this kind, between the mucous membrane of the lips of the two people concerned, is held in high sexual esteem among many nations (including the most highly civilized ones), in spite of the fact that the parts of the body involved do not form part of the sexual apparatus but constitute the entrance to the digestive tract. Here, then, are factors which provide a point of contact between the perversions and normal sexual life and which can also serve as a basis for their classification. Perversions are sexual activities which either (a) extend, in an anatomical sense, beyond the regions of the body that are designed for sexual union, or (b) linger over the intermediate relations to the sexual object which should normally be traversed rapidly on the path towards the final sexual aim.

(A) ANATOMICAL EXTENSIONS

OVERVALUATION OF THE SEXUAL OBJECT   It is only in the rarest instances that the psychical valuation that is set on the sexual object, as being the goal of the sexual instinct, stops short at its genitals. The appreciation extends to the whole body of the sexual object and tends to involve every sensation derived from it.

The same overvaluation spreads over into the psychological sphere: the subject becomes, as it were, intellectually infatuated (that is, his powers of judgement are weakened) by the mental achievements and perfections of the sexual object and he submits to the latter's judgements with credulity. Thus the credulity of love becomes an important, if not the most fundamental, source of *authority*.

This sexual overvaluation is something that cannot be easily reconciled with a restriction of the sexual aim to union of the actual genitals and it helps to turn activities connected with other parts of the body into sexual aims.

The significance of the factor of sexual overvaluation can be best studied in men, for their erotic life alone has become accessible to research. That of women—partly owing to the stunting effect of civilized conditions and partly owing to their conventional secretiveness and insincerity—is still veiled in an impenetrable obscurity.

SEXUAL USE OF THE MUCOUS MEMBRANE OF THE LIPS AND MOUTH

The use of the mouth as a sexual organ is regarded as a perversion if the lips (or tongue) of one person are brought into contact with the genitals of another, but not if the mucous membranes of the lips of both of them come together. This exception is the point of contact with what is normal. Those who condemn the other practices (which have no doubt been common among mankind from primaeval times) as being perversions, are giving way to an unmistakable feeling of *disgust*, which protects them from accepting sexual aims of the kind. The limits of such disgust are, however, often purely conventional: a man who will kiss a pretty girl's lips passionately, may perhaps be disgusted at the idea of using her tooth-brush, though there are no grounds for supposing that his own oral cavity, for which he feels no disgust, is any cleaner than the girl's. Here, then, our attention is drawn to the factor of disgust, which interferes with the libidinal overvaluation of the sexual object but can in turn be overridden by libido. Disgust seems to be one of the forces which have led to a restriction of the sexual aim. These forces do not as a rule extend to the genitals themselves. But there is no doubt that the genitals of the opposite sex can in themselves be an object of disgust and that such an attitude is one of the characteristics of all hysterics, and especially of hysterical women. The sexual instinct in its strength enjoys overriding this disgust.

SEXUAL USE OF THE ANAL ORIFICE

Where the anus is concerned it becomes still clearer that it is disgust which stamps that sexual aim as a perversion. I hope, however, I shall not be accused of partisanship when I assert that people who try to account for this disgust by saying that the organ in question serves the function of excretion and comes in contact with excrement—a thing which is disgusting in itself—are not much more to the point than hysterical girls who account for their disgust at the male genital by saying that it serves to void urine.

The playing of a sexual part by the mucous membrane of the anus is by no means limited to intercourse between men: preference for it is in no way characteristic of inverted feeling. On the contrary, it seems that *paedicatio* with a male owes its origin to an analogy with a similar act performed with a woman; while mutual masturbation is the sexual aim most often found in intercourse between inverts.

SIGNIFICANCE OF OTHER REGIONS OF THE BODY   The extension of sexual interest to other regions of the body, with all its variations, offers us nothing that is new in principle; it adds nothing to our knowledge of the sexual instinct, which merely proclaims its intention in this way of getting possession of the sexual object in every possible direction. But these anatomical extensions inform us that, besides sexual overvaluation, there is a second factor at work which is strange to popular knowledge. Certain regions of the body, such as the mucous membrane of the mouth and anus, which are constantly appearing in these practices, seem, as it were, to be claiming that they should themselves be regarded and treated as genitals. We shall learn later that this claim is justified by the history of the development of the sexual instinct and that it is fulfilled in the symptomatology of certain pathological states.

UNSUITABLE SUB-STITUTES FOR THE SEXUAL OBJECT— FETISHISM   There are some cases which are quite specially remarkable—those in which the normal sexual object is replaced by another which bears some relation to it, but is entirely unsuited to serve the normal sexual aim. From the point of view of classification, we should no doubt have done better to have mentioned this highly interesting group of aberrations of the sexual instinct among the deviations in respect of the sexual *object*. But we have postponed their mention till we could become acquainted with the factor of sexual overvaluation, on which these phenomena, being connected with an abandonment of the sexual aim, are dependent.

What is substituted for the sexual object is some part of the body (such as the foot or hair) which is in general very inappropriate for sexual purposes, or some inanimate object which bears an assignable relation to the person whom it replaces and preferably to that person's sexuality (e.g. a piece of clothing or underlinen). Such substitutes are with some justice likened to the fetishes in which savages believe that their gods are embodied.

A transition to those cases of fetishism in which the sexual aim, whether normal or perverse, is entirely abandoned is afforded by other cases in which the sexual object is required to fulfil a fetishistic condition—such as the possession of some particular hair-colouring or cloth-

ing, or even some bodily defect—if the sexual aim is to be attained. No other variation of the sexual instinct that borders on the pathological can lay so much claim to our interest as this one, such is the peculiarity of the phenomena to which it gives rise. Some degree of diminution in the urge towards the normal sexual aim (an executive weakness of the sexual apparatus) seems to be a necessary pre-condition in every case. The point of contact with the normal is provided by the psychologically essential overvaluation of the sexual object, which inevitably extends to everything that is associated with it. A certain degree of fetishism is thus habitually present in normal love, especially in those stages of it in which the normal sexual aim seems unattainable or its fulfilment prevented.
* * *

The situation only becomes pathological when the longing for the fetish passes beyond the point of being merely a necessary condition attached to the sexual object and actually *takes the place* of the normal aim, and, further, when the fetish becomes detached from a particular individual and becomes the *sole* sexual object. These are, indeed, the general conditions under which mere variations of the sexual instinct pass over into pathological aberrations.

* * *

In other cases the replacement of the object by a fetish is determined by a symbolic connection of thought, of which the person concerned is usually not conscious. It is not always possible to trace the course of these connections with certainty. (The foot, for instance, is an age-old sexual symbol which occurs even in mythology; no doubt the part played by fur as a fetish owes its origin to an association with the hair of the *mons Veneris*.) None the less even symbolism such as this is not always unrelated to sexual experiences in childhood.[4]

(B) FIXATIONS OF PRELIMINARY SEXUAL AIMS

APPEARANCE   Every external or internal factor that hinders or post-
OF NEW AIMS   pones the attainment of the normal sexual aim (such as
               impotence, the high price of the sexual object or the
danger of the sexual act) will evidently lend support to the tendency to linger over the preparatory activities and to turn them into new sexual aims that can take the place of the normal one. Attentive examination always shows that even what seem to be the strangest of these new aims are already hinted at in the normal sexual process.

---

4. [*Footnoted added* 1910:] Psycho-analysis has cleared up one of the remaining gaps in our understanding of fetishism. It has shown the impor-tance, as regards the choice of a fetish, of a co-prophilic pleasure in smelling which has appeared owing to repression. * * *

TOUCHING AND   A certain amount of touching is indispensable (at
LOOKING   all events among human beings) before the normal
sexual aim can be attained. And everyone knows what
a source of pleasure on the one hand and what an influx of fresh
excitation on the other is afforded by tactile sensations of the skin of the
sexual object. So that lingering over the stage of touching can scarcely
be counted a perversion, provided that in the long run the sexual act is
carried further.

The same holds true of seeing—an activity that is ultimately derived
from touching. Visual impressions remain the most frequent pathway
along which libidinal excitation is aroused; indeed, natural selection
counts upon the accessibility of this pathway—if such a teleological form
of statement is permissible[5]—when it encourages the development of
beauty in the sexual object. The progressive concealment of the body
which goes along with civilization keeps sexual curiosity awake. This curiosity seeks to complete the sexual object by revealing its hidden parts. It
can, however, be diverted ('sublimated') in the direction of art, if its interest can be shifted away from the genitals on to the shape of the body as a
whole.[6] It is usual for most normal people to linger to some extent over
the intermediate sexual aim of a looking that has a sexual tinge to it; indeed, this offers them a possibility of directing some proportion of their
libido on to higher artistic aims. On the other hand, this pleasure in looking [scopophilia] becomes a perversion (a) if it is restricted exclusively to
the genitals, or (b) if it is connected with the overriding of disgust (as in the
case of *voyeurs* or people who look on at excretory functions), or (c) if,
instead of being *preparatory* to the normal sexual aim, it supplants it.
This last is markedly true of exhibitionists, who, if I may trust the findings
of several analyses,[7] exhibit their own genitals in order to obtain a recipro-
cal view of the genitals of the other person.

*   *   *

The force which opposes scopophilia, but which may be overridden
by it (in a manner parallel to what we have previously seen in the case
of disgust), is *shame*.

SADISM AND   The most common and the most significant of all the
MASOCHISM   perversions—the desire to inflict pain upon the sexual
object, and its reverse—received from Krafft-Ebing the

5. [The words in this parenthesis were added in
1915.]
6. There is to my mind no doubt that the concept
of 'beautiful' has its roots in sexual excitation and
that its original meaning was 'sexually stimulating.'
This is related to the fact that we never regard the
genitals themselves, which produce the strongest
sexual excitation, as really 'beautiful.'
7. [*Footnote added* 1920:] Under analysis these

perversions—and indeed most others—reveal a
surprising variety of motives and determinants.
The compulsion to exhibit, for instance, is also
closely dependent on the castration complex: it is
a means of constantly insisting upon the integrity
of the subject's own (male) genitals and it reiterates
his infantile satisfaction at the absence of a penis
in those of women.

names of 'sadism' and 'masochism' for its active and passive forms respectively. Other writers [e.g. Schrenck-Notzing (1899)] have preferred the narrower term 'algolagnia'. This emphasizes the pleasure in *pain*, the cruelty; whereas the names chosen by Krafft-Ebing bring into prominence the pleasure in any form of humiliation or subjection.

As regards active algolagnia, sadism, the roots are easy to detect in the normal. The sexuality of most male human beings contains an element of *aggressiveness*—a desire to subjugate; the biological significance of it seems to lie in the need for overcoming the resistance of the sexual object by means other than the process of wooing. Thus sadism would correspond to an aggressive component of the sexual instinct which has become independent and exaggerated and, by displacement, has usurped the leading position.

* * *

Similarly, the term masochism comprises any passive attitude towards sexual life and the sexual object, the extreme instance of which appears to be that in which satisfaction is conditional upon suffering physical or mental pain at the hands of the sexual object. Masochism, in the form of a perversion, seems to be further removed from the normal sexual aim than its counterpart; it may be doubted at first whether it can ever occur as a primary phenomenon or whether, on the contrary, it may not invariably arise from a transformation of sadism.[8] It can often be shown that masochism is nothing more than an extension of sadism turned round upon the subject's own self, which thus, to begin with, takes the place of the sexual object. Clinical analysis of extreme cases of masochistic perversion show that a great number of factors (such as the castration complex and the sense of guilt) have combined to exaggerate and fixate the original passive sexual attitude.

Pain, which is overridden in such cases, thus falls into line with disgust and shame as a force that stands in opposition and resistance to the libido.

* * *

The history of human civilization shows beyond any doubt that there is an intimate connection between cruelty and the sexual instinct; but nothing has been done towards explaining the connection, apart from laying emphasis on the aggressive factor in the libido. * * *

But the most remarkable feature of this perversion is that its active and passive forms are habitually found to occur together in the same individual. A person who feels pleasure in producing pain in someone else in a sexual relationship is also capable of enjoying as pleasure any

8. [*Footnote added* 1924:] My opinion of masochism has been to a large extent altered by later reflection, based upon certain hypotheses as to the structure of the apparatus of the mind and the classes of instincts operating in it. {Freud is here referring to the "structural theory" of mind that he developed in the early 1920s. See below, pp. 628–58.} I have been led to distinguish a primary or *erotogenic* masochism, out of which two later forms, *feminine* and *moral* masochism, have developed. * * *

pain which he may himself derive from sexual relations. A sadist is always at the same time a masochist, although the active or the passive aspect of the perversion may be the more strongly developed in him and may represent his predominant sexual activity.

We find, then, that certain among the impulses to perversion occur regularly as pairs of opposites; and this, taken in conjunction with material which will be brought forward later, has a high theoretical significance. It is, moreover, a suggestive fact that the existence of the pair of opposites formed by sadism and masochism cannot be attributed merely to the element of aggressiveness. We should rather be inclined to connect the simultaneous presence of these opposites with the opposing masculinity and femininity which are combined in bisexuality— a contrast which often has to be replaced in psycho-analysis by that between activity and passivity.

(3) THE PERVERSIONS IN GENERAL

VARIATION   It is natural that medical men, who first studied per-
AND DISEASE   versions in outstanding examples and under special con-
                     ditions, should have been inclined to regard them, like
inversion, as indications of degeneracy or disease. Nevertheless, it is even easier to dispose of that view in this case than in that of inversion. Everyday experience has shown that most of these extensions, or at any rate the less severe of them, are constituents which are rarely absent from the sexual life of healthy people, and are judged by them no differently from other intimate events. If circumstances favour such an occurrence, normal people too can substitute a perversion of this kind for the normal sexual aim for quite a time, or can find place for the one alongside the other. No healthy person, it appears, can fail to make some addition that might be called perverse to the normal sexual aim; and the universality of this finding is in itself enough to show how inappropriate it is to use the word perversion as a term of reproach. In the sphere of sexual life we are brought up against peculiar and, indeed, insoluble difficulties as soon as we try to draw a sharp line to distinguish mere variations within the range of what is physiological from pathological symptoms.

* * *

In the majority of instances the pathological character in a perversion is found to lie not in the *content* of the new sexual aim but in its relation to the normal. If a perversion, instead of appearing merely *alongside* the normal sexual aim and object, and only when circumstances are unfavourable to *them* and favourable to *it*—if, instead of this, it ousts them completely and takes their place in *all* circumstances—if, in short, a perversion has the characteristics of exclusiveness and fixation—then we shall usually be justified in regarding it as a pathological symptom.

THE MENTAL   It is perhaps in connection precisely with the most
FACTOR IN THE   repulsive perversions that the mental factor must be
PERVERSIONS   regarded as playing its largest part in the transformation
                      of the sexual instinct. It is impossible to deny that in
their case, a piece of mental work has been performed which, in spite
of its horrifying result, is the equivalent of an idealization of the instinct.
The omnipotence of love is perhaps never more strongly proved than
in such of its aberrations as these. The highest and the lowest are always
closest to each other in the sphere of sexuality: 'vom Himmel durch die
Welt zur Hölle' {'From Heaven, through the world, to Hell.'}

TWO   Our study of the perversions has shown us that the
CONCLUSIONS   sexual instinct has to struggle against certain mental
                      forces which act as resistances, and of which shame and
disgust are the most prominent. It is permissible to suppose that these
forces play a part in restraining that instinct within the limits that are
regarded as normal; and if they develop in the individual before the
sexual instinct has reached its full strength, it is no doubt that they will
determine the course of its development.

In the second place we have found that some of the perversions which
we have examined are only made intelligible if we assume the convergence of several motive forces. If such perversions admit of analysis,
that is, if they can be taken to pieces, then they must be of a composite
nature. This gives us a hint that perhaps the sexual instinct itself may
be no simple thing, but put together from components which have come
apart again in the perversions. If this is so, the clinical observation of
these abnormalities will have drawn our attention to amalgamations
which have been lost to view in the uniform behaviour of normal people.

(4) THE SEXUAL INSTINCT IN NEUROTICS

PSYCHO-ANALYSIS   An important addition to our knowledge of the
                      sexual instinct in certain people who at least ap-
proximate to the normal can be obtained from a source which can only
be reached in one particular way. There is only one means of obtaining
exhaustive information that will not be misleading about the sexual life
of the persons known as 'psychoneurotics'—sufferers from hysteria, from
obsessional neurosis, from what is wrongly described as neurasthenia,
and, undoubtedly, from dementia praecox and paranoia as well. They
must be subjected to psycho-analytic investigation, which is employed
in the therapeutic procedure introduced by Josef Breuer and myself in
1893 and known at that time as 'catharsis'.

I must first explain—as I have already done in other writings—that
all my experience shows that these psychoneuroses are based on sexual
instinctual forces. By this I do not merely mean that the energy of the
sexual instinct makes a contribution to the forces that maintain the

pathological manifestations (the symptoms). I mean expressly to assert that that contribution is the most important and only constant source of energy of the neurosis and that in consequence the sexual life of the persons in question is expressed—whether exclusively or principally 'or only partly—in these symptoms. * * * The symptoms constitute the sexual activity of the patient. * * *

The removal of the symptoms of hysterical patients by psycho-analysis proceeds on the supposition that those symptoms are substitutes—transcriptions as it were—for a number of emotionally cathected mental processes, wishes and desires, which, by the operation of a special psychical procedure (repression), have been prevented from obtaining discharge in psychical activity that is admissible to consciousness. These mental processes, therefore, being held back in a state of unconsciousness, strive to obtain an expression that shall be appropriate to their emotional importance—to obtain discharge; and in the case of hysteria they find such an expression (by means of the process of 'conversion') in somatic phenomena, that is, in hysterical symptoms. By systematically turning these symptoms back (with the help of a special technique) into emotionally cathected ideas—ideas that will now have become conscious—it is possible to obtain the most accurate knowledge of the nature and origin of these formerly unconscious psychical structures.

FINDINGS OF   In this manner the fact has emerged that symptoms
PSYCHO-   represent a substitute for impulses the source of whose
ANALYSIS   strength is derived from the sexual instinct. What we
              know about the nature of hysterics before they fall ill—
and they may be regarded as typical of all psychoneurotics—and about the occasions which precipitate their falling ill, is in complete harmony with this view. The character of hysterics shows a degree of sexual repression in excess of normal quantity, an intensification of resistance against the sexual instinct (which we have already met with in the form of shame, disgust and morality), and what seems like an instinctive aversion on their part to any intellectual consideration of sexual problems. As a result of this, in especially marked cases, the patients remain in complete ignorance of sexual matters right into the period of sexual maturity.

On a cursory view, this trait, which is so characteristic of hysteria, is not uncommonly screened by the existence of a second constitutional character present in hysteria, namely the predominant development of the sexual instinct. Psycho-analysis, however, can invariably bring the first of these factors to light and clear up the enigmatic contradiction which hysteria presents, by revealing the pair of opposites by which it is characterized—exaggerated sexual craving and excessive aversion to sexuality.

* * *

NEUROSIS AND   There is no doubt that a large part of the opposition
PERVERSION   to these views of mine is due to the fact that sexuality,
                 to which I trace back psychoneurotic symptoms, is re-
garded as though it coincided with the normal sexual instinct. But
psycho-analytic teachings goes further than this. It shows that it is by
no means only at the cost of the so-called *normal* sexual instinct that
these symptoms originate—at any rate such is not exclusively or mainly
the case; they also give expression (by conversion) to instincts which
would be described as *perverse* in the widest sense of the word if they
could be expressed directly in phantasy and action without being diverted
from consciousness. Thus symptoms are formed in part at the cost of
abnormal sexuality; *neuroses are, so to say, the negative of perversions.*

*   *   *

(5) COMPONENT INSTINCTS AND
EROTOGENIC ZONES

If we put together what we have learned from our investigation of
positive and negative perversions, it seems plausible to trace them back
to a number of 'component instincts', which, however, are not of a
primary nature, but are susceptible to further analysis.[9] By an 'instinct'
is provisionally to be understood the psychical representative of an en-
dosomatic, continuously flowing source of stimulation, as contrasted
with a 'stimulus', which is set up by *single* excitations coming from
without. The concept of instinct is thus one of those lying on the frontier
between the mental and the physical. The simplest and likeliest assumption as to the nature of instincts would seem to be that in itself an
instinct is without quality, and, so far as mental life is concerned, is
only to be regarded as a measure of the demand made upon the mind
for work. What distinguishes the instincts from one another and endows
them with specific qualities is their relation to their somatic sources and
to their aims. The source of an instinct is a process of excitation occurring
in an organ and the immediate aim of the instinct lies in the removal
of this organic stimulus.[1]
There is a further provisional assumption that we cannot escape in
the theory of the instincts. It is to the effect that excitations of two kinds
arise from the somatic organs, based upon differences of a chemical
nature. One of these kinds of excitation we describe as being specifically
sexual, and we speak of the organ concerned as the 'erotogenic zone' of
the sexual component instinct arising from it.
The part played by the erotogenic zones is immediately obvious in

9. [The passage from this point till the end of the
paragraph dates from 1915.]
1. [*Footnote added* 1924:] The theory of the instincts is the most important but at the same time
the least complete portion of psycho-analytic the-

ory. I have made further contributions to it in my
later works *Beyond the Pleasure Principle* (1920)
and *The Ego and the Id* (1923). {For both texts,
see below, pp. 594–626, 628–58.}

the case of those perversions which assign a sexual significance to the oral and anal orifices. These behave in every respect like a portion of the sexual apparatus. In hysteria these parts of the body and the neighbouring tracts of mucous membrane become the seat of new sensations and of changes in innervation—indeed, of processes that can be compared to erection[2]—in just the same way as do the actual genitalia under the excitations of the normal sexual processes.

The significance of the erotogenic zones as apparatuses subordinate to the genitals and as substitutes for them is, among all the psychoneuroses, most clearly to be seen in hysteria; but this does not imply that that significance is any the less in the other forms of illness. It is only that in them it is less recognizable, because in their case (obsessional neurosis and paranoia) the formation of the symptoms takes place in regions of the mental apparatus which are more remote from the particular centres concerned with somatic control. In obsessional neurosis what is more striking is the significance of those impulses which create new sexual aims and seem independent of erotogenic zones. Nevertheless, in scopophilia and exhibitionism the eye corresponds to an erotogenic zone; while in the case of those components of the sexual instinct which involve pain and cruelty the same role is assumed by the skin— the skin, which in particular parts of the body has become differentiated into sense organs or modified into mucous membrane, and is thus the erotogenic zone *par excellence*.

(6) REASONS FOR THE

APPARENT PREPONDERANCE

OF PERVERSE SEXUALITY IN THE

PSYCHONEUROSES

The preceding discussion may perhaps have placed the sexuality of psychoneurotics in a false light. It may have given the impression that, owing to their disposition, psychoneurotics approximate closely to perverts in their sexual behaviour and are proportionately remote from normal people. It may indeed very well be that the constitutional disposition of these patients (apart from their exaggerated degree of sexual repression and the excessive intensity of their sexual instinct) includes an unusual tendency to perversion, using that word in its widest sense. Nevertheless, investigation of comparatively slight cases shows that this last assumption is not absolutely necessary, or at least that in forming a judgement on these pathological developments there is a factor to be considered which weighs in the other direction. Most psychoneurotics only fall ill after the age of puberty as a result of the demands made upon them by normal sexual life. (It is most particularly against the

2. [The phrase in parenthesis was added in 1920.]

latter that repression is directed.) Or else illnesses of this kind set in later, when the libido fails to obtain satisfaction along normal lines. In both these cases the libido behaves like a stream whose main bed has become blocked. It proceeds to fill up collateral channels which may hitherto have been empty. Thus, in the same way, what appears to be the strong tendency (though, it is true, a negative one) of psychoneurotics to perversion may be collaterally determined, and must, in any case, be collaterally intensified. The fact is that we must put sexual repression as an internal factor alongside such external factors as limitation of freedom, inaccessibility of a normal sexual object, the dangers of the normal sexual act, etc., which bring about perversions in persons who might perhaps otherwise have remained normal.

* * *

(7) INTIMATION OF THE INFANTILE

CHARACTER OF SEXUALITY

By demonstrating the part played by perverse impulses in the formation of symptoms in the psychoneuroses, we have quite remarkably increased the number of people who might be regarded as perverts. It is not only that neurotics in themselves constitute a very numerous class, but it must also be considered that an unbroken chain bridges the gap between the neuroses in all their manifestations and normality. After all, Moebius could say with justice that we are all to some extent hysterics. Thus the extraordinarily wide dissemination of the perversions forces us to suppose that the disposition to perversions is itself of no great rarity but must form a part of what passes as the normal constitution.

* * *

We have, however, a further reflection to make. This postulated constitution, containing the germs of all the perversions, will only be demonstrable in *children*, even though in them it is only with modest degrees of intensity that any of the instincts can emerge. A formula begins to take shape which lays it down that the sexuality of neurotics has remained in, or been brought back to, an infantile state. Thus our interest turns to the sexual life of children, and we will now proceed to trace the play of influences which govern the evolution of infantile sexuality till its outcome in perversion, neurosis or normal sexual life.

II

INFANTILE SEXUALITY

NEGLECT OF   One feature of the popular view of the sexual instinct
THE INFANTILE   is that it is absent in childhood and only awakens in
FACTOR   the period of life described as puberty. This, however,
                is not merely a simple error but one that has had grave
consequences, for it is mainly to this idea that we owe our present ignorance of the fundamental conditions of sexual life. A thorough study of
the sexual manifestations of childhood would probably reveal the essential characters of the sexual instinct and would show us the course of its
development and the way in which it is put together from various sources.

It is noticeable that writers who concern themselves with explaining
the characteristics and reactions of the adult have devoted much more
attention to the primaeval period which is comprised in the life of the
individual's ancestors—have, that is, ascribed much more influence to
heredity—than to the other primaeval period, which falls within the
lifetime of the individual himself—that is, to childhood. One would
surely have supposed that the influence of this latter period would be
easier to understand and could claim to be considered before that of
heredity.[3] It is true that in the literature of the subject one occasionally
comes across remarks upon precocious sexual activity in small children—
upon erections, masturbation and even activities resembling coitus. But
these are always quoted only as exceptional events, as oddities or as
horrifying instances of precocious depravity. So far as I know, not a
single author has clearly recognized the regular existence of a sexual
instinct in childhood; and in the writings that have become so numerous
on the development of children, the chapter on 'Sexual Development'
is as a rule omitted.[4]

INFANTILE   The reason for this strange neglect is to be sought, I
AMNESIA   think, partly in considerations of propriety, which the au-
               thors obey as a result of their own upbringing, and partly
in a psychological phenomenon which has itself hitherto eluded explanation. What I have in mind is the peculiar amnesia which, in the case
of most people, though by no means all, hides the earliest beginnings
of their childhood up to their sixth or eighth year. Hitherto it has not
occurred to us to feel any astonishment at the fact of this amnesia,

3. [Footnote added 1915:] Nor is it possible to estimate correctly the part played by heredity until
the part played by childhood has been assessed.
4. The assertion made in the text has since struck
me myself as being so bold that I have undertaken
the task of testing its validity by looking through
the literature once more. The outcome of this is

that I have allowed my statement to stand unaltered. The scientific examination of both the physical and mental phenomena of sexuality in
childhood is still in its earliest beginnings. * * *
In none of the accounts which I have read of the
psychology of this period of life is a chapter to be
found on the erotic life of children. * * *

though we might have had good grounds for doing so. For we learn from other people that during these years, of which at a later date we retain nothing in our memory but a few unintelligible and fragmentary recollections, we reacted in a lively manner to impressions, that we were capable of expressing pain and joy in a human fashion, that we gave evidence of love, jealousy and other passionate feelings by which we were strongly moved at the time, and even that we gave utterance to remarks which were regarded by adults as good evidence of our possessing insight and the beginnings of a capacity for judgement. And of all this we, when we are grown up, have no knowledge of our own! Why should our memory lag so far behind the other activities of our minds? We have, on the contrary, good reason to believe that there is no period at which the capacity for receiving and reproducing impressions is greater than precisely during the years of childhood.

On the other hand we must assume, or we can convince ourselves by a psychological examination of other people, that the very same impressions that we have forgotten have none the less left the deepest traces on our minds and have had a determining effect upon the whole of our later development. There can, therefore, be no question of any real abolition of the impressions of childhood, but rather of an amnesia similar to that which neurotics exhibit for later events, and of which the essence consists in a simple withholding of these impressions from consciousness, viz., in their repression. But what are the forces which bring about this repression of the impressions of childhood? Whoever could solve this riddle would, I think, have explained *hysterical* amnesia as well.

Meanwhile we must not fail to observe that the existence of infantile amnesia provides a new point of comparison between the mental states of children and psychoneurotics. We have already come across another such point in the formula to which we were led, to the effect that the sexuality of psychoneurotics has remained at, or been carried back to, an infantile stage. Can it be, after all, that infantile amnesia, too, is to be brought into relation with the sexual impulses of childhood?

Moreover, the connection between infantile and hysterical amnesia is more than a mere play upon words. Hysterical amnesia, which occurs at the bidding of repression, is only explicable by the fact that the subject is already in possession of a store of memory-traces which have been withdrawn from conscious disposal, and which are now, by an associative link, attracting to themselves the material which the forces of repression are engaged in repelling from consciousness. It may be said that without infantile amnesia there would be no hysterical amnesia.

I believe, then, that infantile amnesia, which turns everyone's childhood into something like a prehistoric epoch and conceals from him the beginnings of his own sexual life, is responsible for the fact that in general no importance is attached to childhood in the development of sexual life. The gaps in our knowledge which have arisen in this way cannot be bridged by a single observer. As long ago as in the year 1896

I insisted on the significance of the years of childhood in the origin of certain important phenomena connected with sexual life, and since then I have never ceased to emphasize the part played in sexuality by the infantile factor.

[1] THE PERIOD OF SEXUAL LATENCY IN
CHILDHOOD AND ITS INTERRUPTIONS

The remarkably frequent reports of what are described as irregular and exceptional sexual impulses in childhood, as well as the uncovering in neurotics of what have hitherto been unconscious memories of childhood, allow us to sketch out the sexual occurrences of that period in some such way as this.

There seems no doubt that germs of sexual impulses are already present in the new-born child and that these continue to develop for a time, but are then overtaken by a progressive process of suppression; this in turn is itself interrupted by periodical advances in sexual development or may be held up by individual peculiarities. Nothing is known for certain concerning the regularity and periodicity of this oscillating course of development. It seems, however, that the sexual life of children usually emerges in a form accessible to observation round about the third or fourth year of life.

SEXUAL   It is during this period of total or only partial latency
INHIBITIONS   that are built up the mental forces which are later to
               impede the course of the sexual instinct and, like dams,
restrict its flow—disgust, feelings of shame and the claims of aesthetic and moral ideals. One gets an impression from civilized children that the construction of these dams is a product of education, and no doubt education has much to do with it. But in reality this development is organically determined and fixed by heredity, and it can occasionally occur without any help at all from education. Education will not be trespassing beyond its appropriate domain if it limits itself to following the lines which have already been laid down organically and to impressing them somewhat more clearly and deeply.

REACTION-   What is it that goes to the making of these construc-
FORMATION   tions which are so important for the growth of a civilized
AND   and normal individual? They probably emerge at the
SUBLIMATION   cost of the infantile sexual impulses themselves. Thus
               the activity of those impulses does not cease even during
this period of latency, though their energy is diverted, wholly or in great part, from their sexual use and directed to other ends. Historians of civilization appear to be at one in assuming that powerful components are acquired for every kind of cultural achievement by this diversion of sexual instinctual forces from sexual aims and their direction to new

ones—a process which deserves the name of 'sublimation'. To this we would add, accordingly, that the same process plays a part in the development of the individual and we would place its beginning in the period of sexual latency of childhood.[5]

It is possible further to form some idea of the mechanism of this process of sublimation. On the one hand, it would seem, the sexual impulses cannot be utilized during these years of childhood, since the reproductive functions have been deferred—a fact which constitutes the main feature of the period of latency. On the other hand, these impulses would seem in themselves to be perverse—that is, to arise from erotogenic zones and to derive their activity from instincts which, in view of the direction of the subject's development, can only arouse unpleasurable feelings. They consequently evoke opposing mental forces (reacting impulses) which, in order to suppress this unpleasure effectively, build up the mental dams that I have already mentioned—disgust, shame and morality.

INTERRUPTIONS OF   We must not deceive ourselves as to the hypo-
THE LATENCY   thetical nature and insufficient clarity of our
PERIOD   knowledge concerning the processes of the infantile
                   period of latency or deferment; but we shall be on
firmer ground in pointing out that such an application of infantile sexuality represents an educational ideal from which individual development usually diverges at some point and often to a considerable degree. From time to time a fragmentary manifestation of sexuality which has evaded sublimation may break through; or some sexual activity may persist through the whole duration of the latency period until the sexual instinct emerges with greater intensity at puberty. In so far as educators pay any attention at all to infantile sexuality, they behave exactly as though they shared our views as to the construction of the moral defensive forces at the cost of sexuality, and as though they knew that sexual activity makes a child ineducable: for they stigmatize every sexual manifestation by children as a 'vice', without being able to do much against it. We, on the other hand, have every reason for turning our attention to these phenomena which are so much dreaded by education, for we may expect them to help us to discover the original configuration of the sexual instincts.

[2] THE MANIFESTATIONS OF INFANTILE

SEXUALITY

THUMB-SUCKING   For reasons which will appear later, I shall take
                 thumb-sucking (or sensual sucking) as a sample of
the sexual manifestations of childhood. * * *

5. Once again, it is from Fliess that I have borrowed the term 'period of sexual latency'.

Thumb-sucking appears already in early infancy and may continue into maturity, or even persist all through life. It consists in the rhythmic repetition of a sucking contact by the mouth (or lips). There is no question of the purpose of this procedure being the taking of nourishment. A portion of the lip itself, the tongue, or any other part of the skin within reach—even the big toe—may be taken as the object upon which this sucking is carried out.* * *

* * * In the nursery, sucking is often classed along with the other kinds of sexual 'naughtiness' of children. This view has been most energetically repudiated by numbers of paediatricians and nerve-specialists, though this is no doubt partly due to a confusion between 'sexual' and 'genital'. Their objection raises a difficult question and one which cannot be evaded: what is the general characteristic which enables us to recognize the sexual manifestations of children? The concatenation of phenomena into which we have been given an insight by psycho-analytic investigation justifies us, in my opinion, in regarding thumb-sucking as a sexual manifestation and in choosing it for our study of the essential features of infantile sexual activity.

AUTO-EROTISM   We are in duty bound to make a thorough examination of this example. It must be insisted that the most striking feature of this sexual activity is that the instinct is not directed towards other people, but obtains satisfaction from the subject's own body. It is 'auto-erotic', to call it by a happily chosen term introduced by Havelock Ellis (1910).

Furthermore, it is clear that the behaviour of a child who indulges in thumb-sucking is determined by a search for some pleasure which has already been experienced and is now remembered. In the simplest case he proceeds to find this satisfaction by sucking rhythmically at some part of the skin or mucous membrane. It is also easy to guess the occasions on which the child had his first experiences of the pleasure which he is now striving to renew. It was the child's first and most vital activity, his sucking at his mother's breast, or at substitutes for it, that must have familiarized him with this pleasure. The child's lips, in our view, behave like an erotogenic zone, and no doubt stimulation by the warm flow of milk is the cause of the pleasurable sensation. The satisfaction of the erotogenic zone is associated, in the first instance, with the satisfaction of the need for nourishment. To begin with, sexual activity attaches itself to functions serving the purpose of self-preservation and does not become independent of them until later.[6] No one who has seen a baby sinking back satiated from the breast and falling asleep with flushed cheeks and a blissful smile can escape the reflection that this picture persists as a prototype of the expression of sexual satisfaction in later life. The need for repeating the sexual satisfaction now becomes detached

6. [This sentence was added in 1915.]

his first 'gift': by producing them he can express his active compliance
with his environment and, by witholding them, his disobedience. From
being a 'gift' they later come to acquire the meaning of 'baby'—for babies,
according to one of the sexual theories of children, are acquired by
eating and are born through the bowels.

The retention of the faecal mass, which is thus carried out intentionally by the child to begin with, in order to serve, as it were, as a
masturbatory stimulus upon the anal zone or to be employed in his
relation to the people looking after him, is also one of the roots of the
constipation which is so common among neuropaths. Further, the whole
significance of the anal zone is reflected in the fact that few neurotics
are to be found without their special scatological practices, ceremonies,
and so on, which they carefully keep secret.

Actual masturbatory stimulation of the anal zone by means of the
finger, provoked by a centrally determined or peripherally maintained
sensation of itching, is by no means rare among older children.

ACTIVITY OF THE   Among the erotogenic zones that form part of the
GENITAL ZONES   child's body there is one which certainly does not
                      play the opening part, and which cannot be the
vehicle of the oldest sexual impulses, but which is destined to great
things in the future. In both male and female children it is brought into
connection with micturition (in the glans and clitoris) and in the former
is enclosed in a pouch of mucous membrane, so that there can be no
lack of stimulation of it by secretions which may give an early start to
sexual excitation. The sexual activities of this erotogenic zone, which
forms part of the sexual organs proper, are the beginning of what is later
to become 'normal' sexual life. The anatomical situation of this region,
the secretions in which it is bathed, the washing and rubbing to which
it is subjected in the course of a child's toilet, as well as accidental
stimulation (such as the movement of intestinal worms in the case of
girls), make it inevitable that the pleasurable feeling which this part of
the body is capable of producing should be noticed by children even
during their earliest infancy, and should give rise to a need for its
repetition. If we consider this whole range of contrivances and bear in
mind that both making a mess and measures for keeping clean are bound
to operate in much the same way, it is scarcely possible to avoid the
conclusion that the foundations for the future primacy over sexual activity exercised by this erotogenic zone are established by early infantile
masturbation, which scarcely a single individual escapes. The action
which disposes of the stimulus and brings about satisfaction consists in
a rubbing movement with the hand or in the application of pressure (no
doubt on the lines of a pre-existing reflex) either from the hand or by
bringing the thighs together. This last method is by far the more common
in the case of girls. The preference for the hand which is shown by boys

is already evidence of the important contribution which the instinct for mastery is destined to make to masculine sexual activity.

It will be in the interests of clarity[8] if I say at once that three phases of infantile masturbation are to be distinguished. The first of these belongs to early infancy, and the second to the brief efflorescence of sexual activity about the fourth year of life; only the third phase corresponds to pubertal masturbation, which is often the only kind taken into account.

SECOND PHASE OF INFANTILE MASTURBATION   The masturbation of early infancy seems to disappear after a short time; but it may persist uninterruptedly until puberty, and this would constitute the first great deviation from the course of development laid down for civilized men. At some point of childhood after early infancy, as a rule before the fourth year, the sexual instinct belonging to the genital zone usually revives and persists again for a time until it is once more suppressed, or it may continue without interruption. This second phase of infantile sexual activity may assume a variety of different forms which can only be determined by a precise analysis of individual cases. But all its details leave behind the deepest (unconscious) impressions in the subject's memory, determine the development of his character, if he is to remain healthy, and the symptomatology of his neurosis, if he is to fall ill after puberty. In the latter case we find that this sexual period has been forgotten and that the conscious memories that bear witness to it have been displaced. (I have already mentioned that I am also inclined to relate normal infantile amnesia to this infantile sexual activity.) Psycho-analytic investigation enables us to make what has been forgotten conscious and thus do away with a compulsion that arises from the unconscious psychical material.

RETURN OF EARLY INFANTILE MASTURBATION   During the years of childhood with which I am now dealing, the sexual excitation of early infancy returns, either as a centrally determined tickling stimulus which seeks satisfaction in masturbation, or as a process in the nature of a nocturnal emission which, like the nocturnal emissions of adult years, achieves satisfaction without the help of any action by the subject The latter case is the more frequent with girls and in the second half of childhood; its determinants are not entirely intelligible and often, though not invariably, it seems to be conditioned by a period of earlier *active* masturbation. The symptoms of these sexual manifestations are scanty; they are mostly displayed on behalf of the still undeveloped sexual apparatus by the *urinary* apparatus, which thus acts, as it were, as the former's trustee. Most of the so-called bladder disorders of this period are sexual disturbances: nocturnal enuresis, unless it represents an epileptic fit, corresponds to a nocturnal emission.

8. [This paragraph was added in 1915.]

The reappearance of sexual activity is determined by internal causes and external contingencies, both of which can be guessed in cases of neurotic illness from the form taken by their symptoms and can be discovered with certainty by psycho-analytic investigation. I shall have to speak presently of the internal causes; great and lasting importance attaches at this period to the accidental *external* contingencies. In the foreground we find the effects of seduction, which treats a child as a sexual object prematurely and teaches him, in highly emotional circumstances, how to obtain satisfaction from his genital zones, a satisfaction which he is then usually obliged to repeat again and again by masturbation. An influence of this kind may originate either from adults or from other children. I cannot admit that in my paper on 'The Aetiology of Hysteria' (1896) I exaggerated the frequency or importance of that influence, though I did not then know that persons who remain normal may have had the same experiences in their childhood, and though I consequently overrated the importance of seduction in comparison with the factors of sexual constitution and development. Obviously seduction is not required in order to arouse a child's sexual life; that can also come about spontaneously from internal causes.

POLYMORPHOUSLY PERVERSE DISPOSITION   It is an instructive fact that under the influence of seduction children can become polymorphously perverse, and can be led into all possible kinds of sexual irregularities. This shows that an aptitude for them is innately present in their disposition. There is consequently little resistance towards carrying them out, since the mental dams against sexual excesses—shame, disgust and morality—have either not yet been constructed at all or are only in course of construction, according to the age of the child. In this respect children behave in the same kind of way as an average uncultivated woman in whom the same polymorphously perverse disposition persists. Under ordinary conditions she may remain normal sexually, but if she is led on by a clever seducer she will find every sort of perversion to her taste, and will retain them as part of her own sexual activities. Prostitutes exploit the same polymorphous, that is, infantile, disposition for the purposes of their profession; and, considering the immense number of women who are prostitutes or who must be supposed to have an aptitude for prostitution without becoming engaged in it, it becomes impossible not to recognize that this same disposition to perversions of every kind is a general and fundamental human characteristic.

COMPONENT INSTINCTS   Moreover, the effects of seduction do not help to reveal the early history of the sexual instinct; they rather confuse our view of it by presenting children prematurely with a sexual object for which the infantile sexual instinct at first shows no need. It must, however, be admitted that infantile sexual life, in spite of the preponderating dominance of erotogenic zones, exhibits components which from the very first involve other people as sexual objects. Such are the instincts of scopophilia, exhibitionism and cruelty, which appear in a sense independently of erotogenic zones; these instincts do not enter into intimate relations with genital[9] life until later, but are already to be observed in childhood as independent impulses, distinct in the first instance from erotogenic sexual activity. Small children are essentially without shame, and at some periods of their earliest years show an unmistakable satisfaction in exposing their bodies, with especial emphasis on the sexual parts. The counterpart of this supposedly perverse inclination, curiosity to see other people's genitals, probably does not become manifest until somewhat later in childhood, when the obstacle set up by a sense of shame has already reached a certain degree of development. Under the influence of seduction the scopophilic perversion can attain great importance in the sexual life of a child. But my researches into the early years of normal people, as well as of neurotic patients, force me to the conclusion that scopophilia can also appear in children as a spontaneous manifestation. Small children whose attention has once been drawn—as a rule by masturbation—to their own genitals usually take the further step without help from outside and develop a lively interest in the genitals of their playmates. Since opportunities for satisfying curiousity of this kind usually occur only in the course of satisfying the two kinds of need for excretion, children of this kind turn into *voyeurs*, eager spectators of the processes of micturition and defaecation. When repression of these inclinations set in, the desire to see other people's genitals (whether of their own or the opposite sex) persists as a tormenting compulsion, which in some cases of neurosis later affords the strongest motive force for the formation of symptoms.

The cruel component of the sexual instinct develops in childhood even more independently of the sexual activities that are attached to erotogenic zones. Cruelty in general comes easily to the childish nature, since the obstacle that brings the instinct for mastery to a halt at another person's pain—namely a capacity for pity—is developed relatively late. The fundamental psychological analysis of this instinct has, as we know, not yet been satisfactorily achieved. It may be assumed that the impulse of cruelty arises from the instinct for mastery and appears at a period of sexual life at which the genitals have not yet taken over their later role. It then dominates a phase of sexual life which we shall later describe as a pregenital organization. Children who distinguish themselves by special cruelty towards animals and playmates usually give rise to a just suspicion of an intense and precocious sexual activity arising from erotogenic zones; and, though all the sexual instincts may display simultaneous precocity, *erotogenic* sexual activity seems, nevertheless, to be the primary one. The absence of the barrier of pity brings with it a

9. ['Sexual' in 1905 and 1910.]

danger that the connection between the cruel and the erotogenic instincts, thus established in childhood, may prove unbreakable in later life. Ever since Jean Jacques Rousseau's *Confessions*, it has been well known to all educationalists that the painful stimulation of the skin of the buttocks is one of the erotogenic roots of the *passive* instinct of cruelty (masochism). The conclusion has rightly been drawn by them that corporal punishment, which is usually applied to this part of the body, should not be inflicted upon any children whose libido is liable to be forced into collateral channels by the later demands of cultural education.[1]

[5] THE SEXUAL RESEARCHES OF CHILDHOOD[2]

THE INSTINCT　　　　At about the same time as the sexual life of chil-
FOR KNOWLEDGE　　dren reaches its first peak, between the ages of three
　　　　　　　　　　and five, they also begin to show signs of the activity which may be ascribed to the instinct for knowledge or research. This instinct cannot be counted among the elementary instinctual components, nor can it be classed as exclusively belonging to sexuality. Its activity corresponds on the one hand to a sublimated manner of obtaining mastery, while on the other hand it makes use of the energy of scopophilia. Its relations to sexual life, however, are of particular importance, since we have learnt from psycho-analysis that the instinct for knowledge in children is attracted unexpectedly early and intensively to sexual problems and is in fact possibly first aroused by them.

THE RIDDLE OF　　　It is not by theoretical interests but by practical ones
THE SPHINX　　　　that activities of research are set going in children.
　　　　　　　　　　The threat to the bases of a child's existence offered by the discovery or the suspicion of the arrival of a new baby and the fear that he may, as a result of it, cease to be cared for and loved, make him thoughtful and clear-sighted. And this history of the instinct's origin is in line with the fact that the first problem with which it deals is not the question of the distinction between the sexes but the riddle of where babies come from. (This, in a distorted form which can easily be rectified, is the same riddle that was propounded by the Theban Sphinx.) On the contrary, the existence of two sexes does not to begin with arouse any

1. [*Footnote added* 1910:] When the account which I have given above of infantile sexuality was first published in 1905, it was founded for the most part on the results of psycho-analytic research upon adults. At that time it was impossible to make full use of direct observation on children: only isolated hints and some valuable pieces of confirmation came from that source. Since then it has become possible to gain direct insight into infantile psychosexuality by the analysis of some cases of neurotic illness during the early years of childhood. It is gratifying to be able to report that direct observation has fully confirmed the conclusions arrived at by psycho-analysis—which is incidentally good evidence of the trustworthiness of that method of research. * * * {Freud is, of course, as he observes later in this long footnote, thinking of 'Analysis of a Phobia in a Five-Year-Old Boy', the famous case nicknamed 'Little Hans', published in 1909.}
2. [The whole of this section on the sexual researches of children first appeared in 1915.]

difficulties or doubts in children. It is self-evident to a male child that a genital like his own is to be attributed to everyone he knows, and he cannot make its absence tally with his picture of these other people.

CASTRATION COMPLEX AND PENIS ENVY   This conviction is energetically maintained by boys, is obstinately defended against the contradictions which soon result from observation, and is only abandoned after severe internal struggles (the castration complex). The substitutes for this penis which they feel is missing in women play a great part in determining the form taken by many perversions.[3]

The assumption that all human beings have the same (male) form of genital is the first of the many remarkable and momentous sexual theories of children. It is of little use to a child that the science of biology justifies his prejudice and has been obliged to recognize the female clitoris as a true substitute for the penis.

Little girls do not resort to denial of this kind when they see that boys' genitals are formed differently from their own. They are ready to recognize them immediately and are overcome by envy for the penis—an envy culminating in the wish, which is so important in its consequences, to be boys themselves.

THEORIES OF BIRTH   Many people can remember clearly what an intense interest they took during the prepubertal period in the question of where babies come from. The anatomical answers to the question were at the time very various: babies come out of the breast, or are cut out of the body, or the navel opens to let them through. Outside analysis, there are very seldom memories of any similar researches having been carried out in the *early* years of childhood. These earlier researches fell a victim to repression long since, but all their findings were of a uniform nature: people get babies by eating some particular thing (as they do in fairy tales) and babies are born through the bowel like a discharge of faeces. These infantile theories remind us of conditions that exist in the animal kingdom—and especially of the cloaca in types of animals lower than mammals.

SADISTIC VIEW OF SEXUAL INTERCOURSE   If children at this early age witness sexual intercourse between adults—for which an opportunity is provided by the conviction of grown-up people that small children cannot understand anything sexual—they inevitably regard the sexual act as a sort of ill-treatment or act of subjugation: they view it, that is, in a sadistic sense. Psycho-analysis also shows us

3. [*Footnote added* 1920:] We are justified in speaking of a castration complex in women as well. Both male and female children form a theory that women no less than men originally had a penis, but that they have lost it by castration. The conviction which is finally reached by males that women have no penis often leads them to an enduringly low opinion of the other sex. {For further discussion of this important and delicate topic, see below, pp. 670–78.}

that an impression of this kind in early childhood contributes a great deal towards a predisposition to a subsequent sadistic displacement of the sexual aim. Furthermore, children are much concerned with the problem of what sexual intercourse—or, as they put it, being married—consists in: and they usually seek a solution of the mystery in some common activity concerned with the function of micturition or defaecation.

TYPICAL FAILURE OF INFANTILE SEXUAL RESEARCHES We can say in general of the sexual theories of children that they are reflections of their own sexual constitution, and that in spite of their grotesque errors the theories show more understanding of sexual processes than one would have given their creators credit for. Children also perceive the alterations that take place in their mother owing to pregnancy and are able to interpret them correctly. The fable of the stork is often told to an audience that receives it with deep, though mostly silent, mistrust. There are, however, two elements that remain undiscovered by the sexual researches of children: the fertilizing role of semen and the existence of the female sexual orifice—the same elements, incidentally, in which the infantile organization is itself undeveloped. It therefore follows that the efforts of the childish investigator are habitually fruitless, and end in a renunciation which not infrequently leaves behind it a permanent injury to the instinct for knowledge. The sexual researches of these early years of childhood are always carried out in solitude. They constitute a first step towards taking an independent attitude in the world, and imply a high degree of alienation of the child from the people in his environment who formerly enjoyed his complete confidence.

[6] THE PHASES OF DEVELOPMENT OF THE SEXUAL ORGANIZATION[4]

The characteristics of infantile sexual life which we have hitherto emphasized are the facts that it is essentially autoerotic (i.e. that it finds its object in the infant's own body) and that its individual component instincts are upon the whole disconnected and independent of one another in their search for pleasure. The final outcome of sexual development lies in what is known as the normal sexual life of the adult, in which the pursuit of pleasure comes under the sway of the reproductive function and in which the component instincts, under the primacy of a single erotogenic zone, form a firm organization directed towards a sexual aim attached to some extraneous sexual object.

4. [The whole of this section, too, first appeared in 1915.]

PREGENITAL ORGANIZATIONS
The study, with the help of psycho-analysis, of the inhibitions and disturbances of this process of development enables us to recognize abortive beginnings and preliminary stages of a firm organization of the component instincts such as this—preliminary stages which themselves constitute a sexual régime of a sort. These phases of sexual organization are normally passed through smoothly, without giving more than a hint of their existence. It is only in pathological cases that they become active and recognizable to superficial observation.

We shall give the name of 'pregenital' to organizations of sexual life in which the genital zones have not yet taken over their predominant part. We have hitherto identified two such organizations, which almost seem as though they were harking back to early animal forms of life.

The first of these is the oral or, as it might be called, cannibalistic pregenital sexual organization. Here sexual activity has not yet been separated from the ingestion of food; nor are opposite currents within the activity differentiated. The *object* of both activities is the same; the sexual *aim* consists in the incorporation of the object—the prototype of a process which, in the form of identification, is later to play such an important psychological part. A relic of this constructed phase of organization, which is forced upon our notice by pathology, may be seen in thumb-sucking, in which the sexual activity, detached from the nutritive activity, has substituted for the extraneous object one situated in the subject's own body.

A second pregenital phase is that of the sadistic-anal organization. Here the opposition between two currents, which runs through all sexual life, is already developed: they cannot yet, however, be described as 'masculine' and 'feminine', but only as 'active' and 'passive'. The *activity* is put into operation by the instinct for mastery through the agency of the somatic musculature; the organ which, more than any other, represents the *passive* sexual aim is the erotogenic mucous membrane of the anus. Both of these currents have objects, which, however, are not identical. Alongside these, other component instincts operate in an auto-erotic manner. In this phase, therefore, sexual polarity and an extraneous object are already observable. But organization and subordination to the reproductive function are still absent.

AMBIVALENCE
This form of sexual organization can persist throughout life and can permanently attract a large portion of sexual activity to itself. The predominance in it of sadism and the cloacal part played by the anal zone give it a quite peculiarly archaic colouring. It is further characterized by the fact that in it the opposing pairs of instincts are developed to an approximately equal extent, a state of affairs described by Bleuler's happily chosen term 'ambivalence'.

The assumption of the existence of pregenital organizations of sexual life is based on the analysis of the neuroses, and without a knowledge of them can scarcely be appreciated. Further analytic investigation may be expected to provide us with far more information on the structure and development of the normal sexual function.

In order to complete our picture of infantile sexual life, we must also suppose that the choice of an object, such as we have shown to be characteristic of the pubertal phase of development, has already frequently or habitually been effected during the years of childhood: that is to say, the whole of the sexual currents have become directed towards a single person in relation to whom they seek to achieve their aims. This then is the closest approximation possible in childhood to the final form taken by sexual life after puberty. The only difference lies in the fact that in childhood the combination of the component instincts and their subordination under the primacy of the genitals have been effected only very incompletely or not at all. Thus the establishment of that primacy in the service of reproduction is the last phase through which the organization of sexuality passes.[5]

DIPHASIC CHOICE OF OBJECT   It may be regarded as typical of the choice of an object that the process is diphasic, that is, that it occurs in two waves. The first of these begins between the ages of two and five, and is brought to a halt or to a retreat by the latency period; it is characterized by the infantile nature of the sexual aims. The second wave sets in with puberty and determines the final outcome of sexual life.

Although the diphasic nature of object-choice comes down in essentials to no more than the operation of the latency period, it is of the highest importance in regard to disturbances of that final outcome. The resultants of infantile object-choice are carried over into the later period. They either persist as such or are revived at the actual time of puberty. But as a consequence of the repression which has developed between the two phases they prove unutilizable. Their sexual aims have become mitigated and they now represent what may be described as the 'affectionate current' of sexual life. Only psycho-analytic investigation can show that behind this affection, admiration and respect there lie concealed the old sexual longings of the infantile component instincts which have now become unserviceable. The object-choice of the pubertal period is obliged to dispense with the objects of childhood and to start afresh as a 'sensual current'. Should these two currents fail to converge, the result is often that one of the ideals of sexual life, the focusing of all desires upon a single object, will be unattainable.

5. [Footnote added 1924:] At a later date (1923) {in "The Infantile Genital Organization [An Interpolation into the Theory of Sexuality]," SE XIX, 141–45.}, I myself modified this account by inserting a third phase in the development of childhood, subsequent to the two pregenital organizations. * * *

[7] THE SOURCES OF INFANTILE SEXUALITY

Our efforts to trace the origins of the sexual instinct have shown us so far that sexual excitation arises (*a*) as a reproduction of a satisfaction experienced in connection with other organic processes, (*b*) through appropriate peripheral stimulation of erotogenic zones and (*c*) as an expression of certain 'instincts' (such as the scopophilic instinct and the instinct of cruelty) of which the origin is not yet completely intelligible. Psycho-analytic investigation, reaching back into childhood from a later time, and contemporary observation of children combine to indicate to us still other regularly active sources of sexual excitation. The direct observation of children has the disadvantage of working upon data which are easily misunderstandable; psycho-analysis is made difficult by the fact that it can only reach its data, as well as its conclusions, after long détours. But by co-operation the two methods can attain a satisfactory degree of certainty in their findings.

We have already discovered in examining the erotogenic zones that these regions of the skin merely show a special intensificaiton of a kind of susceptibility to stimulus which is possessed in a certain degree by the whole cutaneous surface. We shall therefore not be surprised to find that very definite erotogenic effects are to be ascribed to certain kinds of general stimulation of the skin. Among these we may especially mention thermal stimuli, whose importance may help us to understand the therapeutic effects of warm baths.

MECHANICAL EXCITATIONS   At this point we must also mention the production of sexual excitation by rhythmic mechanical agitation of the body. Stimuli of this kind operate in three different ways: on the sensory apparatus of the vestibular nerves, on the skin, and on the deeper parts (e.g. the muscles and articular structures). The existence of these pleasurable sensations—and it is worth emphasizing the fact that in this connection the concepts of 'sexual excitation' and 'satisfaction' can to a great extent be used without distinction, a circumstance which we must later endeavour to explain—the existence, then, of these pleasurable sensations, caused by forms of mechanical agitation of the body, is confirmed by the fact that children are so fond of games of passive movement, such as swinging and being thrown up into the air, and insist on such games being incessantly repeated. It is well known that rocking is habitually used to induce sleep in restless children. The shaking produced by driving in carriages and later by railway-travel exercises such a fascinating effect upon older children that every boy, at any rate, has at one time or other in his life wanted to be an engine driver or a coachman. It is a puzzling fact that boys take such an extraordinarily intense interest in things connected with railways, and, at the age at which the production of phantasies is most active (shortly before puberty), use those things as the nucleus of a symbolism that is peculiarly sexual. A compulsive link of this kind between railway-travel and sexuality is clearly derived from the pleasurable character of the sensations of movement. In the event of repression, which turns so many childish preferences into their opposite, these same individuals, when they are adolescents or adults, will react to rocking or swinging with a feeling of nausea, will be terribly exhausted by a railway journey, or will be subject to attacks of anxiety on the journey and will protect themselves against a repetition of the painful experience by a dread of railway-travel.

Here again we must mention the fact, which is not yet understood, that the combination of fright and mechanical agitation produces the severe, hysteriform, traumatic neurosis. It may at least be assumed that these influences, which, when they are of small intensity, become sources of sexual excitation, lead to a profound disorder in the sexual mechanism or chemistry if they operate with exaggerated force.

MUSCULAR ACTIVITY   We are all familiar with the fact that children feel a need for a large amount of active muscular exercise and derive extraordinary pleasure from satisfying it. Whether this pleasure has any connection with sexuality, whether it itself comprises sexual satisfaction or whether it can become the occasion of sexual excitation— all of this is open to critical questioning, which may indeed also be directed against the view maintained in the previous paragraphs that the pleasure derived from sensations of *passive* movement is of a sexual nature or may produce sexual excitation. It is, however, a fact that a number of people report that they experienced the first signs of excitement in their genitals while they were romping or wrestling with playmates—a situation in which, apart from general muscular exertion, there is a large amount of contact with the skin of the opponent. An inclination to physical struggles with some one particular person, just as in later years an inclination to *verbal* disputes,[6] is a convincing sign that object-choice has fallen on him. One of the roots of the sadistic instinct would seem to lie in the encouragement of sexual excitation by muscular activity. In many people the infantile connection between romping and sexual excitation is among the determinants of the direction subsequently taken by their sexual instinct.

AFFECTIVE PROCESSES   The further sources of sexual excitation in children are open to less doubt. It is easy to establish, whether by contemporary observation or by subsequent research, that all comparatively intense affective processes, including even terrifying ones, trench upon sexuality—a fact which may incidentally help to explain the pathogenic effect of emotions of that kind. In schoolchildren dread of going in for an examination or tension over a difficult piece of work

6. 'Was sich liebt, das neckt sich' {"Those who love each other tease each other."}

can be important not only in affecting the child's relations at school but also in bringing about an irruption of sexual manifestations. For quite often in such circumstances a stimulus may be felt which urges the child to touch his genitals, or something may take place akin to a nocturnal emission with all its bewildering consequences. The behaviour of children at school, which confronts a teacher with plenty of puzzles, deserves in general to be brought into relation with their budding sexuality. The sexually exciting effect of many emotions which are in themselves unpleasurable, such as feelings of apprehension, fright or horror, persists in a great number of people throughout their adult life. There is no doubt that this is the explanation of why so many people seek opportunities for sensations of this kind, subject to the proviso that the seriousness of the unpleasurable feeling is damped down by certain qualifying facts, such as its occurring in an imaginary world, in a book or in a play.

If we assume that a similar erotogenic effect attaches even to intensely painful feelings, especially when the pain is toned down or kept at a distance by some accompanying condition, we should here have one of the main roots of the masochistic-sadistic instinct, into whose numerous complexities we are very gradually gaining some insight.

INTELLECTUAL   Finally, it is an unmistakable fact that concentration
WORK   of the attention upon an intellectual task and intellec-
          tual strain in general produce a concomitant sexual
excitation in many young people as well as adults. This is no doubt the only justifiable basis for what is in other respects the questionable practice of ascribing nervous disorders to intellectual 'overwork'.

If we now cast our eyes over the tentative suggestions which I have made as to the sources of infantile sexual excitation, though I have not described them completely nor enumerated them fully, the following conclusions emerge with more or less certainty. It seems that the fullest provisions are made for setting in motion the process of sexual excitation—a process the nature of which has, it must be confessed, become highly obscure to us. The setting in motion of this process is first and foremost provided for in a more or less direct fashion by the excitations of the sensory surfaces—the skin and the sense organs—and, most directly of all, by the operation of stimuli on certain areas known as erotogenic zones. The decisive element in these sources of sexual excitation is no doubt the *quality* of the stimuli, though the factor of intensity, in the case of pain, is not a matter of complete indifference. But apart from these sources there are present in the organism contrivances which bring it about that in the case of a great number of internal processes sexual excitation arises as a concomitant effect, as soon as the intensity of those processes passes beyond certain quantitative limits. What we have called the component instincts of sexuality are either derived directly from these internal sources or are composed of elements both from those sources and from the erotogenic zones. It may well be that nothing of considerable importance can occur in the organism without contributing some component to the excitation of the sexual instinct.

It does not seem to me possible at present to state these general conclusions with any greater clarity or certainty. For this I think two factors are responsible: first, the novelty of the whole method of approach to the subject, and secondly, the fact that the whole nature of sexual excitation is completely unknown to us. Nevertheless I am tempted to make two observations which promise to open out wide future prospects:

VARIETIES
OF SEXUAL
CONSTITUTION

(a) Just as we saw previously that it was possible to derive a multiplicity of innate sexual constitutions from variety in the development of the erotogenic zones, so we can now make a similar attempt by including the *indirect* sources of sexual excitation. It may be assumed that, although contributions are made from these sources in the case of everyone, they are not in all cases of equal strength, and that further help towards the differentiation of sexual constitutions may be found in the varying development of the individual sources of sexual excitation.[7]

PATHWAYS OF
MUTUAL
INFLUENCE

(b) If we now drop the figurative expression that we have so long adopted in speaking of the 'sources' of sexual excitation, we are led to the suspicion that all the connecting pathways that lead from other functions to sexuality must also be traversable in the reverse direction. If, for instance, the common possession of the labial zone by the two functions is the reason why sexual satisfaction arises during the taking of nourishment, then the same factor also enables us to understand why there should be disorders of nutrition if the erotogenic functions of the common zone are disturbed. Or again, if we know that concentration of attention may give rise to sexual excitation, it seems plausible to assume that by making use of the same path, but in a contrary direction, the condition of sexual excitation may influence the possibility of directing the attention. A good portion of the symptomatology of the neuroses, which I have traced to disturbances of the sexual processes, is expressed in disturbances of other, non-sexual, somatic functions; and this circumstance, which has hitherto been unintelligible, becomes less puzzling if it is only the counterpart of the influences which bring about the production of sexual excitation.

The same pathways, however, along which sexual disturbances trench

---

7. [*Footnote added* 1920:] An inevitable consequence of these considerations is that we must regard each individual as possessing an oral erotism, an anal erotism, a urethral erotism, etc., and that the existence of mental complexes corresponding to these implies no judgement of abnormality or neurosis. The difference separating the normal from the abnormal can lie only in the relative strength of the individual components of the sexual instinct and in the use to which they are put in the course of development.

upon the other somatic functions must also perform another important function in normal health. They must serve as paths for the attraction of sexual instinctual forces to aims that are other than sexual, that is to say, for the sublimation of sexuality. But we must end with a confession that very little is as yet known with certainty of these pathways, though they certainly exist and can probably be traversed in both directions.

III

THE TRANSFORMATIONS OF PUBERTY

With the arrival of puberty, changes set in which are destined to give infantile sexual life its final, normal shape. The sexual instinct has hitherto been predominantly auto-erotic; it now finds a sexual object. Its activity has hitherto been derived from a number of separate instincts and erotogenic zones, which, independently of one another, have pursued a certain sort of pleasure as their sole sexual aim. Now, however, a new sexual aim appears, and all the component instincts combine to attain it, while the erotogenic zones become subordinated to the primacy of the genital zone. Since the new sexual aim assigns very different functions to the two sexes, their sexual development now diverges greatly. That of males is the more straightforward and the more understandable, while that of females actually enters upon a kind of involution. A normal sexual life is only assured by an exact convergence of the affectionate current and the sensual current both being directed towards the sexual object and sexual aim. (The former, the affectionate current, comprises what remains over of the infantile efflorescence of sexuality.)[8] It is like the completion of a tunnel which has been driven through a hill from both directions.

The new sexual aim in men consists in the discharge of the sexual products. The earlier one, the attainment of pleasure, is by no means alien to it; on the contrary, the highest degree of pleasure is attached to this final act of the sexual process. The sexual instinct is now subordinated to the reproductive function; it becomes, so to say, altruistic. If this transformation is to succeed, the original dispositions and all the other characteristics of the instincts must be taken into account in the process. Just as on any other occasion on which the organism should by rights make new combinations and adjustments leading to complicated mechanisms, here too there are possibilities of pathological disorders if these new arrangements are not carried out. Every pathological disorder of sexual life is rightly to be regarded as an inhibition in development.

8. [This sentence was added in 1920.]

[1] THE PRIMACY OF THE GENITAL ZONES AND
FORE-PLEASURE

The starting-point and the final aim of the process which I have described are clearly visible. The intermediate steps are still in many ways obscure to us. We shall have to leave more than one of them as an unsolved riddle.

The most striking of the processes at puberty has been picked upon as constituting its essence: the manifest growth of the external genitalia. (The latency period of childhood is, on the other hand, characterized by a relative cessation of their growth.) In the meantime the development of the internal genitalia has advanced far enough for them to be able to discharge the sexual products or, as the case may be, to bring about the formation of a new living organism. Thus a highly complicated apparatus has been made ready and awaits the moment of being put into operation.

This apparatus is to be set in motion by stimuli, and observation shows us that stimuli can impinge on it from three directions: from the external world by means of the excitation of the erotogenic zones with which we are already familiar, from the organic interior by ways which we have still to explore, and from mental life, which is itself a storehouse for external impressions and a receiving-post for internal excitations. All three kinds of stimuli produce the same effect, namely a condition described as 'sexual excitement', which shows itself by two sorts of indication, mental and somatic. The mental indications consist in a peculiar feeling of tension of an extremely compelling character; and among the numerous somatic ones are first and foremost a number of changes in the genitals, which have the obvious sense of being preparations for the sexual act—the erection of the male organ and the lubrication of the vagina.

SEXUAL   The fact that sexual excitement possesses the character of
TENSION   tension raises a problem the solution of which is no less
                difficult than it would be important in helping us to understand the sexual processes. In spite of all the differences of opinion that reign on the subject among psychologists, I must insist that a feeling of tension necessarily involves unpleasure. What seems to me decisive is the fact that a feeling of this kind is accompanied by an impulsion to make a change in the psychological situation, that it operates in an urgent way which is wholly alien to the nature of the feeling of pleasure. If, however, the tension of sexual excitement is counted as an unpleasurable feeling, we are at once brought up against the fact that it is also undoubtedly felt as pleasurable. In every case in which tension is produced by sexual processes it is accompanied by pleasure; even in the preparatory changes in the genitals a feeling of satisfaction of some kind

is plainly to be observed. How, then, are this unpleasurable tension and this feeling of pleasure to be reconciled?

* * *

Let us begin by casting a glance at the way in which the erotogenic zones fit themselves into the new arrangement. They have to play an important part in introducing sexual excitation. The eye is perhaps the zone most remote from the sexual object, but it is the one which, in the situation of wooing an object, is liable to be the most frequently stimulated by the particular quality of excitation whose cause, when it occurs in a sexual object, we describe as beauty. (For the same reason the merits of a sexual object are described as 'attractions'.) This stimulation is on the one hand already accompanied by pleasure, while on the other hand it leads to an increase of sexual excitement or produces it if it is not yet present. If the excitation now spreads to another erotogenic zone—to the hand, for instance, through tactile sensations—the effect is the same: a feeling of pleasure on the one side, which is quickly intensified by pleasure arising from the preparatory changes [in the genitals], and on the other side an increase of sexual tension, which soon passes over into the most obvious unpleasure if it cannot be met by a further accession of pleasure. Another instance will perhaps make this even clearer. If an erotogenic zone in a person who is not sexually excited (e.g. the skin of a woman's breast) is stimulated by touch, the contact produces a pleasurable feeling; but it is at the same time better calculated than anything to arouse a sexual excitation that demands an increase of pleasure. The problem is how it can come about that an experience of pleasure can give rise to a need for greater pleasure.

THE MECHANISM OF   The part played in this by the erotogenic zones,
FORE-PLEASURE   however, is clear. What is true of one of them is
                      true of all. They are all used to provide a certain
amount of pleasure by being stimulated in the way appropriate to them. This pleasure then leads to an increase in tension which in its turn is responsible for producing the necessary motor energy for the conclusion of the sexual act. The penultimate stage of that act is once again the appropriate stimulation of an erotogenic zone (the genital zone itself, in the glans penis) by the appropriate object (the mucous membrane of the vagina); and from the pleasure yielded by this excitation the motor energy is obtained, this time by a reflex path, which brings about the discharge of the sexual substances. This last pleasure is the highest in intensity, and its mechanism differs from that of the earlier pleasure. It is brought about entirely by discharge: it is wholly a pleasure of satisfaction and with it the tension of the libido is for the time being extinguished.

This distinction between the one kind of pleasure due to the excitation of erotogenic zones and the other kind due to the discharge of the sexual substances deserves, I think, to be made more concrete by a difference in nomenclature. The former may be suitably described as 'fore-pleasure' in contrast to the 'end-pleasure' or pleasure of satisfaction derived from the sexual act. Fore-pleasure is thus the same pleasure that has already been produced, although on a smaller scale, by the infantile sexual instinct; end-pleasure is something new and is thus probably conditioned by circumstances that do not arise till puberty. The formula for the new function of the erotogenic zones runs therefore: they are used to make possible, through the medium of the fore-pleasure which can be derived from them (as it was during infantile life), the production of the greater pleasure of satisfaction.

I was able recently to throw light upon another instance, in a quite different department of mental life, of a slight feeling of pleasure similarly making possible the attainment of a greater resultant pleasure, and thus operating as an 'incentive bonus'. In the same connection I was also able to go more deeply into the nature of pleasure.[9]

DANGERS OF FORE-PLEASURE   The connection between fore-pleasure and infantile sexual life is, however, made clearer by the pathogenic part which it can come to play. The attainment of the normal sexual aim can clearly be endangered by the mechanism in which fore-pleasure is involved. This danger arises if at any point in the preparatory sexual processes the fore-pleasure turns out to be too great and the element of tension too small. The motive for proceeding further with the sexual process then disappears, the whole path is cut short, and the preparatory act in question takes the place of the normal sexual aim. Experience has shown that the pre-condition for this damaging event is that the erotogenic zone concerned or the corresponding component instinct shall already during childhood have contributed an unusual amount of pleasure. If further factors then come into play, tending to bring about a fixation, a compulsion may easily arise in later life which resists the incorporation of this particular fore-pleasure into a new context. Such is in fact the mechanism of many perversions, which consist in a lingering over the preparatory acts of the sexual process.

This failure of the function of the sexual mechanism owing to fore-pleasure is best avoided if the primacy of the genitals too is adumbrated in childhood; and indeed things seem actually arranged to bring this about in the second half of childhood (from the age of eight to puberty). During these years the genital zones already behave in much the same way as in maturity; they become the seat of sensations of excitation and of preparatory changes whenever any pleasure is felt from the satisfaction of other erotogenic zones, though this result is still without a purpose—

9. See my volume on *Jokes and Their Relation to the Unconscious* which appeared in 1905. The 'fore-pleasure' attained by the technique of joking is used in order to liberate a greater pleasure derived from the removal of internal inhibitions.

that is to say, contributes nothing to a continuation of the sexual process. Already in childhood, therefore, alongside of the pleasure of satisfaction there is a certain amount of sexual tension, although it is less constant and less in quantity. We can now understand why, in discussing the sources of sexuality, we were equally justified in saying of a given process that it was sexually satisfying or sexually exciting. It will be noticed that in the course of our enquiry we began by exaggerating the distinction between infantile and mature sexual life, and that we are now setting this right. Not only the deviations from normal sexual life but its normal form as well are determined by the infantile manifestations of sexuality.

[2] THE PROBLEM OF SEXUAL EXCITATION

We remain in complete ignorance both of the origin and of the nature of the sexual tension which arises simultaneously with the pleasure when erotogenic zones are satisfied. The most obvious explanation, that this tension arises in some way out of the pleasure itself, is not only extremely improbable in itself but becomes untenable when we consider that in connection with the greatest pleasure of all, that which accompanies the discharge of the sexual products, no tension is produced, but on the contrary all tension is removed. Thus pleasure and sexual tension can only be connected in an indirect manner.

PART PLAYED   Apart from the fact that normally it is only the
BY THE SEXUAL   discharge of the sexual substances that brings sexual
SUBSTANCES   excitation to an end, there are other points of contact
                             between sexual tension and the sexual products. In
the case of a man living a continent life, the sexual apparatus, at varying intervals, which, however, are not ungoverned by rules, discharges the sexual substances during the night, to the accompaniment of a pleasurable feeling and in the course of a dream which hallucinates a sexual act. And in regard to this process (nocturnal emission) it is difficult to avoid the conclusion that the sexual tension, which succeeds in making use of the short cut of hallucination as a substitute for the act itself, is a function of the accumulation of semen in the vesicles containing the sexual products. Our experience in connection with the exhaustibility of the sexual mechanism argues in the same sense. If the store of semen is exhausted, not only is it impossible to carry out the sexual act, but the susceptibility of the erotogenic zones to stimulus ceases, and their appropriate excitation no longer gives rise to any pleasure. We thus learn incidentally that a certain degree of sexual tension is required even for the excitability of the erotogenic zones.

This would seem to lead to what is, if I am not mistaken, the fairly well-spread hypothesis that the accumulation of the sexual substances creates and maintains sexual tension; the pressure of these products upon the walls of the vesicles containing them might be supposed to act as a stimulus upon a spinal centre, the condition of which would be perceived by higher centres and would then give rise in consciousness to the familiar sensation of tension. If the excitation of the erotogenic zones increases sexual tension, this could only come about on the supposition that the zones in question are in an anatomical connection that has already been laid down with these centres, that they increase the tonus of the excitation in them, and, if the sexual tension is sufficient, set the sexual act in motion or, if it is insufficient, stimulate the production of the sexual substances.

The weakness of this theory, which we find accepted, for instance, in Krafft-Ebing's account of the sexual processes, lies in the fact that, having been designed to account for the sexual activity of adult males, it takes too little account of three sets of conditions which it should also be able to explain. These are the conditions in children, in females and in castrated males. In none of these three cases can there be any question of an accumulation of sexual products in the same sense as in males, and this makes a smooth application of the theory difficult. Nevertheless it may at once be admitted that it is possible to find means by which the theory may be made to cover these cases as well. In any case we are warned not to lay more weight on the factor of the accumulation of the sexual products than it is able to bear.

IMPORTANCE OF   Observations on castrated males seem to show that
THE INTERNAL   sexual excitation can occur to a considerable degree
SEXUAL ORGANS   independently of the production of the sexual sub-
                   stances. The operation of castration occasionally fails
to bring about a limitation of libido, although such limitation, which provides the motive for the operation, is the usual outcome. Moreover, it has long been known that diseases which abolish the production of the masculine sex-cells leave the patient, though he is now sterile, with his libido and potency undamaged.[1] * * *

CHEMICAL   Experiments in the removal of the sex-glands (testes and
THEORY   ovaries) of animals, and in the grafting into vertebrates of
              sex-glands from other individuals of the opposite sex, have
at last thrown a partial light on the origin of sexual excitation, and have at the same time still further reduced the significance of a possible accumulation of cellular sexual products. It has become experimentally possible (E. Steinach) to transform a male into a female, and conversely a female into a male. In this process the psychosexual behaviour of the animal alters in accordance with the somatic sexual characters and simultaneously with them. It seems, however, that this sex-determining influence is not an attribute of that part of the sex-glands which gives rise to the specific sex-cells (spermatozoa and ovum) but of their inter-

1. [This sentence was added in 1920.]

stitial tissue, upon which special emphasis is laid by being described in the literature as the 'puberty-gland'. It is quite possible that further investigation will show that this puberty-gland has normally a hermaphrodite disposition. If this were so, the theory of the bisexuality of the higher animals would be given anatomical foundation. It is already probable that the puberty-gland is not the only organ concerned with the production of sexual excitation and sexual characters. In any case, what we already know of the part played by the thyroid gland in sexuality fits in with this new biological discovery. It seems probable, then, that special chemical substances are produced in the interstitial portion of the sex-glands; these are then taken up in the blood stream and cause particular parts of the central nervous system to be charged with sexual tension. (We are already familiar with the fact that other toxic substances, introduced into the body from outside, can bring about a similar transformation of a toxic condition into a stimulus acting on a particular organ.) The question of how sexual excitation arises from the stimulation of erotogenic zones, when the central apparatus has been previously charged, and the question of what interplay arises in the course of these sexual processes between the effects of purely toxic stimuli and of physiological ones—none of this can be treated, even hypothetically, in the present state of our knowledge. It must suffice us to hold firmly to what is essential in this view of the sexual processes: the assumption that substances of a peculiar kind arise from the sexual metabolism. For this apparently arbitrary supposition is supported by a fact which has received little attention but deserves the closest consideration. The neuroses, which can be derived only from disturbances of sexual life, show the greatest clinical similarity to the phenomena of intoxication and abstinence that arise from the habitual use of toxic, pleasure-producing substances (alkaloids).

[3] THE LIBIDO THEORY[2]

* * * We have defined the concept of libido as a quantitatively variable force which could serve as a measure of processes and transformations occurring in the field of sexual excitation. We distinguish this libido in respect of its special origin from the energy which must be supposed to underlie mental processes in general, and we thus also attribute a *qualitative* character to it. In thus distinguishing between libidinal and other forms of psychical energy we are giving expression to the presumption that the sexual processes occurring in the organism are distinguished from the nutritive processes by a special chemistry. The analysis of the perversions and psychoneuroses has shown us that this sexual excitation is derived not from the so-called sexual parts alone, but from all the bodily organs. We thus reach the idea of a quantity of libido, to the mental representation of which we give the name of 'ego-

2. [This whole section, except for its last paragraph, dates from 1915.]

libido', and whose production, increase or diminution, distribution and displacement should afford us possibilities for explaining the psycho-sexual phenomena observed.

This ego-libido is, however, only conveniently accessible to analytic study when it has been put to the use of cathecting sexual objects, that is, when it has become object-libido. We can then perceive it concentrating upon objects, becoming fixed upon them or abandoning them, moving from one object to another and, from these situations, directing the subject's sexual activity, which leads to the satisfaction, that is, to the partial and temporary extinction, of the libido. The psycho-analysis of what are termed transference neuroses (hysteria and obsessional neurosis) affords us a clear insight at this point.

We can follow the object-libido through still further vicissitudes. When it is withdrawn from objects, it is held in suspense in peculiar conditions of tension and is finally drawn back into the ego, so that it becomes ego-libido once again. In contrast to object-libido, we also describe ego-libido as 'narcissistic' libido. From the vantage-point of psycho-analysis we can look across a frontier, which we may not pass, at the activities of narcissistic libido, and may form some idea of the relation between it and object-libido. Narcissistic or ego-libido seems to be the great reservoir from which the object-cathexes are sent out and into which they are withdrawn once more; the narcissistic libidinal cathexis of the ego is the original state of things, realized in earliest childhood, and is merely covered by the later extrusions of libido, but in essentials persists behind them.

It should be the task of a libido theory of neurotic and psychotic disorders to express all the observed phenomena and inferred processes in terms of the economics of the libido. It is easy to guess that the vicissitudes of the ego-libido will have the major part to play in this connection, especially when it is a question of explaining the deeper psychotic disturbances. We are then faced by the difficulty that our method of research, psycho-analysis, for the moment affords us assured information only on the transformations that take place in the object-libido, but is unable to make any immediate distinction between the ego-libido and the other forms of energy operating in the ego.

For the present, therefore,[3] no further development of the libido theory is possible, except upon speculative lines. It would, however, be sacrificing all that we have gained hitherto from psycho-analytic observation, if we were to follow the example of C. G. Jung and water down the meaning of the concept of libido itself by equating it with psychical instinctual force in general. The distinguishing of the sexual instinctual impulses from the rest and the consequent restriction of the concept of libido to the former receives strong support from the assumption which I have already discussed that there is a special chemistry of the sexual function.

3. [This paragraph was added in 1920.]

[4] THE DIFFERENTIATION BETWEEN MEN
AND WOMEN

As we all know, it is not until puberty that the sharp distinction is established between the masculine and feminine characters. From that time on, this contrast has a more decisive influence than any other upon the shaping of human life. It is true that the masculine and feminine dispositions are already easily recognizable in childhood. The development of the inhibitions of sexuality (shame, disgust, pity, etc.) takes place in little girls earlier and in the face of less resistance than in boys; the tendency to sexual repression seems in general to be greater; and, where the component instincts of sexuality appear, they prefer the passive form. The auto-erotic activity of the erotogenic zones is, however, the same in both sexes, and owing to this uniformity there is no possibility of a distinction between the two sexes such as arises after puberty. So far as the autoerotic and masturbatory manifestations of sexuality are concerned, we might lay it down that the sexuality of little girls is of a wholly masculine character. Indeed, if we were able to give a more definite connotation to the concepts of 'masculine' and 'feminine', it would even be possible to maintain that libido is invariably and necessarily of a masculine nature, whether it occurs in men or in women and irrespectively of whether its object is a man or a woman.[4]

Since I have become acquainted with the notion of bisexuality I have regarded it as the decisive factor, and without taking bisexuality into account I think it would scarcely be possible to arrive at an understanding of the sexual manifestations that are actually to be observed in men and women.

LEADING ZONES   Apart from this I have only the following to add.
IN MEN AND   The leading erotogenic zone in female children is
WOMEN   located at the clitoris, and is thus homologous to the
                 masculine genital zone of the glans penis. All my
experience concerning masturbation in little girls has related to the clitoris and not to the regions of the external genitalia that are important in later sexual functioning. I am even doubtful whether a female child can be led by the influence of seduction to anything other than clitoridal masturbation. If such a thing occurs, it is quite exceptional. The spontaneous discharges of sexual excitement which occur so often precisely in little girls are expressed in spasms of the clitoris. Frequent erections

4. [Footnote added 1915:] It is essential to understand clearly that the concepts of 'masculine' and 'feminine', whose meaning seems so unambiguous to ordinary people, are among the most confused that occur in science. {Freud, in the rest of this note, distinguishes between the sense of "activity and passivity," which is "the essential one and the most serviceable in psycho-analysis." The biological and sociological meanings of this pair are far less plain. One should add that Freud did not consistently heed his own advice. If he had, his writings on female sexuality might have been rather different and, indeed, less offensive to feminists.}

of that organ make it possible for girls to form a correct judgement, even without any instruction, of the sexual manifestations of the other sex: they merely transfer on to boys the sensations derived from their own sexual processes.[5]

* * *

[5] THE FINDING OF AN OBJECT

The processes at puberty, thus establish the primacy of the genital zones; and, in a man, the penis, which has now become capable of erection, presses forward insistently towards the new sexual aim—penetration into a cavity in the body which excites his genital zone. Simultaneously on the psychical side the process of finding an object, for which preparations have been made from earliest childhood, is completed. At a time at which the first beginnings of sexual satisfaction are still linked with the taking of nourishment, the sexual instinct has a sexual object outside the infant's own body in the shape of his mother's breast. It is only later that the instinct loses that object, just at the time, perhaps, when the child is able to form a total idea of the person to whom the organ that is giving him satisfaction belongs. As a rule the sexual instinct then becomes auto-erotic, and not until the period of latency has been passed through is the original relation restored. There are thus good reasons why a child sucking at his mother's breast has become the prototype of every relation of love. The finding of an object is in fact a refinding of it.

THE SEXUAL OBJECT DURING EARLY INFANCY But even after sexual activity has become detached from the taking of nourishment, an important part of this first and most significant of all sexual relations is left over, which helps to prepare for the choice of an object and thus to restore the happiness that has been lost. All through the period of latency children learn to feel for other people who help them in their helplessness and satisfy their needs a love which is on the model of, and a continuation of, their relation as sucklings to their nursing mother. There may perhaps be an inclination to dispute the possibility of identifying a child's affection and esteem for those who look after him with sexual love. I think, however, that a closer psychological examination may make it possible to establish this identity beyond any doubt. A child's intercourse with anyone responsible for his care affords him an unending source of sexual excitation and satisfaction from his erotogenic zones. This is especially so since the person in charge of him, who, after all, is as a rule his mother, herself regards him with feelings that are derived from her own sexual life: she strokes him, kisses him, rocks him and quite clearly treats him as a substitute for a complete

5. {For Freud's later thoughts on this matter, see below, pp. 673–74.}

sexual object.[6] A mother would probably be horrified if she were made aware that all her marks of affection were rousing her child's sexual instinct and preparing for its later intensity. She regards what she does as asexual, 'pure' love, since, after all, she carefully avoids applying more excitations to the child's genitals than are unavoidable in nursery care. As we know, however, the sexual instinct is not aroused only by direct excitation of the genital zone. What we call affection will unfailingly show its effects one day on the genital zones as well. Moreover, if the mother understood more of the high importance of the part played by instincts in mental life as a whole—in all its ethical and psychical achievements—she would spare herself any self-reproaches even after her enlightenment. She is only fulfilling her task in teaching the child to love. After all, he is meant to grow up into a strong and capable person with vigorous sexual needs and to accomplish during his life all the things that human beings are urged to do by their instincts. It is true that an excess of parental affection does harm by causing precocious sexual maturity and also because, by spoiling the child, it makes him incapable in later life of temporarily doing without love or of being content with a smaller amount of it. One of the clearest indications that a child will later become neurotic is to be seen in an insatiable demand for his parents' affection. And on the other hand neuropathic parents, who are inclined as a rule to display excessive affection, are precisely those who are most likely by their caresses to arouse the child's disposition to neurotic illness. Incidentally, this example shows that there are ways more direct than inheritance by which neurotic parents can hand their disorder on to their children.

INFANTILE   Children themselves behave from an early age as though
ANXIETY   their dependence on the people looking after them were in
              the nature of sexual love. Anxiety in children is originally nothing other than an expression of the fact that they are feeling the loss of the person they love. It is for this reason that they are frightened of every stranger. They are afraid in the dark because in the dark they cannot see the person they love; and their fear is soothed if they can take hold of that person's hand in the dark. To attribute to bogeys and blood-curdling stories told by nurses the responsibility for making children timid is to over-estimate their efficacy. The truth is merely that children who are inclined to be timid are affected by stories which would make no impression whatever upon others, and it is only children with a sexual instinct that is excessive or has developed prematurely or has become vociferous owing to too much petting who are inclined to be timid. In this respect a child, by turning his libido into anxiety when he cannot satisfy it, behaves like an adult. On the other hand an adult who has become neurotic owing to his libido being unsatisfied behaves

6. Anyone who considers this 'sacrilegious' may be recommended to read Havelock Ellis's views {*Studies in the Psychology of Sex*, vol. III, *Analysis of the Sexual Impulse . . .*, 2nd ed. (1913).}

in his anxiety like a child: he begins to be frightened when he is alone, that is to say when he is away from someone of whose love he had felt secure, and he seeks to assuage this fear by the most childish measures.[7]

THE BARRIER
AGAINST INCEST   We see, therefore, that the parents' affection for their child may awaken his sexual instinct prematurely (i.e. before the somatic conditions of puberty are present) to such a degree that the mental excitation breaks through in an unmistakable fashion to the genital system. If, on the other hand, they are fortunate enough to avoid this, then their affection can perform its task of directing the child in his choice of a sexual object when he reaches maturity. No doubt the simplest course for the child would be to choose as his sexual objects the same persons whom, since his childhood, he has loved with what may be described as damped-down libido. But, by the postponing of sexual maturation, time has been gained in which the child can erect, among other restraints on sexuality, the barrier against incest, and can thus take up into himself the moral precepts which expressly exclude from his object-choice, as being blood-relations, the persons whom he has loved in his childhood. Respect for this barrier is essentially a cultural demand made by society. Society must defend itself against the danger that the interests which it needs for the establishment of higher social units may be swallowed up by the family; and for this reason, in the case of every individual, but in particular of adolescent boys, it seeks by all possible means to loosen their connection with their family—a connection which, in their childhood, is the only important one.[8]

It is in the world of ideas, however, that the choice of an object is accomplished at first; and the sexual life of maturing youth is almost entirely restricted to indulging in phantasies, that is, in ideas that are not destined to be carried into effect.[9] In these phantasies the infantile

---

7. For this explanation of the origin of infantile anxiety I have to thank a three-year-old boy whom I once heard calling out of a dark room: 'Auntie, speak to me! I'm frightened because it's so dark.' His aunt answered him: 'What good would that do? You can't see me.' 'That doesn't matter,' replied the child, 'if anyone speaks, it gets light.' Thus what he was afraid of was not the dark, but the absence of someone he loved; and he could feel sure of being soothed as soon as he had evidence of that person's presence. {The little boy in question is almost certainly one of Freud's sons, and the "auntie," Freud's sister-in-law Minna Bernays, who spent much time in the Freud household and in the mid-nineties moved to Berggasse 19 altogether.}

8. [Footnote added 1915:] The barrier against incest is probably among the historical acquisitions of mankind, and, like other moral taboos, has no

doubt already become established in many persons by organic inheritance. (Cf. my Totem and Taboo, 1912–13). * * * {See below, pp. 481–513.}

9. [Footnote added 1920:]
* * *

It has justly been said that the Oedipus complex is the nuclear complex of the neuroses, and constitutes the essential part of their content. It represents the peak of infantile sexuality, which, through its after-effects, exercises a decisive influence on the sexuality of adults. Every new arrival on this planet is faced by the task of mastering the Oedipus complex; anyone who fails to do so falls a victim to neurosis. With the progress of psychoanalytic studies the importance of the Oedipus complex has become more and more clearly evident; its recognition has become the shibboleth that distinguishes the adherents of psycho-analysis from its opponents.

tendencies invariably emerge once more, but this time with intensified pressure from somatic sources. Among these tendencies the first place is taken with uniform frequency by the child's sexual impulses towards his parents, which are as a rule already differentiated owing to the attraction of the opposite sex—the son being drawn towards his mother and the daughter towards her father. At the same time as these plainly incestuous phantasies are overcome and repudiated, one of the most significant, but also one of the most painful, psychical achievements of the pubertal period is completed: detachment from parental authority, a process that alone makes possible the opposition, which is so important for the progress of civilization, between the new generation and the old. At every stage in the course of development through which all human beings ought by rights to pass, a certain number are held back; so there are some who have never got over their parents' authority and have withdrawn their affection from them either very incompletely or not at all. They are mostly girls, who, to the delight of their parents, have persisted in all their childish love far beyond puberty. It is most instructive to find that it is precisely these girls who in their later marriage lack the capacity to give their husbands what is due to them; they make cold wives and remain sexually anaesthetic. We learn from this that sexual love and what appears to be non-sexual love for parents are fed from the same sources; the latter, that is to say, merely corresponds to an infantile fixation of the libido.

The closer one comes to the deeper disturbances of psychosexual development, the more unmistakably the importance of incestuous object-choice emerges. In psychoneurotics a large portion or the whole of their psychosexual activity in finding an object remains in the unconscious as a result of their repudiation of sexuality. Girls with an exaggerated need for affection and an equally exaggerated horror of the real demands made by sexual life have an irresistible temptation on the one hand to realize the ideal of asexual love in their lives and on the other hand to conceal their libido behind an affection which they can express without self-reproaches, by holding fast throughout their lives to their infantile fondness, revived at puberty, for their parents or brothers and sisters. Psycho-analysis has no difficulty in showing persons of this kind that they are *in love*, in the everyday sense of the word, with these blood-relations of theirs; for, with the help of their symptoms and other manifestations of their illness, it traces their unconscious thoughts and translates them into conscious ones. In cases in which someone who has previously been healthy falls ill after an unhappy experience in love it is also possible to show with certainty that the mechanism of his illness consists in a turning-back of his libido on to those whom he preferred in his infancy.

AFTER-EFFECTS   Even a person who has been fortunate enough to
OF INFANTILE   avoid an incestuous fixation of his libido does not
OBJECT-CHOICE   entirely escape its influence. It often happens that a
                 young man falls in love seriously for the first time with
a mature woman, or a girl with an elderly man in a position of authority;
this is clearly an echo of the phase of development that we have been
discussing, since these figures are able to re-animate pictures of their
mother or father. There can be no doubt that every object-choice whatever is based, though less closely, on these prototypes. A man, especially,
looks for someone who can represent his picture of his mother, as it has
dominated his mind from his earliest childhood; and accordingly, if his
mother is still alive, she may well resent this new version of herself and
meet her with hostility. In view of the importance of a child's relations
to his parents in determining his later choice of a sexual object, it can
easily be understood that any disturbance of those relations will produce
the gravest effects upon his adult sexual life. Jealousy in a lover is never
without an infantile root or at least an infantile reinforcement. If there
are quarrels between the parents or if their marriage is unhappy, the
ground will be prepared in their children for the severest predisposition
to a disturbance of sexual development or to a neurotic illness.

A child's affection for his parents is no doubt the most important
infantile trace which, after being revived at puberty, points the way to
his choice of an object; but it is not the only one. Other starting-points
with the same early origin enable a man to develop more than one sexual
line, based no less upon his childhood, and to lay down very various
conditions for his object-choice.[1]

PREVENTION OF   One of the tasks implicit in object-choice is that it
INVERSION   should find its way to the opposite sex. This, as we
                 know, is not accomplished without a certain amount
of fumbling. Often enough the first impulses after puberty go astray,
though without any permanent harm resulting. Dessoir has justly remarked upon the regularity with which adolescent boys and girls form
sentimental friendships with others of their own sex. No doubt the
strongest force working against a permanent inversion of the sexual object
is the attraction which the opposing sexual characters exercise upon one
another. Nothing can be said within the framework of the present discussion to throw light upon it. This factor is not in itself, however,
sufficient to exclude inversion; there are no doubt a variety of other
contributory factors. Chief among these is its authoritative prohibition
by society. Where inversion is not regarded as a crime it will be found
that it answers fully to the sexual inclinations of no small number of
people. It may be presumed, in the next place, that in the case of men

1. [*Footnote added* 1915:] The innumerable pe-   in love itself are quite unintelligible except by ref-
culiarities of the erotic life of human beings as well   erence back to childhood and as being residual
as the compulsive character of the process of falling   effects of childhood.

a childhood recollection of the affection shown them by their mother and others of the female sex who looked after them when they were children contributes powerfully to directing their choice towards women; on the other hand their early experience of being deterred by their father from sexual activity and their competitive relation with him deflect them from their own sex. Both of these two factors apply equally to girls, whose sexual activity is particularly subject to the watchful guardianship of their mother. They thus acquire a hostile relation to their own sex which influences their object-choice decisively in what is regarded as the normal direction. The education of boys by male persons (by slaves, in antiquity) seems to encourage homosexuality. The frequency of inversion among the present-day aristocracy is made somewhat more intelligible by their employment of menservants, as well as by the fact that their mothers give less personal care to their children. In the case of some hysterics it is found that the early loss of one of their parents, whether by death, divorce or separation, with the result that the remaining parent absorbs the whole of the child's love, determines the sex of the person who is later to be chosen as a sexual object, and may thus open the way to permanent inversion.

Character and Anal Erotism

As Freud's editors have rightly observed, this short paper of 1908, now among his most quoted presentations, aroused considerable "astonishment and indignation" (SE IX, 68) when it first appeared. What matters more is that it represents one of Freud's few excursions into the question of character formation (he returns to it, apart from casual references, in some important pages in The Ego and the Id [see below, pp. 637–40]). Character may be defined as the fairly stable constellation of traits, or, in psychoanalytic parlance, a cluster of fixations. Freud, one should note, is not arguing that the particular set of traits he is here discussing is universal. There are others. But what struck him most was the "anal character."

Among those whom we try to help by our psycho-analytic efforts we often come across a type of person who is marked by the possession of a certain set of character-traits, while at the same time our attention is drawn to the behaviour in his childhood of one of his bodily functions and the organ concerned in it. I cannot say at this date what particular occasions began to give me an impression that there was some organic connection between this type of character and this behaviour of an organ, but I can assure the reader that no theoretical expectation played any part in that impression.

Accumulated experience has so much strengthened my belief in the existence of such a connection that I am venturing to make it the subject of a communication.

The people I am about to describe are noteworthy for a regular combination of the three following characteristics. They are especially *orderly, parsimonious* and *obstinate*. Each of these words actually covers a small group or series of interrelated character-traits. 'Orderly'[1] covers the notion of bodily cleanliness, as well as of conscientiousness in carrying out small duties and trustworthiness. Its opposite would be 'untidy' and 'neglectful'. Parsimony may appear in the exaggerated form of avarice; and obstinacy can go over into defiance, to which rage and revengefulness are easily joined. The two latter qualities—parsimony and obstinacy—are linked with each other more closely than they are with the first—with orderliness. They are, also, the most constant element of the whole complex. Yet it seems to me incontestable that all three in some way belong together.

It is easy to gather from these people's early childhood history that they took a comparatively long time to overcome their infantile *incontinentia alvi* [faecal incontinence], and that even in later childhood they suffered from isolated failures of this function. As infants, they seem to have belonged to the class who refuse to empty their bowels when they are put on the pot because they derive a subsidiary pleasure from defaecating; for they tell us that even in somewhat later years they enjoyed holding back their stool, and they remember—though more readily about their brothers and sisters than about themselves—doing all sorts of unseemly things with the faeces that had been passed. From these indications we infer that such people are born with a sexual constitution in which the erotogenicity of the anal zone is exceptionally strong. But since none of these weaknesses and idiosyncracies are to be found in them once their childhood has been passed, we must conclude that the anal zone had lost its erotogenic significance in the course of development; and it is to be suspected that the regularity with which this triad of properties is present in their character may be brought into relation with the disappearance of their anal erotism.

I know that no one is prepared to believe in a state of things so long as it appears to be unintelligible and to offer no angle from which an explanation can be attempted. But we can at least bring the underlying factors nearer to our understanding by the help of the postulates I laid down in my *Three Essays on the Theory of Sexuality* in 1905. I there attempted to show that the sexual instinct of man is highly complex and is put together from contributions made by numerous constituents and component instincts. Important contributions to 'sexual excitation' are furnished by the peripheral excitations of certain specially designated parts of the body (the genitals, mouth, anus, urethra), which therefore

---

1. ['*Ordentlich*' in German. The original meaning of the word is 'orderly'; but it has become greatly extended in use. It can be the equivalent of such English terms as 'correct', 'tidy', 'cleanly', 'trustworthy', as well as 'regular', 'decent' and 'proper', in the more colloquial senses of those words.]

deserve to be described as 'erotogenic zones'. But the amounts of excitation coming in from these parts of the body do not all undergo the same vicissitudes, nor is the fate of all of them the same at every period of life. Generally speaking, only a part of them is made use of in sexual life; another part is deflected from sexual aims and directed towards others—a process which deserves the name of 'sublimation'. During the period of life which may be called the period of 'sexual latency'—i.e. from the completion of the fifth year to the first manifestations of puberty (round about the eleventh year)—reaction-formations, or counter-forces, such as shame, disgust and morality, are created in the mind. They are actually formed at the expense of the excitations proceeding from the erotogenic zones, and they rise like dams to oppose the later activity of the sexual instincts. Now anal erotism is one of the components of the [sexual] instinct which, in the course of development and in accordance with the education demanded by our present civilization, have become unserviceable for sexual aims. It is therefore plausible to suppose that these character-traits of orderliness, parsimony and obstinacy, which are so often prominent in people who were formerly anal erotics, are to be regarded as the first and most constant results of the sublimation of anal erotism.[2]

The intrinsic necessity for this connection is not clear, of course, even to myself. But I can make some suggestions which may help towards

2. Since it is precisely the remarks in my *Three Essays on the Theory of Sexuality* about the anal erotism of infants that have particularly scandalized uncomprehending readers, I venture at this point to interpolate an observation for which I have to thank a very intelligent patient. 'A friend of mine,' he told me, 'who has read your *Three Essays on the Theory of Sexuality* was talking about the book. He entirely agreed with it, but there was one passage which—though of course he accepted and understood its meaning like that of the rest—struck him as so grotesque and comic that he sat down and laughed over it for a quarter of an hour. The passage ran: "One of the clearest signs of subsequent eccentricity or nervousness is to be seen when a baby obstinately refuses to empty his bowels when he is put on the pot—that is, when his nurse wants him to—and holds back that function till he himself chooses to exercise it. He is naturally not concerned with dirtying the bed, he is only anxious not to miss the subsidiary pleasure attached to defaecating." {See above, p. 000.} The picture of this baby sitting on the pot and deliberating whether he would put up with a restriction of this kind upon his personal freedom of will, and feeling anxious, too, not to miss the pleasure attached to defaecating,—this caused my friend the most intense amusement. About twenty minutes afterwards, as we were having some cocoa, he suddenly remarked without any preliminary: "I say, seeing the cocoa in front of me has suddenly made me think of an idea that I always had when I was a child. I used always to pretend to myself that I was the cocoa-manufacturer Von Houten" (he pronounced the name Van

"Hauten" [i.e., with the first syllable rhyming with the English word "cow"]) and that I possessed a great secret for the manufacture of this cocoa. Everybody was trying to get hold of this secret that was a boon to humanity but I kept it carefully to myself. I don't know why I should have hit specially upon Van Houten. Probably his advertisements impressed me more than any others." Laughing, and without thinking at the time that my words had any deep meaning, I said: "Wann haut'n die Mutter?" {"When does mother smack?" The first two words in the German phrase are pronounced exactly like 'Van Houten'} It was only later that I realized that my pun in fact contained the key to the whole of my friend's sudden childhood recollection, and I then recognized it as a brilliant example of a screen-phantasy. My friend's phantasy, while keeping to the situation actually involved (the nutritional process) and making use of phonetic associations ("Kakao" ['cocoa'—'Kaka' is the common German nursery word for 'faeces']) * * * pacified his sense of guilt by making a complete reversal in the content of his recollection: there was a displacement from the back of the body to the front, excreting food became taking food in, and something that was shameful and had to be concealed became a secret that was a boon to humanity. I was interested to see how, only a quarter of an hour after my friend had fended the phantasy off (though, it is true, in the comparatively mild form of raising an objection on formal grounds), he was, quite involuntarily, presented with the most convincing evidence by his own unconscious.'

an understanding of it. Cleanliness, orderliness and trustworthiness give exactly the impression of a reaction-formation against an interest in what is unclean and disturbing and should not be part of the body. ('Dirt is matter in the wrong place.')[3] To relate obstinacy to an interest in defaecation would seem no easy task; but it should be remembered that even babies can show self-will about parting with their stool, as we have seen above, and that it is a general practice in children's upbringing to administer painful stimuli to the skin of the buttocks—which is linked up with the erotogenic anal zone—in order to break their obstinacy and make them submissive. An invitation to a caress of the anal zone is still used to-day, as it was in ancient times, to express defiance or defiant scorn, and thus in reality signifies an act of tenderness that has been overtaken by repression. An exposure of the buttocks represents a softening down of this spoken invitation into a gesture; in Goethe's *Götz von Berlichingen* both words and gesture are introduced at the most appropriate point as an expression of defiance.[4]

The connections between the complexes of interest in money and of defaecation, which seem so dissimilar, appear to be the most extensive of all. Every doctor who has practised psycho-analysis knows that the most refractory and long-standing cases of what is described as habitual constipation in neurotics can be cured by that form of treatment. This is less surprising if we remember that that function has shown itself similarly amenable to hypnotic suggestion. But in psycho-analysis one only achieves this result if one deals with the patients' money complex and induces them to bring it into consciousness with all its connections. It might be supposed that the neurosis is here only following an indication of common usage in speech, which calls a person who keeps too careful a hold on his money 'dirty' or 'filthy'.[5] But this explanation would be far too superficial. In reality, wherever archaic modes of thought have predominated or persist—in the ancient civilizations, in myths, fairy tales and superstitions, in unconscious thinking, in dreams, and in neuroses—money is brought into the most intimate relationship with dirt. We know that the gold which the devil gives his paramours turns into excrement after his departure, and the devil is certainly nothing else than the personification of the repressed unconscious instinctual life. We also know about the superstition which connects the finding of treasure with defaecation, and everyone is familiar with the figure of the 'shitter of ducats [*Dukatenscheisser*]'.[6] Indeed, even according to

3. [This sentence is in English in the original.]

4. {See Act III of Goethe's youthful play, completed in its final version in 1773, when Goethe was twenty-four. Under siege, standing at the window hearing the herald calling on him to surrender, Goetz the defiant knight tells him that while he continues to have great respect for His Imperial Majesty, his feelings for the messenger's captain are different: "*Er aber, sags ihm, er kann mich im Arsch lecken*,—tell him that he can lick me in the arse." Then, in an immortal gesture (the stage direction tells us) he "slams the window shut."}

5. {Freud uses the German word '*filzig*' as well as the English 'filthy'.}

6. [A term vulgarly used for a wealthy spendthrift.] {It is also the name for a little wooden toy.}

ancient Babylonian doctrine gold is 'the faeces of Hell' (Mammon = *ilu manman*). Thus in following the usage of language, neurosis, here as elsewhere, is taking words in their original, significant sense, and where it appears to be using a word figuratively it is usually simply restoring its old meaning.

It is possible that the contrast between the most precious substance known to men and the most worthless, which they reject as waste matter ('refuse'), has led to this specific identification of gold with faeces.[7]

Yet another circumstance facilitates this equation in neurotic thought. The original erotic interest in defaecation is, as we know, destined to be extinguished in later years. In those years the interest in money makes its appearance as a new interest which had been absent in childhood. This makes it easier for the earlier impulsion, which is in process of losing its aim, to be carried over to the newly emerging aim.

If there is any basis in fact for the relation posited here between anal erotism and this triad of character-traits, one may expect to find no very marked degree of 'anal character' in people who have retained the anal zone's erotogenic character in adult life, as happens, for instance, with certain homosexuals. Unless I am much mistaken, the evidence of experience tallies quite well on the whole with this inference.

We ought in general to consider whether other character-complexes, too, do not exhibit a connection with the excitations of particular erotogenic zones. At present I only know of the intense 'burning' ambition of people who earlier suffered from enuresis. We can at any rate lay down a formula for the way in which character in its final shape is formed out of the constituent instincts: the permanent character-traits are either unchanged prolongations of the original instincts, or sublimations of those instincts, or reaction-formations against them.

Family Romances

The original appearance of this brief paper (written in late 1908) as an untitled section in Otto Rank's book *The Myth of the Birth of the Hero* (1909) suggests that Freud took little pride in it. But it belongs among a set of interesting papers on childhood that he had recently published, notably "The Sexual Enlightenment of Children" (1907), a plea for candor and honesty on the part of parents, and "On the Sexual Theories of Children" (1908), which, like the present paper, frankly canvasses what Freud calls "childish depravity." Two textual matters deserve comment: the title that Freud gave the paper was "Der Familienroman der Neurotiker." Now, "Roman" is a broader designation than "romance." It means "novel," and much of what the translators have called a "romance" is more complex and less agreeable than the term they have chosen suggests. Their second emendation, leaving

7. [In English in the original.]

out Freud's specification "of neurotics," which severely limits this imaginative fantasy that one's parents are really exalted beings, may claim a certain
justification: the "family novel" is after all not confined to neurotics.

The liberation of an individual, as he grows up, from the authority of
his parents is one of the most necessary though one of the most painful
results brought about by the course of his development. It is quite
essential that that liberation should occur and it may be presumed that
it has been to some extent achieved by everyone who has reached a
normal state. Indeed, the whole progress of society rests upon the opposition between successive generations. On the other hand, there is a
class of neurotics whose condition is recognizably determined by their
having failed in this task.

For a small child his parents are at first the only authority and the
source of all belief. The child's most intense and most momentous wish
during these early years is to be like his parents (that is, the parent of
his own sex) and to be big like his father and mother. But as intellectual
growth increases, the child cannot help discovering by degrees the category to which his parents belong. He gets to know other parents and
compares them with his own, and so acquires the right to doubt the
incomparable and unique quality which he had attributed to them. Small
events in the child's life which make him feel dissatisfied afford him
provocation for beginning to criticize his parents, and for using, in order
to support his critical attitude, the knowledge which he has acquired
that other parents are in some respects preferable to them. The psychology of the neuroses teaches us that, among other factors, the most
intense impulses of sexual rivalry contribute to this result. A feeling of
being slighted is obviously what constitutes the subject-matter of such
provocations. There are only too many occasions on which a child is
slighted, or at least *feels* he has been slighted, on which he feels he is
not receiving the whole of his parents' love, and, most of all, on which
he feels regrets at having to share it with brothers and sisters. His sense
that his own affection is not being fully reciprocated then finds a vent
in the idea, often consciously recollected later from early childhood, of
being a step-child or an adopted child. People who have not developed
neuroses very frequently remember such occasions, on which—usually
as a result of something they have read—they interpreted and responded
to their parent's hostile behaviour in this fashion. But here the influence
of sex is already in evidence, for a boy is far more inclined to feel hostile
impulses towards his father than towards his mother and has a far more
intense desire to get free from *him* than from *her*. In this respect the
imagination of girls is apt to show itself much weaker. These consciously
remembered mental impulses of childhood embody the factor which
enables us to understand the nature of myths.

The later stage in the development of the neurotic's estrangement from his parents, begun in this manner, might be described as 'the neurotic's family romance'. It is seldom remembered consciously but can almost always be revealed by psycho-analysis. For a quite peculiarly marked imaginative activity is one of the essential characteristics of neurotics and also of all comparatively highly gifted people. This activity emerges first in children's play, and then, starting roughly from the period before puberty, takes over the topic of family relations. A characteristic example of this peculiar imaginative activity is to be seen in the familiar day-dreaming which persists far beyond puberty. If these day-dreams are carefully examined, they are found to serve as the fulfilment of wishes and as a correction of actual life. They have two principal aims, an erotic and an ambitious one—though an erotic aim is usually concealed behind the latter too. At about the period I have mentioned, then, the child's imagination becomes engaged in the task of getting free from the parents of whom he now has a low opinion and of replacing them by others, who, as a rule, are of higher social standing. He will make use in this connection of any opportune coincidences from his actual experience, such as his becoming acquainted with the Lord of the Manor or some landed proprietor if he lives in the country or with some member of the aristocracy if he lives in town. Chance occurences of this kind arouse the child's envy, which finds expression in a phantasy in which both his parents are replaced by others of better birth. The technique used in developing phantasies like this (which are, of course, conscious at this period) depends upon the ingenuity and the material which the child has at his disposal. There is also the question of whether the phantasies are worked out with greater or less effort to obtain verisimilitude. This stage is reached at a time at which the child is still in ignorance of the sexual determinants of procreation.

When presently the child comes to know the difference in the parts played by fathers and mothers in their sexual relations, and realizes that *'pater semper incertus est'*, while the mother is *'certissima'*,[1] the family romance undergoes a curious curtailment: it contents itself with exalting the child's father, but no longer casts any doubts on his maternal origin, which is regarded as something unalterable. This second (sexual) stage of the family romance is actuated by another motive as well, which is absent in the first (asexual) stage. The child, having learnt about sexual processes, tends to picture to himself erotic situations and relations, the motive force behind this being his desire to bring his mother (who is the subject of the most intense sexual curiosity) into situations of secret infidelity and into secret love-affairs. In this way the child's phantasies, which started by being, as it were, asexual, are brought up to the level of his later knowledge.

Moreover the motive of revenge and retaliation, which was in the

---

1. [An old legal tag: 'paternity is always uncertain, maternity is most certain.']

foreground at the earlier stage, is also to be found at the later one. It is, as a rule, precisely these neurotic children who were punished by their parents for sexual naughtiness and who now revenge themselves on their parents by means of phantasies of this kind.

A younger child is very specially inclined to use imaginative stories such as these in order to rob those born before him of their prerogatives—in a way which reminds one of historical intrigues; and he often has no hesitation in attributing to his mother as many fictitious love-affairs as he himself has competitors. An interesting variant of the family romance may then appear, in which the hero and author returns to legitimacy himself while his brothers and sisters are eliminated by being bastardized. So too if there are any other particular interests at work they can direct the course to be taken by the family romance; for its many-sidedness and its great range of applicability enable it to meet every sort of requirement. In this way, for instance, the young phantasy-builder can get rid of his forbidden degree of kinship with one of his sisters if he finds himself sexually attracted by her.

If anyone is inclined to turn away in horror from this depravity of the childish heart or feels tempted, indeed, to dispute the possibility of such things, he should observe that these works of fiction, which seem so full of hostility, are none of them really so badly intended, and that they still preserve, under a slight disguise, the child's original affection for his parents. The faithlessness and ingratitude are only apparent. If we examine in detail the commonest of these imaginative romances, the replacement of both parents or of the father alone by grander people, we find that these new and aristocratic parents are equipped with attributes that are derived entirely from real recollections of the actual and humble ones; so that in fact the child is not getting rid of his father but exalting him. Indeed the whole effort at replacing the real father by a superior one is only an expression of the child's longing for the happy, vanished days when his father seemed to him the noblest and strongest of men and his mother the dearest and loveliest of women. He is turning away from the father whom he knows to-day to the father in whom he believed in the earlier years of his childhood; and his phantasy is no more than the expression of a regret that those happy days have gone. Thus in these phantasies the overvaluation that characterizes a child's earliest years comes into its own again. An interesting contribution to this subject is afforded by the study of dreams. We learn from their interpretation that even in later years, if the Emperor and Empress appear in dreams, those exalted personages stand for the dreamer's father and mother. So that the child's overvaluation of his parents survives as well in the dreams of normal adults.

Formulations on the Two Principles
of Mental Functioning

This important paper of 1911, which Freud's editors justly call "one of the classics of psycho-analysis" (*SE* XII, 215), harks back to the unfinished and unpublished "Project" of 1895. In his theoretical seventh chapter of *The Interpretation of Dreams*, too, Freud had adumbrated the idea that mental processes may be divided into "primary" (regulated by the "pleasure principle") and "secondary" (regulated by the "reality principle"). In highly condensed form, this paper deals with the way these processes interact and conflict with one another, and how the mind develops to cope with pressures from within as well as from the outside world. It is a difficult paper, but rewarding and indeed essential to psychoanalytic theory.

We have long observed that every neurosis has as its result, and probably therefore as its purpose, a forcing of the patient out of real life, an alienating of him from reality. Nor could a fact such as this escape the observation of Pierre Janet {of 1909}; he spoke of a loss of '*la fonction du réel*' ['the function of reality'] as being a special characteristic of neurotics, but without discovering the connection of this disturbance with the fundamental determinants of neurosis. By introducing the process of repression into the genesis of the neuroses we have been able to gain some insight into this connection. Neurotics turn away from reality because they find it unbearable—either the whole or parts of it. The most extreme type of this turning away from reality is shown by certain cases of hallucinatory psychosis which seek to deny the particular event that occasioned the outbreak of their insanity (Griesinger).[1] But in fact every neurotic does the same with some fragment of reality.[2] And we are now confronted with the task of investigating the development of the relation of neurotics and of mankind in general to reality, and in this way of bringing the psychological significance of the real external world into the structure of our theories.

In the psychology which is founded on psycho-analysis we have become accustomed to taking as our starting-point the unconscious mental processes, with the peculiarities of which we have become acquainted through analysis. We consider these to be the older, primary processes, the residues of a phase of development in which they were the only kind of mental process. The governing purpose obeyed by these primary processes is easy to recognize; it is described as the pleasure-unpleasure [*Lust-Unlust*] principle, or more shortly the pleasure principle. These

---

1. [W. Griesinger (1817–1868) was a well-known Berlin psychiatrist of an earlier generation, much admired by Freud's teacher, Meynert * * * {who, as early as the 1840s} drew attention to the wish-fulfilling character of both psychoses and dreams.]

2. Otto Rank {"Schopenhauer über den Wahnsinn," *Zentralblatt*} (1910) has recently drawn attention to a remarkably clear prevision of this causation shown in Schopenhauer's *The World as Will and Idea* [Part II (Supplements), Chapter 32].

processes strive towards gaining pleasure; psychical activity draws back from any event which might arouse unpleasure. (Here we have repression.) Our dreams at night and our waking tendency to tear ourselves away from distressing impressions are remnants of the dominance of this principle and proofs of its power.

I shall be returning to lines of thought which I have developed elsewhere[3] when I suggest that the state of psychical rest was originally disturbed by the peremptory demands of internal needs. When this happened, whatever was thought of (wished for) was simply presented in a hallucinatory manner, just as still happens to-day with our dream-thoughts every night. It was only the non-occurrence of the expected satisfaction, the disappointment experienced, that led to the abandonment of this attempt at satisfaction by means of hallucination. Instead of it, the psychical apparatus had to decide to form a conception of the real circumstances in the external world and to endeavour to make a real alteration in them. A new principle of mental functioning was thus introduced; what was presented in the mind was no longer what was agreeable but what was real, even if it happened to be disagreeable.[4] This setting-up of the *reality principle* proved to be a momentous step.

(1) In the first place, the new demands made a succession of adaptations necessary in the psychical apparatus, which, owing to our insufficient or uncertain knowledge, we can only retail very cursorily.

The increased significance of external reality heightened the importance, too, of the sense-organs that are directed towards that external world, and of the *consciousness* attached to them. Consciousness now learned to comprehend sensory qualities in addition to the qualities of pleasure and unpleasure which hitherto had alone been of interest to it. A special function was instituted which had periodically to search the external world, in order that its data might be familiar already if an urgent internal need should arise—the function of *attention*. Its activity meets the sense-impressions half way, instead of awaiting their appearance. At the same time, probably, a system of *notation* was introduced, whose task it was to lay down the results of this periodical activity of consciousness—a part of what we call *memory*.

The place of repression, which excluded from cathexis as productive

3. {In *The Interpretation of Dreams*, chapter VII.}
4. I will try to amplify the above schematic account with some further details. It will rightly be objected that an organization which was a slave to the pleasure principle and neglected the reality of the external world could not maintain itself alive for the shortest time, so that it could not have come into existence at all. The employment of a fiction like this is, however, justified when one considers that the infant—provided one includes with it the care it receives from its mother—does almost realize a psychical system of this kind. It probably hallucinates the fulfillment of its internal needs; it betrays its unpleasure, when there is an increase of stimulus and an absence of satisfaction, by the motor discharge of screaming and beating about with its arms and legs, and it then experiences the satisfaction it has hallucinated. Later, as an older child, it learns to employ these manifestations of discharge intentionally as methods of expressing its feelings. Since the later care of children is modelled on the care of infants, the dominance of the pleasure principle can really come to an end only when a child has achieved complete psychical detachment from its parents. * * *

of unpleasure some of the emerging ideas, was taken by an *impartial passing of judgement*, which had to decide whether a given idea was true or false—that is, whether it was in agreement with reality or not—the decision being determined by making a comparison with the memory-traces of reality.

A new function was now allotted to motor discharge, which, under the dominance of the pleasure principle, had served as a means of unburdening the mental apparatus of accretions of stimuli, and which had carried out this task by sending innervations into the interior of the body (leading to expressive movements and the play of features and to manifestations of affect). Motor discharge was now employed in the appropriate alteration of reality; it was converted into *action*.

Restraint upon motor discharge (upon action), which then became necessary, was provided by means of the process of *thinking*, which was developed from the presentation of ideas. Thinking was endowed with characteristics which made it possible for the mental apparatus to tolerate an increased tension of stimulus while the process of discharge was postponed. It is essentially an experimental kind of acting, accompanied by displacement of relatively small quantities of cathexis together with less expenditure (discharge) of them. For this purpose the conversion of freely displaceable cathexes into 'bound' cathexes was necessary, and this was brought about by means of raising the level of the whole cathectic process. It is probable that thinking was originally unconscious, in so far as it went beyond mere ideational presentations and was directed to the relations between impressions of objects, and that it did not acquire further qualities, perceptible to consciousness, until it became connected with verbal residues.

(2) A general tendency of our mental apparatus, which can be traced back to the economic principle of saving expenditure [of energy], seems to find expression in the tenacity with which we hold on to the sources of pleasure at our disposal, and in the difficulty with which we renounce them. With the introduction of the reality principle one species of thought-activity was split off; it was kept free from reality-testing and remained subordinated to the pleasure principle alone. This activity is *phantasying*, which begins already in children's play, and later, continued as *day-dreaming*, abandons dependence on real objects.

(3) The supersession of the pleasure principle by the reality principle, with all the psychical consequences involved, which is here schematically condensed into a single sentence, is not in fact accomplished all at once; nor does it take place simultaneously all along the line. For while this development is going on in the ego-instincts, the sexual instincts become detached from them in a very significant way. The sexual instincts behave auto-erotically at first; they obtain their satisfaction in the subject's own body and therefore do not find themselves in the situation of frustration which was what necessitated the institution of the reality principle; and when, later on, the process of finding an object

begins, it is soon interrupted by the long period of latency, which delays sexual development until puberty. These two factors—auto-erotism and the latency period—have as their result that the sexual instinct is held up in its psychical development and remains far longer under the dominance of the pleasure principle, from which in many people it is never able to withdraw.

In consequence of these conditions, a closer connection arises, on the one hand, between the sexual instinct and phantasy and, on the other hand, between the ego-instincts and the activities of consciousness. Both in healthy and in neurotic people this connection strikes us as very intimate, although the considerations of genetic psychology which have just been put forward lead us to recognize it as a *secondary* one. The continuance of auto-erotism is what makes it possible to retain for so long the easier momentary and imaginary satisfaction in relation to the sexual object in place of real satisfaction, which calls for effort and postponement. In the realm of phantasy, repression remains all-powerful; it brings about the inhibition of ideas *in statu nascendi* before they can be noticed by consciousness, if their cathexis is likely to occasion a release of unpleasure. This is the weak spot in our psychical organization; and it can be employed to bring back under the dominance of the pleasure principle thought-processes which had already become rational. An essential part of the psychical disposition to neurosis thus lies in the delay in educating the sexual instincts to pay regard to reality and, as a corollary, in the conditions which make this delay possible.

(4) Just as the pleasure-ego can do nothing but *wish*, work for a yield of pleasure, and avoid unpleasure, so the reality-ego need do nothing but strive for what is *useful* and guard itself against damage.[5] Actually the substitution of the reality principle for the pleasure principle implies no deposing of the pleasure principle, but only a safeguarding of it. A momentary pleasure, uncertain in its results, is given up, but only in order to gain along the new path an assured pleasure at a later time. But the endopsychic impression made by this substitution has been so powerful that it is reflected in a special religious myth. The doctrine of reward in the after-life for the—voluntary or enforced—renunciation of earthly pleasures is nothing other than a mythical projection of this revolution in the mind. Following consistently along these lines, *religions* have been able to effect absolute renunciation of pleasure in this life by means of the promise of compensation in a future existence; but they have not by this means achieved a conquest of the pleasure principle. It is *science* which comes nearest to succeeding in that conquest; science too, however, offers intellectual pleasure during its work and promises practical gain in the end.

(5) *Education* can be described without more ado as an incitement

---

5. The superiority of the reality-ego over the pleasure-ego has been aptly expressed by Bernard Shaw in these words: 'To be able to choose the line of greatest advantage instead of yielding in the direction of least resistance.' *(Man and Superman)*. {Act III}.

to the conquest of the pleasure principle, and to its replacement by the reality principle; it seeks, that is, to lend its help to the developmental process which affects the ego. To this end it makes use of an offer of love as a reward from the educators; and it therefore fails if a spoilt child thinks that it possesses that love in any case and cannot lose it whatever happens.

(6) *Art* brings about a reconciliation between the two principles in a peculiar way. An artist is originally a man who turns away from reality because he cannot come to terms with the renunciation of instinctual satisfaction which it at first demands, and who allows his erotic and ambitious wishes full play in the life of phantasy. He finds the way back to reality, however, from this world of phantasy by making use of special gifts to mould his phantasies into truths of a new kind, which are valued by men as precious reflections of reality. Thus in a certain fashion he actually becomes the hero, the king, the creator, or the favourite he desired to be, without following the long roundabout path of making real alterations in the external world. But he can only achieve this because other men feel the same dissatisfaction as he does with the renunciation demanded by reality, and because that dissatisfaction, which results from the replacement of the pleasure principle by the reality principle, is itself a part of reality.

(7) While the ego goes through its transformation from a *pleasure-ego* into a *reality-ego*, the sexual instincts undergo the changes that lead them from their original auto-erotism through various intermediate phases to object-love in the service of procreation. If we are right in thinking that each step in these two courses of development may become the site of a disposition to later neurotic illness, it is plausible to suppose that the form taken by the subsequent illness (the *choice of neurosis*) will depend on the particular phase of the development of the ego and of the libido in which the dispositional inhibition of development has occurred. Thus unexpected significance attaches to the chronological features of the two developments (which have not yet been studied), and to possible variations in their synchronization.

(8) The strangest characteristic of unconscious (repressed) processes, to which no investigator can become accustomed without the exercise of great self-discipline, is due to their entire disregard of reality-testing; they equate reality of thought with external actuality, and wishes with their fulfillment—with the event—just as happens automatically under the dominance of the ancient pleasure principle. Hence also the difficulty of distinguishing unconscious phantasies from memories which have become unconscious. But one must never allow oneself to be misled into applying the standards of reality to repressed psychical structures, and on that account, perhaps, into undervaluing the importance of phantasies in the formation of symptoms on the ground that they are not actualities, or into tracing a neurotic sense of guilt back to some other source because there is no evidence that any actual crime has been

committed. One is bound to employ the currency that is in use in the country one is exploring—in our case a neurotic currency. Suppose, for instance, that one is trying to solve a dream such as this. A man who had once nursed his father through a long and painful mortal illness, told me that in the months following his father's death he had repeatedly dreamt that *his father was alive once more and that he was talking to him in his usual way. But he felt it exceedingly painful that his father had really died, only without knowing it.* The only way of understanding this apparently nonsensical dream is by adding 'as the dreamer wished' or 'in consequence of his wish' after the words 'that his father had really died', and by further adding 'that he [the dreamer] wished it' to the last words. The dream-thought then runs: it was a painful memory for him that he had been obliged to wish for his father's death (as a release) while he was still alive, and how terrible it would have been if his father had had any suspicion of it! What we have here is thus the familiar case of self-reproaches after the loss of someone loved, and in this instance the self-reproach went back to the infantile significance of death-wishes against the father.

The deficiencies of this short paper, which is preparatory rather than expository, will perhaps be excused only in small part if I plead that they are unavoidable. In these few remarks on the psychical consequences of adaptation to the reality principle I have been obliged to adumbrate views which I should have preferred for the present to withhold and whose justification will certainly require no small effort. But I hope it will not escape the notice of the benevolent reader how in these pages too the dominance of the reality principle is beginning.

PART THREE: THERAPY
AND TECHNIQUE

Notes Upon a Case of Obsessional Neurosis ("Rat Man") and Process Notes for the Case History

Freud, following his own injunction, did not take notes during the analytic hour but would record in the evening the details of each session he thought worth preserving: the innumerable cartoons depicting psychoanalysts listening to their patients notebook handy misrepresent psychoanalytic procedure. Unfortunately, Freud destroyed virtually all his process notes; the single exception is the notes for the "Rat Man," of which entries covering virtually the first four months have survived. They deserve to be studied in conjunction with the published case history, showing as they do some interesting departures from the printed text; they afford a fascinating glimpse into Freud's laboratory: the psychoanalytic situation.

The obsessional young lawyer who entered psychoanalytic treatment on October 1, 1907, and concluded it some months later, probably the following spring, was one of Freud's favorites. Freud lectured on the "Rat Man" while he was still analyzing him, first to the informal group that met every Wednesday night in Freud's apartment at Berggasse 19, and then, in a four-hour tour de force, to the first international psychoanalytic congress at Salzburg, where Ernest Jones heard him with undisguised awe. Freud judged the analysis, short as it was, a complete success: the Rat Man's obsessions, he notes with satisfaction at the end of the case history, had disappeared. But, as a footnote added in 1923 to the conclusion somberly reveals, "Like so many other young men of value and promise, {the Rat Man} perished in the Great War."

{PROCESS NOTES}

'*Oct. 1, 07.*—Dr. Lorenz[1], aged 29½, said he suffered from obsessions, particularly intensely since 1903, but dating back to his childhood. The chief feature were fears of something happening to two people of whom he was very fond, his father and a lady whom he admired. Besides this, there were compulsive impulses, e.g. to cut his throat with a razor, and prohibitions, sometimes in connection with quite unimportant things. He had wasted years of his studies, he told me, in fighting these ideas of his, and consequently had only just now passed his final law examination. His ideas only affected his professional work when it was concerned with criminal law. He also suffered from an impulse to do some injury to the lady whom he admired. This impulse was usually silent in her presence, but came to the fore when she was not there. Being away from her, however,—she lives in Vienna—had always done

---

1. {The patient's real name was Ernst Lanzer, as was first established by Patrick J. Mahony in his *Freud and the Rat Man* (1986). It might be worthwhile pointing out to an American audience that the title of doctor, which conjures up visions of medicine or academic status, is also conferred on the Continent to lawyers, who had, after all, received a doctor's degree at the university.}

him good. Of the various treatments he had tried none had been of any use to him, except some hydro-therapeutic treatment in Munich, and this, he thought, had only been because he had made an acquaintance there which had led to regular sexual intercourse. Here he had no opportunities of the sort and he very seldom had intercourse, and that only irregularly, when occasion offered. He was disgusted at prostitutes. His sexual life, he said, had been stunted; masturbation had played only a small part in it, in his 16th–17th year. He had first had intercourse at the age of 26.

'He gave me the impression of being a clear-headed and shrewd person. After I had told him my terms, he said he must consult his mother. The next day he came back and accepted them.'

*   *   *

{FROM THE PUBLISHED CASE HISTORY}

{Freud then made the patient pledge to submit himself to the "fundamental rule" of psychoanalysis: to speak freely, without censorship, no matter how insignificant or senseless or disagreeable it might be. The Rat Man begins by speaking of a friend whose judgment he valued, and then began reciting details of his early sexual life, from his fourth or fifth year, viewing his governesses' private parts and buttocks. He then confesses that he is tormented by the fear that his father might die—although it emerges that his father has been dead for several years—or that something terrible might happen to the young lady he loves.

After this, the Rat Man tries, with many hesitations, to recount his great obsessive fear connected with a terrifying story told him by an officer on maneuvers about a punishment meted out to criminals in the Orient: a pot is turned upside down on the buttocks of the criminal and rats in the pot then bore their way into his anus. Freud conjectures that his patient harbors a secret (unconscious) wish that his father might die, a wish the Rat Man vehemently denies. In addition, the patient tells an immensely involved story about obsessive feelings that Freud listens to patiently and tries to unravel.}

INITIATION INTO THE NATURE OF THE TREATMENT

The reader must not expect to hear at once what light I have to throw upon the patient's strange and senseless obsessions about the rats. The true technique of psycho-analysis requires the physician to suppress his curiosity and leaves the patient complete freedom in choosing the order in which topics shall succeed each other during the treatment. At the fourth session, accordingly, I received the patient with the question: 'And how do you intend to proceed to-day?'

'I have decided to tell you something which I consider most important and which has tormented me from the very first.' He then told me at great length the story of the last illness of his father, who had died of emphysema nine years previously. One evening, thinking that the condition was one which would come to a crisis, he had asked the doctor when the danger could be regarded as over. 'The evening of the day after to-morrow', had been the reply. It had never entered his head that his father might not survive that limit. At half-past eleven at night he had lain down for an hour's rest. He had woken up at one o'clock, and had been told by a medical friend that his father had died. He had reproached himself with not having been present at his death; and the reproach had been intensified when the nurse told him that his father had spoken his name once during the last days, and had said to her as she came up to the bed: 'Is that Paul?' He had thought he noticed that his mother and sisters had been inclined to reproach themselves in a similar way; but they had never spoken about it. At first, however, the reproach had not tormented him. For a long time he had not realized the fact of his father's death. It had constantly happened that, when he heard a good joke, he would say to himself: 'I must tell Father that.' His imagination, too, had been occupied with his father, so that often, when there was a knock at the door, he would think: 'Here comes Father', and when he walked into a room he would expect to find his father in it. And although he had never forgotten that his father was dead, the prospect of seeing a ghostly apparition of this kind had had no terrors for him; on the contrary, he had greatly desired it. It had not been until eighteen months later that the recollection of his neglect had recurred to him and begun to torment him terribly, so that he had come to treat himself as a criminal. The occasion of this happening had been the death of an aunt by marriage and of a visit of condolence that he had paid at her house. From that time forward he had extended the structure of his obsessional thoughts so as to include the next world. The immediate consequence of this development had been that he became seriously incapacitated from working.[2] He told me that the only thing that had kept him going at that time had been the consolation given him by his friend, who had always brushed his self-reproaches aside on the ground that they were grossly exaggerated. Hearing this, I took the opportunity of giving him a first glance at the underlying principles of psycho-analytic therapy. When there is a *mésalliance*, I began, between an affect and its ideational content (in this instance, between the intensity of the self-reproach and the occasion for it), a layman will say that the affect is too great for the occasion—that it is exaggerated—and that

---

2. A more detailed description of the episode, which the patient gave me later on, made it possible to understand the effect that it produced on him. His uncle, lamenting the loss of his wife, had exclaimed: 'Other men allow themselves every possible indulgence, but I lived for this woman alone!' The patient had assumed that his uncle was alluding to his father and was casting doubts upon his conjugal fidelity; and although his uncle had denied this construction of his words most positively, it was no longer possible to counteract their effect.

consequently the inference following from the self-reproach (the inference that the patient is a criminal) is false. On the contrary, the [analytic] physician says: 'No. The affect is justified.' * * *

{PROCESS NOTES}

Oct. 10.—He announced that he wanted to talk about the beginning of his obsessional ideas. It turned out that he meant the beginning of his commands. [They began] while he was working for his State Examination. They were connected with the lady, beginning with senseless little orders (e.g. to count up to a certain figure between thunder and lightning, to run round the room at some precise minute, etc.). In connection with his intention to slim, he was compelled by a command on his walks at Gmunden (in the summer of 1902) to go for a run in the glare of the midday heat. He had a command to take the examination in July, but resisted this on his friend's advice; but later had a command to take it at the first possible opportunity in October, and this he obeyed. He encouraged himself in his studies with the phantasy that he must hurry so as to be able to marry the lady. It appears as though this phantasy was the motive for his command. He seems to have attributed these commands to his father. He once lost several weeks owing to the absence of the lady, who had gone away on account of the illness of her grandmother, a very old woman. He offered to visit her there, but she refused. ('Carrion crow'.) Just as he was up to his eyes in his work, he thought: 'You might manage to obey the command to take your examination at the earliest moment in October. But if you received a command to cut your throat, what then?' He at once became aware that this command had already been given, and was hurrying to the cupboard to fetch his razor when he thought: 'No, it's not so simple as that. You must go and kill the old woman.' Upon that, he fell to the ground, beside himself with horror.—Who was it who gave him this command?

The lady still remains most mysterious. Oaths that he has forgotten. His defensive struggle against them explicit but also forgotten.

Oct. 11.—Violent struggle, bad day. Resistance, because I requested him yesterday to bring a photograph of the lady with him—i.e. to give up his reticence about her. Conflict as to whether he should abandon the treatment or surrender his secrets. His *Cs.* was far from having mastered his oscillating thoughts. He described the way in which he tries to fend off obsessional ideas. During his religious period he had made up prayers for himself which took up more and more time and eventually lasted for an hour and a half—the reason being that something always inserted itself into the simple phrases and turned them into their opposite. E.g. 'May God—not—protect him!' (An inverted Balaam.) I explained the fundamental uncertainty of all measures of reassurance, because what is being fought against gradually slips into them. This he confirmed. On one such occasion the notion occurred to him of cursing: that would certainly not turn into an obsessional idea. (This was the original meaning of what had been repressed.) He had suddenly given all this up eighteen months ago; i.e. he had made up a word out of the initials of some of his prayers—something like 'Hapeltsamen' (I must ask for more details about this)—and said this so quickly that nothing could slip in. All this was strengthened by a certain amount of superstition, a trace of omnipotence, as though his evil wishes possessed power, and this was confirmed by real experiences. E.g. the first time he was in the Munich Sanatorium he had a room next to the girl with whom he had sexual relations. When he went there the second time he hesitated whether to take the same room again as it was very large and expensive. When eventually he told the girl that he had made up his mind to take it, she told him that the Professor had taken it already. 'May he be struck dead for it!' he thought. A fortnight later he was disturbed in his sleep by the idea of a corpse. He put it aside; but in the morning he heard that the Professor had really had a stroke and had been taken up to his room at about that time. He also, so he says, possesses the gift of prophetic dreams. He told me the first of these.

Oct. 12.—He did not tell me the second, but told me how he had spent the day. His spirits rose and he went to the theatre. When he got home he chanced to meet his servant-girl, who is neither young nor pretty but has been showing him attention for some time past. He cannot think why, but he suddenly gave her a kiss and then attacked her. Though she no doubt made only a show of resistance, he came to his senses and fled to his room. It was always the same with him: his fine or happy moments were always spoilt by something nasty. I drew his attention to the analogy between this and assassinations instigated by *agents provocateurs*.

He proceeded with this train of thought and reached the subject of masturbation, which in his case had a strange history. He began it when he was about 21—after his father's death, as I got him to confirm—because he had heard of it and felt a certain curiosity. He repeated it very seldom and was always very much ashamed afterwards. One day, without any provocation, he thought: 'I swear on my blessed soul to give it up!' Though he attached no value whatever to this vow, and laughed at it on account of its peculiar solemnity, he did give it up for the time being. A few years later, at the time at which his lady's grandmother died and he wanted to join her, his own mother said: 'On my soul, you shall not go!' The similarity of this oath struck him, and he reproached himself with bringing the salvation of his mother's soul into danger. He told himself not to be more cowardly on his own account than on other people's and, if he persisted in his intention of going to join the lady, to begin to masturbate again. Subsequently he abandoned the idea of going, because he had a letter telling him not to. From that moment on the masturbation reappeared from time to time. It was provoked when he experienced especially fine moments or when he read fine passages. It occurred once, for instance, on a lovely afternoon when he heard a postilion blowing his horn in the Teinfaltstrasse [in the middle of Vienna]—until it was forbidden by a police officer, probably on the ground of some old Court decree prohibiting the blowing of horns in the city. And another time it happened when he read in *Wahrheit und Dichtung* {really *Dichtung und Wahrheit*} how Goethe had freed himself in a burst of tenderness from the effects of a curse which a mistress had pronounced on whoever should kiss his lips; he had long, almost superstitiously, suffered the curse to hold him back, but now he broke his bonds and kissed his love joyfully again and again. (Lilli Schoenemann?)[3] And he masturbated at this point, as he told me with amazement.

In Salzburg, moreover, there had been a servant-girl who attracted him and whom he had to do with later as well. This led to his masturbating. He told me about it by alluding to the fact that this masturbation had spoilt a short trip to Vienna which he had been looking forward to.

He gave me some further particulars about his sexual life. Intercourse with *puellae*[4] disgusts him. Once when he was with one he made it a condition that she should undress, and, when she demanded 50 per cent extra for this, he paid her and went away, he was so much revolted by it all. On the few occasions on which he had had intercourse with girls (at Salzburg and later with the waitress in Munich) he never felt self-reproachful. How *exalté* he had been when the waitress told him the moving tale of her first love and how she had been called to her lover's death-bed. He regretted having arranged to spend the night with her, and it was only her conscientiousness that compelled him to wrong the dead man. He always sought to make a sharp distinction between relations which consisted only in copulation and everything that was called love; and the idea that she had been so deeply loved made her in his eyes an unsuitable object for his sensuality.

I could not restrain myself here from constructing the material at our disposal into an event: how before the age of six he had been in the habit of masturbating and how his father had forbidden it, using as a threat the phrase 'it would be the death of you' and perhaps also threatening to cut off his penis. This would account for his masturbating in connection with the release from the curse, for the commands and prohibitions in his unconscious and for the threat of death which was now thrown back on to his father. His present suicidal ideas would correspond to a self-reproach of being a murderer. This, he said at the end of the session, brought up a great many ideas in his mind.

---

3. [A girl to whom Goethe was engaged for a short time during his youth.]

4. {Spanish for "girls," it means, of course, "prostitutes" in this context.}

Addenda.—He had been serious, he told me, in his intention to commit suicide, and was only held back by two considerations. One of these was that he could not stand the idea of his mother finding his bleeding remains. But he was able to avoid this by the phantasy of performing the deed on the Semmering[5] and leaving behind a letter requesting that his brother-in-law should be the first to be informed. (The second consideration I have curiously enough forgotten.)

I have not mentioned from earlier sessions three interrelated memories dating from his fourth year, which he describes as his earliest ones and which refer to the death of his elder sister Katherine. The first was of her being carried to bed. The second was of his asking 'Where is Katherine?' and going into the room and finding his father sitting in an arm-chair and crying. The third was of his father bending over his weeping mother. (It is curious that I am not certain whether these memories are his or Ph.'s.)

Oct. 14.—My uncertainty and forgetfulness on these last two points seem to be intimately connected. The memories were really his and the consideration which I had forgotten was that once when he was very young and he and his sister were talking about death, she said: 'On my soul, if you die I shall kill myself.' So that in both cases it was a question of his sister's death. (They were forgotten owing to complexes of my own.) Moreover, these earliest recollections, when he was 3½ and his sister 8, fit in with my construction. Death was brought close to him, and he really believed that you die if you masturbate.

The ideas that were brought up in his mind [at the end of the previous session] were as follows. The idea of his penis being cut off had tormented him to an extraordinary degree, and this had happened while he was in the thick of studying. The only reason he could think of was that at that time he was suffering from the desire to masturbate. Secondly, and this seemed to him far more important, twice in his life, on the occasion of his first copulation (at Trieste) and another time in Munich—he had doubts about the first of these, though it is plausible on internal grounds—, this idea occurred to him afterwards: 'This is a glorious feeling! One might do anything for this—murder one's father, for instance!' This made no sense in his case, since his father was already dead. Thirdly, he described a scene of which he had often been told by other people, including his father, but of which he himself had absolutely no recollection. His whole life long he has been terribly afraid of blows, and feels very grateful to his father for never having beaten him (so far as his memory goes). When other children were beaten, he used to creep away and hide, filled with terror. But when he was quite small (3 years old) he seems to have done something naughty, for which his

5. [The mountain resort near Vienna.]

father hit him. The little boy then flew into a terrible rage and began hurling abuse at his father. But as he knew no bad language, he called him all the names of common objects that he could think of: 'You lamp! You towel! You plate!' and so on. His father is said to have declared 'The child will either be a great man or a great criminal!' This story, the patient admitted, was evidence of anger and revenge dating back to the remote past.

I explained to him the principle of the Adige at Verona,[6] which he found most illuminating. He told me some more in connection with his revengefulness. Once when his brother was in Vienna he thought he had grounds for believing that the lady preferred him. He became so furiously jealous over this that he was afraid he might do him some mischief. He asked his brother to have a wrestle with him, and not until he himself had been defeated did he feel pacified.

He told me another phantasy of revenge upon the lady, which he has no need to feel ashamed of. He thinks she sets store by social position. Accordingly he made up a phantasy that she had married a man of that kind in a government office. He himself then entered the same department and rose more rapidly than her husband. One day this man committed some act of dishonesty. The lady threw herself at his feet and implored him to save her husband. He promised to, and informed her that it had only been for love of her that he had entered the service, because he had foreseen that such a moment would occur. Now his mission was fulfilled, her husband was saved, and he would resign his post. Later he went still further and felt he would prefer to be her benefactor and do her some great service without her knowing that it was he who was doing it. In this phantasy he saw only the evidence of his love and not the magnanimity *à la* Monte Cristo which was designed to repress his vengeance.

Oct. 18.—*Arrears.*

He began by confessing a dishonest action when he was grown up. He was playing *vingt-et-un* and had won a great deal. He announced that he would put everything on the next hand and then stop playing. He got up to 19 and reflected for a moment whether to go any further; he then ruffled through the pack as though unintentionally and saw that the next card was in fact a two, so that when it was turned up he had a twenty-one. A childhood memory followed, of his father having egged him on to take his mother's purse out of her pocket and extract a few *kreuzer* from it.

He spoke of his conscientiousness since that time and his carefulness with money. He has not taken over his inheritance but has left it with his mother, who allows him a very small amount of pocket-money. In

6. [The River Adige makes a loop in Verona, which brings it almost back to the point at which it enters the city.]

this way he is beginning to behave like a miser, though he has no such inclination. He found difficulty, too, in making his friend an allowance. He could not bring himself even to mislay any object that had belonged to his father or the lady.

Next day, continuing his associations, he spoke of his attitude towards someone called 'Reserl', who is engaged to be married but is evidently much attached to him; how he gave her a kiss but at the same time had a distressing compulsive idea that something bad was happening to his lady—something resembling the phantasy connected with Captain Novak [the 'cruel' captain]. His dream during the night said much more distinctly what was thus lightly touched on while he was awake:—

(I) Reserl was stopping with us. She got up as though she was hypnotized, came behind my chair with a pale face and put her arms round me. It was as though I tried to shake off her embrace, as though each time she stroked my head some misfortune would occur to the lady—some misfortune in the next world too. It happened automatically—as though the misfortune occurred at the very moment of the stroking.

(The dream was not interpreted. For it is in fact only a more distinct version of the obsessional idea which he did not dare to become aware of during the day.)

He was greatly affected by to-day's dream, for he sets much store by dreams and they have played a large part in his story and have even led up to crises.

(II) In October, 1906—perhaps after masturbating on the occasion of reading the passage in *Wahrheit und Dichtung* {*Dichtung und Wahrheit*}.

The lady was under some kind of restraint. He took his two Japanese swords and set her free. Clutching them, he hurried to the place where he suspected she was. He knew that they meant 'marriage' and 'copulation'. Both things now came true. He found her leaning up against a wall, with thumbscrews fastened to her. The dream seemed to him now to become ambiguous. Either he set her free from this situation by means of his two swords, 'marriage' and 'copulation': or the other idea was that it was only on account of them that she had got into this situation. (It was clear that he himself did not understand this alternative, though his words could not possibly have any other meaning.)

The Japanese swords really exist. They hang at the head of his bed and are made of a very large number of Japanese coins. They were a present from his eldest sister at Trieste, who (as he told me in answer to an enquiry) is very happily married. It is possible that the maid, who is in the habit of dusting his room while he is still asleep, may have touched the coins and so made a noise which penetrated into his sleep.

(III) He cherished this third dream as though it were his most precious treasure.

Dec.—Jan., 1907. I was in a wood and most melancholy. The lady came to meet me, looking very pale. 'Paul, come with me before it is too late. I know we are both sufferers.' She put her arm through mine and dragged me away by force. I struggled with her but she was too strong. We came to a broad river and she stood there. I was dressed in miserable rags which fell into the stream and were carried away by it. I tried to swim after them but she held me back: 'Let the rags go!' I stood there in gorgeous raiment.

He knew that the rags meant his illness and that the whole dream promised him health through the lady. He was very happy at the time— till other dreams came which made him profoundly wretched.

He could not help believing in the premonitory power of dreams, for he had had several remarkable experiences to prove it. Consciously he does not really believe in it. (The two views exist side by side, but the critical one is sterile.)

(IV) In the summer of 1901 he had written to one of his colleagues to send him 3 kronen's worth of pipe tobacco. Three weeks passed with no reply and no tobacco. One morning he woke up and said he had dreamt of tobacco. Had the postman by any chance brought a parcel for him? No.—Ten minutes later the door-bell rang: the postman had brought his tobacco.

(V) During the summer of 1903, while he was working for his Third State Examination.

He dreamt that he was asked in the examination to explain the difference between a 'Bevollmächtigter' and a 'Staatsorgan'.[7] Some months later, in his Finals, he was actually asked this question. He is quite certain about this dream, but there is no evidence of his having spoken of it during the interval [between the dream and its coming true].

He tried to explain the previous dream by the fact that his friend had no money and that he himself may perhaps have known the date at which he was going to have some. No precise dates could be fixed.

(VI) His eldest sister has very beautiful teeth. But three years ago they began to ache, till they had to be pulled out. The dentist where she lives (a friend) said: 'You will lose all your teeth.' One day he [the patient] suddenly thought: 'Who knows what is happening to Hilde's teeth?' Perhaps he may have been having toothache himself. He had masturbated again that day, and as he was going to sleep he saw in a half-sleeping vision his sister bothered with her teeth. Three days later

---

7. [A 'Bevollmächtigter' is a person who exercises his functions by virtue of special appointment, a 'Staatsorgan' acts by virtue of the nature of his office.]

he had a letter to say that another of her teeth was beginning to hurt; and she subsequently lost it.

He was astonished when I explained that his masturbation was responsible for it.

(VII) A dream while he was staying with Marie Steiner. He had already told it to me but now added some details. She is a kind of childhood love of his. When he was 14 or 15 he had a sentimental passion for her. He insists upon her narrow-minded conceit. In September, 1903, he visited her and saw her seven-year-old idiot brother, who made a fearful impression on him. In December he had a dream of going to his funeral. At about the same time the child died. It was not possible to fix the times more precisely. In the dream he was standing beside Marie Steiner and was encouraging her to bear up. ('Carrion crow', as his eldest sister called him. He is constantly killing people so that afterwards he can make his way into someone's good graces.) The contrast between the mother's doting love for the idiot child and her behaviour before his birth. She seems to have been responsible for the child's infirmity by tight-lacing too much, because she was ashamed of having a baby so late in life.

During his stay at Salzburg he was constantly pursued by premonitions which were amazingly fulfilled. For instance, there was the man whom he heard talking to the waitress at the hotel about burglary—which he took as an augury that he would see the man next as a criminal. And this actually occurred a few months later, when he happened to be transferred to the Criminal Department.—At Salzburg, too, he used to meet people on the bridge whom he had been thinking of a moment earlier. (His sister had already explained this as being accounted for by indirect [peripheral] vision.)—Again, he happened to think of a scene at Trieste when he had been in the Public Library with his sister. A man had entered into conversation with them and had talked very stupidly and said to him: 'You are still at the stage of Jean Paul's *Flegeljahre*' ['Fledgling Years']. An hour later [after thinking of this episode] he was in the Salzburg lending library, and the *Flegeljahre* was one of the first books he picked up. (But not the first. An hour earlier he had formed the intention of going to the library and it was this that reminded him of the scene at Trieste.)

At Salzburg he regarded himself as a seer. But the coincidences were never of any importance and never related to things which he expected but only to trivialities.

(The story about Marie Steiner was interpolated between two stories about his sisters. The lack of clarity of his obsessional ideas is noteworthy; in his dreams they are clearer.)

Oct. 18.—Two dreams that were linked with nothing less than crises. Once before he had had the idea of not washing any more. This had come to him in the form usual with his prohibitions: 'What sacrifice am I prepared to make in order to . . . ?' But he had promptly rejected it. In reply to my questions he told me that up till puberty he had been a regular little pig. After that he had inclined towards overcleanliness and with the onset of his illness had been fanatically clean, etc. (in connection with his commands). Now one day he went for a walk with the lady—he was under the impression that what he was telling me was of no importance. The lady greeted a man (a doctor), she was very friendly with him, too friendly—he admitted he had been a little jealous and had in fact spoken about it. At the lady's house they had played cards; he felt melancholy in the evening; next morning he had this dream:—

(VIII) He was with the lady. She was very nice to him, and he told her about his compulsive idea and prohibition in connection with the Japanese swords—the meaning of which was that he might neither marry her nor have sexual intercourse with her. But that is nonsensical, he said, I might just as well have a prohibition against ever washing again. She smiled and nodded to him. In the dream he took this to mean that she agreed with him that both things were absurd. But when he woke up it occurred to him that she had meant that he need not wash any more. He fell into a violent state of emotion and knocked his head against the bed-post. He felt as though there was a lump of blood in his head. On similar occasions he had already had the idea of making a funnel-shaped hole in his head to let what was diseased in his brain come out; the loss would somehow be made up. He does not understand his state. I explained: The Nuremberg funnel[8]—which in fact his father used often to talk about. And [the patient went on] his father used often to say 'you'll get things into your head some day'. I interpreted this: anger, vengeance on the lady out of jealousy, the connection with the provoking cause [of the dream]—the incident on the walk—which he considered so trivial. He confirmed his anger with the doctor. He did not understand about the conflict as to whether he should marry her or not. He had a sense of liberation in the dream—liberation from her, I put in.

He postponed the command not to wash any more and did not carry it out. The idea was replaced by a number of others, especially of cutting his throat.

Oct. 27.—Arrears. So long as he makes difficulties over giving me the lady's name his account must be incoherent. Detached incidents:—

One evening in June 1907 he was visiting his friend, Braun, whose sister, Adela, played to them. She paid him a lot of attention. He was very much oppressed and thought a great deal about the dream of the

8. [An instrument of torture kept in the Nuremberg museum. Water was poured through it down the victim's throat.]

Japanese swords—the thought of marrying the lady if it were not for the other girl.

Dream at night:—His sister Gerda was very ill. He went to her bedside. Braun came towards him. 'You can only save your sister by renouncing all sexual pleasure', upon which he replied in astonishment (to his shame) '*all* pleasure'.

Braun is interested in his sister. Some months ago, he brought her home once when she was feeling unwell. The idea can only have been that if he married Adela, Gerda's marriage with Braun would become probable, too. So he was sacrificing himself for her. In the dream he was putting himself in a compulsive situation so as to be obliged to marry. His opposition to his lady and his inclination to unfaithfulness are plain. When he was 14 he had homosexual relations with Braun—looking at each other's penis.

At Salzburg in 1906 he had this idea during the day-time. Supposing the lady said to him, 'you must have no sexual pleasure till you have married me', would he take an oath not to have any? A voice in him said 'yes'. (Oath of abstinence in his Ucs.) That night he dreamt that he was engaged to the lady, and as he was walking with her arm through his, he said overjoyed 'I should never have imagined that this could have come true so soon'. (This referred to his compulsive abstinence. This was most remarkable, and correct; and it confirmed the view I took above.) At that moment he saw the lady make a face as though the engagement were of no interest to her. His happiness was quite spoilt by this. He said to himself 'you're engaged and not at all happy. You're pretending to be a bit happy so as to persuade yourself that you are.'

After I had persuaded him to reveal the name of Gisa Hertz and all the details about her, his account became clear and systematic. Her predecessor was Lise O., another Lise. (He always had several interests simultaneously, just as he had several lines of sexual attachments, derived from his several sisters.)

Summer 1898. (Aged 20). Dream:—He was discussing an abstract subject with Lise II. Suddenly the dream-picture vanished and he was looking at a big machine with an enormous number of wheels, so that he was astonished at its complexity.—This has to do with the fact that this Lise always seemed to him very complex compared with Julie whose admirer he also was at that time and who has recently died.

He went on to give me a lengthy account of his relations with his lady. On the evening after she had refused him he had the following dream (Dec. 1900):—'I was going along a street. There was a pearl lying in the road. I stooped to pick it up but every time I stooped it disappeared. Every two or three steps it appeared again. I said to myself, "you mayn't".' He explained this prohibition to himself as meaning that his pride would not allow it, because she had refused him once. Actually it was probably a question of a prohibition by his father which originated in his childhood and extended to marriage. He then called to mind an actual remark of his father's to a similar effect: 'Don't go up there so often.' 'You'll make yourself ridiculous' was another snubbing remark of his. Further to the dream:—A short time before he had seen a pearl necklace in a shop and had thought that if he had the money he would buy it for her. He often called her a pearl among girls. This was a phrase they often used. 'Pearl' also seemed to him to fit her because a pearl is a hidden treasure that has to be looked for in its shell.

A suspicion that it was through his sisters that he was led to sexuality, perhaps not on his own initiative—that he had been seduced.

The speeches in his dreams need not be related to real speeches. His Ucs. ideas—as being internal voices—have the value of real speeches which he hears only in his dreams.

Oct. 27.—His lady's grandmother's illness was a disease of the rectum.

The onset of his illness followed a complaint made by his widowed uncle: 'I lived for this woman alone, whereas other men amuse themselves elsewhere.' He thought his uncle was referring to his father, though this did not occur to him at once, but only a few days later. When he spoke to the lady about it she laughed at him, and on another occasion, when he and his uncle were present, she managed to bring the conversation round to his father, whom his uncle then praised to the skies. But this was not enough for him. A little time afterwards he felt obliged to put a direct question to his uncle as to whether he had meant his father, which his uncle denied in astonishment. The patient was particularly surprised at this episode, since he himself would not have blamed his father in the least if he had had an occasional lapse.

In this context he mentioned a half-joking remark of his mother's about the period when his father had had to live at Pressburg and only came to Vienna once a week. (When he first told me this, he omitted this characteristic connection.)

Remarkable coincidence while he was studying for his Second State Examination. He omitted to read two passages only, each of four pages, and it was precisely on these that he was examined. Afterwards, while he was studying for the Third Examination, he had a prophetic dream. This period saw the beginning proper of his piousness and of phantasies of his father still being in contact with him. He used to leave the door to the passage open at night in the conviction that his father would be standing outside. His phantasies at this time were directly attached to this gap in attainable knowledge. He finally pulled himself together and tried to get the better of himself by a sensible argument—what would his father think of his goings on if he was still alive? But this made no impression on him, he was only brought to a stop by the delirious form of the phantasy—that his father might suffer because of his phantasies even in the after-life.

The compulsions that arose while he was studying for the Third Examination, to the effect that he must positively take it in July, seem to have been related to the arrival from New York of an uncle of the lady's, X., of whom he was fearfully jealous; and perhaps even to his suspicion (afterwards confirmed) that the lady would travel to America.

Oct. 29.—I told him I suspected that his sexual curiosity had been kindled in relation to his sisters. This had an immediate result. He had a memory that he first noticed the difference between the sexes when he saw his deceased sister Katherine (five years his senior) sitting on the pot, or something of the sort.

He told me the dream he had had while studying for the Third Examination. Grünhut[9] made a practice every third or fourth time in the Examination of asking one particular question about drafts payable at a specified place; and when he had been answered he would go on to ask, 'and what is the reason for this law?' To which the correct answer was, 'as a protection against the *Schicanen* of the opposing parties'. His dream was on precisely these lines, but he replied instead, 'as a protection against the *Schügsenen*',[1] etc. It was a joke which he might equally well have made when he was awake.

His father's name was not David but Friedrich. Adela was not Braun's sister; the idea of the double marriage must be dropped.

Nov. 8.—When he was a child he suffered much from worms. He probably used to put his fingers up his behind and was an awful pig, he said, like his brother. Now carries cleanliness to excess.

Phantasy before sleep:—He was married to his cousin [the lady]. He kissed her feet; but they weren't clean. They had black marks on them, which horrified him. During the day he had not been able to wash very carefully and had noticed the same thing on his own feet. He was displacing this on to his lady. During the night he dreamt that he was licking her feet, which were clean, however. This last element is a dream-wish. The perversion here is exactly the same as the one we are familiar with in its undistorted form.

That the behind was particularly exciting to him is shown by the fact that when his sister asked him what it was that he liked about his cousin he replied jokingly 'her behind'. The dressmaker whom he kissed to-day first excited his libido when she bent down and showed the curves of her buttocks especially clearly.

Postscript to the rat-adventure. Captain Novak said that this torture ought to be applied to some members of Parliament. The idea then came to him, that he [N.] must not mention Gisa, and to his horror immediately afterwards he did mention Dr. Hertz, which once more seemed to him a fateful occurrence. His cousin is actually called Hertz and he at once thought that the name Hertz would make him think of

---

9. [Professor of Law in Vienna.]   1. {The Yiddish term, for gentile girls, is better known in the United States as "Schickse".}

his cousin, and he sees the point of this. He tries to isolate his cousin from everything dirty.

He suffers from sacrilegious compulsions, like nuns. A dream had to do with joking terms of abuse used by his friend V.—'son of a whore', 'son of a one-eyed monkey' (*Arabian Nights*).

When he was eleven he was initiated into the secrets of sexual life by his [male] cousin, whom he now detests, and who made out to him that all women were whores, including his mother and sisters. He countered this with the question, 'do you think the same of *your* mother?'

Nov. 11.—During an illness of his cousin's (throat trouble and disturbances of sleep), at the time when his affection and sympathy were at their greatest, she was lying on a sofa and he suddenly thought 'may she lie like this for ever'. He interpreted this as a wish that she should be permanently ill, for his own relief, so that he could be freed from his dread of her being ill. An over-clever misunderstanding! What he has already told me shows that this was connected with a wish to see her defenceless, because of her having resisted him by rejecting his love; and it corresponds crudely to a necrophilic phantasy which he once had consciously but which did not venture beyond the point of looking at the whole body.

He is made up of three personalities—one humorous and normal, another ascetic and religious and a third immoral and perverse.

Inevitable misunderstanding of the *Ucs.* {Unconscious} by the *Cs.* {Conscious}, or rather, distortion of the shape of the *Ucs.* wish.

The hybrid thoughts resulting from these.

Nov. 17.—So far he has been in a period of rising spirits. He is cheerful, untrammelled and active, and is behaving aggressively to a girl, a dressmaker. A good idea of his that his moral inferiority really deserved to be punished by his illness. Confessions followed about his relations to his sisters. He made, so he said, repeated attacks on his next younger sister, Julie, after his father's death; and these—he had once actually assaulted her—must have been the explanation of his pathological changes.

He once had a dream of copulating with Julie. He was overcome with remorse and fear at having broken his vow to keep away from her. He woke up and was delighted to find it was only a dream. He then went into her bedroom and smacked her bottom under the bedclothes. He could not understand it, and could only compare it with his masturbating when he read the passage in *Dichtung und Wahrheit*. From this we conclude that his being chastised by his father was related to assaulting his sisters. But how? Purely sadistically or already in a clearly sexual way? His elder or his younger sisters? Julie is three years his junior, and as the scenes we are in search of must have been when he was three or four, she can scarcely be the one. Katherine, his sister who died?

His sanction to the effect that something would happen to his father in the next world is simply to be understood as an ellipse. What it meant was: 'If my father was still alive and learnt of this he would chastise me again and I should fly into a rage with him once more, and this would cause his death, since my affects are omnipotent.' Thus this belongs to the class: 'If Kraus reads this he'll get his ears boxed.'[2]

Even in recent years, when his youngest sister was sleeping in his room, he took off her bed-clothes in the morning so that he could see the whole of her. Then his mother came into the picture as an obstacle to his sexual activity, having taken over this role since his father's death. She protected him against the well-meaning attempts at his seduction by a housemaid called Lise. He once exhibited to the latter very ingeniously in his sleep. He had fallen asleep, exhausted, after an attack of illness and lay uncovered. When, in the morning, the girl spoke to him she asked him suspiciously if he had laughed in his sleep. He *had* laughed—on account of a most lovely dream in which his cousin had appeared. He admitted that it was a device. In earlier years he had exhibited frankly. When he was thirteen he still did so to [Fräulein] Lina, who came back for a short time. He gave the correct excuse for this that she knew exactly what he was like from his early childhood. (She had been with them while he was between six and ten.)

Nov. 18.—He went into his cousin's neurosis, which was becoming clear to him, in which her step-father, who came on the scene when she was twelve, plays a part. He was an officer, a handsome man, and is now separated from her mother. Gisa treats him very badly when sometimes he comes to visit them, and he always tries to soften her towards him. The details as told to me leave very little doubt that he made a sexual attack on the girl and that something in her, which she was unaware of, went part of the way to meet him—the love transferred from her real father whom she had missed since she was six. Thus the situation between them is, as it were, frozen stiff. It seems as though the patient himself knew this. For he was very upset during the manœuvres when Captain N. mentioned the name of a Gisela Fluss (!!!),[3] as though he wanted to prevent any contact between Gisa and an officer. A year before he had a curious dream about a Bavarian lieutenant whom Gisa rejected as a suitor. This pointed to Munich and his affair with the waitress, but there was no association to the lieutenant, and an addendum to the dream about officers' batmen only pointed to the step-father lieutenant.

2. {Freud is here referring to the celebrated essayist and journalist Karl Kraus, a scathing critic of the linguistic and ethical failings of his culture. His periodical, *Die Fackel* ("The Torch"), was virtually required reading for educated Viennese, including Freud.}

3. [Freud's exclamation marks refer to the fact that this had been the name of a girl by whom he himself had been greatly attracted in his schooldays during his first return to his birthplace in Moravia. The episode is described (though attributed to an anonymous patient) in Freud's paper on screen memories {see above, p. 121}].

Nov. 21.—He admits he himself may have had similar suspicions about his cousin. He was very cheerful and has had a relapse into masturbation, which has hardly disturbed him at all (interpolated latency period). When he first masturbated he had an idea that it would result in an injury to someone he was fond of (his cousin). He therefore pronounced a protective formula constructed as we already know from extracts from various short prayers and fitted with an isolated 'amen'. We examined it. It was Glejisamen:—

gl = *glückliche* [happy], i.e. may L [Lorenz] be happy; also, [may] all [be happy].

e = (meaning forgotten).

j = *jetzt und immer* [now and ever].

i (present faintly beside the j).

s (meaning forgotten).

It is easy to see that this word is made up of

GISELA

S   AMEN

and that he united his '*Samen*' ['semen'] with the body of his beloved, i.e. putting it bluntly, had masturbated with her image. He was of course convinced and added that sometimes the formula had secondarily taken the shape of Giselamen, but that he had only regarded this as being an assimilation to his lady's name (an inverted misunderstanding).

Next day he came in a state of deep depression, and wanted to talk about indifferent subjects; but he soon admitted that he was in a crisis. The most frightful thing had occurred to his mind while he was in the tram yesterday. It was quite impossible to say it. His cure would not be worth such a sacrifice. I should turn him out, for it concerned the transference. Why should I put up with such a thing? None of the explanations I gave him about the transference (which did not sound at all strange to him) had any effect. It was only after a forty minutes' struggle—as it seemed to me—and after I had revealed the element of revenge against me and had shown him that by refusing to tell me and by giving up the treatment he would be taking a more outright revenge on me than by telling me—only after this did he give me to understand that it concerned my daughter. With this, the session came to an end.

It was still hard enough. After a struggle and assertions by him that my undertaking to show that all the material concerned only himself looked like anxiety on my part, he surrendered the first of his ideas.

(*a*) A naked female bottom, with nits (larvae of lice) in the hair.

Source. A scene with his sister Julie which he had forgotten in his confession to me. After their romp she had thrown herself back on the bed in such a way that he saw those parts of her form in front—without lice of course. As regards the lice, he confirmed my suggestion that the word 'nits' indicated that something similar had once occurred long ago in the nursery.

The themes are clear. Punishment for the pleasure he felt at the sight, asceticism making use of the technique of disgust, anger with me for forcing him to [become aware of] this; hence the transference-thought, 'No doubt the same thing happens among your children.' (He has heard of a daughter of mine and knows I have a son. Many phantasies of being unfaithful to Gisa with this daughter and punishment for this.)

After quieting down and a short struggle he made a further difficult start on a whole series of ideas which, however impressed him differently. He realized that he had no need to make use of the transference in their case, but the influence of the first case had made all the others go into the transference.

[?(b)] My mother's body naked. Two swords sticking into her breast from the side (like a decoration, he said later—following the Lucrece *motif*).[4] The lower part of her body and especially her genitals had been entirely eaten up by me and the children.

Source, easy. His cousin's grandmother (he scarcely remembers his own). He came into the room once as she was undressing and she cried out. I said that he must no doubt have felt curiosity about her body. In reply he told me a dream. He had it at the time when he thought his cousin was too old for him. In it, his cousin led him up to the bed-side of his grandmother, whose body and genitals were exposed, and showed him how beautiful she still was at ninety (wish-fulfilment).

The two swords were the Japanese ones of his dreams: marriage and copulation. The meaning is clear. He had allowed himself to be led astray by a metaphor. Was not the content the idea that a woman's beauty was consumed—eaten up—by sexual intercourse and child-birth? This time he himself laughed.

He had a picture of one of the deputy judges, a dirty fellow. He imagined him naked, and a woman was practising 'minette' [*fellatio*] with him. Again my daughter! The dirty fellow was himself—he hopes soon to become a deputy judge himself, so as to be able to marry. He had heard of *minette* with horror; but once when he was with the girl in Trieste he pulled himself so far up her that it was an invitation for her to do it to him, but this did not happen. I repeated my lecture of last Saturday on the perversions.

Nov. 22.—Cheerful, but became depressed when I brought him back to the subject. A fresh transference:—My mother was dead. He was anxious to offer his condolences, but was afraid that in doing so an

4. [Lucrece was the Roman matron who stabbed herself after being raped by Sextus Tarquinius.]

impertinent laugh might break out as had repeatedly happened before in the case of a death. He preferred, therefore, to leave a card on me with 'p.c.' written on it; and this turned into a 'p.f.'

'Hasn't it ever occurred to you that if your mother died you would be freed from all conflicts, since you would be able to marry?' 'You are taking a revenge on me,' he said. 'You are forcing me into this, because you want to revenge yourself on me.'

He agreed that his walking about the room while he was making these confessions was because he was afraid of being beaten by me. The reason he had alleged was delicacy of feeling—that he could not lie comfortably there while he was saying these dreadful things to me. Moreover, he kept hitting himself while he was making these admissions which he still found so difficult.

'Now you'll turn me out.' It was a question of a picture of me and my wife in bed with a dead child lying between us. He knew the origin of this. When he was a little boy (age uncertain, perhaps 5 or 6) he was lying between his father and mother and wetted the bed, upon which the father beat him and turned him out. The dead child can only be his sister Katherine, he must have gained by her death. The scene occurred, as he confirmed, after her death.

His demeanour during all this was that of a man in desperation and one who was trying to save himself from blows of terrific violence; he buried his head in his hands, rushed away, covered his face with his arm, etc. He told me that his father had a passionate temper, and then did not know what he was doing.

Another horrible idea—of ordering me to bring my daughter into the room, so that he could lick her, saying 'bring in the *Miessnick*'.[5] He associated to this a story about a friend who wanted to bring up guns against the café that he used to visit but who wanted first to save the excellent and very ugly waiter with the words, '*Miessnick*, come out'. He was a *Miessnick* compared with his younger brother.

Also play on my name: '*Freudenhaus-Mädchen*' ['girls belonging to a House of Joy'—i.e. prostitutes].

Nov. 23.—Next session was filled with the most frightful transferences, which he found the most tremendous difficulty in reporting. My mother was standing in despair while all her children were being hanged. He reminded me of his father's prophecy that he would be a great criminal. I was not able to guess the explanation he produced for having the phantasy. He knew, he said, that a great misfortune had once befallen my family: a brother of mine, who was a waiter, had committee a murder in Budapest and been executed for it. I asked him with a laugh how he knew that, whereupon his whole affect collapsed. He explained that his brother-in-law, who knows my brother, had told him this, as evidence

5. {Yiddish for an ugly creature.}

that education went for nothing and that heredity was all. His brother-in-law, he added, had a habit of making things up, and had found the paragraph in an old number of the *Presse* [the well-known Vienna newspaper]. He was referring, as I know, to a Leopold Freud, the train-murderer, whose crime dates back to my third or fourth year. I assured him that we never had any relatives in Budapest. He was much relieved and confessed that he had started the analysis with a good deal of mistrust on account of this.

Nov. 25.—He had thought that if there were murderous impulses in my family, I should fall upon him like a beast of prey to search out what was evil in him. He was quite gay and cheerful to-day and told me that his brother-in-law was constantly making up things like this. He at once went on to discover the explanation—that his brother-in-law had not forgotten the stigma attached to his own family, for his father had fled to America on account of fraudulent debts. The patient thought that that was why he had not been made Lecturer in Botany at the University. A moment later he found the explanation of all his hostility to my family. His sister Julie had once remarked that Alex [Freud's brother] would be the right husband for Gisa. Hence his fury. (Just as with the officers.)

Next a dream. He was standing on a hill with a gun which he was training on a town which could be seen from where he was, surrounded by a number of horizontal walls. His father was beside him and they discussed the period in which the town was built—the Ancient East or the German Middle Ages. (It was certain that it was not altogether real.) The horizontal walls then turned into vertical ones which stood up in the air like strings. He tried to demonstrate something upon them, but the strings were not stiff enough and kept on falling down. Addendum; analysis.

Nov. 26.—He interrupted the analysis of the dream to tell me some transferences. A number of children were lying on the ground, and he went up to each of them and did something into their mouths. One of them, my son (his brother who had eaten excrement when he was two years old), still had brown marks round his mouth and was licking his lips as though it was something very nice. A change followed: it was I, and I was doing it to my mother.

This reminded him of a phantasy in which he thought that a badly behaved [female] cousin of his was not even worthy that Gisa should do her business into her mouth, and the picture had then been reversed. Pride and high regard lay behind this. A further recollection that his father was very coarse and liked using words like 'arse' and 'shit', at which his mother always showed signs of being horrified. He once tried to imitate his father, and this involved him in a crime which went unpunished. He was a dirty pig, so once, when he was eleven, his mother decided to give him a thorough good wash. He wept for shame and said, 'Where are you going to scrub me next? On the arse?' This would have brought down the most severe chastisement on him from his father, if his mother had not saved him.

His family pride, to which he admitted with a laugh, probably went along with this self-esteem. 'After all, the Lorenzes are the only nice people,' said one of his sisters. His eldest brother-in-law had become used to it and joked about it. He would be sorry if he were to despise his brothers-in-law simply on account of their families. (Contrast between his own father and those of his brothers-in-law.) His father was a first cousin of his mother, both in very humble circumstances, and he used in a joking way to give an exaggerated picture of the conditions they lived in when they were young. His hatred of me, accordingly, was a special case of his hatred of brothers-in-law.

Yesterday, after having come to the assistance of an epileptic, he was afraid of having an attack of rage. He was furious with his cousin and hurt her feelings by a number of innuendos. Why was he in a rage? Afterwards he had a fit of crying in front of her and his sister.

A further dream in connection with this.

(Aged 29.) A most wonderful anal phantasy. He was lying on his back on a girl (my daughter) and was copulating with her by means of the stool hanging from his anus. This pointed directly to Julie, to whom he said 'nothing about you would be disgusting to me'. During the night he had a severe struggle. He did not know what it was about. It turned out to be about whether he should marry his cousin or my daughter. This oscillation can easily be traced back to one between two of his sisters.

A phantasy that if he won the first prize in the lottery he would marry his cousin and spit in my face showed that he thought that I desired to have him as a son-in-law.—He was probably one of those infants who retain their faeces.

He had an invitation to-day to a *rendezvous*. The thought 'rats' at once occurred to him. In connection with this he told me that when he first met him, Lieutenant D., the step-father, related how, when he was a boy, he went about firing a Flaubert pistol[6] at every living thing and shot himself or his brother in the leg. He remembered this on a later visit when he saw a large rat, but the lieutenant did not. He was always saying 'I will shoot you'. Captain Novak must have reminded him of Lieutenant D., especially as he was in the same regiment as D. had been and the latter said 'I ought to have been a captain by now'.— It was another officer who mentioned the name Gisela; Novak had mentioned the name Hertz.—D. is syphilitic, and it was on this account

6. {As the editors point out, this is a misspelled version of "Flobert," a familiar brand name for fire arms. Obviously, Freud was allowing himself to be misled by the way the author of *Madame Bovary* (whose work Freud knew well) spells his name.}

that the marriage broke down. The patient's aunt is still afraid of having been infected. Rats signify fear of syphilis.

Nov. 29.—He has had a great deal of annoyance over money matters with his friends (giving security, etc.). He would dislike it very much if the situation turned in the direction of money. Rats have a special connection with money. When yesterday he borrowed two florins from his sister, he thought 'for each florin a rat'. When at our first interview I told him my fees he said to himself, 'For each *krone* a rat for the children'. Now '*Ratten*' ['rats'] really meant to him '*Raten*' ['instalments']. He pronounced the words alike,[7] and he justified this by saying that the 'a' in '*ratum*' (from '*rear*') is short; and he was once corrected by a lawyer, who pointed out that '*Ratten*' and '*Raten*' are not the same. A year before, he had offered security for a friend who had to pay a sum of money in twenty instalments, and had got the creditor to promise that he would let him know when each instalment fell due so that he should not become liable under the terms of the agreement to pay the whole amount in one sum. So that money and syphilis converge in 'rats'. He now pays in rats.—Rat currency.

Still more about syphilis. Evidently the idea of syphilis gnawing and eating had reminded him of rats. He in fact gave a number of sources for this, especially from his time of military service, where the subject was discussed. (Analogy with the transferences about genitals having been eaten up.) He had always heard that all soldiers were syphilitic, hence dread of the officer mentioning the name Gisela.

Military life reminded him not only of D. but of his father, who was in the army so long. The idea that his father was syphilitic was not so unfamiliar to him. He had often thought of it. He told me a number of stories of his father's gay life while he was serving. He had often thought that the nervous troubles of all of them might perhaps be due to his father having syphilis.

The rat-idea, as relating to his cousin, ran accordingly:—Fear that she was infected by her step-father; behind this, that she had been made ill by her own father, and behind this again the logical and rational fear that, being the child of a general paralytic, she herself was diseased (he had known of this correlation for years). The outbreak of his illness after his uncle's complaint can now be understood in another way. It must have meant the fulfilment of a wish that his own father should also be syphilitic, so that he might have nothing to reproach his cousin with and might marry her after all.

Nov. 30.—More rat-stories; but, as he admitted in the end, he had only collected them in order to evade the transference phantasies which

7. {Though the two words are *not* pronounced the same way: "Ratten" has a short "a," as in "utter"; "Raten," on the other hand, has a long "a," as in "aha."}

had come up in the meantime and which, as he saw, expressed remorse about the *rendezvous* due for to-day.

Postscript. His cousin and her uncle X. from New York, while they were on a railway journey, found a rat's tail in a sausage, and both of them vomited for hours. (Was he gloating over this?)

New material. Disgusting rat-stories. He knows that rats act as carriers of many infectious diseases. In the Fugbachgasse there was a view over a courtyard into the engine house of the Roman baths. He saw them catching rats and heard that they threw them into the boiler. There were a lot of cats there, too, which made a fearful caterwauling, and once he saw a workman beating something in a sack against the ground. He enquired and was told that it was a cat and that it was thrown into the boiler afterwards.

Other stories of cruelty followed, which finally centred on his father. The sight of the cat gave him the idea that his father was in the sack. When his father was serving with the army, corporal punishment was still in force. He described how he had once and once only, in a fit of temper, struck a recruit with the butt-end of his rifle, and he had fallen down. His father had gone in a great deal for lotteries. One of his fellow-soldiers was in the habit of spending all his money in this way; his father once found a bit of paper which this man had thrown away and on which two numbers were written. He put his money on these numbers and won on both of them. He drew his winnings while he was on the march and ran to catch up the column with the florins jingling in his cartridge pouch. What a cruel irony that the other man had never won anything! On one occasion, his father had ten florins of regimental money in his hands to meet certain expenses. He lost some of it in a game of cards with some other men, let himself be tempted to go on playing and lost the whole of it. He lamented to one of his companions that he would have to shoot himself. 'By all means shoot yourself,' said the other, 'a man who does a thing like this ought to shoot himself,' but then lent him the money. After ending his military service, his father tried to find the man, but failed. (Did he ever pay him back?)

His mother was brought up by the Rubenskys as an adopted daughter, but was very badly treated. She told how one of the sons was so sensitive that he cut off chickens' heads in order to harden himself. This was obviously only an excuse, and it excited him very much.—A dream-picture of a big fat rat which had a name and behaved like a domestic animal. This reminded him at once of one of the two rats (this was the first time he said there were only two) which, according to Captain Novak's story, were put in the pot. Furthermore, rats were responsible for his having gone to Salzburg. His mother related of the same Rubensky how he had once 'koshered' a cat by putting it in the oven and then skinning it. This made him feel so bad that his brother-in-law advised him in a friendly way to do something for his health. His attention is so much fixed on rats that he finds them everywhere. On the occasion when he returned from the manœuvres, he found that Dr. Springer had a colleague with him whom he introduced as Dr. Ratzenstein. The first performance he went to was the *Meistersinger*, where he heard the name of 'David' repeatedly called out. He had used the David *motif* as an exclamation in his family. When he repeats his magic formula 'Gleijsamen' now he adds 'without rats', though he pictures it as spelt with one 't'. He produced this material, and more besides, fluently. The connections are superficial and deeper ones are concealed; evidently he had prepared this as an admission, in order to cover something else. This material seems to contain the connection of money and cruelty, on the one hand with rats, and on the other with his father, and it must point towards his father's marriage. He told another anecdote. When, not many years ago, his father came back from Gleichenberg,[8] he said to his mother, after thirty-three years of married life, that he had seen such an incredible number of bad wives that he must beg her to assure him that she had never been unfaithful to him. When she objected, he said he would only believe her if she swore it on their children's lives; and after she had done so, he was pacified. He thinks highly of his father for this as a sign of his frankness, like his admission of ill-treating the soldier or his lapse over a card-game.—There is important material behind this. The rat-story becomes more and more a nodal point.

Dec. 8.—Much change in the course of one week. His spirits rose greatly on account of his *rendezvous* with the dressmaker, though this ended in a premature ejaculation. Soon afterwards he became gloomy, and this came out in transferences in the treatment. During his meeting with the girl there were only slight indications of the rat-sanction. He felt inclined to refrain from using the fingers that had touched the girl, when he took a cigarette from the cigarette-case given him by his cousin, but he resisted the inclination. More details about his father, his coarseness. His mother called him a 'common fellow' because he was in the habit of breaking wind openly.

Our pursuit of the treatment-transference led along many devious paths. He described a temptation whose significance he seemed to be unaware of. A relative of Rubensky had offered to fit up an office for him in the neighbourhood of the Cattle Market as soon as he had got his doctor's degree—which was at the time only a few months off—and to find him clients there. This fitted in with his mother's old scheme for him to marry one of R.'s daughters, a charming girl who is now seventeen. He had no notion that it was in order to evade this conflict that he took flight into illness—a flight which was facilitated by the infantile problem of his choice between an elder and a younger sister and by his regression to the story of his father's marriage. His father used to give a humorous account of his courtship, and his mother would

8. [The Styrian spa.]

occasionally chaff him by telling how he had earlier on been the suitor of a butcher's daughter. It seemed to him an intolerable idea that his father might have abandoned his love in order to secure his future by an alliance with R. He developed great irritation with me, which was expressed in insults which it was highly distressing for him to utter. He accused me of picking my nose, refused to shake hands with me, thought that a filthy swine like me needed to be taught manners and considered that the postcard I had sent him, and had signed 'cordially', was too intimate.

He was clearly struggling against phantasies of being empted to marry my daughter instead of his cousin, and against insults to my wife and daughter. One of his transferences was straight out that Frau Prof. F. should lick his arse—a revolt against a grander family. Another time he saw my daughter with two patches of dung in the place of eyes. This means that he has not fallen in love with her eyes, but with her money. Emmy [the girl his mother wanted him to marry] has particularly beautiful eyes. In recent days, he has stood up manfully against his mother's lamentation over his having spent 30 florins of pocket-money during the last month instead of 16.

The theme of the rats has lacked any element directed towards his mother, evidently because there is very strong resistance in relation to her. In equating 'Ratten' and 'Raten', he was, among other things, laughing at his father. His father had once said to his friend 'I am only a *Laue*' instead of a '*Laie*'.[9] This, like any other sign of his father's lack of education, greatly embarrassed him. His father made occasional attempts at economizing, along with efforts to institute a Spartan *régime*, but he always gave them up after a short time. It is his mother who is the economical one, but she sets store by comfort in the house. The way in which the patient secretly supports his friend is an identification with his father who behaved in just the same way to their first lodger, whose rent he used to pay, and to other people, too. In point of fact he was a very genuine, downright, kindly man, with a sense of humour, and normally the patient thoroughly appreciated these qualities. Nevertheless, with his over-refined attitude, he was manifestly ashamed of his father's simple and soldierly nature.

Dec. 9.—Cheerful, is falling in love with the girl—talkative—a dream with a neologism, general staff map of WŁK (Polish word).[1] We must go into this tomorrow. Vielka = [in Polish] 'old', L = Lorenz, Gl = abbreviation of Glejsamen = Gisela Lorenz.

Dec. 10.—He told me the whole dream, but understands nothing about it; on the other hand he gave me a few associations to WŁK. My idea that this meant a W.C. not confirmed; but with W ['vay'] he

9. ['*Laie*' = layman; '*lau*' = 'tepid'.]   1. [These letters would be pronounced in German like the English 'vay-ell-ka'.]

associated a song sung by his sister '*In meinem Herzen sitzt ein grosses Weh*'[2] [also pronounced 'vay']. This had often struck him as very comic, and he could not help picturing a big W.

His defensive formula against compulsions is, he tells me, an emphatic '*aber*' ['but']. Recently (only since the treatment?) he has stressed it '*abér*' [the word is normally stressed '*áber*']. He said he had explained this wrong accentuation to himself as serving to strengthen the mute 'e' which was not a sufficient protection against intrusions. It now occurred to him that perhaps the '*abér*' stood for '*Abwehr*' ['defence'] where the missing W was to be found in the WŁK.

His formula 'Glejsamen', in which in a happy hour he fixed by a magic spell what was henceforth to continue unchanged, had held good, he said, for quite a time. But it was nevertheless exposed to the enemy, that is, a reversal into its opposite, and for that reason he endeavoured to shorten it still more, and had replaced it—for reasons unknown—by a short '*Wie*' ['how' pronounced as English 'vee'].

The K corresponds to the '*vielka*' [pronounced as English 'vee-ell-ka'] = 'old'. It also reminded him of his anxiety when at school the letter K [i.e. boys whose name began with a K] was being examined, since it meant that his L was getting very near. It would thus correspond to a wish that K should come after L, so that L would already be passed.

Great reduction in the patient's treatment-transferences. He is much afraid of meeting my daughter. Quite unsuspectingly he told me that one of his testes was undescended, though his potency is very good. In a dream he had met a captain who only had his badge of rank on the right side and one of the three stars was hanging down. He pointed out the analogy with his cousin's operation.

Dec. 12—His 'dirty' transferences continued and more are announced. He turns out to be a *renifleur*. In his youth he was able to recognize people by the smell of their clothes; he could distinguish family smells, and he got positive pleasure from the smell of women's hair. It further appears that he has made a transference of the unconscious struggle which made him fall ill, by displacing his love for his cousin on to the dressmaker; and he is now making the latter compete with my daughter, who figures as the rich and respectable match. His potency with the dressmaker is excellent. To-day he ventured to attack the subject of his mother. He had a very early recollection of her lying on the sofa; she sat up, took something yellow out from under her dress and put it on a chair. At the time he wanted to touch it; but, as he recollected it, it was horrible. Later the thing turned into a secretion, and this led to a transference of all the female members of my family being choked in a sea of revolting secretion of every kind. He assumed that all women had disgusting secretions and was astonished afterwards at finding they

2. ['In my heart there sits a big sorrow.']

were absent in his two *liaisons*. His mother suffered from an abdominal affection and now has a bad smell from her genitals, which makes him very angry. She herself says that she stinks unless she has frequent baths, but that she cannot afford it, and this appalls him.

He told me two charming stories of children. One was about a little girl of five or six who was very curious about Santa Claus. She pretended to be asleep and saw her father and mother filling shoes and stockings with apples and pears. Next morning she said to her governess, 'There's no Santa Claus. Daddy and Mummy do it. Now I don't believe in anything at all any more, not even in the stork. Daddy and Mummy do that, too.' The other story was about his little nephew aged seven. He is a great coward and is frightened of dogs. His father said to him, 'What would you do if *two* dogs came along?' 'I'm not afraid of two. They'd smell each other's bottoms so long that I'd have time to run away.'

Dec. 14.—He is getting on well with the girl, for her naturalness pleases him and he is very potent with her; but it is clear from instances of less severe compulsion which he has brought up that a hostile current of feeling against his mother is present, which he is reacting to with exaggerated consideration for her and which is derived from her educational strictures, especially about his dirtiness. Anecdote of his mother eructating; and he had said, aged twelve, that he could not eat on account of his parents.

Dec. 16.—While he was with the dressmaker he thought 'for every copulation a rat for my cousin'. This shows that rats are something which is payable. The sentence is the product of a compromise between friendly and hostile currents of feeling; for (*a*) every copulation of this kind paves the way for one with his cousin, and (*b*) every copulation is done in defiance of her and to make her angry.

The picture is made up of clear conscious ideas, phantasies, deliria, compulsive associations and transferences.

He told me of a 'terrifying' experience in connection with the rat-story. On one occasion, before he fell ill, while he was visiting his father's grave, he saw a beast like a rat gliding past it. (No doubt it was a weasel, of which there are so many there.) He assumed—as might seem very likely—that the creature had just been having a meal off his father. His ideas in his *Ucs.* about survival after death are as consistently materialistic as those of the Ancient Egyptians. This is bound up with his illusion after Captain N.'s speech about the rats that he saw the ground heave in front of him as though there was a rat under it, which he took as an omen. He had no suspicion of the connection.

Dec. 19.—His miserliness is now explained. He was convinced, from a remark which his mother let fall to the effect that her connection with

Rubensky was worth more than a dowry, that his father had married her and abandoned his love for his material advantage. This, together with his recollection of his father's financial embarrassment during his military service, made him detest the poverty which drives people into such crimes. In this way his low opinion of his mother found satisfaction. He economized, therefore, so as not to have to betray his love. For this reason, too, he hands over all his money to his mother, because he does not want to have anything from her; it belongs to her and there is no blessing on it.

He gets everything that is bad in his nature, he says, from his mother's side. His maternal grandfather was a brutal man who ill-treated his wife. All his brothers and sisters have, like him, gone through a great process of transformation from bad children to very worthy people. This was least true of his brother, who was like a parvenu.

Dec. 21.—He has been identifying himself with his mother in his behaviour and treatment-transferences. Behaviour:—Silly remarks all day long, taking pains to say disagreeable things to all his sisters, critical comments on his aunt and cousin. Transferences:—He had the idea of saying he did not understand me, and had the thought, '20 *kronen* are enough for the *Parch*',[3] etc. He confirmed my construction by saying that he used identically the same words as his mother about his cousin's family. It seems likely that he is also identifying himself with his mother in his criticisms of his father and is thus continuing the differences between his parents within himself. In a dream (an old one) which he told me he drew a direct parallel between his own reasons for hating his father and his mother's:—His father had come back. He was not surprised at this. (Strength of his wish.) He was immensely pleased. His mother said reproachfully, 'Friedrich, why is it such a long time since we've heard from you?' He thought that they would have to cut down expenses after all, as there would be an extra person living in the house now. This thought was in revenge against his father who, he had been told, was in despair over his birth, as he was over each new baby. Something else lay behind this, viz. that his father liked having his permission asked, as though he wanted to abuse his power, although perhaps he was really only enjoying the feeling that everything came from him. His mother's complaint went back to a story of hers that once, when she was in the country, he wrote so seldom that she came back to Vienna to see what was going on. In other words, a complaint at being badly treated.

Dec. 23.—Greatly upset by Dr. Pr. falling ill again. Dr. Pr.'s character is similar to his father's—a man of honour in spite of his roughness. The patient is going through just what he did when his father was ill.

3. {Yiddish for a futile person.}

Incidentally, the illness is the same—emphysema. Moreover, his regrets are not unmixed with feelings of revenge. He can see that this is so, from phantasies of Pr. being dead already. The reason for these feelings may be his having been reproached for a long time in the family for not having insisted strongly enough on his father's retiring from work. The rat-sanction extends to Pr. as well. It occurred to him that a few days before his father's death Pr. said that he himself was ill and intended to hand the case over to Dr. Schmidt. This was evidently because the case was a hopeless one and affected him too deeply on account of his intimate friendship. At that time the patient had thought, 'The rats are leaving the sinking ship'. He had the notion that his wish was killing Pr. and that he could keep him alive—an idea of his omnipotence. He thought that a wish of his had actually kept his cousin alive on two occasions. One of these was last year, when she suffered from sleeplessness and he stayed up all night and she in fact slept better for the first time that night. The other time was when she was suffering from her attacks; whenever she was verging on a state of insensibility, he was able to keep her awake by saying something that would interest her. She reacted, too, to his remarks even while she was in that state.

What is the origin of his idea of his omnipotence? I believe it dates back to the first death in his family, that of Katherine—about which he had three memories. He corrected and enlarged the first of these. He saw her being carried to bed, not by her father, and before it was known that she was ill. For her father was scolding and she was being carried away from her parents' bed. She had for a long time been complaining of feeling tired, which was disregarded. But once, when Dr. Pr. was examining her, he turned pale. He diagnosed a carcinoma (?) to which she later succumbed. While I was discussing the possible reasons for his feeling guilty of her death, he took up another point which was also important because here again he had not previously recalled his omnipotence idea. When he was twenty years old, they employed a dressmaker, to whom he repeatedly made aggressive advances but whom he did not really care for, because she made demands and had an excessive desire to be loved. She complained that people did not like her; she asked him to assure her that he was fond of her and was in despair when he flatly refused. A few weeks later she threw herself out of the window. He said she would not have done it if he had entered into the *liaison*. Thus one's omnipotence is manifested when one gives or withholds one's love, in so far as one possesses the power to make someone happy.

The next day he felt surprised that after making this discovery he had no remorse, but he reflected that it was in fact already there. (Excellent!)

He then proposed to give a historical account of his obsessional ideas. He had his first one in Dec. 1902 when he suddenly thought he must take his examination by a certain date, Jan. 1903, and this he did. (After his aunt's death and his self-reproaches on account of his father's strictures.) He understands this perfectly as being a deferred industriousness.

His father had always been upset because he was not industrious. His idea was, accordingly, that if his father were alive he would be harmed by his laziness, and the same is true now. I pointed out to him that this attempt to deny the reality of his father's death is the basis of his whole neurosis. In Feb. 1903, after the death of an uncle, about whom he felt indifferent, there was a fresh onset of self-reproaches for having slept through the night [of his father's death]. Extreme despair, suicidal ideas, horror at the thought of his own death. What, he wondered, did dying mean? It was as though the sound of the word must tell him. How frightful it must be not to see or hear or feel anything. He completely failed to notice his faulty conclusion and he escaped from these thoughts by assuming that there must be a next world and an immortality. During the summer of the same year, 1903, while he was in a boat crossing the Mondsee, he had a sudden idea of jumping into the water. He was coming back with Julie from a visit to Dr. E. with whom she was in love. In the course of thinking what he would do for his father, he began by having a hypothetical idea, 'if you had to throw yourself into the water in order that no harm might come to him . . .', and this was at once followed by a positive command [to the same effect]. This was analogous, even in its actual phrasing, to his reflections before his father's death as to whether he would give up everything to save him. Hence there was some parallel with his cousin who had treated him badly for the second time during that summer. His fury against her had been tremendous, he remembers suddenly thinking as he lay on the sofa, 'she is a whore', which greatly horrified him. He no longer doubts that he had to expiate similar feelings of rage against his father. His fears were at that time already oscillating between his father and his cousin ('whore' seems to imply a comparison with his mother). The command to jump into the water can thus only have come from his cousin—he was her unsuccessful lover.

Dec. 27.—He began with a correction. It was in Dec. 1902 that he told his friend of his self-reproaches. He took his examination in January and did not at that time give himself any fixed date, as he had wrongly thought; this did not happen till 1903, the date being for July.

In the Spring [?1903] he felt violent self-reproaches (why?). A detail brought the answer. He suddenly fell on his knees, conjured up pious feelings and determined to believe in the next world and immortality. This involved Christianity and going to church in Unterach after he had called his cousin a whore. His father had never consented to be baptized, but much regretted that his forefathers had not relieved him of this unpleasant business. He had often told the patient that he would make no objections if he wanted to become a Christian. Might it be, perhaps, I asked, that a Christian girl had appeared just then as a rival to his cousin? 'No.' 'The Rubenskys are Jews, are they not?' 'Yes, and professing ones.' Indeed, if he had become a Christian it would have meant the end of the whole R. scheme. So, I replied, his kneeling must have been directed against the R. scheme and he must therefore have known of this plan before the scene of the kneeling. He thought not but admitted that there was something he was not clear about. What he definitely remembered was the inception of the scheme—his going with his cousin (and future brother-in-law) Bob St. to visit the R.'s where the plan was mentioned of their being established near the Cattle Market, St. as a lawyer and he as his clerk. St. had insulted him over this. In the course of the conversation he had said 'Mind you're ready by then'. It remains quite possible that his mother had told him of the scheme months before.

He told me that during the Spring of 1903 he had been slack at his studies. He drew up a time-table, but only worked in the evening till twelve or one o'clock. He read for hours then but took in none of it. At this point he interpolated a recollection that in 1900 he had taken an oath never to masturbate again—the only one he remembers. At this time, however, he used, after he had been reading, to turn on a great deal of light in the hall and closet, take off all his clothes and look at himself in front of the looking-glass. He felt some concern as to whether his penis was too small, and during these performances he had some degree of erection, which reassured him. He also sometimes put a mirror between his legs. Moreover he used at that time to have an illusion that someone was knocking at the front door. He thought it was his father trying to get into the flat, and that if the door was not opened he would feel that he was not wanted and would go away again. He thought he often came and knocked. He went on doing this till at last he got frightened at the pathological nature of this idea and freed himself from it by means of the thought 'if I do this, it will do my father harm'.

All of this was disconnected and unintelligible. It falls into place if we suppose that for superstitious reasons he expected a visit from his father between 12 and 1 a.m. and thus arranged to do his work at night so that his father should come upon him while he was working; but that then—after an isolating interval of time and a [   ][4] of uncertainty about time—he carried out what he himself regarded as a substitute for masturbation, and thus defied his father. He confirmed the first of these points, and as regards the second, said he had a feeling as though it were connected with some obscure childhood memory, which, however, did not emerge.

On the evening before he started for the country, at the beginning or middle of June, there occurred the scene of farewell with his cousin who had come home with X., in which he felt he had been disowned by her. During the first weeks of his stay in Unterach[5] he peered through the cracks in the wall of the bathing cabin and saw a quite young girl

4. [Word in MS. illegible.]   5. [In Upper Austria. The Mondsee is a lake close by.]

naked. He suffered the most distressing self-reproaches, wondering how it would affect her if she was aware of being spied upon.

This consecutive account of events swallowed up any reference to current happenings.

Dec. 28.—He was hungry and was fed.[6]

Continuation of his story. Compulsion at Unterach. It suddenly occurred to him that he must make himself slimmer. He began to get up from table—of course he left his pudding—and to run about in the sun till he dripped with perspiration. Then he would pause and afterwards have further bouts of running. He dashed up mountains in this way, too. On the edge of a steep precipice he had the idea of jumping over. This would of course have meant his death. He went on to a memory of his military service. During that time he had not found mountain-climbing easy. During winter manœuvres on the Exelberg he lagged behind, and he tried to spur himself on by imagining that his cousin was standing at the top of the mountain and waiting for him. But this failed in its effect and he continued to lag behind until he found himself among the men who had fallen out. He thought that during his military service—in the year in which his father died—his first obsessions were all hypothetical: 'If you were to do something insubordinate.' He pictured situations as though to take the measure of his love of his father. If he was marching in the ranks and saw his father collapse before his eyes, would he fall out and run up to him to help him? (Recollection of his father pocketing his winnings and running to catch up.) The origin of this phantasy was passing his home on a march from the barracks. During the first difficult weeks after his father's death he had been unable to see his people, as at that time he was confined to barracks for 3 weeks. He had not got on well in the army. He was apathetic and ineffective, and he had a lieutenant who was a bully and who struck them with the flat of his sword if they failed to execute certain movements. Recollection that St. once nerved himself to the pitch of saying 'We can manage without the sword, sir'. The man shrank away but then came up to him and said 'next time I shall bring along a horsewhip'. The patient had to suppress a great deal of rage over this; he had a number of phantasies of challenging him to a duel, but gave it up. In some ways he was glad that his father was no longer alive. As an old soldier he would have been very much upset. His father had provided him with an introduction. When the patient showed him a list of his officers his father recognized

---

6. {This rather flat translation of Freud's "Hungerig und wird gelabt," with its old-fashioned "hungerig" (the modern German would be "hungrig") and its equally old-fashioned "gelabt" for "fed"—better, "nourished" or "refreshed"—misses the formal, elevated diction of this laconic passage. Needless to say, Freud's violation of technique, gratifying in an almost maternal way a patient's physical needs, has caused considerable discussion among psychoanalysts. After all, they are enjoined—by Freud himself—to cultivate far more austere attitudes. Freud feeding the Rat Man reads like a skeptical commentary on his demand, in his papers on technique, that the analyst be as cool as a surgeon, as opaque as a mirror.}

one of the names—the son of an officer under whom he himself had served—and wrote to him. There followed a story of this officer's father. Once, when, at Pressburg, the train could not enter the station owing to a heavy fall of snow, the patient's father armed the Jews with spades, though they were as a rule forbidden access to the market. The officer who was in charge of the commissariat at that time came up to him and said, 'Well done, old comrade, that was a good job', whereupon his father retorted 'You rotter! You call me "old comrade" now because I have helped you, but you treated me very differently in the past.'

(There is evidently an effort to please his father by running.)

Another compulsion at Unterach under the influence of his being disowned by his cousin: compulsion to talk. As a rule he does not talk much to his mother, but now he forced himself while he was on a walk with her to talk incessantly. He passed from one point to another and talked a lot of nonsense. He spoke of it as a general thing, but the example he gave showed that it started from his mother.—A common obsession for counting, e.g. counting up to 40 or 50 between thunder and lightning.—A kind of obsession for protecting. When he was with her in a boat in a stiff breeze he had to put his cap on her head. It was as though he had a command that nothing must happen to her.— Obsession for understanding. He forced himself to understand every syllable spoken to him, as though he might be missing some priceless treasure. Accordingly he kept asking: 'What was it you said?' and when it was repeated, it seemed to him that it sounded different the first time and he was very much amused.

This material needs to be brought into relation with his cousin. She had explained to him that what he had regarded as her discouraging him had really been an attempt on her part to protect him from looking ridiculous in front of X. This explanation must have altered the situation fundamentally. The obsession for protecting evidently expressed remorse and penance. The obsession for understanding also went back to the same situation; for it was these words of hers which had been so precious to him. Actually he had not had this last obsession before his cousin's arrival. It is easy to understand how it became generalized. The other forms of obsession had been there before the *éclaircissement* with his cousin, as he remembers. His counting-anxiety in thunderstorms was in the nature of an oracle, and points to a fear of death—the number of years he would live. Again, his running about in the sun had something suicidal about it, on account of his unhappy love. All of this he confirmed.

Before he left Unterach he told his friend Y. that this time he had a strangely definite feeling that he would not get back to Vienna. From his childhood he has been familiar with clear ideas of suicide. For instance, when he came home with bad school reports which he knew would pain his father. Once, however, when he was eighteen, his mother's sister was visiting them. Her son had shot himself eighteen months earlier on account of an unhappy love affair, it was said, and the patient thought that it was still because of Hilde, with whom the young man had been very much in love at one time, that he had killed himself. This aunt looked so miserable and broken that he swore to himself that, on his mother's account, he would never kill himself whatever happened to him, even if he were disappointed in love. His sister Constanze said to him after he had come back from his run, 'You'll see, Paul, one of these days you'll have a stroke.'

If he had suicidal impulses before the *éclaircissement* they can only have been self-punishments for having wished his cousin dead in his rage. I gave him Zola's *Joie de vivre* to read.[7]

He went on to tell me that on the day on which his cousin left U. he found a stone lying in the roadway and had a phantasy that her carriage might hit up against it and she might come to grief. He therefore put it out of the way, but twenty minutes later it occurred to him that this was absurd and he went back in order to replace the stone in its position. So here again we have a hostile impulse against his cousin remaining alongside a protective one.

Dec. 2 [? *Jan.*]—Interruption owing to Dr. Pr.'s illness and death. He treated him like his father, and so arrived at personal relations with him, in which all sorts of hostile elements emerged. Rat-wishes, derived from the fact that he was their family doctor and was paid money by them. 'So many *kreuzers*, so many rats', he said to himself, as he put money into the collection-plate at the funeral. By identifying himself with his mother, he even found grounds for personal hatred against him; for she had reproached him for not having persuaded his father to retire from business. On the way to the cemetery he once again found himself smiling in the strange way which always disturbed him when he attended funerals. He also mentioned a phantasy of Dr. Pr. assaulting his sister Julie sexually. (This was probably envy over medical examinations.) He went on to a memory that his father must have done something he shouldn't have to her when she was ten. He heard screams from the room and then his father came out and said: 'That girl has an arse like a rock.' Strangely enough, his belief that he really nourished feelings of rage against his father has made no progress in spite of his seeing that there was every logical reason for supposing that he had those feelings.

Connected with this, though it is not clear at what point, there was a transference phantasy. Between two women—my wife and my mother—a herring was stretched, extending from the anus of one to that of the other. A girl cut it in two, upon which the two pieces fell away (as though peeled off). All he could say at first was that he disliked herrings intensely; when he was fed recently he had been given a herring

---

7. [The hero of this novel was perpetually occupied with thoughts of his own and other people's death.] {One might add that for an analyst to lend a patient a book, even as a way of making a clinical point, is only marginally less subversive of strict psychoanalytic technique than giving him lunch.}

and left it untouched. The girl was one he had seen on the stairs and had taken to be my twelve-year-old daughter.

Jan. 2. [1908].—(Undisguised expression.) He was surprised at having been so angry this morning when Constanze had invited him to go to the play with her. He promptly wished her the rats and then began to have doubts as to whether he should go or not and as to which of the two decisions would be giving way to a compulsion. Her invitation had upset a *rendezvous* with the dressmaker and a visit to his cousin, who is ill (these were his own words). His depression to-day must be due to his cousin's illness.

Besides this he apparently had only trivialities to report and I was able to say a great deal to him to-day. While he was wishing Constanze the rats he felt a rat gnawing at his own anus and had a visual image of it. I established a connection which throws a fresh light on the rats. After all, he had had worms. What had he been given against them? 'Tablets.' Not enemas as well? He thought he remembered that he had certainly had them too. If so, no doubt he must have objected to them strongly, since a repressed pleasure lay behind them. He agreed to this, too. Before this he must have had a period of itching in his anus. I told him that the story about the herring reminded me very much of the enemas. (He had just before used the phrase '*wächst ihm zum Hals heraus*'. ['He was fed up with it.' Literally, 'it grew out through his throat'.]) Had he not had other worms besides—tape-worms—for which people give you her-rings, or heard of this at least? He did not think so, but went on about worms. (While he was in Munich he found a large round-worm in his stool, after having had a dream of standing on a spring-board which was turning round with him in a circle. This corresponded to the movements of the worm. He had an irresistible call to defaecate immediately after waking.) Once when he was ten he saw his boy cousin defaecating and the latter showed him a big worm in his stool; he was very much disgusted. With this he associated what he described as the greatest fright of his life. When he was rather less than six, his mother had a stuffed bird from a hat, which he borrowed to play with. As he was running along with it in his hands, its wings moved. He was terrified that it had come to life again, and threw it down. I thought of the connection with his sister's death—this scene certainly took place later—and I pointed out how his having thought this (about the bird) made it easier for him to believe afterwards in his father's resurrection.

As he did not react to this, I gave another interpretation of it, namely as an erection caused by the action of his hands. I traced a connection with death from his having been threatened with death at a prehistoric period if he touched himself and brought about an erection of his penis, and suggested that he attributed his sister's death to masturbating. He entered into this to the extent of wondering at his never having managed to masturbate at puberty, in spite of having been troubled with such constant erections even as a child. He described a scene in which he actually showed his mother an erection. He summed up his sexuality as having been content with merely *looking* at [Fräulein] Peter and other women. Whenever he thought of an attractive woman without any clothes on he had an erection. A clear recollection of being in the women's swimming-bath and seeing two girls of twelve and thirteen whose thighs pleased him so much that he had a definite wish for a sister with such lovely thighs. Then followed a homosexual period with male friends; but there was never mutual contact but only looking and at the most pleasure from it. Looking took the place of touching for him. I reminded him of the scenes in front of the looking-glass after he had been studying at night, in which, according to the interpretation, he had masturbated in defiance of his father, after studying in order to please him—in just the same way as his 'God protect him' was followed by a 'not'. We left it at that.

He went on to tell me the worm dream he had had in Munich, and then some information about his rapid stool in the morning, which connected with his transference phantasy about the herring. As an association to the girl who performed the difficult task [of cutting the herring in half] with 'easy virtuosity', he thought of Mizzi Q., a charming little girl who was eight years old at the time when he saw a good deal of her family, and before he himself had got his doctor's degree. He was taking the 6 a.m. train to Salzburg. He was very grumpy because he knew he would soon want to defaecate, and when in fact he felt the urge he made an excuse and got out in the station. He missed the train, and Frau Q. caught him as he was adjusting his clothes. All the rest of the day he felt disgraced in her eyes. At this point he thought of a bull and then broke off. He went on to an ostensibly irrelevant association. At a lecture given by Schweninger and Harden[8] he met Professor Jodl, whom he greatly admired at that time, and actually exchanged a few words with him. But Jodl stands for bull,[9] as he very well knows. Schönthan[1] had written an article at about that time describing a dream in which he was Schweninger and Harden rolled into one, and thus was able to answer all the questions put to him till someone asked him why fishes have no hair. He sweated with fear till an answer occurred to him and he said it was of course well known how greatly scales interfere with the growth of hair and that was why fishes could not have any. This is what determined the appearance of the herring in the transference phantasy. Once when he had told me that his girl had lain on her stomach and her genital hairs were visible from behind, I had said to him that it was a pity that women nowadays gave no care to them and

8. [Ernst Schweninger (Bismarck's doctor) and Maximilian Harden (the famous {"notorious" might be a more accurate term} German journalist) delivered a lecture jointly in dialogue form on Feb. 5, 1898, in Vienna, on the subject of medicine. No doubt Schönthan's article mentioned below was in the nature of a parody of this lecture.]
9. [Jodl was professor of psychology. The allusion is unexplained.]
1. [Well known at the time in Vienna as a writer of light comedies.]

spoke of them as unlovely; and for that reason he was careful that the two women [in the phantasy] should be without hair.

My mother seems to have stood for his grandmother, whom he had never known himself, but he thought of his cousin's grandmother. A house run by two women. When I brought him something to eat he thought at once that it had been prepared by two women.

Jan. 3.—If the rat is a worm, it is also a penis. I decided to tell him this. If so, his formula is simply a manifestation of a libidinal urge towards sexual intercourse—an urge characterized both by rage and desire and expressed in archaic terms (going back to the infantile sexual theory of intercourse by the anus). This libidinal urge is as double-sided as the Southern Slav curse of arse-fucking. Before this he told me, in high spirits, the solution of the last phantasy. It was my science that was the child which solved the problem with the gay superiority of 'smiling virtuosity', peeled off the disguises from his ideas and so liberated the two women from his herring-wishes.

After I had told him that a rat was a penis, *via* worm (at which point he at once interpolated 'a little penis')—rat's tail—tail,[2] he had a whole flood of associations, not all of which belonged to the context and most of them coming from the wishful side of the structure. He produced something in reference to the prehistory of the rat-idea which he had always regarded as connected with it. Some months before the rat-idea was formed he met a woman in the street whom he at once recognized as a prostitute or at all events as someone who had sexual relations with the man who was with her. She smiled in a peculiar way and he had a strange idea that his cousin was inside her body and that her genitals were placed behind the woman's in such a way that she got something out of it every time the woman copulated. Then his cousin, inside her, blew herself out so that she burst her. Of course this can only mean that the woman was her mother, the patient's Aunt Laura. From these thoughts, which made her not much better than a whore, he finally went on to her brother, his Uncle Alfred, who insulted her straight out and said 'You powder your face like a *chonte*'.[3] This uncle died in frightful pain. After his inhibition he frightened himself with the threat that he himself would be punished in the same way for these thoughts of his. Next came various ideas of having actually wished that his cousin should have sexual intercourse; this had been before the rat-theory with its occasional form of having to attack her with rats. Further, a number of connections with money, and the idea that it had always been his ideal to be in a state of sexual readiness, even immediately after copulating. Perhaps he was thinking of a transposition into the next world? Two years after his father's death his mother told him that she had sworn

2. [The German '*Schwanz*', like its English equivalent 'tail', is often used as a vulgar expression for 'penis.']

3. {Yiddish slang phrase for "whore."}

on his father's grave that in the immediate future she would, by econ-omizing, replace the capital which had been spent. He did not believe that she had taken the oath, but this was the chief motive for his own economizing. Thus he had sworn (in his usual way) that he would not spend more than 50 florins per month in Salzburg. Later he made the inclusion of the words 'in Salzburg' uncertain, so that he might *never* be able to spend more, and *never* be able to marry his cousin. (Like the herring-phantasy, this could be traced back *via* Aunt Laura to the hostile current of feeling towards his cousin.) He had another association, how-ever, to the effect that he need not marry his cousin if she only offered herself to him without marriage, and against this, in turn, the objection that if so he would have to pay for every copulation in florins as with the prostitute. Thus he came back to his delirium of 'so many florins, so many rats': i.e. 'so many florins, so many tails (copulations)'.

Of course the whole whore-phantasy goes back to his mother—the suggestions made when he was twelve years old by his boy cousin who maliciously told him that his mother was a whore and made signs like one. His mother's hair is now very thin, and while she combs it he is in the habit of pulling it and calling it a rat's tail.—When he was a child, while his mother was in bed once, she happened to move about carelessly and showed him her behind; and he had the thought that marriage consisted in people showing each other their bottoms. In the course of homosexual games with his brother he was horrified once when, while they were romping together in bed, his brother's penis came into contact with his anus.

Jan. 4.—Cheerful. A large number of further associations, transfer-ences, etc., which we did not interpret for the moment. In connection with the child (my science) who cleared up the herring-slander, he had a phantasy of kicking it, and afterwards of his father smashing a window-pane. Bearing on this he told me an anecdote which gave a reason for his grudge against his father. When he cut his first Scripture lesson at his secondary school and clumsily denied the fact, his father was very much put out, and when the patient complained of Hans hitting him, his father said, 'Quite right, too; give him a kick.' Another kicking anecdote, about Dr. Pr. The patient's brother-in-law Bob St. hesitated a long time between Julie and Dr. Pr.'s daughter, whose married name is now Z. When a decision had to be made, he was called to a family council and he advised that the girl, who loved him, should put the direct question to him of whether or no. Dr. Pr. said [to her]: 'Very well, if you love him, that's all right. But if to-night' (after her *rendezvous* with him) 'you can show me the mark of his bottom on the sole of your shoe I'll give you a hug.' He did not like him at all. It suddenly occurred to the patient that this marriage story was closely connected with his own Rub. temptation. Pr.'s wife was a Rubensky by birth, and if Bob had married his daughter he would have been the only candidate for the support of the Rubensky family. Continuing about his brother-in-law Bob, he [the patient] said that he [Bob] was very jealous of him. Yesterday there had been scenes with his sister in which he had said this straight out. Even the servants said that she loved him and kissed him [the patient] like a lover, not like a brother. He himself, after having been in the next room with his sister for a while, said to his brother-in-law: 'If Julie has a baby in 9 months' time, you needn't think I am its father; I am innocent.' He had already thought that he ought to behave really badly, so that his sister should have no reason for preferring him in making a choice between husband and brother.

I had told him earlier, by way of clearing up a transference, that he was playing the part of a bad man in relation to me—that is to say, the part of his brother-in-law. This meant, I said to him, that he was sorry not to have Julie as his wife. This transference was the latest of his deliria about behaving badly and he brought it out in a very complicated form. In this transference he thought that I made a profit out of the meal I had given him; for he had lost time through it and the treatment would last longer. As he handed me my fee the thought occurred to him that he ought to pay me for the meal as well, namely 70 *kronen*. This was derived from a farce at a Budapest music hall, in which a weakly bridegroom offered a waiter 70 *kronen* if he would undertake the first copulation with the bride instead of him.

There were signs that he was afraid that the comments made by his friend Springer about the treatment might make him antagonistic to it. He said that whenever I praised any of his ideas he was always very much pleased; but that a second voice went on to say, 'I snap my fingers at the praise', or, more undisguisedly, 'I shit on it'.

The sexual meaning of rats did not come up to-day. His hostility was far clearer, as though he had a bad conscience about me. His young woman's pubic hairs reminded him of a mouse's skin, and this mouse seemed to him to have something to do with rats. He did not realize that this is the significance of the pet name '*Mausi*', which he himself uses. When he was fourteen, a depraved boy-cousin had shown him and his brother his penis and had said, 'Mine houses in a wood' ['*Meiner hauset in einem Vorwald*'], but he had taken him to say 'mousie' ['*Mausel*'].

Jan. 6 and 7.—He was smiling with sly amusement, as though he had something up his sleeve.

A dream and some scraps. He dreamt that he went to the dentist to have a bad tooth pulled out. He pulled one out, but it was not the right one, but one next to it which only had something slightly wrong with it. When it had come out he was astonished at its size. (Two addenda later.)

He had a carious tooth; it did not ache, however, but was only slightly tender, sometimes. He went to the dentist once to have it filled. The dentist, however, said there was nothing to be done except to extract it. He was not usually a coward, but he was kept back by the idea that somehow or other his pain would damage his cousin, and he refused to have it done. No doubt, he added, he had had some slight sensations in the tooth, which led to the dream.

But, I said, dreams can disregard stronger sensations than these and even actual pain. Did he know the meaning of tooth-dreams? He vaguely remembered that it was something to do with the death of relatives. 'Yes, in a certain sense. Tooth-dreams involve a transposition from a lower to an upper part of the body.' 'How is that?' 'Linguistic usage likens the face to the genitals.' 'But there are no teeth down below.' I made him see that that was precisely why, and I told him, too, that pulling a branch off a tree has the same meaning. He said he knew the phrase, 'pulling one down'.[4] But, he objected, he had not pulled out his tooth himself, but had had it pulled out by someone else. He admitted, however, that with the dressmaker he has felt a temptation to get her to take hold of his penis and has known how to bring this about. When I asked him whether he was already getting bored with her he replied 'Yes', with astonishment. He confessed that he was afraid she would ruin him financially and that he was giving her what was rightfully due to his ladylove. It came out he had behaved very carelessly in his money matters. He had not been keeping accounts, so that he did not know how much a month she was costing him; he had also lent his friend 100 florins. He admitted that I had caught him out on the high road to making himself dislike his *liaison* and to going back to abstinence. I said I thought that this was susceptible of other interpretations, but I would not tell him what. What could be the meaning of its not having been the right tooth?

Jan. 7.—He himself had a feeling that his sly illness had something up its sleeve. He had been nice to the dressmaker again. His second copulation did not succeed in producing an emission; he was overtaken by a fear that he would micturate instead of having an emission. When he was a child in the fifth form of his primary school, one of his school-fellows had told him that human reproduction was effected by the man 'piddling' into the woman. He had forgotten his condom. He is clearly looking for ways of spoiling his affair (having uncomfortable feelings?), e.g. by *coitus interruptus*—impotence.

Yesterday he had an addendum to the dream. The tooth did not look at all like one, but like a tulip bulb ['*Zwiebel*'], to which he gave the association of slices of onion [also '*Zwiebel*']. He did not accept the further associations of 'orchids'—his cryptorchism [undescended testis,]—his cousin's operation. In connection with the operation he told me that he was beside himself with jealousy at the time. While he

---

4. [In German a vulgarism for masturbating. * * * This whole passage was added to the work in 1909.]

was with her at the nursing home (in 1899) a young doctor visited her on his round and put his hand on her under the bedclothes. He did not know whether this was a correct thing to do. When he heard how brave she had been under the operation he had the foolish idea that that had been so because she enjoyed showing the beauty of her body to the doctors. He was astonished that I did not consider the idea so foolish.

He had heard of this beauty, when he fell in love with her in 1898, from his sister Hilde. This made all the more impresson on him since Hilde herself has a very lovely body. This may have been the root of his love. His cousin had understood perfectly well what they were talking about and had blushed. The dressmaker T., who killed herself later, said she knew that he regarded his cousin officially as the most beautiful of women, although he really knew quite well that there were other, more beautiful ones.

Yes, the tooth was a penis, he realized that. Then there was another addendum: the tooth had dripped.—Well then, what was the meaning of the dentist having pulled out his 'tooth'? It was only with difficulty that he could be brought to see that it was an operation for pulling out his tail. So, too, with the other obvious fact—that the very large penis could only be his father's; he finally admitted this as being a *tu quoque* and a revenge against his father. Dreams have great difficulty in bringing to light such disagreeable memories.

Jan. 20.—A long interruption. Most cheerful mood. A great deal of material. Advances. No solution. A chance explanation showed that his running about so as to avoid getting fat ['*dick*'] was related to the name of his American cousin, Dick (short for Richard)—*Passwort*—whom he hated. But this idea came from me and he did not accept it. Five dreams to-day, four of which dealt with the army. The first of these revealed a restrained rage against officers and his controlling himself so as not to challenge one of them for hitting the dirty waiter Adolph on his behind. (This Adolph was himself.) This led up to the rat scene *via* the lost pince-nez (nippers ['*Kneifer*']). This also touched on an experience in his first year at the University. He was suspected by a friend of 'funking' ['*Kneifen*'], because he had allowed himself to have his ears boxed by a fellow-student, had challenged him to a duel on Springer's joking advice, and had then done nothing further. There was suppressed anger against his friend Springer, whose authority thus originates from this, and against another man who betrayed him and whom, in return, he had later helped at the cost of sacrifices. Thus we find ever-increasing suppression of the instinct of anger, accompanied by a return of the erotogenic instinct for dirt.

[Here the MS. breaks off.]

'Wild' Psycho-Analysis

The history of psychoanalysis in Freud's lifetime is a history of revisions in theory and refinements in technique. Freud's interest in the question just how to deal with the analytic patient for the sake of both advancing research and fostering the process of cure goes back to his earliest psychological writings. The prepsychoanalytic papers he published in 1895 on hysteria contain hints; his case histories contain exemplary lessons. This is only natural: Freud was, as I have noted, much indebted to his patients, who encouraged him to cultivate what might be called alert passivity. His aggressive handling of his famous hysteric patient, Dora, in the fall of 1900 was then characteristic of his way of pushing patients toward insight, but it was also a pivotal moment for a salutary change of mind. As Freud learned more and more about the psychoanalytic situation, he became less pressing and more distant with his analysands—though always more pressing, and less distant, than his own prescriptions or his later followers.

By 1908, Freud was ready to put his gathered experience on psychoanalytic technique into written form. For some time, as his correspondence (particularly with Ferenczi and Ernest Jones) attests, he planned to publish a comprehensive book on the subject. In the end, other matters supervened, including the vexing business of psychoanalytic politics—his quarrels with Adler and his growing estrangement from Jung—and he was satisfied with publishing a series of papers dealing with most, if not all, aspects of the relations between analyst and analysand. " 'Wild' Psycho-Analysis," a "minor" paper of 1910 on these relations, is not officially counted among that series, but it belongs. It is a terse cautionary tale, indignant and humane.

A few days ago a middle-aged lady, under the protection of a female friend, called upon me for a consultation, complaining of anxiety-states. She was in the second half of her forties, fairly well preserved, and had obviously not yet finished with her womanhood. The precipitating cause of the outbreak of her anxiety-states had been a divorce from her last husband; but the anxiety had become considerably intensified, according to her account, since she had consulted a young physician in the suburb she lived in, for he had informed her that the cause of her anxiety was her lack of sexual satisfaction. He said that she could not tolerate the loss of intercourse with her husband, and so there were only three ways by which she could recover her health—she must either return to her husband, or take a lover, or obtain satisfaction from herself. Since then she had been convinced that she was incurable, for she would not return to her husband, and the other two alternatives were repugnant to her moral and religious feelings. She had come to me, however, because the doctor had said that this was a new discovery for which I was responsible, and that she had only to come and ask me to confirm what he said, and I should tell her that this and nothing else was the truth. The friend who was with her, an older, dried-up and unhealthy-looking woman, then implored me to assure the patient that the doctor was mistaken; it could not possibly be true, for she herself had been a widow for many years, and had nevertheless remained respectable without suffering from anxiety.

I will not dwell on the awkward predicament in which I was placed by this visit, but instead will consider the conduct of the practitioner who sent this lady to me. First, however, let us bear a reservation in mind which may possibly not be superfluous—indeed we will hope so. Long years of experience have taught me—as they could teach everyone else—not to accept straight away as true what patients, especially nervous patients, relate about their physician. Not only does a nerve-specialist easily become the object of many of his patients' hostile feelings, whatever method of treatment he employs; he must also sometimes resign himself to accepting responsibility, by a kind of projection, for the buried repressed wishes of his nervous patients. It is a melancholy but significant fact that such accusations nowhere find credence more readily than among other physicians.

I therefore have reason to hope that this lady gave me a tendentiously distorted account of what her doctor had said, and that I do a man who is unknown to me an injustice by connecting my remarks about 'wild' psycho-analysis with this incident. But by doing so I may perhaps prevent others from doing harm to their patients.

Let us suppose, therefore, that her doctor spoke to the patient exactly as she reported. Everyone will at once bring up the criticism that if a physician thinks it necessary to discuss the question of sexuality with a woman he must do so with tact and consideration. Compliance with this demand, however, coincides with carrying out certain *technical rules* of psycho-analysis. Moreover, the physician in question was ignorant of a number of the *scientific theories* of psycho-analysis or had misapprehended them, and thus showed how little he had penetrated into an understanding of its nature and purposes.

Let us start with the latter, the *scientific* errors. The doctor's advice to the lady shows clearly in what sense he understands the expression 'sexual life'—in the popular sense, namely, in which by sexual needs nothing is meant but the need for coitus or analogous acts producing orgasm and emission of the sexual substances. He cannot have remained unaware, however, that psycho-analysis is commonly reproached with having extended the concept of what is sexual far beyond its usual range. The fact is undisputed; I shall not discuss here whether it may justly be used as a reproach. In psycho-analysis the concept of what is sexual comprises far more; it goes lower and also higher than its popular sense. This extension is justified genetically; we reckon as belonging to 'sexual life' all the activities of the tender feelings which have primitive sexual impulses as their source, even when those impulses have become inhibited in regard to their original sexual aim or have exchanged this aim for another which is no longer sexual. For this reason we prefer to speak of *psychosexuality*, thus laying stress on the point that the mental factor in sexual life should not be overlooked or underestimated. We use the word 'sexuality' in the same comprehensive sense as that in which the German language uses the word *lieben* ['to love']. We have long known, too, that mental absence of satisfaction with all its consequences can exist where there is no lack of normal sexual intercourse; and as therapists we always bear in mind that the unsatisfied sexual trends (whose substitutive satisfactions in the form of nervous symptoms we combat) can often find only very inadequate outlet in coitus or other sexual acts.

Anyone not sharing this view of psychosexuality has no right to adduce psycho-analytic theses dealing with the aetiological importance of sexuality. By emphasizing exclusively the somatic factor in sexuality he undoubtedly simplifies the problem greatly, but he alone must bear the responsibility for what he does.

A second and equally gross misunderstanding is discernible behind the physician's advice.

It is true that psycho-analysis puts forward absence of sexual satisfaction as the cause of nervous disorders. But does it not say more than this? Is its teaching to be ignored as too complicated when it declares that nervous symptoms arise from a conflict between two forces—on the one hand, the libido (which has as a rule become excessive), and on the other, a rejection of sexuality, or a repression which is over-severe? No one who remembers this second factor, which is by no means secondary in importance, can ever believe that sexual satisfaction in itself constitutes a remedy of general reliability for the sufferings of neurotics. A good number of these people are, indeed, either in their actual circumstances or in general incapable of satisfaction. If they were capable of it, if they were without their inner resistances, the strength of the instinct itself would point the way to satisfaction for them even though no doctor advised it. What is the good, therefore, of medical advice such as that supposed to have been given to this lady?

Even if it could be justified scientifically, it is not advice that she can carry out. If she had had no inner resistances against masturbation or against a liaison she would of course have adopted one of these measures long before. Or does the physician think that a woman of over forty is unaware that one can take a lover, or does he over-estimate his influence so much as to think that she could never decide upon such a step without medical approval?

All this seems very clear, and yet it must be admitted that there is one factor which often makes it difficult to form a judgement. Some nervous states which we call the 'actual neuroses', such as typical neurasthenia and pure anxiety neurosis, obviously depend on the somatic factor in sexual life, while we have no certain picture as yet of the part played in them by the psychical factor and by repression. In such cases it is natural that the physician should first consider some 'actual' therapy, some alteration in the patient's somatic sexual activity, and he does so with perfect justification if his diagnosis is correct. The lady who consulted the young doctor complained chiefly of anxiety-states, and so he probably assumed that she was suffering from an anxiety neurosis, and felt justified in recommending a somatic therapy to her. Again a convenient misapprehension! A person suffering from anxiety is not for that reason necessarily suffering from anxiety neurosis; such a diagnosis of it cannot be based on the name [of the symptom]; one has to know what signs constitute an anxiety neurosis, and be able to distinguish it from other pathological states which are also manifested by anxiety. My impression was that the lady in question was suffering from anxiety *hysteria*, and the whole value of such nosographical distinctions, one which quite justifies them, lies in the fact that they indicate a different aetiology and a different treatment. No one who took into consideration the possibility of anxiety hysteria in this case would have fallen into the error of neglecting the mental factors, as this physician did with his three alternatives.

Oddly enough, the three therapeutic alternatives of this so-called psycho-analyst leave no room for—psycho-analysis! This woman could apparently only be cured of her anxiety by returning to her husband, or by satisfying her needs by masturbation or with a lover. And where does analytic treatment come in, the treatment which we regard as the main remedy in anxiety-states?

This brings us to the *technical* errors which are to be seen in the doctor's procedure in this alleged case. It is a long superseded idea, and one derived from superficial appearances, that the patient suffers from a sort of ignorance, and that if one removes this ignorance by giving him information (about the causal connection of his illness with his life, about his experiences in childhood, and so on) he is bound to recover. The pathological factor is not his ignorance in itself, but the root of this ignorance in his *inner resistances*; it was they that first called this ignorance into being, and they still maintain it now. The task of the treatment lies in combating these resistances. Informing the patient of what he does not know because he has repressed it is only one of the necessary preliminaries to the treatment. If knowledge about the unconscious were as important for the patient as people inexperienced in psycho-analysis imagine, listening to lectures or reading books would be enough to cure him. Such measures, however, have as much influence on the symptoms of nervous illness as a distribution of menu-cards in a time of famine has upon hunger. The analogy goes even further than its immediate application; for informing the patient of his unconscious regularly results in an intensification of the conflict in him and an exacerbation of his troubles.

Since, however, psycho-analysis cannot dispense with giving this information, it lays down that this shall not be done before two conditions have been fulfilled. First, the patient must, through preparation, himself have reached the neighbourhood of what he has repressed, and secondly, he must have formed a sufficient attachment (transference) to the physician for his emotional relationship to him to make a fresh flight impossible.

Only when these conditions have been fulfilled is it possible to recognize and to master the resistances which have led to the repression and the ignorance. Psycho-analytic intervention, therefore, absolutely requires a fairly long period of contact with the patient. Attempts to 'rush' him at first consultation, by brusquely telling him the secrets which have been discovered by the physician, are technically objectionable. And they mostly bring their own punishment by inspiring a hearty enmity towards the physician on the patient's part and cutting him off from having any further influence.

Besides all this, one may sometimes make a wrong surmise, and one is never in a position to discover the whole truth. Psycho-analysis provides these definite technical rules to replace the indefinable 'medical tact' which is looked upon as some special gift.

It is not enough, therefore, for a physician to know a few of the findings of psycho-analysis; he must also have familiarized himself with its technique if he wishes his medical procedure to be guided by a psycho-analytic point of view. This technique cannot yet be learnt from books, and it certainly cannot be discovered independently without great sacrifices of time, labour and success. Like other medical techniques, it is to be learnt from those who are already proficient in it. It is a matter of some significance, therefore, in forming a judgement on the incident which I took as a starting-point for these remarks, that I am not acquainted with the physician who is said to have given the lady such advice and have never heard his name.

Neither I myself nor my friends and co-workers find it agreeable to claim a monopoly in this way in the use of a medical technique. But in face of the dangers to patients and to the cause of psycho-analysis which are inherent in the practice that is to be foreseen of a 'wild' psycho-analysis, we have had no other choice. In the spring of 1910 we founded an International Psycho-Analytical Association, to which its members declare their adherence by the publication of their names, in order to be able to repudiate responsibility for what is done by those who do not belong to us and yet call their medical procedure 'psycho-analysis'. For as a matter of fact 'wild' analysts of this kind do more harm to the cause of psycho-analysis than to individual patients. I have often found that a clumsy procedure like this, even if at first it produced an exacerbation of the patient's condition, led to a recovery in the end. Not always, but still often. When he has abused the physician enough and feels far enough away from his influence, his symptoms give way, or he decides to take some step which leads along the path to recovery. The final improvement then comes about 'of itself', or is ascribed to some totally indifferent treatment by some other doctor to whom the patient has later turned. In the case of the lady whose complaint against her physician we have heard, I should say that, despite everything, the 'wild' psycho-analyst did more for her than some highly respected authority who might have told her she was suffering from a 'vasomotor neurosis'. He forced her attention to the real cause of her trouble, or in that direction, and in spite of all her opposition this intervention of his cannot be without some favourable results. But he has done himself harm and helped to intensify the prejudices which patients feel, owing to their natural affective resistances, against the methods of psychoanalysis. And this can be avoided.

Recommendations to Physicians Practicing Psycho-Analysis

Together the six papers on technique that Freud published between 1911 and 1915 (to which, as noted just above, one should add the paper " 'Wild' Psycho-Analysis" of 1910) constitute an impressive array of recommendations. Some aspects of psychoanalytic technique, notably termination of treatment, receive quite skimpy treatment in this series. But they remain classic discussions still eminently worth pondering, and not just as historical documents. Two points are worth emphasizing: Freud is not just being polite when he insists that he is offering recommendations rather than laying down dogma. Variations in technique are inescapable, given the differences among analysts and analysands. At the same time, Freud is severe on those psychoanalysts who display their brilliance by offering quick interpretations. Secondly, as Freud's editors note, Freud did not want these papers to be taken as a substitute for practice: "A proper mastery of the subject could only be acquired from clinical experience and not from books" (SE XII, 87).

The technical rules which I am putting forward here have been arrived at from my own experience in the course of many years, after unfortunate results had led me to abandon other methods. It will easily be seen that they (or at least many of them) may be summed up in a single precept. My hope is that observance of them will spare physicians practising analysis much unnecessary effort and guard them against some oversights. I must however make it clear that what I am asserting is that this technique is the only one suited to my individuality; I do not venture to deny that a physician quite differently constituted might find himself driven to adopt a different attitude to his patients and to the task before him.

(a) The first problem confronting an analyst who is treating more than one patient in the day will seem to him the hardest. It is the task of keeping in mind all the innumerable names, dates, detailed memories and pathological products which each patient communicates in the course of months and years of treatment, and of not confusing them with similar material produced by other patients under treatment simultaneously or previously. If one is required to analyse six, eight, or even more patients daily, the feat of memory involved in achieving this will provoke incredulity, astonishment or even commiseration in uninformed observers. Curiosity will in any case be felt about the technique which makes it possible to master such an abundance of material, and the expectation will be that some special expedients are required for the purpose.

The technique, however, is a very simple one. As we shall see, it rejects the use of any special expedient (even that of taking notes). It consists simply in not directing one's notice to anything in particular and in maintaining the same 'evenly-suspended attention' (as I have called it) in the face of all that one hears. In this way we spare ourselves a strain on our attention which could not in any case be kept up for several hours daily, and we avoid a danger which is inseparable from the exercise of deliberate attention. For as soon as anyone deliberately concentrates his attention to a certain degree, he begins to select from the material before him; one point will be fixed in his mind with particular clearness and some other will be correspondingly disregarded, and in making this selection he will be following his expectations or inclinations. This, however, is precisely what must not be done. In making the selection, if he follows his expectations he is in danger of never finding anything but what he already knows; and if he follows his inclinations he will certainly falsify what he may perceive. It must not be forgotten that the things one hears are for the most part things whose meaning is only recognized later on.

It will be seen that the rule of giving equal notice to everything is the necessary counterpart to the demand made on the patient that he should communicate everything that occurs to him without criticism or selection. If the doctor behaves otherwise, he is throwing away most of the advantage which results from the patient's obeying the 'fundamental rule of psycho-analysis'. The rule for the doctor may be expressed: 'He should withhold all conscious influences from his capacity to attend, and give himself over completely to his "unconscious memory".' Or, to put it purely in terms of technique: 'He should simply listen, and not bother about whether he is keeping anything in mind.'

What is achieved in this manner will be sufficient for all requirements during the treatment. Those elements of the material which already form a connected context will be at the doctor's conscious disposal; the rest, as yet unconnected and in chaotic disorder, seems at first to be submerged, but rises readily into recollection as soon as the patient brings up something new to which it can be related and by which it can be continued. The undeserved compliment of having 'a remarkably good memory' which the patient pays one when one reproduces some detail after a year and a day can then be accepted with a smile, whereas a conscious determination to recollect the point would probably have resulted in failure.

Mistakes in this process of remembering occur only at times and places at which one is disturbed by some personal consideration that is, when one has fallen seriously below the standard of an ideal analyst. Confusion with material brought up by other patients occurs very rarely. Where there is a dispute with the patient as to whether or how he has said some particular thing, the doctor is usually in the right.

(b) I cannot advise the taking of full notes, the keeping of a shorthand record, etc., during analytic sessions. Apart from the unfavourable impression which this makes on some patients, the same considerations as have been advanced with regard to attention apply here too. A detrimental selection from the material will necessarily be made as one writes the notes or shorthand, and part of one's own mental activity is tied up in this way, which would be better employed in interpreting what one has heard. No objection can be raised to making exceptions to this rule in the case of dates, the text of dreams, or particular noteworthy events which can easily be detached from their context and are suitable for independent use as instances. But I am not in the habit of doing this either. As regards instances, I write them down from memory in the evening after work is over; as regards texts of dreams to which I attach importance, I get the patient to repeat them to me after he has related them so that I can fix them in my mind.

(c) Taking notes during the session with the patient might be justified by an intention of publishing a scientific study of the case. On general grounds this can scarcely be denied. Nevertheless it must be borne in mind that exact reports of analytic case histories are of less value than might be expected. Strictly speaking, they only possess the *ostensible* exactness of which 'modern' psychiatry affords us some striking examples. They are, as a rule, fatiguing to the reader and yet do not succeed in being a substitute for his actual presence at an analysis. Experience invariably shows that if readers are willing to believe an analyst they will have confidence in any slight revision to which he has submitted his material; if, on the other hand, they are unwilling to take analysis and the analyst seriously, they will pay no attention to accurate verbatim records of the treatment either. This is not the way, it seems, to remedy the lack of convincing evidence to be found in psycho-analytic reports.

(d) One of the claims of psycho-analysis to distinction is, no doubt, that in its execution research and treatment coincide; nevertheless, after a certain point, the technique required for the one opposes that required for the other. It is not a good thing to work on a case scientifically while treatment is still proceeding—to piece together its structure, to try to foretell its further progress, and to get a picture from time to time of the current state of affairs, as scientific interest would demand. Cases which are devoted from the first to scientific purposes and are treated accordingly suffer in their outcome; while the most successful cases are those in which one proceeds, as it were, without any purpose in view, allows oneself to be taken by surprise by any new turn in them, and always meets them with an open mind, free from any presuppositions. The correct behaviour for an analyst lies in swinging over according to need from the one mental attitude to the other, in avoiding speculation or brooding over cases while they are in analysis, and in submitting the material obtained to a synthetic process of thought only after the analysis is concluded. The distinction between the two attitudes would be meaningless if we already possessed all the knowledge (or at least the essential knowledge) about the psychology of the unconscious and about the structure of the neuroses that we can obtain from psycho-analytic work. At present we are still far from that goal and we ought not to cut ourselves off from the possibility of testing what we have already learnt and of extending our knowledge further.

(e) I cannot advise my colleagues too urgently to model themselves during psycho-analytic treatment on the surgeon, who puts aside all his feelings, even his human sympathy, and concentrates his mental forces on the single aim of performing the operation as skilfully as possible. Under present-day conditions the feeling that is most dangerous to a psycho-analyst is the therapeutic ambition to achieve by this novel and much disputed method something that will produce a convincing effect upon other people. This will not only put him into a state of mind which is unfavourable for his work, but will make him helpless against certain resistances of the patient, whose recovery, as we know, primarily depends on the interplay of forces in him. The justification for requiring this emotional coldness in the analyst is that it creates the most advantageous conditions for both parties: for the doctor a desirable protection for his own emotional life and for the patient the largest amount of help that we can give him to-day. A surgeon of earlier times took as his motto the words: 'Je le pansai, Dieu le guérit.' {"I dressed his wounds, God cured him."} The analyst should be content with something similar.

(f) It is easy to see upon what aim the different rules I have brought forward converge. They are all intended to create for the doctor a counterpart to the 'fundamental rule of psycho-analysis' which is laid down for the patient. Just as the patient must relate everything that his self-observation can detect, and keep back all the logical and affective objections that seek to induce him to make a selection from among them, so the doctor must put himself in a position to make use of everything he is told for the purposes of interpretation and of recognizing the concealed unconscious material without substituting a censorship of his own for the selection that the patient has forgone. To put it in a formula: he must turn his own unconscious like a receptive organ towards the transmitting unconscious of the patient. He must adjust himself to the patient as a telephone receiver is adjusted to the transmitting microphone. Just as the receiver converts back into sound-waves the electric oscillations in the telephone line which were set up by sound-waves, so the doctor's unconscious is able, from the derivatives of the unconscious which are communicated to him, to reconstruct that unconscious, which has determined the patient's free associations.

But if the doctor is to be in a position to use his unconscious in this way as an instrument in the analysis, he must himself fulfil one psychological condition to a high degree. He may not tolerate any resistances in himself which hold back from his consciousness what has been perceived by his unconscious; otherwise he would introduce into the analysis a new species of selection and distortion which would be far more detrimental than that resulting from concentration of conscious attention. It is not enough for this that he himself should be an approximately normal person. It may be insisted, rather, that he should have undergone a psycho-analytic purification and have become aware of those complexes of his own which would be apt to interfere with his grasp of what the patient tells him. There can be no reasonable doubt about the disqualifying effect of such defects in the doctor; every unresolved repression in him constitutes what has been aptly described by Stekel as a 'blind spot' in his analytic perception.

Some years ago I gave as an answer to the question of how one can become an analyst: 'By analysing one's own dreams.' This preparation is no doubt enough for many people, but not for everyone who wishes to learn analysis. Nor can everyone succeed in interpreting his own dreams without outside help. I count it as one of the many merits of the Zurich school of analysis that they have laid increased emphasis on this requirement, and have embodied it in the demand that everyone who wishes to carry out analyses on other people shall first himself undergo an analysis by someone with expert knowledge. Anyone who takes up the work seriously should choose this course, which offers more than one advantage; the sacrifice involved in laying oneself open to another person without being driven to it by illness is amply rewarded. Not only is one's aim of learning to know what is hidden in one's own mind far more rapidly attained and with less expense of affect, but impressions and convictions will be gained in relation to oneself which will be sought in vain from studying books and attending lectures. And lastly, we must not under-estimate the advantage to be derived from the lasting mental contact that is as a rule established between the student and his guide.

An analysis such as this of someone who is practically healthy will, as may be imagined, remain incomplete. Anyone who can appreciate the high value of the self-knowledge and increase in self-control thus acquired will, when it is over, continue the analytic examination of his personality in the form of a self-analysis, and be content to realize that, within himself as well as in the external world, he must always expect to find something new. But anyone who has scorned to take the precaution of being analysed himself will not merely be punished by being incapable of learning more than a certain amount from his patients, he will risk a more serious danger and one which may become a danger to others. He will easily fall into the temptation of projecting outwards some of the peculiarities of his own personality, which he has dimly perceived, into the field of science, as a theory having universal validity; he will bring the psycho-analytic method into discredit, and lead the inexperienced astray.

(g) I shall now add a few other rules, that will serve as a transition from the attitude of the doctor to the treatment of the patient.

Young and eager psycho-analysts will no doubt be tempted to bring their own individuality freely into the discussion, in order to carry the patient along with them and lift him over the barriers of his own narrow personality. It might be expected that it would be quite allowable and indeed useful, with a view to overcoming the patient's existing resistances, for the doctor to afford him a glimpse of his own mental defects and conflicts and, by giving him intimate information about his own life, enable him to put himself on an equal footing. One confidence deserves another, and anyone who demands intimacy from someone else must be prepared to give it in return.

But in psycho-analytic relations things often happen differently from what the psychology of consciousness might lead us to expect. Experience does not speak in favour of an affective technique of this kind. Nor is it hard to see that it involves a departure from psycho-analytic principles and verges upon treatment by suggestion. It may induce the patient to bring forward sooner and with less difficulty things he already knows but would otherwise have kept back for a time through conventional resistances. But this technique achieves nothing towards the uncovering of what is unconscious to the patient. It makes him even more incapable of overcoming his deeper resistances, and in severer cases it invariably fails by encouraging the patient to be insatiable: he would like to reverse the situation, and finds the analysis of the doctor more interesting than his own. The resolution of the transference, too—one of the main tasks of the treatment—is made more difficult by an intimate attitude on the doctor's part, so that any gain there may be at the beginning is more than outweighed at the end. I have no hesitation, therefore, in condemning this kind of technique as incorrect. The doctor should be opaque to his patients and, like a mirror, should show them nothing but what is shown to him. In practice, it is true, there is nothing to be said against a psychotherapist combining a certain amount of analysis with some suggestive influence in order to achieve a perceptible result in a shorter time—as is necessary, for instance, in institutions. But one has a right to insist that he himself should be in no doubt about what he is doing and should know that his method is not that of true psycho-analysis.

(h) Another temptation arises out of the educative activity which, in psycho-analytic treatment, devolves on the doctor without any deliberate intention on his part. When the developmental inhibitions are resolved, it happens of itself that the doctor finds himself in a position to indicate new aims for the trends that have been liberated. It is then no more than a natural ambition if he endeavours to make something specially excellent of a person whom he has been at such pains to free from his neurosis and if he prescribes high aims for his wishes. But here again the doctor should hold himself in check, and take the patient's capacities rather than his own desires as guide. Not every neurotic has a high talent for sublimation; one can assume of many of them that they would not have fallen ill at all if they had possessed the art of sublimating their instincts. If we press them unduly towards sublimation and cut them off from the most accessible and convenient instinctual satisfactions, we shall usually make life even harder for them than they feel it in any case. As a doctor, one must above all be tolerant to the weakness of a patient, and must be content if one has won back some degree of capacity for work and enjoyment for a person even of only moderate worth. Educative ambition is of as little use as therapeutic ambition. It must further be borne in mind that many people fall ill precisely from an attempt to sublimate their instincts beyond the degree permitted by their organization and that in those who have a capacity for sublimation the process usually takes place of itself as soon as their inhibitions have been overcome by analysis. In my opinion, therefore, efforts invariably to make use of the analytic treatment to bring about sublimation of instinct are, though no doubt always laudable, far from being in every case advisable.

(i) To what extent should the patient's intellectual co-operation be sought for in the treatment? It is difficult to say anything of general applicability on this point: the patient's personality is the determining factor. But in any case caution and self-restraint must be observed in this connection. It is wrong to set a patient tasks, such as collecting his memories or thinking over some particular period of his life. On the contrary, he has to learn above all—what never comes easily to anyone—that mental activities such as thinking something over or concentrating the attention solve none of the riddles of a neurosis; that can only be done by patiently obeying the psycho-analytic rule, which enjoins the exclusion of all criticism of the unconscious or of its derivatives. One must be especially unyielding about obedience to that rule with patients who practise the art of sheering off into intellectual discussion during their treatment, who speculate a great deal and often very wisely about their condition and in that way avoid doing anything to overcome it. For this reason I dislike making use of analytic writings as an assistance to my patients; I require them to learn by personal experience, and I assure them that they will acquire wider and more valuable knowledge than the whole literature of psycho-analysis could teach them. I recognize, however, that under institutional conditions it may be of great advantage to employ reading as a preparation for patients in analysis and as a means of creating an atmosphere of influence.

I must give a most earnest warning against any attempt to gain the confidence or support of parents or relatives by giving them psychoanalytic books to read, whether of an introductory or an advanced kind. This well-meant step usually has the effect of bringing on prematurely the natural opposition of the relatives to the treatment—an opposition which is bound to appear sooner or later—so that the treatment is never even begun.

Let me express a hope that the increasing experience of psycho-analysts will soon lead to agreement on questions of technique and on the most effective method of treating neurotic patients. As regards the treatment of their relatives I must confess myself utterly at a loss, and I have in general little faith in any individual treatment of them.

On Beginning the Treatment

This paper is a fascinating mixture of practical recommendations—including the tender subject of the analyst's right to his fee—and of gambits essential to the analytic situation, most notably that of the so-called "fundamental rule," without which no analysis can progress at all. It stands as a reminder that the relationship between analyst and analysand is complex indeed, and that virtually anything the analyst does (or seems to be doing) is likely to have some impact on his patient. The paper dates from 1913.

Anyone who hopes to learn the noble game of chess from books will soon discover that only the openings and end-games admit of an exhaustive systematic presentation and that the infinite variety of moves which develop after the opening defy any such description. This gap in instruction can only be filled by a diligent study of games fought out by masters. The rules which can be laid down for the practice of psychoanalytic treatment are subject to similar limitations.

In what follows I shall endeavour to collect together for the use of practising analysts some of the rules for the beginning of the treatment. Among them there are some which may seem to be petty details, as, indeed, they are. Their justification is that they are simply rules of the game which acquire their importance from their relation to the general plan of the game. I think I am well-advised, however, to call these rules 'recommendations' and not to claim any unconditional acceptance for them. The extraordinary diversity of the psychical constellations concerned, the plasticity of all mental processes and the wealth of determining factors oppose any mechanization of the technique; and they bring it about that a course of action that is as a rule justified may at times prove ineffective, whilst one that is usually mistaken may once in a while lead to the desired end. These circumstances, however, do not prevent us from laying down a procedure for the physician which is effective on the average.

Some years ago I set out the most important indications for selecting patients {in "a Psychotherapy" (1905)} and I shall therefore not repeat them here. They have in the meantime been approved by other psychoanalysts. But I may add that since then I have made it my habit, when I know little about a patient, only to take him on at first provisionally, for a period of one to two weeks. If one breaks off within this period one spares the patient the distressing impression of an attempted cure having failed. One has only been undertaking a 'sounding' in order to get to know the case and to decide whether it is a suitable one for psychoanalysis. No other kind of preliminary examination but this procedure is at our disposal; the most lengthy discussions and questionings in ordinary consultations would offer no substitute. This preliminary experiment, however, is itself the beginning of a psycho-analysis and must conform to its rules. There may perhaps be this distinction made, that in it one lets the patient do nearly all the talking and explains nothing more than what is absolutely necessary to get him to go on with what he is saying.

There are also diagnostic reasons for beginning the treatment with a trial period of this sort lasting for one or two weeks. Often enough, when one sees a neurosis with hysterical or obsessional symptoms, which is not excessively marked and has not been in existence for long—just the type of case, that is, that one would regard as suitable for treatment— one has to reckon with the possibility that it may be a preliminary stage of what is known as dementia praecox ('schizophrenia', in Bleuler's terminology; 'paraphrenia', as I have proposed to call it), and that sooner or later it will show a well-marked picture of that affection. I do not agree that it is always possible to make the distinction so easily. I am aware that there are psychiatrists who hesitate less often in their differential diagnosis, but I have become convinced that just as often they make mistakes. To make a mistake, moreover, is of far greater moment for the psycho-analyst than it is for the clinical psychiatrist, as he is called. For the latter is not attempting to do anything that will be of use, whichever kind of case it may be. He merely runs the risk of making a theoretical mistake, and his diagnosis is of no more than academic interest. Where the psycho-analyst is concerned, however, if the case is unfavourable he has committed a practical error; he has been responsible for wasted expenditure and has discredited his method of treatment. He cannot fulfil his promise of cure if the patient is suffering, not from hysteria or obsessional neurosis, but from paraphrenia, and he therefore has particularly strong motives for avoiding mistakes in diagnosis. In an experimental treatment of a few weeks he will often observe suspicious signs which may determine him not to pursue the attempt any further. Unfortunately I cannot assert that an attempt of this kind always enables us to arrive at a certain decision; it is only one wise precaution the more.

Lengthy preliminary discussions before the beginning of the analytic treatment, previous treatment by another method and also previous acquaintance between the doctor and the patient who is to be analysed, have special disadvantageous consequences for which one must be prepared. They result in the patient's meeting the doctor with a transference attitude which is already established and which the doctor must first slowly uncover instead of having the opportunity to observe the growth and development of the transference from the outset. In this way the patient gains a temporary start upon us which we do not willingly grant him in the treatment.

One must mistrust all prospective patients who want to make a delay before beginning their treatment. Experience shows that when the time agreed upon has arrived they fail to put in an appearance, even though the motive for the delay—i.e. their rationalization of their intention— seems to the uninitiated to be above suspicion.

Special difficulties arise when the analyst and his new patient or their families are on terms of friendship or have social ties with one another. The psycho-analyst who is asked to undertake the treatment of the wife or child of a friend must be prepared for it to cost him that friendship, no matter what the outcome of the treatment may be: nevertheless he must make the sacrifice if he cannot find a trustworthy substitute.

Both lay public and doctors—still ready to confuse psycho-analysis with treatment by suggestion—are inclined to attribute great importance to the expectations which the patient brings to the new treatment. They often believe in the case of one patient that he will not give much trouble, because he has great confidence in psycho-analysis and is fully convinced of its truth and efficacy; whereas in the case of another, they think that he will undoubtedly prove more difficult, because he has a sceptical outlook and will not believe anything until he has experienced its successful results on his own person. Actually, however, this attitude on the part of the patient has very little importance. His initial trust or distrust is almost negligible compared with the internal resistances which hold the neurosis firmly in place. It is true that the patient's happy trustfulness makes our earliest relationship with him a very pleasant one; we are grateful to him for that, but we warn him that his favourable prepossession will be shattered by the first difficulty that arises in the analysis. To the sceptic we say that the analysis requires no faith, that he may be as critical and suspicious as he pleases and that we do not regard his attitude as the effect of his judgement at all, for he is not in a position to form a reliable judgement on these matters; his distrust is only a symptom like his other symptoms and it will not be an interference, provided he conscientiously carries out what the rule of the treatment requires of him.

No one who is familiar with the nature of neurosis will be astonished to hear that even a man who is very well able to carry out an analysis on other people can behave like any other mortal and be capable of producing the most intense resistances as soon as he himself becomes the object of analytic investigation. When this happens we are once again reminded of the dimension of depth in the mind, and it does not surprise us to find that the neurosis has its roots in psychical strata to which an intellectual knowledge of analysis has not penetrated.

Points of importance at the beginning of the analysis are arrangements about *time* and *money*.

In regard to time, I adhere strictly to the principle of leasing a definite hour. Each patient is allotted a particular hour of my available working day; it belongs to him and he is liable for it, even if he does not make use of it. This arrangement, which is taken as a matter of course for teachers of music or languages in good society, may perhaps seem too rigorous in a doctor, or even unworthy of his profession. There will be an inclination to point to the many accidents which may prevent the patient from attending every day at the same hour and it will be expected that some allowance shall be made for the numerous intercurrent ailments which may occur in the course of a longish analytic treatment. But my answer is: no other way is practicable. Under a less stringent régime the 'occasional' non-attendances increase so greatly that the doctor finds his material existence threatened; whereas when the arrangement is adhered to, it turns out that accidental hindrances do not occur at all and intercurrent illnesses only very seldom. The analyst is hardly ever put in the position of enjoying a leisure hour which he is paid for and would be ashamed of; and he can continue his work without interruptions, and is spared the distressing and bewildering experience of finding that a break for which he cannot blame himself is always bound to happen just when the work promises to be especially important and rich in content. Nothing brings home to one so strongly the significance of the psychogenic factor in the daily life of men, the frequency of malingering and the non-existence of chance, as a few years' practice of psycho-analysis on the strict principle of leasing by the hour. In cases of undoubted organic illnesses, which, after all, cannot be excluded by the patient's having a psychical interest in attending, I break off the treatment, consider myself entitled to dispose elsewhere of the hour which becomes free, and take the patient back again as soon as he has recovered and I have another hour vacant.

I work with my patients every day except on Sundays and public holidays—that is, as a rule, six days a week. For slight cases or the continuation of a treatment which is already well advanced, three days a week will be enough. Any restrictions of time beyond this bring no advantage either to the doctor or the patient; and at the beginning of an analysis they are quite out of the question. Even short interruptions have a slightly obscuring effect on the work. We used to speak jokingly of the 'Monday crust' when we began work again after the rest on Sunday. When the hours of work are less frequent, there is a risk of not being able to keep pace with the patient's real life and of the treatment losing contact with the present and being forced into by-paths. Occasionally, too, one comes across patients to whom one must give more than the average time of one hour a day, because the best part of an hour is gone before they begin to open up and to become communicative at all.

An unwelcome question which the patient asks the doctor at the outset is: 'How long will the treatment take? How much time will you need to relieve me of my trouble?' If one has proposed a trial treatment of a few weeks one can avoid giving a direct answer to this question by promising to make a more reliable pronouncement at the end of the trial period. Our answer is like the answer given by the Philosopher to the Wayfarer in Aesop's fable. When the Wayfarer asked how long a journey lay ahead, the Philosopher merely answered 'Walk!' and afterwards explained his apparently unhelpful reply on the ground that he must know the length of the Wayfarer's stride before he could tell how long his journey would take. This expedient helps one over the first difficulties; but the comparison is not a good one, for the neurotic can easily alter his pace and may at times make only very slow progress. In point of fact, the question as to the probable duration of a treatment is almost unanswerable.

As the combined result of lack of insight on the part of patients and disingenuousness on the part of doctors, analysis finds itself expected to fulfil the most boundless demands, and that in the shortest time. * * * No one would expect a man to lift a heavy table with two fingers as if it were a light stool, or to build a large house in the time it would take to put up a wooden hut; but as soon as it becomes a question of the neuroses—which do not seem so far to have found a proper place in human thought—even intelligent people forget that a necessary proportion must be observed between time, work and success. This, incidentally, is an understandable result of the deep ignorance which prevails about the aetiology of the neuroses. * * *

Doctors lend support to these fond hopes. Even the informed among them often fail to estimate properly the severity of nervous disorders. A friend and colleague of mine, to whose great credit I account it that after several decades of scientific work on other principles he became converted to the merits of psycho-analysis, once wrote to me: 'What we need is a short, convenient, out-patient treatment for obsessional neurosis.' I could not supply him with it and felt ashamed; so I tried to excuse myself with the remark that specialists in internal diseases, too, would probably be very glad of a treatment for tuberculosis or carcinoma which combined these advantages.

To speak more plainly, a psycho-analysis is always a matter of long periods of time, of half a year or whole years—of longer periods than the patient expects. It is therefore our duty to tell the patient this before he finally decides upon the treatment. I consider it altogether more honourable, and also more expedient, to draw his attention—without trying to frighten him off, but at the very beginning—to the difficulties and sacrifices which analytic treatment involves, and in this way to deprive him of any right to say later on that he has been inveigled into a treatment whose extent and implications he did not realize. A patient who lets himself be dissuaded by this information would in any case have shown himself unsuitable later on. It is a good thing to institute a selection of this kind before the beginning of the treatment. With the progress of understanding among patients the number of those who successfully meet this first test increases.

I do not bind patients to continue the treatment for a certain length of time; I allow each one to break off whenever he likes. But I do not hide it from him that if the treatment is stopped after only a small amount of work has been done it will not be successful and may easily, like an unfinished operation, leave him in an unsatisfactory state. In the early years of my psycho-analytic practice I used to have the greatest difficulty in prevailing on my patients to continue their analysis. This difficulty has long since been shifted, and I now have to take the greatest pains to induce them to give it up.

To shorten analytic treatment is a justifiable wish, and its fulfilment, as we shall learn, is being attempted along various lines. Unfortunately, it is opposed by a very important factor, namely, the slowness with which deep-going changes in the mind are accomplished—in the last resort, no doubt, the 'timelessness' of our unconscious processes. When patients are faced with the difficulty of the great expenditure of time required for analysis they not infrequently manage to propose a way out of it. They divide up their ailments and describe some as unbearable, and others as secondary, and then say: 'If only you will relieve me from this one (for instance, a headache or a particular fear) I can deal with the other one on my own in my ordinary life.' In doing this, however, they over-estimate the selective power of analysis. The analyst is certainly able to do a great deal, but he cannot determine beforehand exactly what results he will effect. He sets in motion a process, that of the resolving of existing repressions. He can supervise this process, further it, remove obstacles in its way, and he can undoubtedly vitiate much of it. But on the whole, once begun, it goes its own way and does not allow either the direction it takes or the order in which it picks up its points to be prescribed for it. The analyst's power over the symptoms of the disease may thus be compared to male sexual potency. A man can, it is true, beget a whole child, but even the strongest man cannot create in the female organism a head alone or an arm or a leg; he cannot even prescribe the child's sex. He, too, only sets in motion a highly compli- cated process, determined by events in the remote past, which ends with the severance of the child from its mother. A neurosis as well has the character of an organism. Its component manifestations are not inde- pendent of one another; they condition one another and give one another mutual support. A person suffers from one neurosis only, never from several which have accidentally met together in a single individual. The patient freed, according to his wish, from his one unendurable symptom might easily find that a symptom which had previously been negligible had now increased and grown unendurable. The analyst who wishes the treatment to owe its success as little as possible to its elements of sug- gestion (i.e. to the transference) will do well to refrain from making use of even the trace of selective influence upon the results of the therapy which may perhaps be open to him. The patients who are bound to be most welcome to him are those who ask him to give them complete health, in so far as that is attainable, and who place as much time at his disposal as is necessary for the process of recovery. Such favourable conditions as these are, of course, to be looked for in only a few cases.

The next point that must be decided at the beginning of the treatment is the one of money, of the doctor's fee. An analyst does not dispute that money is to be regarded in the first instance as a medium for self- preservation and for obtaining power; but he maintains that, besides this, powerful sexual factors are involved in the value set upon it. He can point out that money matters are treated by civilized people in the same way as sexual matters—with the same inconsistency, prudishness and hypocrisy. The analyst is therefore determined from the first not to fall in with this attitude, but, in his dealings with his patients, to treat of money matters with the same matter-of-course frankness to which he wishes to educate them in things relating to sexual life. He shows them that he himself has cast off false shame on these topics, by voluntarily telling them the price at which he values his time. Ordinary good sense cautions him, furthermore, not to allow large sums of money to ac- cumulate, but to ask for payment at fairly short regular intervals— monthly, perhaps. (It is a familiar fact that the value of the treatment is not enhanced in the patient's eyes if a very low fee is asked.) This is, of course, not the usual practice of nerve specialists or other physicians in our European society. But the psycho-analyst may put himself in the position of a surgeon, who is frank and expensive because he has at his disposal methods of treatment which can be of use. It seems to me more respectable and ethically less objectionable to acknowledge one's actual claims and needs rather than, as is still the practice among physicians, to act the part of the disinterested philanthropist—a position which one is not, in fact, able to fill, with the result that one is secretly aggrieved, or complains aloud, at the lack of consideration and the desire for exploitation evinced by one's patients. In fixing his fee the analyst must also allow for the fact that, hard as he may work, he can never earn as much as other medical specialists.

For the same reason he should also refrain from giving treatment free, and make no exceptions to this in favour of his colleagues or their families. This last recommendation will seem to offend against professional amenities. It must be remembered, however, that a gratuitous treatment means much more to a psycho-analyst than to any other medical man; it means the sacrifice of a considerable portion—an eighth or a seventh part, perhaps—of the working time available to him for earning his living, over a period of many months. A second free treatment carried on at the same time would already deprive him of a quarter or a third of his earning capacity, and this would be comparable to the damage inflicted by a severe accident.

The question then arises whether the advantage gained by the patient would not to some extent counterbalance the sacrifice made by the physician. I may venture to form a judgement about this, since for ten years or so I set aside one hour a day, and sometimes two, for gratuitous treatments, because I wanted, in order to find my way about in the neuroses, to work in the face of as little resistance as possible. The advantages I sought by this means were not forthcoming. Free treatment enormously increases some of a neurotic's resistances—in young women, for instance, the temptation which is inherent in their transference-relation, and in young men, their opposition to an obligation to feel grateful, an opposition which arises from their father-complex and which presents one of the most troublesome hindrances to the acceptance of medical help. The absence of the regulating effect offered by the payment of a fee to the doctor makes itself very painfully felt; the whole relationship is removed from the real world, and the patient is deprived of a strong motive for endeavouring to bring the treatment to an end.

One may be very far from the ascetic view of money as a curse and yet regret that analytic therapy is almost inaccessible to poor people, both for external and internal reasons. Little can be done to remedy this. Perhaps there is truth in the widespread belief that those who are forced by necessity to a life of hard toil are less easily overtaken by neurosis. But on the other hand experience shows without a doubt that when once a poor man has produced a neurosis it is only with difficulty that he lets it be taken from him. It renders him too good a service in the struggle for existence; the secondary gain from illness which it brings him is much too important. He now claims by right of his neurosis the pity which the world has refused to his material distress, and he can now absolve himself from the obligation of combating his poverty by working. * * *

As far as the middle classes are concerned, the expense involved in psycho-analysis is excessive only in appearance. Quite apart from the fact that no comparison is possible between restored health and efficiency on the one hand and a moderate financial outlay on the other, when we add up the unceasing costs of nursing-homes and medical treatment and contrast them with the increase of efficiency and earning capacity which results from a successfully completed analysis, we are entitled to say that the patients have made a good bargain. Nothing in life is so expensive as illness—and stupidity.

Before I wind up these remarks on beginning analytic treatment, I must say a word about a certain ceremonial which concerns the position in which the treatment is carried out. I hold to the plan of getting the patient to lie on a sofa while I sit behind him out of his sight. This arrangement has a historical basis; it is the remnant of the hypnotic method out of which psycho-analysis was evolved. But it deserves to be maintained for many reasons. The first is a personal motive, but one which others may share with me. I cannot put up with being stared at by other people for eight hours a day (or more). Since, while I am listening to the patient, I, too, give myself over to the current of my unconscious thoughts, I do not wish my expressions of face to give the patient material for interpretations or to influence him in what he tells me. The patient usually regards being made to adopt this position as a hardship and rebels against it, especially if the instinct for looking (sco-pophilia) plays an important part in his neurosis. I insist on this pro-cedure, however, for its purpose and result are to prevent the transference from mingling with the patient's associations imperceptibly, to isolate the transference and to allow it to come forward in due course sharply defined as a resistance. I know that many analysts work in a different way, but I do not know whether this deviation is due more to a craving for doing things differently or to some advantage which they find they gain by it.

* * *

What the material is with which one starts the treatment is on the whole a matter of indifference—whether it is the patient's life-history or the history of his illness or his recollections of childhood. But in any case the patient must be left to do the talking and must be free to choose at what point he shall begin. We therefore say to him: 'Before I can say anything to you I must know a great deal about you; please tell me what you know about yourself.'

The only exception to this is in regard to the fundamental rule of psycho-analytic technique which the patient has to observe. This must be imparted to him at the very beginning: 'One more thing before you start. What you tell me must differ in one respect from an ordinary conversation. Ordinarily you rightly try to keep a connecting thread running through your remarks and you exclude any intrusive ideas that may occur to you and any side-issues, so as not to wander too far from the point. But in this case you must proceed differently. You will notice that as you relate things various thoughts will occur to you which you would like to put aside on the ground of certain criticisms and objections. You will be tempted to say to yourself that this or that is irrelevant here, or is quite unimportant, or nonsensical, so that there is no need to say it. You must never give in to these criticisms, but must say it in spite of them—indeed, you must say it precisely *because* you feel an aversion to doing so. Later on you will find out and learn to understand the reason for this injunction, which is really the only one you have to follow. So say whatever goes through your mind. Act as though, for instance, you were a traveller sitting next to the window of a railway carriage and describing to someone inside the carriage the changing views which you see outside. Finally, never forget that you have promised to be absolutely honest, and never leave anything out because, for some reason or other, it is unpleasant to tell it.'[1]

Patients who date their illness from a particular moment usually concentrate upon its precipitating cause. Others, who themselves recognize the connection between their neurosis and their childhood, often begin with an account of their whole life-history. A systematic narrative should never be expected and nothing should be done to encourage it. Every detail of the story will have to be told afresh later on, and it is only with these repetitions that additional material will appear which will supply the important connections that are unknown to the patient.

There are patients who from the very first hours carefully prepare what they are going to communicate, ostensibly so as to be sure of making better use of the time devoted to the treatment. What is thus disguising itself as eagerness is resistance. Any preparation of this sort should be disrecommended, for it is only employed to guard against unwelcome thoughts cropping up. However genuinely the patient may

1. Much might be said about our experiences with the fundamental rule of psycho-analysis. One occasionally comes across people who behave as if they had made this rule for themselves. Others offend against it from the very beginning. It is indispensable, and also advantageous, to lay down the rule in the first stages of the treatment. Later, under the domination of the resistances, obedience to it weakens, and there comes a time in every analysis when the patient disregards it. We must remember from our own self-analysis how irresistible the temptation is to yield to these pretexts put forward by critical judgement for rejecting certain ideas. How small is the effect of such agreements as one makes with the patient in laying down the fundamental rule is regularly demonstrated when something intimate about a third person comes up in his mind for the first time. He knows that he is supposed to say everything, but he turns discretion about other people into a new obstacle. 'Must I really say everything? I thought that only applied to things that concern myself.' It is naturally impossible to carry out analysis if the patient's relations with other people and his thoughts about them are excluded. *Pour faire un omelette il faut casser des oeufs.* * * * .

believe in his excellent intentions, the resistance will play its part in this deliberate method of preparation and will see to it that the most valuable material escapes communication. One will soon find that the patient devises yet other means by which what is required may be withheld from the treatment. He may talk over the treatment every day with some intimate friend, and bring into this discussion all the thoughts which should come forward in the presence of the doctor. The treatment thus has a leak which lets through precisely what is most valuable. When this happens, the patient must, without much delay, be advised to treat his analysis as a matter between himself and his doctor and to exclude everyone else from sharing in the knowledge of it, no matter how close to him they may be, or how inquisitive. In later stages of the treatment the patient is usually not subjected to temptations of this sort.

Certain patients want their treatment to be kept secret, often because they have kept their neurosis secret; and I put no obstacle in their way. That in consequence the world hears nothing of some of the most successful cures is, of course, a consideration that cannot be taken into account. It is obvious that a patient's decision in favour of secrecy already reveals a feature of his secret history.

In advising the patient at the beginning of the treatment to tell as few people as possible about it, we also protect him to some extent from the many hostile influences that will seek to entice him away from analysis. Such influences may be very mischievous at the outset of the treatment; later, they are usually immaterial, or even useful in bringing to the fore resistances which are trying to conceal themselves.

If during the course of the anaylsis the patient should temporarily need some other medical or specialist treatment, it is far wiser to call in a non-analytic colleague than to give this other treatment oneself. Combined treatments for neurotic disorders which have a powerful organic basis are nearly always impracticable. The patients withdraw their interest from analysis as soon as they are shown more than one path that promises to lead them to health. The best plan is to postpone the organic treatment until the psychical treatment is finished; if the former were tried first it would in most cases meet with no success.

To return to the beginning of the treatment. Patients are occasionally met with who start the treatment by assuring us that they cannot think of anything to say, although the whole field of their life-history and the story of their illness is open to them to choose from. Their request that we should tell them what to talk about must not be granted on this first occasion any more than on any later one. We must bear in mind what is involved here. A strong resistance has come to the front in order to defend the neurosis; we must take up the challenge then and there and come to grips with it. Energetic and repeated assurances to the patient that it is impossible for no ideas at all to occur to him at the beginning, and that what is in question is a resistance against the analysis, soon oblige him to make the expected admissions or to uncover a first piece of his complexes. It is a bad sign if he has to confess that while he was listening to the fundamental rule of analysis he made a mental reservation that he would nevertheless keep this or that to himself; it is not so serious if all he has to tell us is how mistrustful he is of analysis or the horrifying things he has heard about it. If he denies these and similar possibilities when they are put before him, he can be driven by our insistence to acknowledge that he has nevertheless overlooked certain thoughts which were occupying his mind. He had thought of the treatment itself, though nothing definite about it, or he had been occupied with the picture of the room in which he was, or he could not help thinking of the objects in the consulting room and of the fact that he was lying here on a sofa—all of which he has replaced by the word 'nothing'. These indications are intelligible enough: everything connected with the present situation represents a transference to the doctor, which proves suitable to serve as a first resistance. We are thus obliged to begin by uncovering this transference; and a path from it will give rapid access to the patient's pathogenic material. Women who are prepared by events in their past history to be subjected to sexual aggression and men with over-strong repressed homosexuality are the most apt thus to withhold the ideas that occur to them at the outset of their analysis.

The patient's first symptoms or chance actions, like his first resistance, may possess a special interest and may betray a complex which governs his neurosis. A clever young philosopher with exquisite aesthetic sensibilities will hasten to put the creases of his trousers straight before lying down for his first hour; he is revealing himself as a former coprophilic of the highest refinement—which was to be expected from the later aesthete. A young girl will at the same juncture hurriedly pull the hem of her skirt over her exposed ankles; in doing this she is giving away the gist of what her analysis will uncover later: her narcissistic pride in her physical beauty and her inclinations to exhibitionism.

A particularly large number of patients object to being asked to lie down, while the doctor sits out of sight behind them. They ask to be allowed to go through the treatment in some other position, for the most part because they are anxious not to be deprived of a view of the doctor. Permission is regularly refused, but one cannot prevent them from contriving to say a few sentences before the beginning of the actual 'session' or after one has signified that it is finished and they have got up from the sofa. In this way they divide the treatment in their own view into an official portion, in which they mostly behave in a very inhibited manner, and an informal 'friendly' portion, in which they speak really freely and say all sorts of things which they themselves do not regard as being part of the treatment. The doctor does not accept this division for long. He takes note of what is said before or after the session and he brings it forward at the first opportunity, thus pulling down the partition which the patient has tried to erect. This partition, once again, will have been put together from the material of a transference-resistance.

So long as the patient's communications and ideas run on without any obstruction, the theme of transference should be left untouched. One must wait until the transference, which is the most delicate of all procedures, has become a resistance.

The next question with which we are faced raises a matter of principle. It is this: When are we to begin making our communications to the patient? When is the moment for disclosing to him the hidden meaning of the ideas that occur to him, and for initiating him into the postulates and technical procedures of analysis?

The answer to this can only be: Not until an effective transference has been established in the patient, a proper *rapport* with him. It remains the first aim of the treatment to attach him to it and to the person of the doctor. To ensure this, nothing need be done but to give him time. If one exhibits a serious interest in him, carefully clears away the resistances that crop up at the beginning and avoids making certain mistakes, he will of himself form such an attachment and link the doctor up with one of the imagos of the people by whom he was accustomed to be treated with affection. It is certainly possible to forfeit this first success if from the start one takes up any standpoint other than one of sympathetic understanding, such as a moralizing one, or if one behaves like a representative or advocate of some contending party—of the other member of a married couple, for instance.

This answer of course involves a condemnation of any line of behaviour which would lead us to give the patient a translation of his symptoms as soon as we have guessed it ourselves, or would even lead us to regard it as a special triumph to fling these 'solutions' in his face at the first interview. It is not difficult for a skilled analyst to read the patient's secret wishes plainly between the lines of his complaints and the story of his illness; but what a measure of self-complacency and thoughtlessness must be possessed by anyone who can, on the shortest acquaintance, inform a stranger who is entirely ignorant of all the tenets of analysis that he is attached to his mother by incestuous ties, that he harbours wishes for the death of his wife whom he appears to love, that he conceals an intention of betraying his superior, and so on.[2] I have heard that there are analysts who plume themselves upon these kinds of lightning diagnoses and 'express' treatments, but I must warn everyone against following such examples. Behaviour of this sort will completely discredit oneself and the treatment in the patient's eyes and will arouse the most violent opposition in him, whether one's guess has been true or not; indeed, the truer the guess the more violent will be the resistance.

2. [Cf. the detailed example of this which Freud had already given in his paper " 'Wild' Psycho-Analysis' {see above, pp. 351–56}.]

As a rule the therapeutic effect will be nil; but the deterring of the patient from analysis will be final. Even in the later stages of analysis one must be careful not to give a patient the solution of a symptom or the translation of a wish until he is already so close to it that he has only one short step more to make in order to get hold of the explanation for himself. In former years I often had occasion to find that the premature communication of a solution brought the treatment to an untimely end, on account not only of the resistances which it thus suddenly awakened but also of the relief which the solution brought with it.

But at this point an objection will be raised. Is it, then, our task to lengthen the treatment and not, rather, to bring it to an end as rapidly as possible? Are not the patient's ailments due to his lack of knowledge and understanding and is it not a duty to enlighten him as soon as possible—that is, as soon as the doctor himself knows the explanations? The answer to this question calls for a short digression on the meaning of knowledge and the mechanism of cure in analysis.

It is true that in the earliest days of analytic technique we took an intellectualist view of the situation. We set a high value on the patient's knowledge of what he had forgotten, and in this we made hardly any distinction between our knowledge of it and his. We thought it a special piece of good luck if we were able to obtain information about the forgotten childhood trauma from other sources—for instance, from parents or nurses or the seducer himself—as in some cases it was possible to do; and we hastened to convey the information and the proofs of its correctness to the patient, in the certain expectation of thus bringing the neurosis and the treatment to a rapid end. It was a severe disappointment when the expected success was not forthcoming. How could it be that the patient, who now knew about his traumatic experience, nevertheless still behaved as if he knew no more about it than before? Indeed, telling and describing his repressed trauma to him did not even result in any recollection of it coming into his mind.

* * *

The strange behaviour of patients, in being able to combine a conscious knowing with not knowing, remains inexplicable by what is called normal psychology. But to psycho-analysis, which recognizes the existence of the unconscious, it presents no difficulty. The phenomenon we have described, moreover, provides some of the best support for a view which approaches mental processes from the angle of topographical differentiation. The patients now know of the repressed experience in their conscious thought, but this thought lacks any connection with the place where the repressed recollection is in some way or other contained. No change is possible until the conscious thought-process has penetrated to that place and has overcome the resistances of repression there. It is just as though a decree were promulgated by the Ministry of Justice to the effect that juvenile delinquencies should be dealt with in a certain lenient manner. As long as this decree has not come to the knowledge of the local magistrates, or in the event of their not intending to obey it but preferring to administer justice by their own lights, no change can occur in the treatment of particular youthful delinquents. For the sake of complete accuracy, however, it should be added that the communication of repressed material to the patient's consciousness is nevertheless not without effect. It does not produce the hoped-for result of putting an end to the symptoms; but it has other consequences. At first it arouses resistances, but then, when these have been overcome, it sets up a process of thought in the course of which the expected influencing of the unconscious recollection eventually takes place.

It is now time for us to take a survey of the play of forces which is set in motion by the treatment. The primary motive force in the therapy is the patient's suffering and the wish to be cured that arises from it. The strength of this motive force is subtracted from by various factors—which are not discovered till the analysis is in progress—above all, by what we have called the 'secondary gain from illness', but it must be maintained till the end of the treatment. Every improvement effects a diminution of it. By itself, however, this motive force is not sufficient to get rid of the illness. Two things are lacking in it for this: it does not know what paths to follow to reach this end; and it does not possess the necessary quota of energy with which to oppose the resistances. The analytic treatment helps to remedy both these deficiencies. It supplies the amounts of energy that are needed for overcoming the resistances by making mobile the energies which lie ready for the transference; and, by giving the patient information at the right time, it shows him the paths along which he should direct those energies. Often enough the transference is able to remove the symptoms of the disease by itself, but only for a while—only for as long as it itself lasts. In this case the treatment is a treatment by suggestion, and not a psycho-analysis at all. It only deserves the latter name if the intensity of the transference has been utilized for the overcoming of resistances. Only then has being ill become impossible, even when the transference has once more been dissolved, which is its destined end.

In the course of the treatment yet another helpful factor is aroused. This is the patient's intellectual interest and understanding. But this alone hardly comes into consideration in comparison with the other forces that are engaged in the struggle; for it is always in danger of losing its value, as a result of the clouding of judgement that arises from the resistances. Thus the new sources of strength for which the patient is indebted to his analyst are reducible to transference and instruction (through the communications made to him). The patient, however, only makes use of the instruction in so far as he is induced to do so by the transference; and it is for this reason that our first communication should be withheld until a strong transference has been established. And this, we may add, holds good of every subsequent communication. In each case we must wait until the disturbance of the transference by the successive emergence of transference-resistances has been removed.

Observations on Transference-Love

Freud designed this paper, of which he thought particularly well, to confront quite directly one of the most embarrassing—probably the most embarrassing—side-effect attendant upon psychoanalytic treatment. Reports of male analysts seducing female patients, taking advantage of their susceptible analysands, were widespread, the cause of snide jokes and grave accusations. They were not solely canards; the anecdotal evidence concerning amorous episodes between the physician and the patient he was supposed only to cure, not make love to, was not wholly imaginary.

In writing on transference, it is important to note, Freud did not confine himself to the excited "positive transference" that mimics real love. He also saw two other types of transference: a "negative transference," which loads the analyst with hostile feelings, and a sensible positive transference, in which the analysand rises above illusions about the analyst and approximates the rational conviction that the analyst is a skilled, sympathetic observer, not a lover or an enemy. These various transferences normally exist side by side; hence Freud welcomed Bleuler's term "ambivalence" to characterize the coexistence of love and hate for the same object in all analysands. (See "The Dynamics of Transference" [1912], SE XII, 99–120, esp. 105–7.) This paper was published in 1915.

Every beginner in psycho-analysis probably feels alarmed at first at the difficulties in store for him when he comes to interpret the patient's associations and to deal with the reproduction of the repressed. When the time comes, however, he soon learns to look upon these difficulties as insignificant, and instead becomes convinced that the only really serious difficulties he has to meet lie in the management of the transference.

Among the situations which arise in this connection I shall select one which is very sharply circumscribed; and I shall select it, partly because it occurs so often and is so important in its real aspects and partly because of its theoretical interest. What I have in mind is the case in which a woman patient shows by unmistakable indications, or openly declares, that she has fallen in love, as any other mortal woman might, with the doctor who is analysing her. This situation has its distressing and comical aspects, as well as its serious ones. It is also determined by so many and such complicated factors, it is so unavoidable and so difficult to clear up, that a discussion of it to meet a vital need of analytic technique has long been overdue. But since we who laugh at other people's failings are not always free from them ourselves, we have not so far been precisely in a hurry to fulfil this task. We are constantly coming up against the obligation to professional discretion—a discretion which cannot be dispensed with in real life, but which is of no service in our science. In so far as psycho-analytic publications are a part of real life, too, we have here an insoluble contradiction. * * *

To a well-educated layman (for that is what the ideal civilized person is in regard to psycho-analysis) things that have to do with love are incommensurable with everything else; they are, as it were, written on a special page on which no other writing is tolerated. If a woman patient has fallen in love with her doctor it seems to such a layman that only two outcomes are possible. One, which happens comparatively rarely, is that all the circumstances allow of a permanent legal union between them; the other, which is more frequent, is that the doctor and the patient part and give up the work they have begun which was to have led to her recovery, as though it had been interrupted by some elemental phenomenon. There is, to be sure, a third conceivable outcome, which even seems compatible with a continuation of the treatment. This is that they should enter into a love-relationship which is illicit and which is not intended to last for ever. But such a course is made impossible by conventional morality and professional standards. Nevertheless, our layman will beg the analyst to reassure him as unambiguously as possible that this third alternative is excluded.

It is clear that a psycho-analyst must look at things from a different point of view.

Let us take the case of the second outcome of the situation we are considering. After the patient has fallen in love with her doctor, they part; the treatment is given up. But soon the patient's condition necessitates her making a second attempt at analysis, with another doctor. The next thing that happens is that she feels she has fallen in love with this second doctor too; and if she breaks off with him and begins yet again, the same thing will happen with the third doctor, and so on. This phenomenon, which occurs without fail and which is, as we know, one of the foundations of the psycho-analytic theory, may be evaluated from two points of view, that of the doctor who is carrying out the analysis and that of the patient who is in need of it.

For the doctor the phenomenon signifies a valuable piece of enlightenment and a useful warning against any tendency to a counter-transference which may be present in his own mind. He must recognize that the patient's falling in love is induced by the analytic situation and is not to be attributed to the charms of his own person; so that he has no grounds whatever for being proud of such a 'conquest', as it would be called outside analysis. And it is always well to be reminded of this.

For the patient, however, there are two alternatives: either she must relinquish psycho-analytic treatment or she must accept falling in love with her doctor as an inescapable fate.

I have no doubt that the patient's relatives and friends will decide as emphatically for the first of these two alternatives as the analyst will for the second. But I think that here is a case in which the decision cannot be left to the tender—or rather, the egoistic and jealous—concern of her relatives. The welfare of the patient alone should be the touchstone; her relatives' love cannot cure her neurosis. The analyst need not push himself forward, but he may insist that he is indispensable for the achievement of certain ends. * * * Moreover, the jealous father or husband is greatly mistaken if he thinks that the patient will escape falling in love with her doctor if he hands her over to some kind of treatment other than analysis for combating her neurosis. The difference, on the contrary, will only be that a love of this kind, which is bound to remain unexpressed and unanalysed, can never make the contribution to the patient's recovery which analysis would have extracted from it.

It has come to my knowledge that some doctors who practise analysis frequently prepare their patients for the emergence of the erotic transference or even urge them to 'go ahead and fall in love with the doctor so that the treatment may make progress'. I can hardly imagine a more senseless proceeding. In doing so, an analyst robs the phenomenon of the element of spontaneity which is so convincing and lays up obstacles for himself in the future which are hard to overcome.

At a first glance it certainly does not look as if the patient's falling in love in the transference could result in any advantage to the treatment. No matter how amenable she has been up till then, she suddenly loses all understanding of the treatment and all interest in it, and will not speak or hear about anything but her love, which she demands to have returned. She gives up her symptoms or pays no attention to them; indeed, she declares that she is well. There is a complete change of scene; it is as though some piece of make-believe had been stopped by the sudden irruption of reality—as when, for instance, a cry of fire is raised during a theatrical performance. No doctor who experiences this for the first time will find it easy to retain his grasp on the analytic situation and to keep clear of the illusion that the treatment is really at an end.

A little reflection enables one to find one's bearings. First and foremost, one keeps in mind the suspicion that anything that interferes with the continuation of the treatment may be an expression of resistance. There can be no doubt that the outbreak of a passionate demand for love is largely the work of resistance. One will have long since noticed in the patient the signs of an affectionate transference, and one will have been able to feel certain that her docility, her acceptance of the analytic explanations, her remarkable comprehension and the high degree of intelligence she showed were to be attributed to this attitude towards her doctor. Now all this is swept away. She has become quite without insight and seems to be swallowed up in her love. Moreover, this change quite regularly occurs precisely at a point of time when one is having to try to bring her to admit or remember some particularly distressing and heavily repressed piece of her life-history. She has been in love, therefore, for a long time; but now the resistance is beginning to make use of her love in order to hinder the continuation of the treatment, to deflect all her interest from the work and to put the analyst in an awkward position.

If one looks into the situation more closely one recognizes the influence of motives which further complicate things—of which some are connected with being in love and others are particular expressions of resistance. Of the first kind are the patient's endeavour to assure herself of her irresistibility, to destroy the doctor's authority by bringing him down to the level of a lover and to gain all the other promised advantages incidental to the satisfaction of love. As regards the resistance, we may suspect that on occasion it makes use of a declaration of love on the patient's part as a means of putting her analyst's severity to the test, so that, if he should show signs of compliance, he may expect to be taken to task for it. But above all, one gets an impression that the resistance is acting as an *agent provocateur*; it heightens the patient's state of being in love and exaggerates her readiness for sexual surrender in order to justify the workings of repression all the more emphatically, by pointing to the dangers of such licentiousness. All these accessory motives, which in simpler cases may not be present, have, as we know, been regarded by Adler as the essential part of the whole process.

But how is the analyst to behave in order not to come to grief over this situation, supposing he is convinced that the treatment should be carried on in spite of this erotic transference and should take it in its stride?

It would be easy for me to lay stress on the universally accepted standards of morality and to insist that the analyst must never under any circumstances accept or return the tender feelings that are offered him: that, instead, he must consider that the time has come for him to put before the woman who is in love with him the demands of social morality and the necessity for renunciation, and to succeed in making her give up her desires, and, having surmounted the animal side of her self, go on with the work of analysis.

I shall not, however, fulfil these expectations—neither the first nor the second of them. Not the first, because I am writing not for patients but for doctors who have serious difficulties to contend with, and also because in this instance I am able to trace the moral prescription back to its source, namely to expediency. I am on this occasion in the happy position of being able to replace the moral embargo by considerations of analytic technique, without any alteration in the outcome.

Even more decidedly, however, do I decline to fulfil the second of the expectations I have mentioned. To urge the patient to suppress, renounce or sublimate her instincts the moment she has admitted her erotic transference would be, not an analytic way of dealing with them, but a senseless one. It would be just as though, after summoning up a spirit from the underworld by cunning spells, one were to send him down again without having asked him a single question. One would have brought the repressed into consciousness, only to repress it once more in a fright. Nor should we deceive ourselves about the success of any such proceeding. As we know, the passions are little affected by sublime speeches. The patient will feel only the humiliation, and she will not fail to take her revenge for it.

Just as little can I advocate a middle course, which would recommend itself to some people as being specially ingenious. This would consist in declaring that one returns the patient's fond feelings but at the same time in avoiding any physical implementation of this fondness until one is able to guide the relationship into calmer channels and raise it to a higher level. My objection to this expedient is that psycho-analytic treatment is founded on truthfulness. In this fact lies a great part of its educative effect and its ethical value. It is dangerous to depart from this foundation. Anyone who has become saturated in the analytic technique will no longer be able to make use of the lies and pretences which a doctor normally finds unavoidable; and if, with the best intentions, he does attempt to do so, he is very likely to betray himself. Since we demand strict truthfulness from our patients, we jeopardize our whole authority if we let ourselves be caught out by them in a departure from the truth. Besides, the experiment of letting oneself go a little way in tender feelings for the patient is not altogether without danger. Our control over ourselves is not so complete that we may not suddenly one day go further than we had intended. In my opinion, therefore, we ought not to give up the neutrality towards the patient, which we have acquired through keeping the counter-transference in check.

I have already let it be understood that analytic technique requires of the physician that he should deny to the patient who is craving for love the satisfaction she demands. The treatment must be carried out in abstinence. By this I do not mean physical abstinence alone, nor yet the deprivation of everything that the patient desires, for perhaps no sick person could tolerate this. Instead, I shall state it as a fundamental principle that the patient's need and longing should be allowed to persist in her, in order that they may serve as forces impelling her to do work and to make changes, and that we must beware of appeasing those forces by means of surrogates. And what we could offer would never be anything else than a surrogate, for the patient's condition is such that, until her repressions are removed, she is incapable of getting real satisfaction.

Let us admit that this fundamental principle of the treatment being carried out in abstinence extends far beyond the single case we are considering here, and that it needs to be thoroughly discussed in order that we may define the limits of its possible application. We will not enter into this now, however, but will keep as close as possible to the situation from which we started out. What would happen if the doctor were to behave differently and, supposing both parties were free, if he were to avail himself of that freedom in order to return the patient's love and to still her need for affection?

If he has been guided by the calculation that this compliance on his part will ensure his domination over his patient and thus enable him to influence her to perform the tasks required by the treatment, and in this way to liberate herself permanently from her neurosis—then experience would inevitably show him that his calculation was wrong. The patient would achieve *her* aim, but he would never achieve *his*. What would happen to the doctor and the patient would only be what happened, according to the amusing anecdote, to the pastor and the insurance agent. The insurance agent, a free-thinker, lay at the point of death and his relatives insisted on bringing a man of God to convert him before he died. The interview lasted so long that those who were waiting outside began to have hopes. At last the door of the sick-chamber opened. The free-thinker had not been converted; but the pastor went away insured.

If the patient's advances were returned it would be a great triumph for her, but a complete defeat for the treatment. She would have succeeded in what all patients strive for in analysis—she would have succeeded in acting out, in repeating in real life, what she ought only to have remembered, to have reproduced as psychical material and to have kept within the sphere of psychical events. In the further course of the love-relationship she would bring out all the inhibitions and pathological reactions of her erotic life, without there being any possibility of correcting them; and the distressing episode would end in remorse and a great strengthening of her propensity to repression. The love-relationship in fact destroys the patient's susceptibility to influence from analytic treatment. A combination of the two would be an impossibility.

It is, therefore, just as disastrous for the analysis if the patient's craving for love is gratified as if it is suppressed. The course the analyst must pursue is neither of these; it is one for which there is no model in real life. He must take care not to steer away from the transference-love, or to repulse it or to make it distasteful to the patient; but he must just as resolutely withhold any response to it. He must keep firm hold of the transference-love, but treat it as something unreal, as a situation which has to be gone through in the treatment and traced back to its unconscious origins and which must assist in bringing all that is most deeply hidden in the patient's erotic life into her consciousness and therefore under her control. The more plainly the analyst lets it be seen that he is proof against every temptation, the more readily will he be able to extract from the situation its analytic content. The patient, whose sexual repression is of course not yet removed but merely pushed into the background, will then feel safe enough to allow all her preconditions for loving, all the phantasies springing from her sexual desires, all the detailed characteristics of her state of being in love, to come to light; and from these she will herself open the way to the infantile roots of her love.

There is, it is true, one class of women with whom this attempt to preserve the erotic transference for the purposes of analytic work without satisfying it will not succeed. These are women of elemental passionateness who tolerate no surrogates. They are children of nature who refuse to accept the psychical in place of the material, who, in the poet's words, are accessible only to 'the logic of soup, with dumplings for arguments'. With such people one has the choice between returning their love or else bringing down upon oneself the full enmity of a woman scorned. In neither case can one safeguard the interests of the treatment. One has to withdraw, unsuccessful; and all one can do is to turn the problem over in one's mind of how it is that a capacity for neurosis is joined with such an intractable need for love.

Many analysts will no doubt be agreed on the method by which other women, who are less violent in their love, can be gradually made to adopt the analytic attitude. What we do, above all, is to stress to the patient the unmistakable element of resistance in this 'love'. Genuine love, we say, would make her docile and intensify her readiness to solve the problems of her case, simply because the man she was in love with expected it of her. In such a case she would gladly choose the road to completion of the treatment, in order to acquire value in the doctor's eyes and to prepare herself for real life, where this feeling of love could find a proper place. Instead of this, we point out, she is showing a stubborn and rebellious spirit, she has thrown up all interest in her treatment, and clearly feels no respect for the doctor's well-founded convictions. She is thus bringing out a resistance under the guise of being in love with him; and in addition to this she has no compunction in placing him in a cleft stick. For if he refuses her love, as his duty and his understanding compel him to do, she can play the part of a woman scorned, and then withdraw from his therapeutic efforts out of revenge and resentment, exactly as she is now doing out of her ostensible love.

As a second argument against the genuineness of this love we advance the fact that it exhibits not a single new feature arising from the present situation, but is entirely composed of repetitions and copies of earlier reactions, including infantile ones. We undertake to prove this by a detailed analysis of the patient's behaviour in love.

If the necessary amount of patience is added to these arguments, it is usually possible to overcome the difficult situation and to continue the work with a love which has been moderated or transformed; the work then aims at uncovering the patient's infantile object-choice and the phantasies woven round it.

I should now like, however, to examine these arguments with a critical eye and to raise the question whether, in putting them forward to the patient, we are really telling the truth, or whether we are not resorting in our desperation to concealments and misrepresentations. In other words: can we truly say that the state of being in love which becomes manifest in analytic treatment is not a real one?

I think we have told the patient the truth, but not the whole truth regardless of the consequences. Of our two arguments the first is the stronger. The part played by resistance in transference-love is unquestionable and very considerable. Nevertheless the resistance did not, after all, *create* this love; it finds it ready to hand, makes use of it and aggravates its manifestations. Nor is the genuineness of the phenomenon disproved by the resistance. The second argument is far weaker. It is true that the love consists of new editions of old traits and that it repeats infantile reactions. But this is the essential character of every state of being in love. There is no such state which does not reproduce infantile proto-types. It is precisely from this infantile determination that it receives its compulsive character, verging as it does on the pathological. Transference-love has perhaps a degree less of freedom than the love which appears in ordinary life and is called normal; it displays its dependence on the infantile pattern more clearly and is less adaptable and capable of modification; but that is all, and not what is essential.

By what other signs can the genuineness of a love be recognized? By its efficacy, its serviceability in achieving the aim of love? In this respect transference-love seems to be second to none; one has the impression that one could obtain anything from it.

Let us sum up, therefore. We have no right to dispute that the state of being in love which makes its appearance in the course of analytic treatment has the character of a 'genuine' love. If it seems so lacking in normality, this is sufficiently explained by the fact that being in love in ordinary life, outside analysis, is also more similar to abnormal than to normal mental phenomena. Nevertheless, transference-love is characterized by certain features which ensure it a special position. In the first place, it is provoked by the analytic situation; secondly, it is greatly intensified by the resistance, which dominates the situation; and thirdly, it is lacking to a high degree in a regard for reality, is less sensible, less concerned about consequences and more blind in its valuation of the loved person than we are prepared to admit in the case of normal love. We should not forget, however, that these departures from the norm constitute precisely what is essential about being in love.

As regards the analyst's line of action, it is the first of these three features of transference-love which is the decisive factor. He has evoked this love by instituting analytic treatment in order to cure the neurosis. For him, it is an unavoidable consequence of a medical situation, like the exposure of a patient's body or the imparting of a vital secret. It is therefore plain to him that he must not derive any personal advantage from it. The patient's willingness makes no difference; it merely throws the whole responsibility on the analyst himself. Indeed, as he must know, the patient had been prepared for no other mechanism of cure. After all the difficulties have been successfully overcome, she will often confess to having had an anticipatory phantasy at the time when she entered the treatment, to the effect that if she behaved well she would be rewarded at the end by the doctor's affection.

For the doctor, ethical motives unite with the technical ones to restrain him from giving the patient his love. The aim he has to keep in view is that this woman, whose capacity for love is impaired by infantile fixations, should gain free command over a function which is of such inestimable importance to her; that she should not, however, dissipate it in the treatment, but keep it ready for the time when, after her treatment, the demands of real life make themselves felt. He must not stage the scene of a dog-race in which the prize was to be a garland of sausages but which some humorist spoilt by throwing a single sausage on to the track. The result was, of course, that the dogs threw themselves upon it and forgot all about the race and about the garland that was luring them to victory in the far distance. I do not mean to say that it is always easy for the doctor to keep within the limits prescribed by ethics and technique. Those who are still youngish and not yet bound by strong ties may in particular find it a hard task. Sexual love is undoubtedly one of the chief things in life, and the union of mental and bodily satisfaction in the enjoyment of love is one of its culminating peaks. Apart from a few queer fanatics, all the world knows this and conducts its life accordingly; science alone is too delicate to admit it. Again, when a woman sues for love, to reject and refuse is a distressing part for a man to play; and, in spite of neurosis and resistance, there is an incomparable fascination in a woman of high principles who confesses her passion. It is not a patient's crudely sensual desires which constitute the temptation. These are more likely to repel, and it will call for all the doctor's tolerance if he is to regard them as a natural phenomenon. It is rather, perhaps, a woman's subtler and aim-inhibited wishes which bring with them the danger of making a man forget his technique and his medical task for the sake of a fine experience.

And yet it is quite out of the question for the analyst to give way. However highly he may prize love he must prize even more highly the opportunity for helping his patient over a decisive stage in her life. She has to learn from him to overcome the pleasure principle, to give up a satisfaction which lies to hand but is socially not acceptable, in favour of a more distant one, which is perhaps altogether uncertain, but which is both psychologically and socially unimpeachable. To achieve this overcoming, she has to be led through the primal period of her mental development and on that path she has to acquire the extra piece of mental freedom which distinguishes conscious mental activity—in the systematic sense—from unconscious.

The analytic psychotherapist thus has a threefold battle to wage—in his own mind against the forces which seek to drag him down from the analytic level; outside the analysis, against opponents who dispute the importance he attaches to the sexual instinctual forces and hinder him from making use of them in his scientific technique; and inside the analysis, against his patients, who at first behave like opponents but later on reveal the overvaluation of sexual life which dominates them, and who try to make him captive to their socially untamed passion.

* * *

A Special Type of Choice of Object Made by Men (Contributions to the Psychology of Love I)

Freud never wrote a book on love though, to be sure, the idea pervades his work. What he produced instead were three papers written between 1910 and 1917 and published separately. He then joined them in 1918 under the collective title "Contributions to the Psychology of Love" in Series IV of his shorter papers on neuroses. While they deal with symptoms such as the separation of the ability to love from the desire for sexual gratification, psychological impotence, fantasies of the mother as whore and rescue fantasies, and other instances accompanying neurosis, these papers also shed much illumination on the "normal" ways of loving. In his definition of love as the confluence of two currents—erotic and affectionate—Freud was for once in tune with respectable opinion.

Up till now we have left it to the creative writer to depict for us the 'necessary conditions for loving' which govern people's choice of an object, and the way in which they bring the demands of their imagination into harmony with reality. The writer can indeed draw on certain qualities which fit him to carry out such a task: above all, on a sensitivity that enables him to perceive the hidden impulses in the minds of other people, and the courage to let his own unconscious speak. But there is one circumstance which lessens the evidential value of what he has to say. Writers are under the necessity to produce intellectual and aesthetic pleasure, as well as certain emotional effects. For this reason they cannot reproduce the stuff of reality unchanged, but must isolate portions of it, remove disturbing associations, tone down the whole and fill in what is missing. These are the privileges of what is known as 'poetic licence'. Moreover they can show only slight interest in the origin and development of the mental states which they portray in their completed form. In consequence it becomes inevitable that science should concern herself with the same materials whose treatment by artists has given enjoyment to mankind for thousands of years, though her touch must be clumsier and the yield of pleasure less. These observations will, it may be hoped, serve to justify us in extending a strictly scientific treatment to the field of human love. Science is, after all, the most complete renunciation of the pleasure principle of which our mental activity is capable.

In the course of psycho-analytic treatment there are ample opportunities for collecting impressions of the way in which neurotics behave in love; while at the same time we can recall having observed or heard of similar behaviour in people of average health or even in those with outstanding qualities. When the material happens to be favourable and thus leads to an accumulation of such impressions, distinct types emerge more clearly. I will begin here with a description of one such type of object-choice—which occurs in men—since it is characterized by a number of 'necessary conditions for loving' whose combination is unintelligible, and indeed bewildering, and since it admits of a simple explanation on psycho-analytic lines.

(1) The first of these preconditions for loving can be described as positively specific: wherever it is found, the presence of the other characteristics of this type may be looked for. It may be termed the precondition that there should be 'an injured third party'; it stipulates that the person in question shall never choose as his love-object a woman who is disengaged—that is, an unmarried girl or an unattached married woman—but only one to whom another man can claim right of possession as her husband, fiancé or friend. In some cases this precondition proves so cogent that a woman can be ignored, or even rejected, so long as she does not belong to any man, but becomes the object of passionate feelings immediately she comes into one of these relationships with another man.

(2) The second precondition is perhaps a less constant one, but it is no less striking. It has to be found in conjunction with the first for the type to be realized, whereas the first precondition seems very often to occur independently as well. This second precondition is to the effect that a woman who is chaste and whose reputation is irreproachable never exercises an attraction that might raise her to the status of a love-object, but only a woman who is in some way or other of bad repute sexually, whose fidelity and reliability are open to some doubt. This latter characteristic may vary within substantial limits, from the faint breath of scandal attaching to a married woman who is not averse to a flirtation up to the openly promiscuous way of life of a *cocotte* or of an adept in the art of love; but the men who belong to our type will not be satisfied without something of the kind. This second necessary condition may be termed, rather crudely, 'love for a prostitute'.

While the first precondition provides an opportunity for gratifying impulses of rivalry and hostility directed at the man from whom the loved woman is wrested, the second one, that of the woman's being like a prostitute, is connected with the experiencing of *jealousy*, which appears to be a necessity for lovers of this type. It is only when they are able to be jealous that their passion reaches its height and the woman acquires her full value, and they never fail to seize on an occasion that allows them to experience these most powerful emotions. What is strange is that it is not the lawful possessor of the loved one who becomes the target of this jealousy, but strangers, making their appearance for the first time, in relation to whom the loved one can be brought under suspicion. In glaring instances the lover shows no wish for exclusive possession of the woman and seems to be perfectly comfortable in the triangular situation. One of my patients, who had been made to suffer terribly by his lady's escapades, had no objection to her getting married, and did all he could to bring it about; in the years that followed he never showed a trace of jealousy towards her husband. Another typical patient had, it is true, been very jealous of the husband in his first love affair, and had forced the lady to stop having marital relations; but in his numerous subsequent affairs he behaved like the other members of this type and no longer regarded the lawful husband as an interference.

So much for the conditions required in the love-object. The following points describe the lover's behaviour towards the object he has chosen.

(3) In normal love the woman's value is measured by her sexual integrity, and is reduced by any approach to the characteristic of being like a prostitute. Hence the fact that women with this characteristic are considered by men of our type to be *love-objects of the highest value* seems to be a striking departure from the normal. Their love-relationships with these women are carried on with the highest expenditure of mental energy, to the exclusion of all other interests; they are felt as the only people whom it is possible to love, and the demand for fidelity which the lover makes upon himself is repeated again and again, however often it may be broken in reality. These features of the love-relationships which I am here describing show their *compulsive* nature very clearly, though that is something which is found up to a certain degree whenever anyone falls in love. But the fidelity and intensity that mark the attachment must not lead one to expect that a single love-relationship of this kind will make up the whole erotic life of the person in question or occur only once in it. On the contrary, passionate attachments of this sort are repeated with the same peculiarities—each an exact replica of the others—again and again in the lives of men of this type; in fact, owing to external events such as changes of residence and environment, the love-objects may replace one another so frequently that a *long series of them is formed*.

(4) What is most startling of all to the observer in lovers of this type is the urge they show to 'rescue' the woman they love. The man is convinced that she is in need of him, that without him she would lose all moral control and rapidly sink to a lamentable level. He rescues her, therefore, by not giving her up. In some individual cases the idea of having to rescue her can be justified by reference to her sexual unreliability and the dangers of her social position: but it is no less conspicuous

where there is no such basis in reality. One man of the type I am describing, who knew how to win his ladies by clever methods of seduction and subtle arguments, spared no efforts in the subsequent course of these affairs to keep the woman he was for the time being in love with on the path of 'virtue' by presenting her with tracts of his own composition.

If we survey the different features of the picture presented here—the conditions imposed on the man that his loved one should not be unattached and should be like a prostitute, the high value he sets on her, his need for feeling jealousy, his fidelity, which is nevertheless compatible with being broken down into a long series of instances, and the urge to rescue the woman—it will seem scarcely probable that they should all be derived from a single source. Yet psycho-analytic exploration into the life-histories of men of this type has no difficulty in showing that there is such a single source. The object-choice which is so strangely conditioned, and this very singular way of behaving in love, have the same psychical origin as we find in the loves of normal people. They are derived from the infantile fixation of tender feelings on the mother, and represent one of the consequences of that fixation. In normal love only a few characteristics survive which reveal unmistakably the maternal prototype of the object-choice, as, for instance, the preference shown by young men for maturer women; the detachment of libido from the mother has been effected relatively swiftly. In our type, on the other hand, the libido has remained attached to the mother for so long, even after the onset of puberty, that the maternal characteristics remain stamped on the love-objects that are chosen later, and all these turn into easily recognizable mother-surrogates. The comparison with the way in which the skull of a newly born child is shaped springs to mind at this point: after a protracted labour it always takes the form of a cast of the narrow part of the mother's pelvis.

We have now to show the plausibility of our assertion that the characteristic features of our type—its conditions for loving and its behaviour in love—do in fact arise from the psychical constellation connected with the mother. This would seem to be easiest where the first precondition is concerned—the condition that the woman should not be unattached, or that there should be an injured third party. It is at once clear that for the child who is growing up in the family circle the fact of the mother belonging to the father becomes an inseparable part of the mother's essence, and that the injured third party is none other than the father himself. The trait of overvaluing the loved one, and regarding her as unique and irreplaceable, can be seen to fall just as naturally into the context of the child's experience, for no one possesses more than one mother, and the relation to her is based on an event that is not open to any doubt and cannot be repeated.

If we are to understand the love-objects chosen by our type as being above all mother-surrogates, then the formation of a series of them, which seems so flatly to contradict the condition of being faithful to one, can now also be understood. We have learnt from psycho-analysis in other examples that the notion of something irreplaceable, when it is active in the unconscious, frequently appears as broken up into an endless series: endless for the reason that every surrogate nevertheless fails to provide the desired satisfaction. This is the explanation of the insatiable urge to ask questions shown by children at a certain age: they have one single question to ask, but it never crosses their lips. It explains, too, the garrulity of some people affected by neurosis; they are under the pressure of a secret which is burning to be disclosed but which, despite all temptation, they never reveal.

On the other hand the second precondition for loving—the condition that the object chosen should be like a prostitute—seems energetically to oppose a derivation from the mother-complex. The adult's conscious thought likes to regard his mother as a person of unimpeachable moral purity; and there are few ideas which he finds so offensive when they come from others, or feels as so tormenting when they spring from his own mind, as one which calls this aspect of his mother in question. This very relation of the sharpest contrast between 'mother' and 'prostitute' will however encourage us to enquire into the history of the development of these two complexes and the unconscious relation between them, since we long ago discovered that what, in the conscious, is found split into a pair of opposites often occurs in the unconscious as a unity. Investigation then leads us back to the time in a boy's life at which he first gains a more or less complete knowledge of the sexual relations between adults, somewhere about the years of pre-puberty. Brutal pieces of information, which are undisguisedly intended to arouse contempt and rebelliousness, now acquaint him with the secret of sexual life and destroy the authority of adults, which appears incompatible with the revelation of their sexual activities. The aspect of these disclosures which affects the newly initiated child most strongly is the way in which they apply to his own parents. This ~pplication is often flatly rejected by him, in some such words as these: 'Your parents and other people may do something like that with one another, but my parents can't possibly do it.'

As an almost invariable corollary to this sexual enlightenment, the boy at the same time gains a knowledge of the existence of certain women who practise sexual intercourse as a means of livelihood, and who are for this reason held in general contempt. The boy himself is necessarily far from feeling this contempt: as soon as he learns that he too can be initiated by these unfortunates into sexual life, which till then he accepted as being reserved exclusively for 'grown-ups', he regards them only with a mixture of longing and horror. When after this he can no longer maintain the doubt which makes his parents an exception to the universal and odious norms of sexual activity, he tells himself with cynical logic that the difference between his mother and a whore is not after all so very great, since basically they do the same thing. The enlightening information he has received has in fact awakened the memory-traces of the impressions and wishes of his early infancy, and these have led to a reactivation in him of certain mental impulses. He begins to desire his mother herself in the sense with which he has recently become acquainted, and to hate his father anew as a rival who stands in the way of this wish; he comes, as we say, under the dominance of the Oedipus complex. [1] He does not forgive his mother for having granted the favour of sexual intercourse not to himself but to his father, and he regards it as an act of unfaithfulness. If these impulses do not quickly pass, there is no outlet for them other than to run their course in phantasies which have as their subject his mother's sexual activities under the most diverse circumstances; and the consequent tension leads particularly readily to his finding relief in masturbation. As a result of the constant combined operation of the two driving forces, desire and thirst for revenge, phantasies of his mother's unfaithfulness are by far the most preferred; the lover with whom she commits her act of infidelity almost always exhibits the features of the boy's own ego, or more accurately, of his own idealized personality, grown up and so raised to a level with his father. What I have elsewhere[2] described as the 'family romance' comprises the manifold ramifications of this imaginative activity and the way in which they are interwoven with various egoistic interests of this period of life.

Now that we have gained an insight into this piece of mental development we can no longer regard it as contradictory and incomprehensible that the precondition of the loved one's being like a prostitute should derive directly from the mother-complex. The type of male love which we have described bears the traces of this evolution and is simple to understand as a fixation on the phantasies formed by the boy in puberty—phantasies which have later after all found a way out into real life. There is no difficulty in assuming that the masturbation assiduously practised in the years of puberty has played its part in the fixation of the phantasies.

To these phantasies which have succeeded in dominating the man's love in real life, the urge to *rescue* the loved one seems to bear merely a loose and superficial relation, and one that is fully accounted for by conscious reasons. By her propensity to be fickle and unfaithful the loved one brings herself into dangerous situations, and thus it is understandable that the lover should be at pains to protect her from these dangers by watching over her virtue and counteracting her bad inclinations. However, the study of people's screen-memories, phantasies and nocturnal dreams shows that we have here a particularly felicitous 'rationalization' of an unconscious motive, a process which may be compared to a

1. [This appears to be Freud's first published use of the actual term. The concept had, of course, long been familiar to him.]

2. In [a discussion included in] Rank's *The Myth of the Birth of the Hero* (1909).

successful secondary revision of a dream. In actual fact the 'rescue-*motif*' has a meaning and history of its own, and is an independent derivative of the mother-complex, or more accurately, of the parental complex. When a child hears that he *owes his life* to his parents, or that his mother *gave him life*, his feelings of tenderness unite with impulses which strive at power and independence, and they generate the wish to return this gift to the parents and to repay them with one of equal value. It is as though the boy's defiance were to make him say: 'I want nothing from my father; I will give him back all I have cost him.' He then forms the phantasy of *rescuing his father from danger and saving his life*; in this way he puts his account square with him. This phantasy is commonly enough displaced on to the emperor, king or some other great man; after being thus distorted it becomes admissible to consciousness, and may even be made use of by creative writers. In its application to a boy's father it is the defiant meaning in the idea of rescuing which is by far the most important; where his mother is concerned it is usually its tender meaning. The mother gave the child life, and it is not easy to find a substitute of equal value for this unique gift. With a slight change of meaning, such as is easily affected in the unconscious and is comparable to the way in which in consciousness concepts shade into one another, rescuing his mother takes on the significance of giving her a child or making a child for her—needless to say, one like himself. This is not too remote from the original sense of rescuing, and the change in meaning is not an arbitrary one. His mother gave him a life—his own life— and in exchange he gives her another life, that of a child which has the greatest resemblance to himself. The son shows his gratitude by wishing to have by his mother a son who is like himself: in other words, in the rescue-phantasy he is completely identifying himself with his father. All his instincts, those of tenderness, gratitude, lustfulness, defiance and independence, find satisfaction in the single wish *to be his own father*. Even the element of danger has not been lost in the change of meaning; for the act of birth itself is the danger from which he was saved by his mother's efforts. Birth is both the first of all dangers to life and the prototype of all the later ones that cause us to feel anxiety, and the experience of birth has probably left behind in us the expression of affect which we call anxiety. Macduff of the Scottish legend, who was not born of his mother but ripped from her womb, was for that reason unacquainted with anxiety.[3]

Artemidorus, the dream-interpreter of antiquity, was certainly right in maintaining that the meaning of a dream depends on who the dreamer happens to be. Under the laws governing the expression of unconscious thoughts, the meaning of rescuing may vary, depending on whether the author of the phantasy is a man or a woman. It can equally mean (in a man) making a child, i.e. causing it to be born, or (in a woman) giving

3. [*Macbeth*, V, 7. This is Freud's first extended allusion to the relation between birth and anxiety. {See below, pp. 773–83.}]

birth oneself to a child. These various meanings of rescuing in dreams and phantasies can be recognized particularly clearly when they are found in connection with water. A man rescuing a woman from the water in a dream means that he makes her a mother, which in the light of the preceding discussion amounts to making her his own mother. A woman rescuing someone else (a child) from the water acknowledges herself in this way as the mother who bore him, like Pharoah's daughter in the legend of Moses (Rank, 1909). At times there is also a tender meaning contained in rescue-phantasies directed towards the father. In such cases they aim at expressing the subject's wish to have his father as a son—that is, to have a son who is like his father.

It is on account of all these connections between the rescue-*motif* and the parental complex that the urge to rescue the loved one forms an important feature of the type of loving which I have been discussing.

* * *

On the Universal Tendency to Debasement in the Sphere of Love
(Contributions to the Psychology of Love II)

Freud's second paper on love, published in 1912, takes up the vexed issue of psychological impotence and offers psychoanalytic thoughts on its etiology. In its references to women, it also raises for the historian some interesting questions about how time-bound Freud's observations on the impact of culture on the psyche may be: things have changed, and are changing, for women in the world, and much of what Freud says about their inhibited lives is no longer quite applicable. He borrows and amends a famous saying of Napoleon's on politics: "Anatomy is destiny," which holds less true than in his day. In the concluding passages not included here, Freud supposes that civilization, frustrating as it does much erotic desire, acts as the enemy of the individual. It is a point he had made before and would make again, extensively, in *Civilization and its Discontents* (see below, pp. 722–72). (One technical cavil on the translation: the original German title of this paper is "Über die allgemeinste Erniedrigung des Liebeslebens," which is, correctly, "On the most common degradation in love life." Freud, then, does not argue, as the English title mistakenly has it, that there is some "universal tendency to debasement.")

I

If the practising psycho-analyst asks himself on account of what disorder people most often come to him for help, he is bound to reply—disregarding the many forms of anxiety—that it is psychical impotence. This singular disturbance affects men of strongly libidinous natures, and manifests itself in a refusal by the executive organs of sexuality to carry out the sexual act, although before and after they may show themselves to be intact and capable of performing the act, and although a strong psychical inclination to carry it out is present. The first clue to understanding his condition is obtained by the sufferer himself on making the discovery that a failure of this kind only arises when the attempt is made with certain individuals; whereas with others there is never any question of such a failure. He now becomes aware that it is some feature of the sexual object which gives rise to the inhibition of his male potency, and sometimes he reports that he has a feeling of an obstacle inside him, the sensation of a counter-will which successfully interferes with his conscious intention. However, he is unable to guess what this internal obstacle is and what feature of the sexual object brings it into operation. If he has had repeated experience of a failure of this kind, he is likely, by the familiar process of 'erroneous connection', to decide that the recollection of the first occasion evoked the disturbing anxiety-idea and so caused the failure to be repeated each time; while he derives the first occasion itself from some 'accidental' impression.

Psycho-analytic studies of psychical impotence have already been carried out and published by several writers. Every analyst can confirm the explanations provided by them from his own clinical experience. It is in fact a question of the inhibitory influence of certain psychical complexes which are withdrawn from the subject's knowledge. An incestuous fixation on mother or sister, which has never been surmounted, plays a prominent part in this pathogenic material and is its most universal content. In addition there is the influence to be considered of accidental distressing impressions connected with infantile sexual activity, and also those factors which in a general way reduce the libido that is to be directed on to the female sexual object.

When striking cases of psychical impotence are exhaustively investigated by means of psycho-analysis, the following information is obtained about the psychosexual processes at work in them. Here again—as very probably in all neurotic disturbances—the foundation of the disorder is provided by an inhibition in the developmental history of the libido before it assumes the form which we take to be its normal termination. Two currents whose union is necessary to ensure a completely normal attitude in love have, in the cases we are considering, failed to combine. These two may be distinguished as the *affectionate* and the *sensual* current.

The affectionate current is the older of the two. It springs from the earliest years of childhood; it is formed on the basis of the interests of the self-preservative instinct and is directed to the members of the family and those who look after the child. From the very beginning it carries along with it contributions from the sexual instincts—components of erotic interest—which can already be seen more or less clearly even in childhood and in any event are uncovered in neurotics by psycho-analysis later on. It corresponds to *the child's primary object-choice*. We learn in this way that the sexual instincts find their first objects by

attaching themselves to the valuations made by the ego-instincts, precisely in the way in which the first sexual satisfactions are experienced
in attachment to the bodily functions necessary for the preservation of
life. The 'affection' shown by the child's parents and those who look
after him, which seldom fails to betray its erotic nature ('the child is an
erotic play-thing'), does a very great deal to raise the contributions made
by erotism to the cathexes of his ego-instincts, and to increase them to
an amount which is bound to play a part in his later development,
especially when certain other circumstances lend their support.

These affectionate fixations of the child persist throughout childhood,
and continually carry along with them erotism, which is consequently
diverted from its sexual aims. Then at the age of puberty they are joined
by the powerful 'sensual' current which no longer mistakes its aims. It
never fails, apparently, to follow the earlier paths and to cathect the
objects of the primary infantile choice with quotas of libido that are now
far stronger. Here, however, it runs up against the obstacles that have
been erected in the meantime by the barrier against incest; consequently
it will make efforts to pass on from these objects which are unsuitable
in reality, and find a way as soon as possible to other, extraneous objects
with which a real sexual life may be carried on. These new objects will
still be chosen on the model (imago) of the infantile ones, but in the
course of time they will attract to themselves the affection that was tied
to the earlier ones. A man shall leave his father and his mother—
according to the biblical command {Genesis ii, 24}—and shall cleave
unto his wife; affection and sensuality are then united. The greatest
intensity of sensual passion will bring with it the highest psychical valuation of the object—this being the normal overvaluation of the sexual
object on the part of a man.

Two factors will decide whether this advance in the developmental
path of the libido is to fail. First, there is the amount of *frustration in
reality* which opposes the new object-choice and reduces its value for
the person concerned. There is after all no point in embarking upon an
object-choice if no choice is to be allowed at all or if there is no prospect
of being able to choose anything suitable. Secondly, there is the amount
of *attraction* which the infantile objects that have to be relinquished are
able to exercise, and which is in proportion to the erotic cathexis attaching to them in childhood. If these two factors are sufficiently strong,
the general mechanism by which the neuroses are formed comes into
operation. The libido turns away from reality, is taken over by imaginative activity (the process of introversion), strengthens the images of
the first sexual objects and becomes fixated to them. The obstacle raised
against incest, however, compels the libido that has turned to these
objects to remain in the unconscious. The masturbatory activity carried
out by the sensual current, which is now part of the unconscious, makes
its own contribution in strengthening this fixation. Nothing is altered

in this state of affairs if the advance which has miscarried in reality is now completed in phantasy, and if in the phantasy-situations that lead to masturbatory satisfaction the original sexual objects are replaced by different ones. As a result of this substitution the phantasies become admissible to consciousness, but no progress is made in the allocation of the libido in reality. In this way it can happen that the whole of a young man's sensuality becomes tied to incestuous objects in the unconscious, or to put it another way, becomes fixed to unconscious incestuous phantasies. The result is then total impotence, which is perhaps further ensured by the simultaneous onset of an actual weakening of the organs that perform the sexual act.

Less severe conditions are required to bring about the state known specifically as psychical impotence. Here the fate of the sensual current must not be that its whole charge has to conceal itself behind the affectionate current; it must have remained sufficiently strong or uninhibited to secure a partial outlet into reality. The sexual activity of such people shows the clearest signs, however, that it has not the whole psychical driving force of the instinct behind it. It is capricious, easily disturbed, often not properly carried out, and not accompanied by much pleasure. But above all it is forced to avoid the affectionate current. A restriction has thus been placed on object-choice. The sensual current that has remained active seeks only objects which do not recall the incestuous figures forbidden to it; if someone makes an impression that might lead to a high psychical estimation of her, this impression does not find an issue in any sensual excitation but in affection which has no erotic effect. The whole sphere of love in such people remains divided in the two directions personified in art as sacred and profane (or animal) love. Where they love they do not desire and where they desire they cannot love. They seek objects which they do not need to love, in order to keep their sensuality away from the objects they love; and, in accordance with the laws of {what Jung calls} 'complexive sensitiveness' and of the return of the repressed, the strange failure shown in psychical impotence makes its appearance whenever an object which has been chosen with the aim of avoiding incest recalls the prohibited object through some feature, often an inconspicuous one.

The main protective measure against such a disturbance which men have recourse to in this split in their love consists in a psychical *debasement* of the sexual object, the overvaluation that normally attaches to the sexual object being reserved for the incestuous object and its representatives. As soon as the condition of debasement is fulfilled, sensuality can be freely expressed, and important sexual capacities and a high degree of pleasure can develop. There is a further factor which contributes to this result. People in whom there has not been a proper confluence of the affectionate and the sensual currents do not usually show much refinement in their modes of behaviour in love; they have retained perverse sexual aims whose nonfulfilment is felt as a serious loss of pleasure, and whose fulfilment on the other hand seems possible only with a debased and despised sexual object.

We can now understand the motives behind the boy's phantasies mentioned in the first of these 'Contributions' which degrade the mother to the level of a prostitute. They are efforts to bridge the gulf between the two currents in love, at any rate in phantasy, and by debasing the mother to acquire her as an object of sensuality.

II

In the preceding section we have approached the study of psychical impotence from a medico-psychological angle of which the title of this paper gives no indication. It will however become clear that this introduction was required by us to provide an approach to our proper subject.

We have reduced psychical impotence to the failure of the affectionate and the sensual currents in love to combine, and this developmental inhibition has in turn been explained as being due to the influences of strong childhood fixations and of later frustration in reality through the intervention of the barrier against incest. There is one principal objection to the theory we advance; it does too much. It explains why certain people suffer from psychical impotence, but it leaves us with the apparent mystery of how others have been able to escape this disorder. Since we must recognize that all the relevant factors known to us—the strong childhood fixation, the incest-barrier and the frustration in the years of development after puberty—are to be found in practically all civilized human beings, we should be justified in expecting psychical impotence to be a universal affliction under civilization and not a disorder confined to some individuals.

It would be easy to escape from this conclusion by pointing to the quantitative factor in the causation of illness—to the greater or lesser extent of the contribution made by the various elements which determine whether a recognizable illness results or not. But although I accept this answer as correct, it is not my intention to make it a reason for rejecting the conclusion itself. On the contrary, I shall put forward the view that psychical impotence is much more widespread than is supposed, and that a certain amount of this behaviour does in fact characterize the love of civilized man.

If the concept of psychical impotence is broadened and is not restricted to failure to perform the act of coitus in circumstances where a desire to obtain pleasure is present and the genital apparatus is intact, we may in the first place add all those men who are described as psychanaesthetic: men who never fail in the act but who carry it out without getting any particular pleasure from it—a state of affairs that is more common than one would think. Psycho-analytic examination of such cases discloses the same aetiological factors as we found in psychical impotence in the narrower sense, without at first arriving at any explanation of the difference between their symptoms. An easily justifiable analogy takes one from these anaesthetic men to the immense number of frigid women; and there is no better way to describe or understand their behaviour in love than by comparing it with the more conspicuous disorder of psychical impotence in men.[1]

If however we turn our attention not to an extension of the concept of psychical impotence, but to the gradations in its symptomatology, we cannot escape the conclusion that the behaviour in love of men in the civilized world to-day bears the stamp altogether of psychical impotence. There are only a very few educated people in whom the two currents of affection and sensuality have become properly fused; the man almost always feels his respect for the woman acting as a restriction on his sexual activity, and only develops full potency when he is with a debased sexual object; and this in its turn is partly caused by the entrance of perverse components into his sexual aims, which he does not venture to satisfy with a woman he respects. He is assured of complete sexual pleasure only when he can devote himself unreservedly to obtaining satisfaction, which with his well-brought-up wife, for instance, he does not dare to do. This is the source of his need for a debased sexual object, a woman who is ethically inferior, to whom he need attribute no aesthetic scruples, who does not know him in his other social relations and cannot judge him in them. It is to such a woman that he prefers to devote his sexual potency, even when the whole of his affection belongs to a woman of a higher kind. It is possible, too, that the tendency so often observed in men of the highest classes of society to choose a woman of a lower class as a permanent mistress or even as a wife is nothing but a consequence of their need for a debased sexual object, to whom, psychologically, the possibility of complete satisfaction is linked.

I do not hesitate to make the two factors at work in psychical impotence in the strict sense—the factors of intense incestuous fixation in childhood and the frustration by reality in adolescence—responsible, too, for this extremely common characteristic of the love of civilized men. It sounds not only disagreeable but also paradoxical, yet it must nevertheless be said that anyone who is to be really free and happy in love must have surmounted his respect for women and have come to terms with the idea of incest with his mother or sister. Anyone who subjects himself to a serious self-examination on the subject of this requirement will be sure to find that he regards the sexual act basically as something degrading, which defiles and pollutes not only the body. The origin of this low opinion, which he will certainly not willingly acknowledge, must be looked for in the period of his youth in which the sensual current in him was already strongly developed but its satisfaction with

---

1. I am at the same time very willing to admit that frigidity in women is a complex subject which can also be approached from another angle. {Freud explores this other angle in the third and last contribution to the psychology of love, "The Taboo of Virginity," SE XI, 191–208.}

an object outside the family was almost as completely prohibited as it was with an incestuous one.

In our civilized world women are under the influence of a similar after-effect of their upbringing, and, in addition, of their reaction to men's behaviour. It is naturally just as unfavourable for a woman if a man approaches her without his full potency as it is if his initial over-valuation of her when he is in love gives place to undervaluation after he has possessed her. In the case of women there is little sign of a need to debase their sexual object. This is no doubt connected with the absence in them as a rule of anything similar to the sexual overvaluation found in men. But their long holding back from sexuality and the lingering of their sensuality in phantasy has another important consequence for them. They are subsequently often unable to undo the connection be-tween sensual activity and the prohibition, and prove to be psychically impotent, that is, frigid, when such activity is at last allowed them. This is the origin of the endeavour made by many women to keep even legitimate relations secret for a while; and of the capacity of other women for normal sensation as soon as the condition of prohibition is re-estab-lished by a secret love affair: unfaithful to their husband, they are able to keep a second order of faith with their lover.

* * *

From the History of an Infantile Neurosis ("Wolf Man")

Freud's case history of the "Wolf Man" did not reach print until 1918. But he had written it down in the fall of 1914, a few months after the Wolf Man had graduated from what Freud once beautifully called, in his case history of the Rat Man, his "school of suffering." The war that erupted in early August 1914 forced a postponement of its publication. With its po-lemical edge—"I was still freshly under the impression of the twisted re-interpretations which C. G. Jung and Alfred Adler were endeavouring to give to the findings of psycho-analysis," Freud wrote in a long introductory footnote to the published case history—it stands as a culmination of his prewar phase. It was to distance himself from Jung and Adler that Freud took particular care to focus on the Wolf Man's *childhood* neurosis, and on the convoluted evolution of his sexuality. Freud's editors have called the history of the Wolf Man "the most elaborate and no doubt the most important of all Freud's case histories" (SE XVII, 3), and one can see why. The question whether the Wolf Man's "observation" of his parents in sexual intercourse was a faithful memory or a fantasy is only one of the fascinating cruxes that abound in this case. Certainly the Wolf Man's dream that proved so pivotal in the unraveling of his complicated and deep-seated neurosis ranks with the most celebrated dreams in psychoanalytic history. It rivals Freud's Irma dream of July 1895, which initiated dream analysis. (See above, pp. 130–42.)

The rich and appealing twenty-three-year-old Russian aristocrat, Sergei Pankeieff, who came to consult Freud in February 1910 after several futile attempts to find relief from his mental misery in treatment with eminent and expensive specialists, was close to psychosis—indeed, later psychoanalysts reanalyzing the case have considered the Wolf Man's suffering to be more severe than Freud had indicated. He was, Freud noted, dependent on his personal attendants and virtually unable to take care of himself. From the outset, the Wolf Man showed himself an interesting but extremely difficult case. After the opening session, Freud noted confidentially on February 13, 1910, in a letter to Sándor Ferenczi, that his new patient had "confessed to me the following transferences: Jewish swindler, he would like to use me from behind and shit on my head" (see Gay, *Freud*, p. 287). Despite this dramatic opening, the Wolf Man participated in his analysis intellectually—but not emotionally: for years, long after he had reported his crucial dream to Freud, the Wolf Man remained, in Freud's words, "unassailably entrenched" in his posture of "submissive indifference. He listened, understood, and did not permit anything to touch him." In this predicament, Freud in the spring of 1913 fixed a termination date for the analysis a year hence. This threat made the Wolf Man give up his resistances and produce new material, thus bringing the analysis to what Freud described as a successful conclusion. Freud had adopted a most risky technique: once set, the terminal date could not be postponed without ruining the analyst's authority. Recalling his unorthodox procedure many years later, Freud put it bluntly: "A lion springs only once" ("Analysis Terminable and Interminable" [1937], *SE* XXIII, 219).

There is still more drama to this case than this. On June 28, 1914, on a hot Viennese Sunday, the Wolf Man, about to conclude his treatment, took a long walk and mused on the analysis that had dominated and changed his life for over four years. He felt well, was about to marry. As he returned to his rooms, the maid presented him with extra editions of the afternoon newspaper featuring screaming headlines: the Archduke Franz Ferdinand and the Archduchess had been assassinated at Sarajevo. A little more than a month later, the world was at war.

---

* * *

* * * The analysis of children's neuroses can claim to possess a specially high theoretical interest. They afford us, roughly speaking, as much help towards a proper understanding of the neuroses of adults as do children's dreams in respect to the dreams of adults. Not, indeed, that they are more perspicuous or poorer in elements; in fact, the difficulty of feeling one's way into the mental life of a child makes them set the physician a particularly difficult task. But nevertheless, so many of the later deposits are wanting in them that the essence of the neurosis springs to the eyes with unmistakable distinctness. In the present phase of the battle which is raging round psycho-analysis the resistance to its findings has, as we know, taken on a new form. People were content formerly to dispute the reality of the facts which are asserted by analysis; and for this purpose the best technique seemed to be to avoid examining them. That procedure appears to be slowly exhausting itself; and people are now adopting another plan—of recognizing the facts, but of eliminating, by means of twisted interpretations, the consequences that follow from them, so that the critics can still ward off the objectionable novelties as efficiently as ever. The study of children's neuroses exposes the complete inadequacy of these shallow or high-handed attempts at re-interpretation. It shows the predominant part that is played in the formation of neuroses by those libidinal motive forces which are so eagerly disavowed, and reveals the absence of any aspirations towards remote cultural aims, of which the child still knows nothing, and which cannot therefore be of any significance for him.

Another characteristic which makes the present analysis noteworthy is connected with the severity of the illness and the duration of the treatment. Analyses which lead to a favourable conclusion in a short time are of value in ministering to the therapeutist's self-esteem and substantiate the medical importance of psycho-analysis; but they remain for the most part insignificant as regards the advancement of scientific knowledge. Nothing new is learnt from them. In fact they only succeed so quickly because everything that was necessary for their accomplishment was already known. Something new can only be gained from analyses that present special difficulties, and to the overcoming of these a great deal of time has to be devoted. Only in such cases do we succeed in descending into the deepest and most primitive strata of mental development and in gaining from there solutions for the problems of the later formations. And we feel afterwards that, strictly speaking, only an analysis which has penetrated so far deserves the name. Naturally a single case does not give us all the information that we should like to have. Or, to put it more correctly, it might teach us everything, if we were only in a position to make everything out, and if we were not compelled by the inexperience of our own perception to content ourselves with a little.

As regards these fertile difficulties the case I am about to discuss left nothing to be desired. The first years of the treatment produced scarcely any change. Owing to a fortunate concatenation, all the external circumstances nevertheless combined to make it possible to proceed with the therapeutic experiment. I can easily believe that in less favourable circumstances the treatment would have been given up after a short time. Of the physician's point of view I can only declare that in a case of this kind he must behave as 'timelessly' as the unconscious itself, if he wishes to learn anything or to achieve anything. And in the end he will succeed in doing so, if he has the strength to renounce any short-sighted therapeutic ambition. It is not to be expected that the amount of patience, adaptability, insight, and confidence demanded of the patient and his relatives will be forthcoming in many other cases. But the analyst has a right to feel that the results which he has attained from such lengthy work in one case will help substantially to reduce the length of the treatment in a subsequent case of equal severity, and that by submitting on a single occasion to the timelessness of the unconscious he will be brought nearer to vanquishing it in the end.

The patient with whom I am here concerned remained for a long time unassailably entrenched behind an attitude of obliging apathy. He listened, understood, and remained unapproachable. His unimpeachable intelligence was, as it were, cut off from the instinctual forces which governed his behaviour in the few relations of life that remained to him. It required a long education to induce him to take an independent share in the work; and when as a result of this exertion he began for the first time to feel relief, he immediately gave up working in order to avoid any further changes, and in order to remain comfortably in the situation which had been thus established. His shrinking from a self-sufficient existence was so great as to outweigh all the vexations of his illness. Only one way was to be found of overcoming it. I was obliged to wait until his attachment to myself had become strong enough to counterbalance this shrinking, and then played off this one factor against the other. I determined—but not until trustworthy signs had led me to judge that the right moment had come—that the treatment must be brought to an end at a particular fixed date, no matter how far it had advanced. I was resolved to keep to the date; and eventually the patient came to see that I was in earnest. Under the inexorable pressure of this fixed limit his resistance and his fixation to the illness gave way, and now in a disproportionately short time the analysis produced all the material which made it possible to clear up his inhibitions and remove his symptoms. All the information, too, which enabled me to understand his infantile neurosis is derived from this last period of the work, during which resistance temporarily disappeared and the patient gave an impression of lucidity which is usually attainable only in hypnosis.

Thus the course of this treatment illustrates a maxim whose truth has long been appreciated in the technique of analysis. The length of the road over which an analysis must travel with the patient, and the quantity of material which must be mastered on the way, are of no importance in comparison with the resistance which is met with in the course of the work, and are only of importance at all in so far as they are necessarily proportional to the resistance. The situation is the same as when to-day an enemy army needs weeks and months to make its way across a stretch of country which in times of peace was traversed by an express train in a few hours and which only a short time before had been passed over by the defending army in a few days.

A third peculiarity of the analysis which is to be described in these pages has only increased my difficulty in deciding to make a report upon it. On the whole its results have coincided in the most satisfactory manner with our previous knowledge, or have been easily embodied into it. Many details, however, seemed to me myself to be so extraordinary and incredible that I felt some hesitation in asking other people to believe them. I requested the patient to make the strictest criticism of his recollections, but he found nothing improbable in his statements and adhered closely to them. Readers may at all events rest assured that I myself am only reporting what I came upon as an independent experience, uninfluenced by my expectation. So that there was nothing left for me but to remember the wise saying that there are more things in heaven and earth than are dreamed of in our philosophy. Anyone who could succeed in eliminating his pre-existing convictions even more thoroughly could no doubt discover even more such things.

* * *

IV

THE DREAM AND THE PRIMAL SCENE

I have already published this dream elsewhere,[1] on account of the quantity of material in it which is derived from fairy tales; and I will begin by repeating what I wrote on that occasion:

' "I dreamt that it was night and that I was lying in my bed. (My bed stood with its foot towards the window; in front of the window there was a row of old walnut trees. I know it was winter when I had the dream, and night-time.) Suddenly the window opened of its own accord, and I was terrified to see that some white wolves were sitting on the big walnut tree in front of the window. There were six or seven of them. The wolves were quite white, and looked more like foxes or sheep-dogs, for they had big tails like foxes and they had their ears pricked like dogs when they pay attention to something. In great terror, evidently of being eaten up by the wolves, I screamed and woke up. My nurse hurried to my bed, to see what had happened to me. It took quite a long while before I was convinced that it had only been a dream; I had had such a clear and life-like picture of the window opening and the wolves sitting on the tree. At last I grew quieter, felt as though I had escaped from some danger, and went to sleep again.

' "The only piece of action in the dream was the opening of the window; for the wolves sat quite still and without making any movement on the branches of the tree, to the right and left of the trunk, and looked at me. It seemed as though they had riveted their whole attention upon me.—I think this was my first anxiety-dream. I was three, four, or at most five years old at the time. From then until my eleventh or twelfth

1. "The Occurrence in Dreams of Material from Fairy Tales" (1913) {SE XII, 279–87}.

year I was always afraid of seeing something terrible in my dreams."

'He added a drawing of the tree with the wolves, which confirmed his description (Fig. 1). The analysis of the dream brought the following material to light.

'He had always connected this dream with the recollection that during these years of his childhood he was most tremendously afraid of the picture of a wolf in a book of fairy tales. His elder sister, who was very much his superior, used to tease him by holding up this particular picture in front of him on some excuse or other, so that he was terrified and began to scream. In this picture the wolf was standing upright, striding out with one foot, with its claws stretched out and its ears pricked. He thought this picture must have been an illustration to the story of "Little Red Riding-Hood".

'Why were the wolves white? This made him think of the sheep, large flocks of which were kept in the neighbourhood of the estate. His father occasionally took him with him to visit these flocks, and every time this happened he felt very proud and blissful. Later on—according to en- quiries that were made it may easily have been shortly before the time of the dream—an epidemic broke out among the sheep. His father sent for a follower of Pasteur's, who inoculated the animals, but after the inoculation even more of them died than before.

'How did the wolves come to be on the tree? This reminded him of a story that he had heard his grandfather tell. He could not remember whether it was before or after the dream, but its subject is a decisive argument in favour of the former view. The story ran as follows. A tailor was sitting at work in his room, when the window opened and a wolf leapt in. The tailor hit after him with his yard—no (he corrected himself), caught him by his tail and pulled it off, so that the wolf ran away in terror. Some time later the tailor went into the forest, and suddenly saw a pack of wolves coming towards him; so he climbed up a tree to escape from them. At first the wolves were in perplexity; but the maimed one, which was among them and wanted to revenge himself on the tailor, proposed that they should climb one upon another till the last one could reach him. He himself—he was a vigorous old fellow—would be the base of the pyramid. The wolves did as he suggested, but the tailor had recognized the visitor whom he had punished, and suddenly called out as he had before: "Catch the grey one by his tail!" The tailless wolf, terrified by the recollection, ran away, and all the others tumbled down.

'In this story the tree appears, upon which the wolves were sitting in the dream. But it also contains an unmistakable allusion to the castration complex. The *old* wolf was docked of his tail by the tailor. The fox-tails of the wolves in the dream were probably compensations for this taillessness.

'Why were there six or seven wolves? There seemed to be no answer to this question, until I raised a doubt whether the picture that had frightened him could be connected with the story of "Little Red Riding-Hood". This fairy tale only offers an opportunity for two illustrations—Little Red Riding-Hood's meeting with the wolf in the wood, and the scene in which the wolf lies in bed in the grandmother's night-cap. There must therefore be some other fairy tale behind his recollection of the picture. He soon discovered that it could only be the story of "The Wolf and the Seven Little Goats". Here the number seven occurs, and also the number six, for the wolf only ate up six of the little goats, while the seventh hid itself in the clock-case. The white, too, comes into this story, for the wolf had his paw made white at the baker's after the little goats had recognized him on his first visit by his grey paw. Moreover, the two fairy tales have much in common. In both there is the eating up, the cutting open of the belly, the taking out of the people who have been eaten and their replacement by heavy stones, and finally in both of them the wicked wolf perishes. Besides all this, in the story of the little goats the tree appears. The wolf lay down under a tree after his meal and snored.

'I shall have, for a special reason, to deal with this dream again elsewhere, and interpret it and consider its significance in greater detail. For it is the earliest anxiety-dream that the dreamer remembered from his childhood, and its content, taken in connection with other dreams that followed it soon afterwards and with certain events in his earliest years, is of quite peculiar interest. We must confine ourselves here to the relation of the dream to the two fairy tales which have so much in common with each other, "Little Red Riding-Hood" and "The Wolf and the Seven Little Goats". The effect produced by these stories was shown in the little dreamer by a regular animal phobia. This phobia was only distinguished from other similar cases by the fact that the anxiety-animal was not an object easily accessible to observation (such as a horse or a dog), but was known to him only from stories and picture-books.

'I shall discuss on another occasion the explanation of these animal phobias and the significance attaching to them. I will only remark in anticipation that this explanation is in complete harmony with the principal characteristic shown by the neurosis from which the present dreamer suffered later in his life. His fear of his father was the strongest motive for his falling ill, and his ambivalent attitude towards every father-surrogate was the dominating feature of his life as well as of his behaviour during the treatment.

'If in my patient's case the wolf was merely a first father-surrogate, the question arises whether the hidden content in the fairy tales of the wolf that ate up the little goats and of "Little Red Riding-Hood" may not simply be infantile fear of the father. Moreover, my patient's father had the characteristic, shown by so many people in relation to their children, of indulging in "affectionate abuse"; and it is possible that during the patient's earlier years his father (though he grew severe later on) may more than once, as he caressed the little boy or played with him, have threatened in fun to "gobble him up". One of my patients told me that her two children could never get to be fond of their grand-father, because in the course of his affectionate romping with them he used to frighten them by saying he would cut open their tummies.'

Leaving on one side everything in this quotation that anticipates the dream's remoter implications, let us return to its immediate interpretation. I may remark that this interpretation was a task that dragged on over several years. The patient related the dream at a very early stage of the analysis and very soon came to share my conviction that the causes of his infantile neurosis lay concealed behind it. In the course of the treatment we often came back to the dream, but it was only during the last months of the analysis that it became possible to understand it completely, and only then thanks to spontaneous work on the patient's part. He had always emphasized the fact that two factors in the dream had made the greatest impression on him: first, the perfect stillness and immobility of the wolves, and secondly, the strained attention with which they all looked at him. The lasting sense of reality, too, which the dream left behind it, seemed to him to deserve notice.

Let us take this last remark as a starting-point. We know from our experience in interpreting dreams that this sense of reality carries a particular significance along with it. It assures us that some part of the latent material of the dream is claiming in the dreamer's memory to possess the quality of reality, that is, that the dream relates to an occurrence that really took place and was not merely imagined. It can naturally only be a question of the reality of something unknown; for instance, the conviction that his grandfather really told him the story of the tailor and the wolf, or that the stories of 'Little Red Riding-Hood' and of 'The Seven Little Goats' were really read aloud to him, would not be of a nature to be replaced by this sense of reality that outlasted the dream. The dream seemed to point to an occurrence the reality of which was very strongly emphasized as being in marked contrast to the unreality of the fairy tales.

If it was to be assumed that behind the content of the dream there lay some such unknown scene—one, that is, which had already been forgotten at the time of the dream—then it must have taken place very early. The dreamer, it will be recalled, said: 'I was three, four, or at most five years old at the time I had the dream.' And we can add: 'And I was reminded by the dream of something that must have belonged to an even earlier period.'

The parts of the manifest content of the dream which were emphasized by the dreamer, the factors of attentive looking and of motionlessness, must lead to the content of this scene. We must naturally expect to find that this material reproduces the unknown material of the scene in some distorted form, perhaps even distorted into its opposite.

There were several conclusions, too, to be drawn from the raw material which had been produced by the patient's first analysis of the dream, and these had to be fitted into the collocation of which we were in search. Behind the mention of the sheep-breeding, evidence was to be expected of his sexual researches, his interest in which he was able to gratify during his visits with his father; but there must also have been allusions to a fear of death, since the greater part of the sheep had died of the epidemic. The most obtrusive thing in the dream, the wolves on the tree, led straight to his grandfather's story; and what was fascinating about this story and capable of provoking the dream can scarcely have been anything but its connection with the theme of castration.

We also concluded from the first incomplete analysis of the dream that the wolf may have been a father-surrogate; so that, in that case, this first anxiety-dream would have brought to light the fear of his father which from that time forward was to dominate his life. This conclusion, indeed, was in itself not yet binding. But if we put together as the result of the provisional analysis what can be derived from the material produced by the dreamer, we then find before us for reconstruction some such fragments as these:

A *real occurrence—dating from a very early period—looking—immobility—sexual problems—castration—his father—something terrible.*

One day the patient began to continue with the interpretation of the dream. He thought that the part of the dream which said that 'suddenly the window opened of its own accord' was not completely explained by its connection with the window at which the tailor was sitting and through which the wolf came into the room. 'It must mean: "My eyes suddenly opened." I was asleep, therefore, and suddenly woke up, and as I woke I saw something: the tree with the wolves.' No objection could be made to this; but the point could be developed further. He had woken up and had seen something. The attentive looking, which in the dream was ascribed to the wolves, should rather be shifted on to him. At a decisive point, therefore, a transposition has taken place; and moreover this is indicated by another transposition in the manifest content of the dream. For the fact that the wolves were sitting on the tree was also a transposition, since in his grandfather's story they were underneath, and were unable to climb on to the tree.

What, then, if the other factor emphasized by the dreamer were also distorted by means of a transposition or reversal? In that case instead of immobility (the wolves sat there motionless; they looked at him, but did not move) the meaning would have to be: the most violent motion. That is to say, he suddenly woke up, and saw in front of him a scene of violent movement at which he looked with strained attention. In the one case the distortion would consist in an interchange of subject and object, of activity and passivity: being looked at instead of looking. In the other case it would consist in a transformation into the opposite; rest instead of motion.

On another occasion an association which suddenly occurred to him carried us another step forward in our understanding of the dream: 'The tree was a Christmas-tree.' He now knew that he had dreamt the dream shortly before Christmas and in expectation of it. Since Christmas Day was also his birthday, it now became possible to establish with certainty the date of the dream and of the change in him which proceeded from it. It was immediately before his fourth birthday. He had gone to sleep, then, in tense expectation of the day which ought to bring him a double quantity of presents. We know that in such circumstances a child may easily anticipate the fulfilment of his wishes. So it was already Christmas in his dream; the content of the dream showed him his Christmas box, the presents which were to be his were hanging on the tree. But instead of presents they had turned into—wolves, and the dream ended by his being overcome by fear of being eaten by the wolf (probably his father), and by his flying for refuge to his nurse. Our knowledge of his sexual development before the dream makes it possible for us to fill in the gaps in the dream and to explain the transformation of his satisfaction into anxiety. Of the wishes concerned in the formation of the dream the most powerful must have been the wish for the sexual satisfaction which he was at that time longing to obtain from his father. The strength of this wish made it possible to revive a long-forgotten trace in his memory of a scene which was able to show him what sexual satisfaction from his father was like; and the result was terror, horror of the fulfilment of the wish, the repression of the impulse which had manifested itself by means of the wish, and consequently a flight from his father to his less dangerous nurse.

The importance of this date of Christmas Day had been preserved in his supposed recollection of having had his first fit of rage because he was dissatisfied with his Christmas presents. The recollection combined elements of truth and of falsehood. It could not be entirely right, since according to the repeated declarations of his parents his naughtiness had already begun on their return in the autumn and it was not a fact that they had not come on till Christmas. But he had preserved the essential connection between his unsatisfied love, his rage, and Christmas.

But what picture can the nightly workings of his sexual desire have conjured up that could frighten him away so violently from the fulfilment for which he longed? The material of the analysis shows that there is one condition which this picture must satisfy. It must have been calculated to create a conviction of the reality of the existence of castration. Fear of castration could then become the motive power for the transformation of the affect.

I have now reached the point at which I must abandon the support I have hitherto had from the course of the analysis. I am afraid it will also be the point at which the reader's belief will abandon me.

What sprang into activity that night out of the chaos of the dreamer's unconscious memory-traces was the picture of copulation between his parents, copulation in circumstances which were not entirely usual and were especially favourable for observation. It gradually became possible to find satisfactory answers to all the questions that arose in connection with this scene; for in the course of the treatment the first dream returned in innumerable variations and new editions, in connection with which the analysis produced the information that was required. Thus in the first place the child's age at the date of the observation was established as being about one and a half years.[2] He was suffering at the time from malaria, an attack of which used to come on every day at a particular hour. From his tenth year onwards he was from time to time subject to moods of depression, which used to come on in the afternoon and reached their height at about five o'clock. This symptom still existed at the time of the analytic treatment. The recurring fits of depression took the place of the earlier attacks of fever or languor; five o'clock was either the time of the highest fever or of the observation of the intercourse, unless the two times coincided.[3] Probably for the very reason of this illness, he was in his parents' bedroom. The illness, the occurrence of which is also corroborated by direct tradition, makes it reasonable to refer the event to the summer, and, since the child was born on Christmas Day, to assume that his age was $n + 1\frac{1}{2}$ years.[4] He had been

2. The age of six months came under consideration as a far less probable, and indeed scarcely tenable, alternative.

3. We may remark in this connection that the patient drew only *five* wolves in his illustration to the dream, although the text mentioned six or seven.

4. [It might perhaps be clearer to say '$n + \frac{1}{2}$.']

sleeping in his cot, then, in his parents' bedroom, and woke up, perhaps because of his rising fever, in the afternoon, possibly at five o'clock, the hour which was later marked out by depression. It harmonizes with our assumption that it was a hot summer's day, if we suppose that his parents had retired, half undressed,[5] for an afternoon *siesta*. When he woke up, he witnessed a coitus *a tergo* [from behind], three times repeated:[6] he was able to see his mother's genitals as well as his father's organ; and he understood the process as well as its significance.[7] Lastly he interrupted his parents' intercourse in a manner which will be discussed later.

There is at bottom nothing extraordinary, nothing to give the impression of being the product of an extravagant imagination, in the fact that a young couple who had only been married a few years should have ended a *siesta* on a hot summer's afternoon with a love-scene, and should have disregarded the presence of their little boy of one and a half, asleep in his cot. On the contrary, such an event would, I think, be something entirely commonplace and *banal*; and even the position in which we have inferred that the coitus took place cannot in the least alter this judgement—especially as the evidence does not require that the intercourse should have been performed from behind each time. A single time would have been enough to give the spectator an opportunity for making observations which would have been rendered difficult or impossible by any other attitude of the lovers. The content of the scene cannot therefore in itself be an argument against its credibility. Doubts as to its probability will turn upon three other points: whether a child at the tender age of one and a half could be in a position to take in the perceptions of such a complicated process and to preserve them so accurately in his unconscious; secondly, whether it is possible at the age of four for a deferred revision of the impressions so received to penetrate the understanding; and finally, whether any procedure could succeed in bringing into consciousness coherently and convincingly the details of a scene of this kind which had been experienced and understood in such circumstances.[8]

Later on I shall carefully examine these and other doubts; but I can

---

5. In white underclothes: the *white* wolves.

6. Why three times? He suddenly one day produced the statement that I had discovered this detail by interpretation. This was not the case. It was a spontaneous association {on the Wolf Man's part}, exempt from further criticism; in his usual way he passed it off on me, and by this projection tried to make it more trustworthy.

7. I mean that he understood it at the time of the dream when he was four years old, not at the time of the observation. He received the impressions when he was one and a half; his understanding of them was deferred, but became possible at the time of the dream owing to his development, his sexual excitations, and his sexual researches.

8. The first of these difficulties cannot be reduced by assuming that the child at the time of his observation was after all probably a year older, that is to say *two* and a half, an age at which he may perhaps have been perfectly capable of talking. All the minor details of my patient's case almost excluded the possibility of shifting the date in this way. Moreover, the fact should be taken into account that these scenes of observing parental intercourse are by no means rarely brought to light in analysis. The condition of their occurrence, however, is precisely that it should be in the earliest period of childhood. The older the child is, the more carefully, with parents above a certain social level, will the child be deprived of the opportunity for this kind of observation.

assure the reader that I am no less critically inclined than he towards an acceptance of this observation of the child's, and I will only ask him to join me in adopting a *provisional* belief in the reality of the scene. We will first proceed with the study of the relations between this 'primal scene' and the patient's dream, his symptoms, and the history of his life; and we will trace separately the effects that followed from the essential content of the scene and from one of its visual impressions.

By the latter I mean the postures which he saw his parents adopt—the man upright, and the woman bent down like an animal. We have already heard that during his anxiety period his sister used to terrify him with a picture from the fairy-book, in which the wolf was shown standing upright, with one foot forward, with its claw stretched out and its ears pricked. He devoted himself with tireless perseverance during the treatment to the task of hunting in the second-hand bookshops till he had found the illustrated fairy-book of his childhood, and had recognized his bogy in an illustration to the story of 'The Wolf and the Seven Little Goats'. He thought that the posture of the wolf in this picture might have reminded him of that of his father during the constructed primal scene. At all events the picture became the point of departure for further manifestations of anxiety. Once when he was in his seventh or eighth year he was informed that next day a new tutor was coming for him. That night he dreamt of this tutor in the shape of a lion that came towards his bed roaring loudly and in the posture of the wolf in the picture; and once again he awoke in a state of anxiety. The wolf phobia had been overcome by that time, so he was free to choose himself a new anxiety-animal, and in this late dream he was recognizing the tutor as a father-surrogate. In the later years of his childhood each of his tutors and masters played the part of his father, and was endowed with his father's influence both for good and for evil.

While he was at his secondary school the Fates provided him with a remarkable opportunity of reviving his wolf phobia, and of using the relation which lay behind it as an occasion for severe inhibitions. The master who taught his form Latin was called Wolf. From the very first he felt cowed by him, and he was once taken severely to task by him for having made a stupid mistake in a piece of Latin translation. From that time on he could not get free from a paralysing fear of this master, and it was soon extended to other masters besides. But the occasion on which he made his blunder in the translation was also to the purpose. He had to translate the Latin word '*filius*', and he did it with the French word '*fils*' instead of with the corresponding word from his own language. The wolf, in fact, was still his father.

The first 'transitory symptom' which the patient produced during the treatment went back once more to the wolf phobia and to the fairy tale of 'The Seven Little Goats'. In the room in which the first sessions were held there was a large grandfather clock opposite the patient, who lay on a sofa facing away from me. I was struck by the fact that from time to time he turned his face towards me, looked at me in a very friendly way as though to propitiate me, and then turned his look away from me to the clock. I thought at the time that he was in this way showing his eagerness for the end of the hour. A long time afterwards the patient reminded me of this piece of dumb show, and gave me an explanation of it; for he recalled that the youngest of the seven little goats hid himself in the case of the grandfather clock while his six brothers were eaten up by the wolf. So what he had meant was: 'Be kind to me! Must I be frightened of you? Are you going to eat me up? Shall I hide myself from you in the clock-case like the youngest little goat?'

The wolf that he was afraid of was undoubtedly his father; but his fear of the wolf was conditional upon the creature being in an upright posture. His recollection asserted most definitely that he had not been terrified by pictures of wolves going on all fours or, as in the story of 'Little Red Riding-Hood', lying in bed. The posture which, according to our construction of the primal scene, he had seen the woman assume, was of no less significance; though in this case the significance was limited to the sexual sphere. The most striking phenomenon of his erotic life after maturity was his liability to compulsive attacks of falling physically in love which came on and disappeared again in the most puzzling succession. These attacks released a tremendous energy in him even at times when he was otherwise inhibited, and they were quite beyond his control. I must, for a specially important reason, postpone a full consideration of this compulsive love; but I may mention here that it was subject to a definite condition, which was concealed from his consciousness and was discovered only during the treatment. It was necessary that the woman should have assumed the posture which we have ascribed to his mother in the primal scene. From his puberty he had felt large and conspicuous buttocks as the most powerful attraction in a woman; to copulate except from behind gave him scarcely any enjoyment. At this point a criticism may justly be raised; it may be objected that a sexual preference of this kind for the hind parts of the body is a general characteristic of people who are inclined to an obsessional neurosis, and that its presence does not justify us in referring it back to a special impression in childhood. It is part of the fabric of the anal-erotic disposition and is one of the archaic traits which distinguish that constitution. Indeed, copulation from behind—*more ferarum* [in the fashion of animals]—may, after all, be regarded as phylogenetically the older form. We shall return to this point too in a later discussion, when we have brought forward the supplementary material which showed the basis of the unconscious condition upon which his falling in love depended.

Let us now proceed with our discussion of the relations between his dream and the primal scene. We should so far have expected the dream to present the child (who was rejoicing at Christmas in the prospect of the fulfilment of his wishes) with this picture of sexual satisfaction afforded through his father's agency, just as he had seen it in the primal scene, as a model of the satisfaction that he himself was longing to obtain from his father. Instead of this picture, however, there appeared the material of the story which he had been told by his grandfather shortly before: the tree, the wolves, and the taillessness (in the over-compensated form of the bushy tails of the putative wolves). At this point some connection is missing, some associative bridge to lead from the content of the primal scene to that of the wolf story. This connection is provided once again by the postures and only by them. In his grandfather's story the tailless wolf asked the others *to climb upon him*. It was this detail that called up the recollection of the picture of the primal scene; and it was in this way that it became possible for the material of the primal scene to be represented by that of the wolf story, and at the same time for the *two* parents to be replaced, as was desirable, by *several* wolves. The content of the dream met with a further transformation, and the material of the wolf story was made to fit in with the content of the fairy tale of 'The Seven Little Goats', by borrowing from it the number seven. [9]

The steps in the transformation of the material, 'primal scene—wolf story—fairy tale of "The Seven Little Goats" ', are a reflection of the progress of the dreamer's thoughts during the construction of the dream: 'longing for sexual satisfaction from his father—realization that castration is a necessary condition of it—fear of his father'. It is only at this point, I think, that we can regard the anxiety-dream of this four-year-old boy as being exhaustively explained.

After what has already been said I need only deal shortly with the pathogenic effect of the primal scene and the alteration which its revival produced in his sexual development. We will only trace that one of its effects to which the dream gave expression. Later on we shall have to make it clear that it was not only a single sexual current that started from the primal scene but a whole set of them, that his sexual life was positively splintered up by it. We shall further bear in mind that the activation of this scene (I purposely avoid the word 'recollection') had the same effect as though it were a recent experience. The effects of the scene were deferred, but meanwhile it had lost none of its freshness in the interval between the ages of one and a half and four years. We shall perhaps find in what follows reason to suppose that it produced certain effects even at the time of its perception, that is, from the age of one and a half onwards.

When the patient entered more deeply into the situation of the primal scene, he brought to light the following pieces of self-observation. He assumed to begin with, he said, that the event of which he was a witness was an act of violence, but the expression of enjoyment which he saw on his mother's face did not fit in with this; he was obliged to recognize

---

9. It says 'six or seven' in the dream. Six is the number of the children that were eaten; the seventh escaped into the clock-case. It is always a strict law of dream-interpretation that an explanation must be found for every detail.

that the experience was one of gratification.[1] What was essentially new for him in his observation of his parents' intercourse was the conviction of the reality of castration—a possibility with which his thoughts had already been occupied previously. (The sight of the two girls micturating, his Nanya's threat, the governess's interpretation of the sugar-sticks, the recollection of his father having beaten a snake to pieces.) For now he saw with his own eyes the wound of which his Nanya had spoken, and understood that its presence was a necessary condition of intercourse with his father. He could no longer confuse it with the bottom, as he had in his observation of the little girls.

The dream ended in a state of anxiety, from which he did not recover until he had his Nanya with him. He fled, therefore, from his father to her. His anxiety was a repudiation of the wish for sexual satisfaction from his father—the trend which had put the dream into his head. The form taken by the anxiety, the fear of 'being eaten by the wolf', was only the (as we shall hear, regressive) transposition of the wish to be copulated with by his father, that is, to be given sexual satisfaction in the same way as his mother. His last sexual aim, the passive attitude towards his father, succumbed to repression, and fear of his father appeared in its place in the shape of the wolf phobia.

And the driving force of this repression? The circumstances of the case show that it can only have been his narcissistic genital libido, which, in the form of concern for his male organ, was fighting against a satisfaction whose attainment seemed to involve the renunciation of that organ. And it was from his threatened narcissism that he derived the masculinity with which he defended himself against his passive attitude towards his father.

We now observe that at this point in our narrative we must make an alteration in our terminology. During the dream he had reached a new phase in his sexual organization. Up to then the sexual opposites had been for him *active* and *passive*. Since his seduction his sexual aim had been a passive one, of being touched on the genitals; it was then transformed, by regression to the earlier stage of the sadistic-anal organization,

---

1. We might perhaps best do justice to this statement of the patient's by supposing that the object of his observation was in the first instance a coitus in the normal position, which cannot fail to produce the impression of being a sadistic act, and that only after this was the position altered, so that he had an opportunity for making other observations and judgements. This hypothesis, however, was not confirmed with certainty, and moreover does not seem to me indispensable. We must not forget the actual situation which lies behind the abbreviated description given in the text: the patient under analysis, at an age of over twenty-five years, was putting the impressions and impulses of his fourth year into words which he would never have found at that time. If we fail to notice this, it may easily seem comic and incredible that a child of four should be capable of such technical judgements and learned notions. This is simply another instance of *deferred action*. At the age of one and a half the child receives an impression to which he is unable to react adequately; he is only able to understand it and to be moved by it when the impression is revived in him at the age of four; and only twenty years later, during the analysis, is he able to grasp with his conscious mental processes what was then going on in him. The patient justifiably disregards the three periods of time, and puts his present ego into the situation which is so long past. And in this we follow him, since with correct self-observation and interpretation the effect must be the same as though the distance between the second and third periods of time could be neglected. Moreover, we have no other means of describing the events of the second period.

into the masochistic aim of being beaten or punished. It was a matter of indifference to him whether he reached this aim with a man or with a woman. He had travelled, without considering the difference of sex, from his Nanya to his father; he had longed to have his penis touched by his Nanya, and had tried to provoke a beating from his father. Here his genitals were left out of account; though the connection with them which had been concealed by the regression was still expressed in his phantasy of being beaten *on the penis*. The activation of the primal scene in the dream now brought him back to the genital organization. He discovered the vagina and the biological significance of masculine and feminine. He understood now that active was the same as masculine, while passive was the same as feminine. His passive sexual aim should now have been transformed into a feminine one, and have expressed itself as 'being copulated with by his father' instead of 'being beaten by him on the genitals or on the bottom'. This feminine aim, however, underwent repression and was obliged to let itself be replaced by fear of the wolf.

We must here break off the discussion of his sexual development until new light is thrown from the later stages of his history upon these earlier ones. For the proper appreciation of the wolf phobia we will only add that both his father and mother became wolves. His mother took the part of the castrated wolf, which let the others climb upon it; his father took the part of the wolf that climbed. But his fear, as we have heard him assure us, related only to the standing wolf, that is, to his father. It must further strike us that the fear with which the dream ended had a model in his grandfather's story. For in this the castrated wolf, which had let the others climb upon it, was seized with fear as soon as it was reminded of the fact of its taillessness. It seems, therefore, as though he had identified himself with his castrated mother during the dream, and was now fighting against that fact. 'If you want to be sexually satisfied by Father', we may perhaps represent him as saying to himself, 'you must allow yourself to be castrated like Mother; but I won't have that.' In short, a clear protest on the part of his masculinity! Let us, however, plainly understand that the sexual development of the case that we are now examining has a great disadvantage from the point of view of research, for it was by no means undisturbed. It was first decisively influenced by the seduction, and was then diverted by the scene of observation of the coitus, which in its deferred action operated like a second seduction.

V
A FEW DISCUSSIONS

The whale and the polar bear, it has been said, cannot wage war on each other, for since each is confined to his own element they cannot meet. It is just as impossible for me to argue with workers in the field of psychology or of the neuroses who do not recognize the postulates of psycho-analysis and who look on its results as artefacts. But during the last few years there has grown up another kind of opposition as well, among people who, in their own opinion at all events, take their stand upon the ground of analysis, who do not dispute its technique or results, but who merely think themselves justified in drawing other conclusions from the same material and in submitting it to other interpretations.

As a rule, however, theoretical controversy is unfruitful. No sooner has one begun to depart from the material on which one ought to be relying, than one runs the risk of becoming intoxicated with one's own assertions and, in the end, of supporting opinions which any observation would have contradicted. For this reason it seems to me to be incomparably more useful to combat dissentient interpretations by testing them upon particular cases and problems.

I have remarked above that it will certainly be considered improbable, firstly, that 'a child at the tender age of one and a half could be in a position to take in the perceptions of such a complicated process and to preserve them so accurately in his unconscious; secondly, that it is possible at the age of four for a deferred revision of this material to penetrate the understanding; and finally, that any procedure could succeed in bringing into consciousness coherently and convincingly the details of a scene of this kind which had been experienced and understood in such circumstances'.

The last question is purely one of fact. Anyone who will take the trouble of pursuing an analysis into these depths by means of the prescribed technique will convince himself that it is decidedly possible. Anyone who neglects this, and breaks off the analysis in some higher stratum, has waived his right of forming a judgement on the matter. But the interpretation of what is arrived at in depth-analysis is not decided by this.

The two other doubts are based on a low estimate of the importance of early infantile impressions and an unwillingness to ascribe such enduring effects to them. The supporters of this view look for the causes of neuroses almost exclusively in the grave conflicts of later life; they assume that the importance of childhood is only held up before our eyes in analysis on account of the inclination of neurotics for expressing their present interests in reminiscences and symbols from the remote past. Such an estimate of the importance of the infantile factor would involve the disappearance of much that has formed part of the most intimate characteristics of analysis, though also, no doubt, of much that raises resistance to it and alienates the confidence of the outsider.

The view, then, that we are putting up for discussion is as follows. It maintains that scenes from early infancy, such as are brought up by an exhaustive analysis of neuroses (as, for instance, in the present case), are not reproductions of real occurrences, to which it is possible to ascribe an influence over the course of the patient's later life and over the formation of his symptoms. It considers them rather as products of the imagination, which find their instigation in mature life, which are intended to serve as some kind of symbolic representation of real wishes and interests, and which owe their origin to a regressive tendency, to a turning-away from the tasks of the present. If that is so, we can of course spare ourselves the necessity of attributing such a surprising amount to the mental life and intellectual capacity of children of the tenderest age.

Besides the desire which we all share for the rationalization and simplification of our difficult problem, there are all sorts of facts that speak in favour of this view. It is also possible to eliminate beforehand one objection to it which may arise, particularly in the mind of a practising analyst. It must be admitted that, if this view of these scenes from infancy were the right one, the carrying-out of analysis would not in the first instance be altered in any respect. If neurotics are endowed with the evil characteristic of diverting their interest from the present and of attaching it to these regressive substitutes, the products of their imagination, then there is absolutely nothing for it but to follow upon their tracks and bring these unconscious productions into consciousness; for, leaving on one side their lack of value from the point of view of reality, they are of the utmost value from our point of view, since they are for the moment the bearers and possessors of the interest which we want to set free so as to be able to direct it on to the tasks of the present. The analysis would have to run precisely the same course as one which had a *naïf* faith in the truth of the phantasies. The difference would only come at the end of the analysis, after the phantasies had been laid bare. We should then say to the patient: 'Very well, then; your neurosis proceeded *as though* you had received these impressions and spun them out in your childhood. You will see, of course, that that is out of the question. They were products of your imagination which were intended to divert you from the real tasks that lay before you. Let us now enquire what these tasks were, and what lines of communication ran between them and your phantasies.' After the infantile phantasies had been disposed of in this way, it would be possible to begin a second portion of the treatment, which would be concerned with the patient's real life.

Any shortening of this course, any alteration, that is, in psychoanalytic treatment, as it has hitherto been practised, would be technically inadmissible. Unless these phantasies are made conscious to the patient to their fullest extent, he cannot obtain command of the interest which is attached to them. If his attention is diverted from them as soon as their existence and their general outlines are divined, support is simply being given to the work of repression, thanks to which they have been put beyond the patient's reach in spite of all his pains. If he is given a premature sense of their unimportance, by being informed, for instance, that it will only be a question of phantasies, which, of course, have no real significance, his co-operation will never be secured for the task of bringing them into consciousness. A correct procedure, therefore, would make no alteration in the technique of analysis, whatever estimate might be formed of these scenes from infancy.

I have already mentioned that there are a number of facts which can be brought up in support of the view of these scenes being regressive phantasies. And above all there is this one: so far as my experience hitherto goes, these scenes from infancy are not reproduced during the treatment as recollections, they are the products of construction. Many people will certainly think that this single admission decides the whole dispute.

I am anxious not to be misunderstood. Every analyst knows—and he has met with the experience on countless occasions—that in the course of a successful treatment the patient brings up a large number of spontaneous recollections from his childhood, for the appearance of which (a first appearance, perhaps) the physician feels himself entirely blameless, since he has not made any attempt at a construction which could have put any material of the sort into the patient's head. It does not necessarily follow that these previously unconscious recollections are always true. They may be; but they are often distorted from the truth, and interspersed with imaginary elements, just like the so-called screen memories which are preserved spontaneously. All that I mean to say is this: scenes, like this one in my present patient's case, which date from such an early period and exhibit a similar content, and which further lay claim to such an extraordinary significance for the history of the case, are as a rule not reproduced as recollections, but have to be divined—constructed—gradually and laboriously from an aggregate of indications. Moreover, it would be sufficient for the purposes of the argument if my admission that scenes of this kind do not become conscious in the shape of recollections applied only to cases of obsessional neurosis, or even if I were to limit my assertion to the case which we are studying here.

I am not of opinion, however, that such scenes must necessarily be phantasies because they do not reappear in the shape of recollections. It seems to me absolutely equivalent to a recollection, if the memories are replaced (as in the present case) by dreams the analysis of which invariably leads back to the same scene and which reproduce every portion of its content in an inexhaustible variety of new shapes. Indeed, dreaming is another kind of remembering, though one that is subject to the conditions that rule at night and to the laws of dream-formation. It is this recurrence in dreams that I regard as the explanation of the fact that the patients themselves gradually acquire a profound conviction of the reality of these primal scenes, a conviction which is in no respect inferior to one based on recollection.

There is naturally no need for those who take the opposite view to abandon as hopeless their fight against such arguments. It is well known that dreams can be guided. And the sense of conviction felt by the person analysed may be the result of suggestion, which is always having new parts assigned to it in the play of forces involved in analytic treatment. The old-fashioned psychotherapist, it might be maintained, used to suggest to his patient that he was cured, that he had overcome his inhibitions, and so on; while the psycho-analyst, on this view, suggests to him that when he was a child he had some experience or other, which he must now recollect in order to be cured. This would be the difference between the two.

Let it be clearly be understood that this last attempt at an explanation on the part of those who take the view opposed to mine results in the scenes from infancy being disposed of far more fundamentally than was announced to begin with. What was argued at first was that they were not realities but phantasies. But what is argued now is evidently that they are phantasies not of the patient but of the analyst himself, who forces them upon the person under analysis on account of some complexes of his own. An analyst, indeed, who hears this reproach, will comfort himself by recalling how gradually the construction of this phantasy which he is supposed to have originated came about, and, when all is said and done, how independently of the physician's incentive many points in its development proceeded; how, after a certain phase of the treatment, everything seemed to converge upon it, and how later, in the synthesis, the most various and remarkable results radiated out from it; how not only the large problems but the smallest peculiarities in the history of the case were cleared up by this single assumption. And he will disclaim the possession of the amount of ingenuity necessary for the concoction of an occurrence which can fulfil all these demands. But even this plea will be without an effect on an adversary who has not experienced the analysis himself. On the one side there will be a charge of subtle self-deception, and on the other of obtuseness of judgement; it will be impossible to arrive at a decision.

Let us turn to another factor which supports this opposing view of these constructed scenes from infancy. It is as follows: There can be no doubt of the real existence of all the processes which have been brought forward in order to explain these doubtful structures as phantasies, and their importance must be recognized. The diversion of interest from the tasks of real life, the existence of phantasies in the capacity of substitutes for unperformed actions, the regressive tendency which is expressed in these productions—regressive in more than one sense, in so far as there is involved simultaneously a shrinking-back from life and a harking-back to the past—all these things hold good, and are regularly confirmed by analysis. One might think that they would also suffice to explain the supposed reminiscences from early infancy which are under discussion; and in accordance with the principle of economy in science such an explanation would have the advantage over one which is inadequate without the support of new and surprising assumptions.

I may here venture to point out that the antagonistic views which are to be found in the psycho-analytic literature of to-day are usually arrived at on the principle of *pars pro toto*. From a highly composite combination one part of the operative factors is singled out and proclaimed as the truth; and in its favour the other part, together with the whole combination, is then contradicted. If we look a little closer, to see which group of factors it is that has been given the preference, we shall find that it is the one that contains material already known from other sources or what can be most easily related to that material. Thus, Jung picks out actuality and regression, and Adler, egoistic motives. What is left over, however, and rejected as false, is precisely what is new in psycho-analysis and peculiar to it. This is the easiest method of repelling the revolutionary and inconvenient advances of psycho-analysis.

It is worth while remarking that none of the factors which are adduced by the opposing view in order to explain these scenes from infancy had to wait for recognition until Jung brought them forward as novelties. The notion of a current conflict, of a turning away from reality, of a substitutive satisfaction obtained in phantasy, of a regression to material from the past—all of this (employed, moreover, in the same context, though perhaps with a slightly different terminology) had for years formed an integral part of my own theory. It was not the whole of it, however. It was only one part of the causes leading to the formation of neuroses—that part which, starting from reality, operates in a regressive direction. Side by side with this I left room for another influence which, starting from the impressions of childhood, operates in a forward direction, which points a path for the libido that is shrinking away from life, and which makes it possible to understand the otherwise inexplicable regression to childhood. Thus on my view the two factors co-operate in the formation of symptoms. But an earlier co-operation seems to me to be of equal importance. I am of opinion that *the influence of childhood makes itself felt already in the situation at the beginning of the formation of a neurosis, since it plays a decisive part in determining whether and at what point the individual shall fail to master the real problems of life.*

What is in dispute, therefore, is the significance of the infantile factor. The problem is to find a case which can establish that significance beyond any doubt. Such, however, is the case which is being dealt with so exhaustively in these pages and which is distinguished by the characteristic that the neurosis in later life was preceded by a neurosis in early childhood. It is for that very reason, indeed, that I have chosen it to report upon. Should any one feel inclined to reject it because the animal phobia strikes him as not sufficiently serious to be recognized as an independent neurosis, I may mention that the phobia was succeeded without any interval by an obsessional ceremonial, and by obsessional acts and thoughts, which will be discussed in the following sections of this paper.

The occurrence of a neurotic disorder in the fourth and fifth years of childhood proves, first and foremost, that infantile experiences are by themselves in a position to produce a neurosis, without there being any need for the addition of a flight from some task which has to be faced in real life. It may be objected that even a child is constantly being confronted with tasks which it would perhaps be glad to evade. That is so; but the life of a child under school age is easily observable, and we can examine it to see whether any 'tasks' are to be found in it capable of determining the causation of a neurosis. But we discover nothing but instinctual impulses which the child cannot satisfy and which it is not old enough to master, and the sources from which these impulses arise.

As was to be expected, the enormous shortening of the interval between the outbreak of the neurosis and the date of the childhood experiences which are under discussion reduces to the narrowest limits the regressive part of the causation, while it brings into full view the portion of it which operates in a forward direction, the influence of earlier impressions. The present case history will, I hope, give a clear picture of this position of things. But there are other reasons why neuroses of childhood give a decisive answer to the question of the nature of primal scenes—the earliest experiences of childhood that are brought to light in analysis.

Let us assume as an uncontradicted premise that a primal scene of this kind has been correctly educed technically, that it is indispensable to a comprehensive solution of all the conundrums that are set us by the symptoms of the infantile disorder, that all the consequences radiate out from it, just as all the threads of the analysis have led up to it. Then, in view of its content, it is impossible that it can be anything else than the reproduction of a reality experienced by the child. For a child, like an adult, can produce phantasies only from material which has been acquired from some source or other; and with children, some of the means of acquiring it (by reading, for instance) are cut off, while the space of time at their disposal for acquiring it is short and can easily be searched with a view to the discovery of any such sources.

In the present case the content of the primal scene is a picture of sexual intercourse between the boy's parents in a posture especially favourable for certain observations. Now it would be no evidence whatever of the reality of such a scene if we were to find it in a patient whose symptoms (the effects of the scene, that is) had appeared at some time or other in the later part of his life. A person such as this might have acquired the impressions, the ideas, and the knowledge on a great number of different occasions in the course of the long interval; he might then have transformed them into an imaginary picture, have projected them back into his childhood, and have attached them to his parents. If, however, the effects of a scene of this sort appear in the child's fourth or fifth year, then he must have witnessed the scene at an age even earlier than that. But in that case we are still faced with all the disconcerting consequences which have arisen from the analysis of this infantile neurosis. The only way out would be to assume that the patient not only unconsciously imagined the primal scene, but also concocted the alteration in his character, his fear of the wolf, and his religious obsession; but such an expedient would be contradicted by his otherwise sober nature and by the direct tradition in his family. It must therefore be left at this (I can see no other possibility): either the analysis based on the neurosis in his childhood is all a piece of nonsense from start to finish, or everything took place just as I have described it above.

At an earlier stage in the discussion we were brought up against an ambiguity in regard to the patient's predilection for female nates and for sexual intercourse in the posture in which they are especially prominent. It seemed necessary to trace this predilection back to the intercourse which he had observed between his parents, while at the same time a preference of this kind is a general characteristic of archaic constitutions which are predisposed to an obsessional neurosis. But the contradiction is easily resolved if we regard it as a case of overdetermination. The person who was the subject of his observation of this posture during intercourse was, after all, his father in the flesh, and it may also have been from him that he had inherited this constitutional predilection. Neither his father's subsequent illness nor his family history contradicts this; as has been mentioned already, a brother of his father's died in a condition which must be regarded as the outcome of a severe obsessional disorder.

In this connection we may recall that, at the time of his seduction as a boy of three and a quarter, his sister had uttered a remarkable calumny against his good old nurse, to the effect that she stood all kinds of people on their heads and then took hold of them by their genitals. We cannot fail to be struck by the idea that perhaps the sister, at a similar tender age, also witnessed the same scene as was observed by her brother later on, and that it was this that had suggested to her her notion about 'standing people on their heads' during the sexual act. This hypothesis would also give us a hint of the reason for her own sexual precocity.

Originally I had no intention of pursuing the discussion of the reality of 'primal scenes' any further in this place. Since, however, I have meanwhile had occasion in my *Introductory Lectures on Psycho-Analysis* [1916–17, Lecture XXIII] to treat the subject on more general lines and with no controversial aim in view, it would be misleading if I omitted to apply the considerations which determined my other discussion of the matter to the case that is now before us. I therefore proceed as follows by way of supplement and rectification.—There remains the possibility of taking yet another view of the primal scene underlying the dream— a view, moreover, which obviates to a large extent the conclusion that has been arrived at above and relieves us of many of our difficulties. But the theory which seeks to reduce scenes from infancy to the level of regressive symbols will gain nothing even by this modification; and indeed that theory seems to me to be finally disposed of by this (as it would be by any other) analysis of an infantile neurosis.

This other view which I have in mind is that the state of affairs can be explained in the following manner. It is true that we cannot dispense with the assumption that the child observed a copulation, the sight of which gave him a conviction that castration might be more than an empty threat. Moreover, the significance which he subsequently came to attach to the postures of men and women, in connection with the development of anxiety on the one hand, and as a condition upon which his falling in love depended on the other hand, leaves us no choice but to conclude that it must have been a *coitus a tergo, more ferarum*. But there is another factor which is not so irreplaceable and which may be dropped. Perhaps what the child observed was not copulation between his parents but copulation between animals, which he then displaced on to his parents, as though he had inferred that his parents did things in the same way.

Colour is lent to this view above all by the fact that the wolves in the dream were actually sheep-dogs and, moreover, appear as such in the drawing. Shortly before the dream the boy was repeatedly taken to visit the flocks of sheep, and there he might see just such large white dogs and probably also observe them copulating. I should also like to bring into this connection the number three, which the dreamer introduced without adducing any further motive, and I would suggest that he had kept in his memory the fact that he had made three such observations with the sheep-dogs. What supervened during the expectant excitement of the night of his dream was the transference on to his parents of his recently acquired memory-picture, with *all* its details, and it was only thus that the powerful emotional effects which followed were made possible. He now arrived at a deferred understanding of the impressions which he may have received a few weeks or months earlier—a process such as all of us perhaps have been through in our own experiences. The transference from the copulating dogs on to his parents was accomplished not by means of his making an inference accompanied by words but by his searching out in his memory a real scene in which his parents had been together and which could be coalesced with the situation of the copulation. All the details of the scene which were established in the analysis of the dream may have been accurately reproduced. It was really on a summer's afternoon while the child was suffering from malaria, the parents were both present, dressed in white, when the child woke up from his sleep, but—the scene was innocent. The rest had been added by the inquisitive child's subsequent wish, based on his experiences with the dogs, to witness his parents too in their love-making; and the scene which was thus imagined now produced all the effects that we have catalogued, just as though it had been entirely real and not fused together out of two components, the one earlier and indifferent, the other later and profoundly impressive.

It is at once obvious how greatly the demands on our credulity are reduced. We need no longer suppose that the parents copulated in the presence of their child (a very young one, it is true)—which was a disagreeable idea for many of us. The period of time during which the effects were deferred is very greatly diminished; it now covers only a few months of the child's fourth year and does not stretch back at all into the first dark years of childhood. There remains scarcely anything strange in the child's conduct in making the transference from the dogs on to his parents and in being afraid of the wolf instead of his father. He was in that phase of the development of his attitude towards the world which I have described in *Totem and Taboo* [1912–13, Essay IV] as the return of totemism. The theory which endeavours to explain the primal scenes found in neuroses as retrospective phantasies of a later date seems to obtain powerful support from the present observation, in spite of our patient being of the tender age of four years. Young though he was, he was yet able to succeed in replacing an impression of his fourth year by an imaginary trauma at the age of one and a half. This regression, however, seems neither mysterious nor tendentious. The scene which was to be made up had to fulfil certain conditions which, in consequence of the circumstances of the dreamer's life, could only be found in precisely this early period; such, for instance, was the condition that he should be in bed in his parents' bedroom.

But something that I am able to adduce from the analytic findings in other cases will seem to most readers to be the decisive factor in favour of the correctness of the view here proposed. Scenes of observing sexual intercourse between parents at a very early age (whether they be real memories or phantasies) are as a matter of fact by no means rarities in the analyses of neurotic mortals. Possibly they are no less frequent among those who are not neurotics. Possibly they are part of the regular store in the—conscious or unconscious—treasury of their memories. But as often as I have been able by means of analysis to bring out a scene of this sort, it has shown the same peculiarity which startled us with our present patient too: it has related to *coitus a tergo*, which alone offers the spectator a possibility of inspecting the genitals. There is surely no need any longer to doubt that what we are dealing with is only a phantasy, which is invariably aroused, perhaps, by an observation of the sexual intercourse of animals. And yet more: I have hinted that my description of the 'primal scene' has remained incomplete because I have reserved for a later moment my account of the way in which the child interrupted his parents' intercourse. I must now add that this method of interruption is also the same in every case.

I can well believe that I have now laid myself open to grave aspersions on the part of the readers of this case history. If these arguments in favour of such a view of the 'primal scene' were at my disposal, how could I possibly have taken it on myself to begin by advocating one which seemed so absurd? Or have I made these new observations, which have obliged me to alter my original view, in the interval between the first draft of the case history and this addition, and am I for some reason or other unwilling to admit the fact? I will admit something else instead: I intend on this occasion to close the discussion of the reality of the primal scene with a *non liquet*.[2] This case history is not yet at an end; in its further course a factor will emerge which will shake the certainty which we seem at present to enjoy. Nothing, I think, will then be left but to refer my readers to the passages in my *Introductory Lectures* in which I have treated the problem of primal phantasies or primal scenes.[3]

2. ['It is not clear'—a verdict where the evidence in a trial is inconclusive.]

3. {In a footnote that Freud added to this case history in 1923, he observed that after the war, a penniless refugee who had lost everything in the Russian Revolution, the Wolf Man had come back into analysis with him for a few months, during which "a piece of the transference which had not hitherto been overcome was successfully dealt with. Since then the patient has felt normal and has behaved unexceptionably." But, in fact, the Wolf Man, who remained in Vienna, experienced several distressing psychotic episodes and spent some time from late 1926 to early 1927 in analysis with Ruth Mack Brunswick, one of Freud's disciples. While the Wolf Man never lived up to his potential and remained subject to intermittent fits of brooding and to depressions, his analysis had at least rendered him capable of a fairly normal social existence, of holding a job and of marrying. He remained immensely grateful to Freud to the end of his life, surviving the Anschluss and the war in Vienna to die in 1979 at the advanced age of ninety-two, always proud of being Freud's most famous patient.}

PART FOUR: PSYCHO-ANALYSIS IN CULTURE

Obsessive Actions and Religious Practices

Almost from the beginning of his psychoanalytic thinking, from the mid-1890s onward, Freud hoped to construct a psychology that would hold good for all of human behavior, normal as much as neurotic. His first papers concentrated, to be sure, on hysteria, on obsessions—in short, on the theory of neurosis. But his unfinished and unpublished "Project" of 1895 was a first ambitious stab at a general psychology, and once he had linked reflections on *Oedipus Rex* and *Hamlet* to his explanations of mental functioning, the aim of devising a grand design for such a psychology never left him. In 1907, the year he published this suggestive paper linking obsessions to religious practices, he psychoanalyzed *Gradiva*, a novella by the German writer Wilhelm Jensen, and began to investigate virtually the whole spectrum of cultural phenomena: the law, education, prehistory, the making of literature and art—and religion. "Obsessive Actions and Religious Practices" thus stands as an early instance of Freud's wider interests, interests that did not wane until his death more than three decades later. Reflections on his patients' ruminations on religion (as in the case histories of the Rat Man or the Wolf Man), *Totem and Taboo*, and the late essay of 1927, *The Future of an Illusion*, further document his preoccupation with psychoanalyzing religion. There can be no doubt that he pursued these analyses with particular engagement: Freud was a consistent, aggressive, dogmatic atheist, a child of the Enlightenment who saw a world at war to the death between science and religion. To study religion, he was convinced, one must take a stand outside it: only the unbeliever can truly understand belief.

I am certainly not the first person to have been struck by the resemblance between what are called obsessive actions in sufferers from nervous affections and the observances by means of which believers give expression to their piety. The term 'ceremonial', which has been applied to some of these obsessive actions, is evidence of this. The resemblance, however, seems to me to be more than a superficial one, so that an insight into the origin of neurotic ceremonial may embolden us to draw inferences by analogy about the psychological processes of religious life.

People who carry out obsessive actions or ceremonials belong to the same class as those who suffer from obsessive thinking, obsessive ideas, obsessive impulses and the like. Taken together, these form a particular clinical entity, to which the name of 'obsessional neurosis' ['*Zwangs-neurose*'] is customarily applied. But one should not attempt to deduce the character of the illness from its name; for, strictly speaking, other kinds of morbid mental phenomena have an equal claim to possessing what are spoken of as 'obsessional' characteristics. In place of a definition we must for the time being be content with obtaining a detailed knowledge of these states, since we have not yet been able to arrive at a criterion of obsessional neuroses; it probably lies very deep, although we seem to sense its presence everywhere in the manifestations of the illness.

Neurotic ceremonials consist in making small adjustments to particular everyday actions, small additions or restrictions or arrangements, which have always to be carried out in the same, or in a methodically varied, manner. These activities give the impression of being mere formalities, and they seem quite meaningless to us. Nor do they appear otherwise to the patient himself; yet he is incapable of giving them up, for any deviation from the ceremonial is visited by intolerable anxiety, which obliges him at once to make his omission good. Just as trivial as the ceremonial actions themselves are the occasions and activities which are embellished, encumbered and in any case prolonged by the ceremonial—for instance, dressing and undressing, going to bed or satisfying bodily needs. The performance of a ceremonial can be described by replacing it, as it were, by a series of unwritten laws. For instance, to take the case of the bed ceremonial: the chair must stand in a particular place beside the bed; the clothes must lie upon it folded in a particular order; the blanket must be tucked in at the bottom and the sheet smoothed out; the pillows must be arranged in such and such a manner, and the subject's own body must lie in a precisely defined position. Only after all this may he go to sleep. Thus in slight cases the ceremonial seems to be no more than an exaggeration of an orderly procedure that is customary and justifiable; but the special conscientiousness with which it is carried out and the anxiety which follows upon its neglect stamp the ceremonial as a 'sacred act'. Any interruption of it is for the most part badly tolerated, and the presence of other people during its performance is almost always ruled out.

Any activities whatever may become obsessive actions in the wider sense of the term if they are elaborated by small additions or given a rhythmic character by means of pauses and repetitions. We shall not expect to find a sharp distinction between 'ceremonials' and 'obsessive actions'. As a rule obsessive actions have grown out of ceremonials. Besides these two, prohibitions and hindrances (abulias) make up the content of the disorder; these, in fact, only continue the work of the obsessive actions, inasmuch as some things are completely forbidden to the patient and others only allowed subject to his following a prescribed ceremonial.

It is remarkable that both compulsions and prohibitions (having to do something and having *not* to do something) apply in the first instance only to the subject's solitary activities and for a long time leave his social behaviour unaffected. Sufferers from this illness are consequently able to treat their affliction as a private matter and keep it concealed for many years. And, indeed, many more people suffer from these forms of obsessional neurosis than doctors hear of. For many sufferers, too, concealment is made easier from the fact that they are quite well able to fulfil their social duties during a part of the day, once they have devoted a number of hours to their secret doings, hidden from view like Mélusine.[1]

It is easy to see where the resemblances lie between neurotic ceremonials and the sacred acts of religious ritual: in the qualms of conscience brought on by their neglect, in their complete isolation from all other actions (shown in the prohibition against interruption) and in the conscientiousness with which they are carried out in every detail. But the differences are equally obvious, and a few of them are so glaring that they make the comparison a sacrilege: the greater individual variability of [neurotic] ceremonial actions in contrast to the stereotyped character of rituals (prayer, turning to the East, etc.), their private nature as opposed to the public and communal character of religious observances, above all, however, the fact that, while the minutiae of religious ceremonial are full of significance and have a symbolic meaning, those of neurotics seem foolish and senseless. In this respect an obsessional neurosis presents a travesty, half comic and half tragic, of a private religion. But it is precisely this sharpest difference between neurotic and religious ceremonial which disappears when, with the help of the psycho-analytic technique of investigation, one penetrates to the true meaning of obsessive actions. In the course of such an investigation the appearance which obsessive actions afford of being foolish and senseless is completely effaced, and the reason for their having that appearance is explained. It is found that the obsessive actions are perfectly significant in every detail, that they serve important interests of the personality and that they give expression to experiences that are still operative and to thoughts that are cathected with affect. They do this in two ways, either by direct or by symbolic representation; and they are consequently to be interpreted either historically or symbolically.

I must give a few examples to illustrate my point. Those who are familiar with the findings of psycho-analytic investigation into the psychoneuroses will not be surprised to learn that what is being represented in obsessive actions or in ceremonials is derived from the most intimate, and for the most part from the sexual, experiences of the patient.

(a) A girl whom I was able to observe was under a compulsion to rinse round her wash-basin several times after washing. The significance of this ceremonial action lay in the proverbial saying: 'Don't throw away dirty water till you have clean.' Her action was intended to give a warning to her sister, of whom she was very fond, and to restrain her from getting divorced from her unsatisfactory husband until she had established a relationship with a better man.

(b) A woman who was living apart from her husband was subject to a compulsion, whenever she ate anything, to leave what was the best of it behind: for example, she would only take the outside of a piece of roast meat. This renunciation was explained by the date of its origin. It

---

1. [A beautiful woman in mediaeval legend, who led a secret existence as a water-nymph.]

appeared on the day after she had refused marital relations with her husband—that is to say, after she had given up what was the best.

(c) The same patient could only sit on one particular chair and could only get up from it with difficulty. In regard to certain details of her married life, the chair symbolized her husband, to whom she remained faithful. She found an explanation of her compulsion in this sentence: 'It is so hard to part from anything (a husband, a chair) upon which one has once settled.'

(d) Over a period of time she used to repeat an especially noticeable and senseless obsessive action. She would run out of her room into another room in the middle of which there was a table. She would straighten the table-cloth on it in a particular manner and ring for the housemaid. The latter had to come up to the table, and the patient would then dismiss her on some indifferent errand. In the attempts to explain this compulsion, it occurred to her that at one place on the table-cloth there was a stain, and that she always arranged the cloth in such a way that the housemaid was bound to see the stain. The whole scene proved to be a reproduction of an experience in her married life which had later on given her thoughts a problem to solve. On the wedding-night her husband had met with a not unusual mishap. He found himself impotent, and 'many times in the course of the night he came hurrying from his room into hers' to try once more whether he could succeed. In the morning he said he would feel ashamed in front of the hotel housemaid who made the beds, and he took a bottle of red ink and poured its contents over the sheet; but he did it so clumsily that the red stain came in a place that was very unsuitable for his purpose. With her obsessive action, therefore, she was representing the wedding-night. 'Bed and board' between them make up marriage.

(e) Another compulsion which she started—of writing down the number of every bank-note before parting with it—had also to be interpreted historically. At a time when she was still intending to leave her husband if she could find another more trustworthy man, she allowed herself to receive advances from a man whom she met at a watering-place, but she was in doubt as to whether his intentions were serious. One day, being short of small change, she asked him to change a five-kronen piece for her. He did so, pocketed the large coin and declared with a gallant air that he would never part with it, since it had passed through her hands. At their later meetings she was frequently tempted to challenge him to show her the five-kronen piece, as though she wanted to convince herself that she could believe in his intentions. But she refrained, for the good reason that it is impossible to distinguish between coins of the same value. Thus her doubt remained unresolved; and it left her with the compulsion to write down the number of each bank-note, by which it *can* be distinguished from all others of the same value.

These few examples, selected from the great number I have met with, are merely intended to illustrate my assertion that in obsessive actions everything has its meaning and can be interpreted. The same is true of ceremonials in the strict sense, only that the evidence for this would require a more circumstantial presentation. I am quite aware of how far our explanations of obsessive actions are apparently taking us from the sphere of religious thought.

It is one of the conditions of the illness that the person who is obeying a compulsion carries it out without understanding its meaning—or at any rate its chief meaning. It is only thanks to the efforts of psychoanalytic treatment that he becomes conscious of the meaning of his obsessive action and, with it, of the motives that are impelling him to it. We express this important fact by saying that the obsessive action serves to express *unconscious* motives and ideas. In this, we seem to find a further departure from religious practices; but we must remember that as a rule the ordinary pious individual, too, performs a ceremonial without concerning himself with its significance, although priests and scientific investigators may be familiar with the—mostly symbolic— meaning of the ritual. In all believers, however, the motives which impel them to religious practices are unknown to them or are represented in consciousness by others which are advanced in their place.

Analysis of obsessive actions has already given us some sort of an insight into their causes and into the chain of motives which bring them into effect. We may say that the sufferer from compulsions and prohibitions behaves as if he were dominated by a consciousness of guilt, of which, however, he knows nothing, so that we must call it an unconscious consciousness of guilt, in spite of the apparent contradiction in terms.[2] This sense of guilt has its source in certain early mental events, but it is constantly being revived by renewed temptations which arise whenever there is a contemporary provocation. Moreover, it occasions a lurking sense of expectant anxiety, an expectation of misfortune, which is linked, through the idea of punishment, with the internal perception of the temptation. When the ceremonial is first being constructed, the patient is still conscious that he must do this or that lest some ill should befall, and as a rule the nature of the ill that is to be expected is still known to his consciousness. But what is already hidden from him is the connection—which is always demonstrable—between the occasion on which this expectant anxiety arises and the danger which it conjures up. Thus a ceremonial starts as an *action for defence* or *insurance*, a *protective measure*.

The sense of guilt of obsessional neurotics finds its counterpart in the protestations of pious people that they know that at heart they are miserable sinners; and the pious observances (such as prayers, invocations, etc.,) with which such people preface every daily act, and in especial

---

2. {I have here changed the rendering of Freud's word—he uses "*Bewusstsein*"—from the editors' "sense" to "consciousness." This is not only closer to Freud's original, but also clearly conveys the apparent contradiction of which Freud speaks—a consciousness that is unconscious—which the translators have lost.}

every unusual undertaking, seem to have the value of defensive or protective measures.

A deeper insight into the mechanism of obsessional neurosis is gained if we take into account the primary fact which lies at the bottom of it. This is always *the repression of an instinctual impulse* (a component of the sexual instinct) which was present in the subject's constitution and which was allowed to find expression for a while during his childhood but later succumbed to suppression. In the course of the repression of this instinct a special *conscientiousness* is created which is directed against the instinct's aims; but this psychical reaction-formation feels insecure and constantly threatened by the instinct which is lurking in the unconscious. The influence of the repressed instinct is felt as a temptation, and during the process of repression itself anxiety is generated, which gains control over the future in the form of *expectant* anxiety. The process of repression which leads to obsessional neurosis must be considered as one which is only partly successful and which increasingly threatens to fail. It may thus be compared to an unending conflict; fresh psychical efforts are continually required to counterbalance the forward pressure of the instinct. Thus the ceremonial and obsessive actions arise partly as a defence against the temptation and partly as a protection against the ill which is expected. Against the temptation the protective measures seem soon to become inadequate; then the prohibitions come into play, with the purpose of keeping at a distance situations that give rise to temptation. Prohibitions take the place of obsessive actions, it will be seen, just as a phobia is designed to avert a hysterical attack. Again, a ceremonial represents the sum of the conditions subject to which something that is not yet absolutely forbidden is permitted, just as the Church's marriage ceremony signifies for the believer a sanctioning of sexual enjoyment which would otherwise be sinful. A further characteristic of obsessional neurosis, as of all similar affections, is that its manifestations (its symptoms, including the obsessive actions) fulfil the condition of being a compromise between the warring forces of the mind. They thus always reproduce something of the pleasure which they are designed to prevent; they serve the repressed instinct no less than the agencies which are repressing it. As the illness progresses, indeed, actions which were originally mostly concerned with maintaining the defence come to approximate more and more to the proscribed actions through which the instinct was able to find expression in childhood.

Some features of this state of affairs may be seen in the sphere of religious life as well. The formation of a religion, too, seems to be based on the suppression, the renunciation, of certain instinctual impulses. These impulses, however, are not, as in the neuroses, exclusively components of the sexual instinct; they are self-seeking, socially harmful instincts, though, even so, they are usually not without a sexual component. A sense of guilt following upon continual temptation and an expectant anxiety in the form of fear of divine punishment have, after all, been familiar to us in the field of religion longer than in that of neurosis. Perhaps because of the admixture of sexual components, perhaps because of some general characteristics of the instincts, the suppression of instinct proves to be an inadequate and interminable process in religious life also. Indeed, complete backslidings into sin are more common among pious people than among neurotics and these give rise to a new form of religious activity, namely acts of penance, which have their counterpart in obsessional neurosis.

We have noted as a curious and derogatory characteristic of obsessional neurosis that its ceremonials are concerned with the small actions of daily life and are expressed in foolish regulations and restrictions in connection with them. We cannot understand this remarkable feature of the clinical picture until we have realized that the mechanism of psychical *displacement*, which was first discovered by me in the construction of dreams, dominates the mental processes of obsessional neurosis. It is already clear from the few examples of obsessive actions given above that their symbolism and the detail of their execution are brought about by a displacement from the actual, important thing on to a small one which takes its place—for instance, from a husband on to a chair. It is this tendency to displacement which progressively changes the clinical picture and eventually succeeds in turning what is apparently the most trivial matter into something of the utmost importance and urgency. It cannot be denied that in the religious field as well there is a similar tendency to a displacement of psychical values, and in the same direction, so that the petty ceremonials of religious practice gradually become the essential thing and push aside the underlying thoughts. That is why religions are subject to reforms which work retroactively and aim at a re-establishment of the original balance of values.

The character of compromise which obsessive actions possess in their capacity as neurotic symptoms is the character least easily detected in corresponding religious observances. Yet here, too, one is reminded of this feature of neuroses when one remembers how commonly all the acts which religion forbids—the expressions of the instincts it has suppressed—are committed precisely in the name of, and ostensibly for the sake of, religion.

In view of these similarities and analogies one might venture to regard obsessional neurosis as a pathological counterpart of the formation of a religion, and to describe that neurosis as an individual religiosity and religion as a universal obsessional neurosis. The most essential similarity would reside in the underlying renunciation of the activation of instincts that are constitutionally present; and the chief difference would lie in the nature of those instincts, which in the neurosis are exclusively sexual in their origin, while in religion they spring from egoistic sources.

A progressive renunciation of constitutional instincts, whose activation might afford the ego primary pleasure, appears to be one of the foundations of the development of human civilization. Some part of this instinctual repression is effected by its religions, in that they require the individual to sacrifice his instinctual pleasure to the Deity: 'Vengeance is mine, saith the Lord.' In the development of the ancient religions one seems to discern that many things which mankind had renounced as 'iniquities' had been surrendered to the Deity and were still permitted in his name, so that the handing over to him of bad and socially harmful instincts was the means by which man freed himself from their domination. For this reason, it is surely no accident that all the attributes of man, along with the misdeeds that follow from them, were to an unlimited amount ascribed to the ancient gods. Nor is it a contradiction of this that nevertheless man was not permitted to justify his own iniquities by appealing to divine example.

Creative Writers and Day-Dreaming

The informal diction Freud employed in this paper is a good instance of his capacity for adjusting his style to his audience. He delivered the paper to about ninety laymen, brought together by one of his publishers, Hugo Heller, late in 1907. The English title misses the main psychoanalytic point of the paper, which connects the play of children with the *fantasies* of "creative writers" (Freud uses the economical, untranslatable German word "Dichter," which embraces story-tellers, novelists, poets, and playwrights). It is interesting to note that Freud gives to aesthetic pleasure the name of "fore-pleasure," which links it to sexual pleasure. Altogether, the paper, however casual its tone, is a serious contribution to the psychology of creativity, and hence part of Freud's effort at constructing a general psychology.

We laymen have always been intensely curious to know—like the Cardinal who put a similar question to Ariosto[1]—from what sources that strange being, the creative writer, draws his material, and how he manages to make such an impression on us with it and to arouse in us emotions of which, perhaps, we had not even thought ourselves capable. Our interest is only heightened the more by the fact that, if we ask him, the writer himself gives us no explanation, or none that is satisfactory; and it is not at all weakened by our knowledge that not even the clearest insight into the determinants of his choice of material and into the nature of the art of creating imaginative form will ever help to make creative writers of *us*.

If we could at least discover in ourselves or in people like ourselves an activity which was in some way akin to creative writing! An examination of it would then give us a hope of obtaining the beginnings of an explanation of the creative work of writers. And, indeed, there is

---

1. [Cardinal Ippolito d'Este was Ariosto's first patron, to whom he dedicated the *Orlando Furioso*. The poet's only reward was the question: 'Where did you find so many stories, Lodovico?']

some prospect of this being possible. After all, creative writers themselves like to lessen the distance between their kind and the common run of humanity; they so often assure us that every man is a poet at heart and that the last poet will not perish till the last man does.

Should we not look for the first traces of imaginative activity as early as in childhood? The child's best-loved and most intense occupation is with his play or games. Might we not say that every child at play behaves like a creative writer, in that he creates a world of his own, or, rather, re-arranges the things of his world in a new way which pleases him? It would be wrong to think he does not take that world seriously; on the contrary, he takes his play very seriously and he expends large amounts of emotion on it. The opposite of play is not what is serious but what is real. In spite of all the emotion with which he cathects his world of play, the child distinguishes it quite well from reality; and he likes to link his imagined objects and situations to the tangible and visible things of the real world. This linking is all that differentiates the child's 'play' from 'phantasying'.

The creative writer does the same as the child at play. He creates a world of phantasy which he takes very seriously—that is, which he invests with large amounts of emotion—while separating it sharply from reality. Language has preserved this relationship between children's play and poetic creation. It gives [in German] the name of '*Spiel*' ['play'] to those forms of imaginative writing which require to be linked to tangible objects and which are capable of representation. It speaks of a '*Lustspiel*' or '*Trauerspiel*' ['comedy' or 'tragedy': literally, 'pleasure play' or 'mourning play'] and describes those who carry out the representation as '*Schauspieler*' ['players': literally 'show-players']. The unreality of the writer's imaginative world, however, has very important consequences for the technique of his art; for many things which, if they were real, could give no enjoyment, can do so in the play of phantasy, and many excitements which, in themselves, are actually distressing, can become a source of pleasure for the hearers and spectators at the performance of a writer's work.

There is another consideration for the sake of which we will dwell a moment longer on this contrast between reality and play. When the child has grown up and has ceased to play, and after he has been labouring for decades to envisage the realities of life with proper seriousness, he may one day find himself in a mental situation which once more undoes the contrast between play and reality. As an adult he can look back on the intense seriousness with which he once carried on his games in childhood; and, by equating his ostensibly serious occupations of to-day with his childhood games, he can throw off the too heavy burden imposed on him by life and win the high yield of pleasure afforded by *humour*.

As people grow up, then, they cease to play, and they seem to give up the yield of pleasure which they gained from playing. But whoever understands the human mind knows that hardly anything is harder for a man than to give up a pleasure which he has once experienced. Actually, we can never give anything up; we only exchange one thing for another. What appears to be a renunciation is really the formation of a substitute or surrogate. In the same way, the growing child, when he stops playing, gives up nothing but the link with real objects; instead of *playing*, he now *phantasies*. He builds castles in the air and creates what are called *day-dreams*. I believe that most people construct phantasies at times in their lives. This is a fact which has long been overlooked and whose importance has therefore not been sufficiently appreciated.

People's phantasies are less easy to observe than the play of children. The child, it is true, plays by himself or forms a closed psychical system with other children for the purposes of a game; but even though he may not play his game in front of the grown-ups, he does not, on the other hand, conceal it from them. The adult, on the contrary, is ashamed of his phantasies and hides them from other people. He cherishes his phantasies as his most intimate possessions, and as a rule he would rather confess his misdeeds than tell anyone his phantasies. It may come about that for that reason he believes he is the only person who invents such phantasies and has no idea that creations of this kind are widespread among other people. This difference in the behaviour of a person who plays and a person who phantasies is accounted for by the motives of these two activities, which are nevertheless adjuncts to each other.

A child's play is determined by wishes: in point of fact by a single wish—one that helps in his upbringing—the wish to be big and grown up. He is always playing at being 'grown up', and in his games he imitates what he knows about the lives of his elders. He has no reason to conceal this wish. With the adult, the case is different. On the one hand, he knows that he is expected not to go on playing or phantasying any longer, but to act in the real world; on the other hand, some of the wishes which give rise to his phantasies are of a kind which it is essential to conceal. Thus he is ashamed of his phantasies as being childish and as being unpermissible.

But, you will ask, if people make such a mystery of their phantasying, how is it that we know such a lot about it? Well, there is a class of human beings upon whom, not a god, indeed, but a stern goddess—Necessity—has allotted the task of telling what they suffer and what things give them happiness.[2] These are the victims of nervous illness, who are obliged to tell their phantasies, among other things, to the doctor by whom they expect to be cured by mental treatment. This is

2. {This sentence, as the editors note, is an allusion (unmistakable to any educated German or Austrian) to Goethe's *Torquato Tasso*: in the concluding scene, the troubled hero of the play exclaims,

"Und wenn der Mensch in seiner Qual verstummt,
Gab mir ein Gott zu sagen, wie ich leide—

And when a man falls silent in his torment / A god granted me to tell how I suffer."}

our best source of knowledge, and we have since found good reason to suppose that our patients tell us nothing that we might not also hear from healthy people.

Let us now make ourselves acquainted with a few of the characteristics of phantasying. We may lay it down that a happy person never phantasies, only an unsatisfied one. The motive forces of phantasies are unsatisfied wishes, and every single phantasy is the fulfilment of a wish, a correction of unsatisfying reality. These motivating wishes vary according to the sex, character and circumstances of the person who is having the phantasy; but they fall naturally into two main groups. They are either ambitious wishes, which serve to elevate the subject's personality; or they are erotic ones. In young women the erotic wishes predominate almost exclusively, for their ambition is as a rule absorbed by erotic trends. In young men egoistic and ambitious wishes come to the fore clearly enough alongside of erotic ones. But we will not lay stress on the opposition between the two trends; we would rather emphasize the fact that they are often united. Just as, in many altar-pieces, the portrait of the donor is to be seen in a corner of the picture, so, in the majority of ambitious phantasies, we can discover in some corner or other the lady for whom the creator of the phantasy performs all his heroic deeds and at whose feet all his triumphs are laid. Here, as you see, there are strong enough motives for concealment; the well-brought-up young woman is only allowed a minimum of erotic desire, and the young man has to learn to suppress the excess of self-regard which he brings with him from the spoilt days of his childhood, so that he may find his place in a society which is full of other individuals making equally strong demands.

We must not suppose that the products of this imaginative activity—the various phantasies, castles in the air and day-dreams—are stereotyped or unalterable. On the contrary, they fit themselves in to the subject's shifting impressions of life, change with every change in his situation, and receive from every fresh active impression what might be called a 'date-mark'. The relation of a phantasy to time is in general very important. We may say that it hovers, as it were, between three times—the three moments of time which our ideation involves. Mental work is linked to some current impression, some provoking occasion in the present which has been able to arouse one of the subject's major wishes. From there it harks back to a memory of an earlier experience (usually an infantile one) in which this wish was fulfilled; and it now creates a situation relating to the future which represents a fulfilment of the wish. What it thus creates is a day-dream or phantasy, which carries about it traces of its origin from the occasion which provoked it and from the memory. Thus past, present and future are strung together, as it were, on the thread of the wish that runs through them.

A very ordinary example may serve to make what I have said clear. Let us take the case of a poor orphan boy to whom you have given the address of some employer where he may perhaps find a job. On his way there he may indulge in a day-dream appropriate to the situation from which it arises. The content of his phantasy will perhaps be something like this. He is given a job, finds favour with his new employer, makes himself indispensable in the business, is taken into his employer's family, marries the charming young daughter of the house, and then himself becomes a director of the business, first as his employer's partner and then as his successor. In this phantasy, the dreamer has regained what he possessed in his happy childhood—the protecting house, the loving parents and the first objects of his affectionate feelings. You will see from this example the way in which the wish makes use of an occasion in the present to construct, on the pattern of the past, a picture of the future.

There is a great deal more that could be said about phantasies; but I will only allude as briefly as possible to certain points. If phantasies become over-luxuriant and over-powerful, the conditions are laid for an onset of neurosis or psychosis. Phantasies, moreover, are the immediate mental precursors of the distressing symptoms complained of by our patients. Here a broad by-path branches off into pathology.

I cannot pass over the relation of phantasies to dreams. Our dreams at night are nothing else than phantasies like these, as we can demonstrate from the interpretation of dreams. Language, in its unrivalled wisdom, long ago decided the question of the essential nature of dreams by giving the name of 'day-dreams' to the airy creations of phantasy. If the meaning of our dreams usually remains obscure to us in spite of this pointer, it is because of the circumstance that at night there also arise in us wishes of which we are ashamed; these we must conceal from ourselves, and they have consequently been repressed, pushed into the unconscious. Repressed wishes of this sort and their derivatives are only allowed to come to expression in a very distorted form. When scientific work had succeeded in elucidating this factor of *dream-distortion*, it was no longer difficult to recognize that night-dreams are wish-fulfilments in just the same way as day-dreams—the phantasies which we all know so well.

So much for phantasies. And now for the creative writer. May we really attempt to compare the imaginative writer with the 'dreamer in broad daylight', and his creations with day-dreams? Here we must begin by making an initial distinction. We must separate writers who, like the ancient authors of epics and tragedies, take over their material ready-made, from writers who seem to originate their own material. We will keep to the latter kind, and, for the purposes of our comparison, we will choose not the writers most highly esteemed by the critics, but the less pretentious authors of novels, romances and short stories, who never-theless have the widest and most eager circle of readers of both sexes. One feature above all cannot fail to strike us about the creations of these story-writers: each of them has a hero who is the centre of interest, for whom the writer tries to win our sympathy by every possible means and whom he seems to place under the protection of a special Providence. If, at the end of one chapter of my story, I leave the hero unconscious and bleeding from severe wounds, I am sure to find him at the beginning of the next being carefully nursed and on the way to recovery; and if the first volume closes with the ship he is in going down in a storm at sea, I am certain, at the opening of the second volume, to read of his miraculous rescue—a rescue without which the story could not proceed. The feeling of security with which I follow the hero through his perilous adventures is the same as the feeling with which a hero in real life throws himself into the water to save a drowning man or exposes himself to the enemy's fire in order to storm a battery. It is the true heroic feeling, which one of our best writers has expressed in an inimitable phrase: 'Nothing can happen to *me*!'[3] It seems to me, however, that through this revealing characteristic of invulnerability we can immediately recognize His Majesty the Ego, the hero alike of every day-dream and of every story.

Other typical features of these egocentric stories point to the same kinship. The fact that all the women in the novel invariably fall in love with the hero can hardly be looked on as a portrayal of reality, but it is easily understood as a necessary constituent of a day-dream. The same is true of the fact that the other characters in the story are sharply divided into good and bad, in defiance of the variety of human characters that are to be observed in real life. The 'good' ones are the helpers, while the 'bad' ones are the enemies and rivals, of the ego which has become the hero of the story.

We are perfectly aware that very many imaginative writings are far removed from the model of the naïve day-dream; and yet I cannot suppress the suspicion that even the most extreme deviations from that model could be linked with it through an uninterrupted series of transitional cases. It has struck me that in many of what are known as 'psychological' novels only one person—once again the hero—is described from within. The author sits inside his mind, as it were, and looks at the other characters from outside. The psychological novel in general no doubt owes its special nature to the inclination of the modern writer to split up his ego, by self-observation, into many part-egos, and, in consequence, to personify the conflicting currents of his own mental life in several heroes. Certain novels, which might be described as 'eccentric', seem to stand in quite special contrast to the type of the day-dream. In these, the person who is introduced as the hero plays only a very small active part; he sees the actions and sufferings of other people pass before him like a spectator. Many of Zola's later works belong to this category. But I must point out that the psychological analysis of individuals who are not creative writers, and who diverge in some respects

3. ['Es kann dir nix g'schehen!' This phrase from Anzengruber, the Viennese dramatist, was a favourite one of Freud's.]

from the so-called norm, has shown us analogous variations of the day-dream, in which the ego contents itself with the role of spectator.

If our comparison of the imaginative writer with the day-dreamer, and of poetical creation with the day-dream, is to be of any value, it must, above all, show itself in some way or other fruitful. Let us, for instance, try to apply to these authors' works the thesis we laid down earlier concerning the relation between phantasy and the three periods of time and the wish which runs through them; and, with its help, let us try to study the connections that exist between the life of the writer and his works. No one has known, as a rule, what expectations to frame in approaching this problem; and often the connection has been thought of in much too simple terms. In the light of the insight we have gained from phantasies, we ought to expect the following state of affairs. A strong experience in the present awakens in the creative writer a memory of an earlier experience (usually belonging to his childhood) from which there now proceeds a wish which finds its fulfilment in the creative work. The work itself exhibits elements of the recent provoking occasion as well as of the old memory.

Do not be alarmed at the complexity of this formula. I suspect that in fact it will prove to be too exiguous a pattern. Nevertheless, it may contain a first approach to the true state of affairs; and, from some experiments I have made, I am inclined to think that this way of looking at creative writings may turn out not unfruitful. You will not forget that the stress it lays on childhood memories in the writer's life—a stress which may perhaps seem puzzling—is ultimately derived from the as-sumption that a piece of creative writing, like a day-dream, is a contin-uation of, and a substitute for, what was once the play of childhood.

We must not neglect, however, to go back to the kind of imaginative works which we have to recognize, not as original creations, but as the re-fashioning of ready-made and familiar material. Even here, the writer keeps a certain amount of independence, which can express itself in the choice of material and in changes in it which are often quite extensive. In so far as the material is already at hand, however, it is derived from the popular treasure-house of myths, legends and fairy tales. The study of constructions of folk-psychology such as these is far from being com-plete, but it is extremely probable that myths, for instance, are distorted vestiges of the wishful phantasies of whole nations, the *secular dreams* of youthful humanity.

You will say that, although I have put the creative writer first in the title of my paper, I have told you far less about him than about phantasies. I am aware of that, and I must try to excuse it by pointing to the present state of our knowledge. All I have been able to do is to throw out some encouragements and suggestions which, starting from the study of phan-tasies, lead on to the problem of the writer's choice of his literary material. As for the other problem—by what means the creative writer achieves the emotional effects in us that are aroused by his creations—we have as yet not touched on it at all. But I should like at least to point out to you the path that leads from our discussion of phantasies to the problems of poetical effects.

You will remember how I have said that the day-dreamer carefully conceals his phantasies from other people because he feels he has reasons for being ashamed of them. I should now add that even if he were to communicate them to us he could give us no pleasure by his disclosures. Such phantasies, when we learn them, repel us or at least leave us cold. But when a creative writer presents his plays to us or tells us what we are inclined to take to be his personal day-dreams, we experience a great pleasure, and one which probably arises from the confluence of many sources. How the writer accomplishes this is his innermost secret; the essential *ars poetica* lies in the technique of overcoming the feeling of repulsion in us which is undoubtedly connected with the barriers that rise between each single ego and the others. We can guess two of the methods used by this technique. The writer softens the character of his egoistic day-dreams by altering and disguising it, and he bribes us by the purely formal—that is, aesthetic—yield of pleasure which he offers us in the presentation of his phantasies. We give the name of an *incentive bonus*, or a *fore-pleasure*, to a yield of pleasure such as this, which is offered to us so as to make possible the release of still greater pleasure arising from deeper psychical sources. In my opinion, all the aesthetic pleasure which a creative writer affords us has the character of a fore-pleasure of this kind, and our actual enjoyment of an imaginative work proceeds from a liberation of tensions in our minds. It may even be that not a little of this effect is due to the writer's enabling us thenceforward to enjoy our own day-dreams without self-reproach or shame. This brings us to the threshold of new, interesting and complicated enquiries; but also, at least for the moment, to the end of our discussion.

Leonardo da Vinci and a Memory of His Childhood

Freud worked on this long paper about Leonardo da Vinci from the fall of 1909 to the spring of 1910 and published it late in May. It was one of his favorite productions. But it has also been a favorite among Freud's critics, for it is plagued by problems severe enough to call his whole chain of argumentation into question. (I comment on the most serious of these below, p. 455.) Freud took particular pleasure in this investigation because he saw it as a stage in psychoanalysis's conquest of culture. "Biography, too, must become ours," he wrote to Jung on October 17, 1909, and added that "the riddle of Leonardo da Vinci's character has suddenly become transparent to me. That, then, would be the first step in biography." (See Gay, *Freud*, p. 268.) Psychoanalytic biography, he was convinced, would humanize the writing of lives. And he took pleasure in this paper, too, because he greatly admired Leonardo as one "among the greatest of the human race." Yet this admiration did not exempt Leonardo from psychoanalytic scrutiny. "There is no one so great," Freud wrote, "as to be disgraced by being subject to the laws which govern both normal and pathological activity with equal cogency." There were other, hidden, aspects to Freud's preoccupation with Leonardo: his study of this artist, whose homosexual inclinations he considered as proved, came at a time when he was analyzing the residues of his own feelings for his former intimate friend Wilhelm Fliess. In any event, quite apart from this autobiographical source of Freud's interest in Leonardo's "case," his discussion of one way to homosexual object-choice remains of great interest. One point should be made about his brilliant, if flawed, performance: Freud strenuously denied that he, or psychoanalysis, could ever penetrate to the sources of creativity. His aim was more modest: to uncover the determinants of Leonardo's "mental and intellectual development." Much later, in a famous disclaimer in his paper "Dostoevsky and Parricide" (1928), he said it again: "Before the problem of the creative artist analysis must, alas, lay down its arms" (SE XXI, 177).

I

When psychiatric research, normally content to draw on frailer men for its material, approaches one who is among the greatest of the human race, it is not doing so for the reasons so frequently ascribed to it by laymen. 'To blacken the radiant and drag the sublime into the dust'[1] is no part of its purpose, and there is no satisfaction for it in narrowing the gulf which separates the perfection of the great from the inadequacy of the objects that are its usual concern. But it cannot help finding worthy of understanding everything that can be recognized in those illustrious models, and it believes there is no one so great as to be disgraced by being subject to the laws which govern both normal and pathological activity with equal cogency.

Leonardo da Vinci (1452–1519) was admired even by his contemporaries as one of the greatest men of the Italian renaissance; yet in their time he had already begun to seem an enigma, just as he does to us today. He was a universal genius 'whose outlines can only be surmised,—never defined'.[2] In his own time his most decisive influence was in painting, and it was left to us to recognize the greatness of the natural scientist (and engineer) that was combined in him with the artist. Though he left behind him masterpieces of painting, while his scientific discoveries remained unpublished and unused, the investigator in him never in the course of his development left the artist entirely free, but often made severe encroachments on him and perhaps in the end suppressed him. In the last hour of his life, according to the words that Vasari gives him, he reproached himself with having offended God and man by his

---

1. {Freud is quoting from a poem of Schiller's, "Das Mädchen von Orleans."}
2. {Freud is here quoting the great Swiss historian of the Italian Renaissance, Jacob Burckhardt, whose awe before Leonardo was as great as Freud's.}

failure to do his duty in his art. And even if this story of Vasari's has neither external nor much internal probability but belongs to the legend which began to be woven around the mysterious Master even before his death, it is still of incontestable value as evidence of what men believed at the time.

What was it that prevented Leonardo's personality from being understood by his contemporaries? The cause of this was certainly not the versatility of his talents and the range of his knowledge, which enabled him to introduce himself to the court of the Duke of Milan, Lodovico Sforza, called Il Moro, as a performer on a kind of lute of his own invention, or allowed him to write the remarkable letter to the same duke in which he boasted of his achievements as architect and military engineer. For the days of the renaissance were quite familiar with such a combination of wide and diverse abilities in a single individual— though we must allow that Leonardo himself was one of the most brilliant examples of this. Nor did he belong to the type of genius who has received a niggardly outward endowment from Nature, and who in his turn places no value on the outward forms of life, but in a spirit of painful gloom flies from all dealings with mankind. On the contrary, he was tall and well-proportioned; his features were of consummate beauty and his physical strength unusual; he was charming in his manner, supremely eloquent, and cheerful and amiable to everyone. He loved beauty in the things that surrounded him; he was fond of magnificent clothing and valued every refinement of living. * * *

It is indeed quite possible that the idea of a radiantly happy and pleasure-loving Leonardo is only applicable to the first and longer period of the artist's life. Afterwards, when the downfall of Lodovico Moro's rule forced him to leave Milan, the city that was the centre of his activity and where his position was assured, and to pursue a life lacking in security and not rich in external successes, until he found his last asylum in France, the sparkle of his temperament may have grown dim and some strange sides of his nature may have been thrown into prominence. Moreover the turning of his interests from his art to science, which increased as time went on, must have played its part in widening the gulf between himself and his contemporaries. All the efforts in which in their opinion he frittered away his time when he could have been industriously painting to order and becoming rich (as, for example, his former fellow-student Perugino did) seemed to them to be merely capricious trifling or even caused him to be suspected of being in the service of the 'black art'. We are in a position to understand him better, for we know from his notes what were the arts that he practised. In an age which was beginning to replace the authority of the Church by that of antiquity and which was not yet familiar with any form of research not based on presuppositions, Leonardo—the forerunner and by no means unworthy rival of Bacon and Copernicus—was necessarily isolated. In his dissection of the dead bodies of horses and human beings, in his construction of flying machines, and in his studies on the nutrition of plants and their reactions to poisons, he certainly departed widely from the commentators on Aristotle, and came close to the despised alchemists, in whose laboratories experimental research had found some refuge at least in those unfavourable times.

The effect that this had on his painting was that he took up his brush with reluctance, painted less and less, left what he had begun for the most part unfinished and cared little about the ultimate fate of his works. And this was what he was blamed for by his contemporaries: to them his attitude towards his art remained a riddle.

Several of Leonardo's later admirers have made attempts to acquit his character of the flaw of instability. In his defence they claim that he is blamed for what is a general feature of great artists: even the energetic Michelangelo, a man entirely given up to his labours, left many of his works incomplete, and it was no more his fault than it was Leonardo's in the parallel instance. Moreover, in the case of some of the pictures, they urge, it is not so much a question of their being unfinished as of his declaring them to be so. What appears to the layman as a masterpiece is never for the creator of the work of art more than an unsatisfactory embodiment of what he intended; he has some dim notion of a perfection, whose likeness time and again he despairs of reproducing. Least of all, they claim, is it right to make the artist responsible for the ultimate fate of his works.

Valid as some of these excuses may be, they still do not cover the whole state of affairs that confronts us in Leonardo. The same distressing struggle with a work, the final flight from it and the indifference to its future fate may recur in many other artists, but there is no doubt that this behaviour is shown in Leonardo in an extreme degree. * *· *

The slowness with which Leonardo worked was proverbial. He painted at the Last Supper in the Convent of Santa Maria delle Grazie in Milan, after the most thorough preparatory studies, for three whole years. One of his contemporaries Matteo Bandelli, the story-writer, who at the time was a young monk in the convent, tells how Leonardo often used to climb up the scaffolding early in the morning and remain there till twilight never once laying his brush aside, and with no thought of eating or drinking. Then days would pass without his putting his hand to it. Sometimes he would remain for hours in front of the painting, merely examining it in his mind. At other times he would come straight to the convent from the court in the castle at Milan, where he was making the model of the equestrian statue for Francesco Sforza, in order to add a few strokes of the brush to a figure, and then immediately break off. According to Vasari he spent four years in painting the portrait of Mona Lisa, the wife of the Florentine Francesco del Giocondo, without being able to bring it to final completion. This circumstance may also account for the fact that the picture was never delivered to the man who commissioned it, but instead remained with Leonardo and was taken to

France by him. It was brought by King Francis I, and to-day forms one of the greatest treasures of the Louvre.

If these reports of the way in which Leonardo worked are compared with the evidence of the extraordinarily numerous sketches and studies which he left behind him and which exhibit every *motif* appearing in his paintings in a great variety of forms, we are bound totally to reject the idea that traits of hastiness and unsteadiness acquired the slightest influence over Leonardo's relation to his art. On the contrary, it is possible to observe a quite extraordinary profundity, a wealth of possibilities between which a decision can only be reached with hesitation, demands which can hardly be satisfied, and an inhibition in the actual execution which is not in fact to be explained even by the artist inevitably falling short of his ideal. The slowness which had all along been conspicuous in Leonardo's work is seen to be a symptom of this inhibition and to be the forerunner of his subsequent withdrawal from painting. It was this too which determined the fate of the Last Supper—a fate that was not undeserved. Leonardo could not become reconciled to fresco painting, which demands rapid work while the ground is still moist, and this was the reason why he chose oil colours, the drying of which permitted him to protract the completion of the painting to suit his mood and leisure. These pigments however detached themselves from the ground on which they were applied and which separated them from the wall. Added to this, the defects in the wall, and the later fortunes of the building itself, determined what seems to be the inevitable ruin of the picture.

The miscarriage of a similar technical experiment appears to have caused the destruction of the Battle of Anghiari, the painting which, in competition with Michelangelo, he began to paint some time afterwards on a wall of the Sala del Consiglio in Florence, and which he also abandoned in an unfinished condition. Here it seems as if an alien interest—in experimentation—at first reinforced the artistic one, only to damage the work later on.

The character of Leonardo the man showed some other unusual traits and apparent contradictions. A certain inactivity and indifference seemed obvious in him. At a time when everyone was trying to gain the widest scope for his activity—a goal unattainable without the development of energetic aggressiveness towards other people—Leonardo was notable for his quiet peaceableness and his avoidance of all antagonism and controversy. He was gentle and kindly to everyone; he declined, it is said, to eat meat, since he did not think it justifiable to deprive animals of their lives; and he took particular pleasure in buying birds in the market and setting them free. He condemned war and bloodshed and described man as not so much the king of the animal world but rather the worst of the wild beasts. But this feminine delicacy of feeling did not deter him from accompanying condemned criminals on their way to execution in order to study their features distorted by fear and to sketch them in his notebook. Nor did it stop him from devising the cruellest offensive weapons and from entering the service of Cesare Borgia as chief military engineer. He often gave the appearance of being indifferent to good and evil, or he insisted on measurement by a special standard. He accompanied Cesare in a position of authority during the campaign that brought the Romagna into the possession of that most ruthless and faithless of adversaries. There is not a line in Leonardo's notebooks which reveals any criticism of the events of those days, or any concern in them. A comparison suggests itself here with Goethe during the French campaign.

If a biographical study is really intended to arrive at an understanding of its hero's mental life it must not—as happens in the majority of biographies as a result of discretion or prudishness—silently pass over its subject's sexual activity or sexual individuality. What is known of Leonardo in this respect is little: but that little is full of significance. In an age which saw a struggle between sensuality without restraint and gloomy asceticism, Leonardo represented the cool repudiation of sexuality—a thing that would scarcely be expected of an artist and a portrayer of feminine beauty. Solmi quotes the following sentence of his which is evidence of his frigidity: 'The act of procreation and everything connected with it is so disgusting that mankind would soon die out if it were not an old-established custom and if there were not pretty faces and sensuous natures.' His posthumous writings, which not only deal with the greatest scientific problems but also contain trivialities that strike us as scarcely worthy of so great a mind (an allegorical natural history, animal fables, jokes, prophecies), are chaste—one might say even abstinent—to a degree that would cause surprise in a work of *belles lettres* even to-day. So resolutely do they shun everything sexual that it would seem as if Eros alone, the preserver of all living things, was not worthy material for the investigator in his pursuit of knowledge. It is well known how frequently great artists take pleasure in giving vent to their phantasies in erotic and even crudely obscene pictures. In Leonardo's case on the contrary we have only some anatomical sketches of the internal female genitals, the position of the embryo in the womb and so on.

It is doubtful whether Leonardo ever embraced a woman in passion; nor is it known that he had any intimate mental relationship with a woman, such as Michelangelo's with Vittoria Colonna. While he was still an apprentice, living in the house of his master Verrocchio, a charge of forbidden homosexual practices was brought against him, along with some other young people, which ended in his acquittal. He seems to have fallen under this suspicion because he had employed a boy of bad reputation as a model. When he had become a Master, he surrounded himself with handsome boys and youths whom he took as pupils. The last of these pupils, Francesco Melzi, accompanied him to France, remained with him up to his death and was named by him as his heir. Without sharing in the certainty of his modern biographers, who naturally reject the possibility that there was a sexual relationship between him and his pupils as a baseless insult to the great man, we may take it as much more probable that Leonardo's affectionate relations with the young men who—as was the custom with pupils at that time—shared his existence did not extend to sexual activity. Moreover a high degree of sexual activity is not to be attributed to him.

There is only one way in which the peculiarity of this emotional and sexual life can be understood in connection with Leonardo's double nature as an artist and as a scientific investigator. Among his biographers, to whom a psychological approach is often very alien, there is to my knowledge only one, Edmondo Solmi, who has approached the solution of the problem; but a writer who has chosen Leonardo as the hero of a great historical novel, Dmitry Sergeyevich Merezhkovsky, has made a similar reading of this unusual man the basis of his portrait and has given clear expression to his conception, not indeed in plain language, but (after the way of writers of imagination) in plastic terms. * * *

In an essay in the *Conferenze Fiorentine* the following pronouncement of Leonardo's is quoted, which represents his confession of faith and provides the key to his nature: * * * One has no right to love or hate anything if one has not acquired a thorough knowledge of its nature. And the same is repeated by Leonardo in a passage in the treatise on painting where he seems to be defending himself against the charge of irreligion: 'But such carping critics would do better to keep silent. For that (line of conduct) is the way to become acquainted with the Creator of so many wonderful things, and this is the way to love so great an Inventor. For in truth great love springs from great knowledge of the beloved object, and if you know it but little you will be able to love it only a little or not at all . . .'

The value of these remarks of Leonardo's is not to be looked for in their conveying an important psychological fact; for what they assert is obviously false, and Leonardo must have known this as well as we do. It is not true that human beings delay loving or hating until they have studied and become familiar with the nature of the object to which these affects apply. On the contrary they love impulsively, from emotional motives which have nothing to do with knowledge, and whose operation is at most weakened by reflection and consideration. Leonardo, then, could only have meant that the love practised by human beings was not of the proper and unobjectionable kind: one *should* love in such a way as to hold back the affect, subject it to the process of reflection and only let it take its course when it has stood up to the test of thought. And at the same time we understand that he wishes to tell us that it happens so in his case and that it would be worth while for everyone else to treat love and hatred as he does.

And in his case it really seems to have been so. His affects were controlled and subjected to the instinct for research; he did not love and hate, but asked himself about the origin and significance of what he was to love or hate. Thus he was bound at first to appear indifferent to good and evil, beauty and ugliness. During this work of investigation love and hate threw off their positive or negative signs and were both alike transformed into intellectual interest. In reality Leonardo was not devoid of passion; he did not lack the divine spark which is directly or indirectly the driving force—*il primo motore*—behind all human activity. He had merely converted his passion into a thirst for knowledge; he then applied himself to investigation with the persistence, constancy and penetration which is derived from passion, and at the climax of intellectual labour, when knowledge had been won, he allowed the long restrained affect to break loose and to flow away freely, as a stream of water drawn from a river is allowed to flow away when its work is done. When, at the climax of a discovery, he could survey a large portion of the whole nexus, he was overcome by emotion, and in ecstatic language praised the splendour of the part of creation that he had studied, or—in religious phraseology—the greatness of his Creator. * * *

Because of his insatiable and indefatigable thirst for knowledge Leonardo has been called the Italian Faust. But quite apart from doubts about a possible transformation of the instinct to investigate back into an enjoyment of life—a transformation which we must take as fundamental in the tragedy of Faust—the view may be hazarded that Leonardo's development approaches Spinoza's mode of thinking.

A conversion of psychical instinctual force into various forms of activity can perhaps no more be achieved without loss than a conversion of physical forces. The example of Leonardo teaches us how many other things we have to take into account in connection with these processes. The postponement of loving until full knowledge is acquired ends in a substitution of the latter for the former. A man who has won his way to a state of knowledge cannot properly be said to love and hate; he remains beyond love and hatred. He has investigated instead of loving And that is perhaps why Leonardo's life was so much poorer in love than that of other great men, and of other artists. The stormy passions of a nature that inspires and consumes, passions in which other men have enjoyed their richest experience, appear not to have touched him.

There are some further consequences. Investigating has taken the place of acting and creating as well. A man who has begun to have an inkling of the grandeur of the universe with all its complexities and its laws readily forgets his own insignificant self. Lost in admiration and filled with true humility, he all too easily forgets that he himself is a part of those active forces and that in accordance with the scale of his personal strength the way is open for him to try to alter a small portion of the destined course of the world—a world in which the small is still no less wonderful and significant than the great.

Leonardo's researches had perhaps first begun, as Solmi believes, in the service of his art; he directed his efforts to the properties and laws of light, colours, shadows and perspective in order to ensure mastery in the imitation of nature and to point the same way to others. It is probable that at that time he already overrated the value to the artist of these branches of knowledge. Still constantly following the lead given by the requirements of his painting he was then driven to investigate the painter's subjects, animals and plants, and the proportions of the human body, and, passing from their exterior, to proceed to gain a knowledge of their internal structure and their vital functions, which indeed also find expression in their appearance and have a claim to be depicted in art. And finally the instinct, which had become overwhelming, swept him away until the connection with the demands of his art was severed, so that he discovered the general laws of mechanics and divined the history of the stratification and fossilization in the Arno valley, and until he could enter in large letters in his book the discovery: *Il sole non si move.*[3] His investigations extended to practically every branch of natural science, and in every single one he was a discoverer or at least a prophet and pioneer. Yet his urge for knowledge was always directed to the external world; something kept him far away from the investigation of the human mind. In the 'Academia Vinciana', for which he drew some cleverly intertwined emblems, there was little room for psychology.

Then, when he made the attempt to return from investigation to his starting point, the exercise of his art, he found himself disturbed by the new direction of his interests and the changed nature of his mental activity. What interested him in a picture was above all a problem; and behind the first one he saw countless other problems arising, just as he used to in his endless and inexhaustible investigation of nature. He was no longer able to limit his demands, to see the work of art in isolation and to tear it from the wide context to which he knew it belonged. After the most exhausting efforts to bring to expression in it everything which was connected with it in his thoughts, he was forced to abandon it in an unfinished state or to declare that it was incomplete.

The artist had once taken the investigator into his service to assist him; now the servant had become the stronger and suppressed his master.

When we find that in the picture presented by a person's character a single instinct has developed an excessive strength, as did the craving for knowledge in Leonardo, we look for the explanation in a special disposition—though about its determinants (which are probably organic) scarcely anything is yet known. Our psycho-analytic studies of neurotic people have however led us to form two further expectations which it would be gratifying to find confirmed in each particular case. We consider it probable that an instinct like this of excessive strength was already active in the subject's earliest childhood, and that its supremacy was established by impressions in the child's life. We make the further assumption that it found reinforcement from what were originally sexual instinctual forces, so that later it could take the place of a part of the

3. ['The sun does not move.' Quaderni d'Anatomia, 1–6, Royal Library, Windsor, V, 25.]

subject's sexual life. Thus a person of this sort would, for example, pursue research with the same passionate devotion that another would give to his love, and he would be able to investigate instead of loving. We would venture to infer that it is not only in the example of the instinct to investigate that there has been a sexual reinforcement, but also in most other cases where an instinct is of special intensity.

Observation of men's daily lives shows us that most people succeed in directing very considerable portions of their sexual instinctual forces to their professional activity. The sexual instinct is particularly well fitted to make contributions of this kind since it is endowed with a capacity for sublimation: that is, it has the power to replace its immediate aim by other aims which may be valued more highly and which are not sexual. We accept this process as proved whenever the history of a person's childhood—that is, the history of his mental development— shows that in childhood this over-powerful instinct was in the service of sexual interests. We find further confirmation if a striking atrophy occurs in the sexual life of maturity, as though a portion of sexual activity had now been replaced by the activity of the over-powerful instinct.

There seem to be special difficulties in applying these expectations to the case of an over-powerful instinct for investigation, since precisely in the case of children there is a reluctance to credit them with either this serious instinct or any noteworthy sexual interests. However, these difficulties are easily overcome. The curiosity of small children is manifested in their untiring love of asking questions; this is bewildering to the adult so long as he fails to understand that all these questions are merely circumlocutions and that they cannot come to an end because the child is only trying to make them take the place of a question which he does *not* ask. When he grows bigger and becomes better informed this expression of curiosity often comes to a sudden end. Psycho-analytic investigation provides us with a full explanation by teaching us that many, perhaps most children, or at least the most gifted ones, pass through a period, beginning when they are about three, which may be called the period of *infantile sexual researches*. So far as we know, the curiosity of children of this age does not awaken spontaneously, but is aroused by the impression made by some important event—by the actual birth of a little brother or sister, or by a fear of it based on external experiences—in which the child perceives a threat to his selfish interests. Researches are directed to the question of where babies come from, exactly as if the child were looking for ways and means to avert so undesired an event. In this way we have been astonished to learn that children refuse to believe the bits of informatioin that are given them— for example that they energetically reject the fable of the stork with its wealth of mythological meaning—, that they date their intellectual independence from this act of disbelief, and that they often feel in serious opposition to adults and in fact never afterwards forgive them for having deceived them here about the true facts of the case. They investigate along their own lines, divine the baby's presence inside its mother's body, and following the lead of the impulses of their own sexuality form theories of babies originating from eating, of their being born through the bowels, and of the obscure part played by the father. By that time they already have a notion of the sexual act, which appears to them to be something hostile and violent. But since their own sexual constitution has not yet reached the point of being able to produce babies, their investigation of where babies come from must inevitably come to nothing too and be abandoned as insoluble. The impression caused by this failure in the first attempt at intellectual independence appears to be of a lasting and deeply depressing kind.

When the period of infantile sexual researches has been terminated by a wave of energetic sexual repression, the instinct for research has three distinct possible vicissitudes open to it owing to its early connection with sexual interests. In the first of these, research shares the fate of sexuality; thenceforward curiosity remains inhibited and the free activity of intelligence may be limited for the whole of the subject's lifetime, especially as shortly after this the powerful religious inhibition of thought is brought into play by education. This is the type characterized by neurotic inhibition. We know very well that the intellectual weakness which has been acquired in this way gives an effective impetus to the outbreak of a neurotic illness. In a second type the intellectual development is sufficiently strong to resist the sexual repression which has hold of it. Some time after the infantile sexual researches have come to an end, the intelligence, having grown stronger, recalls the old association and offers its help in evading sexual repression, and the suppressed sexual activities of research return from the unconscious in the form of compulsive brooding, naturallly in a distorted and unfree form, but sufficiently powerful to sexualize thinking itself and to colour intellectual operations with the pleasure and anxiety that belong to sexual processes proper. Here investigation becomes a sexual activity, often the exclusive one, and the feeling that comes from settling things in one's mind and explaining them replaces sexual satisfaction; but the interminable character of the child's researches is also repeated in the fact that this brooding never ends and that the intellectual feeling, so much desired, of having found a solution recedes more and more into the distance.

In virtue of a special disposition, the third type, which is the rarest and most perfect, escapes both inhibition of thought and neurotic compulsive thinking. It is true that here too sexual repression comes about, but it does not succeed in relegating a component instinct of sexual desire to the unconscious. Instead, the libido evades the fate of repression by being sublimated from the very beginning into curiosity and by becoming attached to the powerful instinct for research as a reinforcement. Here, too, the research becomes to some extent compulsive and a substitute for sexual activity; but owing to the complete difference in the underlying psychical processes (sublimation instead of an irruption from the unconscious) the quality of neurosis is absent; there is no attachment to the original complexes of infantile sexual research, and the instinct can operate freely in the service of intellectual interest. Sexual repression, which has made the instinct so strong through the addition to it of sublimated libido, is still taken into account by the instinct, in that it avoids any concern with sexual themes.

If we reflect on the concurrence in Leonardo of his overpowerful instinct for research and the atrophy of his sexual life (which was restricted to what is called ideal [sublimated] homosexuality) we shall be disposed to claim him as a model instance of our third type. The core of his nature, and the secret of it, would appear to be that after his curiosity had been activated in infancy in the service of sexual interests he succeeded in sublimating the greater part of his libido into an urge for research. But it is not easy, to be sure, to prove that this view is right. To do so we should need some picture of his mental development in the first years of his childhood, and it seems foolish to hope for material of that sort when the accounts of his life are so meagre and so unreliable, and when moreover it is a question of information about circumstances that escape the attention of observers even in relation to people of our own generation.

About Leonardo's youth we know very little. He was born in 1452 in the little town of Vinci between Florence and Empoli; he was an illegitimate child, which in those days was certainly not considered a grave social stigma; his father was Ser Piero da Vinci, a notary and descended from a family of notaries and farmers who took their name from the locality of Vinci; his mother was a certain Caterina, probably a peasant girl, who later married another native of Vinci. * * * The only definite piece of information about Leonardo's childhood comes in an official document of the year 1457; it is a Florentine land-register for the purpose of taxation, which mentions Leonardo among the members of the household of the Vinci family as the five-year-old illegitimate child of Ser Piero. The marriage of Ser Piero with a certain Donna Albiera remained childless, and it was therefore possible for the young Leonardo to be brought up in his father's house. He did not leave this house till—at what age is not known—he entered Andrea del Verrocchio's studio as an apprentice. In the year 1472 Leonardo's name was already to be found in the list of members of the 'Compagnia dei Pittori'. That is all.

II

There is, so far as I know, only one place in his scientific notebooks where Leonardo inserts a piece of information about his childhood. In a passage about the flight of vultures he suddenly interrupts himself to pursue a memory from very early years which had sprung to his mind:
'It seems that I was always destined to be so deeply concerned with

vultures; for I recall as one of my very earliest memories that while I was in my cradle a vulture came down to me, and opened my mouth with its tail, and struck me many times with its tail against my lips.[4]

What we have here then is a childhood memory; and certainly one of the strangest sort. It is strange on account of its content and on account of the age to which it is assigned. That a person should be able to retain a memory of his suckling period is perhaps not impossible, but it cannot by any means be regarded as certain. What, however, this memory of Leonardo's asserts—namely that a vulture opened the child's mouth with its tail—sounds so improbable, so fabulous, that another view of it, which at a single stroke puts an end to both difficulties, has more to commend it to our judgement. On this view the scene with the vulture would not be a memory of Leonardo's but a phantasy, which he formed at a later date and transposed to his childhood.

This is often the way in which childhood memories originate. Quite unlike conscious memories from the time of maturity, they are not fixed at the moment of being experienced and afterwards repeated, but are only elicited at a later age when childhood is already past; in the process they are altered and falsified, and are put into the service of later trends, so that generally speaking they cannot be sharply distinguished from phantasies. Their nature is perhaps best illustrated by a comparison with the way in which the writing of history originated among the peoples of antiquity. As long as a nation was small and weak it gave no thought to the writing of its history. Men tilled the soil of their land, fought for their existence against their neighbours, and tried to gain territory from them and to acquire wealth. It was an age of heroes, not of historians. Then came another age, an age of reflection: men felt themselves to be rich and powerful, and now felt a need to learn where they had come from and how they had developed. Historical writing, which had begun to keep a continuous record of the present, now also cast a glance back to the past, gathered traditions and legends, interpreted the traces of antiquity that survived in customs and usages, and in this way created a history of the past. It was inevitable that this early history should have been an expression of present beliefs and wishes rather than a true picture of the past; for many things had been dropped from the nation's memory, while others were distorted, and some remains of the past were given a wrong interpretation in order to fit in with contemporary ideas. Moreover people's motive for writing history was not objective curiosity but a desire

---

4. [In the German text Freud quotes Herzfeld's translation of the Italian original. * * * There are in fact two inaccuracies in the German: 'nibio' should be 'kite' not 'vulture' * * * and 'dentro', 'within' is omitted. This last omission is in fact rectified by Freud himself below. * * *] {Actually the first inaccuracy is far more portentous than the second. It seduced Freud to undertake lengthy learned excursions into Egyptian hieroglyphics and Christian mysticism, both of which turn out to be wholly indefensible and quite irrelevant. I have therefore omitted these speculations. Freud's reconstruction of Leonardo's early emotional development can be separated from this mistranslation and its consequences. It stands—or falls—on its own account.}

to influence their contemporaries, to encourage and inspire them, or to hold a mirror up before them. A man's conscious memory of the events of his maturity is in every way comparable to the first kind of historical writing [which was a chronicle of current events]; while the memories that he has of his childhood correspond, as far as their origins and reliability are concerned, to the history of a nation's earliest days, which was compiled later and for tendentious reasons.

If, then, Leonardo's story about the vulture that visited him in his cradle is only a phantasy from a later period, one might suppose it could hardly be worth while spending much time on it. One might be satisfied with explaining it on the basis of his inclination, of which he makes no secret, to regard his preoccupation with the flight of birds as pre-ordained by destiny. Yet in underrating this story one would be committing just as great an injustice as if one were carelessly to reject the body of legends, traditions and interpretations found in a nation's early history. In spite of all the distortions and misunderstandings, they still represent the reality of the past: they are what a people forms out of the experience of its early days and under the dominance of motives that were once powerful and still operate to-day; and if it were only possible, by a knowledge of all the forces at work, to undo these distortions, there would be no difficulty in disclosing the historical truth lying behind the legendary material. The same holds good for the childhood memories or phantasies of an individual. What someone thinks he remembers from his childhood is not a matter of indifference; as a rule the residual memories— which he himself does not understand—cloak priceless pieces of evidence about the most important features in his mental development. As we now possess in the techniques of psycho-analysis excellent methods for helping us to bring this concealed material to light, we may venture to fill in the gap in Leonardo's life story by analysing his childhood phantasy. And if in doing so we remain dissatisfied with the degree of certainty which we achieve, we shall have to console ourselves with the reflection that so many other studies of this great and enigmatic man have met with no better fate.

If we examine with the eyes of a psycho-analyst Leonardo's phantasy of the vulture, it does not appear strange for long. We seem to recall having come across the same sort of thing in many places, for example in dreams; so that we may venture to translate the phantasy from its own special language into words that are generally understood. The translation is then seen to point to an erotic content. A tail, 'coda', is one of the most familiar symbols and substitutive expressions for the male organ, in Italian no less than in other languages; the situation in the phantasy, of a vulture opening the child's mouth and beating about inside it vigorously with its tail, corresponds to the idea of an act of *fellatio*, a sexual act in which the penis is put into the mouth of the person involved. It is strange that this phantasy is so completely passive in character; moreover it resembles certain dreams and phantasies found in women or passive homosexuals (who play the part of the woman in sexual relations).

I hope the reader will restrain himself and not allow a surge of indignation to prevent his following psycho-analysis any further because it leads to an unpardonable aspersion on the memory of a great and pure man the very first time it is applied to his case. Such indignation, it is clear, will never be able to tell us the significance of Leonardo's childhood phantasy; at the same time Leonardo has acknowledged the phantasy in the most unambiguous fashion, and we cannot abandon our expectation—or, if it sounds better, our prejudice—that a phantasy of this kind must have *some* meaning, in the same way as any other psychical creation: a dream, a vision or a delirium. Let us rather therefore give a fair hearing for a while to the work of analysis, which indeed has not yet spoken its last word.

The inclination to take a man's sexual organ into the mouth and suck at it, which in respectable society is considered a loathsome sexual perversion, is nevertheless found with great frequency among women of to-day—and of earlier times as well, as ancient sculptures show—, and in the state of being in love it appears completely to lose its repulsive character. Phantasies derived from this inclination are found by doctors even in women who have not become aware of the possibilities of obtaining sexual satisfaction in this way by reading Krafft-Ebing's *Psychopathia Sexualis* or from other sources of information. Women, it seems, find no difficulty in producing this kind of wishful phantasy spontaneously. Further investigation informs us that this situation, which morality condemns with such severity, may be traced to an origin of the most innocent kind. It only repeats in a different form a situation in which we all once felt comfortable—when we were still in our suckling days ('*essendo io in culla*') and took our mother's (or wet-nurse's) nipple into our mouth and sucked at it. The organic impression of this experience—the first source of pleasure in our life—doubtless remains indelibly printed on us; and when at a later date the child becomes familiar with the cow's udder whose function is that of a nipple, but whose shape and position under the belly make it resemble a penis, the preliminary stage has been reached which will later enable him to form the repellent sexual phantasy.

Now we understand why Leonardo assigned the memory of his supposed experience with the vulture to his suckling period. What the phantasy conceals is merely a reminiscence of sucking—or being suckled—at his mother's breast, a scene of human beauty that he, like so many artists, undertook to depict with his brush, in the guise of the mother of God and her child. There is indeed another point which we do not yet understand and which we must not lose sight of: this reminiscence, which has the same importance for both sexes, has been transformed by the man Leonardo into a passive homosexual phantasy. For the time being we shall put aside the question of what there may be to connect homosexuality with sucking at the mother's breast, merely recalling that tradition does in fact represent Leonardo as a man with homosexual feelings. In this connection, it is irrelevant to our purpose whether the charge brought against the young Leonardo was justified or not. What decides whether we describe someone as an invert is not his actual behaviour, but his emotional attitude.

Our interest is next claimed by another unintelligible feature of Leonardo's childhood phantasy. We interpret the phantasy as one of being suckled by his mother, and we find his mother replaced by—a vulture. Where does this vulture come from and how does it happen to be found in its present place?[5]

* * *

Our aim in dissecting a childhood phantasy is to separate the real memory that it contains from the later motives that modify and distort it. In Leonardo's case we believe that we now know the real content of the phantasy: the replacement of his mother by the vulture indicates that the child was aware of his father's absence and found himself alone with his mother. The fact of Leonardo's illegitimate birth is in harmony with his vulture phantasy; it was only on this account that he could compare himself to a vulture child. But the next reliable fact that we possess about his youth is that by the time he was five he had been received into his father's household. We are completely ignorant when that happened—whether it was a few months after his birth or whether it was a few weeks before the drawing-up of the land-register. It is here that the interpretation of the vulture phantasy comes in: Leonardo, it seems to tell us, spent the critical first years of his life not by the side of his father and stepmother, but with his poor, forsaken, real mother, so that he had time to feel the absence of his father. This seems a slender and yet a somewhat daring conclusion to have emerged from our psychoanalytic efforts, but its significance will increase as we continue our investigation. Its certainty is reinforced when we consider the circumstances that did in fact operate in Leonardo's childhood. In the same year that Leonardo was born, the sources tell us, his father, Ser Piero da Vinci, married Donna Albiera, a lady of good birth; it was to the childlessness of this marriage that the boy owed his reception into his father's (or rather his grandfather's) house—an event which had taken place by the time he was five years old, as the document attests. Now it is not usual at the start of a marriage to put an illegitimate offspring into the care of the young bride who still expects to be blessed with children of her own. Years of disappointment must surely first have elapsed before it was decided to adopt the illegitimate child—who had

5. {Freud's speculations about the vulture in ancient Egypt and Christian apologetics begin at this point.}

probably grown up an attractive young boy—as a compensation for the absence of the legitimate children that had been hoped for. It fits in best with the interpretation of the vulture phantasy if at least three years of Leonardo's life, and perhaps five, had elapsed before he could exchange the solitary person of his mother for a parental couple. And by then it was too late. In the first three or four years of life certain impressions become fixed and ways of reacting to the outside world are established which can never be deprived of their importance by later experiences.

If it is true that the unintelligible memories of a person's childhood and the phantasies that are built on them invariably emphasize the most important elements in his mental development, then it follows that the fact which the vulture phantasy confirms, namely that Leonardo spent the first years of his life alone with his mother, will have been of decisive influence in the formation of his inner life. An inevitable effect of this state of affairs was that the child—who was confronted in his early life with one problem more than other children—began to brood on this riddle with special intensity, and so at a tender age became a researcher, tormented as he was by the great question of where babies come from and what the father has to do with their origin. It was a vague suspicion that his researches and the history of his childhood were connected in this way which later prompted him to exclaim that he had been destined from the first to investigate the problem of the flight of birds since he had been visited by a vulture as he lay in his cradle. Later on it will not be difficult to show how his curiosity about the flight of birds was derived from the sexual researches of his childhood.

III

In Leonardo's childhood phantasy we have taken the element of the vulture to represent the real content of his memory, while the context in which Leonardo himself placed his phantasy has thrown a bright light on the importance which that content had for his later life. In proceeding with our work of interpretation we now come up against the strange problem of why this content has been recast into a homosexual situation. The mother who suckles her child—or to put it better, at whose breast the child sucks—has been turned into a vulture that puts its tail into the child's mouth. We have asserted that, according to the usual way in which language makes use of substitutes, the vulture's 'coda' cannot possibly signify anything other than a male genital, a penis. But we do not understand how imaginative activity can have succeeded in endowing precisely this bird which is a mother with the distinguishing mark of masculinity; and in view of this absurdity we are at a loss how to reduce this creation of Leonardo's phantasy to any rational meaning.

However, we should not despair, as we reflect on the number of apparently absurd dreams that we have in the past compelled to give up their meaning. Is there any reason why a memory of childhood should offer us more difficulty than a dream?[6]

* * *

* * * But none of these considerations gives us an explanation of the puzzling psychological fact that the human imagination does not boggle at endowing a figure which is intended to embody the essence of the mother with the mark of male potency which is the opposite of everything maternal.

Infantile sexual theories provide the explanation. There was once a time when the male genital was found compatible with the picture of the mother. When a male child first turns his curiosity to the riddles of sexual life, he is dominated by his interest in his own genital. He finds that part of his body too valuable and too important for him to be able to believe that it could be missing in other people whom he feels he resembles so much. As he cannot guess that there exists another type of genital structure of equal worth, he is forced to make the assumption that all human beings, women as well as men, possess a penis like his own. This preconception is so firmly planted in the youthful investigator that it is not destroyed even when he first observes the genitals of little girls. His perception tells him, it is true, that there is something different from what there is in him, but he is incapable of admitting to himself that the content of this perception is that he cannot find a penis in girls. That the penis could be missing strikes him as an uncanny and intolerable idea, and so in an attempt at a compromise he comes to the conclusion that little girls have a penis as well, only it is still very small; it will grow later. If it seems from later observations that this expectation is not realized, he has another remedy at his disposal: little girls too had a penis, but it was cut off and in its place was left a wound. This theoretical advance already makes use of personal experiences of a distressing kind: the boy in the meantime has heard the threat that the organ which is so dear to him will be taken away from him if he shows his interest in it too plainly. Under the influence of this threat of castration he now sees the notion he has gained of the female genitals in a new light; henceforth he will tremble for his masculinity, but at the same time he will despise the unhappy creatures on whom the cruel punishment has, as he supposes, already fallen.[7]

Before the child comes under the dominance of the castration-complex—at a time when he still holds women at full value—he begins to display an intense desire to look, as an erotic instinctual activity. He wants to see other people's genitals, at first in all probability to compare

6. {Freud takes up Egypt here once again.}

7. [*Footnote added* 1919:] The conclusion strikes me as inescapable that here we may also trace one of the roots of the anti-Semitism which appears with such elemental force and finds such irrational expression among the nations of the West. Circumcision is unconsciously equated with castration. If we venture to carry our conjectures back to the primaeval days of the human race we can surmise that originally circumcision must have been a milder substitute, designed to take the place of castration.

them with his own. The erotic attraction that comes from his mother soon culminates in a longing for her genital organ, which he takes to be a penis. With the discovery, which is not made till later, that women do not have a penis, this longing often turns into its opposite and gives place to a feeling of disgust which in the years of puberty can become the cause of psychical impotence, misogyny and permanent homosexuality. But the fixation on the object that was once strongly desired, the woman's penis, leaves indelible traces on the mental life of the child, who has pursued that portion of his infantile sexual researches with particular thoroughness. Fetishistic reverence for a woman's foot and shoe appears to take the foot merely as a substitutive symbol for the woman's penis which was once revered and later missed; without knowing it, 'coupeurs de nattes'[8] play the part of people who carry out an act of castration on the female genital organ.

People will not reach a proper understanding of the activities of children's sexuality and will probably take refuge in declaring that what has been said here is incredible, so long as they cling to the attitude taken up by our civilization of depreciating the genitals and the sexual functions. To understand the mental life of children we require analogies from primitive times. Through a long series of generations the genitals have been for us the 'pudenda', objects of shame, and even (as a result of further successful sexual repression) of disgust. If one makes a broad survey of the sexual life of our time and in particular of the classes who sustain human civilization, one is tempted to declare that it is only with reluctance that the majority of those alive to-day obey the command to propagate their kind; they feel that their dignity as human beings suffers and is degraded in the process. What is to be found among us in the way of another view of sexual life is confined to the uncultivated lower strata of society; among the higher and more refined classes it is concealed, since it is considered culturally inferior, and it ventures to put itself into practice only in the face of a bad conscience. * * *

* * *

At this point a little reflection will remind us that we ought not to feel satisfied yet with the way the vulture's tail in Leonardo's childhood phantasy has been explained. Something more seems to be contained in it which we do not yet understand. Its most striking feature, after all, was that it changed sucking at the mother's breast into being suckled, that is, into passivity, and thus into a situation whose nature is undoubtedly homosexual. When we remember the historical probability of Leonardo having behaved in his life as one who was emotionally homosexual, the question is forced upon us whether this phantasy does not indicate the existence of a causal connection between Leonardo's relation with his mother in childhood and his later manifest, if ideal [sublimated], homosexuality. We should not venture to infer a connec-

8. [Perverts who enjoy cutting off females' hair.]

tion of this sort from Leonardo's distorted reminiscence if we did not know from the psycho-analytic study of homosexual patients that such a connection does exist and is in fact an intimate and necessary one.

Homosexual men, who have in our times taken vigorous action against the restrictions imposed by law on their sexual activity, are fond of representing themselves, through their theoretical spokesmen, as being from the outset a distinct sexual species, as an intermediate sexual stage, as a 'third sex'. They are, they claim, men who are innately compelled by organic determinants to find pleasure in men and have been debarred from obtaining it in women. Much as one would be glad on grounds of humanity to endorse their claims, one must treat their theories with some reserve, for they have been advanced without regard for the psychical genesis of homosexuality. Psycho-analysis offers the means of filling this gap and of putting the assertions of homosexuals to the test. It has succeeded in the task only in the case of a small number of persons, but all the investigations undertaken so far have yielded the same surprising result. In all our male homosexual cases the subjects had had a very intense erotic attachment to a female person, as a rule their mother, during the first period of childhood, which is afterwards forgotten; this attachment was evoked or encouraged by too much tenderness on the part of the mother herself, and further reinforced by the small part played by the father during their childhood. Sadger emphasizes the fact that the mothers of his homosexual patients were frequently masculine women, women with energetic traits of character, who were able to push the father out of his proper place. I have occasionally seen the same thing, but I was more strongly impressed by cases in which the father was absent from the beginning or left the scene at an early date, so that the boy found himself left entirely under feminine influence. Indeed it almost seems as though the presence of a strong father would ensure that the son made the correct decision in his choice of object, namely someone of the opposite sex.[9]

After this preliminary stage a transformation sets in whose mechanism is known to us but whose motive forces we do not yet understand. The child's love for his mother cannot continue to develop consciously any further; it succumbs to repression. The boy represses his love for his mother: he puts himself in her place, identifies himself with her, and

9. [*Footnote added* 1919:] Psycho-analytic research has contributed two facts that are beyond question {relevant} to the understanding of homosexuality, without at the same time supposing that it has exhausted the causes of this sexual aberration. The first is the fixation of the erotic needs on the mother which has been mentioned above; the other is contained in the statement that everyone, even the most normal person, is capable of making a homosexual object-choice, and has done so at some time in his life, and either still adheres to it in his unconscious or else protects himself against it by vigorous counter-attitudes. These two discoveries put an end both to the claim of homosexuals to be regarded as a 'third sex' and to what has been believed to be the important distinction between innate and acquired homosexuality. The presence of somatic characters of the other sex (the quota provided by physical hermaphroditism) is highly conducive to the homosexual object-choice becoming manifest; but it is not decisive. It must be stated with regret that those who speak for the homosexuals in the field of science have been incapable of learning anything from the established findings of psycho-analysis.

takes his own person as a model in whose likeness he chooses the new objects of his love. In this way he has become a homosexual. What he has in fact done is to slip back to auto-erotism: for the boys whom he now loves as he grows up are after all only substitutive figures and revivals of himself in childhood—boys whom he loves in the way in which his mother loved *him* when he was a child. He finds the objects of his love along the path of *narcissism*, as we say; for Narcissus, according to the Greek legend, was a youth who preferred his own reflection to everything else and who was changed into the lovely flower of that name.[1]

Psychological considerations of a deeper kind justify the assertion that a man who has become a homosexual in this way remains unconsciously fixated to the mnemic image of his mother. By repressing his love for his mother he preserves it in his unconscious and from now on remains faithful to her. While he seems to pursue boys and to be their lover, he is in reality running away from the other women, who might cause him to be unfaithful. In individual cases direct observation has also enabled us to show that the man who gives the appearance of being susceptible only to the charms of men is in fact attracted by women in the same way as a normal man; but on each occasion he hastens to transfer the excitation he has received from women on to a male object, and in this manner he repeats over and over again the mechanism by which he acquired his homosexuality.

We are far from wishing to exaggerate the importance of these explanations of the psychical genesis of homosexuality. It is quite obvious that they are in sharp contrast to the official theories of those who speak for homosexuals, but we know that they are not sufficiently comprehensive to make a conclusive explanation of the problem possible. What is for practical reasons called homosexuality may arise from a whole variety of psychosexual inhibitory processes; the particular process we have singled out is perhaps only one among many, and is perhaps related to only one type of 'homosexuality'. We must also admit that the number of cases of our homosexual type in which it is possible to point to the determinants which we require far exceeds the number of those where the deduced effect actually takes place; so that we too cannot reject the part played by unknown constitutional factors, to which the whole of homosexuality is usually traced. We should not have had any cause at all for entering into the psychical genesis of the form of homosexuality we have studied if there were not a strong presumption that Leonardo, whose phantasy of the vulture was our starting point, was himself a homosexual of this very type.

*   *   *

We cannot expect to find in Leonardo anything more than traces of untransformed sexual inclination. But these point in one direction and

---

1. {Note this reference to narcissism. Freud would explore this vitally important stage in human development in detail in his paper on narcissism of 1914. (See below, pp. 545–62.)}

moreover allow him to be reckoned as a homosexual. It has always been emphasized that he took only strikingly handsome boys and youths as pupils. He treated them with kindness and consideration, looked after them, and when they were ill nursed them himself, just as a mother nurses her children and just as his own mother might have tended him. As he had chosen them for their beauty and not for their talent, none of them—Cesare de Sesto, Boltraffio, Andrea Salaino, Francesco Melzi and others—became a painter of importance. Generally they were unable to make themselves independent of their master, and after his death they disappeared without having left any definite mark on the history of art. The others, whose works entitled them to be called his pupils, like Luini and Bazi, called Sodoma, he probably did not know personally.

* * *

In {his} diary, which, by the way, like the diaries of other mortals, often dismisses the most important events of the day in a few words or else passes them over in complete silence, there are some entries which on account of their strangeness are quoted by all Leonardo's biographers. They are notes of small sums of money spent by the artist—notes recorded with a minute exactness, as if they were made by a pedantically strict and parsimonious head of a household. There is on the other hand no record of the expenditure of larger sums or any other evidence that the artist was at home in keeping accounts. One of these notes has to do with a new cloak which he bought for his pupil Andrea Salaino:

Silver brocade	·	·	·	·	15 lire	4 soldi
Crimson velvet for trimming.		·		9 ,,	– ,,
Braid	·	·	·	·	·	– ,,	9 ,,
Buttons	·	·	·	·	·	– ,,	12 ,,

Another very detailed note brings together all the expenses he incurred through the bad character and thievish habits of another pupil: 'On the twenty-first day of April, 1490, I began this book and made a new start on the horse. Jacomo came to me on St. Mary Magdalen's day, 1490: he is ten years old.' (Marginal note: 'thievish, untruthful, selfish, greedy.') 'On the second day I had two shirts cut out for him, a pair of trousers and a jacket, and when I put the money aside to pay for these things, he stole the money from my purse, and it was never possible to make him own up, although I was absolutely sure of it.' (Marginal note: '4 lire . . .') The report of the child's misdeeds runs on in this way and ends with the reckoning of expenses: 'In the first year, a cloak, 2 lire; 6 shirts, 4 lire; 3 jackets, 6 lire; 4 pairs of stockings, 7 lire; etc.'

Nothing is further from the wishes of Leonardo's biographers than to try to solve the problems in their hero's mental life by starting from his small weaknesses and peculiarities; and the usual comment that they make on these singular accounts is one which lays stress on the artist's kindness and consideration for his pupils. They forget that what calls for explanation is not Leonardo's behaviour, but the fact that he left these pieces of evidence of it behind him. As it is impossible to believe that his motive was that of letting proofs of his good nature fall into our hands, we must assume that it was another motive, an affective one, which led him to write these notes down. What motive it was is not easy to guess, and we should be unable to suggest one if there were not another account found among Leonardo's papers which throws a vivid light on these strangely trifling notes about his pupils' clothing, etc.:

Expenses after Caterina's death for her funeral ·	27 florins
2 pounds of wax · · · · · · ·	18 ,,
For transporting and erecting the cross · · ·	12 ,,
Catafalque · · · · · · · ·	4 ,,
Pall-bearers · · · · · · · ·	8 ,,
For 4 priests and 4 clerks · · · · ·	20 ,,
Bell-ringing · · · · · · ·	2 ,,
For the grave-diggers · · · · · ·	16 ,,
For the licence—to the officials · · · ·	1 ,,

Total   108 florins

Previous expenses

For the doctor	· · ·	4 florins
For sugar and candles	· ·	12 ,,

16 florins

Grand total   124 florins

* * *

* * * He had succeeded in subjecting his feelings to the yoke of research and in inhibiting their free utterance; but even for him there were occasions when what had been suppressed obtained expression forcibly. The death of the mother he had once loved so dearly was one of these. What we have before us in the account of the costs of the funeral is the expression—distorted out of all recognition—of his mourning for his mother. We wonder how such distortion could come about, and indeed we cannot understand it if we treat it as a normal mental process. But similar processes are well known to us in the abnormal conditions of neurosis and especially of what is known as 'obsessional neurosis'. There we can see how the expression of intense feelings, which have however become unconscious through repression, is displaced on to trivial and even foolish actions. The expression of these repressed feelings has been lowered by the forces opposed to them to such a degree that one would have had to form a most insignificant estimate of their intensity; but the imperative compulsiveness with which this trivial expressive act is performed betrays the real force of the impulses—a force which is rooted in the unconscious and which consciousness would like to deny. Only a comparison such as this with what happens in obsessional neurosis can explain Leonardo's account of the expenses of his mother's funeral. In his unconscious he was still tied to her by erotically coloured feelings, as he had been in childhood. The opposition that came from the subsequent repression of this childhood love did not allow him to set up a different and worthier memorial to her in his diary. But what emerged as a compromise from this neurotic conflict had to be carried out; and thus it was that the account was entered in the diary, and has come to the knowledge of posterity as something unintelligible.

It does not seem a very extravagant step to apply what we have learnt from the funeral account to the reckonings of the pupils' expenses. They would then be another instance of the scanty remnants of Leonardo's libidinal impulses finding expression in a compulsive manner and in a distorted form. On that view, his mother and his pupils, the likenesses of his own boyish beauty, had been his sexual objects—so far as the sexual repression which dominated his nature allows us so to describe them—and the compulsion to note in laborious detail the sums he spent on them betrayed in this strange way his rudimentary conflicts. From this it would appear that Leonardo's erotic life did really belong to the type of homosexuality whose psychical development we have succeeded in disclosing, and the emergence of the homosexual situation in his phantasy of the vulture would become intelligible to us: for its meaning was exactly what we have already asserted of that type. We should have to translate it thus: 'It was through this erotic relation with my mother that I became a homosexual.'

IV

We have not yet done with Leonardo's vulture phantasy. In words which only too plainly recall a description of a sexual act ('and struck me many times with its tail against my lips'), Leonardo stresses the intensity of the erotic relations between mother and child. From this linking of his mother's (the vulture's) activity with the prominence of the mouth zone it is not difficult to guess that a second memory is contained in the phantasy. This may be translated: 'My mother pressed innumerable passionate kisses on my mouth.' The phantasy is compounded from the memory of being suckled and being kissed by his mother.

Kindly nature has given the artist the ability to express his most secret mental impulses, which are hidden even from himself, by means of the works that he creates; and these works have a powerful effect on others who are strangers to the artist, and who are themselves unaware of the source of their emotion. Can it be that there is nothing in Leonardo's life work to bear witness to what his memory preserved as the strongest impression of his childhood? One would certainly expect there to be something. Yet if one considers the profound transformations through which an impression in an artist's life has to pass before it is allowed to make its contribution to a work of art, one will be bound to keep any claim to certainty in one's demonstration within very modest limits; and this is especially so in Leonardo's case.

Anyone who thinks of Leonardo's paintings will be reminded of a remarkable smile, at once fascinating and puzzling, which he conjured up on the lips of his female subjects. It is an unchanging smile, on long, curved lips; it has become a mark of his style and the name 'Leonardesque' has been chosen for it.[2] In the strangely beautiful face of the Florentine Mona Lisa del Giocondo it has produced the most powerful and confusing effect on whoever looks at it. This smile has called for an interpretation, and it has met with many of the most varied kinds, none of which has been satisfactory. * * *

* * *

The idea that two distinct elements are combined in Mona Lisa's smile is one that has struck several critics. They accordingly find in the beautiful Florentine's expression the most perfect representation of the contrasts which dominate the erotic life of women; the contrast between reserve and seduction, and between the most devoted tenderness and a sensuality that is ruthlessly demanding—consuming men as if they were alien beings. * * *

Leonardo spent four years painting at this picture, perhaps from 1503 to 1507, during his second period of residence in Florence, when he was over fifty. According to Vasari he employed the most elaborate artifices to keep the lady amused during the sittings and to retain the famous smile on her features. In its present condition the picture has preserved but little of all the delicate details which his brush reproduced on the canvas at that time; while it was being painted it was considered to be the highest that art could achieve, but it is certain that Leonardo himself was not satisfied with it, declaring it to be incomplete, and did not deliver it to the person who had commissioned it, but took it to France with him, where his patron, Francis I, acquired it from him for the Louvre.

Let us leave unsolved the riddle of the expression on Mona Lisa's face, and note the indisputable fact that her smile exercised no less powerful a fascination on the artist than on all who have looked at it for the last four hundred years. From that date the captivating smile reappears in all his pictures and in those of his pupils. As Leonardo's Mona Lisa is a portrait, we cannot assume that he added on his own account such an expressive feature to her face—a feature that she did

2. [*Footnote added* 1919:] The connoisseur of art will think here of the peculiar fixed smile found in archaic Greek sculptures—in those, for example, from Aegina; he will perhaps also discover something similar in the figures of Leonardo's teacher Verrocchio and therefore have some misgivings in accepting the argument that follows.

not herself possess. The conclusion seems hardly to be avoided that he found this smile in his model and fell so strongly under its spell that from then on he bestowed it on the free creations of his phantasy. * * *

* * *

Yet this situation may also have come about in another way. The need for a deeper reason behind the attraction of La Gioconda's smile, which so moved the artist that he was never again free from it, has been felt by more than one of his biographers. Walter Pater, who sees in the picture of Mona Lisa a 'presence . . . expressive of what in the ways of a thousand years men had come to desire', and who writes very sensitively of 'the unfathomable smile, always with a touch of something sinister in it, which plays over all Leonardo's work', leads us to another clue when he declares (loc. cit.):

'Besides, the picture is a portrait. From childhood we see this image defining itself on the fabric of his dreams; and but for express historical testimony, we might fancy that this was but his ideal lady, embodied and beheld at last . . .

* * *

Let us attempt to clarify what is suggested here. It may very well have been that Leonardo was fascinated by Mona Lisa's smile for the reason that it awoke something in him which had for long lain dormant in his mind—probably an old memory. This memory was of sufficient importance for him never to get free of it when it had once been aroused; he was continually forced to give it new expression. Pater's confident assertion that we can see, from childhood, a face like Mona Lisa's defining itself on the fabric of his dreams, seems convincing and deserves to be taken literally.

Vasari mentions that 'teste di femmine, che ridono' formed the subject of Leonardo's first artistic endeavours. The passage—which, since it is not intended to prove anything, is quite beyond suspicion—runs more fully according to Schorn's translation (1843,3,6): 'In his youth he made some heads of laughing women out of clay, which were reproduced in plaster, and some children's heads which were as beautiful as if they had been modelled by the hand of the master . . .'

Thus we learn that he began his artistic career by portraying two kinds of objects; and these cannot fail to remind us of the two kinds of sexual objects that we have inferred from the analysis of his vulture-phantasy. If the beautiful children's heads were reproductions of his own person as it was in his childhood, then the smiling women are nothing other than repetitions of his mother Caterina, and we begin to suspect the possibility that it was his mother who possessed the mysterious smile— the smile that he had lost and that fascinated him so much when he found it again in the Florentine lady.

The painting of Leonardo's which stands nearest to the Mona Lisa in point of time is the so-called 'St. Anne with Two Others', St. Anne with the Madonna and child. [See the Frontispiece.] In it the Leonardesque smile is most beautifully and markedly portrayed on both the women's faces. It is not possible to discover how long before or after the painting of the Mona Lisa Leonardo began to paint this picture. As both works extended over years, it may, I think, be assumed that the artist was engaged on them at the same time. It would best agree with our expectations if it was the intensity of Leonardo's preoccupation with the features of Mona Lisa which stimulated him to create the composition of St. Anne out of his phantasy. For if the Gioconda's smile called up in his mind the memory of his mother, it is easy to understand how it drove him at once to create a glorification of motherhood, and to give back to his mother the smile he had found in the noble lady. We may therefore permit our interest to pass from Mona Lisa's portrait to this other picture—one which is hardly less beautiful, and which to-day also hangs in the Louvre.

St. Anne with her daughter and her grandchild is a subject that is rarely handled in Italian painting. At all events Leonardo's treatment of it differs widely from all other known versions. * * *

* * * In Leonardo's picture Mary is sitting on her mother's lap, leaning forward, and is stretching out both arms towards the boy, who is playing with a young lamb and perhaps treating it a little unkindly. The grandmother rests on her hip the arm that is not concealed and gazes down on the pair with a blissful smile. The grouping is certainly not entirely unconstrained. But although the smile that plays on the lips of the two women is unmistakably the same as that in the picture of Mona Lisa, it has lost its uncanny and mysterious character; what it expresses is inward feeling and quiet blissfulness.

After we have studied this picture for some time, it suddenly dawns on us that only Leonardo could have painted it, just as only he could have created the phantasy of the vulture. The picture contains the synthesis of the history of his childhood: its details are to be explained by reference to the most personal impressions in Leonardo's life. In his father's house he found not only his kind stepmother, Donna Albiera, but also his grandmother, his father's mother, Monna Lucia, who—so we will assume—was no less tender to him than grandmothers usually are. These circumstances might well suggest to him a picture representing childhood watched over by mother and grandmother. Another striking feature of the picture assumes even greater significance. St. Anne, Mary's mother and the boy's grandmother, who must have been a matron, is here portrayed as being perhaps a little more mature and serious than the Virgin Mary, but as still being a young woman of unfaded beauty. In point of fact Leonardo has given the boy two mothers, one who stretches her arms out to him, and another in the background; and both are endowed with the blissful smile of the joy of motherhood.
* * *

Leonardo's childhood was remarkable in precisely the same way as this picture. He had had two mothers: first, his true mother Caterina, from whom he was torn away when he was between three and five, and then a young and tender stepmother, his father's wife, Donna Albiera. By his combining this fact about his childhood with the one mentioned above (the presence of his mother and grandmother) and by his condensing them into a composite unity, the design of 'St. Anne with Two Others' took shape for him. The maternal figure that is further away from the boy—the grandmother—corresponds to the earlier and true mother, Caterina, in its appearance and in its special relation to the boy. The artist seems to have used the blissful smile of St. Anne to disavow and to cloak the envy which the unfortunate woman felt when she was forced to give up her son to her better-born rival, as she had once given up his father as well.

We thus find a confirmation in another of Leonardo's works of our suspicion that the smile of Mona Lisa del Giocondo had awakened in him as a grown man the memory of the mother of his earliest childhood. From that time onward, madonnas and aristocratic ladies were depicted in Italian painting humbly bowing their heads and smiling the strange, blissful smile of Caterina, the poor peasant girl who had brought into the world the splendid son who was destined to paint, to search and to suffer.

If Leonardo was successful in reproducing on Mona Lisa's face the double meaning which this smile contained, the promise of unbounded tenderness and at the same time sinister menace (to quote Pater's phrase), then here too he had remained true to the content of his earliest memory. For his mother's tenderness was fateful for him; it determined his destiny and the privations that were in store for him. The violence of the caresses, to which his phantasy of the vulture points, was only too natural. In her love for her child the poor forsaken mother had to give vent to all her memories of the caresses she had enjoyed as well as her longing for new ones; and she was forced to do so not only to compensate herself for having no husband, but also to compensate her child for having no father to fondle him. So, like all unsatisfied mothers, she took her little son in place of her husband, and by the too early maturing of his erotism robbed him of a part of his masculinity. A mother's love for the infant she suckles and cares for is something far more profound than her later affection for the growing child. It is in the nature of a completely satisfying love-relation, which not only fulfils every mental wish but also every physical need; and if it represents one of the forms of attainable human happiness, that is in no little measure due to the possibility it offers of satisfying, without reproach, wishful impulses which have long been repressed and which must be called perverse. In the happiest young marriage the father is aware that the baby, especially if he is a baby son, has become his rival, and this is the starting-point of an antagonism towards the favourite which is deeply rooted in the unconscious.

When, in the prime of life, Leonardo once more encountered the smile of bliss and rapture which had once played on his mother's lips as she fondled him, he had for long been under the dominance of an inhibition which forbade him ever again to desire such caresses from the lips of women. But he had become a painter, and therefore he strove to reproduce the smile with his brush, giving it to all his pictures (whether he in fact executed them himself or had them done by his pupils under his direction)—to Leda, to John the Baptist, and to Bacchus. The last two are variants of the same type. * * * These pictures breathe a mystical air into whose secret one dares not penetrate; at the very most one can attempt to establish their connection with Leonardo's earlier creations. The figures are still androgynous, but no longer in the sense of the vulture-phantasy. They are beautiful youths of feminine delicacy and with effeminate forms; they do not cast their eyes down, but gaze in mysterious triumph, as if they knew of a great achievement of happiness, about which silence must be kept. The familiar smile of fascination leads one to guess that it is a secret of love. It is possible that in these figures Leonardo has denied the unhappiness of his erotic life and has triumphed over it in his art, by representing the wishes of the boy, infatuated with his mother, as fulfilled in this blissful union of the male and female natures.

V

Among the entries in Leonardo's notebooks there is one which catches the reader's attention owing to the importance of what it contains and to a minute formal error.

In July 1504 he writes:

'Adì 9 di Luglio 1504 mercoledi a ore 7 morì Ser Piero da Vinci, notalio al palazzo del Potestà, mio padre, a ore 7. Era d'età d'anni 80, lasciò 10 figlioli maschi e 2 femmine.'[3]

As we see, the note refers to the death of Leonardo's father. The small error in its form consists of the repetition of the time of day 'a ore 7' [at 7 o'clock], which is given twice, as if Leonardo had forgotten at the end of the sentence that he had already written it at the beginning. It is only a small detail, and anyone who was not a psycho-analyst would attach no importance to it. He might not even notice it, and if his attention was drawn to it he might say that a thing like that can happen to anyone in a moment of distraction or of strong feeling, and that it has no further significance.

The psycho-analyst thinks differently. To him nothing is too small to be a manifestation of hidden mental processes. He has learnt long ago that such cases of forgetting or repetition are significant, and that it

3. ['On July 9, 1504, Wednesday at 7 o'clock died Ser Piero da Vinci, notary at the palace of the Podestà, my father, at 7 o'clock. He was 80 years old, and left 10 sons and 2 daughters.']

is the 'distraction' which allows impulses that are otherwise hidden to be revealed.

We would say that this note, like the account for Caterina's funeral and the bills of the pupils' expenses, is a case in which Leonardo was unsuccessful in suppressing his affect and in which something that had long been concealed forcibly obtained a distorted expression. Even the form is similar: there is the same pedantic exactness, and the same prominence given to numbers.

We call a repetition of this kind a perseveration. It is an excellent means of indicating affective colour. * * *

Without Leonardo's affective inhibition the entry in his diary might have run somewhat as follows: 'To-day at 7 o'clock my father died—Ser Piero da Vinci, my poor father!' But the displacement of the perseveration on to the most indifferent detail in the report of his death, the hour at which he died, robs the entry of all emotion, and further lets us see that here was something to be concealed and suppressed.

Ser Piero da Vinci, notary and descendant of notaries, was a man of great energy who reached a position of esteem and prosperity. He was married four times. His first two wives died childless, and it was only his third wife who presented him with his first legitimate son, in 1476, by which time Leonardo had reached the age of 24 and had long ago exchanged his father's home for the studio of his master Verrocchio. By his fourth and last wife, whom he married when he was already in his fifties, he had nine more sons and two daughters.

It cannot be doubted that his father too came to play an important part in Leonardo's psychosexual development, and not only negatively by his absence during the boy's first childhood years, but also directly by his presence in the later part of Leonardo's childhood. No one who as a child desires his mother can escape wanting to put himself in his father's place, can fail to identify himself with him in his imagination, and later to make it his task in life to gain ascendency over him. When Leonardo was received into his grandfather's house before he had reached the age of five, his young step-mother Albiera must certainly have taken his mother's place where his feelings were concerned, and he must have found himself in what may be called the normal relationship of rivalry with his father. As we know, a decision in favour of homosexuality only takes place round about the years of puberty. When this decision had been arrived at in Leonardo's case, his identification with his father lost all significance for his sexual life, but it nevertheless continued in other spheres of non-erotic activity. We hear that he was fond of magnificence and fine clothes, and kept servants and horses, although, in Vasari's words, 'he possessed almost nothing and did little work'. The responsibility for these tastes is not to be attributed solely to his feeling for beauty: we recognize in them at the same time a compulsion to copy and to outdo his father. His father had been a great gentleman to the poor peasant girl, and the son, therefore, never ceased to feel the spur to play the great gentleman as well, the urge 'to out-herod Herod',[4] to show his father what a great gentleman really looks like.

There is no doubt that the creative artist feels towards his works like a father. The effect which Leonardo's identification with his father had on his paintings was a fateful one. He created them and then cared no more about them, just as his father had not cared about him. His father's later concern could change nothing in this compulsion; for the compulsion derived from the impressions of the first years of childhood, and what has been repressed and has remained unconscious cannot be corrected by later experiences.

In the days of the Renaissance—and even much later—every artist stood in need of a gentleman of rank, a benefactor and patron, who gave him commissions and in whose hands his fortune rested. Leonardo found his patron in Lodovico Sforza, called Il Moro, a man of ambition and a lover of splendour, astute in diplomacy, but of erratic and unreliable character. At his court in Milan Leonardo passed the most brilliant period of his life, and in his service his creative power attained its most uninhibited expansion, to which the Last Supper and the equestrian statue of Francesco Sforza bore witness. He left Milan before catastrophe overtook Lodovico Sforza, who died a prisoner in a French dungeon. When the news of his patron's fate reached Leonardo, he wrote in his diary: 'The duke lost his dukedom and his property and his liberty, and none of the works that he undertook was completed.' It is remarkable, and certainly not without significance, that he here cast the same reproach at his patron which posterity was to bring against himself. It is as if he wanted to make someone from the class of his fathers responsible for the fact that he himself left his works unfinished. In point of fact he was not wrong in what he said about the duke.

But if his imitation of his father did him damage as an artist, his rebellion against his father was the infantile determinant of what was perhaps an equally sublime achievement in the field of scientific research. * * * He dared to utter the bold assertion which contains within itself the justification for all independent research: '*He who appeals to authority when there is a difference of opinion works with his memory rather than with his reason.*' Thus he became the first modern natural scientist, and an abundance of discoveries and suggestive ideas rewarded his courage for being the first man since the time of the Greeks to probe the secrets of nature while relying solely on observation and his own judgement. But in teaching that authority should be looked down on and that imitation of the 'ancients' should be repudiated, and in constantly urging that the study of nature was the source of all truth, he was merely repeating—in the highest sublimation attainable by man—the one-sided point of view which had already forced itself on the little boy as he gazed in wonder on the world. If we translate scientific ab-

4. [The last three words are in English in the original.]

straction back again into concrete individual experience, we see that the 'ancients' and authority simply correspond to his father, and nature once more becomes the tender and kindly mother who had nourished him. In most other human beings—no less to-day than in primaeval times— the need for support from an authority of some sort is so compelling that their world begins to totter if that authority is threatened. Only Leonardo could dispense with that support; he would not have been able to do so had he not learnt in the first years of his life to do without his father. His later scientific research, with all its boldness and independence, presupposed the existence of infantile sexual researches uninhibited by his father, and was a prolongation of them with the sexual element excluded.

When anyone has, like Leonardo, escaped being intimidated by his father during his earliest childhood, and has in his researches cast away the fetters of authority, it would be in the sharpest contradiction to our expectation if we found that he had remained a believer and had been unable to escape from dogmatic religion. Psycho-analysis has made us familiar with the intimate connection between the father-complex and belief in God; it has shown us that a personal God is, psychologically, nothing other than an exalted father, and it brings us evidence every day of how young people lose their religious beliefs as soon as their father's authority breaks down. Thus we recognize that the roots of the need for religion are in the parental complex; the almighty and just God, and kindly Nature, appear to us as grand sublimations of father and mother, or rather as revivals and restorations of the young child's ideas of them. Biologically speaking, religiousness is to be traced to the small human child's long-drawn-out helplessness and need of help; and when at a later date he perceives how truly forlorn and weak he is when confronted with the great forces of life, he feels his condition as he did in childhood, and attempts to deny his own despondency by a regressive revival of the forces which protected his infancy. The protection against neurotic illness, which religion vouchsafes to those who believe in it, is easily explained: it removes their parental complex, on which the sense of guilt in individuals as well as in the whole human race depends, and disposes of it, while the unbeliever has to grapple with the problem on his own.

It does not seem as if the instance of Leonardo could show this view of religious belief to be mistaken. Accusations charging him with unbelief or (what at that time came to the same thing) with apostasy from Christianity were brought against him while he was still alive, and are clearly described in the first biography which Vasari wrote of him. (Müntz, 1899, 292 ff.) In the second (1568) edition of this *Vite* Vasari omitted these observations. In view of the extraordinary sensitiveness of his age where religious matters were in question, we can understand perfectly why even in his notebooks Leonardo should have refrained from directly stating his attitude to Christianity. In his researches he did not allow himself to be led astray in the slightest degree by the account of the Creation in Holy Writ; he challenged, for example, the possibility of a universal Deluge, and in geology he calculated in terms of hundreds of thousands of years with no more hesitation than men in modern times.

* * *

The view has been expressed about Leonardo's art that he took from the sacred figures the last remnant of their connection with the Church and made them human, so as to represent by their means great and beautiful human emotions. * * * In the notes that show Leonardo engrossed in fathoming the great riddles of nature there is no lack of passages where he expresses his admiration for the Creator, the ultimate cause of all these noble secrets; but there is nothing which indicates that he wished to maintain any personal relation with this divine power. The reflections in which he has recorded the deep wisdom of his last years of life breathe the resignation of the human being who subjects himself to 'Ανάγκη, to the laws of nature, and who expects no alleviation from the goodness or grace of God. There is scarcely any doubt that Leonardo had prevailed over both dogmatic and personal religion, and had by his work of research removed himself far from the position from which the Christian believer surveys the world.

The findings, mentioned above, which we have reached concerning the development of the mental life of children suggest the view that in Leonardo's case too the first researches of childhood were concerned with the problems of sexuality. Indeed he himself gives this away in a transparent disguise by connecting his urge for research with the vulture phantasy, and by singling out the problem of the flight of birds as one to which, as the result of a special chain of circumstances, he was destined to turn his attention. A highly obscure passage in his notes which is concerned with the flight of birds, and which sounds like a prophecy, gives a very good demonstration of the degree of affective interest with which he clung to his wish to succeed in imitating the art of flying himself: 'The great bird will take its first flight from the back of its Great Swan; it will fill the universe with stupefaction, and all writings with renown, and be the eternal glory of the nest where it was born.' He probably hoped that he himself would be able to fly one day, and we know from wish-fulfilling dreams what bliss is expected from the fulfilment of that hope.

But why do so many people dream of being able to fly? The answer that psycho-analysis gives is that to fly or to be a bird is only a disguise for another wish, and that more than one bridge, involving words or things, leads us to recognize what it is. When we consider that inquisitive children are told that babies are brought by a large bird, such as the stork; when we find that the ancients represented the phallus as having wings; that the commonest expression in German for male sexual activity is 'vögeln' ['to bird': 'Vogel' is the German for 'bird']; that the male organ is actually called *'l'uccello'* ['the bird'] in Italian—all of these are only small fragments from a whole mass of connected ideas, from which we learn that in dreams the wish to be able to fly is to be understood as nothing else than a longing to be capable of sexual performance. This is an early infantile wish. When an adult recalls his childhood it seems to him to have been a happy time, in which one enjoyed the moment and looked to the future without any wishes; it is for this reason that he envies children. But if children themselves were able to give us information earlier they would probably tell a different story. It seems that childhood is not the blissful idyll into which we distort it in retrospect, and that, on the contrary, children are goaded on through the years of childhood by the one wish to get big and do what grown-ups do. This wish is the motive of all their games. Whenever children feel in the course of their sexual researches that in the province which is so mysterious but nevertheless so important there is something wonderful of which adults are capable but which *they* are forbidden to know of and do, they are filled with a violent wish to be able to do it, and they dream of it in the form of flying, or they prepare this disguise of their wish to be used in their later flying dreams. Thus aviation, too, which in our day is at last achieving its aim, has its infantile erotic roots.

In admitting to us that ever since his childhood he felt bound up in a special and personal way with the problem of flight, Leonardo gives us confirmation that his childhood researches were directed to sexual matters; and this is what we were bound to expect as a result of our investigations on children in our own time. Here was one problem at least which had escaped the repression that later estranged him from sexuality. With slight changes in meaning, the same subject continued to interest him from his years of childhood until the time of his most complete intellectual maturity; and it may very well be that the skill that he desired was no more attainable by him in its primary sexual sense than in its mechanical one, and that he remained frustrated in both wishes.

Indeed, the great Leonardo remained like a child for the whole of his life in more than one way; it is said that all great men are bound to retain some infantile part. Even as an adult he continued to play, and this was another reason why he often appeared uncanny and incomprehensible to his contemporaries. It is only we who are unsatisfied that he should have constructed the most elaborate mechanical toys for court festivities and ceremonial receptions, for we are reluctant to see the artist turning his power to such trifles. He himself seems to have shown no unwillingness to spend his time thus, for Vasari tells us that he made similar things when he had not been commissioned to do so: 'There (in Rome) he got a soft lump of wax, and made very delicate animals out of it, filled with air; when he blew into them they flew around, and when the air ran out they fell to the ground. For a peculiar lizard which was found by the wine-grower of Belvedere he made wings from skin torn from other lizards, and filled them with quicksilver, so that they moved and quivered when it walked. Next he made eyes, a beard and horns for it, tamed it and put it in a box and terrified all his friends with it.' Such ingenuities often served to express thoughts of a serious kind. 'He often had a sheep's intestines cleaned so carefully that they could have been held in the hollow of the hand. He carried them into a large room, took a pair of blacksmith's bellows into an adjoining room, fastened the intestines to them and blew them up, until they took up the whole room and forced people to take refuge in a corner. In this way he showed how they gradually became transparent and filled with air; and from the fact that at first they were limited to a small space and gradually spread through the whole breadth of the room, he compared them to genius.' The same playful delight in harmlessly concealing things and giving them ingenious disguises is illustrated by his fables and riddles. The latter are cast into the form of 'prophecies': almost all are rich in ideas and to a striking degree devoid of any element of wit.

The games and pranks which Leonardo allowed his imagination have in some cases led his biographers, who misunderstood this side of his character, grievously astray. In Leonardo's Milanese manuscripts there are, for example, some drafts of letters to the 'Diodario of Sorio (Syria), Viceroy of the Holy Sultan of Babylonia', in which Leonardo presents himself as an engineer sent to those regions of the East to construct certain works; defends himself against the charge of laziness; supplies geographical descriptions of towns and mountains, and concludes with an account of a great natural phenomenon that occurred while he was there.

* * *

It is probable that Leonardo's play-instinct vanished in his maturer years, and that it too found its way into the activity of research which represented the latest and highest expansion of his personality. But its long duration can teach us how slowly anyone tears himself from his childhood if in his childhood days he has enjoyed the highest erotic bliss, which is never again attained.

VI

It would be futile to blind ourselves to the fact that readers to-day find all pathography unpalatable. They clothe their aversion in the complaint that a pathographical review of a great man never results in an understanding of his importance and his achievements, and that it is therefore a piece of useless impertinence to make a study of things in him that could just as easily be found in the first person one came across. But this criticism is so manifestly unjust that it is only understandable when taken as a pretext and a disguise. Pathography does not in the least aim at making the great man's achievements intelligible; and surely no one should be blamed for not carrying out something he has never promised to do. The real motives for the opposition are different. We can discover them if we bear in mind that biographers are fixated on their heroes in a quite special way. In many cases they have chosen their hero as the subject of their studies because—for reasons of their personal emotional life—they have felt a special affection for him from the very first. They then devote their energies to a task of idealization, aimed at enrolling the great man among the class of their infantile models—at reviving in him, perhaps, the child's idea of his father. To gratify this wish they obliterate the individual features of their subject's physiognomy; they smooth over the traces of his life's struggles with internal and external resistances, and they tolerate in him no vestige of human weakness or imperfection. They thus present us with what is in fact a cold, strange, ideal figure, instead of a human being to whom we might feel ourselves distantly related. That they should do this is regrettable, for they thereby sacrifice truth to an illusion, and for the sake of their infantile phantasies abandon the opportunity of penetrating the most fascinating secrets of human nature.[5]

Leonardo himself, with his love of truth and his thirst for knowledge, would not have discouraged an attempt to take the trivial peculiarities and riddles in his nature as a starting-point, for discovering what determined his mental and intellectual development. We do homage to him by learning from him. It does not detract from his greatness if we make a study of the sacrifices which his development from childhood must have entailed, and if we bring together the factors which have stamped him with the tragic mark of failure.

We must expressly insist that we have never reckoned Leonardo as a neurotic or a 'nerve case', as the awkward phrase goes. Anyone who protests at our so much as daring to examine him in the light of discoveries gained in the field of pathology is still clinging to prejudices which we have to-day rightly abandoned. We no longer think that health and illness, normal and neurotic people, are to be sharply distinguished from each other, and that neurotic traits must necessarily be taken as proofs of a general inferiority. To-day we know that neurotic symptoms are structures which are substitutes for certain achievements of repression that we have to carry out in the course of our development from a child to a civilized human being. We know too that we all produce such substitutive structures, and that it is only their number, intensity and distribution which justify us in using the practical concept of illness and in inferring the presence of constitutional inferiority. From the slight indications we have about Leonardo's personality we should be inclined to place him close to the type of neurotic that we describe as 'obsessional'; and we may compare his researches to the 'obsessive brooding' of neurotics, and his inhibitions to what are known as their 'abulias'.

5. This criticism applies quite generally and is not to be taken as being aimed at Leonardo's biographers in particular.

The aim of our work has been to explain the inhibitions in Leonardo's sexual life and in his artistic activity. With this in view we may be allowed to summarize what we have been able to discover about the course of his psychical development.

* * *

In the preceding chapters I have shown what justification can be found for giving this picture of Leonardo's course of development—for proposing these subdivisions of his life and for explaining his vacillation between art and science in this way. If in making these statements I have provoked the criticism, even from friends of psycho-analysis and from those who are expert in it, that I have merely written a psycho-analytic novel, I shall reply that I am far from over-estimating the certainty of these results. Like others I have succumbed to the attraction of this great and mysterious man, in whose nature one seems to detect powerful instinctual passions which can nevertheless only express themselves in so remarkably subdued a manner.

But whatever the truth about Leonardo's life may be, we cannot desist from our endeavour to find a psycho-analytic explanation for it until we have completed another task. We must stake out in a quite general way the limits which are set to what psycho-analysis can achieve in the field of biography: otherwise every explanation that is not forthcoming will be held up to us as a failure. The material at the disposal of a psycho-analytic enquiry consists of the data of a person's life history: on the one hand the chance circumstances of events and background influences, and, on the other hand, the subject's reported reactions. Supported by its knowledge of psychical mechanisms it then endeavours to establish a dynamic basis for his nature on the strength of his reactions, and to disclose the original motive forces of his mind, as well as their later transformations and developments. If this is successful the behaviour of a personality in the course of his life is explained in terms of the combined operation of constitution and fate, of internal forces and external powers. Where such an undertaking does not provide any certain results—and this is perhaps so in Leonardo's case—the blame rests not with the faulty or inadequate methods of psycho-analysis, but with the uncertainty and fragmentary nature of the material relating to him which tradition makes available. It is therefore only the author who is to be held responsible for the failure, by having forced psycho-analysis to pronounce an expert opinion on the basis of such insufficient material.

But even if the historical material at our disposal were very abundant, and if the psychical mechanisms could be dealt with with the greatest assurance, there are two important points at which a psycho-analytic enquiry would not be able to make us understand how inevitable it was that the person concerned should have turned out in the way he did and in no other way. In Leonardo's case we have had to maintain the view that the accident of his illegitimate birth and the excessive tenderness of his mother had the most decisive influence on the formation of his character and on his later fortune, since the sexual repression which set in after this phase of childhood caused him to sublimate his libido into the urge to know, and established his sexual inactivity for the whole of his later life. But this repression after the first erotic satisfactions of childhood need not necessarily have taken place; in someone else it might perhaps have taken place or might have assumed much less extensive proportions. We must recognize here a degree of freedom which cannot be resolved any further by psycho-analytic means. Equally, one has no right to claim that the consequence of this wave of repression was the only possible one. It is probable that another person would not have succeeded in withdrawing the major portion of his libido from repression by sublimating it into a craving for knowledge; under the same influences he would have sustained a permanent injury to his intellectual activity or have acquired an insurmountable disposition to obsessional neurosis. We are left, then, with these two characteristics of Leonardo which are inexplicable by the efforts of psycho-analysis: his quite special tendency towards instinctual repressions, and his extraordinary capacity for sublimating the primitive instincts.

Instincts and their transformations are at the limit of what is discernible by psycho-analysis. From that point it gives place to biological research. We are obliged to look for the source of the tendency to repression and the capacity for sublimation in the organic foundations of character on which the mental structure is only afterwards erected. Since artistic talent and capacity are intimately connected with sublimation we must admit that the nature of the artistic function is also inaccessible to us along psycho-analytic lines. The tendency of biological research to-day is to explain the chief features in a person's organic constitution as being the result of the blending of male and female dispositions, based on [chemical] substances. Leonardo's physical beauty and his left-handedness might be quoted in support of this view. We will not, however, leave the ground of purely psychological research. Our aim remains that of demonstrating the connection along the path of instinctual activity between a person's external experiences and his reactions. Even if psychoanalysis does not throw light on the fact of Leonardo's artistic power, it at least renders its manifestations and its limitations intelligible to us. It seems at any rate as if only a man who had had Leonardo's childhood experiences could have painted the Mona Lisa and the St. Anne, have secured so melancholy a fate for his works and have embarked on such an astonishing career as a natural scientist, as if the key to all his achievements and misfortunes lay hidden in the childhood phantasy of the vulture.

But may one not take objection to the findings of an enquiry which ascribes to accidental circumstances of his parental constellation so decisive an influence on a person's fate—which, for example, makes Leonardo's fate depend on his illegitimate birth and on the barrenness of his first stepmother Donna Albiera? I think one has no right to do so. If one considers chance to be unworthy of determining our fate, it is simply a relapse into the pious view of the Universe which Leonardo himself was on the way to overcoming when he wrote that the sun does not move. We naturally feel hurt that a just God and a kindly providence do not protect us better from such influences during the most defenceless period of our lives. At the same time we are all too ready to forget that in fact everything to do with our life is chance, from our origin out of the meeting of spermatozoon and ovum onwards—chance which nevertheless has a share in the law and necessity of nature, and which merely lacks any connection with our wishes and illusions. The apportioning of the determining factors of our life between the 'necessities' of our constitution and the 'chances' of our childhood may still be uncertain in detail; but in general it is no longer possible to doubt the importance precisely of the first years of our childhood. We all still show too little respect for Nature which (in the obscure words of Leonardo which recall Hamlet's lines) 'is full of countless causes ['*ragioni*'] that never enter experience'.[6]

Every one of us human beings corresponds to one of the countless experiments in which these '*ragioni*' of nature force their way into experience.

Totem and Taboo

Among all his prewar excursions into the psychoanalysis of culture, Freud's four essays published in *Imago* between 1912 and 1913 and collected in the latter year under its collective title, *Totem and Taboo*, is surely the boldest. Freud's passion for archeology was of long standing; Heinrich Schliemann, the discoverer of Troy, was a man he honestly envied. In this book, one might say, he proposed to prove himself the Schliemann of the mind. The antique objects that crowded his consulting room and his study—plaques, sculptures, fragments mainly from the Near East—eloquently testify to what he called his "partiality for the pre-historic." Surely, too, Jung's interest in mythology was stimulus to Freud's speculations. So was his commitment to the Oedipus complex, which he had been complicating during these years; *Totem and Taboo* is a reconstruction, after all, of the origins of this "nuclear complex." The intellectual pedigree of the work, which includes James G. Frazer and Charles Darwin, is impressive enough, but Freud's speculative energies are perhaps more impressive still. What is no less impressive is the range of material on which he draws: in the first essay, "The Horror of Incest," he enlists Polynesians, the Bantu and the Zulus, neurotic women, and boys traversing the oedipal phase. In the second, "Taboo and Emotional Ambivalence," he connects what he had learned from his ob-

6. [The allusion seems to be to Hamlet's familiar words:

There are more things in heaven and earth, Horatio,
Than are dreamt of in your philosophy.]

sessive patients with leading contemporary theories in sociology and cultural anthropology. In the third, "Animism, Magic and the Omnipotence of Thoughts," he makes similar connections between what he knew of children's beliefs and the magical beliefs so prominent in primitive religions. But the fourth essay, here reprinted, is the most imaginative, almost breathtaking part of the book and has remained, not unnaturally, the most controversial. A majority among cultural anthropologists have rejected Freud's speculative reconstruction of the moment when the human animal became human, though some have argued (not without persuasive reasons) that this reconstruction makes sense if one abandons his notion that he has described a single historical event in favor of the more modest proposition that the dramatic murder and incorporation of the father is, if rarely a reality, a recurrent and virtually universal fantasy.

IV

THE RETURN OF TOTEMISM IN CHILDHOOD

There are no grounds for fearing that psycho-analysis, which first discovered that psychical acts and structures are invariably overdetermined, will be tempted to trace the origin of anything so complicated as religion to a single source. If psycho-analysis is compelled—and is, indeed, in duty bound—to lay all the emphasis upon one particular source, that does not mean it is claiming either that that source is the only one or that it occupies first place among the numerous contributory factors. Only when we can synthesize the findings in the different fields of research will it become possible to arrive at the relative importance of the part played in the genesis of religion by the mechanism discussed in these pages. Such a task lies beyond the means as well as beyond the purposes of a psycho-analyst.

(1)

In the first of this series of essays we became acquainted with the concept of totemism. We heard that totemism is a system which takes the place of a religion among certain primitive peoples of Australia, America and Africa, and provides the basis of their social organization. As we have heard, it was a Scotsman, McLennan, who in 1869 first drew general attention to the phenomena of totemism (which had hitherto been regarded as mere curiosities) by giving voice to a suspicion that a large number of customs and usages current in various societies ancient and modern were to be explained as remnants of a totemic age. Since that date science has fully accepted his estimate of totemism.
* * *

The purpose of the present essays obliges us to enter more deeply into the nature of totemism. For reasons which will presently become clear I will begin with an account given by Reinach, who, in 1900, sketched out a 'Code du totémisme' in twelve Articles—a catechism, as it were, of the totemic religion:

(1) Certain animals may neither be killed nor eaten, but individual members of the species are reared by human beings and cared for by them.

(2) An animal which has died an accidental death is mourned over and buried with the same honours as a member of the clan.

(3) In some instances the eating prohibition extends only to one particular part of the animal's body.

(4) When one of the animals which are usually spared has to be killed under the stress of necessity, apologies are offered to it and an attempt is made by means of various artifices and evasions to mitigate the violation of the taboo—that is to say, the murder.

(5) When the animal is made the victim of a ritual sacrifice, it is solemnly bewailed.

(6) On particular solemn occasions and at religious ceremonies the skins of certain animals are worn. Where totemism is still in force, they are the totem animals.

(7) Clans and individuals adopt the names of animals—viz. of the totem animals.

(8) Many clans make use of representations of animals on their standards and weapons; the men have pictures of animals painted or tattooed on their bodies.

(9) If the totem is a formidable or dangerous animal, it is supposed to spare members of the clan named after it.

(10) The totem animal protects and gives warning to members of its clan.

(11) The totem animal foretells the future to the loyal members of its clan and serves them as guide.

(12) The members of the totemic clan often believe that they are related to the totem animal by the bond of a common ancestry.

This catechism of the totemic religion can only be seen at its proper value if we take into account the fact that Reinach has included in it all the indications and traces from which the earlier existence of a totemic system can be inferred. The author's peculiar attitude to the problem is shown by his partial neglect of the essential features of totemism. As we shall see, he has relegated one of the two principal articles of the totemic catechism to the background and entirely overlooked the other.

To obtain a correct picture of the nature of totemism we must turn to another author, who has devoted a four-volume work to the subject, which combines the fullest collection of the relevant observations with the most detailed discussion of the problems they raise. We shall remain indebted to J. G. Frazer, the author of *Totemism and Exogamy* (1910), both for enjoyment and instruction, even if psycho-analytic research may lead to conclusions which differ widely from his.

* * *

In giving particulars of totemism as a religious system, Frazer begins by stating that the members of a totem clan call themselves by the name of their totem, and *commonly believe themselves to be actually descended from it*. It follows from this belief that they will not hunt the totem animal or kill or eat it and, if it is something other than an animal, they refrain from making use of it in other ways. The rules against killing or eating the totem are not the only taboos; sometimes they are forbidden to touch it, or even to look at it; in a number of cases the totem may not be spoken of by its proper name. Any violation of the taboos that protect the totem are automatically punished by severe illness or death.

Specimens of the totem animal are occasionally reared by the clan and cared for in captivity. A totem animal that is found dead is mourned for and buried like a dead clansman. If it is necessary to kill a totem animal, this is done according to a prescribed ritual of apologies and ceremonies of expiation.

The clan expects to receive protection and care from its totem. If it is a dangerous animal (such as a beast of prey or a venomous snake) there is a presumption that it will do no harm to its clansmen; and if that expectation is not fulfilled the injured man is expelled from the clan. Oaths, in Frazer's opinion, were originally ordeals; thus, many tests of descent and legitimacy were submitted for decision to the totem. The totem gives help in sickness and delivers omens and warnings to its clan. The appearance of the totem in or about a house is often regarded as an omen of death; the totem has come to fetch his kinsman.

In particular important circumstances the clansman seeks to emphasize his kinship with the totem by making himself resemble it externally, by dressing in the skin of the animal, by incising a picture of the totem upon his own body, and so on. This identification with the totem is carried into effect in actions and words on the ceremonial occasions of birth, initiation and burial. Various magical and religious purposes are served by dances in which all the clansmen disguise themselves as their totem and imitate its behaviour. Lastly, there are ceremonies in which the totem animal is ceremoniously killed.

The social aspect of totemism is principally expressed in a severely enforced injunction and a sweeping restriction.

The members of a totem clan are brothers and sisters and are bound to help and protect one another. If a member of a clan is killed by someone outside it, the whole clan of the aggressor is responsible for the deed and the whole clan of the murdered man is at one in demanding satisfaction for the blood that has been shed. The totem bond is stronger than that of the family in our sense. The two do not coincide, since the totem is as a rule inherited through the female line, and it is possible that paternal descent may originally have been left entirely out of account.

The corresponding taboo restriction prohibits members of the same totem clan from marrying or having sexual intercourse with each other. Here we have the notorious and mysterious correlate of totemism— exogamy. I have devoted the whole of the first essay in the present work to that subject, so that here I need only repeat that it originates from the intensification among savages of the horror of incest, that it would be fully explained as an assurance against incest under conditions of group marriage, and that it is primarily aimed at restraining the *younger* generation from incest and that only as a later development does it interfere with the older generation.

* * *

If we seek to penetrate to the original nature of totemism, without regard to subsequent accretions or attenuations, we find that its essential characteristics are these: *Originally, all totems were animals, and were regarded as the ancestors of the different clans. Totems were inherited only through the female line. There was a prohibition against killing the totem* (or—which, under primitive conditions, is the same thing— *against eating it). Members of a totem clan were forbidden to practise sexual intercourse with one another.*

We shall now, perhaps, be struck by the fact that in Reinach's *Code du totémisme* one of the two principal taboos, that of exogamy, is not mentioned at all, while the belief upon which the second one is founded, namely descent from the totem animal, is only referred to in passing. My reason, however, for selecting the account given by Reinach (a writer, incidentally, who has made very valuable contributions to the subject) was to prepare us for the differences of opinion between the authorities—differences into which we must now enter.

(2)

* * * Everything connected with totemism seems to be puzzling: the decisive problems concern the origin of the idea of descent from the totem and the reasons for exogamy (or rather for the taboo upon incest of which exogamy is the expression), as well as the relation between these two institutions, totemic organization and prohibition of incest. Any satisfactory explanation should be at once a historical and a psychological one. It should tell us under what conditions this peculiar institution developed and to what psychical needs in men it has given expression.

* * *

It is plausible to suppose that an understanding of the essential nature of totemism and exogamy would best be arrived at, if it were possible to come nearer to the origins of the two institutions. But in this connection we must bear in mind Andrew Lang's warning that even primitive peoples have not retained the original forms of those institutions nor the conditions which gave rise to them; so that we have nothing whatever but hypotheses to fall back upon as a substitute for the observations which we are without. Some of the attempted explanations seem, in the judgement of a psychologist, inadequate at the very outset: they are too rational and take no account of the emotional character of the matters to be explained. Others are based on assumptions which are unconfirmed by observation. Yet others rely upon material which would be better interpreted in another way. There is generally little difficulty in refuting the various views put forward: the authorities are as usual more effective in their criticisms of one another's work than in their own productions. * * *

(a) *The Origin of Totemism*

* * * How did it come about that primitive men called themselves (and their clans) after animals, plants and inanimate objects?

* * * I propose to divide the published theories on the origin of totemism into three groups—(α) the nominalist, (β) the sociological and (γ) the psychological.

(α) NOMINALIST THEORIES

* * *

Garcilasso de la Vega, a descendent of the Peruvian Incas, who wrote a history of his people in the seventeenth century, seems already to have attributed the origin of what he knew of totemic phenomena to the need felt by clans to distinguish themselves from one another by the use of names. (Land, 1905, 34.) Hundreds of years later the same idea was again proposed. * * *

* * *

(β) SOCIOLOGICAL THEORIES

Reinach, who has been successful in tracing survivals of the totemic system in the cults and usages of later periods but who has always attached small importance to the factor of descent from the totem, remarks confidently in one passage that in his opinion totemism is nothing more than 'une hypertrophie de l'instinct social'. (Reinach, 1905-12,1,41.)[1] A

---

1. {Freud is here referring to Salomon Reinach (1858–1932), one of the world's first field anthropologists. The work in question is *Cultes, mythes et religions*, 4 vols. I might add that the abbreviated presentation, necessary to this *Reader*, slights Freud's many references to, and quotations from, his authorities.}

similar view seems to run through the recent book by Durkheim (1912).[2] The totem, he argues, is the visible representative of social religion among the races concerned: it embodies the community, which is the true object of their worship.

* * *

(γ) PSYCHOLOGICAL THEORIES

* * * The totem, according to this view, represented a safe place of refuge in which the soul could be deposited and so escape the dangers which threatened it. When a primitive man had deposited his soul in his totem he himself was invulnerable, and he naturally avoided doing any injury to the receptable of his soul. Since, however, he did not know in which particular individual of the animal species concerned his own soul was lodged, it was reasonable for him to spare the whole species.

Frazer himself subsequently abandoned this theory that totemism was derived from a belief in souls; and, after coming to know of Spencer and Gillen's observations, adopted the sociological theory which I have already discussed. But he came to see himself that the motive from which that second theory derived totemism was too 'rational' and that it implied a social organization which was too complicated to be described as primitive. The magical co-operative societies now seemed to him to be the fruit rather than the seed of totemism. He sought for some simpler factor, some primitive superstition behind these structures, to which the origin of totemism might be traced back. At last he found this original factor in the Arunta's remarkable story of conception.

* * *

Accordingly, the ultimate source of totemism would be the savages' ignorance of the process by which men and animals reproduce their kind; and, in particular, ignorance of the part played by the male in fertilization. This ignorance must have been facilitated by the long interval between the act of fertilization and the birth of the child (or the first perception of its movements). Thus totemism would be a creation of the feminine rather than of the masculine mind: its roots would lie in 'the sick fancies of pregnant women'. 'Anything indeed that struck a woman at that mysterious moment of her life when she first knows herself to be a mother might easily be identified by her with the child in her womb. Such maternal fancies, so natural

---

2. {The book to which Freud refers is Emile Durkheim's celebrated sociological study of religion, *Les formes élémentaires de la vie religieuse: Le système totémique en Australie.*}

and seemingly so universal, appear to be the root of totemism.' (Frazer, 1910, 4, 63.)[3]

* * *

(b) *and* (c) *The Origin of Exogamy and Its Relation to Totemism*

* * *

The attitude taken by an author on the problems of exogamy must naturally depend to some extent on the position he has adopted towards the various theories of totemism. Some of the explanations of totemism exclude any connection with exogamy, so that the two institutions fall completely apart. Thus we find two opposing views: one which seeks to maintain the original presumption that exogamy forms an inherent part of the totemic system, and the other which denies that there is any such connection and holds that the convergence between these two features of the oldest culture is a chance one. * * *

* * *

As regards the chronological relations between the two institutions, most of the authorities agree that totemism is the older of them and that exogamy arose later.

* * *

Other students of exogamy, on the contrary, and evidently with greater justice, have seen in exogamy an institution for the prevention of incest. When one considers the gradually increasing complication of the Australian restrictions upon marriage, it is impossible not to accept the opinions of {L. H.} Morgan (1877), {James G.} Frazer (1910, 4, 105 ff.), {A. W.} Howitt, and Baldwin Spencer that those regulations bear (in Frazer's words) 'the impress of deliberate design' and that they aimed at achieving the result they have in fact achieved. 'In no other way does it seem possible to explain in all its details a system at once so complex and regular.' (Frazer, ibid., 106.)

It is interesting to observe that the first restrictions produced by the introduction of marriage-classes affected the sexual freedom of the *younger* generation (that is, incest between brothers and sisters and between sons and mothers) whereas incest between fathers and daughters was only prevented by a further extension of the regulations.

But the fact that exogamous sexual restrictions were imposed intentionally throws no light on the motive which led to their imposition. What is the ultimate source of the horror of incest which must be recognized as the root of exogamy? To explain it by the existence of an instinctive dislike of sexual intercourse with blood relatives—that is to

3. {James G. Frazer, *Totemism and Exogamy*, 4 vols.}

say, by an appeal to the fact that there *is* a horror of incest—is clearly unsatisfactory; for social experience shows that, in spite of this supposed instinct, incest is no uncommon event even in our present-day society, and history tells us of cases in which incestuous marriage between privileged persons was actually the rule.

Westermarck (1906–8, 2, 368)[4] has explained the horror of incest on the ground that 'there is an innate aversion to sexual intercourse between persons living very closely together from early youth, and that, as such persons are in most cases related by blood, this feeling would naturally display itself in custom and law as a horror of intercourse between near kin'. Havelock Ellis [1914, 205 f.], though he disputed the instinctiveness of the aversion, subscribed to this explanation in the main: 'The normal failure of the pairing instinct to manifest itself in the case of brothers and sisters, or of boys and girls brought up together from infancy, is a merely negative phenomenon due to the inevitable absence in those circumstances of the conditions which evoke the pairing instinct. . . . Between those who have been brought up together from childhood all the sensory stimuli of vision, hearing and touch have been dulled by use, trained to the calm level of affection, and deprived of their potency to arouse the erethistic excitement which produces sexual tumescence.'

It seems to me very remarkable that Westermarck should consider that this innate aversion to sexual intercourse with those with whom one has been intimate in childhood is also the equivalent in psychical terms of the biological fact that inbreeding is detrimental to the species. A biological instinct of the kind suggested would scarcely have gone so far astray in its psychological expression that, instead of applying to blood-relatives (intercourse with whom might be injurious to reproduction), it affected persons who were totally innocuous in this respect, merely because they shared a common home. I cannot resist referring, too, to Frazer's admirable criticism of Westermarck's theory. Frazer finds it inexplicable that to-day there should be scarcely any sexual aversion to intercourse with house-mates, whereas the horror of incest, which on Westermarck's theory is only a derivative of that aversion, should have increased so enormously. * * *

* * *

I may add to {the} excellent arguments of Frazer that the findings of psycho-analysis make the hypothesis of an innate aversion to incestuous intercourse totally untenable. They have shown, on the contrary, that the earliest sexual excitations of youthful human beings are invariably of an incestuous character and that such impulses when repressed play a part that can scarcely be over-estimated as motive forces of neuroses in later life.

4. {This is Edward A. Westermarck (1862–1939), a well-known Finnish anthropologist teaching in London. The work Freud is citing is Westermarck's widely read *The Origin and Development of the Moral Ideas*, 2 vols. (1906–8).}

Thus the view which explains the horror of incest as an innate instinct must be abandoned. Nor can anything more favourable be said of another, widely held explanation of the law against incest, according to which primitive peoples noticed at an early date the dangers with which their race was threatened by inbreeding and for that reason deliberately adopted the prohibition. There are a host of objections to his theory. (Cf. Durkheim, 1898.) Not only must the prohibition against incest be older than any domestication of animals which might have enabled men to observe the effects of inbreeding upon racial characters, but even to-day the detrimental results of inbreeding are not established with certainty and cannot easily be demonstrated in man. Moreover, everything that we know of contemporary savages makes it highly improbable that their most remote ancestors were already concerned with the question of preserving their later progeny from injury. Indeed it is almost absurd to attribute to such improvident creatures motives of hygiene and eugenics to which consideration is scarcely paid in our present-day civilization.

Lastly, account must be taken of the fact that a prohibition against inbreeding, based upon practical motives of hygiene, on the ground of its tending to racial enfeeblement, seems quite inadequate to explain the profound abhorrence shown towards incest in our society. As I have shown elsewhere,[5] this feeling seems to be even more active and intense among contemporary primitive peoples than among civilized ones.

It might have been expected that here again we should have before us a choice between sociological, biological and psychological explanations. (In this connection the psychological motives should perhaps be regarded as representing biological forces.) Nevertheless, at the end of our inquiry, we can only subscribe to Frazer's resigned conclusion. We are ignorant of the origin of the horror of incest and cannot even tell in what direction to look for it. None of the solutions of the enigma that have been proposed seems satisfactory.

I must, however, mention one other attempt at solving it. It is of a kind quite different from any that we have so far considered, and might be described as 'historical'.

This attempt is based upon a hypothesis of Charles Darwin's upon the social state of primitive men. Darwin deduced from the habits of the higher apes that men, too, originally lived in comparatively small groups or hordes within which the jealousy of the oldest and strongest male prevented sexual promiscuity. 'We may indeed conclude from what we know of the jealousy of all male quadrupeds, armed, as many of them are, with special weapons for battling with their rivals, that promiscuous intercourse in a state of nature is extremely improbable. . . . Therefore, if we look far enough back in the stream of time, . . . judging from the social habits of man as he now exists . . . the most probable

---

5. See the first essay in this work {"The Horror of Incest"}.

view is that primaeval man aboriginally lived in small communities, each with as many wives as he could support and obtain, whom he would have jealously guarded against all other men. Or he may have lived with several wives by himself, like the Gorilla; for all the natives "agree that but one adult male is seen in a band; when the young male grows up, a contest takes place for mastery, and the strongest, by killing and driving out the others, establishes himself as the head of the community". (Dr. Savage, in *Boston Journal of Nat. Hist.*, vol. v, 1845–7, p. 423.) The younger males, being thus expelled and wandering about, would, when at last successful in finding a partner, prevent too close interbreeding within the limits of the same family.' (Darwin, {*The Descent of Man*,} 1871, 2, 362 f.)

Atkinson (1903)[6] seems to have been the first to realize that the practical consequence of the conditions obtaining in Darwin's primal horde must be exogamy for the young males. Each of them might, after being driven out, establish a similar horde, in which the same prohibition upon sexual intercourse would rule owing to its leader's jealousy. In course of time this would produce what grew into a conscious law: 'No sexual relations between those who share a common home.' After the establishment of totemism this regulation would assume another form and would run: 'No sexual relations within the totem.'

Andrew Lang (1905, 114 and 143)[7] accepted this explanation of exogamy. In the same volume, however, he supports the other theory (held by Durkheim), according to which exogamy was a resultant of the totemic laws. It is a little difficult to bring these two points of view into harmony: according to the first theory exogamy would have originated before totemism, while according to the second it would have been derived from it.

(3)

Into this obscurity one single ray of light is thrown by psycho-analytic observation.

There is a great deal of resemblance between the relations of children and of primitive men towards animals. Children show no trace of the arrogance which urges adult civilized men to draw a hard-and-fast line between their own nature and that of all other animals. Children have no scruples over allowing animals to rank as their full equals. Uninhibited as they are in the avowal of their bodily needs, they no doubt feel themselves more akin to animals than to their elders, who may well be a puzzle to them.

Not infrequently, however, a strange rift occurs in the excellent relations between children and animals. A child will suddenly begin to be frightened of some particular species of animal and to avoid touching

6. {J. J. Atkinson, *Primal Law*.}   7. {Lang, *The Secret of the Totem*.}

or seeing any individual of that species. The clinical picture of an animal phobia emerges—a very common, and perhaps the earliest, form of psychoneurotic illness occurring in childhood. As a rule the phobia is attached to animals in which the child has hitherto shown a specially lively interest and it has nothing to do with any particular individual animal. There is no large choice of animals that may become objects of a phobia in the case of children living in towns: horses, dogs, cats, less often birds, and with striking frequency very small creatures such as beetles and butterflies. The senseless and immoderate fear shown in these phobias is sometimes attached to animals only known to the child from picture books and fairy tales. On a few rare occasions it is possible to discover what has led to an unusual choice of this kind * * *.

No detailed analytic examination has yet been made of children's animal phobias, though they would greatly repay study. This neglect has no doubt been due to the difficulty of analysing children of such a tender age. It cannot therefore be claimed that we know the general meaning of these disorders and I myself am of the opinion that this may not turn out to be a uniform nature. But a few cases of phobias of this kind directed towards the larger animals have proved accessible to analysis and have thus yielded their secret to the investigator. It was the same in every case: where the children concerned were boys, their fear related at bottom to their father and had merely been displaced on to the animal.

Everyone with psycho-analytic experience will no doubt have come across cases of the sort and have derived the same impression from them. Yet I can quote only a few detailed publications on the subject. This paucity of literature is an accidental circumstance and it must not be supposed that our conclusions are based on a few scattered observations. I may mention, for instance, a writer who has studied the neuroses of childhood with great understanding—Dr. M. Wulff, of Odessa. In the course of a case history of a nine-year-old boy he reports that at the age of four the patient had suffered from a dog-phobia. 'When he saw a dog running past in the street, he would weep and call out: "Dear doggie, don't bite me! I'll be good!" By "being good" he meant "not playing on the fiddle" '—not masturbating. (Wulff, 1912, 15.) 'The boy's dog-phobia', the author explains, 'was in reality his fear of his father displaced on to dogs; for his curious exclamation "Doggie, I'll be good!"—that is, "I won't masturbate"—was directed to his father, who had forbidden him to masturbate.' Wulff adds a footnote which is in complete agreement with my views and at the same time bears witness to the frequent occurrence of such experiences: 'Phobias of this type (phobias of horses, dogs, cats, fowls and other domestic animals) are, in my opinion, at least as common in childhood as *pavor nocturnus*; and in analysis they almost invariably turn out to be a displacement on to the animals of the child's fear of one of his parents. I should not be prepared to maintain that the same mechanism applies to the widespread phobias of rats and mice.'

I recently published (1909) an 'Analysis of a Phobia in a Five-Year-Old Boy', the material of which was supplied to me by the little patient's father. The boy had a phobia of horses, and as a result he refused to go out in the street. He expressed a fear that the horse would come into the room and bite him; and it turned out that this must be the punishment for a wish that the horse might fall down (that is, die). After the boy's fear of his father had been removed by reassurances, it became evident that he was struggling against wishes which had as their subject the idea of his father being absent (going away on a journey, dying). He regarded his father (as he made all too clear) as a competitor for the favours of his mother, towards whom the obscure foreshadowings of his budding sexual wishes were aimed. Thus he was situated in the typical attitude of a male child towards his parents to which we have given the name of the 'Oedipus complex' and which we regard in general as the nuclear complex of the neuroses. The new fact that we have learnt from the analysis of 'little Hans'—a fact with an important bearing upon totemism—is that in such circumstances children displace some of their feelings from their father on to an animal.

Analysis is able to trace the associative paths along which this displacement passes—both the fortuitous paths and those with a significant content. Analysis also enables us to discover the *motives* for the displacement. The hatred of his father that arises in a boy from rivalry for his mother is not able to achieve uninhibited sway over his mind; it has to contend against his old-established affection and admiration for the very same person. The child finds relief from the conflict arising out of this double-sided, this ambivalent emotional attitude towards his father by displacing his hostile and fearful feelings on to a *substitute* for his father. The displacement cannot, however, bring the conflict to an end, it cannot effect a clear-cut severance between the affectionate and the hostile feelings. On the contrary, the conflict is resumed in relation to the object on to which the displacement has been made: the ambivalence is extended to *it*. There could be no doubt that little Hans was not only *frightened* of horses; he also approached them with admiration and interest. As soon as his anxiety began to diminish, he identified himself with the dreaded creature: he began to jump about like a horse and in his turn bit his father. At another stage in the resolution of his phobia he did not hesitate to identify his parents with some other large animals.

It may fairly be said that in these children's phobias some of the features of totemism reappear, but reversed into their negative. We are, however, indebted to Ferenczi (1913a) for an interesting history of a single case which can only be described as an instance of *positive* totemism in a child. It is true that in the case of little Árpád (the subject of Ferenczi's report) his totemic interests did not arise in direct relation with his Oedipus complex but on the basis of its narcissistic precondition, the fear of castration. But any attentive reader of the story of little Hans will find abundant evidence that he, too, admired his father as possessing a big penis and feared him as threatening his own. The same part is played by the father alike in the Oedipus and the castration complexes— the part of a dreaded enemy to the sexual interests of childhood. The punishment which he threatens is castration, or its substitute, blinding.

When little Árpád was two and a half years old, he had once, while he was on a summer holiday, tried to micturate into the fowl-house and a fowl had pecked, or pecked *at* his penis. A year later, when he was back in the same place, he himself turned into a fowl; his one interest was in the fowl-house and in what went on there and he abandoned human speech in favour of cackling and crowing. At the time at which the observation was made (when he was five years old) he had recovered his speech, but his interests and his talk were entirely concerned with chickens and other kinds of poultry. They were his only toys and he only sang songs that had some mention of fowls in them. His attitude towards his totem animal was superlatively ambivalent: he showed both hatred and love to an extravagant degree. His favourite game was playing slaughtering fowls. 'The slaughtering of poultry was a regular festival for him. He would dance round the animals' bodies for hours at a time in a state of intense excitement.' But afterwards he would kiss and stroke the slaughtered animal or would clean and caress the toy fowls that he had himself ill-treated.

Little Árpád himself saw to it that the meaning of his strange behaviour should not remain hidden. From time to time he translated his wishes from the totemic language into that of everyday life. 'My father's the cock', he said on one occasion, and another time: 'Now I'm small, now I'm a chicken. When I get bigger I'll be a fowl. When I'm bigger still I'll be a cock.' On another occasion he suddenly said he would like to eat some 'fricassee of mother' (on the analogy of fricassee of chicken). He was very generous in threatening other people with castration, just as he himself had been threatened with it for his masturbatory activities.

There was no doubt, according to Ferenczi, as to the sources of Árpád's interest in events in the poultry-yard: 'the continual sexual activity between the cock and hens, the laying of eggs and the hatching out of the young brood' gratified his sexual curiosity, the real object of which was *human* family-life. [Ibid., 250.] He showed that he had formed his own choice of sexual objects on the model of life in the hen-run, for he said one day to the neighbour's wife: 'I'll marry you and your sister and my three cousins and the cook; no, not the cook, I'll marry my mother instead.'

Later on we shall be able to assess the worth of this observation more completely. At the moment I will only emphasize two features in it which offer valuable points of agreement with totemism: the boy's complete identification with his totem animal and his ambivalent emotional attitude to it. These observations justify us, in my opinion, in substituting the father for the totem animal in the formula for totemism (in the case of males). It will be observed that there is nothing new or particularly daring in this step forward. Indeed, primitive men say the very same thing themselves, and, where the totemic system is still in force to-day, they describe the totem as their common ancestor and primal father. All we have done is to take at its literal value an expression used by these people, of which the anthropologists have been able to make very little and which they have therefore been glad to keep in the background. Psycho-analysis, on the contrary, leads us to put special stress upon this same point and to take it as the starting-point of our attempt at explaining totemism.

The first consequence of our substitution is most remarkable. If the totem animal is the father, then the two principal ordinances of totemism, the two taboo prohibitions which constitute its core—not to kill the totem and not to have sexual relations with a woman of the same totem—coincide in their content with the two crimes of Oedipus, who killed his father and married his mother, as well as with the two primal wishes of children, the insufficient repression or the re-awakening of which forms the nucleus of perhaps every psychoneurosis. If this equation is anything more than a misleading trick of chance, it must enable us to throw a light upon the origin of totemism in the inconceivably remote past. In other words, it would enable us to make it probable that the totemic system—like little Hans's animal phobia and little Árpád's poultry perversion—was a product of the conditions involved in the Oedipus complex. In order to pursue this possibility, we shall have, in the following pages, to study a feature of the totemic system (or, as we might say, of the totemic religion) which I have hitherto scarcely found an opportunity of mentioning.

(4)

William Robertson Smith, who died in 1894—physicist, philologist, Bible critic and archaeologist—was a man of many-sided interests, clear-sighted and liberal-minded. In his book on the *Religion of the Semites* (first published in 1889) he put forward the hypothesis that a peculiar ceremony known as the 'totem meal' had from the very first formed an integral part of the totemic system. At that time he had only a single piece of evidence in support of his theory: an account of a procedure of the kind dating from the fifth century A.D. But by an analysis of the nature of sacrifice among the ancient Semites he was able to lend his hypothesis a high degree of probability. Since sacrifice implies a divinity, it was a question of arguing back from a comparatively high phase of religious ritual to the lowest one, that is, to totemism.

* * *

Robertson Smith explains that sacrifice at the altar was the essential feature in the ritual of ancient religions. It plays the same part in all religions, so that its origin must be traced back to very general causes, operating everywhere in the same manner. Sacrifice—the sacred act *par excellence (sacrificium, ἱερουργία)*—originally had a somewhat different meaning, however, from its later one of making an offering to the deity in order to propitiate him or gain his favour. (The non-religious usage of the word followed from this subsidiary sense of 'renunciation'. It can be shown that, to begin with, sacrifice was nothing other than 'an act of fellowship between the deity and his worshippers'.

The materials offered for sacrifice were things that can be eaten or drunk; men sacrificed to their deity the things on which they themselves lived: flesh, cereals, fruit, wine and oil. Only in the case of flesh were there limitations and exceptions. The god shared the animal sacrifices with his worshippers, the vegetable offerings were for him alone. There is no doubt that animal sacrifices were the older and were originally the only ones. Vegetable sacrifices arose from the offering of first-fruits and were in the nature of a tribute to the lord of the earth and of the land; but animal sacrifices are more ancient than agriculture.

*   *   *

The oldest form of sacrifice, then, older than the use of fire or the knowledge of agriculture, was the sacrifice of animals, whose flesh and blood were enjoyed in common by the god and his worshippers. It was essential that each one of the participants should have his share of the meal.

A sacrifice of this kind was a public ceremony, a festival celebrated by the whole clan. Religion in general was an affair of the community and religious duty was a part of social obligation. Everywhere a sacrifice involves a feast and a feast cannot be celebrated without a sacrifice. The sacrificial feast was an occasion on which individuals rose joyously above their own interests and stressed the mutual dependence existing between one another and their god.

The ethical force of the public sacrificial meal rested upon very ancient ideas of the significance of eating and drinking together. Eating and drinking with a man was a symbol and a confirmation of fellowship and mutual social obligations. What was *directly* expressed by the sacrificial meal was only the fact that the god and his worshippers were 'commensals', but every other point in their mutual relations was included in this. Customs still in force among the Arabs of the desert show that what is binding in a common meal is not a religious factor but the act of eating itself. Anyone who has eaten the smallest morsel of food with one of these Bedouin or has swallowed a mouthful of his milk need no longer fear him as an enemy but may feel secure in his protection and help. Not, however, for an unlimited time; strictly speaking, only so long as the food which has been eaten in common remains in the body. Such was the realistic view of the bond of union. It needed repetition in order to be confirmed and made permanent.

But why is this binding force attributed to eating and drinking together? In primitive societies there was only one kind of bond which was absolute and inviolable— that of kinship. The solidarity of such a fellowship was complete. * * *

The sacrificial meal, then, was originally a feast of kinsmen, in accordance with the law that only kinsmen eat together. In our own society the members of a family have their meals in common; but the sacrificial meal bears no relation to the family. Kinship is an older thing than family life, and in the most primitive societies known to us the family contained members of more than one kindred. The man married a woman of another clan and the children inherited their mother's clan; so that there was no communion of kin between the man and the other members of the family. In a family of such a kind there was no common meal. To this day, savages eat apart and alone and the religious food prohibitions of totemism often make it impossible for them to eat in common with their wives and children.

Let us now turn to the sacrificial animal. As we have heard, there is no gathering of a clan without an animal sacrifice, nor—and this now becomes significant—any slaughter of an animal except upon these ceremonial occasions. While game and the milk of domestic animals might be consumed without any qualms, religious scruples made it impossible to kill a domestic animal for private purposes. There cannot be the slightest doubt, says Robertson Smith, that the slaughter of a victim was originally among the acts which '*are illegal to an individual, and can only be justified when the whole clan shares the responsibility of the deed*. So far as I know, there is only one class of actions recognized by early nations to which this description applies, viz. actions which involve an invasion of the sanctity of the tribal blood. In fact, a life which no single tribesman is allowed to invade, and which can be sacrificed only by the consent and common action of the kin, stands on the same footing with the life of the fellow-tribesman.' The rule that every participant at the sacrificial meal must eat a share of the flesh of the victim has the same meaning as the provision that the execution of a guilty tribesman must be carried out by the tribe as a whole. In other words, the sacrificial animal was treated as a member of the tribe; *the sacrificing community, the god and the sacrificial animal were of the same blood and members of one clan.*

* * *

The domestication of animals and the introduction of cattle-breeding seems everywhere to have brought to an end the strict and unadulterated totemism of primaeval days. But such sacred character as remained to domestic animals under what had then become 'pastoral' religion is obvious enough to allow us to infer its original totemic nature. Even in late classical times ritual prescribed in many places that the sacrificial priest must take to flight after performing the sacrifice, as though to escape retribution. The idea that slaughtering oxen was a crime must at one time have prevailed generally in Greece. At the Athenian festival of Buphonia ['ox-murder'] a regular trial was instituted after the sacrifice, and all the participants were called as witnesses. At the end of it, it was agreed that the responsibility for the murder should be placed upon the knife; and this was accordingly cast into the sea.

In spite of the ban protecting the lives of sacred animals in their quality of fellow-clansmen, a necessity arose for killing one of them from time to time in solemn communion and for dividing its flesh and blood among the members of the clan. The compelling motive for this deed reveals the deepest meaning of the nature of sacrifice. We have heard how in later times, whenever food is eaten in common, the participation in the same substance establishes a sacred bond between those who consume it when it has entered their bodies. In ancient times this result seems only to have been effected by participation in the substance of a *sacrosanct* victim. *The holy mystery of sacrificial death 'is justified by the consideration that only in this way can the sacred cement be procured which creates or keeps alive a living bond of union between the worshippers and their god'.*

This bond is nothing else than the life of the sacrificial animal, which resides in its flesh and in its blood and is distributed among all the participants in the sacrificial meal. A notion of this kind lies at the root of all the blood covenants by which men made compacts with each other even at a late period of history. This completely literal way of regarding blood-kinship as identity of substance makes it easy to understand the necessity for renewing it from time to time by the physical process of the sacrificial meal.

At this point I will interrupt my survey of Robertson Smith's line of thought and restate the gist of it in the most concise terms. With the establishment of the idea of private property sacrifice came to be looked upon as a gift to the deity, as a transference of property from men to the god. But this interpretation left unexplained all the peculiarities of the ritual of sacrifice. In the earliest times the sacrificial animal had itself been sacred and its life untouchable; it might only be killed if all the members of the clan participated in the deed and shared their guilt in the presence of the god, so that the sacred substance could be yielded up and consumed by the clansmen and thus ensure their identity with one another and with the deity. The sacrifice was a sacrament and the sacrificial animal was itself a member of the clan. It was in fact the ancient totem animal, the primitive god himself, by the killing and consuming of which the clansmen renewed and assured their likeness to the god.

From this analysis of the nature of sacrifice Robertson Smith draws the conclusion that the periodic killing and eating of the totem in times *before the worship of anthropomorphic deities* had been an important element in totemic religion. * * *

* * *

A feature has been observed in the *intichiuma* ceremonies of the Central Australian tribes which agrees admirably with Robertson Smith's conjectures. Each clan, when it is performing magic for the multiplication of its totem (which it itself is normally prohibited from consuming), is obliged during the ceremony to eat a small portion of its own totem before making it accessible to the other clans. According to Frazer ({1910}, 2, 590) the clearest example of a sacramental consumption of an otherwise prohibited totem is to be found among the Bini of West Africa in connection with their funeral ceremonies.

Accordingly, I propose that we should adopt Robertson Smith's hypothesis that the sacramental killing and communal eating of the totem animal, whose consumption was forbidden on all other occasions, was an important feature of totemic religion.

(5)

Let us call up the spectacle of a totem meal of the kind we have been discussing, amplified by a few probable features which we have not yet been able to consider. The clan is celebrating the ceremonial occasion by the cruel slaughter of its totem animal and is devouring it raw— blood, flesh and bones. The clansmen are there, dressed in the likeness of the totem and imitating it in sound and movement, as though they are seeking to stress their identity with it. Each man is conscious that he is performing an act forbidden to the individual and justifiable only through the participation of the whole clan; nor may anyone absent himself from the killing and the meal. When the deed is done, the slaughtered animal is lamented and bewailed. The mourning is obligatory, imposed by dread of a threatened retribution. As Robertson Smith (1894, 412) remarks of an analogous occasion, its chief purpose is to disclaim responsibility for the killing.

But the mourning is followed by demonstrations of festive rejoicing: every instinct is unfettered and there is licence for every kind of gratification. Here we have easy access to an understanding of the nature of festivals in general. A festival is a permitted, or rather an obligatory, excess, a solemn breach of a prohibition. It is not that men commit the excesses because they are feeling happy as a result of some injunction they have received. It is rather that excess is of the essence of a festival; the festive feeling is produced by the liberty to do what is as a rule prohibited.

What are we to make, though, of the prelude to this festive joy—the mourning over the death of the animal? If the clansmen rejoice over the killing of the totem—a normally forbidden act—why do they mourn over it as well?

As we have seen, the clansmen acquire sanctity by consuming the totem: they reinforce their identification with it and with one another. Their festive feelings and all that follows from them might well be explained by the fact that they have taken into themselves the sacred life of which the substance of the totem is the vehicle.

Psycho-analysis has revealed that the totem animal is in reality a substitute for the father; and this tallies with the contradictory fact that, though the killing of the animal is as a rule forbidden, yet its killing is a festive occasion—with the fact that it is killed and yet mourned. The ambivalent emotional attitude, which to this day characterizes the father-complex in our children and which often persists into adult life, seems to extend to the totem animal in its capacity as substitute for the father.

If, now, we bring together the psycho-analytic translation of the totem with the fact of the totem meal and with Darwin's theories of the earliest state of human society, the possibility of a deeper understanding emerges—a glimpse of a hypothesis which may seem fantastic but which offers the advantage of establishing an unsuspected correlation between groups of phenomena that have hitherto been disconnected.

There is, of course, no place for the beginnings of totemism in Darwin's primal horde. All that we find there is a violent and jealous father who keeps all the females for himself and drives away his sons as they grow up. This earliest state of society has never been an object of observation. The most primitive kind of organization that we actually come across—and one that is in force to this day in certain tribes—consists of bands of males; these bands are composed of members with equal rights and are subject to the restrictions of the totemic system, including inheritance through the mother. Can this form of organization have developed out of the other one? and if so along what lines?

If we call the celebration of the totem meal to our help, we shall be able to find an answer. One day[8] the brothers who had been driven out came together, killed and devoured their father and so made an end of the patriarchal horde. United, they had the courage to do and succeeded in doing what would have been impossible for them individually. (Some cultural advance, perhaps, command over some new weapon, had given them a sense of superior strength.) Cannibal savages as they were, it goes without saying that they devoured their victim as well as killing him. The violent primal father had doubtless been the feared and envied model of each one of the company of brothers: and in the act of devouring him they accomplished their identification with him, and each one of them acquired a portion of his strength. The totem meal, which is

8. {This footnote has been shifted from the end of the next footnote below:} The lack of precision in what I have written in the text above, its abbreviation of the time factor and its compression of the whole subject-matter, may be attributed to the reserve necessitated by the nature of the topic. It would be as foolish to aim at exactitude in such questions as it would be unfair to insist upon certainty.

perhaps mankind's earliest festival, would thus be a repetition and a commemoration of this memorable and criminal deed, which was the beginning of so many things—of social organization, of moral restrictions and of religion.[9]

In order that these latter consequences may seem plausible, leaving their premises on one side, we need only suppose that the tumultuous mob of brothers were filled with the same contradictory feelings which we can see at work in the ambivalent father-complexes of our children and of our neurotic patients. They hated their father, who presented such a formidable obstacle to their craving for power and their sexual desires; but they loved and admired him too. After they had got rid of him, had satisfied their hatred and had put into effect their wish to identify themselves with him, the affection which had all this time been pushed under was bound to make itself felt. It did so in the form of remorse. A sense of guilt made its appearance, which in this instance coincided with the remorse felt by the whole group. The dead father became stronger than the living one had been—for events took the course we so often see them follow in human affairs to this day. What had up to then been prevented by his actual existence was thenceforward prohibited by the sons themselves, in accordance with the psychological procedure so familiar to us in psycho-analyses under the name of 'deferred obedience'. They revoked their deed by forbidding the killing of the totem, the substitute for their father; and they renounced its fruits by resigning their claim to the women who had now been set free. They thus created out of their filial sense of guilt the two fundamental taboos of totemism, which for that very reason inevitably corresponded to the two repressed wishes of the Oedipus complex. Whoever contravened those taboos became guilt of the only two crimes with which primitive society concerned itself.

The two taboos of totemism with which human morality has its beginning are not on a par psychologically. The first of them, the law protecting the totem animal, is founded wholly on emotional motives: the father had actually been eliminated, and in no real sense could the

9. This hypothesis, which has such a monstrous air, of the tyrannical father being overwhelmed and killed by a combination of his exiled sons, was also arrived at by Atkinson (1903, 220f.) as a direct implication of the state of affairs in Darwin's primal horde. * * * Atkinson, who incidentally passed his whole life in New Caledonia and had unusual opportunities for studying the natives, also pointed out that the conditions which Darwin assumed to prevail in the primal horde may easily be observed in herds of wild oxen and horses and regularly led to the killing of the father of the herd. He further supposed that, after the father had been disposed of, the horde would be disintegrated by a bitter struggle between the victorious sons. Thus any new organization of society would be precluded: there would be 'an ever-recurring violent succession to the solitary paternal tyrant, by sons whose parri-cidal hands were so soon again clenched in fratricidal strife.' (Ibid., 228.) Atkinson, who had no psycho-analytic hints to help him and who was ignorant of Robertson Smith's studies, found a less violent transition from the primal horde to the next social stage, at which numbers of males live together in a peaceable community. He believed that through the intervention of maternal love the sons—to begin with only the youngest, but later others as well—were allowed to remain with the horde, and that in return for this toleration the sons acknowledged their father's sexual privilege by renouncing all claim to their mother and sister.

Such is the highly remarkable theory put forward by Atkinson. In its essential features it is in agreement with my own; but its divergence results in its failing to effect a correlation with many other issues. * * *

deed be undone. But the second rule, the prohibition of incest, has a powerful practical basis as well. Sexual desires do not unite men but divide them. Though the brothers had banded together in order to overcome their father, they were all one another's rivals in regard to the women. Each of them would have wished, like his father, to have all the women to himself. The new organization would have collapsed in a struggle of all against all, for none of them was of such over-mastering strength as to be able to take on his father's part with success. Thus the brothers had no alternative, if they were to live together, but—not, perhaps, until they had passed through many dangerous crises—to institute the law against incest, by which they all alike renounced the women whom they desired and who had been their chief motive for despatching their father. In this way they rescued the organization which had made them strong—and which may have been based on homosexual feelings and acts, originating perhaps during the period of their expulsion from the horde. Here, too, may perhaps have been the germ of the institution of matriarchy, described by Bachofen, which was in turn replaced by the patriarchal organization of the family.

On the other hand, the claim of totemism to be regarded as a first attempt at a religion is based on the first of these two taboos—that upon taking the life of the totem animal. The animal struck the sons as a natural and obvious substitute for their father; but the treatment of it which they found imposed on themselves expressed more than the need to exhibit their remorse. They could attempt, in their relation to this surrogate father, to allay their burning sense of guilt, to bring about a kind of reconciliation with their father. The totemic system was, as it were, a covenant with their father, in which he promised them everything that a childish imagination may expect from a father—protection, care and indulgence—while on their side they undertook to respect his life, that is to say, not to repeat the deed which had brought destruction on their real father. Totemism, moreover, contained an attempt at self-justification: 'If our father had treated us in the way the totem does, we should never have felt tempted to kill him.' In this fashion totemism helped to smooth things over and to make it possible to forget the event to which it owed its origin.

Features were thus brought into existence which continued thenceforward to have a determining influence on the nature of religion. Totemic religion arose from the filial sense of guilt, in an attempt to allay that feeling and to appease the father by deferred obedience to him. All later religions are seen to be attempts at solving the same problem. They vary according to the stage of civilization at which they arise and according to the methods which they adopt; but all have the same end in view and are reactions to the same great event with which civilization began and which, since it occurred, has not allowed mankind a moment's rest.

There is another feature which was already present in totemism and which has been preserved unaltered in religion. The tension of ambivalence was evidently too great for any contrivance to be able to counteract it; or it is possible that psychological conditions in general are unfavourable to getting rid of these antithetical emotions. However that may be, we find that the ambivalence implicit in the father-complex persists in totemism and in religions generally. Totemic religion not only comprised expressions of remorse and attempts at atonement, it also served as a remembrance of the triumph over the father. Satisfaction over that triumph led to the institution of the memorial festival of the totem meal, in which the restrictions of deferred obedience no longer held. Thus it became a duty to repeat the crime of parricide again and again in the sacrifice of the totem animal, whenever, as a result of the changing conditions of life, the cherished fruit of the crime—appropriation of the paternal attributes—threatened to disappear. We shall not be surprised to find that the element of filial rebelliousness also emerges, in the *later* products of religion, often in the strangest disguises and transformations.

Hitherto we have followed the developments of the *affectionate* current of feeling towards the father, transformed into remorse, as we find them in religion and in moral ordinances (which are not sharply distinguished in totemism). But we must not overlook the fact that it was in the main with the impulses that led to parricide that the victory lay. For a long time afterwards, the social fraternal feelings, which were the basis of the whole transformation, continued to exercise a profound influence on the development of society. They found expression in the sanctification of the blood tie, in the emphasis upon the solidarity of all life within the same clan. In thus guaranteeing one another's lives, the brothers were declaring that no one of them must be treated by another as their father was treated by them all jointly. They were precluding the possibility of a repetition of their father's fate. To the religiously-based prohibition against killing the totem was now added the socially-based prohibition against fratricide. It was not until long afterwards that the prohibition ceased to be limited to members of the clan and assumed the simple form: 'Thou shalt do no murder.' The patriarchal horde was replaced in the first instance by the fraternal clan, whose existence was assured by the blood tie. Society was now based on complicity in the common crime; religion was based on the sense of guilt and the remorse attaching to it; while morality was based partly on the exigencies of this society and partly on the penance demanded by the sense of guilt.

Thus psycho-analysis, in contradiction to the more recent views of the totemic system but in agreement with the earlier ones, requires us to assume that totemism and exogamy were intimately connected and had a simultaneous origin.

(6)

A great number of powerful motives restrain me from any attempt at picturing the further development of religions from their origin in totemism to their condition to-day. I will only follow two threads whose course I can trace with especial clarity as they run through the pattern: the theme of the totemic sacrifice and the relation of son to father.

Robertson Smith has shown us that the ancient totem meal recurs in the original form of sacrifice. The meaning of the act is the same: sanctification through participation in a common meal. The sense of guilt, which can only be allayed by the solidarity of all the participants, also persists. What is new is the clan deity, in whose supposed presence the sacrifice is performed, who participates in the meal as though he were a clansman, and with whom those who consume the meal become identified. How does the god come to be in a situation to which he was originally a stranger?

The answer might be that in the meantime the concept of God had emerged—from some unknown source—and had taken control of the whole of religious life; and that, like everything else that was to survive, the totem meal had been obliged to find a point of contact with the new system. The psycho-analysis of individual human beings, however, teaches us with quite special insistence that the god of each of them is formed in the likeness of his father, that his personal relation to God depends on his relation to his father in the flesh and oscillates and changes along with that relation, and that at bottom God is nothing other than an exalted father. As in the case of totemism, psycho-analysis recommends us to have faith in the believers who call God their father, just as the totem was called the tribal ancestor. If psycho-analysis deserves any attention, then—without prejudice to any other sources or meanings of the concept of God, upon which psycho-analysis can throw no light— the paternal element in that concept must be a most important one. But in that case the father is represented twice over in the situation of primitive sacrifice: once as God and once as the totemic animal victim. And, even granting the restricted number of explanations open to psycho-analysis, one must ask whether this is possible and what sense it can have.

We know that there are a multiplicity of relations between the god and the sacred animal (the totem or the sacrificial victim.) (1) Each god usually has an animal (and quite often several animals) sacred to him. (2) In the case of certain specially sacred sacrifices—'mystic' sacrifices— the victim was precisely the animal sacred to the god (Smith, 1894). (3) The god was often worshipped in the shape of an animal (or, to look at it in another way, animals were worshipped as gods) long after the age of totemism. (4) In myths the god often transforms himself into an animal, and frequently into the animal that is sacred to him.

It therefore seems plausible to suppose that the god himself was the totem animal, and that he developed out of it at a later stage of religious feeling. But we are relieved from the necessity for further discussion by the consideration that the totem is nothing other than a surrogate of the father. Thus, while the totem may be the *first* form of father-surrogate, the god will be a later one, in which the father has regained his human shape. A new creation such as this, derived from what constitutes the root of every form of religion—a longing for the father—might occur if in the process of time some fundamental change had taken place in man's relation to the father, and perhaps, too, in his relation to animals.

Signs of the occurrence of changes of this kind may easily be seen, even if we leave on one side the beginning of a mental estrangement from animals and the disrupting of totemism owing to domestication. There was one factor in the state of affairs produced by the elimination of the father which was bound in the course of time to cause an enormous increase in the longing felt for him. Each single one of the brothers who had banded together for the purpose of killing their father was inspired by a wish to become like him and had given expression to it by incorporating parts of their father's surrogate in the totem meal. But, in consequence of the pressure exercised upon each participant by the fraternal clan as a whole, that wish could not be fulfilled. For the future no one could or might ever again attain the father's supreme power, even though that was what all of them had striven for. Thus after a long lapse of time their bitterness against their father, which had driven them to their deed, grew less, and their longing for him increased; and it became possible for an ideal to emerge which embodied the unlimited power of the primal father against whom they had once fought as well as their readiness to submit to him. As a result of decisive cultural changes, the original democratic equality that had prevailed among all the individual clansmen became untenable; and there developed at the same time an inclination, based on veneration felt for particular human individuals, to revive the ancient paternal ideal by creating gods. The notion of a man becoming a god or of a god dying strikes us to-day as shockingly presumptuous; but even in classical antiquity there was nothing revolting in it. The elevation of the father who had once been murdered into a god from whom the clan claimed descent was a far more serious attempt at atonement than had been the ancient covenant with the totem.

I cannot suggest at what point in this process of development a place is to be found for the great mother-goddesses, who may perhaps in general have preceded the father-gods. It seems certain, however, that the change in attitude to the father was not restricted to the sphere of religion but that it extended in a consistent manner to that other side of human life which had been affected by the father's removal—to social organization. With the introduction of father-deities a fatherless society gradually changed into one organized on a patriarchal basis. The family was a restoration of the former primal horde and it gave back to fathers a large portion of their former rights. There were once more fathers, but the social achievements of the fraternal clan had not been abandoned; and the gulf between the new fathers of a family and the unrestricted primal father of the horde was wide enough to guarantee the continuance of the religious craving, the persistence of an unappeased longing for the father.

We see, then, that in the scene of sacrifice before the god of the clan the father *is* in fact represented twice over—as the god and as the totemic animal victim. But in our attempts at understanding this situation we must beware of interpretations which seek to translate it in a two-dimensional fashion as though it were an allegory, and which in so doing forget its historical stratification. The two-fold presence of the father corresponds to the two chronologically successive meanings of the scene. The ambivalent attitude towards the father has found a plastic expression in it, and so, too, has the victory of the son's affectionate emotions over his hostile ones. The scene of the father's vanquishment, of his greatest defeat, has become the stuff for the representation of his supreme triumph. The importance which is everywhere, without exception, ascribed to sacrifice lies in the fact that it offers satisfaction to the father for the outrage inflicted on him in the same act in which that deed is commemorated.

As time went on, the animal lost its sacred character and the sacrifice lost its connection with the totem feast; it became a simple offering to the deity, an act of renunciation in favour of the god. God Himself had become so far exalted above mankind that He could only be approached through an intermediary—the priest. At the same time divine kings made their appearance in the social structure and introduced the patriarchal system into the state. It must be confessed that the revenge taken by the deposed and restored father was a harsh one: the dominance of authority was at its climax. The subjugated sons made use of the new situation in order to unburden themselves still further of their sense of guilt. They were no longer in any way responsible for the sacrifice as it now was. It was God Himself who demanded it and regulated it. This is the phase in which we find myths showing the god himself killing the animal which is sacred to him and which is in fact himself. Here we have the most extreme denial of the great crime which was the beginning of society and of the sense of guilt. But there is a second meaning to this last picture of sacrifice which is unmistakable. It expresses satisfaction at the earlier father-surrogate having been abandoned in favour of the superior concept of God. At this point the psycho-analytic interpretation of the scene coincides approximately with the allegorical, surface translation of it, which represents the god as overcoming the animal side of his own nature.

Nevertheless it would be a mistake to suppose that the hostile impulses inherent in the father-complex were completely silenced during this period of revived paternal authority. On the contrary, the first phases of the dominance of the two new father-surrogates—gods and kings—show the most energetic signs of the ambivalence that remains a characteristic of religion.

* * *

The memory of the first great act of sacrifice thus proved indestructible, in spite of every effort to forget it; and at the very point at which men sought to be at the farthest distance from the motives that led to it, its undistorted reproduction emerged in the form of the sacrifice of the god. I need not enlarge here upon the developments of religious thought which, in the shape of rationalizations, made this recurrence possible. Robertson Smith, who had no thought of our derivation of sacrifice from the great event in human prehistory, states that the ceremonies at the festivals in which the ancient Semites celebrated the death of a deity 'were currently interpreted as the commemoration of a mythical tragedy'. 'The mourning', he declares, 'is not a spontaneous expression of sympathy with the divine tragedy, but obligatory and enforced by fear of supernatural anger. And a chief object of the mourners is to disclaim responsibility for the god's death—a point which has already come before us in connection with theanthropic sacrifices, such as the "ox-murder at Athens".' It seems most probable that these 'current interpretations' were correct and that the feelings of the celebrants were fully explained by the underlying situation.

Let us assume it to be a fact, then, that in the course of the later development of religions the two driving factors, the son's sense of guilt and the son's rebelliousness, never became extinct. Whatever attempt was made at solving the religious problem, whatever kind of reconciliation was effected between these two opposing mental forces, sooner or later broke down, under the combined influence, no doubt, of historical events, cultural changes and internal psychical modifications.

The son's efforts to put himself in the place of the father-god became ever more obvious. The introduction of agriculture increased the son's importance in the patriarchal family. He ventured upon new demonstrations of his incestuous libido, which found symbolic satisfaction in his cultivation of Mother Earth. Divine figures such as Attis, Adonis and Tammuz emerged, spirits of vegetation and at the same time youthful divinities enjoying the favours of mother goddesses and committing incest with their mother in defiance of their father. But the sense of guilt, which was not allayed by these creations, found expression in myths which granted only short lives to these youthful favourites of the mother-goddesses and decreed their punishment by emasculation or by the wrath of the father in the form of an animal. Adonis was killed by a wild boar, the sacred animal of Aphrodite; Attis, beloved of Cybele, perished by castration.[1] The mourning for these gods and the rejoicings over their resurrection passed over into the ritual of another son-deity who was destined to lasting success.

When Christianity first penetrated into the ancient world it met with competition from the religion of Mithras and for a time it was doubtful which of the two deities would gain the victory. In spite of the halo of light surrounding his form, the youthful Persian god remains obscure to us. We may perhaps infer from the sculptures of Mithras slaying a bull that he represented a son who was alone in sacrificing his father and thus redeemed his brothers from their burden of complicity in the deed. There was an alternative method of allaying their guilt and this was first adopted by Christ. He sacrificed his own life and so redeemed the company of brothers from original sin.

The doctrine of original sin was of Orphic origin. It formed a part of the mysteries, and spread from them to the schools of philosophy of ancient Greece. (Reinach, 1905–12, 2, 75 ff.) Mankind, it was said, were descended from the Titans, who had killed the young Dionysus-Zagreus and had torn him to pieces. The burden of this crime weighed on them. A fragment of Anaximander relates how the unity of the world was broken by a primaeval sin, and that whatever issued from it must bear the punishment. The tumultuous mobbing, the killing and the tearing in pieces by the Titans reminds us clearly enough of the totemic sacrifice described by St. Nilus—as, for the matter of that, do many other ancient myths, including, for instance, that of the death of Orpheus himself. Nevertheless, there is a disturbing difference in the fact of the murder having been committed on a *youthful* god.

There can be no doubt that in the Christian myth the original sin was one against God the Father. If, however, Christ redeemed mankind from the burden of original sin by the sacrifice of his own life, we are driven to conclude that the sin was a murder. The law of talion, which is so deeply rooted in human feelings, lays it down that a murder can only be expiated by the sacrifice of another life: self-sacrifice points back to blood-guilt. And if this sacrifice of a life brought about atonement with God the Father, the crime to be expiated can only have been the murder of the father.

In the Christian doctrine, therefore, men were acknowledging in the most undisguised manner the guilty primaeval deed, since they found the fullest atonement for it in the sacrifice of this one son. Atonement with the father was all the more complete since the sacrifice was accompanied by a total renunciation of the women on whose account the rebellion against the father was started. But at that point the inexorable psychological law of ambivalence stepped in. The very deed in which the son offered the greatest possible atonement to the father brought

---

1. Fear of castration plays an extremely large part, in the case of the youthful neurotics whom we come across, as an interference in their relations with their father. * * * When our [Jewish] children come to hear of ritual circumcision, they equate it with castration. * * *

him at the same time to the attainment of his wishes *against* the father. He himself became God, beside, or, more correctly, in place of, the father. A son-religion displaced the father-religion. As a sign of this substitution the ancient totem meal was revived in the form of communion, in which the company of brothers consumed the flesh and blood of the son—no longer the father—obtained sanctity thereby and identified themselves with him. Thus we can trace through the ages the identity of the totem meal with animal sacrifice, with theanthropic human sacrifice and with the Christian Eucharist, and we can recognize in all these rituals the effect of the crime by which men were so deeply weighed down but of which they must none the less feel so proud. The Christian communion, however, is essentially a fresh elimination of the father, a repetition of the guilty deed. We can see the full justice of Frazer's pronouncement that 'the Christian communion has absorbed within itself a sacrament which is doubtless far older than Christianity.'

(7)

An event such as the elimination of the primal father by the company of his sons must inevitably have left ineradicable traces in the history of humanity; and the less it itself was recollected, the more numerous must have been the substitutes to which it gave rise. I shall resist the temptation of pointing out these traces in mythology, where they are not hard to find, and shall turn in another direction and take up a suggestion made by Salomon Reinach in a most instructive essay on the death of Orpheus.[2]

In the history of Greek art we come upon a situation which shows striking resemblances to the scene of the totem meal as identified by Robertson Smith, and not less profound differences from it. I have in mind the situation of the most ancient Greek tragedy. A company of individuals, named and dressed alike, surrounded a single figure, all hanging upon his words and deeds: they were the Chorus and the impersonator of the Hero. He was originally the only actor. Later, a second and third actor were added, to play as counterpart to the Hero and as characters split off from him; but the character of the Hero himself and his relation to the Chorus remained unaltered. The Hero of tragedy must suffer; to this day that remains the essence of a tragedy. He had to bear the burden of what was known as 'tragic guilt'; the basis of that guilt is not always easy to find, for in the light of our everyday life it is often no guilt at all. As a rule it lay in rebellion against some divine or human authority; and the Chorus accompanied the Hero with feelings of sympathy, sought to hold him back, to warn him and to sober him, and mourned over him when he had met with what was felt as the merited punishment for his rash undertaking.

2. {In this footnote, Freud aptly quotes Ariel's speech from Shakespeare's *The Tempest*, 'Full fathom five thy father lies. * * * '}

But why had the Hero of tragedy to suffer? and what was the meaning of his 'tragic guilt'? I will cut the discussion short and give a quick reply. He had to suffer because he was the primal father, the Hero of the great primaeval tragedy which was being re-enacted with a tendentious twist; and the tragic guilt was the guilt which he had to take on himself in order to relieve the Chorus from theirs. The scene upon the stage was derived from the historical scene through a process of systematic distortion—one might even say, as the product of a refined hypocrisy. In the remote reality it had actually been the members of the Chorus who caused the Hero's suffering; now, however, they exhausted themselves with sympathy and regret and it was the Hero himself who was responsible for his own sufferings. The crime which was thrown on to his shoulders, presumptuousness and rebelliousness against a great authority, was precisely the crime for which the members of the Chorus, the company of brothers, were responsible. Thus the tragic Hero became, though it might be against his will, the redeemer of the Chorus.

In Greek tragedy the special subject-matter of the performance was the sufferings of the divine goat, Dionysus, and the lamentation of the goats who were his followers and who identified themselves with him. That being so, it is easy to understand how drama, which had become extinct, was kindled into fresh life in the Middle Ages around the Passion of Christ.

At the conclusion, then, of this exceedingly condensed inquiry, I should like to insist that its outcome shows that the beginnings of religion, morals, society and art converge in the Oedipus complex. This is in complete agreement with the psycho-analytic finding that the same complex constitutes the nucleus of all neuroses, so far as our present knowledge goes. It seems to me a most surprising discovery that the problems of social psychology, too, should prove soluble on the basis of one single concrete point—man's relation to his father. It is even possible that yet another psychological problem belongs in this same connection. I have often had occasion to point out that emotional ambivalence in the proper sense of the term—that is, the simultaneous existence of love and hate towards the same object—lies at the root of many important cultural institutions. We know nothing of the origin of this ambivalence. One possible assumption is that it is a fundamental phenomenon of our emotional life. But it seems to me quite worth considering another possibility, namely that originally it formed no part of our emotional life but was acquired by the human race in connection with their father-complex, precisely where the psycho-analytic examination of modern individuals still finds it revealed at its strongest.[3]

3. Since I am used to being misunderstood, I think it worth while to insist explicitly that the derivations which I have proposed in these pages do not in the least overlook the complexity of the phenomena under review. All that they claim is to have added a new factor to the sources, known or still unknown, of religion, morality, and society—a factor based on a consideration of the implications of psychoanalysis. * * *

Before I bring my remarks to a close, however, I must find room to point out that, though my arguments have led to a high degree of convergence upon a single comprehensive nexus of ideas, this fact cannot blind us to the uncertainties of my premises or the difficulties involved in my conclusions. I will only mention two of the latter which may have forced themselves on the notice of a number of my readers.

No one can have failed to observe, in the first place, that I have taken as the basis of my whole position the existence of a collective mind, in which mental processes occur just as they do in the mind of an individual. In particular, I have supposed that the sense of guilt for an action has persisted for many thousands of years and has remained operative in generations which can have had no knowledge of that action. I have supposed that an emotional process, such as might have developed in generations of sons who were ill-treated by their father, has extended to new generations which were exempt from such treatment for the very reason that their father had been eliminated. It must be admitted that these are grave difficulties; and any explanation that could avoid presumptions of such a kind would seem to be preferable.

Further reflection, however, will show that I am not alone in the responsibility for this bold procedure. Without the assumption of a collective mind, which makes it possible to neglect the interruptions of mental acts caused by the extinction of the individual, social psychology in general cannot exist. Unless psychical processes were continued from one generation to another, if each generation were obliged to acquire its attitude to life anew, there would be no progress in this field and next to no development. This gives rise to two further questions: how much can we attribute to psychical continuity in the sequence of generations? and what are the ways and means employed by one generation in order to hand on its mental states to the next one? I shall not pretend that these problems are sufficiently explained or that direct communication and tradition—which are the first things that occur to one—are enough to account for the process. Social psychology shows very little interest, on the whole, in the manner in which the required continuity in the mental life of successive generations is established. A part of the problem seems to be met by the inheritance of psychical dispositions which, however, need to be given some sort of impetus in the life of the individual before they can be roused into actual operation. This may be the meaning of the poet's words:

> Was du ererbt von deinen Vätern hast,
> Erwirb es, um es zu besitzen.[4]

The problem would seem even more difficult if we had to admit that mental impulses could be so completely suppressed as to leave no trace whatever behind them. But that is not the case. Even the most ruthless

4. [Goethe, *Faust*, Part I, Scene 1: 'What thou hast inherited from thy fathers, acquire it to make it thine.']

suppression must leave room for distorted surrogate impulses and for reactions resulting from them. If so, however, we may safely assume that no generation is able to conceal any of its more important mental processes from its successor. For psycho-analysis has shown us that everyone possesses in his unconscious mental activity an apparatus which enables him to interpret other people's reactions, that is, to undo the distortions which other people have imposed on the expression of their feelings. An unconscious understanding such as this of all the customs, ceremonies and dogmas left behind by the original relation to the father may have made it possible for later generations to take over their heritage of emotion.

Another difficulty might actually be brought forward from psycho-analytic quarters. The earliest moral precepts and restrictions in primitive society have been explained by us as reactions to a deed which gave those who performed it the concept of 'crime'. They felt remorse for the deed and decided that it should never be repeated and that its performance should bring no advantage. This creative sense of guilt still persists among us. We find it operating in an asocial manner in neurotics, and producing new moral precepts and persistent restrictions, as an atonement for crimes that have been committed and as a precaution against the committing of new ones. If, however, we inquire among these neurotics to discover what were the deeds which provoked these reactions, we shall be disappointed. We find no deeds, but only impulses and emotions, set upon evil ends but held back from their achievement. What lie behind the sense of guilt of neurotics are always *psychical* realities and never *factual* ones. What characterizes neurotics is that they prefer psychical to factual reality and react just as seriously to thoughts as normal people do to realities.

May not the same have been true of primitive men? We are justified in believing that, as one of the phenomena of their narcissistic organization, they overvalued their psychical acts to an extraordinary degree. Accordingly the mere hostile *impulse* against the father, the mere existence of a wishful *phantasy* of killing and devouring him, would have been enough to produce the moral reaction that created totemism and taboo. In this way we should avoid the necessity for deriving the origin of our cultural legacy, of which we justly feel so proud, from a hideous crime, revolting to all our feelings. No damage would thus be done to the causal chain stretching from the beginning to the present day, for psychical reality would be strong enough to bear the weight of these consequences. To this it may be objected that an alteration in the form of society from a patriarchal horde to a fraternal clan did actually take place. This is a powerful argument, but not a conclusive one. The alteration might have been effected in a less violent fashion and none the less have been capable of determining the appearance of the moral reaction. So long as the pressure exercised by the primal father could be felt, the hostile feelings towards him were justified, and remorse on their account would have to await a later day. And if it is further argued that everything derived from the ambivalent relation to the father—taboo and the sacrificial ordinance—is characterized by the deepest seriousness and the most complete reality, this further objection carries just as little weight. For the ceremonials and inhibitions of obsessional neurotics show these same characteristics and are nevertheless derived only from psychical reality—from intentions and not from their execution. We must avoid transplanting a contempt for what is merely thought or wished from our commonplace world, with its wealth of material values, into the world of primitive men and neurotics, of which the wealth lies only within themselves.

Here we are faced by a decision which is indeed no easy one. First, however, it must be confessed that the distinction, which may seem fundamental to other people, does not in our judgement affect the heart of the matter. If wishes and impulses have the full value of facts for primitive men, it is our business to give their attitude our understanding attention instead of correcting it in accordance with our own standards. Let us, then, examine more closely the case of neurosis—comparison with which led us into our present uncertainty. It is not accurate to say that obsessional neurotics, weighed down under the burden of an excessive morality, are defending themselves only against *psychical* reality and are punishing themselves for impulses which were merely *felt*. *Historical* reality has a share in the matter as well. In their childhood they had these evil impulses pure and simple, and turned them into acts so far as the impotence of childhood allowed. Each of these excessively virtuous individuals passed through an evil period in his infancy—a phase of perversion which was the forerunner and precondition of the later period of excessive morality. The analogy between primitive men and neurotics will therefore be far more fully established if we suppose that in the former instance, too, psychical reality—as to the form taken by which we are in no doubt—coincided at the beginning with factual reality: the primitive men actually *did* what all the evidence shows that they intended to do.

Nor must we let ourselves be influenced too far in our judgement of primitive men by the analogy of neurotics. There are distinctions, too, which must be borne in mind. It is no doubt true that the sharp contrast that *we* make between thinking and doing is absent in both of them. But neurotics are above all *inhibited* in their actions: with them the thought is a complete substitute for the deed. Primitive men, on the other hand, are *uninhibited*: thought passes directly into action. With them it is rather the deed that is a substitute for the thought. And that is why, without laying claim to any finality of judgement, I think that in the case before us it may safely be assumed that 'in the beginning was the Deed'.[5]

5. ['*Im Anfang war die Tat*' (Goethe, *Faust*, Part I, Scene 3.)]

The Theme of the Three Caskets

This is one of the most characteristic, probably the most moving, among Freud's "minor" papers. Ernest Jones called it "charming," and declared it his favorite (*Jones* II, 361). Throughout his life, Freud was haunted— "tormented" is scarcely too strong a word—by certain problems that troubled him until he solved them. Here he attempts to explicate the deeper connection that forcibly struck him, in the spring of 1912, between the scene in *King Lear* in which the aged monarch demands expressions of love from his three daughters, the scene of the three caskets in *The Merchant of Venice*, and the judgment of Paris. In this paper, the Shakespearean scenes are at center stage. We have Freud's private word that one central motive for writing the paper was his growing awareness that his daughter Anna, his third and last daughter, was not only intellectually very remarkable but also emotionally very special to him. He published the paper, without mentioning his daughter, in *Imago* in 1913.

I

Two scenes from Shakespeare, one from a comedy and the other from a tragedy, have lately given me occasion for posing and solving a small problem.

The first of these scenes is the suitors' choice between the three caskets in *The Merchant of Venice*. The fair and wise Portia is bound at her father's bidding to take as her husband only that one of her suitors who chooses the right casket from among the three before him. The three caskets are of gold, silver and lead: the right casket is the one that contains her portrait. Two suitors have already departed unsuccessful: they have chosen gold and silver. Bassanio, the third, decides in favour of lead; thereby he wins the bride, whose affection was already his before the trial of fortune. Each of the suitors gives reasons for his choice in a speech in which he praises the metal he prefers and depreciates the other two. The most difficult task thus falls to the share of the fortunate third suitor; what he finds to say in glorification of lead as against gold and silver is little and has a forced ring. If in psycho-analytic practice we were confronted with such a speech, we should suspect that there were concealed motives behind the unsatisfying reasons produced.

Shakespeare did not himself invent this oracle of the choice of a casket; he took it from a tale in the *Gesta Romanorum*,[1] in which a girl has to make the same choice to win the Emperor's son.[2] Here too the third metal, lead, is the bringer of fortune. It is not hard to guess that we have here an ancient theme, which requires to be interpreted, accounted

---

1. [A mediaeval collection of stories of unknown authorship.]   2. {Georg} Brandes {*William Shakespeare*,} (1896).

for and traced back to its origin. A first conjecture as to the meaning of this choice between gold, silver and lead is quickly confirmed by a statement of Stucken's,[3] who has made a study of the same material over a wide field. He writes: 'The identity of Portia's three suitors is clear from their choice: the Prince of Morocco chooses the gold casket—he is the sun; the Prince of Arragon chooses the silver casket—he is the moon; Bassanio chooses the leaden casket—he is the star youth.' In support of this explanation he cites an episode from the Estonian folk-epic 'Kalewipoeg', in which the three suitors appear undisguisedly as the sun, moon and star youths (the last being 'the Pole-star's eldest boy') and once again the bride falls to the lot of the third.

Thus our little problem has led us to an astral myth! The only pity is that with this explanation we are not at the end of the matter. The question is not exhausted, for we do not share the belief of some investigators that myths were read in the heavens and brought down to earth; we are more inclined to judge with Otto Rank that they were projected on to the heavens after having arisen elsewhere under purely human conditions. It is in this human content that our interest lies.

Let us look once more at our material. In the Estonian epic, just as in the tale from the *Gesta Romanorum*, the subject is a girl choosing between three suitors; in the scene from *The Merchant of Venice* the subject is apparently the same, but at the same time something appears in it that is in the nature of an inversion of the theme: a *man* chooses between three—caskets. If what we were concerned with were a dream, it would occur to us at once that caskets are also women, symbols of what is essential in woman, and therefore of a woman herself—like coffers, boxes, cases, baskets, and so on. If we boldly assume that there are symbolic substitutions of the same kind in myths as well, then the casket scene in *The Merchant of Venice* really becomes the inversion we suspected. With a wave of the wand, as though we were in a fairy tale, we have stripped the astral garment from our theme; and now we see that the theme is a human one, *a man's choice between three women*.

This same content, however, is to be found in another scene of Shakespeare's, in one of his most powerfully moving dramas; not the choice of a bride this time, yet linked by many hidden similarities to the choice of the casket in *The Merchant of Venice*. The old King Lear resolves to divide his kingdom while he is still alive among his three daughters, in proportion to the amount of love that each of them expresses for him. The two elder ones, Goneril and Regan, exhaust themselves in asseverations and laudations of their love for him; the third, Cordelia, refuses to do so. He should have recognized the unassuming, speechless love of his third daughter and rewarded it, but he does not recognize it. He disowns Cordelia, and divides the kingdom between the other two, to his own and the general ruin. Is not this once more

3. {Edmund} Stucken, *Astramythen der Hebräer, Babylonier und Aegypter* (1907), 655.

the scene of a choice between three women, of whom the youngest is the best, the most excellent one?

There will at once occur to us other scenes from myths, fairy tales and literature, with the same situation as their content. The shepherd Paris has to choose between three goddesses, of whom he declares the third to be the most beautiful. Cinderella, again, is a youngest daughter, who is preferred by the prince to her two elder sisters. Psyche, in Apuleius's story, is the youngest and fairest of three sisters. Psyche is, on the one hand, revered as Aphrodite in human form; on the other, she is treated by that goddess as Cinderella was treated by her stepmother and is set the task of sorting a heap of mixed seeds, which she accomplishes with the help of small creatures (doves in the case of Cinderella, ants in the case of Psyche).[4] Anyone who cared to make a wider survey of the material would undoubtedly discover other versions of the same theme preserving the same essential features.

Let us be content with Cordelia, Aphrodite, Cinderella and Psyche. In all the stories the three women, of whom the third is the most excellent one, must surely be regarded as in some way alike if they are represented as sisters. (We must not be led astray by the fact that Lear's choice is between three *daughters*; this may mean nothing more than that he has to be represented as an old man. An old man cannot very well choose between three women in any other way. Thus they become his daughters.)

But who are these three sisters and why must the choice fall on the third? If we could answer this question, we should be in possession of the interpretation we are seeking. We have once already made use of an application of psycho-analytic technique, when we explained the three caskets symbolically as three women. If we have the courage to proceed in the same way, we shall be setting foot on a path which will lead us first to something unexpected and incomprehensible, but which will perhaps, by a devious route, bring us to a goal.

It must strike us that this excellent third woman has in several instances certain peculiar qualities besides her beauty. They are qualities that seem to be tending towards some kind of unity; we must certainly not expect to find them equally well marked in every example. Cordelia makes herself unrecognizable, inconspicuous like lead, she remains dumb, she 'loves and is silent'.[5] Cinderella hides so that she cannot be found. We may perhaps be allowed to equate concealment and dumbness. These would of course be only two instances out of the five we have picked out. But there is an intimation of the same thing to be found, curiously enough, in two other cases. We have decided to compare Cordelia, with her obstinate refusal, to lead. In Bassanio's short speech while he is choosing the casket, he says of lead (without in any way leading up to the remark):

'Thy paleness moves me more than eloquence.'

That is to say: 'Thy plainness moves me more than the blatant nature of the other two.' Gold and silver are 'loud'; lead is dumb—in fact like Cordelia, who 'loves and is silent'.[6]

In the ancient Greek accounts of the Judgement of Paris, nothing is said of any such reticence on the part of Aphrodite. Each of the three goddesses speaks to the youth and tries to win him by promises. But, oddly enough, in a quite modern handling of the same scene this characteristic of the third one which has struck us makes its appearance again. In the libretto of Offenbach's *La Belle Hélène*, Paris, after telling of the solicitations of the other two goddesses, describes Aphrodite's behaviour in this competition for the beauty-prize:

> La troisième, ah! la troisième . . .
> La troisième ne dit rien.
> Elle eut le prix tout de même . . .[7]

If we decide to regard the peculiarities of our 'third one' as concentrated in her 'dumbness', then psycho-analysis will tell us that in dreams dumbness is a common representation of death.

More than ten years ago a highly intelligent man told me a dream which he wanted to use as evidence of the telepathic nature of dreams. In it he saw an absent friend from whom he had received no news for a very long time, and reproached him energetically for his silence. The friend made no reply. It afterwards turned out that he had met his death by suicide at about the time of the dream. Let us leave the problem of telepathy on one side: there seems, however, not to be any doubt that here the dumbness in the dream represented death. Hiding and being unfindable—a thing which confronts the prince in the fairy tale of Cinderella three times, is another unmistakable symbol of death in dreams; so, too, is a marked pallor, of which the 'paleness' of the lead in one reading of Shakespeare's text is a reminder. It would be very much easier for us to transpose these interpretations from the language of dreams to the mode of expression used in the myth that is now under consideration if we could make it seem probable that dumbness must be interpreted as a sign of being dead in productions other than dreams.

At this point I will single out the ninth story in Grimm's *Fairy Tales*, which bears the title 'The Twelve Brothers'. A king and a queen have twelve children, all boys. The king declares that if the thirteenth child is a girl, the boys will have to die. In expectation of her birth he has twelve coffins made. With their mother's help the twelve sons take refuge

---

6. In Schlegel's translation this allusion is quite lost; indeed, it is given the opposite meaning: 'Dein schlichtes Wesen spricht beredt mich an.' [Thy plainness speaks to me with eloquence.] {This footnote is a tribute to Freud's command of English—and well-informed respect for Shakespeare. The famous Tieck-Schlegel translation of Shakespeare's plays into German is normally more reliable than this.}

7. [Literally: 'The third one, ah! the third one . . . the third one said nothing. She won the prize all the same.—The quotation is from Act I, Scene 7. * * *]

in a hidden wood, and swear death to any girl they may meet. A girl is born, grows up, and learns one day from her mother that she has had twelve brothers. She decides to seek them out, and in the wood she finds the youngest; he recognizes her, but is anxious to hide her on account of the brothers' oath. The sister says: 'I will gladly die, if by so doing I can save my twelve brothers.' The brothers welcome her affectionately, however, and she stays with them and looks after their house for them. In a little garden beside the house grow twelve lilies. The girl picks them and gives one to each brother. At that moment the brothers are changed into ravens, and disappear, together with the house and garden. (Ravens are spirit-birds; the killing of the twelve brothers by their sister is represented by the picking of the flowers, just as it is at the beginning of the story by the coffins and the disappearance of the brothers.) The girl, who is once more ready to save her brothers from death, is now told that as a condition she must be dumb for seven years, and not speak a single word. She submits to the test, which brings her herself into mortal danger. She herself, that is, dies for her brothers, as she promised to do before she met them. By remaining dumb she succeeds at last in setting the ravens free.

In the story of 'The Six Swans' the brothers who are changed into birds are set free in exactly the same way—they are restored to life by their sister's dumbness. The girl has made a firm resolve to free her brothers, 'even if it should cost her her life'; and once again (being the wife of a king) she risks her own life because she refuses to give up her dumbness in order to defend herself against evil accusations.

It would certainly be possible to collect further evidence from fairy tales that dumbness is to be understood as representing death. These indications would lead us to conclude that the third one of the sisters between whom the choice is made is a dead woman. But she may be something else as well—namely, Death itself, the Goddess of Death. Thanks to a displacement that is far from infrequent, the qualities that a deity imparts to men are ascribed to the deity himself. Such a displacement will surprise us least of all in relation to the Goddess of Death, since in modern versions and representations, which these stories would thus be forestalling, Death itself is nothing other than a dead man.

But if the third of the sisters is the Goddess of Death, the sisters are known to us. They are the Fates, the Moerae, the Parcae or the Norns, the third of whom is called Atropos, the inexorable.

II

We will for the time being put aside the task of inserting the interpretation that we have found into our myth, and listen to what the mythologists have to teach us about the role and origin of the Fates.[8]

The earliest Greek mythology (in Homer) only knew a single Μοῖρα,

8. What follows is taken from Roscher's lexicon [1884–1937], under the relevant headings.

personifying inevitable fate. The further development of this one Moera into a company of three (or less often two) sister-goddesses probably came about on the basis of other divine figures to which the Moerae were closely related—the Graces and the Horae [the Seasons].

The Horae were originally goddesses of the waters of the sky, dispensing rain and dew, and of the clouds from which rain falls; and, since the clouds were conceived of as something that has been spun, it came about that these goddesses were looked upon as spinners, an attribute that then became attached to the Moerae. In the sun-favoured Mediterranean lands it is the rain on which the fertility of the soil depends, and thus the Horae became vegetation goddesses. The beauty of flowers and the abundance of fruit was their doing, and they were accredited with a wealth of agreeable and charming traits. They became the divine representatives of the Seasons, and it is possibly owing to this connection that there were three of them, if the sacred nature of the number three is not a sufficient explanation. For the peoples of antiquity at first distinguished only three seasons: winter, spring and summer. Autumn was only added in late Graeco-Roman times, after which the Horae were often represented in art as four in number.

The Horae retained their relation to time. Later they presided over the times of day, as they did at first over the times of the year; and at last their name came to be merely a designation of the hours (*heure, ora*). The Norns of German mythology are akin to the Horae and the Moerae and exhibit this time-signification in their names.[9] It was inevitable, however, that a deeper view should come to be taken of the essential nature of these deities, and that their essence should be transposed on to the regularity with which the seasons change. The Horae thus became the guardians of natural law and of the divine Order which causes the same thing to recur in Nature in an unalterable sequence.

This discovery of Nature reacted on the conception of human life. The nature-myth changed into a human myth: the weather-goddesses became goddesses of Fate. But this aspect of the Horae found expression only in the Moerae, who watch over the necessary ordering of human life as inexorably as do the Horae over the regular order of nature. The ineluctable severity of Law and its relation to death and dissolution, which had been avoided in the charming figures of the Horae, were now stamped upon the Moerae, as though men had only perceived the full seriousness of natural law when they had to submit their own selves to it.

The names of the three spinners, too, have been significantly explained by mythologists. Lachesis, the name of the second, seems to denote 'the accidental that is included in the regularity of destiny'—or, as we should say, 'experience'; just as Atropos stands for 'the ineluctable'—Death. Clotho would then be left to mean the innate disposition with its fateful implications.

9. [Their names may be rendered: 'What was', 'What is', 'What shall be'.]

effect of the play rests on the purely formal element of its artistic presentation; but this cannot, so it seems to me, take the place of the understanding brought to us by the explanation we have reached of the theme of the choice between the three sisters.

Lear is an old man. It is for this reason, as we have already said, that the three sisters appear as his daughters. The relationship of a father to his children, which might be a fruitful source of many dramatic situations, is not turned to further account in the play. But Lear is not only an old man: he is a dying man. In this way the extraordinary premises of the division of his inheritance loses all its strangeness. But the doomed man is not willing to renounce the love of women; he insists on hearing how much he is loved. Let us now recall the moving final scene, one of the culminating points of tragedy in modern drama. Lear carries Cordelia's dead body on to the stage. Cordelia is Death. If we reverse the situation it becomes intelligible and familiar to us. She is the Death-goddess who, like the Valkyrie in German mythology, carries away the dead hero from the battlefield. Eternal wisdom, clothed in the primaeval myth, bids the old man renounce love, choose death and make friends with the necessity of dying.

The dramatist brings us nearer to the ancient theme by representing the man who makes the choice between the three sisters as aged and dying. The regressive revision which he has thus applied to the myth, distorted as it was by wishful transformation, allows us enough glimpses of its original meaning to enable us perhaps to reach as well a superficial allegorical interpretation of the three female figures in the theme. We might argue that what is represented here are the three inevitable relations that a man has with a woman—the woman who bears him, the woman who is his mate and the woman who destroys him; or that they are the three forms taken by the figure of the mother in the course of a man's life—the mother herself, the beloved one who is chosen after her pattern, and lastly the Mother Earth who receives him once more. But it is in vain that an old man yearns for the love of woman as he had it first from his mother; the third of the Fates alone, the silent Goddess of Death, will take him into her arms.

The Moses of Michelangelo†

The first time that Freud saw Michelangelo's powerful statue of the seated Moses was in September 1901, after he had overcome his crippling inhibition against seeing Rome, on his very first visit. Thereafter, whenever he spent

† [The following footnote, obviously drafted by Freud himself, was attached to the title when the paper made its first, anonymous, appearance in *Imago*:

'Although this paper does not, strictly speaking, conform to the conditions under which contri-

butions are accepted for publication in this Journal, the editors have decided to print it, since the author, who is personally known to them, moves in psycho-analytic circles, and since his mode of thought has in point of fact a certain resemblance to the methodology of psycho-analysis.']

time in Rome in the late summer, he made a pilgrimage to "his" Moses. No doubt, his preoccupation (perhaps identification) with the hero who, according to him, created Judaism, was persistent. (One of his last writings, after all, would be *Moses and Monotheism*, published in 1938, in which, attempting to establish the origins of the Jewish people, Freud claimed that Moses, the founder, had been an Egyptian.) By 1912, he was telling his intimates that he was planning to write a paper on the meaning of the statue. In the following fall, after much hesitation and several changes of mind, he set to work and published the paper in *Imago* in 1914—anonymously: "by ***," despite Abraham's protest that readers would recognize "the lion's claw." Indeed, the disguise Freud adopted in the first note and the opening paragraphs is feeble, almost coy. But he persisted in calling the paper a "love child;" he saw it as a bastard he loved but hesitated to acknowledge. Indeed, acknowledgment did not come for another decade, in 1924. Freud's argument is lucid and extremely detailed, drawing on art-historical literature and the most minute observations.

I may say at once that I am no connoisseur in art, but simply a layman. I have often observed that the subject-matter of works of art has a stronger attraction for me than their formal and technical qualities, though to the artist their value lies first and foremost in these latter. I am unable rightly to appreciate many of the methods used and the effects obtained in art. I state this so as to secure the reader's indulgence for the attempt I propose to make here.

Nevertheless, works of art do exercise a powerful effect on me, especially those of literature and sculpture, less often of painting. This has occasioned me, when I have been contemplating such things, to spend a long time before them trying to apprehend them in my own way, i.e. to explain to myself what their effect is due to. Wherever I cannot do this, as for instance with music, I am almost incapable of obtaining any pleasure. Some rationalistic, or perhaps analytic, turn of mind in me rebels against being moved by a thing without knowing why I am thus affected and what it is that affects me.

This has brought me to recognize the apparently paradoxical fact that precisely some of the grandest and most overwhelming creations of art are still unsolved riddles to our understanding. We admire them, we feel overawed by them, but we are unable to say what they represent to us. I am not sufficiently well-read to know whether this fact has already been remarked upon; possibly, indeed, some writer on aesthetics has discovered that this state of intellectual bewilderment is a necessary condition when a work of art is to achieve its greatest effects. It would be only with the greatest reluctance that I could bring myself to believe in any such necessity.

I do not mean that connoisseurs and lovers of art find no words with which to praise such objects to us. They are eloquent enough, it seems to me. But usually in the presence of a great work of art each says something different from the other; and none of them says anything that solves the problem for the unpretending admirer. In my opinion, what grips us so powerfully can only be the artist's *intention*, in so far as he has succeeded in expressing it in his work and in getting us to understand it. I realize that this cannot be merely a matter of *intellectual* comprehension; what he aims at is to awaken in us the same emotional attitude, the same mental constellation as that which in him produced the impetus to create. But why should the artist's intention not be capable of being communicated and comprehended in *words*, like any other fact of mental life? Perhaps where great works of art are concerned this would never be possible without the application of psycho-analysis. The product itself after all must admit of such an analysis, if it really is an effective expression of the intentions and emotional activities of the artist. To discover his intention, though, I must first find out the meaning and content of what is represented in his work; I must, in other words, be able to *interpret* it. It is possible, therefore, that a work of art of this kind needs interpretation, and that until I have accomplished that interpretation I cannot come to know why I have been so powerfully affected. I even venture to hope that the effect of the work will undergo no diminution after we have succeeded in thus analysing it.

Let us consider Shakespeare's masterpiece, *Hamlet*, a play now over three centuries old. I have followed the literature of psycho-analysis closely, and I accept its claim that it was not until the material of the tragedy had been traced back by psycho-analysis to the Oedipus theme that the mystery of its effect was at last explained. But before this was done, what a mass of differing and contradictory interpretative attempts, what a variety of opinions about the hero's character and the dramatist's intentions! Does Shakespeare claim our sympathies on behalf of a sick man, or of an ineffectual weakling, or of an idealist who is merely too good for the real world? And how many of these interpretations leave us cold!—so cold that they do nothing to explain the effect of the play and rather incline us to the view that its magical appeal rests solely upon the impressive thoughts in it and the splendour of its language. And yet, do not those very endeavours speak for the fact that we feel the need of discovering in it some source of power beyond them alone?

Another of these inscrutable and wonderful works of art is the marble statue of Moses, by Michelangelo, in the Church of S. Pietro in Vincoli in Rome. As we know, it was only a fragment of the gigantic tomb which the artist was to have erected for the powerful Pope Julius II.[1] It always delights me to read an appreciative sentence about this statue, such as that it is 'the crown of modern sculpture' (Grimm).[2] For no piece of statuary has ever made a stronger impression on me than this.

---

1. According to Henry Thode {*Michelangelo: kritische Untersuchungen über seine Werke*, vol. I (1908), 194} the statue was made between the years 1512 and 1516.

2. {*Leben Michelangelos*, 9th ed. (1900), 189.}

How often have I mounted the steep steps from the unlovely Corso Cavour to the lonely piazza where the deserted church stands, and have essayed to support the angry scorn of the hero's glance! Sometimes I have crept cautiously out of the half-gloom of the interior as though I myself belonged to the mob upon whom his eye is turned—the mob which can hold fast no conviction, which has neither faith nor patience, and which rejoices when it has regained its illusory idols.

But why do I call this statue inscrutable? There is not the slightest doubt that it represents Moses, the Law-giver of the Jews, holding the Tables of the Ten Commandments. That much is certain, but that is all. As recently as 1912 an art critic, Max Sauerlandt, has said, 'No other work of art in the world has been judged so diversely as the Moses with the head of Pan. The mere interpretation of the figure has given rise to completely opposed views. . . .' Basing myself on an essay published only five years ago,[3] I will first set out the doubts which are associated with this figure of Moses; and it will not be difficult to show that behind them lies concealed all that is most essential and valuable for the comprehension of this work of art.

I

The Moses of Michelangelo is represented as seated; his body faces forward, his head with its mighty beard looks to the left, his right foot rests on the ground and his left leg is raised so that only the toes touch the ground. His right arm links the Tables of the Law with a portion of his beard; his left arm lies in his lap. Were I to give a more detailed description of his attitude, I should have to anticipate what I want to say later on. The descriptions of the figure given by various writers are, by the way, curiously inapt. What has not been understood has been inaccurately perceived or reproduced. Grimm says that the right hand, 'under whose arms the Tables rest, grasps his beard'. So also Lübke: 'Profoundly shaken, he grasps with his right hand his magnificent, flowing beard . . .'; and Springer: 'Moses presses one (the left) hand against his body, and thrusts the other, as though unconsciously, into the mighty locks of his beard.' Justi thinks that the fingers of his (right) hand are playing with his beard, 'as an agitated man nowadays might play with his watch-chain'. Müntz, too, lays stress on this playing with the beard. Thode speaks of the 'calm, firm posture of the right hand upon the Tables resting against his side'. He does not recognize any sign of excitement even in the right hand, as Justi and also Boito do. 'The hand remains grasping his beard, in the position it was in before the Titan turned his head to one side.' Jakob Burckhardt complains that 'the celebrated left arm has no other function in reality than to press his beard to his body'.

If mere descriptions do not agree we shall not be surprised to find a

3. Thode (1908).

divergence of view as to the meaning of various features of the statue. In my opinion we cannot better characterize the facial expression of Moses than in the words of Thode, who reads in it 'a mixture of wrath, pain and contempt',—'wrath in his threatening contracted brows, pain in his glance, and contempt in his protruded under-lip and in the down-drawn corners of his mouth'. But other admirers must have seen with other eyes. Thus Dupaty says, 'His august brow seems to be but a transparent veil only half concealing his great mind'. Lübke, on the other hand, declares that 'one would look in vain in that head for an expression of higher intelligence; his down-drawn brow speaks of nothing but a capacity for infinite wrath and an all-compelling energy'. Guillaume differs still more widely in his interpretation of the expression of the face. He finds no emotion in it 'only a proud simplicity, an inspired dignity, a living faith. The eye of Moses looks into the future, he foresees the lasting survival of his people, the immutability of his law.' Similarly, to Müntz, 'the eyes of Moses rove far beyond the race of men. They are turned towards those mysteries which he alone has descried.' To Steinmann, indeed, this Moses is 'no longer the stern Lawgiver, no longer the terrible enemy of sin, armed with the wrath of Jehovah, but the royal priest, whom age may not approach, beneficent and prophetic, with the reflection of eternity upon his brow, taking his last farewell of his people'.[4]

There have even been some for whom the Moses of Michelangelo had nothing at all to say, and who are honest enough to admit it. Thus a critic in the Quarterly Review of 1858 [103, 469]: 'There is an absence of meaning in the general conception, which precludes the idea of a self-sufficing whole. . . .' And we are astonished to learn that there are yet others who find nothing to admire in the Moses, but who revolt against it and complain of the brutality of the figure and the animal cast of the head.

Has then the master-hand indeed traced such a vague or ambiguous script in the stone, that so many different readings of it are possible?

Another question, however, arises, which covers the first one. Did Michelangelo intend to create a 'timeless study of character and mood' in this Moses, or did he portray him at a particular moment of his life and, if so, at a highly significant one? The majority of judges have decided in the latter sense and are able to tell us what episode in his life it is which the artist has immortalized in stone. It is the descent from Mount Sinai, where Moses has received the Tables from God,

---

4. {Freud's authorities are, in order: Herman Grimm, *Leben Michelangelos* (1900), 189; Wilhelm Lübke, *Geschichte der Plastik* (1863), 666; Anton Heinrich Springer, *Raffael und Michelangelo*, vol. 2 (1895), 33; Carl Justi, *Michelangelo* (1900), 326; Eugène Müntz, *Histoire de l'art pendant la Renaissance: Italie* (1895), 391n; Thode, *Michelangelo*, 205; Camillo Boito, *Leonardo, Mi-* *chelangelo, Andrea Palladio*, 2nd ed. (1883); Jakob Burckhardt, *Der Cicerone* (1855; ed. 1927), 634; Lübke, *Geschichte der Plastik*, 666–67; Jean Baptiste Claude Eugène Guillaume, "Michel-Ange, Sculpteur," *Gazette des Beaux-Arts* (1876), 96; Müntz, *Histoire de l'art*, 391; Ernst Steinmann, *Rom in der Renaissance* (1899), 169.}

and it is the moment when he perceives that the people have meanwhile made themselves a Golden Calf and are dancing around it and rejoicing. This is the scene upon which his eyes are turned, this is the spectacle which calls out the feelings depicted in his countenance—feelings which in the next instant will launch his great frame into violent action. Michelangelo has chosen this last moment of hesitation, of calm before the storm, for his representation. In the next instant Moses will spring to his feet—his left foot is already raised from the ground—dash the Tables to the earth, and let loose his rage upon his faithless people.

Once more many individual differences of opinion exist among those who support this interpretation.[5]

* * *

Justi [1900, 326–7] has gone the furthest of all in his interpretation of the statue as Moses in the act of perceiving the Golden Calf, and he has pointed out details hitherto unobserved in it and worked them into his hypothesis. He directs our attention to the position of the two Tables—an unusual one, for they are about to slip down on to the stone seat. 'He' (Moses) 'might therefore be looking in the direction from which the clamour was coming with an expression of evil foreboding, or it might be the actual sight of the abomination which has dealt him a stunning blow. Quivering with horror and pain he has sunk down.[6] He has sojourned on the mountain forty days and nights and he is weary. A horror, a great turn of fortune, a crime, even happiness itself, can be perceived in a single moment, but not grasped in its essence, its depths or its consequences. For an instant it seems to Moses that his work is destroyed and he despairs utterly of his people. In such moments the inner emotions betray themselves involuntarily in small movements. He lets the Tables slip from his right hand on to the stone seat; they have come to rest on their corner there and are pressed by his forearm against the side of his body. His hand, however, comes in contact with his breast and beard and thus, by the turning of the head to the spectator's right, it draws the beard to the left and breaks the symmetry of that masculine adornment. It looks as though his fingers were playing with his beard as an agitated man nowadays might play with his watch-chain. His left hand is buried in his garment over the lower part of his body— in the Old Testament the viscera are the seat of the emotions—but the left leg is already drawn back and the right put forward; in the next instant he will leap up, his mental energy will be transposed from feeling into action, his right arm will move, the Tables will fall to the ground,

5. {Freud here cites a number of specialists, including Burckhardt, Lübke, Springer, Grimm, and others not cited before, who offer various interpretations of Moses's posture which do, however, generally agree that Moses is about to spring to his feet.}

6. It should be remarked that the careful arrangement of the mantle over the knees of the sitting figure invalidates this first part of Justi's view. On the contrary, this would lead us to suppose that Moses is represented as sitting there in calm repose until he is startled by some sudden perception.

and the shameful trespass will be expiated in torrents of blood. . . .'
'This is not yet the moment of tension of an act. Pain of mind still
dominates him and almost paralyses him.'

* * *

It cannot be denied that there is something extraordinarily attractive
about attempts at an interpretation of the kind made by Justi * * *

But two remarks of Thode's deprive us of the knowledge we thought
to have gained. This critic says that to his eye the Tables are not slipping
down but are 'firmly lodged'. He notes the 'calm, firm pose of the right
hand upon the resting Tables'. If we look for ourselves we cannot but
admit unreservedly that Thode is right. The Tables are firmly placed
and in no danger of slipping. Moses' right hand supports them or is
supported by them. This does not explain the position in which they
are held, it is true, but that position cannot be used in favour of the
interpretation of Justi and others. [Thode (1908), 205.]

The second observation is still more final. Thode reminds us that 'this
statue was planned as one of six, and is intended to be seated. Both facts
contradict the view that Michelangelo meant to record a particular historical moment. For, as regards the first consideration, the plan of
representing a row of seated figures as types of human beings—as the
vita activa and the vita contemplativa—excluded a representation of a
particular historic episode. And, as regards the second, the representation
of a seated posture—a posture necessitated by the artistic conception of
the whole monument—contradicts the nature of that episode, namely,
the descent of Moses from Mount Sinai into the camp.'

If we accept Thode's objection we shall find that we can add to its
weight. The figure of Moses was to have decorated the base of the tomb
together with five other statues (or according to a later sketch, with three).
Its immediate counterpart was to have been a figure of Paul. One other
pair, representing the vita activa and the vita contemplativa in the shape
of Leah and Rachel—standing, it is true—has been executed on the
tomb as it still exists in its sadly aborted form. The Moses thus forms
part of a whole and we cannot imagine that the figure was meant to
arouse an expectation in the spectator that it was on the point of leaping
up from its seat and rushing away to create a disturbance on its own
account. If the other figures were not also represented as about to take
violent action—and it seems very improbable that they were—then it
would create a very bad impression for one of them to give us the illusion
that it was going to leave its place and its companions, in fact to abandon
its role in the general scheme. Such an intention would have a chaotic
effect and we could not charge a great artist with it unless the facts drove
us to it. A figure in the act of instant departure would be utterly at
variance with the state of mind which the tomb is meant to induce in
us.

The figure of Moses, therefore, cannot be supposed to be springing to his feet; he must be allowed to remain as he is in sublime repose like the other figures and like the proposed statue of the Pope (which was not, however, executed by Michelangelo himself). But then the statue we see before us cannot be that of a man filled with wrath, of Moses when he came down from Mount Sinai and found his people faithless and threw down the Holy Tables so that they were broken. And, indeed, I can recollect my own disillusionment when, during my first visits to San Pietro in Vincoli, I used to sit down in front of the statue in the expectation that I should now see how it would start up on its raised foot, dash the Tables of the Law to the ground and let fly its wrath. Nothing of the kind happened. Instead, the stone image became more and more transfixed, an almost oppressively solemn calm emanated from it, and I was obliged to realize that something was represented here that could stay without change; that this Moses would remain sitting like this in his wrath for ever.

But if we have to abandon our interpretation of the statue as showing Moses just before his outburst of wrath at the sight of the Golden Calf, we have no alternative but to accept one of the hypotheses which regard it as a study of character. Thode's view seems to be the least arbitrary and to have the closest reference to the meaning of its movements. He says, 'Here, as always, he [Michelangelo] is concerned with representing a certain type of character. He creates the image of a passionate leader of mankind who, conscious of his divine mission as Lawgiver, meets the uncomprehending opposition of men. * * *'

* * *

For myself, I see nothing to object to in Thode's explanation; but I feel the lack of something in it. Perhaps it is the need to discover a closer parallel between the state of mind of the hero as expressed in his attitude, and the contrast above-mentioned between his 'outward' calm and 'inward' emotion.

II

Long before I had any opportunity of hearing about psycho-analysis, I learnt that a Russian art-connoisseur, Ivan Lermolieff,[7] had caused a revolution in the art galleries of Europe by questioning the authorship of many pictures, showing how to distinguish copies from originals with certainty, and constructing hypothetical artists for those works whose former supposed authorship had been discredited. He achieved this by insisting that attention should be diverted from the general impression and main features of a picture, and by laying stress on the significance of minor details, of things like the drawing of the fingernails, of the lobe of an ear, of halos and such unconsidered trifles which the copyist neglects to imitate and yet which every artist executes in his own char-

7. His first essays were published in German between 1874 and 1876.

acteristic way. I was then greatly interested to learn that the Russian pseudonym concealed the identity of an Italian physician called Morelli, who died in 1891 with the rank of Senator of the Kingdom of Italy. It seems to me that his method of inquiry is closely related to the technique of psycho-analysis. It, too, is accustomed to divine secret and concealed things from despised or unnoticed features, from the rubbish-heap, as it were, of our observations.

Now in two places in the figure of Moses there are certain details which have hitherto not only escaped notice but, in fact, have not even been properly described. These are the attitude of his right hand and the position of the two Tables of the Law. We may say that this hand forms a very singular, unnatural link, and one which calls for explanation, between the Tables and the wrathful hero's beard. He has been described as running his fingers through his beard and playing with its locks, while the outer edge of his hand rests on the Tables. But this is plainly not so. It is worth while examining more closely what those fingers of the right hand are doing, and describing more minutely the mighty beard with which they are in contact.

We now quite clearly perceive the following things: the thumb of the hand is concealed and the index finger alone is in effective contact with the beard. It is pressed so deeply against the soft masses of hair that they bulge out beyond it both above and below, that is, both towards the head and towards the abdomen. The other three fingers are propped upon the wall of his chest and are bent at the upper joints; they are barely touched by the extreme right-hand lock of the beard which falls past them. They have, as it were, withdrawn from the beard. It is therefore not correct to say that the right hand is playing with the beard or plunged in it; the simple truth is that the index finger is laid over a part of the beard and makes a deep trough in it. It cannot be denied that to press one's beard with one finger is an extraordinary gesture and one not easy to understand.

The much-admired beard of Moses flows from his cheeks, chin and upper lip in a number of waving strands which are kept distinct from one another all the way down. One of the strands on his extreme right, growing from the cheek, falls down to the inward-pressing index finger, by which it is retained. We may assume that it resumes its course between that finger and the concealed thumb. The corresponding strand on his left side falls practically unimpeded far down over his breast. What has received the most unusual treatment is the thick mass of hair on the inside of this latter strand, the part between it and the middle line. It is not suffered to follow the turn of the head to the left; it is forced to roll over loosely and form part of a kind of scroll which lies across and over the strands on the inner right side of the beard. This is because it is held fast by the pressure of the right index finger, although it grows from the left side of the face and is, in fact, the main portion of the whole left side of the beard. Thus, the main mass of the beard is thrown

Courtesy of Archivi Alinari.

DETAIL OF MICHELANGELO'S MOSES

to the right of the figure, whereas the head is sharply turned to the left. At the place where the right index finger is pressed in, a kind of whorl of hairs is formed; strands of hair coming from the left lie over strands coming from the right, both caught in by that despotic finger. It is only beyond this place that the masses of hair, deflected from their course, flow freely once more, and now they fall vertically until their ends are gathered up in Moses' left hand as it lies open on his lap.

I have no illusions as to the clarity of my description, and venture no opinion whether the sculptor really does invite us to solve the riddle of that knot in the beard of his statue. But apart from this, the fact remains that the pressure of the *right* index finger affects mainly the strands of hair from the *left* side; and that this oblique hold prevents the beard from accompanying the turn of the head and eyes to the left. Now we may be allowed to ask what this arrangement means and to what motives it owes its existence. If it was indeed considerations of linear and spatial design which caused the sculptor to draw the downward-streaming wealth of hair across to the right of the figure which is looking to its left, how strangely unsuitable as a means does the pressure of a single finger appear to be! And what man who, for some reason or other, has drawn his beard over to the other side, would take it into his head to hold down the one half across the other by the pressure of one finger? Yet may not these minute particulars mean nothing in reality, and may we not be racking our brains about things which were of no moment to their creator?

But let us proceed on the assumption that even these details have significance. There is a solution which will remove our difficulties and afford a glimpse of a new meaning. If the *left* side of Moses' beard lies under the pressure of his *right* finger, we may perhaps take this pose as the last stage of some connection between his right hand and the left half of his beard, a connection which was a much more intimate one at some moment before that chosen for representation. Perhaps his hand had seized his beard with far more energy, had reached across to its left edge, and, in returning to that position in which the statue shows it, had been followed by a part of his beard which now testifies to the movement which has just taken place. The loop of the beard would thus be an indication of the path taken by this hand.

Thus we shall have inferred that there had been a retreating motion of the right hand. This one assumption necessarily brings others with it. In imagination we complete the scene of which this movement, established by the evidence of the beard, is a part; and we are brought back quite naturally to the hypothesis according to which the resting Moses is startled by the clamour of the people and the spectacle of the Golden Calf. He was sitting there calmly, we will suppose, his head with its flowing beard facing forward, and his hand in all probability not near it at all. Suddenly the clamour strikes his ear; he turns his head and eyes in the direction from which the disturbance comes, sees the scene and takes it in. Now wrath and indignation lay hold of him; and he would fain leap up and punish the wrongdoers, annihilate them. His rage, distant as yet from its object, is meanwhile directed in a gesture against his own body. His impatient hand, ready to act, clutches at his beard which has moved with the turn of his head, and presses it between his thumb and palm in the iron grasp of his closing fingers. It is a gesture whose power and vehemence remind us of other creations of Michelangelo's. But now an alteration takes place, as yet we do not know how or why. The hand that had been put forward and had sunk into his beard is hastily withdrawn and unclasped, and the fingers let go their hold; but so deeply have they been plunged in that in their withdrawal

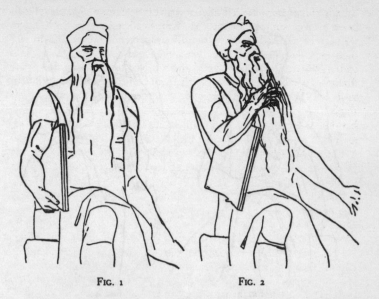

FIG. 1   FIG. 2

they drag a great piece of the left side of the beard across to the right, and this piece remains lodged over the hair of the right under the weight of one finger, the longest and uppermost one of the hand. And this new position, which can only be understood with reference to the former one, is now retained.

It is time now to pause and reflect. We have assumed that the right hand was, to begin with, away from the beard; that then it reached across to the left of the figure in a moment of great emotional tension and seized the beard; and that it was finally drawn back again, taking a part of the beard with it. We have disposed of this right hand as though we had the free use of it. But may we do this? Is the hand indeed so free? Must it not hold or support the Tables? Are not such mimetic evolutions as these prohibited by its important function? And furthermore, what could have occasioned its withdrawal if the motive which made it leave its original position was such a strong one?

Here are indeed fresh difficulties. It is undeniable that the right hand is responsible for the Tables; and also that we have no motive to account for the withdrawal we have ascribed to it. But what if both difficulties could be solved together, and if then and then only they presented a clear and connected sequence of events? What if it is precisely something which is happening to the Tables that explains the movements of the hand?

If we look at the drawing in Fig. 4 we shall see that the Tables present one or two notable features hitherto not deemed worthy of remark. It

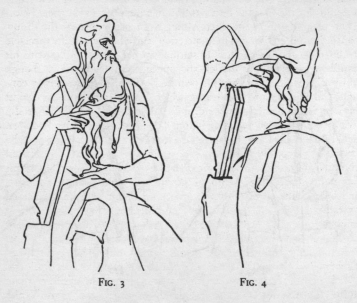

FIG. 3   FIG. 4

has been said that the right hand rests upon the Tables; or again that it
supports them. And we can see at once that the two apposed, rectangular
tablets stand on one corner. If we look closer we shall notice that the
lower edge is a different shape from the upper one, which is obliquely
inclined forward. The upper edge is straight, whereas the lower one has
a protuberance like a horn on the part nearest to us, and the Tables
touch the stone seat precisely with this protuberance. What can be the
meaning of this detail? It can hardly be doubted that this projection is
meant to mark the actual top side of the Tables, as regards the writing.
It is only the top edge of rectangular tablets of this kind that is curved
or notched. Thus we see that the Tables are upside-down. This is a
singular way to treat such sacred objects. They are stood on their heads
and practically balanced on one corner. What consideration of form
could have led Michelangelo to put them in such a position? Or was
this detail as well of no importance to the artist?

We begin to suspect that the Tables too have arrived at their present
position as the result of a previous movement; that this movement was
a consequence of the change of place of the right hand that we have
postulated, and in its turn compelled that hand to make its subsequent
retreat. The movements of the hand and of the Tables can be co-
ordinated in this way: at first the figure of Moses, while it was still sitting
quietly, carried the Tables perpendicularly under its right arm. Its right
hand grasped their lower edge and found a hold in the projection on

their front part. (The fact that this made them easier to carry sufficiently accounts for the upside-down position in which the Tables were held.) Then came the moment when Moses' calm was broken by the disturbance. He turned his head in its direction, and when he saw the spectacle he lifted his foot preparatory to starting up, let go the Tables with his hand and plunged it to the left and upwards into his beard, as though to turn his violence against his own body. The Tables were now consigned to the pressure of his arm, which had to squeeze them against his side. But this support was not sufficient and the Tables began to slip in a forward and downward direction. The upper edge, which had been held horizontally, now began to face forwards and downwards; and the lower edge, deprived of its stay, was nearing the stone seat with its front corner. Another instant and the Tables would have pivoted upon this new point of support, have hit the ground with the upper edge foremost, and been shattered to pieces. It is *to prevent this* that the right hand retreated, let go the beard, a part of which was drawn back with it unintentionally, came against the upper edge of the Tables in time and held them near the hind corner, which had now come uppermost. Thus the singularly constrained air of the whole—beard, hand and tilted Tables—can be traced to that one passionate movement of the hand and its natural consequences. If we wish to reverse the effects of those stormy movements, we must raise the upper front corner of the Tables and push it back, thus lifting their lower front corner (the one with the protuberance) from the stone seat; and then lower the right hand and bring it under the now horizontal lower edge of the Tables.

I have procured from the hand of an artist three drawings to illustrate my meaning. Fig. 3 reproduces the statue as it actually is; Figs. 1 and 2 represent the preceding stages according to my hypothesis—the first that of calm, the second that of highest tension, in which the figure is preparing to spring up and has abandoned its hold of the Tables, so that these are beginning to slip down. Now it is remarkable how the two postures in the imaginary drawings vindicate the incorrect descriptions of earlier writers. Condivi, a contemporary of Michelangelo's, says: 'Moses, the captain and leader of the Hebrews, is seated in the attitude of a contemplative sage, holding the Tables of the Law under his right arm, and leaning his chin on his left hand(!), as one who is weary and full of care.' No such attitude is to be seen in Michelangelo's statue, but it describes almost exactly the view on which the first drawing is based. Lübke writes, together with other critics: 'Profoundly shaken, he grasps with his right hand his magnificent, flowing beard.' This is incorrect if we look at the reproduction of the actual statue, but it is true of the second sketch (Fig. 2). * * *

III

We may now, I believe, permit ourselves to reap the fruits of our endeavours. We have seen how many of those who have felt the influence of this statue have been impelled to interpret it as representing Moses agitated by the spectacle of his people fallen from grace and dancing round an idol. But this interpretation had to be given up, for it made us expect to see him spring up in the next moment, break the Tables and accomplish the work of vengeance. Such a conception, however, would fail to harmonize with the design of making this figure, together with three (or five) more seated figures, a part of the tomb of Julius II. We may now take up again the abandoned interpretation, for the Moses we have reconstructed will neither leap up nor cast the Tables from him. What we see before us is not the inception of a violent action but the remains of a movement that has already taken place. In his first transport of fury, Moses desired to act, to spring up and take vengeance and forget the Tables; but he has overcome the temptation, and he will now remain seated and still, in his frozen wrath and in his pain mingled with contempt. Now will he throw away the Tables so that they will break on the stones, for it is on their especial account that he has controlled his anger; it was to preserve them that he kept his passion in check. In giving way to his rage and indignation, he had to neglect the Tables, and the hand which upheld them was withdrawn. They began to slide down and were in danger of being broken. This brought him to himself. He remembered his mission and for its sake renounced an indulgence of his feelings. His hand returned and saved the unsupported Tables before they had actually fallen to the ground. In this attitude he remained immobilized, and in this attitude Michelangelo has portrayed him as the guardian of the tomb.

As our eyes travel down it the figure exhibits three distinct emotional strata. The lines of the face reflect the feelings which have won the ascendancy; the middle of the figure shows the traces of suppressed movement; and the foot still retains the attitude of the projected action. It is as though the controlling influence had proceeded downwards from above. No mention has been made so far of the left arm, and it seems to claim a share in our interpretation. The hand is laid in the lap in a mild gesture and holds as though in a caress the end of the flowing beard. It seems as if it is meant to counteract the violence with which the other hand had misused the beard a few moments ago.

But here it will be objected that after all this is not the Moses of the Bible. For that Moses did actually fall into a fit of rage and did throw away the Tables and break them. This Moses must be a quite different man, a new Moses of the artist's conception; so that Michelangelo must have had the presumption to emend the sacred text and to falsify the character of that holy man. Can we think him capable of a boldness which might almost be said to approach an act of blasphemy?

The passage in the Holy Scriptures which describes Moses' action at the scene of the Golden Calf is as follows: (Exodus xxxii. 7) 'And the Lord said unto Moses, Go, get thee down; for thy people, which thou broughtest out of the land of Egypt, have corrupted themselves: (8) They have turned aside quickly out of the way which I commanded them: they have made them a molten calf, and have worshipped it, and have sacrificed thereunto, and said, These be thy gods, O Israel, which brought thee up out of the land of Egypt. (9) And the Lord said unto Moses, I have seen this people, and, behold, it is a stiff-necked people: (10) Now therefore let me alone, that my wrath may wax hot against them, and that I may consume them; and I will make of thee a great nation. (11) And Moses besought the Lord his God, and said, Lord, why doth thy wrath wax hot against thy people, which thou hast brought forth out of the land of Egypt with great power, and with a mighty hand? . . .

'(14) And the Lord repented of the evil which he thought to do unto his people. (15) And Moses turned, and went down from the mount, and the two tables of the testimony were in his hand: the tables were written on both their sides; on the one side and on the other were they written. (16) And the tables were the work of God, and the writing was the writing of God, graven upon the tables. (17) And when Joshua heard the noise of the people as they shouted, he said unto Moses, There is a noise of war in the camp. (18) And he said, It is not the voice of them that shout for mastery, neither is it the voice of them that cry for being overcome; but the noise of them that sing do I hear. (19) And it came to pass, as soon as he came nigh unto the camp, that he saw the calf, and the dancing: and Moses' anger waxed hot, and he cast the tables out of his hands, and brake them beneath the mount. (20) And he took the calf which they had made, and burnt it in the fire, and ground it to powder, and strawed it upon the water, and made the children of Israel drink of it. . . .

'(30) And it came to pass on the morrow, that Moses said unto the people, Ye have sinned a great sin: and now I will go up unto the Lord; peradventure I shall make an atonement for your sin. (31) And Moses returned unto the Lord, and said, Oh! this people have sinned a great sin, and have made them gods of gold! (32) Yet now, if thou wilt forgive their sin—; and if not, blot me, I pray thee, out of thy book which thou hast written. (33) And the Lord said unto Moses, Whosoever hath sinned against me, him will I blot out of my book. (34) Therefore now go, lead the people unto the place of which I have spoken unto thee. Behold, mine Angel shall go before thee: nevertheless, in the day when I visit, I will visit their sin upon them. (35) And the Lord plagued the people, because they made the calf which Aaron made.'

It is impossible to read the above passage in the light of modern criticism of the Bible without finding evidence that it has been clumsily put together from various sources. In verse 8 the Lord Himself tells

Moses that his people have fallen away and made themselves an idol; and Moses intercedes for the wrongdoers. And yet he speaks to Joshua as though he knew nothing of this (18), and is suddenly aroused to wrath as he sees the scene of the worshipping of the Golden Calf (19). In verse 14 he has already gained a pardon from God for his erring people, yet in verse 31 he returns into the mountains to implore this forgiveness, tells God about his people's sins and is assured of the postponement of the punishment. Verse 35 speaks of a visitation of his people by the Lord about which nothing more is told us; whereas the verses 20–30 describe the punishment which Moses himself dealt out. It is well known that the historical parts of the Bible, dealing with the Exodus, are crowded with still more glaring incongruities and contradictions.

The age of the Renaissance had naturally no such critical attitude towards the text of the Bible, but had to accept it as a consistent whole, with the result that the passage in question was not a very good subject for representation. According to the Scriptures Moses was already instructed about the idolatry of his people and had ranged himself on the side of mildness and forgiveness; nevertheless, when he saw the Golden Calf and the dancing crowd, he was overcome by a sudden frenzy of rage. It would therefore not surprise us to find that the artist, in depicting the reaction of his hero to that painful surprise, had deviated from the text from inner motives. Moreover, such deviations from the scriptural text on a much slighter pretext were by no means unusual or disallowed to artists. A celebrated picture by Parmigiano possessed by his native town depicts Moses sitting on the top of a mountain and dashing the Tables to the ground, although the Bible expressly says that he broke them 'beneath the mount'. Even the representation of a seated Moses finds no support in the text and seems rather to bear out those critics who maintain that Michelangelo's statue is not meant to record any particular moment in the prophet's life.

More important than his infidelity to the text of the Scriptures is the alteration which Michelangelo has, in our supposition, made in the character of Moses. The Moses of legend and tradition had a hasty temper and was subject to fits of passion. It was in a transport of divine wrath of this kind that he slew an Egyptian who was maltreating an Israelite, and had to flee out of the land into the wilderness; and it was in a similar passion that he broke the Tables of the Law, inscribed by God Himself. Tradition, in recording such a characteristic, is unbiased, and preserves the impression of a great personality who once lived. But Michelangelo has placed a different Moses on the tomb of the Pope, one superior to the historical or traditional Moses. He has modified the theme of the broken Tables; he does not let Moses break them in his wrath, but makes him be influenced by the danger that they will be broken and makes him calm that wrath, or at any rate prevent it from becoming an act. In this way he has added something new and more than human to the figure of Moses; so that the giant frame with its tremendous physical power becomes only a concrete expression of the highest mental achievement that is possible in a man, that of struggling successfully against an inward passion for the sake of a cause to which he has devoted himself.

We have now completed our interpretation of Michelangelo's statue, though it can still be asked what motives prompted the sculptor to select the figure of Moses, and a so greatly altered Moses, as an adornment for the tomb of Julius II. In the opinion of many these motives are to be found in the character of the Pope and in Michelangelo's relations with him. Julius II was akin to Michelangelo in this, that he attempted to realize great and mighty ends, and especially designs on a grand scale. He was a man of action and he had a definite purpose, which was to unite Italy under the Papal supremacy. He desired to bring about single-handed what was not to happen for several centuries, and then only through the conjunction of many alien forces; and he worked alone, with impatience, in the short span of sovereignty allowed him, and used violent means. He could appreciate Michelangelo as a man of his own kind, but he often made him smart under his sudden anger and his utter lack of consideration for others. The artist felt the same violent force of will in himself, and, as the more introspective thinker, may have had a premonition of the failure to which they were both doomed. And so he carved his Moses on the Pope's tomb, not without a reproach against the dead pontiff, as a warning to himself, thus, in self-criticism, rising superior to his own nature.

* * *

Contribution to a Questionnaire on Reading

In 1906, Hugo Heller, the same publisher who would invite Freud to speak on creative writers and day-dreaming, asked a number of eminent writers to list "ten good books." Thirty-two in all—including Hermann Hesse and Arthur Schnitzler—responded, and the results of the questionnaire were published late in the year. Freud was an obvious choice for Heller, who was a faithful member of Freud's Wednesday night society. He answered carefully, making analytical distinctions between the kinds of books he was listing and not listing. His list, and his reasoning, shed interesting light on Freud's habits and tastes. His catholicity is striking: the ten authors listed represent seven different countries. So is his conservatism: no Flaubert, no Strindberg, or, for that matter, no "modernist" Austrian writer like Hugo von Hofmannsthal.

You ask me to name 'ten good books' for you, and refrain from adding to this any word of explanation. Thus you leave to me not only the choice of the books but also the interpretation of your request. Accustomed to paying attention to small signs, I must then trust the wording in which you couch your enigmatical demand. You did not say: 'the ten most magnificent works (of world literature)', in which case I should have been obliged to reply, with so many others: Homer, the tragedies of Sophocles, Goethe's *Faust*, Shakespeare's *Hamlet*, *Macbeth*, etc. Nor did you say the 'ten most significant books', among which scientific achievements like those of Copernicus, of the old physician Johann Weier on the belief in witches, Darwin's *Descent of Man*, and others, would then have found a place. You did not even ask for 'favourite books', among which I should not have forgotten Milton's *Paradise Lost* and Heine's *Lazarus*. I think, therefore, that a particular stress falls on the 'good' in your phrase, and that with this predicate you intend to designate books to which one stands in rather the same relationship as to 'good' friends, to whom one owes a part of one's knowledge of life and view of the world—books which one has enjoyed oneself and gladly commends to others, but in connection with which the element of timid reverence, the feeling of one's own smallness in the face of their greatness, is not particularly prominent.

I will therefore name ten such 'good' books for you which have come to my mind without a great deal of reflection.

> Multatuli, {the Dutch writer Eduard Douwes Dekker}
>   Letters and Works.
> Kipling, *Jungle Book.*
> Anatole France, *Sur la pierre blanche.*
> Zola, *Fécondité.*
> Merezhkovsky, *Leonardo da Vinci.*
> G. Keller, *Leute von Seldwyla.*
> C. F. Meyer, *Huttens letzte Tage.*
> Macaulay, *Essays.*
> Gomperz, *Griechische Denker.*
> Mark Twain, *Sketches.*

I do not know what you intend to do with this list. It seems a most peculiar one even to me; I really cannot let it go without comment. The problem of why precisely these and not other equally 'good' books I will not begin to tackle; I merely wish to throw light on the relation between the author and his work. The connection is not in every case as firm as it is, for instance, with Kipling's *Jungle Book.* For the most part I could just as well have singled out another work by the same author—for instance, in the case of Zola, *Docteur Pascal*—and the like. The same man who has given us one good book has often presented us with several good books. In the case of Multatuli I felt in two minds whether to reject the private letters in favour of the 'Love Letters' or the latter in favour of the former, and for that reason wrote: 'Letters and Works'. Genuinely creative writing of purely poetical value has been excluded from this list, probably because your charge—good books—did not seem exactly aimed at such; for in the case of C. F. Meyer's *Hutten* I must set its 'goodness' far above its beauty: 'edification' above aesthetic enjoyment.

You have touched on something, with your request to name for you 'ten good books', on which an immeasurable amount could be said. And so I will conclude, in order not to become even more informative.

Yours sincerely,

FREUD.

PART FIVE: TRANSITIONS AND REVISIONS

On Narcissism:
An Introduction

This paper is a crucial turning point in the evolution of Freud's thinking. Indeed, the importance of "On Narcissism" cannot be overestimated, though Freud himself minimized its revolutionary implications. His adherents were far more troubled than he: Ernest Jones called the paper "disturbing" (*Jones* II, 302). To be sure, in itself the proposition that a developmental stage of narcissism should be inserted between the infant's primitive auto-eroticism and the child's object love was an innovation but scarcely upsetting. But in contending that there is an "ego-libido" as well as an "object-libido," Freud undercut the theory of drives with which he had been working for almost two decades: according to his traditional theory, the ego drives are not in any way erotic and the libidinal drives are not egotistic. But if the self can be charged with libido—as it became clearer and clearer to Freud that it can be—this sharp division must collapse. It might be that *all* drives are derivatives of libido (which, in a watered-down version, was Jung's view), or it might be that Freud was really what his adversaries charged him with being: a pan-sexualist. To Freud, both of these "solutions" were wholly unpalatable, even though for a time he had no answer to just what theory of the drives he could substitute. That was to be the work of his postwar writings, especially of *Beyond the Pleasure Principle* (1920) (see below, pp. 594–626).

To add to the significant departures that this paper raises, it also introduced the new idea of an "ego ideal," and that, too, foreshadowed the restructuring of Freud's theory of mind, completed in 1923 with *The Ego and the Id* (see below, pp. 628–58). He wrote "On Narcissism" late in 1913 and published it the following year.

I

The term narcissism is derived from clinical description and was chosen by Paul Näcke in 1899 to denote the attitude of a person who treats his own body in the same way in which the body of a sexual object is ordinarily treated—who looks at it, that is to say, strokes it and fondles it till he obtains complete satisfaction through these activities. Developed to this degree, narcissism has the significance of a perversion that has absorbed the whole of the subject's sexual life, and it will consequently exhibit the characteristics which we expect to meet with in the study of all perversions.

Psycho-analytic observers were subsequently struck by the fact that individual features of the narcissistic attitude are found in many people who suffer from other disorders—for instance, as Sadger has pointed out, in homosexuals—and finally it seemed probable that an allocation of the libido such as deserved to be described as narcissism might be present far more extensively, and that it might claim a place in the regular course of human sexual development. Difficulties in psycho-analytic work upon neurotics led to the same supposition, for it seemed as though this kind of narcissistic attitude in them constituted one of the limits to their susceptibility to influence. Narcissism in this sense would not be a perversion, but the libidinal complement to the egoism of the instinct of self-preservation, a measure of which may justifiably be attributed to every living creature.

A pressing motive for occupying ourselves with the conception of a primary and normal narcissism arose when the attempt was made to subsume what we know of dementia praecox (Kraepelin) or schizophre-nia (Bleuler) under the hypothesis of the libido theory. Patients of this kind, whom I have proposed to term paraphrenics,[1] display two fun-damental characteristics: megalomania and diversion of their interest from the external world—from people and things. In consequence of the latter change, they become inaccessible to the influence of psycho-analysis and cannot be cured by our efforts. But the paraphrenic's turning away from the external world needs to be more precisely characterized. A patient suffering from hysteria or obsessional neurosis has also, as far as his illness extends, given up his relation to reality. But analysis shows that he has by no means broken off his erotic relations to people and things. He still retains them in phantasy; i.e. he has, on the one hand, substituted for real objects imaginary ones from his memory, or has mixed the latter with the former; and on the other hand, he has ren-ounced the initiation of motor activities for the attainment of his aims in connection with those objects. * * * It is otherwise with the para-phrenic. He seems really to have withdrawn his libido from people and things in the external world, without replacing them by others in phan-tasy. When he *does* so replace them, the process seems to be a secondary one and to be part of an attempt at recovery, designed to lead the libido back to objects.

The question arises: What happens to the libido which has been withdrawn from external objects in schizophrenia? The megalomania characteristic of these states points the way. This megalomania has no doubt come into being at the expense of object-libido. The libido that has been withdrawn from the external world has been directed to the ego and thus gives rise to an attitude which may be called narcissism. But the megalomania itself is no new creation; on the contrary, it is, as we know, a magnification and plainer manifestation of a condition which had already existed previously. This leads us to look upon the narcissism which arises through the drawing in of object-cathexes as a secondary

1. {Freud's term "paraphrenia" has not survived in the medical literature; Bleuler's "schizophrenia" carried the day.}

one, superimposed upon a primary narcissism that is obscured by a number of different influences.

* * *

This extension of the libido theory—in my opinion, a legitimate one— receives reinforcement from a third quarter, namely, from our observations and views on the mental life of children and primitive peoples. In the latter we find characteristics which, if they occurred singly, might be put down to megalomania: an over-estimation of the power of their wishes and mental acts, the 'omnipotence of thoughts', a belief in the thaumaturgic force of words, and a technique for dealing with the external world—'magic'—which appears to be a logical application of these grandiose premises. In the children of to-day, whose development is much more obscure to us, we expect to find an exactly analogous attitude towards the external world. Thus we form the idea of there being an original libidinal cathexis of the ego, from which some is later given off to objects, but which fundamentally persists and is related to the object-cathexes much as the body of an amoeba is related to the pseudopodia which it puts out. In our researches, taking, as they did, neurotic symptoms for their starting-point, this part of the allocation of libido necessarily remained hidden from us at the outset. All that we noticed were the emanations of this libido—the object-cathexes, which can be sent out and drawn back again. We see also, broadly speaking, an antithesis between ego-libido and object-libido. The more of the one is employed, the more the other becomes depleted. The highest phase of development of which object-libido is capable is seen in the state of being in love, when the subject seems to give up his own personality in favour of an object-cathexis; while we have the opposite condition in the paranoic's phantasy (or self-perception) of the 'end of the world'. Finally, as regards the differentiation of psychical energies, we are led to the conclusion that to begin with, during the state of narcissism, they exist together and that our analysis is too coarse to distinguish between them; not until there is object-cathexis is it possible to discriminate a sexual energy— the libido—from an energy of the ego-instincts.

* * * What is the relation of the narcissism of which we are now speaking to auto-erotism, which we have described as an early state of the libido? Secondly, if we grant the ego a primary cathexis of libido, why is there any necessity for further distinguishing a sexual libido from a non-sexual energy of the ego-instincts? Would not the postulation of a single kind of psychical energy save us all the difficulties of differentiating an energy of the ego-instincts from ego-libido, and ego-libido from object-libido?

As regards the first question, I may point out that we are bound to suppose that a unity comparable to the ego cannot exist in the individual from the start; the ego has to be developed. The auto-erotic instincts, however, are there from the very first; so there must be something added to auto-erotism—a new psychical action—in order to bring about narcissism.

To be asked to give a definite answer to the second question must occasion perceptible uneasiness in every psycho-analyst. One dislikes the thought of abandoning observation for barren theoretical controversy, but nevertheless one must not shirk an attempt at clarification. It is true that notions such as that of an ego-libido, an energy of the ego-instincts, and so on, are neither particularly easy to grasp, nor sufficiently rich in content; a speculative theory of the relations in question would begin by seeking to obtain a sharply defined concept as its basis. But I am of opinion that that is just the difference between a speculative theory and a science erected on empirical interpretation. The latter will not envy speculation its privilege of having a smooth, logically unassailable foundation, but will gladly content itself with nebulous, scarcely imaginable basic concepts, which it hopes to apprehend more clearly in the course of its development, or which it is even prepared to replace by others. For these ideas are not the foundation of science, upon which everything rests: that foundation is observation alone. They are not the bottom but the top of the whole structure, and they can be replaced and discarded without damaging it. The same thing is happening in our day in the science of physics, the basic notions of which as regards matter, centres of force, attraction, etc., are scarcely less debatable than the corresponding notions in psycho-analysis.

The value of the concepts 'ego-libido' and 'object-libido' lies in the fact that they are derived from the study of the intimate characteristics of neurotic and psychotic processes. A differentiation of libido into a kind which is proper to the ego and one which is attached to objects is an unavoidable corollary to an original hypothesis which distinguished between sexual instincts and ego-instincts. At any rate, analysis of the pure transference neuroses (hysteria and obsessional neurosis) compelled me to make this distinction and I only know that all attempts to account for these phenomena by other means have been completely unsuccessful.

In the total absence of any theory of the instincts which would help us to find our bearings, we may be permitted, or rather, it is incumbent upon us, to start off by working out some hypothesis to its logical conclusion, until it either breaks down or is confirmed. There are various points in favour of the hypothesis of there having been from the first a separation between sexual instincts and others, ego-instincts, besides the serviceability of such a hypothesis in the analysis of the transference neuroses. I admit that this latter consideration alone would not be unambiguous, for it might be a question of an indifferent psychical energy which only becomes libido through the act of cathecting an object. But, in the first place, the distinction made in this concept corresponds to the common popular distinction between hunger and love. In the second place, there are biological considerations in its favour. The individual does actually carry on a twofold existence: one to serve his own purposes and the other as a link in a chain, which he serves against his will, or at least involuntarily. The individual himself regards sexuality as one of his own ends; whereas from another point of view he is an appendage to his germ-plasm, at whose disposal he puts his energies in return for a bonus of pleasure. He is the mortal vehicle of a (possibly) immortal substance—like the inheritor of an entailed property, who is only the temporary holder of an estate which survives him. The separation of the sexual instincts from the ego-instincts would simply reflect this twofold function of the individual. Thirdly, we must recollect that all our provisional ideas in psychology will presumably some day be based on an organic substructure. This makes it probable that it is special substances and chemical processes which perform the operations of sexuality and provide for the extension of individual life into that of the species. We are taking this probability into account in replacing the special chemical substances by special psychical forces.

I try in general to keep psychology clear from everything that is different in nature from it, even biological lines of thought. For that very reason I should like at this point expressly to admit that the hypothesis of separate ego-instincts and sexual instincts (that is to say, the libido theory) rests scarcely at all upon a psychological basis, but derives its principal support from biology. But I shall be consistent enough [with my general rule] to drop this hypothesis if psycho-analytic work should itself produce some other, more serviceable hypothesis about the instincts. So far, this has not happened. It may turn out that, most basically and on the longest view, sexual energy—libido—is only the product of a differentiation in the energy at work generally in the mind. But such an assertion has no relevance. It relates to matters which are so remote from the problems of our observation, and of which we have so little cognizance, that it is as idle to dispute it as to affirm it; this primal identity may well have as little to do with our analytic interests as the primal kinship of all the races of mankind has to do with the proof of kinship required in order to establish a legal right of inheritance. All these speculations take us nowhere. Since we cannot wait for another science to present us with the final conclusions on the theory of the instincts, it is far more to the purpose that we should try to see what light may be thrown upon this basic problem of biology by a synthesis of the *psychological* phenomena. Let us face the possibility of error; but do not let us be deterred from pursuing the logical implications of the hypothesis we first adopted of an antithesis between ego-instincts and sexual instincts (a hypothesis to which we were forcibly led by analysis of the transference neuroses), and from seeing whether it turns out to be without contradictions and fruitful, and whether it can be applied to other disorders as well, such as schizophrenia.

It would, of course, be a different matter if it were proved that the libido theory has already come to grief in the attempt to explain the latter disease. This has been asserted by C. G. Jung (1912) and it is on that account that I have been obliged to enter upon this last discussion, which I would gladly have been spared. I should have preferred to follow to its end the course embarked upon in the analysis of the Schreber case without any discussion of its premises. But Jung's assertion is, to say the least of it, premature. The grounds he gives for it are scanty. In the first place, he appeals to an admission of my own that I myself have been obliged, owing to the difficulties of the Schreber analysis, to extend the concept of libido (that is, to give up its sexual content) and to identify libido with psychical interest in general. Ferenczi,[2] in an exhaustive criticism of Jung's work, has already said all that is necessary is correction of this erroneous interpretation. I can only corroborate his criticism and repeat that I have never made any such retraction of the libido theory. Another argument of Jung's, namely, that we cannot suppose that the withdrawal of the libido is in itself enough to bring about the loss of the normal function of reality, is no argument but a dictum. It 'begs the question',[3] and saves discussion; for whether and how this is possible was precisely the point that should have been under investigation. * * * How little this inapt analogy can help us to decide the question may be learnt from the consideration that an anchorite of this kind, who 'tries to eradicate every trace of sexual interest' (but only in the popular sense of the word 'sexual'), does not even necessarily display any pathogenic allocation of libido. He may have diverted his sexual interest from human beings entirely, and yet may have sublimated it into a heightened interest in the divine, in nature, or in the animal kingdom, with his libido having undergone an introversion on to his phantasies or a return to his ego. This analogy would seem to rule out in advance the possibility of differentiating between interest emanating from erotic sources and from others. * * * We may repudiate Jung's assertion, then, that the libido theory has come to grief in the attempt explain dementia praecox, and that it is therefore disposed of for the other neuroses as well.

II

* * *

In estimating the influence of organic disease upon the distribution of libido, I follow a suggestion made to me orally by Sándor Ferenczi. It is universally known, and we take it as a matter of course, that a person who is tormented by organic pain and discomfort gives up his interest in the things of the external world, in so far as they do not concern his suffering. Closer observation teaches us that he also with-

2. {Freud cites the important paper by Sándor Ferenczi, "Entwicklungsstufen des Wirklichkeits-
sinnes," Internationale Zeitschrift für ärztliche
Psychoanalyse, I (1913), tr. as "Stages in the Development of the Sense of Reality," First Contributions to Psychoanalysis (1952), ch. VII.}
3. [In English in the original.]

draws *libidinal* interest from his love-objects: so long as he suffers, he ceases to love. The commonplace nature of this fact is no reason why we should be deterred from translating it into terms of the libido theory. We should then say: the sick man withdraws his libidinal cathexes back upon his own ego, and sends them out again when he recovers. 'Concentrated is his soul', says Wilhelm Busch of the poet suffering from toothache, 'in his molar's narrow hole'.[4] Here libido and ego-interest share the same fate and are once more indistinguishable from each other. The familiar egoism of the sick person covers both. We find it so natural because we are certain that in the same situation we should behave in just the same way. The way in which a lover's feelings, however strong, are banished by bodily ailments, and suddenly replaced by complete indifference, is a theme which has been exploited by comic writers to an appropriate extent.

The condition of sleep, too, resembles illness in implying a narcissistic withdrawal of the positions of the libido on to the subject's own self, or, more precisely, on to the single wish to sleep. The egoism of dreams fits very well into this context. In both states we have, if nothing else, examples of changes in the distribution of libido that are consequent upon a change in the ego.

Hypochondria, like organic disease, manifests itself in distressing and painful bodily sensations, and it has the same effect as organic disease on the distribution of libido. The hypochondriac withdraws both interest and libido—the latter specially markedly—from the objects of the external world and concentrates both of them upon the organ that is engaging his attention. A difference between hypochondria and organic disease now becomes evident: in the latter, the distressing sensations are based upon demonstrable [organic] changes; in the former, this is not so. But it would be entirely in keeping with our general conception of the processes of neurosis if we decided to say that hypochondria must be right: organic changes must be supposed to be present in it, too.

But what could these changes be? We will let ourselves be guided at this point by our experience, which shows that bodily sensations of an unpleasurable nature, comparable to those of hypochondria, occur in the other neuroses as well. I have said before that I am inclined to class hypochondria with neurasthenia and anxiety-neurosis as a third 'actual' neurosis. It would probably not be going too far to suppose that in the case of the other neuroses a small amount of hypochondria was regularly formed at the same time as well. We have the best example of this, I think, in anxiety neurosis with its superstructure of hysteria. Now the familiar prototype of an organ that is painfully tender, that is in some

---

4. {Freud, like most in the German-speaking world, was fond of, and enjoyed quoting, Wilhelm Busch (1832–1908), versifier, illustrator, folksy philosopher, and inventor of immensely popular "wicked" fables and anecdotes.}

way changed and that is yet not diseased in the ordinary sense, is the genital organ in its states of excitation. In that condition it becomes congested with blood, swollen and humected, and is the seat of a multiplicity of sensations. Let us now, taking any part of the body, describe its activity of sending sexually exciting stimuli to the mind as its 'erotogenicity', and let us further reflect that the considerations on which our theory of sexuality was based have long accustomed us to the notion that certain other parts of the body—the 'erotogenic' zones—may act as substitutes for the genitals and behave analogously to them. We have then only one more step to take. We can decide to regard erotogenicity as a general characteristic of all organs and may then speak of an increase or decrease of it in a particular part of the body. For every such change in the erotogenicity of the organs there might then be a parallel change of libidinal cathexis in the ego. Such factors would constitute what we believe to underlie hypochondria and what may have the same effect upon the distribution of libido as is produced by a material illness of the organs.

We see that, if we follow up this line of thought, we come up against the problem not only of hypochondria, but of the other 'actual' neuroses—neurasthenia and anxiety neurosis. Let us therefore stop at this point. * * * We may suspect that the relation of hypochondria to paraphrenia is similar to that of the other 'actual' neuroses to hysteria and obsessional neurosis: we may suspect, that is, that it is dependent on ego-libido just as the others are on object-libido, and that hypochondriacal anxiety is the counterpart, as coming from ego-libido, to neurotic anxiety. Further, since we are already familiar with the idea that the mechanism of falling ill and of the formation of symptoms in the transference neuroses—the path from introversion to regression—is to be linked to a damming-up of object-libido, we may come to closer quarters with the idea of a damming-up of ego-libido as well and may bring this idea into relation with the phenomena of hypochondria and paraphrenia.

At this point, our curiosity will of course raise the question why this damming-up of libido in the ego should have to be experienced as unpleasurable. I shall content myself with the answer that unpleasure is always the expression of a higher degree of tension, and that therefore what is happening is that a quantity in the field of material events is being transformed here as elsewhere into the psychical quality of unpleasure. Nevertheless it may be that what is decisive for the generation of unpleasure is not the absolute magnitude of the material event, but rather some particular function of that absolute magnitude. Here we may even venture to touch on the question of what makes it necessary at all for our mental life to pass beyond the limits of narcissism and to attach the libido to objects. The answer which would follow from our line of thought would once more be that this necessity arises when the cathexis of the ego with libido exceeds a certain amount. A strong egoism is a protection against falling ill, but in the last resort we must begin to love in order not to fall ill, and we are bound to fall ill if, in consequence of frustration, we are unable to love. This follows somewhat on the lines of Heine's picture of the psychogenesis of the Creation:

> Krankheit ist wohl der letzte Grund
> Des ganzen Schöpferdrangs gewesen;
> Erschaffend konnte ich genesen,
> Erschaffend wurde ich gesund.[5]

We have recognized our mental apparatus as being first and foremost a device designed for mastering excitations which would otherwise be felt as distressing or would have pathogenic effects. Working them over in the mind helps remarkably towards an internal draining away of excitations which are incapable of direct discharge outwards, or for which such a discharge is for the moment undesirable. In the first instance, however, it is a matter of indifference whether this internal process of working-over is carried out upon real or imaginary objects. The difference does not appear till later—if the turning of the libido on to unreal objects (introversion) has led to its being dammed up. In paraphrenics, megalomania allows of a similar internal working-over of libido which has returned to the ego; perhaps it is only when the megalomania fails that the damming-up of libido in the ego becomes pathogenic and starts the process of recovery which gives us the impression of being a disease.

* * *

A third way in which we may approach the study of narcissism is by observing the erotic life of human beings, with its many kinds of differentiation in man and woman. Just as object-libido at first concealed ego-libido from our observation, so too in connection with the object-choice of infants (and of growing children) what we first noticed was that they derived their sexual objects from their experiences of satisfaction. The first autoerotic sexual satisfactions are experienced in connection with vital functions which serve the purpose of self-preservation. The sexual instincts are at the outset attached to the satisfaction of the ego-instincts; only later do they become independent of these, and even then we have an indication of that original attachment in the fact that the persons who are concerned with a child's feeding, care, and protection become his earliest sexual objects: that is to say, in the first instance his mother or a substitute for her. Side by side, however, with this type and source of object-choice, which may be called the

---

5. [God is imagined as saying: 'Illness was no doubt the final cause of the whole urge to create. By creating, I could recover; by creating, I became healthy.' {Heinrich Heine,} *Neue Gedichte*, 'Schöpfungslieder VII'.]

'anaclitic' or 'attachment' type,[6] psycho-analytic research has revealed a second type, which we were not prepared for finding. We have discovered, especially clearly in people whose libidinal development has suffered some disturbance, such as perverts and homosexuals, that in their later choice of love-objects they have taken as a model not their mother but their own selves. They are plainly seeking *themselves* as a love-object, and exhibiting a type of object-choice which must be termed 'narcissistic'. In this observation we have the strongest of the reasons which have led us to adopt the hypothesis of narcissism.

We have, however, not concluded that human beings are divided into two sharply differentiated groups, according as their object-choice conforms to the anaclitic or to the narcissistic type; we assume rather that both kinds of object-choice are open to each individual, though he may show a preference for one or the other. We say that a human being has originally two sexual objects—himself and the woman who nurses him—and in doing so we are postulating a primary narcissism in everyone, which may in some cases manifest itself in a dominating fashion in his object-choice.

A comparison of the male and female sexes then shows that there are fundamental differences between them in respect of their type of object-choice, although these differences are of course not universal. Complete object-love of the attachment type is, properly speaking, characteristic of the male. It displays the marked sexual overvaluation which is doubtless derived from the child's original narcissism and thus corresponds to a transference of that narcissism to the sexual object. This sexual overvaluation is the origin of the peculiar state of being in love, a state suggestive of a neurotic compulsion, which is thus traceable to an impoverishment of the ego as regards libido in favour of the love-object. A different course is followed in the type of female most frequently met with, which is probably the purest and truest one. With the onset of puberty the maturing of the female sexual organs, which up till then have been in a condition of latency, seems to bring about an intensification of the original narcissism, and this is unfavourable to the development of a true object-choice with its accompanying sexual overvaluation. Women, especially if they grow up with good looks, develop a certain self-contentment which compensates them for the social restrictions that are imposed upon them in their choice of object. Strictly speaking, it is only themselves that such women love with an intensity comparable to that of the man's love for them. Nor does their need lie in the direction of loving, but of being loved; and the man who

---

6. {The editors comment here, in an elaborate footnote, that they have rendered Freud's "*Anlehnungstypus*"—which, literally, means "leaning-against type"—by this awkward invention. This is one instance of Freud's English translators converting his energetic German, which nearly always draws on ordinary speech, into technical, alien-sounding jargon. James Strachey and his collaborators have been severely criticized for this and related failings—not wholly without justice. But the difficulties of finding appropriate English equivalents for Freud's coinages were formidable, and the Standard Edition remains a heroic achievement.}

fulfils this condition is the one who finds favour with them. The importance of this type of woman for the erotic life of mankind is to be rated very high. Such women have the greatest fascination for men, not only for aesthetic reasons, since as a rule they are the most beautiful, but also because of a combination of interesting psychological factors. For it seems very evident that another person's narcissism has a great attraction for those who have renounced part of their own narcissism and are in search of object-love. The charm of a child lies to a great extent in his narcissism, his self-contentment and inaccessibility, just as does the charm of certain animals which seem not to concern themselves about us, such as cats and the large beasts of prey. Indeed, even great criminals and humorists, as they are represented in literature, compel our interest by the narcissistic consistency with which they manage to keep away from their ego anything that would diminish it. It is as if we envied them for maintaining a blissful state of mind—an unassailable libidinal position which we ourselves have since abandoned. The great charm of narcissistic women has, however, its reverse side; a large part of the lover's dissatisfaction, of his doubts of the woman's love, of his complaints of her enigmatic nature, has its root in this incongruity between the types of object-choice.

Perhaps it is not out of place here to give an assurance that this description of the feminine form of erotic life is not due to any tendentious desire on my part to depreciate women. Apart from the fact that tendentiousness is quite alien to me, I know that these different lines of development correspond to the differentiation of functions in a highly complicated biological whole; further, I am ready to admit that there are quite a number of women who love according to the masculine type and who also develop the sexual overvaluation proper to that type.

Even for narcissistic women, whose attitude towards men remains cool, there is a road which leads to complete object-love. In the child which they bear, a part of their own body confronts them like an extraneous object, to which, starting out from their narcissism, they can then give complete object-love. There are other women, again, who do not have to wait for a child in order to take the step in development from (secondary) narcissism to object-love. Before puberty they feel masculine and develop some way along masculine lines; after this trend has been cut short on their reaching female maturity, they still retain the capacity of longing for a masculine ideal—an ideal which is in fact a survival of the boyish nature that they themselves once possessed.

What I have so far said by way of indication may be concluded by a short summary of the paths leading to the choice of an object.

A person may love:—

(1) According to the narcissistic type:
    (*a*) what he himself is (i.e. himself),
    (*b*) what he himself was,

(c) what he himself would like to be,

(d) someone who was once part of himself.

(2) According to the anaclitic (attachment) type:

(a) the woman who feeds him,

(b) the man who protects him,

and the succession of substitutes who take their place. The inclusion of case (c) of the first type cannot be justified till a later stage of this discussion.

* * *

The primary narcissism of children which we have assumed and which forms one of the postulates of our theories of the libido, is less easy to grasp by direct observation than to confirm by inference from elsewhere. If we look at the attitude of affectionate parents towards their children, we have to recognize that it is a revival and reproduction of their own narcissism, which they have long since abandoned. The trustworthy pointer constituted by overvaluation, which we have already recognized as a narcissistic stigma in the case of object-choice, dominates, as we all know, their emotional attitude. Thus they are under a compulsion to ascribe every perfection to the child—which sober observation would find no occasion to do—and to conceal and forget all his shortcomings. (Incidentally, the denial of sexuality in children is connected with this.) Moreover, they are inclined to suspend in the child's favour the operation of all the cultural acquisitions which their own narcissism has been forced to respect, and to renew on his behalf the claims to privileges which were long ago given up by themselves. The child shall have a better time than his parents; he shall not be subject to the necessities which they have recognized as paramount in life. Illness, death, renunciation of enjoyment, restrictions on his own will, shall not touch him; the laws of nature and of society shall be abrogated in his favour; he shall once more really be the centre and core of creation—'His Majesty the Baby',[7] as we once fancied ourselves. The child shall fulfil those wishful dreams of the parents which they never carried out—the boy shall become a great man and a hero in his father's place, and the girl shall marry a prince as a tardy compensation for her mother. At the most touchy point in the narcissistic system, the immortality of the ego, which is so hard pressed by reality, security is achieved by taking refuge in the child. Parental love, which is so moving and at bottom so childish, is nothing but the parents' narcissism born again, which, transformed into object-love, unmistakably reveals its former nature.

---

7. [In English in the original. Perhaps a reference to a well-known Royal Academy picture of the Edwardian age, which bore that title and showed two London policemen holding up the crowded traffic to allow a nursery-maid to wheel a perambulator across the street.]

III

* * * Psycho-analytic research ordinarily enables us to trace the vicissitudes undergone by the libidinal instincts when these, isolated from the ego-instincts, are placed in opposition to them; but in the particular field of the castration complex, it allows us to infer the existence of an epoch and a psychical situation in which the two groups of instincts, still operating in unison and inseparably mingled, make their appearance as narcissistic interests. It is from this context that Adler [1910] has derived his concept of the 'masculine protest', which he has elevated almost to the position of the sole motive force in the formation of character and neurosis alike and which he bases not on a narcissistic, and therefore still a libidinal, trend, but on a social valuation. Psycho-analytic research has from the very beginning recognized the existence and importance of the 'masculine protest', but it has regarded it, in opposition to Adler, as narcissistic in nature and derived from the castration complex. The 'masculine protest' is concerned in the formation of character, into the genesis of which it enters along with many other factors, but it is completely unsuited for explaining the problems of the neuroses, with regard to which Adler takes account of nothing but the manner in which they serve the ego-instincts. I find it quite impossible to place the genesis of neurosis upon the narrow basis of the castration complex, however powerfully it may come to the fore in men among their resistances to the cure of a neurosis. * * *

Observation of normal adults shows that their former megalomania has been damped down and that the psychical characteristics from which we inferred their infantile narcissism have been effaced. What has become of their ego-libido? Are we to suppose that the whole amount of it has passed into object-cathexes? Such a possibility is plainly contrary to the whole trend of our argument; but we may find a hint at another answer to the question in the psychology of repression.

We have learnt that libidinal instinctual impulses undergo the vicissitude of pathogenic repression if they come into conflict with the subject's cultural and ethical ideas. By this we never mean that the individual in question has a merely intellectual knowledge of the existence of such ideas; we always mean that he recognizes them as a standard for himself and submits to the claims they make on him. Repression, we have said, proceeds from the ego; we might say with greater precision that it proceeds from the self-respect of the ego. The same impressions, experiences, impulses and desires that one man indulges or at least works over consciously will be rejected with the utmost indignation by another, or even stifled before they enter consciousness. The difference between the two, which contains the conditioning factor of repression, can easily be expressed in terms which enable it to be explained by the libido theory. We can say that the one man has set up an *ideal* in himself by which he measures his actual ego, while the other has formed no such ideal. For the ego the formation of an ideal would be the conditioning factor of repression.

This ideal ego is now the target of the self-love which was enjoyed in childhood by the actual ego. The subject's narcissism makes its appearance displaced on to this new ideal ego, which, like the infantile ego, finds itself possessed of every perfection that is of value. As always where the libido is concerned, man has here again shown himself incapable of giving up a satisfaction he had once enjoyed. He is not willing to forgo the narcissistic perfection of his childhood; and when, as he grows up, he is disturbed by the admonitions of others and by the awakening of his own critical judgement, so that he can no longer retain that perfection, he seeks to recover it in the new form of an ego ideal. What he projects before him as his ideal is the substitute for the lost narcissism of his childhood in which he was his own ideal.

We are naturally led to examine the relation between this forming of an ideal and sublimation. Sublimation is a process that concerns object-libido and consists in the instinct's directing itself towards an aim other than, and remote from, that of sexual satisfaction; in this process the accent falls upon deflection from sexuality. Idealization is a process that concerns the *object*; by it that object, without any alteration in its nature, is aggrandized and exalted in the subject's mind. Idealization is possible in the sphere of ego-libido as well as in that of object-libido. For example, the sexual overvaluation of an object is an idealization of it. In so far as sublimation describes something that has to do with the instinct and idealization something to do with the object, the two concepts are to be distinguished from each other.

The formation of an ego ideal is often confused with the sublimation of instinct, to the detriment of our understanding of the facts. A man who has exchanged his narcissism for homage to a high ego ideal has not necessarily on that account succeeded in sublimating his libidinal instincts. It is true that the ego ideal demands such sublimation, but it cannot enforce it; sublimation remains a special process which may be prompted by the ideal but the execution of which is entirely independent of any such prompting. It is precisely in neurotics that we find the highest differences of potential between the development of their ego ideal and the amount of sublimation of their primitive libidinal instincts; and in general it is far harder to convince an idealist of the inexpedient location of his libido than a plain man whose pretensions have remained more moderate. Further, the formation of an ego ideal and sublimation are quite differently related to the causation of neurosis. As we have learnt, the formation of an ideal heightens the demands of the ego and is the most powerful factor favouring repression; sublimation is a way out, a way by which those demands can be met *without* involving repression.

It would not surprise us if we were to find a special psychical agency which performs the task of seeing that narcissistic satisfaction from the ego ideal is ensured and which, with this end in view, constantly watches the actual ego and measures it by that ideal. If such an agency does exist, we cannot possibly come upon it as a *discovery*—we can only *recognize* it; for we may reflect that what we call our 'conscience' has the required characteristics. Recognition of this agency enables us to understand the so-called 'delusions of being noticed' or more correctly, of being *watched*, which are such striking symptoms in the paranoid diseases and which may also occur as an isolated form of illness, or intercalated in a transference neurosis. Patients of this sort complain that all their thoughts are known and their actions watched and supervised; they are informed of the functioning of this agency by voices which characteristically speak to them in the third person ('Now she's thinking of that again', 'now he's going out'). This complaint is justified; it describes the truth. A power of this kind, watching, discovering and criticizing all our intentions, does really exist. Indeed, it exists in every one of us in normal life.

Delusions of being watched present this power in a regressive form, thus revealing its genesis and the reason why the patient is in revolt against it. For what prompted the subject to form an ego ideal, on whose behalf his conscience acts as watchman, arose from the critical influence of his parents (conveyed to him by the medium of the voice), to whom were added, as time went on, those who trained and taught him and the innumerable and indefinable host of all the other people in his environment—his fellow-men—and public opinion.

In this way large amounts of libido of an essentially homosexual kind are drawn into the formation of the narcissistic ego ideal and find outlet and satisfaction in maintaining it. The institution of conscience was at bottom an embodiment, first of parental criticism, and subsequently of that of society—a process which is repeated in what takes place when a tendency towards repression develops out of a prohibition or obstacle that came in the first instance from without. The voices, as well as the undefined multitude, are brought into the foreground again by the disease, and so the evolution of conscience is reproduced regressively. But the revolt against this 'censoring agency' arises out of the subject's desire (in accordance with the fundamental character of his illness) to liberate himself from all these influences, beginning with the parental one, and out of his withdrawal of homosexual libido from them. His conscience then confronts him in a regressive form as a hostile influence from without.

The complaints made by paranoics also show that at bottom the self-criticism of conscience coincides with the self-observation on which it is based. Thus the activity of the mind which has taken over the function of conscience has also placed itself at the service of internal research,

which furnishes philosophy with the material for its intellectual operations. This may have some bearing on the characteristic tendency of
paranoics to construct speculative systems.

*   *   *

We may here recall that we have found that the formation of dreams
takes place under the dominance of a censorship which compels distortion of the dream-thoughts. We did not, however, picture this censorship as a special power, but chose the term to designate one side of
the repressive trends that govern the ego, namely the side which is turned
towards the dream-thoughts. If we enter further into the structure of the
ego, we may recognize in the ego ideal and in the dynamic utterances
of conscience the *dream-censor* as well. If this censor is to some extent
on the alert even during sleep, we can understand how it is that its
suggested activity of self-observation and self-criticism—with such
thoughts as, 'now he is too sleepy to think', 'now he is waking up'—
makes a contribution to the content of the dream.

At this point we may attempt some discussion of the self-regarding
attitude in normal people and in neurotics.

In the first place self-regard appears to us to be an expression of the
size of the ego; what the various elements are which go to determine
that size is irrelevant. Everything a person possesses or achieves, every
remnant of the primitive feeling of omnipotence which his experience
has confirmed, helps to increase his self-regard.

Applying our distinction between sexual and ego-instincts, we must
recognize that self-regard has a specially intimate dependence on narcissistic libido. Here we are supported by two fundamental facts; that in
paraphrenics self-regard is increased, while in the transference neuroses
it is diminished; and that in love-relations not being loved lowers the
self-regarding feelings, while being loved raises them. As we have indicated, the aim and the satisfaction in a narcissistic object-choice is to
be loved.

Further, it is easy to observe that libidinal object-cathexis does not
raise self-regard. The effect of dependence upon the loved object is to
lower that feeling: a person in love is humble. A person who loves has,
so to speak, forfeited a part of his narcissism, and it can only be replaced
by his being loved. In all these respects self-regard seems to remain
related to the narcissistic element in love.

The realization of impotence, of one's own inability to love, in consequence of mental or physical disorder, has an exceedingly lowering
effect upon self-regard. Here, in my judgement, we must look for one
of the sources of the feelings of inferiority which are experienced by
patients suffering from the transference neuroses and which they are so
ready to report. The main source of these feelings is, however, the

impoverishment of the ego, due to the extraordinarily large libidinal cathexes which have been withdrawn from it—due, that is to say, to the injury sustained by the ego through sexual trends which are no longer subject to control.

Adler is right in maintaining that when a person with an active mental life recognizes an inferiority in one of his organs, it acts as a spur and calls out a higher level of performance in him through overcompensation. But it would be altogether an exaggeration if, following Adler's example, we sought to attribute every successful achievement to this factor of an original inferiority of an organ. Not all artists are handicapped with bad eyesight, nor were all orators originally stammerers. And there are plenty of instances of excellent achievements springing from *superior* organic endowment. In the aetiology of neuroses organic inferiority and imperfect development play an insignificant part—much the same as that played by currently active perceptual material in the formation of dreams. Neuroses make use of such inferiorities as a pretext, just as they do of every other suitable factor. We may be tempted to believe a neurotic woman patient when she tells us that it was inevitable she should fall ill, since she is ugly, deformed or lacking in charm, so that no one could love her; but the very next neurotic will teach us better—for she persists in her neurosis and in her aversion to sexuality, although she seems more desirable, and is more desired, than the average woman. The majority of hysterical women are among the attractive and even beautiful representatives of their sex, while, on the other hand, the frequency of ugliness, organic defects and infirmities in the lower classes of society does not increase the incidence of neurotic illness among them.

The relations of self-regard to erotism—that is, to libidinal object-cathexes—may be expressed concisely in the following way. Two cases must be distinguished, according to whether the erotic cathexes are ego-syntonic, or, on the contrary, have suffered repression. In the former case (where the use made of the libido is ego-syntonic), love is assessed like any other activity of the ego. Loving in itself, in so far as it involves longing and deprivation, lowers self-regard; whereas being loved, having one's love returned, and possessing the loved object, raises it once more. When libido is repressed, the erotic cathexis is felt as a severe depletion of the ego, the satisfaction of love is impossible, and the re-enrichment of the ego can be effected only by a withdrawal of libido from its objects. The return of the object-libido to the ego and its transformation into narcissism represents, as it were, a happy love once more; and, on the other hand, it is also true that a real happy love corresponds to the primal condition in which object-libido and ego-libido cannot be distinguished.

* * *

The importance and extensiveness of the topic must be my justification for adding a few more remarks which are somewhat loosely strung together.

* * *

The ego ideal opens up an important avenue for the understanding of group psychology. In addition to its individual side, this ideal has a social side; it is also the common ideal of a family, a class or a nation. It binds not only a person's narcissistic libido, but also a considerable amount of his homosexual libido, which is in this way turned back into the ego. The want of satisfaction which arises from the non-fulfilment of this ideal liberates homosexual libido, and this is transformed into a sense of guilt (social anxiety). Originally this sense of guilt was a fear of punishment by the parents, or, more correctly, the fear of losing their love; later the parents are replaced by an indefinite number of fellow-men. The frequent causation of paranoia by an injury to the ego, by a frustration of satisfaction within the sphere of the ego ideal, is thus made more intelligible, as is the convergence of ideal-formation and sublimation in the ego ideal, as well as the involution of sublimations and the possible transformation of ideals in paraphrenic disorders.

Instincts and Their Vicissitudes

The general war that erupted in early August 1914 was a catastrophe for the culture in which Freud had lived, more or less securely, up to then. Europe, one may say, never really quite recovered from this calamity. Not unnaturally, the war had marked consequences for Freud himself. It was not just that it brought shortages in food and fuel and made his beloved cigars hard to obtain. His private life was severely disrupted as he worried about his three sons in the army; at least two of them, Martin and Ernst, were serving on the Russian front, often in danger. Psychoanalysis, too, suffered, as analytic publications came to a virtual standstill; most of Freud's associates were drafted into the army as physicians; and Freud's schedule of analysands, normally full to bursting, showed sizable gaps. The belligerent powers with their ugly chauvinism, and the military campaigns with their brutality and seemingly interminable blood-letting, gave Freud much to think about. He professed not to be astonished at the dismal scene, with German professors returning English honorary degrees and French publicists maligning Germans as huns, but he confessed to his sadness and disappointment. True, Freud started the war as something of an Austrian patriot and hoped for a victory of the Central Powers. But his enthusiasm gradually waned, and it is significant that throughout the war, he remained in touch with his "enemy" Ernest Jones through neutral channels. It should surprise no one that the prolonged, increasingly senseless slaughter had an impact on Freud's thought, but that impact should not be exaggerated. In any event, it did not manifest itself until well after the conclusion of hostilities in November 1918.

Yet the war proved a boon to Freud in one respect: it gave him a good deal of unexpected, unwelcome, free time. Hence he began to draft a major book on metapsychology that would summarize, and establish, the essential elements of psychoanalytic theory. During the spring and summer of 1915, he wrote the twelve essays he intended to include in the book, rapidly and with little difficulty. Then something happened. Between 1915 and 1917, he did publish the first five of these papers, but after that he resisted persistent pressure by his friends for the whole work. At some point, indeed, he destroyed the other seven. (In 1983, the German psychoanalyst and editor Ilse Grubrich-Simitis discovered in the Ferenczi papers a draft of Freud's twelfth paper, a bold "historical" study of the transference neuroses. It proved a fascinating glimpse into Freud, the speculative thinker. The draft has been beautifully edited by Grubrich-Simitis and is available in an English translation by Alex and Peter T. Hoffer, as *A Phylogenetic Fantasy: Overview of the Transference Neuroses* [1987].) Freud's unwillingness to let the book appear remains mysterious, though it seems most likely that he was increasingly dissatisfied with his old "topographic" scheme and not yet ready to publish the new "structural" theory. The paper of 1914 on narcissism (see above, pp. 545–62) had signalized the need for some rethinking of psychoanalytic theory; Freud's refusal to publish his book on metapsychology strongly hints that he was now fully aware of that need. (See Gay, *Freud*, pp. 373–74.)

The present paper, on the drives, published in late 1915, with its orderly classification of fundamentals and its opening remarks on the nature of psychoanalysis as a science, retains more than historical interest. Yet it, more than the others, would have had to be rewritten if Freud had conceived it in the 1920s.

We have often heard it maintained that sciences should be built up on clear and sharply defined basic concepts. In actual fact no science, not even the most exact, begins with such definitions. The true beginning of scientific activity consists rather in describing phenomena and then in proceeding to group, classify and correlate them. Even at the stage of description it is not possible to avoid applying certain abstract ideas to the material in hand, ideas derived from somewhere or other but certainly not from the new observations alone. Such ideas—which will later become the basic concepts of the science—are still more indispensable as the material is further worked over. They must at first necessarily possess some degree of indefiniteness; there can be no question of any clear delimitation of their content. So long as they remain in this condition, we come to an understanding about their meaning by making repeated references to the material of observation from which they appear to have been derived, but upon which, in fact, they have been imposed. Thus, strictly speaking, they are in the nature of conventions—although everything depends on their not being arbitrarily chosen but determined by their having significant relations to the empirical material, relations that we seem to sense before we can clearly recognize and demonstrate them. It is only after more thorough investigation of the field of observation that we are able to formulate its basic scientific concepts with increased precision, and progressively so to modify them that they become serviceable and consistent over a wide area. Then, indeed, the time may have come to confine them in definitions. The advance of knowledge, however, does not tolerate any rigidity even in definitions. Physics furnishes an excellent illustration of the way in which even 'basic concepts' that have been established in the form of definitions are constantly being altered in their content.

A conventional basic concept of this kind, which at the moment is still somewhat obscure but which is indispensable to us in psychology, is that of an 'instinct.'[1] Let us try to give a content to it by approaching it from different angles.

First, from the angle of *physiology*. This has given us the concept of a 'stimulus' and the pattern of the reflex arc, according to which a stimulus applied to living tissue (nervous substance) *from* the outside is discharged by action *to* the outside. This action is expedient in so far as it withdraws the stimulated substance from the influence of the stimulus, removes it out of its range of operation.

What is the relation of 'instinct' to 'stimulus'? There is nothing to prevent our subsuming the concept of 'instinct' under that of 'stimulus' and saying that an instinct is a stimulus applied to the mind. But we are immediately set on our guard against *equating* instinct and mental stimulus. There are obviously other stimuli to the mind besides those of an instinctual kind, stimuli which behave far more like physiological ones. For example, when a strong light falls on the eye, it is not an instinctual stimulus; it *is* one, however, when a dryness of the mucous membrane of the pharynx or an irritation of the mucous membrane of the stomach makes itself felt.

We have now obtained the material necessary for distinguishing between instinctual stimuli and other (physiological) stimuli that operate on the mind. In the first place, an instinctual stimulus does not arise from the external world but from within the organism itself. For this reason it operates differently upon the mind and different actions are necessary in order to remove it. Further, all that is essential in a stimulus is covered if we assume that it operates with a single impact, so that it can be disposed of by a single expedient action. A typical instance of this is motor flight from the source of stimulation. These impacts may, of course, be repeated and summated, but that makes no difference to our notion of the process and to the conditions for the removal of the stimulus. An instinct, on the other hand, never operates as a force giving

1. ['*Trieb*' in the original.] {There is much respectable psychoanalytic opinion that supports the editors' choice of "instinct" for "*Trieb*," even though "drive" is closer linguistically and, I think, in meaning, to Freud's intentions. Some analysts have compromised by using the term "instinctual drives." In any event, "instinct" and "drive" should be treated as synonyms in this *Reader*.}

a *momentary* impact but always as a *constant* one. Moreover, since it impinges not from without but from within the organism, no flight can avail against it. A better term for an instinctual stimulus is a 'need'. What does away with a need is 'satisfaction'. This can be attained only by an appropriate ('adequate') alteration of the internal source of stimulation.

Let us imagine ourselves in the situation of an almost entirely helpless living organism, as yet unorientated in the world, which is receiving stimuli in its nervous substance. This organism will very soon be in a position to make a first distinction and a first orientation. On the one hand, it will be aware of stimuli which can be avoided by muscular action (flight); these it ascribes to an external world. On the other hand, it will also be aware of stimuli against which such action is of no avail and whose character of constant pressure persists in spite of it; these stimuli are the signs of an internal world, the evidence of instinctual needs. The perceptual substance of the living organism will thus have found in the efficacy of its muscular activity a basis for distinguishing between an 'outside' and an 'inside'.

We thus arrive at the essential nature of instincts in the first place by considering their main characteristics—their origin in sources of stimulation within the organism and their appearance as a constant force—and from this we deduce one of their further features, namely, that no actions of flight avail against them. In the course of this discussion, however, we cannot fail to be struck by something that obliges us to make a further admission. In order to guide us in dealing with the field of psychological phenomena, we do not merely apply certain conventions to our empirical material as basic *concepts*; we also make use of a number of complicated *postulates*. We have already alluded to the most important of these, and all we need now do is to state it expressly. This postulate is of a biological nature, and makes use of the concept of 'purpose' (or perhaps of expediency) and runs as follows: the nervous system is an apparatus which has the function of getting rid of the stimuli that reach it, or of reducing them to the lowest possible level; or which, if it were feasible, would maintain itself in an altogether unstimulated condition. Let us for the present not take exception to the indefiniteness of this idea and let us assign to the nervous system the task—speaking in general terms—of *mastering stimuli*. We then see how greatly the simple pattern of the physiological reflex is complicated by the introduction of instincts. External stimuli impose only the single task of withdrawing from them; this is accomplished by muscular movements, one of which eventually achieves that aim and thereafter, being the expedient movement, becomes a hereditary disposition. Instinctual stimuli, which originate from within the organism, cannot be dealt with by this mechanism. Thus they make far higher demands on the nervous system and cause it to undertake involved and interconnected activities by which the external world is so changed as to afford satisfaction to the internal source of stimulation. Above all, they oblige the nervous system to renounce its ideal intention of keeping off stimuli, for they maintain an incessant and unavoidable afflux of stimulation. We may therefore well conclude that instincts and not external stimuli are the true motive forces behind the advances that have led the nervous system, with its unlimited capacities, to its present high level of development. There is naturally nothing to prevent our supposing that the instincts themselves are, at least in part, precipitates of the effects of external stimulation, which in the course of phylogenesis have brought about modifications in the living substance.

When we further find that the activity of even the most highly developed mental apparatus is subject to the pleasure principle, i.e. is automatically regulated by feelings belonging to the pleasure-unpleasure series, we can hardly reject the further hypothesis that these feelings reflect the manner in which the process of mastering stimuli takes place—certainly in the sense that unpleasurable feelings are connected with an increase and pleasurable feelings with a decrease of stimulus. We will, however, carefully preserve this assumption in its present highly indefinite form, until we succeed, if that is possible, in discovering what sort of relation exists between pleasure and unpleasure, on the one hand, and fluctuations in the amounts of stimulus affecting mental life, on the other. It is certain that many very various relations of this kind, and not very simple ones, are possible.

If now we apply ourselves to considering mental life from a *biological* point of view, an 'instinct' appears to us as a concept on the frontier between the mental and the somatic, as the psychical representative of the stimuli originating from within the organism and reaching the mind, as a measure of the demand made upon the mind for work in consequence of its connection with the body.

We are now in a position to discuss certain terms which are used in reference to the concept of an instinct—for example, its 'pressure', its 'aim', its 'object' and its 'source'.

By the pressure [*Drang*] of an instinct we understand its motor factor, the amount of force or the measure of the demand for work which it represents. The characteristic of exercising pressure is common to all instincts; it is in fact their very essence. Every instinct is a piece of activity; if we speak loosely of passive instincts, we can only mean instincts whose *aim* is passive.

The aim [*Ziel*] of an instinct is in every instance satisfaction, which can only be obtained by removing the state of stimulation at the source of the instinct. But although the ultimate aim of each instinct remains unchangeable, there may yet be different paths leading to the same ultimate aim; so that an instinct may be found to have various nearer or intermediate aims, which are combined or interchanged with one another. Experience permits us also to speak of instincts which are 'inhibited in their aim', in the case of processes which are allowed to make some advance towards instinctual satisfaction but are then inhibited or deflected. We may suppose that even processes of this kind involve a partial satisfaction.

The object [Objekt] of an instinct is the thing in regard to which or through which the instinct is able to achieve its aim. It is what is most variable about an instinct and is not originally connected with it, but becomes assigned to it only in consequence of being peculiarly fitted to make satisfaction possible. The object is not necessarily something extraneous: it may equally well be a part of the subject's own body. It may be changed any number of times in the course of the vicissitudes which the instinct undergoes during its existence; and highly important parts are played by this displacement of instinct. It may happen that the same object serves for the satisfaction of several instincts simultaneously, a phenomenon which Adler has called a 'confluence' of instincts [Triebverschränkung]. A particularly close attachment of the instinct to its object is distinguished by the term 'fixation'. This frequently occurs at very early periods of the development of an instinct and puts an end to its mobility through its intense opposition to detachment.

By the source [Quelle] of an instinct is meant the somatic process which occurs in an organ or part of the body and whose stimulus is represented in mental life by an instinct. We do not know whether this process is invariably of a chemical nature or whether it may also correspond to the release of other, e.g. mechanical, forces. The study of the sources of instincts lies outside the scope of psychology. Although instincts are wholly determined by their origin in a somatic source, in mental life we know them only by their aims. An exact knowledge of the sources of an instinct is not invariably necessary for purposes of psychological investigation; sometimes its source may be inferred from its aim.

Are we to suppose that the different instincts which originate in the body and operate on the mind are also distinguished by different qualities, and that that is why they behave in qualitatively different ways in mental life? This supposition does not seem to be justified; we are much more likely to find the simpler assumption sufficient—that the instincts are all qualitatively alike and owe the effect they make only to the amount of excitation they carry, or perhaps, in addition, to certain functions of that quantity. What distinguishes from one another the mental effects produced by the various instincts may be traced to the difference in their sources. * * *

What instincts should we suppose there are, and how many? There is obviously a wide opportunity here for arbitrary choice. No objection can be made to anyone's employing the concept of an instinct of play or of destruction or of gregariousness, when the subject-matter demands it and the limitations of psychological analysis allow of it. Nevertheless, we should not neglect to ask ourselves whether instinctual motives like these, which are so highly specialized on the one hand, do not admit of further dissection in accordance wih the *sources* of the instinct, so that only primal instincts—those which cannot be further dissected—can lay claim to importance.

I have proposed that two groups of such primal instincts should be distinguished: the *ego*, or *self-preservative*, instincts and the *sexual* instincts. But this supposition has not the status of a necessary postulate, as has, for instance, our assumption about the biological purpose of the mental apparatus; it is merely a working hypothesis, to be retained only so long as it proves useful, and it will make little difference to the results of our work of description and classification if it is replaced by another. The occasion for this hypothesis arose in the course of the evolution of psycho-analysis, which was first employed upon the psychoneuroses, or, more precisely, upon the group described as 'transference neuroses' (hysteria and obsessional neurosis); these showed that at the root of all such affections there is to be found a conflict between the claims of sexuality and those of the ego. It is always possible that an exhaustive study of the other neurotic affections (especially of the narcissistic psychoneuroses, the schizophrenias) may oblige us to alter this formula and to make a different classification of the primal instincts. But for the present we do not know of any such formula, nor have we met with any argument unfavourable to drawing this contrast between sexual and ego-instincts.[2]

* * *

We may sum up by saying that the essential feature in the vicissitudes undergone by instincts lies in *the subjection of the instinctual impulses to the influences of the three great polarities that dominate mental life*. Of these three polarities we might describe that of activity—passivity as the *biological*, that of ego—external world as the *real*, and finally that of pleasure—unpleasure as the *economic* polarity.

The instinctual vicissitude of *repression* will form the subject of an inquiry which follows.

Repression

Freud was very proud of his discovery of repression. We will recall that in his "Autobiographical Study," he linked it to his analysands' resistance: "The expenditure of force on the part of the physician was evidently the measure of a *resistance* on the part of the patient. It was only necessary to translate into words what I myself had observed, and I was in possession of the theory of *repression*. . . . It was a novelty, and nothing like it had ever before been recognized in mental life" (see above, p. 18). He found the concept so

2. {This is precisely what Freud did find it necessary to revise.}

significant that for some years he used it very broadly, to include defensive stratagems of all sorts. Later, he would return to the term "defense" and recognize repression as its archetypal, probably most significant, but not exclusive expression. He published this paper in the issue of the *Zeitschrift* following the one in which its introductory predecessor, "Instincts and Their Vicissitudes," had appeared.

One of the vicissitudes an instinctual impulse may undergo is to meet with resistances which seek to make it inoperative. Under certain conditions, which we shall presently investigate more closely, the impulse then passes into the state of 'repression' ['*Verdrängung*']. If what was in question was the operation of an external stimulus, the appropriate method to adopt would obviously be flight; with an instinct, flight is of no avail, for the ego cannot escape from itself. At some later period, rejection based on judgement (*condemnation*) will be found to be a good method to adopt against an instinctual impulse. Repression is a preliminary stage of condemnation, something between flight and condemnation; it is a concept which could not have been formulated before the time of psycho-analytic studies.

It is not easy in theory to deduce the possibility of such a thing as repression. Why should an instinctual impulse undergo a vicissitude like this? A necessary condition of its happening must clearly be that the instinct's attainment of its aim should produce unpleasure instead of pleasure. But we cannot well imagine such a contingency. There are no such instincts: satisfaction of an instinct is always pleasurable. We should have to assume certain peculiar circumstances, some sort of process by which the pleasure of satisfaction is changed into unpleasure.

* * *

Let us * * * confine ourselves to clinical experience, as we meet with it in psycho-analytic practice. We then learn that the satisfaction of an instinct which is under repression would be quite possible, and further, that in every instance such a satisfaction would be pleasurable in itself; but it would be irreconcilable with other claims and intentions. It would, therefore, cause pleasure in one place and unpleasure in another. It has consequently become a condition for repression that the motive force of unpleasure shall have acquired more strength than the pleasure obtained from satisfaction. Psycho-analytic observation of the transference neuroses, moreover, leads us to conclude that repression is not a defensive mechanism which is present from the very beginning, and that it cannot arise until a sharp cleavage has occurred between conscious and unconscious mental activity—that *the essence of repression lies simply in turning something away, and keeping it at a distance,* *from the conscious.* This view of repression would be made more complete by assuming that, before the mental organization reaches this stage, the task of fending off instinctual impulses is dealt with by the other vicissitudes which instincts may undergo—e.g. reversal into the opposite or turning round upon the subject's own self.

* * *

We have reason to assume that there is a *primal repression*, a first phase of repression, which consists in the psychical (ideational) representative of the instinct being denied entrance into the conscious. With this a *fixation* is established; the representative in question persists unaltered from then onwards and the instinct remains attached to it. This is due to the properties of unconscious processes of which we shall speak later.

The second stage of repression, *repression proper*, affects mental derivatives of the repressed representative, or such trains of thought as, originating elsewhere, have come into associative connection with it. On account of this association, these ideas experience the same fate as what was primally repressed. Repression proper, therefore, is actually an after-pressure. Moreover, it is a mistake to emphasize only the repulsion which operates from the direction of the conscious upon what is to be repressed; quite as important is the attraction exercised by what was primally repressed upon everything with which it can establish a connection. Probably the trend towards repression would fail in its purpose if these two forces did not co-operate, if there were not something previously repressed ready to receive what is repelled by the conscious.

Under the influence of the study of the psychoneuroses, which brings before us the important effects of repression, we are inclined to overvalue their psychological bearing and to forget too readily that repression does not hinder the instinctual representative from continuing to exist in the unconscious, from organizing itself further, putting out derivatives and establishing connections. Repression in fact interferes only with the relation of the instinctual representative to *one* psychical system, namely, to that of the conscious.

Psycho-analysis is able to show us other things as well which are important for understanding the effects of repression in the psychoneuroses. It shows us, for instance, that the instinctual representative develops with less interference and more profusely if it is withdrawn by repression from conscious influence. It proliferates in the dark, as it were, and takes on extreme forms of expression, which when they are translated and presented to the neurotic are not only bound to seem alien to him, but frighten him by giving him the picture of an extraordinary and dangerous strength of instinct. This deceptive strength of instinct is the result of an uninhibited development in phantasy and of the damming-up consequent on frustrated satisfaction. The fact that this last result is bound up with repression points the direction in which the true significance of repression has to be looked for.

Reverting once more, however, to the opposite aspect of repression, let us make it clear that it is not even correct to suppose that repression withholds from the conscious *all* the derivatives of what was primally repressed. If these derivatives have become sufficiently far removed from the repressed representative, whether owing to the adoption of distortions or by reason of the number of intermediate links inserted, they have free access to the conscious. It is as though the resistance of the conscious against them was a function of their distance from what was originally repressed. In carrying out the technique of psycho-analysis, we continually require the patient to produce such derivatives of the repressed as, in consequence either of their remoteness or of their distortion, can pass the censorship of the conscious. Indeed, the associations which we require him to give without being influenced by any conscious purposive idea and without any criticism, and from which we reconstitute a conscious translation of the repressed representative—these associations are nothing else than remote and distorted derivatives of this kind. During this process we observe that the patient can go on spinning a thread of such associations, till he is brought up against some thought, the relation of which to what is repressed becomes so obvious that he is compelled to repeat his attempt at repression. Neurotic symptoms, too, must have fulfilled this same condition, for they are derivatives of the repressed, which has, by their means, finally won the access to consciousness which was previously denied to it.

We can lay down no general rule as to what degree of distortion and remoteness is necessary before the resistance on the part of the conscious is removed. A delicate balancing is here taking place, the play of which is hidden from us; its mode of operation, however, enables us to infer that it is a question of calling a halt when the cathexis of the unconscious reaches a certain intensity—an intensity beyond which the unconscious would break through to satisfaction. Repression acts, therefore, in a *highly individual* manner. Each single derivative of the repressed may have its own special vicissitude; a little more or a little less distortion alters the whole outcome. In this connection we can understand how it is that the objects to which men give most preference, their ideals, proceed from the same perceptions and experiences as the objects which they most abhor, and that they were originally only distinguished from one another through slight modifications. Indeed, as we found in tracing the origin of the fetish, it is possible for the original instinctual representative to be split in two, one part undergoing repression, while the remainder, precisely on account of this intimate connection, undergoes idealization.

The same result as follows from an increase or a decrease in the degree of distortion may also be achieved at the other end of the apparatus, so to speak, by a modification in the condition for the production of pleasure and unpleasure. Special techniques have been evolved, with the purpose of bringing about such changes in the play of mental forces that what would otherwise give rise to unpleasure may on this occasion result in pleasure; and, whenever a technical device of this sort comes into operation, the repression of an instinctual representative which would otherwise be repudiated is removed. These techniques have till now only been studied in any detail in jokes. As a rule the repression is only temporarily removed and is promptly reinstated.

Observations like this, however, enable us to note some further characteristics of repression. Not only is it, as we have just shown, *individual* in its operation, but it is also exceedingly *mobile*. The process of repression is not to be regarded as an event which takes place *once*, the results of which are permanent, as when some living thing has been killed and from that time onward is dead; repression demands a persistent expenditure of force, and if this were to cease the success of the repression would be jeopardized, so that a fresh act of repression would be necessary. We may suppose that the repressed exercises a continuous pressure in the direction of the conscious, so that this pressure must be balanced by an unceasing counter-pressure. Thus the maintenance of a repression involves an uninterrupted expenditure of force, while its removal results in a saving from an economic point of view. The mobility of repression, incidentally, also finds expression in the psychical characteristics of the state of sleep, which alone renders possible the formation of dreams. With a return to waking life the repressive cathexes which have been drawn in are once more sent out.

* * *

The Unconscious

It is significant that among Freud's five published papers on metapsychology, that on the unconscious is by far the longest. "If the series of 'Papers on Metapsychology,' " Freud's English editors write, "may perhaps be regarded as the most important of all Freud's theoretical writings, there can be no doubt that the present essay on 'The Unconscious' is the culmination of that series" (*SE* XIV, 161). Of all the "shibboleths" of psychoanalysis, this is doubtless the one truly indispensable one: it explains how Freud can confidently assert that the mind, which appears so chaotic, contradictory, beyond causation, is ruled by inexorable laws. Mental events are like pearls on an invisible chain, a chain largely invisible precisely because many of the links are unconscious. The evidence for the unconscious, Freud had been arguing since the 1890s, is too powerful to be ignored, and it was one of his grievances against the philosophers that they, he claimed, equated mind with consciousness. He published this long paper in two successive issues of the *Zeitschrift* toward the end of 1915.

We have learnt from psycho-analysis that the essence of the process of repression lies, not in putting an end to, in annihilating, the idea which represents an instinct, but in preventing it from becoming conscious. When this happens we say of the idea that it is in a state of being 'unconscious', and we can produce good evidence to show that even when it is unconscious it can produce effects, even including some which finally reach consciousness. Everything that is repressed must remain unconscious; but let us state at the very outset that the repressed does not cover everything that is unconscious. The unconscious has the wider compass: the repressed is a part of the unconscious.

How are we to arrive at a knowledge of the unconscious? It is of course only as something conscious that we know it, after it has undergone transformation or translation into something conscious. Psycho-analytic work shows us every day that translation of this kind is possible. In order that this should come about, the person under analysis must overcome certain resistances—the same resistances as those which, earlier, made the material concerned into something repressed by rejecting it from the conscious.

I. Justification for the Concept of the Unconscious

Our right to assume the existence of something mental that is unconscious and to employ that assumption for the purposes of scientific work is disputed in many quarters. To this we can reply that our assumption of the unconscious is *necessary* and *legitimate*, and that we possess numerous proofs of its existence.

It is *necessary* because the data of consciousness have a very large number of gaps in them; both in healthy and in sick people psychical acts often occur which can be explained only by presupposing other acts, of which, nevertheless, consciousness affords no evidence. These not only include parapraxes and dreams in healthy people, and everything described as a psychical symptom or an obsession in the sick; our most personal daily experience acquaints us with ideas that come into our head we do not know from where, and with intellectual conclusions arrived at we do not know how. All these conscious acts remain disconnected and unintelligible if we insist upon claiming that every mental act that occurs in us must also necessarily be experienced by us through consciousness; on the other hand, they fall into a demonstrable connection if we interpolate between them the unconscious acts which we have inferred. A gain in meaning is a perfectly justifiable ground for going beyond the limits of direct experience. When, in addition, it turns out that the assumption of there being an unconscious enables us to construct a successful procedure by which we can exert an effective influence upon the course of conscious processes, this success will have given us an incontrovertible proof of the existence of what we have assumed. This being so, we must adopt the position that to require that whatever goes on in the mind must also be known to consciousness is to make an untenable claim.

We can go further and argue, in support of there being an unconscious psychical state, that at any given moment consciousness includes only a small content, so that the greater part of what we call conscious knowledge must in any case be for very considerable periods of time in a state of latency, that is to say, of being psychically unconscious. When all our latent memories are taken into consideration it becomes totally incomprehensible how the existence of the unconscious can be denied. But here we encounter the objection that these latent recollections can no longer be described as psychical, but that they correspond to residues of somatic processes from which what is psychical can once more arise. The obvious answer to this is that a latent memory is, on the contrary, an unquestionable residuum of a *psychical* process. But it is more important to realize clearly that this objection is based on the equation— not, it is true, explicitly stated but taken as axiomatic—of what is conscious with what is mental. This equation is either a *petitio principii* which begs the question whether everything that is psychical is also necessarily conscious; or else it is a matter of convention, of nomenclature. In this latter case it is, of course, like any other convention, not open to refutation. The question remains, however, whether the convention is so expedient that we are bound to adopt it. To this we may reply that the conventional equation of the psychical with the conscious is totally inexpedient. It disrupts psychical continuities, plunges us into the insoluble difficulties of psycho-physical parallelism, is open to the reproach that for no obvious reason it over-estimates the part played by consciousness, and that it forces us prematurely to abandon the field of psychological research without being able to offer us any compensation from other fields.

It is clear in any case that this question—whether the latent states of mental life, whose existence is undeniable, are to be conceived of as conscious mental states or as physical ones—threatens to resolve itself into a verbal dispute. We shall therefore be better advised to focus our attention on what we know with certainty of the nature of these debatable states. As far as their physical characteristics are concerned, they are totally inaccessible to us: no physiological concept or chemical process can give us any notion of their nature. On the other hand, we know for certain that they have abundant points of contact with conscious mental processes; with the help of a certain amount of work they can be transformed into, or replaced by, conscious mental processes, and all the categories which we employ to describe conscious mental acts, such as ideas, purposes, resolutions and so on, can be applied to them. Indeed, we are obliged to say of some of these latent states that the only respect in which they differ from conscious ones is precisely in the absence of consciousness. Thus we shall not hesitate to treat them as objects of psychological research, and to deal with them in the most intimate connection with conscious mental acts.

The stubborn denial of a psychical character to latent mental acts is accounted for by the circumstance that most of the phenomena concerned have not been the subject of study outside psycho-analysis. Anyone who is ignorant of pathological facts, who regards the parapraxes of normal people as accidental, and who is content with the old saw that dreams are froth ['Träume sind Schäume'] has only to ignore a few more problems of the psychology of consciousness in order to spare himself any need to assume an unconscious mental activity. Incidentally, even before the time of psycho-analysis, hypnotic experiments, and especially post-hypnotic suggestion, had tangibly demonstrated the existence and mode of operation of the mental unconscious.

The assumption of an unconscious is, moreover, a perfectly *legitimate* one, inasmuch as in postulating it we are not departing a single step from our customary and generally accepted mode of thinking. Consciousness makes each of us aware only of his own states of mind; that other people, too, possess a consciousness is an inference which we draw by analogy from their observable utterances and actions, in order to make this behaviour of theirs intelligible to us. (It would no doubt be psychologically more correct to put it in this way: that without any special reflection we attribute to everyone else our own constitution and therefore our consciousness as well, and that this identification is a *sine qua non* of our understanding.) This inference (or this identification) was formerly extended by the ego to other human beings, to animals, plants, inanimate objects and to the world at large, and proved serviceable so long as their similarity to the individual ego was overwhelmingly great; but it became more untrustworthy in proportion as the difference between the ego and these 'others' widened. To-day, our critical judgement is already in doubt on the question of consciousness in animals; we refuse to admit it in plants and we regard the assumption of its existence in inanimate matter as mysticism. But even where the original inclination to identification has withstood criticism—that is, when the 'others' are our fellow-men—the assumption of a consciousness in them rests upon an inference and cannot share the immediate certainty which we have of our own consciousness.

Psycho-analysis demands nothing more than that we should apply this process of inference to ourselves also—a proceeding to which, it is true, we are not constitutionally inclined. If we do this, we must say: all the acts and manifestations which I notice in myself and do not know how to link up with the rest of my mental life must be judged as if they belonged to someone else: they are to be explained by a mental life

576 TRANSITIONS AND REVISIONS

ascribed to this other person. Furthermore, experience shows that we understand very well how to interpret in other people (that is, how to fit into their chain of mental events) the same acts which we refuse to acknowledge as being mental in ourselves. Here some special hindrance evidently deflects our investigations from our own self and prevents our obtaining a true knowledge of it.

This process of inference, when applied to oneself in spite of internal opposition, does not, however, lead to the disclosure of an unconscious; it leads logically to the assumption of another, second consciousness which is united in one's self with the consciousness one knows. But at this point, certain criticisms may fairly be made. In the first place, a consciousness of which its own possessor knows nothing is something very different from a consciousness belonging to another person, and it is questionable whether such a consciousness, lacking, as it does, its most important characteristic, deserves any discussion at all. Those who have resisted the assumption of an unconscious *psychical* are not likely to be ready to exchange it for an unconscious *consciousness*. In the second place, analysis shows that the different latent mental processes inferred by us enjoy a high degree of mutual independence, as though they had no connection with one another, and knew nothing of one another. We must be prepared, if so, to assume the existence in us not only of a second consciousness, but of a third, fourth, perhaps of an unlimited number of states of consciousness, all unknown to us and to one another. In the third place—and this is the most weighty argument of all—we have to take into account the fact that analytic investigation reveals some of these latent processes as having characteristics and pe-culiarities which seem alien to us, or even incredible, and which run directly counter to the attributes of consciousness with which we are familiar. Thus we have grounds for modifying our inference about our-selves and saying that what is proved is not the existence of a second consciousness in us, but the existence of psychical acts which lack con-sciousness. We shall also be right in rejecting the term 'subconscious-ness' as incorrect and misleading.[1] The well-known cases of '*double conscience*'[2] (splitting of consciousness) prove nothing against our view. We may most aptly describe them as cases of a splitting of the mental activities into two groups, and say that the same consciousness turns to one or the other of these groups alternately.

In psycho-analysis there is no choice for us but to assert that mental processes are in themselves unconscious, and to liken the perception of them by means of consciousness to the perception of the external world by means of the sense-organs. We can even hope to gain fresh knowledge from the comparison. The psycho-analytic assumption of unconscious

1. {Freud virtually never uses "subconscious" or "subconsciousness." But the term has retained its popularity. When it is employed to say something "Freudian," it is proof that the writer has not read his Freud.}

2. [The French term for 'dual consciousness'.]

mental activity appears to us, on the one hand, as a further expansion of the primitive animism which caused us to see copies of our own consciousness all around us, and, on the other hand, as an extension of the corrections undertaken by Kant of our views on external perception. Just as Kant warned us not to overlook the fact that our perceptions are subjectively conditioned and must not be regarded as identical with what is perceived though unknowable, so psycho-analysis warns us not to equate perceptions by means of consciousness with the unconscious mental processes which are their object. Like the physical, the psychical is not necessarily in reality what it appears to us to be. We shall be glad to learn, however, that the correction of internal perception will turn out not to offer such great difficulties as the correction of external perception—that internal objects are less unknowable than the external world.

II. Various Meanings of 'the Unconscious'—

The Topographical Point of View

Before going any further, let us state the important, though inconvenient, fact that the attribute of being unconscious is only one feature that is found in the psychical and is by no means sufficient fully to characterize it. There are psychical acts of very varying value which yet agree in possessing the characteristic of being unconscious. The unconscious comprises, on the one hand, acts which are merely latent, temporarily unconscious, but which differ in no other respect from conscious ones and, on the other hand, processes such as repressed ones, which if they were to become conscious would be bound to stand out in the crudest contrast to the rest of the conscious processes. It would put an end to all misunderstandings if, from now on, in describing the various kinds of psychical acts we were to disregard the question of whether they were conscious or unconscious, and were to classify and correlate them only according to their relation to instincts and aims, according to their composition and according to which of the hierarchy of psychical systems they belong to. This, however, is for various reasons impracticable, so that we cannot escape the ambiguity of using the words 'conscious' and 'unconscious' sometimes in a descriptive and sometimes in a systematic sense, in which latter they signify inclusion in particular systems and possession of certain characteristics. We might attempt to avoid confusion by giving the psychical systems which we have distinguished certain arbitrarily chosen names which have no reference to the attribute of being conscious. Only we should first have to specify what the grounds are on which we distinguish the systems, and in doing this we should not be able to evade the attribute of being conscious, seeing that it forms the point of departure for all our investigations. Perhaps we may look for some assistance from the proposal to employ, at any rate in writing, the abbreviation *Cs.* for consciousness and *Ucs.* for what is unconscious, when we are using the two words in the systematic sense.[3]

Proceeding now to an account of the positive findings of psycho-analysis, we may say that in general a psychical act goes through two phases as regards its state, between which is interposed a kind of testing (censorship). In the first phase the psychical act is unconscious and belongs to the system *Ucs.*; if, on testing, it is rejected by the censorship, it is not allowed to pass into the second phase; it is then said to be 'repressed' and must remain unconscious. If, however, it passes this testing, it enters the second phase and thenceforth belongs to the second system, which we will call the system *Cs.* But the fact that it belongs to that system does not yet unequivocally determine its relation to consciousness. It is not yet conscious, but it is certainly *capable of becoming conscious* (to use Breuer's expression)—that is, it can now, given certain conditions, become an object of consciousness without any special resistance. In consideration of this capacity for becoming conscious we also call the system *Cs.* the 'preconscious'. If it should turn out that a certain censorship also plays a part in determining whether the preconscious becomes conscious, we shall discriminate more sharply between the systems *Pcs.* and *Cs.* For the present let it suffice us to bear in mind that the system *Pcs.* shares the characteristics of the system *Cs.* and that the rigorous censorship exercises its office at the point of transition from the *Ucs.* to the *Pcs.* (or *Cs.*).

By accepting the existence of these two (or three) psychical systems, psycho-analysis has departed a step further from the descriptive 'psychology of consciousness' and has raised new problems and acquired a new content. Up till now, it has differed from that psychology mainly by reason of its *dynamic* view of mental processes; now in addition it seems to take account of psychical *topography* as well, and to indicate in respect of any given mental act within what system or between what systems it takes place. On account of this attempt, too, it has been given the name of 'depth-psychology'. We shall hear that it can be further enriched by taking yet another point of view into account.

If we are to take the topography of mental acts seriously we must direct our interest to a doubt which arises at this point. When a psychical act (let us confine ourselves here to one which is in the nature of an idea) is transposed from the system *Ucs.* into the system *Cs.* (or *Pcs.*), are we to suppose that this transposition involves a fresh record—as it were, a second registration—of the idea in question, which may thus be situated as well in a fresh psychical locality, and alongside of which the original unconscious registration continues to exist? Or are we rather to believe that the transposition consists in a change in the state of the idea, a change involving the same material and occurring in the same

---

3. {These abbreviations are among the very few concessions Freud made to technical language.}

locality? This question may appear abstruse, but it must be raised if we wish to form a more definite conception of psychical topography, of the dimension of depth in the mind. It is a difficult one because it goes beyond pure psychology and touches on the relations of the mental apparatus to anatomy. We know that in the very roughest sense such relations exist. Research has given irrefutable proof that mental activity is bound up with the function of the brain as it is with no other organ. We are taken a step further—we do not know how much—by the discovery of the unequal importance of the different parts of the brain and their special relations to particular parts of the body and to particular mental activities. But every attempt to go on from there to discover a localization of mental processes, every endeavour to think of ideas as stored up in nerve-cells and of excitations as travelling along nerve-fibres, has miscarried completely. The same fate would await any theory which attempted to recognize, let us say, the anatomical position of the system Cs.—conscious mental activity—as being in the cortex, and to localize the unconscious processes in the subcortical parts of the brain. There is a hiatus here which at present cannot be filled, nor is it one of the tasks of psychology to fill it. Our psychical topography has *for the present* nothing to do with anatomy; it has reference not to anatomical localities, but to regions in the mental apparatus, wherever they may be situated in the body.

In this respect, then, our work is untrammelled and may proceed according to its own requirements. It will, however, be useful to remind ourselves that as things stand our hypotheses set out to be no more than graphic illustrations. The first of the two possibilities which we considered—namely, that the Cs. phase of an idea implies a fresh registration of it, which is situated in another place—is doubtless the cruder but also the more convenient. The second hypothesis—that of a merely *functional* change of state—is *a priori* more probable, but it is less plastic, less easy to manipulate. With the first, or topographical, hypothesis is bound up that of a topographical separation of the systems Ucs. and Cs. and also the possibility that an idea may exist simultaneously in two places in the mental apparatus—indeed, that if it is not inhibited by the censorship, it regularly advances from the one position to the other, possibly without losing its first location or registration.

This view may seem odd, but it can be supported by observations from psycho-analytic practice. If we communicate to a patient some idea which he has at one time repressed but which we have discovered in him, our telling him makes at first no change in his mental condition. Above all, it does not remove the repression nor undo its effects, as might perhaps be expected from the fact that the previously unconscious idea has now become conscious. On the contrary, all that we shall achieve at first will be a fresh rejection of the repressed idea. But now the patient has in actual fact the same idea in two forms in different places in his mental apparatus: first, he has the conscious memory of the auditory trace of the idea, conveyed in what we told him; and secondly, he also has—as we know for certain—the unconscious memory of his experience as it was in its earlier form. Actually there is no lifting of the repression until the conscious idea, after the resistances have been overcome, has entered into connection with the unconscious memory-trace. It is only through the making conscious of the latter itself that success is achieved. On superficial consideration this would seem to show that conscious and unconscious ideas are distinct registrations, topographically separated, of the same content. But a moment's reflection shows that the identity of the information given to the patient with his repressed memory is only apparent. To have heard something and to have experienced something are in their psychological nature two quite different things, even though the content of both is the same.

So for the moment we are not in a position to decide between the two possibilities that we have discussed. Perhaps later on we shall come upon factors which may turn the balance in favour of one or the other. Perhaps we shall make the discovery that our question was inadequately framed and that the difference between an unconscious and a conscious idea has to be defined in quite another way.

* * *

IV. Topography and Dynamics of Repression

We have arrived at the conclusion that repression is essentially a process affecting ideas on the border between the systems Ucs. and Pcs. (Cs.), and we can now make a fresh attempt to describe the process in greater detail.

It must be a matter of a *withdrawal* of cathexis: but the question is, in which system does the withdrawal take place and to which system does the cathexis that is withdrawn belong? The repressed idea remains capable of action in the Ucs., and it must therefore have retained its cathexis. What has been withdrawn must be something else. Let us take the case of repression proper ('after-pressure'), as it affects an idea which is preconscious or even actually conscious. Here repression can only consist in withdrawing from the idea the (pre)conscious cathexis which belongs to the system Pcs. The idea then either remains uncathected, or receives cathexis from the Ucs., or retains the Ucs. cathexis which it already had. Thus there is a withdrawal of the preconscious cathexis, retention of the unconscious cathexis, or replacement of the preconscious cathexis by an unconscious one. We notice, moreover, that we have based these reflections (as it were, without meaning to) on the assumption that the transition from the system Ucs. to the system next to it is not effected through the making of a new registration but through a change in its state, an alteration in its cathexis. The functional hypothesis has here easily defeated the topographical one.

But this process of withdrawal of libido is not adequate to make another characteristic of repression comprehensible to us. It is not clear why the idea which has remained cathected or has received cathexis from the *Ucs.* should not, in virtue of its cathexis, renew the attempt to penetrate into the system *Pcs.* If it could do so, the withdrawal of libido from it would have to be repeated, and the same performance would go on endlessly; but the outcome would not be repression. So, too, when it comes to describing *primal* repression, the mechanism just discussed of withdrawal of preconscious cathexis would fail to meet the case; for here we are dealing with an unconscious idea which has as yet received *no* cathexis from the *Pcs.* and therefore cannot have that cathexis withdrawn from it.

What we require, therefore, is another process which maintains the repression in the first case [i.e. the case of after-pressure] and, in the second [i.e. that of primal repression], ensures its being established as well as continued. This other process can only be found in the assumption of an *anticathexis*, by means of which the system *Pcs.* protects itself from the pressure upon it of the unconscious idea. We shall see from clinical examples how such an anticathexis, operating in the system *Pcs.*, manifests itself. It is this which represents the permanent expenditure [of energy] of a primal repression, and which also guarantees the permanence of that repression. Anticathexis is the sole mechanism of primal repression; in the case of repression proper ('after-pressure') there is in addition withdrawal of the *Pcs.* cathexis. It is very possible that it is precisely the cathexis which is withdrawn from the idea that is used for anticathexis.

We see how we have gradually been led into adopting a third point of view in our account of psychical phenomena. Besides the dynamic and the topographical points of view, we have adopted the *economic* one. This endeavours to follow out the vicissitudes of amounts of excitation and to arrive at least at some *relative* estimate of their magnitude.

It will not be unreasonable to give a special name to this whole way of regarding our subject-matter, for it is the consummation of psychoanalytic research. I propose that when we have succeeded in describing a psychical process in its dynamic, topographical and economic aspects, we should speak of it as a *metapsychological* presentation. We must say at once that in the present state of our knowledge there are only a few points at which we shall succeed in this.

* * *

V. *The Special Characteristics of the System* Ucs.

The distinction we have made between the two psychical systems receives fresh significance when we observe that processes in the one system, the *Ucs.*, show characteristics which are not met with again in the system immediately above it.

The nucleus of the *Ucs.* consists of instinctual representatives which seek to discharge their cathexis; that is to say, it consists of wishful impulses. These instinctual impulses are co-ordinate with one another, exist side by side without being influenced by one another, and are exempt from mutual contradiction. When two wishful impulses whose aims must appear to us incompatible become simultaneously active, the two impulses do not diminish each other or cancel each other out, but combine to form an intermediate aim, a compromise.

There are in this system no negation, no doubt, no degrees of certainty: all this is only introduced by the work of the censorship between the *Ucs.* and the *Pcs.* Negation is a substitute, at a higher level, for repression. In the *Ucs.* there are only contents, cathected with greater or lesser strength.

The cathectic intensities [in the *Ucs.*] are much more mobile. By the process of *displacement* one idea may surrender to another its whole quota of cathexis; by the process of *condensation* it may appropriate the whole cathexis of several other ideas. I have proposed to regard these two processes as distinguishing marks of the so-called *primary psychical process*. In the system *Pcs.* the *secondary process* is dominant. When a primary process is allowed to take its course in connection with elements belonging to the system *Pcs.*, it appears 'comic' and excites laughter.

The processes of the system *Ucs.* are *timeless*; i.e. they are not ordered temporally, are not altered by the passage of time; they have no reference to time at all. Reference to time is bound up, once again, with the work of the system *Cs.*

The *Ucs.* processes pay just a little regard to *reality*. They are subject to the pleasure principle; their fate depends only on how strong they are and on whether they fulfil the demands of the pleasure-unpleasure regulation.

To sum up: *exemption from mutual contradiction, primary process* (mobility of cathexes), *timelessness*, and *replacement of external by psychical reality*—these are the characteristics which we may expect to find in processes belonging to the system *Ucs.*

Unconscious processes only become cognizable by us under the conditions of dreaming and of neurosis—that is to say, when the processes of the higher, *Pcs.*, system are set back to an earlier stage by being lowered (by regression). In themselves they cannot be cognized, indeed are even incapable of carrying on their existence; for the system *Ucs.* is at a very early moment overlaid by the *Pcs.* which has taken over access to consciousness and to motility. Discharge from the system *Ucs.* passes into somatic innervation that leads to development of affect; but even this path of discharge is, as we have seen, contested by the *Pcs.* By itself, the system *Ucs.* would not in normal conditions be able to bring about

any expedient muscular acts, with the exception of those already organized as reflexes.

The full significance of the characteristics of the system *Ucs.* described
above could only be appreciated by us if we were to contrast and compare
them with those of the system *Pcs.* But this would take us so far afield
that I propose that we should once more call a halt and not undertake
the comparison of the two till we can do so in connection with our
discussion of the higher system. Only the most pressing points of all
will be mentioned at this stage.

The processes of the system *Pcs.* display—no matter whether they are
already conscious or only capable of becoming conscious—an inhibition
of the tendency of cathected ideas towards discharge. When a process
passes from one idea to another, the first idea retains a part of its cathexis
and only a small portion undergoes displacement. Displacements and
condensations such as happen in the primary process are excluded or
very much restricted. This circumstance caused Breuer to assume the
existence of two different states of cathectic energy in mental life: one
in which the energy is tonically 'bound' and the other in which it is
freely mobile and presses towards discharge. In my opinion this distinction represents the deepest insight we have gained up to the present
into the nature of nervous energy, and I do not see how we can avoid
making it. A metapsychological presentation would most urgently call
for further discussion at this point, though perhaps that would be too
daring an undertaking as yet.

Further, it devolves upon the system *Pcs.* to make communication
possible between the different ideational contents so that they can influence one another, to give them an order in time, and to set up a
censorship or several censorships; 'reality-testing' too, and the reality-
principle, are in its province. Conscious memory, moreover, seems to
depend wholly on the *Pcs.* This should be clearly distinguished from
the memory-traces in which the experiences of the *Ucs.* are fixed, and
probably corresponds to a special registration such as we proposed (but
later rejected) to account for the relation of conscious to unconscious
ideas. In this connection, also, we shall find means for putting an end
to our oscillations in regard to the naming of the higher system—which
we have hitherto spoken of indifferently, sometimes as the *Pcs.* and
sometimes as the *Cs.*

Nor will it be out of place here to utter a warning against any over-
hasty generalization of what we have brought to light concerning the
distribution of the various mental functions between the two systems.
We are describing the state of affairs as it appears in the adult human
being, in whom the system *Ucs.* operates, strictly speaking, only as a
preliminary stage of the higher organization. The question of what the
content and connections of that system are during the development of
the individual, and of what significance it possesses in animals—these

are points on which no conclusion can be deduced from our description: they must be investigated independently. Moreover, in human beings we must be prepared to find possible pathological conditions under which the two systems alter, or even exchange, both their content and their characteristics.

Mourning and Melancholia

As early as the mid-1890s, Freud had noted the self-reproaches many feel upon the death of loved ones. Such reproaches, he thought, might eventuate in hysteria, obsessions—or depressions, which he called, then and later, by the resonant, tradition-laden term "melancholia." Once he had discovered the mental agency that he called, at this time, the ego ideal—that strict, highly self-critical internal guardian—he could return to methods the mind devises for self-punishment. The idea of the super-ego was not far away. As so often, so here, Freud gains clarity by means of comparing the mental condition he wishes to understand with another, similar, but distinct state. Written like the other metapsychological papers in 1915, it was published in 1917.

* * *

In mourning we found that the inhibition and loss of interest are fully accounted for by the work of mourning in which the ego is absorbed. In melancholia, the unknown loss will result in a similar internal work and will therefore be responsible for the melancholic inhibition. The difference is that the inhibition of the melancholic seems puzzling to us because we cannot see what it is that is absorbing him so entirely. The melancholic displays something else besides which is lacking in mourning—an extraordinary diminution in his self-regard, an impoverishment of his ego on a grand scale. The patient represents his ego to us as worthless, incapable of any achievement and morally despicable; he reproaches himself, vilifies himself and expects to be cast out and punished. He abases himself before everyone and commiserates with his own relatives for being connected with anyone so unworthy. He is not of the opinion that a change has taken place in him, but extends his self-criticism back over the past; he declares that he was never any better. This picture of a delusion of (mainly moral) inferiority is completed by sleeplessness and refusal to take nourishment, and—what is psychologically very remarkable—by an overcoming of the instinct which compels every living thing to cling to life.

It would be equally fruitless from a scientific and a therapeutic point of view to contradict a patient who brings these accusations against his ego. He must surely be right in some way and be describing something that is as it seems to be to him. * * * {Yet it is not} difficult to see that there is no correspondence, so far as we can judge, between the degree of self-abasement and its real justification. A good, capable, conscientious woman will speak no better of herself after she develops melancholia than one who is in fact worthless; indeed, the former is perhaps more likely to fall ill of the disease than the latter, of whom we too should have nothing good to say. Finally, it must strike us that after all the melancholic does not behave in quite the same way as a person who is crushed by remorse and self-reproach in a normal fashion. Feelings of shame in front of other people, which would more than anything characterize this latter condition, are lacking in the melancholic, or at least they are not prominent in him. One might emphasize the presence in him of an almost opposite trait of insistent communicativeness which finds satisfaction in self-exposure.

The essential thing, therefore, is not whether the melancholic's distressing self-denigration is correct, in the sense that his self-criticism agrees with the opinion of other people. The point must rather be that he is giving a correct description of his psychological situation. He has lost his self-respect and he must have good reason for this. It is true that we are then faced with a contradiction that presents a problem which is hard to solve. The analogy with mourning led us to conclude that he had suffered a loss in regard to an object; what he tells us points to a loss in regard to his ego.

Before going into this contradiction, let us dwell for a moment on the view which the melancholic's disorder affords of the constitution of the human ego. We see how in him one part of the ego sets itself over against the other, judges it critically, and, as it were, takes it as its object. Our suspicion that the critical agency which is here split off from the ego might also show its independence in other circumstances will be confirmed by every further observation. We shall really find grounds for distinguishing this agency from the rest of the ego. What we are here becoming acquainted with is the agency commonly called 'conscience'; we shall count it, along with the censorship of consciousness and reality-testing, among the major institutions of the ego, and we shall come upon evidence to show that it can become diseased on its own account. In the clinical picture of melancholia, dissatisfaction with the ego on moral grounds is the most outstanding feature. The patient's self-evaluation concerns itself much less frequently with bodily infirmity, ugliness or weakness, or with social inferiority; of this category, it is only his fears and asseverations of becoming poor that occupy a prominent position.

There is one observation, not at all difficult to make, which leads to the explanation of the contradiction mentioned above [at the end of the last paragraph but one]. If one listens patiently to a melancholic's many and various self-accusations, one cannot in the end avoid the impression that often the most violent of them are hardly at all applicable to the patient himself, but that with insignificant modifications they do fit someone else, someone whom the patient loves or has loved or should love. Every time one examines the facts this conjecture is confirmed. So we find the key to the clinical picture: we perceive that the self-reproaches are reproaches against a loved object which have been shifted away from it on to the patient's own ego.

The woman who loudly pities her husband for being tied to such an incapable wife as herself is really accusing her *husband* of being incapable, in whatever sense she may mean this. There is no need to be greatly surprised that a few genuine self-reproaches are scattered among those that have been transposed back. These are allowed to obtrude themselves, since they help to mask the others and make recognition of the true state of affairs impossible. Moreover, they derive from the *pros* and *cons* of the conflict of love that has led to the loss of love. The behaviour of the patients, too, now becomes much more intelligible. Their complaints are really 'plaints' in the old sense of the word. They are not ashamed and do not hide themselves, since everything derogatory that they say about themselves is at bottom said about someone else. Moreover, they are far from evincing towards those around them the attitude of humility and submissiveness that would alone befit such worthless people. On the contrary, they make the greatest nuisance of themselves, and always seem as though they felt slighted and had been treated with great injustice. All this is possible only because the reactions expressed in their behaviour still proceed from a mental constellation of revolt, which has then, by a certain process, passed over into the crushed state of melancholia.

There is no difficulty in reconstructing this process. An object-choice, an attachment of the libido to a particular person, had at one time existed; then, owing to a real slight or disappointment coming from this loved person, the object-relationship was shattered. The result was not the normal one of a withdrawal of the libido from this object and a displacement of it on to a new one, but something different, for whose coming-about various conditions seem to be necessary. The object-cathexis proved to have little power of resistance and was brought to an end. But the free libido was not displaced on to another object; it was withdrawn into the ego. There, however, it was not employed in any unspecified way, but served to establish an *identification* of the ego with the abandoned object. Thus the shadow of the object fell upon the ego, and the latter could henceforth be judged by a special agency, as though it were an object, the forsaken object. In this way an object-loss was transformed into an ego-loss and the conflict between the ego and the loved person into a cleavage between the critical activity of the ego and the ego as altered by identification.

One or two things may be directly inferred with regard to the pre-conditions and effects of a process such as this. On the one hand, a strong fixation to the loved object must have been present; on the other hand, in contradiction to this, the object-cathexis must have had little power of resistance. * * * The narcissistic identification with the object then becomes a substitute for the erotic cathexis, the result of which is that in spite of the conflict with the loved person the love-relation need not be given up. This substitution of identification for object-love is an important mechanism in the narcissistic affections; Karl Landauer (1914) has lately been able to point to it in the process of recovery in a case of schizophrenia. It represents, of course, a *regression* from one type of object-choice to original narcissism. We have elsewhere shown that identification is a preliminary stage of object-choice, that it is the first way—and one that is expressed in an ambivalent fashion—in which the ego picks out an object. The ego wants to incorporate this object into itself, and, in accordance with the oral or cannibalistic phase of libidinal development in which it is, it wants to do so by devouring it. Abraham is undoubtedly right in attributing to this connection the refusal of nourishment met with in severe forms of melancholia.

The conclusion which our theory would require—namely, that the disposition to fall ill of melancholia (or some part of that disposition) lies in the predominance of the narcissistic type of object-choice—has unfortunately not yet been confirmed by observation. In the opening remarks of this paper, I admitted that the empirical material upon which this study is founded is insufficient for our needs. If we could assume an agreement between the results of observation and what we have inferred, we should not hesitate to include this regression from object-cathexis to the still narcissistic oral phase of the libido in our characterization of melancholia. Identifications with the object are by no means rare in the transference neuroses either; indeed, they are a well-known mechanism of symptom-formation, especially in hysteria. The difference, however, between narcissistic and hysterical identification may be seen in this: that, whereas in the former the object-cathexis is abandoned, in the latter it persists and manifests its influence, though this is usually confined to certain isolated actions and innervations. In any case, in the transference neuroses, too, identification is the expression of there being something in common, which may signify love. Narcissistic identification is the older of the two and it paves the way to an understanding of hysterical identification, which has been less thoroughly studied.

Melancholia, therefore, borrows some of its features from mourning, and the others from the process of regression from narcissistic object-choice to narcissism. It is on the one hand, like mourning, a reaction to the real loss of a loved object; but over and above this, it is marked by a determinant which is absent in normal mourning or which, if it is present, transforms the latter into pathological mourning. The loss of a love-object is an excellent opportunity for the ambivalence in love-relationships to make itself effective and come into the open. Where there is a disposition to obsessional neurosis the conflict due to ambivalence gives a pathological cast to mourning and forces it to express itself in the form of self-reproaches to the effect that the mourner himself is to blame for the loss of the loved object, i.e. that he has willed it. These obsessional states of depression following upon the death of a loved person show us what the conflict due to ambivalence can achieve by itself when there is no regressive drawing-in of libido as well. In melancholia, the occasions which give rise to the illness extend for the most part beyond the clear case of a loss by death, and include all those situations of being slighted, neglected or disappointed, which can import opposed feelings of love and hate into the relationship or reinforce an already existing ambivalence. This conflict due to ambivalence, which sometimes arises more from real experiences, sometimes more from constitutional factors, must not be overlooked among the preconditions of melancholia. If the love for the object—a love which cannot be given up though the object itself is given up—takes refuge in narcissistic identification, then the hate comes into operation on this substitutive object, abusing it, debasing it, making it suffer and deriving sadistic satisfaction from its suffering. The self-tormenting in melancholia, which is without doubt enjoyable, signifies, just like the corresponding phenomenon in obsessional neurosis, a satisfaction of trends of sadism and hate which relate to an object, and which have been turned round upon the subject's own self in the ways we have been discussing. In both disorders the patients usually still succeed, by the circuitous path of self-punishment, in taking revenge on the original object and in tormenting their loved one through their illness, having resorted to it in order to avoid the need to express their hostility to him openly. After all, the person who has occasioned the patient's emotional disorder, and on whom his illness is centred, is usually to be found in his immediate environment. The melancholic's erotic cathexis in regard to his object has thus undergone a double vicissitude: part of it has regressed to identification, but the other part, under the influence of the conflict due to ambivalence, has been carried back to the stage of sadism which is nearer to that conflict.

It is this sadism alone that solves the riddle of the tendency to suicide which makes melancholia so interesting—and so dangerous. So immense is the ego's self-love, which we have come to recognize as the primal state from which instinctual life proceeds, and so vast is the amount of narcissistic libido which we see liberated in the fear that emerges at a threat to life, that we cannot conceive how that ego can consent to its own destruction. We have long known, it is true, that no neurotic harbours thoughts of suicide which he has not turned back upon himself from murderous impulses against others, but we have never been able to explain what interplay of forces can carry such a purpose through to execution. The analysis of melancholia now shows that the ego can kill itself only if, owing to the return of the object-cathexis, it can treat itself as an object—if it is able to direct against itself the hostility which relates to an object and which represents the ego's original reaction to objects in the external world. Thus in regression from narcissistic object-choice the object has, it is true, been got rid of, but it has nevertheless proved more powerful than the ego itself. In the two opposed situations of being most intensely in love and of suicide the ego is overwhelmed by the object, though in totally different ways.

As regards one particular striking feature of melancholia that we have mentioned, the prominence of the fear of becoming poor, it seems plausible to suppose that it is derived from anal erotism which has been torn out of its context and altered in a regressive sense.

Melancholia confronts us with yet other problems, the answer to which in part eludes us. The fact that it passes off after a certain time has elapsed without leaving traces of any gross changes is a feature it shares with mourning. We found by way of explanation that in mourning time is needed for the command of reality-testing to be carried out in detail, and that when this work has been accomplished the ego will have succeeded in freeing its libido from the lost object. We may imagine that the ego is occupied with analogous work during the course of a melancholia; in neither case have we any insight into the economics of the course of events. The sleeplessness in melancholia testifies to the rigidity of the condition, the impossibility of effecting the general drawing-in of cathexes necessary for sleep. The complex of melancholia behaves like an open wound, drawing to itself cathectic energies—which in the transference neuroses we have called 'anticathexes'—from all directions, and emptying the ego until it is totally impoverished. It can easily prove resistant to the ego's wish to sleep.

What is probably a somatic factor, and one which cannot be explained psychogenically, makes itself visible in the regular amelioration in the condition that takes place towards evening. These considerations bring up the question whether a loss in the ego irrespectively of the object— a purely narcissistic blow to the ego—may not suffice to produce the picture of melancholia and whether an impoverishment of ego-libido direclty due to toxins may not be able to produce certain forms of the disease.

* * *

Some Character-Types Met with in Psycho-Analytic Work: [The Exceptions]

In his practice, though intent on grouping his cases under collective diagnostic rubrics like hysteria or paranoia, Freud also cherished the individual differences that made each of his analysands unique or placed them into small, well-defined classes of mental aberrations. Late in 1916, he published three short papers devoted to certain interesting patients, the first of which, on the so-called "exceptions," is reproduced here. The second deals with "Those Wrecked by Success," which draws heavily on Shakespeare's *Mac-*

beth and Ibsen's *Rosmersholm,* and the last, very brief but meaty, with "Criminals from a Sense of Guilt," which once more considers some implications of guilt feelings. The concluding paragraph of the paper on the exceptions raises questions of female psychology that Freud would explore in more depth (and even more controversially) in the following years (see below, ₁ ᵢ. 670–78).

When a doctor carries out the psycho-analytic treatment of a neurotic, his interest is by no means directed in the first instance to the patient's character. He would much rather know what the symptoms mean, what instinctual impulses are concealed behind them and are satisfied by them, and what course was followed by the mysterious path that has led from the instinctual wishes to the symptoms. But the technique which he is obliged to follow soon compels him to direct his immediate curiosity towards other objectives. He observes that his investigation is threatened by resistances set up against him by the patient, and these resistances he may justly count as part of the latter's character. This now acquires the first claim on his interest.

What opposes the doctor's efforts is not always those traits of character which the patient recognizes in himself and which are attributed to him by people round him. Peculiarities in him which he had seemed to possess only to a modest degree are often brought to light in surprisingly increased intensity, or attitudes reveal themselves in him which had not been betrayed in other relations of life. The pages which follow will be devoted to describing and tracing back a few of these surprising traits of characters.

I

THE 'EXCEPTIONS'

Psycho-analytic work is continually confronted with the task of inducing the patient to renounce an immediate and directly attainable yield of pleasure. He is not asked to renounce all pleasure; that could not, perhaps, be expected of any human being, and even religion is obliged to support its demand that earthly pleasure shall be set aside by promising that it will provide instead an incomparably greater amount of superior pleasure in another world. No, the patient is only asked to renounce such satisfactions as will inevitably have detrimental consequences. His privation is only to be temporary; he has only to learn to exchange an immediate yield of pleasure for a better assured, even though a postponed one. Or, in other words, under the doctor's guidance he is asked to make the advance from the pleasure principle to the reality principle by which the mature human being is distinguished from the child. In this educative process, the doctor's clearer insight can hardly be said to play a decisive part; as a rule, he can only tell his patient what the latter's own reason can tell him. But it is not the same to know a thing in one's own mind and to hear it from someone outside. The doctor plays the part of this effective outsider; he makes use of the influence which one human being exercises over another. Or—recalling that it is the habit of psycho-analysis to replace what is derivative and etiolated by what is original and basic—let us say that the doctor, in his educative work , makes use of one of the components of love. In this work of after-education, he is probably doing no more than repeat the process which made education of any kind possible in the first instance. Side by side with the exigencies of life, love is the great educator; and it is by the love of those nearest him that the incomplete human being is induced to respect the decrees of necessity and to spare himself the punishment that follows any infringement of them.

When in this way one asks the patient to make a provisional renunciation of some pleasurable satisfaction, to make a sacrifice, to show his readiness to accept some temporary suffering for the sake of a better end, or even merely to make up his mind to submit to a necessity which applies to everyone, one comes upon individuals who resist such an appeal on a special ground. They say that they have renounced enough and suffered enough, and have a claim to be spared any further demands; they will submit no longer to any disagreeable necessity, for they are *exceptions* and, moreover, intend to remain so. In one such patient this claim was magnified into a conviction that a special providence watched over him, which would protect him from any painful sacrifices of the sort. The doctor's arguments will achieve nothing against an inner confidence which expresses itself as strongly as this; even *his* influence, indeed, is powerless at first, and it becomes clear to him that he must discover the sources from which this damaging prepossession is being fed.

Now it is no doubt true that everyone would like to consider himself an 'exception' and claim privileges over others. But precisely because of this there must be a particular reason, and one not universally present, if someone actually proclaims himself an exception and behaves as such. This reason may be of more than one kind; in the cases I investigated I succeeded in discovering a common peculiarity in the earlier experiences of these patients' lives. Their neuroses were connected with some experience or suffering to which they had been subjected in their earliest childhood, one in respect of which they knew themselves to be guiltless, and which they could look upon as an unjust disadvantage imposed upon them. The privileges that they claimed as a result of this injustice, and the rebelliousness it engendered, had contributed not a little to intensifying the conflicts leading to the outbreak of their neurosis. In one of these patients, a woman, the attitude towards life which I am discussing came to a head when she learnt that a painful organic trouble, which had hindered her from attaining her aims in life, was of congenital origin. So long as she looked upon this trouble as an accidental and late acquisition, she bore it patiently; as soon as she found that it was part of an innate inheritance, she became rebellious. The young man who believed that he was watched over by a special providence had in his infancy been the victim of an accidental infection from his wet-nurse, and had spent his whole later life making claims for compensation, an accident pension, as it were, without having any idea on what he based those claims. In his case the analysis, which constructed this event out of obscure mnemic residues and interpretations of the symptoms, was confirmed objectively by information from his family.

For reasons which will be easily understood I cannot communicate very much about these or other case histories. Nor do I propose to go into the obvious analogy between deformities of character resulting from protracted sickliness in childhood and the behavior of whole nations whose past history has been full of suffering. Instead, however, I will take the opportunity of pointing to a figure created by the greatest of poets—a figure in whose character the claim to be an exception is closely bound up with and is motivated by the circumstance of congenital disadvantage.

In the opening soliloquy to Shakespeare's *Richard III*, Gloucester, who subsequently becomes King, says:

> But I, that am not shaped for sportive tricks,
> Nor made to court an amorous looking-glass;
> I that am rudely stamp'd, and want love's majesty
> To strut before a wanton ambling nymph;
> I, that am curtail'd of this fair proportion,
> Cheated of feature by dissembling Nature,
> Deform'd, unfinish'd, sent before my time
> Into this breathing world, scarce half made up,
> And that so lamely and unfashionable,
> That dogs bark at me as I halt by them;

> * * * * *

> And therefore, since I cannot prove a lover,
> To entertain these fair well-spoken days,
> I am determined to prove a villain,
> And hate the idle pleasures of these days.

At a first glance this tirade may perhaps seem unrelated to our present theme. Richard seems to say nothing more than: 'I find these idle times tedious, and I want to enjoy myself. As I cannot play the lover on account of my deformity, I will play the villain; I will intrigue, murder and do anything else I please.' Such a frivolous motivation could not but stifle any stirring of sympathy in the audience, if it were not a screen for something much more serious. Otherwise the play would be psychologically impossible, for the writer must know how to furnish us with a secret background of sympathy for his hero, if we are to admire his boldness and adroitness without inward protest; and such sympathy can only be based on understanding or on a sense of a possible inner fellow-feeling for him.

I think, therefore, that Richard's soliloquy does not say everything; it merely gives a hint, and leaves us to fill in what it hints at. When we do so, however, the appearance of frivolity vanishes, the bitterness and minuteness with which Richard has depicted his deformity make their full effect, and we clearly perceive the fellow-feeling which compels our sympathy even with a villain like him. What the soliloquy thus means is: 'Nature has done me a grievous wrong in denying me the beauty of form which wins human love. Life owes me reparation for this, and I will see that I get it. I have a right to be an exception, to disregard the scruples by which others let themselves be held back. I may do wrong myself, since wrong has been done to me.' And now we feel that we ourselves might become like Richard, that on a small scale, indeed, we are already like him. Richard is an enormous magnification of something we find in ourselves as well. We all think we have reason to reproach Nature and our destiny for congenital and infantile disadvantages; we all demand reparation for early wounds to our narcissism, our self-love. Why did not Nature give us the golden curls of Balder or the strength of Siegfried or the lofty brow of genius or the noble profile of aristocracy? Why were we born in a middle-class home instead of in a royal palace? We could carry off beauty and distinction quite as well as any of those whom we are now obliged to envy for these qualities.

It is, however, a subtle economy of art in the poet that he does not permit his hero to give open and complete expression to all his secret motives. By this means he obliges us to supplement them; he engages our intellectual activity, diverts it from critical reflection and keeps us firmly identified with his hero. A bungler in his place would give conscious expression to all that he wishes to reveal to us, and would then find himself confronted by our cool, untrammelled intelligence, which would preclude any deepening of the illusion.

Before leaving the 'exceptions', however, we may point out that the claim of women to privileges and to exemption from so many of the importunities of life rests upon the same foundation. As we learn from psycho-analytic work, women regard themselves as having been damaged in infancy, as having been undeservedly cut short of something and unfairly treated; and the embitterment of so many daughters against their mother derives, ultimately, from the reproach against her of having brought them into the world as women instead of as men.

Beyond the Pleasure Principle

While Freud did not explicitly make this claim, one may regard *Beyond the Pleasure Principle* (1920) as the first, still somewhat tentative resolution of the troubling theoretical problem he had raised in the paper on narcissism (see above, pp. 545–62). *The Ego and the Id,* published three years later, was his second, definitive response. He now replaced the pairing of drives—libidinal and egoistic—that had served him for more than a decade of psychoanalytic theorizing and that he had called into question not long before the World War, with a new, more dramatic pair of contestants: life against death. Aggression, to which Freud had earlier devoted a measure of attention that he now deemed inadequate, became from 1920 on the equal adversary of Eros.

As critics have not failed to note, *Beyond the Pleasure Principle* is more remote from Freud's clinical experience than earlier theoretical papers. Freud does adduce some "case material," including veterans suffering from war neuroses, and that famous "fort-da" game that his eighteen-month-old grandson, Ernst Halberstadt—his daughter Sophie's eldest—played while his observant grandfather was watching. But for the rest, as Freud frankly noted, there is a good deal of conjecture in this little, path-breaking book: "What follows," Freud writes after giving his concrete instances of the "compulsion to repeat," is "speculation, often far-fetched speculation." But he thought such speculation unavoidable in the uncharted terrain he was now entering. (In the selections that follow, much of this material, especially about speculative biology, has been omitted.) The essay is a difficult text, but as the first statement of the new "structural" theory of the mind, it is indispensable to an understanding of fundamental shifts in psychoanalytic thinking.

Freud's preoccupation with death, marked in *Beyond the Pleasure Principle* and much of his later writing, has invited the suggestion that his thinking was colored darkly by the death of his charming and attractive daughter Sophie in January 1920, during the great influenza epidemic that claimed so many victims across Europe and the United States. Indeed, Fritz Wittels, an early associate of the Vienna psychoanalytic circle, said so explicitly in his biography of Freud (the first), of which he sent an advance copy to his subject in late 1923. Freud acknowledged that Wittels's argument was plausible enough. But he vigorously denied that he had developed his theory of the death drive as a consequence of grieving for his Sophie: the chronology was against it. He had in fact virtually completed *Beyond the Pleasure Principle* in 1919, and circulated the manuscript among a few intimates, while Sophie was still flourishing and enjoying perfect health. The essay must be read not as an exercise in autobiography, but as a turning point in theory.

I

In the theory of psycho-analysis we have no hesitation in assuming that the course taken by mental events is automatically regulated by the pleasure principle. We believe, that is to say, that the course of those events is invariably set in motion by an unpleasurable tension, and that it takes a direction such that its final outcome coincides with a lowering of that tension—that is, with an avoidance of unpleasure or a production of pleasure. In taking that course into account in our consideration of the mental processes which are the subject of our study, we are introducing an 'economic' point of view into our work; and if, in describing those processes, we try to estimate this 'economic' factor in addition to the 'topographical' and 'dynamic' ones, we shall, I think, be giving the most complete description of them of which we can at present conceive, and one which deserves to be distinguished by the term 'meta-psychological'.

It is of no concern to us in this connection to enquire how far, with this hypothesis of the pleasure principle, we have approached or adopted any particular, historically established, philosophical system. We have arrived at these speculative assumptions in an attempt to describe and to account for the facts of daily observation in our field of study. Priority and originality are not among the aims that psycho-analytic work sets itself; and the impressions that underlie the hypothesis of the pleasure principle are so obvious that they can scarcely be overlooked. On the other hand we would readily express our gratitude to any philosophical or psychological theory which was able to inform us of the meaning of the feelings of pleasure and unpleasure which act so imperatively upon us. But on this point we are, alas, offered nothing to our purpose. This is the most obscure and inaccessible region of the mind, and, since we cannot avoid contact with it, the least rigid hypothesis, it seems to me, will be the best. We have decided to relate pleasure and unpleasure to the quantity of excitation that is present in the mind but is not in any way 'bound'; and to relate them in such a manner that unpleasure corresponds to an *increase* in the quantity of excitation and pleasure to a *diminution*. What we are implying by this is not a simple relation between the strength of the feelings of pleasure and unpleasure and the corresponding modifications in the quantity of excitation; least of all—in view of all we have been taught by psycho-physiology—are we suggesting any directly proportional ratio: the factor that determines the feeling is probably the amount of increase or diminution in the quantity of excitation *in a given period of time*. Experiment might possibly play a part here; but it is not advisable for us analysts to go into the problem further so long as our way is not pointed by quite definite observations.

* * *

The facts which have caused us to believe in the dominance of the pleasure principle in mental life also find expression in the hypothesis that the mental apparatus endeavours to keep the quantity of excitation present in it as low as possible or at least to keep it constant. This latter hypothesis is only another way of stating the pleasure principle; for if the work of the mental apparatus is directed towards keeping the quantity of excitation low, then anything that is calculated to increase that quantity is bound to be felt as adverse to the functioning of the apparatus, that is as unpleasurable. The pleasure principle follows from the principle of constancy: actually the latter principle was inferred from the facts which forced us to adopt the pleasure principle. * * *

It must be pointed out, however, that strictly speaking it is incorrect to talk of the dominance of the pleasure principle over the course of mental processes. If such a dominance existed, the immense majority of our mental processes would have to be accompanied by pleasure or to lead to pleasure, whereas universal experience completely contradicts any such conclusion. The most that can be said, therefore, is that there exists in the mind a strong *tendency* towards the pleasure principle, but that that tendency is opposed by certain other forces or circumstances, so that the final outcome cannot always be in harmony with the tendency towards pleasure. * * *

If we turn now to the question of what circumstances are able to prevent the pleasure principle from being carried into effect, we find ourselves once more on secure and well-trodden ground and, in framing our answer, we have at our disposal a rich fund of analytic experience.

The first example of the pleasure principle being inhibited in this way is a familiar one which occurs with regularity. We know that the pleasure principle is proper to a *primary* method of working on the part of the mental apparatus, but that, from the point of view of the self-preservation of the organism among the difficulties of the external world, it is from the very outset inefficient and even highly dangerous. Under the influence of the ego's instincts of self-preservation, the pleasure principle is replaced by the *reality principle*. This latter principle does not abandon the intention of ultimately obtaining pleasure, but it nevertheless demands and carries into effect the postponement of satisfaction, the abandonment of a number of possibilities of gaining satisfaction and the temporary toleration of unpleasure as a step on the long indirect road to pleasure. The pleasure principle long persists, however, as the method of working employed by the sexual instincts, which are so hard to 'educate', and, starting from those instincts, or in the ego itself, it often succeeds in overcoming the reality principle, to the detriment of the organism as a whole.

There can be no doubt, however, that the replacement of the pleasure principle by the reality principle can only be made responsible for a small number, and by no means the most intense, of unpleasure experiences. Another occasion of the release of unpleasure, which occurs with no less regularity, is to be found in the conflicts and dissensions that take place in the mental apparatus while the ego is passing through its development into more highly composite organizations. Almost all the energy with which the apparatus is filled arises from its innate instinctual impulses. But these are not all allowed to reach the same phases of development. In the course of things it happens again and again that individual instincts or parts of instincts turn out to be incompatible in their aims or demands with the remaining ones, which are able to combine into the inclusive unity of the ego. The former are then split off from this unity by the process of repression, held back at lower levels of psychical development and cut off, to begin with, from the possibility of satisfaction. If they succeed subsequently, as can so easily happen with repressed sexual instincts, in struggling through, by roundabout paths, to a direct or to a substitutive satisfaction, that event, which would in other cases have been an opportunity for pleasure, is felt by the ego as unpleasure. As a consequence of the old conflict which ended in repression, a new breach has occurred in the pleasure principle at the very time when certain instincts were endeavouring, in accordance with the principle, to obtain fresh pleasure. * * *

The two sources of unpleasure which I have just indicated are very far from covering the majority of our unpleasurable experiences. But as regards the remainder it can be asserted with some show of justification that their presence does not contradict the dominance of the pleasure principle. Most of the unpleasure that we experience is *perceptual* unpleasure. It may be perception of pressure by unsatisfied instincts; or it may be external perception which is either distressing in itself or which excites unpleasurable expectations in the mental apparatus—that is, which is recognized by it as a 'danger'. The reaction to these instinctual demands and threats of danger, a reaction which constitutes the proper activity of the mental apparatus, can then be directed in a correct manner by the pleasure principle or the reality principle by which the former is modified. This does not seem to necessitate any far-reaching limitation of the pleasure principle. Nevertheless the investigation of the mental reaction to external danger is precisely in a position to produce new material and raise fresh questions bearing upon our present problem.

II

A condition has long been known and described which occurs after several mechanical concussions, railway disasters and other accidents involving a risk to life; it has been given the name of 'traumatic neurosis'. The terrible war which has just ended gave rise to a great number of illnesses of this kind, but it at least put an end to the temptation to attribute the cause of the disorder to organic lesions of the nervous system brought about by mechanical force.[1] The symptomatic picture presented by traumatic neurosis approaches that of hysteria in the wealth of its similar motor symptoms, but surpasses it as a rule in its strongly marked signs of subjective ailment (in which it resembles hypochondria or melancholia) as well as in the evidence it gives of a far more comprehensive general enfeeblement and disturbance of the mental capacities. No com-

1. Cf. the discussion on the psycho-analysis of war neuroses by Freud, Ferenczi, Abraham, Simmel and Jones {*Psycho-Analysis and the War-Neuroses*, [1919; tr. 1921]}.

plete explanation has yet been reached either of war neuroses or of the traumatic neuroses of peace. In the case of war neuroses, the fact that the same symptoms sometimes came about without the intervention of any gross mechanical force seemed at once enlightening and bewildering. In the case of the ordinary traumatic neuroses, two characteristics emerge prominently: first, that the chief weight in their causation seems to rest upon the factor of surprise, of fright; and secondly, that a wound or injury inflicted simultaneously works as a rule *against* the development of a neurosis. 'Fright', 'fear', and 'anxiety' are improperly used as synonymous expressions; they are in fact capable of clear distinction in their relation to danger. 'Anxiety' describes a particular state of expecting the danger or preparing for it, even though it may be an unknown one. 'Fear' requires a definite object of which to be afraid. 'Fright', however, is the name we give to the state a person gets into when he has run into danger without being prepared for it; it emphasizes the factor of surprise. I do not believe anxiety can produce a traumatic neurosis. There is something about anxiety that protects its subject against fright and so against fright-neuroses. We shall return to this point later.

The study of dreams may be considered the most trustworthy method of investigating deep mental processes. Now dreams occurring in traumatic neuroses have the characteristic of repeatedly bringing the patient back into the situation of his accident, a situation from which he wakes up in another fright. This astonishes people far too little. They think the fact that the traumatic experience is constantly forcing itself upon the patient even in his sleep is a proof of the strength of that experience: the patient is, as one might say, fixated to his trauma. Fixations to the experience which started the illness have long been familiar to us in hysteria. Breuer and Freud declared in 1893 that 'hysterics suffer mainly from reminiscences'. In the war neuroses, too, observers like Ferenczi and Simmel have been able to explain certain motor symptoms by fixation to the moment at which the trauma occurred.

I am not aware, however, that patients suffering from traumatic neurosis are much occupied in their waking lives with memories of their accident. Perhaps they are more concerned with not thinking of it. Anyone who accepts it as something self-evident that their dreams should put them back at night into the situation that caused them to fall ill has misunderstood the nature of dreams. It would be more in harmony with their nature if they showed the patient pictures from his healthy past or of the cure for which he hopes. If we are not to be shaken in our belief in the wish-fulfilling tenor of dreams by the dreams of traumatic neurotics, we still have one resource open to us: we may argue that the function of dreaming, like so much else, is upset in this condition and diverted from its purposes, or we may be driven to reflect on the mysterious masochistic trends of the ego.

* * *

At this point I propose to leave the dark and dismal subject of the traumatic neurosis and pass on to examine the method of working employed by the mental apparatus in one of its earliest *normal* activities— I mean in children's play.

* * * I have been able, through a chance opportunity which presented itself, to throw some light upon the first game played by a little boy of one and a half and invented by himself. It was more than a mere fleeting observation, for I lived under the same roof as the child and his parents for some weeks, and it was some time before I discovered the meaning of the puzzling activity which he constantly repeated.

The child was not at all precocious in his intellectual development. At the age of one and a half he could say only a few comprehensible words; he could also make use of a number of sounds which expressed a meaning intelligible to those around him. He was, however, on good terms with his parents and their one servant-girl, and tributes were paid to his being a 'good boy'. He did not disturb his parents at night, he conscientiously obeyed orders not to touch certain things or go into certain rooms, and above all he never cried when his mother left him for a few hours. At the same time, he was greatly attached to his mother, who had not only fed him herself but had also looked after him without any outside help. This good little boy, however, had an occasional disturbing habit of taking any small objects he could get hold of and throwing them away from him into a corner, under the bed, and so on, so that hunting for his toys and picking them up was often quite a business. As he did this he gave vent to a loud, long-drawn-out 'o-o-o-o', accompanied by an expression of interest and satisfaction. His mother and the writer of the present account were agreed in thinking that this was not a mere interjection but represented the German word *'fort'* ['gone']. I eventually realized that it was a game and that the only use he made of any of his toys was to play 'gone' with them. One day I made an observation which confirmed my view. The child had a wooden reel with a piece of string tied round it. It never occurred to him to pull it along the floor behind him, for instance, and play at its being a carriage. What he did was to hold the reel by the string and very skilfully throw it over the edge of his curtained cot, so that it disappeared into it, at the same time uttering his expressive 'o-o-o-o'. He then pulled the reel out of the cot again by the string and hailed its reappearance with a joyful *'da'* ['there']. This, then, was the complete game—disappearance and return. As a rule one only witnessed its first act, which was repeated untiringly as a game in itself, though there is no doubt that the greater pleasure was attached to the second act.[2]

2. A further observation subsequently confirmed this interpretation fully. One day the child's mother had been away for several hours and on her return was met with the words 'Baby o-o-o-o!' which was at first incomprehensible. It soon turned out, however, that during this long period of solitude the child had found a method of making *himself* disappear. He had discovered his reflection in a full-length mirror which did not quite reach to the ground, so that by crouching down he could make his mirror-image 'gone'.

The interpretation of the game then became obvious. It was related to the child's great cultural achievement—the instinctual renunciation (that is, the renunciation of instinctual satisfaction) which he had made in allowing his mother to go away without protesting. He compensated himself for this, as it were, by himself staging the disappearance and return of the objects within his reach. It is of course a matter of indifference from the point of view of judging the effective nature of the game whether the child invented it himself or took it over on some outside suggestion. Our interest is directed to another point. The child cannot possibly have felt his mother's departure as something agreeable or even indifferent. How then does his repetition of this distressing experience as a game fit in with the pleasure principle? It may perhaps be said in reply that her departure had to be enacted as a necessary preliminary to her joyful return, and that it was in the latter that lay the true purpose of the game. But against this must be counted the observed fact that the first act, that of departure, was staged as a game in itself and far more frequently than the episode in its entirety, with its pleasurable ending.

No certain decision can be reached from the analysis of a single case like this. On an unprejudiced view one gets an impression that the child turned his experience into a game from another motive. At the outset he was in a *passive* situation—he was overpowered by the experience; but, by repeating it, unpleasurable though it was, as a game, he took on an *active* part. These efforts might be put down to an instinct for mastery that was acting independently of whether the memory was in itself pleasurable or not. But still another interpretation may be attempted. Throwing away the object so that it was 'gone' might satisfy an impulse of the child's, which was suppressed in his actual life, to revenge himself on his mother for going away from him. In that case it would have a defiant meaning: 'All right, then, go away! I don't need you. I'm sending you away myself.' A year later, the same boy whom I had observed at his first game used to take a toy, if he was angry with it, and throw it on the floor, exclaiming: 'Go to the fwont!' He had heard at that time that his absent father was 'at the front', and was far from regretting his absence; on the contrary he made it quite clear that he had no desire to be disturbed in his sole possession of his mother.[3] We know of other children who liked to express similar hostile impulses by throwing away objects instead of persons. We are therefore left in doubt as to whether the impulse to work over in the mind some overpowering experience so as to make oneself master of it can find expressions as a primary event, and independently of the pleasure principle. For, in the case we have been discussing, the child may, after all, only

3. When this child was five and three-quarters, his mother died. Now that she was really 'gone' (o-o-o), the little boy showed no signs of grief. It is true that in the interval a second child had been born and had roused him to violent jealousy. {This dry comment is the only direct reflection of Sophie's death in the whole essay.}

have been able to repeat his unpleasant experience in play because the repetition carried along with it a yield of pleasure of another sort but none the less a direct one.

Nor shall we be helped in our hesitation between these two views by further considering children's play. It is clear that in their play children repeat everything that has made a great impression on them in real life, and that in doing so they abreact the strength of the impression and, as one might put it, make themselves master of the situation. But on the other hand it is obvious that all their play is influenced by a wish that dominates them the whole time—the wish to be grown-up and to be able to do what grown-up people do. It can also be observed that the unpleasurable nature of an experience does not always unsuit it for play. If the doctor looks down a child's throat or carries out some small operation on him, we may be quite sure that these frightening experiences will be the subject of the next game; but we must not in that connection overlook the fact that there is a yield of pleasure from another source. As the child passes over from the passivity of the experience to the activity of the game, he hands on the disagreeable experience to one of his playmates and in this way revenges himself on a substitute.

Nevertheless, it emerges from this discussion that there is no need to assume the existence of a special imitative instinct in order to provide a motive for play. Finally, a reminder may be added that the artistic play and artistic imitation carried out by adults, which, unlike children's, are aimed at an audience, do not spare the spectators (for instance, in tragedy) the most painful experiences and can yet be felt by them as highly enjoyable. This is convincing proof that, even under the dominance of the pleasure principle, there are ways and means enough of making what is in itself unpleasurable into a subject to be recollected and worked over in the mind. The consideration of these cases and situations, which have a yield of pleasure as their final outcome, should be undertaken by some system of aesthetics with an economic approach to its subject-matter. They are of no use for *our* purposes, since they presuppose the existence and dominance of the pleasure principle; they give no evidence of the operation of tendencies *beyond* the pleasure principle, that is, of tendencies more primitive than it and independent of it.

III

Twenty-five years of intense work have had as their result that the immediate aims of psycho-analytic technique are quite other to-day than they were at the outset. At first the analysing physician could do no more than discover the unconscious material that was concealed from the patient, put it together, and, at the right moment, communicate it to him. Psycho-analysis was then first and foremost an art of interpreting. Since this did not solve the therapeutic problem, a further aim quickly came in view: to oblige the patient to confirm the analyst's construction from his own memory. In that endeavour the chief emphasis lay upon the patient's resistances: the art consisted now in uncovering these as quickly as possible, in pointing them out to the patient and in inducing him by human influence—this was where suggestion operating as 'transference' played its part—to abandon his resistances.

But it became ever clearer that the aim which had been set up—the aim that what was unconscious should become conscious—is not completely attainable by that method. The patient cannot remember the whole of what is repressed in him, and what he cannot remember may be precisely the essential part of it. Thus he acquires no sense of conviction of the correctness of the construction that has been communicated to him. He is obliged to *repeat* the repressed material as a contemporary experience instead of, as the physician would prefer to see, *remembering* it as something belonging to the past. These reproductions, which emerge with such unwished-for exactitude, always have as their subject some portion of infantile sexual life—of the Oedipus complex, that is, and its derivatives; and they are invariably acted out in the sphere of the transference, of the patient's relation to the physician. When things have reached this stage, it may be said that the earlier neurosis has now been replaced by a fresh, 'transference neurosis'. It has been the physician's endeavour to keep this transference neurosis within the narrowest limits: to force as much as possible into the channel of memory and to allow as little as possible to emerge as repetition. The ratio between what is remembered and what is reproduced varies from case to case. The physician cannot as a rule spare his patient this phase of the treatment. He must get him to re-experience some portion of his forgotten life, but must see to it, on the other hand, that the patient retains some degree of aloofness, which will enable him, in spite of everything, to recognize that what appears to be reality is in fact only a reflection of a forgotten past. If this can be successfully achieved, the patient's sense of conviction is won, together with the therapeutic success that is dependent on it.

In order to make it easier to understand this 'compulsion to repeat', which emerges during the psycho-analytic treatment of neurotics, we must above all get rid of the mistaken notion that what we are dealing with in our struggle against resistances is resistance on the part of the *unconscious*. The unconscious—that is to say, the 'repressed'—offers no resistance whatever to the efforts of the treatment. Indeed, it itself has no other endeavour than to break through the pressure weighing down on it and force its way either to consciousness or to a discharge through some real action. Resistance during treatment arises from the same higher strata and systems of the mind which originally carried out repression. But the fact that, as we know from experience, the motives of the resistances, and indeed the resistances themselves, are unconscious at first during the treatment, is a hint to us that we should correct a shortcoming in our terminology. We shall avoid a lack of clarity if we make our contrast not between the conscious and the unconscious but between the coherent *ego* and the *repressed*. It is certain that much of the ego is itself unconscious, and notably what we may describe as its nucleus; only a small part of it is covered by the term 'preconscious'. Having replaced a purely descriptive terminology by one which is systematic or dynamic, we can say that the patient's resistance arises from his ego, and we then at once perceive that the compulsion to repeat must be ascribed to the unconscious repressed. It seems probable that the compulsion can only express itself after the work of treatment has gone half-way to meet it and has loosened the repression.

There is no doubt that the resistance of the conscious and unconscious ego operates under the sway of the pleasure principle: it seeks to avoid the unpleasure which would be produced by the liberation of the repressed. Our efforts, on the other hand, are directed towards procuring the toleration of that unpleasure by an appeal to the reality principle. But how is the compulsion to repeat—the manifestation of the power of the repressed—related to the pleasure principle? It is clear that the greater part of what is re-experienced under the compulsion to repeat must cause the ego unpleasure, since it brings to light activities of repressed instinctual impulses. That, however, is unpleasure of a kind we have already considered and does not contradict the pleasure principle: unpleasure for one system and simultaneously satisfaction for the other. But we come now to a new and remarkable fact, namely that the compulsion to repeat also recalls from the past experiences which include no possibility of pleasure, and which can never, even long ago, have brought satisfaction even to instinctual impulses which have since been repressed.

The early efflorescence of infantile sexual life is doomed to extinction because its wishes are incompatible with reality and with the inadequate stage of development which the child has reached. That efflorescence comes to an end in the most distressing circumstances and to the accompaniment of the most painful feelings. Loss of love and failure leave behind them a permanent injury to self-regard in the form of a narcissistic scar, which in my opinion * * * contributes more than anything to the 'sense of inferiority' which is so common in neurotics. The child's sexual researches, on which limits are imposed by his physical development, lead to no satisfactory conclusion; hence such later complaints as 'I can't accomplish anything; I can't succeed in anything'. The tie of affection, which binds the child as a rule to the parent of the opposite sex, succumbs to disappointment, to a vain expectation of satisfaction or to jealousy over the birth of a new baby—unmistakable proof of the infidelity of the object of the child's affections. His own attempt to make a baby himself, carried out with tragic seriousness, fails shamefully. The lessening amount of affection he receives, the increasing demands of education, hard words and an occasional punishment—these show him at last the full extent to which he has been scorned. These are a few typical and constantly recurring instances of the ways in which the love characteristic of the age of childhood is brought to a conclusion.

Patients repeat all of these unwanted situations and painful emotions in the transference and revive them with the greatest ingenuity. They seek to bring about the interruption of the treatment while it is still incomplete; they contrive once more to feel themselves scorned, to oblige the physician to speak severely to them and treat them coldly; they discover appropriate objects for their jealousy; instead of the passionately desired baby of their childhood, they produce a plan or a promise of some grand present—which turns out as a rule to be no less unreal. None of these things can have produced pleasure in the past, and it might be supposed that they would cause less unpleasure to-day if they emerged as memories or dreams instead of taking the form of fresh experiences. They are of course the activities of instincts intended to lead to satisfaction; but no lesson has been learnt from the old experience of these activities having led instead only to unpleasure. In spite of that, they are repeated, under pressure of a compulsion.

What psycho-analysis reveals in the transference phenomena of neurotics can also be observed in the lives of some normal people. The impression they give is of being pursued by a malignant fate or possessed by some 'daemonic' power; but psycho-analysis has always taken the view that their fate is for the most part arranged by themselves and determined by early infantile influences. The compulsion which is here in evidence differs in no way from the compulsion to repeat which we have found in neurotics, even though the people we are now considering have never shown any signs of dealing with a neurotic conflict by producing symptoms. Thus we have come across people all of whose human relationships have the same outcome: such as the benefactor who is abandoned in anger after a time by each of his protégés, however much they may otherwise differ from one another, and who thus seems doomed to taste all the bitterness of ingratitude; or the man whose friendships all end in betrayal by his friend; or the man who time after time in the course of his life raises someone else into a position of great private or public authority and then, after a certain interval, himself upsets that authority and replaces him by a new one; or, again, the lover each of whose love affairs with a woman passes through the same phases and reaches the same conclusion. This 'perpetual recurrence of the same thing' causes us no astonishment when it relates to *active* behaviour on the part of the person concerned and when we can discern in him an essential character-trait which always remains the same and which is compelled to find expression in a repetition of the same experiences. We are much more impressed by cases where the subject appears to have a *passive* experience, over which he has no influence, but in which he meets with a repetition of the same fatality. There is the case, for instance, of the woman who married three successive husbands each of whom fell ill soon afterwards and had to be nursed by her on their death-beds.[4] The most moving poetic picture of a fate such as this is given by Tasso in his romantic epic *Gerusalemme Liberata*. Its hero, Tancred, unwittingly kills his beloved Clorinda in a duel while she is disguised in the armour of an enemy knight. After her burial he makes his way into a strange magic forest which strikes the Crusaders' army with terror. He slashes with his sword at a tall tree; but blood streams from the cut and the voice of Clorinda, whose soul is imprisoned in the tree, is heard complaining that he has wounded his beloved once again.

If we take into account observations such as these, based upon behaviour in the transference and upon the life-histories of men and women, we shall find courage to assume that there really does exist in the mind a compulsion to repeat which overrides the pleasure principle. Now too we shall be inclined to relate to this compulsion the dreams which occur in traumatic neuroses and the impulse which leads children to play.

But it is to be noted that only in rare instances can we observe the pure effects of the compulsion to repeat, unsupported by other motives. In the case of children's play we have already laid stress on the other ways in which the emergence of the compulsion may be interpreted; the compulsion to repeat and instinctual satisfaction which is immediately pleasurable seem to converge here into an intimate partnership. The phenomena of transference are obviously exploited by the resistance which the ego maintains in its pertinacious insistence upon repression; the compulsion to repeat, which the treatment tries to bring into its service is, as it were, drawn over by the ego to *its* side (clinging as the ego does to the pleasure principle). A great deal of what might be described as the compulsion of destiny seems intelligible on a rational basis; so that we are under no necessity to call in a new and mysterious motive force to explain it.

The least dubious instance [of such a motive force] is perhaps that of traumatic dreams. But on maturer reflection we shall be forced to admit that even in the other instances the whole ground is not covered by the operation of the familiar motive forces. Enough is left unexplained to justify the hypothesis of a compulsion to repeat—something that seems more primitive, more elementary, more instinctual than the pleasure principle which it over-rides. But if a compulsion to repeat *does* operate in the mind, we should be glad to know something about it, to learn what function it corresponds to, under what conditions it can emerge and what its relation is to the pleasure principle—to which, after all, we have hitherto ascribed dominance over the course of the processes of excitation in mental life.

4. Cf. the apt remark on this subject by C. G. Jung {"The Significance of the Father in the Destiny of the Individual"} (1909) {tr. 1916. This is a virtually unique acknowledgment on Freud's part of Jung's merits—displayed during Jung's "psychoanalytic period"—after his break with Jung}.

IV

What follows is speculation, often far-fetched speculation, which the reader will consider or dismiss according to his individual predilection. It is further an attempt to follow out an idea consistently, out of curiosity to see where it will lead.

Psycho-analytic speculation takes as its point of departure the impression, derived from examining unconscious processes, that consciousness may be, not the most universal attribute of mental processes, but only a particular function of them. Speaking in metapsychological terms, it asserts that consciousness is a function of a particular system which it describes as *Cs*. What consciousness yields consists essentially of perceptions of excitations coming from the external world and of feelings of pleasure and unpleasure which can only arise from within the mental apparatus; it is therefore possible to assign to the system *Pcpt.-Cs.* a position in space. It must lie on the borderline between outside and inside; it must be turned towards the external world and must envelop the other psychical systems. It will be seen that there is nothing daringly new in these assumptions; we have merely adopted the views on localization held by cerebral anatomy, which locates the 'seat' of consciousness in the cerebral cortex—the outermost, enveloping layer of the central organ. Cerebral anatomy has no need to consider why, speaking anatomically, consciousness should be lodged on the surface of the brain instead of being safely housed somewhere in its inmost interior. Perhaps *we* shall be more successful in accounting for this situation in the case of our system *Pcpt.-Cs.*

Consciousness is not the only distinctive character which we ascribe to the processes in that system. On the basis of impressions derived from our psycho-analytic experience, we assume that all excitatory processes that occur in the *other* systems leave permanent traces behind in them which form the foundation of memory. Such memory-traces, then, have nothing to do with the fact of becoming conscious; indeed they are often most powerful and most enduring when the process which left them behind was one which never entered consciousness. We find it hard to believe, however, that permanent traces of excitation such as these are also left in the system *Pcpt.-Cs.* If they remained constantly conscious, they would very soon set limits to the system's aptitude for receiving fresh excitations. If, on the other hand, they were unconscious, we should be faced with the problem of explaining the existence of unconscious processes in a system whose functioning was otherwise accompanied by the phenomenon of consciousness. We should, so to say, have altered nothing and gained nothing by our hypothesis relegating the process of becoming conscious to a special system. Though this consideration is not absolutely conclusive, it nevertheless leads us to suspect that becoming conscious and leaving behind a memory-trace are processes incompatible with each other within one and the same system. Thus we should be able to say that the excitatory process becomes conscious in the system *Cs.* but leaves no permanent trace behind there; but that the excitation is transmitted to the systems lying next within and that it is in *them* that its traces are left. * * * It must be borne in mind that little enough is known from other sources of the origin of consciousness; when, therefore, we lay down the proposition that *consciousness arises instead of a memory-trace*, the assertion deserves consideration, at all events on the ground of its being framed in fairly precise terms.

If this is so, then, the system *Cs.* is characterized by the peculiarity that in it (in contrast to what happens in the other psychical systems) excitatory processes do not leave behind any permanent change in its elements but expire, as it were, in the phenomenon of becoming conscious. An exception of this sort to the general rule requires to be explained by some factor that applies exclusively to that one system. Such a factor, which is absent in the other systems, might well be the exposed situation of the system *Cs.*, immediately abutting as it does on the external world.

* * *

* * * We describe as 'traumatic' any excitations from outside which are powerful enough to break through the protective shield. It seems to me that the concept of trauma necessarily implies a connection of this kind with a breach in an otherwise efficacious barrier against stimuli. Such an event as an external trauma is bound to provoke a disturbance on a large scale in the functioning of the organism's energy and to set in motion every possible defensive measure. At the same time, the pleasure principle is for the moment put out of action. There is no longer any possibility of preventing the mental apparatus from being flooded with large amounts of stimulus, and another problem arises instead—the problem of mastering the amounts of stimulus which have broken in and of binding them, in the psychical sense, so that they can then be disposed of.

The specific unpleasure of physical pain is probably the result of the protective shield having been broken through in a limited area. There is then a continuous stream of excitations from the part of the periphery concerned to the central apparatus of the mind, such as could normally arise only from *within* the apparatus. And how shall we expect the mind to react to this invasion? Cathectic energy is summoned from all sides to provide sufficiently high cathexes of energy in the environs of the breach. An 'anticathexis' on a grand scale is set up, for whose benefit all the other psychical systems are impoverished, so that the remaining psychical functions are extensively paralysed or reduced. We must endeavour to draw a lesson from examples such as this and use them as a basis for our metapsychological speculations. From the present case, then, we infer that a system which is itself highly cathected is capable of taking up an additional stream of fresh inflowing energy and of converting it into quiescent cathexis, that is of binding it psychically. The higher the system's own quiescent cathexis, the greater seems to be its binding force; conversely, therefore, the lower its cathexis, the less capacity will it have for taking up inflowing energy and the more violent must be the consequences of such a breach in the protective shield against stimuli. To this view it cannot be justly objected that the increase of cathexis round the breach can be explained far more simply as the direct result of the inflowing masses of excitation. If that were so, the mental apparatus would merely receive an increase in its cathexes of energy, and the paralysing character of pain and the impoverishment of all the other systems would remain unexplained. Nor do the very violent phenomena of discharge to which pain gives rise affect our explanation, for they occur in a reflex manner—that is, they follow without the intervention of the mental apparatus. The indefiniteness of all our discussions on what we describe as metapsychology is of course due to the fact that we know nothing of the nature of the excitatory process that takes place in the elements of the psychical systems, and that we do not feel justified in framing any hypothesis on the subject. We are consequently operating all the time with a large unknown factor, which we are obliged to carry over into every new formula. It may be reasonably supposed that this excitatory process can be carried out with energies that vary *quantitatively*; it may also seem probable that it has more than one *quality* (in the nature of amplitude, for instance). As a new factor we have taken into consideration Breuer's hypothesis that charges of energy occur in two forms; so that we have to distinguish between two kinds of cathexis of the psychical systems or their elements—a freely flowing cathexis that presses on towards discharge and a quiescent cathexis. We may perhaps suspect that the binding of the energy that streams into the mental apparatus consists in its change from a freely flowing into a quiescent state.

We may, I think, tentatively venture to regard the common traumatic neurosis as a consequence of an extensive breach being made in the protective shield against stimuli. This would seem to reinstate the old, naive theory of shock, in apparent contrast to the later and psychologically more ambitious theory which attributes aetiological importance not to the effects of mechanical violence but to fright and the threat to life. These opposing views are not, however, irreconcilable; nor is the psycho-analytic view of the traumatic neurosis identical with the shock theory in its crudest form. The latter regards the essence of the shock as being the direct damage to the molecular structure or even to the histological structure of the elements of the nervous system; whereas what *we* seek to understand are the effects produced on the organ of the mind by the breach in the shield against stimuli and by the problems that follow in its train. And we still attribute importance to the element of fright. It is caused by lack of any preparedness for anxiety, including lack of hypercathexis of the systems that would be the first to receive the stimulus. Owing to their low cathexis those systems are not in a good position for binding the inflowing amounts of excitation and the consequences of the breach in the protective shield follow all the more easily. It will be seen, then, that preparedness for anxiety and the hypercathexis of the receptive systems constitute the last line of defence of the shield against stimuli. In the case of quite a number of traumas, the difference between systems that are unprepared and systems that are well prepared through being hypercathected may be a decisive factor in determining the outcome; though where the strength of a trauma exceeds a certain limit this factor will no doubt cease to carry weight. The fulfilment of wishes is, as we know, brought about in a hallucinatory manner by dreams, and under the dominance of the pleasure principle this has become their function. But it is not in the service of that principle that the dreams of patients suffering from traumatic neuroses lead them back with such regularity to the situation in which the trauma occurred. We may assume, rather, that dreams are here helping to carry out another task, which must be accomplished before the dominance of the pleasure principle can even begin. These dreams are endeavouring to master the stimulus retrospectively, by developing the anxiety whose omission was the cause of the traumatic neurosis. They thus afford us a view of a function of the mental apparatus which, though it does not contradict the pleasure principle, is nevertheless independent of it and seems to be more primitive than the purpose of gaining pleasure and avoiding unpleasure.

This would seem to be the place, then, at which to admit for the first time an exception to the proposition that dreams are fulfilments of wishes. Anxiety dreams, as I have shown repeatedly and in detail, offer no such exception. Nor do 'punishment dreams', for they merely replace the forbidden wish-fulfilment by the appropriate punishment for it; that is to say, they fulfil the wish of the sense of guilt which is the reaction to the repudiated impulse. But it is impossible to classify as wish-fulfilments the dreams we have been discussing which occur in traumatic neuroses, or the dreams during psycho-analyses which bring to memory the psychical traumas of childhood. They arise, rather, in obedience to the compulsion to repeat, though it is true that in analysis that compulsion is supported by the wish (which is encouraged by 'suggestion') to conjure up what has been forgotten and repressed. Thus it would seem that the function of dreams, which consists in setting aside any motives that might interrupt sleep, by fulfilling the wishes of the disturbing impulses, is not their *original* function. It would not be possible for them to perform that function until the whole of mental life had accepted the dominance of the pleasure principle. If there is a 'beyond the pleasure principle', it is only consistent to grant that there was also a time before the purpose of dreams was the fulfilment of wishes. This would imply no denial of their later function. But if once this general rule has been broken, a further question arises. May not dreams which, with a view to the psychical binding of traumatic impressions, obey the compulsion to repeat—may not such dreams occur *outside* analysis as well? And the reply can only be a decided affirmative.

'War neuroses' (in so far as that term implies something more than a reference to the circumstances of the illness's onset) may very well be traumatic neuroses which have been facilitated by a conflict in the ego. A gross physical injury caused simultaneously by the trauma diminishes the chances that a neurosis will develop, becomes intelligible if one bears in mind two facts which have been stressed by psycho-analytic research: firstly, that mechanical agitation must be recognized as one of the sources of sexual excitation, and secondly, that painful and feverish illnesses exercise a powerful effect, so long as they last, on the distribution of libido. Thus, on the one hand, the mechanical violence of the trauma would liberate a quantity of sexual excitation which, owing to the lack of preparation for anxiety, would have a traumatic effect; but, on the other hand, the simultaneous physical injury, by calling for a narcissistic hypercathexis of the injured organ, would bind the excess of excitation. It is also well known, though the libido theory has not yet made sufficient use of the fact, that such severe disorders in the distribution of libido as melancholia are temporarily brought to an end by intercurrent organic illness, and indeed that even a fully developed condition of dementia praecox is capable of a temporary remission in these same circumstances.

V

The fact that the cortical layer which receives stimuli is without any protective shield against excitations from within must have as its result that these latter transmissions of stimulus have a preponderance in economic importance and often occasion economic disturbances comparable with traumatic neuroses. The most abundant sources of this internal excitation are what are described as the organism's 'instincts'— the representatives of all the forces originating in the interior of the body and transmitted to the mental apparatus—at once the most important and the most obscure element of psychological research.

It will perhaps not be thought too rash to suppose that the impulses arising from the instincts do not belong to the type of *bound* nervous processes but of *freely mobile* processes which press towards discharge. The best part of what we know of these processes is derived from our study of the dream-work. We there discovered that the processes in the unconscious systems were fundamentally different from those in the preconscious (or conscious) systems. In the unconscious, cathexes can easily be completely transferred, displaced and condensed. Such treatment, however, could produce only invalid results if it were applied to preconscious material; and this accounts for the familiar peculiarities exhibited by manifest dreams after the preconscious residues of the preceding day have been worked over in accordance with the laws operating in the unconscious. I described the type of process found in the unconscious as the 'primary' psychical process, in contradistinction to the 'secondary' process which is the one obtaining in our normal waking life. Since all instinctual impulses have the unconscious systems as their point of impact, it is hardly an innovation to say that they obey the primary process. Again, it is easy to identify the primary psychical process with Breuer's freely mobile cathexis and the secondary process with changes in his bound or tonic cathexis. If so, it would be the task of the higher strata of the mental apparatus to bind the instinctual excitation reaching the primary process. A failure to effect this binding would provoke a disturbance analogous to a traumatic neurosis; and only after the binding has been accomplished would it be possible for the dominance of the pleasure principle (and of its modification, the reality principle) to proceed unhindered. Till then the other task of the mental apparatus, the task of mastering or binding excitations, would have precedence—not, indeed, in *opposition* to the pleasure principle, but independently of it and to some extent in disregard of it.

The manifestations of a compulsion to repeat (which we have described as occurring in the early activities of infantile mental life as well as among the events of psycho-analytic treatment) exhibit to a high degree an instinctual[5] character and, when they act in opposition to the pleasure principle, give the appearance of some 'daemonic' force at work. In the case of children's play we seemed to see that children repeat unpleasurable experiences for the additional reason that they can master a powerful impression far more thoroughly by being active than they could by merely experiencing it passively. Each fresh repetition seems to strengthen the mastery they are in search of. Nor can children have their *pleasurable* experiences repeated often enough, and they are inexorable in their insistence that the repetition shall be an identical one. This character trait disappears later on. If a joke is heard for a second time it produces almost no effect; a theatrical production never creates so great an impression the second time as the first; indeed, it is hardly possible to persuade an adult who has very much enjoyed reading a book to re-read it immediately. Novelty is always the condition of enjoyment. But children will never tire of asking an adult to repeat a game that he has shown them or played with them, till he is too exhausted to go on. And if a child has been told a nice story, he will insist on hearing it over and over again rather than a new one; and he will remorselessly stipulate that the repetition shall be an identical one and will correct any alterations of which the narrator may be guilty—though they may actually have been made in the hope of gaining fresh approval. None of this contradicts the pleasure principle; repetition, the re-experiencing of something identical, is clearly in itself a source of pleasure. In the

5. ['*Triebhaft*' here and at the beginning of the next paragraph. The word '*Trieb*' bears much more of a feeling of urgency than the English 'instinct.'] {True, the word conveys a sense of being "driven."}

case of a person in analysis, on the contrary, the compulsion to repeat the events of his childhood in the transference evidently disregards the pleasure principle in every way. The patient behaves in a purely infantile fashion and thus shows us that the repressed memory-traces of his primaeval experiences are not present in him in a bound state and are indeed in a sense incapable of obeying the secondary process. It is to this fact of not being bound, moreover, that they owe their capacity for forming, in conjunction with the residues of the previous day, a wishful phantasy that emerges in a dream. This same compulsion to repeat frequently meets us as an obstacle to our treatment when at the end of an analysis we try to induce the patient to detach himself completely from his physician. It may be presumed, too, that when people unfamiliar with analysis feel an obscure fear—a dread of rousing something that, so they feel, is better left sleeping—what they are afraid of at bottom is the emergence of this compulsion with its hint of possession by some 'daemonic' power.

But how is the predicate of being 'instinctual' related to the compulsion to repeat? At this point we cannot escape a suspicion that we may have come upon the track of a universal attribute of instincts and perhaps of organic life in general which has not hitherto been clearly recognized or at least not explicitly stressed. *It seems, then, that an instinct is an urge inherent in organic life to restore an earlier state of things* which the living entity has been obliged to abandon under the pressure of external disturbing forces; that is, it is a kind of organic elasticity, or, to put it another way, the expression of the inertia inherent in organic life.

This view of instincts strikes us as strange because we have become used to see in them a factor impelling towards change and development, whereas we are now asked to recognize in them the precise contrary— an expression of the *conservative* nature of living substance. On the other hand we soon call to mind examples from animal life which seem to confirm the view that instincts are historically determined. * * *

We shall be met by the plausible objection that it may very well be that, in addition to the conservative instincts which impel towards repetition, there may be others which push forward towards progress and the production of new forms. This argument must certainly not be overlooked, and it will be taken into account at a later stage. But for the moment it is tempting to pursue to its logical conclusion the hypothesis that all instincts tend towards the restoration of an earlier state of things. The outcome may give an impression of mysticism or of sham profundity; but we can feel quite innocent of having had any such purpose in view. We seek only for the sober results of research or of reflection based on it; and we have no wish to find in those results any quality other than certainty.[6]

Let us suppose, then, that all the organic instincts are conservative,

6. [*Footnote added* 1925:] The reader should not overlook the fact that what follows is the development of an extreme line of thought. * * *

are acquired historically and tend towards the restoration of an earlier state of things. It follows that the phenomena of organic development must be attributed to external disturbing and diverting influences. The elementary living entity would from its very beginning have had no wish to change; if conditions remained the same, it would do no more than constantly repeat the same course of life. In the last resort, what has left its mark on development of organisms must be the history of the earth we live in and of its relation to the sun. Every modification which is thus imposed upon the course of the organism's life is accepted by the conservative organic instincts and stored up for further repetition. Those instincts are therefore bound to give a deceptive appearance of being forces tending towards change and progress, whilst in fact they are merely seeking to reach an ancient goal by paths alike old and new. Moreover it is possible to specify this final goal of all organic striving. It would be in contradiction to the conservative nature of the instincts if the goal of life were a state of things which had never yet been attained. On the contrary, it must be an *old* state of things, an initial state from which the living entity has at one time or other departed and to which it is striving to return by the circuitous paths along which its development leads. If we are to take it as a truth that knows no exception that everything living dies for *internal* reasons—becomes inorganic once again—then we shall be compelled to say that '*the aim of all life is death*' and, looking backwards, that '*inanimate things existed before living ones*'.

The attributes of life were at some time evoked in inanimate matter by the action of a force of whose nature we can form no conception. It may perhaps have been a process similar in type to that which later caused the development of consciousness in a particular stratum of living matter. The tension which then arose in what had hitherto been an inanimate substance endeavoured to cancel itself out. In this way the first instinct came into being: the instinct to return to the inanimate state. It was still an easy matter at that time for a living substance to die; the course of its life was probably only a brief one, whose direction was determined by the chemical structure of the young life. For a long time, perhaps, living substance was thus being constantly created afresh and easily dying, till decisive external influences altered in such a way as to oblige the still surviving substance to diverge ever more widely from its original course of life and to make ever more complicated *détours* before reaching its aim of death. These circuitous paths to death, faithfully kept to by the conservative instincts, would thus present us to-day with the picture of the phenomena of life. It we firmly maintain the exclusively conservative nature of instincts, we cannot arrive at any other notions as to the origin and aim of life.

The implications in regard to the great groups of instincts which, as we believe, lie behind the phenomena of life in organisms must appear no less bewildering. The hypothesis of self-preservative instincts, such as we attribute to all living beings, stands in marked opposition to the idea that instinctual life as a whole serves to bring about death. Seen in this light, the theoretical importance of the instincts of self-preservation, of self-assertion and of mastery greatly diminishes. They are component instincts whose function it is to assure that the organism shall follow its own path to death, and to ward off any possible ways of returning to inorganic existence other than those which are immanent in the organism itself. We have no longer to reckon with the organism's puzzling determination (so hard to fit into any context) to maintain its own existence in the face of every obstacle. What we are left with is the fact that the organism wishes to die only in its own fashion. Thus these guardians of life, too, were originally the myrmidons of death. Hence arises the paradoxical situation that the living organism struggles most energetically against events (dangers, in fact) which might help it to attain its life's aim rapidly—by a kind of short-circuit. Such behaviour is, however, precisely what characterizes purely instinctual as contrasted with intelligent efforts.

But let us pause for a moment and reflect. It cannot be so. The sexual instincts, to which the theory of the neuroses gives a quite special place, appear under a very different aspect.

* * * The whole path of development to natural death is not trodden by *all* the elementary entities which compose the complicated body of one of the higher organisms. Some of them, the germ-cells, probably retain the original structure of living matter and, after a certain time, with their full complement of inherited and freshly acquired instinctual dispositions, separate themselves from the organism as a whole. These two characteristics may be precisely what enables them to have an independent existence. Under favourable conditions, they begin to develop—that is, to repeat the performance to which they owe their existence; and in the end once again one portion of their substance pursues its development to a finish, while another portion harks back once again as a fresh residual germ to the beginning of the process of development. These germ-cells, therefore, work against the death of the living substance and succeed in winning for it what we can only regard as potential immortality, though that may mean no more than a lengthening of the road to death. We must regard as in the highest degree significant the fact that this function of the germ-cell is reinforced, or only made possible, if it coalesces with another cell similar to itself and yet differing from it.

The instincts which watch over the destinies of these elementary organisms that survive the whole individual, which provide them with a safe shelter while they are defenceless against the stimuli of the external world, which bring about their meeting with other germ-cells, and so on—these constitute the group of the sexual instincts. They are conservative in the same sense as the other instincts in that they bring back earlier states of living substance; but they are conservative to a higher degree in that they are peculiarly resistant to external influences; and they are conservative too in another sense in that they preserve life itself for a comparatively long period. They are the true life instincts. They operate against the purpose of the other instincts, which leads, by reason of their function, to death; and this fact indicates that there is an opposition between them and the other instincts, an opposition whose importance was long ago recognized by the theory of the neuroses. It is as though the life of the organism moved with a vacillating rhythm. One group of instincts rushes forward so as to reach the final aim of life as swiftly as possible; but when a particular stage in the advance has been reached, the other group jerks back to a certain point to make a fresh start and so prolong the journey. And even though it is certain that sexuality and the distinction between the sexes did not exist when life began, the possibility remains that the instincts which were later to be described as sexual may have been in operation from the very first, and it may not be true that it was only at a later time that they started upon their work of opposing the activities of the 'ego-instincts'.[7]

Let us now hark back for a moment ourselves and consider whether there is any basis at all for these speculations. Is it really the case that, *apart from the sexual instincts*, there are no instincts that do not seek to restore an earlier state of things? that there are none that aim at a state of things which has never yet been attained? I know of no certain example from the organic world that would contradict the characterization I have thus proposed. There is unquestionably no universal instinct towards higher development observable in the animal or plant world, even though it is undeniable that development does in fact occur in that direction. But on the one hand it is often merely a matter of opinion when we declare that one stage of development is higher than another, and on the other hand biology teaches us that higher development in one respect is very frequently balanced or outweighed by involution in another. Moreover there are plenty of animal forms from whose early stages we can infer that their development has, on the contrary, assumed a retrograde character. Both higher developments and involution might well be the consequences of adaptation to the pressure of external forces; and in both cases the part played by instincts might be limited to the retention (in the form of an internal source of pleasure) of an obligatory modification.

It may be difficult, too, for many of us, to abandon the belief that there is an instinct towards perfection at work in human beings, which has brought them to their present high level of intellectual achievement and ethical sublimation and which may be expected to watch over their development into supermen. I have no faith, however, in the existence of any such internal instinct and I cannot see how this benevolent illusion is to be preserved. The present development of human beings requires, as it seems to me, no different explanation from that of animals. What

7. [*Footnote added* 1925:] It should be understood from the context that the term 'ego-instincts' is used here as a provisional description and derives from the earliest psycho-analytical terminology.

appears in a minority of human individuals as an untiring impulsion towards further perfection can easily be understood as a result of the instinctual repression upon which is based all that is most precious in human civilization. The repressed instinct never ceases to strive for complete satisfaction, which would consist in the repetition of a primary experience of satisfaction. No substitutive or reactive formations and no sublimations will suffice to remove the repressed instinct's persisting tension; and it is the difference in amount between the pleasure of satisfaction which is *demanded* and that which is actually *achieved* that provides the driving factor which will permit of no halting at any position attained, but, in the poet's words, *'ungebändigt immer vorwärts dringt'*.[8] The backward path that leads to complete satisfaction is as a rule obstructed by the resistances which maintain the repressions. So there is no alternative but to advance in the direction in which growth is still free—though with no prospect of bringing the process to a conclusion or of being able to reach the goal. The processes involved in the formation of a neurotic phobia, which is nothing else than an attempt at flight from the satisfaction of an instinct, present us with a model of the manner of origin of this supposititious 'instinct towards perfection'—an instinct which cannot possibly be attributed to *every* human being. The *dynamic* conditions for its development are, indeed, universally present; but it is only in rare cases that the *economic* situation appears to favour the production of the phenomenon.

I will add only a word to suggest that the efforts of Eros to combine organic substances into ever larger unities probably provide a substitute for this 'instinct towards perfection' whose existence we cannot admit. The phenomena that are attributed to it seem capable of explanation by these efforts of Eros taken in conjunction with the results of repression.

* * *

Let us turn back * * * to one of the assumptions that we have already made, with the expectation that we shall be able to give it a categorical denial. We have drawn far-reaching conclusions from the hypothesis that all living substance is bound to die from internal causes. We made this assumption thus carelessly because it does not seem to us to *be* an assumption. We are accustomed to think that such is the fact, and we are strengthened in our thought by the writings of our poets. Perhaps we have adopted the belief because there is some comfort in it. If we are to die ourselves, and first to lose in death those who are dearest to us, it is easier to submit to a remorseless law of nature, to the sublime 'Aνάγκη [Necessity], than to a chance which might perhaps have been escaped. It may be, however, that this belief in the internal necessity of dying is only another of those illusions which we have created *'um die*

8. ['Presses ever forward unsubdued.'] Mephistopheles in *Faust*, Part I [Scene 4].

Schwere des Daseins zu ertragen'.[9] It is certainly not a primaeval belief. The notion of 'natural death' is quite foreign to primitive races; they attribute every death that occurs among them to the influence of an enemy or of an evil spirit. We must therefore turn to biology in order to test the validity of the belief.

If we do so, we may be astonished to find how little agreement there is among biologists on the subject of natural death and in fact that the whole concept of death melts away under their hands. The fact that there is a fixed average duration of life at least among the higher animals naturally argues in favour of there being such a thing as death from natural causes. But this impression is countered when we consider that certain large animals and certain gigantic arboreal growths reach a very advanced age and one which cannot at present be computed. According to the large conception of Wilhelm Fliess, all the phenomena of life exhibited by organism—and also, no doubt, their death—are linked with the completion of fixed periods, which express the dependence of two kinds of living substance (one male and the other female) upon the solar year. When we see, however, how easily and how extensively the in-fluence of external forces is able to modify the date of the appearance of vital phenomena (especially in the plant world)—to precipitate them or hold them back—doubts must be cast upon the rigidity of Fliess's formulas or at least upon whether the laws laid down by him are the sole determining factors.

The greatest interest attaches from our point of view to the treatment given to the subject of the duration of life and the death of organisms in the writings of Weismann (1882, 1884, 1892, etc.). It was he who introduced the division of living substance into mortal and immortal parts. The mortal part is the body in the narrower sense—the 'soma'—which alone is subject to natural death. The germ-cells, on the other hand, are potentially immortal, in so far as they are able, under certain favourable conditions, to develop into a new individual, or, in other words, to surround themselves with a new soma. (August Weismann, *Die Dauer des Lebens*, 1884.)

* * *

It will be seen at once that to concede in this way that higher organisms have a natural death is of very little help to us. For if death is a *late* acquisition of organisms, then there can be no question of there having been death instincts from the very beginning of life on this earth. Mul-ticellular organisms may die for internal reasons, owing to defective differentiation or to imperfections in their metabolism, but the matter is of no interest from the point of view of our problem. An account of the origin of death such as this is moreover far less at variance with our

9. ['To bear the burden of existence.' Schiller, *Die Braut von Messina*, I, 8.]

habitual modes of thought than the strange assumption of 'death instincts'.

* * *

Our expectation that biology would flatly contradict the recognition of death instincts has not been fulfilled. We are at liberty to continue concerning ourselves with their possibility, if we have other reasons for doing so. The striking similarity between Weismann's distinction of soma and germ-plasm and our separation of the death instincts from the life instincts persists and retains its significance.

We may pause for a moment over this pre-eminently dualistic view of instinctual life. According to E. Hering's theory, two kinds of processes are constantly at work in living substance, operating in contrary directions, one constructive or assimilatory and the other destructive or dissimilatory. May we venture to recognize in these two directions taken by the vital processes the activity of our two instinctual impulses, the life instincts and the death instincts? There is something else, at any rate, that we cannot remain blind to. We have unwittingly steered our course into the harbour of Schopenhauer's philosophy. For him death is the 'true result and to that extent the purpose of life',[1] while the sexual instinct is the embodiment of the will to live.

Let us make a bold attempt at another step forward. It is generally considered that the union of a number of cells into a vital association—the multicellular character of organisms—has become a means of prolonging their life. One cell helps to preserve the life of another, and the community of cells can survive even if individual cells have to die. We have already heard that conjugation, too, the temporary coalescence of two unicellular organisms, has a life-preserving and rejuvenating effect on both of them. Accordingly, we might attempt to apply the libido theory which has been arrived at in psycho-analysis to the mutual relationship of cells. We might suppose that the life instincts or sexual instincts which are active in each cell take the other cells as their object, that they partly neutralize the death instincts (that is, the processes set up by them) in those cells and thus preserve their life; while the other cells do the same for *them*, and still others sacrifice themselves in the performance of this libidinal function. The germ-cells themselves would behave in a completely 'narcissistic' fashion—to use the phrase that we are accustomed to use in the theory of the neuroses to describe a whole individual who retains his libido in his ego and pays none of it out in object-cathexes. The germ-cells require their libido, the activity of their life instincts, for themselves, as a reserve against their later momentous constructive activity. (The cells of the malignant neoplasms which destroy the organism should also perhaps be described as narcissistic in this same sense: pathology is prepared to regard their germs as innate

1. Schopenhauer (1851) {"Ueber die anscheinende Absichtlichkeit im Schicksale des Einzelnen," from his *Parerga und Paralipomena*}.

and to ascribe embryonic attributes to them.) In this way the libido of our sexual instincts would coincide with the Eros of the poets and philosophers which holds all living things together.

Here then is an opportunity for looking back over the slow development of our libido theory. In the first instance the analysis of the transference neuroses forced upon our notice the opposition between the 'sexual instincts', which are directed towards an object, and certain other instincts, with which we were very insufficiently acquainted and which we described provisionally as the 'ego-instincts'. A foremost place among these was necessarily given to the instincts serving the self-preservation of the individual. It was impossible to say what other distinctions were to be drawn among them. No knowledge would have been more valuable as a foundation for true psychological science than an approximate grasp of the common characteristics and possible distinctive features of the instincts. But in no region of psychology were we groping more in the dark. Everyone assumed the existence of as many instincts or 'basic instincts' as he chose, and juggled with them like the ancient Greek natural philosophers with their four elements—earth, air, fire and water. Psycho-analysis, which could not escape making *some* assumption about the instincts, kept at first to the popular division of instincts typified in the phrase 'hunger and love'. At least there was nothing arbitrary in this; and by its help the analysis of the psychoneuroses was carried forward quite a distance. The concept of 'sexuality', and at the same time of the sexual instinct, had, it is true, to be extended so as to cover many things which could not be classed under the reproductive function; and this caused no little hubbub in an austere, respectable or merely hypocritical world.

The next step was taken when psycho-analysis felt its way closer towards the psychological ego, which it had first come to know only as a repressive, censoring agency, capable of erecting protective structures and reactive formations. Critical and far-seeing minds had, it is true, long since objected to the concept of libido being restricted to the energy of the sexual instincts directed towards an object. But they failed to explain how they had arrived at their better knowledge or to derive from it anything of which analysis could make use. Advancing more cautiously, psycho-analysis observed the regularity with which libido is withdrawn from the object and directed on to the ego (the process of introversion); and, by studying the libidinal development of children in its earliest phases, came to the conclusion that the ego is the true and original reservoir of libido, and that it is only from that reservoir that libido is extended on to objects. The ego now found its position among sexual objects and was at once given the foremost place among them. Libido which was in this way lodged in the ego was described as 'narcissistic'. This narcissistic libido was of course also a manifestation of the force of the sexual instinct in the analytical sense of those words, and it had necessarily to be identified with the 'self-preservative instincts' whose existence had been recognized from the first. Thus the original opposition between the ego-instincts and the sexual instincts proved to be inadequate. A portion of the ego-instincts was seen to be libidinal; sexual instincts—probably alongside others—operated in the ego. Nevertheless we are justified in saying that the old formula which lays it down that psychoneuroses are based on a conflict between ego-instincts and sexual instincts contains nothing that we need reject to-day. It is merely that the distinction between the two kinds of instinct, which was originally regarded as in some sort of way *qualitative*, must now be characterized differently—namely as being *topographical*. And in particular it is still true that the transference neuroses, the essential subject of psycho-analytic study, are the result of a conflict between the ego and the libidinal cathexis of objects.

But it is all the more necessary for us to lay stress upon the libidinal character of the self-preservative instincts now that we are venturing upon the further step of recognizing the sexual instinct as Eros, the preserver of all things, and of deriving the narcissistic libido of the ego from the stores of libido by means of which the cells of the soma are attached to one another. But we now find ourselves suddenly faced by another question. If the self-preservative instincts too are of a libidinal nature, are there perhaps no other instincts whatever but the libidinal ones? At all events there are none other visible. But in that case we shall after all be driven to agree with the critics who suspected from the first that psycho-analysis explains *everything* by sexuality, or with innovators like Jung who, making a hasty judgement, have used the word 'libido' to mean instinctual force in general. Must not this be so?

It was not our *intention* at all events to produce such a result. Our argument had as its point of departure a sharp distinction between ego-instincts, which we equated with death instincts, and sexual instincts, which we equated with life instincts. (We were prepared at one stage to include the so-called self-preservative instincts of the ego among the death instincts; but we subsequently corrected ourselves on this point and withdrew it.) Our views have from the very first been *dualistic*, and to-day they are even more definitely dualistic than before—now that we describe the opposition as being, not between ego-instincts and sexual instincts but between life instincts and death instincts. Jung's libido theory is on the contrary *monistic*; the fact that he has called his one instinctual force 'libido' is bound to cause confusion, but need not affect us otherwise. We suspect that instincts other than those of self-preservation operate in the ego, and it ought to be possible for us to point to them. Unfortunately, however, the analysis of the ego has made so little headway that it is very difficult for us to do so. It is possible, indeed, that the libidinal instincts in the ego may be linked in a peculiar manner with these other ego-instincts which are still strange to us. Even before we had any clear understanding of narcissism, psycho-analysts had a suspicion that the 'ego-instincts' had libidinal components attached to them. But these are very uncertain possibilities, to which our opponents will pay very little attention. The difficulty remains that psycho-analysis has not enabled us hitherto to point to any [ego-] instincts other than the libidinal ones. That, however, is no reason for our falling in with the conclusion that no others in fact exist.

In the obscurity that reigns at present in the theory of the instincts, it would be unwise to reject any idea that promises to throw light on it. We started out from the great opposition between the life and death instincts. Now object-love itself presents us with a second example of a similar polarity—that between love (or affection) and hate (or aggressiveness). If only we could succeed in relating these two polarities to each other and in deriving one from the other! From the very first we recognized the presence of a sadistic component in the sexual instinct. As we know, it can make itself independent and can, in the form of a perversion, dominate an individual's entire sexual activity. It also emerges as a predominant component instinct in one of the 'pregenital organizations', as I have named them. But how can the sadistic instinct, whose aim it is to injure the object, be derived from Eros, the preserver of life? Is it not plausible to suppose that this sadism is in fact a death instinct which, under the influence of the narcissistic libido, has been forced away from the ego and has consequently only emerged in relation to the object? It now enters the service of the sexual function. During the oral stage of organization of the libido, the act of obtaining erotic mastery over an object coincides with that object's destruction; later, the sadistic instinct separates off, and finally, at the stage of genital primacy, it takes on, for the purposes of reproduction, the function of overpowering the sexual object to the extent necessary for carrying out the sexual act. It might indeed be said that the sadism which has been forced out of the ego has pointed the way for the libidinal components of the sexual instinct, and that these follow after it to the object. Wherever the original sadism has undergone no mitigation or intermixture, we find the familiar ambivalence of love and hate in erotic life.

If such an assumption as this is permissible, then we have met the demand that we should produce an example of a death instinct—though, it is true, a displaced one. But this way of looking at things is very far from being easy to grasp and creates a positively mystical impression. It looks suspiciously as though we were trying to find a way out of a highly embarrassing situation at any price. We may recall, however, that there is nothing new in an assumption of this kind. We put one forward on an earlier occasion, before there was any question of an embarrassing situation. Clinical observations led us at that time to the view that masochism, the component instinct which is complementary to sadism, must be regarded as sadism that has been turned round upon the subject's own ego. But there is no difference in principle between an instinct turning from an object to the ego and its turning from the ego to an object—which is the new point now under discussion. Masochism, the turning round of the instinct upon the subject's own ego, would in that case be a return to an earlier phase of the instinct's history, a regression. The account that was formerly given of masochism requires emendation as being too sweeping in one respect: there *might* be such a thing as primary masochism—a possibility which I had contested at that time.[2]

* * *

But we still feel our line of thought appreciably hampered by the fact that we cannot ascribe to the sexual instinct the characteristic of a compulsion to repeat which first put us on the track of the death instincts. The sphere of embryonic developmental processes is no doubt extremely rich in such phenomena of repetition; the two germ-cells that are involved in sexual reproduction and their life history are themselves only repetitions of the beginnings of organic life. But the essence of the processes to which sexual life is directed is the coalescence of two cell-bodies. That alone is what guarantees the immortality of the living substance in the higher organisms.

In other words, we need more information on the origin of sexual reproduction and of the sexual instincts in general. This is a problem which is calculated to daunt an outsider and which the specialists themselves have not yet been able to solve. We shall therefore give only the briefest summary of whatever seems relevant to our line of thought from among the many discordant assertions and opinions.

* * *

* * * Science has so little to tell us about the origin of sexuality that we can liken the problem to a darkness into which not so much as a ray of a hypothesis has penetrated. In quite a different region, it is true, we *do* meet with such a hypothesis; but it is of so fantastic a kind—a myth rather than a scientific explanation—that I should not venture to produce it here, were it not that it fulfils precisely the one condition whose fulfilment we desire. For it traces the origin of an instinct to *a need to restore an earlier state of things*.

What I have in mind is, of course, the theory which Plato put into the mouth of Aristophanes in the *Symposium*, and which deals not only with the *origin* of the sexual instinct but also with the most important of its variations in relation to its object. 'The original human nature was not like the present, but different. In the first place, the sexes were originally three in number, not two as they are now; there was man,

2. A considerable portion of these speculations have been anticipated by Sabina Spielrein (1912) in an instructive and interesting paper {"Die Destruktion als Ursache des Werdens"} which, however, is not entirely clear to me. She there describes the sadistic components of the sexual instinct as 'destructive'. * * * {Spielrein was a brilliant young Russian woman who had gone into analysis with Jung for a severe emotional disorder, became involved with him, but recovered from both. Trained as a psychoanalyst, she spent some time in Freud's circle in Vienna. Upon her return to Russia, she practiced psychoanalysis, but in the late 1930s, her name disappears. She was murdered by German soldiers during the Nazi attack on the Soviet Union.}

woman, and the union of the two. . . . ' Everything about these primaeval men was double: they had four hands and four feet, two faces, two privy parts, and so on. Eventually Zeus decided to cut these men in two, 'like a sorb-apple which is halved for pickling'. After the division had been made, 'the two parts of man, each desiring his other half, came together, and threw their arms about one another eager to grow into one'. [3]

Shall we follow the hint given us by the poet-philosopher, and venture upon the hypothesis that living substance at the time of its coming to life was torn apart into small particles, which have ever since endeavoured to reunite through the sexual instincts? that these instincts, in which the chemical affinity of inanimate matter persisted, gradually succeeded, as they developed through the kingdom of the protista, in overcoming the difficulties put in the way of that endeavour by an environment charged with dangerous stimuli—stimuli which compelled them to form a protective cortical layer? that these splintered fragments of living substance in this way attained a multicellular condition and finally transferred the instinct for reuniting, in the most highly concentrated form, to the germ-cells?—But here, I think, the moment has come for breaking off.

Not, however, without the addition of a few words of critical reflection. It may be asked whether and how far I am myself convinced of the truth of the hypotheses that have been set out in these pages. My answer would be that I am not convinced myself and that I do not seek to persuade other people to believe in them. Or, more precisely, that I do not know how far I believe in them. There is no reason, as it seems to me, why the emo-tional factor of conviction should enter into this question at all. It is surely possible to throw oneself into a line of thought and to follow it wherever it leads out of simple scientific curiosity, or, if the reader prefers, as an *advocatus diaboli*, who is not on that account himself sold to the devil. I do not dispute the fact that the third step in the theory of the instincts, which I have taken here, cannot lay claim to the same degree of certainty as the two earlier ones—the extension of the concept of sexuality and the hypothesis of narcissism. These two innovations were a direct translation of observation into theory and were no more open to sources of error than is inevitable in all such cases. It is true that my assertion of the regressive character of instincts also rests upon observed material—namely on the facts of the compulsion to repeat. It may be, however, that I have overestimated their significance. And in any case it is impossible to pursue an idea of this kind except by repeatedly combining factual material with what is purely speculative and thus diverging widely from empirical observation. The more frequently this is done in the course of constructing a theory, the more untrustworthy, as we know, must be the final result. But the degree of uncertainty is not assignable. One may have made a lucky hit or one may have gone shamefully astray. I do not think a large part is

3. {Freud here thanks his former patient, the philosopher Heinrich Gomperz, for this Platonic myth.}

played by what is called 'intuition' in work of this kind. From what I have seen of intuition, it seems to me to be the product of a kind of intellectual impartiality. Unfortunately, however, people are seldom impartial where ultimate things, the great problems of science and life, are concerned. Each of us is governed in such cases by deep-rooted internal prejudices, into whose hands our speculation unwittingly plays. Since we have such good grounds for being distrustful, our attitude towards the results of our own deliberations cannot well be other than one of cool benevolence. I hasten to add, however, that self-criticism such as this is far from binding one to any special tolerance towards dissentient opinions. It is perfectly legitimate to reject remorselessly theories which are contradicted by the very first steps in the analysis of observed facts, while yet being aware at the same time that the validity of one's own theory is only a provisional one.

We need not feel greatly disturbed in judging our speculation upon the life and death instincts by the fact that so many bewildering and obscure processes occur in it—such as one instinct being driven out by another or an instinct turning from the ego to an object, and so on. This is merely due to our being obliged to operate with the scientific terms, that is to say with the figurative language, peculiar to psychology (or, more precisely, to depth psychology). We could not otherwise describe the processes in question at all, and indeed we could not have become aware of them. The deficiencies in our description would probably vanish if we were already in a position to replace the psychological terms by physiological or chemical ones. It is true that they too are only part of a figurative language; but it is one with which we have long been familiar and which is perhaps a simpler one as well.

On the other hand it should be made quite clear that the uncertainty of our speculation has been greatly increased by the necessity for borrowing from the science of biology. Biology is truly a land of unlimited possibilities. We may expect it to give us the most surprising information and we cannot guess what answers it will return in a few dozen years to the questions we have put to it. They may be of a kind which will blow away the whole of our artificial structure of hypotheses. If so, it may be asked why I have embarked upon such a line of thought as the present one, and in particular why I have decided to make it public. Well—I cannot deny that some of the analogies, correlations and connections which it contains seemed to me to deserve consideration.[4]

---

4. I will add a few words to clarify our terminology, which has undergone some development in the course of the present work. We came to know what the sexual instincts' were from their relation to the sexes and to the reproductive function. We retained this name after we had been obliged by the findings of psycho-analysis to connect them less closely with reproduction. With the hypothesis of narcissistic libido and the extension of the concept of libido to the individual cells, the sexual instinct was transformed for us into Eros, which seeks to force together and hold together the portions of living substance. What are commonly called the sexual instincts are looked upon by us as the part of Eros which is directed towards objects. Our speculations have suggested that Eros operates from the beginning of life and appears as a 'life instinct' in opposition to the 'death instinct' which was brought into being by the coming to life of inorganic substances. These speculations seek to solve the riddle of life by supposing that these two instincts were struggling with each other from the very first.

VII

If it is really the case that seeking to restore an earlier state of things is such a universal characteristic of instincts, we need not be surprised that so many processes take place in mental life independently of the pleasure principle. This characteristic would be shared by all the component instincts and in their case would aim at returning once more to a particular stage in the course of development. These are matters over which the pleasure principle has as yet no control; but it does not follow that any of them are necessarily opposed to it, and we have still to solve the problem of the relation of the instinctual processes of repetition to the dominance of the pleasure principle.

We have found that one of the earliest and most important functions of the mental apparatus is to bind the instinctual impulses which impinge on it, to replace the primary process prevailing in them by the secondary process and convert their freely mobile cathectic energy into a mainly quiescent (tonic) cathexis. While this transformation is taking place no attention can be paid to the development of unpleasure; but this does not imply the suspension of the pleasure principle. On the contrary, the transformation occurs on *behalf* of the pleasure principle; the binding is a preparatory act which introduces and assures the dominance of the pleasure principle.

Let us make a sharper distinction than we have hitherto made between function and tendency. The pleasure principle, then, is a tendency operating in the service of a function whose business it is to free the mental apparatus entirely from excitation or to keep the amount of excitation in it constant or to keep it as low as possible. We cannot yet decide with certainty in favour of any of these ways of putting it; but it is clear that the function thus described would be concerned with the most universal endeavour of all living substance—namely to return to the quiescence of the inorganic world. We have all experienced how the greatest pleasure attainable by us, that of the sexual act, is associated with a momentary extinction of a highly intensified excitation. The binding of an instinctual impulse would be a preliminary function designed to prepare the excitation for its final elimination in the pleasure of discharge.

This raises the question of whether feelings of pleasure and unpleasure can be produced equally from bound and from unbound excitatory processes. And there seems to be no doubt whatever that the unbound or primary processes give rise to far more intense feelings in both directions than the bound or secondary ones. Moreover the primary processes are the earlier in time; at the beginning of mental life there are no others, and we may infer that if the pleasure principle had not already been operative in *them* it could never have been established for the later ones. We thus reach what is at bottom no very simple conclusion, namely that at the beginning of mental life the struggle for pleasure was far more intense than later but not so unrestricted: it had to submit to frequent interruptions. In later times the dominance of the pleasure principle is very much more secure, but it itself has no more escaped the process of taming than the other instincts in general. In any case, whatever it is that causes the appearance of feelings of pleasure and unpleasure in processes of excitation must be present in the secondary process just as it is in the primary one.

Here might be the starting-point for fresh investigations. Our consciousness communicates to us feelings from within not only of pleasure and unpleasure but also of a peculiar tension which in its turn can be either pleasurable or unpleasurable. Should the difference between these feelings enable us to distinguish between bound and unbound processes of energy? or is the feeling of tension to be related to the absolute magnitude, or perhaps to the level, of the cathexis, while the pleasure and unpleasure series indicates a change in the magnitude of the cathexis *within a given unit of time*? Another striking fact is that the life instincts have so much more contact with our internal perception—emerging as breakers of the peace and constantly producing tensions whose release is felt as pleasure—while the death instincts seem to do their work unobtrusively. The pleasure principle seems actually to serve the death instincts. It is true that it keeps watch upon stimuli from without, which are regarded as dangers by both kinds of instincts; but it is more especially on guard against increases of stimulation from within, which would make the task of living more difficult. This in turn raises a host of other questions to which we can at present find no answer. We must be patient and await fresh methods and occasions of research. We must be ready, too, to abandon a path that we have followed for a time, if it seems to be leading to no good end. Only believers, who demand that science shall be a substitute for the catechism they have given up, will blame an investigator for developing or even transforming his views. * * *

Group Psychology and the Analysis of the Ego

While Freud's account of the growth of the ego (and, of course, the superego) implicitly makes a great deal of room for the impact of the external world—society in its varied manifestations—on the individual, Freud wrote little explicit social psychology. One reason for this "neglect" may be found in the extract from his brief study presented here: he thought individual and social psychology to be virtually the same. *Group Psychology* is a far from negligible text, what with its psychoanalytic canvass of the erotic bonds that generate loyalties among the members of a group and between the members and their leader. But it is a somewhat lonely text: neither Freud (nor for that matter his followers) ever systematically followed up the promising leads that he offered in this study written in 1921 and published in the following spring.

It is worth noting (and Freud's translators have noted it without doing anything about it) that "group" is a rather weak translation of the German "*Masse.*" Freud himself spoke in English of "mass," and surely "crowd," with its slightly pejorative connotations, would have rendered his meaning more precisely.

I

INTRODUCTION

The contrast between individual psychology and social or group psychology, which at a first glance may seem to be full of significance, loses a great deal of its sharpness when it is examined more closely. It is true that individual psychology is concerned with the individual man and explores the paths by which he seeks to find satisfaction for his instinctual impulses; but only rarely and under certain exceptional conditions is individual psychology in a position to disregard the relations of this individual to others. In the individual's mental life someone else is invariably involved, as a model, as an object, as a helper, as an opponent; and so from the very first individual psychology, in this extended but entirely justifiable sense of the words, is at the same time social psychology as well.

The relations of an individual to his parents and to his brothers and sisters, to the object of his love, and to his physician—in fact all the relations which have hitherto been the chief subject of psycho-analytic research—may claim to be considered as social phenomena; and in this respect they may be contrasted with certain other processes, described by us as 'narcissistic', in which the satisfaction of the instincts is partially or totally withdrawn from the influence of other people. The contrast between social and narcissistic—Bleuler[1] would perhaps call them 'autistic'—mental acts therefore falls wholly within the domain of individual psychology, and is not well calculated to differentiate it from a social or group psychology.

The individual in the relations which have already been mentioned—to his parents and to his brothers and sisters, to the person he is in love with, to his friend, and to his physician—comes under the influence of only a single person, or of a very small number of persons, each one of whom has become enormously important to him. Now in speaking of social or group psychology it has become usual to leave these relations on one side and to isolate as the subject of inquiry the influencing of an individual by a large number of people simultaneously, people with whom he is connected by something, though otherwise they may in many respects be strangers to him. Group psychology is therefore con-

1. {See Eugen Bleuler, "Das autistische Denken," *Jahrbuch für psychoanalytische und psychopathologische Forschungen* IV (1912).}

cerned with the individual man as a member of a race, of a nation, of a caste, of a profession, of an institution, or as a component part of a crowd of people who have been organized into a group at some particular time for some definite purpose. When once natural continuity has been severed in this way, if a breach is thus made between things which are by nature interconnected, it is easy to regard the phenomena that appear under these special conditions as being expressions of a special instinct that is not further reducible—the social instinct ('herd instinct', 'group mind'),[2] which does not come to light in any other situations. But we may perhaps venture to object that it seems difficult to attribute to the factor of number a significance so great as to make it capable by itself of arousing in our mental life a new instinct that is otherwise not brought into play. Our expectation is therefore directed towards two other possibilities: that the social instinct may not be a primitive one and insusceptible of dissection, and that it may be possible to discover the beginnings of its development in a narrower circle, such as that of the family.

Although group psychology is only in its infancy, it embraces an immense number of separate issues and offers to investigators countless problems which have hitherto not even been properly distinguished from one another. The mere classification of the different forms of group formation and the description of the mental phenomena produced by them require a great expenditure of observation and exposition, and have already given rise to a copious literature. Anyone who compares the narrow dimensions of this little book with the wide extent of group psychology will at once be able to guess that only a few points chosen from the whole material are to be dealt with here. And they will in fact only be a few questions with which the depth-psychology of psychoanalysis is specially concerned.

The Ego and the Id

This text, published in 1923, is as meaty as it is terse. It stands, beyond doubt, as the decisive work of Freud's late years, as the definitive statement of the structural theory that had been so long in the making. Freud himself advertised *The Ego and the Id* to his intimates as the continuation—one might say, the completion—of *Beyond the Pleasure Principle*. But, as he notes in the preface, this essay draws far more from clinical experience, is "closer to psycho-analysis," than its predecessor. Its title, though it promises much, is actually overly modest: *The Ego and the Id* examines not just these two segments of the mental organization, but also gives the super-ego its due of attention. While Freud did not abandon the old classification of conscious, preconscious, and unconscious, he no longer saw it as quite so critical in describing the workings of the mind as he had before. Earlier,

2. [These terms are in English in the original.]

Freud had supposed that the ego stands in opposition to the unconscious. Now he was concerned to emphasize that much of the ego, like much of the superego, is unconscious. This was a most helpful reconceptualization, though Freud did not settle, in this essay or later, just how much power he should assign to the ego, facing as it does its three vigorous adversaries, the id, the super-ego, and the external world. Here he visualizes the ego as a rider who by and large follows where his horse, the id, wants to go. But while he did not finally clarify this important issue—it was left to later psychoanalytic theorists, most notably the so-called "ego psychologists" Heinz Hartmann, Ernst Kris, and Rudolph Loewenstein—to elaborate what Freud had begun; his rethinking had, as Freud's editors rightly observe, "a highly clarifying effect and so made further clinical advances possible" (*SE* XIX, 7). Surely all later psychoanalytic thinking—as well as practice—has taken this text as its fundamental authority. It repays the closest study.

[PREFACE]

The present discussions are a further development of some trains of thought which I opened up in *Beyond the Pleasure Principle*, and to which, as I remarked there, my attitude was one of a kind of benevolent curiosity. In the following pages these thoughts are linked to various facts of analytic observation and an attempt is made to arrive at new conclusions from this conjunction; in the present work, however, there are no fresh borrowings from biology, and on that account it stands closer to psycho-analysis than does *Beyond the Pleasure Principle*. It is more in the nature of a synthesis than of a speculation and seems to have had an ambitious aim in view. I am conscious, however, that it does not go beyond the roughest outline and with that limitation I am perfectly content.

In these pages things are touched on which have not yet been the subject of psycho-analytic consideration, and it has not been possible to avoid trenching upon some theories which have been put forward by non-analysts or by former analysts on their retreat from analysis. I have elsewhere always been ready to acknowledge what I owe to other workers; but in this instance I feel burdened by no such debt of gratitude. If psycho-analysis has not hitherto shown its appreciation of certain things, this has never been because it overlooked their achievement or sought to deny their importance, but because it followed a particular path, which had not yet led so far. And finally, when it has reached them, things have a different look to it from what they have to others.

I

CONSCIOUSNESS AND WHAT IS
UNCONSCIOUS

In this introductory chapter there is nothing new to be said and it will not be possible to avoid repeating what has often been said before.

The division of the psychical into what is conscious and what is unconscious is the fundamental premise of psycho-analysis; and it alone makes it possible for psycho-analysis to understand the pathological processes in mental life, which are as common as they are important, and to find a place for them in the framework of science. To put it once more, in a different way: psycho-analysis cannot situate the essence of the psychical in consciousness, but is obliged to regard consciousness as a quality of the psychical, which may be present in addition to other qualities or may be absent.

If I could suppose that everyone interested in psychology would read this book, I should also be prepared to find that at this point some of my readers would already stop short and would go no further; for here we have the first shibboleth of psycho-analysis. To most people who have been educated in philosophy the idea of anything psychical which is not also conscious is so inconceivable that it seems to them absurd and refutable simply by logic. I believe this is only because they have never studied the relevant phenomena of hypnosis and dreams, which— quite apart from pathological manifestations—necessitate this view. Their psychology of consciousness is incapable of solving the problems of dreams and hypnosis.

* * *

In the * * * course of psycho-analytic work * * * even these distinctions have proved to be inadequate and, for practical purposes, insufficient. This has become clear in more ways than one; but the decisive instance is as follows. We have formed the idea that in each individual there is a coherent organization of mental processes; and we call this his *ego*. It is to this ego that consciousness is attached; the ego controls the approaches to motility—that is, to the discharge of excitations into the external world; it is the mental agency which supervises all its own constituent processes, and which goes to sleep at night, though even then it exercises the censorship on dreams. From this ego proceed the repressions, too, by means of which it is sought to exclude certain trends in the mind not merely from consciousness but also from other forms of effectiveness and activity. In analysis these trends which have been shut out stand in opposition to the ego, and the analysis is faced with the task of removing the resistances which the ego displays against concerning itself with the repressed. Now we find during analysis that, when we put certain tasks before the patient, he gets into difficulties; his associations fail when they should be coming near the repressed. We then tell him that he is dominated by a resistance; but he is quite unaware of the fact, and, even if he guesses from his unpleasurable feelings that a resistance is now at work in him, he does not know what it is or how to describe it. Since, however, there can be no question but that this resistance emanates from his ego and belongs to it, we find ourselves in an unforeseen situation. We have come upon something in the ego itself which is also unconscious, which behaves exactly like the repressed—that is, which produces powerful effects without itself being conscious and which requires special work before it can be made conscious. From the point of view of analytic practice, the consequence of this discovery is that we land in endless obscurities and difficulties if we keep to our habitual forms of expression and try, for instance, to derive neuroses from a conflict between the conscious and the unconscious. We shall have to substitute for this antithesis another, taken from our insight into the structural conditions of the mind—the antithesis between the coherent ego and the repressed which is split off from it.

For our conception of the unconscious, however, the consequences of our discovery are even more important. Dynamic considerations caused us to make our first correction; our insight into the structure of the mind leads to the second. We recognize that the *Ucs.* does not coincide with the repressed; it is still true that all that is repressed is *Ucs.*, but not all that is *Ucs.* is repressed. A part of the ego, too—and Heaven knows how important a part—may be *Ucs.*, undoubtedly is *Ucs.* And this *Ucs.* belonging to the ego is not latent like the *Pcs.*; for if it were, it could not be activated without becoming *Cs.*, and the process of making it conscious would not encounter such great difficulties. When we find ourselves thus confronted by the necessity of postulating a third *Ucs.*, which is not repressed, we must admit that the characteristic of being unconscious begins to lose significance for us. It becomes a quality which can have many meanings, a quality which we are unable to make, as we should have hoped to do, the basis of far-reaching and inevitable conclusions. Nevertheless we must beware of ignoring this characteristic, for the property of being conscious or not is in the last resort our one beacon-light in the darkness of depth-psychology.

II

THE EGO AND THE ID

Pathological research has directed our interest too exclusively to the repressed. We should like to learn more about the ego, now that we know that it, too, can be unconscious in the proper sense of the word. Hitherto the only guide we have had during our investigations has been the distinguishing mark of being conscious or unconscious; we have finally come to see how ambiguous this can be.

Now all our knowledge is invariably bound up with consciousness. We can come to know even the *Ucs.* only by making it conscious. But stop, how is that possible? What does it mean when we say 'making something conscious'? How can that come about?

We already know the point from which we have to start in this connection. We have said that consciousness is the *surface* of the mental apparatus; that is, we have ascribed it as a function to a system which is spatially the first one reached from the external world—and spatially not only in the functional sense but, on this occasion, also in the sense of anatomical dissection. Our investigations too must take this perceiving surface as a starting-point.

All perceptions which are received from without (sense-perceptions) and from within—what we call sensations and feelings—are *Cs.* from the start. But what about those internal processes which we may— roughly and inexactly—sum up under the name of thought-processes? They represent displacements of mental energy which are effected somewhere in the interior of the apparatus as this energy proceeds on its way towards action. Do they advance to the surface, which causes consciousness to be generated? Or does consciousness make its way to them? This is clearly one of the difficulties that arise when one begins to take the spatial or 'topographical' idea of mental life seriously. Both these possibilities are equally unimaginable, there must be a third alternative.

I have already, in another place {"The Unconscious"}, suggested that the real difference between an *Ucs.* and a *Pcs.* idea (thought) consists in this: that the former is carried out on some material which remains unknown, whereas the latter (the *Pcs.*) is in addition brought into connection with word-presentations. This is the first attempt to indicate distinguishing marks for the two systems, the *Pcs.* and the *Ucs.*, other than their relation to consciousness. The question, 'How does a thing become conscious? would thus be more advantageously stated: 'How does a thing become preconscious?' And the answer would be: 'Through becoming connected with the word-presentations corresponding to it.'

These word-presentations are residues of memories; they were at one time perceptions, and like all mnemic residues they can become conscious again. Before we concern ourselves further with their nature, it dawns upon us like a new discovery that only something which has once been a *Cs.* perception can become conscious, and that anything arising from within (apart from feelings) that seeks to become conscious must try to transform itself into external perceptions: this becomes possible by means of memory-traces.

We think of the mnemic residues as being contained in systems which are directly adjacent to the system *Pcpt.-Cs.*, so that the cathexes of those residues can readily extend from within on to the elements of the latter system. We immediately think here of hallucinations, and of the fact that the most vivid memory is always distinguishable both from a hallucination and from an external perception; but it will also occur to us at once that when a memory is revived the cathexis remains in the mnemic system, whereas a hallucination, which is not distinguishable from a perception, can arise when the cathexis does not merely spread over from the memory-trace on to the *Pcpt.* element, but passes over to it *entirely*.

Verbal residues are derived primarily from auditory perceptions, so that the system *Pcs.* has, as it were, a special sensory source. The visual components of word-presentations are secondary, acquired through reading, and may to begin with be left on one side; so may the motor images of words, which, except with deaf-mutes, play the part of auxiliary indications. In essence a word is after all the mnemic residue of a word that has been heard.

We must not be led, in the interests of simplification perhaps, to forget the importance of optical mnemic residues, when they are of *things*, or to deny that it is possible for thought-processes to become conscious through a reversion to visual residues, and that in many people this seems to be the favoured method. The study of dreams and of preconscious phantasies * * * can give us an idea of the special character of this visual thinking. We learn that what becomes conscious in it is as a rule only the concrete subject-matter of the thought, and that the relations between the various elements of this subject-matter, which is what specially characterizes thoughts, cannot be given visual expression. Thinking in pictures is, therefore, only a very incomplete form of becoming conscious. In some way, too, it stands nearer to unconscious processes than does thinking in words, and it is unquestionably older than the latter both ontogenetically and phylogenetically.

To return to our argument: if, therefore, this is the way in which something that is in itself unconscious becomes preconscious, the queston how we make something that is repressed (pre)conscious would be answered as follows. It is done by supplying *Pcs.* intermediate links through the work of analysis. Consciousness remains where it is, therefore; but, on the other hand, the *Ucs.* does not rise into the *Cs.*

Whereas the relation of *external* perceptions to the ego is quite perspicuous, that of *internal* perceptions to the ego requires special investigation. It gives rise once more to a doubt whether we are really right in referring the whole of consciousness to the single superificial system *Pcpt.-Cs.*

Internal perceptions yield sensations of processes arising in the most diverse and certainly also in the deepest strata of the mental apparatus. Very little is known about these sensations and feelings; those belonging to the pleasure-unpleasure series may still be regarded as the best examples of them. They are more primordial, more elementary, than perceptions arising externally and they can come about even when consciousness is clouded. * * *

Sensations of a pleasurable nature have not anything inherently impelling about them, whereas unpleasurable ones have it in the highest degree. The latter impel towards change, towards discharge, and that is why we interpret unpleasure as implying a heightening and pleasure a lowering of energic cathexis. Let us call what becomes conscious as pleasure and unpleasure a quantitative and qualitative 'something' in the course of mental events; the question then is whether this 'something' can become conscious in the place where it is, or whether it must first be transmitted to the system *Pcpt*.

Clinical experience decides for the latter. It shows us that this 'something' behaves like a repressed impulse. It can exert driving force without the ego noticing the compulsion. Not until there is resistance to the compulsion, a hold-up in the discharge-reaction, does the 'something' at once become conscious as unpleasure. In the same way that tensions arising from physical needs can remain unconscious, so also can pain—a thing intermediate between external and internal perception, which behaves like an internal perception even when its source is in the external world. It remains true, therefore, that sensations and feelings, too, only become conscious through reaching the system *Pcpt*.; if the way forward is barred, they do not come into being as sensations, although the 'something' that corresponds to them in the course of excitation is the same as if they did. We then come to speak, in a condensed and not entirely correct manner, of 'unconscious feelings', keeping up an analogy with unconscious ideas which is not altogether justifiable. Actually the difference is that, whereas with *Ucs. ideas* connecting links must be created before they can be brought into the *Cs.*, with *feelings*, which are themselves transmitted directly, this does not occur. In other words: the distinction between *Cs.* and *Pcs.* has no meaning where feelings are concerned; the *Pcs.* here drops out—and feelings are either conscious or unconscious. Even when they are attached to word-presentations, their becoming conscious is not due to that circumstance, but they become so directly.

The part played by word-presentations now becomes perfectly clear. By their interposition internal thought-processes are made into perceptions. It is like a demonstration of the theorem that all knowledge has its origin in external perception. When a hypercathexis of the process of thinking takes place, thoughts are *actually* perceived—as if they came from without—and are consequently held to be true.

After this clarifying of the relations between external and internal perception and the superficial system *Pcpt.-Cs.*, we can go on to work out our idea of the ego. It starts out, as we see, from the system *Pcpt.*, which is its nucleus, and begins by embracing the *Pcs.*, which is adjacent to the mnemic residues. But, as we have learnt, the ego is also unconscious.

Now I think we shall gain a great deal by following the suggestion of a writer who, from personal motives, vainly asserts that he has nothing to do with the rigours of pure science. I am speaking of Georg Groddeck, who is never tired of insisting that what we call our ego behaves essentially passively in life, and that, as he expresses it, we are 'lived' by unknown and uncontrollable forces.[1] We have all had impressions of the same kind, even though they may not have overwhelmed us to the exclusion of all others, and we need feel no hesitation in finding a place for Groddeck's discovery in the structure of science. I propose to take it into account by calling the entity which starts out from the system *Pcpt.* and begins by being *Pcs.* the 'ego', and by following Groddeck in calling the other part of the mind, into which this entity extends and which behaves as though it were *Ucs.*, the 'id'.[2]

We shall soon see whether we can derive any advantage from this view for purposes either of description or of understanding. We shall now look upon an individual as a psychical id, unknown and unconscious, upon whose surface rests the ego, developed from its nucleus the *Pcpt.* system. If we make an effort to represent this pictorially, we may add that the ego does not completely envelop the id, but only does so to the extent to which the system *Pcpt.* forms its [the ego's] surface, more or less as the germinal disc rests upon the ovum. The ego is not sharply separated from the id; its lower portion merges into it.

But the repressed merges into the id as well, and is merely a part of it. The repressed is only cut off sharply from the ego by the resistances of repression; it can communicate with the ego through the id. We at once realize that almost all the lines of demarcation we have drawn at the instigation of pathology relate only to the superficial strata of the mental apparatus—the only ones known to us. The state of things which we have been describing can be represented diagrammatically (Fig. 1); though it must be remarked that the form chosen has no pretensions to any special applicability, but is merely intended to serve for purposes of exposition.

We might add, perhaps, that the ego wears a 'cap of hearing'—on one side only, as we learn from cerebral anatomy. It might be said to wear it awry.

It is easy to see that the ego is that part of the id which has been modified by the direct influence of the external world through the medium of the *Pcpt.-Cs.*; in a sense it is an extension of the surface-differentiation. Moreover, the ego seeks to bring the influence of the

---

1. {Georg Groddeck (1866–1934), an imaginative maverick physician who ran his own sanatorium at the high-priced southwest German spa of Baden-Baden, had become enthusiastic about Freud's ideas some time during the First World War. For some years before, without being well-informed about psychoanalysis, he had been practicing therapy that in significant ways resembled it, and after his "conversion" he made himself into one of Freud's most energetic, though at times disgruntled, advocates. He was an eccentric, a self-proclaimed "wild analyst," whom Freud repeatedly defended against the somewhat straitlaced strictures of his adherents. In his correspondence with Freud, and in his work, *The Book of the It*, published a few weeks before Freud's *The Ego and the Id*, Groddeck analyzes an unconscious force in humans "by which we are lived." Freud's "id" bears significant resemblances to Groddeck's "it," but the differences, Freud insisted, are no less significant.}

2. Groddeck himself no doubt followed the example of Nietzsche, who habitually used this grammatical term for whatever in our nature is impersonal and, so to speak, subject to natural law.

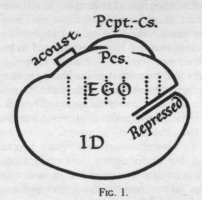

FIG. 1.

external world to bear upon the id and its tendencies, and endeavours to substitute the reality principle for the pleasure principle which reigns unrestrictedly in the id. For the ego, perception plays the part which in the id falls to instinct. The ego represents what may be called reason and common sense, in contrast to the id, which contains the passions. All this falls into line with popular distinctions which we are all familiar with; at the same time, however, it is only to be regarded as holding good on the average or 'ideally'.

The functional importance of the ego is manifested in the fact that normally control over the approaches to motility devolves upon it. Thus in its relation to the id it is like a man on horseback, who has to hold in check the superior strength of the horse; with this difference, that the rider tries to do so with his own strength while the ego uses borrowed forces. The analogy may be carried a little further. Often a rider, if he is not to be parted from his horse, is obliged to guide it where it wants to go; so in the same way the ego is in the habit of transforming the id's will into action as if it were its own.

Another factor, besides the influence of the system *Pcpt.*, seems to have played a part in bringing about the formation of the ego and its differentiation from the id. A person's own body, and above all its surface, is a place from which both external and internal perceptions may spring. It is *seen* like any other object, but to the *touch* it yields two kinds of sensations, one of which may be equivalent to an internal perception. Psycho-physiology has fully discussed the manner in which a person's own body attains its special position among other objects in the world of perception. Pain, too, seems to play a part in the process, and the way in which we gain new knowledge of our organs during painful illnesses is perhaps a model of the way by which in general we arrive at the idea of our body.

The ego is first and foremost a bodily ego; it is not merely a surface entity, but is itself the projection of a surface.[3] If we wish to find an anatomical analogy for it we can best identify it with the 'cortical homunculus' of the anatomists, which stands on its head in the cortex, sticks up its heels, faces backwards and, as we know, has its speech-area on the left-hand side.

The relation of the ego to consciousness has been entered into repeatedly; yet there are some important facts in this connection which remain to be described here. Accustomed as we are to taking our social or ethical scale of values along with us wherever we go, we feel no surprise at hearing that the scene of the activities of the lower passions is in the unconscious; we expect, moreover, that the higher any mental function ranks in our scale of values the more easily it will find access to consciousness assured to it. Here, however, psycho-analytic experience disappoints us. On the one hand, we have evidence that even subtle and difficult intellectual operations which ordinarily require strenuous reflection can equally be carried out preconsciously and without coming into consciousness. Instances of this are quite incontestable; they may occur, for example, during the state of sleep, as is shown when someone finds, immediately after waking, that he knows the solution to a difficult mathematical or other problem with which he had been wrestling in vain the day before.

There is another phenomenon, however, which is far stranger. In our analyses we discover that there are people in whom the faculties of self-criticism and conscience—mental activities, that is, that rank as extremely high ones—are unconscious and unconsciously produce effects of the greatest importance; the example of resistance remaining unconscious during analysis is therefore by no means unique. But this new discovery, which compels us, in spite of our better critical judgement, to speak of an 'unconscious sense of guilt', bewilders us far more than the other and sets us fresh problems, especially when we gradually come to see that in a great number of neuroses an unconscious sense of guilt of this kind plays a decisive economic part and puts the most powerful obstacles in the way of recovery. If we come back once more to our scale of values, we shall have to say that not only what is lowest but also what is highest in the ego can be unconscious. It is as if we were thus supplied with a proof of what we have just asserted of the conscious ego: that it is first and foremost a body-ego.

III

THE EGO AND THE SUPER-EGO (EGO IDEAL)

If the ego were merely the part of the id modified by the influence of the perceptual system, the representative in the mind of the real external

3. [I.e., the ego is ultimately derived from bodily sensations, chiefly from those springing from the surface of the body. It may thus be regarded as a mental projection of the surface of the body, besides, as we have seen above, representing the su-perficies of the mental apparatus.—This footnote first appeared in the English translation of 1927, in which it was described as having been authorized by Freud. It does not appear in the German editions.]

world, we should have a simple state of things to deal with. But there is a further complication.

The considerations that led us to assume the existence of a grade in the ego, a differentiation within the ego, which may be called the 'ego ideal' or 'super-ego', have been stated elsewhere. They still hold good.[4] The fact that this part of the ego is less firmly connected with consciousness is the novelty which calls for explanation.

At this point we must widen our range a little. We succeeded in explaining the painful disorder of melancholia by supposing that [in those suffering from it] an object which was lost has been set up again inside the ego—that is, that an object-cathexis has been replaced by an identification. At that time, however, we did not appreciate the full significance of this process and did not know how common and how typical it is. Since then we have come to understand that this kind of substitution has a great share in determining the form taken by the ego and that it makes an essential contribution towards building up what is called its 'character'.

At the very beginning, in the individual's primitive oral phase, object-cathexis and identification are no doubt indistinguishable from each other. We can only suppose that later on object-cathexes proceed from the id, which feels erotic trends as needs. The ego, which to begin with is still feeble, becomes aware of the object-cathexes, and either acquiesces in them or tries to fend them off by the process of repression.

When it happens that a person has to give up a sexual object, there quite often ensues an alteration of his ego which can only be described as a setting up of the object inside the ego, as it occurs in melancholia; the exact nature of this substitution is as yet unknown to us. It may be that by this introjection, which is a kind of regression to the mechanism of the oral phase, the ego makes it easier for the object to be given up or renders that process possible. It may be that this identification is the sole condition under which the id can give up its objects. At any rate the process, especially in the early phases of development, is a very frequent one, and it makes it possible to suppose that the character of the ego is a precipitate of abandoned object-cathexes and that it contains the history of those object-choices. It must, of course, be admitted from the outset that there are varying degrees of capacity for resistance, which decide the extent to which a person's character fends off or accepts the influences of the history of his erotic object-choices. In women who have had many experiences in love there seems to be no difficulty in finding vestiges of their object-cathexes in the traits of their character. We must also take into consideration cases of simultaneous object-cathexis and identification—cases, that is, in which the alteration in character occurs before the object has been given up. In such cases the

4. Except that I seem to have been mistaken in ascribing the function of 'reality-testing' to the super-ego—a point which needs correction.

alteration in character has been able to survive the object-relation and in a certain sense to conserve it.

From another point of view it may be said that this transformation of an erotic object-choice into an alteration of the ego is also a method by which the ego can obtain control over the id and deepen its relations with it—at the cost, it is true, of acquiescing to a large extent in the id's experiences. When the ego assumes the features of the object, it is forcing itself, so to speak, upon the id as a love-object and is trying to make good the id's loss by saying: 'Look, you can love me too—I am so like the object.'

The transformation of object-libido into narcissistic libido which thus takes place obviously implies an abandonment of sexual aims, a desexualization—a kind of sublimation, therefore. Indeed, the question arises, and deserves careful consideration, whether this is not the univeɪ ɜal road to sublimation, whether all sublimation does not take place through the mediation of the ego, which begins by changing sexual object-libido into narcissistic libido and then, perhaps, goes on to give it another aim.[5] We shall later on have to consider whether other instinctual vicissitudes may not also result from this transformation, whether, for instance, it may not bring about a defusion of the various instincts that are fused together.

Although it is a digression from our aim, we cannot avoid giving our attention for a moment longer to the ego's object-identifications. If they obtain the upper hand and become too numerous, unduly powerful and incompatible with one another, a pathological outcome will not be far off. It may come to a disruption of the ego in consequence of the different identifications becoming cut off from one another by resistances; perhaps the secret of the cases of what is described as 'multiple personality' is that the different identifications seize hold of consciousness in turn. Even when things do not go so far as this, there remains the question of conflicts between the various identifications into which the ego comes apart, conflicts which cannot after all be described as entirely pathological.

But, whatever the character's later capacity for resisting the influences of abandoned object-cathexes may turn out to be, the effects of the first identifications made in earliest childhood will be general and lasting. This leads us back to the origin of the ego ideal; for behind it there lies hidden an individual's first and most important identification, his identification with the father in his own personal prehistory. This is apparently not in the first instance the consequence or outcome of an object-cathexis; it is a direct and immediate identification and takes place earlier than any object-cathexis. But the object-choices belonging to the first sexual period and relating to the father and mother seem normally to

5. Now that we have distinguished between the ego and the id, we must recognize the id as the great reservoir of libido indicated in my paper on narcissism (1914).

find their outcome in an identification of this kind, and would thus reinforce the primary one.

The whole subject, however, is so complicated that it will be necessary to go into it in greater detail. The intricacy of the problem is due to two factors: the triangular character of the Oedipus situation and the constitutional bisexuality of each individual.

In its simplified form the case of a male child may be described as follows. At a very early age the little boy develops an object-cathexis for his mother, which originally related to the mother's breast and is the prototype of an object-choice on the anaclitic model;[6] the boy deals with his father by identifying himself with him. For a time these two relationships proceed side by side, until the boy's sexual wishes in regard to his mother become more intense and his father is perceived as an obstacle to them; from this the Oedipus complex originates. His identification with his father then takes on a hostile colouring and changes into a wish to get rid of his father in order to take his place with his mother. Henceforward his relation to his father is ambivalent; it seems as if the ambivalence inherent in the identification from the beginning had become manifest. An ambivalent attitude to his father and an object-relation of a solely affectionate kind to his mother make up the content of the simple positive Oedipus complex in a boy.

Along with the demolition of the Oedipus complex, the boy's object-cathexis of his mother must be given up. Its place may be filled by one of two things: either an identification with his mother or an intensification of his identification with his father. We are accustomed to regard the latter outcome as the more normal; it permits the affectionate relation to the mother to be in a measure retained. In this way the dissolution of the Oedipus complex would consolidate the masculinity in a boy's character. In a precisely analogous way,[7] the outcome of the Oedipus attitude in a little girl may be an intensification of her identification with her mother (or the setting up of such an identification for the first time)—a result which will be fix the child's feminine character.

These identifications are not what we should have expected, since they do not introduce the abandoned object into the ego; but this alternative outcome may also occur, and is easier to observe in girls than in boys. Analysis very often shows that a little girl, after she has had to relinquish her father as a love-object, will bring her masculinity into prominence and identify herself with her father (that is, with the object which has been lost), instead of with her mother. This will clearly depend on whether the masculinity in her disposition—whatever that may consist in—is strong enough.

It would appear, therefore, that in both sexes the relative strength of the masculine and feminine sexual dispositions is what determines

---

6. * * * In order to simplify my presentation I shall discuss only identification with the father.

7. [The idea that the outcome of the Oedipus complex was 'precisely analogous' in girls and boys was abandoned by Freud not long after this.] {See below, pp. 664–66, 671–76.}

whether the outcome of the Oedipus situation shall be an identification with the father or with the mother. This is one of the ways in which bisexuality takes a hand in the subsequent vicissitudes of the Oedipus complex. The other way is even more important. For one gets an impression that the simple Oedipus complex is by no means its commonest form, but rather represents a simplification or schematization which, to be sure, is often enough justified for practical purposes. Closer study usually discloses the more complete Oedipus complex, which is twofold, positive and negative, and is due to the bisexuality originally present in children: that is to say, a boy has not merely an ambivalent attitude towards his father and an affectionate object-choice towards his mother, but at the same time he also behaves like a girl and displays an affectionate feminine attitude to his father and a corresponding jealousy and hostility towards his mother. It is this complicating element introduced by bisexuality that makes it so difficult to obtain a clear view of the facts in connection with the earliest object-choices and identifications, and still more difficult to describe them intelligibly. It may even be that the ambivalence displayed in the relations to the parents should be attributed entirely to bisexuality and that it is not, as I have represented above, developed out of identification in consequence of rivalry.

In my opinion it is advisable in general, and quite especially where neurotics are concerned, to assume the existence of the complete Oedipus complex. Analytic experience then shows that in a number of cases one or the other constituent disappears, except for barely distinguishable traces; so that the result is a series with the normal positive Oedipus complex at one end and the inverted negative one at the other, while its intermediate members exhibit the complete form with one or other of its two components preponderating. At the dissolution of the Oedipus complex the four trends of which it consists will group themselves in such a way as to produce a father-identification and a mother-identification. The father-identification will preserve the object-relation to the mother which belonged to the positive complex and will at the same time replace the object-relation to the father which belonged to the inverted complex: and the same will be true, *mutatis mutandis*, of the mother-identification. The relative intensity of the two identifications in any individual will reflect the preponderance in him of one or other of the two sexual dispositions.

The broad general outcome of the sexual phase dominated by the Oedipus complex may, therefore, be taken to be the forming of a precipitate in the ego, consisting of these two identifications in some way united with each other. This modification of the ego retains its special position; it confronts the other contents of the ego as an ego ideal or super-ego.

The super-ego is, however, not simply a residue of the earliest object-choices of the id; it also represents an energetic reaction-formation against those choices. Its relation to the ego is not exhausted by the precept: 'You *ought to be* like this (like your father).' It also comprises the prohibition: 'You *may not be* like this (like your father)—that is, you may not do all that he does; some things are his prerogative.' This double aspect of the ego ideal derives from the fact that the ego ideal had the task of repressing the Oedipus complex; indeed, it is to that revolutionary event that it owes its existence. Clearly the repression of the Oedipus complex was no easy task. The child's parents, and especially his father, were perceived as the obstacle to a realization of his Oedipus wishes; so his infantile ego fortified itself for the carrying out of the repression by erecting this same obstacle within itself. It borrowed strength to do this, so to speak, from the father, and this loan was an extraordinarily momentous act. The super-ego retains the character of the father, while the more powerful the Oedipus complex was and the more rapidly it succumbed to repression (under the influence of authority, religious teaching, schooling and reading), the stricter will be the domination of the super-ego over the ego later on—in the form of conscience or perhaps of an unconscious sense of guilt. I shall presently bring forward a suggestion about the source of its power to dominate in this way—the source, that is, of its compulsive character which manifests itself in the form of a categorical imperative.

If we consider once more the origin of the super-ego as we have described it, we shall recognize that it is the outcome of two highly important factors, one of a biological and the other of a historical nature: namely, the lengthy duration in man of his childhood helplessness and dependence, and the fact of his Oedipus complex, the repression of which we have shown to be connected with the interruption of libidinal development by the latency period and so with the diphasic onset of man's sexual life. According to one psycho-analytic hypothesis {by Ferenczi}, the last-mentioned phenomenon, which seems to be peculiar to man, is a heritage of the cultural development necessitated by the glacial epoch. We see, then, that the differentiation of the super-ego from the ego is no matter of chance; it represents the most important characteristics of the development both of the individual and of the species; indeed, by giving permanent expression to the influence of the parents it perpetuates the existence of the factors to which it owes its origin.

Psycho-analysis has been reproached time after time with ignoring the higher, moral, supra-personal side of human nature. The reproach is doubly unjust, both historically and methodologically. For, in the first place, we have from the very beginning attributed the function of instigating repression to the moral and aesthetic trends in the ego, and secondly, there has been a general refusal to recognize that psycho-analytic research could not, like a philosophical system, produce a complete and ready-made theoretical structure, but had to find its way step by step along the path towards understanding the intricacies of the mind by making an analytic dissection of both normal and abnormal phenomena. So long as we had to concern ourselves with the study of what is repressed in mental life, there was no need for us to share in any agitated apprehensions as to the whereabouts of the higher side of man. But now that we have embarked upon the analysis of the ego we can give an answer to all those whose moral sense has been shocked and who have complained that there must surely be a higher nature in man: 'Very true,' we can say, 'and here we have that higher nature, in this ego ideal or super-ego, the representative of our relation to our parents. When we were little children we knew these higher natures, we admired them and feared them; and later we took them into ourselves.'

The ego ideal is therefore the heir of the Oedipus complex, and thus it is also the expression of the most powerful impulses and most important libidinal vicissitudes of the id. By setting up this ego ideal, the ego has mastered the Oedipus complex and at the same time placed itself in subjection to the id. Whereas the ego is essentially the representative of the external world, of reality, the super-ego stands in contrast to it as the representative of the internal world, of the id. Conflicts between the ego and the ideal will, as we are now prepared to find, ultimately reflect the contrast between what is real and what is psychical, between the external world and the internal world.

Through the forming of the ideal, what biology and the vicissitudes of the human species have created in the id and left behind in it is taken over by the ego and re-experienced in relation to itself as an individual. Owing to the way in which the ego ideal is formed, it has the most abundant links with the phylogenetic acquisition of each individual— his archaic heritage. What has belonged to the lowest part of the mental life of each of us is changed, through the formation of the ideal, into what is highest in the human mind by our scale of values. It would be vain, however, to attempt to localize the ego ideal, even in the sense in which we have localized the ego, or to work it into any of the analogies with the help of which we have tried to picture the relation between the ego and the id.

It is easy to show that the ego ideal answers to everything that is expected of the higher nature of man. As a substitute for a longing for the father, it contains the germ from which all religions have evolved. The self-judgement which declares that the ego falls short of its ideal produces the religious sense of humility to which the believer appeals in his longing. As a child grows up, the role of father is carried on by teachers and others in authority; their injunctions and prohibitions re- main powerful in the ego ideal and continue, in the form of conscience, to exercise the moral censorship. The tension between the demands of conscience and the actual performances of the ego is experienced as a sense of guilt. Social feelings rest on identifications with other people, on the basis of having the same ego ideal.

Religion, morality, and a social sense—the chief elements in the higher side of man—were originally one and the same thing. According to the hypothesis which I put forward in *Totem and Taboo* they were acquired phylogenetically out of the father-complex: religion and moral restraint through the process of mastering the Oedipus complex itself, and social feeling through the necessity for overcoming the rivalry that then remained between the members of the younger generation. The male sex seems to have taken the lead in all these moral acquisitions; and they seem to have then been transmitted to women by cross-inheritance. Even to-day the social feelings arise in the individual as a superstructure built upon impulses of jealous rivalry against his brothers and sisters. Since the hostility cannot be satisfied, an identification with the former rival develops. The study of mild cases of homosexuality confirms the suspicion that in this instance, too, the identification is a substitute for an affectionate object-choice which has taken the place of the aggressive, hostile attitude.

With the mention of phylogenesis, however, fresh problems arise, from which one is tempted to draw cautiously back. But there is no help for it, the attempt must be made—in spite of a fear that it will lay bare the inadequacy of our whole effort. The question is: which was it, the ego of primitive man or his id, that acquired religion and morality in those early days out of the father-complex? If it was his ego, why do we not speak simply of these things being inherited by the ego? If it was the id, how does that agree with the character of the id? Or are we wrong in carrying the differentiation between ego, superego, and id back into such early times? Or should we not honestly confess that our whole conception of the processes in the ego is of no help in understanding phylogenesis and cannot be applied to it?

Let us answer first what is easiest to answer. The differentiation between ego and id must be attributed not only to primitive man but even to much simpler organisms, for it is the inevitable expression of the influence of the external world. The super-ego, according to our hypothesis, actually originated from the experiences that led to totemism. The question whether it was the ego or the id that experienced and acquired these things soon comes to nothing. Reflection at once shows us that no external vicissitudes can be experienced or undergone by the id, except by way of the ego, which is the representative of the external world to the id. Nevertheless it is not possible to speak of direct inheritance in the ego. It is here that the gulf between an actual individual and the concept of a species becomes evident. Moreover, one must not take the difference between ego and id in too hard-and-fast a sense, nor forget that the ego is a specially differentiated part of the id. The experiences of the ego seem at first to be lost for inheritance; but, when they have been repeated often enough and with sufficient strength in many individuals in successive generations, they transform themselves, so to say, into experiences of the id, the impressions of which are preserved by heredity. Thus in the id, which is capable of being inherited, are harboured residues of the existences of countless egos; and, when the ego forms its super-ego out of the id, it may perhaps only be reviving shapes of former egos and be bringing them to resurrection.

The way in which the super-ego came into being explains how it is that the early conflicts of the ego with the object-cathexes of the id can be continued in conflicts with their heir, the super-ego. If the ego has not succeeded in properly mastering the Oedipus complex, the energic cathexis of the latter, springing from the id, will come into operation once more in the reaction-formation of the ego ideal. The abundant communication between the ideal and these Ucs. instinctual impulses solves the puzzle of how it is that the ideal itself can to a great extent remain unconscious and inaccessible to the ego. The struggle which once raged in the deepest strata of the mind, and was not brought to an end by rapid sublimation and identification, is now continued in a higher region, like the Battle of the Huns in Kaulbach's painting.[8]

IV

THE TWO CLASSES OF INSTINCTS

We have already said that, if the differentiation we have made of the mind into an id, an ego, and a super-ego represents any advance in our knowledge, it ought to enable us to understand more thoroughly the dynamic relations within the mind and to describe them more clearly. We have also already concluded that the ego is especially under the influence of perception, and that, speaking broadly, perceptions may be said to have the same significance for the ego as instincts have for the id. At the same time the ego is subject to the influence of the instincts, too, like the id, of which it is, as we know, only a specially modified part.

I have lately developed a view of the instincts which I shall here hold to and take as the basis of my further discussions. According to this view we have to distinguish two classes of instincts, one of which, the sexual instincts or Eros, is by far the more conspicuous and accessible to study. It comprises not merely the uninhibited sexual instinct proper and the instinctual impulses of an aim-inhibited or sublimated nature derived from it, but also the self-preservative instinct, which must be assigned to the ego and which at the beginning of our analytic work we had good reason for contrasting with the sexual object-instincts. The second class of instincts was not so easy to point to; in the end we came to recognize sadism as its representative. On the basis of theoretical considerations, supported by biology, we put forward the hypothesis of a death instinct, the task of which is to lead organic life back into the inanimate state; on the other hand, we supposed that Eros, by bringing about a more and more far-reaching combination of the particles into which living

8. [This was the battle, usually known as the Battle of Châlons, in which, in 451, Attila was defeated by the Romans and Visigoths. Wilhelm von Kaulbach (1805–74) made it the subject of one of his mural decorations, originally painted for the Neues Museum in Berlin. In this the dead warriors are represented as continuing their fight in the sky above the battlefield, in accordance with a legend that can be traced back to the fifth century Neo-Platonist, Damascius.]

substance is dispersed, aims at complicating life and at the same time, of course, at preserving it. Acting in this way, both the instincts would be conservative in the strictest sense of the word, since both would be endeavouring to re-establish a state of things that was disturbed by the emergence of life. The emergence of life would thus be the cause of the continuance of life and also at the same time of the striving towards death; and life itself would be a conflict and compromise between these two trends. The problem of the origin of life would remain a cosmological one; and the problem of the goal and purpose of life would be answered dualistically.

On this view, a special physiological process (of anabolism or catabolism) would be associated with each of the two classes of instincts; both kinds of instinct would be active in every particle of living substance, though in unequal proportions, so that some one substance might be the principal representative of Eros.

This hypothesis throws no light whatever upon the manner in which the two classes of instincts are fused, blended, and alloyed with each other; but that this takes place regularly and very extensively is an assumption indispensable to our conception. It appears that, as a result of the combination of unicellular organisms into multicellular forms of life, the death instinct of the single cell can successfully be neutralized and the destructive impulses be diverted on to the external world through the instrumentality of a special organ. This special organ would seem to be the muscular apparatus; and the death instinct would thus seem to express itself—though probably only in part—as an instinct of destruction directed against the external world and other organisms.

Once we have admitted the idea of a fusion of the two classes of instincts with each other, the possibility of a—more or less complete—'defusion' of them forces itself upon us. The sadistic component of the sexual instinct would be a classical example of a serviceable instinctual fusion; and the sadism which has made itself independent as a perversion would be typical of a defusion, though not of one carried to extremes. From this point we obtain a view of a great domain of facts which has not before been considered in this light. We perceive that for purposes of discharge the instinct of destruction is habitually brought into the service of Eros; we suspect that the epileptic fit is a product and indication of an instinctual defusion, and we come to understand that instinctual defusion and the marked emergence of the death instinct call for particular consideration among the effects of some severe neuroses—for instance, the obsessional neuroses. Making a swift generalization, we might conjecture that the essence of a regression of libido (e.g. from the genital to the sadistic-anal phase) lies in a defusion of instincts, just as, conversely, the advance from the earlier phase to the definitive genital one would be conditioned by an accession of erotic components. The question also arises whether ordinary ambivalence, which is so often unusually strong in the constitutional disposition to neurosis, should not be regarded as the product of a defusion; ambivalence, however, is such a fundamental phenomenon that it more probably represents an instinctual fusion that has not been completed.

It is natural that we should turn with interest to enquire whether there may not be instructive connections to be traced between the structures we have assumed to exist—the ego, the super-ego and the id—on the one hand and the two classes of instincts on the other; and, further, whether the pleasure principle which dominates mental processes can be shown to have any constant relation both to the two classes of instincts and to these differentiations which we have drawn in the mind. But before we discuss this, we must clear away a doubt which arises concerning the terms in which the problem itself is stated. There is, it is true, no doubt about the pleasure principle, and the differentiation within the ego has good clinical justification; but the distinction between the two classes of instincts does not seem sufficiently assured and it is possible that facts of clinical analysis may be found which will do away with its pretension.

One such fact there appears to be. For the opposition between the two classes of instincts we may put the polarity of love and hate. There is no difficulty in finding a representative of Eros; but we must be grateful that we can find a representative of the elusive death instinct in the instinct of destruction, to which hate points the way. Now, clinical observation shows not only that love is with unexpected regularity accompanied by hate (ambivalence), and not only that in human relationships hate is frequently a forerunner of love, but also that in a number of circumstances hate changes into love and love into hate. If this change is more than a mere succession in time—if, that is, one of them actually turns into the other—then clearly the ground is cut away from under a distinction so fundamental as that between erotic instincts and death instincts, one which presupposes physiological processes running in opposite directions.

Now the case in which someone first loves and then hates the same person (or the reverse) because that person has given him cause for doing so, has obviously nothing to do with our problem. Nor has the other case, in which feelings of love that have not yet become manifest express themselves to begin with by hostility and aggressive tendencies; for it may be that here the destructive component in the object-cathexis has hurried on ahead and is only later on joined by the erotic one. But we know of several instances in the psychology of the neuroses in which it is more plausible to suppose that a transformation does take place. In persecutory paranoia the patient fends off an excessively strong homosexual attachment to some particular person in a special way; and as a result this person whom he loved most becomes a persecutor, against whom the patient directs an often dangerous aggressiveness. Here we have a right to interpolate a previous phase which has transformed the love into hate. In the case of the origin of homosexuality, and of desexualized social feelings as well, analytic investigation has only recently taught us to recognize that violent feelings of rivalry are present which lead to aggressive inclinations, and that it is only after these have been surmounted that the formerly hated object becomes the loved one or gives rise to an identification. The question arises whether in these instances we are to assume a direct transformation of hate into love. It is clear that here the changes are purely internal and an alteration in the behaviour of the object plays no part in them.

There is another possible mechanism, however, which we have come to know of by analytic investigation of the processes concerned in the change in paranoia. An ambivalent attitude is present from the outset and the transformation is effected by means of a reactive displacement of cathexis, energy being withdrawn from the erotic impulse and added to the hostile one.

Not quite the same thing but something like it happens when the hostile rivalry leading to homosexuality is overcome. The hostile attitude has no prospect of satisfaction; consequently—for economic reasons, that is—it is replaced by a loving attitude for which there is more prospect of satisfaction—that is, possibility of discharge. So we see that we are not obliged in any of these cases to assume a direct transformation of hate into love, which would be incompatible with the qualitative distinction between the two classes of instincts.

It will be noticed, however, that by introducing this other mechanism of changing love into hate, we have tacitly made another assumption which deserves to be stated explicitly. We have reckoned as though there existed in the mind—whether in the ego or in the id—a displaceable energy, which, neutral in itself, can be added to a qualitatively differentiated erotic or destructive impulse, and augment its total cathexis. Without assuming the existence of a displaceable energy of this kind we can make no headway. The only question is where it comes from, what it belongs to, and what it signifies.

The problem of the quality of instinctual impulses and of its persistence throughout their various vicissitudes is still very obscure and has hardly been attacked up to the present. In the sexual component instincts, which are especially accessible to observation, it is possible to perceive a few processes which are in the same category as what we are discussing. We see, for instance, that some degree of communication exists between the component instincts, that an instinct deriving from one particular erotogenic source can make over its intensity to reinforce another component instinct originating from another source, that the satisfaction of one instinct can take the place of the satisfaction of another, and more facts of the same nature—which must encourage us to venture upon certain hypotheses.

In the present discussion, moreover, I am only putting forward a hypothesis; I have no proof to offer. It seems a plausible view that this displaceable and neutral energy, which is no doubt active both in the ego and in the id, proceeds from the narcissistic store of libido—that it is desexualized Eros. (The erotic instincts appear to be altogether more plastic, more readily diverted and displaced than the destructive instincts.) From this we can easily go on to assume that this displaceable libido is employed in the service of the pleasure principle to obviate blockages and to facilitate discharge. In this connection it is easy to observe a certain indifference as to the path along which the discharge takes place, so long as it takes place somehow. We know this trait; it is characteristic of the cathetic processes in the id. It is found in erotic cathexes, where a peculiar indifference in regard to the object displays itself; and it is especially evident in the transferences arising in analysis, which develop inevitably, irrespective of the persons who are their object. Not long ago Rank published some good examples of the way in which neurotic acts of revenge can be directed against the wrong people. Such behaviour on the part of the unconscious reminds one of the comic story of the three village tailors, one of whom had to be hanged because the only village blacksmith had committed a capital offence. Punishment must be exacted even if it does not fall upon the guilty. It was in studying the dream-work that we first came upon this kind of looseness in the displacements brought about by the primary process. In that case it was the objects that were thus relegated to a position of no more than secondary importance, just as in the case we are now discussing it is the paths of discharge. It would be characteristic of the ego to be more particular about the choice both of an object and of a path of discharge.

If this displaceable energy is desexualized libido, it may also be described as *sublimated* energy; for it would still retain the main purpose of Eros—that of uniting and binding—in so far as it helps towards establishing the unity, or tendency to unity, which is particularly characteristic of the ego. If thought-processes in the wider sense are to be included among these displacements, then the activity of thinking is also supplied from the sublimation of erotic motive forces.

Here we arrive again at the possibility which has already been discussed that sublimation may take place regularly through the mediation of the ego. The other case will be recollected, in which the ego deals with the first object-cathexes of the id (and certainly with later ones too) by taking over the libido from them into itself and binding it to the alteration of the ego produced by means of identification. The transformation [of erotic libido] into ego-libido of course involves an abandonment of sexual aims, a desexualization. In any case this throws light upon an important function of the ego in its relation to Eros. By thus getting hold of the libido from the object-cathexes, setting itself up as sole love-object, and desexualizing or sublimating the libido of the id, the ego is working in opposition to the purposes of Eros and placing itself at the service of the opposing instinctual impulses. It has to acquiesce in some of the other object-cathexes of the id; it has, so to speak, to participate in them. We shall come back later to another possible consequence of this activity of the ego.

This would seem to imply an important amplification of the theory of narcissism. At the very beginning, all the libido is accumulated in the id, while the ego is still in process of formation or is still feeble. The id sends part of this libido out into erotic object-cathexes, whereupon the ego, now grown stronger, tries to get hold of this object-libido and to force itself on the id as a love-object. The narcissism of the ego is thus a secondary one, which has been withdrawn from objects.

Over and over again we find, when we are able to trace instinctual impulses back, that they reveal themselves as derivatives of Eros. If it were not for the considerations put forward in *Beyond the Pleasure Principle*, and ultimately for the sadistic constituents which have attached themselves to Eros, we should have difficulty in holding to our fundamental dualistic point of view. But since we cannot escape that view, we are driven to conclude that the death instincts are by their nature mute and that the clamour of life proceeds for the most part from Eros.[9]

And from the struggle against Eros! It can hardly be doubted that the pleasure principle serves the id as a compass in its struggle against the libido—the force that introduces disturbances into the process of life. If it is true that Fechner's principle of constancy governs life, which thus consists of a continuous descent towards death, it is the claims of Eros, of the sexual instincts, which, in the form of instinctual needs, hold up the falling level and introduce fresh tensions. The id, guided by the pleasure principle—that is, by the perception of unpleasure—fends off these tensions in various ways. It does so in the first place by complying as swiftly as possible with the demands of the non-desexualized libido—by striving for the satisfaction of the directly sexual trends. But it does so in a far more comprehensive fashion in relation to one particular form of satisfaction in which all component demands converge—by discharge of the sexual substances, which are saturated vehicles, so to speak, of the erotic tensions. The ejection of the sexual substances in the sexual act corresponds in a sense to the separation of soma and germ-plasm. This accounts for the likeness of the condition that follows complete sexual satisfaction to dying, and for the fact that death coincides with the act of copulation in some of the lower animals. These creatures die in the act of reproduction because, after Eros has been eliminated through the process of satisfaction, the death instinct has a free hand for accomplishing its purposes. Finally, as we have seen, the ego, by sublimating some of the libido for itself and its purposes, assists the id in its work of mastering the tensions.

9. In fact, in our view it is through the agency of Eros that the destructive instincts that are directed towards the external world have been diverted from the self.

V

THE DEPENDENT RELATIONSHIPS

OF THE EGO

The complexity of our subject-matter must be an excuse for the fact that none of the chapter-headings of this book quite correspond to their contents, and that in turning to new aspects of the topic we are constantly harking back to matters that have already been dealt with.

Thus we have said repeatedly that the ego is formed to a great extent out of identifications which take the place of abandoned cathexes by the id; that the first of these identifications always behave as a special agency in the ego and stand apart from the ego in the form of a super-ego, while later on, as it grows stronger, the ego may become more resistant to the influences of such identifications. The super-ego owes its special position in the ego, or in relation to the ego, to a factor which must be considered from two sides: on the one hand it was the first identification and one which took place while the ego was still feeble, and on the other hand it is the heir to the Oedipus complex and has thus introduced the most momentous objects into the ego. The super-ego's relation to the later alterations of the ego is roughly similar to that of the primary sexual phase of childhood to later sexual life after puberty. Although it is accessible to all later influences, it nevertheless preserves throughout life the character given to it by its derivation from the father-complex— namely, the capacity to stand apart from the ego and to master it. It is a memorial of the former weakness and dependence of the ego, and the mature ego remains subject to its domination. As the child was once under a compulsion to obey its parents, so the ego submits to the cat- egorical imperative of its super-ego.

But the derivation of the super-ego from the first object-cathexes of the id, from the Oedipus complex, signifies even more for it. This derivation, as we have already shown, brings it into relation with the phylogenetic acquisitions of the id and makes it a reincarnation of former ego-structures which have left their precipitates behind in the id. Thus the super-ego is always close to the id and can act as its representative vis-à-vis the ego. It reaches deep down into the id and for that reason is farther from consciousness than the ego is.

We shall best appreciate these relations by turning to certain clinical facts, which have long since lost their novelty but which still await theoretical discussion.

There are certain people who behave in a quite peculiar fashion during the work of analysis. When one speaks hopefully to them or expresses satisfaction with the progress of the treatment, they show signs of dis- content and their condition invariably becomes worse. One begins by regarding this as defiance and as an attempt to prove their superiority to the physician, but later one comes to take a deeper and juster view.

One becomes convinced, not only that such people cannot endure any praise or appreciation, but that they react inversely to the progress of the treatment. Every partial solution that ought to result, and in other people does result, in an improvement or a temporary suspension of symptoms produces in them for the time being an exacerbation of their illness; they get worse during the treatment instead of getting better. They exhibit what is known as a 'negative therapeutic reaction'.

There is no doubt that there is something in these people that sets itself against their recovery, and its approach is dreaded as though it were a danger. We are accustomed to say that the need for illness has got the upper hand in them over the desire for recovery. If we analyse this resistance in the usual way—then, even after allowance has been made for an attitude of defiance towards the physician and for fixation to the various forms of gain from illness, the greater part of it is still left over; and this reveals itself as the most powerful of all obstacles to recovery, more powerful than the familiar ones of narcissistic inaccessibility, a negative attitude towards the physician and clinging to the gain from illness.

In the end we come to see that we are dealing with what may be called a 'moral' factor, a sense of guilt, which is finding its satisfaction in the illness and refuses to give up the punishment of suffering. We shall be right in regarding this disheartening explanation as final. But as far as the patient is concerned this sense of guilt is dumb; it does not tell him he is guilty; he does not feel guilty, he feels ill. This sense of guilt expresses itself only as a resistance to recovery which it is extremely difficult to overcome. It is also particularly difficult to convince the patient that this motive lies behind his continuing to be ill; he holds fast to the more obvious explanation that treatment by analysis is not the right remedy for his case.

The description we have given applies to the most extreme instances of this state of affairs, but in a lesser measure this factor has to be reckoned with in very many cases, perhaps in all comparatively severe cases of neurosis. In fact it may be precisely this element in the situation, the attitude of the ego ideal, that determines the severity of a neurotic illness. We shall not hesitate, therefore, to discuss rather more fully the way in which the sense of guilt expresses itself under different conditions.

An interpretation of the normal, conscious sense of guilt (conscience) presents no difficulties; it is based on the tension between the ego and the ego ideal and is the expression of a condemnation of the ego by its critical agency. The feelings of inferiority so well known in neurotics are presumably not far removed from it. In two very familiar maladies the sense of guilt is over-strongly conscious; in them the ego ideal displays particular severity and often rages against the ego in a cruel fashion. The attitude of the ego ideal in these two conditions, obsessional neurosis and melancholia, presents, alongside of this similarity, differences that are no less significant.

In certain forms of obsessional neurosis the sense of guilt is over-noisy but cannot justify itself to the ego. Consequently the patient's ego rebels against the imputation of guilt and seeks the physician's support in repudiating it. It would be folly to acquiesce in this, for to do so would have no effect. Analysis eventually shows that the super-ego is being influenced by processes that have remained unknown to the ego. It is possible to discover the repressed impulses which are really at the bottom of the sense of guilt. Thus in this case the super-ego knew more than the ego about the unconscious id.

In melancholia the impression that the super-ego has obtained a hold upon consciousness is even stronger. But here the ego ventures no objection; it admits its guilt and submits to the punishment. We understand the difference. In obsessional neurosis what were in question were objectionable impulses which remained outside the ego, while in melancholia the object to which the super-ego's wrath applies has been taken into the ego through identification.

It is certainly not clear why the sense of guilt reaches such an extraordinary strength in these two neurotic disorders; but the main problem presented in this state of affairs lies in another direction. We shall postpone discussion of it until we have dealt with the other cases in which the sense of guilt remains unconscious.

It is essentially in hysteria and in states of a hysterical type that this is found. Here the mechanism by which the sense of guilt remains unconscious is easy to discover. The hysterical ego fends off a distressing perception with which the criticisms of its super-ego threaten it, in the same way in which it is in the habit of fending off an unendurable object-cathexes—by an act of repression. It is the ego, therefore, that is responsible for the sense of guilt remaining unconscious. We know that as a rule the ego carries out repressions in the service and at the behest of its super-ego; but this is a case in which it has turned the same weapon against its harsh taskmaster. In obsessional neurosis, as we know, the phenomena of reaction-formation predominate; but here [in hysteria] the ego succeeds only in keeping at a distance the material to which the sense of guilt refers.

One may go further and venture the hypothesis that a great part of the sense of guilt must normally remain unconscious, because the origin of conscience is intimately connected with the Oedipus complex, which belongs to the unconscious. If anyone were inclined to put forward the paradoxical proposition that the normal man is not only far more immoral than he believes but also far more moral than he knows, psychoanalysis, on whose findings the first half of the assertion rests, would have no objection to raise against the second half.[1]

It was a surprise to find that an increase in this *Ucs.* sense of guilt

1. This proposition is only apparently a paradox; it simply states that human nature has a far greater extent, both for good and for evil, than it thinks it has—i.e. than its ego is aware of through conscious perception.

can turn people into criminals. But it is undoubtedly a fact. In many criminals, especially youthful ones, it is possible to detect a very powerful sense of guilt which existed before the crime, and is therefore not its result but its motive. It is as if it was a relief to be able to fasten this unconscious sense of guilt on to something real and immediate.

In all these situations the super-ego displays its independence of the conscious ego and its intimate relations with the unconscious id. Having regard, now, to the importance we have ascribed to preconscious verbal residues in the ego, the question arises whether it can be the case that the super-ego, in so far as it is *Ucs.*, consists in such word-presentations and, if it does not, what else it consists in. Our tentative answer will be that it is as impossible for the super-ego as for the ego to disclaim its origin from things heard; for it is a part of the ego and remains accessible to consciousness by way of these word-presentations (concepts, abstractions). But the *cathectic energy* does not reach these contents of the super-ego from auditory perception (instruction or reading) but from sources in the id.

The question which we put off answering runs as follows: How is it that the super-ego manifests itself essentially as a sense of guilt (or rather, as criticism—for the sense of guilt is the perception in the ego answering to this criticism) and moreover develops such extraordinary harshness and severity towards the ego? If we turn to melancholia first, we find that the excessively strong super-ego which has obtained a hold upon consciousness rages against the ego with merciless violence, as if it had taken possession of the whole of the sadism available in the person concerned. Following our view of sadism, we should say that the destructive component had entrenched itself in the super-ego and turned against the ego. What is now holding sway in the super-ego is, as it were, a pure culture of the death instinct, and in fact it often enough succeeds in driving the ego into death, if the latter does not fend off its tyrant in time by the change round into mania.

The reproaches of conscience in certain forms of obsessional neurosis are as distressing and tormenting, but here the situation is less perspicuous. It is noteworthy that the obsessional neurotic, in contrast to the melancholic, never in fact takes the step of self-destruction; it is as though he were immune against the danger of suicide, and he is far better protected from it than the hysteric. We can see that what guarantees the safety of the ego is the fact that the object has been retained. In obsessional neurosis it has become possible, through a regression to the pregenital organization, for the love-impulses to transform themselves into impulses of aggression against the object. Here again the instinct of destruction has been set free and it seeks to destroy the object, or at least it appears to have that intention. These purposes have not been adopted by the ego and it struggles against them with reaction-formations and precautionary measures; they remain in the id. The super-ego, however, behaves as if the ego were responsible for them and shows at the same time by the seriousness with which it chastises these destructive intentions that they are no mere semblance evoked by regression but an actual substitution of hate for love. Helpless in both directions, the ego defends itself vainly, alike against the instigations of the murderous id and against the reproaches of the punishing conscience. It succeeds in holding in check at least the most brutal actions of both sides; the first outcome is interminable self-torment, and eventually there follows a systematic torturing of the object, in so far as it is within reach.

The dangerous death instincts are dealt with in the individual in various ways: in part they are rendered harmless by being fused with erotic components, in part they are diverted towards the external world in the form of aggression, while to a large extent they undoubtedly continue their internal work unhindered. How is it then that in melancholia the super-ego can become a kind of gathering-place for the death instincts?

From the point of view of instinctual control, of morality, it may be said of the id that it is totally non-moral, of the ego that it strives to be moral, and of the super-ego that it can be super-moral and then become as cruel as only the id can be. It is remarkable that the more a man checks his aggressiveness towards the exterior the more severe—that is aggressive—he becomes in his ego ideal. The ordinary view sees the situation the other way round: the standard set up by the ego ideal seems to be the motive for the suppression of aggressiveness. The fact remains, however, as we have stated it: the more a man controls his aggressiveness, the more intense becomes his ideal's inclination to aggressiveness against his ego. It is like a displacement, a turning round upon his own ego. But even ordinary normal morality has a harshly restraining, cruelly prohibiting quality. It is from this, indeed, that the conception arises of a higher being who deals out punishment inexorably.

I cannot go further in my consideration of these questions without introducing a fresh hypothesis. The super-ego arises, as we know, from an identification with the father taken as a model. Every such identification is in the nature of a desexualization or even of a sublimation. It now seems as though when a transformation of this kind takes place, an instinctual defusion occurs at the same time. After sublimation the erotic component no longer has the power to bind the whole of the destructiveness that was combined with it, and this is released in the form of an inclination to aggression and destruction. This defusion would be the source of the general character of harshness and cruelty exhibited by the ideal—its dictatorial 'Thou shalt'.

Let us again consider obsessional neurosis for a moment. The state of affairs is different here. The defusion of love into aggressiveness has not been effected by the work of the ego, but is the result of a regression which has come about in the id. But this process has extended beyond the id to the super-ego, which now increases its severity towards the innocent ego. It would seem, however, that in this case, no less than in that of melancholia, the ego, having gained control over the libido by means of identification, is punished for doing so by the super-ego through the instrumentality of the aggressiveness which was mixed with the libido.

Our ideas about the ego are beginning to clear, and its various relationships are gaining distinctness. We now see the ego in its strength and in its weaknesses. It is entrusted with important functions. By virtue of its relation to the perceptual system it gives mental processes an order in time and submits them to 'reality-testing'. By interposing the processes of thinking, it secures a postponement of motor discharges and controls the access to motility. This last power is, to be sure, a question more of form than of fact; in the matter of action the ego's position is like that of a constitutional monarch, without whose sanction no law can be passed but who hesitates long before imposing his veto on any measure put forward by Parliament. All the experiences of life that originate from without enrich the ego; the id, however, is its second external world, which it strives to bring into subjection to itself. It withdraws libido from the id and transforms the object-cathexes of the id into ego-structures. With the aid of the super-ego, in a manner that is still obscure to us, it draws upon the experiences of past ages stored in the id.

There are two paths by which the contents of the id can penetrate into the ego. The one is direct, the other leads by way of the ego ideal; which of these two paths they take may, for some mental activities, be of decisive importance. The ego develops from perceiving instincts to controlling them, from obeying instincts to inhibiting them. In this achievement a large share is taken by the ego ideal, which indeed is partly a reaction-formation against the instinctual processes of the id. Psycho-analysis is an instrument to enable the ego to achieve a progressive conquest of the id.

From the other point of view, however, we see this same ego as a poor creature owing service to three masters and consequently menaced by three dangers: from the external world, from the libido of the id, and from the severity of the super-ego. Three kinds of anxiety correspond to these three dangers, since anxiety is the expression of a retreat from danger. As a frontier-creature, the ego tries to mediate between the world and the id, to make the id pliable to the world and, by means of its muscular activity, to make the world fall in with the wishes of the id. In point of fact it behaves like the physician during an analytic treatment: it offers itself, with the attention it pays to the real world, as a libidinal object to the id, and aims at attaching the id's libido to itself. It is not only a helper to the id; it is also a submissive slave who courts his master's love. Whenever possible, it tries to remain on good terms with the id; it clothes the id's *Ucs.* commands with its *Pcs.* rationalizations; it pretends that the id is showing obedience to the admonitions of reality, even when in fact it is remaining obstinate and unyielding; it disguises the id's conflicts with reality and, if possible, its conflicts with the super-ego too. In its position midway between the id and reality, it only too often yields to the temptation to become sycophantic, opportunist and lying, like a politician who sees the truth but wants to keep his place in popular favour.

Towards the two classes of instincts the ego's attitude is not impartial. Through its work of identification and sublimation it gives the death instincts in the id assistance in gaining control over the libido, but in so doing it runs the risk of becoming the object of the death instincts and of itself perishing. In order to be able to help in this way it has had itself to become filled with libido; it thus itself becomes the representative of Eros and thenceforward desires to live and to be loved.

But since the ego's work of sublimation results in a defusion of the instincts and a liberation of the aggressive instincts in the super-ego, its struggle against the libido exposes it to the danger of maltreatment and death. In suffering under the attacks of the super-ego or perhaps even succumbing to them, the ego is meeting with a fate like that of the protista which are destroyed by the products of decomposition that they themselves have created. From the economic point of view the morality that functions in the super-ego seems to be a similar product of decomposition.

Among the dependent relationships in which the ego stands, that to the super-ego is perhaps the most interesting.

The ego is the actual seat of anxiety. Threatened by dangers from three directions, it develops the flight-reflex by withdrawing its own cathexis from the menacing perception or from the similarly regarded process in the id, and emitting it as anxiety. This primitive reaction is later replaced by the carrying-out of protective cathexes (the mechanism of the phobias). What it is that the ego fears from the external and from the libidinal danger cannot be specified; we know that the fear is of being overwhelmed or annihilated, but it cannot be grasped analytically. The ego is simply obeying the warning of the pleasure principle. On the other hand, we can tell what is hidden behind the ego's dread of the super-ego, the fear of conscience. The superior being, which turned into the ego ideal, once threatened castration, and this dread of castration is probably the nucleus round which the subsequent fear of conscience has gathered; it is this dread that persists as the ear of conscience.

The high-sounding phrase, 'every fear is ultimately the fear of death', has hardly any meaning, and at any rate cannot be justified. It seems to me, on the contrary, perfectly correct to distinguish the fear of death from dread of an object (realistic anxiety) and from neurotic libidinal anxiety. It presents a difficult problem to psycho-analysis, for death is an abstract concept with a negative content for which no unconscious correlative can be found. It would seem that the mechanism of the fear of death can only be that the ego relinquishes its narcissistic libidinal cathexis in a very large measure—that is, that it gives up itself, just as it gives up some *external* object in other cases in which it feels anxiety.

I believe that the fear of death is something that occurs between the ego and the super-ego.

We know that the fear of death makes its appearance under two conditions (which, moreover, are entirely analogous to situations in which other kinds of anxiety develop), namely, as a reaction to an external danger and as an internal process, as for instance in melancholia. Once again a neurotic manifestation may help us to understand a normal one.

The fear of death in melancholia only admits of one explanation: that the ego gives itself up because it feels itself hated and persecuted by the super-ego, instead of loved. To the ego, therefore, living means the same as being loved—being loved by the super-ego, which here again appears as the representative of the id. The super-ego fulfils the same function of protecting and saving that was fulfilled in earlier days by the father and later by Providence or Destiny. But, when the ego finds itself in an excessive real danger which it believes itself unable to overcome by its own strength, it is bound to draw the same conclusion. It sees itself deserted by all protecting forces and lets itself die. Here, moreover, is once again the same situation as that which underlay the first great anxiety-state of birth and the infantile anxiety of longing—the anxiety due to separation from the protecting mother.

These considerations make it possible to regard the fear of death, like the fear of conscience, as a development of the fear of castration. The great significance which the sense of guilt has in the neuroses makes it conceivable that common neurotic anxiety is reinforced in severe cases by the generating of anxiety between the ego and the super-ego (fear of castration, of conscience, of death).

The id, to which we finally come back, has no means of showing the ego either love or hate. It cannot say what it wants; it has achieved no unified will. Eros and the death instinct struggle within it; we have seen with what weapons the one group of instincts defends itself against the other. It would be possible to picture the id as under the domination of the mute but powerful death instincts, which desire to be at peace and (prompted by the pleasure principle) to put Eros, the mischief-maker, to rest; but perhaps that might be to undervalue the part played by Eros.

PART SIX:
THE LAST CHAPTER

The Dissolution of the Oedipus Complex

The vigorous rhetoric characterizing this short paper of 1924, which re-affirms the centrality of the Oedipus complex, was in part a response to the new and increasingly disturbing notion of the "birth trauma" advanced by Otto Rank. Freud's amanuensis and, until around 1923, perhaps his most uncritical follower, Rank was moving off on his own in matters of psychoanalytic technique and theory. At first, Freud had taken an interest in Rank's departures and defended them against the suspicions, even anger, of his closest adherents. But after thinking the matter through, he rejected Rank's demotion of the Oedipus complex and installation of the birth trauma as the archetypal and crucial human experience (Rank fully developed this aspect of his thought in *The Trauma of Birth* [1924; tr. 1929]). But while this may have helped to determine its tone, the essential importance of the paper lies elsewhere. For long years, Freud had portrayed the sexual evolution of boys and girls as parallel. Investigations of the early 1920s, prompted by his growing sense that female sexuality is more mysterious than male sexuality and that he knew too little about the evolution of women, had persuaded him to modify his ideas on development and stress the differences rather than the resemblances between the sexes. He returned to his revised views on this sensitive subject more than once and worked them out in greater detail, most notably in 1925, with "Some Psychical Consequences of the Anatomical Distinction Between the Sexes" (see below, pp. 670–78) and in 1931, with "Female Sexuality." But some of the formulations that would—rightly—offend feminists, and the laconic assertion that anatomy is destiny, are already contained in the present paper.

To an ever-increasing extent the Oedipus complex reveals its importance as the central phenomenon of the sexual period of early childhood. After that, its dissolution takes place; it succumbs to repression, as we say, and is followed by the latency period. It has not yet become clear, however, what it is that brings about its destruction. Analyses seem to show that it is the experience of painful disappointments. The little girl likes to regard herself as what her father loves above all else; but the time comes when she has to endure a harsh punishment from him and she is cast out of her fool's paradise. The boy regards his mother as his own property; but he finds one day that she has transferred her love and solicitude to a new arrival. Reflection must deepen our sense of the importance of those influences, for it will emphasize the fact that distressing experiences of this sort, which act in opposition to the content of the complex, are inevitable. Even when no special events occur, like those we have mentioned as examples, the absence of the satisfaction hoped for, the continued denial of the desired baby, must in the end lead the small lover to turn away from his hopeless longing. In this way the Oedipus complex would go to its destruction from its lack of success, from the effects of its internal impossibility.

Another view is that the Oedipus complex must collapse because the time has come for its disintegration, just as the milk-teeth fall out when the permanent ones begin to grow. Although the majority of human beings go through the Oedipus complex as an individual experience, it is nevertheless a phenomenon which is determined and laid down by heredity and which is bound to pass away according to programme when the next pre-ordained phase of development sets in. This being so, it is of no great importance what the occasions are which allow this to happen, or, indeed, whether any such occasions can be discovered at all.

The justice of both these views cannot be disputed. Moreover, they are compatible. There is room for the ontogenetic view side by side with the more far-reaching phylogenetic one. It is also true that even at birth the whole individual is destined to die, and perhaps his organic disposition may already contain the indication of what he is to die from. Nevertheless, it remains of interest to follow out how this innate programme is carried out and in what way accidental noxae exploit his disposition.

* * * A child's sexual development advances to a certain phase at which the genital organ has already taken over the leading role. But this genital is the male one only, or, more correctly, the penis; the female genital has remained undiscovered. This phallic phase, which is contemporaneous with the Oedipus complex, does not develop further to the definitive genital organization, but is submerged, and is succeeded by the latency period. Its termination, however, takes place in a typical manner and in conjunction with events that are of regular recurrence.

When the (male) child's interest turns to his genitals he betrays the fact by manipulating them frequently; and he then finds that the adults do not approve of this behaviour. More or less plainly, more or less brutally, a threat is pronounced that this part of him which he values so highly will be taken away from him. Usually it is from women that the threat emanates; very often they seek to strengthen their authority by a reference to the father or the doctor, who, so they say, will carry out the punishment. In a number of cases the women will themselves mitigate the threat in a symbolic manner by telling the child that what is to be removed is not his genital, which actually plays a passive part, but his hand, which is the active culprit. It happens particularly often that the little boy is threatened with castration, not because he plays with his penis with his hand, but because he wets his bed every night and cannot be got to be clean. Those in charge of him behave as if this nocturnal incontinence was the result and the proof of his being unduly concerned with his penis, and they are probably right. In any case, long-continued bed-wetting is to be equated with the emissions of adults. It is an expression of the same excitation of the genitals which has impelled the child to masturbate at this period.

Now it is my view that what brings about the destruction of the child's phallic genital organizaton is this threat of castration. Not immediately, it is true, and not without other influences being brought to bear as well. For to begin with the boy does not believe in the threat or obey it in the least. Psycho-analysis has recently attached importance to two experiences which all children go through and which, it is suggested, prepare them for the loss of highly valued parts of the body. These experiences are the withdrawal of the mother's breast—at first intermittently and later for good—and the daily demand on them to give up the contents of the bowel. But there is no evidence to show that, when the threat of castration takes place, those experiences have any effect. It is not until a *fresh* experience comes his way that the child begins to reckon with the possibility of being castrated, and then only hesitatingly and unwillingly, and not without making efforts to depreciate the significance of something he has himself observed.

The observation which finally breaks down his unbelief is the sight of the female genitals. Sooner or later the child, who is so proud of his possession of a penis, has a view of the genital region of a little girl, and cannot help being convinced of the absence of a penis in a creature who is so like himself. With this, the loss of his own penis becomes imaginable, and the threat of castration takes its deferred effect.

We should not be as short-sighted as the person in charge of the child who threatens him with castration, and we must not overlook the fact that at this time masturbation by no means represents the whole of his sexual life. As can be clearly shown, he stands in the Oedipus attitude to his parents; his masturbation is only a genital discharge of the sexual excitation belonging to the complex, and throughout his later years will owe its importance to that relationship. The Oedipus complex offered the child two possibilities of satisfaction, an active and a passive one. He could put himself in his father's place in a masculine fashion and have intercourse with his mother as his father did, in which case he would soon have felt the latter as a hindrance; or he might want to take the place of his mother and be loved by his father, in which case his mother would become superfluous. The child may have had only very vague notions as to what constitutes a satisfying erotic intercourse; but certainly the penis must play a part in it, for the sensations in his own organ were evidence of that. So far he had had no occasion to doubt that women possessed a penis. But now his acceptance of the possibility of castration, his recognition that women were castrated, made an end of both possible ways of obtaining satisfaction from the Oedipus complex. For both of them entailed the loss of his penis—the masculine one as a resulting punishment and the feminine one as a precondition. If the satisfaction of love in the field of the Oedipus complex is to cost the child his penis, a conflict is bound to arise between his narcissistic interest in that part of his body and the libidinal cathexis of his parental objects. In this conflict the first of these forces normally triumphs: the child's ego turns away from the Oedipus complex.

I have described elsewhere how this turning away takes place. The object-cathexes are given up and replaced by identifications. The authority of the father or the parents is introjected into the ego, and there it forms the nucleus of the super-ego, which takes over the severity of the father and perpetuates his prohibition against incest, and so secures the ego from the return of the libidinal object-cathexis. The libidinal trends belonging to the Oedipus complex are in part desexualized and sublimated (a thing which probably happens with every transformation into an identification) and in part inhibited in their aim and changed into impulses of affection. The whole process has, on the one hand, preserved the genital organ—has averted the danger of its loss—and, on the other, has paralysed it—has removed its function. This process ushers in the latency period, which now interrupts the child's sexual development.

I see no reason for denying the name of a 'repression' to the ego's turning away from the Oedipus complex, although later repressions come about for the most part with the participation of the super-ego, which in this case is only just being formed. But the process we have described is more than a repression. It is equivalent, if it is ideally carried out, to a destruction and an abolition of the complex. We may plausibly assume that we have here come upon the borderline—never a very sharply drawn one—between the normal and the pathological. If the ego has in fact not achieved much more than a *repression* of the complex, the latter persists in an unconscious state in the id and will later manifest its pathogenic effect.

Analytic observation enables us to recognize or guess these connections between the phallic organization, the Oedipus complex, the threat of castration, the formation of the super-ego and the latency period. These connections justify the statement that the destruction of the Oedipus complex is brought about by the threat of castration. But this does not dispose of the problem; there is room for a theoretical speculation which may upset the results we have come to or put them in a new light. Before we start along this new path, however, we must turn to a question which has arisen in the course of this discussion and has so far been left on one side. The process which has been described refers, as has been expressly said, to male children only. How does the corresponding development take place in little girls?

At this point our material—for some incomprehensible reason—becomes far more obscure and full of gaps. The female sex, too, develops an Oedipus complex, a super-ego and a latency period. May we also attribute a phallic organization and a castration complex to it? The answer is in the affirmative; but these things cannot be the same as they are in boys. Here the feminist demand for equal rights for the sexes does not take us far, for the morphological distinction is bound to find expression in differences of psychical development. 'Anatomy is Destiny', to vary a saying of Napoleon's. The little girl's clitoris behaves just like a penis to begin with; but, when she makes a comparison with a playfellow of the other sex, she perceives that she has 'come off badly' and she feels this as a wrong done to her and as a ground for inferiority. For a while still she consoles herself with the expectation that later on, when she grows older, she will acquire just as big an appendage as the boy's. Here the masculinity complex of women branches off. A female child, however, does not understand her lack of a penis as being a sex character; she explains it by assuming that at some earlier date she had possessed an equally large organ and had then lost it by castration. She seems not to extend this inference from herself to other, adult females, but, entirely on the lines of the phallic phase, to regard them as possessing large and complete—that is to say, male—genitals. The essential difference thus comes about that the girl accepts castration as an accomplished fact, whereas the boy fears the possibility of its occurrence.

The fear of castration being thus excluded in the little girl, a powerful motive also drops out for the setting-up of a super-ego and for the breaking-off of the infantile genital organization. In her, far more than in the boy, these changes seem to be the result of upbringing and of intimidation from outside which threatens her with a loss of love. The girl's Oedipus complex is much simpler than that of the small bearer of the penis; in my experience, it seldom goes beyond the taking of her mother's place and the adopting of a feminine attitude towards her father. Renunciation of the penis is not tolerated by the girl without some attempt at compensation. She slips—along the line of a symbolic equation, one might say—from the penis to a baby. Her Oedipus complex culminates in a desire, which is long retained, to receive a baby from her father as a gift—to bear him a child. One has an impression that the Oedipus complex is then gradually given up because this wish is never fulfilled. The two wishes—to possess a penis and a child—remain strongly cathected in the unconscious and help to prepare the female creature for her later sexual role. The comparatively lesser strength of the sadistic contribution to her sexual instinct, which we may no doubt connect with the stunted growth of her penis, makes it easier in her case for the direct sexual trends to be transformed into aim-inhibited trends of an affectionate kind. It must be admitted, however, that in general our insight into these developmental processes in girls is unsatisfactory, incomplete and vague.

I have no doubt that the chronological and causal relations described here between the Oedipus complex, sexual intimidation (the threat of castration), the formation of the super-ego and the beginning of the latency period are of a typical kind; but I do not wish to assert that this type is the only possible one. Variations in the chronological order and in the linking-up of these events are bound to have a very important bearing on the development of the individual.

Since the publication of Otto Rank's interesting study, *The Trauma of Birth* [1924], even the conclusion arrived at by this modest investigation, to the effect that the boy's Oedipus complex is destroyed by the fear of castration, cannot be accepted without further discussion. Nevertheless, it seems to me premature to enter into such a discussion at the present time, and perhaps inadvisable to begin a criticism or an appreciation of Rank's view at this juncture.

Negation

This short paper of 1925 sums up one of Freud's persistent preoccupations: the meaning of "no" in the analytic setting. His comments on the nature of thinking, brief as they are, are of considerable interest as well. There is one issue raised by an analysand's negations that Freud did not address until near the end of his life, in "Constructions in Analysis" (1937): if the patient's "yes" means "yes," and his "no" means "yes" as well, does this not guarantee the accuracy of *all* the analyst's pronouncements? And if he cannot ever be successfully challenged, can he claim to be anything better than a faith healer? Scientific propositions, after all, can be falsified, but the infallible pronouncements of the analyst by definition do not lend themselves to this test. In the paper on constructions, Freud quotes an unnamed critic of psychoanalysis: "He said that in giving interpretations to a patient we treat him upon the famous principle of 'Heads I win, tails you lose.' That is to say, if the patient agrees with us, then the interpretation is right; but if he contradicts us, that is only a sign of his resistance, which again shows that we are right. In this way we are always in the right against the poor helpless wretch whom we are analysing, no matter how he may respond to what we may put forward." But, Freud objects, this is not how analysts proceed. "No" may indeed mean "yes"—in the manner that his paper on negation had demonstrated. But there are far more reliable ways in which an analyst finds his interpretations confirmed: forms of expression, emotional vehemence, puzzling comments, and the like. Nor should an analyst ever claim infallibility: "There is no justification for the reproach that we neglect or underestimate the importance of the attitude taken up by those under analysis towards our constructions. We pay attention to them and often derive valuable information from them. . . . We do not pretend that an individual construction is anything more than a conjecture which awaits examination, confirmation or rejection. We claim no authority for it . . ." (*SE* XXIII, 257, 265). It would have been tactically extremely useful for the defense of psychoanalysis, if Freud had said all of this, clearly and often, in earlier years.

The manner in which our patients bring forward their associations during the work of analysis gives us an opportunity for making some interesting observations. 'Now you'll think I mean to say something insulting, but really I've no such intention.' We realize that this is a rejection, by projection, of an idea that has just come up. Or: 'You ask who this person in the dream can be. It's *not* my mother.' We emend this to: 'So it *is* his mother.' In our interpretation, we take the liberty of disregarding the negation and of picking out the subject-matter alone of the association. It is as though the patient had said: 'It's true that my mother came into my mind as I thought of this person, but I don't feel inclined to let the association count.'

There is a very convenient method by which we can sometimes obtain a piece of information we want about unconscious repressed material. 'What', we ask, 'would you consider the most unlikely imaginable thing in that situation? What do you think was furthest from your mind at that time?' If the patient falls into the trap and says what he thinks is most incredible, he almost always makes the right admission. A neat counterpart to this experiment is often met with in an obsessional neurotic who has already been initiated into the meaning of his symptoms. 'I've got a new obsessive idea,' he says, 'and it occurred to me at once that it might mean so and so. But no; that can't be true, or it couldn't have occurred to me.' What he is repudiating, on grounds picked up from his treatment, is, of course, the correct meaning of the obsessive idea.

Thus the content of a repressed image or idea can make its way into consciousness, on condition that it is *negated*. Negation is a way of taking cognizance of what is repressed; indeed it is already a lifting of the repression, though not, of course, an acceptance of what is repressed. We can see how in this the intellectual function is separated from the affective process. With the help of negation only one consequence of the process of repression is undone—the fact, namely, of the ideational content of what is repressed not reaching consciousness. The outcome of this is a kind of intellectual acceptance of the repressed, while at the same time what is essential to the repression persists.[1] In the course of analytic work we often produce a further, very important and somewhat strange variant of this situation. We succeed in conquering the negation as well, and in bringing about a full intellectual acceptance of the repressed; but the repressive process itself is not yet removed by this.

Since to affirm or negate the content of thoughts is the task of the function of intellectual judgement, what we have just been saying has led us to the psychological origin of that function. To negate something in a judgement is, at bottom, to say: 'This is something which I should prefer to repress.' A negative judgement is the intellectual substitute for repression; its 'no' is the hall-mark of repression, a certificate of origin—

---

[1]. The same process is at the root of the familiar superstition that boasting is dangerous. 'How nice not to have had one of my headaches for so long.' But this is in fact the first announcement of an attack, of whose approach the subject is already sensible, although he is as yet unwilling to believe it.

like, let us say, 'Made in Germany'.[2] With the help of the symbol of negation, thinking frees itself from the restrictions of repression and enriches itself with material that is indispensable for its proper functioning.

The function of judgement is concerned in the main with two sorts of decisions. It affirms or disaffirms the possession by a thing of a particular attribute; and it asserts or disputes that a presentation has an existence in reality. The attribute to be decided about may originally have been good or bad, useful or harmful. Expressed in the language of the oldest—the oral—instinctual impulses, the judgement is: 'I should like to eat this', or 'I should like to spit it out'; and, put more generally: 'I should like to take this into myself and to keep that out.' That is to say: 'It shall be inside me' or 'it shall be outside me'. As I have shown elsewhere, the original pleasure-ego wants to introject into itself everything that is good and to eject from itself everything that is bad. What is bad, what is alien to the ego and what is external are, to begin with, identical.

The other sort of decision made by the function of judgement—as to the real existence of something of which there is a presentation (reality-testing)—is a concern of the definitive reality-ego, which develops out of the initial pleasure-ego. It is now no longer a question of whether what has been perceived (a thing) shall be taken into the ego or not, but of whether something which is in the ego as a presentation can be rediscovered in perception (reality) as well. It is, we see, once more a question of *external* and *internal*. What is unreal, merely a presentation and subjective, is only internal; what is real is also there *outside*. In this stage of development regard for the pleasure principle has been set aside. Experience has shown the subject that it is not only important whether a thing (an object of satisfaction for him) possesses the 'good' attribute and so deserves to be taken into his ego, but also whether it is there in the external world, so that he can get hold of it whenever he needs it. In order to understand this step forward we must recollect that all presentations originate from perceptions and are repetitions of them. Thus originally the mere existence of a presentation was a guarantee of the reality of what was presented. The antithesis between subjective and objective does not exist from the first. It only comes into being from the fact that thinking possesses the capacity to bring before the mind once more something that has once been perceived, by reproducing it as a presentation without the external object having still to be there. The first and immediate aim, therefore, of reality-testing is, not to *find* an object in real perception which corresponds to the one presented, but to *refind* such an object, to convince oneself that it is still there. Another capacity of the power of thinking offers a further contribution to the differentiation between what is subjective and what is objective. The

2. [In English in the original.]

reproduction of a perception as a presentation is not always a faithful one; it may be modified by omissions, or changed by the merging of various elements. In that case, reality-testing has to ascertain how far such distortions go. But it is evident that a precondition for the setting up of reality-testing is that objects shall have been lost which once brought real satisfaction.

Judging is the intellectual action which decides the choice of motor action, which puts an end to the postponement due to thought and which leads over from thinking to acting. This postponement due to thought has also been discussed by me elsewhere. It is to be regarded as an experimental action, a motor palpating, with small expenditure of discharge. Let us consider where the ego has used a similar kind of palpating before, at what place it learnt the technique which it now applies in its processes of thought. It happened at the sensory end of the mental apparatus, in connection with sense perceptions. For, on our hypothesis, perception is not a purely passive process. The ego periodically sends out small amounts of cathexis into the perceptual system, by means of which it samples the external stimuli, and then after every such tentative advance it draws back again.

The study of judgement affords us, perhaps for the first time, an insight into the origin of an intellectual function from the interplay of the primary instinctual impulses. Judging is a continuation, along lines of expediency, of the original process by which the ego took things into itself or expelled them from itself, according to the pleasure principle. The polarity of judgement appears to correspond to the opposition of the two groups of instincts which we have supposed to exist. Affirmation—as a substitute for uniting—belongs to Eros; negation—the successor to expulsion—belongs to the instinct of destruction. The general wish to negate, the negativism which is displayed by some psychotics, is probably to be regarded as a sign of a defusion of instincts that has taken place through a withdrawal of the libidinal components. But the performance of the function of judgement is not made possible until the creation of the symbol of negation has endowed thinking with a first measure of freedom from the consequences of repression and, with it, from the compulsion of the pleasure principle.

This view of negation fits in very well with the fact that in analysis we never discover a 'no' in the unconscious and that recognition of the unconscious on the part of the ego is expressed in a negative formula. There is no stronger evidence that we have been successful in our effort to uncover the unconscious than when the patient reacts to it with the words 'I didn't think that', or 'I didn't (ever) think of that'.

Some Psychical Consequences of the Anatomical Distinction Between the Sexes

This paper, published late in 1925, was read to the International Psychoanalytic Congress at Homburg by Freud's daughter Anna. Since his cancer operations in 1923, Freud, somewhat hampered in his speech, refused to appear at these congresses, much as he missed them. There is some irony in a woman presenting a paper that many women have since found profoundly offensive. "Some Psychical Consequences" makes explicit, with technical particulars, what Freud had adumbrated briefly, aphoristically, the year before (see above, pp. 661–66). While through the decades, Freud had treated a large number of women patients, the riddle that is woman—an antique cliché about women repeated by Freud in modern language—did not yield easily to his analytic efforts. Ernest Jones reports that Freud once exclaimed to Princess Marie Bonaparte, *"Was will das Weib?"*—What does woman want?" (*Jones* II, 421). The present paper outlines a large part of his answer.

Freud returned to the important and controversial theme of woman's development in two later papers, "Female Sexuality" (1931) and "Femininity" (1933), the latter a chapter in his *New Introductory Lectures on Psycho-Analysis*. Essentially, they do little more than restate the arguments he had advanced in the present paper. But in "Female Sexuality" Freud made more than he had earlier of the little girl's pre–Oedipal attachment to her mother. And in "Femininity," though he stressed the active part of woman in life, he confessed that what he had to say about the subject "is certainly incomplete and fragmentary and does not always sound friendly" (*S.E.*, XXII, 135). It is worth noting that in the 1920s and early 1930s some psychoanalysts, notably Ernest Jones and Karen Horney (then still considering herself a good Freudian), did not accept Freud's verdict that women are virtually failed men, and said so in private and in print.

In my own writings and in those of my followers more and more stress is laid on the necessity that the analyses of neurotics shall deal thoroughly with the remotest period of their childhood, the time of the early efflorescence of sexual life. It is only by examining the first manifestations of the patient's innate instinctual constitution and the effects of his earliest experiences that we can accurately gauge the motive forces that have led to his neurosis and can be secure against the errors into which we might be tempted by the degree to which things have become remodelled and overlaid in adult life. This requirement is not only of theoretical but also of practical importance, for it distinguishes our efforts from the work of those physicians whose interests are focused exclusively on therapeutic results and who employ analytic methods, but only up to a certain point. An analysis of early childhood such as we are considering is tedious and laborious and makes demands both upon the physician and upon the patient which cannot always be met. Moreover, it leads us into dark regions where there are as yet no signposts. Indeed, analysts may feel reassured, I think, that there is no risk of their work becoming mechanical, and so of losing its interest, during the next few decades.

In the following pages I bring forward some findings of analytic research which would be of great importance if they could be proved to apply universally. Why do I not postpone publication of them until further experience has given me the necessary proof, if such proof is obtainable? Because the conditions under which I work have undergone a change, with implications which I cannot disguise. Formerly, I was not one of those who are unable to hold back what seems to be a new discovery until it has been either confirmed or corrected. My *Interpretation of Dreams* (1900*a*) and my 'Fragment of an Analysis of a Case of Hysteria' (1905*e*) (the case of Dora) were suppressed by me—if not for the nine years enjoined by Horace—at all events for four or five years before I allowed them to be published. But in those days I had unlimited time before me—'oceans of time'[1] as an amiable author puts it—and material poured in upon me in such quantities that fresh experiences were hardly to be escaped. Moreover, I was the only worker in a new field, so that my reticence involved no danger to myself and no loss to others.

But now everything has changed. The time before me is limited. The whole of it is no longer spent in working, so that my opportunities for making fresh observations are not so numerous. If I think I see something new, I am uncertain whether I can wait for it to be confirmed. And further, everything that is to be seen upon the surface has already been exhausted; what remains has to be slowly and laboriously dragged up from the depths. Finally, I am no longer alone. An eager crowd of fellow-workers is ready to make use of what is unfinished or doubtful, and I can leave to them that part of the work which I should otherwise have done myself. On this occasion, therefore, I feel justified in publishing something which stands in urgent need of confirmation before its value or lack of value can be decided.

In examining the earliest mental shapes assumed by the sexual life of children we have been in the habit of taking as the subject of our investigations the male child, the little boy. With little girls, so we have supposed, things must be similar, though in some way or other they must nevertheless be different. The point in development at which this difference lay could not be clearly determined.

In boys the situation of the Oedipus complex is the first stage that can be recognized with certainty. It is easy to understand, because at that stage a child retains the same object which he previously cathected with his libido—not as yet a genital one—during the preceding period

1. [In English in the original.]

while he was being suckled and nursed. The fact, too, that in this situation he regards his father as a disturbing rival and would like to get rid of him and take his place is a straightforward consequence of the actual state of affairs. I have shown elsewhere[2] how the Oedipus attitude in little boys belongs to the phallic phase, and how its destruction is brought about by the fear of castration—that is, by narcissistic interest in their genitals. The matter is made more difficult to grasp by the complicating circumstance that even in boys the Oedipus complex has a double orientation, active and passive, in accordance with their bisexual constitution; a boy also wants to take his *mother's* place as the love-object of his *father*—a fact which we describe as the feminine attitude.

As regards the prehistory of the Oedipus complex in boys we are far from complete clarity. We know that that period includes an identification of an affectionate sort with the boy's father, an identification which is still free from any sense of rivalry in regard to his mother. Another element of that stage is invariably, I believe, a masturbatory activity in connection with the genitals, the masturbation of early childhood, the more or less violent suppression of which by those in charge of the child sets the castration complex in action. It is to be assumed that this masturbation is attached to the Oedipus complex and serves as a discharge for the sexual excitation belonging to it. It is, however, uncertain whether the masturbation has this character from the first, or whether on the contrary it makes its first appearance spontaneously as an activity of a bodily organ and is only brought into relation with the Oedipus complex at some later date; this second possibility is by far the more probable. Another doubtful question is the part played by bedwetting and by the breaking of that habit through the intervention of training measures. We are inclined to make the simple connection that continued bed-wetting is a result of masturbation and that its suppression is regarded by boys as an inhibition of their genital activity—that is, as having the meaning of a threat of castration; but whether we are always right in supposing this remains to be seen. Finally, analysis shows us in a shadowy way how the fact of a child at a very early age listening to his parents copulating may set up his first sexual excitation, and how 'hat event may, owing to its after-effects, act as a starting-point for the child's whole sexual development. Masturbation, as well as the two attitudes in the Oedipus complex, later on become attached to this early experience, the child having subsequently interpreted its meaning. It is impossible, however, to suppose that these observations of coitus are of universal occurrence, so that at this point we are faced with the problem of 'primal phantasies'. Thus the prehistory of the Oedipus complex, even in boys, raises all of these questions for sifting and explanation; and there is the further problem of whether we are to suppose that the process

---

2. 'The Dissolution of the Oedipus Complex' (1924).

invariably follows the same course, or whether a great variety of different preliminary stages may not converge upon the same terminal situation.

In little girls the Oedipus complex raises one problem more than in boys. In both cases the mother is the original object; and there is no cause for surprise that boys retain that object in the Oedipus complex. But how does it happen that girls abandon it and instead take their father as an object? In pursuing this question I have been able to reach some conclusions which may throw light precisely on the prehistory of the Oedipus relation in girls.

Every analyst has come across certain women who cling with especial intensity and tenacity to the bond with their father and to the wish in which it culminates of having a child by him. We have good reason to suppose that the same wishful phantasy was also the motive force of their infantile masturbation, and it is easy to form an impression that at this point we have been brought up against an elementary and un-analysable fact of infantile sexual life. But a thorough analysis of these very cases brings something different to light—namely, that here the Oedipus complex has a long prehistory and is in some respects a sec-ondary formation.

The old paediatrician Lindner [1879] once remarked that a child discovers the genital zones (the penis or the clitoris) as a source of pleasure while indulging in sensual sucking (thumb-sucking). I shall leave it an open question whether it is really true that the child takes the newly found source of pleasure in exchange for the recent loss of the mother's nipple—a possibility to which later phantasies (fellatio) seem to point. Be that as it may, the genital zone is discovered at some time or other, and there seems no justification for attributing any psychical content to the first activities in connection with it. But the first step in the phallic phase which begins in this way is not the linking-up of the masturbation with the object-cathexes of the Oedipus complex, but a momentous discovery which little girls are destined to make. They notice the penis of a brother or playmate, strikingly visible and of large proportions, at once recognize it as the superior counterpart of their own small and inconspicuous organ, and from that time forward fall a victim to envy for the penis.

There is an interesting contrast between the behaviour of the two sexes. In the analogous situation, when a little boy first catches sight of a girl's genital region, he begins by showing irresolution and lack of interest; he sees nothing or disavows what he has seen, he softens it down or looks about for expedients for bringing it into line with his expectations. It is not until later, when some threat of castration has obtained a hold upon him, that the observation becomes important to him: if he then recollects or repeats it, it arouses a terrible storm of emotion in him and forces him to believe in the reality of the threat which he has hitherto laughed at. This combination of circumstances leads to two reactions, which may become fixed and will in that case, whether separately or together or in conjunction with other factors, permanently determine the boy's relations to women: horror of the mutilated creature or triumphant contempt for her. These developments, however, belong to the future, though not to a very remote one.

A little girl behaves differently. She makes her judgement and her decision in a flash. She has seen it and knows that she is without it and wants to have it.[3]

Here what has been named the masculinity complex of women branches off. It may put great difficulties in the way of their regular development towards femininity, if it cannot be got over soon enough. The hope of some day obtaining a penis in spite of everything and so of becoming like a man may persist to an incredibly late age and may become a motive for strange and otherwise unaccountable actions. Or again, a process may set in which I should like to call a 'disavowal', a process which in the mental life of children seems neither uncommon nor very dangerous but which in an adult would mean the beginning of a psychosis. Thus a girl may refuse to accept the fact of being castrated, may harden herself in the conviction that she *does* possess a penis, and may subsequently be compelled to behave as though she were a man.

The psychical consequences of envy for the penis, in so far as it does not become absorbed in the reaction-formation of the masculinity complex, are various and far-reaching. After a woman has become aware of the wound to her narcissism, she develops, like a scar, a sense of inferiority. When she has passed beyond her first attempt at explaining her lack of a penis as being a punishment personal to herself and has realized that that sexual character is a universal one, she begins to share the contempt felt by men for a sex which is the lesser in so important a respect, and, at least in holding that opinion, insists on being like a man.[4]

Even after penis-envy has abandoned its true object, it continues to exist: by an easy displacement it persists in the character-trait of *jealousy*. Of course, jealousy is not limited to one sex and has a wider foundation than this, but I am of opinion that it plays a far larger part in the mental life of women than of men and that that is because it is enormously reinforced from the direction of displaced penis-envy. While I was still unaware of this source of jealousy and was considering the phantasy 'a child is being beaten', which occurs so commonly in girls, I constructed

3. This is an opportunity for correcting a statement which I made many years ago. I believed that the sexual interest of children, unlike that of pubescents, was aroused, not by the difference between the sexes, but by the problem of where babies came from. We now see that, at all events with girls, this is certainly not the case. With boys it may no doubt happen sometimes one way and sometimes the other; or with both sexes, chance experiences may determine the event.

4. In my first critical account of the 'History of the Psycho-Analytic Movement' (1914) I recognized that this fact represents the core of truth contained in Adler's theory. That theory has no hesitation in explaining the whole world by this single point ('organ-inferiority', the 'masculine protest', 'breaking away from the feminine line') and prides itself upon having in this way robbed sexuality of its importance and put the desire for power in its place! * * *

a first phase for it in which its meaning was that another child, a rival of whom the subject was jealous, was to be beaten. This phantasy seems to be a relic of the phallic period in girls. The peculiar rigidity which struck me so much in the monotonous formula 'a child is being beaten' can probably be interpreted in a special way. The child which is being beaten (or caressed) may ultimately be nothing more nor less than the clitoris itself, so that at its very lowest level the statement will contain a confession of masturbation, which has remained attached to the content of the formula from its beginning in the phallic phase till later life.

A third consequence of penis-envy seems to be a loosening of the girl's relation with her mother as a love-object. The situation as a whole is not clear, but it can be seen that in the end the girl's mother, who sent her into the world so insufficiently equipped, is almost always held responsible for her lack of a penis. The way in which this comes about historically is often that soon after the girl has discovered that her genitals are unsatisfactory she begins to show jealousy of another child on the ground that her mother is fonder of it than of her, which serves as a reason for her giving up her affectionate relation to her mother. It will fit in with this if the child which has been preferred by her mother is made into the first object of the beating-phantasy which ends in masturbation.

There is yet another surprising effect of penis-envy, or of the discovery of the inferiority of the clitoris, which is undoubtedly the most important of all. In the past I had often formed an impression that in general women tolerate masturbation worse than men, that they more frequently fight against it and that they are unable to make use of it in circumstances in which a man would seize upon it as a way of escape without any hesitation. Experience would no doubt elicit innumerable exceptions to this statement, if we attempted to turn it into a rule. The reactions of human individuals of both sexes are of course made up of masculine and feminine traits. But it appeared to me nevertheless as though masturbation were further removed from the nature of women than of men, and the solution of the problem could be assisted by the reflection that masturbation, at all events of the clitoris, is a masculine activity and that the elimination of clitoridal sexuality is a necessary precondition for the development of femininity. Analyses of the remote phallic period have now taught me that in girls, soon after the first signs of penis-envy, an intense current of feeling against masturbation makes its appearance, which cannot be attributed exclusively to the educational influence of those in charge of the child. This impulse is clearly a forerunner of the wave of repression which at puberty will do away with a large amount of the girl's masculine sexuality in order to make room for the development of her femininity. It may happen that this first opposition to auto-erotic activity fails to attain its end. And this was in fact the case in the instances which I analysed. The conflict continued, and both then and later the girl did everything she could to free herself from the compulsion to masturbate. Many of the later manifestations of sexual life in women remain unintelligible unless this powerful motive is recognized.

I cannot explain the opposition which is raised in this way by little girls to phallic masturbation except by supposing that there is some concurrent factor which turns her violently against that pleasurable activity. Such a factor lies close at hand. It cannot be anything else than her narcissistic sense of humiliation which is bound up with penis-envy, the reminder that after all this is a point on which she cannot compete with boys and that it would therefore be best for her to give up the idea of doing so. Thus the little girl's recognition of the anatomical distinction between the sexes forces her away from masculinity and masculine masturbation on to new lines which lead to the development of femininity.

So far there has been no question of the Oedipus complex, nor has it up to this point played any part. But now the girl's libido slips into a new position along the line—there is no other way of putting it—of the equation 'penis-child'. She gives up her wish for a penis and puts in place of it a wish for a child: and *with that purpose in view* she takes her father as a love-object. Her mother becomes the object of her jealousy. The girl has turned into a little woman. If I am to credit a single analytic instance, this new situation can give rise to physical sensations which would have to be regarded as a premature awakening of the female genital apparatus. When the girl's attachment to her father comes to grief later on and has to be abandoned, it may give place to an identification with him and the girl may thus return to her masculinity complex and perhaps remain fixated in it.

I have now said the essence of what I had to say: I will stop, therefore, and cast an eye over our findings. We have gained some insight into the prehistory of the Oedipus complex in girls. The corresponding period in boys is more or less unknown. In girls the Oedipus complex is a secondary formation. The operations of the castration complex precede it and prepare for it. As regards the relation between the Oedipus and castration complexes there is a fundamental contrast between the two sexes. *Whereas in boys the Oedipus complex is destroyed by the castration complex, in girls it is made possible and led up to by the castration complex.* This contradiction is cleared up if we reflect that the castration complex always operates in the sense implied in its subject-matter: it inhibits and limits masculinity and encourages femininity. The difference between the sexual development of males and females at the stage we have been considering is an intelligible consequence of the anatomical distinction between their genitals and of the psychical situation involved in it; it corresponds to the difference between a castration that has been carried out and one that has merely been threatened. In their essentials, therefore, our findings are self-evident and it should have been possible to foresee them.

The Oedipus complex, however, is such an important thing that the manner in which one enters and leaves it cannot be without its effects. In boys (as I have shown at length in the paper to which I have just referred [1924d] and to which all of my present remarks are closely related) the complex is not simply repressed, it is literally smashed to pieces by the shock of threatened castration. Its libidinal cathexes are abandoned, desexualized and in part sublimated; its objects are incorporated into the ego, where they form the nucleus of the super-ego and give that new structure its characteristic qualities. In normal, or, it is better to say, in ideal cases, the Oedipus complex exists no longer, even in the unconscious; the super-ego has become its heir. Since the penis (to follow Ferenczi [1924]) owes its extraordinarily high narcissistic cathexis to its organic significance for the propagation of the species, the catastrophe to the Oedipus complex (the abandonment of incest and the institution of conscience and morality) may be regarded as a victory of the race over the individual. This is an interesting point of view when one considers that neurosis is based upon a struggle of the ego against the demands of the sexual function. But to leave the standpoint of individual psychology is not of any immediate help in clarifying this complicated situation.

In girls the motive for the demolition of the Oedipus complex is lacking. Castration has already had its effect, which was to force the child into the situation of the Oedipus complex. Thus the Oedipus complex escapes the fate which it meets with in boys: it may be slowly abandoned or dealt with by repression, or its effects may persist far into women's normal mental life. I cannot evade the notion (though I hesitate to give it expression) that for women the level of what is ethically normal is different from what it is in men. Their super-ego is never so inexorable, so impersonal, so independent of its emotional origins as we require it to be in men. Character-traits which critics of every epoch have brought up against women—that they show less sense of justice than men, that they are less ready to submit to the great exigencies of life, that they are more often influenced in their judgements by feelings of affection or hostility—all these would be amply accounted for by the modification in the formation of their super-ego which we have inferred above. We must not allow ourselves to be deflected from such conclusions by the denials of the feminists, who are anxious to force us to regard the two sexes as completely equal in position and worth; but we shall, of course, willingly agree that the majority of men are also far behind the masculine ideal and that all human individuals, as a result of their bisexual disposition and of cross-inheritance, combine in themselves both masculine and feminine characteristics, so that pure masculinity and femininity remain theoretical constructions of uncertain content.

I am inclined to set some value on the considerations I have brought forward upon the psychical consequences of the anatomical distinction between the sexes. I am aware, however, that this opinion can only be maintained if my findings, which are based on a handful of cases, turn out to have general validity and to be typical. If not, they would remain no more than a contribution to our knowledge of the different paths along which sexual life develops.

In the valuable and comprehensive studies on the masculinity and castration complexes in women by Karl Abraham (1921), Karen Horney (1923) and Helene Deutsch (1925)[5] there is much that touches closely on what I have written but nothing that coincides with it completely, so that here again I feel justified in publishing this paper.

The Question of Lay Analysis

Freud published this vigorous and persuasive pamphlet in 1926, when he was seventy. The postscript, first published in 1927 as a contribution to an international symposium on lay analysis, was attached to his original polemic in the eleventh volume of his *Gesammelte Schriften* in 1928. Freud had been complaining for a number of years that he was getting old and losing his grip, but this little book amply demonstrates that his lawyer's argumentative skill and his debating vigor were undiminished. The immediate instigator of *The Question of Lay Analysis* was a suit for quackery brought against one of followers, Theodor Reik, an analyst without a medical degree. This suit was eventually dismissed, but Freud's pamphlet was not addressed to Vienna alone. He was happy to make his position on the matter, already well known in his intimate circle, available to a wider public.

The question of lay analysis had been occupying Freud for years, and the flood of American physicians aspiring to become psychoanalysts in the 1920s only sharpened his appetite for controversy: the Americans, beset by faith healers and frauds claiming to be practicing psychoanalysts, and in desperate search of respectability, were particularly unbending in their demand that anyone qualifying as a psychoanalyst must have a medical degree. Freud, himself of course a physician, thought otherwise. The attitude of the Americans, far from inducing him to change his mind, only strengthened his notorious anti-Americanism. Through the years he had persuaded a number of his followers (his Swiss friend, the pastor Oskar Pfister; his daughter Anna; as well as Theodor Reik) to forego medical training and move directly into psychoanalytic training instead. He had no regrets. Yet Freud's insistence in *The Question of Lay Analysis* that a physician practicing psychoanalysis untrained in it is a charlatan, and that lay people do not need a medical education to become responsible and effective analysts, was not a belated apology for the advice he had so freely given years earlier. Nor did it originate with his fondness for his promising daughter, or for his friends. As early as

5. {The papers in question are: Karl Abraham, "Manifestations of the Female Castration Complex" (1921; tr. 1927, in *Selected Papers on Psychoanalysis*, ch. XXII); Karen Horney, "On the Genesis of the Castration Complex in Women" (1923; tr. 1924, in *Int. J. Psycho-Anal.*, V); Helene Deutsch, *Psychoanalysis of the Sexual Function of Women* (1925).}

1913, in his introduction to Pfister's *The Psycho-Analytic Method*, he had already asserted flatly: "The practice of psycho-analysis calls much less for medical training than for psychological instruction and a free human outlook. The majority of doctors are not equipped to practise psycho-analysis and have completely failed to grasp the value of that therapeutic procedure" (*SE* XII, 331). But while he argued with his European colleagues and railed at the Americans, while he insisted right to the end of his life that he did not want to see psychoanalysis degraded into the handmaiden of psychiatry, his success was indifferent. Great Britain proved more open to Freud's persuasions than other countries, and the debate over lay analysis has not died down yet. But Freud's own position never wavered.

POSTSCRIPT

The immediate occasion of my writing the small volume which was the starting-point of the present discussion was a charge of quackery brought against a non-medical member of our Society, Dr. Theodor Reik, in the Vienna Courts. It is generally known, I think, that after all the preliminary proceedings had been completed and a number of expert opinions had been received, the charge was dropped. I do not believe that this was a result of my book. No doubt the prosecution's case was too weak, and the person who brought the charge as an aggrieved party proved an untrustworthy witness. So that the quashing of the proceedings against Dr. Reik is probably not to be regarded as a considered judgement of the Vienna Courts on the general question of lay analysis. When I drew the figure of the 'Impartial Person' who was my interlocutor in my tract, I had before my mind one of our high officials. This was a man with a friendly attitude and a mind of unusual integrity, to whom I had myself talked about Reik's case and for whom I had, at his request, written a confidential opinion on the subject. I knew I had not succeeded in converting him to my views, and that was why I made my dialogue with the Impartial Person end without agreement too.

Nor did I expect that I should succeed in bringing about unanimity in the attitude of analysts themselves towards the problem of lay analysis. Anyone who compares the views expressed by the Hungarian Society in this discussion with those of the New York group will perhaps conclude that my book has produced no effect whatever and that everyone persists in his former opinion. But I do not believe this either. I think that many of my colleagues have modified their extreme *parti pris* and that the majority have accepted my view that the problem of lay analysis ought not to be decided along the lines of traditional usage but that it arises from a novel situation and therefore demands a fresh judgement.

Again, the turn which I gave to the whole discussion seems to have met with approval. My main thesis was that the important question is not whether an analyst possesses a medical diploma but whether he has had the special training necessary for the practice of analysis. This served as the starting-point for a discussion, which was eagerly embarked upon, as to what is the training most suitable for an analyst. My own view was and still remains that it is not the training prescribed by the University for future doctors. What is known as medical education appears to me to be an arduous and circuitous way of approaching the profession of analysis. No doubt it offers an analyst much that is indispensable to him. But it burdens him with too much else of which he can never make use, and there is a danger of its diverting his interest and his whole mode of thought from the understanding of psychical phenomena. A scheme of training for analysts has still to be created. It must include elements from the mental sciences, from psychology, the history of civilization and sociology, as well as from anatomy, biology and the study of evolution. There is so much to be taught in all this that it is justifiable to omit from the curriculum anything which has no direct bearing on the practice of analysis and only serves indirectly (like any other study) as a training for the intellect and for the powers of observation. It is easy to meet this suggestion by objecting that analytic colleges of this kind do not exist and that I am merely setting up an ideal. An ideal, no doubt. But an ideal which can and must be realized. And in our training institutes, in spite of all their youthful insufficiencies, that realization has already begun.

It will not have escaped my readers that in what I have said I have assumed as axiomatic something that is still violently disputed in the discussion. I have assumed, that is to say, that psycho-analysis is not a specialized branch of medicine. I cannot see how it is possible to dispute this. Psycho-analysis is a part of psychology; not of medical psychology in the old sense, not of the psychology of morbid processes, but simply of psychology. It is certainly not the whole of psychology, but its substructure and perhaps even its entire foundation. The possibility of its application to medical purposes must not lead us astray. Electricity and radiology also have their medical application, but the science to which they both belong is none the less physics. Nor can their situation be affected by historical arguments. The whole theory of electricity had its origin in an observation of a nerve-muscle preparation; yet no one would dream to-day of regarding it as a part of physiology. It is argued that psycho-analysis was after all discovered by a physician in the course of his efforts to assist his patients. But that is clearly neither here nor there. Moreover, the historical argument is double-edged. We might pursue the story and recall the unfriendliness and indeed the animosity with which the medical profession treated analysis from the very first. That would seem to imply that it can have no claims over analysis to-day. And though I do not accept that implication, I still feel some doubts as to whether the present wooing of psycho-analysis by the doctors is based, from the point of view of the libido theory, upon the first or upon the second of Abraham's sub-stages—whether they wish to take possession of their object for the purpose of destroying or of preserving it.

I should like to consider the historical argument a moment longer. Since it is with me personally that we are concerned, I can throw a little light, for anyone who may be interested, on my own motives. After forty-one years of medical activity, my self-knowledge tells me that I have never really been a doctor in the proper sense. I became a doctor through being compelled to deviate from my original purpose; and the triumph of my life lies in my having, after a long and roundabout journey, found my way back to my earliest path. I have no knowledge of having had any craving in my early childhood to help suffering humanity. My innate sadistic disposition was not a very strong one, so that I had no need to develop this one of its derivatives. Nor did I ever play the 'doctor game'; my infantile curiosity evidently chose other paths. In my youth I felt an overpowering need to understand something of the riddles of the world in which we live and perhaps even to contribute something to their solution. The most hopeful means of achieving this end seemed to be to enrol myself in the medical faculty; but even after that I experimented—unsuccessfully—with zoology and chemistry, till at last, under the influence of Brücke, who carried more weight with me than any one else in my whole life, I settled down to physiology, though in those days it was too narrowly restricted to histology. By that time I had already passed all my medical examinations; but I took no interest in anything to do with medicine till the teacher whom I so deeply respected warned me that in view of my impoverished material circumstances I could not possibly take up a theoretical career. Thus I passed from the histology of the nervous system to neuropathology and then, prompted by fresh influences, I began to be concerned with the neuroses. I scarcely think, however, that my lack of a genuine medical temperament has done much damage to my patients. For it is not greatly to the advantage of patients if their doctor's therapeutic interest has too marked an emotional emphasis. They are best helped if he carries out his task coolly and keeping as closely as possible to the rules.

No doubt what I have just said throws little light on the problem of lay analysis; it was only intended to exhibit my personal credentials as being myself a supporter of the inherent value of psycho-analysis and of its independence of its application to medicine. But it will be objected at this point that whether psycho-analysis, regarded as a science, is a subdivision of medicine or of psychology is a purely academic question and of no practical interest. The real point at issue, it will be said, is a different one, namely the application of analysis to the treatment of patients; in so far as it claims to do this it must be content, the argument will run, to be accepted as a specialized branch of medicine, like radiology, for instance, and to submit to the rules laid down for all therapeutic methods. I recognize that that is so; I admit it. I only want to feel assured that the therapy will not destroy the science. Unluckily analogies never carry one more than a certain distance; a point is soon reached at which the subjects of the comparison take divergent paths. The case of analysis differs from that of radiology. A physicist does not require to have a patient in order to study the laws that govern X-rays. But the only subject-matter of psycho-analysis is the mental processes of human beings and it is only in human beings that it can be studied. For reasons which can easily be understood, neurotic human beings offer far more instructive and accessible material than normal ones, and to withhold that material from anyone who wishes to study and apply analysis is to dock him of a good half of his training possibilities. I have, of course, no intention of asking that the interests of neurotic patients should be sacrificed to those of instruction and scientific research. The aim of my small volume on the question of lay analysis was precisely to show that, if certain precautions are observed, the two interests can quite easily be brought into harmony and that the interests of medicine, as rightly understood, will not be the last to profit by such a solution.

I myself brought forward all the necessary precautions and I can safely say that the discussion added nothing on this point. But I should like to remark that the emphasis was often placed in a manner which did not do justice to the facts. What was said about the difficulties of differential diagnosis and the uncertainty in many cases in deciding about somatic symptoms—situations, that is, in which medical knowledge and medical intervention are necessary—this is all of it perfectly true. Nevertheless, the number of cases in which doubts of this kind never arise at all and in which a doctor is *not* required is surely incomparably greater. These cases may be quite uninteresting scientifically, but they play an important enough part in life to justify the activity of lay analysts, who are perfectly competent to deal with them. Some time ago I analysed a colleague who gave evidence of a particularly strong dislike of the idea of anyone being allowed to engage in a medical activity who was not himself a medical man. I was in a position to say to him: 'We have now been working for more than three months. At what point in our analysis have I had occasion to make use of my medical knowledge?' He admitted that I had had no such occasion.

Again, I attach no great importance to the argument that a lay analyst, because he must be prepared to consult a doctor, will have no authority in the eyes of his patients and will be treated with no more respect than such people as bone-setters or masseurs. Once again, the analogy is an imperfect one—quite apart from the fact that what governs patients in their recognition of authority is usually their emotional transference and that the possession of a medical diploma does not impress them nearly so much as doctors believe. A professional lay analyst will have no difficulty in winning as much respect as is due to a secular pastoral worker. Indeed, the words, 'secular pastoral worker', might well serve as a general formula for describing the function which the analyst, whether he is a doctor or a layman, has to perform in his relation to the public. Our friends among the protestant clergy, and more recently among the catholic clergy as well, are often able to relieve their parishioners of the inhibitions of their daily life by confirming their faith—after having first offered them a little analytic information about the nature of their conflicts. Our opponents, the Adlerian 'individual psychologists', endeavour to produce a similar result in people who have become unstable and inefficient by arousing their interest in the social community—after having first thrown some light upon a single corner of their mental life and shown them the part played in their illness by their egoistic and distrustful impulses. Both of these procedures, which derive their power from being based on analysis, have their place in psychotherapy. We who are analysts set before us as our aim the most complete and profoundest possible analysis of whoever may be our patient. We do not seek to bring him relief by receiving him into the catholic, protestant or socialist community. We seek rather to enrich him from his own internal sources, by putting at the disposal of his ego those energies which, owing to regression, are inaccessibly confined in his unconscious, as well as those which his ego is obliged to squander in the fruitless task of maintaining these repressions. Such activity as this is pastoral work in the best sense of the words. Have we set ourselves too high an aim? Are the majority of our patients worth the pains that this work requires of us? Would it not be more economical to prop up their weaknesses from without rather than to rebuild them from within? I cannot say; but there is something else that I do know. In psychoanalysis there has existed from the very first an inseparable bond between cure and research. Knowledge brought therapeutic success. It was impossible to treat a patient without learning something new; it was impossible to gain fresh insight without perceiving its beneficent results. Our analytic procedure is the only one in which this precious conjunction is assured. It is only by carrying on our analytic pastoral work that we can deepen our dawning comprehension of the human mind. This prospect of scientific gain has been the proudest and happiest feature of analytic work. Are we to sacrifice it for the sake of any considerations of a practical sort?

Some remarks that have been made in the course of this discussion have led me to suspect that, in spite of everything, my book on lay analysis has been misunderstood in one respect. The doctors have been defended against me, as though I had declared that they were in general incompetent to practise analysis and as though I had given it out as a password that medical reinforcements were to be rejected. That was not my intention. The idea probably arose from my having been led to declare in the course of my observations (which had a controversial end in view) that untrained medical analysts were even more dangerous than laymen. I might make my true opinion on this question clear by echoing a cynical remark about women that once appeared in Simplicissimus. One man was complaining to another about the weaknesses and troublesome nature of the fair sex. 'All the same,' replied his companion, 'women are the best thing we have of the kind.' I am bound to admit that, so long as schools such as we desire for the training of analysts are not yet in existence, people who have had a preliminary education in medicine are the best material for future analysts. We have a right to demand, however, that they should not mistake their preliminary education for a complete training, that they should overcome the one-sidedness that is fostered by instruction in medical schools and that they should resist the temptation to flirt with endocrinology and the autonomic nervous system, when what is needed is an apprehension of psychological facts with the help of a framework of psychological concepts. I also share the view that all those problems which relate to the connection between psychical phenomena and their organic, anatomical and chemical foundations can be approached only by those who have studied both, that is, by medical analysts. It should not be forgotten, however, that this is not the whole of psycho-analysis, and that for its other aspect we can never do without the co-operation of people who have had a preliminary education in the *mental* sciences. For practical reasons we have been in the habit—and this is true, incidentally, of our publications as well—of distinguishing between medical and applied analysis. But that is not a logical distinction. The true line of division is between *scientific* analysis and its *applications* alike in medical and in non-medical fields.

In these discussions the bluntest rejection of lay analysis has been expressed by our American colleagues. A few words to them in reply will, I think, not be out of place. I can scarcely be accused of making a misuse of analysis for controversial purposes if I express an opinion that their resistance is derived wholly from practical factors. They see how in their own country lay analysts put analysis to all kinds of mischievous and illegitimate purposes and in consequence cause injury both to their patients and to the good name of analysis. It is therefore not to be wondered at if in their indignation they give the widest possible berth to such unscrupulous mischief-makers and try to prevent any laymen from having a share in analysis. But these facts are already enough to diminish the significance of the American position; for the question of lay analysis must not be decided on practical considerations alone, and local conditions in America cannot be the sole determining influence on our views.

The resolution passed by our American colleagues against lay analysts, based as it essentially is upon practical reasons, appears to me nevertheless to be unpractical; for it cannot affect any of the factors which govern the situation. It is more or less equivalent to an attempt at repression. If it is impossible to prevent the lay analysts from pursuing their activities and if the public does not support the campaign against them, would it not be more expedient to recognize the fact of their existence by offering them opportunities for training? Might it not be possible in this way to gain some influence over them? And, if they were offered as an inducement the possibility of receiving the approval of the medical profession and of being invited to co-operate, might they not have some interest in raising their own ethical and intellectual level?

VIENNA, *June* 1927

The Future of an Illusion

Freud's scientific concern with religion reaches back well before the First World War. During the years of his friendship with Jung, he sent Jung word of his great discovery that religion is derived from the early helplessness of the child. In *Totem and Taboo*, he offered a complementary interpretation of the origins of religious ritual, this time appealing to the Oedipus complex. In some of his case histories, notably that of the Rat Man and of the Wolf Man, he called particular attention to the religious ruminations of his patients, which he read as symptoms. And in 1907, in a brilliant short paper, "Obsessive Actions and Religious Practices," he dwelt on the resemblances, and more than resemblances, between the ceremonies of obsessives and the ceremonies of believers. "In view of these similarities and analogies," he wrote there, "one might venture to regard obsessional neurosis as a pathological counterpart of the formation of a religion, and to describe that neurosis as an individual religiosity and religion as a universal obsessional neurosis" (*SE* IX, 126–27). These are strong words, but Freud meant them literally.

His professional interest in the phenomenon of religion was anything but abstract. It was fueled by his principled, highly aggressive, anti-religious stance. Except for a brief spell during his university career, when one of his professors, the persuasive philosopher Franz Brentano, lured him into a tentative flirtation with theism, Freud was a convinced, uncompromising atheist. As noted, a true heir of the Enlightenment, Freud saw history as a great war between science and religion and rejected all compromise between the two contending forces. This pervasive attitude did not prevent him from thinking himself a Jew. But he was, as he told Oskar Pfister, a "godless Jew," as remote from the religion of his forefathers as from all others. *The Future of an Illusion* is thus a far from surprising venture. One of its devices, familiar from several other writings of Freud's, is the use of dialogue to make some crucial points. This underscores Freud's deliberate informality, the wish to reach a broader public than sheer technical papers ever could. The little book is at once one of Freud's most ambitious explorations of culture from a psychoanalyst's perspective, and a highly personal expression of faith—or, rather, unfaith. It is here reproduced complete.

I

When one has lived for quite a long time in a particular civilization and has often tried to discover what its origins were and along what path it has developed, one sometimes also feels tempted to take a glance in the other direction and to ask what further fate lies before it and what transformations it is destined to undergo. But one soon finds that the value of such an enquiry is diminished from the outset by several factors. Above all, because there are only a few people who can survey human activity in its full compass. Most people have been obliged to restrict themselves to a single, or a few, fields of it. But the less a man knows about the past and the present the more insecure must prove to be his judgement of the future. And there is the further difficulty that precisely in a judgement of this kind the subjective expectations of the individual play a part which it is difficult to assess; and these turn out to be dependent on purely personal factors in his own experience, on the greater or lesser optimism of his attitude to life, as it has been dictated for him by his temperament or by his success or failure. Finally, the curious fact makes itself felt that in general people experience their present naïvely, as it were, without being able to form an estimate of its contents; they have first to put themselves at a distance from it—the present, that is to say, must have become the past—before it can yield points of vantage from which to judge the future.

Thus anyone who gives way to the temptation to deliver an opinion on the probable future of our civilization will do well to remind himself of the difficulties I have just pointed out, as well as of the uncertainty that attaches quite generally to any prophecy. It follows from this, so far as I am concerned, that I shall make a hasty retreat before a task that is too great, and shall promptly seek out the small tract of territory which has claimed my attention hitherto, as soon as I have determined its position in the general scheme of things.

Human civilization, by which I mean all those respects in which human life has raised itself above its animal status and differs from the life of beasts—and I scorn to distinguish between culture and civiliza-tion—, presents, as we know, two aspects to the observer. It includes on the one hand all the knowledge and capacity that men have acquired in order to control the forces of nature and extract its wealth for the satisfaction of human needs, and, on the other hand, all the regulations necessary in order to adjust the relations of men to one another and especially the distribution of the available wealth. The two trends of civilization are not independent of each other: firstly, because the mutual relations of men are profoundly influenced by the amount of instinctual satisfaction which the existing wealth makes possible; secondly, because an individual man can himself come to function as wealth in relation to another one, in so far as the other person makes use of his capacity for work, or chooses him as a sexual object; and thirdly, moreover, because every individual is virtually an enemy of civilization, though civilization is supposed to be an object of universal human interest. It is remarkable that, little as men are able to exist in isolation, they should nevertheless feel as a heavy burden the sacrifices which civilization expects of them in order to make a communal life possible. Thus civilization has to be defended against the individual, and its regulations, institutions and commands are directed to that task. They aim not only at effecting a certain distribution of wealth but at maintaining that distribution; indeed, they have to protect everything that contributes to the conquest of nature and the production of wealth against men's hostile impulses. Human creations are easily destroyed, and science and technology, which have built them up, can also be used for their annihilation.

One thus gets an impression that civilization is something which was imposed on a resisting majority by a minority which understood how to obtain possession of the means to power and coercion. It is, of course, natural to assume that these difficulties are not inherent in the nature of civilization itself but are determined by the imperfections of the cultural forms which have so far been developed. And in fact it is not difficult to indicate those defects. While mankind has made continual advances in its control over nature and may expect to make still greater ones, it is not possible to establish with certainty that a similar advance has been made in the management of human affairs; and probably at all periods, just as now once again, many people have asked themselves whether what little civilization has thus acquired is indeed worth defending at all. One would think that a re-ordering of human relations should be possible, which would remove the sources of dissatisfaction with civilization by renouncing coercion and the suppression of the instincts, so that, undisturbed by internal discord, men might devote themselves to the acquisition of wealth and its enjoyment. That would be the golden age, but it is questionable if such a state of affairs can be realized. It seems rather that every civilization must be built up on coercion and renunciation of instinct; it does not even seem certain that if coercion were to cease the majority of human beings would be prepared to undertake to perform the work necessary for acquiring new wealth. One has, I think, to reckon with the fact that there are present in all men destructive, and therefore anti-social and anti-cultural, trends and that in a great number of people these are strong enough to determine their behaviour in human society.

This psychological fact has a decisive importance for our judgement of human civilization. Whereas we might at first think that its essence lies in controlling nature for the purpose of acquiring wealth and that the dangers which threaten it could be eliminated through a suitable distribution of that wealth among men, it now seems that the emphasis has moved over from the material to the mental. The decisive question is whether and to what extent it is possible to lessen the burden of the instinctual sacrifices imposed on men, to reconcile men to those which must necessarily remain and to provide a compensation for them. It is just as impossible to do without control of the mass by a minority as it is to dispense with coercion in the work of civilization. For masses are lazy and unintelligent; they have no love for instinctual renunciation, and they are not to be convinced by argument of its inevitability; and the individuals composing them support one another in giving free rein to their indiscipline. It is only through the influence of individuals who can set an example and whom masses recognize as their leaders that they can be induced to perform the work and undergo the renunciations on which the existence of civilization depends. All is well if these leaders are persons who possess superior insight into the necessities of life and who have risen to the height of mastering their own instinctual wishes. But there is a danger that in order not to lose their influence they may give way to the mass more than it gives way to them, and it therefore seems necessary that they shall be independent of the mass by having means to power at their disposal. To put it briefly, there are two widespread human characteristics which are responsible for the fact that the regulations of civilization can only be maintained by a certain degree of coercion—namely, that men are not spontaneously fond of work and that arguments are of no avail against their passions.

I know the objections which will be raised against these assertions. It will be said that the characteristic of human masses depicted here, which is supposed to prove that coercion cannot be dispensed with in the work of civilization, is itself only the result of defects in the cultural regulations, owing to which men have become embittered, revengeful and inaccessible. New generations, who have been brought up in kindness and taught to have a high opinion of reason, and who have experienced the benefits of civilization at an early age, will have a different attitude to it. They will feel it as a possession of their very own and will be ready for its sake to make the sacrifices as regards work and instinctual satisfaction that are necessary for its preservation. They will be able to do without coercion and will differ little from their leaders. If no culture has so far produced human masses of such a quality, it is because no culture has yet devised regulations which will influence men in this way, and in particular from childhood onwards.

It may be doubted whether it is possible at all, or at any rate as yet, at the present stage of our control over nature, to set up cultural regulations of this kind. It may be asked where the number of superior, unswerving and disinterested leaders are to come from who are to act as educators of the future generations, and it may be alarming to think of the enormous amount of coercion that will inevitably be required before these intentions can be carried out. The grandeur of the plan and its importance for the future of human civilization cannot be disputed. It is securely based on the psychological discovery that man is equipped with the most varied instinctual dispositions, whose ultimate course is determined by the experiences of early childhood. But for the same reason the limitations of man's capacity for education set bounds to the effectiveness of such a transformation in his culture. One may question whether, and in what degree, it would be possible for a different cultural environment to do away with the two characteristics of human masses which make the guidance of human affairs so difficult. The experiment has not yet been made. Probably a certain percentage of mankind (owing to a pathological disposition or an excess of instinctual strength) will always remain asocial; but if it were feasible merely to reduce the majority that is hostile towards civilization to-day into a minority, a great deal would have been accomplished—perhaps all that *can* be accomplished.

I should not like to give the impression that I have strayed a long way from the line laid down for my enquiry. Let me therefore give an express assurance that I have not the least intention of making judgements on the great experiment in civilization that is now in progress in the vast country that stretches between Europe and Asia. I have neither the special knowledge nor the capacity to decide on its practicability, to test the expediency of the methods employed or to measure the width of the inevitable gap between intention and execution. What is in preparation there is unfinished and therefore eludes an investigation for which our own long-consolidated civilization affords us material.

II

We have slipped unawares out of the economic field into the field of psychology. At first we were tempted to look for the assets of civilization in the available wealth and in the regulations for its distribution. But with the recognition that every civilization rests on a compulsion to work and a renunciation of instinct and therefore inevitably provokes opposition from those affected by these demands, it has become clear that civilization cannot consist principally or solely in wealth itself and the means of acquiring it and the arrangements for its distribution; for these things are threatened by the rebelliousness and destructive mania of the participants in civilization. Alongside of wealth we now come upon the means by which civilization can be defended—measures of coercion and other measures that are intended to reconcile men to it and to recompense them for their sacrifices. These latter may be described as the mental assets of civilization.

For the sake of a uniform terminology we will describe the fact that an instinct cannot be satisfied as a 'frustration', the regulation by which this frustration is established as a 'prohibition' and the condition which is produced by the prohibition as a 'privation'. The first step is to distinguish between privations which affect everyone and privations which do not affect everyone but only groups, classes or even single individuals. The former are the earliest; with the prohibitions that established them, civilization—who knows how many thousands of years ago?—began to detach man from his primordial animal condition. We have found to our surprise that these privations are still operative and still form the kernel of hostility to civilization. The instinctual wishes that suffer under them are born afresh with every child; there is a class of people, the neurotics, who already react to these frustrations with asocial behaviour. Among these instinctual wishes are those of incest, cannibalism and lust for killing. It sounds strange to place alongside one another wishes which everyone seems united in repudiating and others about which there is so much lively dispute in our civilization as to whether they shall be permitted or frustrated; but psychologically it is justifiable to do so. Nor is the attitude of civilization to these oldest instinctual wishes by any means uniform. Cannibalism alone seems to be universally proscribed and—to the non-psycho-analytic view—to have been completely surmounted. The strength of the incestuous wishes can still be detected behind the prohibition against them; and under certain conditions killing is still practised, and indeed commanded, by our civilization. It is possible that cultural developments lie ahead of us in which the satisfaction of yet other wishes, which are entirely permissible to-day, will appear just as unacceptable as cannibalism does now.

These earliest instinctual renunciations already involve a psychological factor which remains important for all further instinctual renunciations as well. It is not true that the human mind has undergone no development since the earliest times and that, in contrast to the advances of science and technology, it is the same to-day as it was at the beginning of history. We can point out one of these mental advances at once. It is in keeping with the course of human development that external coercion gradually becomes internalized; for a special mental agency, man's super-ego, takes it over and includes it among its commandments. Every child presents this process of transformation to us; only by that means does it become a moral and social being. Such a strengthening of the super-ego is a most precious cultural asset in the psychological field. Those in whom it has taken place are turned from being opponents of civilization into being its vehicles. The greater their number is in a cultural unit the more secure is its culture and the more it can dispense with external measures of coercion. Now the degree of this internalization differs greatly between the various instinctual prohibitions. As regards the earliest cultural demands, which I have mentioned, the internalization seems to have been very extensively achieved, if we leave out of account the unwelcome exception of the neurotics. But the case is altered when we turn to the other instinctual claims. Here we observe with surprise and concern that a majority of people obey the cultural prohibitions on these points only under the pressure of external coercion—that is, only where that coercion can make itself effective and so long as it is to be feared. This is also true of what are known as the *moral* demands of civilization, which likewise apply to everyone. Most of one's experiences of man's moral untrustworthiness fall into this category. There are countless civilized people who would shrink from murder or incest but who do not deny themselves the satisfaction of their avarice, their aggressive urges or their sexual lusts, and who do not hesitate to injure other people by lies, fraud and calumny, so long as they can remain unpunished for it; and this, no doubt, has always been so through many ages of civilization.

If we turn to those restrictions that apply only to certain classes of society, we meet with a state of things which is flagrant and which has always been recognized. It is to be expected that these underprivileged classes will envy the favoured ones their privileges and will do all they can to free themselves from their own surplus of privation. Where this is not possible, a permanent measure of discontent will persist within the culture concerned and this can lead to dangerous revolts. If, however, a culture has not got beyond a point at which the satisfaction of one portion of its participants depends upon the suppression of another, and perhaps larger, portion—and this is the case in all present-day cultures—it is understandable that the suppressed people should develop an intense hostility towards a culture whose existence they make possible by their work, but in whose wealth they have too small a share. In such conditions an internalization of the cultural prohibitions among the suppressed people is not to be expected. On the contrary, they are not prepared to acknowledge the prohibitions, they are intent on destroying the culture itself, and possibly even on doing away with the postulates on which it is based. The hostility of these classes to civilization is so obvious that it has caused the more latent hostility of the social strata that are better provided for to be overlooked. It goes without saying that a civilization which leaves so large a number of its participants unsatisfied and drives them into revolt neither has nor deserves the prospect of a lasting existence.

The extent to which a civilization's precepts have been internalized—to express it popularly and unpsychologically: the moral level of its participants—is not the only form of mental wealth that comes into consideration in estimating a civilization's value. There are in addition its assets in the shape of ideals and artistic creations—that is, the satisfactions that can be derived from those sources.

People will be only too readily inclined to include among the psychical assets of a culture its ideals—its estimates of what achievements are the highest and the most to be striven after. It will seem at first as though these ideals would determine the achievements of the cultural unit; but the actual course of events would appear to be that the ideals are based on the first achievements which have been made possible by a combination of the culture's internal gifts and external circumstances, and that these first achievements are then held on to by the ideal as something to be carried further. The satisfaction which the ideal offers to the participants in the culture is thus of a narcissistic nature; it rests on their pride in what has already been successfully achieved. To make this satisfaction complete calls for a comparison with other cultures which have aimed at different achievements and have developed different ideals. On the strength of these differences every culture claims the right to look down on the rest. In this way cultural ideals become a source of discord and enmity between different cultural units, as can be seen most clearly in the case of nations.

The narcissistic satisfaction provided by the cultural ideal is also among the forces which are successful in combating the hostility to culture within the cultural unit. This satisfaction can be shared in not only by the favoured classes, which enjoy the benefits of the culture, but also by the suppressed ones, since the right to despise the people outside it compensates them for the wrongs they suffer within their own unit. No doubt one is a wretched plebeian, harassed by debts and military service; but, to make up for it, one is a Roman citizen, one has one's share in the task of ruling other nations and dictating their laws. This identification of the suppressed classes with the class who rules and exploits them is, however, only part of a larger whole. For, on the other hand, the suppressed classes can be emotionally attached to their masters; in spite of their hostility to them they may see in them their ideals; unless such relations of a fundamentally satisfying kind subsisted, it would be impossible to understand how a number of civilizations have survived so long in spite of the justifiable hostility of large human masses.

A different kind of satisfaction is afforded by art to the participants in a cultural unit, though as a rule it remains inaccessible to the masses, who are engaged in exhausting work and have not enjoyed any personal education. As we discovered long since, art offers substitutive satisfactions for the oldest and still most deeply felt cultural renunciations, and for that reason it serves as nothing else does to reconcile a man to the sacrifices he has made on behalf of civilization. On the other hand, the creations of art heighten his feelings of identification, of which every cultural unit stands in so much need, by providing an occasion for sharing highly valued emotional experiences. And when those creations picture the achievements of his particular culture and bring to his mind its ideals in an impressive manner, they also minister to his narcissistic satisfaction.

No mention has yet been made of what is perhaps the most important item in the psychical inventory of a civilization. This consists in its religious ideas in the widest sense—in other words (which will be justified later) in its illusions.

III

In what does the peculiar value of religious ideas lie?

We have spoken of the hostility to civilization which is produced by the pressure that civilization exercises, the renunciations of instinct which it demands. If one imagines its prohibitions lifted—if, then, one may take any woman one pleases as a sexual object, if one may without hesitation kill one's rival for her love or anyone else who stands in one's way, if, too, one can carry off any of the other man's belongings without asking leave—how splendid, what a string of satisfactions one's life would be! True, one soon comes across the first difficulty: everyone else has exactly the same wishes as I have and will treat me with no more consideration than I treat him. And so in reality only one person could be made unrestrictedly happy by such a removal of the restrictions of civilization, and he would be a tyrant, a dictator, who had seized all the means to power. And even he would have every reason to wish that the others would observe at least one cultural commandment: 'thou shalt not kill'.

But how ungrateful, how short-sighted after all, to strive for the abolition of civilization! What would then remain would be a state of nature, and that would be far harder to bear. It is true that nature would not demand any restrictions of instinct from us, she would let us do as we liked; but she has her own particularly effective method of restricting us. She destroys us—coldy, cruelly, relentlessly, as it seems to us, and possibly through the very things that occasioned our satisfaction. It was precisely because of these dangers with which nature threatens us that we came together and created civilization, which is also, among other things, intended to make our communal life possible. For the principal task of civilization, its actual *raison d'être*, is to defend us against nature.

We all know that in many ways civilization does this fairly well already, and clearly as time goes on it will do it much better. But no one is under the illusion that nature has already been vanquished; and few dare hope that she will ever be entirely subjected to man. There are the elements, which seem to mock at all human control: the earth, which quakes and is torn apart and buries all human life and its works; water, which deluges and drowns everything in a turmoil; storms, which blow everything before them; there are diseases, which we have only recently recognized as attacks by other organisms; and finally there is the painful riddle of death, against which no medicine has yet been found, nor probably will be. With these forces nature rises up against us, majestic, cruel and inexorable; she brings to our mind once more our weakness and helplessness, which we thought to escape through the work of civilization. One of the few gratifying and exalting impressions which mankind can offer is when, in the face of an elemental catastrophe, it forgets the discordancies of its civilization and all its internal difficulties and animosities, and recalls the great common task of preserving itself against the superior power of nature.

For the individual, too, life is hard to bear, just as it is for mankind in general. The civilization in which he participates imposes some amount of privation on him, and other men bring him a measure of suffering, either in spite of the precepts of his civilization or because of its imperfections. To this are added the injuries which untamed nature—he calls it Fate—inflicts on him. One might suppose that this condition of things would result in a permanent state of anxious expectation in him and a severe injury to his natural narcissism. We know already how the individual reacts to the injuries which civilization and other men inflict on him: he develops a corresponding degree of resistance to the regulations of civilization and of hostility to it. But how does he defend himself against the superior powers of nature, of Fate, which threaten him as they threaten all the rest?

Civilization relieves him of this task; it performs it in the same way for all alike; and it is noteworthy that in this almost all civilizations act alike. Civilization does not call a halt in the task of defending man against nature, it merely pursues it by other means. The task is a manifold one. Man's self-regard, seriously menaced, calls for consolation; life and the universe must be robbed of their terrors; moreover his curiosity, moved, it is true, by the strongest practical interest, demands an answer.

A great deal is already gained with the first step: the humanization of nature. Impersonal forces and destinies cannot be approached; they remain eternally remote. But if the elements have passions that rage as they do in our own souls, if death itself is not something spontaneous but the violent act of an evil Will, if everywhere in nature there are Beings around us of a kind that we know in our own society, then we can breathe freely, can feel at home in the uncanny and can deal by psychical means with our senseless anxiety. We are still defenceless, perhaps, but we are no longer helplessly paralysed; we can at least react. Perhaps, indeed, we are not even defenceless. We can apply the same methods against these violent supermen outside that we employ in our own society; we can try to adjure them, to appease them, to bribe them, and, by so influencing them, we may rob them of a part of their power. A replacement like this of natural science by psychology not only provides immediate relief, but also points the way to a further mastering of the situation.

For this situation is nothing new. It has an infantile prototype, of which it is in fact only the continuation. For once before one has found oneself in a similiar state of helplessness: as a small child, in relation to one's parents. One had reason to fear them, and especially one's father; and yet one was sure of his protection against the dangers one knew. Thus it was natural to assimilate the two situations. Here, too, wishing played its part, as it does in dream-life. The sleeper may be seized with a presentiment of death, which threatens to place him in the grave. But the dream-work knows how to select a condition that will turn even that dreaded event into a wish-fulfilment: the dreamer sees himself in an ancient Etruscan grave which he has climbed down into, happy to find his archaeological interests satisfied. In the same way, a man makes the forces of nature not simply into persons with whom he can associate as he would with his equals—that would not do justice to the overpowering inpression which those forces make on him—but he gives them the character of a father. He turns them into gods, following in this, as I have tried to show {in *Totem and Taboo*}, not only an infantile prototype but a phylogenetic one.

In the course of time the first observations were made of regularity and conformity to law in natural phenomena, and with this the forces of nature lost their human traits. But man's helplessness remains and along with it his longing for his father, and the gods. The gods retain their threefold task: they must exorcize the terrors of nature, they must reconcile men to the cruelty of Fate, particularly as it is shown in death, and they must compensate them for the sufferings and privations which a civilized life in common has imposed on them.

But within these functions there is a gradual displacement of accent. It was observed that the phenomena of nature developed automatically according to internal necessities. Without doubt the gods were the lords of nature; they had arranged it to be as it was and now they could leave it to itself. Only occasionally, in what are known are miracles, did they intervene in its course, as though to make it plain that they had relinquished nothing of their original sphere of power. As regards the apportioning of destinies, an unpleasant suspicion persisted that the perplexity and helplessness of the human race could not be remedied. It was here that the gods were most apt to fail. If they themselves created Fate, then their counsels must be deemed inscrutable. The notion dawned on the most gifted people of antiquity that Moira [Fate] stood above the gods and that the gods themselves had their own destinies. And the more autonomous nature became and the more the gods withdrew from it, the more earnestly were all expectations directed to the third function of the gods—the more did morality become their true domain. It now became the task of the gods to even out the defects and evils of civilization, to attend to the sufferings which men inflict on one another in their life together and to watch over the fulfilment of the precepts of civilization, which men obey so imperfectly. Those precepts themselves were credited with a divine origin; they were elevated beyond human society and were extended to nature and the universe.

And thus a store of ideas is created, born from man's need to make his helplessness tolerable and built up from the material of memories of the helplessness of his own childhood and the childhood of the human race. It can clearly be seen that the possession of these ideas protects him in two directions—against the dangers of nature and Fate, and against the injuries that threaten him from human society itself. Here is the gist of the matter. Life in this world serves a higher purpose; no doubt it is not easy to guess what that purpose is, but it certainly signifies a perfecting of man's nature. It is probably the spiritual part of man, the soul, which in the course of time has so slowly and unwillingly detached itself from the body, that is the object of this elevation and exaltation. Everything that happens in this world is an expression of the intentions of an intelligence superior to us, which in the end, though its ways and byways are difficult to follow, orders everything for the best—that is, to make it enjoyable for us. Over each one of us there watches a benevolent Providence which is only seemingly stern and which will not suffer us to become a plaything of the over-mighty and pitiless forces of nature. Death itself is not extinction, is not a return to inorganic lifelessness, but the beginning of a new kind of existence which lies on the path of development to something higher. And, looking in the other direction, this view announces that the same moral laws which our civilizations have set up govern the whole universe as well, except that they are maintained by a supreme court of justice with incomparably more power and consistency. In the end all good is rewarded and all evil punished, if not actually in this form of life then in the later exis- tences that begin after death. In this way all terrors, the sufferings and the hardships of life are destined to be obliterated. Life after death, which continues on earth just as the invisible part of the spectrum joins on to the visible part, brings us all the perfection that we may perhaps have missed here. And the superior wisdom which directs this course of things, the infinite goodness that expresses itself in it, the justice that achieves its aim in it—these are the attributes of the divine beings who also created us and the world as a whole, or rather, of the one divine being into which, in our civilization, all the gods of antiquity have been condensed. The people which first succeeded in thus concentrating the divine attributes was not a little proud of the advance. It had laid open to view the father who had all along been hidden behind every divine figure as its nucleus. Fundamentally this was a return to the historical beginnings of the idea of God. Now that God was a single person, man's relations to him could recover the intimacy and intensity of the child's relation to his father. But if one had done so much for one's father, one wanted to have a reward, or at least to be his only beloved child, his Chosen People. Very much later, pious America laid claim to being 'God's own Country'; and, as regards one of the shapes in which men worship the deity, the claim is undoubtedly valid.

The religious ideas that have been summarized above have of course passed through a long process of development and have been adhered to in various phases by various civilizations. I have singled out one such phase, which roughly corresponds to the final form taken by our present- day white Christian civilization. It is easy to see that not all the parts of this picture tally equally well with one another, that not all the questions that press for an answer receive one, and that it is difficult to dismiss the contradiction of daily experience. Nevertheless, such as they are, those ideas—ideas which are religious in the widest sense—are prized as the most precious possession of civilization, as the most precious thing it has to offer its participants. It is far more highly prized than all the devices for winning treasures from the earth or providing men with sustenance or preventing their illnesses, and so forth. People feel that life would not be tolerable if they did not attach to these ideas the value that is claimed for them. And now the question arises: what are these ideas in the light of psychology? Whence do they derive the esteem in which they are held? And, to take a further timid step, what is their real worth?

IV

An enquiry which proceeds like a monologue, without interruption, is not altogether free from danger. One is too easily tempted into pushing aside thoughts which threaten to break into it, and in exchange one is left with a feeling of uncertainty which in the end one tries to keep down by over-decisiveness. I shall therefore imagine that I have an opponent who follows my arguments with mistrust, and here and there I shall allow him to interject some remarks.

I hear him say: 'You have repeatedly used the expressions "civilization creates these religious ideas", "civilization places them at the disposal of its participants". There is something about this that sounds strange to me. I cannot myself say why, but it does not sound so natural as it does to say that civilization has made rules about distributing the products of labour or about rights concerning women and children.'

I think, all the same, that I am justified in expressing myself in this way. I have tried to show that religious ideas have arisen from the same need as have all the other achievements of civilization: from the necessity of defending oneself against the crushingly superior force of nature. To this a second motive was added—the urge to rectify the shortcomings of civilization which made themselves painfully felt. Moreover, it is especially apposite to say that civilization gives the individual these ideas, for he finds them there already; they are presented to him ready-made, and he would not be able to discover them for himself. What he is entering into is the heritage of many generations, and he takes it over as he does the multiplication table, geometry, and similar things. There is indeed a difference in this, but that difference lies elsewhere and I cannot examine it yet. The feeling of strangeness that you mention may be partly due to the fact that this body of religious ideas is usually put forward as a divine revelation. But this presentation of it is itself a part of the religious system, and it entirely ignores the known historical development of these ideas and their differences in different epochs and civilizations.

'Here is another point, which seems to me to be more important. You argue that the humanization of nature is derived from the need to put an end to man's perplexity and helplessness in the face of its dreaded forces, to get into a relation with them and finally to influence them. But a motive of this kind seems superfluous. Primitive man has no choice, he has no other way of thinking. It is natural to him, something innate, as it were, to project his existence outwards into the world and to regard every event which he observes as the manifestation of beings who at bottom are like himself. It is his only method of comprehension. And it is by no means self-evident, on the contrary it is a remarkable coincidence, if by thus indulging his natural disposition he succeeds in satisfying one of his greatest needs.'

I do not find that so striking. Do you suppose that human thought has no practical motives, that it is simply the expression of a disinterested curiosity? That is surely very improbable. I believe rather that when man personifies the forces of nature he is again following an infantile model. He has learnt from the persons in his earliest environment that the way to influence them is to establish a relation with them; and so, later on, with the same end in view, he treats everything else that he comes across in the same way as he treated those persons. Thus I do not contradict your descriptive observation; it is in fact natural to man to personify everything that he wants to understand in order later to control it (psychical mastering as a preparation for physical mastering); but I provide in addition a motive and a genesis for this peculiarity of human thinking.

'And now here is yet a third point. You have dealt with the origin of religion once before, in your book *Totem and Taboo*. But there it appeared in a different light. Everything was the son-father relationship. God was the exalted father, and the longing for the father was the root of the need for religion. Since then, it seems, you have discovered the factor of human weakness and helplessness, to which indeed the chief role in the formation of religion is generally assigned, and now you transpose everything that was once the father complex into terms of helplessness. May I ask you to explain this transformation?'

With pleasure. I was only waiting for this invitation. But is it really a transformation? In *Totem and Taboo* it was not my purpose to explain the origin of religions but only of totemism. Can you, from any of the views known to you, explain the fact that the first shape in which the protecting deity revealed itself to men should have been that of an animal, that there was a prohibition against killing and eating this animal and that nevertheless the solemn custom was to kill and eat it communally once a year? This is precisely what happens in totemism. And it is hardly to the purpose to argue about whether totemism ought to be called a religion. It has intimate connections with the later god-religions. The totem animals become the sacred animals of the gods; and the earliest, but most fundamental moral restrictions—the prohibitions against murder and incest—originate in totemism. Whether or not you accept the conclusions of *Totem and Taboo*, I hope you will admit that a number of very remarkable, disconnected facts are brought together in it into a consistent whole.

The questions of why in the long run the animal god did not suffice, and was replaced by a human one, was hardly touched on in *Totem and Taboo*, and other problems concerning the formation of religion were not mentioned in the book at all. Do you regard a limitation of that kind as the same thing as a denial? My work is a good example of the strict isolation of the particular contribution which psycho-analytic discussion can make to the solution of the problem of religion. If I am now trying to add the other, less deeply concealed part, you should not accuse me of contradicting myself, just as before you accused me of being one-sided. It is, of course, my duty to point out the connecting links between what I said earlier and what I put forward now, between the deeper and the manifest motives, between the father-complex and man's helplessness and need for protection.

These connections are not hard to find. They consist in the relation of the child's helplessness to the helplessness of the adult which continues it. So that, as was to be expected, the motives for the formation of religion which psycho-analysis revealed now turn out to be the same as the infantile contribution to the *manifest* motives. Let us transport ourselves into the mental life of a child. You remember the choice of object according to the anaclitic [attachment] type, which psycho-analysis talks of? The libido there follows the paths of narcissistic needs and attaches itself to the objects which ensure the satisfaction of those needs. In this way the mother, who satisfies the child's hunger, becomes its first love-object and certainly also its first protection against all the undefined dangers which threaten it in the external world—its first protection against anxiety, we may say.

In this function [of protection] the mother is soon replaced by the stronger father, who retains that position for the rest of childhood. But the child's attitude to its father is coloured by a peculiar ambivalence. The father himself constitutes a danger for the child, perhaps because of its earlier relation to its mother. Thus it fears him no less than it longs for him and admires him. The indications of this ambivalence in the attitude to the father are deeply imprinted in every religion, as was shown in *Totem and Taboo*. When the growing individual finds that he is destined to remain a child for ever, that he can never do without protection against strange superior powers, he lends those powers the features belonging to the figure of his father; he creates for himself the gods whom he dreads, whom he seeks to propitiate, and whom he nevertheless entrusts with his own protection. Thus his longing for a father is a motive identical with his need for protection against the consequences of his human weakness. The defence against childish helplessness is what lends its characteristic features to the adult's reaction to the helplessness which *he* has to acknowledge—a reaction which is precisely the formation of religion. But it is not my intention to enquire any further into the development of the idea of God; what we are concerned with here is the finished body of religious ideas as it is transmitted by civilization to the individual.

V

Let us now take up the thread of our enquiry. What, then, is the psychological significance of religious ideas and under what heading are we to classify them? The question is not at all easy to answer immediately. After rejecting a number of formulations, we will take our stand on the following one. Religious ideas are teachings and assertions about facts and conditions of external (or internal) reality which tell one something one has not discovered for oneself and which lay claim to one's belief. Since they give us information about what is most important and interesting to us in life, they are particularly highly prized. Anyone who knows nothing of them is very ignorant; and anyone who has added them to his knowledge may consider himself much the richer.

There are, of course, many such teachings about the most various things in the world. Every school lesson is full of them. Let us take geography. We are told that the town of Constance lies on the Bodensee.[1] A student song adds: 'if you don't believe it, go and see.' I happen to have been there and can confirm the fact that that lovely town lies on the shore of a wide stretch of water which all those who live round it call the Bodensee; and I am not completely convinced of the correctness of this geographical assertion. In this connection I am reminded of another, very remarkable, experience. I was already a man of mature years when I stood for the first time on the hill of the Acropolis in Athens, between the temple ruins, looking out over the blue sea. A feeling of astonishment mingled with my joy. It seemed to say: 'So it really *is* true, just as we learnt at school!' How shallow and weak must have been the belief I then acquired in the real truth of what I heard, if I could be so astonished now! But I will not lay too much stress on the significance of this experience; for my astonishment could have had another explanation, which did not occur to me at the time and which is of a wholly subjective nature and has to do with the special character of the place.[2]

All the teachings like these, then, demand belief in their contents, but not without producing grounds for their claim. They are put forward as the epitomized result of a longer process of thought based on observation and certainly also on inferences. If anyone wants to go through this process himself instead of accepting its result, they show him how to set about it. Moreover, we are always in addition given the source of the knowledge conveyed by them, where that source is not self-evident, as it is in the case of geographical assertions. For instance, the earth is shaped like a sphere; the proofs adduced for this are Foucault's pendulum

1. [The German name for what we call the Lake of Constance.]
2. [This had happened in 1904, when Freud was almost fifty. He wrote a full account of the episode in an open letter to Romain Rolland some ten years after the present work {"A Disturbance of Memory on the Acropolis. An Open Letter to Romain Rolland on the Occasion of His Seventieth Birthday" (1936), SE XXII, 239–48.}]

experiment,[3] the behaviour of the horizon and the possibility of circumnavigating the earth. Since it is impracticable, as everyone concerned realizes, to send every schoolchild on a voyage round the world, we are satisfied with letting what is taught at school be taken on trust; but we know that the path to acquiring a personal conviction remains open.

Let us try to apply the same test to the teachings of religion. When we ask on what their claim to be believed is founded, we are met with three answers, which harmonize remarkably badly with one another. Firstly, these teachings deserve to be believed because they were already believed by our primal ancestors; secondly, we possess proofs which have been handed down to us from those same primaeval times; and thirdly, it is forbidden to raise the question of their authentication at all. In former days anything so presumptuous was visited with the severest penalties, and even to-day society looks askance at any attempt to raise the question again.

This third point is bound to rouse our strongest suspicions. After all, a prohibition like this can only be for one reason—that society is very well aware of the insecurity of the claim it makes on behalf of its religious doctrines. Otherwise it would certainly be very ready to put the necessary data at the disposal of anyone who wanted to arrive at conviction. This being so, it is with a feeling of mistrust which it is hard to allay that we pass on to an examination of the other two grounds of proof. We ought to believe because our forefathers believed. But these ancestors of ours were far more ignorant than we are. They believed in things we could not possibly accept to-day; and the possibility occurs to us that the doctrines of religion may belong to that class too. The proofs they have left us are set down in writings which themselves bear every mark of untrustworthiness. They are full of contradictions, revisions and falsifications, and where they speak of factual confirmations they are themselves unconfirmed. It does not help much to have it asserted that their wording, or even their content only, originates from divine revelation; for this assertion is itself one of the doctrines whose authenticity is under examination, and no proposition can be a proof of itself.

Thus we arrive at the singular conclusion that of all the information provided by our cultural assets it is precisely the elements which might be of the greatest importance to us and which have the task of solving the riddles of the universe and of reconciling us to the sufferings of life—it is precisely those elements that are the least well authenticated of any. We should not be able to bring ourselves to accept anything of so little concern to us as the fact that whales bear young instead of laying eggs, if it were not capable of better proof than this.

This state of affairs is in itself a very remarkable psychological problem. And let no one suppose that what I have said about the impossibility of

3. [J. B. L. Foucault (1819–68) demonstrated the diurnal motion of the earth by means of a pendulum in 1851.]

proving the truth of religious doctrines contains anything new. It has been felt at all times—undoubtedly, too, by the ancestors who bequeathed us this legacy. Many of them probably nourished the same doubts as ours, but the pressure imposed on them was too strong for them to have dared to utter them. And since then countless people have been tormented by similar doubts, and have striven to suppress them, because they thought it was their duty to believe; many brilliant intellects have broken down over this conflict, and many characters have been impaired by the compromises with which they have tried to find a way out of it.

If all the evidence put forward for the authenticity of religious teachings originates in the past, it is natural to look round and see whether the present, about which it is easier to form judgements, may not also be able to furnish evidence of the sort. If by this means we could succeed in clearing even a single portion of the religious system from doubt, the whole of it would gain enormously in credibility. The proceedings of the spiritualists meet us at this point; they are convinced of the survival of the individual soul and they seek to demonstrate to us beyond doubt the truth of this one religious doctrine. Unfortunately they cannot succeed in refuting the fact that the appearance and utterances of their spirits are merely the products of their own mental activity. They have called up the spirits of the greatest men and of the most eminent thinkers, but all the pronouncements and information which they have received from them have been so foolish and so wretchedly meaningless that one can find nothing credible in them but the capacity of the spirits to adapt themselves to the circle of people who have conjured them up.

I must now mention two attempts that have been made—both of which convey the impression of being desperate efforts—to evade the problem. One, of a violent nature, is ancient; the other is subtle and modern. The first is the 'Credo quia absurdum' of the early Father of the Church.[4] It maintains that religious doctrines are outside the jurisdiction of reason—are above reason. Their truth must be felt inwardly, and they need not be comprehended. But this Credo is only of interest as a self-confession. As an authoritative statement it has no binding force. Am I to be obliged to believe every absurdity? And if not, why this one in particular? There is no appeal to a court above that of reason. If the truth of religious doctrines is dependent on an inner experience which bears witness to that truth, what is one to do about the many people who do not have this rare experience? One may require every man to use the gift of reason which he possesses, but one cannot erect, on the basis of a motive that exists only for a very few, an obligation that shall apply to everyone. If one man has gained an unshakable conviction of the true reality of religious doctrines from a state of ecstasy which has deeply moved him, of what significance is that to others?

4. ['I believe because it is absurd.' This is attributed to Tertullian.]

The second attempt is the one made by the philosophy of 'As if'. This asserts that our thought-activity includes a great number of hypotheses whose groundlessness and even absurdity we fully realize. They are called 'fictions', but for a variety of practical reasons we have to behave 'as if' we believed in these fictions. This is the case with religious doctrines because of their incomparable importance for the maintenance of human society.[5] This line of argument is not far removed from the *'Credo quia absurdum'*. But I think the demand made by the 'As if' argument is one that only a philosopher could put forward. A man whose thinking is not influenced by the artifices of philosophy will never be able to accept it; in such a man's view, the admission that something is absurd or contrary to reason leaves no more to be said. It cannot be expected of him that precisely in treating his most important interests he shall forgo the guarantees he requires for all his ordinary activities. I am reminded of one of my children who was distinguished at an early age by a peculiarly marked matter-of-factness. When the children were being told a fairy story and were listening to it with rapt attention, he would come up and ask: 'Is that a true story?' When he was told it was not, he would turn away with a look of disdain. We may expect that people will soon behave in the same way towards the fairy tales of religion, in spite of the advocacy of 'As if'.

But at present they still behave quite differently; and in past times religious ideas, in spite of their incontrovertible lack of authentication, have exercised the strongest possible influence on mankind. This is a fresh psychological problem. We must ask where the inner force of those doctrines lies and to what it is that they owe their efficacy, independent as it is of recognition by reason.

VI

I think we have prepared the way sufficiently for an answer to both these questions. It will be found if we turn our attention to the psychical origin of religious ideas. These, which are given out as teachings, are not precipitates of experience or end-results of thinking: they are illusions, fulfilments of the oldest, strongest and most urgent wishes of mankind. The secret of their strength lies in the strength of those wishes. As we already know, the terrifying impression of helplessness in childhood aroused the need for protection—for protection through love—which was provided by the father; and the recognition that this helplessness lasts throughout life made it necessary to cling to the existence of a father, but this time a more powerful one. Thus the benevolent rule of

5. I hope I am not doing him an injustice if I take the philosopher of 'As if' as the representative of a view which is not foreign to other thinkers. 'We include as fictions not merely indifferent theoretical operations but ideational constructs emanating from the noblest minds, to which the noblest part of mankind cling and of which they will not allow themselves to be deprived. Nor is it our object so to deprive them—for as *practical fictions* we leave them all intact; they perish only as *theoretical truths.*' Hans Vaihinger {*The Philosophy of 'As if,'* [1911; 7th and 8th ed., 1922; tr. 1924]}.

a divine Providence allays our fear of the dangers of life; the establishment of a moral world-order ensures the fulfilment of the demands of justice, which have so often remained unfulfilled in human civilization; and the prolongation of earthly existence in a future life provides the local and temporal framework in which these wish-fulfilments shall take place. Answers to the riddles that tempt the curiosity of man, such as how the universe began or what the relation is between body and mind, are developed in conformity with the underlying assumptions of this system. It is an enormous relief to the individual psyche if the conflicts of its childhood arising from the father-complex—conflicts which it has never wholly overcome—are removed from it and brought to a solution which is universally accepted.

When I say that these things are illusions, I must define the meaning of the word. An illusion is not the same thing as an error; nor is it necessarily an error. Aristotle's belief that vermin are developed out of dung (a belief to which ignorant people still cling) was an error; so was the belief of a former generation of doctors that *tabes dorsalis* is the result of sexual excess. It would be incorrect to call these errors illusions. On the other hand, it was an illusion of Columbus's that he had discovered a new sea-route to the Indies. The part played by his wish in this error is very clear. One may describe as an illusion the assertion made by certain nationalists that the Indo-Germanic race is the only one capable of civilization; or the belief, which was only destroyed by psycho-analysis, that children are creatures without sexuality. What is characteristic of illusions is that they are derived from human wishes. In this respect they come near to psychiatric delusions. But they differ from them, too, apart from the more complicated structure of delusions. In the case of delusions, we emphasize as essential their being in contradiction with reality. Illusions need not necessarily be false—that is to say, unrealizable or in contradiction to reality. For instance, a middle-class girl may have the illusion that a prince will come and marry her. This is possible; and a few such cases have occurred. That the Messiah will come and found a golden age is much less likely. Whether one classifies this belief as an illusion or as something analogous to a delusion will depend on one's personal attitude. Examples of illusions which have proved true are not easy to find, but the illusion of the alchemists that all metals can be turned into gold might be one of them. The wish to have a great deal of gold, as much gold as possible, has, it is true, been a good deal damped by our present-day knowledge of the determinants of wealth, but chemistry no longer regards the transmutation of metals into gold as impossible. Thus we call a belief an illusion when a wish-fulfilment is a prominent factor in its motivation, and in doing so we disregard its relations to reality, just as the illusion itself sets no store by verification.

Having thus taken our bearings, let us return once more to the question of religious doctrines. We can now repeat that all of them are illusions and insusceptible of proof. No one can be compelled to think them true, to believe in them. Some of them are so improbable, so incompatible with everything we have laboriously discovered about the reality of the world, that we may compare them—if we pay proper regard to the psychological differences—to delusions. Of the reality value of most of them we cannot judge; just as they cannot be proved, so they cannot be refuted. We still know too little to make a critical approach to them. The riddles of the universe reveal themselves only slowly to our investigation; there are many questions to which science to-day can give no answer. But scientific work is the only road which can lead us to a knowledge of reality outside ourselves. It is once again merely an illusion to expect anything from intuition and introspection; they can give us nothing but particulars about our own mental life, which are hard to interpret, never any information about the questions which religious doctrine finds it so easy to answer. It would be insolent to let one's own arbitrary will step into the breach and, according to one's personal estimate, declare this or that part of the religious system to be less or more acceptable. Such questions are too momentous for that; they might be called too sacred.

At this point one must expect to meet with an objection. 'Well, then, if even obdurate sceptics admit that the assertions of religion cannot be refuted by reason, why should I not believe in them, since they have so much on their side—tradition, the agreement of mankind, and all the consolations they offer?' Why not, indeed? Just as no one can be forced to believe, so no one can be forced to disbelieve. But do not let us be satisfied with deceiving ourselves that arguments like these take us along the road of correct thinking. If ever there was a case of a lame excuse we have it here. Ignorance is ignorance; no right to believe anything can be derived from it. In other matters no sensible person will behave so irresponsibly or rest content with such feeble grounds for his opinions and for the line he takes. It is only in the highest and most sacred things that he allows himself to do so. In reality these are only attempts at pretending to oneself to other people that one is still firmly attached to religion, when one has long since cut oneself loose from it. Where questions of religion are concerned, people are guilty of every possible sort of dishonesty and intellectual misdemeanour. Philosophers stretch the meaning of words until they retain scarcely anything of their original sense. They give the name of 'God' to some vague abstraction which they have created for themselves; having done so they can pose before all the world as deists, as believers in God, and they can even boast that they have recognized a higher purer concept of God, notwithstanding that their God is now nothing more than an insubstantial shadow and no longer the mighty personality of religious doctrines. Critics persist in describing as 'deeply religious' anyone who admits to a sense of man's insignificance or impotence in the face of the universe, although what constitutes the essence of the religious attitude is not this feeling but only the next step after it, the reaction to it which seeks a remedy for it. The man who goes no further, but humbly acquiesces in the small part which humans beings play in the great world—such a man is, on the contrary, irreligious in the truest sense of the word.

To assess the truth-value of religious doctrines does not lie within the scope of the present enquiry. It is enough for us that we have recognized them as being, in their psychological nature, illusions. But we do not have to conceal the fact that this discovery also strongly influences our attitude to the question which must appear to many to be the most important of all. We know approximately at what periods and by what kind of men religious doctrines were created. If in addition we discover the motives which led to this, our attitude to the problem of religion will undergo a marked displacement. We shall tell ourselves that it would be very nice if there were a God who created the world and was a benevolent Providence, and if there were a moral order in the universe and an after-life; but it is a very striking fact that all this is exactly as we are bound to wish it to be. And it would be more remarkable still if our wretched, ignorant and downtrodden ancestors had succeeded in solving all these difficult riddles of the universe.

VII

Having recognized religious doctrines as illusions, we are at once faced by a further question: may not other cultural assets of which we hold a high opinion and by which we let our lives be ruled be of a similar nature? Must not the assumptions that determine our political regulations be called illusions as well? and is it not the case that in our civilization the relations between the sexes are disturbed by an erotic illusion or a number of such illusions? And once our suspicion has been aroused, we shall not shrink from asking too whether our conviction that we can learn something about external reality through the use of observation and reasoning in scientific work—whether this conviction has any better foundation. Nothing ought to keep us from directing our observation to our own selves or from applying our thought to criticism of itself. In this field a number of investigations open out before us, whose results could not but be decisive for the construction of a 'Weltanschauung'. We surmise, moreover, that such an effort would not be wasted and that it would at least in part justify our suspicion. But the author does not dispose of the means for undertaking so comprehensive a task; he needs must confine his work to following out one only of these illusions—that, namely, of religion.

But now the loud voice of our opponent brings us to a halt. We are called to account for our wrong-doing:

'Archaeological interests are no doubt most praiseworthy, but no one undertakes an excavation if by doing so he is going to undermine the habitations of the living so that they collapse and bury people under their ruins. The doctrines of religion are not a subject one can quibble about like any other. Our civilization is built up on them, and the maintenance of human society is based on the majority of men's believing in the truth of those doctrines. If men are taught that there is no almighty and all-just God, no divine world-order and no future life, they will feel exempt from all obligation to obey the precepts of civilization. Everyone will, without inhibition or fear, follow his asocial, egoistic instincts and seek to exercise his power; Chaos, which we have banished through many thousands of years of the work of civilization, will come again. Even if we knew, and could prove, that religion was not in possession of the truth, we ought to conceal the fact and behave in the way prescribed by the philosophy of "As if"—and this in the interest of the preservation of us all. And apart from the danger of the undertaking, it would be a purposeless cruelty. Countless people find their one consolation in religious doctrines, and can only bear life with their help. You would rob them of their support, without having anything better to give them in exchange. It is admitted that so far science has not achieved much, but even if it had advanced much further it would not suffice for man. Man has imperative needs of another sort, which can never be satisfied by cold science; and it is very strange—indeed, it is the height of inconsistency—that a psychologist who has always insisted on what a minor part is played in human affairs by the intelligence as compared with the life of the instincts—that such a psychologist should now try to rob mankind of a precious wish-fulfilment and should propose to compensate them for it with intellectual nourishment.'

What a lot of accusations all at once! Nevertheless I am ready with rebuttals for them all; and, what is more, I shall assert the view that civilization runs a greater risk if we maintain our present attitude to religion than if we give it up.

But I hardly know where to begin my reply. Perhaps with the assurance that I myself regard my undertaking as completely harmless and free of risk. It is not I who am overvaluing the intellect this time. If people are as my opponents describe them—and I should not like to contradict them—then there is no danger of a devout believer's being overcome by my arguments and deprived of his faith. Besides, I have said nothing which other and better men have not said before me in a much more complete, forcible and impressive manner. Their names are well known, and I shall not cite them, for I should not like to give an impression that I am seeking to rank myself as one of them. All I have done—and this is the only thing that is new in my exposition—is to add some psychological foundation to the criticisms of my great predecessors. It is hardly to be expected that precisely this addition will produce the effect which was denied to those earlier efforts. No doubt I might be asked here what is the point of writing these things if I am certain that they will be ineffective. But I shall come back to that later.

The one person this publication may injure is myself. I shall have to listen to the most disagreeable reproaches for my shallowness, narrow-mindedness and lack of idealism or of understanding for the highest interests of mankind. But on the one hand, such remonstrances are not new to me; and on the other, if a man has already learnt in his youth to rise superior to the disapproval of his contemporaries, what can it matter to him in his old age when he is certain soon to be beyond the reach of all favour or disfavour? In former times it was different. Then utterances such as mine brought with them a sure curtailment of one's earthly existence and an effective speeding-up of the opportunity for gaining a personal experience of the afterlife. But, I repeat, those times are past and to-day writings such as this bring no more danger to their author than to their readers. The most that can happen is that the translation and distribution of his book will be forbidden in one country or another—and precisely, of course, in a country that is convinced of the high standard of its culture. But if one puts in any plea at all for the renunciation of wishes and for acquiescence in Fate, one must be able to tolerate this kind of injury too.

The further question occurred to me whether the publication of this work might not after all do harm. Not to a person, however, but to a cause—the cause of psycho-analysis. For it cannot be denied that psycho-analysis is my creation, and it has met with plenty of mistrust and ill-will. If I now come forward with such displeasing pronouncements, people will be only too ready to make a displacement from my person to psycho-analysis. 'Now we see,' they will say, 'where psycho-analysis leads to. The mask has fallen; it leads to a denial of God and of a moral ideal, as we always suspected. To keep us from this discovery we have been deluded into thinking that psycho-analysis has no *Weltanschauung* and never can construct one.

An outcry of this kind will really be disagreeable to me on account of my many fellow-workers, some of whom do not by any means share my attitude to the problems of religion. But psycho-analysis has already weathered many storms and now it must brave this fresh one. In point of fact psycho-analysis is a method of research, an impartial instrument, like the infinitesimal calculus, as it were. If a physicist were to discover with the latter's help that after a certain time the earth would be destroyed, we would nevertheless hesitate to attribute destructive tendencies to the calculus itself and therefore to proscribe it. Nothing that I have said here against the truth-value of religions needed the support of psycho-analysis; it had been said by others long before analysis came into existence. If the application of the psycho-analytic method makes it possible to find a new argument against the truths of religion, *tant pis* for religion; but defenders of religion will by the same right make use of psycho-analysis in order to give full value to the affective significance of religious doctrines.

And now to proceed with our defence. Religion has clearly performed great services for human civilization. It has contributed much towards the taming of the asocial instincts. But not enough. It has ruled human society for many thousands of years and has had time to show what it can achieve. If it had succeeded in making the majority of mankind happy, in comforting them, in reconciling them to life and in making them into vehicles of civilization, no one would dream of attempting to alter the existing conditions. But what do we see instead? We see that an appallingly large number of people are dissatisfied with civilization and unhappy in it, and feel it as a yoke which must be shaken off; and that these people either do everything in their power to change that civilization, or else go so far in their hostility to it that they will have nothing to do with civilization or with a restriction of instinct. At this point it will be objected against us that this state of affairs is due to the very fact that religion has lost a part of its influence over human masses precisely because of the deplorable effect of the advances of science. We will note this admission and the reason given for it, and we shall make use of it later for our own purposes; but the objection itself has no force.

It is doubtful whether men were in general happier at a time when religious doctrines held unrestricted sway; more moral they certainly were not. They have always known how to externalize the precepts of religion and thus to nullify their intentions. The priests, whose duty it was to ensure obedience to religion, met them half-way in this. God's kindness must lay a restraining hand on His justice. One sinned, and then one made a sacrifice or did penance and then one was free to sin once more. Russian introspectiveness has reached the pitch of concluding that sin is indispensable for the enjoyment of all the blessings of divine grace, so that, at bottom, sin is pleasing to God. It is no secret that the priests could only keep the masses submissive to religion by making such large concessions as these to the instinctual nature of man. Thus it was agreed: God alone is strong and good, man is weak and sinful. In every age immorality has found no less support in religion than morality has. If the achievements of religion in respect to man's happiness, susceptibility to culture and moral control are no better than this, the question cannot but arise whether we are not over-rating its necessity for mankind, and whether we do wisely in basing our cultural demands upon it.

Let us consider the unmistakable situation as it is to-day. We have heard the admission that religion no longer has the same influence on people that it used to. (We are here concerned with European Christian civilization.) And this is not because its promises have grown less but because people find them less credible. Let us admit that the reason—though perhaps not the only reason—for this change is the increase of the scientific spirit in the higher strata of human society. Criticism has whittled away the evidential value of religious documents, natural science has shown up the errors in them, and comparative research has been struck by the fatal resemblance between the religious ideas which we revere and the mental products of primitive peoples and times.

The scientific spirit brings about a particular attitude towards worldly matters; before religious matters it pauses for a little, hesitates, and finally there too crosses the threshold. In this process there is no stopping; the greater the number of men to whom the treasures of knowledge become accessible, the more widespread is the falling-away from religious belief—at first only from its obsolete and objectionable trappings, but later from its fundamental postulates as well. The Americans who instituted the 'monkey trial' at Dayton have alone shown themselves consistent. Elsewhere the inevitable transition is accomplished by way of half-measures and insincerities.

Civilization has little to fear from educated people and brain-workers. In them the replacement of religious motives for civilized behaviour by other, secular motives would proceed unobtrusively; moreover, such people are to a large extent themselves vehicles of civilization. But it is another matter with the great mass of the uneducated and oppressed, who have every reason for being enemies of civilization. So long as they do not discover that people no longer believe in God, all is well. But they will discover it, infallibly, even if this piece of writing of mine is not published. And they are ready to accept the results of scientific thinking, but without the change having taken place in them which scientific thinking brings about in people. Is there not a danger here that the hostility of these masses to civilization will throw itself against the weak spot that they have found in their task-mistress? If the sole reason why you must not kill your neighbour is because God has forbidden it and will severely punish you for it in this or the next life— then, when you learn that there is no God and that you need not fear His punishment, you will certainly kill your neighbour without hesitation, and you can only be prevented from doing so by mundane force. Thus either these dangerous masses must be held down most severely and kept most carefully away from any chance of intellectual awakening, or else the relationship between civilization and religion must undergo a fundamental revision.

VIII

One might think that there would be no special difficulties in the way of carrying out this latter proposal. It is true that it would involve a certain amount of renunciation, but more would perhaps be gained than lost, and a great danger would be avoided. Everyone is frightened of it, however, as though it would expose civilization to a still greater danger. When St. Boniface[6] cut down the tree that was venerated as sacred by the Saxons the bystanders expected some fearful event to follow upon

6. [The eighth-century, Devonshire-born, 'Apostle of Germany'.]

the sacrilege. But nothing happened, and the Saxons accepted baptism.

When civilization laid down the commandment that a man shall not kill the neighbour whom he hates or who is in his way or whose property he covets, this was clearly done in the interest of man's communal existence, which would not otherwise be practicable. For the murderer would draw down on himself the vengeance of the murdered man's kinsmen and the secret envy of others, who within themselves feel as much inclined as he does for such acts of violence. Thus he would not enjoy his revenge or his robbery for long, but would have every prospect of soon being killed himself. Even if he protected himself against his single foes by extraordinary strength and caution, he would be bound to succumb to a combination of weaker men. If a combination of this sort did not take place, the murdering would continue endlessly and the final outcome would be that men would exterminate one another. We should arrive at the same state of affairs between individuals as still persists in Corsica between families, though elsewhere only between nations. Insecurity of life, which is an equal danger for everyone, now unites men into a society which prohibits the individual from killing and reserves to itself the right to communal killing of anyone who violates the prohibition. Here, then, we have justice and punishment.

But we do not publish this rational explanation of the prohibition against murder. We assert that the prohibition has been issued by God. Thus we take it upon ourselves to guess His intentions, and we find that He, too, is unwilling for men to exterminate one another. In behaving in this way we are investing the cultural prohibition with a quite special solemnity, but at the same time we risk making its observance dependent on belief in God. If we retrace this step—if we no longer attribute to God what is our own will and if we content ourselves with giving the social reason—then, it is true, we have renounced the transfiguration of the cultural prohibition, but we have also avoided the risk to it. But we gain something else as well. Through some kind of diffusion or infection, the character of sanctity and inviolability—of belonging to another world, one might say—has spread from a few major prohibitions on to every other cultural regulation, law and ordinance. But on these the halo often looks far from becoming: not only do they invalidate one another by giving contrary decisions at different times and places, but apart from this they show every sign of human inadequacy. It is easy to recognize in them things that can only be the product of short-sighted apprehensiveness or an expression of selfishly narrow interests or a conclusion based on insufficient premisses. The criticism which we cannot fail to level at them also diminishes to an unwelcome extent our respect for other, more justifiable cultural demands. Since it is an awkward task to separate what God Himself has demanded from what can be traced to the authority of an all-powerful parliament or a high judiciary, it would be an undoubted advantage if we were to leave God out altogether and honestly admit the purely human origin of all the regulations and precepts of civilization. Along with their pretended sanctity, these commandments and laws would lose their rigidity and unchangeableness as well. People could understand that they are made, not so much to rule them as, on the contrary, to serve their interests; and they would adopt a more friendly attitude to them, and instead of aiming at their abolition, would aim only at their improvement. This would be an important advance along the road which leads to becoming reconciled to the burden of civilization.

But here our plea for ascribing purely rational reasons to the precepts of civilization—that is to say, for deriving them from social necessity—is interrupted by a sudden doubt. We have chosen as our example the origin of the prohibition against murder. But does our account of it tally with historical truth? We fear not; it appears to be nothing but a rationalistic construction. With the help of psycho-analysis, we have made a study of precisely this piece of the cultural history of mankind, and, basing ourselves on it, we are bound to say that in reality things happened otherwise. Even in present-day man purely reasonable motives can effect little against passionate impulses. How much weaker then must they have been in the human animal of primaeval times! Perhaps his descendants would even now kill one another without inhibition, if it were not that among those murderous acts there was one—the killing of the primitive father—which evoked an irresistible emotional reaction with momentous consequences. From it arose the commandment: Thou shalt not kill. Under totemism this commandment was restricted to the father-substitute; but it was later extended to other people, though even to-day it is not universally obeyed.

But, as was shown by arguments which I need not repeat here, the primal father was the original image of God, the model on which later generations have shaped the figure of God. Hence the religious explanation is right. God actually played a part in the genesis of that prohibition; it was His influence, not any insight into social necessity, which created it. And the displacement of man's will on-to God is fully justified. For men knew that they had disposed of their father by violence, and in their reaction to that impious deed, they determined to respect his will thenceforward. Thus religious doctrine tells us the historical truth—though subject, it is true, to some modification and disguise—whereas our rational account disavows it.

We now observe that the store of religious ideas includes not only wish-fulfilments but important historical recollections. The concurrent influence of past and present must give religion a truly incomparable wealth of power. But perhaps with the help of an analogy yet another discovery may begin to dawn on us. Though it is not a good plan to transplant ideas far from the soil in which they grew up, yet here is a conformity which we cannot avoid pointing out. We know that a human child cannot successfully complete its development to the civilized stage without passing through a phase of neurosis sometimes of greater and sometimes of less distinctness. This is because so many instinctual demands which will later be unserviceable cannot be suppressed by the rational operation of the child's intellect but have to be tamed by acts of repression, behind which, as a rule, lies the motive of anxiety. Most of these infantile neuroses are overcome spontaneously in the course of growing up, and this is especially true of the obsessional neuroses of childhood. The remainder can be cleared up later still by psycho-analytic treatment. In just the same way, one might assume, humanity as a whole, in its development through the ages, fell into states analogous to the neuroses, and for the same reasons—namely because in the times of its ignorance and intellectual weakness the instinctual renunciations indispensable for man's communal existence had only been achieved by it by means of purely affective forces. The precipitates of these processes resembling repression which took place in prehistoric times still remained attached to civilization for long periods. Religion would thus be the universal obsessional neurosis of humanity; like the obsessional neurosis of children, it arose out of the Oedipus complex, out of the relation to the father. If this view is right, it is to be supposed that a turning-away from religion is bound to occur with the fatal inevitability of a process of growth, and that we find ourselves at this very juncture in the middle of that phase of development. Our behaviour should therefore be modelled on that of a sensible teacher who does not oppose an impending new development but seeks to ease its paths and mitigate the violence of its irruption. Our analogy does not, to be sure, exhaust the essential nature of religion. If, on the one hand, religion brings with it obsessional restrictions, exactly as an individual obsessional neurosis does, on the other hand it comprises a system of wishful illusions together with a disavowal of reality, such as we find in an isolated form nowhere else but in amentia, [7] in a state of blissful hallucinatory confusion. But these are only analogies, by the help of which we endeavour to understand a social phenomenon; the pathology of the individual does not supply us with a fully valid counterpart.

It has been repeatedly pointed out (by myself and in particular by Theodor Reik) in how great detail the analogy between religion and obsessional neurosis can be followed out, and how many of the peculiarities and vicissitudes in the formation of religion can be understood in that light. And it tallies well with this that devout believers are safeguarded in a high degree against the risk of certain neurotic illnesses; their acceptance of the universal neurosis spares them the task of constructing a personal one.

Our knowledge of the historical worth of certain religious doctrines increases our respect for them, but does not invalidate our proposal that they should cease to be put forward as the reasons for the precepts of civilization. On the contrary! Those historical residues have helped us

7. ['Meynert's amentia': a state of acute hallucinatory confusion.]

to view religious teachings, as it were, as neurotic relics, and we may now argue that the time has probably come, as it does in an analytic treatment, for replacing the effects of repression by the results of the rational operation of the intellect. We may foresee, but hardly regret, that such a process of remoulding will not stop at renouncing the solemn transfiguration of cultural precepts, but that a general revision of them will result in many of them being done away with. In this way our appointed task of reconciling men to civilization will to a great extent be achieved. We need not deplore the renunciation of historical truth when we put forward rational grounds for the precepts of civilization. The truths contained in religious doctrines are after all so distorted and systematically disguised that the mass of humanity cannot recognize them as truth. The case is similar to what happens when we tell a child that new-born babies are brought by the stork. Here, too, we are telling the truth in symbolic clothing, for we know what the large bird signifies. But the child does not know it. He hears only the distorted part of what we say, and feels that he has been deceived; and we know how often his distrust of the grown-ups and his refractoriness actually take their start from this impression. We have become convinced that it is better to avoid such symbolic disguisings of the truth in what we tell children and not to withhold from them a knowledge of the true state of affairs commensurate with their intellectual level.

IX

'You permit yourself contradictions which are hard to reconcile with one another. You begin by saying that a piece of writing like yours is quite harmless: no one will let himself be robbed of his faith by considerations of the sort put forward in it. But since it is nevertheless your intention, as becomes evident later on, to upset that faith, we may ask why in fact you are publishing your work? In another passage, moreover, you admit that it may be dangerous, indeed very dangerous, for someone to discover that people no longer believe in God. Hitherto he has been docile, but now he throws off his obedience to the precepts of civilization. Yet your whole contention that basing the commandments of civilization on religious grounds constitutes a danger for civilization rests on the assumption that the believer can be turned into an unbeliever. Surely that is a complete contradiction.

'And here is another. On the one hand you admit that men cannot be guided through their intelligence, they are ruled by their passions and their instinctual demands. But on the other hand you propose to replace the affective basis of their obedience to civilization by a rational one. Let who can understand this. To me it seems that it must be either one thing or the other.

'Besides, have you learned nothing from history? Once before an attempt of this kind was made to substitute reason for religion, officially and in the grand manner. Surely you remember the French Revolution and Robespierre? And you must also remember how short-lived and miserably ineffectual the experiment was? The same experiment is being repeated in Russia at the present time, and we need not feel curious as to its outcome. Do you not think we may take it for granted that men cannot do without religion?

'You have said yourself that religion is more than an obsessional neurosis. But you have not dealt with this other side of it. You are content to work out the analogy with a neurosis. Men, you say, must be freed from a neurosis. What else may be lost in the process is of no concern to you.'

The appearance of contradiction has probably come about because I have dealt with complicated matters too hurriedly. But we can remedy this to some extent. I still maintain that what I have written is quite harmless in one respect. No believer will let himself be led astray from his faith by these or any similar arguments. A believer is bound to the teachings of religion by certain ties of affection. But there are undoubtedly countless other people who are not in the same sense believers. They obey the precepts of civilization because they let themselves be intimidated by the threats of religion, and they are afraid of religion so long as they have to consider it as a part of the reality which hems them in. They are the people who break away as soon as they are allowed to give up their belief in the reality-value of religion. But they too are unaffected by arguments. They cease to fear religion when they observe that others do not fear it; and it was of them that I asserted that they would get to know about the decline of religious influence even if I did not publish my work.

But I think you yourself attach more weight to the other contradiction which you charge me with. Since men are so little accessible to reasonable arguments and are so entirely governed by their instinctual wishes, why should one set out to deprive them of an instinctual satisfaction and replace it by reasonable arguments? It is true that men are like this; but have you asked yourself whether they *must* be like this, whether their innermost nature necessitates it? Can an anthropologist give the cranial index of a people whose custom it is to deform their children's heads by bandaging them round from their earliest years? Think of the depressing contrast between the radiant intelligence of a healthy child and the feeble intellectual powers of the average adult. Can we be quite certain that it is not precisely religious education which bears a large share of the blame for this relative atrophy? I think it would be a very long time before a child who was not influenced began to trouble himself about God and things in another world. Perhaps his thoughts on these matters would then take the same paths as they did with his forefathers. But we do not wait for such a development; we introduce him to the doctrines of religion at an age when he is neither interested in them nor capable of grasping their import. Is it not true that the two main points in the programme for the education of children to-day are retardation of sexual development and premature religious influence? Thus by the time the child's intellect awakens, the doctrines of religion have already become unassailable. But are you of opinion that it is very conducive to the strengthening of the intellectual function that so important a field should be closed against it by the threat of Hell-fire? When a man has once brought himself to accept uncritically all the absurdities that religious doctrines put before him and even to over-look the contradictions between them, we need not be greatly surprised at the weakness of his intellect. But we have no other means of controlling our instinctual nature but our intelligence. How can we expect people who are under the dominance of prohibitions of thought to attain the psychological ideal, the primacy of the intelligence? You know, too, that women in general are said to suffer from 'physiological feeble-mindedness'[8]—that is, from a lesser intelligence than men. The fact itself is disputable and its interpretation doubtful, but one argument in favour of this intellectual atrophy being of a secondary nature is that women labour under the harshness of an early prohibition against turning their thoughts to what would most have interested them—namely, the problems of sexual life. So long as a person's early years are influenced not only by a sexual inhibition of thought but also by a religious inhi-bition and by a loyal inhibition derived from this, we cannot really tell what in fact he is like.

But I will moderate my zeal and admit the possibility that I, too, am chasing an illusion. Perhaps the effect of the religious prohibition of thought may not be so bad as I suppose; perhaps it will turn out that hu-man nature remains the same even if education is not abused in order to subject people to religion. I do not know and you cannot know either. It is not only the great problems of this life that seem insoluble at the present time; many lesser questions too are difficult to answer. But you must ad-mit that here we are justified in having a hope for the future—that per-haps there is a treasure to be dug up capable of enriching civilization and that it is worth making the experiment of an irreligious education. Should the experiment prove unsatisfactory I am ready to give up the reform and to return to my earlier, purely descriptive judgement that man is a crea-ture of weak intelligence who is ruled by his instinctual wishes.

On another point I agree with you unreservedly. It is certainly senseless to begin by trying to do away with religion by force and at a single blow. Above all, because it would be hopeless. The believer will not let his belief be torn from him, either by arguments or by prohibitions. And even if this did succeed with some it would be cruelty. A man who has been taking sleeping draughts for tens of years is naturally unable to sleep if his sleeping draught is taken away from him. That the effect of

8. {This phrase stems from P. J. Moebius, "Ueber den physiologischen Schwachsinn des Weibes (5th ed., 1903). Freud more than once objected to Moebius's notion that women are constitutionally inferior.}

religious consolations may be likened to that of a narcotic is well illustrated by what is happening in America. There they are now trying—obviously under the influence of petticoat government—to deprive people of all stimulants, intoxicants, and other pleasure-producing substances, and instead, by way of compensation, are surfeiting them with piety. This is another experiment as to whose outcome we need not feel curious.[9]

Thus I must contradict you when you go on to argue that men are completely unable to do without the consolation of the religious illusion, that without it they could not bear the troubles of life and the cruelties of reality. That is true, certainly, of the men into whom you have instilled the sweet—or bitter-sweet—poison from childhood onwards. But what of the other men, who have been sensibly brought up? Perhaps those who do not suffer from the neurosis will need no intoxicant to deaden it. They will, it is true, find themselves in a difficult situation. They will have to admit to themselves the full extent of their helplessness and their insignificance in the machinery of the universe; they can no longer be the centre of creation, no longer the object of tender care on the part of a beneficent Providence. They will be in the same position as a child who has left the parental house where he was so warm and comfortable. But surely infantilism is destined to be surmounted. Men cannot remain children for ever; they must in the end go out into 'hostile life'. We may call this *education to reality*. Need I confess to you that the sole purpose of my book is to point out the necessity for this forward step?

You are afraid, probably, that they will not stand up to the hard test? Well, let us at least hope they will. It is something, at any rate, to know that one is thrown upon one's own resources. One learns then to make a proper use of them. And men are not entirely without assistance. Their scientific knowledge has taught them much since the days of the Deluge, and it will increase their power still further. And, as for the great necessities of Fate, against which there is no help, they will learn to endure them with resignation. Of what use to them is the mirage of wide acres in the moon, whose harvest no one has ever yet seen? As honest smallholders on this earth they will know how to cultivate their plot in such a way that it supports them. By withdrawing their expectations from the other world and concentrating all their liberated energies into their life on earth, they will probably succeed in achieving a state of things in which life will become tolerable for everyone and civilization no longer oppressive to anyone. Then, with one of our fellow-unbelievers, they will be able to say without regret:

> Den Himmel überlassen wir
> Den Engeln und den Spatzen.[1]

9. {Freud, of course, was writing during Prohibition, and his irritation with and contempt for such a policy was perfectly justified. But his derisive tone is characteristic of his inveterate anti-Americanism.}

1. ['We leaven Heaven to the angels and the sparrows.' From {Heinrich} Heine's poem *Deutschland* (Caput I).]

X

'That sounds splendid! A race of men who have renounced all illusions and have thus become capable of making their existence on earth tolerable! I, however, cannot share your expectations. And that is not because I am the obstinate reactionary you perhaps take me for. No, it is because I am sensible. We seem now to have exchanged roles: you emerge as an enthusiast who allows himself to be carried away by illusions, and I stand for the claims of reason, the rights of scepticism. What you have been expounding seems to me to be built upon errors which, following your example, I may call illusions, because they betray clearly enough the influence of your wishes. You pin your hope on the possibility that generations which have not experienced the influence of religious doctrines in early childhood will easily attain the desired primacy of the intelligence over the life of the instincts. This is surely an illusion: in this decisive respect human nature is hardly likely to change. If I am not mistaken—one knows so little about other civilizations— there are even to-day peoples which do not grow up under the pressure of a religious system, and yet they approach no nearer to your ideal than the rest. If you want to expel religion from our European civilization, you can only do it by means of another system of doctrines; and such a system would from the outset take over all the psychological characteristics of religion—the same sanctity, rigidity and intolerance, the same prohibition of thought—for its own defence. You have to have something of the kind in order to meet the requirements of education. And you cannot do without education. The path from the infant at the breast to the civilized man is a long one; too many human young would go astray on it and fail to reach their life-tasks at the proper time if they were left without guidance to their own development. The doctrines which had been applied in their upbringing would always set limits to the thinking of their riper years—which is exactly what you reproach religion with doing to-day. Do you not observe that it is an ineradicable and innate defect of our and every other civilization, that it imposes on children, who are driven by instinct and weak in intellect, the making of decisions which only the mature intelligence of adults can vindicate? But civilization cannot do otherwise, because of the fact that mankind's age-long development is compressed into a few years of childhood; and it is only by emotional forces that the child can be induced to master the task set before it. Such, then, are the prospects for your "primacy of the intellect".

'And now you must not be surprised if I plead on behalf of retaining the religious doctrinal system as the basis of education and of man's communal life. This is a practical problem, not a question of reality-value. Since, for the sake of preserving our civilization, we cannot postpone influencing the individual until he has become ripe for civilization (and many would never become so in any case), since we are obliged to impose on the growing child some doctrinal system which shall operate in him as an axiom that admits of no criticism, it seems to me that the religious system is by far the most suitable for the purpose. And it is so, of course, precisely on account of its wish-fulfilling and consolatory power, by which you claim to recognize it as an "illusion". In view of the difficulty of discovering anything about reality—indeed, of the doubt whether it is possible for us to do so at all—we must not overlook the fact that human needs, too, are a piece of reality, and, in fact, an important piece and one that concerns us especially closely.

'Another advantage of religious doctrine resides, to my mind, in one of its characteristics to which you seem to take particular exception. For it allows of a refinement and sublimation of ideas, which make it possible for it to be divested of most of the traces which it bears of primitive and infantile thinking. What then remains is a body of ideas which science no longer contradicts and is unable to disprove. These modifications of religious doctrine, which you have condemned as half-measures and compromises, make it possible to avoid the cleft between the uneducated masses and the philosophic thinker, and to preserve the common bond between them which is so important for the safeguarding of civilization. With this, there would be no need to fear that the men of the people would discover that the upper strata of society "no longer believe in God". I think I have now shown that your endeavours come down to an attempt to replace a proved and emotionally valuable illusion by another one, which is unproved and without emotional value.'

You will not find me inaccessible to your criticism. I know how difficult it is to avoid illusions; perhaps the hopes I have confessed to are of an illusory nature, too. But I hold fast to one distinction. Apart from the fact that no penalty is imposed for not sharing them, my illusions are not, like religious ones, incapable of correction. They have not the character of a delusion. If experience should show—not to me, but to others after me, who think as I do—that we have been mistaken, we will give up our expectations. Take my attempt for what it is. A psychologist who does not deceive himself about the difficulty of finding one's bearings in this world, makes an endeavour to assess the development of man, in the light of the small portion of knowledge he has gained through a study of the mental processes of individuals during their development from child to adult. In so doing, the idea forces itself upon him that religion is comparable to a childhood neurosis, and he is optimistic enough to suppose that mankind will surmount this neurotic phase, just as so many children grow out of their similar neurosis. These discoveries derived from individual psychology may be insufficient, their application to the human race unjustified, and his optimism unfounded. I grant you all these uncertainties. But often one cannot refrain from saying what one thinks, and one excuses oneself on the ground that one is not giving it out for more than it is worth.

And there are two points that I must dwell on a little longer. Firstly, the weakness of my position does not imply any strengthening of yours. I think you are defending a lost cause. We may insist as often as we like that man's intellect is powerless in comparison with his instinctual life, and we may be right in this. Nevertheless, there is something peculiar about this weakness. The voice of the intellect is a soft one, but it does not rest till it has gained a hearing. Finally, after a countless succession of rebuffs, it succeeds. This is one of the few points on which one may be optimistic about the future of mankind, but it is in itself a point of no small importance. And from it one can derive yet other hopes. The primacy of the intellect lies, it is true, in a distant, distant future, but probably not in an *infinitely* distant one. It will presumably set itself the same aims as those whose realization you expect from your God (of course within human limits—so far as external reality,' Aνάγκη, allows it), namely the love of man and the decrease of suffering. This being so, we may tell ourselves that our antagonism is only a temporary one and not irreconcilable. We desire the same things, but you are more impatient, more exacting, and—why should I not say it?—more self-seeking than I and those on my side. You would have the state of bliss begin directly after death; you expect the impossible from it and you will not surrender the claims of the individual. Our God, Λόγος,[2] will fulfil whichever of these wishes nature outside us allows, but he will do it very gradually, only in the unforeseeable future, and for a new generation of men. He promises no compensation for us, who suffer grievously from life. On the way to this distant goal your religious doctrines will have to be discarded, no matter whether the first attempts fail, or whether the first substitutes prove to be untenable. You know why: in the long run nothing can withstand reason and experience, and the contradiction which religion offers to both is all too palpable. Even purified religious ideas cannot escape this fate, so long as they try to preserve anything of the consolation of religion. No doubt if they confine themselves to a belief in a higher spiritual being, whose qualities are indefinable and whose purposes cannot be discerned, they will be proof against the challenge of science; but then they will also lose their hold on human interest.

And secondly: observe the difference between your attitude to illusions and mine. You have to defend the religious illusion with all your might. If it becomes discredited—and indeed the threat to it is great enough—then your world collapses. There is nothing left for you but to despair of everything, of civilization and the future of mankind. From that bondage I am, we are, free. Since we are prepared to renounce a good part of our infantile wishes, we can bear it if a few of our expectations turn out to be illusions.

Education freed from the burden of religious doctrines will not, it

<hr>

2. The twin gods Λόγος [*Logos*: Reason] and Aνάγκη [*Ananke*: Necessity] of the Dutch writer Multatuli {for whom, see above, p. 540}.

may be, effect much change in men's psychological nature. Our god Λόγος is perhaps not a very almighty one, and he may only be able to fulfil a small part of what his predecessors have promised. If we have to acknowledge this we shall accept it with resignation. We shall not on that account lose our interest in the world and in life, for we have one sure support which you lack. We believe that it is possible for scientific work to gain some knowledge about the reality of the world, by means of which we can increase our power and in accordance with which we can arrange our life. If this belief is an illusion, then we are in the same position as you. But science has given us evidence by its numerous and important successes that it is no illusion. Science has many open enemies, and many more secret ones, among those who cannot forgive her for having weakened religious faith and for threatening to overthrow it. She is reproached for the smallness of the amount she has taught us and for the incomparably greater field she has left in obscurity. But, in this, people forget how young she is, how difficult her beginnings were and how infinitesimally small is the period of time since the human intellect has been strong enough for the tasks she sets. Are we not all at fault, in basing our judgements on periods of time that are too short? We should make the geologists our pattern. People complain of the unreliability of science—how she announces as a law to-day what the next generation recognizes as an error and replaces by a new law whose accepted validity lasts no longer. But this is unjust and in part untrue. The transformations of scientific opinion are developments, advances, not revolutions. A law which was held at first to be universally valid proves to be a special case of a more comprehensive uniformity, or is limited by another law, not discovered till later; a rough approximation to the truth is replaced by a more carefully adapted one, which in turn awaits further perfectioning. There are various fields where we have not yet surmounted a phase of research in which we make trial with hypotheses that soon have to be rejected as inadequate; but in other fields we already possess an assured and almost unalterable core of knowledge. Finally, an attempt has been made to discredit scientific endeavour in a radical way, on the ground that, being bound to the conditions of our own organization, it can yield nothing else than subjective results, whilst the real nature of things outside ourselves remains inaccessible. But this is to disregard several factors which are of decisive importance for the understanding of scientific work. In the first place, our organization—that is, our mental apparatus—has been developed precisely in the attempt to explore the external world, and it must therefore have realized in its structure some degree of expediency; in the second place, it is itself a constituent part of the world which we set out to investigate, and it readily admits of such an investigation; thirdly, the task of science is fully covered if we limit it to showing how the world must appear to us in consequence of the particular character of our organization; fourthly, the ultimate findings of science, precisely because of the way in which they are acquired, are determined not only by our organization but by the things which have affected that organization; finally, the problem of the nature of the world without regard to our percipient mental apparatus is an empty abstraction, devoid of practical interest.

No, our science is no illusion. But an illusion it would be to suppose that what science cannot give us we can get elsewhere.

Civilization and Its Discontents

For many, this late essay, in which Freud sums up his long-held theories of culture, is the only Freudian text they ever read. The choice of *Civilization and Its Discontents* as *the* representative of his work is, for all its brevity, quite defensible: the little book is a fertile and original meditation on the irreparable conflict between the individual and his institutional surroundings. Hence it may claim a place on the short list of essential writings on political theory. Admittedly Freud's venture into such theory, however impressive, is fragmentary; it lacks the sheer range of Plato's *Republic* or Hobbes's *Leviathan*. But like these historic masterworks, *Civilization and Its Discontents* argues—and demonstrates—that the study of human institutions must begin with the study of human nature. And Freud offers a unique contribution to this study: the psychoanalytic perspective. At the same time, those who know only this epitome of Freud's thoughts on culture miss not only his clinical, technical, and metapsychological contributions; they must of necessity overlook the foundations of this essay in Freud's earlier work. It draws above all, as it must, on his well articulated ideas of the 1920s, notably his new theories of aggression and the superego. *Civilization and Its Discontents* is witness, and tribute, to his structural theory of mind.

Freud wrote the essay in the summer of 1929 and published it as a small book early in 1930. It has been suggested that its grim tone owes much to the growing power of Nazism both in Germany and in Austria. Certainly the last sentence of *Civilization and Its Discontents* (added in the second edition of 1931, virtually unchanged from the first edition) may be understood to mirror Freud's dismay over the electoral triumph of Hitler's NSDAP in the elections to the German Reichstag the previous September. But Freud's gloom is more than a response to newspaper headlines; it is implicit in his view of the human animal at war with civilization—and itself.

I

It is impossible to escape the impression that people commonly use false standards of measurement—that they seek power, success and wealth for themselves and admire them in others, and that they underestimate what is of true value in life. And yet, in making any general judgement of this sort, we are in danger of forgetting how variegated the human world and its mental life are. There are a few men from whom their contemporaries do not withhold admiration, although their greatness rests on attributes and achievements which are completely foreign to the aims and ideals of the multitude. One might easily be inclined to suppose that it is after all only a minority which appreciates these great men, while the large majority cares nothing for them. But things are probably not as simple as that, thanks to the discrepancies between people's thoughts and their actions, and to the diversity of their wishful impulses.

One of these exceptional few calls himself my friend in his letters to me. I had sent him my small book that treats religion as an illusion,[1] and he answered that he entirely agreed with my judgement upon religion, but that he was sorry I had not properly appreciated the true source of religious sentiments. This, he says, consists in a peculiar feeling, which he himself is never without, which he finds confirmed by many others, and which he may suppose is present in millions of people. It is a feeling which he would like to call a sensation of 'eternity', a feeling as of something limitless, unbounded—as it were, 'oceanic'. This feeling, he adds, is a purely subjective fact, not an article of faith; it brings with it no assurance of personal immortality, but it is the source of the religious energy which is seized upon by the various Churches and religious systems, directed by them into particular channels, and doubtless also exhausted by them. One may, he thinks, rightly call oneself religious on the ground of this oceanic feeling alone, even if one rejects every belief and every illusion.

The views expressed by the friend whom I so much honour, and who himself once praised the magic of illusion in a poem,[2] caused me no small difficulty. I cannot discover this 'oceanic' feeling in myself. It is not easy to deal scientifically with feelings. One can attempt to describe their physiological signs. Where this is not possible—and I am afraid that the oceanic feeling too will defy this kind of characterization—nothing remains but to fall back on the ideational content which is most readily associated with the feeling. If I have understood my friend rightly, he means the same thing by it as the consolation offered by an original and somewhat eccentric dramatist to his hero who is facing a self-inflicted death. 'We cannot fall out of this world.'[3] That is to say, it is a feeling of an indissoluble bond, of being one with the external world as a whole. I may remark that to me this seems something rather in the nature of an intellectual perception, which is not, it is true, without an accompanying feeling-tone, but only such as would be present with any other act of thought of equal range. From my own experience I could not convince myself of the primary nature of such a feeling. But this gives

---

1. [*The Future of an Illusion* {see above, pp. 685–722}.]

2. [*Footnote added* 1931:] *Liluli* [1919].—Since the publication of his two books *La vie de Ramakrishna* [1929] and *La vie die Vivekananda* (1930), I need no longer hide the fact that the friend spoken of in the text is Romain Rolland.

3. Christian Dietrich Grabbe [1801–36], *Hannibal*: 'Ja, aus der Welt werden wir nicht fallen. Wir sind einmal darin.' ['Indeed, we shall not fall out of this world. We are in it once and for all.']

me no right to deny that it does in fact occur in other people. The only question is whether it is being correctly interpreted and whether it ought to be regarded as the *fons et origo* of the whole need for religion.

I have nothing to suggest which could have a decisive influence on the solution of this problem. The idea of men's receiving an intimation of their connection with the world around them through an immediate feeling which is from the outset directed to that purpose sounds so strange and fits in so badly with the fabric of our psychology that one is justified in attempting to discover a psycho-analytic—that is, a genetic—explanation of such a feeling. The following line of thought suggests itself. Normally, there is nothing of which we are more certain than the feeling of our self, of our own ego. This ego appears to us as something autonomous and unitary, marked off distinctly from everything else. That such an appearance is deceptive, and that on the contrary the ego is continued inwards, without any sharp delimitation, into an unconscious mental entity which we designate as the id and for which it serves as a kind of façade—this was a discovery first made by psycho-analytic research, which should still have much more to tell us about the relation of the ego to the id. But towards the outside, at any rate, the ego seems to maintain clear and sharp lines of demarcation. There is only one state—admittedly an unusual state, but not one that can be stigmatized as pathological—in which it does not do this. At the height of being in love the boundary between ego and object threatens to melt away. Against all the evidence of his senses, a man who is in love declares that 'I' and 'you' are one, and is prepared to behave as if it were a fact. What can be temporarily done away with by a physiological [i.e. normal] function must also, of course, be liable to be disturbed by pathological processes. Pathology has made us acquainted with a great number of states in which the boundary lines between the ego and the external world become uncertain or in which they are actually drawn incorrectly. There are cases in which parts of a person's own body, even portions of his own mental life—his perceptions, thoughts and feelings—, appear alien to him and as not belonging to his ego; there are other cases in which he ascribes to the external world things that clearly originate in his own ego and that ought to be acknowledged by it. Thus even the feeling of our own ego is subject to disturbances and the boundaries of the ego are not constant.

Further reflection tells us that the adult's ego-feeling cannot have been the same from the beginning. It must have gone through a process of development, which cannot, of course, be demonstrated but which admits of being constructed with a fair degree of probability. An infant at the breast does not as yet distinguish his ego from the external world as the source of the sensations flowing in upon him. He gradually learns to do so, in response to various promptings. * * *

In this way, then, the ego detaches itself from the external world. Or, to put it more correctly, originally the ego includes everything, later it separates off an external world from itself. Our present ego-feeling is, therefore, only a shrunken residue of a much more inclusive—indeed, an all-embracing—feeling which corresponded to a more intimate bond between the ego and the world about it. If we may assume that there are many people in whose mental life this primary ego-feeling has persisted to a greater or less degree, it would exist in them side by side with the narrower and more sharply demarcated ego-feeling of maturity, like a kind of counterpart to it. In that case, the ideational contents appropriate to it would be precisely those of limitless and of a bond with the universe—the same ideas with which my friend elucidated the 'oceanic' feeling.

But have we a right to assume the survival of something that was originally there, alongside of what was later derived from it? Undoubtedly. There is nothing strange in such a phenomenon, whether in the mental field or elsewhere. In the animal kingdom we hold to the view that the most highly developed species have proceeded from the lowest; and yet we find all the simple forms still in existence to-day. The race of the great saurians is extinct and has made way for the mammals; but a true representative of it, the crocodile, still lives among us. This analogy may be too remote, and it is also weakened by the circumstance that the lower species which survive are for the most part not the true ancestors of the present-day more highly developed species. As a rule the intermediate links have died out and are known to us only through reconstruction. In the realm of the mind, on the other hand, what is primitive is so commonly preserved alongside of the transformed version which has arisen from it that it is unnecessary to give instances as evidence. When this happens it is usually in consequence of a divergence in development: one portion (in the quantitative sense) of an attitude or instinctual impulse has remained unaltered, while another portion has undergone further development.

This brings us to the more general problem of preservation in the sphere of the mind. The subject has hardly been studied as yet; but it is so attractive and important that we may be allowed to turn our attention to it for a little, even though our excuse is insufficient. Since we overcame the error of supposing that the forgetting we are familiar with signified a destruction of the memory-trace—that is, its annihilation—we have been inclined to take the opposite view, that in mental life nothing which has once been formed can perish—that everything is somehow preserved and that in suitable circumstances (when, for instance, regression goes back far enough) it can once more be brought to light. Let us try to grasp what this assumption involves by taking an analogy from another field. We will choose as an example the history of the Eternal City. Historians tell us that the oldest Rome was the *Roma Quadrata*, a fenced settlement on the Palatine. Then followed the phase of the *Septimontium*, a federation of the settlements on the different hills; after that came the city bounded by the Servian wall; and later still, after all the transformations during the periods of the republic and the early Caesars, the city which the Emperor Aurelian surrounded with his walls. We will not follow the changes which the city went through any further, but we will ask ourselves how much a visitor, whom we will suppose to be equipped with the most complete historical and topographical knowledge, may still find left of these early stages in the Rome of to-day. Except for a few gaps, he will see the wall of Aurelian almost unchanged. In some places he will be able to find sections of the Servian wall where they have been excavated and brought to light. If he knows enough— more than present-day archaeology does—he may perhaps be able to trace out in the plan of the city the whole course of that wall and the outline of the *Roma Quadrata*. Of the buildings which once occupied this ancient area he will find nothing, or only scanty remains, for they exist no longer. The best information about Rome in the republican era would only enable him at the most to point out the sites where the temples and public buildings of that period stood. Their place is now taken by ruins, but not by ruins of themselves but of later restorations made after fires or destruction. It is hardly necessary to remark that all these remains of ancient Rome are found dovetailed into the jumble of a great metropolis which has grown up in the last few centuries since the Renaissance. There is certainly not a little that is ancient still buried in the soil of the city or beneath its modern buildings. This is the manner in which the past is preserved in historical sites like Rome.

Now let us, by a flight of imagination, suppose that Rome is not a human habitation but a psychical entity with a similarly long and copious past—an entity, that is to say, in which nothing that has once come into existence will have passed away and all the earlier phases of development continue to exist alongside the latest one. This would mean that in Rome the palaces of the Caesars and the Septizonium of Septimius Severus would still be rising to their old height on the Palatine and that the castle of S. Angelo would still be carrying on its battlements the beautiful statues which graced it until the siege by the Goths, and so on. But more than this. In the place occupied by the Palazzo Caffarelli would once more stand—without the Palazzo having to be removed— the Temple of Jupiter Capitolinus; and this not only in its latest shape, as the Romans of the Empire saw it, but also in its earliest one, when it still showed Etruscan forms and was ornamented with terra-cotta antefixes. Where the Coliseum now stands we could at the same time admire Nero's vanished Golden House. On the Piazza of the Pantheon we should find not only the Pantheon of to-day, as it was bequeathed to us by Hadrian, but, on the same site, the original edifice erected by Agrippa; indeed, the same piece of ground would be supporting the church of Santa Maria sopra Minerva and the ancient temple over which it was built. And the observer would perhaps only have to change the direction of his glance or his position in order to call up the one view or the other.

There is clearly no point in spinning our phantasy any further, for it leads to things that are unimaginable and even absurd. If we want to represent historical sequence in spatial terms we can only do it by juxtaposition in space: the same space cannot have two different contents. Our attempt seems to be an idle game. It has only one justification. It shows us how far we are from mastering the characteristics of mental life by representing them in pictorial terms.

* * *

* * * Perhaps we ought to content ourselves with asserting that what is past in mental life *may* be preserved and is not *necessarily* destroyed. It is always possible that even in the mind some of what is old is effaced or absorbed—whether in the normal course of things or as an exception—to such an extent that it cannot be restored or revivified by any means; or that preservation in general is dependent on certain favourable conditions. It is possible, but we know nothing about it. We can only hold fast to the fact that it is rather the rule than the exception for the past to be preserved in mental life.

Thus we are perfectly willing to acknowledge that the 'oceanic' feeling exists in many people, and we are inclined to trace it back to an early phase of ego-feeling. The further question then arises, what claim this feeling has to be regarded as the source of religious needs.

To me the claim does not seem compelling. After all, a feeling can only be a source of energy if it is itself the expression of a strong need. The derivation of religious needs from the infant's helplessness and the longing for the father aroused by it seems to me incontrovertible, especially since the feeling is not simply prolonged from childhood days, but is permanently sustained by fear of the superior power of Fate. I cannot think of any need in childhood as strong as the need for a father's protection. Thus the part played by the oceanic feeling, which might seek something like the restoration of limitless narcissism, is ousted from a place in the foreground. The origin of the religious attitude can be traced back in clear outlines as far as the feeling of infantile helplessness. There may be something further behind that, but for the present it is wrapped in obscurity.

I can imagine that the oceanic feeling became connected with religion later on. The 'oneness with the universe' which constitutes its ideational content sounds like a first attempt at a religious consolation, as though it were another way of disclaiming the danger which the ego recognizes as threatening it from the external world. Let me admit once more that it is very difficult for me to work with these almost intangible quantities.
* * *

II

* * *

Let us return to the common man and to his religion—the only religion which ought to bear that name. The first thing that we think of is the well-known saying of one of our great poets and thinkers concerning the relation of religion to art and science:

Wer Wissenschaft und Kunst besitzt, hat auch Religion;
Wer jene beide nicht besitzt, der habe Religion![4]

This saying on the one hand draws an antithesis between religion and the two highest achievements of man, and on the other, asserts that, as regards their value in life, those achievements and religion can represent or replace each other. If we also set out to deprive the common man [who has neither science nor art] of his religion, we shall clearly not have the poet's authority on our side. We will choose a particular path to bring us nearer an appreciation of his words. Life, as we find it, is too hard for us; it brings us too many pains, disappointments and impossible tasks. In order to bear it we cannot dispense with palliative measures. 'We cannot do without auxiliary constructions', as Theodor Fontane tells us. There are perhaps three such measures: powerful deflections, which cause us to make light of our misery; substitutive satisfactions, which diminish it; and intoxicating substances, which make us insensitive to it. Something of the kind is indispensable.[5] Voltaire has deflections in mind when he ends *Candide* with the advice to cultivate one's garden; and scientific activity is a deflection of this kind, too. The substitutive satisfactions, as offered by art, are illusions in contrast with reality, but they are none the less psychically effective, thanks to the role which phantasy has assumed in mental life. The intoxicating substances influence our body and alter its chemistry. It is no simple matter to see where religion has its place in this series. We must look further afield.

The question of the purpose of human life has been raised countless times; it has never yet received a satisfactory answer and perhaps does not admit of one. Some of those who have asked it have added that if it should turn out that life has *no* purpose, it would lose all value for them. But this threat alters nothing. It looks, on the contrary, as though one had a right to dismiss the question, for it seems to derive from the human presumptuousness, many other manifestations of which are already familiar to us. Nobody talks about the purpose of the life of animals, unless, perhaps, it may be supposed to lie in being of service to man. But this view is not tenable either, for there are many animals of which

---

4. ['He who possesses science and art also has religion; but he who possesses neither of those two, let him have religion!']—Goethe, *Zahme Xenien* IX (Gedichte aus dem Nachlass).

5. In *Die Fromme Helene* {Freud's favorite German humorist} Wilhelm Busch has said the same thing on a lower plane: 'Wer Sorgen hat, hat auch Likör.' ['He who has cares has brandy too.]

man can make nothing, except to describe, classify and study them; and innumerable species of animals have escaped even this use, since they existed and became extinct before man set eyes on them. Once again, only religion can answer the question of the purpose of life. One can hardly be wrong in concluding that the idea of life having a purpose stands and falls with the religious system.

We will therefore turn to the less ambitious question of what men themselves show by their behaviour to be the purpose and intention of their lives. What do they demand of life and wish to achieve in it? The answer to this can hardly be in doubt. They strive after happiness; they want to become happy and to remain so. This endeavour has two sides, a positive and a negative aim. It aims, on the one hand, at an absence of pain and unpleasure, and, on the other, at the experiencing of strong feelings of pleasure. In its narrower sense the word 'happiness' only relates to the last. In conformity with this dichotomy in his aims, man's activity develops in two directions, according as it seeks to realize—in the main, or even exclusively—the one or the other of these aims.

As we see, what decides the purpose of life is simply the programme of the pleasure principle. This principle dominates the operation of the mental apparatus from the start. There can be no doubt about its efficacy, and yet its programme is at loggerheads with the whole world, with the macrocosm as much as with the microcosm. There is no possibility at all of its being carried through; all the regulations of the universe run counter to it. One feels inclined to say that the intention that man should be 'happy' is not included in the plan of 'Creation'. What we call happiness in the strictest sense comes from the (preferably sudden) satisfaction of needs which have been dammed up to a high degree, and it is from its nature only possible as an episodic phenomenon. When any situation that is desired by the pleasure principle is prolonged, it only produces a feeling of mild contentment. We are so made that we can derive intense enjoyment only from a contrast and very little from a state of things. Thus our possibilities of happiness are already restricted by our constitution. Unhappiness is much less difficult to experience. We are threatened with suffering from three directions: from our own body, which is doomed to decay and dissolution and which cannot even do without pain and anxiety as warning signals; from the external world, which may rage against us with overwhelming and merciless forces of destruction; and finally from our relations to other men. The suffering which comes from this last source is perhaps more painful to us than any other. We tend to regard it as a kind of gratuitous addition, although it cannot be any less fatefully inevitable than the suffering which comes from elsewhere.

It is no wonder if, under the pressure of these possibilities of suffering, men are accustomed to moderate their claims to happiness—just as the pleasure principle itself, indeed, under the influence of the external world, changed into the more modest reality principle—, if a man thinks himself happy merely to have escaped unhappiness or to have survived his suffering, and if in general the task of avoiding suffering pushes that of obtaining pleasure into the background. Reflection shows that the accomplishment of this task can be attempted along very different paths; and all these paths have been recommended by the various schools of worldly wisdom and put into practice by men. An unrestricted satisfaction of every need presents itself as the most enticing method of conducting one's life, but it means putting enjoyment before caution, and soon brings its own punishment. The other methods, in which avoidance of unpleasure is the main purpose, are differentiated according to the source of unpleasure to which their attention is chiefly turned. Some of these methods are extreme and some moderate; some are one-sided and some attack the problem simultaneously at several points. Against the suffering which may come upon one from human relationships the readiest safeguard is voluntary isolation, keeping oneself aloof from other people. The happiness which can be achieved along this path is, as we see, the happiness of quietness. Against the dreaded external world one can only defend oneself by some kind of turning away from it, if one intends to solve the task by oneself. There is, indeed, another and better path: that of becoming a member of the human community and, with the help of a technique guided by science, going over to the attack against nature and subjecting her to the human will. Then one is working with all for the good of all. But the most interesting methods of averting suffering are those which seek to influence our own organism. In the last analysis, all suffering is nothing else than sensation; it only exists in so far as we feel it, and we only feel it in consequence of certain ways in which our organism is regulated.

The crudest, but also the most effective among these methods of influence is the chemical one—intoxication. I do not think that anyone completely understands its mechanism, but it is a fact that there are foreign substances which, when present in the blood or tissues, directly cause us pleasurable sensations; and they also so alter the conditions governing our sensibility that we become incapable of receiving unpleasurable impulses. The two effects not only occur simultaneously, but seem to be intimately bound up with each other. But there must be substances in the chemistry of our own bodies which have similar effects, for we know at least one pathological state, mania, in which a condition similar to intoxication arises, without the administration of any intoxicating drug. Besides this, our normal mental life exhibits oscillations between a comparatively easy liberation of pleasure and a comparatively difficult one, parallel with which there goes a diminished or an increased receptivity to unpleasure. It is greatly to be regretted that this toxic side of mental processes has so far escaped scientific examination. The service rendered by intoxicating media in the struggle for happiness and in keeping misery at a distance is so highly prized as a benefit that individuals and peoples alike have given them an established place in the economics of their libido. We owe to such media not merely the immediate yield of pleasure, but also a greatly desired degree of independence from the external world. * * *

The complicated structure of our mental apparatus admits, however, of a whole number of other influences. Just as a satisfaction of instinct spells happiness for us, so severe suffering is caused us if the external world lets us starve, if it refuses to sate our needs. One may therefore hope to be freed from a part of one's sufferings by influencing the instinctual impulses. This type of defence against suffering is no longer brought to bear on the sensory apparatus; it seeks to master the internal sources of our needs. The extreme form of this is brought about by killing off the instincts, as is prescribed by the worldly wisdom of the East and practised by Yoga. If it succeeds, then the subject has, it is true, given up all other activities as well—he has sacrificed his life; and, by another path, he has once more only achieved the happiness of quietness. We follow the same path when our aims are less extreme and we merely attempt to *control* our instinctual life. In that case, the controlling elements are the higher psychical agencies, which have subjected themselves to the reality principle. Here the aim of satisfaction is not by any means relinquished; but a certain amount of protection against suffering is secured, in that non-satisfaction is not so painfully felt in the case of instincts kept in dependence as in the case of uninhibited ones. As against this, there is an undeniable diminution in the potentialities of enjoyment. The feeling of happiness derived from the satisfaction of a wild instinctual impulse untamed by the ego is incomparably more intense than that derived from sating an instinct that has been tamed. The irresistibility of perverse instincts, and perhaps the attraction in general of forbidden things, finds an economic explanation here.

Another technique for fending off suffering is the employment of the displacements of libido which our mental apparatus permits of and through which its function gains so much in flexibility. The task here is that of shifting the instinctual aims in such a way that they cannot come up against frustration from the external world. In this, sublimation of the instincts lends its assistance. One gains the most if one can sufficiently heighten the yield of pleasure from the sources of psychical and intellectual work. When that is so, fate can do little against one. A satisfaction of this kind, such as an artist's joy in creating, in giving his phantasies body, or a scientist's in solving problems or discovering truths, has a special quality which we shall certainly one day be able to characterize in metapsychological terms. At present we can only say figuratively that such satisfactions seem 'finer and higher'. * * * The weak point of this method is that it is not applicable generally: it is accessible to only a few people. It presupposes the possession of special dispositions and gifts which are far from being common to any practical degree. And even to the few who do possess them, this method cannot give complete protection from suffering. It creates no impenetrable armour against the arrows of fortune, and it habitually fails when the source of suffering is a person's own body.[6]

While this procedure already clearly shows an intention of making oneself independent of the external world by seeking satisfaction in internal, psychical processes, the next procedure brings out those features yet more strongly. In it, the connection with reality is still further loosened; satisfaction is obtained from illusions, which are recognized as such without the discrepancy between them and reality being allowed to interfere with enjoyment. The region from which these illusions arise is the life of the imagination; at the time when the development of the sense of reality took place, this region was expressly exempted from the demands of reality-testing and was set apart for the purpose of fulfilling wishes which were difficult to carry out. At the head of these satisfactions through phantasy stands the enjoyment of works of art—an enjoyment which, by the agency of the artist, is made accessible even to those who are not themselves creative. People who are receptive to the influence of art cannot set too high a value on it as a source of pleasure and consolation in life. Nevertheless the mild narcosis induced in us by art can do no more than bring about a transient withdrawal from the pressure of vital needs, and it is not strong enough to make us forget real misery.

Another procedure operates more energetically and more thoroughly. It regards reality as the sole enemy and as the source of all suffering, with which it is impossible to live, so that one must break off all relations with it if one is to be in any way happy. The hermit turns his back on the world and will have no truck with it. But one can do more than that; one can try to re-create the world, to build up in its stead another world in which its most unbearable features are eliminated and replaced by others that are in conformity with one's own wishes. But whoever, in desperate defiance, sets out upon this path to happiness will as a rule attain nothing. Reality is too strong for him. He becomes a madman, who for the most part finds no one to help him in carrying through his delusion. * * * The religions of mankind must be classed among the mass-delusions of this kind. No one, needless to say, who shares a delusion ever recognizes it as such.

I do not think that I have made a complete enumeration of the methods by which men strive to gain happiness and keep suffering away and I know, too, that the material might have been differently arranged. One

---

6. * * * No other technique for the conduct of life attaches the individual so firmly to reality as laying emphasis on work; for his work at least gives him a secure place in a portion of reality, in the human community. The possibility it offers of displacing a large amount of libidinal components, whether narcissistic, aggressive or even erotic, on to professional work and on to the human relations connected with it lends it a value by no means second to what it enjoys as something indispensable to the preservation and justification of exis- tence in society. Professional activity is a source of special satisfaction if it is a freely chosen one—if, that is to say, by means of sublimation, it makes possible the use of existing inclinations, of per- sisting or constitutionally reinforced instinctual impulses. And yet, as a path to happiness, work is not highly prized by men. They do not strive after it as they ao after other possibilities of satisfaction. The great majority of people only work under the stress of necessity, and this natural human aversion to work raises most difficult social problems.

procedure I have not yet mentioned {: work.} * * * {It} locates satisfaction in internal mental processes, making use, in so doing, of the displaceability of the libido of which we have already spoken. But it does not turn away from the external world; on the contrary, it clings to the objects belonging to that world and obtains happiness from an emotional relationship to them. Nor is it content to aim at an avoidance of unpleasure—a goal, as we might call it, of weary resignation; it passes this by without heed and holds fast to the original, passionate striving for a positive fulfilment of happiness. And perhaps it does in fact come nearer to this goal than any other method. I am, of course, speaking of the way of life which makes love the centre of everything, which looks for all satisfaction in loving and being loved. A psychical attitude of this sort comes naturally enough to all of us; one of the forms in which love manifests itself—sexual love—has given us our most intense experience of an overwhelming sensation of pleasure and has thus furnished us with a pattern for our search for happiness. What is more natural than that we should persist in looking for happiness along the path on which we first encountered it? The weak side of this technique of living is easy to see; otherwise no human being would have thought of abandoning this path to happiness for any other. It is that we are never so defenceless against suffering as when we love, never so helplessly unhappy as when we have lost our loved object or its love. But this does not dispose of the technique of living based on the value of love as a means to happiness. There is much more to be said about it.

We may go on from here to consider the interesting case in which happiness in life is predominantly sought in the enjoyment of beauty, wherever beauty presents itself to our senses and our judgement—the beauty of human forms and gestures, of natural objects and landscapes and of artistic and even scientific creations. This aesthetic attitude to the goal of life offers little protection against the threat of suffering, but it can compensate for a great deal. The enjoyment of beauty has a peculiar, mildly intoxicating quality of feeling. Beauty has no obvious uses; nor is there any clear cultural necessity for it. Yet civilization could not do without it. * * * The love of beauty seems a perfect example of an impulse inhibited in its aim. 'Beauty' and 'attraction' are originally attributes of the sexual object. It is worth remarking that the genitals themselves, the sight of which is always exciting, are nevertheless hardly ever judged to be beautiful; the quality of beauty seems, instead, to attach to certain secondary sexual characters.

In spite of the incompleteness [of my enumeration], I will venture on a few remarks as a conclusion to our enquiry. The programme of becoming happy, which the pleasure principle imposes on us, cannot be fulfilled; yet we must not—indeed, we cannot—give up our efforts to bring it nearer to fulfilment by some means or other. Very different paths may be taken in that direction, and we may give priority either to the positive aspect of the aim, that of gaining pleasure, or to its negative one, that of avoiding unpleasure. By none of these paths can we attain all that we desire. Happiness, in the reduced sense in which we recognize it as possible, is a problem of the economics of the individual's libido. There is no golden rule which applies to everyone: every man must find out for himself in what particular fashion he can be saved.[7] All kinds of different factors will operate to direct his choice. It is a question of how much real satisfaction he can expect to get from the external world, how far he is led to make himself independent of it, and, finally, how much strength he feels he has for altering the world to suit his wishes. In this, his psychical constitution will play a decisive part, irrespectively of the external circumstances. The man who is predominantly erotic will give first preference to his emotional relationships to other people; the narcissistic man, who inclines to be self-sufficient, will seek his main satisfactions in his internal mental processes; the man of action will never give up the external world on which he can try out his strength. As regards the second of these types, the nature of his talents and the amount of instinctual sublimation open to him will decide where he shall locate his interests. Any choice that is pushed to an extreme will be penalized by exposing the individual to the dangers which arise if a technique of living that has been chosen as an exclusive one should prove inadequate. Just as a cautious business-man avoids tying up all his capital in one concern, so, perhaps, worldly wisdom will advise us not to look for the whole of our satisfaction from a single aspiration. Its success is never certain, for that depends on the convergence of many factors, perhaps on none more than on the capacity of the psychical constitution to adapt its function to the environment and then to exploit that environment for a yield of pleasure. A person who is born with a specially unfavourable instinctual constitution, and who has not properly undergone the transformation and rearrangement of his libidinal components which is indispensable for later achievements, will find it hard to obtain happiness from his external situation, especially if he is faced with tasks of some difficulty. As a last technique of living, which will at least bring him substitutive satisfactions, he is offered that of a flight into neurotic illness—a flight which he usually accomplishes when he is still young. The man who sees his pursuit of happiness come to nothing in later years can still find consolation in the yield of pleasure of chronic intoxication; or he can embark on the desperate attempt at rebellion seen in a psychosis.

Religion restricts this play of choice and adaptation, since it imposes equally on everyone its own path to the acquisition of happiness and protection from suffering. Its technique consists in depressing the value of life and distorting the picture of the real world in a delusional manner—which presupposes an intimidation of the intelligence. At this price, by forcibly fixing them in a state of psychical infantilism and by

7. [The allusion is to a saying attributed to Frederick the Great, {King of Prussia, 1740–1786}: 'In my State every man can be saved after his own fashion.']

drawing them into a mass-delusion, religion succeeds in sparing many people an individual neurosis. But hardly anything more. There are, as we have said, many paths which *may* lead to such happiness as is attainable by men, but there is none which does so for certain. Even religion cannot keep its promise. If the believer finally sees himself obliged to speak of God's 'inscrutable decrees', he is admitting that all that is left to him as a last possible consolation and source of pleasure in his suffering is an unconditional submission. And if he is prepared for that, he could probably have spared himself the *détour* he has made.

III

Our enquiry concerning happiness has not so far taught us much that is not already common knowledge. And even if we proceed from it to the problem of why it is so hard for men to be happy, there seems no greater prospect of learning anything new. We have given the answer already by pointing to the three sources from which our suffering comes: the superior power of nature, the feebleness of our own bodies and the inadequacy of the regulations which adjust the mutual relationships of human beings in the family, the state and society. In regard to the first two sources, our judgement cannot hesitate long. It forces us to acknowledge those sources of suffering and to submit to the inevitable. We shall never completely master nature; and our bodily organism, itself a part of that nature, will always remain a transient structure with a limited capacity for adaptation and achievement. This recognition does not have a paralysing effect. On the contrary, it points the direction for our activity. If we cannot remove all suffering, we can remove some, and we can mitigate some: the experience of many thousands of years has convinced us of that. As regards the third source, the social source of suffering, our attitude is a different one. We do not admit it at all; we cannot see why the regulations made by ourselves should not, on the contrary, be a protection and a benefit for every one of us. And yet, when we consider how unsuccessful we have been in precisely this field of prevention of suffering, a suspicion dawns on us that here, too, a piece of unconquerable nature may lie behind—this time a piece of our own psychical constitution. * * *

How has it happened that so many people have come to take up this strange attitude of hostility to civilization? I believe that the basis of it was a deep and long-standing dissatisfaction with the then existing state of civilization and that on that basis a condemnation of it was built up, occasioned by certain specific historical events. * * *

There is also an added factor of disappointment. During the last few generations mankind has made an extraordinary advance in the natural sciences and in their technical application and has established his control over nature in a way never before imagined. The single steps of this advance are common knowledge and it is unnecessary to enumerate them. Men are proud of those achievements, and have a right to be. But they seem to have observed that this newly-won power over space and time, this subjugation of the forces of nature, which is the fulfilment of a longing that goes back thousands of years, has not increased the amount of pleasurable satisfaction which they may expect from life and has not made them feel happier. From the recognition of this fact we ought to be content to conclude that power over nature is not the *only* precondition of human happiness, just as it is not the *only* goal of cultural endeavour; we ought not to infer from it that technical progress is without value for the economics for our happiness. One would like to ask: is there, then, no positive gain in pleasure, no unequivocal increase in my feeling of happiness, if I can, as often as I please, hear the voice of a child of mine who is living hundreds of miles away or if I can learn in the shortest possible time after a friend has reached his destination that he has come through the long and difficult voyage unharmed? Does it mean nothing that medicine has succeeded in enormously reducing infant mortality and the danger of infection for women in childbirth, and, indeed, in considerably lengthening the average life of a civilized man? And there is a long list that might be added to benefits of this kind which we owe to the much-despised era of scientific and technical advances. * * * If there had been no railway to conquer distances, my child would never have left his native town and I should need no telephone to hear his voice; if travelling across the ocean by ship had not been introduced, my friend would not have embarked on his sea-voyage and I should not need a cable to relieve my anxiety about him. What is the use of reducing infantile mortality when it is precisely that reduction which imposes the greatest restraint on us in the begetting of children, so that, taken all round, we nevertheless rear no more children than in the days before the reign of hygiene, while at the same time we hae created difficult conditions for our sexual life in marriage, and have probably worked against the beneficial effects of natural selection? And, finally, what good to us is a long life if it is difficult and barren of joys, and if it is so full of misery that we can only welcome death as a deliverer?

It seems certain that we do not feel comfortable in our present-day civilization, but it is very difficult to form an opinion whether and in what degree men of an earlier age felt happier and what part their cultural conditions played in the matter. We shall always tend to consider people's distress objectively—that is, to place ourselves, with our own wants and sensibilities, in *their* conditions, and then to examine what occasions we should find in them for experiencing happiness or unhappiness. This method of looking at things, which seems objective because it ignores the variations in subjective sensibility, is, of course, the most subjective possible, since it puts one's own mental states in the place of any others, unknown though they may be. Happiness, however, is something essentially subjective. No matter how much we may shrink with horror from certain situations—of a galley-slave in antiquity, of a peasant during the Thirty Years' War, of a victim of the Holy Inquisition, of a Jew awaiting a pogrom—it is nevertheless impossible for us to feel our way into such people—to divine the changes which original obtuseness of mind, a gradual stupefying process, the cessation of expectations, and cruder or more refined methods of narcotization have produced upon their receptivity to sensations of pleasure and unpleasure. Moreover, in the case of the most extreme possibility of suffering, special mental protective devices are brought into operation. It seems to me unprofitable to pursue this aspect of the problem any further.

It is time for us to turn our attention to the nature of this civilization on whose value as a means to happiness doubts have been thrown. * * *

The first stage is easy. We recognize as cultural all activities and resources which are useful to men for making the earth serviceable to them, for protecting them against the violence of the forces of nature, and so on. As regards this side of civilization, there can be scarcely any doubt. If we go back far enough, we find that the first acts of civilization were the use of tools, the gaining of control over fire and the construction of dwellings. Among these, the control over fire stands out as a quite extraordinary and unexampled achievement, while the others opened up paths which man has followed ever since, and the stimulus to which is easily guessed. With every tool man is perfecting his own organs, whether motor or sensory, or is removing the limits to their functioning. Motor power places gigantic forces at his disposal, which, like his muscles, he can employ in any direction; thanks to ships and aircraft neither water nor air can hinder his movements; by means of spectacles he corrects defects in the lens of his own eye; by means of the telescope he sees into the far distance; and by means of the microscope he overcomes the limits of visibility set by the structure of his retina. In the photographic camera he has created an instrument which retains the fleeting visual impressions, just as a gramophone disc retains the equally fleeting auditory ones; both are at bottom materializations of the power he possesses of recollection, his memory. With the help of the telephone he can hear at distances which would be respected as unattainable even in a fairy tale. Writing was in its origin the voice of an absent person; and the dwelling-house was a substitute for the mother's womb, the first lodging, for which in all likelihood man still longs, and in which he was safe and felt at ease.

These things that, by his science and technology, man has brought about on this earth, on which he first appeared as a feeble animal organism and on which each individual of his species must once more make its entry ('oh inch of nature'[8]) as a helpless suckling—these things do not only sound like a fairy tale, they are an actual fulfilment of every—or of almost every—fairy-tale wish. All these assets he may lay

8. [In English in the original.]

claim to as his cultural acquisition. Long ago he formed an ideal conception of omnipotence and omniscience which he embodied in his gods. To these gods he attributed everything that seemed unattainable to his wishes, or that was forbidden to him. One may say, therefore, that these gods were cultural ideals. To-day he has come very close to the attainment of this ideal, he has almost become a god himself. Only, it is true, in the fashion in which ideals are usually attained according to the general judgement of humanity. Not completely; in some respects not at all, in others only half way. Man has, as it were, become a kind of prosthetic God.[9] When he puts on all his auxiliary organs he is truly magnificent; but those organs have not grown on to him and they still give him much trouble at times. Nevertheless, he is entitled to console himself with the thought that this development will not come to an end precisely with the year 1930 A.D. Future ages will bring with them new and probably unimaginably great advances in this field of civilization and will increase man's likeness to God still more. But in the interests of our investigations, we will not forget that present-day man does not feel happy in his Godlike character.

We recongize, then, that countries have attained a high level of civilization if we find that in them everything which can assist in the exploitation of the earth by man and in his protection against the forces of nature—everything, in short, which is of use to him—is attended to and effectively carried out. In such countries rivers which threaten to flood the land are regulated in their flow, and their water is directed through canals to places where there is a shortage of it. The soil is carefully cultivated and planted with the vegetation which it is suited to support; and the mineral wealth below ground is assiduously brought to the surface and fashioned into the required implements and utensils. The means of communication are ample, rapid and reliable. Wild and dangerous animals have been exterminated, and the breeding of domesticated animals flourishes. But we demand other things from civilization besides these, and it is a noticeable fact that we hope to find them realized in these same countries. As though we were seeking to repudiate the first demand we made, we welcome it as a sign of civilization as well if we see people directing their care too to what has no practical value whatever, to what is useless—if, for instance, the green spaces necessary in a town as playgrounds and as reservoirs of fresh air are also laid out with flower-beds, or if the windows of the houses are decorated with pots of flowers. We soon observe that this useless thing which we expect civilization to value is beauty. We require civilized man to reverence beauty wherever he sees it in nature and to create it in the objects of his handiwork so far as he is able. But this is far from exhausting our demands on civilization. We expect besides to see the

9. {Freud is here poignantly alluding to himself. He had been forced to wear a prosthesis, an enlarged cumbersome, chafing, often painful plate, since his cancer operations on his palate and jaw in 1923.}

signs of cleanliness and order. We do not think highly of the cultural level of an English country town in Shakespeare's time when we read that there was a big dung-heap in front of his father's house in Stratford; we are indignant and call it 'barbarous' (which is the opposite of civilized) when we find the paths in the Wiener Wald[1] littered with paper. Dirtiness of any kind seems to us incompatible with civilization. We extend our demand for cleanliness to the human body too. We are astonished to learn of the objectionable smell which emanated from the *Roi Soleil*;[2] and we shake our heads on the Isola Bella[3] when we are shown the tiny wash-basin in which Napoleon made his morning toilet. Indeed, we are not surprised by the idea of setting up the use of soap as an actual yardstick of civilization. The same is true of order. It, like cleanliness, applies solely to the works of man. But whereas cleanliness is not to be expected in nature, order, on the contrary, has been imitated from her. Man's observation of the great astronomical regularities not only furnished him with a model for introducing order into his life, but gave him the first points of departure for doing so. Order is a kind of compulsion to repeat which, when a regulation has been laid down once and for all, decides when, where and how a thing shall be done, so that in every similar circumstance one is spared hesitation and indecision. The benefits of order are incontestable. It enables men to use space and time to the best advantage, while conserving their psychical forces. We should have a right to expect that order would have taken its place in human activities from the start and without difficulty; and we may well wonder that this has not happened—that, on the contrary, human beings exhibit an inborn tendency to carelessness, irregularity and unreliability in their work, and that a laborious training is needed before they learn to follow the example of their celestial models.

Beauty, cleanliness and order obviously occupy a special position among the requirements of civilization. No one will maintain that they are as important for life as control over the forces of nature or as some other factors with which we shall become acquainted. And yet no one would care to put them in the background as trivialities. That civilization is not exclusively taken up with what is useful is already shown by the example of beauty, which we decline to omit from among the interests of civilization. The usefulness of order is quite evident. With regard to cleanliness, we must bear in mind that it is demanded of us by hygiene as well, and we may suspect that even before the days of scientific prophylaxis the connection between the two was not altogether strange to man. Yet utility does not entirely explain these efforts; something else must be at work besides.

No feature, however, seems better to characterize civilization than its esteem and encouragement of man's higher mental activities—his in-

1. [The wooded hills on the outskirts of Vienna.]   3. [The well-known island in Lake Maggiore.]
2. [Louis XIV of France.]

tellectual, scientific and artistic achievements—and the leading role that it assigns to ideas in human life. Foremost among those ideas are the religious systems, on whose complicated structure I have endeavoured to throw light elsewhere. Next come the speculations of philosophy; and finally what might be called man's 'ideals'—his ideas of a possible perfection of individuals, or of peoples or of the whole of humanity, and the demands he sets up on the basis of such ideas. The fact that these creations of his are not independent of one another, but are on the contrary closely interwoven, increases the difficulty not only of describing them but of tracing their psychological derivation. If we assume quite generally that the motive force of all human activities is a striving towards the two confluent goals of utility and a yield of pleasure, we must suppose that this is also true of the manifestations of civilization which we have been discussing here, although this is easily visible only in scientific and aesthetic activities. But it cannot be doubted that the other activities, too, correspond to strong needs in men—perhaps to needs which are only developed in a minority. Nor must we allow ourselves to be misled by judgements of value concerning any particular religion, or philosophic system, or ideal. Whether we think to find in them the highest achievements of the human spirit, or whether we deplore them as aberrations, we cannot but recognize that where they are present, and, in especial, where they are dominant, a high level of civilization is implied.

The last, but certainly not the least important, of the characteristic features of civilization remains to be assessed: the manner in which the relationships of men to one another, their social relationships, are regulated—relationships which affect a person as a neighbour, as a source of help, as another person's sexual object, as a member of a family and of a State. Here it is especially difficult to keep clear of particular ideal demands and to see what is civilized in general. Perhaps we may begin by explaining that the element of civilization enters on the scene with the first attempt to regulate these social relationships. If the attempt were not made, the relationships would be subject to the arbitrary will of the individual: that is to say, the physically stronger man would decide them in the sense of his own interests and instinctual impulses. Nothing would be changed in this if this stronger man should in his turn meet someone even stronger than he. Human life in common is only made possible when a majority comes together which is stronger than any separate individual and which remains united against all separate individuals. The power of this community is then set up as 'right' in opposition to the power of the individual, which is condemned as 'brute force'. This replacement of the power of the individual by the power of a community constitutes the decisive step of civilization. The essence of it lies in the fact that the members of the community restrict themselves in their possibilities of satisfaction, whereas the individual knew no such restrictions. The first requisite of civilization, therefore, is that of justice— that is, the assurance that a law once made will not be broken in favour of an individual. This implies nothing as to the ethical value of such a law. The further course of cultural development seems to tend towards making the law no longer an expression of the will of a small community—a caste or a stratum of the population or a racial group—which, in its turn, behaves like a violent individual towards other, and perhaps more numerous, collections of people. The final outcome should be a rule of law to which all—except those who are not capable of entering a community—have contributed by a sacrifice of their instincts, and which leaves no one—again with the same exception—at the mercy of brute force.

The liberty of the individual is no gift of civilization. It was greatest before there was any civilization, though then, it is true, it had for the most part no value, since the individual was scarcely in a position to defend it. The development of civilization imposes restrictions on it, and justice demands that no one shall escape those restrictions. What makes itself felt in a human community as a desire for freedom may be their revolt against some existing injustice, and so may prove favourable to a further development of civilization; it may remain compatible with civilization. But it may also spring from the remains of their original personality, which is still untamed by civilization and may thus become the basis in them of hostility to civilization. The urge for freedom, therefore, is directed against particular forms and demands of civilization or against civilization altogether. It does not seem as though any influence could induce a man to change his nature into a termite's. No doubt he will always defend his claim to individual liberty against the will of the group. A good part of the struggles of mankind centre round the single task of finding an expedient accommodation—one, that is, that will bring happiness—between this claim of the individual and the cultural claims of the group; and one of the problems that touches the fate of humanity is whether such an accommodation can be reached by means of some particular form of civilization or whether this conflict is irreconcilable.

By allowing common feeling to be our guide in deciding what features of human life are to be regarded as civilized, we have obtained a clear impression of the general picture of civilization; but it is true that so far we have discovered nothing that is not universally known. At the same time we have been careful not to fall in with the prejudice that civilization is synonymous with perfecting, that it is the road to perfection pre-ordained for men. But now a point of view presents itself which may lead in a different direction. The development of civilization appears to us as a peculiar process which mankind undergoes, and in which several things strike us as familiar. We may characterize this process with reference to the changes which it brings about in the familiar instinctual dispositions of human beings, to satisfy which is, after all, the economic task of our lives. A few of these instincts are used up in such a manner that something appears in their place which, in an individual, we describe as a character-trait. The most remarkable example of such a process is found in the anal erotism of young human beings. Their original interest in the excretory function, its organs and products, is changed in the course of their growth into a group of traits which are familiar to us as parsimony, a sense of order and cleanliness—qualities which, though valuable and welcome in themselves, may be intensified till they become markedly dominant and produce what is called the anal character. How this happens we do not know, but there is no doubt about the correctness of the finding. Now we have seen that order and cleanliness are important requirements of civilization, although their vital necessity is not very apparent, any more than their suitability as sources of enjoyment. At this point we cannot fail to be struck by the similarity between the process of civilization and the libidinal development of the individual. Other instincts [besides anal erotism] are induced to displace the conditions for their satisfaction, to lead them into other paths. In most cases this process coincides with that of the *sublimation* (of instinctual aims) with which we are familiar, but in some it can be differentiated from it. Sublimation of instinct is an especially conspicuous feature of cultural development; it is what makes it possible for higher psychical activities, scientific, artistic or ideological, to play such an important part in civilized life. If one were to yield to a first impression, one would say that sublimation is a vicissitude which has been forced upon the instincts entirely by civilization. But it would be wiser to reflect upon this a little longer. In the third place, finally, and this seems the most important of all, it is impossible to overlook the extent to which civilization is built up upon a renunciation of instinct, how much it presupposes precisely the non-satisfaction (by suppression, repression or some other means?) of powerful instincts. This 'cultural frustration' dominates the large field of social relationships between human beings. As we already know, it is the cause of the hostility against which all civilizations have to struggle. It will also make severe demands on our scientific work, and we shall have much to explain here. It is not easy to understand how it can become possible to deprive an instinct of satisfaction. Nor is doing so without danger. If the loss is not compensated for economically, one can be certain that serious disorders will ensue.

* * *

IV

* * *

After primal man had discovered that it lay in his own hands, literally, to improve his lot on earth by working, it cannot have been a matter of indifference to him whether another man worked with or against him.

The other man acquired the value for him of a fellow-worker, with whom it was useful to live together. Even earlier, in his ape-like pre-history, man had adopted the habit of forming families, and the members of his family were probably his first helpers. One may suppose that the founding of families was connected with the fact that a moment came when the need for genital satisfaction no longer made its appearance like a guest who drops in suddenly, and, after his departure, is heard of no more for a long time, but instead took up its quarters as a permanent lodger. When this happened, the male acquired a motive for keeping the female, or, speaking more generally, his sexual objects, near him; while the female, who did not want to be separated from her helpless young, was obliged, in their interests, to remain with the stronger male. In this primitive family one essential feature of civilization is still lacking. The arbitrary will of its head, the father, was unrestricted. In *Totem and Taboo* I have tried to show how the way led from this family to the succeeding stage of communal life in the form of bands of brothers. In overpowering their father, the sons had made the discovery that a com-bination can be stronger than a single individual. The totemic culture is based on the restrictions which the sons had to impose on one another in order to keep this new state of affairs in being. The taboo-observances were the first 'right' or 'law'. The communal life of human beings had, therefore, a two-fold foundation: the compulsion to work, which was created by external necessity, and the power of love, which made the man unwilling to be deprived of his sexual object—the woman—, and made the woman unwilling to be deprived of the part of herself which had been separated off from her—her child. Eros and Ananke [Love and Necessity] have become the parents of human civilization too. The first result of civilization was that even a fairly large number of people were now able to live together in a community. And since these two great powers were co-operating in this, one might expect that the further development of civilization would proceed smoothly towards an even better control over the external world and towards a further extension of the number of people included in the community. Nor is it easy to understand how this civilization could act upon its participants otherwise than to make them happy.

Before we go on to enquire from what quarter an interference might arise, this recognition of love as one of the foundations of civilization may serve as an excuse for a digression which will enable us to fill in a gap which we left in an earlier discussion. We said there that man's discovery that sexual (genital) love afforded him the strongest experiences of satisfaction, and in fact provided him with the prototype of all hap-piness, must have suggested to him that he should continue to seek the satisfaction of happiness in his life along the path of sexual relations and that he should make genital erotism the central point of his life. We went on to say that in doing so he made himself dependent in a most dangerous way on a portion of the external world, namely, his chosen love-object, and exposed himself to extreme suffering if he should be rejected by that object or should lose it through unfaithfulness or death. For that reason the wise men of every age have warned us most emphatically against this way of life; but in spite of this it has not lost its attraction for a great number of people.

A small minority are enabled by their constitution to find happiness, in spite of everything, along the path of love. But far-reaching mental changes in the function of love are necessary before this can happen. These people make themselves independent of their object's acquiescence by displacing what they mainly value from being loved on to loving; they protect themselves against the loss of the object by directing their love, not to single objects but to all men alike; and they avoid the uncertainties and disappointments of genital love by turning away from its sexual aims and transforming the instinct into an impulse with an *inhibited aim*. What they bring about in themselves in this way is a state of evenly suspended, steadfast, affectionate feeling, which has little external resemblance any more to the stormy agitations of genital love, from which it is nevertheless derived. Perhaps St. Francis of Assisi went furthest in thus exploiting love for the benefit of an inner feeling of happiness. Moreover, what we have recognized as one of the techniques for fulfilling the pleasure principle has often been brought into connection with religion; this connection may lie in the remote regions where the distinction between the ego and objects or between objects themselves is neglected. According to one ethical view, whose deeper motivation will become clear to us presently, this readiness for a universal love of mankind and the world represents the highest standpoint which man can reach. Even at this early stage of the discussion I should like to bring forward my two main objections to this view. A love that does not discriminate seems to me to forfeit a part of its own value, by doing an injustice to its object; and secondly, not all men are worthy of love.

The love which founded the family continues to operate in civilization both in its original form, in which it does not renounce direct sexual satisfaction, and in its modified form as aim-inhibited affection. In each, it continues to carry on its function of binding together considerable numbers of people, and it does so in a more intensive fashion than can be effected through the interest of work in common. The careless way in which language uses the word 'love' has its genetic justification. People give the name 'love' to the relation between a man and a woman whose genital needs have led them to found a family; but they also give the name 'love' to the positive feelings between parents and children, and between the brothers and sisters of a family, although *we* are obliged to describe this as 'aim-inhibited love' or 'affection'. Love with an inhibited aim was in fact originally fully sensual love, and it is so still in man's unconscious. Both—fully sensual love and aim-inhibited love—extend outside the family and create new bonds with people who before were strangers. Genital love leads to the formation of new families, and aim-inhibited love to 'friendships' which become valuable from a cultural standpoint because they escape some of the limitations of genital love, as, for instance, its exclusiveness. But in the course of development the relation of love to civilization loses its unambiguity. On the one hand love comes into opposition to the interests of civilization; on the other, civilization threatens love with substantial restrictions.

This rift between them seems unavoidable. The reason for it is not immediately recognizable. It expresses itself at first as a conflict between the family and the larger community to which the individual belongs. We have already perceived that one of the main endeavours of civilization is to bring people together into large unities. But the family will not give the individual up. The more closely the members of a family are attached to one another, the more often do they tend to cut themselves off from others, and the more difficult is it for them to enter into the wider circle of life. The mode of life in common which is phylogenetically the older, and which is the only one that exists in childhood, will not let itself be superseded by the cultural mode of life which has been acquired later. Detaching himself from his family becomes a task that faces every young person, and society often helps him in the solution of it by means of puberty and initiation rites. We get the impression that these are difficulties which are inherent in all psychical—and, indeed, at bottom, in all organic—development.

Furthermore, women soon come into opposition to civilization and display their retarding and restraining influence—those very women who, in the beginning, laid the foundations of civilization by the claims of their love. Women represent the interests of the family and of sexual life. The work of civilization has become increasingly the business of men, it confronts them with ever more difficult tasks and compels them to carry out instinctual sublimations of which women are little capable. Since a man does not have unlimited quantities of psychical energy at his disposal, he has to accomplish his tasks by making an expedient distribution of his libido. What he employs for cultural aims he to a great extent withdraws from women and sexual life. His constant association with men, and his dependence on his relations with them, even estrange him from his duties as a husband and father. Thus the woman finds herself forced into the background by the claims of civilization and she adopts a hostile attitude towards it.

The tendency on the part of civilization to restrict sexual life is no less clear than its other tendency to expand the cultural unit. Its first, totemic, phase already brings with it the prohibition against an incestuous choice of object, and this is perhaps the most drastic mutilation which man's erotic life has in all time experienced. Taboos, laws and customs impose further restrictions, which affect both men and women. Not all civilizations go equally far in this; and the economic structure of the society also influences the amount of sexual freedom that remains. Here, as we already know, civilization is obeying the laws of economic necessity, since a large amount of the psychical energy which it uses for its own purposes has to be withdrawn from sexuality. In this respect civilization behaves towards sexuality as a people or a stratum of its population does which has subjected another one to its exploitation. Fear of a revolt by the suppressed elements drives it to stricter precautionary measures. A high-water mark in such a development has been reached in our Western European civilization. A cultural community is perfectly justified, psychologically, in starting by proscribing manifestations of the sexual life of children, for there would be no prospect of curbing the sexual lusts of adults if the ground had not been prepared for it in childhood. But such a community cannot in any way be justified in going to the length of actually *disavowing* such easily demonstrable, and, indeed, striking phenomena. As regards the sexually mature individual, the choice of an object is restricted to the opposite sex, and most extra-genital satisfactions are forbidden as perversions. The requirement, demonstrated in these prohibitions, that there shall be a single kind of sexual life for everyone, disregards the dissimilarities, whether innate or acquired, in the sexual constitution of human beings; it cuts off a fair number of them from sexual enjoyment, and so becomes the source of serious injustice. The result of such restrictive measures might be that in people who are normal—who are not prevented by their constitution—the whole of their sexual interests would flow without loss into the channels that are left open. But heterosexual genital love, which has remained exempt from outlawry, is itself restricted by further limitations, in the shape of insistence upon legitimacy and monogamy. Present-day civilization makes it plain that it will only permit sexual relationships on the basis of a solitary, indissoluble bond between one man and one woman, and that it does not like sexuality as a source of pleasure in its own right and is only prepared to tolerate it because there is so far no substitute for it as a means of propagating the human race.

This, of course, is an extreme picture. Everybody knows that it has proved impossible to put it into execution, even for quite short periods. Only the weaklings have submitted to such an extensive encroachment upon their sexual freedom, and stronger natures have only done so subject to a compensatory condition, which will be mentioned later. Civilized society has found itself obliged to pass over in silence many transgressions which, according to its own rescripts, it ought to have punished. But we must not err on the other side and assume that, because it does not achieve all its aims, such an attitude on the part of society is entirely innocuous. The sexual life of civilized man is notwithstanding severely impaired; it sometimes gives the impression of being in process of involution as a function, just as our teeth and hair seem to be as organs. * * *

V

Psycho-analytic work has shown us that it is precisely these frustrations of sexual life which people known as neurotics cannot tolerate. The neurotic creates substitutive satisfactions for himself in his symptoms, and these either cause him suffering in themselves or become sources of suffering for him by raising difficulties in his relations with his environment and the society he belongs to. The latter fact is easy to understand; the former presents us with a new problem. But civilization demands other sacrifices besides that of sexual satisfaction.

We have treated the difficulty of cultural development as a general difficulty of development by tracing it to the inertia of the libido, to its disinclination to give up an old position for a new one. We are saying much the same thing when we derive the antithesis between civilization and sexuality from the circumstance that sexual love is a relationship between two individuals in which a third can only be superfluous or disturbing, whereas civilization depends on relationships between a considerable number of individuals. When a love-relationship is at its height there is no room left for any interest in the environment; a pair of lovers are sufficient to themselves, and do not even need the child they have in common to make them happy. In no other case does Eros so clearly betray the core of his being, his purpose of making one out of more than one; but when he has achieved this in the proverbial way through the love of two human beings, he refuses to go further.

So far, we can quite well imagine a cultural community consisting of double individuals like this, who, libidinally satisfied in themselves, are connected with one another through the bonds of common work and common interests. If this were so, civilization would not have to withdraw any energy from sexuality. But this desirable state of things does not, and never did, exist. Reality shows us that civilization is not content with the ties we have so far allowed it. It aims at binding the members of the community together in a libidinal way as well and employs every means to that end. It favours every path by which strong identifications can be established between the members of the community, and it summons up aim-inhibited libido on the largest scale so as to strengthen the communal bond by relations of friendship. In order for these aims to be fulfilled, a restriction upon sexual life is unavoidable. But we are unable to understand what the necessity in which forces civilization along this path and which causes its antagonism to sexuality. There must be some disturbing factor which we have not yet discovered.

The clue may be supplied by one of the ideal demands, as we have called them, of civilized society. It runs: 'Thou shalt love thy neighbour as thyself.' It is known throughout the world and is undoubtedly older than Christianity, which puts it forward as its proudest claim. Yet it is certainly not very old; even in historical times it was still strange to mankind. Let us adopt a naïve attitude towards it, as though we were hearing it for the first time; we shall be unable then to suppress a feeling of surprise and bewilderment. Why should we do it? What good will it do us? But, above all, how shall we achieve it? How can it be possible? My love is something valuable to me which I ought not to throw away without reflection. It imposes duties on me for whose fulfilment I must be ready to make sacrifices. If I love someone, he must deserve it in some way. (I leave out of account the use he may be to me, and also his possible significance for me as a sexual object, for neither of these two kinds of relationship comes into question where the precept to love my neighbour is concerned.) He deserves it if he is so like me in important ways that I can love myself in him; and he deserves it if he is so much more perfect than myself that I can love my ideal of my own self in him. Again, I have to love him if he is my friend's son, since the pain my friend would feel if any harm came to him would be my pain too—I should have to share it. But if he is a stranger to me and if he cannot attract me by any worth of his own or any significance that he may already have acquired for my emotional life, it will be hard for me to love him. Indeed, I should be wrong to do so, for my love is valued by all my own people as a sign of my preferring them, and it is an injustice to them if I put a stranger on a par with them. But if I am to love him (with this universal love) merely because he, too, is an inhabitant of this earth, like an insect, an earth-worm or a grass-snake, then I fear that only a small modicum of my love will fall to his share— not by any possibility as much as, by the judgement of my reason, I am entitled to retain for myself. What is the point of a precept enunciated with so much solemnity if its fulfilment cannot be recommended as reasonable?

On closer inspection, I find still further difficulties. Not merely in this stranger in general unworthy of my love; I must honestly confess that he has more claim to my hostility and even my hatred. He seems not to have the least trace of love for me and shows me not the slightest consideration. If it will do him any good he has no hesitation in injuring me, nor does he ask himself whether the amount of advantage he gains bears any proportion to the extent of the harm he does to me. Indeed, he need not even obtain an advantage; if he can satisfy any sort of desire by it, he thinks nothing of jeering at me, insulting me, slandering me and showing his superior power; and the more secure he feels and the more helpless I am, the more certainly I can expect him to behave like this to me. If he behaves differently, if he shows me consideration and forbearance as a stranger, I am ready to treat him in the same way, in any case and quite apart from any precept. Indeed, if this grandiose commandment had run 'Love thy neighbour as thy neighbour loves thee', I should not take exception to it. And there is a second commandment, which seems to me even more incomprehensible and arouses still stronger opposition in me. It is 'Love thine enemies'. If I think it over, however, I see that I am wrong in treating it as a greater imposition. At bottom it is the same thing.[4]

I think I can now hear a dignified voice admonishing me: 'It is precisely because your neighbour is not worthy of love, and is on the contrary your enemy, that you should love him as yourself.' I then understand that the case is one like that of *Credo quia absurdum.*

Now it is very probable that my neighbour, when he is enjoined to love me as himself, will answer exactly as I have done and will repel me for the same reasons. I hope he will not have the same objective grounds for doing so, but he will have the same idea as I have. Even so, the behaviour of human beings shows differences, which ethics, disregarding the fact that such differences are determined, classifies as 'good' or 'bad'. So long as these undeniable differences have not been removed, obedience to high ethical demands entails damage to the aims of civilization, for it puts a positive premium on being bad. One is irresistibly reminded of an incident in the French Chamber when capital punishment was being debated. A member had been passionately supporting its abolition and his speech was being received with tumultuous applause, when a voice from the hall called out: 'Que messieurs les assassins commencent!'[5]

The element of truth behind all this, which people are so ready to disavow, is that men are not gentle creatures who want to be loved, and who at the most can defend themselves if they are attacked; they are, on the contrary, creatures among whose instinctual endowments is to be reckoned a powerful share of aggressiveness. As a result, their neighbour is for them not only a potential helper or sexual object, but also someone who tempts them to satisfy their aggressiveness on him, to exploit his capacity for work without compensation, to use him sexually without his consent, to seize his possessions, to humiliate him, to cause him pain, to torture and to kill him. *Homo homini lupus.*[6] Who, in the face of all his experience of life and of history, will have the courage to dispute this assertion? As a rule this cruel aggressiveness waits for some provocation or puts itself at the service of some other purpose, whose goal might also have been reached by milder measures. In circumstances that are favourable to it, when the mental counter-forces which ordinarily inhibit it are out of action, it also manifests itself spontaneously and

---

4. A great imaginative writer may permit himself to give expression—jokingly, at all events—to psychological truths that are severely proscribed. Thus Heine confesses: 'Mine is a most peaceable disposition. My wishes are: a humble cottage with a thatched roof, but a good bed, good food, the freshest milk and butter, flowers before my window, and a few fine trees before my door; and if God wants to make my happiness complete, he will grant me the joy of seeing some six or seven of my enemies hanging from those trees. Before their death I shall, moved in my heart, forgive them all the wrong they did me in their lifetime. One must, it is true, forgive one's enemies—but not before they have been hanged.' (*Gedanken und Einfälle* [Section I].)

5. ['It's the murderers who should make the first move.']

6. ['Man is a wolf to man.' Derived from Plautus, *Asinaria*, II, iv, 88.] {This harsh saying evokes the tough-minded, realistic political thought of Thomas Hobbes, with which Freud's ideas are often congruent.}

reveals man as a savage beast to whom consideration towards his own kind is something alien. Anyone who calls to mind the atrocities committed during the racial migrations or the invasions of the Huns, or by the people known as Mongols under Jenghiz Khan and Tamerlane, or at the capture of Jerusalem by the pious Crusaders, or even, indeed, the horrors of the recent World War—anyone who calls these things to mind will have to bow humbly before the truth of this view.

The existence of this inclination to aggression, which we can detect in ourselves and justly assume to be present in others, is the factor which disturbs our relations with our neighbour and which forces civilization into such a high expenditure [of energy]. In consequence of this primary mutual hostility of human beings, civilized society is perpetually threatened with disintegration. The interest of work in common would not hold it together; instinctual passions are stronger than reasonable interests. Civilization has to use its utmost efforts in order to set limits to man's aggressive instincts and to hold the manifestations of them in check by psychical reaction-formations. Hence, therefore, the use of methods intended to incite people into identifications and aim-inhibited relationships of love, hence the restriction upon sexual life, and hence too the ideal's commandment to love one's neighbour as oneself—a commandment which is really justified by the fact that nothing else runs so strongly counter to the original nature of man. In spite of every effort, these endeavours of civilization have not so far achieved very much. It hopes to prevent the crudest excesses of brutal violence by itself assuming the right to use violence against criminals, but the law is not able to lay hold of the more cautious and refined manifestations of human aggressiveness. The time comes when each one of us has to give up as illusions the expectations which, in his youth, he pinned upon his fellowmen, and when he may learn how much difficulty and pain has been added to his life by their ill-will. At the same time, it would be unfair to reproach civilization with trying to eliminate strife and competition from human activity. These things are undoubtedly indispensable. But opposition is not necessarily enmity; it is merely misused and made an *occasion* for enmity.

The communists believe that they have found the path to deliverance from our evils. According to them, man is wholly good and is well-disposed to his neighbour; but the institution of private property has corrupted his nature. The ownership of private wealth gives the individual power, and with it the temptation to ill-treat his neighbour; while the man who is excluded from possession is bound to rebel in hostility against his oppressor. If private property were abolished, all wealth held in common, and everyone allowed to share in the enjoyment of it, ill-will and hostility would disappear among men. Since everyone's needs would be satisfied, no one would have any reason to regard another as his enemy; all would willingly undertake the work that was necessary. I have no concern with any economic criticisms of the communist system; I cannot enquire into whether the abolition of private property is expedient or advantageous.[7] But I am able to recognize that the psychological premises on which the system is based are an untenable illusion. In abolishing private property we deprive the human love of aggression of one of its instruments, certainly a strong one, though certainly not the strongest; but we have in no way altered the differences in power and influence which are misused by aggressiveness, nor have we altered anything in its nature. Aggressiveness was not created by property. It reigned almost without limit in primitive times, when property was still very scanty, and it already shows itself in the nursery almost before property has given up its primal, anal form; it forms the basis of every relation of affection and love among people (with the single exception, perhaps, of the mother's relation to her male child). If we do away with personal rights over material wealth, there still remains prerogative in the field of sexual relationships, which is bound to become the source of the strongest dislike and the most violent hostility among men who in other respects are on an equal footing. If we were to remove this factor, too, by allowing complete freedom of sexual life and thus abolishing the family, the germ-cell of civilization, we cannot, it is true, easily foresee what new paths the development of civilization could take; but one thing we can expect, and that is that this indestructible feature of human nature will follow it there.

It is clearly not easy for men to give up the satisfaction of this inclination to aggression. They do not feel comfortable without it. The advantage which a comparatively small cultural group offers of allowing this instinct an outlet in the form of hostility against intruders is not to be despised. It is always possible to bind together a considerable number of people in love, so long as there are other people left over to receive the manifestations of their aggressiveness. I once discussed the phenomenon that it is precisely communities with adjoining territories, and related to each other in other ways as well, who are engaged in constant feuds and in ridiculing each other—like the Spaniards and Portuguese, for instance, the North Germans and South Germans, the English and Scotch, and so on. I gave this phenomenon the name of 'the narcissism of minor differences', a name which does not do much to explain it. We can now see that it is a convenient and relatively harmless satisfaction of the inclination to aggression, by means of which cohesion between

---

7. Anyone who has tasted the miseries of poverty in his own youth and has experienced the indifference and the arrogance of the well-to-do, should be safe from the suspicion of having no understanding or good will towards endeavours to fight against the inequality of wealth among men and all that it leads to. To be sure, if an attempt is made to base this fight upon an abstract demand, in the name of justice, for equality for all men, there is a very obvious objection to be made—that nature, by endowing individuals with extremely unequal physical attributes and mental capacities, has introduced injustices against which there is no remedy. {This is one of a small handful of isolated passages (another may be found in *The Future of an Illusion*, above, p. 687–89) in which Freud makes perfectly clear that, for all his social conservatism, he is not infatuated with the status quo, and understands—even to some measure shares—the revolutionary impulses agitating his time. It should be added that the absolute egalitarianism which he tries to refute in this note was not a serious political program but a utopian vision; it is really a straw man.}

the members of the community is made easier. In this respect the Jewish people, scattered everywhere, have rendered most useful services to the civilizations of the countries that have been their hosts; but unfortunately all the massacres of the Jews in the Middle Ages did not suffice to make that period more peaceful and secure for their Christian fellows. When once the Apostle Paul had posited universal love between men as the foundation of his Christian community, extreme intolerance on the part of Christendom towards those who remained outside it became the inevitable consequence. To the Romans, who had not founded their communal life as a State upon love, religious intolerance was something foreign, although with them religion was a concern of the State and the State was permeated by religion. Neither was it an unaccountable chance that the dream of a Germanic world-dominion called for anti-semitism as its complement; and it is intelligible that the attempt to establish a new, communist civilization in Russia should find its psychological support in the persecution of the bourgeois. One only wonders, with concern, what the Soviets will do after they have wiped out their bourgeois.

If civilization imposes such great sacrifices not only on man's sexuality but on his aggressivity, we can understand better why it is hard for him to be happy in that civilization. In fact, primitive man was better off in knowing no restrictions of instinct. To counterbalance this, his prospects of enjoying this happiness for any length of time were very slender. Civilized man has exchanged a portion of his possibilities of happiness for a portion of security. We must not forget, however, that in the primal family only the head of it enjoyed this instinctual freedom; the rest lived in slavish suppression. In that primal period of civilization, the contrast between a minority who enjoyed the advantages of civilization and a majority who were robbed of those advantages was, therefore, carried to extremes. As regards the primitive peoples who exist to-day, careful researches have shown that their instinctual life is by no means to be envied for its freedom. It is subject to restrictions of a different kind but perhaps of greater severity than those attaching to modern civilized man.

When we justly find fault with the present state of our civilization for so inadequately fulfilling our demands for a plan of life that shall make us happy, and for allowing the existence of so much suffering which could probably be avoided—when, with unsparing criticism, we try to uncover the roots of its imperfection, we are undoubtedly exercising a proper right and are not showing ourselves enemies of civilization. We may expect gradually to carry through such alterations in our civilization as will better satisfy our needs and will escape our criticisms. But perhaps we may also familiarize ourselves with the idea that there are difficulties attaching to the nature of civilization which will not yield to any attempt at reform. Over and above the tasks of restricting the instincts, which we are prepared for, there forces itself on our notice the danger of a state of things which might be termed 'the psychological poverty of groups'. This danger is most threatening where the bonds of a society are chiefly constituted by the identification of its members with one another, while individuals of the leader type do not acquire the importance that should fall to them in the formation of a group. The present cultural state of America would give us a good opportunity for studying the damage to civilization which is thus to be feared. But I shall avoid the temptation of entering upon a critique of American civilization; I do not wish to give an impression of wanting myself to employ American methods. [8]

VI

* * *

* * * Of all the slowly developed parts of analytic theory, the theory of the instincts is the one that has felt its way the most painfully forward. And yet that theory was so indispensable to the whole structure that something had to be put in its place. In what was at first my utter perplexity, I took as my starting-point a saying of the poet-philosopher, Schiller, that 'hunger and love are what moves the world'. Hunger could be taken to represent the instincts which aim at preserving the individual; while love strives after objects, and its chief function, favoured in every way by nature, is the preservation of the species. Thus, to begin with, ego-instincts and object-instincts confronted each other. * * *

Every analyst will admit that even to-day this view has not the sound of a long-discarded error. Nevertheless, alterations in it became essential, as our enquiries advanced from the repressed to the repressing forces, from the object-instincts to the ego. The decisive step forward was the introduction of the concept of narcissism—that is to say, the discovery that the ego itself is cathected with libido, that the ego, indeed, is the libido's original home, and remains to some extent its headquarters. This narcissistic libido turns towards objects, and thus becomes object-libido; and it can change back into narcissistic libido once more. The concept of narcissism made it possible to obtain an analytic understanding of the traumatic neuroses and of many of the affections bordering on the psychoses, as well as of the latter themselves. It was not necessary to give up our interpretation of the transference neuroses as attempts made by the ego to defend itself against sexuality; but the concept of libido was endangered. Since the ego-instincts, too, were libidinal, it seemed for a time inevitable that we should make libido coincide with instinctual energy in general, as C. G. Jung had already advocated earlier. Nevertheless, there still remained in me a kind of conviction, for which I was not as yet able to find reasons, that the instincts could not all be of the same kind. My next step was taken in *Beyond the Pleasure Principle* (1920), when the compulsion to repeat and the con-

8. {A gratuitous observation which once again exhibits Freud's persistent and unreasoning anti-Americanism. On this point, see Gay, *Freud*, pp. 553–70.}

servative character of instinctual life first attracted my attention. Starting from speculations on the beginning of life and from biological parallels, I drew the conclusion that, besides the instinct to preserve living substance and to join it into ever larger units, there must exist another, contrary instinct seeking to dissolve those units and to bring them back to their primaeval, inorganic state. That is to say, as well as Eros there was an instinct of death. The phenomena of life could be explained from the concurrent or mutually opposing action of these two instincts. It was not easy, however, to demonstrate the activities of this supposed death instinct. The manifestations of Eros were conspicuous and noisy enough. It might be assumed that the death instinct operated silently within the organism towards its dissolution, but that, of course, was no proof. A more fruitful idea was that a portion of the instinct is diverted towards the external world and comes to light as an instinct of aggressiveness and destructiveness. In this way the instinct itself could be pressed into the service of Eros, in that the organism was destroying some other thing, whether animate or inanimate, instead of destroying its own self. Conversely, any restriction of this aggressiveness directed outwards would be bound to increase the self-destruction, which is in any case proceeding. * * *

The assumption of the existence of an instinct of death or destruction has met with resistance even in analytic circles; I am aware that there is a frequent inclination rather to ascribe whatever is dangerous and hostile in love to an original bi-polarity in its own nature. To begin with it was only tentatively that I put forward the views I have developed here, but in the course of time they have gained such a hold upon me that I can no longer think in any other way. To my mind, they are far more serviceable from a theoretical standpoint than any other possible ones; they provide that simplification, without either ignoring or doing violence to the facts, for which we strive in scientific work. I know that in sadism and masochism we have always seen before us manifestations of the destructive instinct (directed outwards and inwards), strongly alloyed with erotism; but I can no longer understand how we can have overlooked the ubiquity of non-erotic aggressivity and destructiveness and can have failed to give it its due place in our interpretation of life. (The desire for destruction when it is directed *inwards* mostly eludes our perception, of course, unless it is tinged with erotism.) I remember my own defensive attitude when the idea of an instinct of destruction first emerged in psycho-analytic literature, and how long it took before I became receptive to it. That others should have shown, and still show, the same attitude of rejection surprises me less. For 'little children do not like it'[9] when there is talk of the inborn human inclination to 'badness', to aggressiveness and destructiveness, and so to cruelty as well. God has made them in the image of His own perfection; nobody wants

---

9. ['Denn die Kindlein, sie hören es nicht gerne.' A quotation from Goethe's poem 'Die Ballade vom vertriebenen und heimgekehrten Grafen'.]

to be reminded how hard it is to reconcile the undeniable existence of evil—despite the protestations of Christian Science—with His all-powerfulness or His all-goodness. The Devil would be the best way out as an excuse for God; in that way he would be playing the same part as an agent of economic discharge as the Jew does in the world of the Aryan ideal. But even so, one can hold God responsible for the existence of the Devil just as well as for the existence of the wickedness which the Devil embodies. In view of these difficulties, each of us will be well advised, on some suitable occasion, to make a low bow to the deeply moral nature of mankind; it will help us to be generally popular and much will be forgiven us for it.[1]

The name 'libido' can once more be used to denote the manifestations of the power of Eros in order to distinguish them from the energy of the death instinct. It must be confessed that we have much greater difficulty in grasping that instinct; we can only suspect it, as it were, as something in the background behind Eros, and it escapes detection unless its presence is betrayed by its being alloyed with Eros. It is in sadism, where the death instinct twists the erotic aim in its own sense and yet at the same time fully satisfies the erotic urge, that we succeed in obtaining the clearest insight into its nature and its relation to Eros. But even where it emerges without any sexual purpose, in the blindest fury of destructiveness, we cannot fail to recognize that the satisfaction of the instinct is accompanied by an extraordinarily high degree of narcissistic enjoyment, owing to its presenting the ego with a fulfilment of the latter's old wishes for omnipotence. The instinct of destruction, moderated and tamed, and, as it were, inhibited in its aim, must, when it is directed towards objects, provide the ego with the satisfaction of its vital needs and with control over nature. Since the assumption of the existence of the instinct is mainly based on theoretical grounds, we must also admit that it is not entirely proof against theoretical objections. But this is how things appear to us now, in the present state of our knowledge; future research and reflection will no doubt bring further light which will decide the matter.

In all that follows I adopt the standpoint, therefore, that the inclination to aggression is an original, self-subsisting instinctual disposition in man, and I return to my view that it constitutes the greatest impediment to civilization. At one point in the course of this enquiry I was led to the idea that civilization was a special process which mankind undergoes, and I am still under the influence of that idea. I may now add that civilization is a process in the service of Eros, whose purpose is to combine single human individuals, and after that families, then races, peoples and nations, into one great unity, the unity of mankind. Why

1. In Goethe's Mephistopheles {Faust's eloquent antagonist in *Faust*} we have a quite exceptionally convincing identification of the principle of evil with the destructive instinct. {And Freud then quotes Mephistopheles' lines arguing that everything that has been created is worth being destroyed, and that what Faust calls sin or destruction, "in short evil," is his "proper element." In contrast, the devil's true adversary is the power of nature to create and produce—"that is, Eros." See *Faust*, part I, scene 3.}

this has to happen, we do not know; the work of Eros is precisely this. These collections of men are to be libidinally bound to one another. Necessity alone, the advantages of work in common, will not hold them together. But man's natural aggressive instinct, the hostility of each against all and of all against each, opposes this programme of civilization. This aggressive instinct is the derivative and the main representative of the death instinct which we have found alongside of Eros and which shares world-dominion with it. And now, I think, the meaning of the evolution of civilization is no longer obscure to us. It must present the struggle between Eros and Death, between the instinct of life and the instinct of destruction, as it works itself out in the human species. This struggle is what all life essentially consists of, and the evolution of civilization may therefore be simply described as the struggle for life of the human species. And it is this battle of the giants that our nurse-maids try to appease with their lullaby about Heaven.[2]

VII

* * *

* * * What means does civilization employ in order to inhibit the aggressiveness which opposes it, to make it harmless, to get rid of it, perhaps? We have already become acquainted with a few of these methods, but not yet with the one that appears to be the most important. This we can study in the history of the development of the individual. What happens in him to render his desire for aggression innocuous? Something very remarkable, which we should never have guessed and which is nevertheless quite obvious. His aggressiveness is introjected, internalized; it is, in point of fact, sent back to where it came from—that is, it is directed towards his own ego. There it is taken over by a portion of the ego, which sets itself over against the rest of the ego as super-ego, and which now, in the form of 'conscience', is ready to put into action against the ego the same harsh aggressiveness that the ego would have liked to satisfy upon other, extraneous individuals. The tension between the harsh super-ego and the ego that is subjected to it, is called by us the sense of guilt; it expresses itself as a need for punishment. Civilization, therefore, obtains mastery over the individual's dangerous desire for aggression by weakening and disarming it and by setting up an agency within him to watch over it, like a garrison in a conquered city.

As to the origin of the sense of guilt, the analyst has different views from other psychologists; but even he does not find it easy to give an account of it. To begin with, if we ask how a person comes to have a sense of guilt, we arrive at an answer which cannot be disputed: a person feels guilty (devout people would say 'sinful') when he has done some-

2. ['*Eiapopeia vom Himmel.*' A quotation from Heine's poem *Deutschland*, Caput I {using a nonsense word familiar in German-speaking nurseries}.]

thing which he knows to be 'bad'. But then we notice how little this answer tells us. Perhaps, after some hesitation, we shall add that even when a person has not actually *done* the bad thing but has only recognized in himself an *intention* to do it, he may regard himself as guilty; and the question then arises of why the intention is regarded as equal to the deed. Both cases, however, presuppose that one had already recognized that what is bad is reprehensible, is something that must not be carried out. How is this judgement arrived at? We may reject the existence of an original, as it were natural, capacity to distinguish good from bad. What is bad is often not at all what is injurious or dangerous to the ego; on the contrary, it may be something which is desirable and enjoyable to the ego. Here, therefore, there is an extraneous influence at work, and it is this that decides what is to be called good or bad. Since a person's own feelings would not have led him along this path, he must have had a motive for submitting to this extraneous influence. Such a motive is easily discovered in his helplessness and his dependence on other people, and it can best be designated as fear of loss of love. If he loses the love of another person upon whom he is dependent, he also ceases to be protected from a variety of dangers. Above all, he is exposed to the danger that this stronger person will show his superiority in the form of punishment. At the beginning, therefore, what is bad is whatever causes one to be threatened with loss of love. For fear of that loss, one must avoid it. This, too, is the reason why it makes little difference whether one has already done the bad thing or only intends to do it. In either case the danger only sets in if and when the authority discovers it, and in either case the authority would behave in the same way.

This state of mind is called a 'bad conscience'; but actually it does not deserve this name, for at this stage the sense of guilt is clearly only a fear of loss of love, 'social' anxiety. In small children it can never be anything else, but in many adults, too, it has only changed to the extent that the place of the father or the two parents is taken by the larger human community. Consequently, such people habitually allow themselves to do any bad thing which promises them enjoyment, so long as they are sure that the authority will not know anything about it or cannot blame them for it; they are afraid only of being found out. Present-day society has to reckon in general with this state of mind.

A great change takes place only when the authority is internalized through the establishment of a super-ego. The phenomena of conscience then reach a higher stage. Actually, it is not until now that we should speak of conscience or a sense of guilt. At this point, too, the fear of being found out comes to an end; the distinction, moreover, between doing something bad and wishing to do it disappears entirely, since nothing can be hidden from the super-ego, not even thoughts. It is true that the seriousness of the situation from a real point of view has passed away, for the new authority, the super-ego, has no motive that we know of for ill-treating the ego, with which it is intimately bound up; but genetic influence, which leads to the survival of what is past and has been surmounted, makes itself felt in the fact that fundamentally things remain as they were at the beginning. The super-ego torments the sinful ego with the same feeling of anxiety and is on the watch for opportunities of getting it punished by the external world.

At this second stage of development, the conscience exhibits a peculiarity which was absent from the first stage and which is no longer easy to account for. For the more virtuous a man is, the more severe and distrustful is its behaviour, so that ultimately it is precisely those people who have carried saintliness furthest who reproach themselves with the worst sinfulness. This means that virtue forfeits some part of its promised reward; the docile and continent ego does not enjoy the trust of its mentor, and strives in vain, it would seem, to acquire it. The objection will at once be made that these difficulties are artificial ones, and it will be said that a stricter and more vigilant conscience is precisely the hallmark of a moral man. Moreover, when saints call themselves sinners, they are not so wrong, considering the temptations to instinctual satisfaction to which they are exposed in a specially high degree—since, as is well known, temptations are merely increased by constant frustration, whereas an occasional satisfaction of them causes them to diminish, at least for the time being. The field of ethics, which is so full of problems, presents us with another fact: namely that ill-luck—that is, external frustration—so greatly enhances the power of the conscience in the super-ego. As long as things go well with a man, his conscience is lenient and lets the ego do all sorts of things; but when misfortune befalls him, he searches his soul, acknowledges his sinfulness, heightens the demands of his conscience, imposes abstinences on himself and punishes himself with penances.[3] Whole peoples have behaved in this way, and still do. This, however, is easily explained by the original infantile stage of conscience, which, as we see, is not given up after the introjection into the super-ego, but persists alongside of it and behind it. Fate is regarded as a substitute for the parental agency. If a man is unfortunate it means that he is no longer loved by this highest power; and, threatened by such a loss of love, he once more bows to the parental representative in his super-ego—a representative whom, in his days of good fortune, he was ready to neglect. This becomes especially clear where Fate is looked upon in the strictly religious sense of being nothing else than an expression of the Divine Will. The people of Israel had believed themselves to be the favourite child of God, and when the great Father caused misfortune after misfortune to rain down upon this people of his, they were never shaken in their belief in his relationship to them

3. This enhancing of morality as a consequence of ill-luck has been illustrated by Mark Twain in a delightful little story, *The First Melon I ever Stole*. The first melon happened to be unripe. I heard Mark Twain tell the story himself in one of his public readings. After he had given out the title, he stopped and asked himself as though he was in doubt: 'Was it the first?' With this, everything had been said. The first melon was evidently not the only one.

or questioned his power or righteousness. Instead, they produced the prophets, who held up their sinfulness before them; and out of their sense of guilt they created the over-strict commandments of their priestly religion. It is remarkable how differently a primitive man behaves. If he has met with a misfortune, he does not throw the blame on himself but on his fetish, which has obviously not done its duty, and he gives it a thrashing instead of punishing himself.

Thus we know of two origins of the sense of guilt: one arising from fear of an authority, and the other, later on, arising from fear of the super-ego. The first insists upon a renunciation of instinctual satisfactions; the second, as well as doing this, presses for punishment, since the continuance of the forbidden wishes cannot be concealed from the super-ego. We have also learned how the severity of the super-ego—the demands of conscience—is to be understood. It is simply a continuation of the severity of the external authority, to which it has succeeded and which it has in part replaced. We now see in what relationship the renunciation of instinct stands to the sense of guilt. Originally, renunciation of instinct was the result of fear of an external authority: one renounced one's satisfactions in order not to lose its love. If one has carried out this renunciation, one is, as it were, quits with the authority and no sense of guilt should remain. But with fear of the super-ego the case is different. Here, instinctual renunciation is not enough, for the wish persists and cannot be concealed from the super-ego. Thus, in spite of the renunciation that has been made, a sense of guilt comes about. This constitutes a great economic disadvantage in the erection of a super-ego, or, as we may put it, in the formation of a conscience. Instinctual renunciation now no longer has a completely liberating effect; virtuous continence is no longer rewarded with the assurance of love. A threatened external unhappiness—loss of love and punishment on the part of the external authority—has been exchanged for a permanent internal unhappiness, for the tension of the sense of guilt.

These interrelations are so complicated and at the same time so important that, at the risk of repeating myself, I shall approach them from yet another angle. The chronological sequence, then, would be as follows. First comes renunciation of instinct owing to fear of aggression by the *external* authority. (This is, of course, what fear of the loss of love amounts to, for love is a protection against this punitive aggression.) After that comes the erection of an *internal* authority, and renunciation of instinct owing to fear of it—owing to fear of conscience. In this second situation bad intentions are equated with bad actions, and hence come a sense of guilt and a need for punishment. The aggressiveness of conscience keeps up the aggressiveness of the authority. So far things have no doubt been made clear; but where does this leave room for the reinforcing influence of misfortune (of renunciation imposed from without), and for the extraordinary severity of conscience in the best and most tractable people? We have already explained both these peculiarities of conscience, but we probably still have an impression that those explanations do not go to the bottom of the matter, and leave a residue still unexplained. And here at last an idea comes in which belongs entirely to psycho-analysis and which is foreign to people's ordinary way of thinking. This idea is of a sort which enables us to understand why the subject-matter was bound to seem so confused and obscure to us. For it tells us that conscience (or more correctly, the anxiety which later becomes conscience) is indeed the cause of instinctual renunciation to begin with, but that later the relationship is reversed. Every renunciation of instinct now becomes a dynamic source of conscience and every fresh renunciation increases the latter's severity and intolerance. If we could only bring it better into harmony with what we already know about the history of the origin of conscience, we should be tempted to defend the paradoxical statement that conscience is the result of instinctual renunciation, or that instinctual renunciation (imposed on us from without) creates conscience, which then demands further instinctual renunciation.

The contradiction between this statement and what we have previously said about the genesis of conscience is in point of fact not so very great, and we see a way of further reducing it. In order to make our exposition easier, let us take as our example the aggressive instinct, and let us assume that the renunciation in question is always a renunciation of aggression. (This, of course, is only to be taken as a temporary assumption.) The effect of instinctual renunciation on the conscience then is that every piece of aggression whose satisfaction the subject gives up is taken over by the super-ego and increases the latter's aggressiveness (against the ego). This does not harmonize well with the view that the original aggressiveness of conscience is a continuance of the severity of the external authority and therefore has nothing to do with renunciation. But the discrepancy is removed if we postulate a different derivation for this first instalment of the super-ego's aggressivity. A considerable amount of aggressiveness must be developed in the child against the authority which prevents him from having his first, but none the less his most important, satisfactions, whatever the kind of instinctual deprivation that is demanded of him may be; but he is obliged to renounce the satisfaction of this revengeful aggressiveness. He finds his way out of this economically difficult situation with the help of familiar mechanisms. By means of identification he takes the unattackable authority into himself. The authority now turns into his super-ego and enters into possession of all the aggressiveness which a child would have liked to exercise against it. The child's ego has to content itself with the unhappy role of the authority—the father—who has been thus degraded. Here, as so often, the [real] situation is reversed: 'If I were the father and you were the child, I should treat you badly.' The relationship between the super-ego and the ego is a return, distorted by a wish, of the real relationships between the ego, as yet undivided, and an external object.

That is typical, too. But the essential difference is that the original severity of the super-ego does not—or does not so much—represent the severity which one has experienced from it [the object], or which one attributes to it; it represents rather one's own aggressiveness towards it. If this is correct, we may assert truly that in the beginning conscience arises through the suppression of an aggressive impulse, and that it is subsequently reinforced by fresh suppressions of the same kind.

Which of these two views is correct? The earlier one, which genetically seemed so unassailable, or the newer one, which rounds off the theory in such a welcome fashion? Clearly, and by the evidence, too, of direct observations, both are justified. They do not contradict each other, and they even coincide at one point, for the child's revengeful aggressiveness will be in part determined by the amount of punitive aggression which he expects from his father. Experience shows, however, that the severity of the super-ego which a child develops in no way corresponds to the severity of treatment which he has himself met with.[4] The severity of the former seems to be independent of that of the latter. A child who has been very leniently brought up can acquire a very strict conscience. But it would also be wrong to exaggerate this independence; it is not difficult to convince oneself that severity of upbringing does also exert a strong influence on the formation of the child's super-ego. What it amounts to is that in the formation of the super-ego and the emergence of a conscience innate constitutional factors and influences from the real environment act in combination. This is not at all surprising; on the contrary, it is a universal aetiological condition for all such processes.[5]

It can also be asserted that when a child reacts to his first great instinctual frustrations with excessively strong aggressiveness and with a correspondingly severe super-ego, he is following a phylogenetic model and is going beyond the response that would be currently justified; for the father of prehistoric times was undoubtedly terrible, and an extreme amount of aggressiveness may be attributed to him. Thus, if one shifts over from individual to phylogenetic development, the differences between the two theories of the genesis of conscience are still further diminished. On the other hand, a new and important difference makes its appearance between these two developmental processes. We cannot get away from the assumption that man's sense of guilt springs from the Oedipus complex and was acquired at the killing of the father by the brothers banded together. On that occasion an act of aggression was not suppressed but carried out; but it was the same act of aggression whose

4. As has rightly been emphasized by Melanie Klein and by other English writers.

5. The two main types of pathogenic methods of upbringing—overstrictness and spoiling—have been accurately assessed by Franz Alexander in his book *The Psychoanalysis of the Total Personality* (1927) in connection with {August} Aichhorn's study of delinquency [*Wayward Youth*, 1925]. The 'unduly lenient and indulgent father' is the cause of children's forming an over-severe super-ego, because, under the impression of the love that they receive, they have no other outlet for their aggressiveness but turning it inwards. * * *

suppression in the child is supposed to be the source of his sense of guilt. At this point I should not be surprised if the reader were to exclaim angrily: 'So it makes no difference whether one kills one's father or not—one gets a feeling of guilt in either case! We may take leave to raise a few doubts here. Either it is not true that the sense of guilt comes from suppressed aggressiveness, or else the whole story of the killing of the father is a fiction and the children of primaeval man did not kill their fathers any more often than children do nowadays. Besides, if it is not fiction but a plausible piece of history, it would be a case of something happening which everyone expects to happen—namely, of a person feeling guilty because he really has done something which cannot be justified. And of this event, which is after all an everyday occurrence, psycho-analysis has not yet given any explanation.'

That is true, and we must make good the omission. Nor is there any great secret about the matter. When one has a sense of guilt after having committed a misdeed, and because of it, the feeling should more properly be called *remorse*. It relates only to a deed that has been done, and, of course, it presupposes that a *conscience*—the readiness to feel guilty—was already in existence before the deed took place. Remorse of this sort can, therefore, never help us to discover the origin of conscience and of the sense of guilt in general. What happens in these everyday cases is usually this: an instinctual need acquires the strength to achieve satisfaction in spite of the conscience, which is, after all, limited in its strength; and with the natural weakening of the need owing to its having been satisfied, the former balance of power is restored. Psycho-analysis is thus justified in excluding from the present discussion the case of a sense of guilt due to remorse, however frequently such cases occur and however great their practical importance.

But if the human sense of guilt goes back to the killing of the primal father, that was after all a case of 'remorse'. Are we to assume that [at that time] a conscience and a sense of guilt were not, as we have pre-supposed, in existence before the deed? If not, where, in this case, did the remorse come from? There is no doubt that this case should explain the secret of the sense of guilt to us and put an end to our difficulties. And I believe it does. This remorse was the result of the primordial ambivalence of feeling towards the father. His sons hated him, but they loved him, too. After their hatred had been satisfied by their act of aggression, their love came to the fore in their remorse for the deed. It set up the super-ego by identification with the father; it gave that agency the father's power, as though as a punishment for the deed of aggression they had carried out against him, and it created the restrictions which were intended to prevent a repetition of the deed. And since the inclination to aggressiveness against the father was repeated in the following generations, the sense of guilt, too, persisted, and it was reinforced once more by every piece of aggressiveness that was suppressed and carried over to the super-ego. Now, I think, we can at last grasp two things perfectly clearly: the part played by love in the origin of conscience and the fatal inevitability of the sense of guilt. Whether one has killed one's father or has abstained from doing so is not really the decisive thing. One is bound to feel guilty in either case, for the sense of guilt is an expression of the conflict due to ambivalence, of the eternal struggle between Eros and the instinct of destruction or death. This conflict is set going as soon as men are faced with the task of living together. So long as the community assumes no other form than that of the family, the conflict is bound to express itself in the Oedipus complex, to establish the conscience and to create the first sense of guilt. When an attempt is made to widen the community, the same conflict is continued in forms which are dependent on the past; and it is strengthened and results in a further intensification of the sense of guilt. Since civilization obeys an internal erotic impulsion which causes human beings to unite in a closely-knit group, it can only achieve this aim through an ever-increasing reinforcement of the sense of guilt. What began in relation to the father is completed in relation to the group. If civilization is a necessary course of development from the family to humanity as a whole, then—as a result of the inborn conflict arising from ambivalence, of the eternal struggle between the trends of love and death—there is inextricably bound up with it an increase of the sense of guilt, which will perhaps reach heights that the individual finds hard to tolerate. * * *

VII

Having reached the end of his journey, the author must ask his readers' forgiveness for not having been a more skilful guide and for not having spared them empty stretches of road and troublesome *détours*. There is no doubt that it could have been done better. I will attempt, late in the day, to make some amends.

In the first place, I suspect that the reader has the impression that our discussions on the sense of guilt disrupt the framework of this essay: that they take up too much space, so that the rest of its subject-matter, with which they are not always closely connected, is pushed to one side. This may have spoilt the structure of my paper; but it corresponds faithfully to my intention to represent the sense of guilt as the most important problem in the development of civilization and to show that the price we pay for our advance in civilization is a loss of happiness through the heightening of the sense of guilt.[6] Anything that still sounds strange about this statement, which is the final conclusion to our in-

---

6. 'Thus conscience does make cowards of us all . . .'

That the education of young people at the present day conceals from them the part which sexuality will play in their lives is not the only reproach which we are obliged to make against it. Its other sin is that it does not prepare them for the aggressiveness of which they are destined to become the objects. In sending the young out into life with such a false psychological orientation, education is behaving as though one were to equip people starting on a Polar expedition with summer clothing and maps of the Italian Lakes. * * *

vestigation, can probably be traced to the quite peculiar relationship—as yet completely unexplained—which the sense of guilt has to our consciousness. In the common case of remorse, which we regard as normal, this feeling makes itself clearly enough perceptible to consciousness. Indeed, we are accustomed to speak of a 'consciousness of guilt' instead of a '{consciousness} of guilt'. Our study of the neuroses, to which, after all, we owe the most valuable pointers to an understanding of normal conditions, brings us up against some contradictions. In one of those affections, obsessional neurosis, the sense of guilt makes itself noisily heard in consciousness; it dominates the clinical picture and the patient's life as well, and it hardly allows anything else to appear alongside of it. But in most other cases and forms of neurosis it remains completely unconscious, without on that account producing any less important effects. Our patients do not believe us when we attribute an 'unconscious sense of guilt" to them. In order to make ourselves at all intelligible to them, we tell them of an unconscious need for punishment, in which the sense of guilt finds expression. But its connection with a particular form of neurosis must not be over-estimated. Even in obsessional neurosis there are types of patients who are not aware of their sense of guilt, or who only feel it as a tormenting uneasiness, a kind of anxiety, if they are prevented from carrying out certain actions. It ought to be possible eventually to understand these things; but as yet we cannot. Here perhaps we may be glad to have it pointed out that the sense of guilt is at bottom nothing else but a topographical variety of anxiety; in its later phases it coincides completely with *fear of the super-ego*. And the relations of anxiety to consciousness exhibit the same extraordinary variations. Anxiety is always present somewhere or other behind every symptom; but at one time it takes noisy possession of the whole of consciousness, while at another it conceals itself so completely that we are obliged to speak of unconscious anxiety or, if we want to have a clearer psychological conscience, since anxiety is in the first instance simply a feeling, of possibilities of anxiety. Consequently it is very conceivable that the sense of guilt produced by civilization is not perceived as such either, and remains to a large extent unconscious, or appears as a sort of *malaise*,[7] a dissatisfaction, for which people seek other motivations. Religions, at any rate, have never overlooked the part played in civilization by a sense of guilt. Furthermore—a point which I failed to appreciate elsewhere—they claim to redeem mankind from this sense of guilt, which they call sin. From the manner in which, in Christianity, this redemption is achieved—by the sacrificial death of a single person, who in this manner takes upon himself a guilt that is common to everyone—we have been able to infer what the first occasion may have been on which this primal guilt, which was also the beginning of civilization, was acquired.

7. {Freud here uses the word *Unbehagen*, which the translators, when they encountered it in the title of this essay, rendered as "discontents." One might argue that *malaise* would have been equally felicitous, perhaps even more felicitous.}

Though it cannot be of great importance, it may not be superfluous to elucidate the meaning of a few words such as 'super-ego', 'conscience', 'sense of guilt', 'need for punishment' and 'remorse', which we have often, perhaps, used too loosely and interchangeably. They all relate to the same state of affairs, but denote different aspects of it. The super-ego is an agency which has been inferred by us, and conscience is a function which we ascribe, among other functions, to that agency. This function consists in keeping a watch over the actions and intentions of the ego and judging them, in exercising a censorship. The sense of guilt, the harshness of the super-ego, is thus the same thing as the severity of the conscience. It is the perception which the ego has of being watched over in this way, the assessment of the tension between its own strivings and the demands of the super-ego. The fear of this critical agency (a fear which is at the bottom of the whole relationship), the need for punishment, is an instinctual manifestation on the part of the ego, which has become masochistic under the influence of a sadistic super-ego; it is a portion, that is to say, of the instinct towards internal destruction present in the ego, employed for forming an erotic attachment to the super-ego. We ought not to speak of a conscience until a super-ego is demonstrably present. As to a sense of guilt, we must admit that it is in existence before the super-ego, and therefore before conscience, too. At that time it is the immediate expression of fear of the external authority, a recognition of the tension between the ego and that authority. It is the direct derivative of the conflict between the need for the authority's love and the urge towards instinctual satisfaction, whose inhibition produces the inclination to aggression. The superimposition of these two strata of the sense of guilt—one coming from fear of the *external* authority, the other from fear of the *internal* authority—has hampered our insight into the position of conscience in a number of ways. Remorse is a general term for the ego's reaction in a case of sense of guilt. It contains, in little altered form, the sensory material of the anxiety which is operating behind the sense of guilt; it is itself a punishment and can include the need for punishment. Thus remorse, too, can be older than conscience.

Nor will it do any harm if we once more review the contradictions which have for a while perplexed us during our enquiry. Thus, at one point the sense of guilt was the consequence of acts of aggression that had been abstained from; but at another point—and precisely at its historical beginning, the killing of the father—it was the consequence of an act of aggression that had been carried out. But a way out of this difficulty was found. For the institution of the internal authority, the super-ego, altered the situation radically. Before this, the sense of guilt coincided with remorse. (We may remark, incidentally, that the term 'remorse' should be reserved for the reaction after an act of aggression has actually been carried out.) After this, owing to the omniscience of the super-ego, the difference between an aggression intended and an aggression carried out lost its force. Henceforward a sense of guilt could be produced not only by an act of violence that is actually carried out (as all the world knows), but also by one that is merely intended (as psycho-analysis has discovered). Irrespectively of this alteration in the psychological situation, the conflict arising from ambivalence—the conflict between the two primal instincts—leaves the same result behind. We are tempted to look here for the solution of the problem of the varying relation in which the sense of guilt stands to consciousness. It might be thought that a sense of guilt arising from remorse for an evil *deed* must always be conscious, whereas a sense of guilt arising from the perception of an evil *impulse* may remain unconscious. But the answer is not so simple as that. Obsessional neurosis speaks energetically against it.

The second contradiction concerned the aggressive energy with which we suppose the super-ego to be endowed. According to one view, that energy merely carries on the punitive energy of the external authority and keeps it alive in the mind; while, according to another view, it consists, on the contrary, of one's own aggressive energy which has not been used and which one now directs against that inhibiting authority. The first view seemed to fit in better with the *history*, and the second with the *theory*, of the sense of guilt. Closer reflection has resolved this apparently irreconcilable contradiction almost too completely; what remained as the essential and common factor was that in each case we were dealing with an aggressiveness which had been displaced inwards. Clinical observation, moreover, allows us in fact to distinguish two sources for the aggressiveness which we attribute to the super-ego; one or the other of them exercises the stronger effect in any given case, but as a general rule they operate in unison.

* * * In the most recent analytic literature a predilection is shown for the idea that any kind of frustration, any thwarted instinctual satisfaction, results, or may result, in a heightening of the sense of guilt.[8] A great theoretical simplification will, I think, be achieved if we regard this as applying only to the *aggressive* instincts, and little will be found to contradict this assumption. For how are we to account, on dynamic and economic grounds, for an increase in the sense of guilt appearing in place of an unfulfilled *erotic* demand? This only seems possible in a round-about way—if we suppose, that is, that the prevention of an erotic satisfaction calls up a piece of aggressiveness against the person who has interfered with the satisfaction, and that this aggressiveness has itself to be suppressed in turn. But if this is so, it is after all only the aggressiveness which is transformed into a sense of guilt, by being suppressed and made over to the super-ego. I am convinced that many processes will admit of a simpler and clearer exposition if the findings of psycho-analysis with regard to the derivation of the sense of guilt are restricted to the aggressive

8. This view is taken in particular by Ernest Jones, Susan Isaacs and Melanie Klein; and also, I understand, by {Theodor} Reik and {Franz} Alexander.

instincts. Examination of the clinical material gives us no unequivocal answer here, because, as our hypothesis tells us, the two classes of instinct hardly ever appear in a pure form, isolated from each other; but an investigation of extreme cases would probably point in the direction I anticipate.

I am tempted to extract a first advantage from this more restricted view of the case by applying it to the process of repression. As we have learned, neurotic symptoms are, in their essence, substitutive satisfactions for unfulfilled sexual wishes. In the course of our analytic work we have discovered to our surprise that perhaps every neurosis conceals a quota of unconscious sense of guilt, which in its turn fortifies the symptoms by making use of them as a punishment. It now seems plausible to formulate the following proposition. When an instinctual trend undergoes repression, its libidinal elements are turned into symptoms, and its aggressive components into a sense of guilt. Even if this proposition is only an average approximation to the truth, it is worthy of our interest.

Some readers of this work may further have an impression that they have heard the formula of the struggle between Eros and the death instinct too often. It was alleged to characterize the process of civilization which mankind undergoes but it was also brought into connection with the development of the individual, and, in addition, it was said to have revealed the secret of organic life in general. We cannot, I think, avoid going into the relations of these three processes to one another. The repetition of the same formula is justified by the consideration that both the process of human civilization and of the development of the individual are also vital processes—which is to say that they must share in the most general characteristic of life. On the other hand, evidence of the presence of this general characteristic fails, for the very reason of its general nature, to help us to arrive at any differentiation [between the processes], so long as it is not narrowed down by special qualifications. We can only be satisfied, therefore, if we assert that the process of civilization is a modification which the vital process experiences under the influence of a task that is set it by Eros and instigated by Ananke— by the exigencies of reality; and that this task is one of uniting separate individuals into a community bound together by libidinal ties. When, however, we look at the relation between the process of human civilization and the developmental or educative process of individual human beings, we shall conclude without much hesitation that the two are very similar in nature, if not the very same process applied to different kinds of object. The process of the civilization of the human species is, of course, an abstraction of a higher order than is the development of the individual and it is therefore harder to apprehend in concrete terms, nor should we pursue analogies to an obsessional extreme; but in view of the similarity between the aims of the two processes—in the one case

the integration of a separate individual into a human group, and in the
other case the creation of a unified group out of many individuals—we
cannot be surprised at the similarity between the means employed and
the resultant phenomena.

In view of its exceptional importance, we must not long postpone the
mention of one feature which distinguishes between the two processes.
In the developmental processes of the individual, the programme of the
pleasure principle, which consists in finding the satisfaction of happiness,
is retained as the main aim. Integration in, or adaptation to, a human
community appears as a scarcely avoidable condition which must be
fulfilled before this aim of happiness can be achieved. If it could be
done without that condition, it would perhaps be preferable. To put it
in other words, the development of the individual seems to us to be a
product of the interaction between two urges, the urge towards happiness,
which we usually call 'egoistic', and the urge towards union with others
in the community, which we call 'altruistic'. Neither of these descriptions
goes much below the surface. In the process of individual development,
as we have said, the main accent falls mostly on the egoistic urge (or
the urge towards happiness); while the other urge, which may be described as a 'cultural' one, is usually content with the role of imposing
restrictions. But in the process of civilization things are different. Here
by far the most important thing is the aim of creating a unity out of the
individual human beings. It is true that the aim of happiness is still
there, but it is pushed into the background. It almost seems as if the
creation of a great human community would be most successful if no
attention had to be paid to the happiness of the individual. The developmental process of the individual can thus be expected to have special
features of its own which are not reproduced in the process of human
civilization. It is only in so far as the first of these processes has union
with the community as its aim that it need coincide with the second
process.

Just as a planet revolves around a central body as well as rotating on
its own axis, so the human individual takes part in the course of development of mankind at the same time as he pursues his own path in
life. But to our dull eyes the play of forces in the heavens seems fixed
in a never-changing order; in the field of organic life we can still see
how the forces contend with one another, and how the effects of the
conflict are continually changing. So, also, the two urges, the one
towards personal happiness and the other towards union with other
human beings, must struggle with each other in every individual; and
so, also, the two processes of individual and of cultural development
must stand in hostile opposition to each other and mutually dispute the
ground. But this struggle between the individual and society is not a
derivative of the contradiction—probably an irreconcilable one—between the primal instincts of Eros and death. It is a dispute within the

economics of the libido, comparable to the contest concerning the distribution of libido between ego and objects; and it does admit of an eventual accommodation in the individual, as, it may be hoped, it will also do in the future of civilization, however much that civilization may oppress the life of the individual to-day.

The analogy between the process of civilization and the path of individual development may be extended in an important respect. It can be asserted that the community, too, evolves a super-ego under whose influence cultural development proceeds. It would be a tempting task for anyone who has a knowledge of human civilizations to follow out this analogy in detail. I will confine myself to bringing forward a few striking points. The super-ego of an epoch of civilization has an origin similar to that of an individual. It is based on the impression left behind by the personalities of great leaders—men of overwhelming force of mind or men in whom one of the human impulsions has found its strongest and purest, and therefore often its most one-sided, expression. In many instances the analogy goes still further, in that during their lifetime these figures were—often enough, even if not always—mocked and maltreated by others and even despatched in a cruel fashion. In the same way, indeed, the primal father did not attain divinity until long after he had met his death by violence. The most arresting example of this fateful conjunction is to be seen in the figure of Jesus Christ—if, indeed, that figure is not a part of mythology, which called it into being from an obscure memory of that primal event. Another point of agreement between the cultural and the individual super-ego is that the former, just like the latter, sets up strict ideal demands, disobedience to which is visited with 'fear of conscience'. Here, indeed, we come across the remarkable circumstance that the mental processes concerned are actually more familiar to us and more accessible to consciousness as they are seen in the group than they can be in the individual man. In him, when tension arises, it is only the aggressiveness of the super-ego which, in the form of reproaches, makes itself noisily heard; its actual demands often remain unconscious in the background. If we bring them to conscious knowledge, we find that they coincide with the precepts of the prevailing cultural super-ego. At this point the two processes, that of the cultural development of the group and that of the cultural development of the individual, are, as it were, always interlocked. For that reason some of the manifestations and properties of the super-ego can be more easily detected in its behaviour in the cultural community than in the separate individual.

The cultural super-ego has developed its ideals and set up its demands. Among the latter, those which deal with the relations of human beings to one another are comprised under the heading of ethics. People have at all times set the greatest value on ethics, as though they expected that it in particular would produce especially important results. And it does in fact deal with a subject which can easily be recognized as the sorest spot in every civilization. Ethics is thus to be regarded as a therapeutic attempt—as an endeavour to achieve, by means of a command of the super-ego, something which has so far not been achieved by means of any other cultural activities. As we already know, the problem before us is how to get rid of the greatest hindrance to civilization—namely, the constitutional inclination of human beings to be aggressive towards one another; and for that very reason we are especially interested in what is probably the most recent of the cultural commands of the super-ego, the commandment to love one's neighbour as oneself. In our research into, and therapy of, a neurosis, we are led to make two reproaches against the super-ego of the individual. In the severity of its commands and prohibitions it troubles itself too little about the happiness of the ego, in that it takes insufficient account of the resistances against obeying them—of the instinctual strength of the id [in the first place], and of the difficulties presented by the real external environment [in the second]. Consequently we are very often obliged, for therapeutic purposes, to oppose the super-ego, and we endeavour to lower its demands. Exactly the same objections can be made against the ethical demands of the cultural super-ego. It, too, does not trouble itself enough about the facts of the mental constitution of human beings. It issues a command and does not ask whether it is possible for people to obey it. On the contrary, it assumes that a man's ego is psychologically capable of anything that is required of it, that his ego has unlimited mastery over his id. This is a mistake; and even in what are known as normal people the id cannot be controlled beyond certain limits. If more is demanded of a man, a revolt will be produced in him or a neurosis, or he will be made unhappy. The commandment, 'Love thy neighbour as thyself', is the strongest defence against human aggressiveness and an excellent example of the unpsychological proceedings of the cultural super-ego. The commandment is impossible to fulfil; such an enormous inflation of love can only lower its value, not get rid of the difficulty. Civilization pays no attention to all this; it merely admonishes us that the harder it is to obey the precept the more meritorious it is to do so. But anyone who follows such a precept in present-day civilization only puts himself at a disadvantage *vis-à-vis* the person who disregards it. What a potent obstacle to civilization aggressiveness must be, if the defence against it can cause as much unhappiness as aggressiveness itself! 'Natural' ethics, as it is called, has nothing to offer here except the narcissistic satisfaction of being able to think oneself better than others. At this point the ethics based on religion introduces its promises of a better after-life. But so long as virtue is not rewarded here on earth, ethics will, I fancy, preach in vain. I too think it quite certain that a real change in the relations of human beings to possessions would be of more help in this direction than any ethical commands; but the recognition of this fact among socialists has been obscured and made useless for practical purposes by a fresh idealistic misconception of human nature.

I believe the line of thought which seeks to trace in the phenomena of cultural development the part played by a super-ego promises still further discoveries. I hasten to come to a close. But there is one question which I can hardly evade. If the development of civilization has such a far-reaching similarity to the development of the individual and if it employs the same methods, may we not be justified in reaching the diagnosis that, under the influence of cultural urges, some civilizations, or some epochs of civilization—possibly the whole of mankind—have become 'neurotic'? An analytic dissection of such neuroses might lead to therapeutic recommendations which could lay claim to great practical interest. I would not say that an attempt of this kind to carry psychoanalysis over to the cultural community was absurd or doomed to be fruitless. But we should have to be very cautious and not forget that, after all, we are only dealing with analogies and that it is dangerous, not only with men but also with concepts, to tear them from the sphere in which they have originated and been evolved. Moreover, the diagnosis of communal neuroses is faced with a special difficulty. In an individual neurosis we take as our starting-point the contrast that distinguishes the patient from his environment, which is assumed to be 'normal'. For a group all of whose members are affected by one and the same disorder no such background could exist; it would have to be found elsewhere. And as regards the therapeutic application of our knowledge, what would be the use of the most correct analysis of social neuroses, since no one possesses authority to impose such a therapy upon the group? But in spite of all these difficulties, we may expect that one day someone will venture to embark upon a pathology of cultural communities.

For a wide variety of reasons, it is very far from my intention to express an opinion upon the value of human civilization. I have endeavoured to guard myself against the enthusiastic prejudice which holds that our civilization is the most precious thing that we possess or could acquire and that its path will necessarily lead to heights of unimagined perfection. I can at least listen without indignation to the critic who is of the opinion that when one surveys the aims of cultural endeavour and the means it employs, one is bound to come to the conclusion that the whole effort is not worth the trouble, and that the outcome of it can only be a state of affairs which the individual will be unable to tolerate. My impartiality is made all the easier to me by my knowing very little about all these things. One thing only do I know for certain and that is that man's judgements of value follow directly his wishes for happiness—that, accordingly, they are an attempt to support his illusions with arguments. I should find it very understandable if someone were to point out the obligatory nature of the course of human civilization and were to say, for instance, that the tendencies to a restriction of sexual life or to the institution of a humanitarian ideal at the expense of natural selection were developmental trends which cannot be averted or turned aside and to which it is best for us to yield as though they were necessities of nature. I know, too, the objection that can be made against this, to the effect that in the history of mankind, trends such as these, which were considered unsurmountable, have often been thrown aside and replaced by other trends. Thus I have not the courage to rise up before my fellow-men as a prophet, and I bow to their reproach that I can offer them no consolation: for at bottom that is what they are all demanding—the wildest revolutionaries no less passionately than the most virtuous believers.

The fateful question for the human species seems to me to be whether and to what extent their cultural development will succeed in mastering the disturbance of their communal life by the human instinct of aggression and self-destruction. It may be that in this respect precisely the present time deserves a special interest. Men have gained control over the forces of nature to such an extent that with their help they would have no difficulty in exterminating one another to the last man. They know this, and hence comes a large part of their current unrest, their unhappiness and their mood of anxiety. And now it is to be expected that the other of the two 'Heavenly Powers', eternal Eros, will make an effort to assert himself in the struggle with his equally immortal adversary. But who can foresee with what success and with what result?

Letter to the Burgomaster of Příbor

This touching autobiographical document, which Freud composed and his daughter Anna read out in his behalf, is a vivid and eloquent reminder of Freud's childhood happiness. In this letter, he briefly recalls his "first indelible impressions from this air, from this soil" in, and around, his birthplace, Freiberg in Moravia. By the time the seventy-five-year-old Freud wrote it, Freiberg had become Příbor (as the Czechs already called the place in his youth) in Czechoslovakia. The occasion was the festive unveiling, on October 25, 1931, of a plaque at the house in which Freud had been born on May 6, 1856.

I offer my thanks to the Burgomaster of the town of Příbor-Freiberg, to the organizers of this celebration and to all those who are attending it, for the honour they have done me in marking the house of my birth with this commemorative tablet from an artist's hand—and this during my lifetime and while the world around us is not yet agreed in its estimate of my work.

I left Freiberg at the age of three and visited it when I was sixteen, during my school holidays, as a guest of the Fluss family,[1] and I have never returned to it again. Since that time much has befallen me; my labours have been many, I have experienced some suffering and happiness as well, and I have had a share of success—the common medley of human life. At seventy-five it is not easy for me to put myself back into those early times; of their rich experiences but few relics remain in my memory. But of one thing I can feel sure: deeply buried within me there still lives the happy child of Freiberg, the first-born son of a youthful mother, who received his first indelible impressions from this air, from this soil. Thus I may be allowed to end my words of thanks with a heartfelt wish for the happiness of this place and of those who live in it.

Lecture XXXII
Anxiety and Instinctual Life

In 1932, as the psychoanalytic publishing house in Vienna was in deep financial troubles once again—it had been struggling for years—Freud, its surest drawing card, decided to help out by writing a series of general introductory papers that would not be actually delivered but would be in the form of lectures. He had taken a strong paternal interest in this publishing venture for years, and, to appeal to the educated general public, he designed these "lectures" to resemble, and ostensibly follow upon, the celebrated, widely read introductory lectures he had delivered, and published, during the years of the First World War.

Among these new presentations, which took full account of the revisions Freud had undertaken in his theories during the 1920s, one offers a detailed survey of his new views on anxiety, which he had first published in a book of 1926, *Inhibitions, Symptoms and Anxiety*. In his early writings on anxiety predating this work, Freud had seen it as transformed libido: "Neurotic anxiety," he had written in a note of 1920 to his *Three Essays on the Theory of Sexuality*, "arises out of libido . . . is a transformation of it, and . . . is thus related to it in the same kind of way as vinegar is to wine" (*SE* VII, 224). By this theory, repression produces anxiety. But in 1926, he reversed field and argued instead that anxiety produces repression; it is a signal, whether appropriate or inappropriate, realistic or neurotic, of danger ahead. The ego is issuing a warning that there is some traumatic situation that will need to be coped with. Freud suggested that the first situation producing anxiety is the trauma of birth, but unlike his one-time follower Otto Rank, who, in his much debated book *The Trauma of Birth* (1924), devalued the Oedipus complex and took the birth trauma to be the most significant of all anxiety-producing experiences, Freud developed a schedule of anxieties that succeed—or, rather, pile upon—one another. In his book of 1926,

1. {Emil Fluss was one of Freud's schoolmates, and his sister Gisela was briefly the target of his adolescent infatuation, which, as he freely confessed, was really a displacement of his immense fondness for Emil and Gisela's charming and hospitable mother. Freud had already exploited his memories of these years in "Screen Memories" (see above, pp. 117–26).}

Freud had stated his new views forcefully but, at the same time, rather diffusely. *Inhibitions, Symptoms and Anxiety* is a most useful book, but it is most interesting when it deals with defensive stratagems. The present paper summarizes Freud's revised ideas on anxiety just as forcefully and, in many ways, more manageably. See also above, pp. 661–66.

Ladies and gentlemen, * * *

I devoted a lecture (the twenty-fifth) to anxiety in my previous series; and I must briefly recapitulate what I said in it. We described anxiety as an affective state—that is to say, a combination of certain feelings in the pleasure-unpleasure series with the corresponding innervations of discharge and a perception of them, but probably also the precipitate of a particular important event, incorporated by inheritance—something that may thus be likened to an individually acquired hysterical attack. The event which we look upon as having left behind it an effective trace of this sort is the process of birth, at the time of which effects upon the heart's action and upon respiration characteristic of anxiety were expedient ones. The very first anxiety would thus have been a toxic one. We then started off from a distinction between realistic anxiety and neurotic anxiety, of which the former was a reaction, which seemed intelligible to us, to a danger—that is, to an expected injury from outside—while the latter was completely enigmatic, and appeared to be pointless.

In an analysis of realistic anxiety we brought it down to the state of increased sensory attention and motor tension which we describe as 'preparedness for anxiety'. It is out of this that the anxiety reaction develops. Here two outcomes are possible. Either the generation of anxiety—the repetition of the old traumatic experience—is limited to a signal, in which case the remainder of the reaction can adapt itself to the new situation of danger and can proceed to flight or defence; or the old situation can retain the upper hand and the total reaction may consist in no more than a generation of anxiety, in which case the affective state becomes paralysing and will be inexpedient for present purposes.

We then turned to neurotic anxiety and pointed out that we observe it under three conditions. We find it first as a freely floating, general apprehensiveness, ready to attach itself temporarily, in the form of what is known as 'expectant anxiety', to any possibility that may freshly arise—as happens, for instance, in a typical anxiety neurosis. Secondly, we find it firmly attached to certain ideas in the so-called 'phobias', in which it is still possible to recognize a relation to external danger but in which we must judge the fear exaggerated out of all proportion. Thirdly and lastly, we find anxiety in hysteria and other forms of severe neurosis, where it either accompanies symptoms or emerges independently as an attack or more persistent state, but always without any visible basis in an external danger. We then asked ourselves two questions: 'What are people afraid of in neurotic anxiety?' and 'How are we to bring it into relation with realistic anxiety felt in the face of external dangers?'

Our investigations were far from remaining unsuccessful: we reached a few important conclusions. In regard to anxious expectation clinical experience revealed that it had a regular connection with the libidinal economics of sexual life. The commonest cause of anxiety neurosis is unconsummated excitation. Libidinal excitation is aroused but not satisfied, not employed; apprehensiveness then appears instead of this libido that has been diverted from its employment. I even thought I was justified in saying that this unsatisfied libido was directly changed into anxiety. This view found support in some quite regularly occurring phobias of small children. Many of these phobias are very puzzling to us, but others, such as the fear of being alone and the fear of strangers, can be explained with certainty. Loneliness as well as a strange face arouse the child's longing for his familiar mother; he is unable to control this libidinal excitation, he cannot hold it in suspense but changes it into anxiety. This infantile anxiety must therefore be regarded not as of the realistic but as of the neurotic kind. Infantile phobias and the expectation of anxiety in anxiety neurosis offer us two examples of one way in which neurotic anxiety originates: by a direct transformation of libido. * * *

For we consider that what is responsible for the anxiety in hysteria and other neuroses is the process of repression. We believe it is possible to give a more complete account of this than before, if we separate what happens to the idea that has to be repressed from what happens to the quota of libido attaching to it. It is the idea which is subjected to repression and which may be distorted to the point of being unrecognizable; but its quota of affect is regularly transformed into anxiety—and this is so whatever the nature of the affect may be, whether it is aggressiveness or love. It makes no essential difference, then, for what reason a quota of libido has become unemployable: whether it is on account of the infantile weakness of the ego, as in children's phobias, or on account of somatic processes in sexual life, as in anxiety neurosis, or owing to repression, as in hysteria. Thus in reality the two mechanisms that bring about neurotic anxiety coincide.

In the course of these investigations our attention was drawn to a highly significant relation between the generation of anxiety and the formation of symptoms—namely, that these two represent and replace each other. For instance, an agoraphobic patient may start his illness with an attack of anxiety in the street. This would be repeated every time he went into the street again. He will now develop the symptom of agoraphobia; this may also be described as an inhibition, a restriction of the ego's functioning, and by means of it he spares himself anxiety attacks. We can witness the converse of this if we interfere in the formation of symptoms, as is possible, for instance, with obsessions. If we prevent a patient from carrying out a washing ceremonial, he falls into a state of anxiety which he finds hard to tolerate and from which he had evidently been protected by his symptom. And it seems, indeed, that the generation of anxiety is the earlier and the formation of symptoms the later of the two, as though the symptoms are created in order to avoid the outbreak of the anxiety state. This is confirmed too by the fact that the first neuroses of childhood are phobias—states in which we see so clearly how an initial generation of anxiety is replaced by the later formation of a symptom; we get an impression that it is from these interrelations that we shall best obtain access to an understanding of neurotic anxiety. And at the same time we have also succeeded in answering the question of what it is that a person is afraid of in neurotic anxiety and so in establishing the connection between neurotic and realistic anxiety. What he is afraid of is evidently his own libido. The difference between this situation and that of realistic anxiety lies in two points: that the danger is an internal instead of an external one and that it is not consciously recognized.

In phobias it is very easy to observe the way in which this internal danger is transformed into an external one—that is to say, how a neurotic anxiety is changed into an apparently realistic one. In order to simplify what is often a very complicated business, let us suppose that the ago-raphobic patient is invariably afraid of feelings of temptation that are aroused in him by meeting people in the street. In his phobia he brings about a displacement and henceforward is afraid of an external situation. What he gains by this is obviously that he thinks he will be able to protect himself better in that way. One can save oneself from an external danger by flight; fleeing from an internal danger is a difficult enterprise.

At the conclusion of my earlier lecture on anxiety I myself expressed the opinion that, although these various findings of our enquiry were not mutually contradictory, somehow they did not fit in with one another. Anxiety, it seems, in so far as it is an affective state, is the reproduction of an old event which brought a threat of danger; anxiety serves the purposes of self-preservation and is a signal of a new danger; it arises from libido that has in some way become unemployable and it also arises during the process of repression; it is replaced by the formation of a symptom, is, as it were, psychically bound—one has a feeling that something is missing here which would bring all these pieces together into a whole.

Ladies and Gentlemen, the dissection of the mental personality into a super-ego, an ego and an id, which I put before you in my last lecture, has obliged us to take our bearings afresh in the problem of anxiety as well. With the thesis that the ego is the sole seat of anxiety—that the ego alone can produce and feel anxiety—we have established a new and stable position from which a number of things take on a new aspect. And indeed it is difficult to see what sense there would be in speaking of an 'anxiety of the id' or in attributing a capacity for apprehensiveness to the super-ego. On the other hand, we have welcomed a desirable element of correspondence in the fact that the three main species of anxiety, realistic, neurotic and moral, can be so easily connected with the ego's three dependent relations—to the external world, to the id and to the super-ego. Along with this new view, moreover, the function of anxiety as a signal announcing a situation of danger (a notion, incidentally, not unfamiliar to us) comes into prominence, the question of what the material is out of which anxiety is made loses interest, and the relations between realistic and neurotic anxiety have become surprisingly clarified and simplified. It is also to be remarked that we now understand the apparently complicated cases of the generation of anxiety better than those which were considered simple.

For we have recently been examining the way in which anxiety is generated in certain phobias which we class as anxiety hysteria, and have chosen cases in which we were dealing with the typical repression of wishful impulses arising from the Oedipus complex. We should have expected to find that it was a libidinal cathexis of the boy's mother as object which, as a result of repression, had been changed into anxiety and which now emerged, expressed in symptomatic terms, attached to a substitute for his father. I cannot present you with the detailed steps of an investigation such as this; it will be enough to say that the surprising result was the opposite of what we expected. It was not the repression that created the anxiety; the anxiety was there earlier; it was the anxiety that made the repression. But what sort of anxiety can it have been? Only anxiety in the face of a threatening external danger—that is to say, a realistic anxiety. It is true that the boy felt anxiety in the face of a demand by his libido—in this instance, anxiety at being in love with his mother; so the case was in fact one of neurotic anxiety. But this being in love only appeared to him as an internal danger, which he must avoid by renouncing that object, because it conjured up an external situation of danger. And in every case we examine we obtain the same result. It must be confessed that we were not prepared to find that internal instinctual danger would turn out to be a determinant and preparation for an external, real, situation of danger.

But we have not made any mention at all so far of what the real danger is that the child is afraid of as a result of being in love with his mother. The danger is the punishment of being castrated, of losing his genital organ. You will of course object that after all that is not a real danger. Our boys are not castrated because they are in love with their mothers during the phase of the Oedipus complex. But the matter cannot be dismissed so simply. Above all, it is not a question of whether castration is really carried out; what is decisive is that the danger is one that threatens from outside and that the child believes in it. He has some ground for this, for people threaten him often enough with cutting off his penis during the phallic phase, at the time of his early masturbation, and hints at that punishment must regularly find a phylogenetic rein-forcement in him. It is our suspicion that during the human family's primaeval period castration used actually to be carried out by a jealous and cruel father upon growing boys, and that circumcision, which so frequently plays a part in puberty rites among primitive peoples, is a clearly recognizable relic of it. We are aware that here we are diverging widely from the general opinion; but we must hold fast to the view that fear of castration is one of the commonest and strongest motives for repression and thus for the formation of neuroses. The analysis of cases in which circumcision, though not, it is true, castration, has been carried out on boys as a cure or punishment for masturbation (a far from rare occurrence in Anglo-American society) has given our conviction a last degree of certainty. It is very tempting at this point to go more deeply into the castration complex, but I will stick to our subject.

Fear of castration is not, of course, the only motive for repression: indeed, it finds no place in women, for though they have a castration complex they cannot have a fear of being castrated. Its place is taken in their sex by a fear of loss of love, which is evidently a later prolongation of the infant's anxiety if it finds its mother absent. You will realize how real a situation of danger is indicated by this anxiety. If a mother is absent or has withdrawn her love from her child, it is no longer sure of the satisfaction of its needs and is perhaps exposed to the most distressing feelings of tension. Do not reject the idea that these determinants of anxiety may at bottom repeat the situation of the original anxiety at birth, which, to be sure, also represented a separation from the mother. Indeed, if you follow a train of thought suggested by Ferenczi, you may add the fear of castration to this series, for a loss of the male organ results in an inability to unite once more with the mother (or a substitute for her) in the sexual act. I may mention to you incidentally that the very frequent phantasy of returning into the mother's womb is a substitute for this wish to copulate. There would be many interesting things and surprising connections to tell you at this point, but I cannot go outside the framework of an introduction to psycho-analysis. I will only draw your attention to the fact that here psychological researchers trench upon the facts of biology.

Otto Rank, to whom psycho-analysis is indebted for many excellent contributions, also has the merit of having expressly emphasized the significance of the act of birth and of separation from the mother. Nevertheless we have all found it impossible to accept the extreme inferences which he has drawn from this factor as bearing on the theory of the neuroses and even on analytic therapy. The core of his theory—that the experience of anxiety at birth is the model of all later situations of danger—he found already there. If we dwell on these situations of danger for a moment, we can say that in fact a particular determinant of anxiety (that is, situation of danger) is allotted to every age of devel-opment as being appropriate to it. The danger of psychical helplessness fits the stage of the ego's early immaturity; the danger of loss of an object (or loss of love) fits the lack of self-sufficiency in the first years of child-hood; the danger of being castrated fits the phallic phase; and finally fear of the super-ego, which assumes a special position, fits the period of latency. In the course of development the old determinants of anxiety should be dropped, since the situations of danger corresponding to them have lost their importance owing to the strengthening of the ego. But this only occurs most incompletely. Many people are unable to surmount the fear of loss of love; they never become sufficiently independent of other people's love and in this respect carry on their behaviour as infants. Fear of the super-ego should normally never cease, since, in the form of moral anxiety, it is indispensable in social relations, and only in the rarest cases can an individual become independent of human society. A few of the old situations of danger, too, succeed in surviving into later periods by making contemporary modifications in their determinants of anxiety. Thus, for instance, the danger of castration persists under the mark of syphilidophobia. It is true that as an adult one knows that castration is no longer customary as a punishment for the indulgence of sexual desires, but on the other hand one has learnt that instinctual liberty of that kind is threatened by serious diseases. There is no doubt that the people we describe as neurotics remain infantile in their attitude to danger and have not surmounted obsolete determinants of anxiety. We may take this as a factual contribution to the characterization of neurotics; it is not so easy to say why it should be so.

I hope you have not lost the thread of what I am saying and remember that we are investigating the relations between anxiety and repression. In the course of this we have learnt two new things: first, that anxiety makes repression and not, as we used to think, the other way round, and [secondly] that the instinctual situation which is feared goes back ultimately to an external situation of danger. The next question will be: how do we now picture the process of a repression under the influence of anxiety? The answer will, I think, be as follows. The ego notices that the satisfaction of an emerging instinctual demand would conjure up one of the well-remembered situations of danger. This instinctual ca-thexis must therefore be somehow suppressed, stopped, made powerless. We know that the ego succeeds in this task if it is strong and has drawn the instinctual impulse concerned into its organization. But what happens in the case of repression is that the instinctual impulse still belongs to the id and that the ego feels weak. The ego thereupon helps itself by a technique which is at bottom identical with normal thinking. Thinking is an experimental action carried out with small amounts of energy, in the same way as a general shifts small figures about on a map before setting his large bodies of troops in motion. Thus the ego anticipates the satisfaction of the questionable instinctual impulse and permits it to bring about the reproduction of the unpleasurable feelings at the begin-ning of the feared situation of danger. With this the automatism of the pleasure-unpleasure principle is brought into operation and now carries out the repression of the dangerous instinctual impulse.

'Stop a moment!' you will exclaim; 'we can't follow you any further there!' You are quite right; I must add a little more before it can seem acceptable to you. First, I must admit that I have tried to translate into the language of our normal thinking what must in fact be a process that is neither conscious nor preconscious, taking place between quotas of energy in some unimaginable substratum. But that is not a strong objection, for it cannot be done in any other way. What is more important is that we should distinguish clearly what happens in the ego and what happens in the id when there is a repression. We have just said what the ego does: it makes use of an experimental cathexis and starts up the pleasure-unpleasure automatism by means of a signal of anxiety. After that, several reactions are possible or a combination of them in varying proportions. Either the anxiety attack is fully generated and the ego withdraws entirely from the objectionable excitation; or, in place of the experimental cathexis it opposes the excitation with an anticathexis, and this combines with the energy of the repressed impulse to form a symptom; or the anticathexis is taken up into the ego as a reaction-formation, as an intensification of certain of the ego's dispositions, as a permanent alteration of it. The more the generation of anxiety can be restricted to a mere signal, so much the more does the ego expend on actions of defence which amount to the psychical binding of the repressed [impulse], and so much the closer, too, does the process approximate to a normal working-over of it, though no doubt without attaining to it.

Incidentally, here is a point on which we may dwell for a moment. You yourselves have no doubt assumed that what is known as 'character', a thing so hard to define, is to be ascribed entirely to the ego. We have already made out a little of what it is that creates character. First and foremost there is the incorporation of the former parental agency as a super-ego, which is no doubt its most important and decisive portion, and, further, identifications with the two parents of the later period and with other influential figures, and similar identifications formed as precipitates of abandoned object-relations. And we may now add as contributions to the construction of character which are never absent the reaction-formations which the ego acquires—to begin with in making its repressions and later, by a more normal method, when it rejects unwished-for instinctual impulses.

Now let us go back and turn to the id. It is not so easy to guess what occurs during repression in connection with the instinctual impulse that is being fought against. The main question which our interest raises is as to what happens to the energy, to the libidinal charge, of that excitation—how is it employed? You recollect that the earlier hypothesis was that it is precisely this that is transformed by repression into anxiety. We no longer feel able to say that. The modest reply will rather be that what happens to it is probably not always the same thing. There is probably an intimate correspondence which we ought to get to know about between what is occurring at the time in the ego and in the id in connection with the repressed impulse. For since we have decided that the pleasure-unpleasure principle, which is set in action by the signal of anxiety, plays a part in repression, we must alter our expectations. That principle exercises an entirely unrestricted dominance over what happens in the id. We can rely on its bringing about quite profound changes in the instinctual impulse in question. We are prepared to find that repression will have very various consequences, more or less far-reaching. In some cases the repressed instinctual impulse may retain its libidinal cathexis, and may persist in the id unchanged, although subject to constant pressure from the ego. In other cases what seems to happen is that it is totally destroyed, while its libido is permanently diverted along other paths. I expressed the view that this is what happens when the Oedipus complex is dealt with normally—in this desirable case, therefore, being not simply repressed but destroyed in the id. Clinical experience has further shown us that in many cases, instead of the customary result of repression, a degradation of the libido takes place— a regression of the libidinal organization to an earlier stage. This can, of course, only occur in the id, and if it occurs it will be under the influence of the same conflict which was introduced by the signal of anxiety. The most striking example of this kind is provided by the obsessional neurosis, in which libidinal regression and repression operate together.

I fear, Ladies and Gentlemen, that you will find this exposition hard to follow, and you will guess that I have not stated it exhaustively. I am sorry to have had to rouse your displeasure. But I can set myself no other aim than to give you an impression of the nature of our findings and of the difficulties involved in working them out. The deeper we penetrate into the study of mental processes the more we recognize their abundance and complexity. A number of simple formulas which to begin with seemed to meet our needs have later turned out to be inadequate. We do not tire of altering and improving them. In my lecture on the theory of dreams [the first in the present series] I introduced you to a region in which for fifteen years there has scarcely been a new discovery. Here, where we are dealing with anxiety, you see everything in a state of flux and change. These novelties, moreover, have not yet been thoroughly worked through and perhaps this too adds to the difficulties of demonstrating them. But have patience! We shall soon be able to take leave of the subject of anxiety. I cannot promise that it will have been settled to our satisfaction, but it is to be hoped that we shall have made a little bit of progress. And in the meantime we have made all sorts of new discoveries. Now, for instance, our study of anxiety leads us to add a new feature to our description of the ego. We have said that the ego is weak in comparison with the id, that it is its loyal servant, eager to carry out its orders and to fulfil its demands. We have no intention of withdrawing this statement. But on the other hand this same ego is the better organized part of the id, with its face turned towards reality. We must not exaggerate the separation between the two of them too much, and we must not be surprised if the ego on its part can bring its influence to bear on the processes in the id. I believe the ego exercises this influence by putting into action the almost omnipotent pleasure-unpleasure principle by means of the signal of anxiety. On the other hand, it shows its weakness again immediately afterwards, for by the act of repression it renounces a portion of its organization and has to allow the repressed instinctual impulse to remain permanently withdrawn from its influence.

And now, only one more remark on the problem of anxiety. Neurotic anxiety has changed in our hands into realistic anxiety, into fear of particular external situations of danger. But we cannot stop there, we must take another step—though it will be a step backward. We ask ourselves what it is that is actually dangerous and actually feared in a situation of danger of this kind. It is plainly not the injury to the subject as judged objectively, for this need be of no significance psychologically, but something brought about by it in the mind. Birth, for instance, our model for an anxiety state, can after all scarcely be regarded on its own account as an injury, although it may involve a danger of injuries. The essential thing about birth, as about every situation of danger, is that it callls up in mental experience a state of highly tense excitation, which is felt as unpleasure and which one is not able to master by discharging it. Let us call a state of this kind, before which the efforts of the pleasure principle break down, a 'traumatic' moment. Then, if we take in succession neurotic anxiety, realistic anxiety and the situation of danger, we arrive at this simple proposition: what is feared, what is the object of the anxiety, is invariably the emergence of a traumatic moment, which cannot be dealt with by the normal rules of the pleasure principle. We understand at once that our endowment with the pleasure principle does not guarantee us against objective injuries but only against a particular injury to our psychical economics. It is a long step from the pleasure principle to the self-preservative instinct; the intentions of the two of them are very far from coinciding from the start. But we see something else besides; perhaps it is the solution we are in search of. Namely, that in all this it is a question of relative quantities. It is only the magnitude of the sum of excitation that turns an impression into a traumatic mo-ment, paralyses the function of the pleasure principle and gives the situation of danger its significance. And if that is how things are, if these puzzles can be solved so prosaically, why should it not be possible for similar traumatic moments to arise in mental life without reference to hypothetical situations of danger—traumatic moments, then, in which anxiety is not aroused as a signal but is generated anew for a fresh reason. Clinical experience declares decidedly that such is in fact the case. It is only the *later* repressions that exhibit the mechanism we have described, in which anxiety is awakened as a signal of an earlier situation of danger. The first and original repressions arise directly from traumatic moments, when the ego meets with an excessively great libidinal demand; they construct their anxiety afresh, although, it is true, on the model of birth. The same may apply to the generation of anxiety in anxiety neurosis owing to somatic damage to the sexual function. We shall no longer maintain that it is the libido itself that is turned into anxiety in such cases. But I can see no objection to there being a twofold origin of anxiety—one as a direct consequence of the traumatic moment and the other as a signal threatening a repetition of such a moment.

* * *

Lecture XXXV
The Question of a *Weltanschauung*

It is highly significant that Freud reserved the concluding "lecture" of his *New Introductory Lectures* for the question of a *Weltanschauung*—the question of just what fundamental view of the world is appropriate to psychoanalysis. Freud's English editors observe (*SE* XXII, 4) that this lecture, like several others in that series, is "only indirectly related to psychoanalysis," though they concede that it is interesting. That view is, I submit, unduly narrow, unduly technical. In actuality, this paper on a *Weltanschauung* sums up a lifetime of Freud's reflections on the relation of scientific to religious thinking and of the place that psychoanalysis may claim among the sciences. The point Freud wants to make, and make emphatically, is that his creation, psychoanalysis, is one among the sciences and neither needs, nor could generate, a world view of its own.

Ladies and Gentlemen,—At our last meeting we were occupied with little everyday concerns—putting our own modest house in order, as it were. I propose that we should now take a bold leap and venture upon answering a question which is constantly being asked in other quarters: does psycho-analysis lead to a particular *Weltanschauung* and, if so, to which?

'*Weltanschauung*' is, I am afraid, a specifically German concept, the translation of which into foreign languages might well raise difficulties. If I try to give you a definition of it, it is bound to seem clumsy to you. In my opinion, then, a *Weltanschauung* is an intellectual construction which solves all the problems of our existence uniformly on the basis of one overriding hypothesis, which, accordingly, leaves no question unanswered and in which everything that interests us finds its fixed place. It will easily be understood that the possession of a *Weltanschauung* of this kind is among the ideal wishes of human beings. Believing in it one can feel secure in life, one can know what to strive for, and how one can deal most expediently with one's emotions and interests.

If that is the nature of a *Weltanschauung*, the answer as regards psycho-analysis is made easy. As a specialist science, a branch of psychology—a depth-psychology or psychology of the unconscious—it is quite unfit to construct a *Weltanschauung* of its own: it must accept the scientific one. But the *Weltanschauung* of science already departs noticeably from our definition. It is true that it too assumes the *uniformity* of the explanation of the universe; but it does so only as a programme, the fulfilment of which is relegated to the future. Apart from this it is marked by negative characteristics, by its limitation to what is at the moment knowable and by its sharp rejection of certain elements that are alien to it. It asserts that there are no sources of knowledge of the universe other than the intellectual working-over of carefully scrutinized observations—in other words, what we call research—and alongside of it no knowledge derived from revelation, intuition or divination. It seems as though this view came very near to being generally recognized in the course of the last few centuries that have passed; and it has been left to *our* century to discover the presumptuous objection that a *Weltanschauung* like this is alike paltry and cheerless, that it overlooks the claims of the human intellect and the needs of the human mind.

This objection cannot be too energetically repudiated. It is quite without a basis, since the intellect and the mind are objects for scientific research in exactly the same way as any nonhuman things. Psycho-analysis has a special right to speak for the scientific *Weltanschauung* at this point, since it cannot be reproached with having neglected what is mental in the picture of the universe. Its contribution to science lies precisely in having extended research to the mental field. And, inci-dentally, without such a psychology science would be very incomplete. If, however, the investigation of the intellectual and emotional functions of men (and of animals) is included in science, then it will be seen that nothing is altered in the attitude of science as a whole, that no new sources of knowledge or methods of research have come into being. Intuition and divination would be such, if they existed; but they may safely be reckoned as illusions, the fulfilments of wishful impulses. It is easy to see, too, that these demands upon a *Weltanschauung* are only based on emotion. Science takes notice of the fact that the human mind produces these demands and is ready to examine their sources; but it has not the slightest reason to regard them as justified. On the contrary it sees this as a warning carefully to separate from knowledge everything that is illusion and an outcome of emotional demands like these.

This does not in the least mean that these wishes are to be pushed contemptuously on one side or their value for human life under-estimated. We are ready to trace out the fulfilments of them which they have created for themselves in the products of art and in the systems of religion and philosophy; but we cannot nevertheless overlook the fact that it would be illegitimate and highly inexpedient to allow these demands to be transferred to the sphere of knowledge. For this would be to lay open the paths which lead to psychosis, whether to individual or group psychosis, and would withdraw valuable amounts of energy from endeavours which are directed towards reality in order, so far as possible, to find satisfaction in it for wishes and needs.

From the standpoint of science one cannot avoid exercising one's critical faculty here and proceeding with rejections and dismissals. It is not permissible to declare that science is one field of human mental activity and that religion and philosophy are others, at least its equal in value, and that science has no business to interfere with the other two: that they all have an equal claim to be true and that everyone is at liberty to choose from which he will draw his convictions and in which he will place his belief. A view of this kind is regarded as particularly superior, tolerant, broad-minded and free from illiberal prejudices. Unfortunately it is not tenable and shares all the pernicious features of an entirely unscientific *Weltanschauung* and is equivalent to one in practice. It is simply a fact that the truth cannot be tolerant, that it admits of no compromises or limitations, that research regards every sphere of human activity as belonging to it and that it must be relentlessly critical if any other power tries to take over any part of it.

Of the three powers which may dispute the basic position of science, religion alone is to be taken seriously as an enemy. Art is almost always harmless and beneficent; it does not seek to be anything but an illusion. Except for a few people who are spoken of as being 'possessed' by art, it makes no attempt at invading the realm of reality. Philosophy is not opposed to science, it behaves like a science and works in part by the same methods; it departs from it, however, by clinging to the illusion of being able to present a picture of the universe which is without gaps and is coherent, though one which is bound to collapse with every fresh advance in our knowledge. It goes astray in its method by over-estimating the epistemological value of our logical operations and by accepting other sources of knowledge such as intuition. * * *

But philosophy has no direct influence on the great mass of mankind; it is of interest to only a small number even of the top layer of intellectuals and is scarcely intelligible to anyone else. On the other hand, religion is an immense power which has the strongest emotions of human beings at its service. It is well known that at an earlier date it comprised everything that played an intellectual part in men's lives, that it took the place of science when there was scarcely yet such a thing as science, and that it constructed a *Weltanschauung*, consistent and self-contained to an unparalleled degree, which, although it has been profoundly shaken, persists to this day.

If we are to give an account of the grandiose nature of religion, we must bear in mind what it undertakes to do for human beings. It gives them information about the origin and coming into existence of the universe, it assures them of its protection and of ultimate happiness in the ups and downs of life and it directs their thoughts and actions by precepts which it lays down with its whole authority. Thus it fulfils three functions. With the first of them it satisfies the human thirst for knowledge; it does the same thing that science attempts to do with *its* means, and at that point enters into rivalry with it. It is to its second function that it no doubt owes the greatest part of its influence. Science can be no match for it when it soothes the fear that men feel of the dangers and vicissitudes of life, when it assures them of a happy ending and offers them comfort in unhappiness. It is true that science can teach us how to avoid certain dangers and that there are some sufferings which it can successfully combat; it would be most unjust to deny that it is a powerful helper to men; but there are many situations in which it must leave a man to his suffering and can only advise him to submit to it. In its third function, in which it issues precepts and lays down prohibitions and restrictions, religion is furthest away from science. For science is content to investigate and to establish facts, though it is true that from its application rules and advice are derived on the conduct of life. In some circumstances these are the same as those offered by religion, but, when this is so, the reasons for them are different.

* * *

You know how hard it is for anything to die away when once it has achieved psychical expression. So you will not be surprised to hear that many of the utterances of animism have persisted to this day, for the most part as what we call superstition, alongside of and behind religion. But more than this, you will scarcely be able to reject a judgement that the philosophy of today has retained some essential features of the animistic mode of thought—the overvaluation of the magic of words and the belief that the real events in the world take the course which our thinking seeks to impose on them. It would seem, it is true, to be an animism without magical actions. On the other hand, we may suppose that even in those days there were ethics of some sort, precepts upon the mutual relations of men; but nothing suggests that they had any intimate connection with animistic beliefs. They were probably the direct expression of men's relative powers and of their practical needs.

* * *

This being the prehistory of the religious *Weltanschauung*, let us turn now to what has happened since then and to what is still going on before our eyes. The scientific spirit, strengthened by the observation of natural processes, has begun, in the course of time, to treat religion as a human affair and to submit it to a critical examination. Religion was not able to stand up to this. What first gave rise to suspicion and scepticism were its tales of miracles, for they contradicted everything that had been taught by sober observation and betrayed too clearly the influence of the activity of the human imagination. After this its doctrines explaining the origin of the universe met with rejection, for they gave evidence of an ignorance which bore the stamp of ancient times and to which, thanks to their increased familiarity with the laws of nature, people knew they were superior. The idea that the universe came into existence through acts of copulation or creation analogous to the origin of individual people had ceased to be the most obvious and self-evident hypothesis since the distinction between animate creatures with a mind and an inanimate Nature had impressed itself on human thought—a distinction which made it impossible to retain belief in the original animism. Nor must we overlook the influence of the comparative study of different religious systems and the impression of their mutual exclusiveness and intolerance.

Strengthened by these preliminary exercises, the scientific spirit gained enough courage at last to venture on an examination of the most important and emotionally valuable elements of the religious *Weltanschauung*. People may always have seen, though it was long before they dared to say so openly, that the pronouncements of religion promising men protection and happiness if they would only fulfil certain ethical requirements had also shown themselves unworthy of belief. It seems not to be the case that there is a Power in the universe which watches over the well-being of individuals with parental care and brings all their affairs to a happy ending. On the contrary, the destinies of mankind can be brought into harmony neither with the hypothesis of a Universal Benevolence nor with the partly contradictory one of a Universal Justice. * * * Obscure, unfeeling and unloving powers determine men's fate; the system of rewards and punishments which religion ascribes to the government of the universe seems not to exist. Here once again is a reason for dropping a portion of the animistic theory which had been rescued from animism by religion.

The last contribution to the criticism of the religious *Weltanschauung* was effected by psycho-analysis, by showing how religion originated from the helplessness of children and by tracing its contents to the survival into maturity of the wishes and needs of childhood. This did not precisely mean a contradiction of religion, but it was nevertheless a necessary rounding-off of our knowledge about it, and in one respect at least it was a contradiction, for religion itself lays claim to divine origin. And, to be sure, it is not wrong in this, provided that our interpretation of God is accepted.

In summary, therefore, the judgement of science on the religious *Weltanschauung* is this. While the different religions wrangle with one another as to which of them is in possession of the truth, our view is that the question of the truth of religious beliefs may be left altogether on one side. Religion is an attempt to master the sensory world in which we are situated by means of the wishful world which we have developed within us as a result of biological and psychological necessities. But religion cannot achieve this. Its doctrines bear the imprint of the times in which they arose, the ignorant times of the childhood of humanity. Its consolations deserve no trust. Experience teaches us that the world is no nursery. The ethical demands on which religion seeks to lay stress need, rather, to be given another basis; for they are indispensable to human society and it is dangerous to link obedience to them with religious faith. It we attempt to assign the place of religion in the evolution of mankind, it appears not as a permanent acquisition but as a counterpart to the neurosis which individual civilized men have to go through in their passage from childhood to maturity.

* * *

The struggle of the scientific spirit against the religious *Weltanschauung* is, as you know, not at an end: it is still going on to-day under our eyes. Though as a rule psycho-analysis makes little use of the weapon of controversy, I will not hold back from looking into this dispute. In doing so I may perhaps throw some further light on our attitude to *Weltanschauung*. You will see how easily some of the arguments brought forward by the supporters of religion can be answered, though it is true that others may evade refutation.

The first objection we meet with is to the effect that it is an impertinence on the part of science to make religion a subject for its investigations, for religion is something sublime, superior to any operation of the human intellect, something which may not be approached with hair-splitting criticisms. In other words, science is not qualified to judge religion: it is quite serviceable and estimable otherwise, so long as it keeps to its own sphere. But religion is not its sphere, and it has no business there. If we do not let ourselves be put off by this brusque repulse and enquire further what is the basis of this claim to a position exceptional among all human concerns, the reply we receive (if we are thought worthy of any reply) is that religion cannot be measured by human measurements, for it is of divine origin and was given us as a revelation by a Spirit which the human spirit cannot comprehend. One would have thought that there was nothing easier than the refutation of this argument: it is a clear case of *petitio principii*, of 'begging the question'[1]—I know of no good German equivalent expression. The actual question raised is whether there *is* a divine spirit and a revelation by it; and the matter is certainly not decided by saying that this question cannot be asked, since the deity may not be put in question. The position here is what it occasionally is during the work of analysis. If a usually

1. [In English in the original.]

sensible patient rejects some particular suggestion on specially foolish grounds, this logical weakness is evidence of the existence of a specially strong motive for the denial—a motive which can only be of an affective nature, an emotional tie.

We may also be given another answer, in which a motive of this kind is openly admitted: religion may not be critically examined because it is the highest, most precious, and most sublime thing that the human spirit has produced, because it gives expression to the deepest feelings and alone makes the world tolerable and life worthy of men. We need not reply by disputing this estimate of religion but by drawing attention to another matter. What we do is to emphasize the fact that what is in question is not in the least an invasion of the field of religion by the scientific spirit, but on the contrary an invasion by religion of the sphere of scientific thought. Whatever may be the value and importance of religion, it has no right in any way to restrict thought—no right, therefore, to exclude itself from having thought applied to it.

Scientific thinking does not differ in its nature from the normal activity of thought, which all of us, believers and unbelievers, employ in looking after our affairs in ordinary life. It has only developed certain features: it takes an interest in things even if they have no immediate, tangible use; it is concerned carefully to avoid individual factors and affective influences; it examines more strictly the trustworthiness of the sense-perceptions on which it bases its conclusions; it provides itself with new perceptions which cannot be obtained by everyday means and it isolates the determinants of these new experiences in experiments which are deliberately varied. Its endeavour is to arrive at correspondence with reality—that is to say, with what exists outside us and independently of us and, as experience has taught us, is decisive for the fulfilment or disappointment of our wishes. This correspondence with the real external world we call 'truth'. It remains the aim of scientific work even if we leave the practical value of that work out of account. When, therefore, religion asserts that it can take the place of science, that, because it is beneficent and elevating, it must also be true, that is in fact an invasion which must be repulsed in the most general interest. It is asking a great deal of a person who has learnt to conduct his ordinary affairs in accordance with the rules of experience and with a regard to reality, to suggest that he shall hand over the care of what are precisely his most intimate interests to an agency which claims as its privilege freedom from the precepts of rational thinking. And as regards the protection which religion promises its believers, I think none of us would be so much as prepared to enter a motor-car if its driver announced that he drove, unperturbed by traffic regulations, in accordance with the impulses of his soaring imagination.

The prohibition against thought issued by religion to assist in its self-preservation is also far from being free from danger either for the individual or for human society. Analytic experience has taught us that a prohibition like this, even if it is originally limited to a particular field, tends to widen out and thereafter to become the cause of severe inhibitions in the subject's conduct of life. This result may be observed, too, in the female sex, following from their being forbidden to have anything to do with their sexuality even in thought. Biography is able to point to the damage done by the religious inhibition of thought in the life stories of nearly all eminent individuals in the past. On the other hand intellect—or let us call it by the name that is familiar to us, reason—is among the powers which we may most expect to exercise a unifying influence on men—on men who are held together with such difficulty and whom it is therefore scarcely possible to rule. It may be imagined how impossible human society would be, merely if everyone had his own multiplication table and his own private units of length and weight. Our best hope for the future is that intellect— the scientific spirit, reason—may in process of time establish a dictatorship in the mental life of man. The nature of reason is a guarantee that afterwards it will not fail to give man's emotional impulses and what is determined by them the position they deserve. But the common compulsion exercised by such a dominance of reason will prove to be the strongest uniting bond among men and lead the way to further unions. Whatever, like religion's prohibition against thought, opposes such a development, is a danger for the future of mankind.

* * *

So the struggle is not at an end. The supporters of the religious *Weltanschauung* act upon the ancient dictum: the best defence is attack. 'What', they ask, 'is this science which presumes to disparage our religion—our religion which has brought salvation and consolation to millions of people over many thousands of years? What has it accomplished so far? What can we expect from it in the future? On its own admission it is incapable of bringing consolation and exaltation. Let us leave them on one side then, though that is no light renunciation. But what about its theories? Can it tell us how the universe came about and what fate lies before it? Can it even draw us a coherent picture of the universe, or show us where we are to look for the unexplained phenomena of life or how the forces of the mind are able to act upon inert matter? If it could do this we should not refuse it our respect. But none of these, no problem of this kind, had been solved by it hitherto. It gives us fragments of alleged discovery, which it cannot bring into harmony with one another; it collects observations of uniformities in the course of events which it dignifies with the name of laws and submits to its risky interpretations. And consider the small degree of certainty which it attaches to its findings! Everything it teaches is only provisionally true: what is praised to-day as the highest wisdom will be rejected to-morrow and replaced by something else, though once more only tentatively. The latest error is then described as the truth. And for this truth we are to sacrifice our highest good!'

* * *

* * * The path of science is indeed slow, hesitating, laborious. This fact cannot be denied or altered. No wonder the gentlemen in the other camp are dissatisfied. They are spoilt: revelation gave them an easier time. Progress in scientific work is just as it is in an analysis. We bring expectations with us into the work, but they must be forcibly held back. By observation, now at one point and now at another, we come upon something new; but to begin with the pieces do not fit together. We put forward conjectures, we construct hypotheses, which we withdraw if they are not confirmed, we need much patience and readiness for any eventuality, we renounce early convictions so as not to be led by them into overlooking unexpected factors, and in the end our whole expenditure of effort is rewarded, the scattered findings fit themselves together, we get an insight into a whole section of mental events, we have completed our task and now we are free for the next one. In analysis, however, we have to do without the assistance afforded to research by experiment.

Moreover, there is a good deal of exaggeration in this criticism of science. It is not true that it staggers blindly from one experiment to another, that it replaces one error by another. It works as a rule like a sculptor at his clay model, who tirelessly alters his rough sketch, adds to it and takes away from it, till he has arrived at what he feels is a satisfactory degree of resemblance to the object he sees or imagines. Besides, at least in the older and more mature sciences, there is even to-day a solid ground-work which is only modified and improved but no longer demolished. Things are not looking so bad in the business of science.

And what, finally, is the aim of these passionate disparagements of science? In spite of its present incompleteness and of the difficulties attaching to it, it remains indispensable to us and nothing can take its place. It is capable of undreamt-of improvements, whereas the religious *Weltanschauung* is not. This is complete in all essential respects; if it was a mistake, it must remain one for ever. No belittlement of science can in any way alter the fact that it is attempting to take account of our dependence on the real external world, while religion is an illusion and it derives its strength from its readiness to fit in with our instinctual wishful impulses.

* * *

The first of {other} *Weltanschauungen* is as it were a counterpart to political anarchism, and is perhaps a derivative of it. There have certainly been intellectual nihilists of this kind in the past, but just now the relativity theory of modern physics seems to have gone to their head. They start out from science, indeed, but they contrive to force it into self-abrogation, into suicide; they set it the task of getting itself out of the way by refuting its own claims. One often has an impression in this connection that this nihilism is only a temporary attitude which is to be retained until this task has been performed. Once science has been disposed of, the space vacated may be filled by some kind of mysticism or, indeed, by the old religious *Weltanschauung*. According to the anarchist theory there is no such thing as truth, no assured knowledge of the external world. What we give out as being scientific truth is only the product of our own needs as they are bound to find utterance under changing external conditions: once again, they are illusion. Fundamentally, we find only what we need and see only what we want to see. We have no other possibility. Since the criterion of truth—correspondence with the external world—is absent, it is entirely a matter of indifference what opinions we adopt. All of them are equally true and equally false. And no one has a right to accuse anyone else of error.

A person of an epistemological bent might find it tempting to follow the paths—the sophistries—by which the anarchists succeed in enticing such conclusions from science. No doubt we should come upon situations similar to those derived from the familiar paradox of the Cretan who says that all Cretans are liars.[2] But I have neither the desire nor the capacity for going into this more deeply. All I can say is that the anarchist theory sounds wonderfully superior so long as it relates to opinions about abstract things: it breaks down with its first step into practical life. Now the actions of men are governed by their opinions, their knowledge; and it is the same scientific spirit that speculates about the structure of atoms or the origin of man and that plans the construction of a bridge capable of bearing a load. If what we believe were really a matter of indifference, if there were no such thing as knowledge distinguished among our opinions by corresponding to reality, we might build bridges just as well out of cardboard as out of stone, we might inject our patients with a decagram of morphine instead of a centigram, and might use tear-gas as a narcotic instead of ether. But even the intellectual anarchists would violently repudiate such practical applications of their theory.

The other opposition has to be taken far more seriously, and in this instance I feel the liveliest regret at the inadequacy of my information. I suspect that you know more about this business than I do and that you took up your position long ago in favour of Marxism or against it. Karl Marx's investigations into the economic structure of society and into the influence of different economic systems upon every department of human life have in our days acquired an undeniable authority. How far his views in detail are correct or go astray, I cannot of course tell. I understand that this is not an easy matter even for others better instructed

2. [The simplest form of this paradox (known as the 'Epimenides') is provided by a man who says 'I am lying'. If he is lying, he is speaking the truth; and if he is speaking the truth, he is lying.]

than I am. There are assertions contained in Marx's theory which have struck me as strange: such as that the development of forms of society is a process of natural history, or that the changes in social stratification arise from one another in the manner of a dialectical process. I am far from sure that I understand these assertions aright; nor do they sound to me 'materialistic' but, rather, like a precipitate of the obscure Hegelian philosophy in whose school Marx graduated. I do not know how I can shake off my lay opinion that the class structure of society goes back to the struggles which, from the beginning of history, took place between human hordes only slightly differing from each other. Social distinctions, so I thought, were originally distinctions between clans or races. Victory was decided by psychological factors, such as the amount of constitutional aggressiveness, but also by the firmness of the organization within the horde, and by material factors, such as the possession of superior weapons. Living together in the same area, the victors became the masters and the vanquished the slaves. There is no sign to be seen in this of a natural law or of a conceptual [dialectical] evolution. On the other hand the influence exercised upon the social relations of mankind by progressive control over the forces of Nature is unmistakable. For men always put their newly acquired instruments of power at the service of their aggressiveness and use them against one another. The introduction of metals—bronze and iron—made an end to whole epochs of civilization and their social institutions. I really believe that it was gunpowder and fire-arms that abolished chivalry and aristocratic rule, and that the Russian despotism was already doomed before it lost the War, because no amount of inbreeding among the ruling families of Europe could have produced a race of Tsars capable of withstanding the explosive force of dynamite.

* * *

I am almost ashamed to comment to you on a subject of such importance and complexity with these few inadequate remarks, and I know too that I have told you nothing that is new to you. I merely want to draw your attention to the fact that the relation of mankind to their control over Nature, from which they derive their weapons for fighting their fellow-men, must necessarily also affect their economic arrangements. We seem to have come a long way from the problem of a *Weltanschauung*, but we shall very soon be back to it. The strength of Marxism clearly lies, not in its view of history or the prophecies of the future that are based on it, but in its sagacious indication of the decisive influence which the economic circumstances of men have upon their intellectual, ethical and artistic attitudes. A number of connections and implications were thus uncovered, which had previously been almost totally overlooked. But it cannot be assumed that economic motives are the only ones that determine the behaviour of human beings in society. The undoubted fact that different individuals, races and nations behave differently under the same economic conditions is alone enough to show that economic motives are not the sole dominating factors. It is altogether incomprehensible how psychological factors can be overlooked where what is in question are the reactions of living human beings; for not only were these reactions concerned in establishing the economic conditions, but even under the domination of those conditions men can only bring their original instinctual impulses into play—their self-preservative instinct, their aggressiveness, their need to be loved, their drive towards obtaining pleasure and avoiding unpleasure. In an earlier enquiry I also pointed out the important claims made by the super-ego, which represents tradition and the ideals of the past and will for a time resist the incentives of a new economic situation. And finally we must not forget that the mass of human beings who are subjected to economic necessities also undergo the process of cultural development—of civilization as other people may say—which, though no doubt influenced by all the other factors, is certainly independent of them in its origin, being comparable to an organic process and very well able on its part to exercise an influence on the other factors. It displaces instinctual aims and brings it about that people become antagonistic to what they had previously tolerated. Moreover, the progressive strengthening of the scientific spirit seems to form an essential part of it. If anyone were in a position to show in detail the way in which these different factors—the general inherited human disposition, its racial variations and its cultural transformations—inhibit and promote one another under the conditions of social rank, profession and earning capacity—if anyone were able to do this, he would have supplemented Marxism so that it was made into a genuine social science. For sociology too, dealing as it does with the behaviour of people in society, cannot be anything but applied psychology. Strictly speaking there are only two sciences: psychology, pure and applied, and natural science.

The newly achieved discovery of the far-reaching importance of economic relations brought with it a temptation not to leave alterations in them to the course of historical development but to put them into effect oneself by revolutionary action. Theoretical Marxism, as realized in Russian Bolshevism, has acquired the energy and the self-contained and exclusive character of a *Weltanschauung*, but at the same time an uncanny likeness to what it is fighting against. Though originally a portion of science and built up, in its implementation, upon science and technology, it has created a prohibition of thought which is just as ruthless as was that of religion in the past. Any critical examination of Marxist theory is forbidden, doubts of its correctness are punished in the same way as heresy was once punished by the Catholic Church. The writings of Marx have taken the place of the Bible and the Koran as a source of revelation, though they would seem to be no more free from contradictions and obscurities than those older sacred books.

And although practical Marxism has mercilessly cleared away all idealistic systems and illusions, it has itself developed illusions which are no less questionable and unprovable than the earlier ones. It hopes in the course of a few generations so to alter human nature that people will live together almost without friction in the new order of society, and that they will undertake the duties of work without any compulsion. Meanwhile it shifts elsewhere the instinctual restrictions which are essential in society; it diverts the aggressive tendencies which threaten all human communities to the outside and finds support in the hostility of the poor against the rich and of the hitherto powerless against the former rulers. But a transformation of human nature such as this is highly improbable. The enthusiasm with which the mass of the people follow the Bolshevist instigation at present, so long as the new order is incomplete and is threatened from outside, gives no certainty for a future in which it would be fully built up and in no danger. In just the same way as religion, Bolshevism too must compensate its believers for the sufferings and deprivations of their present life by promises of a better future in which there will no longer be any unsatisfied need. This Paradise, however, is to be in this life, instituted on earth and thrown open within a foreseeable time. But we must remember that the Jews as well, whose religion knows nothing of an after-life, expected the arrival of a Messiah on earth, and that the Christian Middle Ages at many times believed that the Kingdom of God was at hand.

There is no doubt of how Bolshevism will reply to these objections. It will say that so long as men's nature has not yet been transformed it is necessary to make use of the means which affect them to-day. It is impossible to do without compulsion in their education, without the prohibition of thought and without the employment of force to the point of bloodshed; and if the illusions were not awakened in them, they could not be brought to acquiesce in this compulsion. And we should be politely asked to say how things could be managed differently. This would defeat us. I could think of no advice to give. I should admit that the conditions of this experiment would have deterred me and those like me from undertaking it; but we are not the only people concerned. There are men of action, unshakable in their convictions, inaccessible to doubt, without feeling for the sufferings of others if they stand in the way of their intentions. We have to thank men of this kind for the fact that the tremendous experiment of producing a new order of this kind is now actually being carried out in Russia. At a time when the great nations announce that they expect salvation only from the maintenance of Christian piety, the revolution in Russia—in spite of all its disagreeable details—seems none the less like the message of a better future. Unluckily neither our scepticism nor the fanatical faith of the other side gives a hint as to how the experiment will turn out. The future will tell us; perhaps it will show that the experiment was undertaken prematurely, that a sweeping alteration of the social order has little prospect of success until new discoveries have increased our control over the forces of Nature and so made easier the satisfaction of our needs. Only then perhaps may it become possible for a new social order not only to put an end to the material need of the masses but also to give a hearing to the cultural demands of the individual. Even then, to be sure, we shall still have to struggle for an incalculable time with the difficulties which the untameable character of human nature presents to every kind of social community.

Ladies and Gentlemen,—Allow me in conclusion to sum up what I had to say of the relation of psycho-analysis to the question of a *Weltanschauung*. Psycho-analysis, in my opinion, is incapable of creating a *Weltanschauung* of its own. It does not need one; it is a part of science and can adhere to the scientific *Weltanschauung*. This, however, scarcely deserves such a grandiloquent title, for it is not all-comprehensive, it is too incomplete and makes no claim to being self-contained and to the construction of systems. Scientific thought is still very young among human beings; there are too many of the great problems which it has not yet been able to solve. A *Weltanschauung* erected upon science has, apart from its emphasis on the real external world, mainly negative traits, such as submission to the truth and rejection of illusions. Any of our fellow-men who is dissatisfied with this state of things, who calls for more than this for his momentary consolation, may look for it where he can find it. We shall not grudge it him, we cannot help him, but nor can we on his account think differently.

Postscript

With his flat affirmation, written down in 1932 and published the year after, that psychoanalysis shares the world view of natural science, Freud as it were shut up shop. He was seventy-seven; the threat of Hitler in neighboring Germany and the unsettled conditions of Austria were continuing worries, as was his health. Yet he continued writing. In the summer of 1934, he completed a draft of a speculative little book he then called *The Man Moses, A Historical Novel*, which was to haunt him the rest of the five years he still had to live: the final, complete version was published in early 1939 under the more neutral title *Moses and Monotheism: Three Essays*. It was just one more provocative work from the pen of a man who had spent his life being provocative. Freud argued that the Moses known to readers of the Old Testament had not been a Jew at all but an Egyptian who had tried to press his severe monotheism on the primitive ancient Hebrews. He was assassinated for his pains, and the Jews did not adopt his religion until several centuries later, when another figure, taking the name of Moses, finally brought them under the yoke of a strict, demanding single deity. The book brought outcries of rage and despair from Jewish scholars and little sympathy from gentile ones. Yet Freud insisted on publishing it—he had spent his life following the lead of his ideas and he would not give up on that now.

Then, in 1937, he wrote a rather somber paper on technique, "Analysis Terminable and Interminable," and began, in the summer of 1938, a terse and by no means elementary *Outline of Psychoanalysis*, a fascinating fragment that was not published until 1940, the year after his death. By the time he began work on the outline, he and most of his family were safe in England. After the Anschluss to Germany in early March 1938 and the enthusiastic welcome of the German Nazi invaders on the part of most Austrians, even Freud, unwilling to move before, was persuaded that it was time to leave. He came to England in June 1938, "to die in freedom," as he put it, and died on September 23, 1939, in freedom, as he had hoped.

Selected Bibliography

It hardly needs saying that the literature about Freud is vast and steadily growing. Here I can only suggest the most interesting titles, many of which have sizable bibliographies of their own.

I. BIOGRAPHIES AND GENERAL ASSESSMENTS

The standard biography has long been, and for some purposes remains, Ernest Jones, *The Life and Work of Sigmund Freud*, 3 vols. (1953–57; one-volume abridgment by Lionel Trilling and Steven Marcus, 1961), by one of Freud's closest collaborators. Ronald W. Clark's *Freud: The Man and the Cause* (1980) is diligently researched but derivative on the ideas. Peter Gay's *Freud: A Life for Our Time* (1988) unites life and work and is based on much hitherto unpublished materials, with a substantial and combative bibliographical essay. William J. McGrath, *Freud's Discovery of Psychoanalysis: The Politics of Hysteria* (1986) has much valuable material and interpretation on Freud's younger years. *Sigmund Freud: His Life in Pictures and Words*, eds. Ernst Freud, Lucie Freud, and Ilse Grubrich-Simitis (1976; tr. Christine Trollope, 1978) offers a bouquet of unhackneyed illustrations. Max Schur, *Freud, Living and Dying* (1972), by Freud's personal physician, himself a psychoanalyst, is informed and illuminating. Richard Wollheim, *Freud* (1971) is a compact, brilliant biography of Freud's ideas. See also Philip Rieff's *Freud: The Mind of the Moralist* (1959; paperback ed., 1961), an intelligent essay. Ilse Grubrich-Simitis's sensitive "Einleitung" to Sigmund Freud, '*Selbstdarstellung,*' 7–33, deserves translation. Hanns Sachs, one of Freud's closest and wittiest followers, has some unique and touching reminiscences in *Freud: Master and Friend* (1945); Didier Anzieu, *Freud's Self-Analysis* (2nd ed., 1975; tr. Peter Graham, 1986), carefully examines Freud's dreams to light up his early life. Martin Freud's affectionate memoir of his father, *Sigmund Freud: Man and Father* (1958), has valuable and intimate domestic details.

The international authority of the twenty-four-volume *Standard Edition of the Complete Psychological Works of Sigmund Freud*, translated under the general editorship of James Strachey in collaboration with Anna Freud, assisted by Alix Strachey and Alan Tyson (1953–75), remains, with its extensive notes, despite some cavils, assured. The most exciting recent discovery, the draft of one of the metapsychological papers Freud destroyed, was discovered and authoritatively edited and introduced by Ilse Grubrich-Simitis: *A Phylogenetic Fantasy: Overview of the Transference Neuroses* (1985; trans. Axel and Peter T. Hoffer, 1987).

Among special treatments illuminating Freud's life, I single out K. R. Eissler's *Sigmund Freud und die Wiener Universität: Über die Pseudo-Wissenschaftlichkeit der jüngsten Wiener Freud-Biographik* (1966), which proves that Freud's academic advancement was indeed held up for years. Edmund Engelman's photographs, collected in *Berggasse 19: Sigmund Freud's Home and Offices, Vienna 1938* (1976), amply document Freud's bourgeois conventional tastes.

II. THE DEBATE OVER THE STATUS OF FREUD'S IDEAS

The most careful (and sympathetic) study of Freud's claims for psychoanalysis is Paul Kline, *Fact and Fantasy in Freudian Theory* (1972; 2nd ed., 1981). Seymour Fisher and Roger P. Greenberg's *The Scientific Credibility of Freud's Theories and Therapy* (1977) is less positive but informative; to be supplemented by the same authors' evenhanded anthology, *The Scientific Evaluation of Freud's Theories and Therapy* (1978). See also Joseph Masling, ed., *Empirical Studies of Psychoanalytic Theories*, 2 vols. (1983–85), with interesting material on experimental work by such psychoanalytic researchers as Hartvig Dahl. For a highly critical (but to my mind unacceptable if tenaciously argued) philosophical assessment, see Adolf Grünbaum, *The Foundations of Psychoanalysis: A Philosophical Critique* (1984). For a criticism of that book, Edwin R. Wallace IV, "The Scientific Status of Psychoanalysis: A Review of Grünbaum's *The Foundations of Psychoanalysis*," *The Journal of Nervous and Mental Disease*, CLXXIV (1986), 379–86. Another critical appraisal of psychoanalysis by a philosopher is B. A. Farrell, *The Standing*

of Psychoanalytic Theory (1981). An important philosophical collection is Richard Wollheim and
J. Hopkins, *Philosophical Essays on Freud* (1983).

III. STUDIES OF FREUD'S CASE HISTORIES AND TECHNIQUE

Mark Kanzer and Jules Glenn, eds., *Freud and His Patients* (1980), present a compendious
collection of essays on all his major analysands, with a full bibliography. Other informative
treatments of Freud's case histories include Patrick J. Mahony, *Cries of the Wolf Man* (1984),
and the same author's *Freud and the Rat Man* (1986). The most carefully researched analysis of
the Schreber case is Han Israëls, *Schreber, Father and Son*, tr. from the Dutch original by
H. S. Lake (1981), which places the famous paranoid into his family context. The book modifies
but does not wholly supersede William G. Niederland, *The Schreber Case: Psychoanalytic Profile
of a Paranoid Personality* (1974). For the Wolf Man see (in addition to Mahony), Muriel Gardiner,
ed., *The Wolf-Man by the Wolf-Man* (1971), which includes the Wolf Man's reminiscences.
There is as yet no book-length study of "Little Hans." "Anna O.," Josef Breuer's famous hysterical
patient and in many respects the founding patient of psychoanalysis has been thoroughly explored
in Albrecht Hirschmüller, *Physiologie und Psychoanalyse im Leben und Werk Josef Breuers* (1978).

Most writings on psychoanalytic technique after Freud lean heavily on his work. In the absence
of a specific study exclusively devoted to his papers, these remain quite helpful. The best texts
are Edward Glover, *Technique of Psycho-Analysis* (1955); Karl Menninger, *Theory of Psychoanalytic Technique* (1958); Leo Stone, *The Psychoanalytic Situation: An Examination of Its Development and Essential Nature* (1961); Ralph R. Greenson, *The Technique and Practice of
Psychoanalysis*, vol. I (1967), the only to appear. There are also important discussions on technique
in the collection of Phyllis Greenacre's papers, *Emotional Growth: Psychoanalytic Studies of the
Gifted and a Great Variety of Other Individuals*, 2 vols. (1971). I should add Janet Malcolm's
amusing, brilliant introduction to contemporary psychoanalytic technique—and politics, *Psycho-
analysis: The Impossible Profession* (1981).

IV. APPLIED PSYCHOANALYSIS

By far the best overview of Freud's aesthetic theories is Jack J. Spector, *The Aesthetics of Freud:
A Study in Psychoanalysis and Art* (1972). There are interesting discussions in Harry Trosman,
Freud and the Imaginative World (1985). Among other psychoanalysts' ventures into this field,
see Eduard Hitschmann, *Great Men: Psychoanalytic Studies* (1957), and also Ernest Jones, *Hamlet
and Oedipus* (1949). Otto Rank's *The Myth of the Birth of the Hero* (1909; tr. F. Robbins and
Smith Ely Jelliffe, 1914) remains an interesting effort. Rank's huge study of incest in literature,
Das Inzest-Motiv in Dichtung und Sage (1912; 2nd ed., 1926) is a valiant compendium. Another
instance of (somewhat flat though far from tedious) Freudian psychobiography is Marie Bonaparte,
The Life and Works of Edgar Allan Poe: A Psycho-Analytic Interpretation (1933; tr. John Rodker,
1949). More recent work has been rich. See Gilbert J. Rose, *The Power of Form: A Psychoanalytic
Approach to Aesthetic Form* (1980); D. W. Winnicott's perceptive and immensely suggestive
papers, gathered in *Playing and Reality* (1971); Robert Waelder, *Psychoanalytic Avenues to Art*
(1965); and John E. Gedo, *Portraits of the Artist: Psychoanalysis of Creativity and Its Vicissitudes*
(1983), which ventures into a field from which Freud himself shied away. On Freud's paper on
Leonardo da Vinci, see especially Meyer Schapiro, "Leonardo and Freud: An Art-Historical
Study," *Journal of the History of Ideas*, XVII (1956), 147–78; K. R. Eissler's response, *Leonardo
da Vinci: Psycho-Analytic Notes on the Enigma* (1961), suffers from overkill but has interesting
thoughts on psychoanalysis and art. On *Totem and Taboo*, see Edwin R. Wallace IV's lucid
Freud and Anthropology: A History and a Reappraisal (1983). The best defense of Freud's
controversial speculative venture into prehistory is Derek Freeman, "Totem and Taboo: A Reappraisal," in *Man and His Culture: Psychoanalytic Anthropology after 'Totem and Taboo'*, ed.
Warner Muensterberger (1970), 53–78.

V. PSYCHOANALYSIS IN THE MAKING AND IN COMBAT

The several collections of Freud's immense correspondence are of varying value, but they all,
even the highly selected ones, throw significant light on the making of Freud's thought, on its
development, and on Freud's battle with the world and with his followers. By far the most revealing
collection of these letters is *The Complete Letters of Sigmund Freud to Wilhelm Fliess, 1887–
1904*, ed. and tr. Jeffrey Moussaieff Masson (1985). A close second is *The Freud/Jung Letters:
The Correspondence Between Sigmund Freud and C. G. Jung*, ed. William McGuire and Wolfgang
Sauerländer, tr. Ralph Manheim (Freud's letters) and R. F. C. Hull (Jung's); the first edition of
1974 has been slightly revised in the third (1987). Among others, do not neglect Sigmund Freud,
Karl Abraham, *A Psychoanalytic Dialogue: The Letters of Sigmund Freud and Karl Abraham,*

1907–1926, ed., Hilda Abraham and Ernst L. Freud, tr. Bernard Marsh and Hilda Abraham (1965); Sigmund Freud, Lou Andreas-Salomé, *Letters*, ed., Ernst Pfeiffer, tr. William and Elaine Robson-Scott (1972); Sigmund Freud, Oscar Pfister, *Psychoanalysis and Faith: The Letters of Sigmund Freud and Oskar Pfister*, ed. Ernst L. Freud and Heinrich Meng, tr. William and Elaine Robson-Scott (1970).

On the evolution of Freud's ideas, there is Kenneth Levin, *Freud's Early Psychology of the Neuroses: A Historical Perspective* (1978). Henri F. Ellenberger's vast *The Discovery of the Unconscious: The History and Evolution of Dynamic Psychiatry* (1970) puts Freud into a large historical context. For Freud's theory of dreams and his own dreams on which he drew so freely, see, in addition to Anzieu, Alexander Grinstein, *On Sigmund Freud's Dreams* (1968; 2nd ed., 1980). Ernest Jones has some interesting early papers on dream theory, collected in *Papers on Psycho-Analysis* (3rd ed., 1923, and later editions). Franz Alexander, Samuel Eisenstein, and Martin Grotjahn have edited *Psychoanalytic Pioneers* (1966), a generally useful but still very uneven collection surveying Freud's early followers. The only book-length, far from adequate biography of Karl Abraham is Hilda Abraham, *Karl Abraham: An Unfinished Biography* (1974). E. James Lieberman's *Acts of Will: The Life and Work of Otto Rank* (1985) is superior but, to my mind, too favorable. Ernest Jones's unfinished autobiography, *Free Associations: Memories of a Psycho-Analyst* (1959), shows Jones opinionated but well-informed and informative.

On Freud's decisive paper on narcissism, see Sydney Pulver, "Narcissism: The Term and the Concept," *Journal of the American Psychoanalytic Association*, XVIII (1970), 319–41, and, among a large literature, Otto F. Kernberg, *Borderline Conditions and Pathological Narcissism* (1975). The emergence of aggression as an independent drive in Freud's system is economically traced in Paul E. Stepansky, *A History of Aggression in Freud* (1977), to be supplemented by Anna Freud, "Aggression in Relation to Emotional Development: Normal and Pathological," *Psychoanalytic Study of the Child*, III/IV (1949), 37–42, and Beata Rank, "Aggression," ibid., 43–48. For the contentious literature on Freud's theories of female sexuality, see two illuminating surveys by Zenia Odes Fliegel, "Feminine Psychosexual Development in Freudian Theory: A Historical Reconstruction," *Psychoanalytic Quarterly*, XLII (1973), 385–408; and "Half a Century Later: Current Status of Freud's Controversial Views on Women," *Psychoanalytic Review*, LXIX (1982), 7–28. There is a useful anthology of articles in the *Journal of the American Psychoanalytic Association, Female Psychology: Contemporary Psychoanalytic Views*, ed., Harold P. Blum (1977).

For Freud's views on matters of faith—Jewishness in particular and religion in general—see Peter Gay, *A Godless Jew: Freud, Atheism, and the Making of Psychoanalysis* (1987). As for Freud (and psychoanalysis) on politics: a really authoritative study is still wanted. Meanwhile there is the interesting long essay by Robert Bocock, *Freud and Modern Society: An Outline and Analysis of Freud's Sociology* (1976). See also J. C. Flugel, *Man, Morals and Society: A Psycho-Analytic Study* (1945); R. E. Money-Kyrle, *Psychoanalysis and Politics: A Contribution to the Psychology of Politics and Morals* (1951).

Index

Abraham, Karl, xxvii, 33, 140 *n.*, 587, 678 and *n.*
abreaction, 13
abstinence, 285
"actual" neuroses, 551–52
  sexual etiology of, 15, 353–54
  See also anxiety-neuroses; hypochondria; neurasthenia
Adige River, 316 and *n.*
Adler, Alfred, xiiin, xxviii, 32, 351, 683
  theories of, disputed, xxvi, 33, 381, 400, 421, 557, 561, 674 *n.*
Adonis, 507
aesthetic pleasure, 443, 738, 739, 740.
  See also art
aetiology, sexual. *See* sexual etiology of mental illness
Aetiology of Hysteria, The (1896), 96–111
  cited by Freud, 268
affect
  its appropriateness of intensity, in analysis, 311–12
  in infantile sexuality, 276–77
  reversal of, 184, 185
affectionate and sexual currents of libido, 274, 279, 395–96, 397–98
afterlife, 304, 696, 704, 706, 707, 717
aggression, xxviii, xxix, 722, 749–52
  and death-instincts, 655
  vs. Eros, 594
  vs. love, 621, 647
  Marxism and, 793, 794, 795
  in sexuality, 252, 253
  in super-ego and, 766–67
  suppressed, 655–56, 750, 756, 759, 760–61, 772
  See also destructive instinct; killing; sadism
agoraphobia, 775
Aichhorn, August: *Wayward Youth*, 761 *n.*

aim-inhibited love. *See* inhibited aim
algolagnia, 252
Alexander, Franz: *Psychoanalysis of the Total Personality, The*, 761, 766 *n.*
alienation, Freud's. *See* isolation/alienation, Freud's
ambiguity, verbal, 207 *n.*
ambivalence, 32, 245 *n.*, 646–47
  and bisexuality, 641
  toward father, 493, 500, 503, 506, 507, 508–9, 510, 513, 640, 699, 762–63
  as incomplete instinctual function, 647
  and infantile sexual organization, 273–74
  of love and death, 520
  in love relationships and mourning, 587–88
  and taboos, 40
  in transference-love, 378
America. *See* anti-Americanism, Freud's; United States
amnesia, infantile, 29, 259–60
amnesia, hysterical, 260
anaclitic object-choice, 532–54
anaesthesia, 7, 8
anal character, 293, 294–97, 742
anal eroticism, 245, 248–49, 278 *n.*, 742
  and character, 293–97
  infantile, 22
  and melancholia, 589
anal-sadistic phase, 273
analysands. *See* patients, psychoanalytic
analysis, 176, 177
  Here are entered aspects of the individual therapeutic process.
  See *psychoanalysis* for the discipline in general; *psychoanalytic method and techniques* for the methodology; *psychoanalytic movement* for history of the dis-